Connections in the

History and Systems

of Psychology

CONNECTIONS IN THE HISTORY AND SYSTEMS OF PSYCHOLOGY

B. MICHAEL THORNE

TRACY B. HENLEY

Mississippi State University

HOUGHTON MIFFLIN COMPANY

Boston   New York

To Wanda, my wife and life companion, and to my children, Dean and Erin—B. M. T.

To the memory of Michael Tinsley (1951–1993) and his love for the history of psychology—T. B. H.

Sponsoring Editor: David C. Lee

Senior Associate Editor: Jane Knetzger

Assistant Editor: Gwyneth V. Fairweather

Senior Project Editor: Janet Edmonds

Associate Production/Design Coordinator: Jennifer Meyer

Senior Manufacturing Coordinator: Priscilla J. Bailey

Marketing Manager: Pamela J. Laskey

Cover design: Deborah Azerrad Savona
Cover images (clockwise): Wilhelm Wundt, Corbis-Bettmann; Margaret Floy Washburn, Archives of the History of American Psychology, University of Akron, Ohio; Karl Lashley, Archives of the History of American Psychology, University of Akron, Ohio; René Descartes (from the painting by Frans Hals, in the gallery of the Louvre), North Wind Picture Archives

Chapter 7: Excerpts from Boring, E. G., "Edward Bradford Titchener: 1867–1927," 1927. *The American Journal of Psychology*, 38, 488–506; Chapter 10: Excerpts from Ross, D. (1972) *G. Stanley Hall: The Psychologist as Prophet.* Chicago: The University of Chicago Press. Copyright © 1972 by The University of Chicago Press. Reprinted by permission; excerpt from letter by Dr. B.F. Skinner is reprinted with permission of the B.F. Skinner Foundation, Morgantown, WV. (Credits continued on page 624.)

Printed in the U.S.A.

Library of Congress Catalog Card Number: 96-76968

ISBN: 0-395-67084-5

123456789-DH-00 99 98 97

Brief Contents

Contents

Preface

Most students close their undergraduate careers—and open their graduate ones—with a course over the history of their field. With this in mind, we set out to write a book for such a course in psychology. In writing this book, we have been guided by three goals: (1) to make the work as scholarly and comprehensive as any on the market; (2) to incorporate as many pedagogical aids as possible; and (3) to make the subject as interesting and entertaining as it can be, consistent with current, accurate, and comprehensive scholarship.

An early reviewer of this book actually criticized our writing as too entertaining and too interesting and asked the question: "What effect will this have on students?" We hope that the effect will be to stimulate student interest in pursuing the subject further and in greater depth. If the reviewer's assessment was correct, we look forward to helping create a generation of students who are motivated to learn more about the history of the field that we love.

Because students (and their instructors) like to learn about people—about their lives as well as their ideas—we have made our biographical information as three-dimensional as possible. For example, from our book, readers can get a sense of William James as a person, that he agonized over a career and suffered from depression before finding his true calling in teaching, that he had a lifelong interest in the paranormal, in addition to the standard facts that he lived from 1842 to 1910 and wrote perhaps psychology's most famous book. We have also introduced information that reveals the struggle of women early in the history of American psychology, including the efforts of pioneers such as Mary Calkins, Milicent Shinn, and Margaret Floy Washburn. This, and the special coverage we have given to minorities in the history of psychology, reflects our awareness of two important facts: First, women and minorities have made historically significant contributions to psychology; and, second, psychology is a discipline that is increasingly attractive to women and minorities.

In addition to the rich biographical coverage we have provided, our book is about connections—emphasized even in the title we have chosen: *Connections in the History and Systems of Psychology*. We have been struck by the fascinating and substantive connections that permeate the history of psychology and we have made such connections an integrating feature of this book. All too often students leave their history of psychology courses without a sense of who was contemporary with whom, who influenced whom, and whose ideas affected which system of psychology, thereby missing out on the overarching themes in the history of our field. As noted below, the book incorporates several special features designed to facilitate the drawing of connections.

In Chapter 1 we talk about how historical facts are often biased by the filters through which they pass (e.g., historians and/or the people involved). It is undoubtedly true that we have "filtered" this survey of the history of psychology. You do not have to be an ardent behaviorist to appreciate that the social and educational contexts from which we emerge shape our thoughts and actions. Nevertheless, although some historians write a book from some particular perspective—for example, behaviorism or cognitive psychology—we have attempted to avoid this. Likewise, some historians clearly endorse a certain view of the history of science: that it must be thematic, that it is paradigmatic, that it often is socially constructed, and so on. Although we are aware of many such theories, we have attempted to favor none of them.

TEXT ORGANIZATION: THREE BOOKS IN ONE

The book you hold in your hands is really three books in one—that is, it is broken into three distinct sections. Part I covers the philosophical and physiological roots from which psychology developed. Part II is devoted to psychology's "great schools." Part III covers by topic important, mostly 20th-century, developments in such areas as physiology, intelligence testing and psychometrics, social psychology, and cognition.

Because this book is actually three books in one, if instructors choose to emphasize psychology's recent past, they can cover Parts II and III and encourage students to read Part I as needed. If instructors are primarily interested in the history of psychology's schools, then a focus on Parts I and II will include the schools and their philosophical antecedents. Part III could then be optional, although students may find it particularly helpful when preparing for the subject portion of the Graduate Record Examination (GRE). In other words, our outline and coverage permit the flexibility that teachers with different approaches to the history and systems course require.

In Part I, "Philosophical and Physiological Beginnings," the philosophical coverage begins with the ancient Greeks, emphasizing the main currents of thought during the "Golden Age" of Greece (e.g., of the philosophers Socrates, Plato, and Aristotle).

Next, we explore the development of philosophy and science through the Roman period, the Middle Ages, and into the Renaissance. We focus particularly on Descartes as a major transitional figure leading toward the modern era. From Descartes and his immediate successors on the Continent (e.g., Spinoza and Leibniz), we examine the major philosophical antecedents to the beginning of psychology as a separate discipline. We emphasize the British empiricists and associationists (e.g., Locke, Berkeley, Hume, and James and John Stuart Mill), the French empiricists (e.g., La Mettrie, Condillac, and Cabanis), and the Continental rationalists (e.g., Kant, Hegel, and Herbart). We also examine the influences from positivism and romanticism.

Part I ends with a survey of the 19th-century (and earlier) effects on psychology from physiology. The theme of "demystification of the nervous system" is seen particularly in the work of Helmholtz, who measured the speed of the nerve impulse; Flourens, who developed the ablation method as a way to disprove experimentally the contentions of phrenology; and such early stimulators of brain tissue as Fritsch and Hitzig, Ferrier, and Hughlings Jackson. The 19th-century physiological influences also include the development of psychophysics by Weber and Fechner.

In Part II, "The Schools of Psychology," after describing Wundt's voluntarism and Titchener's structuralism, we study the individuals who offered a phenomenological alternative to Wundt's view of psychology, including Brentano, Stumpf, Külpe, and G. E. Müller.

Next, we examine the antecedents and founding of the first school that developed in opposition to voluntarism and structuralism—functionalism. Evolution was central to the thinking of the functionalists, and Darwin and Galton are particularly emphasized in our look at the British forerunners. We cover extensively American anticipators such as James, Hall, and Cattell, and the founders and developers of the school—Dewey, Angell, Carr, Thorndike, and Woodworth—conclude the chapters devoted to the formation of American psychology.

Russian objective psychology—culminating with Pavlov—and the pragmatic approach of Watson are highlighted in our examination of behaviorism's founding. Reflecting behaviorism's belief in the importance of the environment for the development of behavior, we focus on learning theory in the contributions of neobehaviorists such as Guthrie, Tolman, Hull, and Skinner, whose lives and work are considered in some detail.

Part II closes with separate chapters on the schools of Gestalt psychology and psychoanalysis. The lives and thought of Gestalt's founders—Wertheimer, Koffka, and Köhler—are highlighted in the Gestalt chapter, along with the contributions of Kurt Lewin to the development of experimental social psychology. Freud, his disciples, and his successors are the focus of the chapters on psychoanalysis and on personality theory and clinical psychology beyond psychoanalysis. This last chapter also includes a detailed review of existential and humanistic psychology.

In Part III, "Beyond the Schools," the chapter on physiological (particularly neurophysiological) developments emphasizes the work of Sherrington, Loewi, Lashley, Hebb, Olds, and Sperry, as well as others, many of whom are very much part of the contemporary scene. Particularly emphasized in our look at the history of intelligence testing are the contributions of Binet, Terman, and Wechsler. In our examination of psychometrics in the 20th century, we highlight the work of Thurstone, Anastasi, Cronbach, and Eysenck and discuss the development of a number of psychological assessment instruments, including the MMPI and the Rorschach test.

Our survey of social psychology examines many people, including the Allports and the Murphys. Some of the topics covered are the study of attitudes (e.g., by Hovland, Newcomb, and Sherif), obedience by Milgram, bystander "apathy" by Latané and Darley, and race and gender (e.g., by Clark, Bem, and Maccoby).

Focusing on cognitive psychology, the book's final chapter looks at early contributors (e.g., Bartlett, Vygotsky, and Piaget) and explores the work of such contemporaries as Chomsky, Bruner, Miller, and Neisser. Some of the topics of interest are memory, categorization, reasoning, and artificial intelligence.

PEDAGOGICAL FEATURES: DRAWING CONNECTIONS

To stimulate reader interest and to help students draw thematic and biographical connections, this book incorporates a number of special features.

Extensive and carefully selected illustrations. Images help bring history to life, and we have consciously tried to include such material whenever appropriate. Several of the photos are rare and show the individual at a younger age.

Chapter outlines. Each chapter begins with an outline of the chapter's major topics, giving the reader an overview of the chapter's contents.

Chronologies. The timelines at the start of each chapter are designed to orient the reader to the period of history discussed in the chapter. They enable the reader to see when the chapter's major characters lived within the context of major world events. This should facilitate seeing the connections—some substantive, others merely fascinating coincidence—among people, ideas, and the times.

Concept maps. For each of the chapters after the first, we have created a diagram that shows how the chapter's major ideas and concepts are related. Instead of including these with the chapters, we have invited the reader in an end-of-chapter question to draw his or her own concept maps and then to compare them with ours, which are located at the end of the book. The goal of the concept map is to help the reader form the all-important connections we perceive in the history of psychology.

Connections questions. To further aid the reader's development of connections in the material, we have supplied several synthetic questions—questions that draw together many related concepts—at the end of each chapter. Although the questions are not intended to be critical thinking exercises per se, they can serve much the same function.

Chapter summaries. Good summaries help reinforce the information the reader has been exposed to in the chapter. In writing the summaries, we have tried to present enough information to refresh and help organize the reader's learning without inviting laziness.

Annotated suggested readings. For the reader whose interest in the subject has been piqued by our presentation, we have provided a brief, annotated list of suggested readings for each chapter. Many of the articles/books were chosen as particularly readable examples of the work of the chapter's key individuals.

Key terms and glossary. Throughout the book, we have highlighted key terms by boldfacing them. All boldfaced terms appear in a comprehensive glossary of terms at the end of the book.

ACKNOWLEDGMENTS

At each stage of development, certain individuals played facilitating roles in this project. At Houghton Mifflin, Mike DeRocco signed the project, and Jane Knetzger nurtured us along. At home, Wanda Thorne was an early reader and Lani Lyman-Henley supplied some draft illustrations. At Mississippi State University, our department head, Steve Klein, helped us in myriad ways. Both Keith Noland and Charlie Spirrison (and several graduate assistants) tracked down source material for us. As the project matured, several reviewers provided helpful criticism. They included:

Tom Allaway, Algoma University College
C. George Boeree, Shippensburg University
Charles L. Brewer, Furman University
Gerald S. Clack, Loyola University New Orleans
Philip W. Compton, Ohio Northern University
George M. Diekhoff, Midwestern State University

Wallace E. Dixon, Heidelberg College
Charles E. Early, Roanoke College
Kathleen M. Galleher, St. Mary's University of Minnesota
Harvey J. Ginsburg, Southwest Texas State University
Bruce B. Henderson, Western Carolina University
Stephen Hoyer, Pittsburg State University
Deborah Johnson, University of Southern Maine
Donald McBurney, University of Pittsburgh
John Rickards, University of Connecticut
Michael J. Scavio, California State University, Fullerton
David J. Schneider, Rice University
Ronald D. Taylor, University of Kentucky
W. Scott Terry, The University of North Carolina at Charlotte
Catherine M. Wehlburg, Stephens College

B. Michael Thorne
Tracy B. Henley

Connections in the

History and Systems

of Psychology

Introduction

Why is the year 1879 considered so important for the history of psychology? What famous person in psychology's history wrote a serious work on the spiritual life of plants? Whose novel—*Walden Two*—popularized the behaviorist approach to learning? Whose train ride along the German Rhine led to the insights that produced Gestalt psychology? Why was the accident in which a tamping rod was blown through Phineas P. Gage's head important for psychology?

You are probably thinking that a list of questions is an odd way to open a textbook, and you are right. But hold on—we have even more questions that might pique your interest in psychology's history.

When his mind-reading experiments in children were prohibited, what famous psychologist decided to study animal intelligence, thereby producing some of psychology's most enduring and important "laws"? Why was the prefrontal lobotomy's originator, Egas Moniz, involved in only a small number of operations

when others did hundreds or even thousands? What woman was the only student in the class that first used William James's (1890) now classic *Principles of Psychology* as a textbook? Who was the first woman to earn a Ph.D. in psychology, and who directed her dissertation?

As you might imagine, there are literally thousands more questions we might ask, but a textbook devoted solely to questions would not be very informative. All of these questions will be answered in this book—at least some of them in this chapter—so you have interesting reading ahead.

WHY STUDY THE HISTORY OF PSYCHOLOGY?

Although it may be true, we do not believe that it is enough to say "This course is required to graduate, so that is why you have to take it!" Nor do we believe that tradition provides enough justification, that is, we had to suffer through history courses so you have to as well. (Actually, we *enjoyed* our history courses.) At any rate, teachers often feel an obligation to justify their courses to students, and here are some better reasons for this course.

As Harvard historian, philosopher, and poet George Santayana (Chapter 10) said, "Those who do not know history are doomed to repeat it." In other words, if we learn about the mistakes of our predecessors, perhaps we can avoid making the same or similar mistakes. But, first we have to know about the mistakes, and this requires the study of history.

For example, structuralism (Chapter 7), an approach that sought to discover the contents or elements of consciousness by using introspective analysis, is today generally considered one of psychology's digressions. Still, it was an important system both because it revealed introspection as a method of study

not to pursue and because it gave more flexible systems like functionalism (Chapter 11) and Gestalt psychology (Chapter 14) something to oppose.

Another reason we think a course in the history of psychology is important has to do with connections. Too often psychology students have little conception of how the modern ideas they are exposed to evolved, or even how the ideas are related. If there is one thing about psychology that we can say with complete assurance, it is that the field is incredibly diverse. History is the one course that cuts across all the subfields of our science and ties them together, allowing you to see the evolution of ideas within them. You begin your study of the field with a course of broad scope—introductory psychology—and we believe that near the end of your coursework you should have a similar integrative experience. By synthesizing psychology's disparate elements, a history course provides the breadth we feel you need to complete your training. In this book, we will examine topics in cognition, sensation and perception, physiological psychology, learning, intelligence testing, psychoanalysis, social psychology, developmental psychology, and other areas. We will discuss all of these different areas from the unifying perspective of history.

Finally, history is interesting in its own right. Little justification is necessary when a topic is as fascinating as the history of psychology. Like so many famous figures through the ages, most of the people who made psychology what it is had one thing in common—they were not dull. In fact, they were more often "characters" with interesting lives, amazing accomplishments, and sometimes incredible insights. We hope that our treatment of psychology's important people and their ideas will stimulate you to pursue further the study of psychology's history.

THOUGHTS ABOUT HISTORY

Unfortunately for the students of history and the writers of history textbooks, history's "facts" are often elusive and frequently cannot be verified. An event occurs and may or may not be recorded, and even when it is registered, the record may be distorted by the perspective of the recorder. To illustrate how this biasing effect can work, Albert Hastorf and Hadley Cantril (1954) conducted an important study of perspective. Their work followed that season's Dartmouth-Princeton football game. Both schools' newspapers devoted much space for several weeks after the game to the particular events surrounding the injury to the Princeton quarterback. The Princeton paper discussed Dartmouth's *clear* strategy of putting the quarterback out of commission early in the game, whereas the Dartmouth paper reported only a roughly fought, fair contest with unfortunate, but accidental, injuries. Which paper was right?

Hastorf and Cantril (1954) showed students at both schools clips of the game film and asked them a number of questions, some designed to determine which fouls, if any were "flagrant." Not surprisingly, students from the two schools reported seeing different things. Think of the last televised football game

you watched. If you supported a particular team and there was a controversial play, your perception of the play probably favored your team. The same thing is true of many historical facts—they were recorded by people with perspectives that probably influenced their perceptions.

As one example, much of what the modern world knows of the psychology of Wilhelm Wundt (Chapter 7), the man usually credited with founding psychology as a science in 1879, comes from the writings of one of psychology's most famous historians, **Edwin Garrigues Boring** (1886–1968). Did Boring write an unbiased record of the historical facts available to him? The answer is almost certainly no. Boring (1950) dedicated his classic work, *A History of Experimental Psychology,* to his mentor, Edward Bradford Titchener (Chapter 7). Titchener received his Ph.D. under Wundt and modeled his psychology after what he perceived as the most important aspects of his teacher's system. Actually, Titchener adopted only a part of Wundt's system and downplayed or ignored much of the rest. Influenced by Titchener, Boring perpetuated this restricted view of Wundt, which has only recently been revised (e.g., Blumenthal, 1979; Danziger, 1979; Leahey, 1981).

Our point here is not to criticize unduly Boring's most important work but rather to recognize some of the sources of bias that can infect any historian's efforts. One nearly ubiquitous form is called the **presentist bias**. That is, there is always the tendency to discuss and analyze past ideas, people, and events in terms of the present. For example, if we refer to a past psychologist (e.g., Titchener) as a male chauvinist—as someone who treated his female students less seriously than their male counterparts—we are imposing our present sensitivities on a bygone era. We are forgetting that during most of our history such bias against women (religions, ethnic groups) was the cultural norm, and the person we are describing was probably just reflecting the milieu in which he or she lived.

Also, any history textbook will reflect the idiosyncrasies of its author(s). That is, the authors decide to include and emphasize certain events, ideas, topics, and people and to ignore or deemphasize others. A classic work by a philosopher of science, Thomas Kuhn (1970), suggested a reason for this phenomenon of history.

Kuhn (1970) wrote that once a particular theory has become widely accepted, proponents of that theory receive a certain degree of power. By controlling the journals that publish current research, they are in a position to downplay competing theories. Proponents of the dominant theory may also write the textbooks (including history texts) for that generation. An analysis of psychology textbooks shows omissions and highlightings in keeping with the theoretical leanings of the writer(s) (Henley, Johnson, Herzog, & Jones, 1989). Historical segments in some textbooks suggest that past theories were merely stepping-stones to the modern "correct" way of thinking. However, Kuhn believes that there is little evidence for this stepwise ideal of how history marches forward. Such depictions of history's progress are often historical fictions intended to lend credibility to existing ideas.

We admit our own agendas in selecting material to include in this text. We are biased in favor of the famous (and infamous) people important in psychology's history. We are biased in favor of interesting and colorful material, although we have provided appropriate coverage of other less interesting, but undeniably important, facts in the history of our field. We are biased in favor of people and events that seem relevant to contemporary American psychology, although we appreciate that many parallel insights arose in the East (e.g., China, Japan). We are somewhat biased in favor of the *Zeitgeist* (spirit of the times) theory of history, and this is why the first word in our title is "Connections." In other words, we believe that discoveries, new ideas, and inventions do not arise in a vacuum and that it is important to place them in historical perspective. Our effort to provide historical perspective is evident in the chronologies at the beginning of each chapter following this one, in the sample concept maps collected at the end of the book, and in the Connections Questions posed after every chapter. Still, despite our bias in favor of the *Zeitgeist* theory, the text is primarily organized around people.

Boring (1950) argued persuasively for the *Zeitgeist*, or, as he sometimes called it, the naturalistic theory of history, as opposed to the personalistic, or great person, view. Are important historical contributions the sole property of great minds, or do great minds make such contributions because of the cultural and intellectual context in which they find themselves? For example, was Wundt the founder of psychology as a separate scientific discipline because of his genius, or would psychology have arisen as a science in the late 19th century even if Wundt had chosen to remain a politician?

There is much evidence to support the idea that the latter part of the 19th century was the right time for the birth of scientific psychology. For example, Franz Brentano (Chapter 8), Wundt's contemporary, had a competing system based on his *Psychologie vom empirischen Standpunkte* (*Psychology from an Empirical Standpoint*), which was published in 1874, the same year Wundt finished publishing his work calling for a separate science of psychology, *Grundzüge der physiologischen Psychologie* (*Principles of Physiological Psychology*).

Further evidence favoring the *Zeitgeist* theory includes independent contributions occurring at nearly the same time. For example, calculus was developed (ca. 1675) independently by Gottfried Wilhelm von Leibniz and Sir Isaac Newton (both Chapter 3). The spur that goaded Charles Darwin (Chapter 9) to publish his theory of evolution in 1859 was a paper sent to him the year before by Alfred Russel Wallace (Chapter 9), a young naturalist. In the paper, Wallace outlined a theory remarkably similar to the one on which Darwin had labored for 20 years. In a letter to a friend dated June 18, 1858, the day on which Wallace's paper arrived, Darwin wrote: "[I]f Wallace had my MS. sketch written out in 1842, he could not have made a better short abstract! Even his terms now stand as heads of my chapters" (Darwin, 1898, p. 473).

Additional evidence for the naturalistic theory of history comes from ideas that foundered or had to be "rediscovered" because the intellectual climate was not right for their acceptance. For example, consider the use of systematic desensitization as a method for removing pathological fears. (In systematic desensitization, the person being treated is gradually exposed in a nonthreatening context either to ideas of the feared object or to the feared object itself.) John Locke (1693/1964; Chapter 4) gave instructions for the removal of "vain terrors" in children that sound remarkably like the method "discovered" by Joseph

Wolpe (Chapter 4) in 1958 and actually used by Mary Cover Jones (and reported by John Watson, 1928; Chapter 12) in removing a child's fears of white, furry animals.

According to Boring (1950), "You get the personalistic view when you ignore the [antecedents] of the great man, and you get the naturalistic view back again when you ask what made the great man great" (p. 4). We will ask what made the great person great in our look at the history of psychology. That is, we will explore wherever possible the "connections" between one person's great idea and the ideas of his or her predecessors and contemporaries. Note that what Boring (and others) called the "great man" view we are calling the "great person" approach. We strongly believe that women have also shaped the history of psychology. Wherever possible, we will discuss the contributions of women who have often been omitted in other treatments of psychology's history.

Yet another problem in writing about history is that historical facts are not like scientific facts; we cannot verify them experimentally. All we have to go on are the writings of observers at the time or the later writings of people who got their "evidence" by word of mouth, from people's memories of the events. Sometimes the observers were the people themselves—that is, the writings are autobiographical. But how accurate are autobiographies?

Although getting the words directly from the source would seem to be ideal, there are several reasons why autobiographical material might be distorted. For example, most people write autobiographies long after the events they record have taken place. Human memory is notoriously fallible and often changes with the passage of time.

Events and sequences of events are often remembered as being "better"—more orderly—than they really were. That is, an autobiographer may inadvertently "clean up" certain memories to make the narrative of his or her life history more cohesive. Modern cognitive psychologists (Chapter 20) have studied autobiographical memories, including our tendency to "re-construct," as opposed to "re-view," the information we remember. These reconstructions can change our memory based on events in the present or during the intervening period.

Although these effects have been known for a long time (Bartlett, 1932), modern research on the topic is particularly illuminating. For example, Ulric Neisser's (1982) book, *Memory Observed,* presents research that shows this influence in everyday events. In one study, subjects were asked to recall whether they saw any broken glass in a film of an automobile accident. Subjects who were asked if they saw glass after the two cars "smashed" said yes 32% of the time, whereas subjects who were asked if they saw glass after the two cars "hit" said yes only 14% of the time. Actually, there was no broken glass in the film (see Loftus & Palmer, 1974, for the complete study).

In addition, much of what we remember relates to us. Because we have a set of beliefs about ourselves, our memory of autobiographical events tends to conform to our self-perceptions, even when they conflict with what actually happened. If you have watched reruns of "The Andy Griffith Show," you may have noticed that one recurrent theme was for Andy's blundering deputy, Barney, to cause a series of disasters that allowed a crook to escape. Invariably, Andy would catch the crook and save Barney from his folly. How did Barney remember the events? In his retelling at the end of the show, he was always the hero. Was Barney consciously pulling our legs, or did he remember the events differently? According to Neisser's research, we tend to remember information in ways that support our self-image. Furthermore, we may unconsciously reorganize information to make it consistent with beliefs about how we should have acted in a given situation.

It is also possible for autobiographical material to present events in a poorer light than they deserve. For example, written at the end of his life, G. Stanley Hall's (Chapter 10) autobiography (Hall, 1923) perhaps reflects in its bitterness the author's age and health. Likewise, we know that Wundt's autobiography contained several factual errors (Hilgard, 1987), and to hear John Watson (1936)—one of the central figures of American behaviorism (Chapter 12)—tell it, it is a miracle he ever finished college.

So, historical facts may become distorted by the people involved, and sometimes this may even be recognized at the time the autobiography is written. For example, pharmacologist Otto Loewi (Chapter 17) wrote at the beginning of an autobiographical sketch:

"An advantage of autobiography may be that its author reports more competently than others on his inner experience and its effects; yet, even so, fiction may come into play because a retrospective report may not always truly reflect the past as it happened" (Loewi, 1960, p. 3).

Recognizing the limitations of biographical and autobiographical material, Innes (1969) suggested that biographies and autobiographies should contain extensive details about the family life and social background of the subject. This perhaps excessive detail is necessary for future historians to examine the effects of the early environment on a person's subsequent life and thought. Although we certainly have not included as much biographical detail on major individuals as you would find in dedicated biographies, we have tried to present enough information to give you at least the flavor of the life and times of the individual.

Before we leave our "thoughts about history," we should temper our discussion of the difficulties of verifying the truth of historical facts by noting that the answer to much of the problem lies in the use of multiple sources and methods. For example, even though much of Watson's (1936) autobiographical essay is negative in tone, we can assess the truth or falsity of what he wrote by examining archival material that may be available, by perusing the excellent Watson biographies, by reading other contemporary writings by Watson and others, and so forth. In other words, even though any given source may be biased or just plain inaccurate, the historian often does not have to depend on a single source of information. The list of references at the end of this book gives a hint of the myriad sources available for the student in search of historical "truth."

For further discussion of some of the issues involved in writing about the history of psychology, see Hilgard, Leary, and McGuire (1991). In addition to E. G. Boring, any list of noteworthy historians of psychology would have to include **Robert I. Watson** (1909–1980) and **Ernest R. Hilgard** (1905–). Among other contributions, Watson implemented the first doctoral degree program in the history of psychology in the United States at the University of New Hampshire in 1967, helped plan the Archives of the History of American Psychology, and aided in launching the *Journal of the History of the Behavioral*

Sciences, an invaluable source of information on the history of psychology and other behavioral sciences (Ross, 1981). Perhaps Hilgard's most important contribution to the field is his monumental *Psychology in America: A Historical Survey* (Hilgard, 1987).

WHERE DO WE START?

Lapointe (1970) studied the evolution of the term *psychology* and traced the word to Melanchthon in the 16th century, although the Greek root *psyche* is clearly much older. So, where should we start our look at the history of psychology? We could start with the 1879 founding of psychology's first experimental laboratory by Wilhelm Wundt or with the 1816 publication of Johann Friedrich Herbart's *Lehrbuch zur Psychologie* (*Textbook of Psychology*), which is often considered the first textbook in psychology.

Perhaps we should journey back even farther to the time of René Descartes (Chapter 3), the philosopher/mathematician who is associated with the period historians consider the beginning of the "modern era" (17th century). In the work of the ancient Greeks, we can find the antecedents of many contemporary ideas, as we will illustrate in Chapter 2. But why start with the Greeks? It is possible to imagine prehistoric people studying the behavior of prey animals (and predators, as well). In that sense, prehistoric people were the first comparative psychologists. In addition, early men and women undoubtedly studied the behavior of their fellows, making them all psychologists of a sort.

In fact, the Cambridge ethologist Nicholas Humphrey (1983) suggested that modern humans should perhaps be known as *Homo psychologicus* rather than *Homo sapiens*. Humphrey argued that what makes humans different from all other animals is their ability to decipher what other humans must be feeling and thinking both by studying their behavior and by imagining what it would be like to be in their position. Indeed, Humphrey believes that consciousness evolved just for the capacity to "do psychology."

But prehistoric is, after all, *pre*historic. We obviously cannot begin our look at the history of psychology before recorded history began. Still, the idea that humans have always been interested in psychological topics is nicely captured in Hermann Ebbinghaus's (1910) famous quotation from his *Abriss der Psychologie* (*A Summary of Psychology*): "Psychology has a long past, but only a short history" (p. 9). The "long past" referred to thought about psychological topics throughout recorded history, whereas "short history" recognized the founding of psychology as a distinct scientific discipline in the latter half of the 19th century. Unfortunately, Ebbinghaus's own history came to an untimely end in 1909 with his death from pneumonia at the age of 59 (Chapter 8).

As we hinted above, we will begin our look at psychology's history with the ancient Greeks. Many of them were concerned with questions and topics that are still debated by modern psychologists. Some of the questions they tried to answer were: What are the senses, and how do they work? What (and where) is the mind, and how is it related to the body? What are the principles of human learning and memory? Are there chemical (humoral) causes for human behavior? What are the relative contributions of nature (heredity) and nurture (the environment) to behavior? Next, we will take a further look at some of these ancient questions and recurring issues.

SOME OF PSYCHOLOGY'S RECURRING ISSUES

In the history of psychology, many issues have surfaced repeatedly and have led to much debate. Some of the main ones are the **mind-body problem,** **reductionism** versus **nonreductionism,** and the **nature-nurture controversy.** Each of these issues has a rich history and, in some modern guise, remains with us today.

The Mind-Body Problem

Some philosophers have suggested that people have both a body and a mind; others have contended that there is only body or only mind. If there is both a body and a mind, are they connected or are they separate? The issue has often had religious overtones—in some languages the words for mind and soul are the same. Because the body is obviously mortal, a belief in immortality requires a soul (mind). The various "solutions" to the mind-body problem generally fall into two categories: monism and dualism.

Monism assumes that there is only one underlying reality, either mind or body, but not both. The major forms of monism are materialism and mentalism. **Materialism** assumes that the only underlying reality is physical; there is only body. Critics of this position say that the materialists have lost their minds. From ancient times, Democritus (ca. 400 B.C.; Chapter 2) exemplifies this position, and the claim that all thought and action can be reduced to the electrochemical activity of the brain is a more recent example. **Mentalism** (also called **immaterialism** or **subjective idealism**) is a version of monism that holds that reality ultimately exists in the mind. Without a mind to perceive it, the physical world is irrelevant (or perhaps does not exist). Although this position can be traced to antiquity, modern versions are often based on the writings of the philosopher George Berkeley (ca. 1710; Chapter 4). Other mentalists want to maintain a primary role for the mind but also acknowledge the brain's importance, which makes them dualists of one sort or another.

Dualism is the mind-body position that says that both mind and body exist. The major forms of dualism are interactionism and parallelism. Another mind-body position, double aspectism, is sometimes classified as a form of dualism and sometimes as a form of monism, which illustrates that the categories are not always mutually exclusive. **Interactionism** is the position that mind and body are separate, but they interact. Mind can influence body and vice versa, according to this solution's chief proponent, René Descartes (ca. 1640).

Parallelism, or **psychophysical parallelism,** is the view that mind and body are separate entities that do not interact. They appear to interact because they are perfectly constructed and are set into motion at the same time. The analogy often given is of two perfect clocks started simultaneously; they would always have the same time even though they have no effect on each other. Psychophysical parallelism was the position taken by Gottfried Wilhelm von Leibniz (ca. 1695).

Double aspectism is the mind-body solution that holds that mind and body are just two aspects of the same thing, like the obverse and reverse of a coin. From this definition, you can probably see the difficulty in classifying the solution. Mind and body both exist simultaneously; they are inseparable without interacting. This position was originally proposed by Baruch Spinoza (ca. 1665; Chapter 3).

There are several other positions on the mind-body problem, but probably the most interesting of these is epiphenomenalism. Closely related to materialism, **epiphenomenalism** holds that the brain's activity produces mind as a sort of by-product. The mind does not influence the brain or behavior any more than the noise of a car's engine influences the way it runs. The origin of epiphenomenalism is often attributed to Thomas Hobbes (Chapter 4), and a variety of contemporary versions are popular today.

The mind-body positions we have presented here do not exhaust the possibilities but may exhaust the reader. (If not, a good source for further reading is Paul Churchland's [1988] *Matter and Consciousness,* which is further described in the suggested readings.) In fact, so many different views exist, and so much time has been devoted to their discussion, that some philosophers (e.g., Ryle, 1949; Wittgenstein, 1953) have wondered whether the whole mind-body issue is simply a "bad" question.

Reductionism versus Nonreductionism

The main idea of **reductionism** is to look for increasingly more basic explanations of psychological phenomena, whereas **nonreductionism** takes the position that psychological phenomena should stand on their own, without the need for biological or biochemical explanations. For example, suppose a rat learns a maze. A nonreductionist would say it is sufficient to explain the rat's behavior in terms of stimuli in the maze, the responses the animal makes to those stimuli, the presence or absence of rewards, and so forth. By contrast, a reductionist would look for the brain areas involved in the behavior and, once those were found, would perhaps search for the transmitter substances involved in the activity.

Physiological psychologists are reductionists, and many of them would argue that psychology is just a branch of biology. By contrast, the Gestalt psychologists tended toward nonreductionism, believing that behavior should be studied as intact, meaningful wholes and rejecting the search for simpler, more elemental explanations.

The Nature-Nurture Controversy

There are many other terms related to this long-standing issue: nativism-empiricism, heredity-environment, innate-learned, and so forth. The basic question is, How much of behavior is instinctive or unlearned, and how much is learned or acquired through experience with the environment?

Actually, the most extreme positions have been taken by **nurturists**, people who argued for the nurture, or learning side, of the issue. For example, John Locke viewed the mind as "white paper" on which experience writes. John Watson and other behaviorists were also outspoken proponents of the nurture idea.

Nativists, by contrast, have usually taken less extreme positions in the discussion, often accepting that much of behavior is indeed learned while pointing to elements that seem innate. For example, René Descartes believed that most of the mind's ideas come from experience, but he also thought that some ideas are so clear and perfect that they have to be innate, put there by God. Examples of Descartes's innate ideas included unity, infinity, the geometrical axioms, and God. Others of interest to psychology who are generally classified as nativists include Socrates and Plato (Chapter 2), Leibniz, Kant (Chapter 5), and such relatively recent psychologists as William McDougall (Chapter 12), Eleanor Gibson (Chapter 13), and the Gestalt psychologists.

All of these issues have been important elements in the history of psychology and especially in its philosophical past. Even today, psychologists can be characterized by their stances on the debates we have introduced here. Particularly in Part I of this book—because of its primary focus on psychology's philosophical antecedents—we will make explicit connections between theorists and these thematic issues. To a lesser extent, we will continue to make such connections in Parts II and III. As you learn more about where thinkers of the past have stood on the different issues, you may want to begin to consider your positions on the various questions.

ORGANIZATION OF THE BOOK

A history of psychology textbook could be organized in many different ways. For example, we might take a strictly chronological approach, beginning at some time in the distant past (460 B.C., perhaps, because that was about the time that the Greek philosopher Anaxagoras introduced the concept of *nous*, or mind) and working our way by centuries at first and then by decades until we come to the present day. Unfortunately, this would be an unsatisfactory way to look at history, because in taking a strictly chronological approach we would probably miss history's patterns.

The approach we will use is roughly chronological, emphasizing the contributions of important people in the history of philosophy, psychology, and science in general. We will begin our survey with the ancient Greeks, and our organization after the beginnings of scientific psychology will focus on psychology's major systems and schools. Although the terms *system* and *school* are often used interchangeably, a distinction can be made. A **system** refers to a collection of ideas defining what is psychological and the methods that will be used to study the psychological, whereas a **school** consists of the people who more or less agree with the system. For example, the system of structuralism—as the term is used in the history of psychology—defined psychology as the study of the contents of the conscious mind of normal adult humans using introspection. The school of structuralism consisted of all psychologists who agreed with the system (e.g., Titchener).

As psychology grew and matured, its systems and schools became so diffuse that today they no longer exist. Thus, when we finish discussing the last of the great schools, we will then take a look at more recent history in the context of several important topics in the 20th century. Still, at the beginning of scientific psychology, the systems and their associat-

ed schools held sway, with most developing in opposition to one or ones already in place. Most standard history texts cover and define the classical systems of psychology as follows:

Structuralism. Using introspection, psychology should study the contents of adult, human consciousness, searching for the irreducible elements that comprise consciousness.

Functionalism. Psychology should study the functions of mind and behavior in the context of the organism's adaptation to the environment.

Behaviorism. Using objective methods, psychology should study the behavior of the organism in relation to its environment.

Gestalt psychology. Psychologists should study and discover useful and meaningful laws about the relations between parts and wholes of experience.

Psychoanalysis. Psychology should study personality and motivation, recognizing that much of it is unconscious and concerned with power and sex. The methods include the analysis of dreams, errors, and free associations.

Of the major systems, functionalism and Gestalt psychology developed in opposition to structuralism—which itself grew out of Wundt's system called voluntarism—whereas behaviorism developed in opposition to both structuralism and functionalism.

We would like to end this chapter with a tale of the rise and fall of the prefrontal lobotomy. Although we have read Ken Kesey's *One Flew Over the Cuckoo's Nest* (and enjoyed the movie of the same name) and shudder at the thought of a lobotomy, the following story illustrates how fascinating the history of psychology can be. However, despite the anecdote's interest value, there are definitely cautionary messages to be drawn from it. One message is that premature application to humans of techniques taken from animal research may have devastating consequences. Another message is that treatments for mental disorders should not be adopted in wholesale fashion until their effectiveness and safety have been thoroughly studied. The obvious moral is that history can—and should—be both mesmerizing and educational at the same time.

EGAS MONIZ AND THE PREFRONTAL LOBOTOMY

In 1935, **Egas Moniz** (1874–1955), a Portuguese neurologist, heard a conference paper about the effects of frontal lobe damage on a memory task in chimpanzees. The damage caused poor performance in the chimps, but what most fascinated Moniz was the probably incidental comment by presenter Carlyle Jacobsen that one chimpanzee was more manageable postoperatively (i.e., the operation had a "taming" effect). Later, Moniz (1956) claimed that hearing of the animal work had nothing to do with his introduction of the prefrontal lobotomy—that he had been thinking of trying that kind of treatment on mental patients long before 1935.

Nevertheless, not long after the conference, Moniz and Almeida Lima performed the first **prefrontal lobotomies**—brain operations in which the prefrontal lobes were severed from other brain areas—on humans. In 1936, Moniz published a report on the results from his first 20 patients, claiming that 7 were cured, 7 were improved, and 6 were unchanged. The best results were obtained with depressed patients with agitation; schizophrenics were not helped.

From this beginning, lobotomy became a widely used technique for treating the mentally ill. One of the leading popularizers of the new technique was the American neuropsychiatrist, **Walter Freeman** (1895–1972), who, along with the neurosurgeon James Watts, performed over 1,000 operations by 1950. Before his retirement, Freeman claimed to have done more than 3,500 lobotomies.

In 1949, Moniz (Figure 1–1) shared the Nobel Prize in Physiology and Medicine "for his discovery of the therapeutic value of prefrontal [lobotomy] in certain psychoses" (Valenstein, 1973, p. 54).

The incidence of prefrontal lobotomies peaked in the late 1940s and declined precipitously in the mid-1950s. Some interesting historical questions we might ask at this point are: Why did the operation become so popular? What contributed to its rapid demise? Also, it is noteworthy that Moniz himself was only involved in about 100 operations. Why did the originator of this new treatment method do so few operations?

One of the main reasons for the popularity of the prefrontal lobotomy is that when it was introduced,

FIGURE 1–1. Egas Moniz, the originator of the prefrontal lobotomy.

Source: National Library of Medicine.

there were no effective methods for treating severely disturbed mental patients. World War II produced many psychiatric casualties, and army and Veterans Administration hospitals contained a large number of patients who seemed to be permanently insane. An efficient, beneficial technique was badly needed, and the prefrontal lobotomy seemed to fulfill the need.

Additionally, the medical community may have embraced the lobotomy quickly because Moniz was a prestigious scientist. In 1927, he had developed cerebral angiography, a method for visualizing the brain through X-ray pictures following the injection of a dye into the brain's arteries.

Another reason for the rapid growth in lobotomies was that neurosurgery was relatively new as a separate medical specialty. As Valenstein (1980) put it, "[T]he field of neurosurgery was particularly responsive to influence from a small number of its more prominent members, who persuaded their fellow neurosurgeons that [lobotomies] produced desirable results and that there was a reasonably good scientific rationale to explain why these operations worked" (p. 25).

Given its rapid growth, why did the operation decline so rapidly in the mid-1950s? We would like to be able to say that negative side effects—some of the most common were seizures, partial paralysis, incontinence, and huge weight gain—and mortality rates ranging up to 6% convinced neurosurgeons to give up the practice. However, the truth is that the introduction of the first effective antipsychotic drug, chlorpromazine, was primarily responsible for the dramatic decline in the use of lobotomies.

If Walter Freeman did over 3,500 lobotomies, why did Moniz do no more than 100? The answer is that Moniz was rendered a paraplegic by a bullet wound to the spine—he was shot by a patient who had had a prefrontal lobotomy! If you look back at the beginning of this story, you will note that what most intrigued Moniz about the operation was that it had a "taming" effect on a chimpanzee.

The story also illustrates how the details of history can be distorted. A recent edition of a popular introductory psychology textbook claimed, for example, that Moniz and Freeman shared the Nobel Prize (McConnell & Philipchalk, 1992). Our purpose here is not to criticize the authors but merely to show how easy it is for errors of fact to creep into lengthy works produced by human beings. Actually, Moniz shared the Nobel Prize with W. R. Hess, a neuroscientist who did pioneering work with electrical brain stimulation in animals. More of a showman than a scientist, Freeman once performed an operation with a hammer and an ice pick for shock value and is rumored to have worked with gold-plated instruments.

CONCLUSIONS

We have tried to stimulate your interest in this introductory chapter, and we have also provided you with some thoughts on history in general and the history of psychology in particular. Because we have introduced some important terms and ideas, you will find a summary at the end of the chapter (and in other chapters) to underscore the material covered. In addition, we mentioned quite a few important people (Wundt, Ebbinghaus, Descartes, etc.), and we will have much more to say about most of them later.

The question might be raised at this point, Is the history of psychology about ideas, events, or people? For us, it is about all three. Although it is possible to write a history of psychology that emphasizes ideas while deemphasizing the lives and historical times of the people with the ideas, we feel that such a history misses both what is important for understanding the context in which the ideas arose and what makes the historical figures real to the reader. We have tried to strike a balance in our presentation, sketching the lives and times of the most important figures in psychology's history while covering their major ideas in some depth.

We have provided a glossary of terms and names at the end of the book that includes all the boldfaced items from this and the remaining chapters. Finally, in case we have you hooked on the history of psychology, we have included a set of suggested readings about some of the more interesting topics and people we have discussed in this chapter.

S U M M A R Y

Why Study the History of Psychology?

Reasons to study the history of psychology include the idea that people who do not know history are likely to repeat the mistakes of the past, the fact that a history course can integrate many of the disparate elements in psychology, and the idea that the history of psychology is interesting.

Thoughts about History

History's "facts" are often elusive and hard to verify. One reason for this is that historians are often biased reporters. Autobiographies may be biased as well, either because of a person's faulty memory or because the person, consciously or unconsciously, makes the story different than it actually was.

This text somewhat favors the *Zeitgeist,* or spirit of the times, theory of history in contrast to the great person viewpoint, although the book will contain much information on psychology's "great people," as well. Although the truth about the lives and ideas of people important for psychology is sometimes difficult to verify, the answer to much of the problem lies in using multiple sources and methods in historical research.

Where Do We Start?

Candidates for where to start our look at psychology include Wundt's 1879 founding of psychology's first experimental laboratory and Herbart's first textbook of psychology. However, remembering Ebbinghaus's famous statement, "Psychology has a long past, but only a short history," we will begin with the ancient Greeks because they tried to answer many questions that are still with us today.

Some of Psychology's Recurring Issues

Some of psychology's recurring issues are the mind-body problem, reductionism versus nonreductionism, and the nature-nurture controversy. We will revisit these issues in many places in the book.

The main positions taken on the mind-body problem were monism—there is only one underlying reality, either mind (mentalism) or body (materialism)—and dualism. Dualism is the mind-body solution that says that both mind and body exist. The mind and the body either interact (interactionism) or they do not interact (psychophysical parallelism). Double aspectism is the solution that holds that mind and body are two aspects of the same thing, like the two sides of a coin. Epiphenomenalism is a mind-body position that holds that the brain's activity produces mind as a by-product.

Reductionists look for increasingly elemental explanations for psychological phenomena, whereas nonreductionists believe that psychological phenomena can stand on their own, without the need for more elemental explanations. The nature-nurture controversy is concerned with the extent to which behavior patterns are instinctive or inherited (nature) or are learned through interaction with the environment (nurture).

Organization of the Book

The organization of this text is roughly chronological, looking at psychology's development from the Greeks through the major systems or schools of psychology. A psychological system is a collection of ideas defining what is psychological and the methods that will be used to study it, whereas a school consists of the people who display allegiance to the system. The classical systems of psychology include structuralism, functionalism, behaviorism, Gestalt psychology, and psychoanalysis.

Egas Moniz and the Prefrontal Lobotomy

In 1935, Egas Moniz introduced the prefrontal lobotomy as a method for treating mental patients. Lobotomy was widely adopted mainly because there was nothing better available at the time, although a variety of problems soon became apparent. The introduction of the major antipsychotic drugs in the 1950s resulted in a rapid decline in the use of prefrontal lobotomies. Although the story illustrates the fascinating nature of the history of psychology, it also contains a cautionary message.

SUGGESTED READINGS

Churchland, P. (1988). *Matter and consciousness: A contemporary introduction to the philosophy of mind.* Cambridge, MA: MIT Press. This is an extremely readable book with excellent coverage of the mind-body problem and many other issues related to "philosophical" psychology.

Hilgard, E. R., Leary, D. E., & McGuire, G. R. (1991). The history of psychology: A survey and critical assessment. *Annual Review of Psychology, 42,* 79–107. This is an excellent overview of the approaches to the study of psychology's history and of the outstanding people who have studied that history.

Kuhn, T. (1970). *The structure of scientific revolutions* (Rev. ed.). Chicago: University of Chicago Press. This is the classic work on the nature of science. It is also a good starting point if you are interested in the topic, and we will revisit it in Chapter 20.

Neisser, U. (1982). *Memory observed.* San Francisco: Freeman. Although somewhat dated, this anthology contains many of the finest works pertaining to the psychology of memory. Original studies on reconstructive memory, in addition to other fascinating topics, can be found in *Memory Observed.*

Valenstein, E. S. (1973). *Brain control.* New York: Wiley.

Valenstein, E. S. (Ed.) (1980). *The psychosurgery debate.* San Francisco: Freeman. Entertainingly written, *Brain Control* and *The Psychosurgery Debate* will tell you everything you ever wanted to know about the history of psychosurgery.

Philosophical and Physiological Beginnings

In Chapter 1, we discussed some of the reasons why it is important to study the history of psychology (e.g., ignorance of history can lead to needless repetition, history is interesting in its own right), some of the issues and problems facing writers of history textbooks (e.g., biased reporting of historical events), some of psychology's recurring themes (e.g., the mind-body problem, nature vs. nurture), and where to start an examination of the past. We also indicated that we would begin our coverage of psychology's history with a discussion of the ancient Greeks.

One reason for starting with the Greeks is that they left a substantial body of literature that allows us to construct a reasonable portrait of their lives and their thought. That is, unlike the legions of undoubtedly fascinating *prehistoric* people, the ancient Greeks are historical figures. In addition, the Greeks are important for our look at the beginnings of psychology because in much of their work we can find topics and speculation about those topics that today we would recognize as being truly psychological. For example, Aristotle wrote about such phenomena as learning, motivation, dreaming, and the contents of the mind at birth. Finally, we can also find in the ancient Greeks the beginnings of thinking about psychology's perennial issues, such as reductionism versus nonreductionism.

In Chapter 3, we will explore the progress of philosophy and of science through the Roman period, the Middle ages, and particularly the Renaissance. We will examine in detail the lives and thinking of René Descartes, Baruch Spinoza, and Gottfried Wilhelm von Leibniz. Because of his many important and original contributions and his break with the philosophies of the past, Descartes is the major transitional figure between the "ancient" and the "modern" worlds.

In Chapters 4 and 5, we will consider further the major philosophical antecedents to the development of psychology as a discipline. Chapter 4 will examine the empirical approach to science and the mind, both in its British and French incarnations, which is contrasted with Chapter 5's focus on the various rationalistic philosophies. The empiricist-rationalist debate to some extent continues in the tension between modern behaviorists and cognitive psychologists.

As we will see in Part II, the birth of the science of psychology resulted from the union of philosophy and physiology. Because of this, it is fitting that the first chapter in Part I, devoted to the ancient Greeks, looks at both philosophy and physiology, the middle chapters focus on philosophy, whereas the final chapter (6) examines the major developments in physiology that helped establish psychology as a separate science.

Precursors to Psychology in Ancient Greece

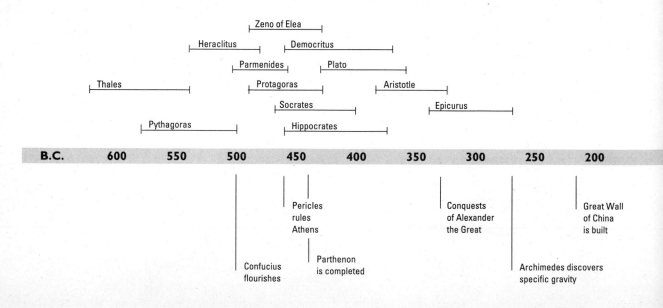

THE GOLDEN AGE OF GREECE

Although some historians of psychology devote little or no attention to ancient philosophers and physiologists, there are several important reasons why we have elected to put them first. For example, scholars in many other disciplines (e.g., physics, physiology, philosophy) recognize the pre-Socratic Greeks as the authors of the oldest body of ideas clearly related to philosophy and science. Although older sources exist, and some of them may even be of interest to psychology (e.g., Laver, 1972), for the most part they concern religious, accounting, or political matters.

A more substantive reason—which gives the connection between ancient philosophy and physiology and modern psychology—is that the basic categories, questions, and foundations for subsequent Western thought are first articulated in the work of the Greeks. For example, many have observed (e.g., Lakoff, 1987)

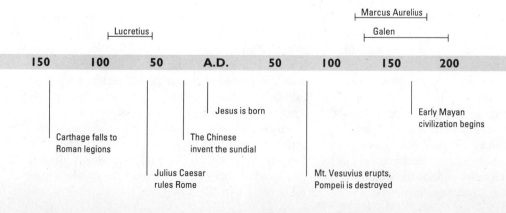

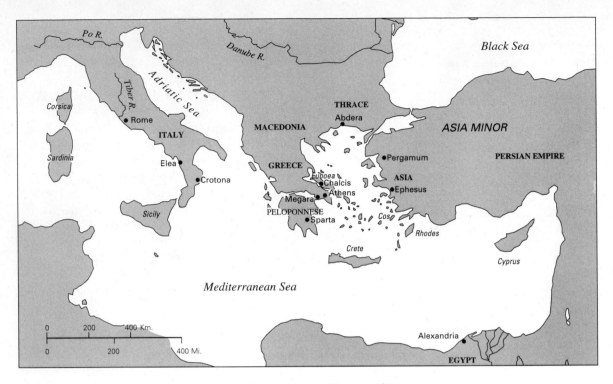

FIGURE 2–1.   Map of ancient Greece and its outposts.
Although this map does not correspond to any specific date, it is representative of Greece's Golden Age.

that the basic categories that organize thinking in the Western world (i.e., distinctions such as living and dead, plant and animal, real and imaginary) are not recognized by all cultures. Such distinctions at the heart of modern Western science originated in the speculations of the pre-Socratic philosophers.

In Chapter 1, we noted that the history of psychology, particularly the earlier and more philosophical history, can be viewed in terms of several key issues. In contemporary terms, the issues are the mind-body problem, the nature-nurture controversy, and so forth. Virtually all of these issues were first considered by the ancient Greeks, and the outline of the answers adopted by modern philosophers and scientists can often be found in their writings.

Of particular interest to us in psychology, some of the first speculations about such topics as motivation, learning, sensation and perception, and personality can be found in the teachings of the ancients. We encourage you to look for what might be recognizable as truly psychological material in our

survey of the classical contributions to philosophy and in our review of the early advances in physiology and medicine.

Thales (ca. 624–545 B.C.), often considered the "first" Greek philosopher, nicely illustrates the search for knowledge that became philosophy and science. Thales proposed the first natural (as opposed to supernatural) explanation for the universe, with his belief that water is the essence of all things. A talented thinker, Thales used mathematics to predict a solar eclipse. This feat earned him popular acclaim and demonstrated that a knowledge of nature brought power over the environment. This search for knowledge soon blossomed in the period called the **Golden Age of Greece**. Figure 2–1 shows a map of ancient Greece and its outposts.

Historian Will Durant (1939) considered the century and a half between the birth of the ruler Pericles (ca. 490 B.C.) and the death of the philosopher Aristotle (322 B.C.) the most memorable period in the history of the world. We will use some of Durant's thoughts as color commentary to our consideration of this period.

Born of distinguished parents, **Pericles** (ca. 490–429 B.C.) was carefully educated. He heard the lectures of the philosopher Zeno of Elea (discussed later) and studied with the philosopher Anaxagoras (ca. 500–428 B.C.), who was prosecuted for arguing that the sun was a red-hot mass of rock at a time when the sun was a god to many. Under Pericles' rule, Athens enjoyed the privileges of both democracy and a benign dictatorship. "History through [Pericles] illustrated again the principle that liberal reforms are most ably executed . . . by the cautious and moderate leadership of an aristocrat enjoying popular support. Greek civilization was at its best when democracy had grown sufficiently to give it variety and vigor, and aristocracy survived sufficiently to give it order and taste" (Durant, 1939, p. 249).

Sparta, Athens's chief rival, was in disarray from internal problems and natural disasters. Because the struggle between Greece and Persia flared up periodically, for their protection the Greek cities organized the Delian Confederacy under Athenian leadership (477 B.C.). Through its sea power, Athens soon dominated its allies, and the Confederacy became the Athenian Empire.

PHILOSOPHY IN THE GOLDEN AGE

Greek philosophy reached its zenith in the age of Pericles, and "in Periclean Athens the 'dear delight' of philosophy captured the imagination of the educated classes; . . . philosophers were lionized, and clever arguments were applauded like sturdy blows at the Olympic games" (Durant, 1939, p. 349). One important philosophical debate contrasted the theories of materialism and idealism. As we noted in Chapter 1, materialism is the belief that matter is the only reality and that the universe, including thoughts and feelings, can be explained only in terms of matter. By contrast, **idealism (immaterialism, mentalism)** is the view that ideas are the ultimate reality (hence idea-lism) and it is impossible to know whether reality exists apart from the mind. The debate between materialism and idealism in

many ways is the foundation for the tension between empirical and rational conceptions of psychology explored in Chapter 8.

Pythagoras and the Pythagoreans

In the 6th century B.C., **Pythagoras** (ca. 580–500 B.C.) founded a mystical cult society in which philosophy and mathematics constituted a lifestyle aimed at salvation. His life is shrouded by myth and legend, and we know of him through the writings of other Greeks.

After much travel, Pythagoras settled in Crotona, a Greek colony in southern Italy, where he founded a successful school that operated on the principle of equality of the sexes. Trained in philosophy, literature, and domestic skills, "Pythagorean women" were honored in antiquity as the epitome of Greek femininity.

Pythagoras believed that the soul was immortal, undergoing reincarnation in different forms of animal life (transmigration of the soul). Hence, meat eating was prohibited, and there were additional rules of abstinence, including the mysterious dictum "Do not eat beans." To be freed from the cycle of rebirth, the Pythagoreans believed that the soul had to be purified, which was best achieved through studying science and mathematics. The chain of transmigration could only be ended by living a completely virtuous life. This was undoubtedly Pythagoras's aim, as "We are told . . . that the Master never drank wine by day, and lived for the most part on bread and honey, with vegetables as dessert; . . . that he was never known to eat too much, or to make love; that he never indulged in laughter, or jests, or stories; that he never chastised any one, not even a slave" (Durant, 1939, pp. 162–163).

Pythagoras is associated with mathematical discoveries, most importantly the relation between music and numbers (e.g., modern-day octaves and scales) and the Pythagorean theorem (the square of the hypotenuse of a right triangle is equal to the sum of the squares of the other two sides). In fact, Pythagoras believed that the explanation for everything could be found through numbers and their relations. The Pythagoreans "assumed that the book of nature . . . is written in the language of mathematics" (Allen, 1966, p. 6), and it is no exaggeration to say that the Pythagoreans laid the foundations of present-day mathematics.

In the Golden Age, Plato was enamored with the mystical figure of Pythagoras and took from him such things as his scorn of democracy, his love of geometry, and his ideas of the nature and destiny of the soul. Additionally, early "scientific" physicians such as Alcmaeon (discussed later) are believed to have been influenced by Pythagoras. Some historians credit Pythagoras with founding both science and philosophy in Western civilization. Indeed, the word *philosophy* may have been his creation: "He rejected the term *sophia,* or wisdom, as pretentious, and described his own pursuit of understanding as *philosophia*—the love of wisdom" (Durant, 1939, p. 164).

Heraclitus

Born in Ephesus of an aristocratic family, **Heraclitus** (ca. 540–480 B.C.) was a younger contemporary of Pythagoras. Heraclitus was known in antiquity by such unflattering terms as "the obscure" and "the riddler" because of his tendency to express himself circuitously. To illustrate Heraclitus's obscurity in his own time, there is a story that the playwright Euripides gave a copy of Heraclitus's work to the philosopher Socrates and later asked Socrates' opinion of it. Socrates replied, "What I understand is excellent, as is no doubt the part I don't understand. But it takes a Delian [inhabitant of Delos] diver to get to the bottom of it" (from Diogenes Laertius; MacLennan, 1990).

Heraclitus's fascination with the changing nature of things led to his most famous statement, which is often paraphrased, "You can never step into the same river twice." That is, because the water continuously flows, the water you enter a second time will not be the same water you stepped into originally (in psychology, no two experiences can ever be identical).

Heraclitus expressed his reliance on the senses: "The things of which there is seeing and hearing and perception, these do I prefer" (Kirk, Raven, & Schofield, 1983, p. 188). But Heraclitus also said, "Evil witnesses are eyes and ears for men, if they have souls that do not understand their language" (p. 188), by which he meant that understanding required the ability to interpret sensory information correctly. For understanding to occur, sensory information must be tempered with *logos,* or reason.

The concept of *logos* was extremely important in ancient Greek philosophy. The word was derived from the expression "to say," and its most fundamental meaning was "saying" or "speaking" in the sense of giving a reason or providing an explanation. However, the term also meant to calculate a ratio—the basis of Pythagorean mathematics and religion—or to show the true form of a thing. For the Pythagoreans, these seemingly different meanings were really identical: To explain something was to be able to provide a mathematical account of it. This idea is a part of much modern science, including some areas of psychology, where the most convincing explanation for a phenomenon is thought to be provided by a mathematical model.

MacLennan (1990) argued that in Heraclitus we see a different conception of *logos* and, in turn, rationality, understanding, and science. With his focus on change, Heraclitus provided an image of the world not easily captured by mathematical or rational structures. Thus, MacLennan suggested that in Heraclitus we see the birth of a different explanatory tradition that can be traced through history to modern chaos theory. **Chaos theory** holds that complex systems (e.g., behavioral phenomena) create unpredictability (chaos), and random events (hence, chaotic) have an order of their own.

Heraclitus believed that the essence of all things was fire, because fire is ever-changing. Fire is either going down through progressive condensation into moisture, water, and earth or going up from earth to water to moisture to fire. Everything is constantly "becoming," changing between pairs of opposites such as night and day, life and death, and so on. For Heraclitus there was unity in opposites. In fact, Heraclitus considered strife from the tension of opposites necessary for development. Each member of an opposing pair was necessary for the existence of its opposite.

In sum, Heraclitus's philosophy contained three major principles: fire, constant change, and the unity of opposites. These principles have been incorporated into subsequent philosophies: for example, the divinity of fire into the Christian final conflagration; the idea of struggle and change as necessary for development reappears in the writings of Charles Darwin and Herbert Spencer (both in Chapter 9) and Friedrich Nietzsche (Chapter 16).

Parmenides

Parmenides (ca. 504–456 B.C.) was born in Elea, a Greek city on the Italian coast. In his youth, Parmenides studied with a Pythagorean, but there is little evidence for strict Pythagorean ideas in the thought of the mature Parmenides. Parmenides is usually credited with founding the Eleatic school.

The purpose of Parmenides' work was to show that belief in the reality of the physical world of change and plurality is mistaken. Instead, Parmenides proposed an indestructible, static, ungenerated, spherical One. Where Heraclitus said *Panta rei* (all things change), Parmenides said *Hen ta panta* (all things are one and never change).

In rejecting change, Parmenides argued that there is no state of nonbeing from which something can arise. If something "comes to be," then it must "not have been," but Parmenides argued that this state of "nonbeing" was impossible. "How could it come to be? For if it came into being, it is not. . . . Thus coming to be [change] is extinguished and perishing [is] unheard of " (Kirk et al., 1983, p. 250). That is, something can neither be generated (come to be) nor can it perish.

Change assumes that something changes from nonbeing to being or from being to being, and Parmenides argued that this assumption makes no sense. If something arises from being, then it already is, and there is no change. If something arises from nonbeing, then the assumption is that nonbeing is something. Parmenides believed this assumption to be a contradiction because every something has being, and if something has being, then it cannot be "non-being."

Although Parmenides believed that he had demonstrated logically that change does not exist, he recognized that things appear to be in a state of flux. His answer for this apparent contradiction lay in the distinction between appearances and reality. Reality is the basis of truth, whereas appearances from sensory experience can result in no more than

opinion. Opinions based on sensation must yield to reason, which tells us that if there is a single substance comprising everything, then movement or change cannot occur.

Thus, for Parmenides our experience is invalid. The way of truth is knowledge from the gods, and the way of seeming is what comes through our senses. Parmenides' position is obvious—given the choice, he would select truth, or reason, rather than the appearances of the senses.

Parmenides' method for seeking truth was extreme **rationalism**, or the use of reason. Thought implanted by the gods contained truth. Any object of thought must exist because we have thought of it, and we cannot think of nothing. In the philosopher's words: "What is there to be said and thought must needs be: for it is there for being, but nothing is not" (Kirk et al., 1983, p. 247). That is, if you can think of something and speak of it, then it must exist. Parmenides denied the existence of nothingness, arguing that because thoughts must be of something, then nothingness (the void) cannot exist.

Parmenides' differentiation of appearance and reality, of opinion and knowledge, became the basis for Platonism. His objections to plurality and change inspired Plato's belief that the sensory world is a lower form of reality than the world known through reason. Parmenides' chief defender was Zeno.

Zeno's Paradoxes

Little is known about **Zeno of Elea** (ca. 490–430 B.C.) other than that he was a follower of Parmenides. According to one account, Zeno and Parmenides traveled together to Athens, where Socrates met them, but this is contradicted by another ancient writer, Diogenes Laertius, who noted that Zeno so loved Elea that he never left the city. Zeno's end is equally mysterious, and the details of his attempted overthrow of a tyrant at Elea, his capture, torture, and murder, vary so much that it is impossible to reconstruct what really happened.

Parmenides believed that the senses give information about appearances and not about reality, and Zeno proved this to his satisfaction in his millet seed example (millet is a cereal grass with tiny seeds). The fall of a single millet seed to the ground makes no sound; empty a half-bushel of seeds, and there will be a sound. Our senses have fooled us, because either the single falling seed made a sound or the many falling made no sound. Either way, Zeno concluded that it was more profitable to seek the truth through reason than to use sensory information.

To defend Parmenides against critics who argued for change and plurality, Zeno composed a series of paradoxes, of which nine have survived. One paradox describes a runner traversing a racecourse. According to the Pythagoreans, the distance around a racecourse is divisible into units. Suppose the distance is 400 meters. The 400 meters can be divided in half, the first half divided in half, and so on, *ad infinitum*. In other words, there is an infinity of units into which the racecourse can be divided, and this infinite number of units must be traveled by a runner in a finite amount of time, which Zeno argued was impossible. Thus, he reasoned, there is no motion.

One answer to Zeno's paradox is that time itself can be divided into an infinite number of units, so that the time to travel the racecourse is infinite in its divisibility, just as is the distance. Given this assumption, the paradox disappears. Still, Zeno's paradoxes have been revived as serious philosophical issues in modern times by Nobel laureate Bertrand Russell (Chapter 13), the famous Welsh philosopher and mathematician; by Lewis Carroll, the pseudonym of mathematician Charles Dodgson (1832–1898), who wrote *Alice's Adventures in Wonderland;* and by cognitive scientist Douglas Hofstadter (1979) in the Pulitzer Prize–winning book, *Gödel, Escher, Bach: An Eternal Golden Braid.*

To refute Parmenides' theory of the unchanging, motionless, indivisible One, defended by Zeno's paradoxes, Leucippus developed the philosophy of **atomism**—the idea that the universe is made of tiny, indivisible particles (atoms, from the Greek *atomos,* meaning indivisible). His theory was developed in greater detail by his pupil or associate, Democritus.

Democritus

Democritus (ca. 460–370 B.C.) was born in Abdera, a town in northeast Greece. From his father,

Democritus inherited a large sum of money, much of which he spent in travel. Although Democritus was a prolific writer, few of his works have survived. He is best known for his theory that there were only atoms and the void.

Unlike many of the ancient Greeks, Democritus believed that the senses can be trusted, for all practical purposes. Sensations are caused by atoms leaving an object and contacting our sense organs. However, the only qualities of objects in the outside world that can be perceived directly are weight (heavy or light) and texture (hard or soft). All other qualities represent the interaction of our atoms with the atoms we have received from the object. Thus, sensory experience is relative to the individual. In a frequently quoted passage, Democritus wrote that "By convention sweet is sweet, bitter is bitter, hot is hot, cold is cold, color is color; but in truth there are only atoms and the void."

Thus, except for weight and texture, all the qualities of objects we experience (e.g., taste, color) are secondary qualities, or qualities that depend on a perceiver. The analysis of secondary qualities was central to early modern philosophers such as John Locke and George Berkeley (Chapter 4). Also, Democritus believed that all sensations are reducible to touch, because the atoms emitted by objects are interpreted as having contacted or touched the body atoms of the perceiver.

The atoms comprising the world differ in size, shape, and weight, with mind atoms being tiny, round, and smooth, like the atoms of fire. The mind atoms receive an image (*eidolon*) of the object being sensed, but in storage the *eidola* rub against each other and are altered, resulting in errors in our memory.

Many different labels can be attached to Democritus. For example, he is called a materialist because he believed that all matter, including the soul, was made of the same atomic material. Additionally, because Democritus believed that the behavior of atoms is lawful and determines both physical and mental events, he has been called a **determinist**. Determinism is the belief that all events are determined by prior causes, and we will encounter many determinists in future chapters. For example, John Watson (Chapter 12) and B. F. Skinner (Chapter 13) believed in environmental determinism, whereas Sigmund Freud (Chapter 15) embraced a psychological determinism. On the issue of reductionism versus nonreductionism, Democritus was clearly a reductionist, because he believed that everything on the observable level could be explained by the interaction of things (atoms) at a more fundamental level. Finally, on the nature-nurture issue, Democritus is labeled a nurturist, believing that the mind's contents come from the *eidola* received by the senses.

In Democritus's completely naturalistic, deterministic theory, there was no need for a deity as a prime mover, and Democritus thought that bodily atoms became part of some other form with a person's death. Without spiritual survival after death, there was no higher state to which humans might aspire—hence, no absolute standard of action. Despite this, Democritus believed that the atoms comprising the mind (or soul; they were the same for him) were the body's noblest part, and a wise person would free himself or herself from bodily passions, superstition, and ignorance and would seek through contemplation such happiness as was humanly possible. For Democritus, happiness did not come from things, but rather from culture. Sensual pleasure is only briefly satisfying, and no pleasure can outweigh the gaining of knowledge. Thus, Democritus counseled a life of moderation, good cheer, and serenity of the soul. Presumably taking his own advice, he lived to the age of either 90 or 109, depending on the source. When asked the secret of his longevity, Democritus supposedly answered that he ate honey daily and bathed with oil.

In the atomists we find much of relevance for modern science: in their conception of a universe consisting of elemental particles, in their distinction between primary and secondary qualities, and in their insistence on determinism. However, we should note that their beliefs were not based on scientific inquiry, but rather on their efforts to challenge Parmenides and Zeno's rationalistic position.

The Sophists

The Greek philosophers to this point were searching for a general principle or principles to explain the universe. For Heraclitus, the general principle was change, whereas for Parmenides and Zeno it was the lack of change. Parmenides denied the existence of empty space and thus of movement, because movement can only occur when an object occupies a void. To counter Parmenides' argument for a static universe, Democritus conceived a universe consisting of atoms and the void.

Obviously the search for universal explanations had produced no agreement, and the various theoretical treatments appeared irreconcilably different. Lack of agreement on a universal principle prompted the Sophists and Socrates to focus on issues more relevant to human behavior, that is, on the study of people.

The **Sophists** (from *sophistes,* which means "wise man") were traveling teachers who played an important role in educating young men aspiring to leadership positions in Periclean Athens. Under Pericles, aristocracy was replaced with democracy, and this meant that free citizens became eligible for public office. However, the old style of education had not prepared men for the changing conditions of political life. Without a university system, the Sophists were needed to teach logic, science, philosophy, and particularly rhetoric, or persuasive speaking.

At first the Sophists enjoyed a favorable reputation, but it soon became clear that the art of persuasion could be used both for good and for ill. "Rhetoric aims at persuasion, not truth, and the popular charge that the Sophists undertook to make the weak argument stronger and the strong argument weak was quite correct" (Allen, 1966, p. 18). Today, *sophistry* is defined as the use of misleading but clever arguments.

The Sophists' reputation was further tarnished by the justified claim that they took young men from good families and taught them to analyze skeptically their ancestors' religion and ethics. The Sophists' *skepticism* is the philosophical position that absolute knowledge is impossible and inquiry must be a process of doubting in order to obtain even relative certainty.

In addition, far from being disinterested thinkers, some of the Sophists levied high fees for their teaching, which meant that only the wealthy could profit from it. The relatively poor Socrates could only afford the Sophists' "short course." What might he have accomplished if his education had been more complete?

Protagoras

Protagoras was among the most famous of the Sophists, and we will consider his ideas as an illustration of Sophist thought. Born in Abdera, **Protagoras** (ca. 490–420 B.C.) was an older contemporary of Democritus and during his lifetime was better known and more influential than the younger man. Protagoras was a frequent visitor to Athens and a friend of Pericles.

Most of our knowledge of Protagoras comes from Plato's dialogues—discussions of Plato's ideas and thoughts written in the form of conversations between two people—one of which is named for Protagoras. Although Plato despised the Sophists in general, his treatment of Protagoras was respectful. In fact, in Plato's account of an exchange with Socrates, Protagoras makes the superior showing, appearing more the gentlemanly philosopher whereas Socrates appears more the Sophist.

Although Parmenides rejected sensation as the avenue to truth, Protagoras accepted it as the source of knowledge, refusing to theorize any higher reality. Truth, goodness, and beauty are subjective, relative to the individual. This is the main point of Protagoras's famous saying: "[M]an is the measure of all things, of the things that are, that they are, and of the things that are not, that they are not" (Stumpf, 1989, p. 32). Whatever knowledge humans can achieve is limited by human capacities. Protagoras did accept one thing as true, however—that there are no ultimate truths. Protagoras's philosophical position is called **relativism**, which is the theory that conceptions of truth and moral values are not absolute but are relative to their possessors.

Protagoras concluded that knowledge is relative to each person, which makes it impossible to discover the "true" nature of anything. Your "truth" may be different from mine. Thus, Protagoras's approach could not readily be used to build a system of knowledge, because each person would perceive things differently. However, such ideas remain a part of contemporary psychology, as reflected in various movements in social psychology (Chapter 19).

Protagoras also believed that moral judgments are relative and that there is no absolute code that all humans should adopt. Laws and moral rules are based on convention, not on nature. However, Protagoras did not teach that each person was free to decide for himself or herself what was moral or right. Instead, he taught that the state makes the laws, and we should conform to them in order to have a peaceful, orderly society.

Protagoras also took a relativistic approach to religion, saying that it was impossible for anyone to know with certainty about the existence and nature of the gods. Because of this statement, the Athenian Assembly banished Protagoras and ordered his works burned in the marketplace. It is said that he fled for Sicily but drowned on the way.

Although Protagoras himself supported the rule of law by convention, his teaching of cultural relativity led many to conclude that no behavior is absolutely right or wrong. Socrates' mission in life was to expose the fallacies in the Sophists' reasoning and to reestablish some concept of truth and a basis for moral judgments.

Socrates

Paradoxically, although Socrates was one of the Sophists' most constant critics, many Athenians considered him a Sophist because his approach—unrelenting analysis of a subject—was similar to that of the Sophists. The difference was that Socrates used argumentation and analysis to discover fundamental concepts of truth and goodness, whereas the Sophists believed that there were no absolute truths. Also, Socrates refused to take pay for his instruction, although he did accept help occasionally from his wealthy friends.

Except for military service, Athenian-born **Socrates** (469–399 B.C.) spent nearly his whole life within the city's walls. Although he wrote nothing and did not found a school, Socrates is considered one of the greatest philosophers, his pivotal influence illustrated by the frequent classification of all earlier Greek philosophers as pre-Socratic. We know about him from three sources—Plato, Aristophanes, and Xenophon—each undoubtedly biased in his own way.

The comic playwright Aristophanes portrayed Socrates as a professional Sophist in *The Clouds,* whereas Xenophon, abandoning philosophy for the military, described his revered teacher as a practical figure—like Xenophon himself. But Plato is the source of most of our knowledge of Socrates, through a series of dialogues that have preserved Socrates' memory.

In the early dialogues, Socrates was often the leading figure, and some feel that Plato described the historical Socrates and that all the ideas expressed in Plato's dialogues were really those of his teacher. On the other hand, Aristotle attributed to Socrates the universal definitions and inductive arguments—that is, the method—and attributed to Plato the development of some of the particulars, such as the theory of Forms. The **theory of Forms** is the belief that there are universal Ideas, or Forms, that underlie what we know through our senses. These Forms can be realized only through rational, deductive, logical means. The most widely accepted view is that Plato's early dialogues portray the philosophical activities of Socrates, whereas the later dialogues express Plato's views.

Socrates' father was a sculptor, and his mother was a midwife. At Socrates' birth, Pericles was a young man, and Euripides and Sophocles were boys who later wrote great tragic plays that Socrates may have seen. The building of the Parthenon occurred during his lifetime, which spanned Greece's Golden Age.

Socrates participated in three military campaigns, distinguishing himself by bravery, physical endurance, and indifference to climate and alcohol. According to one source, Socrates (Figure 2–2) was walleyed, snub-nosed, bald in later life, with a walk like a duck (Allen, 1966). Perhaps because of his odd gait, he was portrayed in *The Clouds* as a strutting waterfowl.

Socrates was forced by what he called his *daimon,* or inner guiding spirit, to examine the moral attitudes of his contemporaries. To overcome the Sophists' relativism and skepticism, Socrates sought a foundation on which to build knowledge, which he found in the *psyche,* or soul. For Socrates, the soul was the human capacity for intelligence and character. A person's aim should be to make the soul as good as possible, in keeping with knowledge of true moral values. Before Socrates, Apollo's motto, "Know Thyself," inscribed

FIGURE 2–2.   Socrates.

Source: Corbis-Bettmann.

on the entrance to the temple at Delphi, was interpreted to mean that a person should know and stay in his or her place in society. Socrates interpreted the words more literally, believing that human happiness comes from spiritual perfection, which requires self-knowledge. Only with self-knowledge can a person know good from evil, and for Socrates, "the unexamined life is not worth living."

Like the Sophists, Socrates used **dialectic,** or logical argumentation, to uncover the truth of an issue. Unlike the Sophists, who often used dialectic simply to train orators, Socrates used it to achieve creative ideas of goodness and truth. The "Socratic method" began with Socrates asking a fellow citizen to define something like beauty, truth, or justice. He would then point out contradictions and problems in the definitions, claiming all the while to be as ignorant as the person questioned. By correcting a person's incomplete or inaccurate notions, Socrates believed he could tease out the truth, and in one of the demonstrations of the method's power, Socrates coaxes the Pythagorean theorem from an ignorant lad.

A person cannot be taught virtue, although facts about virtue, what people in the past have thought, can be taught. In order truly to understand virtue, a person must "discover" it for himself or herself, and this was the point of the Socratic method. Personal discovery produces insight, which can never be taken away. When Socrates said "virtue is knowledge" (or "knowledge is virtue"), he meant that virtue is self-knowledge, knowledge of the soul's nature and of the true goal in life and how to achieve it.

Socrates distinguished between two objects of thought, the particular (e.g., a beautiful flower) and the general or universal (e.g., the Idea of Beauty), which are related to the distinction between appearances and reality, respectively. Only by a rigorous process of definition does the mind grasp the distinction between the particular and the general, and the goal of the process is to uncover the clear and fixed concepts Socrates sought.

The end of the 5th century B.C. was a time of upheaval in Athens, and many Athenians longed for a return to the old order of things. Socrates had spent his adult life questioning the old concepts and was brought to trial on the charges of not worshipping the State's gods and of corrupting youth. Convicted, Socrates was permitted to suggest his own punishment. When he proposed that Athens should reward him by according him "public maintenance in the prytaneum," his arrogance resulted in a death sentence. Still, his friends could have arranged for Socrates' escape, but having examined escape dialectically, he chose instead to drink the poison hemlock.

Although Socrates' enemies removed him from Athenian life, they could not remove his influence. The dialectic technique was passed on through Plato to Aristotle, who developed it into a system of logic that survives unchanged today. Through his pupils, Socrates' many ideas—for example, the importance of self-knowledge, personal discovery produces insight, the distinction between the particular and the general—form the backbone of most later Western philosophies.

Plato

A year after Pericles' death, **Plato** (427–347 B.C.) was born into an aristocratic Athenian family. He was named Aristocles, meaning "best and renowned," and later acquired the nickname Plato because of his broad shoulders. True to his original name, Plato excelled in virtually every field from philosophy to sports and, at 20, considered careers either as a poet or as a politician before succumbing to Socrates and philosophy. As a philosopher, Plato's influence has been so great that English mathematician and philosopher Alfred North Whitehead (1861–1947) once characterized the history of Western philosophy as but a series of "footnotes to Plato."

After Socrates' trial and death, Plato and other Socratic disciples took temporary refuge with the philosopher Euclides at Megara. From there, Plato traveled in Greece, Egypt, southern Italy—where he probably studied with Pythagoreans—and Sicily before returning to Athens in about 387 B.C. With financial aid from friends, Plato founded the **Academy** in a grove of trees (the grove of *Akademos,* a figure in Greek legend) outside Athens. Plato directed the Academy for the rest of his life, and it survived over 900 years before being closed by the Christian emperor Justinian in 529 A.D.

The Academy's chief subjects were philosophy and mathematics, the latter subject considered so important that the warning, "Let no one without geometry enter here," was inscribed over the portal. Perhaps knowledge of geometry was required for admission, or, more likely, the inscription reflected the Pythagorean belief in the primacy of mathematics in all understanding.

Plato's writings consist primarily of some 30 dialogues customarily categorized as early, middle, and late. In most of the early dialogues (e.g., the *Laches* and the *Apology*), Socrates, cast as the main character, engages in dialectics with his fellow Greeks to ascertain the definition of different moral virtues. In the *Apology,* Socrates defends himself against the charges for which he was sentenced to die.

The middle dialogues (e.g., the *Phaedo* and the *Republic*) show Socrates expressing more positive, systematic views, which some modern scholars assume to be Plato's. In these dialogues, we find Plato's theory of knowledge as recollection, the theory of Forms, and his ideas on the immortality of the soul. The *Republic* describes Plato's famous political utopia.

The third group, less literary than the earlier dialogues, is a series of sophisticated criticisms of the metaphysical and logical assumptions of doctrines from the middle group. Examples include the *Parmenides* and the *Laws*.

Theory of Forms

For Plato, there were two worlds—a world of Knowledge and a world of Opinion—which correspond to Parmenides' "Way of Truth" and "Way of Seeming," respectively. The world of Knowledge contains the **Forms**, or Ideas, which are the universals known only through reason. By contrast, the world of Opinion contains the changing particulars of the material world that are conveyed to us by our senses. Because the senses are inaccurate, the body actually hinders us in acquiring knowledge of the Forms.

To Plato, the relation between the two worlds is one of imitation. The particulars are to the universals as the shadows of objects are to the objects that cast them. To illustrate this analogy, in Book VII of the *Republic,* Plato presented his famous parable of men in a cave or den. It begins with Socrates saying:

> Behold! human beings living in an underground den, which has a mouth open towards the light and reaching all along the den; here they have been from their childhood, and have their legs and necks chained so that they cannot move, and can only see before them, being prevented by the chains from turning round their heads. Above and behind them a fire is blazing at a distance, and between the fire and the prisoners there is a raised way; and you will see, if you look, a low wall built along the way, like the screen which marionette players have in front of them, over which they show the puppets. (Plato, *Republic;* Loomis, 1942, p. 398)

Along the raised way, walking men carry various objects and animals, which project shadows onto the cave wall before the chained people. To the chained people, "the truth would be literally nothing but the shadows of the images" (Plato, *Republic;* Loomis, 1942, p. 399). For Plato, the flickering shadows on the cave's wall are like our sensations, providing us with unreliable images of a reality we can know only from reasoning.

It is a reality we have known before, because our souls originally resided in purity and bliss in the throng of human souls that God distributed among the stars. Attracted to the earth, each soul is joined to a body for a lifetime. During this earthly life, the soul has reminders of the world of true Being and perfect Form in which it once dwelled. Learning to understand and appreciate the perfect Forms is a matter of **anamnesis**, or recollection of information we already possess.

For Plato, the truth of things is always in the soul, even though we may be unaware of it. Note that Plato's belief that Truth and Knowledge are present in the soul before birth is an extreme nature position that lays the foundation for other philosophers such as Kant (Chapter 5) and for psychologists such as Eleanor Gibson (Chapter 13).

Education's purpose is to lead people from the cave into the world of light, to turn them from the world of appearance to the world of reality. Once a person has been freed from the cave and has achieved a higher knowledge of reality, the person must not be permitted to stay in the world of contemplation. Instead, the educated person is obligated to return to the cave to participate in the life of the prisoners.

Unlike most of his contemporaries, Plato did not limit education to men, and women were admitted into the Academy. In the *Republic,* he noted that many women are superior to men in many things. For example, they may have greater musical skills and be better at curing disease. Thus, Plato concluded that girls and boys should receive the same education, and women should be permitted to secure positions in the state commensurate with their abilities. In earlier writings, Plato appealed for female political participation, and "as far as we know, Plato was the first to argue seriously that women should share as equals with men in the public life of the state" (Loomis, 1942, p. 17).

Plato's Tripartite Soul

As Plato described it in the *Republic,* the soul has three parts (hence **tripartite soul**): reason, spirit, and appetite. Reason is the rational part of the soul, whereas spirit and appetite are the irrational parts. The rational and irrational parts have different origins. The rational comes from the same receptacle as the World Soul, which means that it originally has a clear vision of the Forms. Because the soul's irrational part is created by the gods who form the body, it has a tendency to pull the soul toward the earth and away from heaven's purity. The conflicting natures of the rational and irrational parts of the soul are beautifully illustrated in the *Phaedrus* by the image of a charioteer driving two horses. The charioteer represents reason, and the two horses, a well-trained thoroughbred and a wild brute, represent spirit and appetite, respectively. We see Plato's rational and irrational parts of the soul echoed over 2,000 years later in Sigmund Freud's ego and id, rational and irrational parts of the mind, respectively.

For Plato, bodily stimulation enables the irrational part of the soul to overcome its rational counterpart. This leads to the search for pleasure and the exaggeration of such drives as hunger and sex. Thus, because of the susceptibility of the spirit and appetites of the soul to the body's influences, the soul's harmony is disturbed and reason is prevented from recalling the truth it once knew. By exposing the soul to many sensations, the body is responsible for ignorance, imprudence, and lust.

Morality comes when the soul's lost inner harmony is reestablished. Reason must regain control over the irrational. Whereas the Sophists had taught that a culture could define the good life however it wished, Plato taught that virtue is grounded in the nature of the soul. Virtue is attained when each of the soul's parts is performing the function for which it was created, and this requires that reason work to keep the spirit and the appetites in check. Success in reasoning's function produces the virtue of wisdom.

By the same token, the appetites and the spirit have their functions to play in the good life. When the appetites are restrained, avoiding the excesses that would defeat the sovereignty of reason, the virtue of temperance results. The virtue of courage is produced when the spirit is restrained. When each of the soul's parts is fulfilling its particular function, the result is the virtue of justice. Justice reflects a person's achievement of inner harmony, which only comes when all of the soul's parts are performing their special functions.

Plato's Contributions

Plato gave us some fundamental rules of logical reasoning, although logic itself was systematized by his pupil Aristotle. In Plato's dialogues, Socrates insists on defining terms, on distinguishing between mere opinion and true knowledge, and on differentiating words from the objects they represent. Plato's Forms are also related to contemporary use of the term *concept* to refer to something abstracted from physical reality. We will encounter the modern study of concepts in our discussion of cognitive psychology (Chapter 20).

Plato was the father of all idealistic philosophers who see behind the visible, inconstant world an invisible world of order, intelligence, and purpose striving to reveal itself. He was also the forerunner of many rationalists who have argued for innate knowledge—for example, Descartes (Chapter 3), Leibniz (Chapter 3), and Kant.

Aristotle

Unlike Socrates and Plato, **Aristotle** (384–322 B.C.) was not born in Athens. Instead, he hailed from Stagira, a Greek colony in Macedonia, which was a country north of Greece. Aristotle's father was the court physician to Amyntas II, Macedonia's ruler, the father of Philip, and Alexander the Great's grandfather. As a boy, Aristotle was undoubtedly exposed by his father to the biological sciences, and Aristotle's most abundant observations were in biology. Plato and Aristotle are shown in Figure 2–3.

In 368 B.C., Aristotle journeyed to Athens to study under Plato at the Academy. It is believed that he stayed at the Academy, first as a student and later as a teacher, until Plato died in 347 B.C. After Plato's death, Aristotle went to the court of Hermeias—a former Academy pupil—where in 344 B.C., he married Pythias, Hermeias's niece and

FIGURE 2–3.   Plato and Aristotle.

Source: "School of Athens" by Raphael; Corbis-Bettmann.

adopted daughter. Pythias bore Aristotle a daughter and then died. After Pythias's death, Aristotle began a lasting but never legalized relation with Herpyllis, with whom he had a son they called Nicomachus. One of Aristotle's most popular works, the *Nicomachean Ethics,* was named after the boy. Tradition holds that Nicomachus collected and edited the notes that became the *Ethics* from a set of Aristotle's lectures.

In 343 B.C., Philip of Macedon invited Aristotle to be the teacher of his 13-year-old son Alexander, who later became the conqueror known as Alexander the Great. Aristotle taught the lad until Alexander took the throne upon his father's assassination.

Returning to Athens, Aristotle founded the **Lyceum**, which took its name from its proximity to buildings devoted to *Apollo Lyceus* (God of Shepherds). The Lyceum's students were called "peripatics," which means "to walk about," perhaps because of their master's tendency to pace while lecturing, or because of the type of open-air porch (*peripaté*) on which Aristotle often lectured. Like

the Academy, the Lyceum survived until closed by the emperor Justinian.

With Alexander's death in 323, a wave of anti-Macedonian feeling swept Athens, and Aristotle was accused of impiety. Aristotle fled Athens to settle in Chalcis on Euboea, a Greek island in the Aegean, and died a year later.

Aristotle's writings can be divided into two main groups: the 27 nonsurviving dialogues for which Aristotle was known in antiquity, and treatises based on Aristotle's lecture notes, which were unknown outside the Lyceum until published in the 1st century B.C. The surviving writings are extraordinary in their range and originality, including discussions of logic, physics and metaphysics, astronomy, biology and physiology, psychology, ethics, and politics. They profoundly influenced medieval Islamic philosophy and Christian philosophy (Chapter 3).

Aristotle and Plato Compared

In some ways the thought of Aristotle was the opposite of that of his former teacher. Plato was more of a rationalist, believing that reality could only be known through the exercise of reason and that the role of perception is merely to remind us of what we have already known. By contrast, Aristotle was more like an empiricist who believed that perception is a direct avenue to reality and that all concepts are derived from sense experience.

Plato was an idealist who taught that reality consists not of what we can know through our senses, but in the transcendent Forms. Aristotle believed the world to be a blend of the material and the ideal. The material world, an object of opinion for Plato, was an object of knowledge for Aristotle.

Plato relied on **deductive reasoning**, that is, reasoning from a known principle to an unknown. In addition to deduction, Aristotle applied the **inductive reasoning** method, or reasoning from the particular to the general. Thus, Aristotle sometimes used experience and observation to test deduced principles, and at other times he arrived at general principles inductively, through the prior application of observation.

Although Plato and Aristotle disagreed on many important points, they both opposed Democritus, who held that the universe could be explained in purely mechanical terms. Both Plato and Aristotle believed that God, Aristotle's Unmoved Mover, exists independently of material form.

Aristotle and the Scientific Method

As we noted, Aristotle, like Plato, used reasoning to arrive at general principles. Unlike Plato, Aristotle was always ready to modify his theories if experience or observation showed them to be incorrect.

In the *Organon* (Greek for "tool" or "instrument"), Aristotle systematically demonstrated the reasoning process that leads to sure knowledge, beginning from certain fundamental axioms assumed to be true. Aristotle called this path of reasoning the **syllogism**; beginning with a fundamental, unarguable, general statement, additional statements about particular instances follow of necessity. If all A are B, and C is an example of A, then C must be B. Aristotle's standard example is: All men (A) are mortal (B). Because Socrates (C) is a man (A), then Socrates (C) is mortal (B). Syllogistic reasoning as an avenue to knowledge became something of an obsession with Western philosophers after Aristotle's rediscovery in the later Middle Ages (Chapter 3).

In syllogistic or deductive reasoning, the basic statement from which we are reasoning must be both correct and comprehensive. Lack of either condition may invalidate the conclusions, but if the initial premises are true, then a valid conclusion necessarily follows.

Aristotle also systematized inductive argument, a second form of reasoning that can lead to valid conclusions. If many observations all point to the same general conclusion, then the conclusion may well be correct. For example, every morning we have observed that the sun rises in the east and sets in the west. From this, we may be justified in concluding that the sun *always* rises in the east and sets in the west. Still, we must remain vigilant to the exception that will negate the principle, and we must not be too hasty in drawing conclusions. With inductive reason-

ing, there is always the danger that sweeping conclusions may be drawn from limited data, and Aristotle himself was often guilty of this type of error.

In searching for the fundamental principles of the universe, Aristotle first began his work *Metaphysics* (meaning "after physics") with a review of the theories of previous Greek thinkers. He rejected all of the earlier theories as being insufficiently analytical. They had failed to incorporate the four basic **causes**: material, formal, efficient, and final. To understand anything completely, we must know its four causes.

The *material cause* answers the question, Of what is a thing made? For example, a statue's material cause is the marble from which it is chiselled. Aristotle criticized many of the earlier philosophers for being content with simply naming the material(s) comprising an object and for not recognizing that there was more to causation. The *formal cause* answers the question, What is it? When we say an object is a statue of Aphrodite, we have identified its form, the pattern its material has assumed. The *efficient cause* answers the question, By whom or by what is the object made? In the case of the statue, we say the efficient cause is the sculptor, wielding his hammer and chisel. The *final cause* answers the question, What is the purpose or end for which the object was made? A statue's final cause may be to satisfy the sculptor's creative urges, to provide something the sculptor can sell to put food on the table, or to please its viewers.

By noting and emphasizing final cause, Aristotle revealed his belief in **teleology**, the idea that everything is directed toward a definite end and a final purpose. For Aristotle, this built-in goal or function was **entelechy**, defined as actuality rather than potentiality. An acorn has the potential to become an oak tree, and its entelechy keeps it moving toward its appropriate end. Aristotle believed in the priority of actuality over potentiality. Although a girl is potentially a woman, before a girl could exist with that potentiality, there first had to be an actual woman.

To explain the constantly changing world of potential striving toward an end that perishes, Aristotle assumed the existence of a pure actuality that was above the world of potential, or dying things. Thus, he postulated a Being of pure actuality, motionless because change is a kind of motion. This was the Unmoved Mover, which Aristotle considered more from a scientific standpoint than from a theological one. The Unmoved Mover was the final cause toward which everything strives.

Aristotle did not think of the Unmoved Mover as a conscious entity prescribing purposes or goals for the world. Instead he conceived of It as the unconscious principle of motion inherent in the universe. Later Christian philosophers, particularly St. Thomas Aquinas (Chapter 3), equated Aristotle's Unmoved Mover with the God of Christianity.

Aristotle's Biology

Aristotle's observations in biology were abundant, but often wrong. Aristotle made many contributions, however; he was the first to construct a rational classification scheme for the animal kingdom. He divided it into *anaima* and *enaima*—bloodless and blooded—animals, which correspond approximately to our invertebrates and vertebrates, respectively. Aristotle separated animals with blood into fishes, amphibians, birds, and mammals.

Aristotle's theory of analogous organs demonstrated his recognition of the interrelations of animals throughout the animal kingdom. Thus, he saw a bird's feather as the analogue of a fish's scale and a nail as the analogue of a claw. Aristotle at times even approached the concept of evolution:

> Nature proceeds little by little from things lifeless to animal life in such a way that it is impossible to determine the exact line of demarcation. . . . Thus, next after lifeless things in the upward scale comes the genus of plants, relatively lifeless as compared with animals, but alive as compared with corporeal objects. There is in plants a continuous scale of ascent towards the animal. There are certain objects in the sea concerning which one would be at a loss to determine whether they be animal or vegetable. . . . In regard to sensibility, some animals give no sign of it, others indicate it obscurely. . . . And so throughout the animal scale there is a graduated differentiation. (Aristotle, *History of Animals;* Durant, 1939, p. 530)

Aristotle's conception of the world of nature consisting of a hierarchy from the simplest entity, barely alive, to the most complex creature, man, was a powerful influence on later European thinking. Charles Darwin found the principle of natural selection foreshadowed in the following passage from Aristotle's *Physicae Auscultationes*:

> Wheresoever, therefore, all things together (that is all the parts of one whole) happened like as if they were made for the sake of something, these were preserved, having been appropriately constituted by an internal spontaneity; and whatsoever things were not thus constituted, perished, and still perish. (Aristotle, *Physicae Auscultationes;* Appleman, 1979, p. 19)

To further acknowledge Aristotle's influence, Darwin wrote: "Linnaeus and Cuvier have been my two gods, . . . but they were mere schoolboys compared to old Aristotle" (Loomis, 1943, p. xxvii).

Aristotle's notion that animals might be arranged on a graded scale of complexity led many later scholars to accept the idea that animals could be ranked on a continuous dimension known as the *scala naturae,* or Great Chain of Being (Lovejoy, 1936). At the lowest position were animals like sponges that were essentially formless, whereas humans were at the top of the scale. The phylogenetic scale is a modern version of this natural scale, and it has been suggested that many comparative psychologists and other psychologists who study animals (e.g., neuroanatomists, physiologists, etc.) have mistakenly adopted the Aristotle-inspired scale instead of the more appropriate Darwinian phylogenetic tree (Hodos & Campbell, 1969). According to Hodos and Campbell, this mistaken choice led to a lack of theory in comparative psychology.

In addition to Aristotle's sometimes brilliant observations and suggestions, there are many errors in the *History of Animals,* some simply amusing (e.g., the only diseases from which elephants suffer are runny nose and flatulence) and others of more consequence. One of his more consequential errors was his conclusion that the heart was the source of the blood and the seat of sensations, emotions, intelligence, and most importantly, of the *psyche.*

Aristotle's Psychology

Although the word *psyche* means soul, Aristotle meant it in the sense of a vital principle that differentiates the living and the nonliving. All living things possess **psyche**, but there are three different grades: vegetative (or nutritive), sensitive, and rational. Plants have only a vegetative *psyche,* which allows them to take in matter, grow, and reproduce. In addition, animals and humans have a sensitive *psyche* that allows them to sense and to perceive their environments. To the five traditional senses—vision, audition, olfaction, gustation, and touch—Aristotle proposed a common sense that assimilates the information from the other senses. The sensitive *psyche* also allows the qualities sensed to continue after the object sensed is no longer present. In other words, it is responsible for memory and imagination. Only humans possess a rational *psyche,* which permits thinking and reasoning.

Several observations led Aristotle to put *psyche* in the heart. First, he knew that diseases of the heart are fatal, and *psyche* is only present in the living. Also, feelings such as anger and fear produce changes experienced as sensations in the chest. Aristotle also observed that the heart is the first organ formed in the embryonic chicken, and its beating signals life. Finally, Aristotle rejected the brain as the organ of the *psyche,* because cerebral tissue is insensitive to direct stimulation. For Aristotle, the brain probably cooled the blood. Aristotle was not alone in making this mistake: "Twenty-five centuries before Aristotle, Egyptians, too, identified the heart with psychological activity, and . . . they also treated the brain, insofar as they noted it all, as a more or less useless substance" (Laver, 1972, p. 181).

Because one definition Aristotle gave the *psyche* was that it was a substance with the capacity to receive knowledge, what is the source of this knowledge? Unlike Plato, who held that knowledge was already present from the time the soul dwelled among the Forms, Aristotle believed that sensation preceded thought and that mind without thought was like a blank slate. The blank slate metaphor will reappear in the work of the British empiricists

(especially John Locke) and in all the psychologists who have taken the nurture position on the nature-nurture issue.

For Aristotle, humans were the only animals with thought, even though other animals have sensations that produce images (mental representations created by sensations that outlast the sensations) that may become memories (the retention of the mental representations). Remembering is the recalling of some previously created image, and Aristotle explicitly stated that memory does not take place without an image.

Aristotle also held that thought, in addition to memory, requires images: "Now we have already discussed imagination [the formation of images] in the treatise *On the Soul* and we concluded there that thought is impossible without an image" (Aristotle, *Parva Naturalia;* Sahakian, 1968, p. 11). Similarly, the founder of scientific psychology, Wilhelm Wundt (Chapter 7), and his student, Edward Bradford Titchener (Chapter 7), believed that "imageless" thought was impossible. Wundt's and Titchener's adherence to Aristotelian dogma created controversy in the late 19th and early 20th centuries with members of the Würzburg School (Chapter 8) and others who believed that thought sometimes occurs without images.

Recollection, or recall, is not the same thing as remembering. Remembering is a spontaneous reproduction of past experiences, whereas recall involves an active search that attempts to recover previous perceptions. In describing the process of recall, Aristotle touched on principles that have been incorporated into the doctrine of association held by most learning theorists in modern times (Chapter 13). Aristotle's **principles of association** are similarity, contrast, and contiguity. That is, the recall of an object or event tends to evoke the memory of one like it (similar to it), one opposite to it (contrasted to it), or one that occurred at the same time or place (contiguous to it) in the original learning.

Aristotle also named additional factors important in recollection that have been incorporated into modern learning theory (see Maniou-Vakali, 1974). For example, he recognized that repetition improves our ability to recall something. Also, Aristotle noted that some things are easier to remember than others; some experiences are better remembered after one or a few repetitions than others often experienced. In addition to the many psychological reasons for this phenomenon—for example, meaningfulness, strong emotional coloring—it fits nicely with modern ideas on biological predispositions and constraints on learning (e.g., Timberlake & Lucas, 1989) and with some less modern but historically significant ideas (see Thorndike, Chapter 12).

Dreaming is related to the same processes we see in remembering and recollection. Images created from sensations that are retained by the mind are aroused during sleep and become the dream. It is noteworthy that Aristotle recognized the similarity between dreams during sleep and hallucinations produced by illness in the waking state. "So much is clear on this subject that the same agency which in disease produces illusion while we are awake, also produces the condition of illusion in sleep" (Aristotle, *Parva Naturalia;* Sahakian, 1968, p. 13).

Aristotle was the first to recognize the phenomenon of psychological **catharsis** (from the Greek *katharsis,* which means purification), although the term had been used earlier by the physician Hippocrates (for the evacuation of morbid humors) and by Plato (for the purification of the soul by philosophy). Aristotle believed that tragic drama allows the viewer to purify or purge negative emotions, through the process of identification with the tragic hero. Sigmund Freud made catharsis a basic component of psychoanalysis.

Aristotle's Influence

Aristotle dared much and failed at times, but with all his errors, Aristotle is truly the forerunner of the "scientific method." He gave us advanced logic, an empirical approach to knowledge in contrast to Plato's extreme rationalism, and many of his observations anticipated more modern conceptions (e.g., evolution, principles of association, the mind as a blank slate). Aristotle wrote about many other things that have undoubtedly influenced directly or indirectly modern psychology. For example, Aristotle's writings on art and tragedy shaped the structure of Shakespeare's plays, and the idea of his "lost work" on comedy has served to advance one modern linguistic theory—semiotics, or the study of signs and sign systems (Eco, 1983).

Even with all his accomplishments, it can be argued that Aristotle had a negative influence on science for several hundred years (although it was not Aristotle's fault). Scholars in the Middle Ages considered Aristotle's concept of the Unmoved Mover evidence that he was a divinely inspired monotheist. As such, his writings became the final authority on worldly matters. Because Aristotle's monotheism indicated his divine inspiration, the argument went, there was no need to continue scientific exploration. Scholars should concentrate on spiritual matters.

Eventually, Renaissance scientists such as Copernicus, Galileo, Newton, and Harvey (all Chapter 3) challenged Aristotle on so many points that his monopoly on scientific thought expired. However, "as philosopher, moral and political thinker, and author of the earliest canons of literary criticism, he still commands the world's respectful attention" (Loomis, 1943, p. xxxvii).

MEDICINE IN THE GOLDEN AGE AND BEYOND

Both in the distant past and in recent times, psychology arose from philosophy and physiology. After our examination of philosophy in the Golden Age, we now turn to physiology and medicine in the same period. We will begin with Alcmaeon, an important precursor to Hippocrates, considered by many the most famous physician of all time. Hippocrates lived during Greece's Golden Age, and his development of rational medicine—medicine based on reason rather than religion—was anticipated by Alcmaeon.

Alcmaeon

At the time of **Alcmaeon** (ca. 500 B.C.), Greek medicine was largely tied to religion. Treatment occurred in the temples of Asclepius (the Greek god of medicine), where the priests subjected patients to ritual and suggestion, extracted large sums of money, and probably cured patients whose symptoms were largely psychological and those for whom a period of rest was needed.

Alcmaeon was one of the first recorded anatomists. In his animal dissections he located the optic nerves and discovered the eustachian tubes connecting the throat with the middle ears. Unlike some, Alcmaeon believed that the brain was the organ of thought. Following the lead of the Pythagoreans, Alcmaeon considered health a matter of harmonious balance of such opposites as dry/wet, hot/cold, and bitter/sweet, with disease resulting from an imbalance. Although Alcmaeon has been called the founder of Greek medicine, his is a relatively late name in a long line of secular physicians originating before recorded history.

Hippocrates

The son of a physician, **Hippocrates** (ca. 460–377 B.C.) was born on Cos, an island in the Aegean Sea, off the southwest coast of present-day Turkey. Although Hippocrates is often called the father of medicine and there are literally dozens of treatises penned under his name, most of these works were almost certainly written by Hippocrates' followers. One of the most important of the Hippocratic works is *On the Sacred Disease,* a discussion of epilepsy. Unlike his contemporaries, Hippocrates did not think epilepsy was caused by the gods stealing a victim's mind, attributing it instead to natural causes and in particular to an imbalance in the four humors.

The four **humors** (bodily fluids) of Hippocrates were black bile, yellow bile, blood, and phlegm, which Hippocrates thought were distilled from the poet and philosopher Empedocles' (ca. 490–430 B.C.) four basic elements: earth, air, fire, and water, respectively. Humoral imbalance resulted in disease, whereas balance was essential to health. Naturalistic treatments were used to restore humoral balance, and Hippocrates prescribed such remedies as purgatives, bloodletting, exercise, and special diets.

Hippocrates described the symptoms of a number of mental disorders, including phobias, postpartum depression (depression after childbirth), and hysteria (a physical disorder without organ pathology). Believing it only occurred in women, Hippocrates attributed hysteria to the "wandering uterus." For example, Hippocrates thought hysterical blindness was produced when the uterus lodged behind the eyes. Treatment was designed to restore the uterus to its normal location; thus, he prescribed marriage and pregnancy. Hippocrates' mistaken notion that hysteria (a somatoform disorder in current clinical terminology) was exclusively a disorder of women held until challenged in modern times by Freud and others.

Probably Hippocrates' greatest contribution was his continuing fight to free medicine from philosophical and religious influences. Although he occasionally prescribed prayer, Hippocrates insisted that theology per se had no place in medicine. Remnants of Hippocratic treatment can be seen even in relatively modern times—bleeding was widely practiced until at least the middle of the 19th century—and George Washington's death may have been hastened by excessive bloodletting.

Galen

We know of Hippocrates largely through **Galen** (ca. 130–200 A.D.). Galen was born in Pergamum, where he discovered philosophy at 14, remaining always under its spell despite turning to medicine at 17. Galen served for a time as a surgeon in the Pergamum school for gladiators, which probably exposed him to internal human anatomy. Galen's extensive travels took him eventually to Rome, where he practiced until his success in exposing the dishonesty of many Roman physicians resulted in his having to flee the city temporarily.

Living some 600 years after Hippocrates, Galen was strongly influenced by Hippocratic medicine and by Aristotle's biology. Like Hippocrates, Galen believed in the brain as the organ of the mind, strongly opposing Aristotle's notion that the mind was located in the heart. Drawing on the writings of his predecessors, especially Hippocrates, and on his own experiments, Galen produced some 500 volumes, of which over 100 have survived. These volumes cover all branches of medicine and many areas of philosophy.

Roman law forbade human dissection, so Galen dissected and vivisected (dissections on the living) a variety of animals, sometimes generalizing too readily to humans (Sarton, 1954). From his investigations, Galen can be said to have founded experimental neurology. He recognized 7 of the 12 pairs of cranial nerves, demonstrated that injuries to one side of the brain resulted in functional impairment on the opposite side of the body, and distinguished between motor and sensory nerves, a distinction lost until finally established in the early 19th century (Chapter 6). In addition, Galen named such neural structures as the corpus callosum, the pineal and pituitary glands, and the ventricles. He believed that the ventricles serve as the reservoir for **animal spirits**, the mysterious substance that many Greeks felt distinguished the living from the dead.

Galen incorporated Hippocrates' humoral theory into a primitive personality theory, in which the predominance of each humor is associated with a particular temperament. For example, Galen believed that an excess of blood is related to being cheerful or sanguine (from the Latin *sanguineus,* meaning blood). Excessive black bile makes a person melancholic or sad, whereas too much yellow bile gives a person a choleric or fiery temperament. Finally, an excess of phlegm produces a sluggish or dull individual—that is, one who is phlegmatic. (How did you feel the last time you had a runny nose and a productive cough?)

Galen rejected the mechanistic interpretations of biology held by atomists such as Democritus. In his studies, Galen was struck by the beauty and functional utility of the body's parts, which he believed showed purpose in the body's design. For Galen, purpose in the origin, structure, and function of organs revealed divine influence in the workings of the universe. Early Christians were as impressed with Galen's monotheism as they were with Aristotle's, and until the Renaissance, Galen was the unquestioned authority in physiology. Galen became "an Aristotle for medieval medicine" (Durant, 1944, p. 507).

OTHER SCHOOLS OF THOUGHT

Greece's Golden Age did not end simply because Aristotle died. Its decline really began much earlier with Athens's defeat in the Peloponnesian War by Sparta and its allies (with help from the Persians). This 404 B.C. defeat led to a dismantling of the Athenian Empire and to the installation in Athens of a Spartan-backed puppet regime. After a year of terror, the Thirty Tyrants were overthrown and democracy was reestablished, but the city-state of Athens did not recover its former glory.

Just as Greece's Golden Age did not end with Aristotle's death, neither did Greek philosophy. After Aristotle, **Theophrastus** (ca. 372–286 B.C.) became the head of the Lyceum. Theophrastus tended to be more empirical than Aristotle, and his special interest was in botany, where his contributions have led many to label him the founder of the science of plants. In a work on the senses and sensation, Theophrastus described in detail the observable processes of the mind, which he placed in the brain, unlike Aristotle. Theophrastus described such processes as sensation and perception, pain and pleasure, and emotions in a work that some consider an early discussion of physiological psychology (e.g., Stratton, 1917).

In addition to the work and study at the Lyceum, several other schools of thought flourished in the Greco-Roman period, including Skepticism, Cynicism, Epicureanism, and Stoicism.

Skepticism

Skepticism was founded by **Pyrrho** (ca. 365–270 B.C.), who traveled in Persia and India with Alexander the Great. Like Socrates, Pyrrho wrote nothing yet had a great effect on his students and contemporaries. Pyrrho's extreme version of **Skepticism** held that we are never in a position to have definitive beliefs about anything, including Skepticism itself. The only way to avoid believing in something that may be false is to not believe in anything. This does not mean that you should not conform to the rules of the society of which you are a part, however. It just means that you should not believe there is any rational basis for such rules.

Cynicism

The school of **Cynicism** was cofounded by **Antisthenes** (ca. 455–360 B.C.) and his pupil **Diogenes** (ca. 410–320 B.C.). Antisthenes was one of the people with Socrates when he died. Together, Diogenes and Antisthenes taught a back-to-nature life free from society's conventions. Diogenes became famous for his disregard of creature comforts and social niceties. According to legend, when Alexander the Great asked what he, Alexander, could do for Diogenes, the Cynic replied, "You could move out of the sun and not cast a shadow on me." Supposedly Diogenes lived in a barrel, "like a dog," thereby earning the title *kynikos,* which means "like a dog." From *kynikos* came the term *cynic.*

The Cynics not only dropped out of society, they attacked its precepts, seeing in society only hypocrisy, envy, greed, and hate. Another story tells of Diogenes wandering the streets of Athens by day carrying a lamp, searching for an honest man. Much of Cynicism was incorporated into Stoicism, but, unlike the Cynics, the Stoics did not reject society's comforts.

Stoicism

Zeno of Citium (ca. 333–262 B.C.) was the founder of Stoicism, named for the *Stoa Poikile* (painted colonnade, or porch) in which Zeno began his school. The chief themes of **Stoicism**—that the world functions according to a divine plan, that there are no accidents, and that whatever happens is just part of the plan—were developed by Zeno's successor, Cleänthes of Assos. Because life's events cannot be changed, it is best just to accept them. Acceptance is aided by a detached or indifferent attitude—by being stoic.

Stoicism gained such diverse adherents as the philosopher Seneca, the slave (and later noted teacher) Epictetus, and the Roman emperor **Marcus Aurelius** (121–180 A.D.). Marcus Aurelius was one of the best of the Roman emperors, and his *Meditations* reveal his innermost thoughts and are a delight to read. Being stoical was particularly adaptive under the Roman Empire, which emphasized fidelity to law and order. As the Roman Empire began to crumble, however, people sought other answers to how to cope with life. As we will see in Chapter 3, many found the answer in the new religion of Christianity.

Epicureanism

Epicureanism, the philosophy of **Epicurus** (ca. 341–270 B.C.), can be traced back to the atomism of Democritus. Like Democritus, Epicurus rejected the idea of an afterlife or of supernatural influences. In fact, Epicurus's disciple **Lucretius** (ca. 99–55 B.C.) proudly called Epicurus the "destroyer of religion."

Today, "epicure" is used to describe a person who is especially fond of luxury and sensuous pleasure, although this was not the life Epicurus endorsed. Epicurus refined **hedonism**—the search for pleasure and the avoidance of pain—by looking for pleasure in serenity and freedom from fear, not from sensuality, which he recognized was often followed by pain. For example, overindulgence in alcohol usually leads to a hangover. True pleasure, the absence of pain and anxiety, is to be found in simplicity and moderation.

CONCLUSIONS

Our survey of the philosophical traditions of the ancient Greeks has been designed to lay the foundation for our look in the next chapter at philosophy (and psychology) from the time of the Roman Empire into the Renaissance. In addition, important work in philosophy occurred in places other than the city-states of ancient Greece. For example, Egypt and Babylon were known for their rich philosophical traditions, and precursors of psychology can be seen in ancient Egypt (Laver, 1972). Alexandria, Egypt, in particular, was home to important thinkers, including the anatomists Herophilus and Erasistratus. Erasistratus is sometimes said to have been the first to distinguish between motor and sensory nerves and to have been the first to do *in vivo* work on the nervous system. However, historical events like the development of key trade routes, the spread of certain religions, and the ravages of wars made the philosophical systems of Periclean Greece and not Assyria (or elsewhere) of direct importance for modern psychology.

The Golden Age of Greece was a time in which medicine, philosophy, and science flourished, and it is possible for us to see connections from the Golden Age to the 20th century. Examples include the struggle begun by Alcmaeon and Hippocrates to develop medicine as a rational science, the debate between materialism and idealism, and the belief, begun by Pythagoras, that to know a thing is to be able to capture it mathematically. In addition, we see the origins of some of the most fundamental concepts of modern science (e.g., atomic theory) in the writings of the ancient Greeks.

Socrates, Plato's mentor, is still considered by some the most impressive thinker of all time. Although he was not a scientist, his ideas and methods provided the foundation for productive inquiry.

We will see that the writings of Plato and Aristotle shaped the scientific and intellectual pursuits of Western civilization for centuries. Aristotelian thought, especially on matters of biological and astro-geological science, became dogma after its rediscovery in the medieval period and provided a system to attack for the scientists and philosophers of the Renaissance. Still, a variety of concepts from both Plato and Aristotle can be seen clearly in more modern psychology (e.g., mental representations, catharsis, principles of association).

Clearly, medicine, philosophy, and science did not end with the decline in importance of the Greek city-states. As we have seen, several schools (e.g., Stoicism, Cynicism) emerged and were popular during the Roman era. In the next chapter, we will trace philosophy and science through the Middle Ages into the stimulative turmoil of the Renaissance.

S U M M A R Y

The Golden Age of Greece

The period between the birth of Pericles and the death of Aristotle is sometimes called the Golden Age of Greece. During much of this time, Athens flourished under democratic rule.

Philosophy in the Golden Age

The philosophical positions of materialism and idealism were debated during Greece's Golden Age. An idealist, Plato was the end of a line of development beginning with Pythagoras and Parmenides, whereas Democritus was a materialist. Plato also took much from Pythagoras, who is strongly associated with mathematical discoveries, particularly of the relations between music and numbers.

Heraclitus was intrigued by the changing nature of things, and his fascination with change can be linked to modern chaos theory. Parmenides rejected Heraclitus's idea of change, which he explained by distinguishing appearances from reality. Appearances we know from sensory experience, whereas reality we know from reason. Parmenides' extreme rationalism became the basis for Platonism. Parmenides was defended by Zeno of Elea,

who composed a series of paradoxes to show that change and movement are impossible.

In order to refute Parmenides' theory of the unchanging One, Democritus developed the theory of atomism, in which the universe consists of atoms (tiny, indivisible particles) and the void. Democritus held that all the qualities of objects we experience, except for weight and texture, are secondary qualities. He has been called a materialist, a determinist, a reductionist, and a nurturist.

The Sophists taught young men logic, science, philosophy, and rhetoric. Protagoras accepted sensation as the source of knowledge, refusing to theorize a higher reality. One of the greatest of the ancient philosophers, Socrates was sometimes accused of being a Sophist because of his "Socratic method" of logical argumentation to achieve creative ideas of concepts like beauty and truth. Socratic suggestions such as the importance of self-knowledge and the distinction between the general and the particular are the foundation of most later Western philosophies.

Socrates' pupil Plato founded the Academy. Like Parmenides, Plato believed in a world of Knowledge (containing the Forms, or Ideas) and a world of Opinion, using the parable of men chained in a cave to illustrate the differences between the two worlds. Learning to understand the Forms requires the recollection of knowledge we already possess, and Plato believed that knowledge is in the soul before birth. Plato's tripartite soul consisted of reason, spirit, and appetite.

Plato's student Aristotle founded a school to rival the Academy—the Lyceum. Whereas Plato was a rationalist, Aristotle was more of an empiricist who sought knowledge through the senses. In addition to Plato's deductive reasoning, Aristotle used the inductive method. Aristotle discovered the form of reasoning called the syllogism and wrote about four basic causes: material, formal, efficient, and final.

Aristotle's belief that animals might be arranged on a hierarchy of complexity led to the *scala naturae*. For Aristotle, all living things possessed *psyche*, but there were three different grades: vegetative, sensitive, and rational. Aristotle placed the mind in the heart, held that the mind without thought was like a blank slate, suggested three principles of association for recall, and recognized catharsis.

Medicine in the Golden Age and Beyond

Alcmaeon and Hippocrates practiced rational medicine rather than medicine tied to religion. Alcmaeon discovered the eustachian tubes and considered the brain the organ of thought. Hippocrates attributed epilepsy to natural causes and described the symptoms of several mental disorders. He believed that an imbalance in the four humors caused disease. Galen incorporated humoral theory into a personality theory and wrote extensively on the brain's ventricles, considering them the reservoir for animal spirits. Because of his monotheism, the early Christians made Galen the unquestioned authority in physiology.

Other Schools of Thought

Other Greek schools of thought included Skepticism, founded by Pyrrho; Cynicism, founded by Antisthenes and Diogenes; Epicureanism, founded by Epicurus and mostly known through the efforts of Lucretius; and Stoicism, founded by Zeno of Citium and popularized by Marcus Aurelius.

CONNECTIONS QUESTIONS

1. How might Greece's political system in the Age of Pericles be connected with the rise of the Sophists?
2. Why is the debate between the ideas of Heraclitus and Parmenides of importance to psychology?
3. Contrast and compare Plato and Aristotle across as many dimensions as you can.
4. Locate as many connections as you can between the thought of the ancient Greek physicians and philosophers and the psychologists in the 19th and 20th centuries.
5. Should the history of psychology begin with the Greeks? Some point earlier? Later? Why?
6. Draw a concept map connecting rational medicine, Pythagoras, Heraclitus, Parmenides, Zeno, Democritus, Protagoras, Socrates, Plato, and Aristotle, and compare your results with one possible solution provided on p. 561.
7. What connections might you draw between Galen and modern neurotransmitter research?

SUGGESTED READINGS

Allen, R. E. (Ed.) (1966). *Greek philosophy: Thales to Aristotle.* New York: Macmillan. This commonly used reader has short original passages by classical Greek philosophers, including Plato and Aristotle. In addition, there is a brief introduction that contains biographical information for the major Greek philosophers.

Durant, W. (1939). *The life of Greece.* New York: Simon and Schuster. This is the second volume in a monumental 10-volume work by Will and Ariel Durant. Like all the volumes, *The Life of Greece*

is highly readable and extensively referenced. Although modern historians question elements of Durant's work, it remains a delightful introduction.

Kirk, G. S., Raven, J. E., & Schofield, M. (Eds.) (1983). *The Presocratic philosophers* (2nd ed.). Cambridge: Cambridge University Press. This is one of the standard texts for the study of pre-Socratic philosophy. It provides detailed coverage of all the pre-Socratics, including several we did not examine in this chapter.

Sahakian, W. S. (Ed.) (1968). *History of psychology: A source book in systematic psychology.* Itasca, IL: F. E. Peacock Publishers, Inc. Sahakian's book contains brief excerpts from the writings of most of the major Greek philosophers, including passages from Democritus, Socrates and Plato, Aristotle, Zeno of Citium, and Epicurus. A variety of other volumes like Sahakian's book can be found, each providing an economical introduction to many original works.

Saunders, J. L. (Ed.) (1966). *Greek and Roman philosophy after Aristotle.* New York: The Free Press. This is a nice anthology containing short selections by the Cynics, Stoics, and so on. You will be surprised to see that much of the wisdom of these schools remains with us today.

Books of readings from Plato and Aristotle—as well as the later traditions such as Stoicism—are always in print. A good starting place for Plato would be one of the dialogues such as *Meno* or the *Republic.* One of Aristotle's most popular and readable works is the *Nicomachean Ethics,* which should be readily available. You will find *Meditations* by Marcus Aurelius amazingly relevant as a personal philosophy for the 21st century. When Bill Clinton was asked to name one book, other than the Bible, that has proven to be most important to him, he chose *The Meditations* of Marcus Aurelius.

The Roman Period, the Middle Ages, and the Renaissance

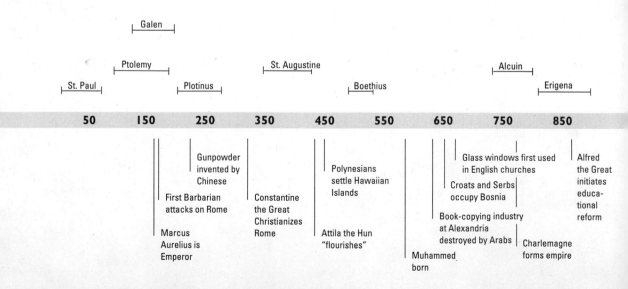

| Galen |
| Ptolemy | St. Augustine | Alcuin |
| St. Paul | Plotinus | Boethius | Erigena |

| 50 | 150 | 250 | 350 | 450 | 550 | 650 | 750 | 850 |

Gunpowder invented by Chinese

Glass windows first used in English churches

Alfred the Great initiates educational reform

Croats and Serbs occupy Bosnia

First Barbarian attacks on Rome

Constantine the Great Christianizes Rome

Polynesians settle Hawaiian Islands

Book-copying industry at Alexandria destroyed by Arabs

Marcus Aurelius is Emperor

Attila the Hun "flourishes"

Charlemagne forms empire

Muhammed born

Lull

Maimonides   St. Thomas Aquinas

Spinoza

Newton

Roger Bacon   William of Ockham

Galileo

Erasmus   Francis Bacon   Leibniz

St. Anselm   Grosseteste   Petrarch

Machiavelli   Harvey

Averroës

Duns Scotus

Copernicus   Descartes

Avicenna   Abélard   St. Albert Magnus

Luther   Gassendi

| 950 | 1050 | 1150 | 1250 | 1350 | 1450 | 1550 | 1650 | 1750 |

"Leaning" Tower of Pisa built

Cromwell dissolves parliament

Advanced hospitals built by Moslems

Marco Polo travels to China

Gutenberg begins printing

Bethlehem Hospital, London, becomes an asylum

Vikings discover Greenland

First recorded use of gondolas in Venice

William Shakespeare writes plays

Black Death devastates Europe

Martin Luther begins the Reformation (1517)

Macbeth becomes King of Scotland

Kublai Khan rules Mongol Empire

Columbus arrives in America (1492)

PHILOSOPHICAL AND THEOLOGICAL THOUGHT DURING THE ROMAN PERIOD

The material in this chapter can be divided into two major parts, the first part encompassing roughly the millenium and a half from the time of Christ until Descartes in the first half of the 17th century. The second part explores the key 17th-century Continental philosophers. The major theme of the pre-Descartes material can be seen as the slow progression of thought from the ancient Greeks and attempts to reconcile this scholarship with contemporary spiritual ideas. Descartes's primary significance lay in his effort to break completely withthe philosophies of the past, particularly with Aristotelianism, to establish a new approach to knowledge unfettered by dogma. The philosophies of Spinoza and Leibniz can be viewed as alternatives to Descartes's.

At the end of Chapter 2, we outlined the principal schools of thought during the Roman Empire. As we noted, some well-known figures, such as the Emperor Marcus Aurelius, made important contributions. However, the greatest influence on modern psychology during this period came from religious writers such as St. Paul. Before the Roman Empire fell, Christianity and what we call "Western Thought" became virtually synonymous. Much of our folk wisdom about human behavior, whether we are aware of it or not, comes from Pauline writings.

St. Paul

Paul (originally Saul; 10–64 A.D.) was born in Tarsus, a city now in southern Turkey, then part of the Roman Empire. Paul trained as a rabbi under a religious teacher in Jerusalem, even though there was a respected "university" in Tarsus, where he may have begun his classical education. He was probably executed by the Roman Emperor Nero.

Paul was extremely knowledgeable about Jewish theology and Greek philosophy. During Paul's day, Christianity was still viewed as a minor Jewish sect—Christ being a Jew—and it was largely through Paul's efforts that the Christian community became established. New Testament study reveals that Paul provided much of the actual theology that became Christianity's foundation. Much of what Paul wrote in his letters to individuals and to numerous early Christian churches was practical advice about daily matters and does not concern us here.

Paul considered the human body evil and the spirit (or soul) divine, and, in fact, many writers have suggested that Western civilization's notion of the body as "dirty," particularly the sexual body, can be traced to Paul. The rational mind is caught between the body and the spirit, sometimes serving one and sometimes serving the other. Like Plato, Paul saw the body as the major source of our problems. Humans are forced into a perpetual struggle between God's law and corrupt bodily urges, a conflict created by our spark of divinity. Unlike Plato, for Paul, reason was not the solution to the conflict. Faith in God was the answer. It is noteworthy that Paul authored much of Christian thought, and Christianity exerted a profound influence for centuries on how science and human behavior were viewed.

Plotinus

Plotinus (ca. 205–270) was a Neoplatonist philosopher who greatly influenced early Christian thought. Probably born in Egypt of Roman parentage, he received a Greek education and studied in Alexandria under Ammonius Saccas, the founder of Neoplatonic philosophy. Beginning in Alexandria, **Neoplatonism** was a school that tried to combine Plato's views with ethical concepts from Christianity, Judaism, and Near Eastern mysticism.

Although Plotinus accepted much of Plato's philosophy, his own opinion of sensory experience was less negative than Plato's. For Plotinus, although there was much of beauty in the sensory world, it was less perfect than the spiritual world. Because the spiritual world was the early Christians' chief concern, it was a short journey for some from Neoplatonism to Christianity. Thus, through the link of the Church, Neoplatonism became the dominant European philosophy for generations, bridging the gap between ancient and medieval thought.

CHRISTIANITY, ISLAM, AND JEWISH PHILOSOPHY OF THE MEDIEVAL ERA

As we have noted, the period from the Roman Empire until the Renaissance was dominated by religious thought, although not all of it was Christian. This medieval period—parts of which are sometimes called the Dark Ages because of the relative lack of philosophical and scientific development—contains several points of interest for psychology, beginning with St. Augustine.

St. Augustine

The most influential Christian scholar since St. Paul, **St. Augustine** of Hippo (or, Aurelius Augustinus; 354–430) was born in Tagaste, part of the Roman province of Numidia, which is in modern Tunisia. According to Copleston (1950), the "African Doctor . . . came of a pagan father, Patricius, and a Christian mother, St. Monica" (p. 55). Augustine's mother introduced him to Christianity at an early age, and at 16 his father sent him to Carthage to study rhetoric and law. In Carthage, Augustine read Cicero's *Hortensius* and wrote of it that "I was inflamed by such a love of philosophy." In addition, he took a mistress, later remarking: "Give me chastity and continency, but not yet." His mistress gave him a son.

In 383, Augustine traveled to Rome, and the following year he went to Milan to teach rhetoric. In 387, Augustine and his son were baptized by St. Ambrose. Augustine returned to Africa and became Bishop of Hippo in 396. Augustine (Figure 3–1) died in 430, as the Vandals were besieging Hippo.

Like Descartes would do over a thousand years later, Augustine sought one certain aspect of human experience, and, like Descartes, he found it in the fact that he doubted. For Augustine, this proved the validity of inner experience, which could be studied through **introspection** (literally to look within). Introspection in some form has been a major method for studying the mind's contents since St. Augustine's time.

FIGURE 3–1.   St. Augustine reading St. Paul's Epistles.

Source: Philosophical Library, New York.

Augustine's *Confessions* (ca. 400) is both a spiritual autobiography and an original work of philosophy that is considered a classic of world literature. In addition, he wrote about such matters of relevance to psychology as free will, reason, and memory. Augustine believed that our freedom to choose explains evil in the world. People choose evil, thereby denying themselves an afterlife. During life, incorrect choices lead to guilt, which, along with feelings of virtue for having chosen correctly, operates as an internal control over behavior.

Augustine considered extensively the nature of human knowledge, including scientific knowledge. Using Thales (Chapter 2) as his prototypical scientist, Augustine was not totally sympathetic to "knowledge" unconnected with religion. For

Augustine, reason without faith was possible, but necessarily incomplete. Humans have an ultimate spiritual destiny, and the human condition cannot be understood unless viewed from the standpoint of the Christian faith. In fact, Augustine believed that the world must be considered from this perspective, which meant that science and philosophy not in the service of theology were suspect (St. Augustine, 412–427/1931). Augustine's influence set the tone of Christian thinking for the next millenium and may have been important in the pervasive distrust in science characteristic of the Christian Church.

The Middle Ages

The **Middle Ages** are often said to have begun with the collapse of the Roman Empire around 500 and to have lasted until the Renaissance, which began about 1500. Although little scholarship closely connected to contemporary psychology was produced in the first half of this medieval period, we will briefly mention some of the important thinkers who served as transitional figures between the ancient world and the later Middle Ages.

For example, around the year 500, a still-unknown writer produced work that stimulated debate and discussion for the next 1,500 years. Originally, scholars attributed the writings to a disciple of St. Paul, Dionysius the Areopagite, but it is now assumed that the author used a pseudonym. As a result, modern scholars call the author of these works **Pseudo-Dionysius**. Although the writings are mostly theological, they greatly influenced scholars of the Middle Ages, because of the author's systematic attempts to relate Neoplatonic views with Christian thought.

By contrast, the writings of **Anicius Manlius Severinus Boethius** (ca. 480–525) were primarily Aristotelian. Boethius's most famous work was *De consolatione philosophiae* (*The Consolation of Philosophy*), written while the author was in prison awaiting execution (ca. 525). Boethius had been an important political figure whose goals included translating the Greek classics into Latin and reforming education. During his lifetime, the state

of Roman science and philosophy was low, with virtually none of the works of Plato or Aristotle available. Although Boethius's plans for educational reform were cut short by his execution, he was responsible for much of the Greek wisdom that survived into the medieval period. For the next millenium, the *Consolation* was probably the most widely read book after the Bible. Pseudo-Dionysius and Boethius are important because they connect later medieval scholarship with the classical Greek philosophies.

Alcuin (ca. 735–804) was another beacon of learning during the early Middle Ages. Born and educated at York, Alcuin was invited to the court of Charlemagne (Charles the Great, 742–814), King of the Franks, where he became the court philosopher/physician/astrologer/magician. Under Charlemagne's direction, Alcuin founded the Palatine school in the capital at Aachen, now a German city. The Palatine school may have been the conceptual model for the University of Paris.

Alcuin's impact on education during the Carolingian Empire (Charlemagne's empire) is undisputed. He may also have been involved in scientific information exchanges with Islamic philosophers, medical information exchanges with Jewish scholars, and the introduction of Arabic numerals into Western Civilization (perhaps to facilitate computations in astrology and astronomy, as Roman numerals are tedious for advanced calculations).

John Scotus Erigena (ca. 810–877) was also one of the key thinkers of the early medieval period. Erigena was born in "Scotia" (now Ireland); Eriugena means "born of the peoples of Erin," and Erin is another name for Ireland (Wippel & Wolter, 1969). Like Alcuin under Charlemagne, Erigena was the master of the Palatine school under Charles the Bald. In his major writings, Erigena attempted to fuse Neoplatonism with Christian doctrines and to reconcile faith and reason. He is also considered to have anticipated aspects of both Hegelian rationalism (Chapter 5) and scholasticism (discussed later). Supposedly, Erigena's students killed him with their writing pens, for the "sin of trying to make them think."

Islamic and Jewish Philosophy

During the period after the Roman Empire's fall, for the most part the wisdom of the ancient Greeks was lost to Europe. However, at the same time the Arabs were able to make great advances in philosophy, medicine, and science by building directly on the classical works, particularly those of Aristotle.

In the Arab world, Islam was the predominant religion, arising from the teachings of the prophet Muhammed (also Mohammed). Muhammed (ca. 570–632) was born in Mecca, the Islamic holy city in Saudia Arabia. Orphaned at 6, he was raised by relatives and trained to be a merchant. When he was about 40, Muhammed began to receive revelations from Allah (God), which are now contained in the Koran (Qur'an). By 630, Muhammed and his followers had gained control over all Arabia, and within 100 years of his death, the Muslim (or Moslem) sphere of influence was larger than the Roman Empire had been at its height.

Although there were many well-known Arabic philosophers, we will focus on Avicenna and Averroës. A Persian, Avicenna represents the "Eastern" tradition, whereas Averroës is more "Western," having lived and worked in Cordova, Spain. Although both men were Muslims and wrote in Arabic, neither was an Arab, illustrating the Islamic world's scope. Both men were important for Western philosophy because they preserved and transmitted the teachings of Aristotle and other Greek thinkers and because they wrote interpretations of the Greeks that led to controversy (and ultimately to change) in medieval philosophy. Without Avicenna and Averroës, Aristotelian revival in the West would have been almost unimaginable.

Avicenna

Avicenna (Arabic name, ibn Sina; 980–1037) was precocious, memorizing the Koran by the age of 10 and becoming a practicing physician at 16. Centering on Aristotle, Avicenna's philosophy also contained original elements and Neoplatonic influences. Much of Avicenna's work involved making

FIGURE 3–2. Avicenna.

Source: Philosophical Library, New York.

Aristotle compatible with the prevailing theology. Avicenna is shown in Figure 3–2.

In order to explain human intellectual activity, Avicenna distinguished between the possible intellect and the Agent Intellect. According to Avicenna, God creates a single effect called an *Intelligence,* which, in turn, creates a subordinate Intelligence. There are nine Intelligences, with the ninth creating the final Intelligence, which is the Agent Intellect. The Agent Intellect creates the minds (souls) of humans.

However, in the beginning humans have only a possible intellect, in the sense of a potential. Although the human intellect has the potential to know, it is not created with knowledge, which reflects Aristotle's nurture position on the nature-nurture issue. The intellect's acquisition of knowledge requires the bodily senses, the power to retain images in memory, and the ability to discover the essence of things through abstraction.

Once discovered, Avicenna's work interested Christian scholars. For example, in the 13th century, Siger de Brabant at the University of Paris came under suspicion for teaching Arabic "psychology." Christian theologian St. Bonaventura thought that Avicenna's psychology, as taught by Siger de Brabant, threatened the notion of personal individuality, although Avicenna had not intended this interpretation. The problem for Christian writers was that the Agent Intellect, and not God, enlightened the human intellect. Although Siger de Brabant was eventually acquitted by the Inquisitor, he was apparently murdered by his secretary while being held for surveillance.

Averroës

Like Avicenna, **Averroës** (1126–1198) was a prodigious scholar. Averroës thought Aristotle was the greatest of all philosophers and considered him a model of human perfection. Although they both generally started from the same Aristotelian source, Averroës did not always agree with Avicenna. For example, Averroës did not believe that humans have possible intellects separate from the Agent Intellect. He denied the doctrine of immortality and had little respect for theology, which explains why many pre-Renaissance Christian theologians found his teachings heretical. Averroës's (Figure 3–3) primary importance came from his belief that philosophy and theology could be independent, another foreshadowing of scholasticism, the major intellectual movement of the late Middle Ages.

Maimonides

Jews were treated inconsistently in Europe. At times their knowledge (often medical) brought them fame and fortune, whereas at other times they were persecuted as pagans. Like Arabic thought, Jewish philosophy was more advanced than Christian scholarship through the Middle

FIGURE 3–3.   Averroës.
Source: Philosophical Library, New York.

Ages. Of the Jewish thinkers from this era, **Maimonides**, or Moses Ben Maimon (1135–1204), was the most influential. He was born at nearly the same time and in the same place (Cordova, Spain) as Averroës. Maimonides was forced to emigrate from Spain to Morocco and then to Egypt, where he practiced medicine. In his medical writings, he anticipated modern ideas of bodily afflictions caused by both psychological factors and allergies. His *The Guide of the Perplexed* (1190) still stands as an excellent treatise on the relation between reason (or science) and faith (or religion). In *Guide*, Maimonides's intention was to harmonize Judaism and Aristotle, and his doctrines were paralleled by later theologians, most importantly by Thomas Aquinas (discussed later). Through Aquinas, Maimonides's insights were probably transmitted to later *Thomists* (followers of *Thom*as Aquinas).

CHRISTIAN PHILOSOPHY IN THE LATER MIDDLE AGES

Gradually Western scholars (often monks) became familiar with Greek and Roman thought, often through reading Jewish and Islamic writers. In turn, a renewed interest in philosophy and science emerged to become the foundation for the Renaissance. In the Augustinian tradition, some of these scholars were skeptical of science or philosophy that did not serve theology. This skepticism has often been misinterpreted as an anti-intellectualism, and many of the most gifted thinkers of the Middle Ages—such as St. Peter Damian (1007–1072)—have been erroneously portrayed as mindlessly against philosophy and science. In fact, at issue was the place of, and not the use of, this newly acquired wisdom. Several generations were required to clarify the relation between reason and faith, and St. Anselm was one of the important early contributors.

St. Anselm

Born into a noble family, **St. Anselm** (1033–1109) became a Benedictine monk against his father's wishes. He eventually became the Archbishop of Canterbury (Figure 3–4), a position he held until his death. Anselm believed strongly that dialectics and other rational aspects of formal philosophy were important to theologians. His belief in the value of reason for understanding God directly conflicts with the Christian tradition emphasizing acceptance on faith. Because of his beliefs, Anselm is often considered the founder of **scholasticism**, a system of thought that dominated the later Middle Ages. Based on Aristotelian logic and the writings of the early Christian thinkers, scholasticism's adherents were called schoolmen.

St. Anselm is also known for his **ontological argument** for God's existence, which states that God is "that than which nothing greater can be thought." If God did not exist, then something greater than He could be thought; thus, God must exist. Anselm's ontological argument was used by Descartes and others.

FIGURE 3–4.   Anselm, the Archbishop of Canterbury.

Source: Philosophical Library, New York.

Peter Abélard

Peter Abélard (1079–1142) was perhaps the most brilliant of the Western philosophers between Aristotle and Descartes, but not the most saintly. The eldest son of a noble family in Brittany, Abélard sought out intellectual debate, forsaking a military career for the love of "dialectical disputation" (Wipple & Wolter, 1969). He studied first under a nominalist, and then later under a realist. **Nominalists** believed that universals exist in name only, that words like "goodness" and "beauty" are merely labels allowing the categorization of objects with similar traits. By contrast, **realists** believed that there are universals like "goodness" and "beauty" that are independent of specific examples and have a real existence not unlike Plato's Forms.

Abélard's school endorsed a "moderate realism" position in the nominalist-realist debate. His position was that there is a reality behind the universals, whose ground is the way similar things strike our minds. Although this is an objective ground for the universals, it is not something real in the sense of a thing, as the "exaggerated" realists contended. Abélard also rejected the strict nominalist view that the universal is just a subjective ideal for which there is no objective ground.

Abélard's moderate position on universals was victorious over the extremes of realism and nominalism, and the next major treatment of the problem of universals did not come until William of Ockham nearly 2 centuries later. Although he was sometimes critical of Aristotle, Abélard was also one of the persons most responsible for the high esteem in which the Greek master was held by the Church for centuries. Additionally, some of Abélard's Aristotelian reflections are directly important for psychology. For example, Abélard held that the act of thinking and the content of thought are distinct from each other. The importance of this point for understanding the nature of human thought was still being considered as recently as the late 19th century by William James (Chapter 10).

Abélard became the most celebrated teacher in Paris, and his particular dialectical techniques are said to have revolutionized the teaching of theology. However, Abélard's reputation for publicly debating and often ridiculing other well-known teachers and church figures eventually proved costly. First, there was the matter of his love affair with Héloïse, the 17-year-old niece of the canon Fulbert, with whom Abélard was lodging. Although the couple was secretly married after Héloïse gave birth to Abélard's son, her relatives broke into Abélard's bedroom one night and castrated him. When two of Abélard's assailants were captured, they lost their genitals *and* their eyes, which shows that some sympathized with Abélard. Still, Abélard's career in the Church was tarnished. "He felt a certain unpoetic justice in his fall: he had been maimed in the flesh that had sinned, and had been betrayed by the man whom he had betrayed" (Durant, 1950, p. 938).

Near the end of his life, St. Bernard accused him of heresy, arranged for his condemnation, and thwarted his attempts at a papal appeal. Banned from teaching, Abélard was condemned to live in bitter silence at the Cluny monastery. At his death, Héloïse had Abélard's remains interred at the monastic school he founded and then gave to Héloïse and a sisterhood (Figure 3–5). When Héloïse died in 1164, she was placed in the same tomb. Their remains were taken to Paris in 1800, and in 1817 the two historic lovers were buried in the same sepulchre.

St. Thomas Aquinas

Born in the castle of Roccasecca (in Italy), **St. Thomas Aquinas** (1225–1274) was educated by the Benedictines of Monte-Cassino and at the University of

FIGURE 3–5.   Peter Abélard installs his mistress Héloïse as the abbess of the Convent of the Paraclete.

Source: Philosophical Library, New York.

Naples. When he entered the Dominican order in 1243, his brothers kidnapped him and imprisoned him in the family castle for 2 years. He escaped to Cologne, where he became a pupil of **St. Albertus Magnus** (ca. 1193–1280), the era's major Aristotelian scholar.

At Naples, Aquinas read Aristotle and probably Avicenna, Averroës, and Maimonides. Aquinas became such an Aristotelian devotee that it is not clear if it makes sense to talk about a separate Thomistic psychology. Basically, Aquinas's main contribution was to reintroduce the West to Aristotle's psychology through Christianity's filter.

Aquinas also championed the view that reason and faith are compatible, arguing that all true paths should lead to the same result. Therefore, faith and reason could be considered independently, and a philosophy separate from theology was suggested as a possibility for the first time in almost 1,000 years in the Christian world. Aquinas himself continued to blend faith and reason in good scholastic fashion.

Aquinas (Figure 3–6) wrote about a variety of matters of psychological relevance: for example, the relation between the soul and the body (in some ways anticipating Descartes); "faculties" (rational, sensitive, nutritive, etc.); and the *agens intellectus* (Avicenna's Agent Intellect), or the part of us concerned with understanding, judgment, and reason. Between Aquinas and the Renaissance, the Church remained the major factor in determining proper behavior and proper topics of scholarship. John Duns Scotus and William of Ockham, two Franciscan friars associated with Oxford, are the last medieval thinkers in the Christian tradition we will consider. Although they held some different views (e.g., on nominalism and realism), both are remembered for working to separate philosophy from theology, the trend in the latter part of the Middle Ages.

John Duns Scotus

Known as the Subtle Doctor, **John Duns Scotus** (ca. 1265–1308) was born in Scotland at the Duns estate, near the present town of Duns. He was educated and taught at Oxford, Paris, possibly at Cambridge,

FIGURE 3–6.   St. Thomas Aquinas.
Source: Corbis-Bettmann.

and at Cologne, where he died. His associates collected and edited his writings after his death.

Widely disparaged, Duns Scotus's philosophy represented a strong reaction against both Aristotle and Aquinas. His followers were called Dunsmen, Duncemen, and eventually Dunces, a term first applied to any opponent of education and then later to any stupid person. Whereas Aquinas argued for the supremacy of reason, Duns Scotus argued for the supremacy of the will, and his view became known as *voluntarism,* a term Wilhelm Wundt, considered the creator of a separate science of psychology, used to describe his system (Chapter 7).

William of Ockham

William of Ockham (also Occam, ca. 1285–1349) was born in the town of Ockham, near present-day

London. Ockham studied at Oxford as an "inceptor," or beginner, and never attained a higher position because of his controversial views (Ockham is sometimes called "the Venerable Inceptor"). Pope John XXII summoned Ockham to answer charges of heresy, and he was excommunicated. Fleeing to Bavaria in 1328, Ockham died in Munich, probably from the Black Death.

Ockham is known for having rejected more central assumptions of the Church and of philosophy than anyone else of his time. In the struggle to find universals, Ockham held that universality can be attributed only to terms, not to things, which is the nominalist position. Ockham is best known in philosophy for his successful defense of nominalism against realism.

In psychology, Ockham is known for **Ockham's razor**. Ockham believed that arguments should have their extraneous assumptions shaved away, a point sometimes called the *Law of Parsimony*, which holds that if two explanations are equally plausible, the simplest explanation—usually the one with the fewest assumptions—is preferred. Ockham chose the nominalist position because it did not require him to assume that universals have an independent reality. That is, nominalism required fewer assumptions than realism. In the late 19th century, C. Lloyd Morgan (Chapter 9) applied a principle like Ockham's razor to explanations of animal behavior.

MEDIEVAL SCIENCE BEFORE THE RENAISSANCE

Although pre-Renaissance scientific achievement was limited, a few names deserve mention. For example, the Englishman **Robert Grosseteste** (ca. 1175–1253) was the first chancellor of Oxford University, and a catalog of his works includes treatises on sound, motion, and color—all topics of interest to psychology (Southern, 1986). **Roger Bacon** (ca. 1214–1292) studied at Oxford and Paris and gained a reputation for knowledge that led some to call him *Doctor mirabilis* (wonderful doctor). His interest in learning nature's secrets aroused the suspicions of his fellow Franciscans, and Bacon was denounced as a sorcerer and imprisoned for 10 years with neither books nor scientific instruments. Bacon's name is associated with inventions like the magnifying glass and gunpowder and with speculations on lighter-than-air flying machines, telescopes, and microscopes. Despite his years of confinement and the censorship of the Franciscans, Bacon managed to publish important works on mathematics, philosophy, and logic.

Raymond (or Ramon) Lull (ca. 1232–1315) was a Spanish theologian and mystic known as *Doctor Illuminatus* (enlightened doctor, see Figure 3–7) because of his great learning. Lull was perhaps the only person of this period to have been more ambitious than Roger Bacon. Born in Majorca, he led a dissolute life as a soldier and troubadour poet in his youth (a troubadour was a poet-musician). In 1266, Lull became an ascetic

FIGURE 3–7. Raymond Lull (*Doctor Illuminatus*).

Source: Philosophical Library, New York.

and began a crusade to convert the Muslims to Christianity. Toward this end, he presented a system for acquiring knowledge and solving all possible problems by manipulating fundamental ideas using Aristotelian logic. Lull assumed, as would Leibniz several hundred years later, a kind of logical atomism—that is, that certain elementary concepts exist from which all knowledge is constructed. Lull aimed to build a device "programmed" with the atomic concepts and logical rules of reasoning and then to let the machine generate all there was to know. Some modern commentators (MacLennan, 1990; Moody, 1967) have suggested that Lull was the father of computer programming.

Lull was an adversary of Averroës and lectured against Averroës's principles at the University of Paris. After this, he returned to Algeria to continue his mission to convert Muslims. Twice banished from Algeria, on his third mission Lull was stoned and died a few days later.

UNIVERSITIES IN THE MIDDLE AGES

Before we enter the Renaissance and encounter the explosion of knowledge it brought, we will survey briefly the early universities. In Chapter 2, we noted the "universities" founded by Plato (the Academy) and Aristotle (the Lyceum), both closed by the Emperor Justinian in 529. In the first century A.D., St. Paul probably studied at a university in Tarsus, then part of the Roman Empire.

These early universities were not universities as we think of them today, and we should probably look to the later Middle Ages for the first true universities. The first European universities were Italy's University of Bologna, founded in 1119, and the University of Paris (with a controversial date of founding). Oxford University was also founded in the 12th century, and its development was hastened by the exclusion of Englishmen from the University of Paris in 1167. Other early universities were at Cambridge (first college founded in 1284) in England, Toulouse (1229) and Orléans (1309) in France, and Lisbon (1290) in Portugal.

Many of the early universities originally followed a curriculum suggested by Boethius and established by Alcuin at the Palatine. It consisted of an arts course—actually, the study of the seven liberal arts (arithmetic, geometry, astronomy, music, grammar, rhetoric, and dialectic) plus natural philosophy or science, ethics, and metaphysics—and advanced courses in law, medicine, and theology. After becoming truly important in the 13th century, universities became a powerful intellectual force during the Renaissance, both for preserving and spreading knowledge and for producing it.

RENAISSANCE HUMANISM

Although there were other renaissances (e.g., the 8th- and 9th-century Carolingian Empire, the 12th-century foundation of the first true universities), when we speak of the Renaissance (literally "rebirth"), we are referring to the revival of classical art, architecture, literature, and learning that originated in Italy and spread throughout Europe in the period from the 14th through the 16th centuries. Contemporaneous with this revival and contributing to it were such things as the invention of printing, the discovery of America, the religious Reformation, and astronomical discoveries that changed our understanding of the universe and of our place in it.

Major changes in the social order produced the *Zeitgeist* that fostered and encouraged the scientific achievements that were part of the Renaissance. For example, **humanism**—a focus on human interests—is considered a primary factor contributing to the Renaissance. Several themes characterized Renaissance humanism, including curiosity about human abilities and accomplishments; a desire to make religion more individualistic and less ceremonial; historical interest, particularly in the works of the leading Greek and Roman poets, philosophers, and politicians; and opposition to the mindless support of Aristotle as the authority on all matters of secular science.

Early people whose work embodied one or more of humanism's themes include Petrarch,

Juan Luis Vives, and Giovanni Pico. **Petrarch** (1304–1374), or Francesco Petrarca, was an Italian poet and scholar whose writings arguably signal the beginning of the Renaissance. Petrarch wrote much of his work in opposition to Averroës's reliance on Aristotle, a philosopher Petrarch found suspect. Petrarch's opposition to scholasticism and to religious authority aided challenges to Aristotelian scientific dogma.

The Spaniard **Juan Luis Vives** (1492–1540) is important for his views on education and for his three-volume work on psychology and the scientific method, *De anima et Vita* (1538). Vives can be credited with applying a biomedical approach to fields such as education and psychology. For example, in psychology, Vives relied on Hippocratic humoral explanations for mental phenomena rather than using scholastic arguments about the nature and essence of the soul and its faculties. Because of his emphasis on the physiological aspects of the life processes, Vives perhaps deserves consideration as "The Father of Modern Psychology" (Clements, 1967).

The work of Italian philosopher and humanist **Giovanni Pico della Mirandola** (1463–1494) emphasized individualism. Although Pico's range of influence was broad, his work on human dignity was his most enduring contribution. Pico's important philosophical works included an attempted reconciliation of Platonic and Aristotelian doctrines and a document on free will.

Another major social change leading to and sustaining the Renaissance involved **Martin Luther** (1483–1546), the German founder of the Protestant Reformation. Although most of Luther's actions were motivated by his disgust over conditions within the Catholic Church, humanism's themes can be seen in his works. For example, Luther argued that the assimilation of Aristotle was a major cause of the Church's decline, and he also sought a more personalized and less ritualistic religion. Clearly the Reformation changed Western society, in part by challenging the Pope's authority as well as Aristotelian dogma. Both challenges added to the *Zeitgeist* that produced psychology's most immediate philosophic antecedents.

Desiderius Erasmus (1466–1536) was another early Renaissance social philosopher. Ordained a priest in 1492, Erasmus was already being drawn away from scholasticism toward humanism. Erasmus was a "debunker," who, among other things, tried to dispel the myth of better life through alchemy (chemistry of the Middle Ages whose principal aims were to discover the potion for eternal youth and to change base metals into gold). He sided with neither the Catholics nor the Protestants in their conflicts and managed to become an enemy of both sides. Without approving of Luther's theology, Erasmus defended him for the sake of freedom of conscience and helped save Luther's life at the beginning of the latter's challenge of the Catholic Church.

Niccolò Machiavelli (1469–1527) achieved the dubious honor of having his name become a word, *Machiavellian,* which refers to the use of deceit and duplicity to achieve goals. It also refers to a psychological construct (e.g., Christie & Geis, 1960; Wilson, Near, & Miller, 1996). Machiavelli's reputation rests largely on *Il Principe* (*The Prince*), published 5 years after his death. His torture by the Medici (a banking family that ruled Florence and funded much of the artistic Renaissance) gave Machiavelli firsthand experience of human cruelty. *The Prince* is basically a handbook for rulers, and its main theme is that "the ends justify the means."

Machiavelli wrote other works—for example, *Discourses*—that are not as cynical as *The Prince.* In *Discourses,* Machiavelli presented an analysis of republican government in which he praised democracy. In turn, Machiavelli's admirers lauded him for his realism about human nature, whereas his more numerous and more vocal critics saw him as dangerously cynical and amoral. Interestingly, Machiavelli's disciples may have been Machiavellian in their public pronouncements about him. For example, King Frederick II of Prussia (1712–1786) wrote a book opposing Machiavelli at the same time that he practiced Machiavelli's ideas. Machiavelli's views contributed to an image of human nature that has remained part of psychology in some form ever since.

RENAISSANCE SCIENCE

At the beginning of the Renaissance, ancient and conventional wisdom began to be questioned, and much was found to be wrong. This era marks the birth of many ideas central to modern science, and we will survey briefly some of the key contributions that provided an important foundation for all subsequent sciences, including psychology. One change in our way of thinking of ourselves, the universe, and of our place in the universe came with the publication by **Nicolas Copernicus** (1473–1543), modern astronomy's Polish founder, of a heliocentric (sun-centered) view of the universe. Before Copernicus, Ptolemy's (ca. 90–168) geocentric (earth-centered) view prevailed, because it agreed with the theological idea of the central place of humans in creation. Thus, Copernicus's work, *De revolutionibus orbium coelestium* (*On the Revolutions of the Celestial Spheres*), received a hostile reception when it was published in 1543. Tradition holds that Copernicus delayed publication and first saw the book on his deathbed.

Italian philosopher **Giordano Bruno** (1548–1600) extended the Copernican system to include an infinity of suns like ours, with each circled by planets possibly inhabited by sentient beings. Bruno traveled widely in Europe, lecturing about a pantheistic philosophy in which God animated all of creation. Arrested in Venice by the Inquisition, Bruno was burned at the stake in Rome after an 8-year trial. Although the Renaissance favored change, there was still resistance to ideas too different from long-held beliefs.

Another scientist who ran afoul of the Inquisition was Italian astronomer, mathematician, and natural scientist **Galileo Galilei** (1564–1642). Perfecting the refracting telescope invented in Holland, Galileo used it to make observations that convinced him that Copernicus's theory was correct. He proclaimed the Milky Way to be a track of limitless stars and inferred the sun's rotation from the movement of spots on it. In 1632, Galileo published a work supporting the Copernican system and was called before the Inquisition. After a tedious trial, he was convicted and forced to abjure (recant) his teachings. Under house arrest near Florence, Galileo (Figure

FIGURE 3–8.   Galileo Galilei.

Source: Philosophical Library, New York.

3–8) continued his studies while gradually losing his sight and hearing. Galileo's final discovery was the moon's monthly and annual oscillations, made just before he became totally blind.

In addition to his role as a pioneering natural scientist, Galileo did work directly relevant to psychology. For example, Galileo did not believe that subjective properties such as color, smell, and taste have the same reality as physical properties of objects such as shape and motion. He believed that the former qualities reside in the observer, not in the object observed. Without an observer, the qualities disappear. Galileo called the qualities inherent in matter (e. g., shape, quantity, and motion) **primary qualities**, whereas **secondary qualities** (e.g., color, smell, and taste) arise when the primary qualities contact an observer's sensory apparatus. Galileo's distinction was accepted by many later theorists, including Descartes and Newton (Martinez, 1974), the British empiricists, and the first psychologists.

Further astronomical discoveries were made by **Tycho Brahe** (1564–1601), a Dane, and by the German astronomer **Johann Kepler** (1571–1630), who went to Prague as Brahe's assistant and succeeded him in 1601. At 14, Brahe witnessed a partial solar eclipse and became obsessed with astronomy. Considered the greatest of the pretelescope astronomers, Brahe was brilliant but hot-tempered; at 19, he lost most of his nose in a duel and wore a fake silver nose thereafter. Kepler made discoveries in optics, physics, and geometry and proposed fundamental laws of planetary motion that formed the basis for Isaac Newton's later discoveries.

Galileo's contemporary, **Sir Francis Bacon** (1561–1626), an Englishman, made no signal discoveries, but his unflagging promotion of experimentation for understanding nature gives him an important place in the history of science. Abandoning the deductive logic of his predecessors, Bacon stressed the necessity to be continually on guard for evidence that might refute a previously held belief. For Bacon, truth came not from authority but from experience. Almost singlehandedly, he created the inductive scientific method, which he died pursuing. He caught a fatal cold while stuffing a bird with snow to observe the effects of cold on meat preservation.

Bacon is perhaps best known for his discussion of **Idols,** or preconceived notions that contaminate reasoning. For example, Bacon's Idols of the Cave were based on Plato's cave allegory and refer to limitations placed on the untrained mind by experience (e.g., by books read, by intellectual authorities accepted, etc.). Idols of the Tribe are biases that an individual brings to any experience. Idols of the Market Place are biases that result from carelessly created language, which can weaken knowledge. Finally, Idols of the Theater are the "grand systematic dogmas" we endorse—such as the principles of science—out of custom, gullibility, and laziness.

Another Englishman, **William Harvey** (1578–1657), used the experimental method to study blood's circulation and proved conclusively that the heart was simply a pump. In so doing, Harvey demonstrated that the scientific method could be used to study a biological system as precisely as physical systems are studied by physicists, paving the way for experimental biology.

Sir Isaac Newton (1642–1727) was an English physicist and mathematician and one of the greatest physical scientists of all time. His most important discoveries include the law of gravitation, the idea that white light is a mixture of all colors, and calculus. Newton (Figure 3–9) constructed the first reflecting telescope, and his 1687 publication, *Philosophiae naturalis principia mathematica* (*Mathematical Principles of Natural Philosophy*), inspired John Locke (Chapter 4) to write a work of great importance for psychology (*An Essay Concerning Human Understanding*). Newton was also interested in the relationship between science and religion. A special issue of *The Journal of Mind and Behavior* (Vol. 16, No. 1) recently explored Newton's monumental impact on science, including his influence on psychology.

FIGURE 3–9.   Isaac Newton studying a beam of light.

Source: Philosophical Library, New York.

Newton also was involved in a number of controversies, one of which was with Gottfried Leibniz (discussed later) over the discovery of calculus. It has been speculated that some of Newton's irascible behavior was the result of mercury poisoning (Broad, 1981). Before 1693, Newton had been involved in alchemical experiments often pursued until late at night, and sometimes he fell asleep next to bubbling retorts. During his "madness," Newton wrote many strange letters to his friends, accusing Locke in one letter of trying to embroil him with women. Further evidence for Newton's mercury poisoning comes from samples of his hair, which have been analyzed and found to contain elevated mercury concentrations.

As you can see from this survey of social and scientific changes characterizing the Renaissance, Western Europe was awash with new ideas and creative personalities. Added to this ferment was the danger from the Church, which sought to protect its influence over the spiritual realm and all other aspects of the lives of its faithful. However, no matter how repressive the Church tried to be, there were always people willing to risk everything to defend their perception of the truth. We have noted some who ran afoul of the Inquisition: Bruno, who was burned at the stake for supporting Copernicus and going beyond him; Galileo, who was forced to recant his views; and Luther, who was nearly killed before he could begin the Reformation. Against this backdrop of scientific and social change appeared a man who altered philosophy forever—René Descartes.

RENÉ DESCARTES

His mother died within a few days of his birth, the victim of the tuberculosis she bequeathed to her son. **René Descartes** (1596–1650) himself was so weak that the attending physician had no hope for his survival. In fact, if a nurse had not given him the warmth and nourishment of her body, Descartes would have soon followed his mother.

Descartes was born near Tours, France, in a town now called La Haye-Descartes. His father was a wealthy lawyer who willed his son an annual income that gave Descartes the freedom to live without having to work. In 1604, Descartes entered the Jesuit College of La Flèche, where his teachers recognized his delicate health and his mental precocity and allowed him to stay in bed beyond normal rising hours. Descartes spent the time devouring books. Because of his experiences with them, Descartes never lost his admiration for the Jesuits.

At 17, Descartes went to Paris and from Paris to the University of Poitiers, where he graduated with degrees in civil and canon law. Next, he enlisted in the army of Prince Maurice of Nassau. Descartes continued his studies, particularly in mathematics, through various military campaigns. On November 10, 1619, he had three visions or dreams in which a divine spirit revealed a new philosophy. This experience led Descartes to formulate analytic geometry and to pursue the application of mathematical methodology to philosophy. He conceived of a system of true knowledge modeled on mathematics and supported by rationalism.

Returning to France in 1622, Descartes took care of financial matters, and then set off once again on his travels. In 1628, he settled in Holland, where he spent most of the remainder of his life. Although he moved more than 20 times during the next 2 decades, probably to conceal himself, Descartes was usually near either a university or a library.

In 1649, 23-year-old Queen Christina of Sweden invited Descartes to her court to teach her philosophy. Queen Christina was friends with many academics, including Giles Ménage (1613–1692), known for his *History of Women Philosophers* and for his commentary on Diogenes Läertius's *Lives of the Greek Philosophers*. In response to the queen's summons, Descartes initially hesitated, but he eventually sailed from Amsterdam to Stockholm on the warship she had sent. Descartes found that Christina wanted her instruction at 5 A.M., 3 days a week, in the depths of the Scandinavian winter. He had spent a lifetime lying in a warm bed long after normal hours for rising, and under the queen's regimen he developed a cold, the cold became pneumonia, and on February 11 Descartes (Figure 3–10) died, having received the last rites of the Catholic Church. His final words are said to have been, "ça

FIGURE 3–10. René Descartes.
Source: Archives of the History of American Psychology.

mon âme, il faut partir," which means "so my soul, a time for parting."

The fate of Descartes's body is both grisly and ironic. Buried in Stockholm, his corpse was exhumed 16 years later to be returned to France. Unfortunately, Descartes's body was not treated with the respect it deserved. First, Sweden's French ambassador cut off Descartes's right forefinger as a souvenir. When the coffin brought to transport his remains was found to be too short, his head was removed to be shipped back to France separately. Descartes's headless body was subsequently buried in Paris with a fitting ceremony. However, his head was stolen by an army captain and took 150 years to reach Paris, where it has apparently been in the *Academie des Sciences* ever since (Boakes, 1984). Ironically, Descartes, whose head is perhaps perma-

nently separated from his body, was the chief proponent of a mind-body dualism.

Descartes's Method

In *Discours de la Méthode* (*Discourse on Method,* 1637), Descartes began by rejecting all dogma and authority, particularly that of Aristotle. He resolved to doubt everything, refusing to accept anything as true unless he was absolutely sure of it. But how could he be sure of the existence of anything? Could he be certain of the reality of objects because he sensed them? Unlike Aristotle and Francis Bacon, Descartes put little weight on sensory experience and experimentation as a means of gathering knowledge. Like Plato, Descartes relied mainly on reasoning.

Descartes sought first an idea so clear and distinct to his mind that its truth was beyond question. He could then progress from this starting point through the orderly use of intuition and deduction. By intuition, Descartes meant a vision so clear that it could not be doubted; by deduction, he meant making all possible inferences from facts of which he was certain.

Descartes's search for something absolutely certain led him to perhaps philosophy's most famous statement: *Je pense, donc je suis* in French, and *Cogito ergo sum* in Latin. "I think, therefore I am." Like many ideas we will encounter, this one was not original with its author; St. Augustine had used a similar argument, and Descartes had probably read his work.

Cogito ergo sum asserts the existence of the thinker, which is a thing that thinks. But this thing is not the body, and Descartes still had doubts about the existence of his body and of anything else other than his thinking. How could he proceed from the certainty of his existence as a thinking thing? First, Descartes asked himself what made the statement *Cogito ergo sum* true and certain, concluding that he could safely assume the truth of things that he conceived clearly and distinctly. Descartes now had to prove the existence of God and that God is not a deceiver. If God were a deceiver, then even clear and distinct ideas could be false.

Examining the ideas that passed through his mind, Descartes decided that they originated either from within, from his mind's invention, or from without. Because he was a finite, imperfect being, his conception of God as a perfect Being could only have come from a source outside himself, that is, from God. Further, because experience teaches us that deception comes from some defect, God cannot be a deceiver. If He were a deceiver, God could not be perfect.

Next, Descartes argued for the reality of the physical world and of his bodily self. We all have the experience of moving about, of making contact with objects, and of receiving sense impressions, and these experiences imply a body, which Descartes called "an extended substance." Our belief that these experiences come from contact with something real must come from God, because God would be deceitful if the experiences were produced by objects without physical reality. As God is not deceitful, we must accept the reality of corporeal objects.

At this point, Descartes believed that he had proved the existence of God, the self, and things. Descartes argued for a duality of substances in nature; there were thinking things (the mind; *l'âme*, the French word Descartes used, means either mind or soul) and extended things (the body). This distinction leads to Descartes's **mind-body dualism.**

Mind-Body Dualism

For Descartes, the mind is unextended, free, and without substance. Its ideas have no length, width, position, weight, or any other material quality. The mind is distinct from the body and surely survives the body's death (here the word "soul" is more appropriate). Only humans have mind.

By contrast, the body is extended, limited, and has substance. It operates by purely mechanical principles. For Descartes, the mechanical statues in the gardens of the palace at St. Germain were analogous to the operations of human and animal bodies. The automatons operated by hydraulic pressure so that when a visitor stepped on a pressure plate in a walkway, water coursing through pipes caused the statues to move. Basing his thinking on Galen's ideas (Chapter 2), Descartes envisioned human and animal bodies animated mechanically by means of fluids in tubes (nerves) connected to empty bladders (muscles).

As further evidence for a mind-body dualism, Descartes adopted Galileo's distinction for dealing with the separation of the areas we know as physics and psychology, which was the distinction between primary and secondary qualities. Secondary qualities (sensations) exist only in mind, whereas bodies exist only in shape (extension) and motion.

It was important for Descartes to deny mind to animals, as acceptance of a human-animal continuity could lead to the idea that hedonism is the only rational basis for human conduct. If animals can attain Heaven with little virtuous behavior, there is no reason for humans to be good in order to achieve the same end. Also, if animals are just automata—an idea that antedated Descartes (Bandrés & Llavona, 1992)—then animal dissections are little different from dismantling a piece of machinery. Descartes, who performed many dissections and vivisections, argued that although vivisection might appear to be painful to an animal, this is not the case because the animal has no mind and is not conscious in the way we are.

Descartes realized that many of the human body's activities are as mechanical as the activities of animals or machines. Respiration, digestion, and circulation are all performed automatically, without the mind's influence. But the mind can influence the body and vice versa. Although the body is primarily responsible for physical sensations and perceptions, the mind knows about them, and its thinking can be affected by this knowledge. The mind's influence on the body is evident in the act of will that allows a person to hold his or her hand in a candle's flame. Thus, Descartes believed that there was mind-body interaction, but the interaction was problematic for his strict dualism. Interaction requires contact, which necessitates an extended mind. Of course, Descartes recognized that the mind was unextended and lacking in substance; hence, the mind-body "problem."

Descartes chose the brain's **pineal gland** as the point of interaction between the mind (soul) and the body. In *Passions of the Soul,* Descartes wrote:

Although the soul is joined to the whole body, there is . . . a certain part in which it exercises its functions more particularly than in all the others; and . . . it seems as though . . . the part of the body in which the soul exercises its functions immediately is in nowise the heart, nor the whole of the brain, but merely the most inward of all its parts . . . a certain very small gland [the pineal or *conarium*] which is situated in the middle of its substance and so suspended above the duct whereby the animal spirits in its anterior cavities have communication with those in the posterior, that the slightest movements which take place in it may alter very greatly the course of these spirits; and reciprocally that the smallest changes which occur in the course of the spirits may do much to change the movements of this gland. (Descartes; Wilson, 1969, p. 362)

Why the pineal gland? Our sense organs come in pairs, but our thoughts of an object are unitary, which means that somewhere in the mind the dual messages we have received are combined into one thought. Descartes chose the pineal gland as the point of interaction because he thought it was the brain's only unpaired structure and because he believed it was only present in humans. Actually, anatomists had originally discovered the gland in the brain of an ox, where its pine-cone shape suggested its Latin name, *conarium.* Descartes theorized that the pineal's movements direct the animal spirits through different pores in the brain, resulting in different responses.

The pineal is not, as psychological historian Robert I. Watson (1971) wrote, "a vestigial organ of no functional significance whatsoever . . ." (p. 239). The pineal hormone melatonin is produced and secreted on a light-dark schedule in all mammals, providing a signal of changing daylength. In seasonally breeding mammals, the signal is important for reproductive readiness (Tamarkin, Baird, & Almeida, 1985). Melatonin synthesis decreases with age in humans through puberty, supporting a long-held theory that a pineal secretion suppresses puberty (Kolata, 1984). Thus, although the pineal has a definite and important function, it does not have the significance Descartes suggested for it.

Innate and Derived Ideas

Descartes believed that ideas that come to mind with certainty and inevitability are **innate** and do not come from experience. Self, Descartes's first principle, is an example of an idea he considered innate, along with God, space, time, motion, and certain geometrical axioms.

Descartes did not mean that the innate ideas are completely formed and always present in every person. What he meant was that they represent a potentiality of thought that can be brought forth by experience. Unfortunately, errors in sensory experiences may prevent innate ideas from appearing. Descartes's concept of innate ideas is reminiscent of Plato's (Chapter 2) Forms—innate universals only known through reasoning—and Plato also believed that sensory information (the body) could hinder the development of knowledge already in the mind.

Descartes also recognized **derived ideas** that come from environmental experiences and are stored in memory through an alteration of the nervous system. Descartes proposed that a new experience forces animal spirits through a particular set of the brain's pores, which leaves an imprint analogous to the holes left in linen cloth through which a set of needles has passed. When the experience is repeated, the open or partially open pores more easily allow the passage of the animal spirits. A "memory trace" has been laid down through a change in the brain. Substitute synapses and nerve impulses for pores and animal spirits, and Descartes's idea about memory formation acquires a remarkably modern flavor.

Descartes's Influence

Descartes made further contributions related to psychology, and overall his influence has been enormous. For example, he was the first to describe the retinal image, which is a tiny, inverted model of the scene external to the eye projected by the lens onto the retina. Using a bull's eye, Descartes scraped off the back outer covering, inserted the eye into an opening bored in a shutter, and described the image that he saw on the back of the eyeball (Boring, 1950).

Descartes was also the first to describe reflex action. For him, sensory stimulation causes tiny fibers in the hollow nerves to open specific pores in the brain, which release animal spirits into the appropriate muscles for movement. A particular movement follows predictably from specific sensory stimulation, a conception that anticipates the idea of reflex action. Descartes differentiated two kinds of reflexive responses: the first accounted for automatic and immediate responses, the kind of responses that we call reflexes; the second was a learned reaction in which the response becomes associated with the stimulus in some unspecified way.

Although wrong in detail, Descartes's conception of the reflex as a stimulus-response process occurring through the nervous system became crucial for psychology. The reflex action concept and the view of animals as automatons influenced the development of both animal and physiological psychology.

The late Renaissance fostered a new world view, illustrated through Galileo's conception of the universe as a giant machine in which lawful explanations are possible. Descartes's work was compatible with the new world image, because he saw the human body as a machine capable of affecting and being affected by the mind. Descartes perceived human behavior as lawful and ultimately explainable, and, most importantly, he localized the mind's interaction with the body in the brain.

Because Descartes believed ideas exist in the mind before sensory experience, he is a nativist according to the nature-nurture dichotomy we discussed in Chapter 1. Descartes's nativism is important for stimulating opposition in the British empiricists (e.g., Locke and Berkeley, Chapter 4) and others.

On the mind-body issue, Descartes is classified as an interactive dualist, because he believed that both mind and body exist and interact. However, a review of correspondence in 1643 between Descartes and Princess Elizabeth, later queen of Bohemia, suggests that whether or not Descartes was a dualist depends on the Cartesian work being considered (Tibbetts, 1973). *Passions of the Soul* provides the classical statement of psychophysical dualism, whereas Descartes's letters to Elizabeth indicate a muddled picture. The problem with Descartes's interactive dualism, which Elizabeth addressed in her letters, lay in explaining how the immaterial mind interacts with the material body. Another French philosopher, Pierre Gassendi (discussed later), was also aware of this difficulty.

Descartes used a rationalistic, deductive approach to generate knowledge, which others replaced with an experimental, inductive approach. One of Descartes's most important successors, John Locke, admired Descartes's mechanistic approach to the physical world but rejected rationalism in order to establish the empiricist tradition in psychology.

Descartes's lasting and widespread influence occurred in part because, like Galileo, he wrote in his native tongue rather than in the Latin used in most scholarly books of the period. Unlike Galileo, Descartes avoided trouble with the Inquisition primarily by putting many of his thoughts into manuscripts published after his death. Still, at one point he was attacked by clergy in Holland, who managed to get his books banned from universities because they were considered subversive to religious dogma. The irony is that Descartes was sincere in his religious faith. Hearing of Galileo's condemnation by the Inquisition in 1633, Descartes set aside writings in which he had planned to combine all his scientific work and wrote to a friend that "on no account will I publish anything . . . that might displease the Church" (Fischer, 1887, p. 231).

Pierre Gassendi

One of Descartes's earliest and most ardent critics was French philosopher and scientist **Pierre Gassendi** (1592–1655). Gassendi was so bright that at the age of 16 he was appointed a teacher of rhetoric, and at 25 he became professor of philosophy at the University of Aix. In 1645, Gassendi became professor of mathematics at the Collège Royal in Paris, where his friends included Kepler and Galileo.

Without his moderate conduct and faithfulness in his religious duties, Gassendi's beliefs in Copernican astronomy, the atomism of Democritus, and Epicurean moral philosophy might have caused him problems with the Inquisition. However, he combined his materialism with a belief in the God of the Bible, asserting that atoms were created and given an initial push by God, but from then on everything continued by its own laws. Gassendi considered the greatest pleasures to be mental, and he strongly advocated the experimental approach to science.

Gassendi began his criticism of Descartes by asserting that the unextended, immaterial mind could neither influence nor be influenced by the extended, material body. Only the physical can influence the physical. Further, it was obvious to Gassendi that anything that moves exists, which made him wonder why Descartes had to struggle to conclude that the fact of his thinking proved his existence. Continuing, Gassendi challenged Descartes's notion that animals are purely mechanical and only humans have mind. If movement proves existence, then why do humans need mind to move when, according to Descartes, animals do not? For Gassendi, the mind's operations come from the workings of the brain, and a separate, immaterial mind is not needed to explain our behavior.

Despite critics like Gassendi, Descartes's philosophy continued to influence the thinkers of the Renaissance and beyond. Another challenge came from Baruch Spinoza, a man who adopted some of Descartes's methods, which he used to deduce a mind-body solution that was even less acceptable to the Church than Descartes's interactive dualism.

BARUCH SPINOZA

Baruch (or Benedictus; Baruch is Hebrew for "blessed," which in Latin is Benedictus) **Spinoza** (1632–1677) was born in Amsterdam, where Spinoza's Jewish family had moved from Spain to escape religious persecution. Spinoza's mother died when he was 6, bequeathing him the same consumption (tuberculosis) from which she suffered. (Recall Descartes had a similar inheritance.) When Spinoza's father died in 1654, a sister claimed the estate. Spinoza successfully contested the claim in court and then gave the sister all of the legacy except for a bed, an act typical of Spinoza's generosity and

disinterest in worldly possessions—what he valued most were philosophy and friendships. To support himself, Spinoza (Figure 3–11) ground and polished lenses for microscopes, telescopes, and eyeglasses.

At 23, Spinoza was excommunicated from the synagogue and ostracized from the local Jewish community for revealing doubts about his religious teachings. "[N]o one was to speak or write to him, or do him any service, or read his writings, or come within the space of four cubits' [approximately 20 in. or 50 cm] distance from him" (Durant & Durant, 1963, pp. 622–623).

Like Descartes, Spinoza valued privacy. In 1660, he moved to the village of Rijnsburg, where he wrote several minor works and Book I of his posthumously published *Ethica Ordine Geometrico Demonstrata* (*Ethic Demonstrated in Geometrical Order,* or simply, the *Ethics*). Next, Spinoza moved to a town near The Hague, the capital of the Netherlands, where he con-

FIGURE 3–11. Baruch Spinoza.

Source: Philosophical Library, New York.

tinued grinding lenses and working on the *Ethics*. In 1670, Spinoza moved to The Hague, living his last 6 years in a single room on the top floor of a private home. In 1673, he was offered a philosophy professorship at the University of Heidelberg, where he was to have the freedom to philosophize, as long as he did not say anything to disturb established religion, but he graciously declined.

The great mathematician/philosopher Leibniz came to visit Spinoza in 1676, but Spinoza was in an advanced state of consumption, probably aggravated by the glass dust he had breathed for years. He died in February 1677, and through the efforts of friends and admirers, the *Ethics* and several other works were published toward the end of the year.

Spinoza's Philosophy

Like Descartes, Spinoza thought he could achieve knowledge of reality using the method of geometry. That is, he would begin by developing clear and distinct principles from which he would deduce all knowledge (recall Raymond Lull). Again, the approach was rationalistic and deduction-based as opposed to Francis Bacon's empirical, inductive approach.

In contrast to Descartes's relatively simple system, Spinoza's contained some 250 axioms and theorems. Like Descartes, Spinoza believed that clear and distinct ideas were true. However, instead of starting with the idea of self, Spinoza began with God, because, for him, God must be before everything else.

Spinoza's approach to God is **pantheism**, the belief that God is everything and vice versa. He equated God with Nature, as shown in the Latin phrase *Deus sive Natura* (God or Nature). Spinoza concluded that the ultimate nature of reality is a single substance (God or Nature) with an infinity of attributes. We can know of only two attributes of substance: thought (mind) and extension (body). For Descartes, this meant that there were two substances, mind and body, which interacted, but the problem was that the unextended mind should not be able to affect the extended body. However, Spinoza had no problem with this, because he saw the mind and the body as two different ways of

expressing the activity of a single substance. There is no separation of the mind and the body, because they are just different aspects of the same thing—God. God is both infinite thought and infinite extension. Mind and body do not interact because they are one with God, which is everything. Spinoza's mind-body solution is called **double aspectism**. An analogy often used to express the solution is that mind and body are like two sides of a coin.

In Spinoza's universe, everything is determined. Human behavior is determined according to God's substance. Our feeling of having freedom of will is an illusion caused by our ignorance of prior causes. There is a unity of Nature, and the human species is a part of it. Thus, all our actions, mental and physical, are determined by prior causes.

According to Spinoza, there are three levels of knowledge, and by refining our understanding of things, we can ascend from imagination, to reason, and finally to intuition. At the imagination level, ideas come from sensations and are concrete and specific. Although the ideas are specific, they are inadequate and do not give us true knowledge. At the reason level, we have scientific knowledge. At this level, we can deal with abstract ideas rather than being confined to particular ideas from our sensations. Here, knowledge is adequate and true. Finally, at the intuition level, we become increasingly aware of Nature and of our place in it. Our knowledge at the first level is seen from a new perspective. Where we first saw bodies disconnectedly, we now see them as part of Nature's grand scheme.

Although our behavior is determined, Spinoza believed that morality comes with improving our knowledge by moving from the imagination level to the intuition level. Only through knowledge can we achieve happiness, for it is only through knowledge that we can gain freedom from our passions. Our passions enslave us when they are attached to temporary things and when we do not understand them. The more we understand our emotions, the more we can control them. The kind of knowledge that frees us from the rule of our passions necessarily leads to the knowledge and intellectual love of God. This intellectual love is not the love of God as a divine person but is more like the pleasure from understanding a mathematical formula. Spinoza conceded that his way to morality was difficult.

Spinoza's Influence

Like the Stoics before him, Spinoza believed in a strict determinism, both of psychological and physiological events. His **psychic determinism**—behavior is determined by mental causes—came 300 years before Sigmund Freud's (Chapter 15), and Spinoza is often considered a forerunner of psychoanalysis, because Freud certainly knew of Spinoza's works.

Spinoza's work was at first condemned as atheistic and subversive because of his equating of God and nature, and between "1650 and 1680 there were some fifty edicts, by church authorities, against the reading or circulation of the philosopher's works" (Durant & Durant, 1963, p. 631). However, Spinoza's reputation improved, and he is now considered, along with Descartes and Leibniz, as one of the 17th-century's great rationalist thinkers. In fact, Bernard (1972) argued that because of his influence on relatively modern people (e.g., Freud, Fechner, Wundt), "modern [scientific] psychology owes a far greater historical debt to Spinoza than to Descartes" (p. 215). Many of the same individuals were similarly influenced by one of Spinoza's friends—Gottfried Wilhelm von Leibniz.

GOTTFRIED WILHELM VON LEIBNIZ

The son of a professor at the University of Leipzig, **Gottfried Wilhelm von Leibniz** (1646–1716) was born in Leipzig, Germany. A precocious child, Leibniz read Latin at 8 and Greek at 12, and by then he had read most of the classics in Latin. At 15, he entered the University of Leipzig, and at 20 he applied for the doctorate in law. Instead of waiting a year because of his youth, he went to a smaller university at Altdorf, Switzerland, where he earned his degree in 6 months. The university authorities were so impressed with Leibniz's dissertation that he was offered a professorship, which he declined.

Leibniz spent a year in Nuremberg before moving to Mainz in western Germany, where he became legal advisor to the Elector of Mainz (a German prince authorized to vote to elect the Pope). At Mainz, Leibniz revised and systematically organized laws, wrote plans to unify the Christian religions, and absorbed the philosophy, mathematics, and science of the day.

In 1672, Leibniz went to Paris, where he met **Nicolas Malebranche** (1638–1715), a French philosopher who adopted Descartes's dualism but explained mind-body interaction as the intervention of God. Malebranche's position is called **occasionalism**, because our need to act becomes the occasion for divine intervention. Leibniz also met Christiaan Huygens (1629–1693), a noted Dutch physicist who led him into higher mathematics, and Leibniz began work leading to his discovery of the infinitesimal (integral) calculus.

On a trip to England in 1673, Leibniz showed members of the Royal Society a mathematical calculating machine, which so impressed them that they made him one of the first non-British members. By 1676, Leibniz had discovered both the differential calculus and the infinitesimal calculus. In 1684 and 1686, Leibniz published his two discoveries, unaware that Isaac Newton had made the same observations earlier. Because Newton did not publish his work until 1692, a quarrel over priority erupted between the two. Although Newton was the earlier inventor, Leibniz's notation system proved superior, and we use it today.

Following the death of the Elector of Mainz, Leibniz accepted a position as court councilor to the House of Hanover (a political entity in northern Germany). On a leisurely trip back to Germany, Leibniz stopped in Amsterdam, meeting both Spinoza and Anton van Leeuwenhoek (1632–1723), the modern microscope's inventor. The microorganisms Leibniz saw in van Leeuwenhoek's microscope undoubtedly influenced his conception of a creation composed of living, organic units.

In 1685, Leibniz was assigned to write a history of the House of Hanover. Fortunately, Leibniz's historian duties did not occupy all of his time, and he continued his voluminous correspondence with people all over the Continent. In his lifetime,

Leibniz made original contributions in mathematics, optics, mechanics, statistics, logic, and probability theory; he wrote on history, law, and political theory, and his philosophy was the foundation of 18th-century rationalism.

Despite his accomplishments, Leibniz's life was unfulfilled. His enthusiasms were so many that he rarely finished anything, and it was left to future generations to organize his notes, correspondence, and unpublished manuscripts. Considered almost a clown because of his jet-black wig and his taste in clothes, Leibniz (Figure 3–12) was ridiculed during his lifetime. His overly optimistic philosophy (e.g., this is the best of all possible worlds) made him the model for the asinine philosopher Pangloss in Voltaire's satirical short story *Candide*.

In 1714, Leibniz's patron became George I of England. Because of his priority squabble with Newton, Leibniz was ordered to stay in Hanover and finish the family history. When Leibniz died 2 years later, no one of importance attended his funeral, and his death was unmarked by the society he founded (the Society of the Sciences at Berlin, which later became the Prussian Academy).

Monads

Leibniz was dissatisfied with the mind-body solutions of both Descartes and Spinoza, although he felt a closer affinity to the latter. In fact, according to philosopher/mathematician Bertrand Russell (1937), "Leibniz fell into Spinozism whenever he allowed himself to be logical; in his published works, accordingly, he took care to be illogical" (p. vii). As we have noted, the main problem with Descartes's mind-body solution is that it does not explain the interaction of the immaterial mind with the material body. Spinoza's solution was that there is only one substance, which has the two attributes of mind and body. Leibniz rejected Spinoza's pantheism, which equated God, humans, and nature, because Leibniz wanted to keep the three separate. Instead, Leibniz adopted Spinoza's single-substance theory, but his concept of the single substance was so extraordinary that he was able to use it to speak of God's transcendance, the individuality of people, and the reality of freedom and purpose.

Remember that Leibniz had looked through van Leeuwenhoek's microscope at microorganisms forming a world within a world. Because everything we see can be divided into smaller parts, surely all substances are merely collections of simple substances. Leibniz called these simple substances **monads**, a word that comes from the Greek *monas*, which means "a unit." In Chapter 2, we noted that Democritus believed that all things are composed of indivisible atoms. Atoms and monads differ in that atoms are extended and have substance, whereas monads are force or energy. Also, atoms are lifeless particles of matter, whereas monads are alive and active, with differing degrees of perceptual ability. Monads are unextended, uncreatable, indestructible, immutable, and independent of each other. Leibniz saw the world as an infinite collection of independent monads.

FIGURE 3–12.   Gottfried Wilhelm von Leibniz.

Source: National Library of Medicine.

In this collection, there are four kinds of monads, arranged hierarchically by the clarity and distinctiveness of their consciousness. First, there is a supreme monad, God, from which all other monads are created. All-knowing, the supreme monad is known to varying degrees by its creations, the finite monads.

As the conscious souls of humans, rational monads are closest to God in the clarity and completeness of their consciousness. Rational monads have the capability for simple perception and also for apperception, by which Leibniz meant reasoning ability and self-consciousness. The rational monads of human beings are both conscious and aware of their consciousness.

Sentient monads make up the souls of nonhuman organisms, providing their possessors with simple perceptual ability and memory, but denying them the self-consciousness and reasoning ability of rational monads. Finally, simple monads are the components of both organic and inorganic matter, reacting to the world in an unconscious way.

Pre-Established Harmony

Although independent of each other, the monads act according to a pre-established harmony. For example, although it may appear that the human mind's rational monads and the body's sentient and simple monads interact, this is really not true. Their apparent interaction comes from their parallel and harmonious courses, established by the supreme monad. Leibniz used the metaphor of perfectly constructed clocks started simultaneously, which all keep the same time, but do so independently. For Leibniz, the pre-established harmony of all things was another proof of God's existence. Leibniz's mind-body solution—that mind and body exist and maintain parallel courses without interacting—is called psychophysical parallelism.

The world's harmony convinced Leibniz that God had created the best of all possible worlds. Leibniz recognized the world's disorder and evil but considered it compatible with a benevolent God, reasoning that if God made his creation perfect, then it would be God. Therefore, creation must necessarily be imperfect, and evil is an absence of perfection, not something God created. Furthermore, Leibniz assumed that God constructed the best world possible given the limitation that it could not be perfect.

Levels of Consciousness

Because all substance is made of monads, there are different degrees or levels of consciousness in any substance. The levels range from clear and distinct apperceptions through perceptions that never reach consciousness. Leibniz called these latter perceptions *petite perceptions*, and an example is the sound of Zeno's single millet seed (Chapter 2). The noise is too faint to be registered, but the sound of a half-bushel falling reaches consciousness and is apperceived.

Leibniz's Influence

Leibniz's notion of degrees of consciousness, and thus unconscious ideas, has influenced later psychological thought. For example, Freud made levels of consciousness a major psychoanalytic concept. Leibniz's influence can be seen also in Ernst Weber and Gustav Fechner's just noticeable differences (Chapter 6), in Franz Brentano's act psychology (Chapter 8), and in Wilhelm Wundt's concept of apperception (Chapter 7).

Like the Pythagoreans, Leibniz imagined that all knowledge could be represented mathematically. Building on Lull, and more importantly on English churchman and scientist John Wilkins (1614–1672), Leibniz saw the possibility of computing all knowledge from a device "programmed" with fundamental concepts. Leibniz envisioned the day when "no discussion between two philosophers will be any longer necessary . . . . It will rather be enough for them to . . . say . . . "Calculemus!" (Let us calculate!) (Leibniz, as cited in Bochenski, 1961, p. 275). Leibniz's mathematical calculator improved on mathematician, physicist, and psychological philosopher Blaise Pascal's (1623–1662) earlier machine. Although Leibniz's device was capable of multiplication and division, it could not compute or handle extremely large numbers (MacLennan, 1990). This work establishes Leibniz's claim as a forerunner of cognitive science (Chapter 20).

One of Leibniz's most important works for psychology was *Nouveaux Essais sur l'entendement humain* (*New Essays on Human Understanding*), an essay critical of John Locke's *Essay Concerning Human Understanding*. We will discuss Locke's *Essay* and Leibniz's *New Essays* in the next chapter.

CONCLUSIONS

Historically, the more than 1,700 years from Christ's birth to Leibniz's death encompasses the decline of the Roman Empire and the years before the American and French revolutions. In science, the nearly 2 millenia take us from the superstition and speculation of the ancients to the beginning of what most historians call the Early Modern period. The early 18th century is modern in the sense that some of the broad concepts (e.g., gravitational attraction) and scientific methodologies (e.g., inductive empiricism) used today are in place. Philosophically speaking, there is the decline, resurgence, and, finally, movement beyond the ancient Greeks, their philosophies superseded by the systems stimulated by late Renaissance thinkers such as Descartes, Spinoza, and Leibniz.

One unifying theme during the Middle Ages is the interest in synthesizing Greek philosophical wisdom with theology, which we can see in the writings of St. Paul, Plotinus, and St. Augustine. The decline of the Roman Empire ushered in a period in which interest in and knowledge of classical, secular philosophy was lost in the West. St. Anselm and other scholastics reawakened interest in the philosophers of ancient Greece. The rediscovery of Aristotle in the West was further facilitated by the work of Islamic philosophers such as Avicenna and Averroës. Even St. Aquinas's efforts to reconcile Christianity and Aristotle were anticipated by Maimonides.

The Church's acceptance of Aristotelian ideas had far-reaching implications for Western philosophy and science. One implication, derived from Aristotle's system of formal logic and particularly from the syllogism, was that with the correct initial premise, all knowledge could be determined. This idea is particularly evident in the work of Lull and Leibniz. Descartes also sought the initial premise that would allow him to deduce everything using logic.

Although the acceptance of Aristotelian logic was beneficial for science, the Church's unquestioning adoption of Aristotle's theory of the universe had a more negative impact. Progress in science was frequently handicapped by the Inquisition. In time, concern with human interests rather than with the natural world resulted in a movement away from Aristotelianism. Early humanists such as Petrarch, Pico, and Luther adopted an approach to philosophy that relied less on the wisdom of the Greeks as filtered through the Church and more on individual human experience. Perhaps the clearest expression of this approach is in Shakespeare's work (ca. 1600).

Descartes is often considered the first modern philosopher because of his efforts to break with the philosophies of the past. Rationalism as a philosophical tradition began before Plato, was carried to new heights by Descartes, and was further refined by Spinoza and Leibniz. In the next chapter, we will contrast this rationalism with British empiricism, a system that owes much to Sir Frances Bacon's promotion of experimentation for understanding nature.

S U M M A R Y

Philosophical and Theological Thought during the Roman Period

St. Paul was largely responsible for the establishment of the Christian community through which he continues to exert an influence on science and on thoughts about human behavior. Plotinus established Neoplatonism, a school that sought to combine Plato, Christian and Judaic religious concepts, and Near Eastern mysticism.

Christianity, Islam, and Jewish Philosophy of the Medieval Era

St. Augustine was not totally sympathetic to knowledge unconnected with religion, and this negative attitude became part of the Christian Church's distrust of science. For Augustine, consciousness could be studied by looking within (introspection).

In about 500, an unknown writer called Pseudo-Dionysius attempted systematically to relate Christian thought and Neoplatonism. By contrast, Boethius's writings were mostly Aristotelian.

Under Charlemagne's direction, Alcuin founded the Palatine school. Erigena—noted for attempting to fuse Neoplatonism with Christian doctrines—directed the Palatine school under Charles the Bald.

Avicenna and Averroës were Islamic philosophers whose work centered on Aristotle. Avicenna's philosophy also contained novel elements, including the distinction between the possible intellect and the Agent Intellect. Averroës disagreed with Avicenna's distinction, and he also had little respect for theology. Seeking to harmonize Judaism with Aristotle, Maimonides was the most influential Jewish thinker of the era.

Christian Philosophy in the Later Middle Ages

Because of his support of rationalism's value, St. Anselm is often considered the founder of scholasticism, which is based on Aristotelian logic and the writings of early Christian thinkers. Anselm is also remembered for the ontological argument for God's existence. Peter Abélard took a moderate position in the nominalist-realist debate, which was the argument between people who believed that universals exist in reality (realists) and those who thought that universals exist in name only (nominalists). St. Thomas Aquinas sought the synthesis of Aristotle with Christianity and argued that faith and reason are not incompatible.

The philosophy of John Duns Scotus was a reaction against both Aristotle and Aquinas, and his argument for the will's supremacy was called voluntarism. William of Ockham defended nominalism against realism and is best known for Ockham's razor, which argues for taking the explanation of a phenomenon requiring the fewest assumptions.

Medieval Science Before the Renaissance

Highlights of science in this period include Roger Bacon's inventions of such things as the magnifying glass and gunpowder and his speculations about flying machines, telescopes, and microscopes. Raymond Lull conceived of a machine that would algorithmically generate all knowledge.

Universities in the Middle Ages

Universities at Bologna, Paris, and Oxford were founded in the 12th century. Other important early universities were at Cambridge in England, Toulouse and Orléans in France, and Lisbon in Portugal. Many of the early universities followed the curriculum Alcuin established at the Palatine.

Renaissance Humanism

Focusing on human interests rather than on religion or the natural world, early humanists included Juan Luis Vives. Distrusting Aristotle, Petrarch wrote mostly in opposition to Averroës. Petrarch's opposition to scholasticism and to religious authority helped later challenges to Aristotelian dogma.

Giovanni Pico's philosophical contribution was an attempted reconciliation of Platonic and Aristotelian doctrines. Martin Luther began the Protestant Reformation in opposition to conditions he saw in the Catholic Church. Drawn to humanism, Desiderius Erasmus reacted against scholasticism and defended Luther early in Luther's challenge to the Catholic Church.

"Machiavellian" comes from the name of Niccolò Machiavelli, author of *The Prince,* which is mainly a handbook for rulers who believe "the ends justify the means."

Renaissance Science

Nicolas Copernicus replaced the earth-centered idea of the universe with a sun-centered view. For defending the Copernican system, Giordano Bruno was burned at the stake by the Inquisition. Galileo made many astronomical discoveries and distinguished between primary and secondary qualities of objects. Johann Kepler, Tycho Brahe's assistant and successor, proposed laws of planetary motion fundamental to some of Isaac Newton's work.

Sir Francis Bacon promoted experimentation for understanding nature, and William Harvey used experimentation to show that the heart was just a pump. Physicist and mathematician Newton conceived the law of gravitation, discovered that white light is a mixture of all colors, invented calculus, and constructed the first reflecting telescope.

René Descartes

Descartes began his new philosophy by searching for an idea of which he was certain, which he found summarized in the phrase: *Cogito ergo sum* (I think, therefore I am). From this beginning, Descartes conceived a mind-body dualism in which the mind is unextended and lacks substance, whereas the body is extended and has substance. Descartes believed that the body operates by mechanical principles, and animals have body but not mind. For

Descartes, there were both innate and derived ideas. One of Descartes's early critics, Pierre Gassendi tried to reconcile an atomic materialism with Christian doctrine.

Baruch Spinoza

Spinoza's philosophy equated God with Nature and concluded that the ultimate nature of reality is a single substance (God) with an infinity of attributes. Spinoza saw the mind and the body as two different sides of the same coin, and his solution to the mind-body problem is called double aspectism.

Gottfried Wilhelm von Leibniz

To solve the mind-body problem, Leibniz invented the monad, an unextended, uncreatable, indestructible, immutable substance. Monads are independent, appearing to act in concert because of a pre-established harmony. This mind-body solution is called psychophysical parallelism. Because all substance is made of monads and monads vary in their degrees of consciousness, there are different levels of consciousness in any substance.

CONNECTIONS QUESTIONS

1. What connections can be made between Renaissance scientific advances in areas such as astronomy and the rise of philosophical psychology?
2. What connections can be made between the Greek philosophers and Christian, Jewish, and Islamic scholarship in the Middle Ages?
3. In constructing his theory of mind and body, what connections with the past did Descartes make or break?
4. What are some of the connections between religion and philosophy of the central characters at the end of this chapter; that is, Descartes, Spinoza, Leibniz, and so on?

5. What was the major criticism of Descartes's solution to the mind-body problem and how did Spinoza and Leibniz attempt to resolve it?
6. Draw three concept maps, one connecting the figures from the beginning of the Middle Ages to the Renaissance, one connecting the major Renaissance figures, and one connecting the early modern philosophers through Leibniz, and compare your results with one possible solution provided on p. 562.

SUGGESTED READINGS

Augustine (1963). *Confessions.* New York: New American Library. (Original work published 400) Available in many different editions, St. Augustine's *Confessions* is an autobiographical account of the man's fascinating life and times.

Boakes, R. (1984). *From Darwin to behaviourism: Psychology and the minds of animals.* New York: Cambridge. This book is out of print, but it may be in your library. Boakes's work has excellent pictures of the people discussed and fascinating accounts of their lives (recall his account of the treatment of Descartes's body). The psychological insights are important, as well.

Descartes, R. (1956). *Discourse on method* (L. J. Lafleur, Trans.). Indianapolis: Bobbs-Merrill. (Original work published 1637) This work is available in many different editions and should be read by anyone wishing to explore Descartes in his own words.

Machiavelli, N. (1891). *Il principe.* Oxford: The Clarendon Press. (Original work published 1532) Machiavelli's *The Prince* is available in many different contemporary editions. A delight to read, *The Prince* is a timeless treatise on human nature.

Wilson, M. D. (Ed.) (1969). *The essential Descartes.* New York: Mentor Books. This small book is representative of the many works on Descartes. Such works can be found in bookstores selling used books, usually in the philosophy section. It contains a broad sampling of Descartes's writings, including some of his correspondence with Princess Elizabeth, later queen of Bohemia.

Wippel, J. F., & Wolter, A. B. (1969). *Medieval philosophy.* New York: Free Press. This is a standard textbook on medieval philosophy. The book contains excerpts from the writings of most of the philosophers and theologians covered in the first half of this chapter.

Empiricism, Associationism, and Common-Sense Psychology

David Hartley

George Berkeley

Julien Offrey de La Mettrie

Étienne Bonnot de Condillac

John Locke

David Hume

Thomas Hobbes

Thomas Reid

1575	1600	1625	1650	1675	1700	1725	1750

Bruno
burned as
a heretic

Death of René
Descartes
Charles I is executed

Louis XIV dies

Harvard College is founded

Baruch Spinoza born

Newton publishes
Principia Mathematica

J. S.
Bach
dies

James I dies

British Empiricism
  Thomas Hobbes
  John Locke
  George Berkeley
  David Hume

British Associationism
  David Hartley
  James Mill and John Stuart Mill
  Alexander Bain

French Empiricism
  Julien Offray de La Mettrie
  Étienne Bonnot de Condillac
  Pierre Jean Georges Cabanis

The Scottish School
  Thomas Reid
  Dugald Stewart
  Thomas Brown

Conclusions

In the last two chapters, we presented the material more or less chronologically. After the Renaissance, so many important events happened concurrently but at different locations that a strictly chronological approach is less desirable. For this reason, historians of philosophy and psychology often use a standard set of spatial-topical categories to cover the period from the late 1600s through the early 1800s. These categories include British empiricism, British associationism, and the Scottish School (also known as common-sense psychology), among others.

Bear in mind that these categories are the invention of historians, and the actual people may have considered themselves in very different relations to their predecessors, contemporaries, and successors than we arrange them today. For example, David

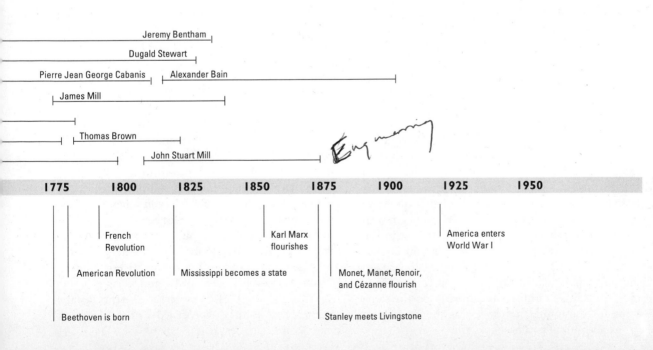

Jeremy Bentham

Dugald Stewart

Pierre Jean George Cabanis | Alexander Bain

James Mill

Thomas Brown

John Stuart Mill

| 1775 | 1800 | 1825 | 1850 | 1875 | 1900 | 1925 | 1950 |

French Revolution

Karl Marx flourishes

America enters World War I

American Revolution

Mississippi becomes a state

Monet, Manet, Renoir, and Cézanne flourish

Beethoven is born

Stanley meets Livingstone

Hume is generally classified as a British empiricist, even though he was Scottish by birth and could be considered the first of the associationists. Also, grouping people thematically is sometimes misleading chronologically. For example, British associationism is almost always presented before either French empiricism or the Scottish School, although it does not actually predate either. Fortunately, the chronological timeline should help you see who was contemporary with whom.

In this chapter, we will present a number of ideas that have been important in the history of psychology and that remain a part of psychological theory today. For example, there is the idea associated with John Locke that our minds are like a blank slate (or white paper) at birth on which experience writes. In addition, several of the chapter's central characters recognized that mental events are combined through the use of a small number of associative principles, with David Hume being perhaps the first to formalize the principles as part of his system. In Julien de La Mettrie's consideration of humans as merely biological machines, we will see one answer to Descartes's mind-body problem.

As we indicated in Chapter 3, once Renaissance thinkers began to break away from the restraints imposed by medieval dogma, knowledge grew rapidly. Challenges came in astronomy, with the work of Copernicus, Galileo, and Kepler successfully overturning the earlier geocentric view. Challenges also came in philosophy, and we saw Descartes, Spinoza, and Leibniz developing systems of thought that were not merely modifications of Plato or Aristotle. Their general approach was rationalistic, and we will explore Continental rationalism after Leibniz in the next chapter. In this chapter, the main theme is **empiricism**, which is the search for knowledge through experience rather than through reasoning. We will begin with the British philosophers who used the empirical approach advocated by Isaac Newton and Francis Bacon. Where Newton had attempted to explain the universe by using a few basic observed principles, the British empiricists aimed to do the same thing for the mind, thereby laying the foundation for experimental psychology.

BRITISH EMPIRICISM

We should note that the British empiricists were not "empirical" in the modern sense of the term. In contemporary psychology, empirical is often used as a shorthand means to indicate formal observations and controlled experiments. The British empiricists were philosophers who used their everyday experiences to obtain principles from which they logically (and rationally) deduced systems. We begin with Thomas Hobbes, who numbered among his friends Francis Bacon, Galileo, and Gassendi.

Thomas Hobbes

Thomas Hobbes was born prematurely on April 5, 1588, his birth supposedly hastened by news of the approaching Spanish Armada. Although Hobbes often attributed his natural timidity to this early exit from the womb, as the most conspicuous heretic of his age, Hobbes may have inherited a combative streak from his father. An Anglican vicar in the southern England town of Malmesbury, Hobbes's father got into a fight at the door of his church and then disappeared, leaving his children's care to a prosperous brother.

At 20, Hobbes graduated from Oxford and became a private tutor to William Cavendish, who became the second Earl of Devonshire. Hobbes's long association with the Cavendish family enabled him to travel, meet important people, and protected him from the criticism that invariably followed his publications.

Hobbes served briefly as Francis Bacon's secretary, an experience perhaps leading to his empirical philosophy. A visit to Galileo in 1636 may have strengthened Hobbes's desire to describe the universe mechanically. Hobbes's political theory was influenced by the conflict between King Charles I and Parliament that sent Hobbes fleeing to the Continent in 1640. As a published defender of an absolute monarchy, Hobbes felt threatened as the struggle progressed into a civil war. Victory went to Oliver Cromwell (1599–1658), and Charles I was executed in 1649. Hobbes served 2 years as the mathematics tutor to the exiled Prince of Wales, who became Charles II.

FIGURE 4–1. Thomas Hobbes.

Source: Corbis-Bettmann.

In 1651, Hobbes published *Leviathan or The Matter, Form and Power of A Commonwealth, Ecclesiastical and Civil,* which led to an outcry in France that forced Hobbes to make peace with Cromwell and return to England, where he again secured the Earl of Devonshire's protection. As *Leviathan* became more widely read, Hobbes was besieged by British critics, and in 1666, a motion was made in Parliament to burn him as a heretic. Hobbes's clerical enemies blamed him for the Plague and the Great Fire of London (1665–1666), which they saw as God's wrath against England for harboring such an outspoken atheist. Newly restored King Charles II came to his aid, gave Hobbes a pension, had his portrait painted, and welcomed him to court.

Sickly as a youth, Hobbes (Figure 4–1) was healthy in old age—he played tennis until he was 75. On December 4, 1679, at 91, Hobbes died after

receiving the Sacrament as an Anglican. Given his reputation as an atheist, this is ironic, although deathbed conversions are not uncommon.

Hobbes's Philosophy

When Hobbes was 40, he happened upon a copy of Greek mathematician Euclid's *Elements*. Hobbes fell in love with the structure of geometry, in which interconnected propositions issue from basic definitions and axioms. Like Descartes and Spinoza (both Chapter 3), Hobbes sought a marriage of philosophy and mathematics.

Hobbes's theory of humans and society was a mechanical model whose main ingredients were bodies and motion. The idea of a world composed of bodies in motion may have come from Galileo or from William Harvey, the discoverer of the circulation of blood. Because he did not believe in the existence of incorporeal beings, Hobbes denied the reality of spirit, or God, if the terms were used to imply beings without bodies. He considered the theologians' view of God as an incorporeal substance a contradiction in terms.

Because Hobbes saw the world as bodies in motion, his mind-body solution was a type of monistic materialism we called epiphenomenalism in Chapter 1. Although Hobbes was somewhat inconsistent in his writings, he most often viewed consciousness as simply an epiphenomenon, or byproduct, of the brain's activity. That is, Hobbes thought mental processes were caused by motions in the brain.

Anticipating Locke, Hobbes saw all knowledge arising from sensation: "For there is no conception in a man's mind, which hath not at first, totally, or by parts, been begotten upon the organs of Sense" (Hobbes, 1651/1914, p. 3). Thus, Hobbes rejected Descartes's belief in innate ideas for a psychological empiricism in which all knowledge comes from sensory experience.

Additionally, there is imagination, which here means the formation of an image. In Hobbes's materialistic explanation, imagination "is nothing but *decaying sense* ..." (Hobbes, 1651/1914, p. 5, italics in the original), the retention of an object's image when the object is removed. Memory is the expression of the decay of the sense experience when it is old and fading. Hobbes concluded that imagination and memory are just different names for the same thing.

For Hobbes, thought was a sequence of imaginations or memories, determined by laws of the association of ideas. To explain how one thought leads to another, Hobbes used contiguity. Memories, imaginations, and sense experiences occurring together in the past are associated with each other, with the result that one can call up the other. Also, free will did not exist for Hobbes. There is an unbroken chain of causes and effects, and if we could see the connections, we would understand that behavior we consider voluntary is actually determined.

Hobbes's mechanical model readily explained dreams. Whereas waking imaginations proceed from external motions (e.g., the contact of an object with a sensory receptor) to internal motions (imaginations), dreams proceed from internal motions in the brain outward. The fantastic nature of dreams occurs because there is no external sensation to provide a reference point.

Hobbes's political beliefs stemmed from his pessimistic view of "human nature," which he saw as basically aggressive and selfish. Without the control of a strong form of government, human life is "solitary, poore, nasty, brutish, and short" (Hobbes, 1651/1914, p. 65). Enlightened selfishness leads to a "social contract," in which people cede the right of aggression to an absolute ruler. "Leviathan" was Hobbes's name for this omnipotent state.

Summarizing Hobbes

In general, we can describe Hobbes's positions with the labels we used for Democritus (Chapter 2). Like Democritus, Hobbes was a *determinist* who believed that all events are set by prior causes. He was a *materialist* because he believed that all existence consists of bodies in motion, and he did not believe in incorporeal substances. Hobbes was a *reductionist* because he thought that events on the observable level could be explained on a more basic level, and all could ultimately be explained by the interaction and motion of bodies. His development of reductionism is perhaps

his most important contribution for modern psychology. Like Democritus, Hobbes was a *nurturist* who rejected innate ideas for the belief that the mind's contents come from sensory experience, which earns him the *empiricist* label. Hobbes, again like Democritus and particularly like Galileo, held that the object qualities we experience do not reside in the objects but rather in ourselves. Qualities such as taste and odor are secondary qualities, in other words.

Hobbes was certainly among the first to apply empirical methods to questions of human nature. From Hobbes's initial speculations, Locke developed a more careful and orderly system in *An Essay Concerning Human Understanding*. Hobbes's materialism also strongly influenced later thought, particularly that of Julien de La Mettrie (discussed later). Although his written views were often incomplete, we can conclude that Hobbes anticipated many subsequent empirical and materialistic images of mind that remain vital to psychology.

John Locke

John Locke (1632–1704) was born in Wrington in the county of Somerset, which is in southwest England. Locke's father was the attorney for a local member of Parliament, who sponsored Locke for admission to London's Westminster School. In Locke's second year at Westminster School, King Charles I was executed in nearby Whitehall Palace yard. Although Locke probably did not see the execution, it undoubtedly influenced his philosophy.

At 20, Locke entered Oxford as a scholarship student. Studying medicine, Locke rejected the approach rooted in the classical Greek and Latin texts for the observational, experimental approach taught and practiced by scientists such as Thomas Willis (1621–1675). Willis was a pioneer student of the brain's anatomy and one of the founders of the Royal Society in 1662. A circuit of blood vessels at the base of the brain is called the circle of Willis in his honor.

Locke also interacted with Robert Boyle (1627–1691), a scientist central to the modernization of chemistry. From Boyle, Locke learned how to approach problems empirically. Boyle also gave

Locke the distinction between primary and secondary qualities, a distinction made many times
previously, as we have noted. Later we will see the
influence of Newton's *Principia* on Locke's most
famous work. Newton had taken an atomistic,
reductionistic approach to understanding the universe, and Locke adopted a similar approach for
the mind.

After receiving a bachelor's and a master's
degree from Oxford, Locke stayed on as a don.
Because he had not taken the medical courses in
the classical vein, Locke never received a medical
degree. However, he did enjoy some success as a
physician, because of a chance encounter with Sir
Anthony Ashley Cooper (1621–1683). Lord Ashley
suffered from a liver cyst, and, when it became
inflamed, Locke inserted a drainage tube into it
through an abdominal incision. The result was so
satisfactory that Ashley lived the rest of his life
with a tube in place.

Ashley became the first Earl of Shaftesbury and
was much involved in British politics until 1681.
Locke, who was more of a trusted adviser and friend
than a physician to Ashley, shared in the Earl's success and found his political philosophy molded in
the process.

In 1679, the Earl encountered difficulties over
the royal succession. Charles II had no legitimate
offspring, his brother James was a Catholic, and
Shaftesbury and his supporters feared a Catholic
king who might owe primary allegiance to the Pope.
Although Shaftesbury successfully steered a bill
through Parliament disqualifying Catholics from
the succession, Charles II stood his ground, and the
battle was joined. Locke wrote papers supporting
his patron's cause, including drafts of *Two Treatises
of Government*.

Briefly imprisoned, Shaftesbury fled to Holland
and Locke prudently followed in 1684. Assuming a
false name and moving frequently, Locke finished
the manuscripts of *An Essay Concerning Human
Understanding* and *Two Treatises*. In 1689, William
III and his wife, Mary II, replaced James II as the
monarchs of Great Britain and Ireland. Locke
returned to England, and the *Essay* and *Two
Treatises* were published in 1690, making Locke the
most renowned philosopher of his day.

FIGURE 4–2. John Locke.
Source: National Library of Medicine.

After 1691, Locke (Figure 4–2) lived mainly at
Oates Manor in Essex with Sir Francis Masham and
his wife. He spent his time writing and rewriting
until he died in 1704, while listening to Lady
Masham reading Psalms.

An Essay Concerning Human Understanding

Ideas: The Mind's Contents. Locke's impetus for
the *Essay* came in 1670, when a philosophical discussion with several friends became hopelessly mired in
difficulties. Locke decided to investigate the more
general question of the origin and nature of human
abilities.

Locke concluded that our knowledge is restricted
to ideas. These were not Plato's innate universals
(Chapter 2), but ideas generated from experience.
There are no innate ideas, as Descartes and others
would have us believe.

Let us then suppose the mind to be, as we say, white paper, void of all characters, without any ideas; how comes it to be furnished? . . . To this I answer, in one word, from *experience.* . . . Our observation employed either about external sensible objects, or about the internal operations of our minds perceived and reflected on by ourselves, is that which supplies our understandings with all the materials of thinking. (Locke, 1690/1964, pp. 89–90, italics in the original)

People who argued for innate ideas often pointed to such universal principles as "it is impossible for the same thing to be and not to be." Even if such ideas are universal—which Locke doubted because children and the retarded do not have them—they do not have to be innate. Locke considered the innateness doctrine unnecessary, because he could explain the presence of "universal" ideas with an empirical description of their source in experience.

Sensation and Reflection. Furthermore, the two sources of ideas from experience are sensation and reflection. By **sensation**, Locke meant the impressions passively received from our sense organs and transmitted to our minds. These impressions constitute **simple ideas**, because they cannot be divided further. For example, in the presence of a rose, we receive a color sensation, an odor sensation, and a feeling of texture if we touch the petals. Although the rose is a combination of qualities, for us the qualities are simple ideas because each enters through a separate sense. Simple ideas have their origin in sensations and also in reflection.

Locke said that **reflection** is the "perception of the operations of our own minds within us, as it is employed about the ideas it has got" (Locke, 1690/1964, p. 90). That is, additional ideas are created by the mind's operations, working on sensations previously received. The mind's operations comprising reflection are "*perception, thinking, doubting, believing, reasoning, knowing, willing,* and all the different actings of our own minds . . ." (Locke, 1690/1964, p. 90, italics in the original). Ideas created by reflection cannot be innate, because reflection

must initially use ideas that have entered the mind through the senses.

In addition to simple ideas from the senses, the mind can use its operations to create other simple ideas. For example, a simple idea created by reflecting on sensations received from a flower might be the idea of pleasure. Locke wrote that pleasure or pain, delight or uneasiness are involved in almost all of our ideas, whether they are ideas of sensation or of reflection.

Whereas simple ideas are received passively by the mind, **complex ideas** are created by combining simple ideas of both kinds. Several simple ideas of sensation, such as the color and smell of a flower, might combine with a simple idea of reflection (e.g., pleasure) to give the complex idea of a rose.

Although Locke is credited with coining the phrase "the association of ideas," it was not added to the *Essay* until the fourth edition. In the chapter in which he discusses "associations," Locke does not refer either to Aristotle (Chapter 2) or to Hobbes, and he does not formulate any "laws of association." He argued that experience can cause ideas to be linked in an infinite variety of combinations and that associations formed "accidentally" can be just as compelling as more "natural" associations. For example, a child repeatedly told not to talk to strangers may come to associate strangers and danger just as strongly as roundness and orangeness are associated with oranges.

Interestingly, Locke considered the association of ideas important for creating pathological aversions. For example, he clearly described what we call **conditioned taste aversion** (e.g., Garcia, Hankins, & Rusiniak, 1974; see also Chapter 12) in the following:

A grown person surfeiting with honey no sooner hears the name of it, but his fancy immediately carries sickness and qualms to his stomach, and he cannot bear the very idea of it; other ideas of dislike, and sickness, and vomiting, presently accompany it, and he is disturbed. . . . (Locke, 1690/1964, p. 252)

Perception. Locke wrote that perception "is the first faculty of the mind exercised about our ideas . . ." and that "it is the first and simplest idea we have from reflection, and is by some called thinking in general" (Locke, 1690/1964, p. 119). Locke also speculated on the form our perceptions would take if, as adults, we were suddenly to gain the use of a sense that we had previously lacked.

Locke quoted a letter from the Irish scientist **William Molyneux** (or Molineux, as Locke spelled it; 1656–1696) in which Molyneux speculated that a person born blind who gained sight as an adult would be unable to make distinctions visually that the person had learned to make with other senses. Locke agreed, predicting that the person would not be able to identify objects visually that had been known previously only by touch. The reason is that visual perception of an object such as a cube depends on visual sensations creating the appropriate ideas in the mind. Until these ideas have been formed, the person will not be able to recognize the object by sight.

Unfortunately, the answer of whether Locke and Molyneux were right is not clear-cut. Several people born blind who gained sight through surgery (e.g., cataract removal) have been studied, and many of the cases have supported Locke and Molyneux's position. Often the people could see little at first and were unable to name even the simplest objects or shapes. For many, a lengthy period of training was needed before there was useful vision, which suggests that it is necessary to have visual ideas before there can be visual perceptions. However, "some did see quite well almost immediately, particularly those who were intelligent and active, and who had received a good education while blind" (Gregory, 1966, p. 193). Gregory concluded that it is "extremely difficult, if not entirely impossible, to use these cases to answer Molyneux's question" (p. 198). An adult learning to use vision is not at all like an infant undergoing initial learning. For one thing, the adult has a vast store of knowledge from other senses. Adults "with restored vision are not living fossils of infants" (p. 198).

Primary and Secondary Qualities. Following the lead of Galileo, Descartes, Boyle, and others, Locke distinguished between primary and secondary qualities of objects. For Locke, the primary qualities were solidity, extension, figure, and mobility. Secondary qualities are "qualities which

in truth are nothing in the objects themselves but powers to produce various sensations in us . . ." (Locke, 1690/1964, p. 112). Examples include color, sound, taste, smell, and temperature, the latter demonstrated by Locke through the use of three bowls of water.

Take three bowls, Locke suggested, and fill the one on the left with cold water, the one on the right with hot water, and the one in the middle with lukewarm water. Place your right hand in the hot water and your left hand in the cold water. Your right hand should feel hot and your left hand cold just as you would expect. Next, place both hands into the middle bowl. Now, your left hand will feel warm and your right hand will feel cool even though both hands are in the same water, which Locke believed demonstrated that the sensation of temperature is not a property of the water but comes from experience (i.e., is a secondary quality).

Actually, if sensation is understood to be the *warming* or *cooling* of the skin, then Locke's demonstration could be of a primary quality. Because the empiricists did not see relations or change as sensations, they missed truths that William James (Chapter 10) and later the Gestaltists (Chapter 14) could see. The empiricists' problem may have been that they were not empirical enough. They adhered to their beliefs in the primacy of sensation rather than allowing themselves to be convinced by the evidence from their experiences. Nevertheless, Locke's demonstration successfully made the point he intended.

By differentiating primary and secondary qualities, Locke was trying to distinguish appearance from reality, a distinction reflecting Newton's influence. Newton explained the appearance of white, for example, by the motions of tiny, invisible particles. Reality is not found in the secondary quality of whiteness but in the movement of the tiny particles themselves. Although the secondary qualities are just appearance, there is something real behind them (particles in motion), and Locke called this underlying reality *substance*. Locke could not precisely describe substance, writing, "if anyone will examine himself concerning his notion of pure substance in general, he will find he has no other idea of it at all, but only a supposition of he knows not what *support* of such qualities which are capable of producing simple ideas in us" (Locke, 1690/1964, p. 185, italics in the original). Despite his inability to describe it, Locke considered substance the explanation for sensation.

Degrees of Knowledge. Because he could not describe substance, Locke was led to consider the extent and validity of our knowledge. First, he defined knowledge as "nothing but *the perception of the connexion and agreement, or disagreement and repugnancy, of any of our ideas*" (Locke, 1690/1964, p. 320, italics in the original). In some cases, the mind immediately perceives the agreement or disagreement of two ideas, and Locke called this *intuitive knowledge.* "Thus the mind perceives that white is not black, that a circle is not a triangle. . . . Such kinds of truths the mind perceives at the first sight of the ideas together by bare intuition" (Locke, 1690/1964, p. 325–326).

Next, the mind again perceives the agreement or disagreement between ideas, but not immediately. Instead, the agreement or disagreement occurs through the intervention of one or more other ideas, and Locke called this *demonstrative knowledge.* An example is proving propositions in geometry.

According to Locke (1690/1964), whatever falls short of intuitive or demonstrative knowledge is "but *faith* or *opinion,* but not knowledge . . ." (p. 330). However, there is another kind of knowledge, which Locke called *sensitive knowledge,* or knowledge of things received through our senses. Sensitive knowledge is less precise and verifiable than intuitive and demonstrative knowledge, which makes it difficult to be sure that things exist. Locke wrote: "of the *real actual existence of things,* we have an intuitive knowledge of *our own existence,* and a demonstrative knowledge of the existence of a *God:* of the existence of *anything else,* we have no other but a sensitive knowledge; which extends not beyond the objects present to our senses" (Locke, 1690/1964, pp. 340–341, italics in the original).

Leibniz's Critique of the Essay

In 1696, Leibniz wrote a 7-page review of Locke's *Essay,* known to him at the time only from an abstract. When Leibniz learned that Locke had "misunderstood" his criticisms, he began to elaborate them. By the time Locke died in 1704, Leibniz's critique was nearly 600 pages long. Having no wish to argue with a dead man, Leibniz did not finish his commentary, which was not published until 1765, nearly 50 years after Leibniz died.

Considered Leibniz's (1765/1949) greatest work, *New Essays on Human Understanding* begins with a summary of the author's psychology, followed by a Socratic dialogue between fictional characters representing Locke's and Leibniz's views. After praising Locke's *Essay* as "one of the most beautiful and esteemed works of this period" (p. 41), Leibniz posed the question central to his criticism, which is

> whether the [mind] in itself is entirely empty as the tablets upon which as yet nothing has been written (*tabula rasa*) according to Aristotle, and the author of the Essay, and whether all that is traced thereon comes solely from the senses and from experience; or whether the [mind] contains originally the principles of many ideas and doctrines which external objects merely call up on occasion, as I believe with Plato. . . (Leibnitz, 1765/1949, pp. 42–43)

In other words, is the mind empty, with all its contents coming from experience à la Aristotle and Locke, or does the mind contain innate "ideas and doctrines" à la Plato and Leibniz? Note that Locke compared the mind at birth to "white paper," not to a *tabula rasa* (clean slate or erased tablet), as a passage in Aristotle was translated (see also Petryszak, 1981).

Leibniz may have been attacking a "straw man" by interpreting Locke's *Essay* as implying that there is nothing in the mind that did not enter through the senses. As we noted, Locke identified the second source of the mind's ideas as reflection, "the perception of the operations of our own minds" (Locke, 1690/1964, p. 90). Because the operations (e.g., perception, thinking, doubting, reasoning, etc.) antedate experience, they are innate. Thus, at least some of Leibniz's criticisms were of a Locke of Leibniz's own construction.

To the empiricist creed, "There is nothing in the intellect that was not first in the senses," Leibniz

(1765/1949, p. 111) added "except the intellect itself." Leibniz then wrote: "the [mind] comprises being, substance, unity, identity, cause, *perception, reason,* and many other notions which the senses cannot give" (p. 111, italics added). Leibniz's innate additions to the mind's contents included Locke's operations. Decades later, Immanuel Kant (Chapter 5) offered a similar rationalist critique of David Hume's (discussed later) empirical philosophy.

Locke and the Education of Children

Although Locke never married, he presented his views on childrearing to Edward and Mary Clarke in letters written while he was in Holland. The Clarkes had asked for advice on educating their son, and as Mary Clarke's cousin, Locke was happy to respond. He used these letters as the basis for *Some Thoughts Concerning Education* (1693).

Not surprisingly, Locke stressed the importance of early education. Although he conceded that some small number of people are constitutionally superior, he wrote:

> Examples of this Kind are but few, and I think I may say, that of all the Men we meet with, Nine Parts of Ten are what they are, Good or Evil, useful or not, by their Education. 'Tis that which makes the great Difference in Mankind. The little, and almost insensible Impressions on our tender Infancies, have very important and lasting Consequences" (Locke, 1705; Axtell, 1968, p. 114)

John B. Watson (Chapter 12) would certainly have agreed.

Locke's letters covered a wide spectrum of educational topics, including passages devoted to reward and punishment, dancing, manners, obstinacy, and so forth. Much of what Locke said is antiquated from our perspective (e.g., he recommended bathing a child's feet in cold water every night and giving the child leaky shoes to wear to toughen the youngster against the sometimes fatal disease that could follow wet feet), but some of his advice sounds remarkably modern. For example, in a passage that might have been taken from a current chapter on treating a phobia with behav-

ior therapy, Locke used a fear of frogs to detail a method that we call **systematic desensitization** and usually attribute to **Joseph Wolpe** (1915–).

> Your Child shrieks, and runs away at the sight of a Frog; Let another catch it, and lay it down at a good distance from him: At first accustom him to look upon it; When he can do that, then to come nearer to it, and see it leap without Emotion; then to touch it lightly when it is held fast in another's hand; and so on, till he can come to handle it as confidently as a Butter-fly, or a Sparrow. By the same way any other vain Terrors may be remov'd; if Care be taken, that you go not too fast, and push not the Child on to a new degree of assurance, till he be thoroughly confirm'd in the former. (Locke, 1705; Axtell, 1968, p. 223)

Locke's emphasis on nurture is echoed in many of John B. Watson's writings, and Locke's method for removing "vain Terrors" was used by Mary Cover Jones working with Watson to treat a fear of animals in a child (see Chapter 12).

Locke and Politics

During Locke's life, the monarchy was first in power, then out of power after a civil war, and finally restored to power. As we indicated, Hobbes's response was to argue for an absolute monarchy because of his low opinion of the natural state of humans. By contrast, Locke favored a constitutional monarchy in *Two Treatises of Government.* His social contract theory defended the natural rights of individuals, justified constitutional law, and called for majority rule.

Further, Locke wrote that if the ruling body violated the natural rights of the governed, the people had the right to overthrow the government. The leaders of both the American Revolution (1776) and the French Revolution (1789) used Locke's writings to defend their actions. Locke's natural rights of the people became the American Constitution's Bill of Rights, and our Declaration of Independence owes much to Locke's political writings. In addition, Locke's political writings were used as justification in his own time for the "Glorious Revolution" of 1689. Durant and Durant (1963) commented that

"Locke's influence on political thought remained supreme till Karl Marx" (p. 582).

Locke's Influence

Locke's *Essay* is often said to mark British empiricism's beginning as an organized system of philosophy. George Berkeley and David Hume were profoundly influenced by the *Essay,* as were 18th-century French philosophers, especially Étienne Bonnot de Condillac (discussed later). It is little exaggeration to say that Locke's philosophy dominated the 18th century as Descartes's did the 17th.

Locke's view of a relatively passive mind largely populated with sensory experiences, as well as his understanding of how perception gives rise to conception, forms the basis of many subsequent psychological theories. For example, in Chapters 12 and 13 we will see Locke's influence in the emphasis of the behaviorists on the importance of conditioning and learning for behavior. In addition, although he did not develop it, Locke's phrase "association of ideas" led to the school of British associationism (discussed later).

Next we will discuss George Berkeley, who took Locke's distinction between primary and secondary qualities to its logical conclusion, which he then used as proof of God's existence.

George Berkeley

George Berkeley, or Bishop Berkeley of Cloyne, was born at Dysert Castle in County Kilkenny, Ireland, on March 12, 1685. Although Berkeley never ventured farther west than Rhode Island, the American town of Berkeley, California, is named after him.

At 15, Berkeley entered Dublin's Trinity College, and he stayed there as student, fellow, and tutor until 1713. After travel abroad, Berkeley returned in 1721 to Trinity College, where he earned further degrees and in 1723 was appointed Hebrew Lecturer. By 1724, Berkeley was obsessed with founding a college in the New World (i.e., the Bermudas) that would promote religion among American Indians. With the promise of 20,000 pounds from Parliament to start St. Paul's College, in 1728, newly married, Berkeley sailed for America,

arriving in Newport, Rhode Island, in 1729. When the promised funding did not appear, Berkeley returned to England in 1731. Although his stay in America was brief, Berkeley was so impressed by what he found that he helped establish the University of Pennsylvania, contributed land and books to Yale, donated books to Harvard, and wrote a poem containing the famous line, "Westward the course of empire takes its way."

In 1734, Berkeley (Figure 4–3) was appointed Bishop of Cloyne. On Sunday evening, January 14, 1753, Berkeley died from a "palsy in the heart" while he was listening to his wife read a sermon. His death went unnoticed until his daughter, handing him a cup of tea, discovered that his body was cold and his joints were stiff.

Berkeley's Contributions

Virtually all of Berkeley's accomplishments for psychology are contained in his three most important books: *An Essay Towards a New Theory of Vision* (1709), *A Treatise Concerning the Principles of Human Knowledge* (1710), and *Three Dialogues Between Hylas and Philonous* (1713). *An Essay Towards a New Theory of Vision* was triggered by Locke's quoting in his *Essay* a letter from William Molyneux (who, not coincidentally, was a tutor at Trinity College, Dublin) predicting that a blind man gaining sight would have to learn to recognize objects visually. Berkeley agreed that experience is necessary for visual perception, but his analysis of depth perception and the judgment of distances took a different tangent from Locke. Locke assumed that visually recognized objects really exist; there must be substance in order for objects to have primary qualities. Further, when we see an object at a distance from ourselves, although we do not directly experience the object and the distance, both are really there.

For Berkeley, our perceptions of distance *and objects* are mental constructs.

> It is, I think, agreed by all, that *distance* of itself, and immediately, cannot be seen. For *distance* being a line directed end-wise to the eye, it projects only one point [to] the eye. Which point

FIGURE 4–3.   George Berkeley (far right) with family.

Source: "Dean Berkeley and His Entourage" by John Smibert from Yale University Art Gallery, Gift of Isaac Lothrop.

remains invariably the same, whether the distance be longer or shorter. (Berkeley, 1709/1837, p. 86, italics in the original)

Because we do not see distance directly, we acquire through experience with distance cues the ability to tell that some objects are farther from us than others. In *New Theory of Vision,* Berkeley clearly recognized three cues to distance perception, although he did not apply our modern names to them. In **interposition**, near objects hide or partially hide more distant objects. Berkeley (1709/1837) wrote: "when I perceive a great number of intermediate *objects,* such as houses, fields, rivers, and the like, which I have experienced to take up a considerable space, I thence form a judgment . . . that the *object* I see beyond them is at a great distance" (p. 86, italics in the original).

The **relative size** cue occurs when two objects of the same size are at different distances from the observer and the near object appears larger than the more distant object. According to Berkeley (1709/1837), "when an *object* appears faint and small, which at a near distance I have experienced to make a vigorous and large appearance, I instantly conclude it to be far off" (p. 86, italics in the original).

Convergence is the inward rotation of our eyes to keep an approaching object in focus. Berkeley's description was explicit:

> when we look at a near *object* with both eyes, according as it approaches or recedes from us, we alter the disposition of our eyes, by lessening or widening the interval between the *pupils.* This . . . turn of the eyes is attended with a sensation, which seems to me to be that which in this case brings the *idea* of greater or lesser distance into the mind. (Berkeley, 1709/1837, pp. 87-88, italics in the original)

Thus, we have extensive experience associating visual cues with objects at different distances from us, and Berkeley clearly recognized the principle of association, without specifically naming it.

> Not that there is any natural or necessary connexion between the sensation we perceive by the turn of the eyes, and greater or lesser distance; but because the mind has by constant *experience* found the different sensations corresponding to the different dispositions of the eyes, to be attended each with a different degree of distance in the *object:* there has grown an habitual or customary connexion between those two sorts of *ideas.* (Berkeley, 1709/1837, p. 88, italics in the original)

This "habitual or customary connexion" between ideas is formed by experience, through their frequent association.

Berkeley's *New Theory of Vision* was followed by *A Treatise Concerning the Principles of Human Knowledge,* published when he was only 25. Again, *Principles* was triggered by Locke's *Essay.* If all ideas come from sensations and our knowledge of the world depends on our perception, then Berkeley drew the obvious conclusion: *esse est percipi*—to be, is to be perceived. In one of the most famous passages in philosophy, Berkeley wrote:

> Some truths there are so near and obvious to the mind that a man need only open his eyes to see them. Such I take this important one to be, to wit, that all the choir of heaven and furniture of the earth, in a word all those bodies which compose the mighty frame of the world, have not any subsistence without a mind, that their being is to be perceived or known. . . (Berkeley, 1710/ 1837, p. 9)

The truth of Berkeley's idea that the world exists only in being perceived was obvious to *his* mind, but it was less obvious to others. In one famous criticism, James Boswell (1740–1795) challenged Samuel Johnson (1709–1784) to refute Berkeley as they were leaving church. Dr. Johnson kicked a large stone, saying, "I refute it thus." Johnson's point was that his pain from kicking the rock proved its existence. If Berkeley had been present,

he would have told Johnson that Johnson's idea of the rock included the associated ideas of solidity and heaviness, both of which would produce the sensation of pain when he kicked the rock.

Although he had written that objects exist in being perceived, Berkeley did not deny the ultimate reality of objects. For him, the world depended for its permanence on God's infinite mind. Like Locke, Berkeley believed that the sensations we receive from an object come from a real object. Unlike Locke, Berkeley thought that the object's ultimate reality occurred because it was perceived by the "ultimate Perceiver."

Berkeley did not need Locke's distinction between primary and secondary qualities. For him, all object qualities were secondary because their existence depends on their being perceived. He wrote, "it is evident from what we have already shewn, that extension, figure and motion are only ideas existing in the mind. . . ." (Berkeley, 1710/1837, p. 9). That is, it is impossible to think of an object's size, shape, or motion independently of our perception of it. These "primary" qualities are just as much ideas in our minds as Locke's secondary qualities. Therefore, objects are the sum of their perceived qualities, which is why Berkeley argued that to be is to be perceived.

Berkeley's Influence

Berkeley's mind-body position has been called mentalism, immaterialism, or subjective idealism. Immaterialism is perhaps most appropriate because Berkeley's aim in much of his writing was to crush the doctrine of materialism that he saw as the "main pillar and support of scepticism, so likewise upon the same foundation have been raised all the impious schemes of Atheism and irreligion" (Berkeley, 1710/1837, p. 25).

However, although he believed he had demolished materialism with his prescription *esse est percipi,* Berkeley did not want to destroy the science of his day, which depended heavily on the concept and study of matter. Rather, he wanted to rid science, particularly physics, of such metaphysical notions as force and gravity, which are used as though they refer to an underlying material substance. Sensed qualities are all that can be shown to exist, and we know about them through experience. All we have to go on are our experiences (empiricism).

Thus, Berkeley's lasting influence came from his strict empirical approach to obtaining knowledge, not from his idealism or immaterialism. Although Berkeley sought to destroy skepticism, some felt his writings had the opposite effect. For example, David Hume (1748/1955) wrote:

> indeed most of the writings of [Berkeley] form the best lessons of scepticism, which are to be found either among the ancient or modern philosophers. . . . But that all his arguments, though otherwise intended, are, in reality, merely sceptical, appears from this, that *they admit of no answer and produce no conviction.* Their only effect is to cause that momentary amazement and irresolution and confusion, which is the result of scepticism. (p. 163, italics in the original)

As a summary of Berkeley's accomplishments, we find Durant and Durant's (1963) comment delightful: "No man ever surpassed him in proving the unreality of the real. In his effort to restore religious belief, and to exorcise the Hobbesian materialism that was infecting England, [Berkeley] turned philosophy outside in . . ." (p. 597).

David Hume

David Hume was born on April 26, 1711, in Edinburgh, Scotland. Although he came from a good family, the Humes were not wealthy, and, as the younger son, Hume's inheritance was meager. Hume's family planned for him to study law, but he was more interested in philosophy. He studied at the University of Edinburgh but did not graduate.

In 1734, Hume had a brief fling in Bristol with the life of commerce but soon realized that this was not for him. He went to France to pursue his studies in a country retreat, perhaps fleeing from Agnes Galbraith's charge that he was the father of the child she carried, and there he established his life's plan: "I resolved to make a very rigid frugality supply my deficiency of fortune, to maintain unimpaired my independence, and to regard every object as con-

temptible except the improvement of my talents in literature" (Hume, 1776/1955, p. 4).

Hume's literary talents needed improving. His first and most important work, *A Treatise of Human Nature,* published anonymously in 1739–1740, "fell *deadborn from the press*" (Hume, 1776/1955, p. 4, italics in the original). A simplified version published under the title *An Inquiry* (or *Enquiry*) *Concerning Human Understanding* (1748) was at least initially no more successful. Although other writings received a more gratifying response, Hume's atheism prevented him from attaining two professorships he sought.

In 1745, Hume spent a year as the tutor to an insane nobleman, a position from which he gained a number of appointments that improved his economic situation. In 1752, Hume became the keeper of the library of the Faculty of Advocates in Edinburgh. Although the position paid little, it provided access to a large library and stimulated Hume to write a history of England. Unfortunately, the first volume of Hume's history was not well received: "I was assailed by one cry of reproach, disapprobation, and even detestation . . . and after the first ebullitions of . . . fury were over, what was still more mortifying, the book seemed to sink into oblivion" (Hume, 1776/1955, p. 7).

As secretary to an ambassador in Paris from 1763 to 1765, Hume was generally treated royally. In fact, the ambassador was amazed to find his secretary more celebrated than he. Hume was much admired and became a favored guest in homes both in Paris and later in London, where he served briefly as undersecretary of state for the Northern Department. Before returning to London from France, Hume befriended Jean-Jacques Rousseau (Chapter 5). Rousseau accompanied Hume back to England, but Rousseau's developing paranoia led him to provoke a quarrel with Hume and flee back to France. Shown in Figure 4–4, Hume was so large he was known to break furniture by sitting on it.

In 1768, Hume returned to Edinburgh to stay. In the spring of 1775, he was "struck with a disorder in my bowels, which at first gave me no alarm, but has since, as I apprehend it, become mortal and incurable" (Hume, 1776/1955, p. 10). Hume died on

FIGURE 4–4.   David Hume.
Source: New York Public Library.

August 25, 1776, and a large crowd attended his funeral despite a heavy downpour.

Hume's Psychology

Although we can find relevant ideas for modern psychology in the writings of Locke, Descartes, and even Plato and Aristotle, they were clearly philosophers, not psychologists. Although the same is true for Hume, a portion of his work is distinctively psychological, and several authors (e.g., Bricke, 1974; Miller, 1971) trace the roots of psychology as an independent science to Hume. Either directly, or indirectly through late British empiricism's influence on psychology's more recognized founders (Wundt, Chapter 7; James), Hume's contributions represent an important milestone in the history of psychology.

Impressions and Ideas. Hume began by accepting the empiricism of Locke and Berkeley: All the mind's contents come from experience through impressions. By **impressions**, Hume (1748/1955) meant "all our more lively perceptions, when we hear, or see, or feel, or love, or hate, or desire, or will" (p. 27). Hume called the second class of the mind's perceptions ideas, which are faint copies of impressions.

Because he believed that there were no ideas without impressions, Hume also predicted that a man born blind and gaining sight as an adult would have to develop visual ideas through experience. He wrote:

> if it happen, from a defect of the organ, that a man is not susceptible of any species of sensation, we always find that he is as little susceptible of the correspondent idea. A blind man can form no notion of colors, a deaf man of sounds. Restore either of them that sense in which he is deficient by opening this new inlet for his sensations, you also open an inlet for the ideas. . . (Hume, 1748/1955, p. 28)

Like Locke, Hume distinguished between simple and complex ideas, and impressions, too, could be either simple or complex. Simple impressions or ideas cannot be further subdivided, whereas complex impressions or ideas can be broken down further. For example, the impression or idea of an apple is a compound of simple impressions or ideas, which include the apple's color, odor, taste, shape, and so forth.

Although there must be a prior impression for every idea, every idea does not reflect a corresponding impression. For example, we may imagine a horse with wings, although we have never seen such a thing. We have seen creatures with wings, and we have seen horses, and when we have an idea of a flying horse, it is through the connection or association of ideas in our mind.

Association of Ideas. Hume (1748/1955) was explicit about the principles of **association of ideas:** "To me there appear to be only three principles of connections among ideas, namely, *Resemblance, Contiguity* in time or place, and *Cause* or *Effect*" (p. 32, italics in the original). To illustrate the three principles, Hume wrote:

A picture naturally leads our thoughts to the original [resemblance]. The mention of one apartment in a building naturally introduces an inquiry . . . concerning the others [contiguity]; and if we think of a wound, we can scarcely forbear reflecting on the pain which follows it [cause and effect]. (Hume, 1748/1955, p. 32)

Causality. Hume's thinking about **causality**, or cause and effect, was both original and influential: He considered cause an idea that could not be shown to have objective reality. We infer that event A causes event B when we have experienced the two events many times in temporal sequence. The idea of a "necessary connection" between the events occurs in our minds, not in the conjunction of the two events. If we consider the two events or objects separately, we see no necessary connection between them. Only by experiencing the two together do we infer that one causes the other. Thus, causality is a habit of the mind that comes from frequent repetitions of A followed by B. Hume did not deny causality, as some have said; rather, he denied that reason is capable of understanding it.

When objects or events have been constantly observed to be conjoined, we immediately infer the existence of one when we experience the other. According to Hume, "habit" is the principle by which this connection of objects or events is formed. He saw habit "as the ultimate principle which we can assign of all our conclusions from experience" (Hume, 1748/1955, p. 57).

Note that Hume saw habit, not reasoning, as the ultimate principle allowing us to draw inferences from our experiences. This is equally true for animals, which,

> as well as men, learn many things from experience and infer that the same events will always follow from the same causes. . . . This is still more evident from the effects of discipline and education on animals, who by the proper application of rewards and punishments may be taught any course of action the most contrary to their natural instincts and propensities. (Hume, 1748/1955, pp. 112–113)

We will see this idea echoed nearly 150 years later in Edward Lee Thorndike's law of effect (Chapter 12).

The Mind and External Reality. For Locke, our experience of objects comes from sensations, and he assumed that the objects have substance. Berkeley argued that things exist only in being perceived, and it is the "ultimate Perceiver" that gives the universe its apparent permanence. Hume went one step further, contending that mind consists only of impressions and their associations, and there is no "ultimate Perceiver" to give things independent existence. As Hume put it, "nothing can ever be present to the mind but an image or perception, and . . . the senses are only the inlets through which these images are conveyed, without being able to produce any immediate intercourse between the mind and the object" (Hume, 1748/1955, pp. 160–161).

If our knowledge of external reality comes from our impressions, which are merely copies of external objects, how can we prove that our perceptions are caused by external objects? Hume raised and discarded several possibilities. First, he suggested experience: "But here experience is and must be entirely silent. The mind has never anything present to it but the perceptions, and cannot possibly reach any experience of their connection with objects" (Hume, 1748/1955, p. 162).

The "veracity of the Supreme Being" will not work either. If "his veracity were at all concerned in this matter, our senses would be entirely infallible, because it is not possible that he can ever deceive" (Hume, 1748/1955, p. 162). In a related matter, Hume agreed with Berkeley that there are only secondary qualities. For Hume, Locke's primary quality of extension "is entirely acquired from the senses of sight and feeling" (p. 163).

In the end, there is no rational or experiential proof of the existence of external things. Instead, we form a belief in the independent existence of certain things through our awareness of the constancy and coherence of our impressions. For example, if you look at the room you are now in and then shut your eyes, when you reopen them you will receive the same impressions you received before. This constancy aids your belief in external reality. Similarly, if you remove the drain plug in a sink full of water and then go for a walk, when you return to find the water gone, you are not surprised, because this is what you have previously observed in similar circumstances. Your impressions are coherent with the process of change. Hume's point is that the constancy and coherence of impressions cause us to believe in the reality of external objects without proving their existence.

Hume's Influence

One of Hume's most important contributions was that he provided a focus for the attacks of his successors. As we noted, Hume took the step beyond Berkeley, who had concluded that God validated the existence of the world. The skeptic Hume concluded that we have direct knowledge only of the mind's processes. This conclusion led him to doubt the existence of the self, God, and the external world and also led other philosophers to try to show the error of Hume's ways. A fellow Scot, Thomas Reid (discussed later) was stimulated to philosophical activities by Hume's skepticism, and, on the Continent, Hume awakened Immanuel Kant from his "dogmatic slumber."

Hume's belief in the importance of association and his specification of the major principles, resemblance (similarity) and contiguity, have been crucial for psychology. Although he initially listed cause and effect as an associative principle, his thinking evolved, and he came to see it as contiguity with a feeling of a necessary connection between two events or objects. He saw habit as the ultimate principle allowing us to generalize from our experiences and believed this principle was equally at work in animals. By recognizing the similarity in the mental lives of animals and people, Hume provided an argument for a comparative approach a century before Darwin (Chapter 9).

For Hume, there had to be a prior impression before there could be an idea, and he believed that any idea could be traced back to the impression(s) that give rise to it. Ideas with no basis in our experience should be discarded, and this included ideas of divinity and metaphysics. As he expressed it:

> When we run over libraries, persuaded of these principles, what havoc must we make? If we take in our hand any volume—of divinity or school metaphysics, for instance—let us ask,

Does it contain any abstract reasoning concerning quantity or number? No. Does it contain any experimental reasoning concerning matter of fact and existence? No. Commit it then to the flames, for it can contain nothing but sophistry and illusion. (Hume, 1748/1955, p. 173)

BRITISH ASSOCIATIONISM

The British empiricists—Hobbes, Locke, Berkeley, and Hume—rejected the Cartesian belief in innate ideas that could be deduced by rational means, assuming instead that the mind's ideas originate in sensory experience. The empiricists incorporated in their theories conceptions of the "association of ideas," a phrase Locke introduced in his *Essay*. However, none of the empiricists elevated the association of ideas to the level of a doctrine, although Hume came close. Beginning with David Hartley, the remaining key British empiricists are also called British associationists because they formalized the association of ideas. Derived from empiricism, **associationism** includes formal rules for the association of ideas in the mind.

David Hartley

David Hartley (1705–1757) was born in Halifax, a city in Yorkshire, England. A minister's son, Hartley initially planned to be a minister himself, but his objection to an article dealing with eternal damnation prevented him from signing a document necessary for Church of England membership. Blocked from becoming a cleric, Hartley studied medicine at Cambridge without taking a degree but became a successful physician.

In his spare time, Hartley (Figure 4–5) worked for 18 years on *Observations on Man, His Frame, His Duty and His Expectations,* which was published in 1749 (see Webb, 1988, for a discussion of the development of *Observations*). Two major influences on Hartley's thinking were Newton and Locke, and *Observations* represents the fusion of Locke's conception of the association of ideas and Newton's theory of vibrations. Although Hume's *Treatise* was

FIGURE 4–5.   David Hartley.
Source: Philosophical Library, New York.

published before *Observations,* Hartley began his work nearly a decade before Hume's publication, and Hartley was probably not directly influenced by Hume.

Hartley's Psychology

Instead of Descartes's hollow nerves containing animal spirits, Hartley adopted Newton's notion of solid nerves in which tiny particles vibrate in response to sensory events (Smith, 1987). The vibrations in the nerves produce miniature vibrations (**vibratiuncles**) in the brain's "medullary particles." Hartley considered the vibratiuncles the physical manifestation of ideas. Where Hume said that ideas were faint copies of impressions (mainly sensations), Hartley said that the vibratiuncles were tiny representations of the sensory vibrations in the nerves. Thus, Hartley's work can be seen as Hume

(and as Smith suggests, Newton) translated to the physiological level.

Following Newton, Hartley noted that the vibratiuncles continue briefly after the sensation producing them has been withdrawn. A **positive afterimage** illustrates this property, which Hartley (1749/1966) called Proposition 3— *"The Sensations remain in the Mind for a short time after the sensible Objects are removed"* (p. 9, italics in the original). As an example, Hartley wrote of continuing to perceive a candle flame for some time after a person has closed his or her eyes.

Thus, ideas (vibratiuncles) are faint copies of sensations and the two—ideas and sensations—are associated through contiguity, which Hartley said could be either synchronous (simultaneous) or successive. Ideas, too, can be associated through contiguity, and a particular sensation may arouse a sequence of ideas with which it has been frequently conjoined. For example, according to Proposition 10,

> *Any Sensations A, B, C, &c. by being associated with one another a sufficient Number of Times, get such a Power over the corresponding Ideas a, b, c, &c. that any one of the Sensations A, when impressed alone, shall be able to excite in the Mind, b, c, &c. the Ideas of the rest.* (Hartley, 1749/1966, p. 65, italics in the original)

Hartley applied his doctrines of vibration and association to an array of psychological topics, including words and associated ideas, emotions and motivation (Mischel, 1966), memory, and imagination. For Hartley, association was the basis of mental compounding, and simple ideas associated together become combinations of ideas and eventually one complex idea. In fact, if enough simple ideas coalesce into a complex idea, each simple idea may no longer be discernible, an idea that foreshadows John Stuart Mill's mental chemistry (discussed later).

Hartley's Influence

According to Webb (1988), Hartley was the first to study psychological phenomena (mind) as a natural science, he was the forerunner of physiological psychology as a recognized subdiscipline, and he was the father of British associationism as a long-standing psychological theory. To name the process by which ideas and sensations are joined, Hartley chose a chapter title from Locke's *Essay*: "Of the association of ideas." However, the impetus for Hartley's thinking about association probably came from the Reverend John Gay's writings about association as the basis of morality.

Along with contiguity as the condition for the association of ideas, Hartley recognized the necessity of repetition, although he did not name or formalize it as a principle. We will see the importance of repetition in Ebbinghaus's memory research (Chapter 8) and in Thorndike's law of exercise (Chapter 12).

With his neurophysiological basis for sensations and ideas, Hartley, along with Descartes who envisioned different nervous mechanisms, anticipated the development of physiological psychology. In addition, Hartley unequivocally stressed the brain's importance for mental activity, a fact that we take for granted but that needed frequent repetition in the 18th and 19th centuries. To illustrate how Hartley connected activity in the brain with mental functions, here is what he wrote about memory:

> Memory depends entirely or chiefly on the State of the Brain. For Diseases, Concussions of the Brain, spirituous Liquors, and some Poisons, impair or destroy it; and it generally returns again with the Return of Health. . . . And all this is peculiarly suitable to the Notion of Vibrations. If Sensations and Ideas arise from peculiar Vibrations . . . in the medullary Substance of the Brain, it is easy to conceive, that the Causes above alleged may so confound the Sensations and Ideas, as that the usual Order and Proportion of the Ideas shall be destroyed. (Hartley, 1749/1966, p. 374)

Hartley also influenced individuals better known for their contributions outside of psychology. For example, Joseph Priestly (1733–1804), the chemist who discovered oxygen, published in 1775 an abridged version of Hartley's *Observations* that included three essays of Priestly's own. The English poet and philosopher Samuel Taylor Coleridge (1772–1834) was so impressed with Hartley's *Observations* that in 1796 he named his first son David Hartley. In the next 2 years, however, Coleridge

lost his enthusiasm for Hartley's mechanical psychology, and he named his second son Berkeley. Interestingly, Coleridge's critical self-examination of such problems as an opium addiction anticipated modern research in psychopathology.

Hartley and Hume were contemporaries, and throughout the 18th century Hartley was at least as influential as Hume. In the introduction to a modern edition of Hartley's *Observations,* Huguelet (1966, p. xii) observed that the "true heir of Hartley's philosophy was the Utilitarian James Mill . . . , who employed the *Observations on Man* as the basis of his . . . *Analysis of the Phenomena of the Human Mind* (1829)."

James Mill and John Stuart Mill

James Mill

James Mill (1773–1836) was a shoemaker's son from Scotland. His brilliance was noticed by Sir John Stuart, a Baron of the Exchequer in Scotland, and Mill attended the University of Edinburgh on a scholarship begun by Lady Jane Stuart and friends for educating young men to be ministers in the Scottish Church.

Licensed as a preacher in 1798, Mill was never able to get a congregation because people did not understand his sermons. He moved to London in 1802 and supported himself for the next 17 years through journalism and editorial work.

James Mill got married in 1805, and the following year a son, John Stuart, named for Mill's benefactor, was born. In John Stuart Mill's autobiography, there is no mention of his mother, although in an early draft he indirectly referred to her as someone whom his father "had not, and never could have supposed that he had, the inducements of kindred intellect, tastes, or pursuits" (J. S. Mill, 1873/1969, p. 4). Although James Mill and his wife were not kindred spirits, they eventually had nine children. Curiously, James Mill (Figure 4–6) was an early proponent of birth control (Mazlish, 1975).

In 1806, James Mill began writing a history of India, which was published in 1817 as *History of British India* and was an immediate success. In

FIGURE 4–6.   James Mill.
Source: The Hulton Getty Picture Collection, London.

1819, James Mill achieved financial security by taking a post at the East India Company, where he remained until his death.

Both James and John Stuart Mill were followers of **Jeremy Bentham** (1748–1832), a pioneer of **Utilitarianism**. The Utilitarian social movement taught that the goal of all behavior and legislation should be to achieve the "greatest good for the greatest number." Bentham and James Mill took leading roles in founding University College, London, where Bentham's stuffed and clothed body, with his preserved head between his feet, remains on permanent display, as stipulated in his will.

The Psychology of James Mill

In *Analysis of the Phenomena of the Human Mind* (1829), James Mill followed Hartley (and Hume with slightly different terminology) in making sen-

sations and ideas the mind's basic elements. To Aristotle's five senses—vision, audition, olfaction, gustation, and touch—Mill added muscular sensations (e.g., feelings of contraction and relaxation), sensations of disorganization in any body part (e.g., itching, burning), and sensations from the alimentary canal (e.g., feelings in the stomach caused by seasickness). These sensations are the primary elements of consciousness, and ideas are just copies of sensations that remain in the mind after the source of a sensation is removed. Unlike Hume, Mill did not think ideas are necessarily weaker than sensations.

In "The Association of Ideas," Mill gave the rules by which ideas are associated in the mind. In one passage, he used his "train of thought" to illustrate how sensations call forth ideas that in turn trigger other ideas, and so on.

> If our senses are awake, we are continually receiving sensations. . . . After sensations, ideas are perpetually excited of sensations formerly received; after those ideas, other ideas: and during the whole of our lives, a series of those two states of consciousness, called sensations, and ideas, is constantly going on. I see a horse: that is a sensation. Immediately I think of his master: that is an idea. The idea of his master makes me think of his office; he is a minister of state: that is another idea. The idea of a minister of state makes me think of public affairs; and I am led into a train of political ideas; when I am summoned to dinner. This is a new sensation. . . (Mill, 1869/1967, p. 70)

According to Mill, the strength of associations may vary because of vividness and frequency. The more vivid the paired ideas, the stronger will be their association. Similarly, the association between ideas that are frequently paired will tend to be stronger than that between ideas that occur together infrequently. Mill considered frequency the most important of the two determinants of the strength of an association. Vividness and frequency can be found today as part of most theories of conception and categorization (e.g., Matlin, 1989). The strength of associations can be seen in their permanence, certainty, and facility. More permanent associations are stronger than less permanent ones; more certain (i.e., more correct) associations are stronger; and easily formed associations are stronger.

Mill also believed that all associations occur from contiguity alone. Of causation, Mill (1869/1967) wrote: "Causation, the second of Mr. Hume's principles, is the same [as] contiguity in time, or the order of succession. Causation is only a name for the order established between an antecedent and a consequent . . ." (p. 110). Mill also reduced resemblance to contiguity. That is, we classify alike things together, not necessarily because of their similarity, but because they frequently have been grouped together in our experience. "When we see a tree, we generally see more trees than one; . . . a man, more men than one. From this observation, I think, we may refer resemblance to the law of frequency . . ." (p. 111).

Like Hartley, Mill wrote that contiguity could occur either from successive pairings of ideas or from ideas occurring synchronously. To illustrate, the words you are reading are associated successively, but the books in your bookcase are associated synchronously. Mill thought that many more sensations and ideas were received successively than synchronously.

Mill also distinguished between simple ideas and complex ideas, which are combinations of simple and/or complex ideas. The uniting of two complex ideas, through association, Mill said that Hartley had called a **duplex idea**. In a footnote to the revised edition of his father's work, John Stuart Mill wrote: "I have been unable to trace in Hartley the expression here ascribed to him. In every passage that I can discover, the name [Hartley] gives to a combination of two or more complex ideas is that of a *decomplex* idea" (Mill, 1869/1967, p. 115, italics in the original).

Finally, in a frequently quoted passage, Mill carried the mental compounding model to its logical extreme:

> Brick is one complex idea, mortar is another complex idea; these ideas with ideas of position and quantity, compose my idea of a wall. My idea of a plank is a complex idea, my idea of a rafter is a complex idea, my idea of a nail is a complex idea. These, united with the same ideas of position and quantity, compose my duplex idea of a floor. In the same manner my complex idea of glass, and wood, and others, compose my duplex idea of a window; and these duplex ideas, united together, compose

> my idea of a house, which is made up of various duplex ideas. How many complex, or duplex ideas, are all united in the idea of furniture? . . . How many more in the idea called Every Thing? (Mill, 1869/1967, pp. 115–116)

Although it may be reasonable to conclude that the idea of everything is comprised of all the ideas of things, there is little reason to believe that a consciousness could simultaneously contain a limitless number of ideas. Thus, the passive association of ideas reached its peak in James Mill's mental compounding model. In the process, the model's flaws were exposed, and John Stuart Mill revised his father's views.

John Stuart Mill

Like his intellectual predecessors, James Mill took an extreme nurture approach, and, accordingly, he structured his firstborn son's experience to contain as many intellectual ideas as possible. The result was in one sense a triumph—John Stuart Mill (1873/1969) described himself as someone who "started . . . with an advantage of a quarter of a century over my contemporaries" (p. 20)—and in other ways a failure. John Stuart Mill suffered several episodes of depression, and he attributed his psychological problems to his father's efforts: "My education, which was wholly his work, had been conducted without any regard to the possibility of its ending in this result [depression]; and I saw no use in giving him the pain of thinking that his plans had failed, when the failure was probably irremediable" (p. 82).

Following his father's and Jeremy Bentham's plan for his education, perhaps based on the French empiricist Claude Helvetius's (1715–1771) philosophy, **John Stuart Mill** (1806–1873) learned Greek when he was 3, committing to memory lists of Greek words and their English meanings that his father had written out for him on cards. Note that this feat indicates that Mill already knew how to read English. By the time he was 8, Mill had read a variety of classical Greek works, including Plato's first six dialogues and the writings of several Greek historians. Perhaps wistfully, he wrote, "Of children's books, any more than of playthings, I had scarcely any . . ." (Mill, 1873/1969, p. 7).

At 8, Mill learned Latin, teaching it to a younger sister as he progressed. At this time, he became responsible for the lessons of his siblings, a task that he disliked because he was held accountable for them. Mill's reading continued in Greek, Latin, and English. In addition, he studied mathematics and science. One important book for his education was his father's *History of British India*. During the year before the book was published, when Mill was no more than 11 or 12, he read the manuscript while his father corrected the page proofs.

John Stuart Mill's education with his father as "headmaster" essentially ended at the age of 14, when the boy went to stay with Jeremy Bentham's brother's family in France. Before he left, John Stuart Mill's father told him that he would discover that he had been taught many things that others of his age did not know and that he would be complimented on his great knowledge. However, John Stuart Mill should not take this as an indication of how learned or bright he was, but rather as testimony to his father's trouble and effort.

Was John Stuart Mill (1873/1969) being disingenuous when he wrote that "in all these natural gifts [e.g., quick apprehension, an accurate and retentive memory] I am rather below than above par" (pp. 19–20)? Although it is obvious that John Stuart Mill was extremely intelligent—one estimate put his IQ at 190, the highest estimate for any of 300 "geniuses" (Cox, 1926)—he seems to attribute his accomplishments almost solely to his father's efforts. The reason for John Stuart Mill's self-deprecation is easy to find. In his autobiography, Mill explained that his father persistently prevented him from hearing himself praised by others. "If I thought anything about myself, it was that I was rather backward in my studies, since I always found myself so, in comparison with what my father expected from me" (p. 21).

John Stuart Mill was particularly deficient in his emotions, and he insightfully attributed his inadequacy to the influence of both his parents. Mill (1873/1969) wrote of his father: "The element which was chiefly deficient in his [emotional] relation to his children, was that of tenderness" (p. 32).

In a passage edited from the final document, he noted, "a really warm hearted mother, would in the first place have made my father a totally different being, and in the second would have made the children grow up loving and being loved. . . . [T]o make herself loved . . . required qualities which she unfortunately did not possess" (p. 33).

Still, John Stuart Mill was able to love at least one person, Harriet Taylor, whom he met in 1830, when he was 25 and she was 23. Harriet Taylor was married and the mother of two children at the time. For slightly more than 2 decades, Mill maintained a Platonic but extremely close relationship with Mrs. Taylor, who sometimes lived apart from her husband. In 1851, 2 years after she was widowed, Harriet Taylor became Harriet Mill. She died just 7 years later.

Outwardly impervious to the opinions of their contemporaries, both Mill and Harriet Taylor suffered a variety of ailments, at least some of which were probably psychosomatic. Harriet Taylor Mill died at the relatively young age of 50, and Mill in old age is shown in Figure 4–7.

The Psychology of John Stuart Mill

In 1843, John Stuart Mill published his most important work for psychology—*A System of Logic Ratiocinative and Inductive, Being a Connected View of the Principles of Evidence and the Methods of Scientific Investigation. A System of Logic*, as it is usually known, went through eight editions in Mill's lifetime.

In *A System of Logic*, Mill considered whether a science of human nature is possible. Although Auguste Comte (Chapter 5), whom Mill supported for a time (see Heyd, 1989), denied the possibility, Mill argued for it in a chapter titled "That There is, or May Be, a Science of Human Nature." Mill (1843/1973) wrote, "Any facts are fitted to be a subject of science" (p. 844) and that included psychology's facts. Mill recognized that psychology did not have the exactness of a science such as astronomy, "but there is no reason that it should not be as much a science as. . . Astronomy was when its calculations had only mastered the main phenomena . . ." (p. 846).

FIGURE 4–7. John Stuart Mill in old age.
Source: National Portrait Gallery, London.

Like the earlier British empiricists and associationists, John Stuart Mill divided the mind's contents into impressions and ideas. Unlike his father, Mill returned to Hume's distinction between impressions and ideas, in which ideas are necessarily weaker than the impressions that give rise to them.

To Hume's similarity and contiguity, Mill added intensity. "The third law [of association] is, that greater intensity in either or both of the impressions, is equivalent, in rendering them excitable by one another, to a greater frequency of conjunction" (Mill, 1843/1973, p. 852). By intensity, Mill was referring to the vividness his father mentioned as a factor affecting the strength of an association.

John Stuart Mill's major addition to psychology was the idea of a **mental chemistry**. Using the rules of the association of ideas, James Mill had devised mental compounding, in which all the elements of a complex idea still exist, although they

may have disappeared through a process of associative coalescence. The idea thus formed might appear to be a simple idea, but James Mill believed that it still consisted of all the simple ideas comprising it, even though breaking it into its components would be difficult.

John Stuart Mill extended his father's analysis of the combining of ideas as follows:

> [T]he laws of the phenomena of mind are sometimes analogous to mechanical, but sometimes also to chemical laws. . . . so it appears to me that the Complex Idea, formed by the blending together of several simpler ones, should, when it really appears simple, (that is, when the separate elements are not consciously distinguishable in it,) be said to *result from,* or *be generated by,* the simple ideas, not to *consist* of them. . . . These therefore are cases of mental chemistry: in which it is proper to say that the simple ideas generate, rather than that they compose, the complex ones. (J. S. Mill, 1843/1973, pp. 853–854, italics in the original)

Thus, for John Stuart Mill the whole idea was sometimes the sum of its parts, as his father had written, but sometimes it was an idea *generated* by its simple components, not consisting of them.

The Influence of the Mills

James Mill's mental compounding according to the laws of association is considered the culmination of British associationism and a psychological dead end. His son's mental chemistry, however, was an important concept that we will see reflected in the writings of William James and the Gestalt psychologists. John Stuart Mill's support of the possibility of a science of psychology may have influenced Wundt, who established psychology as a separate scientific discipline shortly after Mill's death. Mill's mental chemistry may also be represented in Wundt's creative synthesis.

The final British associationist was a personal friend of John Stuart Mill, assisted in Mill's revision of his father's *Analysis of the Phenomena of the Human Mind,* wrote a biography of James Mill, has been called the first true psychologist, and brought British associationism to a climax.

Alexander Bain

Like James Mill, a man he greatly admired, **Alexander Bain** (1818–1903) was Scottish. He was born in Aberdeen, the son of a weaver. Bain was perhaps as precocious as John Stuart Mill but without Mill's educational advantages. He worked at the loom to pay for an irregular education and was often forced to borrow books to increase his knowledge. By the age of 17, Bain had taught himself geometry, algebra, trigonometry, and Newtonian calculus. He had studied astronomy, natural philosophy, Hume, and was learning Latin from Newton's *Principia* and an English translation. Bain was fortunate to have been born in perhaps the only country at the time where someone as poor as he, but intellectually gifted, could go to a university fairly easily. Taking advantage of the opportunity, Bain entered Marischal College, where he shared with another student the school's highest honors upon graduation.

For the next 20 years, Bain (Figure 4–8) supported himself in London and Scotland with freelance writing. Attempts to secure a university position were rebuffed partly because of his youthful radicalism and partly because he never became a church member. Finally, in 1860 he was appointed Professor of Logic at the University of Aberdeen, where he remained for the rest of his life. His appointment was aided by the publication of his two most important works: *The Senses and the Intellect* (1855) and *The Emotions and the Will* (1859).

Bain's Psychology

Bain's two books were really a systematic treatise on psychology, published separately because the first volume failed to find a ready market. Despite their initial lack of success, Bain spent much of his last 40 years revising the works that became the standard British psychological text.

Like Hartley, Bain linked psychology with physiological processes. Unlike Hartley, Bain used physiological processes that were as real as contemporary knowledge could make them rather than being based on speculative Newtonian physiology. For Bain, mental and bodily events occurred in parallel, without a causal relation between them. However,

FIGURE 4–8.   Alexander Bain.

Source: National Library of Medicine. © Open Court Trades & Academic Books, a division of Carus Publishing.

contrary to what some have stated, Bain did not originate psychophysical parallelism. In Chapter 3, we noted that Leibniz's view of the harmony between the mind's monads and the body's monads is an earlier version of psychophysical parallelism.

One of Bain's most original contributions to psychology was his discussion of the origin and development of voluntary behavior. Bain combined the effects of pleasure and pain (hedonic effects) with spontaneous behavior to produce what is formalized in Thorndike's law of effect. It was probably significant for Bain's development that his friend John Stuart Mill applied his "greatest happiness principle" to politics and to personal morals. Mill derived the principle by adapting the criterion of utility of his father and Jeremy Bentham.

Bain's linkage of spontaneous behavior with the "greatest happiness principle" apparently stemmed from observations he made on the behavior of lambs during their first few hours of life. Initial movements produce only chance contact with the mother's skin or teat. However, these contacts lead to more direct-ed behavior, and in less than 24 hours, at the sight of its mother, the lamb approaches her, finds the teat, and begins to feed. An association has been made between a particular stimulus (i.e., the sight of the mother's teat) and the movements needed to reach it. Bain provided other examples of this "trial and error" behavior to suggest that the process "was the universal means by which voluntary control over spontaneous activity is first achieved" (Boakes, 1984, p. 9). He was unable to suggest a physiological basis for the process, writing:

> I cannot descend deeper into the . . . cerebral organization than to state . . . that when pain co-exists with an accidental alleviating move-ment, or when pleasure co-exists with a plea-sure-sustaining movement, such movements become subject to the control of the respective feelings which they occur in company with. . . . Turn it over as we may on every side, some such ultimate connexion between the two great primary manifestations of our nature—plea-sure and pain, with active instrumentality—must be assumed as the basis of our ability to work out ends. (Bain, 1859, p. 349)

Bain's statement contains all the elements of the law of effect, the idea that successful behaviors tend to be repeated, but unsuccessful behaviors drop out. We can trace a connection between Bain and Thorndike through C. Lloyd Morgan (Chapter 9), a British comparative psychologist Bain influenced. In 1896, Morgan lectured at Harvard on his learn-ing studies with chickens. A graduate student at Harvard, Thorndike soon began his own studies on the intelligence of chickens and other animals, which led to his 1898 statement of the law of effect.

Bain's Influence

In 1876, Bain founded the journal *Mind*, which, despite its philosophical bent, may be considered the world's first journal of psychology. Bain sup-ported the journal financially until 1892. *Mind* was not a journal of experimental results, probably because Bain was not an experimentalist. As we will see, the beginning of experimental psychology

occurred in Germany, and the first journal of modern experimental psychology was started by Wundt 7 years after *Mind's* appearance. *Mind* remains a respected vehicle for essays in the philos-ophy of psychology and the philosophy of mind.

Some authorities consider Alexander Bain the first true psychologist, although the same claim could be made about many others we have dis-cussed (e.g., Hume, Hartley, James Mill). Boakes (1984) suggested that Bain is the first psychologist because he devoted almost his entire career to the study of mind and behavioral phenomena.

Although Descartes and Hartley both attempted to give neurological explanations for actions, their explanatory mechanisms were fanciful. Because Bain applied known physiological mechanisms in his explanations, he is also often considered the first physiological psychologist.

In his interest in and explanations for voluntary behavior, we see much that probably influenced psychologists who became the founders of behav-iorism. Bain's work signals the end of philosophical associationism, the armchair associationism of Hartley, the Mills, and Bain himself. After Bain—whose most important publications for psychology came in the 1850s—we will see the growth of the experimental approach to psychology. For now, we will continue the chapter's main theme with a look at French empiricism.

FRENCH EMPIRICISM

In France, as in England, some philosophers sought to explain the mind as Newton had explained the universe, through the use of a few basic elements and principles. As we noted in Chapter 3, in Descartes's mind-body dualism, people had minds as well as bodies, but animals were mechanical, without a mind (or soul) and thus effectively sepa-rated from humans. However, the French empiri-cists thought that a mechanistic explanation for animal actions might be generalized to human behavior as well. Julien de La Mettrie was one of the most important French empiricists (or mechanists).

Julien Offray de La Mettrie

Julien Offray de La Mettrie (1709–1751) was born on Christmas Day in St. Malo, a seaport in Brittany, France. Rather than becoming a priest, as his father wanted, in 1725 La Mettrie became a doctor. In 1733 he went to Leyden to study under the famous Dutch physiologist Hermann Boerhaave. A year later La Mettrie published a translation of Boerhaave's *Aphrodisiacus,* adding to it his own work on venereal diseases. After publishing a treatise on vertigo, La Mettrie was criticized for his presumption in publishing his own thoughts so early in his career.

In 1742 La Mettrie went to Paris, where he met the Duke of Gramont. The Duke got him commissioned as the physician to his guards, and La Mettrie accompanied the Duke to war. At a siege, La Mettrie had an attack of fever, about which La Mettrie's eulogizer, Frederick the Great of Prussia, wrote:

> For a philosopher an illness is a school of physiology; [La Mettrie] believed that he could clearly see that thought is but a consequence of the organization of the machine, and that the disturbance of the springs has considerable influence on that part of us which the metaphysicians call soul. (La Mettrie, 1748/1912, p. 6)

In 1745 La Mettrie published *The Natural History of the Soul,* which expressed his materialistic philosophy. In it La Mettrie formulated his belief in the similarity of animals and humans. For him there was as much evidence for the capacity of feeling in animals as there was in people.

Spurred by the outcry against him because of *The Natural History of the Soul,* La Mettrie fled France for Holland's more liberal climate. With the publication of *Man a Machine,* Calvinists, Catholics, and Lutherans forgot their dividing issues and united in their outrage. This time La Mettrie fled to Prussia, where Frederick the Great gave him a pension and membership in the Berlin Academy of Sciences.

La Mettrie's first theme in *Man a Machine* was his view of the direct relation between physical factors and mental states. For La Mettrie, Descartes's dualism came from a lack of evidence from clinical medicine. From his fever La Mettrie had observed that bodily changes can have profound effects on the mind. Then there are the mental effects of substances such as opium. Not only does opium produce sleep, it "even alters the will, forcing the [mind] which wished to wake and to enjoy life, to sleep in spite of itself" (La Mettrie, 1748/1912, p. 93). "Thus, the diverse states of the [mind] are always correlative with those of the body" (p. 97).

The book's second major theme is the continuity of intelligence in the animal kingdom, which argues against a discontinuity between humans and their closest relatives, the great apes. Animals have varying capacities to learn, and La Mettrie asked: "[W]ould it be absolutely impossible to teach the ape a language?" (La Mettrie, 1748/1912, p. 100) La Mettrie thought it would be possible and sketched a plan for an ape's education that he believed would produce "a perfect man, a little gentleman, with as much matter or muscle as we have, for thinking and profiting by his education" (p. 103).

Is it possible to teach language to an ape? The first modern attempts to teach chimpanzees to talk were failures (e.g., Hayes, 1951), and later efforts avoided the lack of chimp vocal ability by requiring the animals to use nonverbal expression (e.g., American Sign Language, manipulation of plastic symbols). In the first such effort, Gardner and Gardner (1969) trained a chimp to use over 130 different signs. However, many believe that language-taught apes have not become the "perfect men" La Mettrie envisioned (e.g., Terrace, 1979). After 5 years of attempts to teach a chimp sign language, Terrace concluded that the ape could learn to imitate his trainers but was unable to acquire grammar rules and could not spontaneously generate sentences.

More recent research by Sue Savage-Rumbaugh and her colleagues (e.g., Savage-Rumbaugh, Murphy, Sevcik, Brakke, Williams, & Rumbaugh, 1993) is better controlled than earlier work, and the experimenters claim that their pigmy chimp has used keyboard symbols to solve problems creatively and even to describe future actions, which he then performed. Earlier critics of ape language, Herbert Terrace and MIT linguist Noam Chomsky (Chapter 20), are not

FIGURE 4–9.   Julien Offray de La Mettrie.
Source: National Library of Medicine.

disarmed by the new research, however. In fact, Chomsky "ridicules the notion that any species would have a capacity highly advantageous to survival but not use it until a researcher taught them to" (Gibbons, 1991, p. 1562). We still do not have a definitive answer to La Mettrie's question, but it appears to be unlikely that an ape can learn human language (Thorne, in press).

Man a Machine's third theme concerns morality. La Mettrie wrote that "Some say that there is in man a natural law, a knowledge of good and evil, which has never been imprinted on the heart of animals" (La Mettrie, 1748/1912, p. 114). La Mettrie disagreed with this belief, first arguing from examples that animals possess natural law. Conversely, if we deny the knowledge of good and evil to animals, then we must also deny it in people, for humans are "not moulded from a costlier clay; nature has used but one dough, and has merely varied the leaven" (p. 117).

"Nature has created us all solely to be happy," La Mettrie (1748/1912, p. 121) wrote. Many believe

that La Mettrie's death illustrates the proper reward for unbridled hedonism: He supposedly died from indigestion after overindulging in a meal of pheasant and truffles. In public, Frederick the Great claimed that La Mettrie died from a fever that first deprived him of his intelligence. "It seems that the disease, knowing with whom it had to deal, was clever enough to attack his brain first, so that it would more surely confound him" (p. 9). In private, Frederick admitted the truth of popular legend. Whatever the cause, La Mettrie (Figure 4–9) died on November 11, 1751, not quite 42 years old.

La Mettrie's Legacy

According to Boakes (1984), La Mettrie's writings and the circumstances of his death combined to give him "a monstrous reputation" (p. 92), which meant that his works were never cited, even by late 18th-century writers he influenced. His ideas on the importance of an individual's environment undoubtedly crossed the Atlantic to influence the author of the *Declaration of Independence* in 1776. Thomas Jefferson's appeal to self-evident truths hearkens back to Descartes, but the ideas that all people are created equal and that one of our inalienable rights is the pursuit of happiness bear La Mettrie's imprint.

La Mettrie's discussion of animal continuity in *Man a Machine* anticipated much that would be claimed by the English evolutionists a century later. In addition, La Mettrie's conviction that training could convert an ape into a perfect little person and that human behavior can be understood mechanically dovetails nicely with American behaviorism. With his rejection of Descartes's mind-body problem by focusing on the body, La Mettrie's ideas were important as a beacon lighting the way from spiritualism toward materialism and physiological interpretations of mind.

Étienne Bonnot de Condillac

Étienne Bonnot (1715–1780) was a French Jesuit priest who became the Abbot of Condillac; hence, **Étienne Bonnot de Condillac**. Condillac was a friend of French social philosopher Jean-Jacques Rousseau, and although he did not read English, he greatly admired John Locke. As a priest, Condillac (Figure 4–10) probably would not have been allowed to read La Mettrie, although his work is often reminiscent enough of La Mettrie's to suggest its author was familiar with the latter's mechanistic writings.

At first, Condillac's writings on reflection and sensation as the sources of knowledge basically parroted Locke in French. Later, Condillac's work assumed a more mechanistic tone in which he argued that logically only sensation could be a source of knowledge. This argument appeared in *Treatise on Sensation,* published in 1754. In *Treatise,* Condillac asked his readers to picture a marble statue, internally organized like themselves, but with a mind free of ideas. The *sentient statue* has only the sense of smell and can distinguish pleasure from pain. From this, Condillac showed that all forms of thought could be derived from sensations alone. With four other senses, the statue would develop a complex mind.

In short, Condillac suggested that the higher mental processes used in Locke's reflection originated from sensation. Condillac also rejected the prevailing notion of instinct as an innate process blind to experience. His extreme nurture position fits our modern "blank slate" conception of Locke's empiricism better than Locke himself fits it.

Like La Mettrie, Condillac held that the study of animals should be useful in understanding man because the same mechanisms and processes give rise to sensation and knowledge in both. Thus, Condillac can be seen as further marking the departure from Descartes's philosophical disinterest in animals toward empirical psychology's wide use of animals to explore general principles of learning and motivation.

By the late 18th century, Condillac's mechanistic empiricism had replaced Descartes's rationalistic philosophy in French schools, the replacement aided by Cartesian critics such as Nicholas de Malebranche and Pierre Gassendi (both Chapter 3). Condillac influenced other important Continental empiricists and mechanists, such as **Charles Étienne Bonnet** (1720–1793), a Swiss empiricist impressed by the sentient statue's logic. Bonnet was

FIGURE 4–10.   Étienne Bonnot de Condillac.
Source: Philosophical Library, New York.

a naturalist until failing eyesight forced him to abandon experimentation with insects and turn to philosophy. Trained in biology, Bonnet added physiology to Condillac's statue. Condillac also influenced **Antoine Destutt de Tracy** (1754–1836), a French mechanist who believed that mental phenomena were mechanistically caused by biological phenomena. For him, understanding how sensations led to knowledge required understanding how the brain received and processed sensory experience. However, Destutt de Tracy's contemporary, Pierre Cabanis, was the premier French mechanist.

Pierre Jean Georges Cabanis

Pierre Jean Georges Cabanis (1757–1808) was such an indifferent student that his father sent him to Paris to fend for himself. In Paris, he read the classics and more contemporary writings by Descartes, La Mettrie, Condillac, Locke, and

Goethe (Chapter 5). Adding Hippocrates and Galen to his reading, Cabanis became a physician and was briefly the personal physician to Mirabeau (1749–1791), a leader of the French Revolution. Cabanis was a member of the Committee of Five Hundred, the revolutionary ruling body of France, before becoming a professor of medicine at the University of Paris in 1799.

Although Cabanis is considered primarily a mechanist and empiricist, his writings contain elements of **vitalism**, the notion that life is caused by a principle distinct from chemical and physical forces. A move toward **panpsychism**, the idea that mind or soul pervades everything, is also evident in Cabanis's work and later in Gustav Fechner's (Chapter 6). However, Cabanis is best known for his views on the biological basis of mental events.

Cabanis's interest in the mind-body relation apparently began when he was given the gruesome task of determining whether the victims of the guillotine were still conscious after being beheaded. Although there were reports of eye movements in disembodied heads and of headless bodies standing up and moving around, Cabanis concluded that neither the heads nor the bodies were conscious after execution. The brain was necessary for consciousness, and the movements were just reflex actions.

For Cabanis, the brain was the organ designed to produce thought, just as the stomach and intestines perform digestion. Cabanis expressed a modern view of the relation between mental events and brain processes when he suggested that mental events *are* brain processes. This view led to the 19th-century interest in the localization of mental functions in specific brain areas (Chapter 6) and also to the demystification of mental abnormality and to its eventual reconceptualization as "mental illness." Although there are many candidates for the title of the first physiological psychologist (e.g., Descartes, Hartley, Bain), Cabanis fits this label as well as any and better than most.

A contemporary of Cabanis, **François-Pierre Maine de Biran** (1766–1824), was, like Cabanis, part vitalist philosopher and part physiologist. He advocated a type of "experimental psychology," which, nevertheless, was quite different from that of Wilhelm Wundt. In time, Maine de Biran drifted from experimental psychology toward a Cartesian spiritualism (i.e., toward an interest in the soul as separate from the body and deserving of study). Freud was probably influenced by Maine De Biran's belief that much of importance in life is not experienced consciously.

Two other French empiricists are noteworthy: Hippolyte Taine and Théodule Ribot. **Hippolyte Adolphe Taine** (1828–1893) is sometimes called the French Bain. Taine's 1875 work, *On Intelligence,* was reportedly used by William James at Harvard. Taine's similarities to Bain include a belief in psychophysical parallelism and in associationism and an interest in the physiology of mental events. Although Taine's academic position was in aesthetics, he strongly influenced the development of French empirical psychology.

Taine's 1876 journal article on children's language acquisition stimulated the interest of the journal's publisher, **Théodule Armand Ribot** (1839–1916), in child development. Ribot was important for the establishment of psychology as a scientific discipline in France, and his journal, *Revue Philosophique,* was the French equivalent of Bain's *Mind* (Hilgard, 1987).

THE SCOTTISH SCHOOL

As we noted earlier, Hume's skepticism stimulated a fellow Scot, Thomas Reid, into philosophical activity (see Robinson, 1989). Reid was the first member of what became known as the Scottish School because its major members were all professors at Scottish universities.

Thomas Reid

Thomas Reid (1710–1796) was born into an important and well-educated Scottish family in Strachen, near Aberdeen. Reid (Figure 4–11) spent much of his life and career affiliated with the University of Aberdeen, from which he graduated at 16. He worked there as a librarian, a minister, and a professor before he took Glasgow's chair of moral philosophy in 1764. (A "chair" is normally the pinnacle rank of academia.)

FIGURE 4–11.   Thomas Reid.

Source: Philosophical Library, New York.

Like Hume, Reid was for a time a librarian, but his connection to Hume was not limited to a common Scottish ancestry or vocation. Although he admitted the soundness of Hume's logic, Reid disagreed with Hume's thesis that the mind knows only its own processes and can only infer the existence of anything outside itself. This premise offended common-sense, and Reid's position is called either "common sense" psychology or the Scottish School of moral philosophy ("moral philosophy" was the name given to psychological theory until almost the 20th century). Note that the term *common sense* also can be used as Aristotle (Chapter 2) used it, to refer to a sense beyond the traditional five that integrates or assimilates information from the other senses.

Reid replaced the empiricist's view of the mind as a passive collection of ideas with a faculty-based, action-oriented psychology (e.g., Brooks, 1976). For Reid, the mind was an active entity containing a variety of powers. He identified 24 such powers (e.g., self-preservation, hunger) and 6 intellectual powers (e.g., judgment, memory, perception). The phrenologist Franz Joseph Gall (Chapter 6) took the faculties that he localized in brain areas from Reid and his followers. Reid's approach is sometimes called **faculty psychology**.

We can see in Reid many connections to subsequent philosophical and psychological positions. For example, in repudiating Hume's skepticism, Reid adopted a common-sense method that involved an analysis of ordinary language. Reid's approach is similar to modern-day ordinary-language philosophy (e.g., Wittgenstein, 1953; Chapter 20). Reid's view of perceptual acts as contacting real objects heralds Franz Brentano's act psychology (Chapter 8). Reid assumed that many of the mind's faculties are innate, and his nativism will be found in Gestalt psychology and in the writings of a host of early American psychologists. Reid's chief popularizer was his student, Dugald Stewart.

Dugald Stewart

Dugald Stewart (1753–1828) was born, reared, and educated in Edinburgh, where his father was Professor of Mathematics. Stewart also studied in Glasgow under Reid and for 35 years was Professor of Moral Philosophy at Edinburgh. Scottish philosophers with ties to this chair shaped and influenced early psychology in America (Chapter 10).

Dugald Stewart was Reid's chief interpreter and expositor, lecturing at Edinburgh to classrooms filled with people seeking intellectual expansion. In addition to popularizing Reid's faculty psychology, Stewart is known for his two Scottish students at Edinburgh: James Mill and Thomas Brown, the latter eventually claiming Stewart's Edinburgh chair.

Thomas Brown

Thomas Brown (1778–1820) first studied law and then medicine at Edinburgh. He was initially Stewart's disciple, then a colleague, and finally his successor. Stewart's early enthusiasm for Brown cooled because of Brown's willingness to compromise Scottish common-sense psychology with British associationism.

By Brown's time, Scottish distaste for Hume's atheistic skepticism had become a general aversion to associationism itself. Brown realized that he needed a mechanism like association to account for the way the mind deals with its elements. He called his principle **suggestion** to avoid association's passive connotations. Brown's primary laws of suggestion were resemblance, contrast, and nearness in time and space. You may remember these as Aristotle's principles (similarity, contrast, contiguity) mentioned as important for the recall of an event.

Unlike the British associationists, Brown also identified secondary laws of suggestion (association), which he used to explain why one particular idea might be aroused rather than another, when both seem equally likely. Brown's secondary laws included the relative duration of sensations, their relative liveliness, their relative recency, and their relative frequency. James Mill, Stewart's other famous student, cited vividness (i.e., relative liveliness) and frequency as determinants of the strength of associations. Although we covered Mill earlier, Brown's work precedes Mill's.

As we noted, Reid's solution to the doubt Hume had cast on the reality of external objects was to appeal to a common-sense notion of external validity. It makes common sense for us to trust the impressions we receive from the external world. Brown's approach was to argue that our belief in the existence of external objects comes from the felt resistance of muscular exertion. The smell of a rose is initially pure sensation, but when the smell accompanies the muscular effort required to move the flower, the sensations come to suggest resistance, with the result that we have the perception of a real object. Brown's theory of perception directly anticipated that of Lotze (Chapter 5).

In his lectures, Brown also talked about a "mental chemistry," using the term to refer to the outcome of a psychological combination that no longer resembled its components. Somewhat later

in time, John Stuart Mill further developed, and is recognized for, the mental chemistry idea.

Because of Brown's compromises with associationism, it is difficult to know whether to keep him with the Scottish School or to classify him as a British associationist whose work slightly preceded that of the Mills. Further, Mills (1987) established connections between Brown and the French empiricists Condillac and Destutt de Tracy. Perhaps because he stayed in Scotland and because he was so closely associated with Stewart, he is generally considered part of the Scottish School.

CONCLUSIONS

Beginning with Hobbes, we see the unification of themes that provided the groundwork for empirical psychology. These themes—determinism, materialism, reductionism, and a nurturist approach to the origin of ideas—were not original with empiricism. However, against the backdrop of scientists such as Galileo and Newton, Hobbes's appropriated themes presaged a new era for psychology.

Locke, Berkeley, and Hume each built on Hobbes's themes and reshaped them into the philosophy that we call British empiricism. Although each of the British empiricists held unique views about the nature of mind and humans, two features of their work emerged to spark later traditions: the association of ideas and a strong nurturist philosophy.

Although associationist overtures can be found in Hobbes and Locke, Hume is the transitional figure between the *philosophy* of British empiricism and the *psychology* of the British associationists Hartley, the Mills, and Bain. We can characterize British associationism as an early form of "modern" psychology because of the clear influence that the associationists had on such later empirical psychologists as James and Wundt.

The strong nurturist viewpoint of the British empiricists—that all the mind's ideas come through experience with the external world—was the second feature that figured prominently in other traditions. As we have seen, the nurturist idea spread to France where it was pushed to logical extremes in the works of La Mettrie (*Man a Machine*) and Condillac (the sentient statue). During this period, we can see the waning of Descartes's influence on French thought and the rise of French psychology through the efforts of Cabanis, Taine, and Ribot. As is true of the British, we more clearly recognize as psychological the theorists with interests in physiology and association.

French empiricism (or materialism) and British associationism were not the only products of British empiricism. There was also the Scottish School under the direction of Reid, Stewart, and Brown. The Scottish School advocated faculty psychology, a view that in modern dress continues to be a viable alternative as a theory of mind (see Fodor, 1983).

Many of the people covered in this chapter were contemporaries, both of each other and of the "Continentals" we will cover in the next chapter. This chapter, in conjunction with the next, lays out the empiricism-rationalism debate along which many subsequent issues in psychology can be mapped.

S U M M A R Y

The chapter's main theme is empiricism, or the search for knowledge through experience rather than through reasoning. The British empiricists (Hobbes, Locke, Berkeley, and Hume) sought to explain the mind through a few basic, observed principles.

British Empiricism

Thomas Hobbes sought the union of philosophy and geometry. He rejected Descartes's belief in innate ideas for the belief that sensations produce all the mind's ideas, which are linked by contiguity. Like Democritus, Hobbes was a determinist, a materialist, a reductionist, a nurturist, and an empiricist.

In *An Essay Concerning Human Understanding,* John Locke described the mind as initially like "white paper," devoid of ideas. Experience provides sensations and reflection (the operations of the mind on the ideas from sensation). Simple ideas cannot be further divided, and complex ideas are a combination of simple ideas. Locke distinguished primary and secondary qualities of objects and believed that there is substance behind secondary qualities.

Leibniz objected to Locke's characterization of the mind at birth as "white paper." To the empiricist creed, "There is nothing in the intellect that was not first in the senses," Leibniz added, "except the intellect itself." However, Leibniz may have attacked a Locke who never existed.

George Berkeley gave an empiricist account of the development of visual depth perception in *An Essay Towards a New Theory of Vision.* In *A Treatise Concerning the Principles of Human Knowledge,* Berkeley concluded that "to be, is to be perceived," and he attributed the ultimate reality of objects to God's infinite mind. Only secondary qualities existed for Berkeley, whose mind-body position has been called mentalism, immaterialism, or subjective idealism.

David Hume accepted Locke's and Berkeley's empiricism, dividing the mind's contents into impressions (lively perceptions) and ideas (faint copies of impressions). Hume explicitly named the principles of the association of ideas: resemblance and contiguity. He attributed causality to a habit of the mind rather than to a "necessary connection" between events.

British Associationism

The British associationists elevated the association concept to the level of a doctrine. David Hartley founded associationism with *Observations on Man, His Frame, His Duty and His Expectations.* Because of his medical background, Hartley gave his associationist ideas a physiological basis, and his work can be seen as a translation of Hume to the physiological level.

James Mill took passive associationism to its logical conclusion. Ideas were copies of sensations; through contiguity, simple ideas unite to become complex ideas and the union of complex ideas produces duplex ideas. James Mill's son, John Stuart Mill, added the concept of mental chemistry—an idea is generated by its simple components rather than consisting of them—to mental compounding.

Alexander Bain's *The Senses and the Intellect* and *The Emotions and the Will* became the standard British psychological texts for nearly 50 years. Bain's linkage of spontaneous behavior with the "greatest happiness principle" anticipated Thorndike's law of effect. Bain's journal *Mind* can be considered the world's first journal of psychology.

French Empiricism

Like their British counterparts, French empiricists sought to explain the mind through the use of basic components and principles. The French empiricists thought it might be possible to generalize a mechanical explanation of animal behavior to the behavior of humans.

In his writings, Julien de La Mettrie expressed his belief in human and animal similarity. In *Man a Machine,* La Mettrie discussed the direct relation between mental states and physical factors, the continuity of intelligence in the animal kingdom, and man's capacity to recognize good and evil, which he thought was no greater than that of animals.

In *Treatise on Sensation,* Étienne Bonnot de Condillac created a "sentient statue," with only one sense (smell) and the ability to distinguish pleasure from pain. From this, Condillac tried to show that all forms of thought could be derived from sensations alone. Charles Étienne Bonnet added physiology to Condillac's statue, and Antoine Destutt de Tracy believed that mental phenomena were caused by biological phenomena.

Pierre Jean Georges Cabanis concluded that the brain is necessary for consciousness and that mental events are brain processes. Cabanis's contemporary, François-Pierre Maine de Biran, advocated an introspective method he called "experimental psychology."

Hippolyte Adolphe Taine is sometimes called the French Bain because of similarities in the two men. One of Taine's papers stimulated Théodule Armand Ribot's interest in child development.

The Scottish School

Thomas Reid, Dugald Stewart, and Thomas Brown, professors at Scottish universities, comprised the common-sense or Scottish School of psychology. Reid was stimulated by Hume's empirical skepticism to found a common-sense psychology in which the mind was seen as an entity containing 24 active powers and 6 intellectual powers. Stewart popularized Reid's faculty psychology and is perhaps best known for his students, James Mill and Thomas Brown. Brown compromised common-sense psychology with British associationism, calling his mechanism for combining the mind's elements suggestion rather than association.

CONNECTIONS QUESTIONS

1. How many different connections can you make between Aristotle's ideas and the ideas of the various philosophers in this chapter?
2. How does the mind-body problem connect to empiricism?
3. What connections can you make between the empirical psychologists and contemporary psychological theory?
4. In what ways did political events connect to philosophical psychology during this period?
5. Draw a concept map describing the connections between British empiricism, British associationism, French empiricism, and common-sense psychology, and compare your results with one possible solution provided on p. 562.

SUGGESTED READINGS

Hartley, D. (1966). *Observations on man, his frame, his duty, and his expectations.* Gainesville, FL: Scholars' Facsimiles & Reprints. (Original work published 1749)

Hobbes, T. (1914). *Leviathan.* London: J.M. Dent & Sons Ltd. (Original work published 1651)

Hume, D. (1955). *An inquiry concerning human understanding.* Indianapolis, IN: Bobbs-Merrill. (Original work published 1748; "My own life," a brief autobiographical sketch, was originally published 1776)

La Mettrie, J. O. d. (1912). *Man a machine* (M. W. Calkins, Trans.). La Salle, IL: Open Court. (Original work published 1748)

Leibnitz, G. W. (1949). *New essays concerning human understanding.* (A. G. Langley, Trans.). La Salle, IL: Open Court. (Original work published 1765)

Locke, J. (1964). *An essay concerning human understanding.* New York: New American Library. (Original work published 1690)

Mill, J. (1967). *Analysis of the phenomena of the human mind* (2nd ed.). New York: Augustus M. Kelley, Publishers. (Original work published 1869) It is frequently rewarding to read the original writings of famous historical figures, and several original works cited in this chapter are listed here. Although specific editions have been given, there are often other reprints available. If you have access to used-book bookstores, you may be able to find inexpensive paperback editions of the above in the philosophy section.

Mazlish, B. (1975). *James and John Stuart Mill.* New York: Basic Books. This book of "psychohistory" recounts the incredibly complex relations between one of history's most famous father-son pairs.

Mill, J. S. (1969). *Autobiography.* Boston: Houghton Mifflin. (Original work published 1873) This remarkable document details Mill's unusual education, his mental crisis, and his special love, Harriet Taylor.

Continental Philosophies: Rationalism, Positivism, and Romanticism

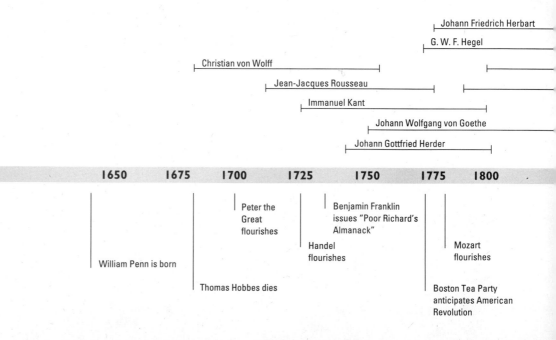

Johann Friedrich Herbart

G. W. F. Hegel

Christian von Wolff

Jean-Jacques Rousseau

Immanuel Kant

Johann Wolfgang von Goethe

Johann Gottfried Herder

1650	1675	1700	1725	1750	1775	1800

Peter the Great flourishes

Benjamin Franklin issues "Poor Richard's Almanack"

Handel flourishes

Mozart flourishes

William Penn is born

Thomas Hobbes dies

Boston Tea Party anticipates American Revolution

In this chapter, the theme will be the Continental (mainly German) reaction to and contrast with British empiricism and associationism. Specifically, we will examine **rationalism** (the use of reason to develop knowledge), positivism (a system based on observable scientific facts and their relations to each other), and romanticism (an emphasis on the whole person and particularly on the person's feelings). Each of these philosophical systems was an important part of the 19th-century *Zeitgeist,* and all remain active approaches today. In fact, with the rise of cognitive psychology (Chapter 20), rationalism is perhaps more influential on the actual practice of psychology than ever before.

In addition, although some developments in quantum physics have challenged elements of positivism as a philosophy of science, many of positivism's basic principles for theory development

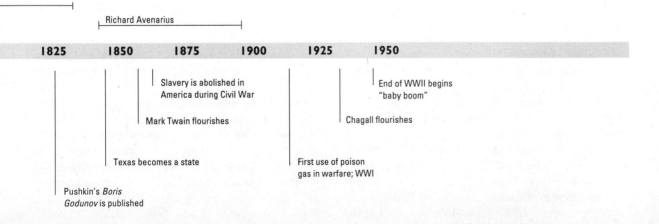

| 1825 | 1850 | 1875 | 1900 | 1925 | 1950 |

Ernst Mach

Auguste Comte

Arthur Schopenhauer

Rudolf Hermann Lotze

Richard Avenarius

Slavery is abolished in America during Civil War

Mark Twain flourishes

End of WWII begins "baby boom"

Chagall flourishes

Texas becomes a state

First use of poison gas in warfare; WWI

Pushkin's *Boris Godunov* is published

and evaluation are firmly established as part of psychology's experimental method. For better or worse, Comte's vision of science (discussed later) as a more fundamental basis for social change than religion is with us today. To illustrate, ask yourself this question: If a televangelist and a perceptual researcher both announce that playing too many video games will make you go blind, which are you more likely to believe?

Romanticism, too, is still found on college campuses, although more often in departments of English and philosophy than in psychology. We will begin our examination of these three important traditions with rationalism.

RATIONALISM

Rationalism matured as a philosophical system in Germany in the period just before the birth of psychology as a formal academic discipline. Many historians draw close connections between German rationalism and the rise of psychology (e.g., Boring, 1950; Leary, 1978), and the legacy of rationalism remains a central part of psychology today. At the end of Chapter 4, we reviewed some of the elements of empiricism that were important for psychology—for example, the passive mind, the primacy of experiences. Other psychologists, with roots in rationalism, have held that the mind actively structures sensory experiences into meaningful perceptions and have tended to favor more nativist than nurturist explanations for psychological processes.

The empirical-rational debate is still active in philosophy, where empiricism and rationalism represent competing views on the origin of knowledge. Likewise, in psychology, where the terms stand as shorthand for nurturistic, passive-mind, behavioral (empirical) views in contrast to nativistic, active-mind, cognitive (rational) views, the debate is still an issue. To examine this debate and its implications for modern psychology more completely, we will now survey some of the major rationalist philosophers as contrasts to the empiricists we covered in Chapter 4. We have already looked at the reaction of one German philosopher (Leibniz) to

Locke's empiricism, and we will begin our look at rationalism with a review of the response of a later German rationalist (Kant) to a later British empiricist (Hume).

Immanuel Kant

Immanuel Kant (1724–1804) was born in the university town of Königsberg, Prussia, and lived there all his life except for a brief period of tutoring in a nearby village. Kant entered the University of Königsberg in 1740, eventually earning his doctoral degree in 1755. He lectured at the university for 15 years as a *Privatdozent* (private teacher), all his pay coming from his students' fees. During this time, he was twice denied promotion, and he remained so poor that he never married.

In 1770, Kant assumed the chair of logic and metaphysics at the university. [A German professorship (or chair) includes a permanent salary that is continued in full even in retirement.] At about this time, he was awakened by Hume from his "dogmatic slumbers" and began work on the book that brought him his greatest fame as a philosopher, the *Critique of Pure Reason,* published in 1781. After 1781, students flocked to his classes, young philosophers made pilgrimages to Königsberg to see Kant, and he had to continually change restaurants for his midday meal because the public came to watch him eat.

Despite his fame, the diminutive Kant (he was barely 5 feet tall) led a life of regularity and order. When Kant left his house for a stroll along "The Philosopher's Walk," his neighbors knew that it was precisely 3:30 P.M. Kant walked in every season, sunshine or rain, although if rain threatened, his servant could be seen walking behind, a large umbrella under his arm. Never healthy, Kant attributed his survival to his regimen. One of his favorite principles was to breathe only through his nose, particularly when he was outdoors. During the cool seasons, Kant allowed no one to talk to him during his walks, considering silence preferable to a cold.

Kant (Figure 5–1) resigned his university chair in 1797 and entered a long period of physical decline. He was buried in the Königsberg cathedral, although he had cared little for organized religion and had

FIGURE 5–1.   Immanuel Kant.
Source: Philosophical Library, New York.

only attended church when his academic responsibilities required it. Over his grave were inscribed his words: "The starry heavens above me; the moral law within me."

Critique of Pure Reason

Before reading Hume—probably *An Inquiry Concerning Human Understanding,* which appeared in German in 1755—Kant spent time familiarizing himself with and elaborating on the work of **Christian von Wolff** (1679–1754). Wolff was a contemporary and pupil of Leibniz and was twice a professor at the University of Halle, the first time on Leibniz's recommendation. Wolff is an important transitional figure in the development of German psychological philosophy. As several historians have noted (e.g., Leary, 1982), Wolff was an early German proponent of faculty psychology, and

he identified empirical psychology and rational psychology as distinct approaches in content and method. Elements of his distinction remain with us today as part of the "empiricism versus rationalism" debate. The term *psychology* gained stature through its frequent use by Wolff in *Psychologia Empirica* and in *Psychologia Rationalis* (Boring, 1966). Another of Wolff's contributions was his influence on Kant, who considered him the greatest of the dogmatic philosophers, that is, philosophers who were relatively inflexible proponents of rationalism.

Hume's exposition of causality stimulated Kant. Hume had argued that because all our knowledge comes from experience, and we never experience causality, we cannot use our present experience to predict future events. "Causality" is just an idea that comes from our habit of associating events because we experience them together. Without causality, we can never conclude that experimentally administered event A causes resulting event B (i.e., there can be no guaranteed inductive inferences). Because science is built up from inductive inference, Hume was in effect saying there could be no certain scientific knowledge. Impressed by the scientific advances in his day, Kant thought that he needed to rescue science from Hume's skepticism. He needed to salvage causality from the humble status of uncertain conjecture to which Hume had banished it.

To rescue causality, Kant made it part of the mind's inherent structure. That is, he accepted and then bypassed Hume's argument that we can never directly experience cause-effect relations. The problem that followed in Hume's argument stemmed from the basic empiricist assumption that all knowledge comes from sensations. "There can be no doubt that all our knowledge begins with experience," Kant wrote. "But though all our knowledge *begins* with experience, it does not follow that it all arises *out of* experience" (Kant, 1787/1929, p. 41, italics added).

Knowledge of causality (and certain other knowledge, as well) must exist for us before experience and must not arise from experience. Consider the following: We are willing to accept the proposition that every change must have a cause. Yet, the truth of this proposition can never be verified by our experience, because we will never experience *every* change. Because it is always finite, experience can never give us knowledge about the universality of propositions.

Kant agreed with the British empiricists that sensations precede knowledge. However, as soon as we have sensations, they are molded by the mind's structure, which is a priori—that is, before the sensations. The mind for Kant was not a passive entity shaped by experience. Rather, the mind is an active agent, coordinating sensations into perceptions and perceptions into knowledge, changing manifold experiences into the unity of thought.

Sensations are things like a taste on the tongue, a sound in the ear, a touch on the skin, that the mind takes and classifies according to its inherent forms of "intuition" (perception), which are the forms of space and time. That is, the mind attributes a set of sensations to some object *here* or to some object *there,* to an object that is *now* before us or to one that *was* before us or *will be* before us. Perceptions are sensations that pass through the mind's categories of space and time.

Perceptions become knowledge through their transformation by the mind's inherent forms of conception. Like the space and time forms, the forms of conception are independent of experience. Kant called them **categories of thought**, and they included reality, totality, cause and effect, and existence and nonexistence. Kant believed that we have 12 such innate categories of thought that shape our experiences. Because these categories are part of the mind's structure, they permit us to conceptualize totality, for example, even though we can never experience *all* of anything. Similarly, because cause and effect are categories of the mind, we are willing to believe that one event causes another even though we never directly experience causality. Finally, it makes no sense for the mind initially to be a "blank slate," because without a priori knowledge of space and time, how could sensations themselves be sensibly organized?

Thus, for Kant our experience of the outside world, which he called the **noumenal world**, is always filtered through the structure of our minds to give us the **phenomenal world**, our inner world. The noumenal world consists of "things-in-themselves," which we can never experience directly. Our phenomenal world is created by the intuitions and conceptions (the categories) of our minds. Most modern cognitive psychologists adhere to Kant's distinction between the noumenal and phenomenal worlds and thus study the nature and structure of the mental representations that we form through experience, which in turn direct our behaviors.

Kant's categories of thought can be seen as analogous, in some ways, to the faculties of the Scottish School (Chapter 4), and, in fact, Kant was attracted to Reid's faculty psychology. However, Kant's categories did not have any particular location in the mind or brain and thus were incompatible with the faculty psychology espoused by the phrenologists (Chapter 6).

Just as Kant sought to rescue causality (and science) with his categories of thought, he also sought to rescue morality from utilitarianism (Chapter 4). Kant believed that moral knowledge was based on a priori judgments just as was scientific knowledge. Kant called his supreme a priori principle of morality the **categorical imperative**, which is categorical in the sense of applying to all rational beings and imperative because it is the principle according to which we should act. The basic formulation of the categorical imperative is that a person should act in such a way that the rule behind his or her actions could serve as a universal law for all to follow. Although the categorical imperative is innate, humans can choose whether or not to act in accordance with it (we have free will, in other words). Kant's axiomatic (rule-based) approach to ethical matters still represents the major alternative to utilitarianism's "greatest good for the greatest number" principle.

Kant's Influence

Like all rationalistic philosophers, Kant saw the mind not as a passive recipient of sensations like the empiricists had thought, but as an active contributor to the experience of the world. The immediate objects of perception depend both on sensations *and* on perceptual apparatus, which orders and structures sensations into intelligible unities. In Chapter 14 we will argue that Gestalt psychology was indebted to Kant—specifically, to his conception of perception and cognitive structure. Kant's influence is also evident in the work of James J. and Eleanor Gibson (Chapter 13), and through the Gestaltists and the Gibsons, it flavors much of cognitive psychology.

Kant's more immediate influence was on the German physiologists we will cover in Chapter 6—particularly Johannes Müller and Hermann von Helmholtz—as they considered the implications of the law of specific nerve energies, which held that each nerve imparts its own particular quality to the sensations it receives. The idea of specific nerve energies can be seen as analogous to Kant's predispositions in the mind, which impart their particular qualities on the information the mind receives.

Kant did not think the study of the mind and its organizing properties—psychology—would ever acquire the status of a true science. Among his objections was the belief that mental phenomena could neither be manipulated experimentally nor described mathematically. One 19th-century German who was not deterred by Kant's conjectures was Gustav Fechner, who was 3 years old when Kant died. Fechner aimed to develop a mathematical equation to express the relation between physical stimuli and the mental experience of the stimuli, and we will review his work in the next chapter.

The generation of German philosophers following Kant can be viewed as his "disciples." Thus, the work of Hegel, Herbart, Fichte, and Schopenhauer—all post-Kantian philosophers discussed later—began with or passed through a period of Kantian commentary and extension. With this in mind, it is difficult to overestimate Kant's influence on later philosophy and psychology. The subject of psychology interested Kant throughout his life (Gouaux, 1972), and it is fair to say that he, "more than any other philosopher of the eighteenth century, has profoundly influenced that science since his time" (Buchner, 1897, p. 14).

Georg Wilhelm Friedrich Hegel

Born in Stuttgart, Germany, **Georg Wilhelm Friedrich Hegel** (1770–1831) was educated at Tübingen University, where he studied theology. As an academician, he taught at several locations and

FIGURE 5–2. Georg Wilhelm Friedrich Hegel.
Source: Stock Montage.

was briefly a newspaper editor before being elevated in 1818 to the most prestigious academic position in Europe—the chair in philosophy at the University of Berlin. He stayed in Berlin until his death from cholera in 1831. Hegel is shown in Figure 5–2.

Hegel's writings can be incredibly difficult to read, and most of what is available either comes from his lecture notes or from notes taken by students attending his lectures. Given the obscurity of Hegel's style and the wealth of ideas he embraced, it is easy to see why so many different people after him found relevance for their own positions in his work.

Following Kant, Hegel accepted the categories of thought, but with a twist: Hegel gave objective status to Kant's concepts of the mind. That is, for Hegel, the categories exist independently of any individual's thought, which is not all that strange if you consider that most of us assume naively that concepts like time and space are "out there" in the world and not "in here" in our minds. For Hegel, the categories have their being in the Absolute. Like Spinoza (Chapter 3), who saw God in everything and everything in God, Hegel saw the universe as an interconnected unity, which he called the Absolute (God).

Unlike psychologists, who tend to focus on the individual, Hegel's system typically dealt with larger units, such as nations and populations. His interest in psychology centered on the nature of *Geist,* the German word for mind or spirit (we encountered it in *Zeitgeist,* or spirit of the times). Although Hegel's "macroscopic focus" on large units served Darwin and Marx well in their understanding of species and society, respectively, this element of Hegel's philosophy alienated others, such as Kierkegaard (Chapter 15).

Evolution was central to Hegel's philosophy, and everything, including humanity, is evolving toward the Absolute. Hegel's mechanism for evolution was **dialectical movement**, in which every condition (thought, thing) leads inexorably to its opposite, and from the conflict of opposites a new, higher whole emerges. Hegel called the initial condition the *thesis,* its opposite the *antithesis,* and the emerging whole the *synthesis.* Each synthesis becomes the thesis in a progression toward the Absolute. Dialectical movement is illustrated in Figure 5–3 in the development of theories by the ancient Greeks. Thus, Heraclitus believed that all is change (thesis), which led Parmenides to propose that nothing changes (antithesis). Plato's view that some things change (world of opinion) but some things are constant (world of knowledge) can be viewed as a synthesis of Heraclitus and Parmenides.

Hegel's dialectical process can be seen clearly throughout the works of Sigmund Freud. As one example, the instinctual id can be seen as thesis, the superego (conscience) can be seen as antithesis, and the ego, which tries to reconcile the id-superego conflict, can be seen as synthesis. Sören Kierkegaard and Karl Marx (1818–1883) were educated in the

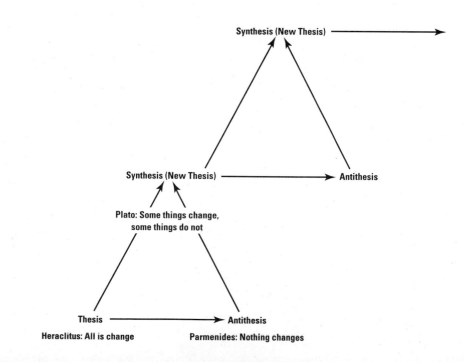

FIGURE 5–3.   Dialectical Movement.

German university system at the height of Hegel's influence. Although each became a major philosopher in his own right—Kierkegaard as the founder of existentialism and Marx through the social and economic philosophy for communism—both were importantly influenced by Hegel. Kierkegaard's existentialism, with its emphasis on the experience of individuals, emerged in response to Hegel's system that highlighted abstract concepts such as "nation," "people," or "spirit." By contrast, Marx developed a materialistic version of Hegel that Marx said "turned Hegel on his head," and his economic theory can be seen as an extension of Hegel's dialectical reasoning into economics.

The evolutionary focus in Hegel undoubtedly was part of the *Zeitgeist* that influenced Darwin (Chapter 9), and a connection exists between Hegel and several of the major figures of American psychology. G. Stanley Hall's (Chapter 10) initial interest in psychology, as well as many elements of John Dewey's (Chapter 10) functionalism, were closely connected to Hegelian ideas.

Johann Friedrich Herbart and Rudolf Hermann Lotze

Conventional wisdom assigns the "founding" of modern psychology to either Gustav Fechner (Chapter 6), Wilhelm Wundt (Chapter 7), or William James (Chapter 10), and a strong case can be made for each man. However, most historians of psychology like to note an earlier figure who seems pivotal in the transition from either physiology or philosophy (or both) to psychology, someone other than the "big three" whose contributions seem crucial to the founding of modern psychology. Although some of the figures in Chapter 4 (e.g., Alexander Bain) are sometimes assigned such a pivotal role, Johann Friedrich Herbart and Rudolf Hermann Lotze are two German thinkers more often accorded the distinction.

Johann Friedrich Herbart

Johann Friedrich Herbart (1776–1841) was born in Oldenburg, Germany. Because of an accident in infancy, he was a frail child who was educated at home by his mother until the age of 12. At 16, Herbart became profoundly impressed by Kant, who, in 1792, was at the height of his power and influence. Two years later, Herbart entered the university at Jena to study under one of Kant's disciples, the philosopher Johann Gottlieb Fichte (1762–1814). After 3 years, Herbart left Jena to become a private tutor in Switzerland. While there, he developed a lifelong interest in education per se, and before leaving, he visited Johann Heinrich Pestalozzi (1746–1827), the famous Swiss educational reformer. Given Herbart's later research on pedagogy, Boring (1950) called him "the 'father' of scientific pedagogy" (p. 250). Because his pedagogy was grounded in psychology, many authorities consider him the founder of educational psychology.

Next, Herbart spent 3 years in Bremen before enrolling at the University of Göttingen. After receiving his doctoral degree in philosophy, Herbart was invited to remain at Göttingen, which he did until 1809. At Göttingen, Herbart's interests shifted from Kant to Leibniz (Chapter 3). The influence of Leibniz's mathematics and his monadology is obvious in Herbart's psychological writings.

Herbart left Göttingen to fill Kant's philosophy chair at Königsberg, a position that attests to his stature among other German philosopher-psychologists of the day. Herbart remained at Königsberg for almost 25 years before he returned to Göttingen. Herbart (Figure 5–4) remained in the chair at Göttingen until his death in 1841. Three years after Herbart's death, Lotze assumed the chair.

As primarily a rationalist philosopher, Herbart had clear ideas about psychology. One of his claims to the status of the first psychologist is that he was the first person to write a textbook on psychology as a so-named and independent discipline (*Lehrbuch zur Psychologie* or *Textbook of Psychology*, published in 1816). Herbart conceived of psychology not as "moral philosophy," but as a separate science. However, like Kant, he saw psychology as a science that was not conducive to experimentation. "What Herbart gave to psychology was status. He took it out of both philosophy and physiology and sent it forth with a mission of its own" (Boring, 1950, p. 252).

FIGURE 5–4. Johann Friedrich Herbart.

Source: Philosophical Library, New York.

It now sounds strange to speak of something being a science but not being conducive to experimentation. Although Herbart thought of psychology as being *empirical,* it was empirical in the sense of being grounded in experience. Only through later positivist conceptions would empirical come to be nearly synonymous with experimental.

Herbart also thought of psychology as being mathematical, but it was a mathematics divorced from quantitative experimental observations. Historical developments have shown that Herbart's approach was not the only possible mathematical psychology, nor even the most useful. However, "it was the first to be recognized as a viable alternative; and it inspired the further evolution of mathematical psychology" (Leary, 1980, p. 159). As we will see in Chapter 6, Fechner successfully united Herbart's use of mathematics with an experimental approach to sensory phenomena.

Herbart's influence on Fechner also included his conception of the **threshold**, or **limen of conscious-**

ness. By threshold of consciousness, Herbart meant a limit that an idea had to surpass in order to become conscious. In this, he was influenced by Leibniz, whose monads had different levels of consciousness, with *petite perceptions* never reaching consciousness. For Leibniz, perceptions that reached consciousness were apperceived, and Herbart also used the concept of apperception, referring to the **apperceptive mass** as a group of compatible ideas that forms in consciousness—it is what you are attending to at any moment in time. In order for an unconscious idea to enter the apperceptive mass, it must be compatible with the ideas already there. Otherwise, it will be prevented from entering the mass by being repressed.

Herbart's conception of ideas striving to enter consciousness but being prevented through repression became a central feature of Freud's psychoanalysis. Wundt's thinking was also influenced by Herbart, but perhaps Herbart's greatest effect on him came through Wundt's attempts to disprove Herbart's belief that psychology could not be an experimental science.

Herbart's writing also anticipates some of the themes and concepts central to Gestalt psychology (Chapter 14), and Heider (1970) made the point that Herbart's ideas were overlooked until the Gestaltists embraced them, because the time was not right for them. "It took Wertheimer [Gestalt psychology's founder] to teach us to understand Herbart's remarks on perception as it took Freud to give meaning to what Herbart said about repression and other phenomena. There are probably still many insightful passages in Herbart . . . with which the spirit of the times will eventually catch up" (p. 139).

As we indicated, Herbart was interested in education, or pedagogy. One of his suggestions was that material to be learned is best learned when it is first previewed, then presented, and finally, reviewed. Herbart also observed that relating or connecting new information to older, more familiar information is important to learning. Take another look at the organization of each chapter in this book, and we think you will find that we have applied Herbart's principles.

You might also reflect on the good lecturers you have had. Did they use the "Tell them what you are going to tell them, tell them, and then tell them what you told them" approach? Did they connect new material to things with which you were already familiar, such as experiences you may have had or previous course material?

Rudolf Hermann Lotze

Rudolf Hermann Lotze (1817–1881) was born in Bautzen, Sacony (a former kingdom in southern Germany), the son of a military physician. At 17, Lotze entered the University of Leipzig, where he earned a medical degree. Although trained as a physician, he was always interested in philosophy and the arts, and his first publication after his dissertation was a book of poems.

At Leipzig, Lotze had contact with both Ernst Weber and Gustav Fechner, and Boring (1950) described him as a "silent listener in Fechner's circle" (p. 263). After a year of "private practice," Lotze returned to Leipzig, where he had simultaneous appointments in both the medical and philosophy faculties.

In 1844, Lotze went to Göttingen to fill the chair in philosophy that had opened with Herbart's death. Lotze retained the chair for over 35 years, and it passed to his student, G. E. Müller (Chapter 8). In 1852, Lotze produced his magnum opus, *Medicinische Psychologie oder Physiologie der Seele* (*Medical Psychology or Physiology of the Soul*), in which the phrase *physiological psychology* first appeared. In 1881, Lotze was persuaded by Hermann von Helmholtz (Chapter 6) and others to accept the chair of philosophy at Berlin. Three months later, Lotze (Figure 5–5) died of pneumonia.

In large part, Lotze's influence on the development of psychology came through his students and friends. For example, his student, G. E. Müller, who succeeded him at Göttingen, did much to further experimental psychology. Another student, Carl Stumpf (Chapter 8), developed a laboratory at the University of Berlin to rival Wundt's Leipzig laboratory. Franz Brentano (Chapter 8), philosopher, psychologist, and important countervoice to Wundt, was helped by Lotze to gain a position at the

FIGURE 5–5. Rudolf Hermann Lotze.
Source: Philosophical Library, New York.

University of Vienna during one of Brentano's periods of difficulty with the Catholic Church.

Lotze's major direct contribution to psychology came in his theory of space perception. In some ways, Lotze's theory continued the empirical tradition from Thomas Brown (Chapter 4), while rejecting the Kantian approach, which considered space perception inherent in the mind. Actually, Lotze's theory also had nativist elements (i.e., he believed that the mind possesses the tendency to arrange its sensory contents spatially); but the space perception that develops comes from experience with nonspatial input.

To illustrate Lotze's theory, consider the development of space perception through tactual sensations. According to Lotze, every tactual sensation produces a **local sign**, or "sensory address," which for touch is a pattern of intensities that is different for touches anywhere on the body. For example, a touch on the arm produces a different pattern than a touch on the leg, which provides a different pattern than a touch on the back, and so on. Similarly, a touch at one point on the arm results in a different pattern than a touch at another point on the arm. In general, local signs are patterns of stimulation that convey some sense of location. In Lotze's theory, the conscious perception of space develops from experience and movement. Movement changes the place of stimulation by an object, which changes the local signs. Because the mind has the tendency to arrange its inputs spatially, the movement-produced changes in local signs create the perception of space. We will encounter Lotze's empirical version of space perception again when we discuss Carl Stumpf, who used Lotze's theory as the starting point for his own nativist theory, and when we consider the Helmholtz-Hering debate (empiricist-nativist, respectively) in Chapter 6.

Psychology's Founder Reconsidered

We began this section by suggesting that either Herbart or Lotze can be considered to have been pivotal to the founding of psychology. In some respects, both men remind us of William James, another leading candidate for the title of first psychologist. Like James, Lotze was the mentor of students who distinguished themselves in psychology (e.g., Carl Stumpf, G.E. Müller). Also like James, Lotze was part-physician and part-philosopher in his interests and training. Like James, Lotze was not a psychologist, yet was essential to psychology (see Henley & Thorne, 1992).

Comparing Herbart and James, Herbart contributed the first textbook in psychology, whereas William James's (1890) *Principles of Psychology* is widely credited with being the greatest textbook in the history of psychology. Like Herbart's, James's conception of empiricism did not lead to the type of scientific research that would be the hallmark of experimental psychology (e.g., Johnson & Henley, 1990; Robinson, 1993). In short, although we too are tempted by Lotze and Herbart (and William James), we will honor Wundt as the first true psychologist in

the modern sense of that term. In Chapter 7 we will examine the reasons for Wundt's signal place in the history of psychology. Continuing our look at the philosophical threads leading to psychology's founding, we will now consider positivism.

POSITIVISM

British empiricists, French mechanists, and to some degree even the later German rationalists (i.e., Herbart) shared the belief that knowledge comes from experience. By Wundt's time (i.e., the latter part of the 19th century), empiricism's focus on experience had begun to shape the understanding of science itself. One variation of empiricism was based only on empirical observation—on observable scientific facts and their logical relations to each other. Called **positivism**, this system originated with the ideas of Auguste Comte.

Auguste Comte

Auguste Marie François Xavier Comte (1798–1857) was born at Montpellier, in southern France. Benjamin Franklin (1706–1790), whom Comte called the modern Socrates, was the idol of his youth. The France of Comte's boyhood had just endured the Revolution, and it was a time of political upheaval. This instability influenced Comte's main philosophical goal, which was the total reorganization of society in accordance with science.

Comte's personal life was also filled with turmoil and upheaval. Twice he was committed to an insane asylum. The first commitment resulted from a brief, unhappy marriage and attempted suicide in the Seine, and the second followed the death of the love of his life, Clotilde de Vaux.

Comte's major work, *Cours de Philosophie Positive* (*Course of Positive Philosophy*), was published in several volumes between 1830 and 1842. The work won Comte a number of adherents, including John Stuart Mill (Chapter 4), who for a time helped support Comte financially. After de Vaux's death, Comte alienated many of his admirers with his efforts to establish his positive philosophy

FIGURE 5–6.   Auguste Comte.

Source: Stock Montage.

as a religion. In his Religion of Humanity, Comte exalted the human being as an object of worship. As one wag put it, his religion had all the trappings of the Catholic Church (e.g., a priesthood, sacraments, saints, etc.) without Christianity. Comte (Figure 5–6) himself was the High Priest.

Although Comte is credited with originating positive philosophy, or positivism, the ideas were part of the *Zeitgeist,* according to John Stuart Mill. Positivism can be understood as a movement that rejects the notion of some ultimate goal or purpose to nature, just as it rejects the idea that there are secret causes of things (it is antimetaphysical). Positivism seeks to replace not only religion, but philosophy itself, with science. It is reductionistic, seeking explanations of phenomena at progressively more basic levels, and its aim is to formulate the laws of science as the laws of constant relations among phenomena. Positivism's facts are to be gathered through empirical, objective observations.

Comte's philosophical approach stemmed from his **Law of Three Stages**. According to Comte, in each field of thought a historian of ideas could

observe a movement through three stages. First comes the *theological stage,* in which phenomena are explained by the dictates of some deity. Thought next moves to the *metaphysical stage,* in which divine concepts are replaced by impersonal abstractions. For example, in astronomy's metaphysical stage, stars were thought to move in circles because the circle was considered the most perfect geometric shape. The third stage is the *positivistic,* or *scientific stage,* which Comte said implies experiment, observation, and the explanation of phenomena through the laws of natural cause and effect.

Before Comte began to propagandize his Religion of Humanity, he sought to establish a science of society whose goal was to serve humanity. He called this science sociology, and he placed it at the apex of the sciences, which were, in order of decreasing generality and increasing complexity: mathematics, astronomy, physics, chemistry, biology, and sociology. Comte intentionally omitted psychology because, as we noted when we discussed John Stuart Mill, Comte did not think a science of the mind was possible, particularly if that science used introspection as its principal method (Wilson, 1991). According to Comte,

> the mind may observe all phenomena but its own. . . . In order to observe, your intellect must pause from activity; yet it is this very activity that you want to observe. If you cannot effect the pause, you cannot observe: if you do effect it, there is nothing to observe. The results of such a method are in proportion to its absurdity. After two thousand years of psychological pursuit, no one proposition is established to the satisfaction of its followers. They are divided, to this day, into a multitude of schools, still disputing about the very elements of their doctrine. This interior observation gives birth to almost as many theories as there are observers. We ask in vain for any one discovery, great or small, which has been made under this method. (Comte; Commins & Linscott, 1954, p. 234)

John B. Watson (Chapter 12) similarly criticized introspection in 1913, and the success that Watson and later behaviorists earned by emphasizing the observation of behavior owed much to positivism.

Comte's later writings were strongly influenced by his brief love affair with Clotilde de Vaux.

Although he had stressed the role of the intellect as a reforming force in his early writings, he placed feelings above intellect after 1845. Still, he considered the aim of human effort to be the improvement of the human condition. Comte believed that the altruistic nature of people was an established fact. The phrenologist Franz Joseph Gall (Chapter 6) claimed that there was a benevolence organ in the human brain, and Comte believed in phrenology.

We can see Comte as a member of the list of thinkers concerned with scientific method, empiricism, objectivism, and the acceptance only of absolutely certain facts. This list begins with Francis Bacon (Chapter 3) and Thomas Hobbes (Chapter 4) and includes most of the empiricists and associationists. In some ways, this early form of positivism can be seen as culminating in the writings of another English psychological philosopher, Herbert Spencer (Chapter 9). The list also suggests why Comte's positivist movement gained more adherents in England than it did in France. Another version of positivism arose in Germany—Ernst Mach's.

Ernst Mach

Ernst Mach (1838–1916) was born in Turas, Moravia, then a part of Austria. Mach (Figure 5–7) studied at Vienna, became professor of mathematics at Graz for 3 years, physics professor at Prague for 28 of his most productive years, and then professor of physics at Vienna.

Although he was a physicist, Mach published a variety of observations relevant for psychology, including work on visual space perception, the perception of bodily rotation, and a theory of hearing. His most important work for psychology was published in 1886, *Analyse der Empfindungen* (*Analysis of Sensations*), although there were other contributions (Arens, 1985).

Mach, who had studied time estimation and visual space perception, wrote of space-sensations and time-sensations in *Analyse*. From Mach, Kant's space and time categories became experiential data, and, in this form, were influential in the development of Gestalt psychology.

In *Analyse,* Mach also established what has been called early modern positivism, or, sometimes,

FIGURE 5–7.   Ernst Mach.
Source: Bidarchiv der Osterreichischen Nationalbibliothek, NB519.971.

Machian positivism. The purpose of Machian positivism was to establish a set of basic rules that would ensure the integrity of science. The main idea is that sensations are the basic data of science. That is, science is public and observational, and the data of observation are sensory experiences. Positivism under Mach was evolving into a set of guidelines for the proper conduct of legitimate science. Interestingly, Mach saw data from the observation of consciousness as legitimate, thereby justifying the use of introspection, which Comte had ruled out.

Independently of Mach, **Richard Avenarius** (1843–1896) expressed similar ideas about the proper conduct of science, worked out in careful detail. According to Boring (1950), Zürich professor of philosophy Avenarius "was as difficult, uninspiring and involved a thinker as Mach was simple, dramatic and clear" (p. 395). Furthermore, Avenarius's books "were even more difficult to write than to read, for they broke Avenarius's health and he died not long after their publication" (p. 396). Still, Avenarius was admired by Titchener (Chapter 7), who organized his conception of structural psychology in accordance with positivistic principles.

Somewhat after Mach and Avenarius, Rudolf Carnap (Chapter 13), **Moritz Schlick** (1882–1936), and other members of the **Vienna Circle** continued positivism's refinement through a systematic investigation of the logic of science. Carnap and Schlick's movement became known as **logical positivism**, and it rejected most traditional metaphysics as giving meaningless solutions to pseudoproblems. In psychology, both modern and logical positivism set the stage for behaviorism. As we will see in Chapters 12 and 13, the objective approach to science required by positivism favored behaviorism's takeover of psychology, and Watson was simply part of that movement (Mackenzie, 1972).

Note that a common goal of all positivistic philosophies has been to make science primary. Because of this, Comte, "modern" positivism, and logical positivism are three connected, but different, attempts to bolster the nature and status of science. In turn, the alliance of positivism and behaviorism greatly enhanced psychology's standing as a scientific discipline.

As we have seen through our discussion of positivism in the 19th century, science was in the air, and a positivistic version of psychology was about to be born. In addition to the empiricist-rationalist debate we examined at the beginning of this chapter, there were other competing ideas concerning the scope and nature of psychology. For example, the pioneer Belgian psychologist, Desiré Mercier (1851–1926), advocated a return to Aristotle and scholasticism. Romanticism was another Continental movement influencing art, literature, music, philosophy, and psychology in the late 18th and 19th centuries.

ROMANTICISM

Romanticism in philosophy was a reaction against both empiricism and rationalism. Whereas empiricism tended to diminish humans as unemotional machines, rational thought often produced equally unappealing conceptions of human nature as under the control of abstract forces. Thus, the romantics thought that what was needed was a consideration of the whole person, and particularly the person's feelings. Romanticism's foundation lay in the views of Johann Gottfried Herder.

Johann Gottfried Herder

Johann Gottfried Herder (1744–1803) was a German critic and poet, born in East Prussia. He studied at Königsberg, where he became a disciple of Kant. In his later years, Herder (Figure 5–8) opposed Kant, particularly the idea of a "depraved nature" in humans because of "original sin."

By contrast to Kant, Herder was entranced with unsophisticated human nature. For example, his love for the music of the people led him to collect folksongs, which he published. Herder saw adoration of the historical past as a means to refresh the

FIGURE 5–8.   Johann Gottfried Herder.
Source: Philosophical Library, New York.

sentiments of modern society and stressed the importance of the historical method for understanding humankind.

In his reverence for history and a belief in the historical method's importance, Herder was anticipated by a man whose views were remarkably similar, although Herder's were formed independently. Herder's forerunner was **Giambattista Vico** (1668–1744), who died the year Herder was born. Vico was an Italian philosopher and historian, born in Naples. In Vico's major work, *Scienza Nuova* (*The New Science,* 1725), he distinguished between historical and scientific explanations, rejected the idea of an unchanging human nature, and argued that recurring historical developments can only be understood by studying the changes in human nature as expressed through language, myth, and culture.

In his focus on the study of cultures, language, and myth, Herder influenced Wundt. Wundt's monumental *Völkerpsychologie* (*Cultural Psychology*) was the study of such things as language, myths, and social customs through historical records and literature. In addition, Wundt saw the new science of psychology as lying somewhere between the social sciences (*Geisteswissenschaften*) and the natural or physical sciences (*Naturwissenschaften*), which also were distinguished by Herder.

Herder, who considered change, growth, and development of fundamental importance to his view of the world, also in some ways anticipated evolutionary theory. However, he is perhaps best remembered for his influence on Goethe, whom he met in Strassburg in 1770, and the development of German romanticism. Although Herder laid much of the groundwork for romanticism in philosophy, we must look to a man with a "delicate and neurotic nature . . ." (Durant, 1961, p. 259) for a complete understanding of romanticism.

Jean-Jacques Rousseau

Jean-Jacques Rousseau (1712–1778) was born in Geneva, Switzerland. His mother died at his birth, and Rousseau had little early family life and less formal education. At 16, he fled to Italy and Savoy (part of the former empire of Sardinia), where he lived with and eventually became the lover of Baronne Louise de Warens. In 1741, Rousseau was replaced in her affections, and he moved to Paris, where he thrived. In Paris, he began an "association" with an illiterate servant, Thérése le Vasseur, by whom he fathered five children, all consigned to a foundling home. Ironically, Rousseau is well known for his influential essay on the education of children.

In 1755, Rousseau published *Discours sur l'Origine et les Fondements de l'Inégalité Parmi les Hommes* (*Discourse on the Origin and Foundations of Inequality Amongst Men*), in which he stressed the natural goodness of humans and society's corrupting influence. Recall that Hobbes's view of human nature was exactly the opposite of this. Hobbes saw the natural condition of humans as a state of mutual warfare and thought that enlightened selfishness would lead people to form a "social contract" giving the right of aggression to an absolute ruler.

In 1762, Rousseau published his masterpiece, *Du Contrat Social* (*The Social Contract*), in which he discussed the social contract that is present wherever there is a legitimate government. Under Rousseau's social contract, all people modify their conduct to be in accord with the freedom of others. All individuals surrender their rights to the collective "general will." Individuals thereby lose individual liberty and a right to everything, but they gain civil liberty and property rights. *Du Contrat Social,* with its slogan "Liberty, Equality, Fraternity," became the bible of the French Revolution, which began a decade after Rousseau's death. The slogan still graces French coins.

Also in 1762, Rousseau published *Émile,* an essay on education, written as a novel. [Excerpts from it can be found in more contemporary works, such as Archer (1964).] In *Émile,* Rousseau included the "Confession of Faith of the Savoyard Vicar," whose central argument was that reason is against belief in God and immortality, but feeling strongly favors such belief. Hence, it is better to trust feeling than to yield to the despair of skepticism.

Émile greatly affected the educationists of the time, particularly Pestalozzi, who, as we noted, influenced Herbart. Kant, too, was profoundly influenced by *Émile,* omitting his daily walk in order to finish it. *Émile* so inflamed the political and religious establishment that Rousseau was forced to flee to

Switzerland and then to England at Hume's invitation, as we noted in Chapter 4. While working on his autobiographical *Confessions,* Rousseau became seriously unstable, provoking fights with his friends, particularly Hume. He returned to France in 1767, where he eked out a living copying music, something he had done before he became famous. He finished writing his *Confessions* and several other works, while continuing to decline emotionally. Rousseau (Figure 5–9) died in Ermenonville in 1778.

To summarize, Rousseau's writings began the romantic movement by stressing the importance of feelings and deemphasizing reason, suggesting a new direction for education, and profoundly influencing subsequent philosophies. After the inauguration of romanticism through Rousseau's writings, German romanticism was exemplified by the work

FIGURE 5–9. Jean-Jacques Rousseau.
Source: © Houghton Mifflin Company.

of a man of towering intellect—Johann Wolfgang von Goethe.

Johann Wolfgang von Goethe

Johann Wolfgang von Goethe (1749–1832) was born in Frankfurt-am-Main. Privately educated, he studied reluctantly for a law profession until a love affair stimulated him to write his first two plays. Following an illness, he returned to the study of law at Strassburg, where he came under Herder's influence.

In 1771, Goethe returned to Frankfurt and became a newspaper critic. He began work on his most famous literary masterpiece, *Faust* (Goethe, 1808, 1832/1967), which was eventually published in two parts in 1808 and 1832. An earlier triumph came with the publication of *Leiden des jungen Werthers* (*The Sorrows of Young Werther,* 1774), which is the tale of a young man in a hopeless love affair. *Werther* solves the problem of dissonant obligations by nobly committing suicide; Goethe's powerful writing actually triggered a number of suicides.

With age, Goethe increasingly disapproved of the German romanticism that he had crystallized. He particularly disliked the romantics' enthusiasm for the French Revolution, which he satirized in several works. In addition, he disliked what he considered the German romantics' disregard for style, and he attempted to correct this problem by example.

Goethe (Figure 5–10) apparently lived life to the fullest, spurred on by the desire to explore whatever can be explored, to inquire as far as possible, and not to give up too quickly. He died at Weimar, a town in central Germany.

Goethe influenced psychology in a number of ways. For example, both Sigmund Freud and Carl Jung (Chapter 16) acknowledged a debt to him. Freud indicated that Goethe's essay on nature and Darwin's evolutionary theory were in part responsible for his decision to go into medicine. Aspects of Freud's libido (psychic energy) theory are traceable to Goethe.

Apparently, modern behavior therapy owes an unrecognized debt to Goethe. As a 20-year-old law student, Goethe developed an irritability to loud sounds and fears of heights and dark places, all of

FIGURE 5–10.   Johann Wolfgang von Goethe.

Source: Philosophical Library, New York.

which he treated with what we call implosive therapy. For example, to treat his fear of heights, he forced himself to climb to the highest part of a church tower, and he repeated this procedure until he was no longer afraid. Similar methods were successfully used on his other symptoms (Bringmann, Krichev, & Balance, 1970).

Goethe's influence also came through his scientific pursuits. Unlike many of the romantics, Goethe was also a scientist, and he made contributions in such diverse fields as anatomy, mineralogy, meteorology, botany, zoology, and optics. Although many of his observations were excellent, Goethe unwisely attempted to refute Newton's then-prevailing theory of color vision (ca. 1810), finding it impossible to think of white light as a mixture of all colors. In this respect, Newton was right and Goethe was wrong, but Goethe's methodology was important for psychology. Goethe believed in exact observation of phenomena, and his desire to study intact, meaning-

ful experiences rather than fragmented, artificial ones led to refinements in phenomenology, an important element of Gestalt psychology.

Helmholtz, the famous German physiologist, knew of Goethe's phenomenological approach to the study of vision. Unfortunately, by focusing on Goethe's errors of observation (e.g., his erroneous conclusion about white light), Helmholtz overlooked valid observations (e.g., the prominence of red-green and blue-yellow color pairs) that led to the development of an alternative theory of color vision to his own.

Goethe's observations on vision also stimulated research by other scientists, particularly by **Jan Purkinje** (1787–1869). Purkinje was the Czechoslovakian physiologist after whom the Purkinje shift, the change from cone vision to rod vision in twilight, is named. Following Goethe, Purkinje promoted the phenomenological tradition in psychology. Goethe also interested his friend Arthur Schopenhauer in color vision. We will examine Schopenhauer's life and contributions next.

Arthur Schopenhauer

Arthur Schopenhauer (1788–1860) was born in Danzig, a seaport in Poland. His family was historically wealthy and well-connected, as illustrated by the fact that when Russia's Peter the Great and the Empress Catherine visited Danzig, they stayed in Schopenhauer's great-grandfather's house. Schopenhauer's father was a banker, and his mother was one of the leading novelists of her day. The young Schopenhauer accompanied his parents in their travels throughout Europe, and the experience broadened his horizons but interrupted the continuity of his early education. However, Schopenhauer was so intellectually gifted that he was able to compensate quickly for his lack of systematic study.

At first, Schopenhauer was educated to become a merchant, but he soon showed a strong interest in philosophy. After his father's apparent suicide, the 17-year-old was on his own. He and his mother were temperamentally opposites; she was optimistic and pleasure-loving, whereas he was pessimistic and distrustful. Goethe exacerbated problems between the mother and son by telling the mother that her boy would become famous. Schopenhauer's mother was irritated because she had never heard of two geniuses in the same family. "Finally, in some culminating quarrel, the mother pushed the son and rival down the stairs; whereupon [Schopenhauer] bitterly informed her that she would be known to posterity only through him" (Durant, 1961, p. 303). He never saw his mother again, and his prophetic curse has largely been realized.

In 1809, Schopenhauer embarked on a university education. Although his doctoral dissertation at the University of Jena was published in 1813 and received praise from Goethe, it attracted little attention and few copies were sold. Undeterred, Schopenhauer immediately began writing what became his masterpiece, and everything he did after it can be seen as merely commentaries on *Die Welt als Wille und Vorstellung* (*The World as Will and Representation,* 1819). Again, the world was not ready for Schopenhauer's message, and 16 years after the book's publication, the author was told that most of the edition had been sold as waste paper.

In 1822, Schopenhauer had the chance to present his philosophy at the University of Berlin. Like his publications, this attempt to gain recognition for his ideas was unsuccessful. In part, Schopenhauer defeated himself by scheduling his lectures opposite those of Hegel, with the result that he found himself lecturing to an empty classroom. Schopenhauer resigned and sought revenge by his bitterly negative comments about Hegel in his later publications. For example, in the preface to the second edition of *The World as Will and Representation,* Schopenhauer (1844/1969) wrote: "How could minds strained and ruined in the freshness of youth by the nonsense of Hegelism still be capable of following Kant's profound investigations?" (p. xxiv).

Perhaps Schopenhauer also considered it poetic justice that he fled Berlin at the onset of a cholera epidemic in 1831 and never returned, but Hegel returned too soon and was a victim of the disease. Schopenhauer (Figure 5–11) lived the remainder of his life in Frankfurt, his only companion a poodle, which the townspeople dubbed "Young Schopenhauer."

In the mid-19th century, disillusioned with efforts to achieve lasting peace and stability, Europeans eventually embraced Schopenhauer's dark philosophy. Fame at last found the great pessimist, and on the occasion of his 70th birthday in 1858, Schopenhauer received congratulations from every continent. He died 2 years later.

Schopenhauer's philosophy was inspired by Plato, Kant, Goethe, and ancient Indian philosophy known as the *Vedas* (sacred literature of Hinduism). *The World as Will and Representation* begins with the apparently egotistical statement: "The world is my representation" [or, as it is sometimes translated, "The world is my idea"]. By this, Schopenhauer was conveying his acceptance of Kant's position that the world is known to us only through our sensations and ideas. The world presents itself to us as an object to a subject, and as subjects we know only the

FIGURE 5–11. Arthur Schopenhauer and "friend."

Source: Philosophical Library, New York.

world of our perception. The world of objects is but representation or idea, completely determined by the subject. Thus, the world is my (or your, or Schopenhauer's) idea. Note the similarity to Berkeley's (Chapter 4) subjective idealism—to be, is to be perceived.

Schopenhauer also accepted Kant's belief that the human mind organizes its inputs according to certain a priori categories. Having accepted rationalistic idealism, Schopenhauer vigorously attacked materialism, the philosophical doctrine that matter is the only reality and that everything can be explained as matter. When we know matter only through mind, through ideas, how can we explain mind as matter? Schopenhauer wrote that "the materialist was like Baron von Münchausen [1720–1797, the German soldier who told tall tales of his exploits], who, when swimming in water on horseback, drew his horse up by his legs, and himself by his upturned pigtail" (Schopenhauer, 1844/1969, p. 27). Von Münchausen's feat was as stupendous in Schopenhauer's opinion as the materialists' attempt to explain living phenomena by physical and chemical forces.

Thus, the world is idea, and the world is also **will**, which is the central theme of Schopenhauer's philosophy. Note that by "will," Schopenhauer meant something more like Freud's "libido," or driving force behind human action, than he did "decision making" or "choice." Here is where we find a major disagreement between Kant and Schopenhauer. Kant had said that we can never directly know the noumenal world, the world outside ourselves, the world of "things-in-themselves." Schopenhauer thought there was one exception to the notion that we are always on the outside of things, and that is the knowledge each of us has of his or her own "willing." Although we ordinarily think of our bodily actions as the product of willing, Schopenhauer saw willing and action as the same thing: The body's actions are nothing but the "act of the will objectified." What we know of ourselves is that we belong to the inner nature of what is to be known. We are the "thing-in-itself," and the thing-in-itself is will. Thus, the essence of each of us is will. Further, will is the inner nature of

everything, of the world, and we arrive at the conclusion with which this paragraph began: The world is will.

Note that the will is in everything, not just in rational beings. It is in animals and even in inanimate objects. In fact, there is only one will, and each thing is just a specific example of it. The driving impulse of all nature is will, and this endless striving is the "will to live," whose enemy is death. But the will can defeat death through the ultimate martyrdom of reproduction. Like a modern evolutionary biologist, for Schopenhauer the only purpose of the will to live is to continue the cycle of life.

Remember that Schopenhauer was the ultimate philosopher of pessimism. Thinking like the merchant he was almost trained to be, Schopenhauer equated life to a business whose proceeds did not come close to covering its cost. There can be no true happiness because happiness is only a temporary respite from pain. Pain results from desires, most of which go unfulfilled.

For Schopenhauer, there were at least two avenues of potential escape from the will's dictates: asceticism and aesthetics. Like the Epicureans and the Stoics (both Chapter 2), Schopenhauer understood that self-control and avoiding worldly temptations was one route to psychological health. By being an ascetic and practicing abstinence and self-denial, we can thwart the will as much as possible and come close to freeing ourselves from it. Of course, death is the ultimate freedom from the will, and the only reason suicide is not more often practiced is that it is the opposite of the will to survive.

Another way to at least partially escape the will's dictates is through aesthetics (i.e., through the contemplation of artistic beauty). When we examine a work of art, we become knowing, as opposed to willing, people. What we see is the universal element in a painting. If we happen to study a painting of a person, we may see the painting as the representation of some element of humanity we all share. This view is close to Plato's concept of the Idea (or Form).

In the end, we cannot win. With the beginning of our greater understanding and wisdom, the body begins its inevitable decay. Eventually, we meet death, which has been playing with us as a cat plays with a mouse.

Schopenhauer's pessimism was pervasive, and part of its origin came from the romantic movement, with its emphasis on feelings rather than rationality or experience. In a letter to Sir Horace Mann, Horace Walpole wrote, "This world is a comedy to those who think, a tragedy to those who feel" (Henry, 1955, p. 524). "Perhaps no movement has been so prolific of melancholy as emotional romanticism" (Durant, 1961, p. 345).

Possibly Schopenhauer's greatest influence on psychology can be seen in Freud's writings. Schopenhauer's concept of will as a blind driving force is similar to the Freudian id. In addition, Schopenhauer wrote of repression of unwanted thoughts into the unconscious and of the resistance that occurs with any attempt to retrieve the repressed thoughts. Freud credited Schopenhauer with being the first to discover these unconscious processes, although Freud contended that he had discovered them independently.

Wundt, scientific psychology's founder, also shows Schopenhauer's influence in his psychology of consciousness. Like Kant and Schopenhauer, Wundt stressed the mind's ability to organize its elements. Schopenhauer's philosophy clearly influenced many existential philosophers, especially Nietzsche (Chapter 15), and he is often seen as a transitional figure between romanticism and existentialism.

CONCLUSIONS

Three points that define rationalism's legacy for psychology stand out: First, and most generally, we have the "rationalism versus empiricism" debate. Unlike the empiricists, who often conceived of mind as a passive receptacle of environmental sensations, the rationalists tended to view mind as an active, structuring agent and grounded "reality" in it, not in the world. Both an "active" mind and the study of mental representations are the hallmarks of many subsequent psychological theories.

Second, we have the nativist-nurturist conflict introduced in the first chapter. Rationalism is usually a philosophy supportive of nativist positions, and psychology and psychological theories have never entirely escaped this debate. As early as Lotze, it was clear that most psychological phenomena have both nativist (innate mental or biological structures) and nurturist (learning) components. Intelligence (Chapter 18) provides perhaps the best example of this conflict in modern psychology.

Third, we have the contrast between faculty psychology and associationism. Here, we find Kant aligned with the Scottish School on the side that saw various components of mind (e.g., language, memory, reasoning) as more or less discrete entities in opposition to the idea that one general principle—the association of ideas—characterizes the nature of mind. William James's *Principles of Psychology* is, to some extent, organized around this contrast, as are many contemporary theories in psychology.

Another important rationalist covered in this chapter was Hegel, whose evolutionary approach to phenomena (dialectical movement) sowed the seeds for many ideas in biology, psychology, and economics. In addition to Hegel, several others come close to earning the label of the first "true" psychologist, such as Herbart and Lotze.

Psychology as a science owes an enormous debt to positivism, which traces its roots to Auguste Comte. Positivism matured into an important philosophy of science under Mach and Avenarius and came to stand as the gatekeeper of all the sciences from physics to psychology by the time of the Vienna Circle. By establishing the ground rules for what constituted proper science during an era in which science rose from hobby to religion, the gatekeeping function that positivism served cannot be overestimated. In psychology, behaviorism under Watson, Skinner (Chapter 13), and Hull (Chapter 13) allied itself with positivistic conceptions of science in order to flourish.

Finally, with a focus on humans themselves, romanticism as seen in the philosophies of Herder, Rousseau, and Goethe represented a reaction to the materialism and mechanism of the age. We will see its influence again in the more person-centered approaches to psychology, such as phenomenology and humanistic psychoanalysis (Chapter 16).

Last but not least, it can be argued that rationalism itself evolves directly into modern cognitive psychology through the transitional phase of Gestalt psychology. As we will see in Chapter 14, the Gestaltists were able to create a productive synthesis between rational philosophy and the growing body of psychologically relevant physiological phenomena to which we turn next.

S U M M A R Y

The chapter's theme was the Continental reaction to and contrast with British empiricism and associationism.

Rationalism

Reading Hume stimulated Immanuel Kant to write *Critique of Pure Reason.* Reacting against Hume, Kant made causality part of the mind's inherent structure, along with such things as space and time forms, totality, and existence and nonexistence. After the mind coordinates sensations into perceptions, the perceptions are changed into knowledge by Kant's innate categories of thought. Our experience of the outside world (noumenal world) is filtered through the structure of our minds to give us the phenomenal world. Kant's work particularly influenced Gestalt psychology and the German physiologists Müller and Helmholtz.

Georg Wilhelm Friedrich Hegel accepted Kant's categories of thought and gave them objective status in the Absolute (God). In Hegel's philosophy, everything evolves toward the Absolute through dialectical movement in which a thesis leads to its opposite (antithesis), which begets an emerging whole (synthesis).

Johann Friedrich Herbart studied under a Kantian disciple and visited the educational reformer Johann Heinrich Pestalozzi. Herbart's application of psychology to education earns him the title of the founder of educational psychology. By writing the first textbook on psychology, Herbart becomes a candidate for the honor of being the founder of psychology as a science. However, like Kant, Herbart saw psychology as a nonexperimental science. Herbart's conception of the threshold of consciousness and the repression of incompatible ideas influenced Fechner and Freud, respectively.

Trained as a physician, Rudolf Hermann Lotze eventually filled Herbart's chair in philosophy at Göttingen. Lotze indirectly influenced psychology through his students and friends, including Ernst Weber and Gustav Fechner, G.E. Müller, Carl Stumpf, and Franz Brentano.

His major direct contribution came through his theory of space perception in the empirical tradition.

Positivism

Positivism is a philosophical system based only on empirical observation, on observable scientific facts and their interrelations, which was originated by Auguste Comte. For Comte, the development of each field of thought moved through three stages: the theological stage, the metaphysical stage, and the positivistic or scientific stage. Comte did not think a science of the mind using introspection was possible.

The physicist Ernst Mach worked on visual space perception and audition, and his *Analysis of Sensations* established Machian positivism, whose central idea is that sensations are the basic data of all science. Independently, Richard Avenarius expressed similar ideas. Later, Rudolf Carnap and Moritz Schlick developed logical positivism, a movement that rejected most traditional metaphysics and aided the rise of behaviorism in psychology.

Romanticism

In philosophy, romanticism was a reaction against both empiricism and rationalism and emphasized the whole person, particularly the person's feelings. An early romanticist, Johann Gottfried Herder was fascinated by unsophisticated human nature and stressed the importance of the historical method for understanding people. Herder influenced Wundt, whose *Völkerpsychologie* included the study of language, myths, and social customs through historical records.

Jean-Jacques Rousseau discussed the social contract between people and their legitimate government in *The Social Contract,* which became the bible of the French Revolution. Rousseau's *Émile* influenced the leading educationists and Kant, who saw in Rousseau's appeal to feelings the answer to the era's irreligion.

Johann Wolfgang von Goethe was a writer, critic, and scientist whose belief in the study of intact, meaningful phenomena led to phenomenology, which was an important antecedent of Gestalt psychology. Goethe's color vision observations stimulated the work of Jan Purkinje, of Purkinje shift fame.

In *The World as Will and Representation*, Arthur Schopenhauer presented his philosophy. For Schopen-

hauer, the world is idea and the world is will. The "will to live" is the driving impulse of nature, whose purpose is to enable us to live long enough to reproduce. Escape from the will's dictates can come through asceticism or aesthetics. Schopenhauer's pessimistic philosophy influenced Freud, Wundt, and the existential philosophers.

CONNECTIONS QUESTIONS

1. How does rationalism connect with, and contrast with, empiricism?
2. Of the individuals we have encountered so far, which seem most important for the rise of psychology as an independent discipline?
3. How is positivism connected to psychology?
4. What is the nativist-empiricist debate, and why has it been so important for psychology?

5. In what ways was romanticism a part of psychology's beginning?
6. Draw a concept map showing the relationships among Continental rationalism, positivism, and romanticism, and compare your results with one possible solution provided on p. 563.

SUGGESTED READINGS

Archer, R. L. (Ed.) (1964). *Jean Jacques Rousseau: His educational theories selected from Émile, Julie and other writings.* Woodbury, NY: Barron's Educational Series, Inc. This is an excellent introduction to Rousseau's educational theories.

Comte, A. (1954). The positive philosophy. In S. Commins & R. N. Linscott (Eds.), *Man & the universe: The philosophers of science* (pp. 223–241). New York: Pocket Books, Inc. In addition to the reading from Comte, this little paperback contains readings from Copernicus, Francis Bacon, Descartes, Darwin, Freud, and Albert Einstein, as well as others. Most anthologies on the philosophy of science will include a selection from Comte.

Durant, W. (1961). *The story of philosophy.* New York: Washington Square Press. Durant's chapters on Kant and Schopenhauer are entertaining and informative. The chapter on Schopenhauer is full of quotes from the philosopher, and Kant's chapter contains much *about* Kant but little *by* Kant. The reason for this, Durant noted, is that "Kant is the last person in the world whom we should read on Kant" (p. 253). The chapter on Kant ends with "A Note on Hegel."

Goethe, J.W.v. (1967) *Faust: A tragedy.* New York: Modern Library. (Original work published 1808, 1832) Perhaps Goethe's best known work, it demonstrates not only the author's writing talents but his interest in such diverse topics as science and the occult. It is widely available in many formats and editions.

Kant, I. (1929). *Critique of pure reason* (N. K. Smith, Trans.). New York: St. Martin's Press. (Original work published 1787) Kant is an important thinker for both ethics and the philosophy of mind and perhaps the premier philosopher in this chapter. If you are interested in rationalism, it will be well worth your effort to read at least some of Kant's *Critique.*

Schopenhauer, A. (1969). *The world as will and representation* (E. F. J. Payne, Trans.). New York: Dover Publications, Inc. (Original work published 1844) Schopenhauer is more readable than Hegel and Kant, and this two-volume work is a good place to begin any investigation of his philosophy.

Nineteenth-Century Physiological Influences on the Development of Psychology

Johann Caspar Spurzheim

Robert Whytt

Sir Charles Bell

Alessandro Volta

François Magendie

Franz Joseph Gall

Luigi Galvani

1700	1720	1740	1760	1780	1800

Frederick the Great is born

Erasmus Darwin is born

David Hume flourishes

Josiah Wedgwood founds pottery works

Immanuel Kant flourishes

America wins independence

Goethe and Napoleon meet

Realistically, all the early physiologists and philosophers could do was speculate about the nature and locus of "mind," because the technology necessary to achieve valid insights into the operations of the nervous system were often centuries in the future. Within their limitations, some of the ancients guessed correctly, but others had ideas that were amusing and, from our late 20th-century perspective, nonsensical. Before we congratulate ourselves too quickly, we should bear in mind that our current theories may seem as outmoded to neuroscientists 100 years from now as many of the early theories of nervous system structure and function seem to us today. However, neuroscience has made great strides in the last 2 centuries, and in this chapter we will examine the people and the ideas that laid the foundation for our current knowledge.

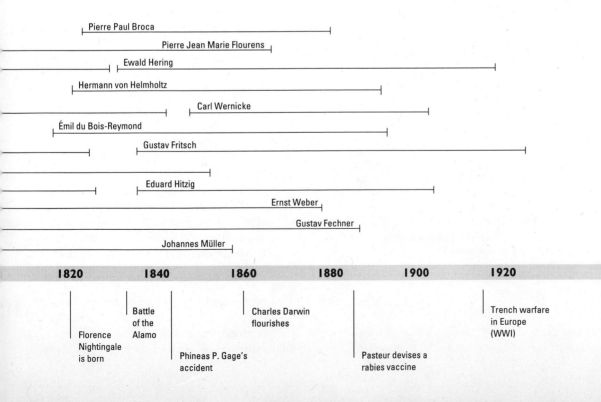

One theme stands out in the early study of the physiological basis of mind: the demystification of the nervous system. This can be seen in the finally accepted conclusion that the brain is the organ of mind, emphasized by the phrenologists, supported by the animal research of Flourens, and dramatically demonstrated by the personality changes in accident-victim P. P. Gage. This demystification will be revealed further with the recognition of the electrical nature of many nervous system activities and in the experimental recording by Helmholtz of the speed of the nerve impulse. Helmholtz's demonstrations of the susceptibility of the nervous system to investigation were amplified by the 19th-century development of the major investigative techniques of ablation and electrical stimulation. This 19th-century development of major methods to study the mind-body connection also includes Fechner's refinement of psychophysics. As a final example of the demystification, we will examine the controversy over the localization or the nonlocalization of function in the nervous system, which eventually produced definitive evidence that some functions are localized in particular nervous system areas.

REVIEW OF EARLY SPECULATION

As certain as we are today that behavior is ultimately a function of brain activity, we have difficulty comprehending that in the past there was considerably less certainty about the primacy of this organ. For example, Aristotle (Chapter 2) taught that the brain functioned to cool the blood and that the mind was in the heart, even though 50 years earlier Hippocrates had said:

> Men ought to know that from the brain and from the brain only, arise our pleasures, joys, laughter and jests, as well as our sorrows, pains, griefs and tears. Through it, in particular, we think, see, hear, and distinguish the ugly from the beautiful, the bad from the good, the pleasant from the unpleasant. (Jones, 1923, p. 129)

Herophilus (ca. 335–280 B.C.), an anatomist and founder of the anatomy school at Alexandria (mentioned in Chapter 2), may have been the first to dissect the human body in order to compare it with the anatomy of other animals. Although Herophilus believed that the brain was the main organ of the nervous system and the seat of intelligence, he thought the mind was located in the brain's cavities or ventricles. In addition, Herophilus distinguished between sensory and motor nerves.

Galen also thought that the brain was the organ of the mind and was strongly opposed to Aristotle's placing it in the heart. Galen wrote extensively about the brain's ventricles, believing they were the reservoir for the animal spirits, which many ancient Greeks felt distinguished the living from the nonliving.

As we noted in Chapter 2, Galen's views and those of Aristotle were important because they were accepted and systematized by the early Christian Church, becoming dogma that was propounded and defended until the Renaissance. According to the model of mind the Church developed, nutrients were absorbed from the intestines and passed to the liver, which converted them into a fluid called *natural spirit*. Natural spirit journeyed from the liver to the heart where it was changed to *vital spirit*. Finally, vital spirit traveled to a network of blood vessels at the base of the brain, where it was converted to *animal spirit* and stored in the ventricles.

The Church's model of mind focused on the fluid-filled ventricles. Although anatomically inaccurate, the ventricles were seen as three chambers, one behind the other, and in 1490 Leonardo da Vinci (1452–1519) drew anatomical studies of the head incorporating the ventricular scheme (Figure 6–1). Note how the optic nerves converge on the first chamber in both the side view and the view from above. As you might guess, sensory analysis was believed to occur in the first ventricle. Images formed there were passed to the middle ventricle, which was considered to be the seat of reason, thought, and judgment. The last ventricle held memory.

Between 1504 and 1507, da Vinci dissected the brain of an ox. Instead of finding the nerves from the sense organs all ending in the first ventricle pair, da Vinci found that many terminated around the middle ventricle, in the brain area we call the

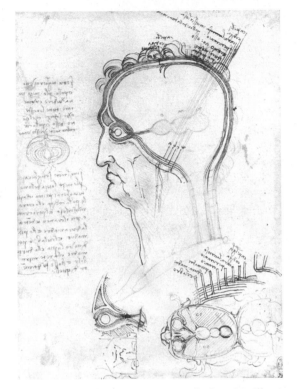

FIGURE 6–1. Leonardo da Vinci's drawing illustrating the Church's ventricular scheme.

Source: The Royal Collection © Her Majesty Queen Elizabeth II.

thalamus. As a result, he decided that sensory analysis took place in the middle ventricle. Although it was still incorrect, da Vinci's conclusion cast doubt on the model the Church had so vigorously defended.

René Descartes (Chapter 3) broke completely with the prevailing model, conceptualizing the nervous system as a hydraulic affair, with hollow tubes (nerves) leading to empty bladders (muscles). Descartes believed that the nerves contained threads connecting the sensory receptors to the brain. Stimulation of a sense organ tightened the threads, which caused a "pore" to open in the brain, releasing animal spirits that flowed back to the appropriate muscle. Expanding from the animal spirits, the muscle caused movement. Descartes's model resembles the workings of the lifelike statues in the gardens of St. Germain (Chapter 3).

Probably the best thing about Descartes's hydraulic model was that it was easy to test. Early experiments by Jan Swammerdam (1637–1680) and Francis Glisson (ca. 1597–1677) did not support Descartes's nervous system model. Later, Luigi Galvani (discussed later) found that frog muscles could still contract after separation from the frog's body. Obviously, this is impossible if animal spirits from the brain produce muscle contraction.

Meanwhile, other investigators such as **Robert Whytt** (1714–1766) and George Prochaska (1749–1820) were overhauling Descartes's understanding of reflex action. Whytt studied frog spinal reflexes, demonstrating that automatic movements were possible with stimulation of only a small portion of the spinal cord. He emphasized the difference between voluntary movements that depend on an act of will and involuntary movements that occur too rapidly to involve reason. However, even though Whytt believed that reflex movements were involuntary and depended on the spinal cord, he thought the nervous tissue contained a sentient (conscious) principle. Thus, reflexes were not quite unconscious for Whytt. In 1751, Whytt described the reflexive contraction of the pupil to light, which is sometimes called **Whytt's Reflex**.

Scottish physician and physiologist **Marshall Hall** (1790–1857) performed experiments to clarify knowledge of reflex action in the first half of the 19th century. Hall distinguished voluntary movement (which depends on consciousness and higher brain centers), respiratory movement (which is involuntary and depends on lower brain areas), involuntary movement (which depends on muscular irritability when muscle is directly stimulated), and reflex movement. For Hall, reflex movement depended only on the spinal cord; that is, it was independent of consciousness and the brain. Hall's conception of the reflex paved the way for modern conceptions of the reflex arc (e.g., John Dewey, Chapter 11; Ivan Pavlov, Chapter 12).

By the end of the 18th century, the hydraulic model was completely overturned, and the ancient concept of animal spirits was replaced with something that seemed equally farfetched—electricity.

ELECTRICITY AND NERVE FUNCTION

In 1600, English physicist and physician William Gilbert (1540–1603) published *De Magnete,* a pioneering work on electricity that introduced the terms *electric force, electric attraction,* and *magnetic pole.* Interest in this mysterious force grew rapidly, and the 18th century has been called the "Age of Electricity." Scientists soon speculated that electricity might be the force responsible for nerve function, but testing this speculation was a problem. Early investigators could neither reliably generate electricity nor measure it, but matters began to improve toward the end of the 18th century.

An Italian lecturer in anatomy and professor of obstetrics at the University of Bologna, **Luigi Galvani** (1737–1798) began experiments on electricity in about 1780. The results of his experiments were published in 1791, when they appeared in *De viribus electricitatis in motu muscularis commentarius* (*A Commentary on the Role of Electricity in Muscular Contractions*).

Galvani found that a frog's leg twitched when one of its nerves received an electrical charge, and he also found that twitching occurred when the leg muscles hung between two different metals. For example, iron and silver produced a vigorous reaction, and the leg would continue to twitch as long as it was suspended. Galvani had made an organic battery, because an electrical current is produced when a salt solution connects two dissimilar metals, and the frog's leg and motor nerve are essentially salt solutions.

Although Galvani's conclusion that his frogs had generated electricity was soon challenged, his belief that nervous energy has an electrical component was important. The **galvanic skin response** (GSR, a change in the skin's electrical conductivity) is named after him.

Italian physicist **Count Alessandro Volta** (1745–1827) concluded that Galvani's frogs had merely conducted electricity, which was actually generated by the two metals and the attached frog leg. In 1800, Volta made the first battery that did not include animal tissue. The Voltaic pile consisted of alternating layers of disks of silver, brine-moistened cardboard, and zinc. By his construction of an inorganic battery, Volta believed he had disproved the notion that animals generated electricity, but other eminent scientists of the period did not abandon the idea (e.g., Johannes Müller, discussed later).

Volta's construction of a reliable way to produce a "galvanic current" led physicists to make an instrument—called, appropriately enough, a galvanometer—to measure the current. As Galvani would have expected, an electrical current was observed when a galvanometer was applied to nervous tissue. This observation so captivated German-born Swiss physician **Émil du Bois-Reymond** (1818–1896) that he devoted his life to electrophysiology, the field that he created.

While studying the electrical nature of nervous tissue, du Bois-Reymond formulated the idea that nervous and muscle tissue are charged with positive and negative particles. He demonstrated that when nerves are electrically stimulated, the charged particles reverse their positions. We call this reversal the **action potential**, and it is considered to be the nervous system's basic means of long-distance communication.

In keeping with this chapter's central theme, note that du Bois-Reymond's work demystified the nerve impulse, bringing it from the realm of animal spirits into the real world of science. This suggested to Hermann von Helmholtz that the speed of a nerve impulse might actually be measurable.

Hermann Ludwig von Helmholtz

Although Helmholtz is considered one of the greatest scientists of the 19th century, this may be doing him a disservice. In fact, it is no exaggeration to say that Helmholtz was one of the greatest scientists of all time. Shortly after Helmholtz's death, Carl Stumpf (Chapter 8) wrote: "Since the death of Darwin, the loss of no one in the scientific world has made such a deep impression as that of Helmholtz. . . . Whenever he smote the rock of nature, there gushed forth the living waters of knowledge" (1895, p. 1). Following his interests, Helmholtz made outstanding contributions in physics (he mathematically formulated the law of conservation of energy when he was only 26), neural physiology (he measured the speed of the nerve impulse), optics (he invented the ophthalmoscope and was cofounder of a theory of color vision considered viable today), and acoustics (he proposed a "place" theory of pitch perception). Although Helmholtz was primarily a physicist, some have considered him a physiological psychologist as well (e.g., Stumpf, 1895).

Hermann Ludwig Ferdinand von Helmholtz (1821–1894) was born in Potsdam, Germany, which is near Berlin. His father was a teacher of philology (the study of language and culture) and philosophy at a Potsdam *Gymnasium.* Helmholtz's mother was Caroline Penne, a descendant of William Penn, the English Quaker reformer who founded Pennsylvania.

A weak child, Helmholtz was first tutored at home by his father. Although he did not do well in his studies, "his apparent mediocrity seems to have been due to his independence of thought rather than to any lack of ability" (Boring, 1950, p. 298). In fact, Helmholtz worked out many geometrical principles by playing with a set of wooden blocks. By the time he graduated from the *Gymnasium,* Helmholtz had decided to become a physicist.

Financially unable to pursue his interest in physics, Helmholtz entered a Berlin medical institute that charged no tuition to young men who promised to serve as Prussian Army surgeons. Although he was not a student at the University of Berlin, he was greatly influenced by a physiology professor there—Johannes Müller—and several of Müller's students, particularly du Bois-Reymond.

After graduating from the medical institute in 1842, Helmholtz began work in Potsdam as an army surgeon. However, he continued his studies in mathematics and physics, and in 1847 he read his famous paper on the conservation of energy to the *Physikalische Gesellschaft* (Physical Society) in Berlin. Conservation of energy was important for psychology because it raised further doubts about the possibility of an immaterial mind affecting a material body. Accepting the principle leads to the conclusion that all physical changes have physical causes, which in turn suggests a materialistic, deter-

ministic psychology. Helmholtz's mathematical formulation made it clear to his fellow scientists that he belonged in academia, not in the military.

In 1849, Helmholtz went to the University of Königsberg as professor of physiology and general pathology. In his 7 years at Königsberg, Helmholtz measured the speed of the nerve impulse, invented the ophthalmoscope, and revised an earlier theory of color vision. The ophthalmoscope permitted direct examination of the retina, which is actually part of the central nervous system. In fact, the retina is the only central nervous system structure that can be examined noninvasively without elaborate and expensive equipment.

From Königsberg, Helmholtz went to Bonn for 2 years as professor of physiology. Next, Helmholtz became professor of physiology at Heidelberg, where he stayed until 1871. Finally, Helmholtz was called to be professor of physics at the University of Berlin, the peak of German academia.

Helmholtz traveled to America in 1893 to see the Chicago World's Fair. On the return voyage, he fell down a stairway and never fully recovered. Helmholtz (Figure 6–2) died in 1894.

Measuring the Speed of the Nerve Impulse

In his *Handbook of Human Physiology,* Müller (discussed later) listed three different estimates for the speed of the nerve impulse, which ranged from 9,000 feet per minute (at 150 feet per second, this was reasonable) to 57,600 million feet per second, which is nearly 60 times the speed of light! Although Müller disagreed with the fastest estimate, he thought that the speed was extremely rapid, perhaps approaching the speed of light, and would never be measured.

Helmholtz soon proved Müller wrong. Using the frog motor nerve and attached leg muscle preparation, Helmholtz stimulated the nerve and recorded the resulting muscle contraction on a drum rotating at a constant speed. Because he knew the time of stimulation, the distance the impulse traveled (i.e., the length of the motor nerve), and the time of muscle contraction, it was a simple matter to compute the speed of the impulse, which Helmholtz found to be about 90 feet per second.

FIGURE 6–2.   Helmholtz at about the time he first measured the speed of the nerve impulse.

Source: From Boakes, From Darwin to Behaviourism *(1984); by courtesy Harvard College Library.*

Helmholtz next measured the speed of transmission in sensory nerves by stimulating a man on either the toe or the thigh and requiring the man to respond by pushing a button. Helmholtz found that the man's reaction time was longer with the greater distance traveled. By subtracting the shorter reaction time from the longer, Helmholtz arrived at transmission speeds for impulses along sensory nerves ranging from approximately 50–100 meters per second (165–330 feet per second).

Although du Bois-Reymond later measured the speeds more precisely, the importance of the discovery that nervous transmission was not nearly instantaneous was incalculable. As Boring (1950) put it, "The most important effect of the experiment and all the research that followed upon it was. . . that it brought the soul to time, . . . [it]

actually captured the essential agent of mind in the toils of natural science" (p. 42).

Other Contributions of Helmholtz

Young-Helmholtz Theory. In 1798, John Dalton (1766–1844), the famed English chemist who developed atomic theory, wrote on color deficiencies shared by him and his brother. Dalton's work was followed in 1802 by English physician and physicist **Thomas Young**'s (1773–1829) proposal that color sensations come from some pattern of stimulation of three different receptor types in the eye. Fifty years later, Helmholtz rediscovered Young's relatively ignored theory, modified it slightly, and it became known as the **Young-Helmholtz theory**, or as **trichromatic theory** (trichromatic means three colors).

Helmholtz stated that there are three different sets of fibers in the eye, the stimulation of each producing a different color sensation (i.e., red, green, and violet). A color other than one of the primaries stimulates some combination of the three fibers, resulting in a perceived color other than one of the primaries. For example, looking at a ripe banana would activate some combination of red and green fibers, resulting in the perception of yellow. (If you think that the combination of red and green results in brown, you are thinking of mixing pigments, which produces a subtractive color mixture. The eye's receptors perform an additive color mixture, which you obtain by combining colored lights.)

Critics of the Young-Helmholtz theory pointed out that the most common form of color defect is the inability to differentiate red and green. According to trichromatic theory, yellow results from stimulation of red fibers and green fibers, which are assumed to be defective in red-green "blindness." Thus, the theory would predict incorrectly that a person with a red-green defect should also have trouble seeing yellow. Such incorrect predictions led to other theories of color vision, the most successful of which was proposed by Helmholtz-contemporary Ewald Hering (discussed later).

Place Theory of Pitch Perception. In studying the auditory system, Helmholtz was primarily concerned with accounting for the ability to discriminate between different pitched sounds. Helmholtz sought the mechanism we use to tell the difference between a high-pitched sound (e.g., a fingernail pulled across a blackboard) and a low-pitched sound (e.g., a foghorn).

The inner ear's cochlea contains a structure called the basilar membrane. Normally coiled, uncoiled the basilar membrane looks like a harp—narrow at one end and wide at the other. Helmholtz assumed that the membrane was important for pitch perception and that fibers at the narrow end resonate to high-pitched sounds, whereas fibers at the wide end resonate to low-pitched sounds. Thus, Helmholtz's theory was an early version of place theory, which holds that the place of basilar stimulation determines a sound's pitch. In Chapter 17, we will describe Georg von Békésy's research leading to a modern **place theory of pitch perception**.

Ewald Hering and Opponent-Process Theory

As a student of medicine at the University of Leipzig, **Ewald Hering** (1834–1918) was instructed by both Weber and Fechner (discussed later). Although Hering did not study with Johannes Müller, he was greatly influenced by Müller's work. Hering earned his M.D. but practiced for only 2 years before settling on physiology as a career. In 1870, Hering succeeded Jan Purkinje (Chapter 5) at Prague. In 1895, Hering accepted a professorship at Leipzig, where he became a colleague of Wundt (Chapter 7).

Hering proposed **opponent-process theory** in 1874. For Hering, there were four primaries, with the fourth being yellow. In his theory, three receptor complexes each respond in one of two opposing ways. The three complexes signal either red or green, yellow or blue, or black or white. An example of a red-green system would be a retinal unit whose activity increased in the presence of red and decreased in the presence of green. Similarly, a yellow-blue complex might increase its activity when stimulated by blue and decrease its activity to yellow. The black-white process is intended to account for brightness perception.

Hering's opponent-process idea better accounts for color defect phenomena than does trichromatic theory. With Hering's theory, a person with a red-green weakness should have no trouble with blue and yellow. Also, color weaknesses tend to come in pairs—there are red-green weaknesses and blue-yellow weaknesses—and this too is a feature of opponent-process theory.

Hering's theory also readily explains the **negative afterimage**, which is the perception of the complementary or opposite color after prolonged stimulation with a particular hue. For example, if you stare at a picture of a red dog for 2 minutes and then look at a white space, you will see a green dog in the space. According to opponent-process theory, fatiguing the red response in a complex by staring at a red image causes the green system to account for more activity of the complex when you look at the white space. Hence, you see a green dog.

Helmholtz-Hering Debate

In addition to opposing Helmholtz's view of color vision, Hering was critical of Helmholtz's theory of visual space perception. Taking the nativist approach, Hering thought that each retinal point has from the beginning three local signs: one for height, one for lateral position, and one for depth. As an empiricist, Helmholtz believed that space forms develop from experience and that the location of local signs is learned.

Hering's nativism was at least partly the result of Johannes Müller's influence; Müller was Kantian (Chapter 5) in his treatment of space as one of the innate intuitions. Hering, in turn, influenced Carl Stumpf, and through him, the Gestaltists (Chapter 14). On the other side of the debate, Helmholtz was following the lead of Lotze (Chapter 5) and the British empiricists (Chapter 4), and in this he influenced Wundt—briefly his assistant—and Wundt influenced Titchener (Chapter 7) and Külpe (Chapter 8). We mention these connections because the **Helmholtz-Hering debate** became representative of the larger empiricist-nativist debate about the nature of perception, which remains with us today.

LOCALIZATION OF FUNCTION

In addition to the interest in the electrical nature of nervous activity, another thread running through 19th-century neuroscience was interest in localization of function. **Localizationists** believe that specific functions reside in specific nervous system areas, whereas **nonlocalizationists** have been more impressed with the way the nervous system works as a coordinated unit. The central question is, Are neural functions tied to one specific nervous system location?

The Bell-Magendie Law

A distinction between sensory nerves and motor nerves had been made by some (e.g., Herophilus, Galen) over the centuries, but by the beginning of the 19th century the distinction was not usually made. The spinal and cranial nerves were all assumed to have both sensory and motor functions, a nonlocalizationist position. Sir Charles Bell in England and François Magendie in France independently performed research that led to the distinction between sensory nerves and motor nerves known as the **Bell-Magendie law**. The law states that the dorsal roots of spinal nerves bring in sensory information, and the ventral roots of the spinal nerves carry motor fibers to the muscles (dorsal means "pertaining to the back of an organism," referring to the top of the spinal cord in a vertebrate; ventral refers to the lower surface of an animal).

Born in Edinburgh, Scotland, **Sir Charles Bell** (1774–1842) was a brilliant neurologist, surgeon, and physiologist whose fame eventually extended to the Continent. One story tells of a French physiologist who, on the occasion of a visit from Bell, dismissed his class without a lecture, saying to the students, *"C'est assez, messieurs, vous avez vu Charles Bell!"* ("That's enough, gentlemen, you have seen Charles Bell!")

In 1811, Bell gave 100 copies of a privately published pamphlet to his friends. In it, he told of experiments with rabbits in which cutting the dorsal root of spinal nerves resulted in no movement, whereas touching the ventral root with his knife produced violent muscle contractions. Bell correctly

FIGURE 6–3.   Sir Charles Bell.

Source: National Library of Medicine.

surmised that the dorsal root was sensory and the ventral root was motor. Extending his research to cranial nerves (nerves entering the brain directly), Bell later demonstrated that some are entirely sensory, some entirely motor, and some are mixed.

In 1822, French physiologist **François Magendie** (1783–1855) published experiments on the spinal nerves of puppies. (Antivivisectionists—people opposed to surgical research on live animals—often cite Magendie's research as a particularly horrible example of science's cruelty to animals, because it was performed without anesthesia, like all the animal work of this period.) When Magendie cut the dorsal root, pinching the animal's affected limb produced no reaction, although the limb still moved spontaneously. Magendie concluded that the limb was anesthetized, not paralyzed, and the cut dorsal root had carried sensory information. Cutting a ventral root paralyzed the limb, indicating that the ventral root was motor.

FIGURE 6–4. François Magendie.
Source: National Library of Medicine.

Magendie's publication stimulated a battle over priority. Although Magendie's research was more thorough and convincing than Bell's, the fact that most historians call the discovery the Bell-Magendie law suggests that Bell and his supporters were victorious. Bell and Magendie are shown in Figures 6–3 and 6–4, respectively.

Magendie was also the teacher of **Claude Bernard** (1813–1878), whom some consider the "father" of experimental physiology (and psychology) in France. Bernard disliked philosophy, and his efforts in establishing experimentation in France greatly influenced William James's (Chapter 10) conception of psychology (Taylor, 1990).

The Bell-Magendie law supports localization of function, because it says that sensory and motor functions are separated in spinal nerve roots. Bell also speculated that the separation in the roots was maintained in the spinal cord and in the brain, which might therefore contain separate sensory and motor regions.

In addition to differentiating the sensory and motor nerves, Bell anticipated Johannes Müller's later doctrine of specific nerve energies. Bell said that each of the senses is mediated by its own kind of nerve. We don't see or hear or feel or taste or smell anything directly. Instead, an object makes an impression upon a sense organ and then the sensory nerve acts as an intermediary between the object and the brain. This idea had been held by a number of Greek philosophers and had been familiar doctrine since Galen.

The Doctrine of Specific Nerve Energies

Born in Koblenz, Germany, **Johannes Müller** (1801–1858) became professor of physiology at the University of Berlin in 1833. He is best known for his *Handbuch der Physiologie des Menschen* (*Handbook of Human Physiology*), which appeared from 1833 to 1840. The *Handbuch* summarized the physiology of the day and included many original observations and speculations. In the *Handbuch,* Müller formulated the **doctrine of specific nerve energies**, whose central principle is that we are directly aware only of the activity in our nerves, not of the external world itself. The nerves impose their own specific qualities on the mind (e.g., stimulation of the optic nerve always leads to a visual experience). Müller also considered and rejected the possibility that the specific sensory quality was imparted by the area of the brain to which the nerve travels.

You can demonstrate Müller's doctrine to yourself. According to the doctrine, no matter how a particular sensory nerve is stimulated, the sensation will be appropriate to the stimulated nerve. For example, visual sensations result from stimulation of the optic nerve, even if the nerve is stimulated mechanically, electrically, or in some other way. Close your eyes and *gently* press the right side of your right eye. The resulting visual sensation in your left visual field is a pressure phosphene, and it shows that mechanical stimulation of the optic nerve produces a visual sensation.

Note that Müller's doctrine is consistent with one of the primary elements of German rationalism, which is that the mind (brain, in this context) is an active agent that structures, organizes, and interprets sensory information. Although you touched the side of your eye, your brain interpreted the sensation as visual, demonstrating that you are not just a passive receiver of information as it appears in the world.

Another corollary of the doctrine is that the same stimulus applied to different sensory nerves results in different sensations, with each nerve giving the sensation appropriate to itself. For example, a tactile stimulus on your arm results in the sensation of touch, whereas the same stimulus applied to your optic nerve gives a visual sensation.

Müller's doctrine of specific nerve energies also supports the concept of localization of function, because as we have indicated, visual sensations result from optic nerve stimulation alone, auditory sensations result only from stimulation of the auditory nerve, and so on. For Müller, the doctrine of specific nerve energies differentiated the various sensory modalities. Influenced by Müller, Helmholtz went one step further and applied the doctrine *within* a sense modality, arriving at what Boring (1950) called a doctrine of specific fiber energies.

As you will recall, the Young-Helmholtz theory of color vision theorized that there were three different sets of fibers in the eye, each set giving rise to a different color sensation. Thus, not only does stimulation of the optic nerve produce visual sensations, stimulation of particular fibers within the optic nerve should lead to specific color sensations. Because Young had the idea of different color qualities before Helmholtz, Young in a sense anticipated both Bell and Müller on the doctrine of specific nerve energies.

Bell, Magendie, Müller, and Helmholtz all supported the idea that nervous functions were localized, with the sensory theories of Helmholtz arguing for many specific nerve qualities. For a while, localization of function in the nervous system received even greater support from the writings and lectures of Franz Joseph Gall and an associate, Johann Caspar Spurzheim.

Phrenology

Franz Joseph Gall (1758–1828) was born in Tiefenbrunn in Baden, a region in southwestern

FIGURE 6–5.   Franz Joseph Gall.
Source: National Library of Medicine.

Germany. As a physician and anatomist, Gall made some excellent contributions to 19th-century science. For example, Gall examined the brains of many different animal species and of humans of different ages and mental status and concluded that the higher mental functions are associated with the size and integrity of the brain and particularly with its outer covering, or cortex. In fact, "Gall was the first to claim that mental activities were localized in the cortex alone; the white matter he relegated to the role of a system of conduction and projection" (Neuburger, 1897/1981, p. 268). Unfortunately, despite his scientific contributions, Gall (Figure 6–5) is most remembered for founding the pseudo-science that became known as **phrenology** (the "science of the mind").

As a youth, Gall was often irritated by the superior performance of some of his schoolmates whom Gall considered to be less intelligent than he. What they lacked in intelligence, his schoolmates compensated for by being better "memorizers." These better memorizers all seemed to have one common physical feature: large and protuberant eyes. Perhaps their eyes protruded because the area of the brain behind the eyes was enlarged. Because these boys all had excellent memories, Gall reasoned that verbal memory resides in the part of the frontal lobes behind the eyes. And if one function or faculty of the mind can be localized to a particular brain area, perhaps others can be similarly localized.

In his "research," Gall made three questionable assumptions. First, he assumed that the skull's outer contours correspond to the contours of the underlying brain. Gall believed that the form of the brain is determined early in life, and the skull conforms to the brain's shape. Further, he thought that enlargements in a particular brain area are reflected in a bump on the skull, whereas a smaller than normal brain area might cause an indentation. Gall's second assumption was that the mind can be analyzed or divided into a limited number of faculties or functions. This assumption was neither novel nor necessarily wrong, and Gall selected his faculties from the lists of the Scottish philosophers Thomas Reid and Dugald Stewart (both Chapter 4). Gall's third assumption, which is at least partly correct, was that the mind's functions are located in different places in the brain.

Armed with these assumptions, Gall specifically studied the heads of people with special qualities. To locate people with unusual characteristics, Gall traveled to foundling homes, prisons, and mental asylums and gradually accumulated a catalog of "relations" between mental abilities and bumps on the skull. For example, Gall observed a number of people with strong sexual drives and concluded that they all had well-developed necks and unusually thick skull bases. Because the cerebellum is at the base of the brain, Gall concluded that the faculty of "amativeness" (love, particularly sexual love) resides there.

Gall eventually settled on 27 highly specific faculties, including such abilities as acquisitiveness, benevolence, mirthfulness, and secretiveness, in addition to amativeness. Later phrenologists added more faculties to Gall's list, and the arbitrary choice of faculties was one of phrenology's great defects. Ironically, there is little more agreement today on

the basic dimensions of personality than there was in Gall's time (see Chapter 16).

Another methodological defect was the way Gall tested his hypotheses. Observations that did not fit the system—for example, a generous person with a bulge in the acquisitiveness area—were explained away rather than being allowed to cast doubt on the system's validity. With 27 or more potentially interacting faculties, Gall could easily dismiss discrepant findings, and the generous person might have an enlarged "benevolence" area, which would obviously counteract any acquisitive tendencies.

Gall was a model of experimental propriety compared to some of his followers, however. To illustrate this, Fancher (1990) wrote:

> When a cast of Napoleon's right skull predicted qualities markedly at variance with the emperor's known personality, one phrenologist replied that his dominant side had been the left—a cast of which was conveniently missing. When Descartes's skull was examined and found deficient in the regions for reason and reflection, phrenologists retorted that the philosopher's rationality had always been overrated. (p. 79)

It is perhaps poetic justice that a story widely circulated after Gall's death held that his skull had been found to be twice as thick as average.

Gall began lecturing about what he called either craniology (the study of skulls) or physiognomy (the art of judging mental qualities by facial features) in Vienna, where his teaching soon attracted a large following. The most important of his disciples was **Johann Caspar Spurzheim** (1776–1832). The first great work on phrenology was authored by Gall, with Spurzheim's collaboration on the first two of four volumes. Appearing between 1810 and 1819, the publication was titled *Anatomie et Physiologie du Système Nerveux en Général, et du Cerveau en Particulier, avec Observations sur la Possibilité de Reconnaître Plusieurs Dispositions Intellectuelles et Morales de l'Homme et des Animaux par la Configuration de Leurs Têtes* (*The Anatomy and Physiology of the Nervous System in General, and of the Brain in Particular, with Observations on the Possibility of Discovering the*

Number of Intellectual and Moral Dispositions of Men and Animals Through the Configurations of Their Heads). Obviously, this was intended to be a serious work.

Spurzheim was phrenology's great popularizer. In fact, it was he who adopted the term "phrenology" in 1815, 2 years after he and Gall separated in Paris. Gall and Spurzheim's parting came because of their disagreements over the nature of phrenology. One of their main points of disagreement concerned the number of faculties into which the mind could be divided. Spurzheim wanted to add to Gall's list, but Gall resisted, believing that if more faculties were added, the whole process would get out of control. On his own, Spurzheim adopted a list of 37, subdivided into affective and intellectual faculties. Examples of affective qualities included destructiveness and benevolence, whereas the intellectual faculties included calculation and language. A typical phrenological chart is shown in Figure 6–6.

Gall stayed in Paris, but Spurzheim took phrenology's message all over Europe, Great Britain, and even to the United States. Phrenology was popular in America, and Orson and Lorenzo Fowler, along with their brother-in-law, Samuel Wells, established the successful firm of Fowler and Wells in New York City. Fowler and Wells also published books on phrenology, including the widely used text by Drayton and McNeill (1879). The Institute of Phrenology was still in business in New York as late as 1912 (Boring, 1950), and Jesse Fowler continued to give phrenological examinations until her death in 1932 (Risse, 1976).

Phrenologists came to serve much the same function as today's applied psychologists. After performing an examination, the phrenologist could make predictions about a child's intellectual ability, about a couple's prospects for marital happiness, or about the honesty of a prospective employee. In Chapter 1, we noted that the prefrontal lobotomy was replaced by a better treatment method, not because people realized its ineffectiveness. This was also true for phrenology, which was replaced early in the 20th century by the psychological testing movement (Chapter 18). In fact, the "firm of Fowler and Wells was the historical antecedent of The Psychology Corporation" (Bakan, 1966, p. 211).

Founded by James McKeen Cattell (Chapter 10), The Psychological Corporation publishes widely used intelligence tests and other psychological instruments.

Although widely accepted by the public, phrenology was not well received by scientists. In fact, most in the scientific community viewed phrenology as a joke, much as the scientific community today views astrology. However, phrenology did serve in a number of ways to further the study of the brain. First and foremost, phrenology established the brain as the source of the mind. By doing this, it concentrated scientific efforts on understanding neural physiology and the psychophysics of sensation.

Phrenology also reinforced the idea that functions can be localized in the brain. Although the phrenologists were essentially incorrect about their choice of faculties and where these faculties were located, still it remained for empirical studies to prove them wrong. Some of the most important of these studies were performed by Pierre Flourens, whose work is often viewed as supporting the nonlocalization position. In fact, Flourens handicapped the development of cortical localization theory by his successful attacks on Gall and phrenological localization of function (e.g., Neuburger, 1897/1981).

Pierre Flourens and the Ablation Method

Born near Montpellier in southern France, **Pierre Jean Marie Flourens** (1794–1867) graduated from Montpellier's medical school at the age of 19, having already published his first scientific article. Moving to Paris, he soon became the protégé of Georges Cuvier (1769–1832), a French anatomist known as the founder of comparative anatomy and paleontology. Flourens (Figure 6–7) was elected to the *Académie des Sciences* in 1828, and at Cuvier's dying request, he was appointed its permanent secretary.

An ardent opponent of phrenology, Flourens performed experiments to show that the functions the phrenologists had assigned to specific brain areas could not actually reside there. In his attack, Flourens used the ablation method, or, as it is some-

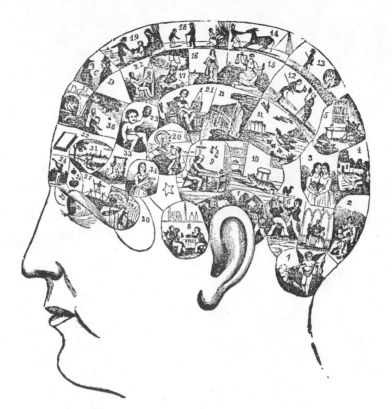

NUMBERING AND DEFINITION OF THE ORGANS.

1. AMATIVENESS, Sexual and connubial love.	21. IDEALITY, Refinement—taste—purity.
2. PHILOPROGENITIVENESS, Parental love.	B. SUBLIMITY, Love of grandeur.
3. ADHESIVENESS, Friendship—sociability.	22. IMITATION, Copying—patterning.
A. UNION FOR LIFE, Love of one only.	23. MIRTHFULNESS, Jocoseness—wit—fun.
4. INHABITIVENESS, Love of home.	24. INDIVIDUALITY, Observation.
5. CONTINUITY, One thing at a time.	25. FORM, Recollection of shape.
6. COMBATIVENESS, Resistance—defence.	26. SIZE, Measuring by the eye.
7. DESTRUCTIVENESS, Executiveness-force.	27. WEIGHT, Balancing—climbing.
8. ALIMENTIVENESS, Appetite, hunger.	28. COLOR, Judgment of colors.
9. ACQUISITIVENESS, Accumulation.	29. ORDER, Method—system—arrangement.
10. SECRETIVENESS, Policy—management.	30. CALCULATION, Mental arithmetic.
11. CAUTIOUSNESS, Prudence, provision.	31. LOCALITY. Recollection of places.
12. APPROBATIVENESS, Ambition—display.	32. EVENTUALITY, Memory of facts.
13. SELF-ESTEEM, Self-respect—dignity.	33. TIME, Cognizance of duration.
14. FIRMNESS, Decision—perseverance.	34. TUNE, MUSIC—melody by ear.
15. CONSCIENTIOUSNESS, Justice—equity	35. LANGUAGE, Expression of ideas.
16. HOPE, Expectation—enterprise.	36. CAUSALITY, Applying causes to effects
17. SPIRITUALITY, Intuition—spiritual revery.	37. COMPARISON, inductive reasoning.
18. VENERATION, Devotion—respect.	C. HUMAN NATURE, perception of motives.
19. BENEVOLENCE, Kindness—goodness.	D. AGREEABLENESS, Pleasantness—suavity
20. CONSTRUCTIVNESS. Mechanical ingenuity	

FIGURE 6–6.   A typical phrenological chart.

Source: Courtesy, The Francis A. Countway Library of Medicine, Harvard University.

times called, the extirpation method. (**Ablation** is the surgical removal of part of the body.) Although Flourens did not actually invent the technique, he refined it greatly and has been called its father (e.g., Boring, 1950). The ablation method was widely used to study the functions of the nervous system through at least the 1970s, and several important discoveries made with it will be presented in Chapter 17.

FIGURE 6–7.   Pierre Flourens.

Source: National Library of Medicine.

Flourens's method involved the complete surgical removal of one of what he considered the nervous system's six basic anatomical units: the cerebral hemispheres or cerebrum, the cerebellum, the corpora quadrigemina, the medulla oblongata, the spinal cord, and the nerves themselves. Once he had removed one of the six units, Flourens nursed the animal back to health, if possible, and carefully noted any changes in the animal's abilities. If a particular ability was permanently lost following the injury, Flourens inferred that the part of the nervous system removed normally controlled that ability.

Flourens found that removal of the **cerebral lobes**—the outer part of the brain, lying immediately beneath the skull—abolished voluntary movements and perception. A pigeon without its cortex was kept alive by force feeding, but it never moved voluntarily and appeared insensitive to visual or auditory stimulation. Flourens concluded that the cerebrum was the site of perception, intelligence, and the will.

After removing a dog's **cerebellum** (brain structure below and behind the cerebral lobes), Flourens observed that the animal still possessed all its intellectual faculties and its perceptual abilities. What was destroyed was the animal's ability to coordinate its movements. Obviously, uncoordinated movement had nothing to do with Gall's amativeness organ.

Without its **corpora quadrigemina** (an area in the center of the animal's brain), a bird was blind, even though the cerebral lobes were intact, and Flourens concluded that the structures were necessary for vision. Damage to the **medulla oblongata**—the first brain structure after the spinal cord—resulted in an animal's death. Thus, the medulla was called the "vital knot," even before Flourens's investigations.

Finally, Flourens concluded that the function of the spinal cord was conduction, whereas the function of the nerves was excitation. Although Flourens had found that each of the six units has a specific function—which he called the *action propre* or appropriate action of the part—he was more impressed by the nervous system's ability to function as a unitary system. In addition to the *action propre,* the units were subjected to an *action commune* or common action of the system working as a whole. Within each of the nervous system's major parts, Flourens thought there was no differentiation of function. For example, he believed that perception and willing were properties of the whole cerebrum—a nonlocalizationist position—not of any specific areas within it.

Flourens found evidence for this communal action in animals subjected to ablation in which there was recovery of a lost function over time. Knowing that brain tissue does not regenerate, Flourens reasoned that other brain areas must have assumed some of the ablated areas' lost functions. This phenomenon of **neural plasticity** is still investigated today (e.g., Finger, 1988).

Phineas P. Gage—A Case of Accidental Ablation

Although Flourens deliberately damaged the nervous system in animals in order to study its func-

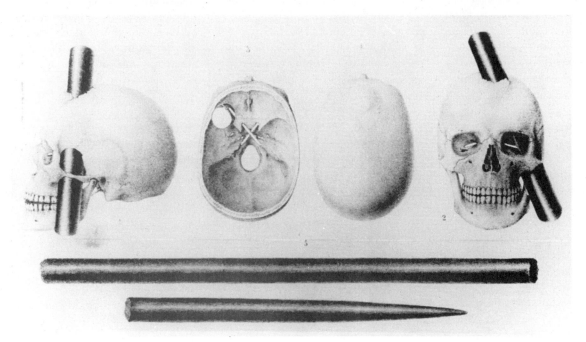

FIGURE 6–8.   This photo illustrates the size of the tamping rod and Phineas Gage's skull.

Source: National Library of Medicine.

tions, a case of accidental brain damage provided clues to human prefrontal lobe function and helped establish the brain as the organ of mind once and for all. This was the celebrated case of railroad construction supervisor **Phineas P. Gage**.

On September 13, 1848, as Gage prepared a hole for blasting powder, a premature explosion blew an iron tamping rod through his head. The bar (Figure 6–8) entered Gage's left cheek and exited above his right temple. To the amazement of his crew, Gage almost immediately sat up and asked for the rod. The physician to whom Gage was taken, Dr. John Harlow, proved to himself the story of Gage's injury with the observation that his two index fingers touched when he inserted them into the entry and exit wounds. Harlow (1868) later reported the accident and its aftermath.

Although Gage recovered physically, his personality was dramatically altered. According to Dr. Harlow (1868),

His physical health is good, and I am inclined to say that he has recovered. . . . Applied for his situation as foreman, but is undecided whether to work or travel. His contractors, who regarded him as the most efficient and capable foreman in their employ previous to his injury, considered the change in his mind so marked that they could not give him his place again. The equilibrium . . . between his intellectual faculties and animal propensities, seems to have been destroyed. He is fitful, irreverent, indulging at times in the grossest profanity (which was not previously his custom), manifesting but little deference for his fellows, impatient of restraint or advice when it conflicts with his desires, at times pertinaciously obstinate, yet capricious and vacillating, devising many plans of future operation, which are no sooner arranged than they are abandoned in turn for others appearing more feasible. . . . [H]is mind was radically changed, so decidedly that his friends and acquaintances said he was "no longer Gage." (pp. 339-340)

Gage lived for several years after his accident, flitting from one occupation to another and at one point exhibiting himself at Barnum's Museum in New York City. His lack of initiative and inability to carry through plans are characteristic of people with prefrontal lobe damage (e.g., Valenstein, 1973).

In summary, Gage's accident definitively showed the importance of the brain for the mind. After his injury, Gage was "no longer Gage." Also, Gage's experience argued against Flourens's nonlocalizationist position by showing that specific human abilities depended on the integrity of the frontal lobes. Further evidence supporting localization of function appeared in Paul Broca's clinical work.

Localization of Language Areas

Although Flourens's nonlocalizationist beliefs held center stage through the mid-1850s because of the precision of his experiments and his opposition to phrenology, the tide of scientific opinion soon took a localizationist turn. The evidence for localization came from Paul Broca's study in 1861 of a patient sometimes called Tan. As is often the case, Broca's study was anticipated by earlier work.

Jean Baptiste Bouillaud (1796–1881) was a physician and an admirer of Gall and phrenology. In 1825, Bouillaud reported clinical evidence supporting Gall's claim for a language "organ" in the brain's frontal area. Because of the general acceptance of Flourens's antilocalizationist beliefs, Bouillaud's claim was discounted, and his offer of 500 francs for proof that he was wrong failed to elicit a challenge.

Bouillaud was supported by his son-in-law Ernest Aubertin (1825–1893). Aubertin was most convinced by a patient who had recovered from a gunshot wound to the left front of the head. Pressing the soft spot over the man's wound caused him to lose the power of speech. Aubertin had another patient who had lost his speech, and he predicted that this patient, who was near death, would be found to have frontal lobe damage.

Before Aubertin could test his prediction, another speechless but otherwise intelligent patient came to the attention of **Pierre Paul Broca** (1824–1880; Figure 6–9), the 37-year-old chief of surgery at the

Bicêtre hospital near Paris. Broca's patient was a 51-year-old man named Leborgne who had been at the hospital for 21 years. Although the man apparently could understand everything said to him, all he could say was either "*tan, tan*" or, in times of great frustration over his inability to communicate, he would utter the curse "*Sacré nom de Dieu*" (Sacred name of God). His fellow patients considered him "an egoist, vindictive and objectionable, and his associates, who detested him, even accused him of stealing" (Broca, 1861; in Benjamin, 1988, p. 94).

Leborgne was transferred to Broca's ward after an infection in his paralyzed right leg became gangrenous. Broca realized both the hopelessness of the case and its importance for science. After satisfying himself that there was nothing wrong with Leborne's larynx and tongue muscles, Broca asked Aubertin if the case was a suitable test of Aubertin's hypothesized frontal lobe language center. Aubertin agreed that it was, and Leborgne died 6 days after admission

FIGURE 6–9.   Pierre Paul Broca.

Source: National Library of Medicine.

FIGURE 6–10.   Carl Wernicke.

Source: National Library of Medicine.

to Broca's ward. Broca's autopsy revealed a lesion about the size of a hen's egg to the third convolution of the frontal lobe on the brain's left side. He presented the brain to the *Société d'Anthropologie* a few hours after the autopsy.

If this were Broca's only contribution to the discovery of a left frontal lobe language area, we might conclude that Aubertin and Bouillaud deserve a kinder historical fate than to be almost completely overlooked. However, "while Broca may have been lucky to steal Aubertin's thunder in producing the first demonstration case, he proved his real mettle as a scientist by collecting more supportive evidence" (Fancher, 1990, p. 88).

Today we honor Broca by attaching his name to the left frontal lobe area, where damage produces an expressive aphasia (aphasia refers to a language defect). Damage to Broca's area is associated with labored, agrammatical speech—a difficulty in

expressing himself or herself—in a person with relatively intact language comprehension.

Slightly more than a decade after Broca's discovery, in 1874, German neurologist **Carl Wernicke** (1848–1905) reported an aphasia from damage to the superior (top) portion of the left temporal lobe. The symptoms include poor language comprehension and fluent, but meaningless, speech. Wernicke's aphasia is sometimes called receptive aphasia, because language meaning is poorly received. Wernicke is shown in Figure 6–10, and Figure 6–11 shows Broca's area and Wernicke's area in the context of Wernicke's model.

Wernicke's model for the neural control of language forms the basis for current neural models of language. Because Wernicke's area is adjacent to the primary auditory cortex, Wernicke concluded that it converts speech sounds into meaning. Broca's area, close to the motor cortex areas controlling the

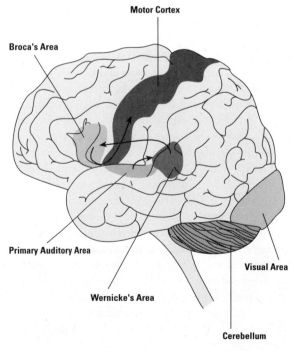

FIGURE 6–11.   Lateral view of the left human neocortex, showing Wernicke's model as discussed in the text.

Source: Adapted from Saul Kassin, Psychology *(Boston: Houghton Mifflin Company, 1995), figure 2.18.*

face and neck region, converts temporal lobe language representations from Wernicke's area into speech. Wernicke predicted that disconnection of the two areas would result in fluent, but nonsensical, speech in a person with intact language comprehension. His prediction was found to be correct when people were discovered with damage to the arcuate fasciculus—fibers interconnecting Broca's area and Wernicke's area—which produces a language deficit called a conduction aphasia. The person cannot "conduct" language information from Wernicke's area to Broca's area.

Electrical Brain Stimulation and Localization of Function

By the end of the 19th century, two major techniques had been developed for studying the nervous system: ablation and electrical stimulation. In this section, we will see how electrical brain stimulation provided further evidence for functional localization.

Working with epileptic patients, English neurologist **John Hughlings Jackson** (1835–1911) guessed that there were discrete motor areas in the cerebral cortex. Perhaps stimulation of these motor areas would result in motor movements. His speculation was soon verified by investigators applying electrical stimulation to the cortex of animals.

Electrical stimulation of the brain was initially hindered by the belief that the cortex, and perhaps the rest of the brain as well, was insensitive to stimulation. Several observations had contributed to this belief, held by Magendie, Flourens, and others. Specifically, operations on the brains of conscious people had produced no sensory phenomena; mechanical brain stimulation rarely caused motor movements; and cortical stimulation immediately after death was ineffective, even though it was known that the motor nerves briefly retained their excitability (recall Cabanis's conclusions in Chapter 4 about guillotine victims).

A major turning point in the study of the brain occurred when German scientists **Gustav Fritsch** (1838–1927) and **Eduard Hitzig** (1838–1907) reported in 1870 that electrical stimulation of part of the cortex of a dog resulted in motor movements. Fritsch

and Hitzig had discovered the motor cortex, working with homemade instruments under crude conditions.

Fritsch and Hitzig's results were soon replicated and extended by the Scottish neurologist **David Ferrier** (1843–1928). Ferrier had studied with Alexander Bain for his M.A. degree, and in Chapter 4 we noted that Bain may be considered an early physiological psychologist. Ferrier was eventually knighted for his studies of cortical localization of function. Working with monkeys, Ferrier found vision in the occipital lobes, where stimulation produced scanning eye movements, and ablation caused blindness. Ferrier thought that removal of one occipital lobe caused blindness in the eye opposite the side of the lesion. However, German physiologist **Hermann Munk** (1839–1912) demonstrated that the loss of one occipital lobe produces blindness not in the opposite eye, but in the opposite visual field. For example, destruction of the right occipital lobe causes blindness in the left visual field, not in the left eye.

Munk and Ferrier both found an auditory center in the temporal lobes, and the skin senses (e.g., touch, temperature) were localized in the parietal lobes. For both the motor cortex and somatosensory cortex (parietal lobe representation of skin senses), investigators found that the amount of neural representation of a body part corresponded to the body part's functional importance, not to its actual size. For example, the brain area devoted to the torso is small, but the areas corresponding to the hands, fingers, and face are quite large. As a result, the sensory and motor homunculi (literally "little men") are distorted, with tiny bodies and huge hands and faces.

Electrical stimulation results tended to refute Flourens's nonlocalization position, but the evidence did not support phrenology. Functions were localized in the brain, but the functions localized and where they were found bore no resemblance to phrenology's teachings.

Electrical Stimulation of the Human Brain

In 1874, Cincinnati physician **Roberts Bartholow** (1831–1904) had the opportunity to electrically stimulate the exposed brain of one of his patients—

a 30-year-old, somewhat feeble-minded woman named Mary Rafferty. Cancer had eaten a 2-inch hole in the top of her skull, which exposed the pulsations of her brain. Apparently this hole was all the invitation Bartholow needed, and he inserted a needle insulated except for its tip in order to prevent the widespread distribution of the electrical current passed through the needle. In this, Bartholow was guided by the earlier work of Fritsch and Hitzig and of Ferrier.

At first, the study went well and Bartholow was able to elicit some sensations and motor movements. For example, Bartholow (1874) reported that his third application of electric current triggered "muscular contraction of the right upper and lower extremities. . . . Mary complained of a very strong and unpleasant feeling of tingling in both extremities, especially in the right arm, which she seized with the opposite hand and rubbed vigorously. Notwithstanding the very evident pain . . . , she smiled as if much amused" (p. 310).

Hoping to increase Rafferty's reaction, Bartholow strengthened the current. As a result, Rafferty had a violent convulsion on her left side and lost consciousness. Twenty minutes after the seizure, Rafferty awakened, complaining of dizziness and weakness. Two days later, Bartholow brought Rafferty into the electrical room for further stimulation but decided to abandon the experiment, as Rafferty "was pale and depressed; her lips were blue; and she had evident difficulty in locomotion" (Bartholow, 1874, p. 311). Mary Rafferty died 2 days later.

Although Bartholow did not think Rafferty's death was caused by his stimulation experiments, the report of the investigation produced a scandal. Bartholow had to resign from his staff position at a hospital in Cincinnati and was eventually forced to leave the city. Interestingly, he later developed a positive reputation for his books on practical medical therapeutics (Valenstein, 1973).

The lack of a therapeutic rationale clearly separates Bartholow's experiment and the later investigations of the American-born Canadian neurosurgeon **Wilder Graves Penfield** (1891–1976), whose work is further discussed in Chapter 17. In his operations on conscious epileptic patients, Penfield electrically stimulated their exposed brains to search for the locus of epileptic seizures (so that he could remove it) and for the locus of language areas (so that he could avoid damaging them as much as possible). Still, we must give Bartholow credit for anticipating the later work of the "surgeon-experimenter."

So far, we have examined research designed to uncover the mind-body connections by directly assaulting the brain, either by stimulating it or by damaging it (or by studying the sequelae to naturally occurring damage). Another 19th-century physiological approach to the mind-body problem produced psychophysics, and its inventor is considered a leading contender for the honor of having originated psychology as a science. His name is Gustav Fechner, and we will begin our look at psychophysics with an examination of the anticipatory work of Ernst Weber, Fechner's colleague.

PSYCHOPHYSICS

Ernst Weber

Ernst Heinrich Weber (1795–1878) was born in Wittenberg, a city in eastern Germany on the Elbe River. Weber's long career began and ended at the University of Leipzig, where he earned his Ph.D. in 1815, was appointed *Dozent* in physiology in 1817, became Professor of Anatomy in 1818, Professor of Physiology in 1840, and retired in 1871. Weber is shown in Figure 6-12.

As an anatomist and physiologist, Weber's special interest lay in two little-investigated sensory mechanisms: touch and kinesthesis (the sense of movement or the position of body parts). Weber was one of the first to demonstrate that touch is actually more than one sense. For him, the sense of touch provided three classes of sensation: pressure, temperature, and locality, with the sense of locality being secondary to, and its arousal dependent on, other sensations. That is, Weber held that sensation varies only in quality and intensity. Localization in space depends on the mind's actions and the relations among sensations.

Although Weber attributed the sense of locality in part to the actions of the mind, this did not prevent

FIGURE 6–12. Ernst Weber.
Source: Archives of the History of American Psychology.

him from attempting its investigation. The investigation of locality led to the first of his major contributions to psychology, the measurement of the two-point threshold.

The Two-Point Threshold

Using a compass-like instrument (it has two points that can be separated greater or lesser distances), Weber mapped the body's sensitivity to dual, simultaneous touches. With the points slightly apart, a portion of the body is touched and the subject asked to report whether one or two touches has been felt. Weber found that sensitivity varied greatly for different body parts. For example, an observer could detect two touches on the tongue when the points were only about 1 mm apart, whereas separate touches on the back were not perceived until the points were separated by approximately 60 mm. Weber attributed this difference to differential receptor density. Spatial discrimination is most

accurate where the receptors are many and closely packed (e.g., on the tongue).

Although Weber was interested in measuring the sensitivity of spatial discrimination on the body, his "compass test" has become synonymous with the measurement of the **two-point threshold**, or limen. This research was important because it showed that for every change in stimulation (e.g., spreading apart the points) there is not always a corresponding change in sensation. On the back, only one touch is felt whether the points are 10 mm, 20 mm, or 30 mm apart. Apparently gross differences in stimulation result in no change in sensation. Do you remember Zeno's millet seed example in Chapter 2?

Weber's most important investigations of sensitivity dealt with judgments of lifted weights and gave rise to a mathematical relation Fechner called Weber's law. These were Weber's studies of the just noticeable difference (jnd) in weight judgments.

The Just Noticeable Difference

On each trial, Weber required a subject to lift an unvarying standard weight and a comparison weight, which varied in measured amounts from the standard. The subject then reported whether the comparison weight felt lighter, heavier, or the same as the standard. Weber found that the difference that could be reliably detected, the **just noticeable difference**, depended on the standard weight. With a light standard weight, small changes were detected. With a heavy standard, a relatively large change was needed for detection.

Although the absolute size of the jnd varied, Weber believed it varied by a constant ratio of the standard stimulus. For judgments of lifted weights, Weber found the ratio to be 1/40. That is, if the standard weighed 40 g, a change of at least 1 g was needed to detect a difference. A 39-g weight would be felt as lighter and a 41-g weight heavier, but a 39.5-g weight or a 40.5-g weight would appear to weigh the same as the standard. With an 80-g standard, a change of at least 2 g (2/80 = 1/40) would be needed for the difference to be detected.

Weber determined the jnds for other types of discriminations and found them also to be constant ratios of the standard stimulus, although the ratios varied for the different types of judgments. As we have seen, for lifted weights, the ratio was 1/40; it was 1/30 for weights passively felt and 1/100 for judgments of the length of two lines.

Following Fechner, we call the ratios **Weber fractions**, and they fit data reasonably well, deviating only at extreme intensities of the standard stimulus. However, Weber is important not for the accuracy of his fractions, but for having a valid claim to being the first to quantitatively measure the mind. Although Weber did not recognize the importance of his research for psychology, a fellow scientist at Leipzig did.

Gustav Theodor Fechner

Gustav Theodor Fechner (1801–1887) was born in the village of Gross Särchen in southeastern Germany. His father was the local pastor, a man who shocked his congregation by installing a lightning rod on the church steeple, as the congregation considered this a lack of faith in the Lord's protection. The father's freethinking also extended to preaching without a wig, which, he argued, Jesus must also have done. If the father's ability to think for himself extended to his son, it was either through his genes or through his early interactions with the boy—Pastor Fechner died when Gustav was 5.

Fechner enrolled at the University of Leipzig to study medicine in 1817, the same year that Weber was appointed *Dozent* in physiology. Fechner's study was largely completed on his own, from books, although he did attend lectures in Weber's physiology course. Despite passing the required examinations for an undergraduate degree, Fechner did not obtain the doctorate that would have allowed him to practice medicine, confessing later that he had not learned any of the requisite skills for such practice (e.g., how to apply a bandage or how to deliver a baby).

However, Fechner had learned enough about the medicine of his day to satirize it. Under the pseudonym Dr. Mises, Fechner's first publication was *Beweiss, dass der Mond aus Iodine bestehe* (*Proof that the Moon is Made of Iodine,* 1821), in which he lampooned the use of iodine to treat virtually every ill-

ness. Dr. Mises also commented on the *Vergleichende Anatomie der Engel* (*The Comparative Anatomy of Angels*), noting that the "basic angelic form is always the sphere, and we regard the sphere as no more than the basic form of Beauty" (Fechner, 1825/1969, p. 137). In this comment, Fechner revealed his interest in aesthetics, a topic he returned to late in life. Dr. Mises published 14 times between 1821 and 1876, revealing Fechner's lifelong tendency to follow his own mind rather than accepting the dogma of authority. For a commentary on *Comparative Anatomy,* see Marshall (1969).

With no academic appointment, Fechner stayed at Leipzig to study physics and mathematics, supplementing his meager income by translating a French physics textbook into German. In 1824, he began lecturing at the university, and he also started experiments on electricity. By 1834, Fechner's reputation was such that he was made a full professor of physics at Leipzig, a position that commanded a good salary and a lifetime pension.

Fechner married in 1833, and his life settled into a frenetic pace of intellectual and social activity that soon took its toll. He began to have headaches and difficulty sleeping, and his worry about his health turned to depression. Fechner's eyesight began to deteriorate, undoubtedly aggravated by an experiment on afterimages in which he stared at the sun through colored glasses. Finally, his health almost gone, Fechner resigned his chair in physics and retired on his pension.

Fechner's illness remains something of a mystery, with obvious psychological components. In the beginning, he experienced a deep depression accompanied by a loss of interest in eating. Various remedies were tried, including laxatives, electricity, and violent counterirritants. Nothing worked, and Fechner was nearly dead from starvation and the remedies when an acquaintance offered him a dish of spiced raw ham soaked in Rhine wine and lemon juice whose recipe had appeared to her in a dream. Fechner accepted it, and his illness entered a new phase involving the wild flight of ideas, mutism, and a fear of light. During this period, Fechner sat in a darkened room, while his mother read to him through an opening in the door. His recovery came suddenly in October 1843, and the sight of flowers on his first venture outside without a blindfold led to another of Dr. Mises's books, *Nanna, oder über das Seelenleben der Pflanzen* (*Nanna, or Concerning the Mental Life of Plants*, 1848).

Nanna reveals a deepening of Fechner's religious convictions and argues against the scientific materialism of his day. "Miraculously" recovered, Fechner now considered he had a mission, which was to reveal to all that consciousness pervaded the world of nature (panpsychism). *Nanna* was intended to be the wake-up call in Fechner's mission to inform a sleeping public. His next call came in *Zend-Avesta, oder über die Dinge des Himmels und des Jenseits* (*Zend-Avesta, or Concerning Matters of Heaven and the Hereafter*, 1851). Although the public continued to sleep, *Zend-Avesta* was important because in it Fechner outlined psychophysics. Thus, *Zend-Avesta* anticipated Fechner's famous *Elemente der Psychophysik* (*Elements of Psychophysics*, 1860). Fechner's panpsychism is described in Woodward (1972).

Elements of Psychophysics

Fechner sought the relation between the spiritual and the material worlds, the relation between the mind and the body. According to him, the insight for how to determine the relation came on the morning of October 22, 1850, while he was still in bed. (The importance of precise dates of discovery is a matter of conjecture [e.g., Rosenzweig, 1987].) He would develop a method to measure the relation between sensation (the mental) and the stimulus giving rise to it (the physical), and he would call the method and associated theory **psychophysics**. According to Fechner (1860/1966), "Psychophysics should be understood . . . as an exact theory of the functionally dependent relations of body and soul or, more generally, . . . of the physical and the psychological worlds" (p. 7).

Without Fechner's insight in 1850, a truly experimental psychology probably would have been only slightly delayed. The time was ripe for the birth of scientific psychology, and Fechner was in the right place at the right time with the right preparation. First, from Herbart (Chapter 5), Fechner had obtained the conception of psychology as an enterprise to which mathematics could be applied. More importantly, Herbart gave Fechner the idea that mind might be analyzed through the exploration of the threshold of consciousness, an idea Herbart had gotten from Leibniz (Chapter 3).

Weber's work on the measurement of the just noticeable difference also influenced Fechner. As we noted, Weber had found that the jnd for at least three sensory modalities was a constant ratio of the standard stimulus. Fechner gave Weber's relation mathematical form and called the result **Weber's law**, which may be written

$$\frac{\delta R}{R} = \text{a constant,}$$

where R stands for the stimulus magnitude (the German word for stimulus is *Reiz*), and δR is the amount of stimulus change needed for detection (the jnd). Weber's law shows that the jnd is a constant ratio of the standard stimulus and that "the magnitude of the stimulus increment must increase in precise proportion to the stimulus already present, in order to bring about an equal increase in sensation . . ." (Fechner, 1860/1966, p. 54).

Fechner did not claim that the function relating stimulus intensity and sensation magnitude originated either with him or with Weber. He noted that the relation had been recognized in other contexts by mathematicians such as Pierre Simon Laplace (1749–1827), Siméon Denis Poisson (1781–1840), and particularly by Daniel Bernoulli (1700–1782). Bernoulli pointed out that the same monetary stimulus has dramatically different effects on people depending on their state of wealth. A dollar is meaningless to a rich man but cause for celebration to a beggar.

Through a series of mathematical exercises, Fechner changed Weber's law into what we call **Fechner's law**, which is

$$S = \text{k log } R,$$

where S is the psychological sensation, which is equal to a constant (k) times the logarithm of physical stimulus intensity (log R). As you can see from Figure 6–13, a graph of Fechner's law, with low levels of stimulus intensity, even a small change produces a change in sensation. However, as the

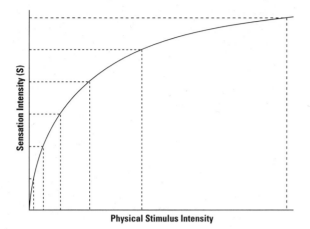

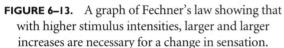

FIGURE 6–13. A graph of Fechner's law showing that with higher stimulus intensities, larger and larger increases are necessary for a change in sensation.

intensity of *R* increases, larger and larger changes are required for a change in sensation.

In recent years, Fechner's logarithmic relation between stimulus intensity and sensation has been modified into a power relation called **Stevens's law** (Stevens, 1956; Chapter 18). Still, Fechner had at least indirectly measured sensation. He had shown that it is possible to measure the mind and had either developed or systematized psychophysics' major methods: the **method of limits**, the method of constant stimuli, and the method of average error.

To illustrate the methods, we will consider the method of limits, which can be used to determine thresholds of detection. Suppose you want to know the least intense sound that someone can detect. Beginning with an undetectable sound, you gradually increase its volume until the person reports hearing the sound, noting the intensity at which the person's report changes from "I do not hear it" to "I hear it." Then, you start with a clearly detectable sound, decreasing it until the person says "I no longer hear it." After several ascending and descending presentations, the average intensity at which the judgment changes is found and called the detection threshold. The name *method of limits* was coined in 1891 by Emil Kraepelin (Chapter 7), one

of Wundt's most famous students. The name refers to the fact that a stimulus series ends when the tested person reaches a limit or point of change in his or her judgments.

Other Contributions

After psychophysics, Fechner turned to art. His first publication in **experimental aesthetics** (the study of beauty) concerned the "golden section," the most aesthetically pleasing ratio of length to width in an object. To study their proportions, Fechner measured 20,000 paintings in 22 art museums. In 1876, he published *Vorschule der Aesthetik* (*Preparatory School of Aesthetics*), which became the foundation of experimental aesthetics.

One of Fechner's most interesting speculations dealt with the function of the brain's major interconnecting structure, the **corpus callosum**. Because Fechner believed that consciousness is one of the brain's properties, he theorized that consciousness would be separated into two streams if the corpus callosum were cut (Blakemore, 1977). Nearly 100 years later, the chance to test his speculation came in patients receiving split-brain operations as treatment for epilepsy, and Fechner may have been correct. Roger Sperry, co-winner of the 1981 Nobel Prize for medicine or physiology, studied these surgical patients, and we will review his work in Chapter 17.

Fechner's Influence

Response to Fechner's *Elements of Psychophysics* was immediate, and many of psychology's founders (e.g., Helmholtz and Wundt) conducted experiments similar to those of Weber and Fechner. As we will see in Chapter 7, one of Wundt's major research areas was the study of sensation and perception using Fechner's psychophysical methods. Inspired by a used copy of *Elements*, Hermann Ebbinghaus (Chapter 8) applied Fechner's experimental methods in an elegant investigation of human memory.

Although Fechner's *Elements* stimulated the development of a scientific, experimental psychology, some scientists disagreed with various details of psychophysics (e.g., the use of the jnd as a unit of measurement or the validity of Weber's law and the mathematical transformations leading to Fechner's law). One who saw little of value in Fechner's work was William James. Three years after Fechner's death, James wrote:

> Fechner himself indeed was a German *Gelehrter* [scholar] of the ideal type, at once simple and shrewd, a mystic and an experimentalist, homely and daring, and as loyal to facts as to his theories. But it would be terrible if even such a dear old man as this could saddle our Science forever with his patient whimsies, and, in a world so full of more nutritious objects of attention, compel all future students to plough through the difficulties, not only of his own works, but of the still drier ones written in his refutation. . . . The only amusing part . . . is that Fechner's critics should always feel bound, after smiting his theories hip and thigh and leaving not a stick of them standing, to wind up by saying that nevertheless to him belongs the *imperishable glory* of first formulating them and thereby turning psychology into an *exact science*(!). (James, 1890, Vol. 1, p. 549, italics in the original)

Boring (1950) certainly did not agree with James's (1890) negative characterization of Fechner's work, concluding:

> Fechner, because of what he did and the time at which he did it, set experimental quantitative psychology off upon the course which it has followed. One may call him the 'founder' of experimental psychology, or one may assign that title to Wundt. It does not matter. Fechner had a fertile idea which grew and brought forth fruit abundantly. (p. 295)

Fechner is shown in Figure 6–14.

CONCLUSIONS

By the end of the 19th century, great strides had been made in demystifying the nervous system. The brain had been established unequivocally as the mind's substrate, in part thanks to phrenology

FIGURE 6-14.   Gustav Theodor Fechner.

Source: Philosophical Library, New York.

and to Phineas Gage's accident, and the nerve impulse had been shown to have an electrical component through the studies of Galvani, Volta, and du Bois-Reymond. Helmholtz had measured the speed of the nerve impulse, demonstrating that at least one of the nervous system's functions was amenable to experimental study. In addition, two of the methods that would be used so successfully for studying the brain and its functions in the 20th century were well established by the end of the 19th century (i.e., the ablation and electrical stimulation methods). The phrenologists' extreme localizationist position had given way to the nonlocalizationist beliefs of Flourens, which, in turn, were superseded by the evidence for localization (but not the localization preached by the phrenologists) discovered by Broca, Wernicke, Fritsch and Hitzig, Ferrier, Munk, and others. A major motor area had been mapped in the cortex of the brain, along with sensory areas for all the senses except olfaction and taste. Language centers had been found. The study of the brain and its functions was on the threshold of the century of progress that we will examine in Chapter 17.

The 19th century also saw the development of another approach to the mind-body problem. Building on earlier experimental investigations of mind-body relations, particularly those of his Leipzig colleague Ernst Weber, Gustav Fechner developed the science of psychophysics. His 1860 publication, *Elements of Psychophysics,* coming nearly 2 decades before Wundt organized his laboratory, is considered by some to mark the beginning of psychology as an experimental science.

S U M M A R Y

Review of Early Speculation

Except for Aristotle, most of the ancient philosophers guessed correctly that the brain was the biological substrate of thought and behavior. Early interest focused on the brain's ventricles as the reservoir for the animal spirits. In the Christian Church's three-chambered model of mind, the first chamber was the site of sensory analysis, the middle chamber was responsible for reason and thought, and the third chamber held memory. Leonardo da Vinci's anatomical studies of an ox brain cast serious doubt on the Church's model.

A century after da Vinci, Descartes viewed the nervous system as a hydraulic affair in which sensory stimulation opens pores in the brain, releasing animal spirits that fill the muscles. Descartes's model was quickly shown to be impossible by such investigators as Jan Swammerdam and Francis Glisson.

Electricity and Nerve Function

In the 18th century, electricity replaced animal spirits as the nervous system's activating substance. Electrical stimulation of a motor nerve caused contraction of a frog's leg muscle, which led Luigi Galvani to conclude that the frogs had generated electricity. By contrast, Alessandro Volta, inventor of an inorganic battery, believed that Galvani's frogs had conducted electricity instead of generating it. Studying the electrical nature of nervous tissue, Émil du Bois-Reymond demonstrated the reversal of the positions of positively and negatively charged particles with nerve stimulation. With this research, du Bois-Reymond brought the nerve impulse into the world of science and paved the way for Helmholtz to measure its speed.

As a student in Berlin, Helmholtz was greatly influenced by Johannes Müller (famous for his *Handbook of Human Physiology*) and his students, particularly du Bois-Reymond. At the University of Königsberg, Helmholtz measured the speed of the nerve impulse, invented the ophthalmoscope, and revised Thomas Young's trichromatic theory of color vision. Helmholtz also developed a place theory of auditory pitch perception.

Criticisms of trichromatic theory led Ewald Hering to propose opponent-process theory in which three receptor complexes signal either red or green, yellow or blue, or black or white. Helmholtz and Hering also disagreed on visual space perception, with Hering taking a nativist approach, whereas Helmholtz believed that space forms develop from experience.

Localization of Function

Localizationists believe that specific functions are located in specific areas of the nervous system, whereas nonlocalizationists are more impressed by the way the nervous system functions as a whole. The Bell-Magendie law—the dorsal roots of spinal nerves are sensory and the ventral roots are motor—supported localization of function and suggested that discrete sensory and motor areas might be found in the brain.

Johannes Müller formulated the doctrine of specific nerve energies, whose central tenet is that we are aware only of the activity in our nerves, not of the external world itself. Helmholtz was greatly influenced by the doctrine, extending the concept to vision and audition.

Phrenology, the idea that bumps and indentations on the skull reflect functional areas underneath, took an extreme localizationist position. Founded by Franz Joseph Gall and supported by Johann Caspar Spurzheim, phrenology was important in its emphasis on the brain as the organ of mind and in teaching that behavioral functions can be localized in the brain.

One of phrenology's chief opponents, Pierre Flourens used the ablation method to study brain function in animals. From his studies, Flourens discovered the specific functions of individual nervous system parts, but he was most impressed by the common action of the separate parts and of the whole system.

In 1848, accidental damage to the prefrontal lobes of Phineas P. Gage demonstrated the importance of the brain for human behavior and gave clues to the functions of the brain's prefrontal area. Further evidence for functional localization came from the discoveries by Pierre Broca and Carl Wernicke of language areas in the brain. Broca's area in the frontal lobe is concerned with speech production, whereas damage to Wernicke's area in the temporal lobe results in fluent speech that is not meaningful. Wernicke's model connects Wernicke's area to Broca's area through the arcuate fasciculus.

Gustav Fritsch and Eduard Hitzig electrically stimulated a dog's brain and discovered the motor cortex. Their animal work was extended by scientists such as David Ferrier and Hermann Munk. Ferrier localized vision in the occipital lobes, and both Ferrier and Munk found a temporal lobe auditory center. Neural areas important for the skin senses were found in the parietal lobes. Cincinnati physician Roberts Bartholow electrically stimulated the exposed brain of a patient, marking the beginning of the clinical investigations of the surgeon-experimenter.

Psychophysics

Leipzig physiologist Ernst Weber mapped the two-point threshold in studying the sense of touch. Of even greater importance was his study of the just noticeable difference (jnd), which he found to vary by a constant ratio of a standard stimulus when a subject compared the standard with a comparison stimulus.

After recovering from a mysterious physical and mental breakdown, Leipzig physicist/philosopher Gustav Fechner set out to define an equation that would express the relation between the body and the mind. Fechner gave Weber's relation between the jnd and the standard stimulus mathematical form, which he called Weber's law. Next, Fechner mathematically derived Fechner's law, which states that there is a logarithmic relation between sensation and stimulus magnitude. Fechner also developed or systematized the major methods of psychophysics, and his *Elements of Psychophysics* stimulated the development of a scientific, experimental psychology.

CONNECTIONS QUESTIONS

1. What connections can you make between physics and physiology/psychology?
2. What connections exist between the study of color blindness and color vision?
3. Discuss the connections between psychophysics and the emergence of psychology as a science.
4. In what ways was phrenology important for psychology?
5. In what sense does psychology emerge from the connection between physiology and philosophy?
6. Connect the signal physiological discoveries in the 19th century with the localization/nonlocalization of function controversy.
7. Draw a concept map connecting the major physiological developments discussed in this chapter, and compare your results with one possible solution provided on p. 563.

SUGGESTED READINGS

Benjamin, L. T., Jr. (1988). *A history of psychology: Original sources and contemporary research.* New York: McGraw-Hill Book Company. Chapter 4 of this book of readings, "The Physiological Roots of Psychology," contains original works by Broca and Helmholtz. Broca's account of his discovery of the speech area that bears his name is entertaining. Benjamin's compilation is only one of several books of readings that provide convenient sources for original material.

Blakemore, C. (1977). *Mechanics of the mind.* Cambridge: Cambridge University Press. This is an excellent treatment of the development of scientific investigation of the brain. The illustrations are outstanding.

Fechner, G. (1966). *Elements of psychophysics* (Vol. 1) (H. E. Adler, Trans.). New York: Holt, Rinehart and Winston, Inc. (Original work published 1860) Despite James's negative view of Fechner's work, it is always worthwhile to read the original writings of psychology's founders, if not in the original, at least in translation.

Hilgard, E. R. (1987). *Psychology in America: A historical survey.* San Diego: Harcourt Brace Jovanovich. Chapter 12 of Hilgard's book, "Physiological Psychology as Neuroscience," is a readable and informative look at neuroscience, mainly in America and mainly in the 20th century. In many cases, Hilgard draws from his own experience to give fascinating anecdotes about key neuroscientists.

Stumpf, C. (1895). Hermann von Helmholtz and the new psychology. *Psychological Review, 2,* 1–12. Written by one of the key figures in the history of psychology, this is a good summary of Helmholtz's contributions to psychology.

The Schools of Psychology

As an experimental science, psychology had its beginning in the latter part of the 19th century. At this point, we will briefly review the context in which the new science of experimental psychology arose.

As we saw in Chapter 5, the spirit of positivism was in the air in Europe at this time, begun by Auguste Comte and supported and extended by John Stuart Mill, Ernst Mach, Richard Avenarius, and others. Positivism accepted as real only things that could be known, while rejecting anything that could not be supported by observation. People who endorsed this philosophy found certain other intellectual positions especially appealing. Thus, positivists naturally gravitated toward empiricism because of the empiricists' belief that the only source of knowledge is sensory experience. Positivists also found their position supported by materialists, who hold that everything can be explained only in terms of matter. Evolution was also an important part of the positivist philosophy: Comte saw civilization evolving through stages—theological, metaphysical, and positive or scientific.

Even in its early form, we saw empiricism in concert with materialism. For example, in the mid-18th century, David Hartley developed a materialistic model of the human mind based on Newton's vibratory theory. By the latter half of the 19th century, advances in physiology had shown that mechanical vibrations were not involved in nervous system activity but that electrical and chemical processes were. Most physiologists and physicians of the time were convinced that all human acts ultimately could be explained materially—by physical and electrochemical principles.

As we saw in Chapter 6, great strides in understanding sensory physiology had been made by the second half of the 19th century. Much of this work had been done in Germany by such people as Weber, Fechner, Helmholtz, and Hering. The *Zeitgeist* was compatible with the successful emergence of a man trained in physiology but with an affinity for philosophy, an assistant of the great Helmholtz—Wilhelm Wundt. The result was the inception of psychology as an experimental science.

As we indicated in the first chapter, the early history of psychology as a separate science was dominated by the development of schools or systems of thought. "System" refers to a collection of ideas about what is psychological and how it will be studied, whereas a "school" is a collection of people who more or less subscribe to the system. Although Wundt, generally recognized as the founder of scientific psychology, called his system voluntarism, the first school is often considered to be structuralism, which was initiated by one of Wundt's students, Edward Bradford Titchener. We will study the lives and ideas of both Wundt and Titchener in Chapter 7. In Chapter 8, we will examine several of Wundt's contemporaries and sometimes opponents, one of whom, Franz Brentano, conceived a system to rival Wundt's voluntarism, which is called act psychology. In Chapters 9 through 11 we will examine the antecedents of and the first school that developed in opposition to voluntarism and structuralism, the school of functionalism. Chapters 12 and 13 will describe the forerunners, founders, and later adherents of behaviorism, whereas Chapter 14 considers the school of Gestalt psychology. Finally, Chapters 15 and 16 will focus on psychoanalysis and personality theory and clinical psychology beyond psychoanalysis.

Voluntarism and Structuralism: The First Schools

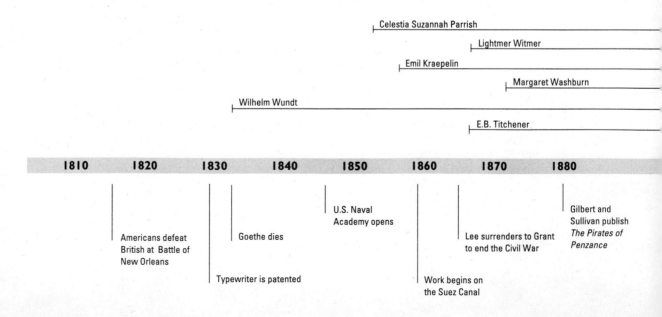

Celestia Suzannah Parrish

Lightmer Witmer

Emil Kraepelin

Margaret Washburn

Wilhelm Wundt

E.B. Titchener

| 1810 | 1820 | 1830 | 1840 | 1850 | 1860 | 1870 | 1880 |

Americans defeat British at Battle of New Orleans

Goethe dies

U.S. Naval Academy opens

Lee surrenders to Grant to end the Civil War

Gilbert and Sullivan publish *The Pirates of Penzance*

Typewriter is patented

Work begins on the Suez Canal

In the last five chapters, we have explored the events in philosophy and physiology (or medicine) that laid the foundation for psychology. In this chapter, we will see that scientific psychology arose when the experimental methods of physiology were applied to certain philosophical problems. This combination of influences—an interest in philosophy and a knowledge of physiology—have often been seen in the same person. For example, in Chapter 4, Locke, Hartley, La Mettrie, and Cabanis all had medical backgrounds. In Chapter 5, we saw that Lotze earned a medical degree while retaining his interest in philosophy and the arts. Fechner (Chapter 6), whose 1860 *Elements of Psychophysics* is sometimes considered the beginning of scientific psychology, studied medicine before becoming a physicist, psychophysicist, and philosopher. In fact, of the men who have received some support as the "founders"

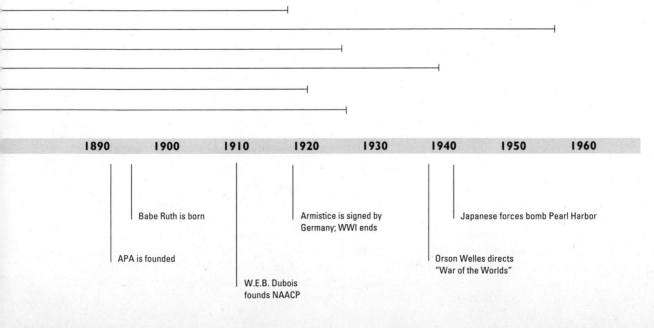

| 1890 | 1900 | 1910 | 1920 | 1930 | 1940 | 1950 | 1960 |

Babe Ruth is born

Armistice is signed by
Germany; WWI ends

Japanese forces bomb Pearl Harbor

APA is founded

Orson Welles directs
"War of the Worlds"

W.E.B. Dubois
founds NAACP

of psychology, almost all had medical backgrounds plus strong interests in philosophy.

In Chapter 10, we will see that William James, trained as a physician, devoted his professional life to psychology and philosophy. His 1875 demonstration laboratory at Harvard establishes his claim for the distinction as experimental psychology's founder, but James was never really an experimentalist. Because the theme of this chapter is the founding of psychology as an experimental science, as distinct from psychology as a philosophical enterprise of the sort we reviewed previously, we will focus on Wilhelm Wundt and his laboratory at the University of Leipzig. Wundt is the man and Leipzig the location that most historians of psychology associate with the founding of a separate science of psychology.

Before we begin, you might be curious about why psychology as an experimental science arose in Germany rather than in England or France or some other country. Was there something about Germany's university system in the 19th century that fostered the development of psychology as a science? The answer is probably yes. According to several authors (e.g., Dobson & Bruce, 1972), German universities particularly encouraged scholarship through "freedom of teaching" and "freedom of learning." Freedom of teaching meant that instructors were free to choose their topics, to present them in their own styles, and to express their views without fear of interference from an outside party. By the same token, students were free to attend lectures on whatever topics interested them, taught by teachers they liked, and as frequently (or infrequently) as they wished. Examinations were not given by semesters but were held at the end of a course of study, another approach that fostered freedom of learning by allowing study of whatever interested an individual as long as the person could pass a comprehensive examination.

In addition, the Germany university system's research emphasis may have been critical for giving psychology its scientific approach (Hilgard, 1987). "Original research as part of university training, in all fields, was a major innovation by the German universities" (p. 15). Wilhelm Wundt was trained in this German research tradition and took advan-

tage of it to create a new synthesis of philosophy and physiology that has become modern scientific psychology.

WILHELM MAXIMILIAN WUNDT AND VOLUNTARISM

Wilhelm Maximilian Wundt (1832–1920) was born in the village of Neckarau, part of Baden, which is a division of southwestern Germany. His parents' fourth child, Wundt had only one living brother, who was 8 years older. Wundt's father was a Lutheran minister, characterized by Wundt as a good-humored spendthrift. By contrast, his mother was a frugal shopper whose bargain hunting embarrassed her husband. On his father's side, two of Wundt's ancestors had been presidents of the University of Heidelberg, whereas others had scholarly interests in economics, geography, and history. On his mother's side, there had been scientists, governmental administrators, and physicians.

Despite his erudite ancestors, Wundt's daydreaming produced a mediocre academic record. On one occasion, Wundt's father visited his class as the school inspector and became so angered at Wundt's inattentiveness "that he slapped him in the face" (Bringmann, Balance, & Evans, 1975, p. 288). In his autobiography, Wundt noted that this incident stood in marked contrast to the treatment he normally received from his father.

When he was 13, Wundt spent a year at the Catholic *Gymnasium* at Bruchsal, where one of his teachers implied in front of the class that Wundt was qualified, at best, to be a mail carrier. Wundt's winter of 1845 was a "school of suffering."

Next, his parents sent him to the Lyceum in Heidelberg. Wundt's father died during the school year, and Wundt finally overcame his daydreaming tendency. At Heidelberg, the previously shy Wundt developed friendships for the first time in his life. Although he continued to dislike school, he became an avid reader and found it reinforcing when a teacher read his essays to the class as examples of good writing.

When Wundt graduated in 1851, he and his mother were barely existing on her widow's pension. With his poor academic record, Wundt did not qualify for the scholarship normally available to ministers' sons. After a year studying medicine at Tübingen University, Wundt returned to Heidelberg and completed his medical training in just 3 years. Having finally learned how to apply himself to his work, Wundt ranked first in the medical state board examinations in 1855.

As a Heidelberg medical student, Wundt also developed an interest in research. Supervised by noted chemist Robert Bunsen (1811–1899), of Bunsen burner fame, Wundt deprived himself of salt in order to study the effect on the salt concentration of his urine. Wundt considered the resulting publication more enjoyable than any other because it was his first. Another piece of independent research earned Wundt a prize from the medical school faculty.

For 6 months after completing the state board examination, Wundt worked as the clinical assistant to one of his former teachers. Although the work was at times exhausting, Wundt continued his research. He considered his observations on the touch sensitivity of hysterical patients as the first steps on his journey toward experimental psychology. This investigation became Wundt's medical dissertation, and on November 10, 1855, Wundt received his M.D., *summa cum laude.*

Next, Wundt spent a semester studying physiology in Berlin with Johannes Müller and Émil du Bois-Reymond (Chapter 6). Wundt returned to Heidelberg, where he applied for the second doctorate (*Habilitation*) to enable him to offer courses of his own. After initially turning him down, the faculty changed its mind and allowed Wundt to teach his first course in experimental physiology in the summer of 1857 as a *Privatdozent.*

Although his initial class contained only four students and was held in his mother's apartment, the stress resulted in a near-fatal lung hemorrhage. Wundt went to the Swiss Alps to recover, and, perhaps deciding that teaching was too demanding, applied for a position as assistant to Helmholtz (Chapter 6) in the newly established physiological institute at Heidelberg. He held the position from 1858 until 1864, and, as one of Helmholtz's assistants, Wundt shared a room with Ivan Sechenov (Chapter 12), a Russian physiologist who greatly influenced Ivan Pavlov (Chapter 12). Sechenov later recalled that Wundt never spoke either to him or to the other three men who shared the room and that he had never even heard Wundt's voice!

According to G. Stanley Hall (Chapter 10), a visitor to Wundt in Leipzig who later wrote a biography of Wundt, Helmholtz fired Wundt for mathematical incompetence. However, Wundt disputed Hall's claim, and Helmholtz wrote several recommendation letters for his former assistant "in which he praised Wundt for his teaching skills, his publication record and especially the integrity of his research methods" (Bringmann et al., 1975, p. 292).

In 1862, Wundt published *Beiträge zur Theorie der Sinneswahrnehmung* (*Contributions Toward a Theory of Sense Perception*). In *Contributions,* Wundt outlined his plans for psychology, which he envisioned as a science that would establish the facts of consciousness. Wundt planned to create an experimental psychology, a scientific metaphysics (i.e., "a philosophy which makes the results of all the other sciences the object of its own special investigations" [Titchener, 1921, p. 167]), and a social psychology. Two physiology textbooks followed the *Contributions,* and Wundt's income from his writings allowed him to leave the physiological institute and start a small laboratory in his home, where he continued his experimentation.

After leaving Helmholtz, Wundt also had a brief political career. As president of the Heidelberg Workmen's Educational Association, he traveled and lectured on popular scientific topics. Appointed to serve in the Baden Parliament in 1866, Wundt was elected in 1867, but he resigned the next year when he realized that the position deserved his full attention, and he was still primarily interested in research.

In 1871, Wundt received a salaried appointment (*ausserordentlicher Professor* or *Professor extraordinarius*) at Heidelberg with an income nearly twice the amount he had received as Helmholtz's assistant. With his improved economic situation, Wundt married Sophie Mau, his fiancée of several years.

In 1873 and 1874, Wundt published the two volumes of the first edition of his most important and influential book, *Grundzüge der physiologischen Psychologie* (*Principles of Physiological Psychology*). Note that "physiological psychology" did not mean the same thing to Wundt that it does to us. To Wundt, it meant experimental or laboratory psychology rather than psychological neuroscience. The word "physiological" referred to the use of physiology's methods, not to what was studied.

From Heidelberg, Wundt went to the University of Zurich to assume a professorship in philosophy. Zurich was considered to be a stopover for young scholars on their way up the academic ladder, and Wundt added to this reputation. In little more than a year, he was called to the chair of philosophy at the University of Leipzig, where he remained for the next 42 years. Note that Wundt accepted positions in philosophy at Zurich and Leipzig, despite the fact that he had taken only one philosophy course as an undergraduate. Wundt had established his credentials in philosophy with a book on the philosophical analysis of the physical basis of causality, written primarily for the income it might bring.

At Leipzig, Wundt established psychology as an experimental science through his voluminous publications, his teaching and research, a journal, and the graduate students he trained. But all of this was in the future when he arrived in 1875. To store the equipment he had brought from Zurich, Wundt was assigned a small room in the dining hall, and it was here in 1879 that Wundt began some independent psychological research. It was also here that much of the famous research by Wundt's students was later performed.

Although generally accepted as the date of scientific psychology's founding, the year 1879 is not etched in stone (Boring, 1965). In fact, a variety of other years have appeared in print, including 1874, 1875, and 1878. Sometimes more than one date has been given in the same article: for example, 1878 and 1879 in Baldwin (1894). However, Wundt himself spoke of the autumn of 1879 as the time when experimentation began in the Leipzig laboratory space, and there is a wealth of supporting documentation (e.g., Bringmann, Bringmann, & Ungerer, 1980) for the 1879 date.

For 2 years, Wundt supported his "institute" with his own money, and his laboratory was not recognized in the university catalog until 1883. This belated official recognition was stimulated by an offer Wundt had received from another university, which provided the leverage Wundt needed to persuade the administration to give him more resources.

Soon, Wundt was able to expand his laboratory into rooms vacated by the school of pharmacy. In 1892, the laboratory moved to 11 rooms in a building that had previously housed the department of gynecology. Finally, 5 years later, Wundt and his laboratory moved to a building constructed to his specifications. This building served as a model for the construction of many similar laboratories until its destruction during World War II.

During his career, Wundt taught more than 24,000 students. Wundt was a popular lecturer at Leipzig, and his lecture style has been described by one of his American students as follows:

> As soon as his familiar figure appeared, applause in the form of shuffling feet on the part of his hundreds of students would greet him. . . . Utterly unmoved, as if he had not heard us, Wundt would glide to his place on the dais, assume his accustomed position, fix his eyes on vacancy and begin his discourse. There could not be a better scientific lecturer. Without a scrap of writing, he would speak for three-quarters of an hour so clearly, concisely, and to the point, that, in listening to him, one would imagine one were reading a well-written book in which the paragraphs, the important text of the page, the small print, and the footnotes were plainly indicated. Wundt told no stories, gave few illustrations, scorned any attempt at popularity. His only thought was to deal with the topic of the day as thoroughly and exhaustively as the time permitted. . . . With all this, he was followed almost breathlessly, sometimes by eight hundred students, and, if the lecture had been unusually amazing, they would burst into spontaneous applause. (Worcester, 1932, p. 90)

Wundt supervised a large number of doctoral dissertations and apparently had close relationships with many of his graduate students. He also maintained friendly relations with former students who disagreed with his views, such as Hugo Münsterberg (Chapter 10), with whom he corresponded regularly and recommended to the University of Zurich after a major disagreement.

Liked by his university colleagues, Wundt "regarded himself fortunate to have personally known the two psychophysicists [Ernst] Weber . . . and Gustav Theodor Fechner . . . and to have been a guest in their homes" (Bringmann et al., 1975, p. 295). Friedrich Sander (1889–1972), Wundt's last assistant, recalled a mellow Wundt, tired of controversy, who enjoyed their intimate conversations.

In addition, Wundt's home life was apparently pleasant and conventional. With his wife, he entertained faculty and students, and the Wundts went to the theater, to the opera, and to concerts. His wife also helped him professionally, and he kept her informed about his research and his classes (Hilgard, 1987). Wundt (Figure 7–1) died in 1920 shortly after

FIGURE 7–2. Wundt's pendulum-clock experiment.

Source: R. E. Fancher, Pioneers of Psychology *(2nd edition, © 1990).*

his 88th birthday and just 8 days after completing his autobiography, *Erlebtes und Erkanntes* (*What I Have Experienced and Discovered*).

Wundt's Psychology

In 1861, Wundt rigged a pendulum clock into an apparatus (Figure 7–2) that he used to perform an interesting experiment (Wundt, 1862). Below the pendulum (B), Wundt had placed a calibrated scale (M). As the pendulum swung, a knitting needle (S) struck a bell (g) when the pendulum reached either position b or d. However, Wundt found that when he tried to attend to both the sound of the bell and the position of the pendulum, the pendulum was never precisely at b or d at the moment he heard the bell—it was always on its way back toward the center of the scale. In fact, he determined that it

FIGURE 7–1. Wilhelm Wundt.

Source: Archives of the History of American Psychology.

took him approximately 1/10 of a second to switch his attention from the bell's sound to the pendulum's location or vice versa. Although the sound of the bell and the extreme position of the pendulum occurred simultaneously, Wundt had not consciously experienced the two sensations together. He had experienced the sensations successively, indicating that separate acts of attention were necessary.

The importance of this experiment was that Wundt, like Fechner, had experimentally measured a psychological process. As we noted, in the same year that he published the results of this experiment, Wundt published *Contributions Toward a Theory of Sense Perception* in which he proposed to create a field of experimental psychology. Wundt's experimental psychology did not develop overnight, however, and 17 years passed before he began the Leipzig studies honored by the American Psychological Association in 1979. In the meantime, he published the first edition, in two volumes, of *Principles of Physiological Psychology.* To keep up with the work pouring from his laboratory, Wundt revised the *Principles* five times, with the last two editions expanded to three volumes.

In the *Principles,* it is evident that Wundt was seeking to establish psychology as a "new domain of science," but not necessarily one completely independent of philosophy (Brock, 1993). In calling for a science of psychology, Wundt was refuting the claims of Comte and Kant (both Chapter 5) that psychology could not be a science. By arguing for an experimental psychology, Wundt was disagreeing with Herbart's (Chapter 5) belief that psychology could not be an experimental endeavor. In fact, Herbart "provided much of the background against which Wundt rebelled" (Blumenthal, 1979, p. 549).

Despite his regular revisions of the *Principles,* Wundt realized that he needed a journal to provide more timely publication of his experimental results. In 1881, he began publishing *Philosophische Studien* (*Philosophical Studies*). Wundt initially planned to call the journal *Psychologische Studien* (*Psychological Studies*), but a journal with that title already existed, and, worse, it dealt with parapsychology and spiritism. According to Brock (1993), Wundt wrote in his autobiography that he deliberately chose the title *Philosophische Studien* to emphasize that psychology was part of philosophy. However, citing let-

ters written in 1880 from Wundt to Emil Kraepelin (discussed later), Bringmann et al. (1980) reported that there is no question that Wundt initially planned to call his journal *Psychologische Studien.* We use this slight discrepancy as a reminder of our Chapter 1 discussion of the difficulties of pinning down a completely accurate history. Questions of its intended title aside, this was the first journal devoted primarily to psychological experiments.

Wundt's Two Psychologies

For Wundt, the mind could be seen as a collection of conscious experiences produced by the interaction of external stimuli and higher mental processes. Psychology was the science of mind: that is, a science of conscious experiences. Wundt further assumed that consciousness could be experienced either directly or indirectly. For example, experienced directly, an apple produces sensations of redness and a rounded shape along with a feeling of mild pleasure. Wundt called this direct experience **immediate experience**, because it is based on an "immediate" reaction, uninfluenced by previous knowledge of the stimulus. Immediate experience gives the data for experimental psychology, which was one of Wundt's two psychologies.

By contrast, you may use a light meter to measure the amount of light the apple's surface reflects or a scale to determine its weight. This experience of the apple is indirect, mediated by the instruments used to collect the data. Wundt called this type of experience **mediate experience**, which produces data for physics and other natural sciences.

The part of Wundt's psychology with which most contemporary psychologists are familiar studied the lower mental processes—for example, sensing and feeling—using the methods of physiology. Wundt treated his physiological (experimental) psychology as a natural science (*Naturwissenschaft*).

Wundt did not believe that the higher mental processes—for example, language, memory, and thinking—could be studied experimentally, treating them instead as a cultural science (*Geisteswissenschaft*). Thus, he studied the *products* of the processes rather than the mental processes themselves, and the result grew into the 10 volumes of

Völkerpsychologie: Eine Untersuchung der Entwick-lungsgesetz von Sprache, Mythus, und Sitte (*Cultural Psychology: An Investigation of the Developmental Laws of Language, Myth, and Morality*). Consisting of 2 volumes on language, 2 on myth and religion, 2 on society, and 1 each on art, culture, law, and history, the **Völkerpsycholo-gie** was published during the last 2 decades of Wundt's life and remains largely undiscovered by most American psychologists.

Wundt's Use of Internal Perception

One of the most enduring misconceptions about Wundt's methodology concerns the use of intro-spection (*Selbstbeobachtung*, self-study or looking inward). "Wundt was not an introspectionist as that term is popularly applied today [as looking into one's own mind to contemplate one's thoughts, sensations, and feelings]. The thrust behind his entire experimental program was the claim that progress in psychology had been slow because of reliance on casual, unsystematic introspection, which had led invariably to unresolvable debates" (Blumenthal, 1975, p. 1082). That is, Wundt did not use the type of introspection (Chapter 3) that is implied by the term, although this use is often attributed to him.

Wundt distinguished between introspection and **internal perception** (*innere Wahrnehmung*). In principle, Wundt thought that internal perceptions could be as valid as external perceptions. Recognizing that conscious experiences are continually changing, Wundt developed specific rules for reporting them. First, the observer needed proper training in order to insure that he or she described immediate experience rather than mediate experience. Second, the observer needed to know when the stimulus would be presented so that he or she would not be caught by surprise. One reason for this is that the report was supposed to occur as soon as the observations were made instead of being based on memory. Third, the observer must be primed to experience the stimulus, in a state of strained attention. Fourth, the observations must be repeated many times, in order to reveal any problems that might have occurred with early presentations. Finally,

the experimental conditions should be varied systematically to enhance the generality of the observations. Given the lengthy training needed to become a proficient user of internal perception and the stringent rules for its use, it is easy to see why William James wrote that Wundt's experimental method "hardly could have arisen in a country whose natives could be *bored*" (1890, Vol. 1, p. 192, italics in the original).

Although it is sometimes implied that internal perception was the *only* technique Wundt and his students used, its use was limited to studies of sensation and perception in which the different rules could be applied. Wundt's disapproval of introspection (as opposed to internal perception) is clear from an analysis of nearly 180 studies published in 20 years of *Philosophische Studien,* which revealed that only 4 had produced qualitative introspective data of the kind gathered in other laboratories in the first decade of the 20th century (Danziger, 1980). Danziger noted that 2 of the 4 were specifically criticized by Wundt, and a third concerned data not gathered in his laboratory.

Wundt's Research

Wundt's research was remarkable for its wide range of topics. Because Wundt assigned the research problems to his students, an analysis of the research contents of *Philosophische Studien* (e.g., Boring, 1950) provides an indication of the scope and nature of the studies done in Wundt's laboratory.

Sensation and Perception. Approximately half of the studies from Wundt's laboratory between 1881 and 1903 investigated topics in sensation and perception, with most of the work being done in vision. For example, there were studies on the psychophysics of light and color, studies of negative afterimages, studies of color defects, and studies of optical illusions. There were also psychophysical studies of auditory sensations and studies of Weber's two-point threshold (Chapter 6).

Reaction-Time Studies. With his clock experiment in 1861, Wundt had revealed an interest in how long it took to react to sensory stimulation. Probably this interest was fueled by Wundt's having been Helmholtz's assistant: As we noted in Chapter 6, Helmholtz used a reaction-time difference to measure the speed of the nerve impulse. However, an interest in reaction-time measurement antedated Helmholtz's work by over half a century.

In 1796 at Greenwich Observatory, British astronomer-royal Nevil Maskelyne (1732–1811) fired his assistant, Kinnebrook, because of a significant difference in the two men's readings of the times of stellar transit—the time noted when an observed star crossed grid lines in the telescope. Stellar transit was measured by the "eye and ear" method, where an observer watched the movement of the star across a grid while counting the beats of a clock. This information was then used to make a complex judgment, and, not surprisingly, the differences in judgments made by Maskelyne and his assistant were attributed to faults in Kinnebrook, not in the astronomer-royal.

Twenty years later, German astronomer Friedrich Wilhelm Bessel (1784–1846) learned of the Kinnebrook-Maskelyne incident and decided to see if there were differences between himself and other astronomers and to investigate the differences, if they existed. Following Bessel's work, the difference between any two astronomers became known as a "personal equation." Bessel's discovery forced astronomers to determine their personal equations and to correct for them. In addition, the Dutch physiologist Franciscus Cornelius Donders (1818–1889) took over the reaction experiment from the astronomers.

In the measurement of a "simple" reaction time, a subject reacts to a predetermined stimulus with a predetermined movement. In 1868, Donders complicated the simple reaction task by adding other stimuli to which the subject either responded or did not respond. Complicating the task should lengthen the reaction time, presumably by the time it takes the subject to make additional judgments. Donders's **mental chronometry** method was based on the following assumptions: It takes time to perform mental acts; complicated reaction times are the sum of the reaction times for each of the different mental acts involved; and

it is possible to determine the time required for a particular mental act by subtraction. To illustrate, suppose it takes a subject 0.2 seconds to release a telegraph key when a blue light appears. As a complication, the subject is given two telegraph keys and must now release the left key when a blue light appears and the right key when a yellow light appears. The result is a 0.3 second reaction time. Donders assumed that the time needed mentally to categorize the color of the light (blue or yellow) and to make the appropriate response (release the left key or the right key) is 0.1 second $(0.3 - 0.2 = 0.1)$.

At first, reaction-time experiments appeared to be the answer to a true mental chronometry—a measure of the amount of time each mental process took—and about 17% of the studies from Wundt's laboratory involved the reaction experiment. For example, James McKeen Cattell (Chapter 10), Wundt's first assistant, worked extensively with reaction times, performing experiments with ingenious equipment he designed. Whereas in earlier studies the measurement of reaction times required a subject to either press or release a telegraph key, for later experiments Cattell invented keys activated by lip movements or by sound vibrations from a subject's voice. In one series of observations, Cattell presented letters or words and required subjects to name the stimuli by speaking. The finding that subjects took about the same time to name short words as they did individual letters led Cattell to the valid conclusion that people perceive words as wholes rather than perceiving each letter separately.

Wundt, and later his critics, were particularly interested in the 1888 reaction-time experiment by **Ludwig Lange** (1863–1936). Lange compared simple reaction times when the subject attended either to the expected stimulus or to the response to be made. Generally, reactions were about 1/10 of a second longer when the focus was on the stimulus. The personal equation problem appeared to have been solved: Astronomers who attend to the stimulus take longer to respond than astronomers who attend to making the response.

Wundt attributed the difference to a distinction made by Leibniz (Chapter 3) between simple perception and apperception. When concentrating on the response, the subject merely perceives the stimulus, leading to a quick response. When concentrating on the stimulus, the subject apperceives it, and apperception (or attention) requires an extra 1/10 of a second. Thus, Lange's study led to a third major research area in Wundt's laboratory—attention.

Perhaps Wundt should have taken Helmholtz's experience with reaction times as instructive: Helmholtz abandoned them because of unreliability. "Unfortunately the promise of the method was not realized," Boring (1950) wrote, "for the constancy of the measured times was not great, and later introspection [by Külpe and his followers] showed that in a more complicated reaction the entire conscious pattern is changed and that the alteration is not merely the insertion of another link in a chain" (p. 342). Nevertheless, the recording of reaction times has proved useful in such areas as sensation and perception (e.g., Coren, Ward, & Enns, 1994), intelligence testing (e.g., Vernon, 1987), and cognitive psychology (e.g., Posner, 1978).

Attention. The study of attention accounted for about 10% of the studies in *Philosophische Studien*. In order to appreciate the importance of attention for Wundt, we must examine his system more closely.

For Wundt, there were three mental acts involved in simple reaction time: First, the sensory stimulus enters consciousness (**apprehension**). Next, attention is focused on the sensory impression (**apperception**). Finally, there is a voluntary release of the response (voluntary behavior). Wundt believed that there are two zones of consciousness: The first, larger zone is the background of impressions that have entered consciousness but are not clearly perceived. These impressions are apprehended. The second zone consists of material on which attention is focused, which results in clear perception or apperception. Think of a stage on which a spotlight is trained. At the center of the spotlight, characters and objects are apperceived, whereas the dimly illuminated objects and characters outside the spotlight are merely apprehended.

Wundt assumed that apprehension occurs passively, determined by the actual stimulation and the individual's physiology and experiences. By contrast, Wundt thought of apperception as an act of will, as an active desire to pay attention. You may recall the centrality of the concept of the will in Schopenhauer's philosophy (Chapter 5). Rejecting Schopenhauer's metaphysics, Wundt made the voluntary nature of attention his "paradigm [model or pattern] psychological phenomenon." Because of this, Wundt called his system **voluntarism** and by the end of the century had placed it in opposition to Titchener's **structuralism** (discussed later), a term Wundt never applied to his own psychology (Blumenthal, 1979).

Wundt further held that different rules of organization and combination apply to apprehended and apperceived ideas. Apprehended ideas are organized automatically and mechanically, based on channels carved by experience, whereas apperceived ideas may be combined in novel ways. In other words, a **creative synthesis** of ideas may take place at the focus of attention. Although it has been suggested (see Chapter 4) that Wundt's creative synthesis is related to John Stuart Mill's mental chemistry, Blumenthal (1975) argued against making too much of the relationship.

> Wundt did in his early years make brief, passing references to J. S. Mill's use of a chemical analogy to describe certain perceptual processes. . . . Similarly, the qualities of a perception are not directly given in its underlying elements.
>
> But Wundt points out that this analogy does not go far enough, and by the end of the century he is describing it as a false analogy because the chemical synthesis is . . . wholly determined by its elements while the psychological synthesis is "truly a new formation, not merely the result of a chemical-like formation." . . . What the chemical analogy lacks is the independent, constructive, attentional process which in the psychological case is the source of the synthesis. (p. 1083)

Some of Wundt's students experimentally measured the apperception span to determine the number of stimulus elements that could be clearly fixed in consciousness with a single exposure. Random letters, numbers, or words were flashed briefly on a screen, and subjects tried to recall as many of the stimuli as possible. The number of recalled stimuli generally ranged from four to six, and this was true whether the stimuli were individual letters or familiar words. For example, if the brief stimulus was a four-by-four array of random letters, four to six letters were normally apperceived. However, if the random array consisted of 16 six-letter words, 4 to 6 words were recalled, supporting Cattell's finding that words are treated as wholes rather than as individual letters. Note that this works with *familiar* words; with unfamiliar words, apperception occurs at the level of individual letters.

As Wundt's student, the German-born psychiatrist **Emil Kraepelin** (1856–1926) applied Wundt's attentional theory to schizophrenia, which he called *dementia praecox* (insanity of the young). He considered the abnormal behavior of schizophrenics the result of "flaws in the central control process that may take the form of either highly reduced attentional scanning, or highly erratic scanning, or extremes of attentional focusing" (Blumenthal, 1975, p. 1085). More recently, the importance of defective attention in schizophrenia has been discussed, reviving Kraepelin's analysis (e.g., Silverman, 1964).

Feelings. As we noted above, Wundt divided the contents of consciousness into sensations and feelings. In the 1890s, a great deal of Wundt's research focused on feelings, and an analysis of *Philosophische Studien* reveals that such studies constituted about 10% of the experimental reports.

Based on his own internal perceptions to the clicking of a metronome—an instrument for keeping time in music—Wundt concluded that there are three different dimensions of feelings.

> *Three* such chief directions may be distinguished; we will call them the direction of *pleasurable* and *unpleasurable* feelings, that of *arousing* and *subduing* (exciting and depressing) feelings, and finally that of feelings of *strain* and *relaxation*. Any concrete feeling may belong to all of these directions or only two or even only one of them. (Wundt, 1897; Sahakian, 1968, p. 127, italics in the original)

Figure 7–3 illustrates Wundt's three-dimensional theory of feelings.

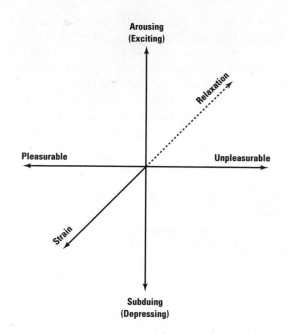

FIGURE 7–3. Wundt's three-dimensional theory of feeling.

Research at Leipzig tried to relate the three dimensions to unique bodily response patterns using the **method of expression**. According to Boring (1950), "there were half a dozen researches on the method of expression, relating changes of pulse, breathing, muscular strength and so on, to correlated feelings. . . . Most of these papers sought to support Wundt's new theory and are now seen, with the theory, to have failed" (p. 343). However, more recent research, using the factor analytic statistical techniques (Chapter 18), has identified dimensions similar to Wundt's. For example, Schlosberg (1954) described three affective dimensions as "pleasantness-unpleasantness," "high-low activation," and "attention-rejection," whereas Osgood, Suci, and Tannenbaum's (1957) three dimensions were "good-bad," "active-passive," and "strong-weak."

Wundt's Students

As we have seen, Wundt's Leipzig laboratory quickly became a busy place, and Wundt directed 186 dissertations, with 116 on psychological problems and the rest on philosophical topics. Although many of Wundt's Ph.D. recipients disappeared into the *Gymnasium* system without affecting psychology, there are still many important names in the roster of Wundt's students.

For example, American visitors to Wundt's laboratory included William James and G. Stanley Hall. Americans who earned a Ph.D. with Wundt included James McKeen Cattell; **Edward W. Scripture** (1864–1945), an early director of the Yale Psychological Laboratory; **Lightner Witmer** (1867–1956), founder of the world's first psychological clinic in 1896 at the University of Pennsylvania (see the March 1996 issue of *American Psychologist* for further information on Witmer and his contributions); and **Charles H. Judd** (1873–1946), a pioneer educational and social psychologist at the University of Chicago. Wundt's important Continental students included Oswald Külpe (Chapter 8); Emil Kraepelin; Hugo Münsterberg; **Theodor Lipps** (1851–1914), best remembered for his empathy theory of aesthetic enjoyment; and Vladimir Bekhterev (Chapter 12). Edward Bradford Titchener was a famous British student.

As you can see from the brief listing of names, Wundt's influence on psychology's development was strong through his students. Although his experimentally trained American students quickly lost most vestiges of whatever version of Wundt's system they were taught, what they brought from Leipzig was an enthusiasm for laboratory psychology and a commitment to psychological research (Benjamin, Durkin, Link, Vestal, & Accord, 1992). Several founded laboratories of psychology, including Cattell (University of Pennsylvania and Columbia University), Harry K. Wolfe (University of Nebraska; Chapter 13), Frank Angell (Cornell and Stanford University; Chapter 11), **George Stratton** (1865–1957; University of California-Berkeley), and Charles Judd (Wesleyan and New York Universities).

The Resurrection of Wundt

Over 2 decades have passed since Arthur Blumenthal began his pioneering reappraisal of Wundt (Blumen-

thal, 1970). Since 1970, Blumenthal (e.g., Blumenthal, 1975, 1979), Wolfgang Bringmann (e.g., Bringmann et al., 1975; Bringmann & Balk, 1992; Bringmann et al., 1980), Kurt Danziger (e.g., Danziger, 1979, 1980), and Thomas Leahey (e.g., Leahey, 1979, 1981) have been instrumental in revising our portrait of experimental psychology's founder.

As we indicated in Chapter 1, the traditional way to view Wundt was as Boring (1950), influenced by Titchener, portrayed him—as an introspectionist primarily concerned with unearthing the elements of consciousness. According to this view, Wundt's work led to the development of structuralism, the school of psychology fleshed out by Titchener, who was responsible for bringing Wundt's psychology to America. Leahey (1981) and others (e.g., Koch, 1992) have written convincingly on the differences between the psychologies of Wundt and Titchener, and we will explore these differences in more detail shortly.

As we indicated, much of Wundt's research did not use introspection, and we have carefully referred to one of his methods as "internal perception" rather than introspection. In fact, Danziger (1980) wrote:

> Wundt would have been appalled to find himself categorized as an "introspective psychologist," not only because of his scorn for the introspectionist tradition, but also because of the implication that the reach of psychology was for him coextensive with the scope of introspection, an inference that was totally at variance with his whole approach to psychology. Quite apart from the ten volumes of his social psychology (*Völkerpsychologie*), his major text of experimental psychology, the *Grundzüge der physiologischen Psychologie*, contains a great deal of psychology that goes well beyond the data provided by experimental introspection. (p. 249)

Further, "Wundt [the introspectionist] became a convenient straw-man for behaviorists who wanted to demonstrate the superiority of their approach" (Brock, 1993, p. 236), and Wundt's modern reappraisal has come with behaviorism's declining influence and the growing importance of cognitive psychology (e.g., Blumenthal, 1975; Danziger, 1979). As Blumenthal put it, "Strange as it may seem, Wundt may be more easily understood today than he could have been just a few years ago. This is because of the current milieu of modern cognitive psychology and of the recent research on human information processing" (p. 1087). By acknowledging that Wundt can be more easily interpreted in the era of cognitive psychology than he could be in a period dominated by behaviorism, Blumenthal's statement may illustrate the "presentist bias" we discussed in Chapter 1—that is, the tendency to reinterpret people from the past in present-day terms.

According to Danziger (1979), at the beginning of psychology's development as a separate science, two models were proposed: First, there was Wundt's model, in which psychology kept at most one foot in the natural science camp. This observes Wundt's distinction between a *Naturwissenschaften* (experimental psychology) and a *Geisteswissenschaften* (social psychology or *Völkerpsychologie*). As we noted in Chapter 5, Johann Gottfried Herder earlier distinguished between *Naturwissenschaften* and *Geisteswissenschaften,* and his belief in the importance of the historical method influenced Wundt's *Völkerpsychologie.*

The main proponents of psychology wholly as a natural science (the second model) were Oswald Külpe, Hermann Ebbinghaus, and E. B. Titchener, men committed to the positivist philosophy associated with Mach and Avenarius. Külpe and his contemporaries aimed for psychology to have a scientific status equal to that of the physical sciences. In order to facilitate this process, Külpe rejected the "psychical individual" as an explanatory principle, opting instead for the "corporeal individual." Psychological explanations should be replaced as soon as possible with physiological explanations (reductionism).

Wundt was adamantly opposed to any positivistic or reductionistic approach that challenged his conception of psychology, arguing insightfully that psychology can be an independent science only if the psychical processes are interpreted in psychical terms, not in physical terms. If the psychical can be interpreted physiologically, then there is no need for an independent science of psychology. Ironically, the same positivist *Zeitgeist* that influenced Wundt's promotion of experimental psychology

also set the stage for behaviorism and its repudiation of Wundt.

Wundt's Legacy

Although first trained in physiology and often employed as a philosopher, Wundt is considered the first modern psychologist. His Leipzig laboratory qualifies as the first experimental psychology laboratory, and he trained many of the first generation of psychologists, several of whom established programs and/or laboratories in which an experimental approach to psychology was taught. Despite its title, Wundt's *Philosophische Studien* was the first experimental journal devoted primarily to psychology. Overlooked for many years, Wundt's surprisingly modern ideas in the *Völkerpsychologie* have been rediscovered with the burgeoning interest in all things cognitive.

Wundt's incredible publication record has been the subject of frequent commentaries, many based on Boring's (1950) analysis. Boring stated that "Wundt's penchant for writing can be statisticized, though one must not lose one's sense of humor in so doing" (p. 345). Boring then noted that "the adding-machine shows that Wundt . . . wrote about 53,375 pages in the sixty-eight years between 1853 and 1920 inclusive. . . . Wundt wrote or revised at the average rate of 2.2 pages a day . . . which comes to about one word every two minutes, day and night, for the entire sixty-eight years" (p. 345).

Cattell suggested the secret to Wundt's productivity in a letter to his parents cited in Bringmann and Balk (1992): "[Wundt] works with great regularity, so in the course of a year accomplishes a great deal . . ." (p. 52). Cattell also contributed to Wundt's output by introducing him to the typewriter, a "new American invention." Although Cattell (1928) later claimed to have given Wundt his typewriter when he left Leipzig, "Wundt had already purchased his own machine in the summer of 1885 . . ." (Bringmann & Balk, p. 53).

Despite all of Wundt's well-documented accomplishments, there were detractors. G. Stanley Hall characterized Wundt's writing style as solid and as lusterless as lead. In a letter to Carl Stumpf (Chapter 8), William James devoted four pages to Wundt, writing that he was trying to be

> a Napolean of the intellectual world. Unfortunately he will never have a Waterloo, for he is a Napoleon without genius and with no central idea which, if defeated, brings down the whole fabric in ruin.

Concerning Wundt and his critics, James wrote:

> Whilst they make mincemeat of some of his views by their criticisms, he is meanwhile writing a book on an entirely different subject. Cut him up like a worm, and each fragment crawls; there is no *noeud vital* in his mental medulla oblongata, so that you can't kill him all at once. (James, 1887; Perry, 1935, Vol. II, p. 68)

In analyzing the quantity of Wundt's writings, Bringmann and Balk (1992) essentially agreed with Boring's (1950) assessment. Their interpretation of Wundt's productivity was more flattering, however. In common with other particularly productive natural and social scientists, Bringmann and Balk noted that Wundt began publishing at an early age (not quite 21), which is comparable with Freud (21), Darwin (22), and Einstein (22). Like other eminent scientists, Wundt had a lengthy period of productivity (68 years), which is actually longer than Darwin (51+ years), Einstein (53 years), and Freud (55+ years). Albert (1975) defined a genius as someone who produces over a long period of time a large body of work, which has a significant influence on many people for many years. By this definition, Wundt was indeed a genius.

We will close our examination of Wundt's contributions to psychology with the words of one of his most famous students—Edward Bradford Titchener (1921):

> I take Wundt to be the first great figure in the history of thought whose temperament—disposition, attitude, habitual mode of approach to scientific problems—is that of the scientific psychologist. . . . I believe that when Wundt's special theories have utterly perished his fame will still endure; it will endure because . . . he established a new point of view and from it surveyed the whole scientific and philosophical domain. In this sense I am prepared to say that

Wundt is the founder, not of experimental psychology alone, but of psychology. (pp. 176–177)

In our continuing examination of scientific psychology's beginnings, we turn to Titchener and the version of Wundt's experimental psychology he brought to America.

EDWARD BRADFORD TITCHENER AND STRUCTURALISM

Edward Bradford Titchener (1867–1927) was born in the Roman-established town of Chichester, which is in West Sussex in the south of England. Titchener (Figure 7–4) was from an old English family steeped in tradition but not wealthy. Titchener's father went to America on an adventure at the time of the

FIGURE 7–4. Edward Bradford Titchener.

Source: From the Collection of Rand B. Evans.

American Civil War, fought with the Confederate army, returned to England, married, sired Titchener, and died while still in his 30s. Fortunately, Titchener's intellectual gifts earned him scholarships first to Malvern College and then to Oxford. At Malvern, he won so many academic prizes that the presenter remarked when Titchener appeared for yet another award, "I am tired of seeing you, Mr. Titchener."

Although his family wanted him to go to Cambridge, the independent-minded Titchener chose Brasenose College, Oxford, instead. During his first 4 years at Oxford, Titchener studied philosophy and the classics. As a temporary devotee of Herbert Spencer (Chapter 9), Titchener was attracted to Darwinian biology and developed an interest in comparative animal psychology. His publication of several articles on the topic is ironic, given his later indifference to animal psychology.

With a firm grounding in British philosophy, Titchener stayed an extra year to learn more science, working as a research student with noted experimental physiologist Sir John Scott Burdon Sanderson (1828–1905). Titchener was impressed with Burdon Sanderson's careful experimental technique and so respected the physiologist that he later dedicated two of his books to him.

Titchener also learned of Wundt's new physiological psychology while at Oxford but received no encouragement from his friends for his idea to go to Leipzig. Undeterred, Titchener translated Wundt's third edition of *Grundzüge der physiologischen Psychologie* into English and took the translation to Leipzig in 1890, only 3 years after the book's publication. However, the fourth edition was nearly finished, so Titchener's translation was obsolete. The same thing happened with the fourth and nearly with the fifth editions; Titchener translated the fourth edition only to learn that Wundt had completed the fifth. Persevering, Titchener translated the first volume of the fifth edition and published it immediately (Wundt, 1902/1904).

At Leipzig in the fall of 1890, Titchener roomed with **Ernst Meumann** (1862–1915), who became an outstanding educational psychologist before his untimely death from influenza. Oswald Külpe was Wundt's assistant, and the Americans there were Edward Pace, Edward W. Scripture, and Frank Angell, with whom Titchener formed a lifelong friendship. The next year the three Americans returned home and were replaced by Lightner Witmer and **Howard C. Warren** (1867–1934), the latter best known as the founder of the Psychological Review Company, which published such journals as *Psychological Review* and *Psychological Bulletin.*

At Leipzig, Külpe was developing his *Grundriss der Psychologie* (*Outline of Psychology*), which we will examine in Chapter 8, and Titchener was involved in its planning. The *Grundriss* was published in 1893, and Titchener translated it into English in 1895 and wrote his own *Outline of Psychology* in 1896. Both Külpe and Titchener were enormously influenced by the recently published works on positivism by the philosopher Avenarius and by the physicist Mach.

After receiving the Ph.D. with Wundt, Titchener returned briefly to Oxford as an extension lecturer in biology, having published 10 biology papers in *Nature* since 1889. Titchener would have liked to establish experimental psychology at Oxford, but the university was not interested in the new discipline. Besides, Titchener had already committed himself to a position at Cornell University in Ithaca, New York. "I remember well the day when Titchener received the call to Cornell; we were in Wundt's lecture hall during the 'academic quarter-hour' waiting for the lecturer, and T. asked me whether Cornell really ranked as a first-class university" (Warren, 1930, p. 451).

Titchener's Cornell offer came by way of Frank Angell, who had returned to America to found a laboratory at Cornell. When he left after a year to go to Stanford University, Angell suggested Titchener as his replacement. Titchener came to Cornell planning to stay just a year or two but stayed instead for the remaining 35 years of his life. In 1917, he rejected what he considered the best position in America, Münsterberg's Harvard professorship. Perhaps he would have gone to Oxford, but the call never came. In fact, it could be argued that German-style experimental psychology was slow to develop in England, although there were exceptions (e.g., James Ward; see Hilgard, 1987).

At Cornell, Titchener patterned his professorial style after that of his mentor. Although Titchener spent only 2 years at Leipzig, and his relationship with Wundt was not particularly close, Boring (1927)—one of Titchener's students—detailed a number of ways in which the pupil came to resemble the master. Like Wundt, Titchener ruled his laboratory autocratically. Also like Wundt, Titchener required his students to maintain a unified front, to work together with him in pursuing his goal of the analysis of consciousness. Like Wundt, Titchener believed in formal psychological apparatus and the need to equip his laboratory with standardized pieces. Titchener adopted the Wundtian practice of using experimental demonstrations in his elementary lectures and of dramatizing his lectures. One dramatic device was to speak in his Oxford master's gown, because it gave him "the right to be dogmatic." Like Wundt, Titchener required his staff to attend the elementary lectures, where they listened "with suppressed excitement to hear how, after some new discovery at Cornell, [Titchener] would alter the familiar treatment of the subject" (pp. 492–493).

Like his mentor, Titchener felt the need for a journal to express his views on what he considered true scientific psychology. Unlike Wundt, Titchener never achieved sole responsibility and ownership of a journal. For many years, he was one of the principal editors of *The American Journal of Psychology,* along with Edmund Clark Sanford (Chapter 10) and the journal's founder, G. Stanley Hall. When **Karl Dallenbach** (1887–1971), one of Titchener's Ph.D. students, bought the journal in 1921, Titchener became its sole editor. In 1925, Dallenbach suggested that the journal might begin to include some dignified advertising. In response, Titchener resigned and was replaced by an editorial board consisting of four of his Ph.D. students.

In 1894, Titchener married Sophie K. Bedlow, and she provided invaluable assistance in his laboratory and with drawings for the books that poured from his prolific pen. As we noted, he translated and published Külpe's *Grundriss* in 1895, his own *Outlines* in 1896, *Primer of Psychology* in 1898, and started work on his monumental *Experimental Psychology,* which was published in four volumes in 1901 and 1905. Also, with assistance, Titchener

translated some of Wundt's books (and subsequent editions) between 1894 and 1902. Meanwhile, he was developing his laboratory and publishing 62 articles between 1893 and 1900 (Boring, 1927). With this record of productivity, Titchener became a full professor in 1895, when he was only 28.

The claim is sometimes made that Titchener was a male chauvinist, yet this is curious given his training and encouragement of female students. Of the Titchener-directed Cornell Ph.D. students in psychology listed in Boring's (1927) tribute, over a third are women, and Titchener's first Ph.D. student was Margaret Floy Washburn (discussed later).

Even before Washburn received her Ph.D., Titchener had shown his support for women in academia by helping **Celestia Suzannah Parrish** (1853–1918) learn about the new experimental psychology. "Parrish persuaded Edward Bradford Titchener, newly appointed Professor of Psychology at Cornell, to accept her as a student in the 1893 summer school. During this summer she also persuaded Titchener to provide her with a tailor-made correspondence course that she could take while teaching at R-MWC [Randolph-Macon Woman's College] that fall" (Rowe & Murray, 1979, p. 282). Parrish established the first psychology laboratory in the South at R-MWC in Lynchburg, Virginia, using the notes she had taken from Titchener as the textbook for her class until 1896, when he published his *Outline of Psychology.* Parrish's first publication in psychology was based on work she did at Cornell in the summers of 1894 and 1895. Parrish moved on from R-MWC to the chair in psychology and pedagogy at the State Normal School, which later became part of the University of Georgia.

The evidence for Titchener's misogynism comes mainly from his founding of **The Experimentalists**, an informal club of psychology laboratory directors. Titchener intended for the men he invited (or whose invitation he approved when the meeting was to be held away from Cornell) to meet annually to discuss their research with each other and with their most promising graduate students. Titchener "wanted oral reports that could be interrupted, dissented from and criticized, in a smoke-filled room with no women present—for in 1904, when the Experimentalists was founded, women were considered too pure to smoke" (Boring, 1967, p. 315). "Trapped by the social norms existing in his time, Titchener did exclude women from the meetings of the Experimentalists but this is something quite different from misogyny" (Evans, 1991, p. 90).

The impetus for The Experimentalists was Titchener's disaffection with the American Psychological Association (APA), founded in 1892 (Chapter 10), and its failure to censure E. W. Scripture for what Titchener considered plagiarism. In 1895, Scripture published a popular introduction to the new experimental psychology in which he closely paraphrased J. E. Creighton and Titchener's translation of Wundt's *Vorlesungen über die Menschen- und Thierseele* (*Human and Animal Psychology*) too closely, according to Titchener. When the APA failed to act, Titchener resigned in protest. Beginning in 1904, The Experimentalists continued to meet throughout Titchener's lifetime, omitting only the war year of 1918. After Titchener's death, The Experimentalists reorganized as The Society of Experimental Psychologists, breaking two of the earlier association's taboos first by permitting the discussion of animal research and then by inviting women. Fittingly, Washburn was the first woman elected to membership. Now more formally organized than when it began, Titchener's creation continues to this day.

Titchener was never fully integrated into American psychology, but the reason for this had more to do with Titchener himself than it did with American psychology. British by birth, Titchener's Leipzig years molded his character to the point where he was often considered a German, once even by a visiting British psychologist. After 35 years in the United States, "his work was generally spiced with German phrases and even German sentences. In fact, Titchener published a German-English dictionary of psychological terms that were essential to the understanding of his writings" (Hindeland, 1971, p. 23). Titchener never became an American citizen, and during World War I, "his 'we' meant Great Britain and his 'you' America" (Boring, 1927, p. 490).

Boring (1927) speculated that Titchener's declining productivity (and perhaps interest) in psychology after 1910 was a response to the loss of external drive.

"It was becoming plain that Titchener would find no one who would carry on his torch as he had been carrying Wundt's, and he always wanted an able successor-disciple" (p. 502). As an alien, he was ineligible for election into the National Academy of Sciences, and, as a "psychologist in the colonies," Titchener never became a Fellow of the Royal Society. Thus, Boring believed that Titchener found it easy to allow himself to be distracted by other interests.

Titchener and his wife were collectors of many things, including live reptiles, and he and "Mrs. Titchener early agreed that the house should be a museum. In it was a place for anything that represented the intimate habits of other times or other peoples; . . . devil's masks and idols, pewter galore and old American hardware, hair wreaths, chest handles, the ancestral furniture and silver—I mention only what occurs to me" (Boring, 1927, p. 495). There was much more, including a collection of semiprecious stones, which Titchener began by giving one to his wife during their engagement. At the time, he overheard someone tell her

> "You had better accept jewelry now because when you marry a college professor he won't be able to give you any more." [Titchener] vowed at that time that whenever he had any supplementary income . . . he would buy her a semiprecious stone for her collection, and he remained true to his word. (Hilgard, 1987, p. 76)

Titchener also developed an interest in Greek and Roman numismatics and in working out the inscriptions on ancient coins. He enjoyed puzzles, and this was a pursuit that allowed him to use his linguistic ability (Thorne, 1996). According to Boring (1927),

> He retained his training in Greek and Latin from the Oxford days, when he studied classics; he used to make up Latin verses for fun. He was most fluent in German, which he read incessantly and could speak well. He also read French constantly, and spoke it well in his younger days. He could read Italian, but used an Italian-German dictionary when he wished to be accurate. . . . He knew some Sanskrit on account of his interest in philology. The numismatics took him into Arabic and even a little Chinese. (p. 503)

Obviously, Titchener was a complex and fascinating individual. Boring (1967) later characterized him as

> brilliant, erudite, kindly, paternal, insultable, flexible yet intransigeant, [someone] whose insistent contradictions were matched only by the ambivalences of his disciples, some of whom ultimately became his hesitant critics and detractors. (pp. 315–316)

In Titchener's structuralism, psychologists of all types found something to criticize.

Titchener's Structural Psychology

When psychologists discuss Titchener's system, they are generally referring to the thoughts in Titchener's 1910 work, *A Text-Book of Psychology*. After 1910, followers and critics alike waited for Titchener's *magnum opus*, finding at his death "only three chapters, and those dealt with general and introductory considerations. The important chapter on method, which was to be the final chapter of the first volume, the *Prolegomena*, was never written and no trace of notes on the other volumes has been found" (Evans, 1972, p. 168). The three chapters were published as *Systematic Psychology: Prolegomena* in 1929. Before exploring how Titchener's system changed, we will first consider its form in the first half of Titchener's career.

Science of the Mind

A reading of Ernst Mach (Chapter 5) laid the foundation for Titchener's conception of science and also for his science of psychology. For Titchener, psychology was the science of the generalized, normal, human, adult mind. He was not interested in abnormal minds, animal minds, the minds of children, or in individual minds—he was interested in mind in an idealized sense. Titchener saw his task as cataloging the elements (the structure) of consciousness, discovering how they are connected, and investigating the underlying physiological processes. Most of his career was devoted to the first chore, the enumeration and description of the components of conscious experience.

As Titchener saw it, Wundt's distinction between immediate experience (direct experience uninfluenced by previous knowledge or instrumentation) and mediate experience (indirect experience that provides the data for the natural sciences) makes psychology's subject matter different from that of the natural sciences. This means that psychology can never be a natural science. Thus, Titchener rejected Wundt's distinction for a position that he felt allowed psychology to be on a par with the other natural sciences.

"All human knowledge is derived from human experience," Titchener (1910, p. 6) wrote, "there is no other source of knowledge. But human experience . . . may be considered from different points of view." Although there are other possibilities, consider the following points of view: One is that an experience is independent of any particular individual—that is, an experience occurs whether or not anyone experiences it. This is the question of a tree falling in the woods: If no ear hears it, does it make a sound? From the viewpoint independent of an experiencing individual (e.g., of physics), the answer is clearly yes. Physics defines sound as transmitted vibrations, which can be detected and recorded even if no ear hears them.

The second viewpoint is that the experience is completely dependent upon an individual. From this perspective, without a conscious mind to perceive it, the claim that the falling tree makes a sound is meaningless. Therefore, the answer to the falling tree question depends on the point of view taken.

As another example, consider the familiar Müller-Lyer Illusion in Figure 7–5. From the point of view independent of an individual, the vertical lines are equal, as shown by a ruler. However, from the perspective of an experiencing individual—your perspective—they appear to be different.

The psychological description in which Titchener was interested is that you see two visual extents, and one is longer than the other. Because you know that the two lines are actually the same length, you might be tempted to describe the illusion as consisting of two equal lines, one of which *appears* longer. In this description, you have mixed the physical and the psychological perspectives. You have committed Titchener's **stimulus error**, which is describing the

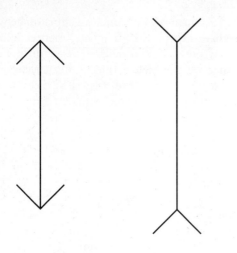

FIGURE 7–5. Müller-Lyer Illusion.

stimulus itself rather than reporting the immediate sensations or feelings the stimulus produces.

Another example that Titchener (1910) used to show the different points of view is that of time. As he put it, "The hour that you spend in the waiting-room of a village station and the hour that you spend in watching an amusing play are physically equal; they measure alike in units of 1 sec. To you, the one hour goes slowly, the other quickly; they are not equal" (p. 7).

To summarize, Wundt had said there were two different kinds of experience, one peculiar to the natural sciences and the other specific to psychology, which for Titchener meant that psychology could never wholly be a natural science. Titchener believed that by insisting on only one kind of experience, viewed from different perspectives, he was ensuring that psychology was a natural science.

Introspection and the Elements of Consciousness

To investigate conscious experiences, Titchener used an "analytical or anatomical introspection. Unlike Wundt's, Titchener's subjects did not just briefly report an experimentally controlled experience, they had to dissect it, attempting to discover the sensation-elements given at that moment in

consciousness" (Leahey, 1981, p. 275). Experience would thereby be reduced to meaningless elements identical with the sensory elements forming the basis of physical science, the difference being in the point of view. Psychology studies the elements in their dependence on a mind, whereas physics studies them independently (Danziger, 1980).

The Basic Elements. Using analytical introspection, Titchener identified three basic elements of consciousness: sensations, images, and affections or feelings. Sensations are the elements of perceptions and are the basis for everything else in the mind. Titchener concluded that there were more than 44,000 different sensations: 32,000+ visual and nearly 12,000 auditory. In keeping with modern research on taste (e.g., see Kalat, 1995), he found only 4 specifiable taste sensations—salt, sweet, sour, and bitter.

Images are the elements of ideas, which arise when a particular sensation has been experienced previously. We can form an image of an apple in the absence of the actual fruit, although the image is less distinct than its template. Similarly, feelings are the emotions' elements. Recall that for Wundt, there were three dimensions of feelings: pleasantness-unpleasantness (pleasurable-unpleasurable), arousing-subduing, and strain-relaxation. Titchener's introspections produced only the pleasantness-unpleasantness dimension.

Attributes. Sensations, images, and feelings all have certain attributes, and, in fact, a mental element does not exist apart from its attributes. According to Titchener, the basic **attributes** are quality, intensity, duration, clearness, and extent. Quality allows us to differentiate sensations, and examples include the "redness" of an apple and the "coldness" of ice. Intensity refers to the strength of an experience: for example, the loudness of a sound or the brightness of a light. Duration is the length of an experience, and clearness refers to how much an experience stands out from the background against which it appears. Extent gives an experience a spatial dimension that tells how "spread out" the image or sensation is.

For sensations and images, all of the attributes apply, except that extent generally applies only to sight and touch sensations. Feelings are accompanied by quality, intensity, and duration attributes but not by attributes of clearness or extent.

Attention. For Wundt, attention was related to apperception, which he saw as an active desire to pay attention. Whatever is at the point of apperception is clearly perceived. Titchener simplified **attention** by making it an attribute of sensations, equating it with clearness. "Where Wundt had explained sensory clarity by appealing to the process of attention, Titchener argued that 'attention' is just a descriptive label given to what we experience with clarity" (Leahey, 1981, p. 275). Because he considered it just a label attached to a clear sensation, Titchener believed attention could not be directly observed. In his system, he first called clearness *vividness* and then later *attensity.*

Meaning. Like attention, meaning cannot be directly observed. In fact, Titchener exhorted his observers to avoid confusing the meaning of a stimulus with the direct experience it produces, and, in this sense, giving the meaning of an observation rather than the immediate experience of it is analogous to committing the stimulus error. Both mistakes come from mixing the physical and psychological points of view.

According to Titchener, "[m]eaning, psychologically, is always context; one mental process is the meaning of another mental process if it is that other's context. And context, in this sense, is simply the mental process which accrues to the given process through the situation in which the organism finds itself" (Titchener, 1910, p. 367). Like attention, **meaning** is something we attribute to our conscious experiences based on the context in which we experience them. A shoulder tap has a different meaning to a person reading a horror novel than it does to the same person at a party. Although the core experience is the same, the different contexts produce different meanings.

Interestingly, Henle (1971) argued that Titchener himself may have committed the stimulus error in his conception of meaning. Using an example

from Titchener's (1915) *A Beginner's Psychology,* Henle identified at least one type of experience as meaningful without the aid of Titchener's context theory, which suggests that other experiences may be similarly meaningful. Perhaps, she concluded, Boring's (1927) attribution of Titchener's declining productivity in later years to a lack of external incentives was incorrect. It is possible that "inconsistencies such as the ones I have mentioned were beginning to arise out of the inadequacies of his approach" (p. 282), were recognized by Titchener, and he chose not to start over.

Changes in Titchener's System

During the second half of Titchener's career, his system changed, although the changes were never systematized in the publication psychologists awaited. Now that we have sketched Titchener's structuralism through the first decade of the 20th century, we can speculate on how it might have looked if Titchener had had the nearly 3 extra decades allotted to Wundt.

As we indicated, by 1915, Titchener's system had just two elements: sensations and feelings. Titchener's thinking on the mental elements continued to evolve, and in a 1923 letter to Boring, "Titchener announced . . . that he was ready to shelve the concept of elements [for] . . . attributive dimensions" (Evans, 1972, p. 172). Thus, images were the first of the mental elements to go, followed by sensations and affections. "So the first level of Titchener's old system reduced to the five dimensions of quality, intensity, protensity [duration], extensity, and attensity, with quality taking precedence over the others" (p. 174). Further, intensity as a dimension separate from quality was suspect. Where would Titchener have gone with this had he lived?

Titchener's questioning even included his introspective method, and he apparently came to believe that a more flexible introspection might be fruitful for studying qualitative dimensions. Perhaps the arduous training of observers was unnecessary. In fact, Titchener (1912) may have been considering a phenomenological approach like that of Stumpf or Husserl (Chapter 8) for the study of consciousness when he wrote: "a roughly phenomenological account, a description of consciousness as it shows itself to common sense, may be useful or even necessary as the starting-point of a truly psychological description" (p. 490).

Actually, the last thesis Titchener edited for publication was a study by F. L. Bixby using a phenomenological methodology (Evans, 1972). Although the method had changed, the subject of study was still the contents of consciousness, however. As we will see in Chapter 14, the phenomenological approach was an important antecedent to Gestalt psychology, but there is no hint before 1925 that Titchener was modifying his negative attitude toward Gestalt psychology. He called it a fad and said in a 1924 letter cited in Evans, "There is really no remedy for all these eccentric movements except time and the general logic involved in the progress of science all round" (p. 178). Still later, after one of Gestalt psychology's founders visited Cornell, Titchener's attitude softened considerably, and he acknowledged that the Gestaltists had done "much good work, and some brilliant work."

Titchener and Wundt Compared

In 1981, Leahey wrote: "It is widely believed by American psychologists that Edward Bradford Titchener was a loyal pupil of Wilhelm Wundt who acted as a kind of English-speaking double for the founder of psychology" (p. 273). Do contemporary psychologists really believe in the similarity of which Leahey spoke? That some still do is evident from the following statement from a recent introductory psychology textbook: "The school of thought associated with Wundt and his student E. B. Titchener is called structuralism, or the science of the structure of the mind" (Pettijohn, 1992, p. 9). Not only are Wundt and Titchener equated, Wundt's school is called structuralism rather than voluntarism, which Wundt used to contrast his approach with Titchener's.

Although voluntarism and structuralism clearly differed both in detail and in substance, it is also apparent that Titchener owed much to his former teacher. In the preface to *Experimental Psychology* (Vol. 1, *Qualitative Experiments:* Part II, *Instructor's Manual*), Titchener (1901) wrote: "My greatest

debt, here as elsewhere, is to Wundt" (p. vii). Continuing, he acknowledged that his system was diverging from Wundt's: "If my recent writing has seemed rather to be directed against Wundtian doctrines, that is but the natural reaction of a pupil who cannot swear to the literal teaching of the Master" (pp. vii–viii). What are some of the major differences between the two systems?

As we noted, Wundt called for two psychologies, one to study lower mental processes (e.g., sensing, feeling) and another to study higher mental processes (e.g., language, thought). Wundt believed that the lower mental processes could be studied experimentally, whereas the higher processes could not. For Wundt, a "complete psychology thus had to include [experimental] psychology as a direct study of outer mental phenomena given in consciousness, and *Völkerpsychologie* as an indirect study of the inner phenomena of mind" (Leahey, 1981, p. 274). By not making Wundt's distinction, Titchener largely deleted the *Völkerpsychologie* from his system. Like Külpe, Titchener made a frontal assault on the higher mental processes, which he viewed as "completely analyzable complexes of conscious sensations to be reduced to their elemental constituents" (Leahey, p. 275).

As noted, Wundt distinguished between immediate experience and mediate experience, whereas Titchener argued that this is but one type of experience viewed from different perspectives. Where Titchener advocated a meaning-free depiction of the elements of consciousness, a structuralism, Wundt stressed the voluntary operation of the mind, a voluntarism. Wundt's voluntarism was particularly evident in his concept of apperception, attention through an act of will. By contrast, Titchener viewed attention as one of the attributes of sensations and images. Instead of an act of will, he saw attention as just a label we apply to anything we experience with clarity.

As we have seen, Wundt's use of internal perception (*innere Wahrnehmung*) was different from Titchener's use of introspection (*Selbstbeobachtung*). Wundt's use of the internal perception method was quite circumscribed, and he would have bristled at the notion that he was an "introspective psychologist," a label that better fit Titchener.

From this description of some of the Wundt-Titchener contrasts, it is evident that the two systems differed significantly, and, given the difference in backgrounds of the two men, it is clear *why* they differed. "Although Titchener studied with Wundt, Titchener's earlier grounding in philosophy in England undoubtedly kept him from absorbing the Wundtian paradigm, and predisposed him to accept the Machian positivism espoused by some . . ." (Leahey, 1981, p. 276). After 2 years with Wundt, Titchener journeyed to America to establish himself, where, faced with a totally new environment, "he reverted to what he knew" (p. 276), which was traditional English psychology.

Titchener's Contribution

Titchener's primary contribution was the strict, empirical, experimental approach he brought to American psychology. More specifically, he wrote *Experimental Psychology,* the first two volumes of which, the *Student's* and *Instructor's Qualitative Manuals,* appeared in 1901. Publication of the *Student's* and *Instructor's Quantitative Manuals* was delayed until 1905 by the 1904 appearance of G. E. Müller's *Psychophysische Methodik* (Chapter 8), which forced Titchener to revise his nearly completed manuscripts. Even with the hasty revision, "Külpe is said to have called them the most erudite psychological work in the English language" (Boring, 1950, p. 413). In relation to the extant psychological literature, "they are encyclopedic, and also astonishingly accurate" (Boring, 1927, p. 497). The books were widely used for decades, and many psychologists who would never have identified with Titchener's structuralism (e.g., John Watson) learned experimental psychology from them.

Titchener's influence was also significant through the large number of Ph.D. students he trained, 56 according to Boring's (1927) listing, including several Oriental students. Some of Titchener's students later rose to prominence in American psychology, and over a third of his Ph.D. students were women, as we noted earlier. In 1950, Boring included Margaret Floy Washburn, Walter Pillsbury, Karl Dallenbach, and John Wallace Baird in his list of Titchener-trained Ph.D. students of importance. We must not forget that Titchener trained Boring himself, the dean of historians of psychology, and J. Paul Guilford (Chapter 18), the famous psychometrician, was one of Titchener's last students.

Titchener's first Ph.D. student, Vassar-trained **Margaret Floy Washburn** (1871–1939), worked briefly with James McKeen Cattell at Columbia before going to Cornell, noted for its liberal stance in admissions. Under Titchener, she became the first woman to earn a Ph.D. in psychology. Washburn (Figure 7–6) remained an active "structuralist" researcher across a career that saw her teaching at several colleges and universities before returning to Vassar in 1903. Her most noted interests included animal motivation (see Chapter 12) and a motor theory of consciousness. Wash-

FIGURE 7–6. Margaret Floy Washburn.
Source: Archives of the History of American Psychology.

burn's honors included being elected APA president in 1921 and being elected to the National Academy of Sciences in 1931. In each case, Washburn was the second woman so honored; Mary Calkins (Chapter 10) was the first.

Beyond his students, Titchener was important for his willingness to argue against findings and theoretical matters that he considered in error. Two controversies will illustrate Titchener's role as a gadfly. The first concerns "imageless thought."

To investigate thought, Oswald Külpe—one of Titchener's friends and teachers at Leipzig—and his Würzburg associates developed an experiment in which observers introspected on the thought processes that occurred when they solved complex problems. Most of the Würzburg subjects reported images and feelings while they performed higher mental activities, but for some, the solutions seemed to appear suddenly in consciousness without images or feelings. They had experienced **imageless thought**, which Wundt and Titchener considered impossible.

Wundt rejected Külpe's results in part because he did not believe that higher mental processes could be studied experimentally. Titchener accepted the experimental study of higher mental processes but rejected the Würzburgers' findings because Cornell researchers always obtained images in their analysis of thought. In other words, he rejected "imageless thought" as an artifact of improper introspection. When introspection was done Titchener's way, images were always obtained. Ironically, by 1915, the year Külpe died, Titchener and the Cornell researchers had abandoned images as a basic element of consciousness (Evans, 1972).

A second controversy was with James Mark Baldwin (Chapter 10). In the discussion of Wundt, we noted that when trained observers attended either to the presentation of a stimulus or to making a response, the sensorial reaction time was about 1/10 second longer than the muscular reaction time, and Titchener agreed with this result. Using untrained observers, Baldwin sometimes observed just the opposite result, finding that the muscular reaction time was longer than the sensorial reaction

time. Further, he accused Titchener of being blind to a fact of nature—the Leipzig/Cornell reaction-time difference depended on trained observers. Titchener responded that his experimental psychology was concerned with the laws of the generalized mind, not with individual minds, and that Baldwin's individual differences led to no general law. The controversy served to further isolate Titchener in America, because one effect of it was that he avoided the *Psychological Review Publications,* which were begun by Baldwin and Cattell.

At a more general level, Titchener's development of structuralism in America was important because it gave competing approaches something to attack. Rebellion is always more effective with something to rebel against, and Titchener provided a convenient target until his sudden death in 1927.

> The death of no other psychologist could so alter the psychological picture in America. Not only was he unique among American psychologists as a personality and in his scientific attitude, but he was a cardinal point in the national systematic orientation. The clear-cut opposition between behaviorism and its allies, on the one hand, and something else, on the other, remains clear only when the opposition is between behaviorism and Titchener, mental tests and Titchener, or applied psychology and Titchener. His death thus . . . creates a classificatory chaos in American systematic psychology. (Boring, 1927, p. 489)

With Titchener's death, structuralism "suddenly collapsed, dwindling rapidly from the status of a vital faith in the importance of consciousness to the equally essential but wholly inglorious state of having been an unavoidable phase of historical development" (Boring, 1950, p. 420).

CONCLUSIONS

Scientific psychology, which began in 1879 with Wundt at Leipzig, arose from physiology and philosophy. Philosophy provided the issues—for example, the nature of perception, the structure of consciousness—and research in the tradition of physiology was used to seek the answers. Wundt converted this from a possibility to an actuality, taking psychology from the philosopher's armchair to the laboratory. Psychology under Wundt became an empirical science, not just in the philosophical sense that Herbart had noted, but in the modern sense of that phrase.

Because of the early dominance of behaviorism in America, we often assume that John Watson (Chapter 12) brought psychology in line with the other, more mature sciences (e.g., physics). In fact, it was Titchener who went beyond Wundt and first argued that the subject matter of psychology is no different in kind from that of physics. The subject matter of both physics and psychology is simply experience. Viewed from the individual's perspective, the experience is psychological, but viewed from a perspective independent of an individual, the experience is physical.

Despite the effects of several phenomenological alternatives that we will consider in Chapter 8, psychology became a positivist enterprise just as Titchener desired. Wundt and Titchener, and whatever common elements of "structuralism" existed between them, formed the first schools of psychology and gave psychology its legacy. Today, psychology remains situated midway between philosophy and physiology, which a cursory glance at modern-day cognitive neuroscience will confirm. In addition, psychology continues to advance as an empirical science, adhering to the methods and conventions—although no longer positivistic—of the wider scientific community. As Koch (1992, p. 8) noted:

> What Wundt effectuated . . . was the stabilization of *a* meaning of a word that had been invited and worked toward over several prior centuries and an arrogation of that "new" meaning to sovereign status relative to all prior usages in the history of thought. Henceforward the core meaning of "psychology" would be dominated by the adjectives *scientific* and *experimental.*

Wundt and Titchener both trained many of the next generation of psychologists. In Wundt's case, his students formed laboratories all across Europe and America, making him in a nontrivial sense the "father" of psychology.

S U M M A R Y

Psychological topics have interested individuals trained in physiology and medicine throughout history. Of the potential "founders" of psychology, all were philosophers and almost all were trained in physiology. Wilhelm Wundt, credited with founding scientific psychology through the establishment of his laboratory at Leipzig in 1879, applied the methods of physiology to philosophical problems.

Wilhelm Maximilian Wundt and Voluntarism

In 1873 and 1874, Wundt published the first edition of *Principles of Physiological Psychology,* in which it was evident that he was seeking to create a new science. Founding his Leipzig laboratory in 1879, Wundt eventually supervised 186 doctoral dissertations. So rapidly did his experimental psychology create new results that in 1881 Wundt started the journal *Philosophical Studies.*

Wundt distinguished between the immediate experience of a stimulus, which provides the data for psychology, and mediate experience, which provides data for physics and other natural sciences. Wundt saw the need for two psychologies: one to study the lower mental processes with the methods of physiology and another to study the products of the higher mental functions, because he thought the higher mental functions could not be studied experimentally. Wundt treated his physiological (experimental) psychology as a natural science, whereas he conceived his indirect study of the higher mental processes as a cultural or mental science. Wundt's work in experimental psychology is better known than the *Völkerpsychologie,* his study of culture and language.

Wundt believed that the basic elements of consciousness were sensations and feelings and that subjects could be trained to report their internal perceptions. Other

Wundt experimental techniques included the recording of reaction times and the method of expression, in which recording devices assessed the subject's physiological changes.

The bulk of the studies done in Wundt's laboratory concerned sensation and perception, reaction times, feelings, and attention. Studies of attention led Wundt to distinguish between apprehension, apperception, and voluntary behavior. For Wundt, the focusing of attention in apperception contained an act of will, and he used the term *voluntarism* to describe his system of psychology. Some of Wundt's students measured the span of apperception, and Emil Kraepelin, a psychiatrist, extended Wundt's attentional theory to schizophrenia.

Based on his own internal perceptions, Wundt developed a three-dimensional theory of feelings: pleasurable and unpleasurable, strain and relaxation, and arousing and subduing. Using the method of expression, Wundt tried to relate the dimensions to specific physiological responses.

Influenced by Titchener, E. G. Boring contributed, along with American behaviorism, to an overly narrow conception of Wundt. In recent years, we have discovered that much of the misinformation about Wundt came from confusing him with Titchener. In addition, Wundt was opposed to a reductionistic approach based on positivism. When behaviorism, by way of positivism, gained ascendancy in psychology, Wundt's contribution was seen as unimportant. With behaviorism's declining influence and the growing importance of cognitive psychology, Wundt has been favorably reappraised. For developing the first laboratory of experimental psychology and training many of the first generation of psychologists, Wundt is honored as the founder of psychology as a separate scientific discipline.

Edward Bradford Titchener and Structuralism

Edward Bradford Titchener was an Oxford-educated Englishman who studied with Wundt for 2 years at Leipzig. Similarities between Wundt and Titchener include the following: Both were autocratic in their laboratories; both required a unified front among their students; both believed in apparatus and used experimental demonstrations in their lectures; and both sought a journal for the publication of their findings. Titchener was long associated with *The American Journal of Psychology*.

For Titchener, psychology was the science of the generalized, normal, human, adult mind, and he spent much of his career cataloging the elements (or structure) of consciousness. Unlike Wundt, Titchener did not distin-

guish between immediate and mediate experience, a distinction that Titchener thought prevented psychology from being wholly a natural science. By insisting on only one kind of experience, viewed from different perspectives, Titchener made psychology a natural science. Describing an experience from the wrong perspective led to the stimulus error, which for Titchener was a description of the stimulus itself rather than reporting the sensations or feelings the stimulus produced.

Using an analytical introspection, Titchener sought to reduce experience to its most basic elements: sensations, images, and feelings. Titchener found more than 44,000 different sensations. For him, images were the elements of ideas, and feelings were the elements of the emotions. Titchener reduced Wundt's three-dimensional theory of feelings to the dimension of pleasantness-unpleasantness.

The basic elements have certain attributes, which Titchener reported to be quality, intensity, duration, clearness, and extent. Quality allows us to differentiate sensations, and intensity describes the strength of an experience. Duration is how long an experience lasts, and clearness indicates how much an experience stands out from its background. Extent gives an experience spatial dimension. For Titchener, attention was equated with clearness, and meaning is something we attribute to our experiences based on the context of the experience.

Over the second half of his time in America, Titchener's system changed, although the changes were not systematized. By 1923, Titchener was ready to abandon the three basic elements of consciousness for attributive dimensions, and he initiated a phenomenological approach to the study of consciousness.

Wundt's voluntarism and Titchener's structuralism were decidedly different. Where Wundt called for separate psychologies to study lower mental processes and higher mental processes, Titchener advocated a frontal assault on both processes. Instead of an act of will, Titchener saw attention as an attribute of sensation. For Titchener, feelings had only one dimension instead of Wundt's three dimensions.

Titchener brought a strict, empirical, experimental approach to American psychology, and his structuralism was important in that it gave other approaches a convenient target. Titchener's style invited controversy. One of his controversies was over imageless thought, and another controversy with James Mark Baldwin served to isolate Titchener further in America.

Titchener's influence was felt through the large number of Ph.D. students he trained. With Titchener's death, structuralism dwindled rapidly in importance.

CONNECTIONS QUESTIONS

1. What are the connections between Wundt and Titchener?
2. How would you contrast the conceptions of psychology held by Wundt and Titchener?
3. Given the differences in the systems of Wundt and Titchener, why was Titchener's structuralism considered to be just an Americanized version of voluntarism for half a century?
4. What evidence would you cite to support the claim that Wundt was the founder of scientific psychology?

5. Based on our description of the systems of Wundt and Titchener, reflect on how a person's definition of psychology both creates and constrains that person's research program.
6. Draw a concept map connecting the major ideas of Wundt and Titchener, and compare your results with one possible solution provided on p. 564.

SUGGESTED READINGS

Blumenthal, A. L. (1975). A reappraisal of Wilhelm Wundt. *American Psychologist, 30,* 1081–1088.

Blumenthal, A. L. (1979). The founding father we never knew. *Contemporary Psychology, 24,* 547–550.

Bringmann, W. G., Balance, W. D. G., & Evans, R. B. (1975). Wilhelm Wundt 1832–1920: A brief biographical sketch. *Journal of the History of the Behavioral Sciences, 11,* 287–297.

Leahey, T. H. (1981). The mistaken mirror: On Wundt and Titchener's psychologies. *Journal of the History of the Behavioral Sciences, 17,* 273–282. In recent years, there has been a "rediscovery" of Wilhelm Wundt and a reappraisal of his contributions. These articles will help you see psychology's "founding father" in this modern light. Leahey's article will help you understand the similarities and differences between Titchener and Wundt.

Boring, E. G. (1927). Edward Bradford Titchener: 1867–1927. *American Journal of Psychology, 38,* 488–506. Written by arguably his most famous student, this obituary of Titchener must be read by anyone interested in learning more about the man.

Danziger, K. (1980). The history of introspection reconsidered. *Journal of the History of the Behavioral Sciences, 16,* 241–262. Danziger's article traces the history of the use of introspection to explore the conscious mind. One particularly important focus is on the differences in the methods used by Wundt and Titchener, even though both are often uncritically called introspection.

Evans, R. B. (1972). E. B. Titchener and his lost system. *Journal of the History of the Behavioral Sciences, 8,* 168–180. What changes in his system was Titchener contemplating in the last 2 decades of his life? This article explores the possibilities.

Evans, R. B. (1991). E. B. Titchener on scientific psychology and technology. In G. A. Kimble, M. Wertheimer, & C. White, (Eds.), *Portraits of pioneers in psychology* (pp. 89–103). Hillsdale, NJ: Lawrence Erlbaum Associates, Publishers. In this reading, Rand Evans, Titchener's biographer, presents Titchener's thoughts on the relationship between scientific psychology and applied psychology in the form of a lecture that Titchener might have given. The sources of Titchener's "address" are a speech to the 1909 Clark Conference, a paper published in a popular magazine, and two letters from Titchener to psychiatrist Adolf Meyer.

Titchener, E. B. (1910). *A text-book of psychology.* New York: Macmillan. This book provides a readable overview of Titchener's psychological system.

Wundt, W. (1904). *Principles of physiological psychology* (5th ed.; Vol. 1; E. B. Titchener, Trans.). New York: Macmillan. (Original work published 1902). Translated by Titchener, this book provides an overview of the scientific psychology created by Wundt. Excerpts are often included in anthologies of readings in the history of psychology (e.g., Dennis, 1948).

Competing Approaches to Psychology's First Schools

Oswald Külpe

Alexius Meinong

Christian von Ehrenfels

Franz Brentano

Edmund Husserl

G. E. Müller

Hermann Ebbinghaus

Carl Stumpf

1800	1810	1820	1830	1840	1850	1860	1870

First steamship crosses the Atlantic

William James is born

Jefferson begins his second term

Hans Christian Anderson publishes his first tales

Slavery abolished in British Empire

William Tecumseh Sherman devastates the South in the Civil War

Charles Babbage builds a calculating machine

In the last chapter, we examined the life and psychology of Wilhelm Wundt, who is credited with founding psychology as an experimental science. From the *Zeitgeist* view of history, the fact that Wundt successfully began psychology as a separate scientific discipline implies that the time was right for its beginning. In this chapter, we will explore further the *Zeitgeist* that produced psychology through an inspection of the efforts of Wundt's contemporaries. What was the atmosphere that facilitated a productive synthesis of physiology and philosophy? If the time was truly right for experimental psychology's founding, who would have filled the void if Wundt had not become a researcher? What would the first psychology have been like?

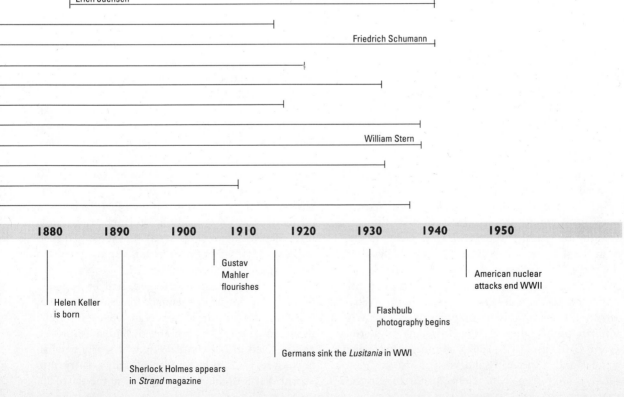

Erich Jaensch

Friedrich Schumann

William Stern

| 1880 | 1890 | 1900 | 1910 | 1920 | 1930 | 1940 | 1950 |

Gustav Mahler flourishes

American nuclear attacks end WWII

Helen Keller is born

Flashbulb photography begins

Germans sink the *Lusitania* in WWI

Sherlock Holmes appears in *Strand* magazine

To answer these questions, we will examine the lives and work of several individuals, all of whom—interestingly enough—may have been more recognized as Germany's leading psychologists than was Wundt at the turn of the century. The most prominent name on this list is that of Franz Brentano, the man who published his system of psychology in 1874, the year that Wundt completed the publication of *Principles of Physiological Psychology*.

FRANZ BRENTANO

Franz Clemens Brentano (1838–1917) was born in Marienburg, Germany, into a family of renown and ability. An uncle was a poet/novelist and a leader in German romanticism, and an aunt was such an imaginative writer that she was known as the "Sibyl of romanticism." Both Brentano's father and mother achieved some stature as writers of religious works (Rancurello, 1968), and a brother, Lujo Brentano (1844–1931), was a prominent pacifist and German political economist.

Brentano's early education came from a Catholic priest hired by his parents. He completed his secondary education at the local *Gymnasium,* where he showed a talent for classical languages and mathematics. After a spiritual crisis, Brentano chose philosophy over mathematics hoping that philosophy could solve his religious quandary. At this point, Brentano decided to become a priest.

After three semesters at the *Lyceum* in Aschaffenburg, Brentano studied successively at the Universities of Munich, Würzburg, and Berlin, as well as at the Academy of Münster, before receiving his doctorate in philosophy from the University of Tübingen in 1862, with a dissertation on Aristotle (Chapter 2). Frederick Trendelenburg (1802–1872), the leading German philologist and Aristotelian philosopher at the University of Berlin; Franz Clemens (1815–1862), another Aristotelian scholar and a modern scholastic at Münster; and Ignatius Döllinger (1799–1890), historian and theologian at the University of Munich, all significantly influenced Brentano.

Brentano became a priest in 1864 and was habilitated (accredited as a university lecturer) as a *Dozent* at Würzburg in 1866 based on his excellent studies of Aristotle's psychology. Brentano was also an outstanding teacher, and his ultimate influence on psychology was at least as great through his students as through his writings. Although he was popular with students, Brentano was less popular with some of the Würzburg faculty. The "liberal circles" saw him as a mystic, a scholastic, and even as a disguised Jesuit and successfully blocked his promotion to professor in 1872 on the grounds that he was a priest. His opponents were undoubtedly pleased when Brentano resigned from the university in 1873 following another religious crisis.

In the 1860s, a split in the Catholic Church occurred over the doctrine of papal infallibility, which is the idea that the Pope is infallible when he defines doctrines of faith or morals from the throne of St. Peter. Asked to perform a comprehensive study of the doctrine, Brentano's highly critical analysis was published before the vote of the First Vatican Council. However, in the summer of 1870, the Council voted 533 to 2 for the doctrine, and after an agonizing 3 years, Brentano resigned from the priesthood and from the University of Würzburg.

With no clerical or university commitments, in 1874 Brentano published the book that established his fame in psychology, *Psychologie vom empirischen Standpunkte* (*Psychology from an Empirical Standpoint*). Also, with Lotze's (Chapter 5) recommendation Brentano secured a professorship at the University of Vienna, which he lost in 1880 because of his marriage to a Catholic (former priests were forbidden to marry in Austria). Brentano returned to the university as a *Privatdozent,* hoping in vain to be reinstated to his former position.

In 1894, Brentano's wife died, and he resigned from the University of Vienna. After leaving Austria, Brentano settled in Florence in 1896. In 1897, Brentano (Figure 8–1) married Emilia Ruprecht, and he lived in Italy until 1915, when, as a pacifist, he moved to Zurich because of Italy's entry into World War I. Brentano died in 1917 at the age of 80.

FIGURE 8–1. Franz Brentano.
Source: Philosophical Library, New York.

Brentano's Psychology

The first half of Wundt's *Principles of Physiological Psychology* appeared in 1873, and Brentano addressed it in his *Psychology from an Empirical Standpoint,* written at the end of 1873 and the beginning of 1874. However, Brentano was not simply motivated by opposition to Wundt. "The real reason behind his work was that he had something worth saying in its own right and he said it when the time was ripe for him" (Rancurello, 1968, p. 14).

Brentano's psychology was empirical primarily in the philosophical sense. He used the empirical method of comparing philosophic insights on a particular topic and then used his experience to try to resolve conflicts. Thus, it was empirical because it was based on experience, but it was not empirical in the sense in which the term is often used—as being experimental. Although Brentano's repeatedly unsuccessful attempts to secure an institute and

a laboratory in Vienna indicate his continuing interest in research, Titchener (1921) was probably correct in asserting that Brentano would not have performed Wundtian-type experiments even if he had had a laboratory.

Brentano intended for his completed *Psychology* to have six "books," the first two of which—"psychology as a science" and "psychic phenomena in general"—comprised the 1874 publication. The other books—which he never completed—"would have investigated 'the properties and laws' of representation . . . , of judgment . . . , and of 'affective and volitional states,' and 'the relationship between mind and body' . . ." (Rancurello, 1968, p. 15).

Act Psychology

For Brentano, psychic phenomena were characterized by their "intentional in-existence" or their "immanent objectivity." Psychic phenomena, or **acts**, are directed toward an object, which then exists within the act. The act has immanent objectivity, that is, contains an object within itself. According to Brentano,

> Every mental phenomenon includes something as object within itself. . . . In presentation something is presented, in judgment something is affirmed or denied, in love loved, in hate hated, in desire desired and so on . . . (Watson, 1979, p. 138)

As a further example, the act of seeing contains within it what is seen. If you see a red patch, seeing is the act, the psychic phenomenon, and the color red is the content. Brentano's psychology was an **act psychology,** whereas Wundt's (and later Titchener's) was a psychology of content. Brentano's act psychology was also a holistic approach (e.g., act of seeing plus what is seen) compared to the elementism (e.g., only what is seen) of Wundt and Titchener.

According to Brentano, the mental acts occur in three main categories: acts of *presentation* (or sometimes *ideating*), acts of *judging,* and acts of *desire* (sometimes *loving* and *hating*). Sensing and imagining are examples of the acts of presentation, and the acts of judging include rejecting, perceiving, and recalling. Examples of the acts of loving and hating include feeling, wishing, and intending. The object of an act may be either a real object, a fictional object (e.g., we can imagine a unicorn), or another act (e.g., we can imagine loving someone or we can reject our feelings).

Brentano's Method. According to Brentano, "Psychology, like the natural sciences, has its basis in perception and experience. Above all, however, its source is to be found in the *inner perception* of our own mental phenomena" (Watson, 1979, p. 139, italics in the original). Like Wundt, Brentano distinguished between inner or internal perception (*innere Wahrnehmung*) and inner observation or introspection (*Selbstbeobachtung*), selecting internal perception as the "primary and essential source of psychology." Danziger (1980) has suggested that Wundt may have adopted Brentano's terminology without giving him credit for it. Nevertheless, Brentano's inner perception method was decidedly different from Wundt's. Although we can direct our full attention to objects perceived externally, this is impossible for objects of inner perception. In the attempt, we change the object of study. Brentano wrote:

> If someone is in a state in which he wants to observe his own anger raging within him, the anger must already be somewhat diminished, and so his original object of observation would have disappeared. (Watson, 1979, p. 140)

If we cannot use inner observation to study mental states such as anger directly, Brentano suggested that we can use our inner perception indirectly:

> It is only while our attention is turned toward a different object that we are able to perceive, incidentally, the mental processes which are directed toward that object. . . . Indeed, turning one's attention to physical phenomena in our imagination is, if not the only source of our knowledge of laws governing the mind, at least the immediate and principal source. . . (Watson, 1979, p. 140)

In addition to the indirect inner perception of our mental phenomena when they occur, we can observe past mental phenomena in memory. If our observation of anger as it occurs diminishes the anger, this is not a problem with anger remembered.

> Furthermore, we could say that it is even possible to undertake experimentation on our own mental phenomena in this manner. For we can, by various means, arouse certain mental phenomena in ourselves intentionally, in order to find out whether this or that other phenomenon occurs as a result. We can then contemplate the result of the experiment calmly and attentively in our memory. (Watson, 1979, p. 141)

A third Brentano method can be called "objective observation." We can observe the "*externalization* of the psychic life of other persons" in their speech, autobiographies, achievements, and voluntary acts. Further, this observation can include the behavior of animals, children, people in primitive societies, the mentally ill, and "the physiological antecedents of our psychic states and outer behavior" (Rancurello, 1968, p. 32). However, lest these "objective observations" be seen as advocating a kind of behaviorism (Chapter 12), Brentano cautioned "that these techniques can never be more than supplemental" (Fancher, 1977, p. 219) to the use of inner perception in adult humans.

Undoubtedly, Brentano's greatest contribution to philosophy and to psychology was his conception of intentionality. **Intentionality** is the defining feature of consciousness—consciousness always intends something—and the act of being conscious of something manifests the property of intentionality. For Aristotelian expert Brentano, the recognition of intentionality as the central element of consciousness represented a restoration of Aristotle's concept of final cause as it underscored the purposefulness of cognitive acts.

Following Brentano, intentionality has been central to the philosophy of mind. Both his students Alexius Meinong and Edmund Husserl further developed the concept, and some modern philosophers of psychology have continued to argue for the centrality of intentionality in this era of cognitive science (e.g., Chisholm, 1981; Searle, 1983).

As psychology has matured, it has become clear that Brentano's general conception of a holistic psychology and his influence through his students were of more importance than the actual details of his system of act psychology. Thus, without further detailing his system, we will review Brentano's influences on the development of psychology as a prelude to our consideration of some of his best-known students.

Brentano's Influence

First and foremost, Brentano had a developed system different from Wundt's—but contemporaneous with it—to which non-Wundtians could turn for support. People who could not accept Wundt's content psychology had the alternative of Brentano's act psychology. By contrast with Wundt the researcher and educator, Brentano was a scholar and teacher. Some of his students of importance for psychology are Carl Stumpf and Edmund Husserl (discussed later), **Christian von Ehrenfels** (1859–1932), and **Alexius Meinong** (1853–1920; founder of the first psychological laboratory in Austria at Graz in 1894). Von Ehrenfels—devotee of Wagner, friend of Freud, and advocate of legalized polygamy (Heider, 1970)—developed the concept of *Gestaltqualität* as an extension of Ernst Mach's (Chapter 5) writings on perception. Meinong and others advanced this idea, which anticipated (or matured into) Gestalt theory (Chapter 14).

Others who found Brentano's system more appealing than Wundt's include Oswald Külpe (discussed later); the American pioneer William James (Chapter 10), a forerunner of functionalism and a friend of Stumpf; and the Gestalt psychologists. As students of Brentano, Husserl and Stumpf were greatly influenced by his descriptive psychology, which Brentano subtitled "descriptive phenomenology" when he taught it in 1888–1889 (Rancurello, 1968). With Goethe (Chapter 5), we defined phenomenology as the study of intact, meaningful experiences, which is precisely what Brentano advocated. Husserl is considered the founder of philosophical phenomenology as a discipline, and both

Husserl and Stumpf clearly influenced Gestalt psychology. As we suggested in Chapter 7, in his later years, Titchener may even have been drifting toward Brentano's phenomenological orientation.

Brentano's view of consciousness as an intentional, goal-directed activity was shared by the functionalists that we will consider in Chapters 10 and 11. Sigmund Freud (Chapter 15) also has been called a functionalist, and as Freud took all his nonmedical courses from Brentano, it should not be surprising to find similarities between the two. Fancher (1977) detailed some important similarities between Brentano's system in 1874 and Freud's metapsychology as revealed in his 1895 *Project for a Scientific Psychology*. Brentano's influence on existential psychology (Chapter 19) will be apparent in our later discussion and has been noted by others (e.g., Gilbert, 1968).

Finally, as the patriarch of the phenomenological alternatives to Wundt that foreshadowed cognitive psychology, Brentano can be credited with at least an indirect influence on the modern study of cognition. In addition, at least one theorist (MacNamara, 1993) has suggested that Brentano displayed a better understanding of cognition than some modern psychologists.

CARL STUMPF

Carl Stumpf (1848–1936) was born in Wiesenthied, a hamlet in the Bavarian province that contains Würzburg. Like Brentano, Stumpf came from an accomplished family. His father was the County Court Physician, his paternal grandfather was a well-known Bavarian historian, and two paternal uncles were active scientists. His mother's family also contained many physicians, and in his autobiography, Stumpf (Figure 8–2) concluded that "it may be that the love of medicine and natural science was in my blood" (Stumpf, 1930, p. 389).

Stumpf and his family were also talented musicians. Stumpf learned to play the violin at 7 and five other instruments "with more or less success." He began composing at 10, and his first work was

FIGURE 8–2.   Carl Stumpf.

Source: Philosophical Library, New York.

an oratorio for three male voices. After a normal elementary and secondary education, he entered the University of Würzburg, with, as he reported, a greater love of music than of learning.

In Stumpf's second semester, Brentano joined the faculty, and Stumpf was captivated by his personality, his teaching, and his style of thinking. Under Brentano's tutelage, Stumpf learned to think like a philosopher. Brentano encouraged Stumpf to take natural science courses, because he considered that the true philosophical method was the same as that for natural science. Working in a chemistry laboratory, Stumpf caused a fire that prompted him to remark later: "I never attained manual cleverness" (Stumpf, 1930, p. 392).

Taking Brentano's advice, Stumpf went to Göttingen to study with Lotze, and he earned his Ph.D. in 1868. Stumpf (1930) noted that Lotze's "mental attitude had greater influence on me than

Brentano really wished" (p. 392). Following graduation, Stumpf returned to Würzburg for further study with Brentano and also to prepare for the priesthood. For Stumpf, just as for Brentano, the controversy over papal infallibility intervened, and Stumpf "took off the black robe."

In 1870, Stumpf continued his friendship with Lotze as an instructor at Göttingen. In addition, he met the two elderly psychophysicists from Leipzig—Weber and Fechner (Chapter 6). At his brother Wilhelm Weber's house, Ernst demonstrated sensory fields on Stumpf's body, and on a field trip to Leipzig, Stumpf and a friend served as subjects for one of Fechner's experiments.

In 1872, Stumpf began work on the origin of space perception that led to his first psychological book *Über den psychologischen Ursprung der Raumvorstellung* (*On the Psychological Origin of Space Perception*). Stumpf's theory was nativistic, and he "argued that both color and extension are equally primitive part-contents of visual sensation" (Boring, 1950, p. 363). The book came at a good time, and with Lotze's and Brentano's recommendations, Stumpf secured a professorship in philosophy at Würzburg. Unfortunately, Stumpf found that he was essentially the whole department of philosophy.

In 1875, Stumpf began work that combined his interests in music and psychology and resulted in the publication in two volumes in 1883 and 1890 of *Tonpsychologie* (*Tone Psychology*). Between 1873 and 1894, Stumpf went from Würzburg to Prague to Halle to Munich, and then finally to Berlin. At Prague, he was stimulated by contact with Ernst Mach and Ewald Hering (Chapter 6) and by a visit from William James, with whom he began a correspondence that lasted until James's death.

In 1890, while at Munich, Stumpf began a quarrel with Wundt by criticizing the work on tonal distances of one of Wundt's students. Wundt quickly made the controversy personal, spicing his comments "with the most scathing invectives" (Stumpf, 1930, p. 401). Stumpf based his argument on his superior musical knowledge, whereas Wundt relied on laboratory results with apparatus and psychophysical methods. In the end, Stumpf concluded that he must have been correct because the offending experiments were never mentioned again, except in Wundt's textbook. "Wundt's methods . . . had been repellent to me since his Heidelberg days, . . . although I admire his extraordinary breadth of vision and his literary productivity, even in his extreme old age" (Stumpf, 1930, p. 401).

At Berlin, Stumpf was at the peak of German psychology, in a position that might more properly have gone to Wundt as Germany's senior psychologist. Stumpf's productivity dramatically increased as his inherited laboratory grew into a large and important institute, and the demands on his energies drew him into many activities. For example, in 1900, he founded the Archive for Phonograms, which made recordings of primitive music, but much of the credit for developing this archive belongs to his student, Erich von Hornbostel (1877–1936). In the same year, Stumpf and a school principal began the Berlin *Gesellschaft für Kinderpsychologie* (Society for Child Psychology). Through the Society, Stumpf hoped to encourage the study and observation of the mental life of the child. Stumpf kept a careful record of his own children, and he often studied child prodigies.

In 1904, Stumpf was involved in the celebrated case of Clever Hans (discussed later). Stumpf served as Rector of the University of Berlin in 1907–1908, and the position gave him access to "the leading personalities of all circles," including Kaiser Wilhelm II. In 1909, Stumpf represented the University at the centenary of Darwin's birth at Cambridge. "[T]he idea of evolution had been bred in my very bones— as was the case with all my contemporaries" (Stumpf, 1930, p. 409). In Chapter 9, we will examine Darwinian evolution and the *Zeitgeist*, noted here by Stumpf, that favored its acceptance.

In 1913, Stumpf was asked to select someone to head an anthropoid (ape) research station on Tenerife, an island off the west coast of Africa. He suggested a former student, Wolfgang Köhler (Chapter 14), who was successful in his investigations and eventually succeeded Stumpf as Director of the Berlin Psychological Institute.

During World War I, although Stumpf was heavily involved in organizing German psychologists for the war effort, he admitted that the German psychologists' cooperation was not as great as that of the Americans. However, in the recording "of the native dialects, songs, and other musical productions of the prisoners-of-war . . ." (Stumpf, 1930, p. 410) from all over the world, Stumpf felt that Germany had surpassed other countries. Again, we see Stumpf's interest in music.

Stumpf retired in 1921 but continued lecturing until 1923. He also continued his research in tone psychology until he was well into his 80s, and a former student noted that it "was rather impressive to see the old gentleman well over eighty come from time to time to the institute . . . to make personal observations on the elaborate instrument he had built for the synthetic production of vowels" (Lewin, 1937, p. 190). Stumpf died on Christmas Day in 1936.

Stumpf's Psychology

As Brentano's student, Stumpf developed within an atmosphere of rigorous philosophy that culminated with Husserl's phenomenology. Stumpf's own focus concerned the classification of experience. Stumpf's first class of experiences was that of phenomena such as tones, colors, and tastes, which comprise sensations and images. Appropriately, Stumpf called the study of such phenomena as sensations and images "phenomenology." Stumpf considered the study of phenomena to be preparatory to the study of the second class of experiences—the functions. Stumpf's functions were Brentano's acts, such things as perceiving, grouping, and willing. "Observation of the functions is the foundation of the mental sciences . . ." (Stumpf, 1930, p. 424). Stumpf devoted most of his career to his phenomenology, which, like Husserl, he considered antecedent to the real work of psychology.

Stumpf and Clever Hans

Owned by Herr von Osten, a former mathematics teacher, *der kluge Hans* (**Clever Hans**) was ostensibly a horse genius. Hans was actually Hans II, Hans I having died before attaining the abilities of his successor (Candland, 1993). Hans had apparently been taught to perform mathematical calculations and to read and spell, answering questions put to him by tapping his hoof or by pointing his head toward an appropriate card or object. Hans's apparent intelligence was considered important support for the continuity of mental ability stressed by Darwin's theory of evolution. Hans and von Osten are shown in Figure 8–3.

As the Director of the Psychological Institute at the University of Berlin, Stumpf was included on a commission charged with investigating Hans's abilities. In 1904, the commission concluded that in all likelihood Hans was not being intentionally aided by von Osten. Additionally, the commission could not determine any unintentional cueing, and Stumpf selected his student **Oskar Pfungst** (1874–1932) to assist him in further investigating Hans. The series of experiments Pfungst conducted represent "the first application of sophisticated methods to the study of animal behaviour . . . and read, even now, like a textbook illustration of how to apply experimental methods to a psychological problem" (Boakes, 1984, p. 78).

After determining that Hans could correctly answer questions asked by people other than his owner, Pfungst then had a questioner present items to Hans for which the questioner either knew or did not know the answer. Pfungst found that Hans correctly answered the questions over 90% of the time in the "tester-with-knowledge" condition but no more than 10% of the time when the tester did not know the answer. Somehow a tester who knew the correct answer was giving Hans that information. Note that Pfungst's "tester-without-knowledge" condition possibly represents the first use of something like a double-blind procedure to control for experimenter effects.

With "keen eyes and iron patience" (Stumpf, 1930, p. 407), Pfungst discovered that questioner movement was the key: "von Osten would make a barely discriminable downward movement when the horse began tapping and an equally small upward jerk when the correct number had been reached" (Boakes, 1984, p. 79). Other movements that would

FIGURE 8–3.   Testing Clever Hans.
Herr von Osten is the gentleman with a full beard wearing a long coat and a light-colored hat.
Source: Archives of the History of American Psychology.

cue Hans to stop tapping included slight motions of the eyebrows and even dilation of the nostrils.

Once he knew Hans's "secret," Pfungst was able to demonstrate the same phenomenon in the laboratory with himself as the horse. Including a young psychology student named Kurt Koffka (Chapter 14), subjects were asked to think of a number and Pfungst then tapped it out with his hand, stopping when he saw the kind of signal Hans had responded to. Unaware of having cued Pfungst, many of the subjects saw the test as an effective demonstration of mind reading.

Although Pfungst did not fully appreciate them, a number of important learning phenomena were demonstrated in the study of Clever Hans. At first, von Osten rewarded Hans for each correct response, but as the horse became more proficient, he was rewarded for a gradually decreasing proportion of successful responses. This anticipates B. F. Skinner's (Chapter 13) work on partial reinforcement by several decades.

Pfungst's laboratory modeling of Hans's behavior enabled Pfungst to demonstrate what has since been called "conditioning without awareness." Pfungst told a subject to think of "left" or "right" in any order, and Pfungst would try to indicate the subject's thought by lowering his arm if the thought was "right" or raising it if the subject was thinking "left." After several trials, Pfungst found that the subject began to raise his eyes when thinking "left" and lower them when thinking "right." The subject had apparently learned to anticipate Pfungst's arm movements, upward to "left" and downward to "right."

> Afterwards the people taking part in these experiments reported that they had simply tried to imagine the objects; they claimed that they never thought about the related arm movement of the experimenter and were completely unaware of the changes that had occurred in their own behaviour. (Boakes, 1984, p. 80)

Herr von Osten, Hans's owner, was apparently blameless in the episode, believing unconditionally in his horse's reasoning capability. He was deeply disturbed by Pfungst's findings and died within a few months of the publication of *Clever Hans (The*

Horse of Mr. von Osten) by Pfungst (1911/1965). Pfungst's fine research was not even rewarded with a degree (Candland, 1993).

Stumpf's Influence

Like Brentano, Stumpf's greatest legacy was his students. Unlike the authoritarian Wundt, Stumpf took a less directive approach in assigning research topics. As he wrote at the end of his autobiography,

> I have never endeavored to found a school in the strict sense; and have found it almost pleasanter, certainly more interesting, to have my students reach different conclusions than to have them merely corroborate my theorems. I derive all the more joy and gratitude from the loyalty of the young people who, in the same scientific spirit, but by their own independent plans, continue the work of research. (Stumpf, 1930, p. 441)

This style is corroborated by one of the last of his students, Kurt Lewin (Chapter 14).

> Stumpf gave his students an unusual amount of freedom. For example, I selected my topic for a thesis and it was presented to Stumpf by the assistant while I waited in another room. The assistant came out to tell me that the topic was accepted and during the next three or four years I spent on this work, I do not remember having ever discussed the matter with Stumpf previous to my final presentation. . . . In respect to the guidance of students, as in most points, Stumpf's views were quite different from those of Wundt whose name was nearly taboo in the Berlin Institute. (Lewin, 1937, pp. 193–194)

Stumpf's influence was most evident on the men who made his rather than Husserl's phenomenology the basis for Gestalt psychology, and we can view Stumpf as an important link between Brentano and Gestalt psychology. Two of Gestalt psychology's three founders, Kurt Koffka and Wolfgang Köhler, took their Ph.D.s with Stumpf, and the man often listed as the fourth major Gestalt psychologist, Kurt Lewin, did also. As we noted, Köhler succeeded Stumpf at Berlin when the latter retired, and "the center for the new Gestalt school was seen to be where Stumpf's laboratory had been" (Boring, 1950, p. 370). Stumpf "remained a psychological theorist who formulated a system of act psychology friendly to experimentalism, and a student of the psychology of music" (p. 371).

Never a large subfield, the psychology of music is still being studied (e.g., Handel, 1989). Although Stumpf is recognized as the area's pioneer, other important early contributors included **Carl Emil Seashore** (1866–1949), the 1911 president of the American Psychological Association, who worked primarily at the University of Iowa.

EDMUND HUSSERL

Edmund Gustav Albrecht Husserl (1859–1938) was born in Prossnitz, Moravia, then part of the Austro-Hungarian Empire and today a province within the Czech Republic. At 17, Husserl began his higher education at the University of Leipzig, where he studied under Wundt. After 2 years, Wundt had failed "to make any special impression on him" (Misiak & Sexton, 1966, p. 406), and Husserl went to Berlin. First at Berlin, then at Vienna, Husserl studied mathematics, completing his degree in 1883. He returned to Berlin, where he briefly taught mathematics before moving to Vienna to study logic with Brentano.

Husserl remained a lifelong friend of Brentano, and it was Brentano who suggested that he should work with Stumpf at Halle. Although Husserl considered Brentano his "one and only teacher," Husserl completed his philosophy degree as Stumpf's first graduate student.

Husserl's career as a philosopher of psychology began with his appointment at Halle in 1887. After 14 years at Halle, Husserl moved to Göttingen, where he taught until 1916. During his lifetime, phenomenology "was in the air, and so were Husserl's views" (Boring, 1950, p. 368). His Göttingen colleagues, David Katz and G. E. Müller (both discussed later), as well as Alexius Meinong and Carl Stumpf, all held similar phenomenological views about how to progress in psychology. In addition, through either Husserl or his friend Karl

Bühler (Chapter 14), phenomenology's influence spread to Külpe's Würzburg laboratory. Although there were differences between the various "phenomenologies," Husserl's system was largely victorious, and it remains an active, although uncommon, approach to psychology today (e.g., Buytendijk, 1959; Giorgi, 1970; Spiegelberg, 1960).

In 1916, Husserl moved to the University of Freiburg, where he retired in 1929. Although he was a Lutheran, Husserl had been born a Jew, and in 1933 the Nazis stripped him of his titles and forbade him to lecture or to attend any academic conferences.

Husserl's Freiburg chair passed to Martin Heidegger (Chapter 16), his best-known pupil, and a man considered along with Ludwig Wittgenstein (Chapter 20) one of this century's most important philosophers. Husserl was clearly at the center of an important and far-reaching philosophical movement, and his impact on psychology (more indirect than direct) should not be underestimated.

Edmund Husserl (Figure 8–4) died in 1938, undoubtedly frustrated that large quantities of his own work remained unpublished or untranslated. His personal library was considered such a fine collection that his wife Malvine went to great lengths to keep it from the Nazis as she fled. After failing to get nuns to transport the material across the Swiss border, Malvine convinced Belgium's prime minister to declare the material Belgian property. Fortunately, she and most of Husserl's books and papers escaped to Belgium, and much of the material can be found at the Husserl Archives in Louvain, Belgium.

Husserl's Phenomenology

The term *phenomenology* may be among the most misunderstood words in the history of psychology. Hegel's most important work, *The Phenomenology of Mind,* popularized the concept, and we first indicated that it is the study of intact, meaningful experiences in our discussion of Goethe. For Husserl and his contemporaries, the term had a more circumscribed and technical meaning, however. Heidegger, and many other philosophers and psychologists in the generation after Husserl (e.g., the

FIGURE 8–4.   Edmund Husserl.
Source: Philosophical Library, New York.

Gestalt psychologists), shaped the term into the meaning that it carries for most modern-day philosophers and psychologists.

According to Husserl, **phenomenology** is the science of examining the data of conscious experience. As such, phenomenology seems neither overly complex nor unrelated to psychology, as critics have argued. In fact, Husserl's understanding of phenomenology closely resembles William James's conception of psychology, and several publications have explored the similarity between Husserl, phenomenology, and James (e.g., Edie, 1987; Linschoten, 1968; Stevens, 1974; Wilshire, 1968).

Despite this similarity with James, Husserl did not see phenomenology as a type of psychology, but as a separate science, which logically came before psychology. Husserl's critics have made much of this "separateness" and have used Husserl's own

words to argue that he should be of no interest to psychologists (e.g., Jennings, 1986; see Henley, 1988, for a reply).

Husserl's phenomenology first appeared in earnest with the publication of *Logical Investigations*. A popular variation of this work was published in 1913, with an English translation in 1931 known as the *Ideas* (Husserl, 1913/1931). Husserl also wrote the phenomenology entry for the *Encyclopedia Britannica*, which is considered one of the finest presentations of phenomenology.

Husserl set the stage for his phenomenology by examining many of the philosophers we have reviewed. According to Husserl, beginning with Descartes, the history of philosophy and of psychology can be viewed as an attempt to find a suitably scientific system to structure further inquiry. Tracing the search through the works of Brentano and Stumpf, Husserl concluded that phenomenology was the appropriate system.

Husserl's phenomenology can be seen as a methodology for further inquiry into the structure and content of conscious experience. Husserl's system has several "steps," with the most essential being **description**, which involves intense concentration on, analysis of, and the depiction of a given phenomenon. Thus, careful description became central to Husserl's program, and it remains the primary feature of modern-day phenomenological psychology (e.g., Pollio, Henley, & Thompson, in press).

Another important step in Husserl's system is *Wesensschau*, or the cognition of essence. *Wesensschau's* purpose is to apprehend something's essence through a consideration of phenomena. For example, looking at many green objects leads to the apprehension of greenness or color. Both *Wesensschau* and Husserl's notion of intentionality continue to be popular in various philosophical theories of perception and other mental events (e.g., Føllesdal, 1974).

Although Husserl was a logician and a philosopher, the relation between phenomenology and psychology is central to most of his later writings. In fact, from his day until this, psychological philosophers have made the most use of Husserl's work. Husserl was critical of positivism (Chapter 5) and of the sort of "mechanistic" psychology that endorsed it (e.g., associationism and behaviorism). Similarly, he was never impressed with Wundt's efforts or with Wundtian-style empirics.

For Husserl, phenomenology and psychology should be mutually beneficial enterprises. Phenomenology offered psychology a methodology for analyzing the data of consciousness and a structured program to guide the analysis. In turn, psychology was expected to provide new discoveries and factual data about the nature of conscious experience that could be used to refine phenomenology further. Examples of contemporary studies linked to Husserl's approach include topics such as learning and memory (e.g., Giorgi, 1989) and consumer behavior (e.g., Thompson, Locander, & Pollio, 1989).

More than a particular philosophical methodology, phenomenology represented a statement about how psychology should progress and what should count as its proper subject matter. Despite the efforts of various "phenomenological" contingents (e.g., the Gestaltists, James, the Würzburgers), no version of phenomenology ever became dominant in psychology. In fact, over Husserl's admonitions, Wundt's empiricism and positivistic forms of associationism and behaviorism gained center stage in the new science of psychology.

Husserl's Influence

Without being dominant, the phenomenological tradition in psychology was, and remains, influential. We have noted Husserl's impact on such contemporaries as Katz and Bühler, and through them on the Gestaltists and the Würzburgers, respectively. We have also mentioned the similarity between Husserl and James and have made connections to important philosophers, such as Heidegger. Through the French psychologist Maurice Merleau-Ponty, we can trace a direct connection between Husserl and much of modern-day phenomenological psychology (e.g., Pollio, 1982). In Chapter 16, we will examine further the connections between later phenomenologists like Merleau-Ponty and existentialists such as Jean-Paul Sartre, with "humanistic" psychology.

Although there are significant differences between Husserl's phenomenology and cognitive

psychology, Dreyfus (1982) suggested that without Husserl modern-day cognitive science might not exist. According to Dreyfus, Husserl anticipated several concepts pivotal to cognitive psychology, particularly issues concerning the nature and structure of mental representations. As we noted, Husserl's views on perception and conception have remained popular among philosophical psychologists, many of whom helped start the "cognitive revolution" we will explore in Chapter 20.

From Brentano and his students, we move to a psychologist who did his most important work outside the university system, using himself as his only subject. Despite its limitations, the work of Hermann Ebbinghaus remains as relevant today as it was over a century ago.

HERMANN EBBINGHAUS

Hermann Ebbinghaus (1850–1909) was born in Barmen, near Bonn, the son of a wealthy merchant. Ebbinghaus attended the Barmen *Gymnasium* and then went to the University of Bonn at 17. Planning to study history and philology, over the next 3 years Ebbinghaus spent time at Halle and Berlin. At Berlin, philosophy became his major interest.

In 1873, following a brief tour with the Prussian Army in the Franco-Prussian War, Ebbinghaus obtained the Ph.D. degree with a dissertation on Eduard von Hartmann's (1842–1906) influential *Philosophie des Unbewussten* (*Philosophy of the Unconscious*), published just 4 years earlier. Ebbinghaus spent the next 7 years in independent study, first in Berlin, where he read science in keeping with the academic tradition of the time. From 1875 to 1878, Ebbinghaus traveled in France and England, studying and tutoring. In a used bookstore in London—not Paris as reported in E. R. Jaensch's obituary of Ebbinghaus (Traxel, 1985)—he purchased a copy of Fechner's *Elements of Psychophysics*. Its effect on him was so great that Ebbinghaus dedicated a 1902 book to Fechner, saying "*ich hab' es nur von Euch*" (I owe everything to you).

Ebbinghaus was impressed by the advances Fechner made in studying sensation and perception with his psychophysical methods, and he was convinced that he could use similar methods to study the higher mental processes that Wundt had said could not be studied experimentally. Thus, he undertook the study of memory, a problem he had gotten from the British associationists. In this, he was treating psychology as *Naturwissenschaft* (natural science), something he did throughout his career (Shakow, 1930) and something that led him into controversy with famed philosopher Wilhelm Dilthey (1833–1911), a former teacher.

Converted to psychology early, Ebbinghaus essentially abandoned philosophy in order to make psychology a quantitative natural science. By contrast, Dilthey argued that the "new" psychology—apparently meaning Herbart's psychology—could never be more than descriptive, and the mind could not be analyzed. Ebbinghaus responded in part through his use of laboratory methods to study memory successfully. In this, Ebbinghaus was also showing that higher mental functions could be investigated directly and that Wundt's *Völkerpsychologie* was not the only approach to their study.

In 1880, Ebbinghaus was habilitated as an instructor at Berlin, and in 1885, he published the results of his studies of human memory in *Über das Gedächtnis: Untersuchungen zur experimentellen Psychologie* (*Concerning Memory: An Investigation in Experimental Psychology*). Shortly thereafter, Ebbinghaus was promoted, and, probably in the late 1880s, he founded the laboratory that Stumpf took over when he moved to Berlin in 1894. Shakow (1930) noted that Ebbinghaus's Berlin laboratory was probably the third in Germany, after Wundt's at Leipzig and G. E. Müller's at Göttingen.

One of Ebbinghaus's most significant contributions to psychology occurred in 1890, when he and the physicist Arthur König founded the *Zeitschrift für Psychologie und Physiologie der Sinnesorgane* (*Journal of Psychology and Physiology of the Sense Organs*). The cooperating editors included Helmholtz, Hering, Müller, and Stumpf, and the journal represented a German alternative to Wundt's *Philosophische Studien*. The journal is still being published as *Zeitschrift für Psychologie,* and a 1985 volume celebrated the centennial of the publication of Ebbinghaus's *Über das Gedächtnis* with a variety of papers on Ebbinghaus and his legacy.

In 1894, Ebbinghaus was passed over for promotion to professor at Berlin, probably because of his dearth of publications, and Stumpf got the position. Ebbinghaus departed for a professorship at the University of Breslau. In Breslau, Ebbinghaus was on a commission charged with testing school children to see if their mental prowess declined over the 5-hour school sessions. Although the central question got lost, the "Ebbinghaus Completion Test" proved useful for measuring general intellectual ability. For example, a child might be asked to complete the statement, "Children are _____ than their parents," with both the accuracy and speed of the child's answer important in scoring. Performance was highly correlated with the students' ranks in class, an indication of the test's potential for measuring intelligence. Partly because of the success of the Ebbinghaus Completion Test, Alfred Binet (Chapter 18) later used similar tasks in developing the first intelligence tests.

In 1902, Ebbinghaus published *Grundzüge der Psychologie* (*Principles of Psychology*), which was an immediate success, primarily because of its readability. Demands for revisions came soon after the book's publication and continued after Ebbinghaus's death, with first E. Dürr doing the honors and then Karl Bühler after Dürr's death.

Abriss der Psychologie (*Outline of Psychology*), a brief sketch of psychology that opens with Ebbinghaus's famous line, "Psychology has a long past, but only a short history," was published in 1908, and it too was successful. The book averaged a new edition every 2 years through its eighth edition in 1922.

By all accounts, Ebbinghaus was an exceptional lecturer. "His ever-youthful personality, his natural humor, and the unusual clarity and ease of his presentation assured him of an overflowing audience and of considerable influence on his auditors" (Shakow, 1930, pp. 507–508). According to Schwartz (1986), Ebbinghaus was also well liked as a person. Given his obvious attractiveness, it is perhaps surprising that there were so few "Ebbinghausians." In his obituary of Ebbinghaus, E. R. Jaensch

(1909) accounted for the lack of disciples by writing that Ebbinghaus had no desire to create them.

Two of the better-known people who worked with Ebbinghaus were William Stern and William Lowe Bryan. One of Ebbinghaus's Ph.D. students, **William Stern** (1871–1938) made important contributions in cognition, developmental psychology, applied psychology, and individual differences. His suggestion for dividing mental age by chronological age as a measure of intelligence was adopted by Lewis Terman for the Stanford-Binet test (Chapter 18). **William Lowe Bryan** (1860–1955) worked with Ebbinghaus in Berlin for a year, subsequently earned his Ph.D. with G. Stanley Hall (Chapter 10), and later worked with Külpe at Würzburg. An APA president, Bryan was a longtime president of Indiana University, where he established the oldest continuing psychological laboratory in the United States.

In 1905, Ebbinghaus (Figure 8–5) went from Breslau to Halle. In 1909, he developed pneumonia and died unexpectedly at 59. R. S. Woodworth (1909) expressed the feelings of many when he wrote:

> The sudden death, on February 26 . . . of Dr. Hermann Ebbinghaus . . . is felt as a severe loss throughout the psychological world, for few psychologists were more international in their reputation and sympathies. Nowhere, perhaps, will the loss be keener felt than on this side of the water, where his work has long been held in high esteem, and where his great book, the "Grundzüge der Psychologie," is by many regarded as the best general treatment of the subject. (p. 253)

Although the *Grundzüge* was an excellent general treatment of psychology, the work for which Ebbinghaus is justifiably famous is his work on memory.

Ebbinghaus's Memory Research

Following Fechner's lead, Ebbinghaus decided that objective research methods were needed to study memory, and he also believed that simplification of psychological problems was essential. His greatest simplification was an invention that would have the

FIGURE 8–5. Hermann Ebbinghaus.
Source: Archives of the History of American Psychology.

characteristics of a word without being contaminated by previous experience. Ebbinghaus's invention is often called the **nonsense syllable**, or **CVC trigram** (two consonants with a vowel between). However, the actual term Ebbinghaus used to refer to his material was "*sinnlose Silben,*" which literally means "meaningless syllable," and even this may be a misnomer because in one passage Ebbinghaus (1885/1964) wrote: "the differences between sense and nonsense material were not nearly so great as one would be inclined a priori to imagine" (p. 23). Although Ebbinghaus gave no examples, his "meaningless syllables" have been found in archival material (Hoffman, Bringmann, Bamberg, & Klein, 1987). According to Hoffman et al.,

> [Ebbinghaus] first prepared a pool of 2300 syllables, but these were not consonant-vowel-consonant trigrams, as is reported in most history of psychology texts. . . . The stimuli

were syllables, but quite a few were words or were at least very word-like. Here are some examples: *heim, beis, ship, dush, noir, noch, dach, wash, born, for, zuch, dauch, shok, hal, dauf, fich, theif, haum, shish,* and *rur.*[2] In discussing the materials, Ebbinghaus referred to their simplicity or homogeneity and to the ease with which they could be systematically varied, but not to their "meaninglessness." (pp. 66–67, italics and footnote in the original)

Many texts report that Ebbinghaus invented the nonsense syllable, because Ebbinghaus wrote that he constructed his syllables by placing a vowel sound between two consonants. His footnote specifying the vowels and consonants explains why some of the syllables unearthed by Hoffman et al. (1987) consisted of more than three letters.

The vowel sounds employed were a, e, i, o, u, ä, ö, ü, au, ei, eu. For the beginning of the syllables the following consonants were employed: b, d, f, g, h, j, k, l, m, n, p, r, s, (= sz), t, w, and in addition ch, sch, soft s, and the French j (19 altogether); for the end of the syllables f, k, l, m, n, p, r, s, (= sz), t, ch, sch (11 altogether). For the final sound fewer consonants were employed than for the initial sound, because a German tongue even after several years practice in foreign languages does not quite accustom itself to the correct pronunciation of the mediae at the end. (Ebbinghaus, 1885/1964, p. 22)

G. E. Müller and F. Schumann later made the rules for constructing nonsense syllables even more explicit. In a review of their work, Bergström (1894) indicated that the following rules were used:

The seventeen initial and twelve end consonants, and the twelve vowels and diphthongs used were written on cards and placed in three boxes. A syllable was made by taking one card haphazard from each box. Since [Müller and Schumann] only used twelve syllable series, this method enabled them to construct . . . normal series, each of which has the following properties: All initial and end consonants and vowels are different. The initial consonant is not the same as the end consonant of the preceding syllable, or the end consonant of the second syllable of the same measure. Successive syllables do not form familiar words. (p. 299)

According to this description, Müller and Schumann's method produced syllables consisting of an initial consonant and an end consonant with either a vowel or a combination of two vowel sounds—the German umlaut (e.g., ü)—between them. That is, the method resulted in CVC syllables.

For 2 years, Ebbinghaus learned and relearned lists of syllables using a "complete mastery" procedure. Specifically, he read through a list at a set rate, timed with either a metronome or a watch, until he had completely mastered the list and could recite it from memory. Then he would measure his retention of the list after varying time periods by relearning it and computing a percentage savings score with the formula

$$\frac{OL - RL \times 100}{OL}$$

In the formula, OL stands for the number of repetitions to mastery in original learning, RL refers to the same value in relearning, and the difference between OL and RL is multiplied by 100 to avoid a fractional answer. For example, if it took Ebbinghaus 40 repetitions to learn a list on one day and only 20 repetitions to relearn it the next day, his percentage savings was 50% (40 − 20 × 100 = 2000/40 = 50). Using this procedure and himself as the experimental subject, Ebbinghaus investigated several important questions, including the effect of practice (number of repetitions) on memory and the effect of time on memory.

Amount of Practice and Memory

You readily assume that the amount of time you spend studying some material translates into better retention of it later, but is this true? Ebbinghaus answered the question by learning and relearning lists of 16 syllables each. He found that the number of repetitions in original learning was inversely related to the number of repetitions in relearning. That is, the more times he rehearsed a list originally, the fewer the number of repetitions required to relearn the list to an errorless repetition 24 hours later.

This experiment also demonstrated the importance of **overlearning**—continued rehearsal beyond mastery—for retention. Once Ebbinghaus could say a 16-word list without error, continuing practice constituted overlearning, and he found that over-learned lists were better retained than nonover-learned lists. Further, the greater the overlearning, the greater the savings after 24 hours. Take it from Ebbinghaus: If you want to be sure that you retain material for a test, overlearn it. Specifically, once you can recite it from memory, rehearse it some more.

Memory and the Passage of Time

To determine the function relating forgetting to time since learning, Ebbinghaus learned 13-syllable lists to complete mastery and then tested his reten-tion by relearning the lists after different periods of time. Plotting savings scores over time, Ebbinghaus obtained the classic forgetting curve (Figure 8–6), which reveals a large initial drop in retention fol-lowed by decreasing losses over longer periods. As you can see, there was only 58% retention after 20 minutes and by an hour after learning, there was a savings of less than half (44 %). However, the curve also shows that most forgetting occurs within 24 hours, with relatively little forgetting beyond that.

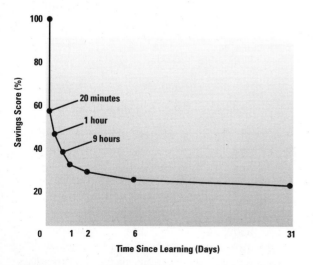

FIGURE 8–6.   The classical Ebbinghaus forgetting curve.

Source: Schwartz, Classic studies in psychology. *Mayfield.*

Additional Observations

Some of Ebbinghaus's almost incidental observa-tions are important and widely cited. For example, Ebbinghaus noted that, "With any considerable number of repetitions a suitable distribution of them over a space of time is decidedly more advantageous than the massing of them at a single time" (Ebbinghaus, 1885/1964, p. 89). In other words, Ebbinghaus found that for learning lists of syllables, **distributed practice** was better than **massed practice**. In addition, Ebbinghaus's work foreshadows various serial position effects (e.g., recency and primacy).

Discussing the results of several experiments, Ebbinghaus concluded that "the number of syllables which I can repeat without error after a single read-ing is about seven. One can, with a certain justifica-tion, look upon this number as a measure of the ideas of this sort which I can grasp in a single uni-tary conscious act" (Ebbinghaus, 1885/1964, p. 109). This passage anticipates modern short-term memory discussions. One example of such a discus-sion is in Miller's (1956) paper appropriately titled, "The magical number seven plus or minus two: Some limits on our capacity for processing informa-tion." Miller's paper is sometimes viewed as the start of the cognitive revolution (Chapter 20).

Ebbinghaus's Influence

Ebbinghaus's memory research not only refuted Wundt's claim that higher mental functions could not be studied experimentally, his experimental findings are still considered valid and are cited alongside much more recent work. In part, this continuing relevance had to do with his careful experimental procedures, some of which we have described. Unlike some of his contemporaries (e.g., Wundt, Titchener, G. E. Müller), Ebbinghaus did not rush his findings into print. The following Ebbinghaus statement, quoted in Woodworth (1909), explains why:

"the individual has to make innumerable stud-ies for his own sake. He tests and rejects, tests once more and once more rejects. For certainly not every happy thought, bolstered up perhaps by a few rough-and-ready experiments, should be brought before the public. But sometimes the individual reaches a point where he is permanently clear and satisfied with his interpretation. Then the matter belongs to the scientific public for their further judgment." (p. 255)

Although Ebbinghaus completed his memory studies by 1880, he did not publish *Über das Gedächtnis* until 1885. He was replicating and extending his original findings in the meantime.

When considering the originality of Ebbinghaus's memory research, note that there was no precedent for it. There were no others doing similar research; Ebbinghaus had no subject pool of undergraduate students; he had no colleagues to consult when he encountered a problem; his simplifying syllables were his own creation. This makes his accomplishment all the more remarkable.

Of course, not all of the influences of Ebbinghaus's memory studies have been unequivocally positive. In 1985, the *Journal of Experimental Psychology: Learning, Memory, and Cognition* published commentaries on the article, "Ebbinghaus: Some Associations" (Slamecka, 1985). In one, Kintsch (1985) decried the invention of the nonsense syllable, writing:

> What a terrible struggle our field has had just to overcome the nonsense syllable! Decades to discover the "meaningfulness" of nonsense syllables, and decades more to finally turn away from the seductions of this chimera. (p. 461)

Young (1985) criticized Ebbinghaus for doing research that was too good, with the result that "he . . . put a stamp on this field which resulted in rigidifying, for nearly 80 years, the paradigms used to study human learning" (p. 491). According to Young, Ebbinghaus's simplifying methodology ruled out the study of mnemonics (memory aids) for almost 80 years.

If his only contribution to psychology had been his memory research, that would be enough to cement Ebbinghaus's place in the history of psychology. As we noted, he did two additional things of importance: The first was his cofounding of the *Zeitschrift,* which provided a place to publish psychological research outside Wundt's sphere. His

second contribution was the discovery that complex tasks are useful for assessing mental ability.

In summary, Ebbinghaus did highly original work, which has stood the test of time. He was not the type of researcher who hits upon a useful method and problem and then mines it for all it is worth. Instead, he was content to show the way and leave the "mopping up" to others. One of those "others" was Georg Elias Müller, who devoted a considerable portion of his research career to extending and refining Ebbinghaus's work on memory.

GEORG ELIAS MÜLLER

In his obituary of Stumpf, Kurt Lewin (1937) wrote: "For a German graduate student of psychology around 1910, like myself, two men held the highest rank and dignity within the pyramid of psychologists actively participating in research . . . Stumpf and . . . G. E. Müller" (p. 189). Boring (1950), too, held a high opinion of Müller, referring to him as the "last of the 'giants,' except for Stumpf . . ." (p. 379) and as one of the "pioneers in a very important undertaking, the bringing of the impalpable mind into the experimental laboratory" (Boring, 1935, p. 348). Despite the accolades, Müller is often given short shrift in histories of psychology, but we feel that he deserves better.

Georg Elias Müller (1850–1934) was born in the town of Grimma, which is not far from Leipzig. After an early humanistic education that included little mathematics or science, Müller (Figure 8–7) developed a philosophical bent by reading such works as Goethe's *Faust* and the poetry of Byron and Shelley. Reading Gotthold Ephraim Lessing (1729–1781), a philosophically minded poet, playwright, essayist, and critic, taught Müller the value of careful, rigorous thought, much as Stumpf learned it from Brentano.

Müller's higher education included study at Leipzig, Berlin, and Göttingen, with a year off for the Franco-Prussian War. At Göttingen, Lotze completed Müller's training in precise thinking, and he also reinforced further the need to ground philosophy in

FIGURE 8–7.   G. E. Müller.

Source: Archives of the History of American Psychology.

science. Although the philosophers interested in psychology at this time believed that psychology should be grounded in the scientific method, they rarely became experimentalists. Müller, Ebbinghaus, and Wundt were the exceptions.

At Leipzig, Müller had become acquainted with Fechner, and he maintained a scientific correspondence with the psychophysicist. Müller revised and extended the methodology of psychophysics and used the work to secure an instructor's position at the University of Göttingen. Unlike Stumpf, who worked at five universities before settling in Berlin, Müller was professor of philosophy at Göttingen for 40 years, long enough to make him an institution there, much as Wundt was at Leipzig.

At Göttingen, Müller continued his psychophysical research, becoming the leader in the field with Fechner's death in 1887. As we noted in Chapter 7, the 1903 publication of Müller's handbook of psy-

chophysics forced Titchener to delay publication of the second volumes of his *Experimental Psychology.*

In 1887, Müller seized on another research topic—the investigation of human memory. Two years after Ebbinghaus's publication of *Über das Gedächtnis,* Müller and his assistant, **Friedrich Schumann** (1863–1940), began work on memory using Ebbinghaus's complete mastery method. To standardize the presentation of lists of nonsense syllables, Müller and Schumann invented the **memory drum** (Figure 8–8), which consists of a rotating piece of paper on which are printed verbal materials to be learned. Each verbal item appears for a set time in the window or slot facing the subject.

An important behind-the-scenes psychologist, Schumann earned his degree at Göttingen with Müller and worked with him on memory. Schumann then went to Berlin, where he served as Stumpf's right-hand man for 11 years, doing important work on visual space perception. With Ebbinghaus's death, Schumann assumed the editorship of *Zeitschrift für Psychologie.* In 1910, Schumann was at Frankfurt in time to give laboratory space and equipment to Max Wertheimer, so that Wertheimer, working with Kurt Koffka and Wolfgang Köhler, could do the experiments that led to Gestalt psychology.

Müller verified and extended Ebbinghaus's verbal learning research. His addition of introspective reports to Ebbinghaus's method convinced Müller

FIGURE 8–8.   A memory drum.

Source: Archives of the History of American Psychology.

that subjects did not learn nonsense syllable lists passively, that there were attempts to group items in the lists and to find meaning even in meaningless material, an observation usually associated with later researchers (e.g., Bousfield, 1953). In addition, a subject's preparatory set (*Anlage*) affected the memory processes, a finding we will see further investigated in Oswald Külpe's Würzburg laboratory. Külpe spent some time with Müller.

With Alfons Pilzecker, Müller developed the **interference theory of forgetting**, finding that new learning can interfere with the memory of material learned earlier. They called this source of interference **retroactive inhibition**, because it acts back upon (retro-active) an earlier memory. Interference theory became and continues to be an important explanation for forgetting.

In addition, Müller was interested in the problems of vision. In a series of articles, he detailed and defended a theory of color vision that advanced Ewald Hering's opponent-process theory (Chapter 6). Hering's theory predicts that when there is equal stimulation of the black-white, blue-yellow, and red-green systems, the result should be that we see nothing, a visual "silence." In reality, we see gray, and Müller accounted for this by proposing that there is a constant gray caused by molecular activity in the cortex (cortical gray).

A number of additional people who worked in Müller's laboratory figure prominently in the history of psychology. For example, **Erich R. Jaensch** (1883–1940), **David Katz** (1884–1957), and **Edgar Rubin** (1886–1951) all worked on or published phenomenological investigations at approximately the same time that Wertheimer, Koffka, and Köhler were engaged in the similar research that led to Gestalt psychology. This further demonstrates the persuasive power of the phenomenological *Zeitgeist* in non-Wundtian German psychology.

After earning her Ph.D. with Titchener in 1898, Eleanor Acheson McCulloch Gamble was Müller's student in 1906–1907. She subsequently published a classic work on the reconstruction method for measuring memory, which was based primarily on research performed at Wellesley before she went to Göttingen. In midlife, **Lillien Jane Martin**

(1851–1943) discovered the work of Wilhelm Wundt. Deciding to go to Germany to study, Martin arrived at Göttingen in 1894 and spent 4 years there, failing to earn a Ph.D. because the university was not granting them to women at the time. In 1898, Martin joined the faculty at Stanford University, where in 1915 she became the first woman to head a Stanford department. Finally, working with Müller, Adolph Jost published memory research that produced Jost's law, which states that "when two associations are of equal strength, a repetition strengthens the older more than the younger" (Boring, 1950, p. 375).

Müller's Influence

As you can see, Müller was a gifted researcher who made substantial contributions in the areas of psychophysics, memory, and vision. In addition, he provided a laboratory at Göttingen to rival Wundt's at Leipzig. As Boring (1950) put it, "Within experimental psychology he exhibited a broad interest and a fertile mind. His students received from him more than their meed of inspiration and help, and through his own work and through theirs he exerted a great influence upon experimental psychology in its formative years. As a power and an institution he was second only to Wundt" (p. 379).

We will conclude with an examination of the career and influence of a man who worked under both "institutions" in German psychology in the late 19th century, who found Brentano's psychology more appealing than that of the man whose assistant he had been, and who went on to found a research program with a lasting influence—Oswald Külpe.

OSWALD KÜLPE

Oswald Külpe (1862–1915) was born in Candau in Courland, Latvia, which at the time was part of Russia. However, both his family and his native tongue were German, and Külpe did not learn Russian until he entered the *Gymnasium* at Libau. Although the Külpes were probably not affluent, they were well educated.

From the *Gymnasium,* Külpe went in 1881 to the University of Leipzig to study history. He attended Wundt's lectures, but Wundt's laboratory was just getting underway, so Külpe transferred to Berlin to again study history. From Berlin, Külpe went to Göttingen, where he studied under G. E. Müller, who supplied his dissertation topic. With a digression in Russia, Külpe returned to Leipzig and Wundt's seminar, and in 1887, he had his doctoral examination. In 1888, Külpe defended a second dissertation and became a *Privatdozent* at the university. He also became Wundt's second assistant, James McKeen Cattell (Chapter 10) having returned to America.

In the early 1890s, Külpe planned to write a textbook of psychology that would present the results of the experimental work that had been done and that would be simpler than Wundt's *Principles.* Much of the planning involved discussions with Titchener, and Titchener translated Külpe's *Grundriss der Psychologie* into *Outlines of Psychology,* which was published only 2 years after *Grundriss* appeared (Külpe, 1895). Although Külpe dedicated his book to Wundt, Wundt did not approve of it and promptly wrote his own *Grundriss der Psychologie.*

Külpe was promoted at Leipzig shortly after the publication of the *Grundriss,* but in the same year (1894) he went to the chair of philosophy at the University of Würzburg. At Würzburg, Külpe developed a laboratory that soon rivaled Wundt's Leipzig laboratory in quality. In 1909, Külpe moved to Bonn, and then in 1913, he moved to Munich, establishing laboratories at both universities. Before Christmas in 1915, Külpe had a bout with influenza, and he died on December 30, 1915, at only 53.

According to R. M. Ogden (1951; Chapter 14), one of his Ph.D. students, "Oswald Külpe was both an impressive and a lovable character. . . . Külpe's character is best described, I think, as that of an esthetic personality in a factual world" (pp. 6–7). Külpe (Figure 8–9) never married and often said "with a twinkle in his eye: 'Science is my bride'" (p. 4).

Külpe's Psychology

While still at Leipzig, Külpe and Titchener were strongly influenced by the positivistic writings of Mach and Avenarius. As a result, Titchener and

FIGURE 8–9.   Oswald Külpe.

Source: Philosophical Library, New York.

Külpe accepted the view that any mental state, no matter how complex, could be reduced to elementary states. This allowed them to study higher and lower mental processes with the same methodology, experimental introspection, rather than reserving experimental methodology only for the study of the lower processes, as Wundt taught.

Külpe (1895) defined psychology as "a science of the facts of experience in their dependency upon experiencing individuals . . ." (p. 3), thus avoiding Wundt's distinction between immediate experience as the province of psychology and mediate experience as the property of physics. Külpe could then define physics as a science of experience that was independent of an experiencing individual.

Külpe's *Outlines* attempted to cover all that was known of experimental psychology at the time it was written, omitting discussion of unresearched topics. Thus, he wrote nothing on the study of thought, as Wundt considered thought a subject that was not amenable to experimental investigation. At Würzburg, Külpe and his students made thought a major topic of study and soon discovered that not all thought is accompanied by images. As we noted, this resulted in the imageless thought controversy with Wundt and Titchener.

The Würzburg School

Note that "none of the articles in the traditional Würzburg canon were written by the founder and father figure of the school, Oswald Külpe" (Lindenfeld, 1978, p. 132), which leads to the question: What was Külpe's relationship to the school associated with his name? Boring (1950) wrote that Külpe was the inspiration for all the work issuing from his laboratory, and Ogden (1951) agreed:

> Unlike G. E. Müller, [Külpe] published no extensive experimental studies of his own. It should be noted, however, that he was intimately engaged in all that went on in his laboratory. It was a matter of principle with him to act as observer in the experimental work of his students. . . . His influence upon his students was never dominating. Instead, they were engaged together in a joint enterprise of scientific discovery. (p. 9)

The method used by the **Würzburg school** was **systematic experimental introspection**. Using this method, people performed a complex task that involved such mental events as thinking, remembering, or judging and were then required to make a retrospective report of their mental experiences during the task. The mental events *during* the solution were what interested the Würzburgers, not the task solution itself.

One of the Würzburg school's first studies was reported in 1901 by **Karl Marbe** (1869–1953). Marbe required subjects first to judge the heavier of two lifted weights and then to report what happened in consciousness during the judgment. He found that the subjects were usually correct in their judgments, but they did not know how the judgments got into their minds. Marbe concluded that judgment in this case was not a conscious process, attributing it to *Bewusstseinslagen* or "conscious attitudes." Conscious

attitude then became a new element of the mind, distinct from Wundt's sensations, images, and feelings.

The next key study was performed by **Henry Jackson Watt** (1879–1925), Külpe's Scottish doctoral student. In 1904, Watt asked subjects to make partially restricted associations to stimulus words. For example, the subject might be required to make a superordinate response or a subordinate response to the word "dog." An appropriate superordinate response might be "animal," whereas an appropriate subordinate response might be "bulldog." As before, Watt was interested in the thought processes leading to the response, and he found that subjects produced appropriate associations without conscious effort.

Without solving the problem of thought, Watt introduced two important things to the Würzburg investigations. First, he began the technique of **fractionating** the introspections into four periods: (1) the preparatory period, (2) the period when the stimulus word was presented, (3) the period of search for the associated word, and (4) the period when the response was made. The second important contribution was that Watt's research placed the emphasis on the *Aufgabe,* or task. Once the subject was given and had accepted the task, Watt found that the response followed the stimulus word automatically, without conscious content. That is, Watt found little conscious content in period 3, the period when there should be the search for the response. The *Aufgabe* created an *Einstellung,* or "set" to respond.

Watt's work was followed in 1905 by the work of Külpe's junior colleague, **Narziss Ach** (1871–1946). Ach gave his subjects pairs of numbers, after first giving them the instruction to either add, subtract, multiply, or divide the numbers. If 8 and 2 are printed on a piece of paper, with 8 above and 2 below, the typical associations are 10, 6, 16, and 4. However, the instruction to add strengthens one association so that the result is almost inevitably 10. The *Aufgabe,* or, as Ach called it, the **determining tendency**, effectively predetermines the result.

This idea of predetermining tendency was foreshadowed by Külpe's interpretation of Ludwig Lange's reaction-time studies (Chapter 7) in Wundt's laboratory. Recall that Lange found that subjects concentrating on making a response showed shorter reaction times than subjects concentrating on the presentation of the stimulus. Wundt's interpretation was that concentrating on the stimulus added apperception to the perceptual-response sequence, and apperception of the stimulus required an extra 1/10 of a second beyond simply apprehending it. By contrast, Külpe argued in his *Grundriss* that changing the set did not merely add another element: It changed the whole process. Ach's research, and Watt's before it, showed that Külpe was right.

In addition to the "determining tendency," Ach's research uncovered an element of conscious content that was neither image nor sensation, which Ach called *Bewusstheit* (awareness). This "was the birth of an 'imageless thought content' . . ." (Ogden, 1951, p. 10).

Imageless Thought Controversy. Both Wundt and Titchener assumed that thinking depended on mental images, and thought without images, with *unanschauliche Bewusstheiten* (vague awareness), questioned this basic assumption. Neither man believed that studies from the Würzburg school damaged his position. Wundt rejected imageless thought as the result of faulty methodology—thought cannot be observed while one is thinking. The Würzburgers' retrospective introspection failed to observe the actual thought processes that occurred during the search-for-response period. After the response is made, the original thought processes cannot recur.

Although Titchener believed that thought could be studied introspectively, he objected to imageless thought because at Cornell, introspectively analyzed thought always produced images. Titchener tried to reduce the Würzburgers' *unanschauliche Bewusstheiten* to kinesthetic sensations (sensations of position, movement, etc., of parts of the body). "The introspective [reports] kept showing, for example, that the kinesthesis of an incipient smile or of a relaxed chest could mean familiarity. 'The great god kinesthesis,' exclaimed someone on reading a set of such [records], so pervasive were these somesthetic sensory processes in the stream of consciousness" (Boring, 1969, p. 28).

In addition to the Würzburgers, Robert S. Woodworth (Chapter 11) in America soon reported

imageless thought, and it was also "seen" by Alfred Binet in France. Binet even claimed that the "method of Würzburg" should be called the "method of Paris." Külpe responded by pointing to the early studies from his laboratory by Marbe and Ach, which antedated Binet's work.

Probably the most important effect of the imageless thought controversy was that it undermined confidence in introspection as a method. The data generated by introspection were unreliable, open to alternative interpretations, and, perhaps, too easily biased by the observer's viewpoint.

Külpe's Influence

Perhaps most important, Külpe's Würzburg program generated controversy, which is excellent for stimulating research. Controversy prevents the establishment of orthodoxy, which works to stifle dissent. Unfortunately for Külpe, there was a heavy personal price to pay: His unorthodox findings generated criticism, even attack, from the men he admired and liked the most.

> His break with Wundt over matters of principle, which occurred even in his Leipzig days, failed to weaken his reverent regard for his master teacher. He published three tributes to Wundt and was active in the preparation of the *Festschrift* that brought to a close the publication of Wundt's *Philosophische Studien*. Külpe retained a like regard for Müller, his second teacher, though he was deeply hurt when Müller saw fit to attack the methods and results of the Würzburg school. It was sadness rather than resentment that characterized his feelings when Titchener, his friend and companion of Leipzig days, turned the guns of his laboratory at Cornell against the Würzburg investigations of the thought-processes. "If I could only sit down with Titchener," he said to me, "I am sure I could make him see what we are driving at." (Ogden, 1951, p. 6)

Like Ebbinghaus's and Müller's memory experiments, Külpe's studies of thought showed that higher mental processes could be examined experimentally and that Wundt's "two psychologies" (experimental to study lower mental processes and cultural to study higher mental processes) were unnecessary. In addition, the Würzburgers' demonstration that mental operations frequently occur without definite images undermined the basic assumption of Wundt's and Titchener's approaches that the elements of consciousness are sensations, images, and feelings.

Throughout, Külpe's work showed the importance of mental set. Given the appropriate instructions, subjects extracted relevant information from a stimulus while failing to extract other, equally apparent, information. Thus, the stimulus did not automatically produce sensations that in turn became images, again showing a deficiency in Wundt's and Titchener's systems.

The Würzburgers' studies stressed the importance of motivation in terms like *Aufgabe* (task), *Einstellung* (set), and determining tendency. The subjects were not consciously aware of these directing tendencies, indicating that they operated unconsciously. However, the Würzburgers viewed the tendencies as vague conscious elements, and it remained for Freud to make the unconscious control of behavior a vital concept.

Külpe's research sharpened the distinction between mental content and mental acts or functions, which brought him closer to Brentano than to Wundt. Because so many of Brentano's students were important for Gestalt psychology's development, it is not surprising that one of Külpe's doctoral students, Max Wertheimer, had the seminal insight that led to Gestalt psychology. The basic compatibility was there in the Würzburgers' tendency toward the holistic approach in contrast to Wundtian elementism.

Finally, the inconsistencies in the introspective reports that led to the imageless thought controversy hastened the demise of introspection as an experimental method of psychology.

CONCLUSIONS

In this chapter, we have explored contemporary alternatives in Germany to Wundtian psychology. Except for Ebbinghaus, all the major people we examined—Brentano, Stumpf, Husserl, Müller, and Külpe—can be considered "phenomenological" psychologists. As we indicated, phenomenological ideas were a major part of the era's *Zeitgeist.*

As presented in *Psychology from an Empirical Standpoint,* Brentano's system stands as the backdrop to the various phenomenologies (e.g., Stumpf's, Husserl's) and phenomenological approaches to psychology (e.g., the Würzburg school, Gestalt psychology) that came later. Like Brentano, Stumpf and Husserl were more important as philosophers of psychology than as experimental psychologists. By contrast, Müller and Külpe (and later the Gestaltists) made substantial laboratory contributions. We can only speculate about how the tension that began between Wundt's psychology and Brentano's psychology would have been resolved if World War II had not intervened. As we will see, the Gestaltists and other students of Stumpf seemed poised to control the field in German universities before the rise of the Nazis.

Of course, the Nazis did come to power, and individuals such as Husserl suffered as a result. Whether we blame it on the Nazis or not, Brentano's system and its descendants faded from mainstream psychology, which turned to America, first to Titchener's structuralism and then to behaviorism. Both structuralism and behaviorism were steeped in the positivist and empirical traditions attacked often by subsequent phenomenologists (e.g., Husserl). Remnants of Brentano's alternate vision for psychology can be found in Freud and in functionalism (Chapter 11), mostly in the form of active conceptions of mind, which stand in contrast to the empirical behaviorists' view.

The legacy of men Boring (1950) called giants (e.g., Stumpf and Müller) remained alive in Gestalt psychology and phenomenology for decades and has recently been "rediscovered" by cognitive psychologists. In fact, modern-day cognitive science, with its central interest in memory and thinking, owes much to the efforts of not only the various phenomenologists but to Ebbinghaus as well. Although the non-Wundtians in this chapter may not have strongly influenced American psychology's history, they may still shape its future.

S U M M A R Y

The success of Wundt's founding efforts reveal that the *Zeitgeist* was right for the development of psychology as a separate science. However, if Wundt had not developed his psychological system, there were numerous alternatives.

Franz Brentano

Franz Brentano's most important work for psychology was *Psychology from an Empirical Standpoint* (1874). Brentano's psychology was empirical in the sense of being based on experience.

Brentano's psychology was an act psychology, where acts are psychic phenomena falling into three broad categories: presentation (or ideating); judging; and desire, loving, and hating. Brentano's method included indirect inner perception, the observation of past mental phenomena in memory, and "objective observation," in which others are studied through their speech, autobiographies, and voluntary acts.

Brentano was important in establishing intentionality as a central issue for the philosophy of mind and through his influence on such students as Christian von Ehrenfels, Alexius Meinong, Carl Stumpf, Edmund Husserl, and Sigmund Freud. Stumpf, Husserl, Külpe, the Gestaltists, and such functionalists as Freud and James all found in Brentano's act psychology an attractive alternative to Wundt's experimental psychology.

Carl Stumpf

Carl Stumpf studied under Brentano and then Lotze. In 1873, he published a nativistic theory of space perception, and in 1875, he began work that combined his interests in psychology and music, which culminated in *Tone Psychology*.

Stumpf classified experience into phenomena and functions. Phenomena were such things as tones and colors, and Stumpf called their study "phenomenology." Stumpf's functions were Brentano's acts, and although he considered study of the functions to be the foundation of psychology, Stumpf devoted most of his career to investigating phenomena, which he considered preparatory to psychology. Stumpf's greatest influence came through the students who made his phenomenology the basis for Gestalt psychology: Koffka, Köhler, and Lewin.

Edmund Husserl

Edmund Husserl was a respected logician and philosopher whose phenomenology was the most detailed and eventually the most accepted of the "phenomenologies." Husserl's phenomenology was defined as the science of examining the data of conscious experience, and he considered phenomenology a science separate from psychology and preparatory to it. Husserl's approach examines the structure and content of conscious experience through a series of steps, of which description is the most important. *Wesensschau*—the cognition of essence—is another important step.

Husserl was a critic of positivism and of the mechanistic psychologies that endorsed it, and his influence extended to subsequent "phenomenological" approaches to psychology, including the Gestalt school and the Würzburg school. Similarly, he influenced existential-phenomenological philosophers and psychologists such as Martin Heidegger and Maurice Merleau-Ponty.

Hermann Ebbinghaus

A used copy of Fechner's *Elements of Psychophysics* inspired Hermann Ebbinghaus to use Fechner's psychophysical methods in the study of the higher mental function of memory. In 1885, Ebbinghaus published the results of his memory research in *Concerning Memory*.

To simplify the learning of verbal material, Ebbinghaus invented nonsense material, from which he constructed lists. Ebbinghaus found that the more time he spent practicing a list originally, the less time it took to relearn it later. Ebbinghaus also found that overlearning was important for retention and that there is a large drop in retention soon after learning that is followed by a more gradual decline over time. Ebbinghaus found that distributed practice was superior to massed practice and anticipated modern discussions of short-term memory span with his observation that he could remember a maximum of seven syllables after a single reading.

Ebbinghaus's memory research showed that it was possible to study a higher mental function experimentally and produced many findings still considered valid. The *Zeitschrift für Psychologie* and the "Ebbinghaus completion method" were further significant contributions to psychology.

Georg Elias Müller

Georg Elias Müller's first experimental efforts gave him the leadership of psychophysics after Fechner's death. Following Ebbinghaus's lead, Müller began research on human memory. To aid in this research, Müller and Friedrich Schumann invented the memory drum. In further studies of human memory, Müller and Alfons Pilzecker developed the interference theory of forgetting, which says that new learning can interfere with the memory of material learned earlier. Müller also worked on vision, producing a theory of color vision that included Hering's theory. Müller was second only to Wundt as an institution in the early days of psychology.

Oswald Külpe

Oswald Külpe developed the Würzburg school, whose major method was systematic experimental introspection, in which subjects performed a task that involved higher mental processes and were then asked to report their mental experiences during the task. Working at Würzburg, Karl Marbe attributed subjects' weight judgments to "conscious attitudes." Henry Watt found that partially restricted associations to stimulus words were made without conscious effort because the task created a set to respond. Narziss Ach also showed the importance of the determining tendency in his work and uncovered a conscious element that led to the imageless thought controversy with Wundt and Titchener. The controversy undermined confidence in introspection, and Külpe's research program showed that it was possible to study higher mental processes experimentally.

CONNECTIONS QUESTIONS

1. Compare and contrast Brentano's psychology with Wundt's. List and discuss as many ways that they differed as you can.
2. What similarities (connections) can you see between Ebbinghaus and Müller?
3. In what ways did Külpe extend experimental psychology beyond the limits imposed on it by Wundt?
4. What was the context in which the study of Clever Hans became important for psychology?
5. Compare and contrast the phenomenologies of Husserl and Stumpf.
6. Compare and contrast Wundt's and Brentano's *innere Wahrnehmung.* How would Brentano and Wundt have approached the study of the phenomenon of anger?
7. Draw a concept map connecting the major ideas and individuals discussed in this chapter; and compare your results to one possible solution provided on p. 564.

SUGGESTED READINGS

Dreyfus, H. (1982). *Husserl, intentionality, and cognitive science.* Cambridge, MA: MIT Press. This is a fine collection of essays on Husserl and his connection to modern-day cognitive psychology and the philosophy of mind.

Ebbinghaus, H. (1964). *Memory: A contribution to experimental psychology.* New York: Dover. (Original work published 1885; translated 1913) Widely available, this slender book is must reading for anyone interested in the study of memory. Remembering that the research that led to this work was almost completely novel will help you appreciate Ebbinghaus's genius.

Føllesdal, D. (1974). Phenomenology. In E. Carterette & M. Friedman (Eds.), *Handbook of perception: Vol. 1* (pp. 377–386). New York: Academic Press. This is perhaps the best short introduction to phenomenology available for the interested student with little background. Føllesdal uses a variety of examples to illustrate many of Husserl's most important concepts.

Lewin, K. (1937). Carl Stumpf. *Psychological Review, 44,* 188–194. Obituaries are often excellent sources of information about historical figures, and this is no exception. Lewin, as we will see, is an important historical figure in his own right.

Ogden, R. M. (1951). Oswald Külpe and the Würzburg school. *American Journal of Psychology, 64,* 4–19. Written by one of his doctoral students, this paper is an excellent overview of Külpe and the research of the Würzburg school.

Pfungst, O. (1965). *Clever Hans (The horse of Mr. von Osten).* New York: Holt, Rinehart and Winston, Inc. (Original work published 1911) This is the report of Pfungst's efforts to discover and test the cues Hans used to answer questions put to him. There are introductions by Robert Rosenthal and Carl Stumpf as well as supplements giving the reports from the commissions organized to study Hans and a detailing of von Osten's teaching methods.

Rancurello, A. C. (1968). *A study of Franz Brentano: His psychological standpoint and his significance in the history of psychology.* New York: Academic Press. This is an excellent monograph on a pivotal figure in the history of psychology.

Shakow, D. (1930). Hermann Ebbinghaus. *American Journal of Psychology, 17,* 504–518. Shakow's article is almost always cited in any treatment of Ebbinghaus—with good reason.

Stumpf, C. (1930). Carl Stumpf. In C. Murchison (Ed.), *A history of psychology in autobiography* (Vol. 1, pp. 389–441). Worcester, MA: Clark University Press. Any in-depth study of Stumpf should begin with his remarkably readable and candid autobiography.

British Forerunners of Functionalism

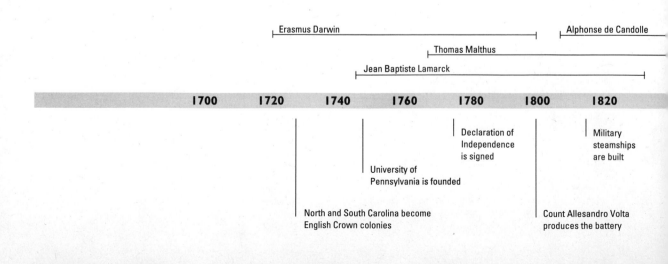

Charles Darwin

Charles Lyell

Erasmus Darwin

Alphonse de Candolle

Thomas Malthus

Jean Baptiste Lamarck

| 1700 | 1720 | 1740 | 1760 | 1780 | 1800 | 1820 |

Declaration of
Independence
is signed

Military
steamships
are built

University of
Pennsylvania is founded

North and South Carolina become
English Crown colonies

Count Allesandro Volta
produces the battery

In Chapter 7, we examined Wundt's initiation of psychology as a separate science and reviewed Titchener's version of Wundt's system. Titchener's structuralism never achieved dominance in America, despite Titchener's efforts and the large number of psychologists he trained. More viable, at least for a time, was the psychology of function to which Titchener compared his psychology of structure in 1898 (Titchener, 1898). Instead of having Titchener's concern with the identification of the mind's elements, many of America's first psychological theorists (e.g., William James, G. Stanley Hall, John Dewey) were more interested in the mind's functions. In large part, this interest in function had been stimulated by the concept of evolution, which gained scientific acceptance through the efforts of Charles Darwin.

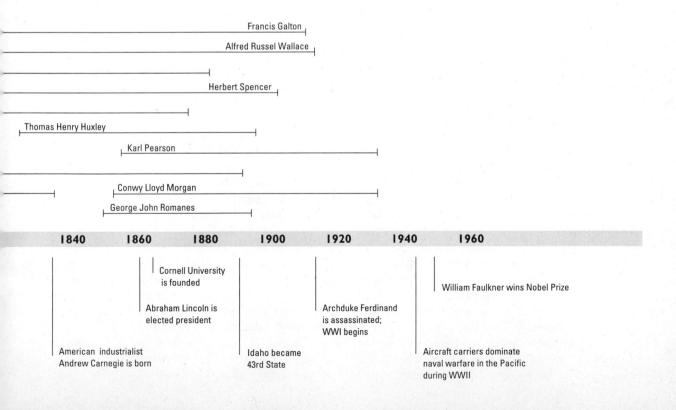

In Chapter 8, we indicated that phenomenology was "in the air" in the 19th century; evolution is another idea that was part of that *Zeitgeist* and is this chapter's primary theme. The concept of organic evolution, in which structures or systems gradually change in response to external pressures, was important for psychology in many ways. For example, presumably consciousness has evolved, and thus the study of the mind's role in adaptation becomes a relevant concern. In addition, Darwinian evolution requires variability within a species, and the study of this variability in the human species led to the examination of individual differences, which was pursued with great vigor by Darwin's cousin, Francis Galton (discussed later). Finally, evolution puts humans in the animal kingdom and makes the study of animal behavior—comparative psychology—an important enterprise. In this chapter, we will review the beginnings of comparative psychology in the work of John Romanes and C. Lloyd Morgan. In addition to the idea of evolution, another common link between this chapter's major people is that they were all British, which gives us our title—"British Forerunners of Functionalism."

Although we tend to think of Charles Darwin as the discoverer of the concept of evolution, Darwin, for all his admirable qualities, was definitely a product of his age. Other scientists, some of whom we have already mentioned, were important antecedents of Darwin.

PRE-DARWINIAN EVOLUTION

We have suggested previously that a concept of evolution first appeared with the ancient Greeks (e.g., Aristotle, Heraclitus), but we will not go back that far. In Chapter 5, we encountered three early contributors to the evolutionary *Zeitgeist* of the 19th century—Hegel, Comte, and Goethe. An idea of evolution was central to the philosophies of Hegel and Comte. For Goethe—author, philosopher, and scientist—there was a fascination with the metamorphosis of parts. From careful observation of plants, Goethe concluded that different plant forms can be established by the modification of one part

into another, and he extended this principle from plants to the animal kingdom.

A Darwin before Charles, **Erasmus Darwin** (1721–1802), reached similar conclusions independently of Goethe about the transmutation (change) of species. A popular physician known for his free-thinking opinions, his poetry, his botanical garden, and his mechanical inventions, Darwin saw evidence for the mutability of species in the changes that occur during embryonic development, in the changes that resulted from domestication and hybridization, and in the similarity in the structural plan of vertebrates. Darwin speculated that change in species occurs through adaptations to the environment that result from the struggle for survival, and many of these adaptations are transmitted to descendants. As a poet, Darwin set his ideas to verse, which weakened their power by making them seem less scientific than they might have seemed in prose. Erasmus Darwin was Charles Darwin's grandfather by his first wife and Francis Galton's grandfather by his second wife.

The French naturalist **Jean-Baptiste Lamarck** (1744–1829) was another important pre-Darwinian evolutionist. Lamarck was the descendant of an impoverished noble family. He joined the French army at 17 and became interested in Mediterranean plants as a soldier, publishing in 1778 *Flore français* (*French Flowers*). Resigning from the military after an injury, he became a clerk in a Paris bank, using his income to study medicine and botany.

For a time, Lamarck was the tutor of the sons of the **Comte de Buffon** (1707–1788), a famous French naturalist. Buffon theorized that the earth was much older than the Biblical account indicates, and his writings also foreshadowed a theory of evolution. At Buffon's death, Lamarck became keeper of the herbarium in the *Jardin du Roi* (the royal botanical gardens in Paris). With the onset of the French Revolution in 1789, the designation "*du Roi*" (of the King) fell from favor, and Lamarck's suggestion to rename the garden the *Jardin des Plantes* (Garden of Plants) was accepted.

Lamarck's interest moved from plants to animals and especially to animals without backbones, which he called *invertébrés* (invertebrates). Given the task of classifying animal collections in the Paris

Museum of Natural History, Lamarck was struck by the similarities in closely related species. Perhaps if enough closely related species were studied together, the differences between them would be so small as to be undetectable. Although this is not exactly true, the idea led Lamarck to develop a theory of evolution in which there was the descent of species from other species over long periods of time.

According to Lamarck, the action of two factors accounted for evolution. The first factor was a supposed tendency in organisms toward perfection and increased complexity, a concept Lamarck considered so self-evident that it required no proof. This factor led him to suggest that simple organisms must have arisen recently by spontaneous generation, because if they had arisen earlier, they would be more perfect and complex.

Lamarck's second factor was intended to account for the deviations in a perfect ordering of organisms from the lowliest at the bottom to humans at the top. The anomalies must reflect environmental interference. As he wrote in *Philosophie Zoologique* (*Zoological Philosophy*),

> Every considerable alteration in the local circumstances in which each race of animals exists causes a change in their wants, and these new wants excite them to new actions and habits. These actions require the more frequent [use] of some parts before but slightly exercised, and then greater development follows as a consequence of their more frequent use. Other organs no longer in use are impoverished and diminished in size, nay, are sometimes entirely annihilated, while in their place new parts are insensibly produced for the discharge of new functions. (Lamarck, 1809/1914, p. 234)

These acquired alterations are then passed on to offspring.

Lamarckism has been distilled into the phrase "the inheritance of acquired characteristics," as if an animal whose tail has been amputated should produce tailless progeny. The oft-repeated phrase is a disservice to Lamarck, because it implies more than he intended. Lamarck stressed the transformation of body parts through efforts by the animal to adapt to its environment, with the subsequent inheritance of these changes. The heritable changes

are wrought by an organism's internal need and effort, not by something imposed externally.

> It is, however, only fair to say that Lamarck has been treated with less than justice by history, for his name is associated with a hypothetic cause of evolution that he did not invent and that is unacceptable, whereas it was his genius in proposing a scheme of evolution that deserves commemoration in the term Lamarckism. (Sir Gavin de Beer; Appleman, 1979, p. 5)

At the end of his life, Lamarck (Figure 9–1) lost his eyesight and became nearly destitute. "His life was a tribute to his courage, and his old age was a disgrace to his government" (Durant & Durant, 1975, p. 328).

In his view of the mutability of species, Lamarck was vigorously opposed by French naturalist Georges Cuvier (mentioned in Chapter 6), who believed in the orthodox Biblical account of the creation of species. The weight of Cuvier's opinion effectively prevented wide acceptance of Lamarck's ideas, much

FIGURE 9–1. Jean-Baptiste Lamarck.

Source: Wellcome Institute Library, London.

as Flourens's stature inhibited the search for and belief in the localization of function espoused by Gall and phrenology (Chapter 6). However, at least one important evolutionist embraced a type of Lamarckism—Herbert Spencer.

Herbert Spencer

Herbert Spencer (1820–1903) was born in Derby, an industrial town in central England. He was intermittently educated by an uncle and by his father, a schoolmaster, and this nontraditional education was perhaps responsible for Spencer's tendency to champion unorthodox beliefs and to form strong opinions without careful study.

After 10 years spent employed by a variety of small railway companies, in 1848 Spencer went to London to work as a journalist. In London, Spencer acquired a circle of friends that included writer George Henry Lewes, novelist Marian Evans (better known as George Eliot), and **Thomas Henry Huxley** (1825–1895), a biologist who became one of Darwin's chief defenders. Huxley's relatives included Aldous Huxley (1894–1963), the author of *Brave New World* (1932), Sir Julian Huxley (1887–1975), biologist and humanist, and Sir Andrew Fielding Huxley (1917–), a co-winner of the 1963 Nobel Prize for physiology or medicine.

Spencer's interest in evolution began in 1839 when a reading of **Sir Charles Lyell**'s (1797–1875) criticism of Lamarck in *Principles of Geology* paradoxically convinced Spencer of Lamarck's validity. In his 1855 work, *The Principles of Psychology*, Spencer detailed an evolutionary doctrine that anticipated Darwin's *The Origin of Species* (1859). Note that Spencer's *Principles* antedated by nearly 25 years the establishment of Wundt's laboratory at Leipzig. However, Spencer's views on evolution had little impact in the 1850s because they were based on Lamarckism, which was already familiar, and Spencer himself—at least initially—had little credibility with the scientific community because of his lack of training in science. The later scientific acceptance of Darwin's work resulted in greater acceptance of Spencer's more general ideas, as scientists and nonscientists alike became interested in reading about evolution. Spencer (Figure 9–2) is

FIGURE 9–2. Herbert Spencer at about the age at which he wrote *The Principles of Psychology*.
Source: National Library of Medicine.

shown at about the age at which he wrote his *Principles*.

By the early 1860s, Spencer had decided on his life's work: Inspired by Darwin's publication of *The Origin of Species*, he would produce a comprehensive philosophy of science based on evolutionary concepts. In some ways similar to Comte's ambitious enterprise, Spencer's **synthetic philosophy** aimed at an examination of the problems of sociology, psychology, biology, education, and ethics from the standpoint of evolution, in which an indefinite homogeneity becomes a differentiated heterogeneity.

Through funds generated from a syllabus sent to prospective subscribers and frugal living, Spencer was able to produce 10 volumes of *The System of Synthetic Philosophy*. Spencer's productivity was aided by his unusual habit of dictating his books. His work on psychology for the synthetic philosophy was actually the revision of his 1855 *Principles*, which encompassed two volumes published in 1870 and 1872. These works "were largely dictated on a boat, in between vigorous bouts of rowing on a lake in a London park" (Boakes, 1984, p. 12).

In Spencer's revised *Principles of Psychology,* the key concept for us is his **evolutionary association- ism**. To Alexander Bain's (Chapter 4) development of voluntary behavior through the action of plea- surable or unpleasurable events, Spencer added a Lamarckian tendency for frequently made associa- tions to be passed on to future generations. Thus, Bain's account of the development of voluntary behavior became known as the **Spencer-Bain prin- ciple**. Spencer saw his evolutionary association- ism operating phylogenetically: Simple creatures respond in simple, undifferentiated ways to gross stimuli. Their behavior is analogous to reflex actions in higher organisms. On a higher level, instinct is "compound reflex action," capable of mediating an organism's response to more com- plex and differentiated conditions. Memory and cognition arise from instincts, and we see Spencer's evolutionary hierarchy of mental states.

Although there was little direct response to his 1855 *Principles,* by 1870 Spencer had developed a considerable reputation, particularly in America. His teleological approach to evolution—the idea that evolution has a final purpose or end toward which change is heading and that evolutionary change is always in the direction of progress—found favor with American functional psychology. Ameri- can business particularly liked **social Darwinism**, which resulted from Spencer's application of evolu- tionary ideas to ethics and social phenomena. Social Darwinism was the notion that societies and the institutions within them evolve like species and that the **survival of the fittest**—Spencer's phrase, not Darwin's—is morally justified. Because social Dar- winism suggests that progress will be maximized when free enterprise prevails in all spheres, Ameri- can capitalists applauded Spencer.

Reviews of Spencer's work from other sources were often mixed (at best). About him, Darwin wrote in his autobiography, edited by his grand- daughter, Nora Barlow:

> After reading any of his books, I generally feel enthusiastic admiration for his transcendent tal- ents, and have often wondered whether in the distant future he would rank with such great men as Descartes, Leibnitz, etc., about whom, howev- er, I know very little. Nevertheless I am not con- scious of having profited in my own work by Spencer's writings. (Barlow, 1958, pp. 108–109)

William James (Chapter 10) used Spencer's *Principles of Psychology* as his text in 1876 in the first course in America on the new physiological (experi- mental) psychology and cited Spencer extensively in his own *Principles of Psychology* (James, 1890). However, James was also sometimes critical of Spencer's abilities (e.g., Boring, 1950).

Almost universally recognized as a brilliant thinker, Spencer was interested in discovering the relations between facts. By contrast, Darwin was a great observer, a man of dazzling insight, and was among functionalism's most important antecedents. He is certainly one of the key figures in the history of Western science.

CHARLES ROBERT DARWIN

Charles Robert Darwin (1809–1882) was the son of Robert Darwin, a wealthy physician, and Susannah Wedgwood Darwin, the granddaughter of Josiah Wedgwood, the famous potter. As noted, Darwin's paternal grandfather was Erasmus Darwin, a distin- guished thinker in his own right. Darwin was born in Shrewsbury, England, on February 12, 1809, the same day as Abraham Lincoln.

Darwin was an indifferent student who seemed fated not to fulfill the destiny of his heritage. After grammar school at Shrewsbury, Darwin was sent by his father to medical school at the University of Edinburgh, where he found the lectures dull and the clinical experiences horrifying. In the days before anesthesia, surgery was swift and gory, and Darwin fled from his second visit to an operation, never to return.

With the clergy in mind, Darwin next went to Cambridge, where he formed friendships with the Reverends Adam Sedgwick (1785–1873) and John Stevens Henslow (1796–1861). Sedgwick was a Cambridge professor of geology, and Darwin accompanied him on a geological tour of north Wales after his graduation in 1831.

Botany professor Henslow encouraged Darwin's interest in zoology and geology, and the two men were often seen walking the streets of the town together. At this point, Darwin saw his future in his friend: "More than anyone, Henslow was the kind of man he yearned to be—a clerical naturalist or professor—the sort that even [his father] might approve of" (Desmond & Moore, 1991, p. 89). Fate had other plans for Darwin, however: Henslow recommended that he accompany **Captain Robert FitzRoy** (1805–1865) on the HMS *Beagle*'s planned 2-year surveying voyage of South America. FitzRoy was looking for a "gentleman" to share his table and to give him someone other than the crew to talk to. If the gentleman happened to be a naturalist, there would be opportunity aplenty on the trip.

After an uncle convinced Darwin's father of the trip's benefits, it became a matter of convincing FitzRoy that Darwin was right for the position. However, FitzRoy believed in physiognomy, the notion that a person's character can be deduced from his or her features, "and [FitzRoy] doubted whether anyone with [Darwin's] nose could possess sufficient energy and determination for the voyage. But I think he was afterwards well-satisfied that my nose had spoken falsely" (Barlow, 1958, p. 72). Darwin's amiability won over FitzRoy, who, ironically, saw the voyage as "a grand opportunity to substantiate the Bible, especially the book of Genesis. As a naturalist, Darwin might easily find many evidences of the Flood and the first appearance of all created things upon the earth. He could perform a valuable service by interpreting his scientific discoveries in the light of the Bible" (Moorehead, 1969, p. 37). Note that Darwin himself was earnestly religious at the beginning of the voyage, often "quoting the Bible as an unanswerable authority on some point of morality" (Barlow, p. 85).

For Darwin, the trip was the experience of a lifetime, although he suffered from seasickness throughout the voyage. Not long into the trip, Darwin read the first volume of Lyell's *Principles of Geology*. Lyell advocated a controversial geological theory called uniformitarianism, which holds that the earth's major features are the result of processes occurring

over eons. In Chile, Darwin experienced an earthquake, which convinced him that Lyell was correct: The earth is far older than the Biblical account suggests, and the processes that have shaped it are still occurring. Lyell and uniformitarianism were critical for encouraging Darwin to think in the kind of time frames required by a gradual process of change.

In addition to his geological investigations, Darwin was fascinated by his biological studies. The *Beagle*'s frequent landings gave Darwin opportunities to explore exotic and varied species of animal and plant life. As a passionate collector from an early age, he "seemed . . . intent on putting the South American continent into specimen bottles" (Irvine, 1955, p. 47).

In the Galápagos Islands, Darwin found striking evidence for the changeability of species. Some 500 miles off the northwestern coast of South America, the Galápagos Islands lie on the equator and are home to species found nowhere else on earth. *Galápagos* is Spanish for "giant tortoise," one of the island chain's more well-known inhabitants, and Darwin discovered that each island contained its own tortoise variety. A local Englishman remarked to him that he could tell at a glance which island a particular tortoise came from by the design of its shell.

Even more striking were the varieties of finches on the islands. There were finches on one island with thick, strong beaks for cracking nuts, finches on another island with smaller beaks designed to catch insects, and so on. Apparently the finches on a particular island, separated by miles of ocean from other finches, had changed to fit the requirements of the island they inhabited. Although Darwin did not immediately recognize all the implications of what he had observed on the Galápagos Islands, his ideas about the immutability of species were undermined by his observations.

Arriving home in the fall of 1836, Darwin found that he was already well regarded in scientific circles. The specimens he had shipped back to England had been well received, and Henslow had taken the liberty of publishing geological excerpts from Darwin's letters. In short order, Darwin became a fellow of the Royal Geological and Zoological Societies and began editing for publication the journal of his experiences on the voyage. He also found time in 1839 to marry his cousin, Emma Wedgwood (1808–1896). Finding the pace of London life too exhausting, in 1842 the Darwins moved to Down House near the village of Downe.

Now convinced of the mutability of species, in October of 1838 Darwin read "for amusement" **Thomas Malthus**'s 1798 *Essay on the Principle of Population.* In it, Malthus (1766–1834), an economist and clergyman, discussed the tendency of the human population to increase faster than the means to support it. The result is a population suppressed by famine, disease, and war.

From his studies of the selective breeding of animal species, Darwin had already grasped the idea of selection. Obviously, humans select domestic animals for particular qualities. The question of how nature selects was answered by Malthus's essay: Nature selects by breeding an oversupply of a species and then killing off individuals whose characteristics fail to match the needs of their environments. Animals that are better adapted to the environment are more likely to survive to procreate. There is a continual struggle for existence in which the fittest survive.

Struck with this insight, Darwin did not rush to publish it. In fact, it was not until 1842 that he wrote a 35-page sketch. In 1844, the sketch was expanded to 231 pages, which he gave to his wife with instructions on publishing it if he died. Given Darwin's ill health, an early demise was distinctly possible.

Some historians wonder if Darwin's illness was a psychosomatic response to his theory's implications, or if it was the result of a then-undiagnosed malady to which he had been exposed on the *Beagle*'s voyage. The leading candidate for a "real" illness is Chagas disease, something Darwin might have contracted from handling the South American Benchuga bug. Whatever their cause, Darwin's symptoms included weakness, fatigue, headache, and insomnia, and as he grew older, any change from a set routine proved disastrous. His routine included 3 hours of scientific work (8 to 9:30 A.M. and 10:30 to noon), walking, resting, thinking, answering letters, and long hours of reading.

Although he had communicated his ideas to his closest friends and had given Emma a sketch,

Darwin had still not published a paper on evolution by the mid-1850s. Lyell urged him to publish at least a brief account of his theory of organic evolution, which Lyell did not fully accept, to establish his priority. The botanist **Joseph Hooker** (1817–1911) advised Darwin instead to publish an authoritative treatise, and Darwin was working on this project when he received the now-famous letter and essay in 1858 from **Alfred Russel Wallace** (1823–1913). As we noted in Chapter 1, Wallace's theory, developed in some 3 years, was remarkably similar to the one on which Darwin had been laboring for decades.

Darwin's immediate reaction was to have Wallace's paper published and to give him credit for the discovery, but this idea was rejected by Lyell and Hooker, who believed that Darwin should have priority. After an agonizing exchange of letters with Lyell and Hooker, Darwin, prostrated with despair at the death of one of his children, left the problem in the hands of his friends. Their solution was to have Wallace's paper read at the next meeting of the Linnean Society along with a paper by Darwin. To ensure that Darwin got the credit he deserved, his paper was accompanied by "a copy of Darwin's letter to Asa Gray [describing natural selection in some detail], written the previous year, and a statement certifying that Hooker had known of Darwin's work fifteen years earlier" (Rachels, 1986, p. 23). Although Rachels contends that Darwin and his friends acted badly in the affair, Wallace was quite pleased with the turn of events and apparently never considered that he should have received priority over Darwin. In fact, he called one of the many books he wrote during his lengthy career *Darwinism.* Actually, Wallace made several contributions to our understanding of evolution, and some of his thoughts on matters such as the evolution of the human brain and the intelligence of native peoples were more enlightened than Darwin's (Eiseley, 1961).

Darwin's thinking about evolution began soon after he returned to England, and in 1837 he started his first notebook on the transmutation problem. As we indicated, in 1838 he read Malthus and got the idea of natural selection through a struggle for survival. Why did Darwin wait until 1858, and then only under the pressure of Wallace's letter, to go public? Some of the suggested causes for the delay include work on other publications, fear of the theory's social consequences, and time to accumulate supporting evidence. However, perhaps the best explanation is that Darwin delayed because of what he considered a possibly fatal difficulty for his theory (Richards, 1983).

From Darwin's reading in the early 1840s, he knew that theologians were enthusiastic about one particular example from the animal kingdom that appeared to reveal God's hand—the instincts of worker bees and slave-making ants. If not for God's intervention, how else could the ants' ability to select the best servants be explained? What other explanation would apply to the ability of bees to make perfectly hexagonal cells to house their larvae?

In the 1840s, Darwin's explanation for instinctive behavior was that—like anatomical structures—it evolved through natural selection. Unfortunately, this explanation appeared invalid for the neuter insects, who leave no offspring to inherit favorable variations. In fact, Darwin at first considered this an insurmountable problem, and he said as much in *The Origin of Species.* Thus, Darwin delayed until he felt he had resolved the issue. "Darwin came to recognize the solution to his difficulty [kin selection rather than selection at the individual level] and to flesh it out only in late December of 1857, as he wrote what would become the chapter on instinct in *The Origin of Species*" (Richards, 1983, p. 52). Darwin realized that evolution may have as its basic unit something bigger than the individual. That is, a kinship group such as a hive, a colony, or a family could be what was struggling to survive and propagate itself. As with earlier insights, Darwin's essentially correct understanding in the absence of a well-articulated genetic theory was remarkable.

Darwin and Wallace's joint papers to the Linnean Society in July 1858 attracted little attention. However, there was a decidedly different reaction to the publication a little over a year later of *On the Origin of Species by Means of Natural Selection, or the Preservation of Favoured Races in the Struggle for Life.* The first edition's 1,250 printed copies sold out on the day of publication. Darwin is shown in Figure 9–3 at about the age at which he wrote *The Origin of Species.*

FIGURE 9–3.   Charles Darwin at about the age at which he wrote *The Origin of Species.*

Source: Stock Montage.

The reaction was predictably negative. Darwin's *The Origin of Species* "became a kind of anti-Bible" (Irvine, 1955, p. 107). Fortunately, Darwin had chosen his allies well. In addition to Lyell and Hooker, there was Thomas Huxley, Spencer's friend. Before the *Origin,* Huxley reacted to Darwin's ideas by giving up his belief in the Biblical account of creation without fully accepting evolution. After reading *The Origin of Species,* his first reaction was to exclaim: "How extremely stupid not to have thought of that" (Irvine, p. 106). Huxley soon proved his mettle in the battle with the forces arrayed against Darwin.

In June of 1860, the British Association for the Advancement of Science met at Oxford to debate Darwin's evolutionary theory. The chief opponents were Bishop of Oxford Samuel Wilberforce (1805–1873), whose oratorical skills had earned him the nickname of "Soapy Sam," and Huxley and Hooker. As usual, Darwin was ill and did not attend. However, the attendance from Oxford undergraduates, clergy, and scientists and their wives was so great that the meeting had to be moved from its usual venue.

After two days of meetings, Wilberforce began an oration against Darwinism, which he unwisely punctuated with a jab at Huxley sitting on the speaker's platform, demanding to know whether it was through his grandfather or his grandmother that he claimed to be descended from the apes. Huxley, speaking in an undertone, said, "The Lord hath delivered him into my hands." He then stood and "announced that he would certainly prefer to be descended from an ape rather than from a cultivated man who prostituted the gifts of culture and eloquence to the service of prejudice and falsehood. The Bishop in short did not know what he was talking about" (Moorehead, 1969, p. 263).

Pandemonium ensued, and in its midst a slight, grey-haired man stood, waving a Bible. "Here was the truth, he cried, here and nowhere else. Long ago he had warned Darwin about his dangerous thoughts. Had he but known then that he was carrying in his ship such a . . ." (Moorehead, 1969, p. 266). It was Robert FitzRoy, the skipper of the *Beagle*. Less than 5 years later, he committed suicide.

The Origin of Species

Although the main ideas of the book came as a revelation to some and a threat to many, Darwin's most famous work is not exactly exciting. Instead, he marshals fact after fact to lead inevitably to the conclusion that species change over time in response to natural selection. Given the overabundance of life and the limited supply of essential ingredients to support it, any variation in a species that gives its possessor an advantage will increase the chances that the individual survives to breed and pass on the advantage.

Darwin's chapter on instinct is particularly important for psychology. In it, he treats behavior patterns in the same way he treats bodily structure, as something inheritable. Behavior, even instinctual behavior, varies within a species. If an individual's

behavior confers a reproductive advantage, then this too will be passed on to its offspring.

Given Darwin's evidence, it is difficult to imagine how a thoughtful person would not have reached the same conclusion that he expressed succinctly in the second paragraph of the final chapter of *The Origin of Species*:

> That many and serious objections may be advanced against the theory of descent with modification through variation and natural selection, I do not deny. . . . Nothing at first can appear more difficult to believe than that the more complex organs and instincts have been perfected, not by means superior to, though analogous with, human reason, but by the accumulation of innumerable slight variations, each good for the individual possessor. Nevertheless, this difficulty, though appearing to our imagination insuperably great, cannot be considered real if we admit the following propositions, namely, that all parts of the organisation and instincts offer, at least, individual differences— that there is a struggle for existence leading to the preservation of profitable deviations of structure or instinct—and, lastly, that gradations in the state of perfection of each organ may have existed, each good of its kind. The truth of these propositions cannot, I think, be disputed. (Darwin, 1859/1958, p. 426)

But the truth of the propositions was, and sometimes still is, disputed, particularly by the nonscientific community. This illustrates that what is commonly accepted by scientists may be rejected or unknown to the majority of laypersons.

As important as it was, *The Origin of Species* did not mark the end of Darwin's career, and, in fact, two of his later books are of even more direct relevance for psychology. They are *The Descent of Man, and Selection in Relation to Sex* and *The Expression of the Emotions in Man and Animals*.

The Descent of Man

Near the end of *The Origin of Species*, Darwin wrote that "In the future . . . [m]uch light will be thrown on the origin of man and his history" (Darwin, 1859/1958, p. 449). In the first part of *The Descent of*

Man, Darwin aimed natural selection's light on humankind, presenting evidence that humans, like other species, had evolved from some "lower" form. He began by pointing to the similarity in structure between humans and the "higher" mammals:

> It is notorious that man is constructed on the same general type or model as other mammals. All the bones in his skeleton can be compared with corresponding bones in a monkey, bat, or seal. So it is with his muscles, nerves, blood-vessels, and internal viscera. The brain . . . follows the same law, as shown by Huxley and other anatomists. Bischoff, who is a hostile witness, admits that every chief fissure and fold in the brain of man has its analogy in that of the orang . . . (Darwin, 1874, p. 6)

The similarity in structure that Darwin noted between the human brain and the brain of an orangutan points to a similarity in mental ability, and he wrote: "My object . . . is to show that there is no fundamental difference between man and the higher mammals in their mental faculties" (Darwin, 1874, p. 74). Innumerable examples of animal behavior are then used to illustrate that animals exhibit the qualities typically attributed to humans: for example, jealousy, which illustrates that animals love and need to be loved; excitement and boredom; curiosity; imitation; memory; reason; sense of beauty; and so on. Darwin concluded that "the difference in mind between man and the higher animals, great as it is, certainly is one of degree and not of kind" (p. 143).

Darwin's conclusion that there is continuity of mental ability in the animal kingdom sent his supporters, such as George Romanes (discussed later), to search for evidence of reasoning in animals. This was the context for the interest in animal geniuses like Clever Hans (Chapter 8). Another way to support the continuity was to search for animal origins of human behavior, and Darwin took this approach in his next work of importance for psychology.

The Expression of the Emotions in Man and Animals

In *The Descent of Man,* Darwin planned to include a chapter on emotions, but he set the chapter aside when it grew too large. The expanded chapter became *The Expression of the Emotions in Man and Animals,* first published in 1872. In the book, Darwin sought to demonstrate that human emotional expressions are inherited and have evolved because they have survival value.

Darwin used several methods for gathering information, including the observation of infants to see emotional expression at the earliest stage of life; the study of the expressions of the insane, because "they are liable to the strongest passions, and give uncontrolled vent to them" (Darwin, 1872/1979, p. 13); the study of cultural variations and similarities in emotional expression; and the examination of the emotional expressions in "some of the commoner animals." For information on the expressions of the insane, Darwin relied heavily on material he received from James Crichton Browne (1840–1938), a psychiatrist, amateur photographer, and the director of the West Riding Asylum (Gilman, 1979).

Darwin concluded that three principles account for most of the emotional expressions used by humans and animals: the *principle of serviceable associated habits,* the *principle of antithesis,* and the *principle of the direct action of the nervous system.* According to the principle of serviceable associated habits, movements, facial expressions, and the like that have been long associated with some particular set of stimuli will tend to be performed when the associated stimuli are encountered, even though the movements are useless. Wrinkling the nose in a sneer in response to an offensive smell is an illustration.

The principle of antithesis is seen in the submissive posture of a dog who, moments before discovering that an intruder is its master, had bristled with hostility toward the approaching human. Instead of an upright posture with erected fur, bared fangs, and ears tight against the head, the dog now crouches with smooth fur, covered teeth, and formerly stiff tail wagging at its master's approach. The dog assumes postures that are the opposite (antithesis) of postures indicating hostility and aggressiveness.

Finally, there is the principle of the direct action of the nervous system. In highly aroused states, Darwin believed that the "nerve-force" spills over and produces movements without functional benefit. For example, Darwin noted that either fear, anger, or joy might produce trembling. "I remember once seeing a boy who had just shot his first snipe on the wing, and his hands trembled to such a degree from delight, that he could not for some time reload his gun" (Darwin, 1872/1979, p. 67). In his autobiography, Darwin revealed the hunter's identity: "How well I remember killing my first snipe, and my excitement was so great that I had much difficulty in reloading my gun from the trembling of my hands" (Barlow, 1958, p. 44).

In *Expression of the Emotions,* Darwin devoted great effort to showing that human emotional expressions are similar in all humans, no matter what their culture or race. From this, he concluded that all races "descended from a single parent-stock, which must have been almost completely human in structure, and to a large extent in mind, before the period at which the races diverged from each other" (Darwin, 1872/1979, p. 361). In 1872, as in 1859, Darwin was still proselytizing, and in the book's last paragraph, he wrote: "We have seen that the study of the theory of expression confirms to a certain limited extent the conclusion that man is derived from some lower animal form . . . but as far as my judgment serves, such confirmation was hardly needed" (p. 367).

Darwin's Influence

The Origin of Species changed forever our view of the world and the place of humans in it. No longer could we see a Cartesian split in the animal kingdom, with animals as automatons and humans as possessors of mind and reason. To an even greater degree, *The Descent of Man* made explicit the continuity between humans and animals, making the study of animals a legitimate enterprise for learning about humans. Darwin's encouragement of a young naturalist, George John Romanes, began comparative psychology, which was ably developed further by a committed Darwinian, C. Lloyd Morgan (Burghardt, 1985).

The "animal nature" of humans undoubtedly influenced Sigmund Freud (Chapter 15) and his conception of the id as a storehouse for biological drives. Interestingly, Darwin recognized his own

tendency to use repression (motivated forgetting), a mechanism Freud saw as central to our attempts to keep ourselves from experiencing injurious self-revelations. In fact, Darwin attributed at least part of the success of *The Origin of Species* to his ability to *avoid* repression:

> I had, also, during many years, followed a golden rule, namely, that whenever a published fact, a new observation or thought came across me, which was opposed to my general results, to make a memorandum of it without fail and at once; for I had found by experience that such facts and thoughts were far more apt to escape from the memory than favourable ones. Owing to this habit, very few objections were raised against my views which I had not at least noticed and attempted to answer. (Barlow, 1958, p. 123)

In 1877, Darwin published "Biographical sketch of an infant," which was based on his records of the early development of his first child. This can be seen as one of the first papers in child psychology. Darwin suggested that the stages through which his son developed roughly approximated the stages through which humans may have proceeded in their evolution. For example, in language development the boy learned to connect names with important people or objects before inventing words for himself and stringing them together; Darwin wrote that this is what we might expect, because we know that some animals can learn to understand spoken words. In the development of locomotion, the boy first crawled (moved in a quadrupedal fashion) before learning to walk (moved bipedally), again illustrating the stages through which our ancestors may have evolved. The idea that an individual's development repeats in some fashion the development of the species ("ontogeny recapitulates phylogeny") was later popularized by the German naturalist and Darwinian, **Ernst Haeckel** (1834–1919). The same idea was the key to G. Stanley Hall's developmental theories (Chapter 10).

How can you summarize the influence of a man about whom so much has been written, both in support and in refutation? Darwin's key contribution has to be his idea of evolution by natural selection, about which Dennett (1995) wrote:

If I were to give an award for the single best idea anyone has ever had, I'd give it to Darwin, ahead of Newton and Einstein and everyone else. In a single stroke, the idea of evolution by natural selection unifies the realm of life, meaning, and purpose with the realm of space and time, cause and effect, mechanism and physical law. (p. 21)

Darwin, for all his limitations, left behind an enormous amount of published work of high quality.

The strongest proof of his greatness is that he—not Wallace, Huxley, nor anybody else—was the center of Darwinism. Despite his illnesses and his limitations, he had the largeness, sobriety, and concentration of mind to retain leadership within his own broad area of investigation. (Irvine, 1955, p. 73)

Darwin died at three o'clock on the morning of April 19, 1882. His family wanted him to be buried at Downe, but his friends and supporters had another idea: Because his country had not awarded him a knighthood (ironically, three of his sons were knighted), he would be canonized by burial in Westminster Abbey. With Huxley, Hooker, and Wallace among his pallbearers, Darwin was buried next to Sir Isaac Newton. Francis Galton "was sufficiently impressed [by Darwin's funeral] to urge in a letter to *The Pall Mall Gazette* that the old creation window [in Westminster Abbey] . . . be replaced by an evolutionary one in honor of his famous cousin" (Irvine, 1955, p. 229).

GEORGE JOHN ROMANES

As we noted, *The Descent of Man* stimulated the search for humanlike abilities in animals. None searched more ardently for such abilities than the man who became Darwin's protégé, George John Romanes. Darwin had seen a letter by Romanes in *Nature*, and he responded by sending Romanes a friendly note and an invitation to pay a visit. Romanes's wife later called that visit an epoch event in her husband's life (E. Romanes, 1896).

Born in Canada, **George John Romanes** (1848–1894) was the son of a minister who received a major inheritance the year Romanes was born and moved the family back to England. After a spotty education at home, where he was considered a "shocking dunce," in 1867 Romanes entered Cambridge, initially planning to take Holy Orders. In 1870, he took his tests, earning a Second Class degree. He gave no answer to a question on natural selection, not having read Darwin at this time. In fact, he did not read Darwin until about 1873 and paid his first visit in about 1874, the same year he began to work in the physiology laboratory of Dr. Burdon Sanderson, Titchener's first mentor (Chapter 7). By this time, Romanes had decided to devote himself to scientific research.

Although Romanes was a prolific researcher, with many and varied publications, he is most remembered for *Animal Intelligence,* which appeared in 1881. This and his later book, *Mental Evolution in Animals,* were "designed to prove that the law of evolution is universal, and applies to the mind of man as well as to his bodily organisation" (E. Romanes, 1896, p. 170). *Animal Intelligence* quite literally began the field of comparative psychology: "I have thought it desirable that there should be something resembling a textbook of the facts of Comparative Psychology . . ." (Romanes, 1881/1895, p. v).

Although he made many positive contributions to the psychology of animal behavior (Burghardt, 1985), Romanes feared that *Animal Intelligence* might be judged badly, and he was right. Today, if Romanes is mentioned at all, it is usually in a negative fashion as "the archetypal purveyor of anecdotes about animals" (Boakes, 1984, p. 25). In reality, Romanes was more critical of the anecdotes he collected than many of his contemporaries, including Darwin. Romanes used only stories reported by observers he knew to be competent (anything reported by Darwin was automatically incorporated), reports based on careful observation, and anecdotes that described an animal ability that had been noted by independent observers. Despite these stringent criteria, *Animal Intelligence* contains much that would be rejected today. As Boakes put it, "In many cases the observed behaviour was interesting and believable; it was the observer's rich interpretation in terms of current ideas from human psychology that was wide open to objection" (p. 26).

To illustrate, Romanes carefully described a cat that had learned to open a door with a half-hoop handle and a thumb-latch. Because he had observed this behavior himself, there is little reason to question its authenticity. There followed an example of Romanes's "rich interpretation":

> Hence we can only conclude that the cats in such cases have a very definite idea as to the mechanical properties of a door; they know that to make it open, even when unlatched, it requires to be *pushed.* . . . The whole psychological process, therefore, implied by the fact of a cat opening a door in this way is really most complex. First the animal must have observed that the door is opened by the hand grasping the handle and moving the latch. Next she must reason . . . If a hand can do it, why not a paw? Then, strongly moved by this idea, she makes the first trial. The steps which follow have not been observed, so we cannot certainly say whether she learns by a succession of trials that depression of the thumb-piece constitutes the essential part of the process, or, perhaps more probably, that her initial observations supplied her with the idea of clicking the thumb-piece. (Romanes, 1881/1895, pp. 421–422)

Unfortunately, Romanes had not made the earlier observations. If he had, perhaps he would have been less inclined to credit his cat with so much reasoning ability. Edward Lee Thorndike (Chapter 12) made just such observations and concluded from his cats' trial-and-error behavior that the animals did not use reasoning.

The fact that Romanes is remembered mainly for the anecdotes in *Animal Intelligence* was in part caused by his steadfast loyalty to Darwin and to his unquestioning acceptance of Darwin's addition of a Lamarckian principle to natural selection to explain the development of instincts. By the 1880s, Wallace's position that evolution could be explained by natural selection, without resort to Lamarckism, was called "Neo-Darwinism" by Romanes. Neo-Darwinism was strongly supported by German biologist August Weismann's (1834-1914) "germ-plasm" theory of heredity, which contributed to the modern theory of genetics (see Johnston, 1995).

Note that Darwin had no real understanding of genetics as the vehicle of inheritance, which explains his attachment to some Lamarckian concepts and underscores the remarkable insights he had into the evolutionary process. Ironically, Austrian monk and botanist **Gregor Johann Mendel** (1822–1884) had published work on the genetics of pea plants that would have solved problems of inheritance that Darwin agonized over both before and after publication of *The Origin of Species*. It is one of those vagaries of history that Mendel's research appeared in an obscure journal and was not discovered until 1900, many years after both he and Darwin had died.

Like Romanes, C. Lloyd Morgan—who became Romanes's protégé although he was only 4 years younger than Romanes—supported the "unadulterated" Darwinism (i.e., with some Lamarckism), at least during the period of his friendship with Romanes. In the last year of his life, Romanes summoned Morgan and gave him instructions about unfinished work that Morgan carried out with diligence (E. Romanes, 1896). Romanes (Figure 9–4)

FIGURE 9–4. George John Romanes.

Source: National Library of Medicine.

was still devising plans for experiments bearing on Weismann's theory in his final days. He died on May 23, 1894, just 3 days after his 46th birthday.

CONWY LLOYD MORGAN

Reminiscent of Romanes's experience with Darwin, Morgan's relationship with Romanes began through a letter Morgan sent to *Nature* criticizing a passage in *Animal Intelligence* suggesting that scorpions commit suicide in times of stress. Morgan's experiments suggested instead that the animals' tail movements were reflexive attempts to rid themselves of sources of irritation, which only incidentally resulted in their being stung.

Thomas Huxley, Darwin's friend and supporter, played a major role in **Conwy Lloyd Morgan**'s (1852–1936) intellectual development. Too poor to attend Oxford, the school of his forebears, Morgan was sent to London's Royal School of Mines to be trained as a mining engineer. At one of the school's annual dinners, Huxley, professor of natural history, engaged him in conversation and ended the evening by suggesting that Morgan "put in a year under him" (Morgan, 1932, p. 241), which Morgan did following a 3-month trip to America.

After a series of temporary jobs, Morgan obtained a teaching post in South Africa, where he made the scorpion observations. In addition, he continued the self-education that had begun in his teens when the parish rector had advised him to read Berkeley (Chapter 4) in the original rather than accepting someone's second- or third-hand opinion. Berkeley was followed by many of the philosophers we have encountered, and eventually Morgan read Darwin's *Origin of Species*, "browsed in Romanes' *Animal Intelligence*; and resolutely tackled Herbert Spencer" (Morgan, 1932, p. 247). In regard to Romanes's anecdotes, Morgan

> felt, as no doubt he did, that not on such anecdotal foundations could a science of comparative psychology be built. . . . I then entertained doubts whether one could extract from the minds of animals (wholly inferential from their observable behavior) the data requisite for a

FIGURE 9–5.   Conwy Lloyd Morgan and family.

Source: From Boakes From Darwin to Behaviourism (1984) by courtesy of Mary Denniston and Harvard College Library.

> science. . . . Did one get out of the animal mind aught else than that which one put into it? (pp. 247–248)

In 1884, Morgan (Figure 9–5) returned to England to teach at University College, Bristol. Approximately 10 years later, he began research designed to enable him to "get into the animal mind." Reasoning that instinctive behavior is characterized by "*like* performance on the first and on all subsequent occasions" (Morgan, 1932, p. 249), Morgan made sure that he was studying behavior on its first occasion. To this end, he studied, among other species, chickens hatched in an incubator. In one study, Morgan gave chicks the opportunity to peck and consume edible caterpillars. Next, he exposed them to bad tasting and brilliantly decorated caterpillars of the cinnabar moth. After a few pecks, the chicks avoided these caterpillars. Morgan considered the chicks' behavior an example of the Spencer-Bain principle, in which behavior is modified by its consequences. As we noted in Chapter 4,

Morgan's lectures on his research on the Spencer-Bain principle at Harvard in 1896 undoubtedly influenced Thorndike.

By 1900, Morgan's support for "unadulterated Darwinism" had waned, and he now rejected any appeal to Lamarckism because of the success of Weismann's germ-plasm doctrine of heredity, which precluded any effect on heritable material of an individual's bodily or psychological changes. Although he rejected Lamarckism, Morgan could not accept a second assumption that was part of Neo-Darwinism: the Cartesian perception of the organism as an automaton. In Chapter 3, we noted that Descartes believed that animals were totally mechanical, without a mind or soul. Huxley, the modern pioneer of the notion of animals as automatons, accepted that animals have consciousness while he treated them like machines; he believed their consciousness was merely a side effect (epiphenomenon) of a certain amount of neural tissue.

Supported by the more Lamarckian James Mark Baldwin (Chapter 12), Morgan developed a theory of organic selection as "an attempt to repair evolutionary theory by treating evolution not as a random, mechanical process, but as reflecting the organism's *intentional* relation to its environment" (Costall, 1993, p. 115, emphasis added). Morgan and Baldwin saw their theory as an extension of Darwin that Darwin would have approved.

However, Lloyd Morgan was also the author of what we call **Morgan's Canon**, which was supposedly an effort to avoid the dangers of Romanes's anecdotal method by invoking the Law of Parsimony or Ockham's razor, named for William of Ockham (Chapter 3). In this context, the Law of Parsimony states that we should explain behavior by the simplest mental processes that will account for the facts. The Canon is usually stated as follows:

> In no case may we interpret an action as the outcome of the exercise of a higher psychical faculty, if it can be interpreted as the outcome of one which stands lower in the psychological scale. (Morgan, 1894, p. 53)

How can we reconcile Morgan's Canon, generally interpreted as an attempt to eliminate mind or consciousness in animals, with Morgan's theory of organic selection, which stresses the importance of mind (intentionality) in the evolutionary process?

According to Costall (1993), Morgan did not intend for the Canon to be a rigid prohibition against *any* explanation of animal behavior in terms of higher mental processes. Morgan's main concern was that Darwin's supporters, in their zeal to prove the evolution of mental abilities, had read too much into their accounts of animal behavior in order to find continuity of mental abilities. "The real aim of Morgan's Canon was to alert the Darwinians to the need to establish the existence of modes of relations between organisms and environments other than that of reflective, rational thought . . ." (p. 117). Rather than being a revolt against Romanes, as it is usually portrayed, Costall contends that Morgan's Canon was

> an acceptance of Romanes's conception of a true comparative psychology, as opposed to a mere study of animal conduct . . . Contrary to Morgan's original intentions, [Morgan's Canon] has been used with great rhetorical effect to perpetuate exactly the kind of psychology and biology Morgan sought to displace, the essentially Cartesian notion of the animal as "a mere puppet in the hand of circumstances," . . . (pp. 120–121)

We can conclude our look at Romanes and Morgan by noting that Romanes began comparative psychology in support of Darwin, and Morgan developed it experimentally. As we indicated, Romanes was more than an uncritical anecdotalist, and the interpretation of Morgan's Canon as a refutation of Romanes's interpretations needs to be more closely examined.

Following Darwin, "mind" itself could be seen as something that evolved because it facilitated the individual's adaptation to the environment; mind had, and has, function. In order for mind to have evolved, there must be variability of mental ability within human populations, and the study of individual differences thus became a legitimate focus for psychologists. One of the most important early workers in the study of individual differences was Darwin's cousin and friend, Francis Galton.

FRANCIS GALTON

Of all the individuals affected by Darwin's theory of evolution, perhaps none was more influenced than Francis Galton. Galton, responding to a letter from Darwin giving his positive reaction to Galton's book, *Hereditary Genius* (1869), penned the following:

> It would be idle to speak of the delight your letter has given me, as there is no one in the world whose approbation in these matters can have the same weight as yours. Neither is there any one whose approbation I prize more highly, . . . because I always think of you in the same way as converts from barbarism think of the teacher who first relieved them from the intollerable (sic) burden of their superstition. I used to be wretched under the weight of the old fashioned 'arguments [of Creation] from design', of which I felt though I was unable to prove it myself, the worthlessness. Consequently the appearance of your 'Origin of Species' formed a real crisis in my life; your book drove away the constraint of my old superstition as if it had been a nightmare and was the first to give me freedom of thought. (Galton, 1869, reproduced in Pearson, 1914–1930, Vol. 1, Plate II)

From his first reading of *The Origin of Species,* Galton's interest in the "natural history of human faculty" never diminished (McClearn, 1991). Galton, seeking to supply the evidence of human variability in mental and physical abilities required for human evolution, studied individual differences in contrast to the Continental studies of Fechner and Wundt, which aimed to discover the general principles of human nature. Studies of individual differences proved to be of paramount importance for American psychology. Galton's (Figure 9–6) talents, experiences, and interests before 1859 prepared him admirably for his subsequent study of human abilities.

Francis Galton (1822–1911) was born in Birmingham, England, the ninth and youngest child in an upper-class British family that included the founders of the Quaker religion on his father's side and the Darwins on his mother's side. He was the grandson of Erasmus Darwin, and his mother was the half-sister of Charles Darwin's father. Galton's father was a wealthy banker, and when he died,

FIGURE 9–6. Francis Galton.
Source: Archives of the History of American Psychology.

Galton's inheritance freed him from the need to acquire a profession.

Galton's early education was directed by an invalid sister, Adèle. By all accounts, Galton was incredibly precocious. His letter to Adèle written shortly before his 5th birthday well illustrates his early abilities.

> My Dear Adèle,
>
> I am four years old and I can read any English book. I can say all the Latin Substantives and Adjectives and active verbs besides 52 lines of Latin poetry. I can cast up any sum in addition and can multiply by 2, 3, 4, 5, 6, 7, 8, [9], 10, [11]. I can also say the pence table. I read French a little and I know the Clock.
>
> Francis Galton.
> Feb[r]uary-15-1827

(Pearson, 1914–1930, Vol. 1, p. 66)

Pearson explained that the numbers 9 and 11 were removed by Galton, the first with a penknife and the second with a piece of paper pasted over it. Galton knew he had claimed too much.

In comments that could easily have been said of the adult Francis Galton, his mother wrote of him when he was 8, "His activity of body could only be equalled by the activity of his mind. He was a boy never known to be idle. His habit was always to be doing something" (Violetta Galton, in an 1830 letter to her son Benjamin, as cited in Pearson, 1914–1930, Vol. 1, p. 67). That same year Galton began his education away from home, some of which he hated and some of which he enjoyed. Galton's experience at King Edward's School, Birmingham, which he entered at 13, began badly when he contracted scarlet fever. The illness proved to be an educational setback from which his biographer said he probably never completely recovered. Finally, at the age of 16, Galton was freed from the strictures of the private schools he had been attending and enrolled as a House Pupil at the General Hospital, Birmingham. His father had decided he would become a physician.

Little better suited to be a physician than his cousin had been, Galton proudly informed his father in early 1844 that he had earned his B.A. from Cambridge, placing third in mathematics (misunderstanding one question cost him a first-place standing). In May, Galton was back in Cambridge to resume his medical studies, but they were interrupted for good when his father died in October.

Following his father's death, Galton entered his "fallow years," during which he pursued "travel and sport for pure amusement's sake . . ." (Pearson, 1914–1930, Vol. 1, p. 209). By the summer of 1849, he had "sown his wild oats," and in 1850 he went to Africa, where for 2 years he explored uncharted territory in what today is Namibia. During this journey, he began to indulge in what became an obsession—measurement. To illustrate, at one point in his travels, Galton wanted to measure the form of a particularly well-endowed Hottentot maiden. There was a problem, however: He knew not a word of Hottentot and did not want to ask his missionary host to translate.

The object of my admiration stood under a tree, and was turning herself about . . . as ladies who wish to be admired usually do. Of a sudden my eye fell upon my sextant; the bright thought struck me, and I took a series of observations upon her figure in every direction, up and down, crossways, diagonally, and so forth, and I registered them carefully upon an outline drawing for fear of any mistake; this being done I boldly pulled out my measuring-tape, and measured the distance from where I was to the place where she stood, and having thus obtained both base and angles, I worked out the results by trigonometry and logarithms. (Galton, 1853/1971, p. 88)

Galton returned to England as one of Great Britain's renowned 19th-century explorers (e.g., Sir Richard Burton, David Livingstone). However, his health and his marriage dimmed his wanderlust and for the rest of his life Galton confined his travel to the occasional vacation ramble. Before abandoning geography altogether, Galton published *Art of Travel* (1855), a small volume that went through many editions and, according to Pearson (1914–1930, Vol. 2), "remains still a treasury not only for the professed traveller, but for the leaders of the boy-scouts and girl-guides; nay, there are methods to be learnt in the *Art of Travel* which may bring profit to the ordinary household of to-day" (p. 2).

Along with Galton's geographical explorations, there was a parallel interest in meteorology, stemming first from a consideration of the effect of climate on the explorer. With his penchant for measuring, Galton prepared tables of climate, and these led him to construct meteorological maps. From his wind and pressure charts, he discovered the anticyclone, a weather system the opposite of the already recognized cyclone. Although the term quickly caught on, few associate it with Francis Galton. Daily weather forecasts in England actually developed from storm warnings initiated by HMS *Beagle*'s Robert FitzRoy, who, unlike Galton, "had more enthusiasm than science" (Pearson, 1914–1930, Vol. 2, p. 43).

Hereditary Genius

Turning from the environment to humans themselves, Galton (1865) published a paper that anticipated the larger work to follow. In "Hereditary Talent and Character," he expressed his belief in the inheritance of both physical and mental characters and rejected the inheritance of acquired characteristics. Using biographical dictionaries and other sources, Galton demonstrated that distinguished fathers had many more distinguished sons than would be found in the general population. Anticipating by more than half a century Lewis Terman's results from his longitudinal study of gifted children (Chapter 18), Galton concluded that high intelligence was not associated with physical weakness. In fact, quite the opposite was true.

Galton followed his preliminary essay with the work for which he is best known, *Hereditary Genius: An Inquiry into Its Laws and Consequences,* published in 1869. His purpose was clear from the outset: "I propose to show in this book that a man's natural abilities are derived by inheritance, under exactly the same limitations as are the form and physical features of the whole organic world" (Galton, 1892, p. 1).

Galton began by contradicting the notion that babies are born pretty much alike, contending that there is wide variability in human ability. In his argument, Galton made his first appeal to statistical method, using the "very curious theoretical law of 'deviation from an average'" (Galton, 1892, p. 22) of **Jacques Quételet**. A Belgian astronomer and statistician, Quételet (1796–1874) had shown that the distributions of such heritable physical characteristics as the heights of French conscripts conformed to a curve with a peak in the center and symmetrical tails on either side, which we call the **normal curve**. Galton found that the distribution of scores on a Cambridge mathematical examination fit Quételet's distribution, which suggested to him that mental characteristics, like physical, were inherited. It should be noted that Galton's assumption of a correspondence between a normal distribution and the inheritance of a particular characteristic may not be valid.

Next, Galton examined the family trees of people eminent in different areas, his subjects including judges, statesmen, military commanders, literary men, scientists, poets, and wrestlers. Galton found that there were nearly 1,000 eminent men in the 300 families he studied. Because he had defined eminence as a position attained by only 1 out of 4,000, his discovery of so many men of eminence in a small number of families supported his belief in the inheritance of ability.

Further, Galton found that the incidence of eminence was greater the closer the kinship. Thus, the

> eminent sons are almost invariably more numerous than the eminent brothers, and these are a trifle more numerous than the eminent fathers. . . . [W]e come to a sudden dropping off of the numbers at the second grade of kinship, namely, at the grandfathers, uncles, nephews, and grandsons. . . . On reaching the third grade of kinship, another abrupt dropping off in numbers is again met with, but the first cousins are found to occupy a decidedly better position than other relations within the third grade. (Galton, 1892, p. 309)

Galton also found that there was a tendency for relatives to exhibit their abilities in the same fields. For example, the relatives of eminent painters were often painters themselves, and the relatives of eminent writers were often writers.

Galton concluded that his results provided evidence for the inheritance of abilities, but the possibility of environmental influences was high and not addressed in *Hereditary Genius.* The offspring of eminent parents in the Victorian era were afforded the best educational opportunities, the best medical treatment, and the best nutrition available, all of which might have contributed to their eventual success. Also, the model of a parent successful in science or music could easily encourage a child to develop skills similar to those of the parent.

Although Darwin and Wallace perceived the value of *Hereditary Genius,* their view was not universal. One critic was the Swiss botanist, **Alphonse de Candolle** (1806–1893). De Candolle was more impressed with environmental influences on the development of eminence in families, and Galton's book stimulated him to publish *Histoire des Sciences et des Savants depuis deux Siècle (History of the Sciences and Scientists over Two Centuries)* in 1872. Examining biographical information on over 300 eminent European scientists, de Candolle found that heredity played a role in their success, but he also found conclusive evidence for environmental influences such as the size and climate of a country, its type of government, and the degree of religious tolerance.

Galton's response to de Candolle's book began a correspondence with de Candolle that stimulated Galton to investigate further the heredity-environment question in scientists. For this purpose, he developed an extensive questionnaire that he sent to nearly 200 distinguished Fellows of the Royal Society. This instrument, which marked the first use of the **questionnaire**, asked for information ranging from the respondent's political and social background to such physical information as hair color and hat size. The scientists were also asked to describe their educational experiences, particularly experiences that might have interested them in science. In a question he considered crucial, Galton asked whether or not the respondents felt their interest in science was innate.

Although most of the responding Fellows thought their interest in science was innate, there was also evidence for the importance of the environment. For example, Galton observed that a relatively large number of the scientists were Scottish, and many of the Scots noted the value of their educational experiences in fostering an interest in science. Acknowledging this environmental influence, Galton called for a reform of the English schools to make them more like schools in Scotland.

In the 1874 book that addressed his study of eminent British scientists, Galton used the phrase "**nature and nurture**" and clearly described the issues involved.

> The phrase "nature and nurture" is a convenient jingle of words, for it separates under two distinct heads the innumerable elements of which personality is composed. Nature is all that a man brings with himself into the world; nurture is every influence that affects him after his birth. (Galton, 1874, p. 12)

The phrase was even part of the book's title: *English Men of Science: Their Nature and Nurture*. Although the phrase may have been stimulated by Galton's awareness of de Candolle's work (Fancher, 1979),

and its origin may be much earlier—for example, Shakespeare (Conley, 1984) or Richard Mulcaster, an early writer of educational treatises (Teigen, 1984)—there is no question that Galton deserves credit for popularizing it.

Having recognized an environmental influence on the development of eminent scientists, Galton introduced the **study of twins** in his attempt to measure the relative effect of nature and nurture. Twins are important because monozygotic (identical) twins share both their genes and their environments (if raised together), whereas dizygotic (fraternal) twins share their environments but only half of their genes. Particularly important are cases of identical twins separated soon after birth. If the twins turn out to be very similar, the similarity may be attributed to heredity. As we will see in Chapter 18, twin studies continue to be a powerful methodology for psychologists.

Galton gathered detailed case histories from nearly 100 twin pairs, finding that the pairs separated into two broad categories: pairs of like-sex twins with evidence for close similarity and pairs of twins in which there were marked dissimilarities. He concluded: "The impression that all this evidence leaves on the mind is one of some wonder whether nurture can do anything at all beyond giving instruction and professional training" (Galton, 1876, p. 404).

Galton's "Intelligence" Tests

Galton's hereditarian position led to his interest, or perhaps obsession, with the idea of **eugenics**, which is the improvement of the human race by selectively breeding the "best" people. Ironically, Galton and his wife had no children. But how would the most "fit" people be determined? If we waited until a person became eminent, the person might be too old to be used as breeding stock. Galton needed a test to identify the brightest and best people while they were still in their reproductive prime. This led him to establish the first **anthropometric laboratory** at the International Health Exhibition in London in 1884. For a small fee, a person could have a variety of measurements performed. The measurements were primarily physiological, as Galton assumed that the ablest individuals would have the best sensory acuity and the quickest reaction times. During the Exhibition, 9,337 people were measured, and when the Exhibition closed, the laboratory was moved to the Science Museum in South Kensington. Galton's monumental set of data is still considered worth analyzing (e.g., Johnson et al., 1985). Although Galton's physiological measurements failed to provide the measure of intelligence he sought—later studies found the relationship between physiological measures and measures of intelligence to be discouragingly low (Chapter 10)—they did stimulate him to develop an important statistical method—correlation.

Correlation and Regression

Faced with mountains of data relating height to weight, the height of parents to the height of their offspring, and so forth, Galton eventually began to try to visualize with graphs the relationship between such variables. That is, he plotted his data as **scatter plots**, graphs with one variable on the *x* axis and the other variable on the *y* axis. From the graphs, Galton concluded that there was reversion or **regression toward the mean**. For example, although children of tall parents tend to be tall themselves, they tend to be closer to the average height than their parents. Similarly, short parents tend to have short offspring, but their children tend to be closer to the average, that is, taller, than their parents.

At Galton's urging, **Karl Pearson** (1857–1936), a devoted disciple, developed a mathematical formula to calculate an index of correlation. Pearson's index is called the **Pearson product-moment correlation coefficient,** or **Pearson r,** the *r* standing for regression. Karl Pearson and his contemporary rival Sir Ronald Fisher (Chapter 18) are sometimes called the founders of modern statistics.

Other Contributions to Psychology

In addition to the contributions we have discussed, Galton is also recognized for his study of word associations, mental imagery, and comparative sensory abilities. His first attempt to study associations

came on a leisurely walk down Pall Mall in London. During his stroll, he was struck by the large number of associations stimulated by the objects he saw. A second walk a few days later also stimulated a variety of associations, but many were repetitions from the previous outing. Fascinated, Galton developed a method for studying his associations more scientifically.

Galton made a list of 75 different words, each written on a separate piece of paper. Next, he exposed the words one at a time, recording the associations and, with a stopwatch, the length of time it took him to produce two associations. He repeated this procedure on four different occasions at intervals of a month.

Again, he found that there were many repetitions. Of greater importance, Galton was able to identify in 124 cases when the association had occurred in his life. He found that 39% had occurred in his boyhood and youth, 46% in adulthood, and only 15% in the recent past. This was an early demonstration of the importance of the experiences of childhood for adult behavior.

Galton's **word-association experiment** was appropriated and developed extensively by Wundt and his students. Carl Jung (Chapter 16) also developed a word-association test based on Galton's work. In addition, Freud's development of free association may have been influenced by Galton's experiment. Finally, association-based studies of language and memory can be found in both the behaviorist and cognitive traditions (e.g., Crovitz, 1970).

In studying word associations, Galton found that imagery—picturing something in his mind—was more likely to be the second association to a word than the first. This observation stimulated his interest in mental imagery, which Galton studied with a questionnaire that asked his respondents to visualize the morning's breakfast table and then to answer questions about their images. He then asked whether the respondents could visualize such concrete objects as furniture, people, and scenery.

Galton was amazed to find that many scientists claimed to have no imagery at all. In fact, he found wide individual differences and concluded that there was a continuum of imaging ability, from people who form clear and distinct mental images to people with no ability. In the middle there are the majority of people who have some, but not much, imaging ability.

Because of his interest in measuring human sensory abilities, Galton invented a whistle that produced sounds of different frequencies. In addition to testing human auditory acuity with his whistle, Galton performed animal experiments with it. Attaching a whistle to the end of a walking stick, Galton would produce a sound in the vicinity of an animal and observe whether or not the animal responded. In this way, Galton found that little dogs were more likely to respond than big dogs and that cats were superior to all other animals he tested. He attributed the cats' better ability to natural selection, reasoning that cats who heard the high-pitched squeaks of mice and other small animals fared better in the search for food and were more likely to breed and pass on this ability to future generations.

Galton's Influence

Blessed with a long life, high intelligence (recall his precocity as a child), independent means, and unending curiosity, Sir Francis Galton—he was knighted in 1909—achieved an enviable record of innovations. Before developing an interest in psychology, Galton was an explorer who wrote a popular book of practical suggestions for travellers. Stemming from his interest in exploration, he was the inventor of weather maps and the discoverer of the anticyclone. Later in his life, Galton developed fingerprinting as a means of identification (Pearson, 1914–1930, Vol. 3) and the technique of **composite portraiture**. Composite photographs are made by combining several images onto one photograph; Galton was interested in producing a picture of the "average" criminal of a particular type—for example, a murderer.

In the spirit of Galton, modern psychological researchers have adapted Galton's method to the study of physical attractiveness. For example, Langlois and Roggman (1990) found that composite faces, produced by averaging samples of faces, were judged as more attractive than almost all of the individual faces comprising the composites. The

researchers concluded that this is consistent with evolutionary forces that favor characteristics close to the population mean. Galton would have endorsed the conclusion.

Galton was a methodological innovator of exceptional ability. An avid user of statistics, his development of the idea of correlation and regression has immensely benefited not only psychology but other sciences as well. Additionally, Galton was the originator of the questionnaire, which we will see extensively used by G. Stanley Hall, another of functionalism's forerunners. Galton was also the inventor of the word-association test, which became an important research tool in Wundt's laboratory and beyond. Further, the use of twins to investigate the effects of inheritance on physiology and/or behavior was first employed by Galton in his efforts to study the relative contributions of "nature and nurture," a phrase he popularized. Strongly influenced by Galton, Sir Cyril Burt (Chapter 18) later used (and possibly misused) twin studies to argue for the inheritance of intelligence.

It is interesting to compare Galton with some of his more famous contemporaries. For example, Darwin employed a more "Baconian" method (Chapter 3), collecting facts without having a theory in mind. Then, with the facts in hand, he searched for a law that would explain them. By contrast, Galton first formed a problem and then devised experiments to answer it. Obviously, in capable hands, both methods can be successful.

Comparing Galton to Wundt, Pearson (1914–1930, Vol. 2) observed that Wundt progressed from psychology to anthropology (folk or cultural psychology), whereas Galton went the other way—from anthropology to psychology. Their work was independent, and Wundt was the pioneer of experimental psychology in Germany, Galton the pioneer in England. On another point of comparison, Wundt's interest was in the generalized human mind, whereas Galton's interest was in the mental ability of individuals. Galton's creative methods to study human capabilities became part of American functional psychology, earning Galton an important place as a forerunner of functionalism.

Although Galton never had an academic position, he did have disciples, as we have noted. One was Karl Pearson, his biographer, and another was James McKeen Cattell (Chapter 10), sometimes called a "Galtonian" in America.

CONCLUSIONS

In Chapter 8, we saw that phenomenology was "in the air" at the birth of psychology, and in this chapter, we have described how evolution was another part of the *Zeitgeist* of the late 18th century and the 19th century. Although evolutionary ideas have a long history, the modern concept of evolution presented in different versions by Lamarck, Spencer, Wallace, and Darwin was particularly important for psychology and all the life sciences. In the absence of an understanding of genetics, the details of evolutionary theory were subject to debate—as evidenced by the "Neo-Darwinians" and other movements favoring one mechanism over another—but the broad outline of evolution and its implications for psychology were readily embraced.

With its interest in comparative animal studies, American functionalism was the foremost benefactor of evolutionary theory in psychology. The acceptance of evolution led to a concern with the function of consciousness and behavior. As we will see in the next two chapters, the focus on function and on the

application of psychological knowledge was part of what made a psychology of function more popular in America than Titchener's structuralist approach. In addition, the theory of evolution bridged the Cartesian split between humans and animals, making the study of animals—such as in ethology (Chapter 12) and in the comparative study of animals and people—a respectable enterprise for psychology (see Armstrong, 1993, for an examination of Darwin as an ethologist).

In addition to Darwin and evolution, this chapter examined the work of Darwin's cousin, Sir Francis Galton. Galton was remarkable for the scope and nature of his accomplishments, many of which—for example, the formalization of the nature versus nurture debate, the use of questionnaires, twin studies, the study of individual differences—remain as defining features of modern-day psychology. Together with Alexander Bain and Herbert Spencer, Galton represents an important landmark in the development of a true science of psychology in Great Britain. Although England has produced many other noted psychologists—for example, James Ward (1843–1925), W. H. R. Rivers (1864–1922), and Sir Frederic Bartlett (Chapter 20)—Galton's contributions stand out.

After looking at the British forerunners of functionalism, our examination of psychology's history is now ready to consider American developments.

S U M M A R Y

This chapter begins our examination of the school of functionalism to which Titchener compared his structuralism. Just as phenomenology was part of the *Zeitgeist* that produced scientific psychology, so too was the concept of evolution.

Pre-Darwinian Evolution

The concept of evolution first appeared with the ancient Greeks, but more recently it can be found in the writings of Hegel, Comte, and Goethe. Charles Darwin's grandfather, Erasmus Darwin, was another early evolutionary theorist.

The French naturalist, Jean-Baptiste Lamarck, was among the first of several important precursors to Darwin and modern evolutionary theory. For Lamarck, the princi-

pal factors accounting for evolution were a striving for perfection and environmental influences. Lamarck's ideas are often distilled into the phrase "the inheritance of acquired characteristics," and his ideas were vigorously opposed by Georges Cuvier.

Evolution formed the centerpiece for Herbert Spencer's comprehensive philosophy of science. Spencer's synthetic philosophy included a revision of his 1855 *Principles of Psychology* in which he introduced an evolutionary associationism by adding an evolutionary principle to Bain's account of voluntary behavior. In addition to the Spencer-Bain principle, Spencer is famous for social Darwinism, which is the idea that society and its institutions evolve like animal species.

Charles Robert Darwin

Charles Darwin accompanied Captain Robert FitzRoy on the HMS *Beagle*'s surveying voyage of South America. On the trip, Darwin became convinced that the earth was far older than the Biblical account of creation suggested. In the Galápagos Islands, Darwin found compelling evidence for the mutability of species. Malthus's *Essay on the Principle of Population* gave Darwin the insight that nature selects by breeding an excess of a species and then murdering members that are not well adapted to their environment.

Botanist Joseph Hooker advised Darwin to publish an authoritative treatise on evolution, and Darwin was working on this when he received a letter and essay from Alfred Russel Wallace, which expressed a theory virtually identical to Darwin's. At the urging of his friends, Darwin allowed Wallace's paper along with one of his own to be read to the Linnean Society in July of 1858.

Although the first public exposure of Darwin's ideas drew little attention, there was an enormous reaction to the later publication of *On the Origin of Species by Means of Natural Selection, or the Preservation of Favoured Races in the Struggle for Life*. In *The Origin of Species,* Darwin presented the facts he had amassed that lead almost inevitably to the conclusion that species change over time in response to natural selection.

In *Descent of Man,* Darwin argued that humans, like other species, have evolved through the mechanism of natural selection. In *The Expression of the Emotions in Man and Animals,* Darwin sought to demonstrate that human emotional expressions have evolved because of their survival value.

The Origin of Species forever changed our view of the world and the place of humans in it. The *Origin* and to a greater extent *The Descent of Man* abolished the Cartesian split in the animal kingdom, making explicit the continuity between humans and animals. Following Darwin, mind too could be seen as something that evolved because it facilitated adaptation.

George John Romanes

George Romanes was the pioneer of comparative psychology. Romanes is most remembered for *Animal Intelligence,* which has been criticized as a collection of animal anecdotes. Actually, Romanes's problem was his tendency to interpret animal behavior in human terms. Romanes remained a staunch defender of Darwin in the face of several competing Neo-Darwinian explanations.

Conwy Lloyd Morgan

When he was over 40, C. Lloyd Morgan began research to "get him into the animal mind." Morgan's study of the behavior of newly hatched chickens led him to conclude that the birds learned to avoid a bad-tasting caterpillar through the action of the Spencer-Bain principle. Supported by James Mark Baldwin, Morgan developed a theory of organic selection, which treated evolution as a process reflecting the organism's intentional relation to its environment, thus stressing the importance of mind. Morgan's Canon—do not attribute to the animal mind higher mental abilities than are necessary to explain its behavior—seems to contradict his theory of organic selection. However, the interpretation of Morgan's Canon as a prohibition against Romanes's excesses needs closer examination.

Francis Galton

Perhaps no one was more influenced by Darwin's *The Origin of Species* than his cousin, Francis Galton. Galton focused much of his energy on the collection of data to substantiate his belief in eugenics—the improvement of mankind through selective breeding. In *Hereditary Genius,* Galton tried to show that the natural abilities of humans are subject to inheritance just as are the form and physical features of the organic world.

Galton's interest in human ability made him a pioneer in the study of individual differences and facilitated his development of methodological and statistical techniques. Galton purportedly found evidence for a relationship between kinship and eminence. In order to study further the nature and nurture issue, Galton created a questionnaire that he distributed to the Fellows of the Royal Society. He also introduced the study of twins as a method to assess the relative contributions of nature and nurture.

In an effort to identify the most "fit" people for eugenics, Galton developed measures of human ability that he administered to people visiting his Anthropometric Laboratory in London. Galton's physiological measurements stimulated him to develop the method of correlation. At Galton's urging, Karl Pearson invented the Pearson product-moment correlation coefficient.

Galton's other contributions to psychology include the word-association experiment, the study of visual imagery, and a whistle that produced sounds of different frequencies, which Galton used to test human and animal auditory acuity. As the pioneer of experimental psychology in England, Galton can be compared with Wundt, who was a similar developer in Germany.

✦✦✦
✦✦✦

CONNECTIONS QUESTIONS

1. Trace the connections between Alfred Russel Wallace and Charles Darwin. Should Wallace have been given credit for the theory of evolution, as Rachels (1986) implies, or do you think Darwin deserved the credit he received?

2. Connect all the elements you can that contributed to Darwin's development of the concept of organic evolution.

3. Describe the context in which Romanes collected his animal anecdotes and critique his interpretations. Have you been guilty of similar interpretations of the behavior of your own pets? How was Morgan's Canon designed to prevent extravagant interpretations of animal rationality?

4. Compare and contrast Wundt and Galton.

5. What are the connections between Galton and Darwin?

6. How many connections can you make between Galton's work and contemporary methods/issues in the social sciences?

7. Draw a concept map showing the "evolution" of the concept of evolution. Connect as many different theorists as you can, and compare your results to one possible solution provided on p. 565.

SUGGESTED READINGS

Barlow, N. (Ed.) (1958). *The autobiography of Charles Darwin, 1809–1882.* New York: W. W. Norton. (Original work published as part of *Life and letters of Charles Darwin* in 1887) Edited by his granddaughter, Nora Barlow, Darwin's autobiography was written for his family and for himself and reveals an intelligent, witty, and ultimately very human individual. The picture is of a singularly unconceited man who was comforted by the thought that "I have worked as hard and as well as I could, and no man can do more than this" (p. 126).

Darwin, C. (1958). *The origin of species, by means of natural selection or the preservation of favoured races in the struggle for life.* New York: New American Library. (Original work published 1859)

Darwin, C. (1874). *The descent of man, and selection in relation to sex* (2nd ed.). New York: A. L. Burt, Publisher.

Darwin, C. (1979). *The expression of emotions in man and animals.* London: Julian Friedmann Publishers. (Original work published 1872) There are many different modern reprints of Darwin's major works. You will find that his writing is remarkably clear and understandable and just as relevant today as it was over a century ago.

Desmond, A., & Moore, J. (1991). *Darwin.* New York: Warner Books. Stephen Jay Gould, an acclaimed science writer himself, called this "the finest [biography] ever written about Darwin." In it, the callow youth becomes a famous naturalist and then the tortured purveyor of a theory that changed his world and ours. The book's 90 pictures alone are worth its price.

Galton, F. (1892). *Hereditary genius: An inquiry into its laws and consequences* (2nd ed.). London: Watts & Co. Galton's most famous book, this is a good introduction to the man's thoughts and interests.

Irvine, W. (1955). *Apes, angels, and Victorians.* Cleveland, OH: The World Publishing Co. This is the well-researched but eminently readable story of the lives and time of two famous men of the Victorian era, Charles Darwin and Thomas Henry Huxley. In many ways, Huxley was the more brilliant of the two, but it was Darwin who had the ultimate insight and the perseverance to ensure the near-total scientific acceptance of the idea of evolution.

Morgan, C. L. (1932). C. Lloyd Morgan. In C. Murchison (Ed.), *A history of psychology in autobiography* (Vol. 2, pp. 237–264). Worcester, MA: Clark University Press. Morgan's autobiographical account is readable and entertaining, whereas his psychology is worthwhile but will require careful reading in order to be fully grasped.

Pearson, K. (1914–1930). *The life, letters and labours of Francis Galton* (Vols. 1–3). Cambridge, England: Cambridge University Press. Pearson's three volumes constitute the definitive biography of an extraordinary Victorian, Sir Francis Galton.

Romanes, E. (1896). *The life and letters of George John Romanes.* London: Longmans, Green, and Co.

Romanes, G. J. (1895). *Animal intelligence.* New York: D. Appleton and Company. (Original work published 1881) *The life and letters of George John Romanes* is a readable and very sympathetic account of the brief life of Romanes, edited and written by his wife. Before condemning Romanes as the quintessential anecdotalist, be sure to read this book and *Animal Intelligence*, Romanes's most famous work.

American Forerunners of Functionalism

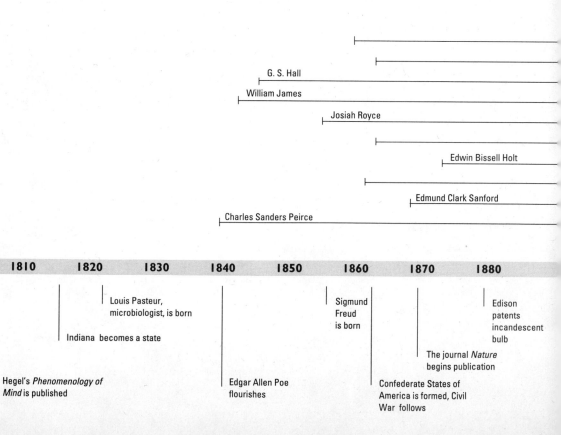

1810	1820	1830	1840	1850	1860	1870	1880

Louis Pasteur, microbiologist, is born

Indiana becomes a state

Sigmund Freud is born

Edison patents incandescent bulb

The journal *Nature* begins publication

Hegel's *Phenomenology of Mind* is published

Edgar Allen Poe flourishes

Confederate States of America is formed, Civil War follows

As we noted in Chapter 9, evolution was a major theme during the 19th century, not only in England but also in the United States. As a result of the *Zeitgeist*, Herbert Spencer's social Darwinism—the idea that institutions and societies evolve—met with great favor on this side of the Atlantic. When Spencer came to America in 1882, he was enthusiastically received. His principle of survival of the fittest captured the mood of our developing nation by stressing the importance of individual initiative, of independence from regulation, and of the ability of the more successful among us to adapt to an often harsh and demanding environment.

By 1882, Spencer's evolutionary message was Darwinism, and few were more influenced by Darwinian evolution than two early American

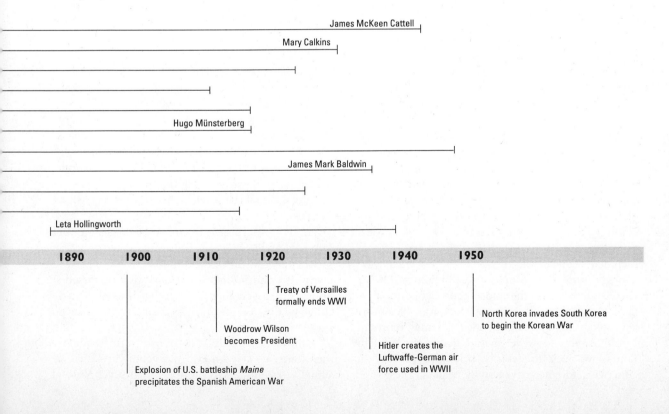

psychologists—William James and G. Stanley Hall (both discussed later). Both believed in the idea that consciousness has a function, which is to aid its possessor in the struggle for survival. Although psychologists of function, neither was quite a functionalist in the formal sense of the term.

Both the forerunners of functionalism we discussed in Chapter 9 and the ones we will survey in this chapter established the foundation for functionalism by taking psychology into fields of study avoided by "pure" psychologists (i.e., psychologists interested in understanding the generalized mind, not in applying psychological knowledge to practical problems) such as Titchener (Chapter 7). Again, the mood in America in the 19th century favored a more practical psychology. Psychology, like so many things in our young nation, needed to be useful. As we saw in the last chapter, Galton pioneered the study and testing of individual differences, and we will see this interest in individual differences continued in America by James McKeen Cattell (discussed later) and others. After Darwinian evolution had legitimized the study of animal behavior, Romanes and Lloyd Morgan (both Chapter 9) established comparative psychology, which was further developed by the research of functionalists such as Harvey A. Carr (Chapter 11). Following Morgan's lead, Edward Lee Thorndike (Chapters 11 and 12) performed the animal studies that cemented his fame for psychology.

The central theme of this chapter will be an examination of the origins of American psychology. Our main characters will be William James and G. Stanley Hall. Although neither really had the personality to become a laboratory scientist, James and Hall were instrumental in moving American psychology away from its philosophical origins toward the science it became. Both had backgrounds that included study in the disciplines from which psychology arose—philosophy and physiology. Of the two, Hall became the more thoroughgoing psychologist. After establishing American scientific psychology almost singlehandedly, James returned to philosophy. However, before discussing William James, we need to describe briefly psychology in America before he arrived on the scene.

EARLY PHILOSOPHY AND PSYCHOLOGY IN AMERICA

It sometimes seems that American psychology sprang full-blown from William James's pen, with the 1890 publication of *The Principles of Psychology,* and that before James's text, American psychology simply did not exist. Published statements reinforce this view: For example, Boring (1950) wrote that "James began psychology in America with his recognition of the significance of the new physiological [experimental] psychology of Germany" (p. 505). Without specifically mentioning James, Cattell told the Ninth International Congress of Psychology in 1929 that a history of psychology in America before the 1880s "would be as short as a book on snakes in Ireland since the time of St. Patrick" (Cattell, 1929, p. 336; according to legend, St. Patrick rid Ireland of snakes in the 5th century).

Although it is true that James taught the first courses in the new scientific psychology in America and that his *Principles* effectively communicated this psychology to a waiting and willing audience, there was some "psychology" in America before James. America's early psychology was primarily the story of moral philosophy.

Jonathan Edwards (1703–1758) is perhaps America's first noteworthy philosopher. Educated at Yale, where he read Locke's *An Essay Concerning Human Understanding* (Chapter 4), Edwards preached a hardline Calvinism as minister of the Congregationalist Church at Northampton, Massachusetts. As a theologian, he urged people to return to God's absolute rule; humanity, born with nothing (Locke's mind as "white paper, void of all characters"), has received everything from God.

Locke's *Essay* also influenced America's **Samuel Johnson** (1696–1772), Columbia University's first president. Johnson wrote a book that popularized many of empiricism's ideas and also discussed a number of psychological topics such as child psychology, the use of introspection, consciousness, and perception.

Although Edwards and Johnson are frequently mentioned as early American psychologists, neither actually "attempted to present a real psychological point of view . . ." (Harms, 1972, p. 120). The distinction between theologians or moral philosophers with some relevance to psychology and ones who were "doing psychology" emerged less clearly in America than in Europe, but we can see it in the comparison of Edwards and Johnson with **Laurens Perseus Hickok** (1798–1888). Hickok's work differed from many of his contemporaries in that he attempted to provide a system of scientific psychology based on his analysis of philosophical positions from Aristotle through Kant. In *Empirical Psychology,* Hickok stressed "observation, investigation, and experiment," by which he meant the study of consciousness through introspection. Harms concluded that "Hickok's whole psychology and this book are . . . unique in the psychology of the 19th century, claiming to be an exact and fully worthy psychology based totally upon self observation" (p. 122).

After the American Revolution, psychology in America fell largely under the influence of Scottish common-sense philosophy (Chapter 4). Textbooks written by the Scottish philosophers included such traditionally psychological topics as sensation, perception, association, memory, and thinking. Written by Dugald Stewart (Chapter 4), such a textbook was used at Yale in the early part of the 19th century. As we will see, the textbooks that provided competition to James's *Principles* included one by Princeton's President James McCosh, who was a leader in America of Scottish philosophical psychology. There were also textbooks based on the rational psychology of Germany, and the ideas of Hegel and Herbart (both Chapter 5) form part of the background for functionalism in America. In part, James's genius lay in his ability to synthesize such diverse elements.

WILLIAM JAMES

With the publication of *The Principles of Psychology,* William James almost overnight became America's foremost psychologist. In addition to its literary quality, the *Principles* is noted for its scope and its tolerant tone. The origin of that tolerance can per-

haps be found in James's unusual childhood in a family that also produced one of America's most brilliant novelists—Henry James (1843–1916).

William James (1842–1910) was the oldest of five children born to Henry James, often called Henry James Senior to distinguish him from his novelist son. Henry Senior was the son of an Irish immigrant, the original William James, who had amassed a fortune through land speculation. Among his purchases was the village of Syracuse, New York, for $30,000. As a result of his inheritance, Henry Senior never had to work for a living.

After initially planning to be a Methodist minister, in his zeal Henry Senior managed to become permanently alienated from organized religion. At 35, a friend introduced him to the writings of Emanuel Swedenborg (1688–1772), a Swedish scientist/mystic/theologian, and in Swedenborg, Henry Senior found his calling. For the rest of his life, he devoted himself to the study of Swedenborg and to the spread of his doctrines by lecturing and writing. At times, Henry Senior's writing was not very enlightening. After the publication of *The Secret of Swedenborg,* a friend joked that Henry had not only found the secret, he had kept it.

An affectionate and permissive parent, Henry Senior allowed his brood almost complete freedom of expression. Meals were often characterized by intellectual combat, where each youngster learned to think for himself or herself. Such free-for-alls took place in a spirit of loving togetherness.

Another constant in the James's household was travel, which was used both for the children's education and as a remedy for illness. William James took his first trip to Europe when he was 2, and later in life any crisis calling for a decision or any refractory ailment sent him across the Atlantic. One positive result of all the travel was that James "became adept in French and passable in German and Italian, languages that would aid him in his scholarly life. He also spoke a little Portuguese and read Latin and Greek" (Evans, 1990, p. 12).

James's nomadic childhood produced a markedly abnormal education: a series of governesses until he was 9; three different New York schools between the ages of 9 and 13; and schools in Paris, Boulogne,

Geneva, Bonn, and Rhode Island between 13 and 18. James emerged well read and intellectually curious, with a dislike of mathematics and logic, ready to become an artist. Perhaps realizing that his son's interest in art would be brief, James's father surreptitiously ordered a dissecting microscope, saying, "Willy needs it and will be much obliged" (Lewis, 1991, p. 108).

In 1861, James enrolled as a chemistry student at the Lawrence Scientific School at Harvard. His chemistry instructor, Charles W. Eliot (1834–1926), was a neighbor of the Jameses and soon became Harvard's president. Eliot had little influence on William James as a chemistry teacher, however, and James's interest in chemistry soon waned, perhaps because of illness.

Influenced by Harvard's brilliant Swiss-born naturalist Louis Agassiz (1807–1873), James next shifted toward biology. Fearing that a biologist's income would not allow him to support a family, he opted for medicine, entering Harvard Medical School in 1864. However, his interest in medicine was never wholehearted, and James accompanied Agassiz on an expedition to Brazil in 1865. The experience was valuable mainly because it taught James that he was not cut out to be a field naturalist.

James returned to his medical studies but dropped out once again in the spring of 1867, beset by ailments that included "insomnia, digestive disorders, eye-troubles, weakness of the back, and sometimes deep depression . . ." (James, 1920, Vol. I, p. 84). These may have been psychosomatic, as James was 25 years old, without a vocation, and uncertain that he was suited for medicine. To partake of the medicinal baths and to perfect his German while studying the physiology of the nervous system, James went to Europe.

James spent the next 2 years mainly in Germany, much of the time suffering from depression so deep he thought often of suicide. In this season of melancholy, two events stand out: James had his first literary effort published, and he revealed a burgeoning interest in psychology. In a letter to a friend, he wrote:

> I have blocked out some reading in physiology and psychology which I hope to execute this winter. . . . It seems to me that perhaps the time

has come for psychology to begin to be a science. . . . I am going on to study what is already known, and perhaps may be able to do some work at it. Helmholtz and a man named Wundt at Heidelberg are working at it, and I hope I live through this winter to go to them in the summer. (James, 1920, Vol. I, pp. 118–119)

James heard lectures on physiology by du Bois-Reymond in Berlin and Helmholtz in Heidelberg (both Chapter 6) before returning to America and medical studies at Harvard in November 1868. During this period, he also became something of a disciple of the French physiologist Claude Bernard (Chapter 6) and may have considered psychiatry as a profession (Howard, 1992; Taylor, 1990). James wrote his father of his interest in physiology: "I find myself getting more interested in physiology and nourishing a hope that I may be able to make its study (and perhaps its teaching) my profession . . ." (James, 1920, Vol. I, p. 134). In June 1869, James finally received his Harvard medical degree.

For the next 3 years, James lived at home, reading voraciously, writing an occasional article or review, and spending "most of the time in a state of hypochondriacal misery" (Knight, 1950, p. 29). He was finally rescued from his morbid preoccupations by reading the French philosopher **Charles Bernard Renouvier** (1815–1903). In one of his notebooks, James wrote:

> I think that yesterday was a crisis in my life. I finished the first part of Renouvier's second "Essais" and see no reason why his definition of Free Will—"the sustaining of a thought *because I choose to* when I might have other thoughts"— need be the definition of an illusion. At any rate, I will assume for the present—until next year—that it is no illusion. My first act of free will shall be to believe in free will. (James, 1920, Vol. I, p. 147)

Before this "crisis," James had believed in the material or physical basis of his mental states, which led him to seek physiological remedies. When these failed, he had come to view his depression and its manifestations as something to be endured. Renouvier had shown him that perhaps he had the ability (Free Will) to sustain a thought of his own choosing.

Two years after the worst of his depression was over, former chemistry instructor Charles W. Eliot, now Harvard's president, asked James to teach the physiology portion of an undergraduate course in anatomy and physiology. James taught the course and thereby found the vocation he had sought. Not only was he good at teaching, teaching was good for him. In February 1873, James wrote:

> I find the work very interesting and stimulating. It presents two problems, the intellectual one—how best to state your matter to [the students]; and the practical one—how to govern them, stir them up, not bore them, yet make them work, etc. I should think it not unpleasant as a permanent thing. . . . So far, I seem to have succeeded in interesting them, for they are admirably attentive, and I hear expressions of satisfaction on their part. (James, 1920, Vol. I, p. 168)

According to Ross (1991), James was an excellent teacher because of his unusual education, his personal philosophy, and his age and experience.

> Having been included in intellectual discussions from an early age in his liberal household, James was at ease with students and they with him. His varied background and his attempts to relate class material to life situations were appealing to students. The breadth of his experiences and reading, his ability to communicate, and his engaging style added to his popularity. (p. 18)

Eliot offered James a permanent appointment to teach a course in physiology and another in anatomy. For the next 3 years, James taught the courses with increasing success and self-confidence, his morbid hypochondriasis almost completely behind him.

In 1875, James added to his teaching repertoire a course in physiological psychology, teaching it first to graduate students and then the next year to undergraduates. In conjunction with the new course, James obtained the use of two rooms to house psychological apparatus, which became the first experimental psychology "laboratory" in America. Although James did produce a few carefully designed studies (see Taylor, 1992), experimental research was not his true love.

In 1876, James met Alice Howe Gibbens, and they were married in 1878. James began to draft the opening chapters of the *Principles* on his honeymoon. In correspondence with Henry Holt, the publisher, James had said that he did not think he would be able to complete the book in under 2 years—it actually took him nearly 12.

The *Principles* was finally finished in May of 1890, and in a letter to Holt, James, perhaps disingenuously, expressed his feelings about the manuscript:

> No one could be more disgusted than I at the sight of the book. *No* subject is worth being treated of in 1000 pages! Had I ten years more, I could rewrite it in 500; but as it stands it is this or nothing—a loathsome, distended, tumefied, bloated, dropsical mass, testifying to nothing but two facts: *1st,* that there is no such thing as a *science* of psychology, and *2nd,* that W.J. is an incapable. (James, 1920, Vol. I, p. 294, italics in the original)

The "James," as it came to be known, was an immediate success, and it took James only another 2 years to complete his 500-page abridgement entitled *Psychology: The Briefer Course.* A letter to his publisher amusingly summarized how James condensed the *Principles* and his expectations about the new book's potential for financial success.

> I expect to send you within ten days the MS. of my "Briefer Course," boiled down to possibly 400 pages. By adding some twaddle about the senses, by leaving out all polemics and history, all bibliography and experimental details, all metaphysical subtleties and digressions, all quotations, all humor and pathos, all *interest* in short, and by blackening the tops of all the paragraphs, I think I have produced a tome of pedagogic classic which will enrich both you and me, if not the student's mind. (James, 1920, Vol. I, p. 314)

The "Jimmy" proved to be an excellent introductory textbook, and for years it remained the most widely used psychology textbook in the English language. In Figure 10–1, James is shown with his daughter, Margaret Mary, in 1892, the year the Jimmy was published.

FIGURE 10–1. William James and daughter in 1892, the year the "Jimmy" was published.

Source: By permission of the Houghton Library, Harvard University.

The Principles of Psychology

Competition and Criticism

The Principles of Psychology entered a textbook market in which there were several competitors. As Holt waited for James's manuscript, three major books appeared in 1886 alone: James McCosh's *Psychology: The Cognitive Powers;* John Dewey's *Psychology;* and Bordon P. Bowne's *Introduction to Psychological Theory.* In 1887, Yale philosophy professor **George Trumbull Ladd** (1842–1920) published *Elements of Physiological Psychology,* which was well received. Like James's, Ladd's psychology was largely self-taught. His 1887 book was based on Wundt's system of psychology, as revealed in Wundt's *Principles of Physiological Psychology* (Chapter 7). Although Ladd's *Elements* was a work

about experimental psychology by someone who had never done a psychological experiment, it was widely used as a textbook in the United States and in England and was revised in 1911. For further details about Ladd and his textbook writing, see Mills (1974).

Praise for the *Principles* was swift, but not universal. Reviewers like **James Sully** (1842–1923), a British textbook writer and a friend of Alexander Bain (Chapter 4), found James's style too brilliant, contending that a textbook should be duller. Perhaps Sully realized how much competition his own *Outlines of Psychology* (1884) would receive from the *Principles.*

More recently, B. F. Skinner (Chapter 13), writing from William James Hall, praised the writer but not his message in a 1986 letter to one of this book's authors:

> William James is generally accepted as the last important figure in the history of mentalistic psychology. He was a careful thinker and a *charming writer* but my own feeling is that *those traits are to be regretted.* He made altogether too good a case for what could be said at the time about the human mind. (italics added)

Reviewers also criticized the *Principles'* unsystematic arrangement. For example, James's chapter on sensation does not appear until Chapter 17. The discussion of perception, which often follows the discussion of sensation, occurs in Chapters 15 ("The Perception of Time"), 19 ("The Perception of Things"), 20, ("The Perception of Space"), and 21 ("The Perception of Reality"). The instinct chapter, which might logically appear before a discussion of habit (Chapter 4), is delayed until Chapter 24.

There are several possible reasons for James's apparently random arrangement of chapters. For one thing, some of the grouping may simply reflect James's personal interests and priorities; that is, topics of greater interest were covered earlier. More importantly, the arrangement may have stemmed from James's attempts to be inclusive and systematic of both a phenomenological account of psychology and a physiological account.

Some reviewers criticized James's physiological approach, objecting that the *Principles* was "materialistic to the core." Although the book offers a careful balance of phenomenology and physiology, in his materialistic moments James was merely incorporating the view he had expressed many years earlier to President Eliot—that psychology could not be taught as a living science by anyone who did not have a knowledge of nervous physiology.

Selected Topics from the Principles

Instead of attempting an overview of the *Principles'* nearly 1,400 pages, we will discuss briefly three of James's most influential concepts—the stream of consciousness, habit, and his theory of emotions—citing liberally from the *Principles* to give the flavor of his writing. For further information on James and the many important contributions he made to psychology through the *Principles,* we direct your attention to Blanshard and Schneider (1942), Donnelly (1992), Johnson and Henley (1990), and McLeod (1969). Each of these works examines several topics in which James's views were pioneering, such as the mind-body problem, association, will and free will, and the self, which we will not treat in detail here.

Stream of Consciousness. As we noted in Chapter 7, Wundt and Titchener approached the study of consciousness by seeking to identify its elements, beginning with sensations. According to James, this is the wrong place to start.

> It is astonishing what havoc is wrought in psychology by admitting at the outset apparently innocent suppositions, that nevertheless contain a flaw. . . . The notion that sensations, being the simplest things, are the first things to take up in psychology is one of these suppositions. The only thing which psychology has a right to postulate at the outset is the fact of thinking itself, and that must first be taken up and analyzed. If sensations then prove to be amongst the elements of the thinking, we shall be no worse off as respects them than if we had taken them for granted at the start. (James, 1890, Vol. 1, p. 224)

If we begin with thinking, James suggested, we find that thought is a continuous stream rather than a collection of bits and pieces susceptible to the analysis to which Wundt and Titchener and others

had subjected it. James's analysis revealed that thought has five characteristics:

1. Our thoughts are part of a personal consciousness. My thoughts are mine; your thoughts are yours.
2. Thought is always changing. As Heraclitus (Chapter 2) believed, you cannot step into the same stream twice, or as James expressed it, " . . . *no state once gone can recur and be identical with what it was before*" (James, 1890, Vol. 1, p. 230, italics in the original).
3. Our thoughts are sensibly continuous. As long as we are not unconscious, we are unaware of gaps or divisions in our consciousness.
4. Our consciousness appears to deal with objects outside of itself. That is, we believe that our thoughts deal with objects having an external reality. The reason for this belief "is that there are *many* human thoughts, each with the *same* objects. . . . The judgment that *my* thought has the same object as *his* thought is what makes the psychologist call my thought cognitive of an outer reality" (Vol. 1, pp. 271–272, italics in the original).
5. Our consciousness is concerned with some parts of the objects rather than others at any point in time. Consciousness is selective; attention is focused more on some elements of our experiences than on others.

James believed that consciousness evolved because it has a function, which is to aid in its possessor's adaptation. He wrote:

> It is very generally admitted . . . that consciousness grows the more complex and intense the higher we rise in the animal kingdom. That of a man must exceed that of an oyster. From this point of view it seems an organ, superadded to the other organs which maintain the animal in the struggle for existence; and the presumption . . . is that it helps him in some way in the struggle, just as they do. But it cannot help him without being in some way efficacious and influencing the course of his bodily history. If now it could be shown in what consciousness might help him, and if . . . the defects of his other organs . . . are such as to make them need

just the kind of help that consciousness would bring provided it were efficacious; why, then the plausible inference would be that it came just because of its efficacy. . . (James, 1890, Vol. 1, pp. 138–139)

In summary, consciousness is a continuous, ever-changing, yet selective, stream that is unique to its possessor. In addition, consciousness has a purpose or function, which is to aid in its possessor's adaptation to the environment.

James's contributions to our understanding of consciousness cannot be overstated, and the image of consciousness James offered remains the view of modern psychology. For a discussion of the stream of consciousness concept since James, see Pollio (1990).

Habit. For James, habit was a well-learned pattern of behavior that results from the malleability of our nervous systems, and he described the process of habit formation as follows:

> It is to the infinitely attenuated currents that pour in through [the sensory nerve-roots] that the hemispherical cortex shows itself to be so peculiarly susceptible. The currents, once in, must find a way out. In getting out they leave their traces in the paths which they take. The only thing they *can* do, in short, is to deepen old paths or to make new ones. . . . The most complex habits . . . are . . . nothing but *concatenated* discharges in the nerve-centres, due to the presence there of systems of reflex paths, so organized as to wake each other up successively—the impression produced by one muscular contraction serving as a stimulus to provoke the next, until a final impression inhibits the process and closes the chain. (James, 1890, Vol. 1, pp. 107–108, italics in the original)

For James, the anatomical substrate of habit was a pathway in the brain, so altered that it could be more easily traversed in the future.

Habits are essential for maintaining society's integrity, according to James, and in a frequently cited passage, he wrote:

> Habit is thus the enormous fly-wheel of society, its most precious conservative agent. It alone is what keeps us all within the bounds of ordi-

nance, and saves the children of fortune from the envious uprisings of the poor. It alone prevents the hardest and most repulsive walks of life from being deserted by those brought up to tread therein. It keeps the fisherman and the deck-hand at sea through the winter; it holds the miner in his darkness, and nails the country-man to his log-cabin and his lonely farm through all the months of snow. . . . It dooms us all to fight out the battle of life upon the lines of our nurture or our early choice. . . . (James, 1890, Vol. 1, p. 121)

Later, James offered some practical suggestions on how to acquire new habits or to remove old ones, following Bain's advice. First, "we must take care to *launch ourselves with as strong and decided an initiative as possible*" (James, 1890, Vol. 1, p. 123, italics in the original). In other words, use every means to strengthen your resolve. For example, if you want to quit smoking, you might make a public pledge that you are going to stop, or you might spend as much of your time as possible in a nonsmoking environment. These actions "will give your new beginning such a momentum that the temptation to break down will not occur as soon as it otherwise might; and every day during which a breakdown is postponed adds to the chances of its not occurring at all" (p. 123).

Second, "*Never suffer an exception to occur till the new habit is securely rooted in your life*" (James, 1890, Vol. 1, p. 123, italics in the original). Practice your new habit (or the absence of an old one) until it becomes second nature, for each "lapse is like the letting fall of a ball of string which one is carefully winding up; a single slip undoes more than a great many turns will wind again" (p. 123). How many times has your latest diet been undone by eating a single snack or dessert? "*Continuity* of training is the great means of making the nervous system act infallibly right" (p. 123). James offered further suggestions, but this should give you a feeling for the importance he attached to the habit concept.

Although today James is more often associated with cognitive psychology than with behaviorism, his discussion of habit proved to be central to functionalism (behaviorism's parent) and to learning theory. At the same time that behaviorists (Chapters

12 and 13) distanced themselves from James's mentalism, his analysis of habit was fundamental to all subsequent American psychology.

Emotion. In 1884, James described a novel theory of emotion that reversed the sequence of events usually thought to occur in an emotion-producing situation. In 1885, Danish physiologist **Carl Lange** (1834–1900) independently published a similar theory, with the result that we call it the **James-Lange theory of emotion**.

Normally, we believe that a stimulus (e.g., telephone call saying that you have won a sweepstakes) produces an emotion (e.g., joy), and the emotion triggers your response (e.g., increased heart rate, shouting, hugging family members). James altered the sequence, saying that the stimulus first triggers the response, and awareness of the response constitutes the emotion. As he colorfully expressed it:

> Common-sense says, we lose our fortune, are sorry and weep; we meet a bear, are frightened and run; we are insulted by a rival, are angry and strike. The hypothesis here to be defended says that this order of sequence is incorrect, that the one mental state is not immediately induced by the other, that the bodily manifestations must first be interposed between, and that the more rational statement is that we feel sorry because we cry, angry because we strike, afraid because we tremble, and not that we cry, strike, or tremble, because we are sorry, angry, or fearful, as the case may be. (James, 1890, Vol. 2, pp. 449–450)

One criterion of a good theory is that it can be tested, and by this criterion the James-Lange theory succeeded. In 1927, Harvard physiologist and former student of James **Walter B. Cannon** (1871–1945) attacked the theory on several fronts, with apparent success. Among his many contributions, Cannon argued that stimulation of the sympathetic nervous system prepares an organism for "fight or flight," and he coined the word *homeostasis* to describe the body's relatively constant internal conditions. Let us consider two of Cannon's objections to the James-Lange theory and how they might be reinterpreted today. Although Cannon (1927) had additional criticisms, none was any more telling than the ones we will discuss here.

James had argued that an emotion-producing stimulus triggers a bodily response, and awareness of the response is the emotional feeling. In addition to the external manifestations of the response (e.g., laughing, crying, running), there are less visible, but no less important, "internal" bodily changes, such as heart rate changes and inhibition of digestive processes. If an emotional feeling occurs because of feedback from bodily changes, then blocking the feedback should prevent the emotional feeling.

Thus, Cannon's (1927) first criticism was that "*Total separation of the viscera* [internal organs] *from the central nervous system does not alter emotional behavior*" (p. 108, italics in the original). In support, Cannon reviewed research that showed that emotional responses continued in animals after the sensory nerves between the viscera and the central nervous system had been cut. Cannon concluded that "operations which largely or completely destroy emotional feeling, nevertheless leave the animals behaving as angrily, as joyfully, as fearfully as ever" (p. 109).

However, the fact that cats with no feedback from their viscera still manifest external signs of rage does not mean that they still *feel* rage. Obviously, cats cannot tell us what they feel, and they might *appear* angry without any corresponding *feeling*. More importantly, James did not say that *all* emotional feelings depend on visceral feedback. He also thought muscular feedback was important, and Cannon's operations did not abolish feedback from the muscles.

But what about emotional feelings in humans with altered feedback from their bodies? Hohman (1966) asked people with spinal cord injuries about the intensity of their feelings, and, supporting the James-Lange theory, he found a clear correlation between level of injury and intensity of feelings. That is, people with high spinal injuries (less bodily feedback) reported less intense feelings than people with lower spinal damage (greater bodily feedback).

Another Cannon objection was that the "*Artificial induction of the visceral changes typical of strong emotions does not produce them*" (Cannon, 1927, p. 113, italics in the original). In support, Cannon reported studies in which people injected with adrenalin—which produces the bodily changes that normally accompany strong emotions—generally did not experience any emotions, although associated "with these sensations there was in certain cases an indefinite affective state coldly appreciated, and without real emotion" (p. 113). In other words, artificially inducing the physiological changes that accompany an emotion usually failed to cause a true emotional feeling.

But is the criticism valid? Stanley Schachter and Jerome Singer (1962) studied subjects who received either a placebo or adrenalin, were either told what to expect physiologically or were misinformed about what to expect, and were exposed either to a euphoric confederate or to an angry confederate while they responded to a questionnaire. Although the results were less clear-cut than the experimenters might have wished, Schachter and Singer concluded that they supported a two-factor theory of emotion: A stimulus causes arousal, and our emotional feeling depends on how we label the stimulus. Presumably, subjects in the studies Cannon reviewed did not feel any particular emotion because they experienced their physiological changes in a neutral environment to which they could not attach a label (see also Zillmann, Katcher, & Milavsky, 1972).

Because the James-Lange theory argues that the bodily expression precedes and determines the experience of an emotion, one corollary is that simulating the emotion (e.g., smiling when you are unhappy) should produce the appropriate feeling. James had actually used this technique to combat his grief following his parents' deaths, and he was speaking from personal experience when he wrote:

> Whistling to keep up courage is no mere figure of speech. On the other hand, sit all day in a moping posture, sigh, and reply to everything with a dismal voice, and your melancholy lingers. There is no more valuable precept in moral education than this, as all who have experience know: if we wish to conquer undesirable emotional tendencies in ourselves, we must assiduously . . . go through the *outward movements* of those contrary dispositions which we prefer to cultivate. The reward of persistency will infallibly come, in the fading out of the sullenness or depression, and the advent of real cheerfulness and kindliness in

> their stead. Smooth the brow, brighten the eye, . . . and speak in a major key, pass the genial compliment, and your heart must be frigid indeed if it do not gradually thaw! (James, 1890, Vol. 2, p. 463)

Carlson (1994) reported that "several experiments suggest that feedback from the contraction of facial muscles can affect people's moods and even alter the activity of the autonomic nervous system" (p. 351). A physiological mechanism for the effect has been proposed: By influencing blood flow to the brain, facial expressions may alter the release of neurotransmitter substances that affect our moods (Zajonc, Murphy, & Ingelhart, 1989). As you can see, the James-Lange theory of emotion is still capable of generating research long after it was first proposed, and it is still discussed in almost all of the current physiological psychology and introductory psychology textbooks.

After the *Principles*

Having virtually created American scientific psychology with his book, James, never a laboratory scientist, wanted to be freed from it. To gain his freedom, he needed someone to take charge of his Harvard laboratory. The scientist he chose was a young German who had received his Ph.D. from Leipzig, working under Wundt—Hugo Münsterberg (discussed later).

As time passed, James also became increasingly interested in being freed from psychology, calling it "a nasty little subject" and turning instead toward philosophy. Nevertheless, in his last 2 decades, James continued to engage in psychological activities and to write books with a strong psychological flavor. For example, he served twice as APA president (1894, 1904). In 1899, he published *Talks to Teachers*, which represented the application of his psychological ideas to pedagogy. Three years later, there was *The Varieties of Religious Experience*, a book that examined, among other things, the relations between religious experience and abnormal psychology. In 1909, although gravely ill, he traveled to Clark University to hear and meet Sigmund Freud during Freud's only visit to America. According to

Freud's colleague and biographer Ernest Jones (Chapter 15), James responded to Freud and his associates on the occasion of their meeting by saying, "The future of psychology belongs to your work" (Jones, 1955, p. 57). About the man himself, James wrote, "I confess that [Freud] made on me personally the impression of a man obsessed with fixed ideas" (James, 1920, Vol. 2, p. 328).

But it is also true that James increasingly thought of himself as a philosopher after 1890, and the philosophical theory with which he is most closely associated is pragmatism.

James's Pragmatism

Although James first detailed his pragmatism in the 1897 publication, *The Will to Believe and Other Essays in Popular Philosophy,* his thinking about it preceded this publication by at least 2 decades. When he was in his 20s, James had taken part in discussions with an informal group that included Chauncey Wright, Oliver Wendell Holmes, and **Charles Sanders Peirce** (1839–1914). Peirce later called the group the "Metaphysical Club." Only a few years older than James, Peirce became one of his lifelong friends. Philosopher, logician, and mathematician, Peirce was never able to obtain an academic position beyond a half-time appointment as a lecturer in logic at Johns Hopkins from 1879 until 1884. "Despite his universally acknowledged genius, he was considered too difficult to deal with and too abstract to be a good teacher" (Cadwallader, 1974, p. 291). His ideas aided in the establishment of semiotics (a theory of meaning), a concept now central to linguistics and the philosophy of language. Peirce actually introduced the term "**pragmatism**" into philosophy in an article in *Popular Science Monthly* (Peirce, 1878).

At meetings of the Metaphysical Club, Peirce promoted his theory of pragmatism, which, among other things, stressed the uses for science and knowledge. In order to find the meaning of an idea, according to Peirce, we must understand the consequences to which the idea leads. In other words, the pragmatist asks what is the function of an idea? Does the idea work? Further, an idea that works in one context may not work in another, with the result

that ideas, like organisms and societies, evolve. Here, you can see the relation between pragmatism and Darwinian evolution, which was relatively new at the time of the Metaphysical Club's discussions.

Pragmatism's central test—Does it work?—led James to reconsider the nature of truth. For James, truth became, not an objective entity (Truth with a capital "T"), but something that works—that is functional. His decision in the early 1870s to believe in free will was true in the sense that it worked to bring him out of his depression. Truth, according to James, was the value of an idea within a context. If it works in that context, it is true.

In *The Will to Believe,* James defended empirical methods against rationalistic or absolutist methods in philosophy. He was particularly opposed to systems developed by deductive reasoning, such as that of Hegel. Instead, James believed that philosophy could only advance by using the inductive, empirical method of the natural sciences, which means advancing from one working hypothesis to another and abandoning the search for absolute truths.

The main point of *The Will to Believe* is that we may often be justified in embracing a belief as a working hypothesis whose validity cannot be proved. Although few would argue with this idea, James carried it a step further a decade later in *Pragmatism,* when he defined truth in terms of whether or not an idea works. That is, he now believed that an idea that works is true *by definition.* Critics pointed to the circularity of his definition; logically, a true belief becomes a belief that it is to our advantage to regard as true.

Although some critics view *Pragmatism* as James's least satisfactory work, James himself liked it, and it remains widely read and enormously influential. As one illustration of its influence, Thomas Kuhn's philosophy of science that we introduced in Chapter 1 reflects many of the tenets of James's pragmatism. Nevertheless, Peirce tried in vain to relabel his philosophy "pragmaticism" to distinguish it from James's pragmatism.

James's Students

A wide variety of people who became important psychologists were attracted to James. However, as

Robinson (1993) noted, there were never any "Jamesians" as there were "Wundtians," "Titchenerians," and in later generations, "Freudians," "Skinnerians," and so on. Some of the most well known of James's students included philosopher, historian, poet, and novelist **George Santayana** (1863–1952), American writer Gertrude Stein (1874–1946), physiologist Walter B. Cannon, and W. E. B. DuBois (1868–1963). DuBois, a cofounder of the National Association for the Advancement of Colored People in 1909, entered Harvard in 1888 and later wrote movingly of his relationship with James, whom he considered a friend and his guide to clarity of thought (Myers, 1986).

Some of the psychologists who studied with James are Morton Prince (Chapter 16), James Rowland Angell, Edward Lee Thorndike, and Robert S. Woodworth (all in Chapter 11), **Edwin Bissell Holt** (1873–1946), as well as Mary Calkins and G. Stanley Hall (discussed later). Often viewed as an early behaviorist, Holt was one of James's favorite students. First at Harvard, then at Princeton, Holt continued the Jamesian tradition of combining sophisticated philosophical analysis with his psychological inquiries.

James's Influence

We can point to a number of James's specific contributions to psychology: for example, with Lange, his theory of emotion; the importance of habit as an organizing principle of mind; and his stream of consciousness idea, which diverted attention from the atomism of voluntarism and structuralism and anticipated Gestalt psychology's emphasis on wholes (Chapter 14).

The ideas that James expressed in both the *Principles* and his pragmatic philosophical writings led rather directly to functionalism. For example, James saw consciousness as useful and adaptive—functional, in a word. John Dewey (Chapter 11) and James Rowland Angell, considered founders of functionalism, acknowledged their debt to James. James was also influential through the people he attracted

to psychology, foremost among whom were Edward Lee Thorndike and Robert S. Woodworth.

The very qualities that made James so popular—open-mindedness, wide interests—sometimes divided opinion of him as a scientist. One example is his interest in psychical research. In America,

> James for years stood almost alone among men of high intellectual repute, and although he was eminently conservative in his estimate of the results of the work of the [psychical research] society, he nevertheless committed himself to belief in certain mediumistic phenomena in a way which seriously offended many of his professional colleagues. At best, they regarded him as a man whose judgment could not be trusted, at worst as an unwitting backer of quackery and fraud.
>
> His position on the issue was all of a piece with his insistent and never failing protestantism, his passion for fair play, and a just hearing for all sides of every question. . . (Angell, 1911, p. 81)

James, along with Münsterberg and Josiah Royce (discussed later), helped establish Harvard as one of the principal sites for psychology in America. As we will see, R. M. Yerkes (Chapter 12), **Herbert S. Langfeld** (1879–1958), E. B. Holt, and E. G. Boring (Chapter 1)—psychology's best-known historian—all served as part of Harvard's early psychology faculty. Langfeld received his Ph.D. under Stumpf (Chapter 8) in Berlin, and then spent most of his professional life at Princeton, where he directed the psychological laboratory.

James's kindness and creativity are revealed in a visit he paid to Helen Keller (1880–1968), who, blind and deaf from the age of 19 months, achieved distinction as a lecturer, writer, and scholar.

> Helen Keller wrote that James visited her and Anne Sullivan [her teacher] when Keller was a young girl at the Perkins Institution for the Blind in South Boston. Comparing him to Plato and to Francis Bacon, she recalled in 1929 that he had brought her an ostrich feather. "'I thought,' he said, 'you would like the feather, it is soft and light and caressing'". . . . The creative touch in this gesture was another of James's trademarks. (Myers, 1986, p. 42)

In summary,

> William James was that rarest of human beings—a great man who was also simple, kindly, brave and true. His memory will always be with us as an inspiration and a benediction. (Angell, 1911, p. 82)

We will now examine the life and career of an early psychologist who was significantly influenced by James. Her difficulties well illustrate the problems faced by women of her time who wanted to earn the Ph.D. in psychology.

MARY WHITON CALKINS

Mary Whiton Calkins (1863–1930) was the oldest child of Wolcott and Charlotte Calkins. Her father was a strong-willed evangelical minister, once described by his wife as "unconventional." Both of Mary Calkins's parents "were intimately involved in directing the education of their children, sons and daughters alike" (Scarborough & Furumoto, 1987, p. 30).

After earning a B.A. degree with a concentration in the classics from Smith College in western Massachusetts, Calkins was offered an appointment in the Greek Department at Wellesley College, a prestigious women's school near Boston. In 1888, Wellesley decided to introduce the new scientific psychology into its curriculum. Calkins was offered the teaching position, provided that she first complete a year of study in psychology. Initially, Calkins thought of going to Germany, because she was fluent in German and that was the source of the new physiological psychology. However, she was deterred by a letter that gave her a firsthand look at the difficulties—for example, inability to gain access to lectures—she would encounter.

The American schools with graduate psychology programs were few in 1890, and the graduate schools that would admit women were even fewer. Calkins eventually rejected study with John Dewey at Michigan or G. T. Ladd at Yale and sought to take courses at Harvard's "Annex." Not officially part of Harvard, the Annex was a method Harvard faculty

had developed for offering private courses to women. At first, Calkins was encouraged to take regular advanced courses taught by James and Royce. However, this plan ran into President Eliot's opposition. Finally, through the intercession of James and her father, Calkins was allowed to attend the courses taught by Royce and James without registering as a Harvard student. Two days after the favorable decision, James welcomed Calkins into his seminar.

According to Calkins (1930):

> I began the serious study of psychology with William James. Most unhappily for them and most fortunately for me the other members of his seminary in psychology dropped away in the early weeks of the fall of 1890; and James and I were left . . . quite literally at either side of a library fire. The *Principles of Psychology* was warm from the press; and my absorbed study of those brilliant, erudite, and provocative volumes, as interpreted by their writer was my introduction to psychology. (p. 31)

In essence, Calkins had a private tutorial with James, using as a textbook the just-published *Principles*. But there was more: "I was equally fortunate, in this same fall of 1890, in entering on laboratory work under the guidance of Edmund Sanford [at Clark University in Worcester, MA], a teacher unrivalled for the richness and precision of his knowledge of experimental procedure and for the prodigality with which he lavished time and interest upon his students" (p. 32). **Edmund Clark Sanford** (1869–1924) was an innovator of early psychological apparatus and published the first laboratory manual for experimental psychology. Just 3 years older than Calkins, Sanford had earned a Ph.D. at Johns Hopkins.

When Sanford recommended to Calkins that she look to Germany for a Ph.D. and noted that he had seen a picture of Münsterberg and his seminar that contained at least one woman, Calkins considered working with Münsterberg in Freiburg. However, James urged her to delay as long as possible her decision about where to study. The reason for the delay was that Münsterberg was coming to Harvard.

> Chronologically third of my great teachers in psychology was Hugo Münsterberg, a man of deep learning, high originality, and astounding

versatility, interested alike in systematic psychology, in the setting and solution of experimental problems, and, years later, in the applications of psychology. (Calkins, 1930, p. 33)

Calkins worked with Münsterberg from 1893 to 1895, and he sent a letter to the Harvard Corporation describing her as the strongest student working in the laboratory during his tenure and asking if she could be admitted as a Ph.D. candidate. He concluded that a Harvard Ph.D. associated with her name would honor both her and the University. Unfortunately, women graduate students did not become eligible for the Harvard Ph.D. until 1963.

Calkins was granted an unofficial examination for the Ph.D. by the philosophy department. In a letter to one of Calkins's Smith College classmates, James wrote that Calkins's performance far surpassed that of any Harvard doctoral candidate he had examined. The results were reported to the Harvard authorities but had no effect.

Radcliffe College replaced the Harvard Annex in 1894, and in 1902 Radcliffe's governing board offered Calkins a Ph.D. for her Harvard work. Viewing the offer as simply a way for Harvard to continue to deny degree recognition to women, Calkins reluctantly rejected it.

Calkins taught at Wellesley for the rest of her career, retiring in 1929. Her list of publications includes four books and over 100 papers, divided equally between psychology and philosophy. According to Furumoto (1979), Calkins's main contributions to psychology were the establishment of an early laboratory of psychology at Wellesley, the invention of a paired-associates method for studying memory, and the development of a system of self-psychology. Calkins's (1894) report of the **paired-associates method** first appeared in a publication in which she stated that she had shown subjects colors paired with numbers. G. E. Müller (Chapter 8) further refined the method, which Calkins herself did not pursue (Strunk, 1972).

Calkins viewed her **self-psychology** system as having much greater importance. Building on many of James's conceptions of psychology and the self, Calkins's own view of psychology was that it "should be conceived as the science of the self, or person, as related to its environment, physical and social" (Calkins, 1930, p. 42). Self-psychology, or sometimes personalistic psychology, is a type of introspectionist psychology, which has three basic concepts: "that of the self, that of the object, and that of the self's relation or attitude toward its object" (p. 45). Although undefinable, the self has describable characteristics, which include that it is a unique being (I am I and you are you), an identical but changing being (my adult self is the same being as my 10-year-old self, but at the same time the two differ), and "a being related in a distinctive fashion both to itself and its experiences and to environing objects, personal and impersonal." The self's relation to the objects "is called its consciousness of them" (p. 45).

Calkins (1906) proposed to use self-theory as a means of reconciling structural and functional psychology. By 1930, Calkins confidently noted the compatibility of her system with the other systems of psychology proposed to that point: with structuralism; with behaviorism and its forerunner, functionalism; with Gestalt psychology; and with "every one of the psychoanalytic systems" (p. 53). Heidbreder (1972) suggested that Calkins was trying to develop a conceptual scheme that would allow psychology to deal "with its empirical subject-matter, not only as that subject-matter appears when observed under laboratory conditions and by certain approved methods, but as it presents itself in ordinary experience and in common-sense knowledge" (p. 66). Heidbreder concluded that Calkins did not succeed in her conceptual efforts, but her way of perceiving the problem and her approach to it are instructive.

Calkins (Figure 10–2) received many honors during her career. She was elected president of the APA in 1905 and of the American Philosophical Association in 1918, in each case being the first woman to hold the post. In a 1903 ranking of the 50 leading American psychologists, Calkins ranked 12th. Calkins received honorary degrees from Columbia in 1909 and from Smith College in 1910, and she received an honorary membership in the British Psychological Association in 1928 (Furumoto, 1991).

FIGURE 10–2.   Mary Calkins as a young Wellesley faculty memeber.

Source: Photo by Partridge, courtesy of Wellesley College Archives.

We will now examine the contributions of the third of Calkins's major teachers, the man James brought from Germany to supervise the Harvard psychology laboratory—Hugo Münsterberg.

HUGO MÜNSTERBERG

Hugo Münsterberg (1863–1916) was born in Danzig, East Prussia. His father was a prominent Jewish lumber merchant, and his mother was an avid painter and musician. Both of his parents died before Münsterberg (Figure 10–3) was 20, and Münsterberg converted to Protestantism following their deaths (Spillmann & Spillmann, 1993).

Münsterberg attended Wundt's lectures and earned his Ph.D. from Leipzig in 1885. Next, he studied medicine at the University of Heidelberg, receiving his M.D. in 1887. That same year, Mün-

sterberg was appointed a *Dozent* at the University of Freiburg, establishing a laboratory there with equipment purchased with his own money.

In 1888, Münsterberg published the work he had intended as his dissertation but had not used at Wundt's request, *Die Willenshandlung* (*Voluntary Action*), a book that James called "a little masterpiece" in the *Principles.* In it, Münsterberg criticized Wundt's position on will at the same time that he "railed at statistics-gathering empiricism as well. Hence from James's view young Münsterberg had attacked the humbug of an artificial idealism as well as the excesses of a dry positivism" (Bjork, 1983, p. 43). When G. E. Müller brutally reviewed Münsterberg's book, James wrote Münsterberg a letter of "consolation." At the time of Munsterberg's first meeting with James at the First International Congress of Psychology in Paris in 1889, Münsterberg had broken with Wundt, established a laboratory at Freiburg, and was beginning to publish a series of

FIGURE 10–3.   Hugo Münsterberg.

Source: Harvard University Archives, courtesy Harvard College Library.

four volumes entitled *Beiträge zur experimentelle Psychologie* (*Contributions to Experimental Psychology*). In Münsterberg, James believed he had found his director for the Harvard laboratory.

However, Münsterberg spoke no English and was nationalistically German. "He seems to have always seen himself as a missionary of enlightenment amidst naive hosts" (Watkins, 1989, p. 3) and appears never to have considered becoming a United States citizen. Still, he was interested enough in the Harvard position to come to America in 1892 for a 3-year trial.

During Münsterberg's test period, James had gone to Europe on sabbatical, leaving **Josiah Royce** (1855–1916) in charge of the department. Although Royce and James were close personally, Royce was thoroughly a rationalist, a Hegelian, believing in an Absolute Mind. By contrast, James considered Hegel his "philosophic *bête noire* [literally black beast, or "pet peeve"]" (Knight, 1950, p. 39). Keeping in touch with the department through correspondence with Royce, James learned that his new laboratory director was an "immense success."

In 1895, Münsterberg returned to Germany but was unable to find a chair at a major university. Thus, Münsterberg formally joined the Harvard faculty in 1897 and stayed until his 1916 death from a cerebral hemorrhage during a lecture to an introductory psychology class at Radcliffe College. "At the time of his death he was widely despised and ridiculed, and essentially friendless. Harvard refused to pay any pension to his widow. By provision of his will, his remains were returned to Germany" (Watkins, 1989, p. 3). From such a promising beginning—Münsterberg was elected the seventh APA president in 1898—what led to such an ignominious ending?

The problem was that Münsterberg developed and pursued interests beyond the psychological laboratory. Although many of these interests led to important contributions to psychology, they also gave Münsterberg a visibility that became a liability because of his pro-German activities at a time when American sentiment was decidedly anti-German.

Although Münsterberg actively fomented experimentalism among his students in the laborato-

ry, he . . . had heard the siren voice of philosophy and was rapidly becoming more interested in the "principles" of psychology than in the discovery of new facts. He became famous in America for his personal brilliancy, his participation in public affairs, his voluminous popular writings, and his innovating applications of psychology to industry, jurisprudence, and medicine. (Perry, 1935, p. 201)

A listing of just a few of Münsterberg's book titles shows his versatility: *On the Witness Stand* (1909), *Psychology and the Teacher* (1909), *Psychotherapy* (1909), and *Psychology and Industrial Efficiency* (1913). A best seller, *On the Witness Stand* was concerned with what we would call forensic or legal psychology. *Psychology and Industrial Efficiency* was important in the development of industrial psychology in America. *On the Witness Stand* and *Psychology and Industrial Efficiency* established Münsterberg as a pioneer in applied psychology (Chapter 18).

Münsterberg's publications, many aimed at and read by the general public, made him perhaps the best-known psychologist in America in the early part of the 20th century. This was a time of steadily worsening relations between Germany and its Western European neighbors, culminating in World War I. Münsterberg, as a German in America, worked actively to keep America neutral.

The Harvard administration was frequently embarrassed by Münsterberg's pro-German activities, and President Eliot rebuked Münsterberg on a number of occasions. Unfortunately, the irrepressible Münsterberg continued such activities after war began in Europe. In 1914, a former Harvard student, Major Clarence Wiener of London, sent an open letter to the Dean of Harvard College and several newspapers threatening to withdraw his promise of a sizable bequest unless Münsterberg was removed from the faculty. Although the Harvard administration intended to ignore the threat, Münsterberg made matters worse by declaring publicly that he would resign if Wiener would give half the gift immediately. Wiener refused, but the administration found itself having to defend Münsterberg's unpopular antics—such as writing articles and books defending Germany's position. Stemming from Münsterberg's belief system, his activities continued after the 1915 German sinking of the *Lusitania*, with the loss of over 100 Americans. Despite his early promise and the accomplishments of his campaign of applied psychology, in the end, Münsterberg was so despised that no eulogy was published when he died.

Münsterberg and Titchener Compared

It is historically interesting to compare the careers and long-term influence of Münsterberg and Titchener, two of Wundt's students who came to America to take charge of experimental laboratories at major universities. Apparently, neither man considered becoming an American citizen, but the similarity ends there.

Psychology for Titchener was the study of the adult, human, generalized mind in order to determine its basic elements and structure. Münsterberg's psychology was much broader than Titchener's and not as easily characterized. In particular, Münsterberg was interested in the application of psychology to the betterment of life, and he worked vigorously in the last part of his career to this end. "Münsterberg therefore set out to design a system of vocational guidance which combined job satisfaction with maximum achievement, and psychological prediction with psychological control" (Spillmann & Spillmann, 1993, p. 331). As part of this effort, Münsterberg invented a new science that was called psychotechnics, which was a forerunner of today's **ergonomics** (designing equipment that can be more efficiently used by humans; also called human factors engineering) and industrial psychology.

Münsterberg's contributions to applied psychology, an area Titchener considered inappropriate for a "pure" psychology, were profound, and "Hugo Münsterberg is regarded as the founder of applied psychology in the United States, as well as in Europe" (Spillmann & Spillmann, 1993, p. 332). Thus, we can see Münsterberg's influence in such applied areas as business and industry, the legal profession, and the psychological clinic. By contrast, Titchener's structuralism did not long survive him.

Of the two, Münsterberg has had by far the greater impact on contemporary psychology, although this is often not apparent in histories of psychology. For example, although both books contain a chapter on structuralism in which Titchener is treated prominently, neither Kendler's (1987) *Historical Foundations of Modern Psychology* nor Marx and Cronan-Hillix's (1987) *Systems and Theories in Psychology* index Münsterberg's name. Although these are extreme examples, Münsterberg rarely receives the recognition his contributions merit. We can conclude our look at Münsterberg by noting that his applied approach to psychology was consistent with functionalism's emphasis on the functions of consciousness.

Although Münsterberg and Titchener both contributed significantly, perhaps Münsterberg more than Titchener, the person universally recognized as second only to William James in shaping the early course of American psychology was G. Stanley Hall.

GRANVILLE STANLEY HALL

William James's influence on psychology has continued primarily because of his writing of the *Principles*. G. Stanley Hall's influence continues because of his organizational talents, exemplified by the founding of the American Psychological Association, of journals such as *The American Journal of Psychology*, and in the department of psychology at Clark University that Hall, as Clark's first president, developed. Despite all his personal faults, Hall was a pioneering founder of psychology in America. Like James, but for different reasons, Hall's development as a psychologist was circuitous.

Granville Stanley Hall (1844–1924) was born near Ashfield, Massachusetts, the first child of descendants of colonists who arrived on the *Mayflower*. Although both of Hall's parents had been schoolteachers, his father was a farmer at the time Hall was born and remained so for the rest of his life.

Hall's father was harshly puritanical, stern, and quick tempered, whereas his mother was gently pious. Hall's feelings toward his father combined love and admiration with hostility. Perhaps stemming from "these ambivalent feelings [towards his father], Stanley developed a character at once aggressive and constrained" (Ross, 1972, p. 11).

Throughout his life, Hall tended to develop a series of intense interests. As he described it in a letter to a student:

> I sometimes think my life has been a series of fads or crazes. . . . When I got hold of the first edition of Wundt's "Psychology" I became infatuated, resigned my professorship, and rushed over to Leipzig. . . . When I came back, my laboratory was the first in the country, to which I devoted all my time for several years with Dewey, Cattell, Donaldson, Jastrow, and others as my pupils.
>
> Then my child-study craze arose, and for some years at Baltimore and for more years after coming [to Clark University] we did no end of questionnaire work. . . .
>
> Psycho-analysis, merging over into the study of nutrition in the way started by [Pavlov], Turro, and others has been the last obsession, unless I except war psychology, on which I have a book coming out. (Pruette, 1926, pp. 3–4)

With this as a preview, we will examine how Hall became one of American psychology's great founders.

Hall's Early Years

At 23, Hall graduated with Phi Beta Kappa honors from Williams College in Massachusetts. Upon graduation, he wanted to further the philosophical interests he had developed from reading John Stuart Mill (Chapter 4) with study in Germany, but he could not afford to go. Selecting the only advanced educational avenue open to someone of limited means with an interest in philosophy—theology—Hall enrolled in 1867 at New York City's Union Theological Seminary.

Like many other youths of restricted experience, Hall found New York exhilarating. In his spare time,

> He attended all kinds of church services, from Catholic to Seventh-Day Adventist to Spiritist. He tested the city's famous phrenologists and mediums, repeatedly visited the police courts and the morgue, and dabbled in a few of the reform movements of the day. . . . Twice he

went to see "The Black Crook," a popular and scandalous ballet spectacle which featured for the first time on the American stage one hundred female dancers very scantily attired. After the second visit, Hall wrote his parents that he "sat very near and this time was disgusted." (Ross, 1972, pp. 32–33).

Still, Hall dreamed of becoming a professor of philosophy. With a $500 loan from a wealthy patron of Union, he sailed for Europe in June 1869. In Germany, Hall's main studies were as a member of the seminar of Frederick Trendelenburg, the Berlin philosopher who influenced Brentano (Chapter 8). Trendelenburg's emphasis on development encouraged Hall to investigate Hegel, and both Hegel and Trendelenburg confirmed Hall's belief in the value of historical process. Hall also vigorously pursued biological science, and he may have heard du Bois-Reymond lecture. Unfortunately, Hall's money soon ran out, and he reluctantly returned to America in the fall of 1870.

By the time Hall received his Union divinity degree, he had decided to use it to obtain a position teaching philosophy in college rather than to become a minister. Perhaps the result of his trial sermon helped him decide against the ministry: Instead of the usual critique, his professor knelt and prayed for his soul.

After graduation, Hall spent 2 more years in New York, where his religious orthodoxy waned further. Hall found it difficult to obtain a university position teaching philosophy because the topic was usually taught in America by a more traditional cleric. An academic position finally came through an offer for him to teach rhetoric and English literature at Ohio's Antioch College. Because of financial straits at Antioch, Hall was additionally required to teach French, German, and Anglo-Saxon. In his "spare time," he also functioned as the college librarian, debate coach, and drillmaster. During Hall's 4 years at the school, he earned a reputation as one of Antioch's best teachers. However, even with the liberal Unitarian beliefs of the authorities, Hall found his attitudes incompatible with those in Ohio. He chafed at the routine of his teaching post, and his ambitions were unfulfilled.

Hall's philosophy was also evolving. The second edition of Spencer's *Principles of Psychology* (1872) probably provided the unifying principle for Hall's diverse philosophical interests—psychology—and he introduced lectures on psychology into his philosophy course. Soon thereafter, Hall received the first volume of Wundt's *Principles of Physiological Psychology* and was greatly excited by it. Hall's studies in Germany and his independent readings had well prepared him to appreciate Wundt's effort to form a science of psychology from its bases in physiology and philosophy. He decided to take a year's leave of absence from Antioch in order to consider his next move. After being rejected for a teaching position at newly formed Johns Hopkins University, Hall elected to attend lectures at Harvard.

According to Hall, he stayed at Harvard to earn his Ph.D. after he was offered a teaching post in English by President Eliot. "This story is not supported by contemporary evidence. . . . The story appears to reflect Hall's desire to minimize the importance of his debt to William James" (Ross, 1972, p. 61), which was considerable, as Hall took most of his work with James. Note that this illustrates our Chapter 1 discussion of both the reconstructive nature of some autobiographical material and the necessity of consulting multiple sources when attempting to verify historical events.

Although Hall was only 2 years younger than James, his puritanical, conservative religious upbringing was poles apart from the liberal environment in which James developed. Still, the two shared an interest in the new scientific psychology.

Hall's largely theoretical dissertation was on the muscular perception of space, supported by experiments he performed in Henry P. Bowditch's (1840–1911) laboratory at Harvard Medical School. In addition to his 1878 Ph.D.—the first doctorate awarded by Harvard's philosophy department and the first psychology doctorate in America—Hall took from his experience with James a functional and pragmatic approach to the mind. With no immediate employment prospects, Hall pooled his resources and left for a second visit to the German universities and the laboratories of several physiologists we introduced in Chapter 6.

Because of his interest in motor processes, Hall traveled first to du Bois-Reymond's Berlin laboratory. In addition, Hall attended some of Helmholtz's lectures, and the great man's efforts to explain the processes of life physically and chemically caught Hall's imagination. Hall began increasingly to feel that philosophy rested upon psychology and psychology upon physiology, a reductionistic view. Hall also heard and was impressed by Hermann Munk. Finally, Hall's Berlin experience exposed him to the study of psychopathology.

In the fall of 1879, Hall moved to Leipzig, where he spent most of his time working in Karl Ludwig's (1816–1895) physiology laboratory. Hall also worked in Wundt's newly established laboratory, but nothing publishable resulted. Still, Wundt commended his first American student in recommendation letters for carrying on laboratory work "with great zeal and success." By contrast, Hall's opinion of Wundt decreased with greater contact, and in a letter to James, he described Wundt "as a man who has done more speculation and less valuable observing than any man I know who has had his career" (as cited in Ross, 1972, p. 85).

Ernst Haeckel's theories formed a major part of the scientific backdrop during Hall's stay in Germany. Haeckel (Chapter 9) believed that an individual repeats the evolutionary history of the species in its development, and this recapitulation idea became central to Hall's theory of child development (discussed later).

Before returning to America, Hall applied a second time to Johns Hopkins and again was rejected. Hall's subsequent difficulties in finding employment caused him briefly to consider studying medicine. Finally, hitting upon the idea of applying psychology to education, Hall assembled pedagogical materials and quickly toured schools in Germany, France, and England. This tour and his interest in psychology applied to education proved important for his later career.

Hall and Psychology in America

After securing employment as a teacher of the history of philosophy at Williams College, Hall gave a series of lectures on pedagogy on Saturday mornings at the request of Harvard's president. The lectures' success led to an offer for Hall to do a similar series at Johns Hopkins.

Hall gave 10 lectures on the "new" psychology in January of 1882, and in March, Hopkins' President Daniel Gilman offered him a 3-year appointment in the philosophy department as a lecturer in psychology and pedagogy. Hall found himself competing for a professorial slot with a mentor from Union, George Morris, and with James's friend, Charles S. Peirce. After Peirce was dismissed in early 1884, Hall was chosen over Morris, at least partly because of the difference in their personalities: Morris was quiet and retiring, whereas Hall was forceful and dynamic.

Hall considered the principal division of the "new" psychology to be experimental psychology, and most of his efforts at Hopkins were aimed at establishing himself in this area. Thus, in 1883, he developed a small psychological laboratory in the building where he lectured, which some consider the first formally established psychological laboratory in America (e.g., Cattell, 1929). By 1887, Hall's laboratory space had expanded to four rooms in a new building. When he left a year later, Hall took with him the laboratory apparatus, and Johns Hopkins did not re-establish a psychological laboratory until 1903. Even though most of Hall's Ph.D. students at Hopkins did not become experimentalists, his Hopkins' laboratory influenced the development of psychology in America by forcing other universities to create laboratories in order to stay current.

In addition to James McKeen Cattell (discussed later) and John Dewey, a number of Hall's Hopkins' students went on to have significant careers. **Joseph Jastrow** (1863–1944) and Henry Donaldson (Chapter 12) were among the earliest contingent. The founder of the laboratory at the University of Wisconsin and 1900 APA president, Jastrow is perhaps best known for his books that popularized psychology, including *The House that Freud Built,* as well as for his duck-rabbit reversible figure. Jastrow and Donaldson were soon joined by Edmund Sanford, and Sanford and Donaldson accompanied Hall to Clark University.

The most famous of Hall's students at Hopkins was T. W. Wilson, "who spent a long Sunday after-noon walking and debating with Hall whether he should leave the study of politics and history and come definitely into psychology . . ." (Pruette, 1926, p. 91). As history records it, Thomas Woodrow Wilson (1856–1924) became a lawyer, then president of Princeton, governor of New Jersey, and finally, America's 28th president.

Hall's efforts at Hopkins included psychical research, which he had first encountered in Germany. There, Hall had established contact with some of the spiritualists in the Leipzig academic community, which included his neighbor, Gustav Fechner (Chapter 6). The Society for Psychical Research was formed in England in 1882, and William James was a member. In 1884, an American version was founded, with Hall as one of five vice-presidents. Hall was skeptical of the thought trans-ference the British Society claimed to have found, considering that many "psychic phenomena" were created by deception. To help him detect the decep-tion, Hall studied magic, becoming an expert per-former. He used this expertise to expose mediums and became one of the first of the scientific leaders to resign from the Society.

Perhaps Hall's foremost accomplishment at Hop-kins was the founding in 1887 of America's first psy-chological journal, *The American Journal of Psy-chology*. Ironically, some of the funds for the *Journal* came from a gift from a member of the American Society for Psychical Research, who undoubtedly assumed that Hall's *Journal* would be favorably dis-posed toward psychical research. When this proved not to be the case, there were no more contribu-tions. In addition, Hall's enthusiasm for psychology led him to order far more copies of the first volume than he actually sold. Although the *Journal* eventual-ly recovered from Hall's extravagance, he never recovered personally. The need for financial econ-omy became such an overriding concern that, at his death, Hall was found to have over $172,000 in small amounts in 78 different Massachusetts' banks.

At about the time that Hall founded his jour-nal, Jonas Clark and eight other citizens of Worcester, Massachusetts, were petitioning the state legislature to incorporate an institution to be known as Clark University. After earning a fortune as a merchant in the California gold rush in the mid-19th century, Clark (1815–1900) had returned to his birthplace to establish a lasting monument to himself in the form of a university bearing his name. Clark apparently wanted a school that would incorporate both collegiate work and higher graduate work, perhaps in the mold of Johns Hopkins, where there would be maximum freedom in both teaching and scientific investigation. To head his institution, Clark and his board of trustees chose Hall.

At Clark's expense, Hall toured European universities to gather the latest thinking on higher education, using the opportunity to create a positive image of Clark University in the minds of all he met. Before and after his European trip, Hall assembled his faculty, which proved to be a remarkably talented group, with many recruited from Hopkins. In addition, Hall secured their services at minimum cost to Clark. His professors were willing to accept low wages because of Hall's promise of reduced teaching loads, maximum research time, and ample equipment support. As just one example, attracted by the promise of free summers to pursue fieldwork, Franz Boas (1858–1942)—who became the country's premier anthropologist—came to Clark for half the $2,000 he was paid at *Science* magazine.

Clark University opened in the fall of 1889. As promised, teaching duties were light, and the 18 faculty members devoted most of their time to directing the research of 34 students. However, this idyllic situation was short-lived, its ending presaged in 1890 by a personal disaster for Hall. While recuperating in Ashfield from diphtheria, Hall learned that his wife and young daughter had been accidentally asphyxiated by a faulty heater, with only his 9-year-old son surviving. Hall sought solace in a renewed faith in God and in a passion for work. Unfortunately, hard work and faith alone were insufficient to save his dream for Clark University.

In the beginning, the problem was Jonas Clark's unrealistic expectations of the cost of a university. Forced to meet operating expenses out of his own pocket, Clark's ardor for the project cooled rapidly. Hall did think of one way to generate public approval and needed funds for the University, however. In 1891, he opened a summer school for the area's educators. That same year Hall founded the

journal *Pedagogical Seminary,* which later became the *Journal of Genetic Psychology.*

But summer school for educators did not bring in enough money, and Clark became increasingly tight with his funds. Hall responded by becoming increasingly autocratic and devious. Eventually, his alienation of the faculty almost destroyed the University, coming at a time when President William Harper was trying to attract quality personnel to his newly organized University of Chicago. "In the end, two-thirds of all those of faculty rank and 70 percent of the student body left Clark in the spring of 1892" (Ross, 1972, p. 227). With so many students and faculty gone in so many areas, the department of psychology, with its subdivision of pedagogy, came to dominate Clark. After the word spread about the university's problems, Hall found it nearly impossible to hire quality faculty to replace those he had lost.

Despite his problems at Clark, the year 1892 was not all bad for Hall's ambitions. In that year, he was instrumental in founding the American Psychological Association and was elected its first president. It is worth noting that Clark University survived its early hardships and remains a prestigious center for psychological research.

Hall and the Founding of the APA

Hall invited over 25 people interested in scientific psychology to an organizational meeting of the **American Psychological Association** at Clark University on July 8, 1892. The charter members included Hall and Sanford at Clark; James, Royce, and Münsterberg at Harvard; Cattell at Columbia; Witmer (Chapter 7) at Pennsylvania; James Mark Baldwin (discussed later) at Toronto; Titchener at Cornell; Dewey at Michigan; and Jastrow at Wisconsin. As president, Hall presided over the first annual meeting of the APA, which was held at the University of Pennsylvania on December 27, 1892. With his election again in 1924, Hall became only the second person ever to hold the office twice; James was the other.

From the 31 charter members, the membership of the APA has increased rapidly, with the organi-

TABLE 10–1

Presidents of The American Psychological Association

1892 G. Stanley Hall	1927 H. L. Hollingworth	1962 Paul Meehl
1893 G. T. Ladd	1928 E. G. Boring	1963 Charles Osgood
1894 William James	1929 Karl S. Lashley	1964 Quinn McNemar
1895 J. McKeen Cattell	1930 Herbert S. Langfeld	1965 Jerome S. Bruner
1896 G. S. Fullerton	1931 Walter S. Hunter	1966 Nicholas Hobbs
1897 J. M. Baldwin	1932 Walter R. Miles	1967 Gardner Lindzey
1898 Hugo Münsterberg	1933 L. L. Thurstone	1968 Abraham Maslow
1899 John Dewey	1934 Joseph Peterson	1969 George A. Miller
1900 Joseph Jastrow	1935 A. T. Poffenberger	1970 George W. Albee
1901 Josiah Royce	1936 Clark L. Hull	1971 Kenneth B. Clark
1902 E. C. Sanford	1937 Edward C. Tolman	1972 Anne Anastasi
1903 William L. Bryan	1938 J. F. Dashiell	1973 Leona E. Tyler
1904 William James	1939 Gordon Allport	1974 Albert Bandura
1905 Mary W. Calkins	1940 Leonard Carmichael	1975 Donald T. Campbell
1906 James R. Angell	1941 Herbert Woodrow	1976 Wilbert McKeachie
1907 Henry R. Marshall	1942 Calvin P. Stone	1977 Theodore H. Blau
1908 George M. Stratton	1943 John E. Anderson	1978 M. Brewster Smith
1909 Charles H. Judd	1944 Gardner Murphy	1979 Nicholas A. Cummings
1910 Walter B. Pillsbury	1945 Edwin R. Guthrie	1980 Florence L. Denmark
1911 Carl E. Seashore	1946 Henry E. Garrett	1981 John J. Conger
1912 Edward L. Thorndike	1947 Carl R. Rogers	1982 William Bevan
1913 Howard C. Warren	1948 Donald G. Marquis	1983 Max Siegel
1914 R. S. Woodworth	1949 Ernest R. Hilgard	1984 Janet T. Spence
1915 John B. Watson	1950 J. P. Guilford	1985 Robert Perloff
1916 Raymond Dodge	1951 Robert R. Sears	1986 Logan Wright
1917 Robert M. Yerkes	1952 J. McVickers Hunt	1987 Bonnie R. Strickland
1918 J. W. Baird	1953 Laurance F. Shaffer	1988 Raymond D. Fowler
1919 Walter D. Scott	1954 O. Hobart Mowrer	1989 Joseph D. Matarazzo
1920 Shepherd I. Franz	1955 E. Lowell Kelly	1990 Stanley R. Graham
1921 Margaret Washburn	1956 T. M. Newcomb	1991 Charles Spielberger
1922 Knight Dunlap	1957 Lee J. Cronbach	1992 Jack G. Wiggins
1923 Lewis M. Terman	1958 Harry F. Harlow	1993 Frank Farley
1924 G. Stanley Hall	1959 Wolfgang Köhler	1994 Ronald E. Fox
1925 Madison Bentley	1960 D. O. Hebb	1995 Robert J. Resnick
1926 Harvey A. Carr	1961 Neal Miller	1996 Dorothy Cantor

zation claiming over 81,500 members in 1996. Table 10–1 lists the APA presidents, and you will see that most of the people in this chapter are on the list.

Since the APA's founding, a number of rival organizations have formed, generally with the goal of being more accommodating to scientific and academic psychology. Titchener's The Experimentalists (later The Society of Experimental Psychologists) is

one example. Another example is the **Psychonomic Society**, founded in 1959–1960 by Clifford T. Morgan (1915–1976), William Verplanck (1916-), and other well-respected experimentalists. A physiological psychologist, Morgan served as chairman of the organizing committee. Like The Society of Experimental Psychologists, the Psychonomic Society was organized to serve the needs of basic scientists in psychology.

The APA's apparent applied-clinical focus triggered a mass defection in 1988. The resulting **American Psychological Society** (APS) has an explicit focus on scientific psychology. By 1996, the APS had over 16,000 members. More than anything, the various professional organizations for psychologists highlight the diversity in the field, which is well illustrated by the over 40 different APA divisions to which a member can belong. In addition to the organizations we have mentioned, other groups of psychologists have formed over the years, including the following with which the authors have been or are affiliated: Cheiron (The International Society for the History of the Behavioral and Social Sciences), the International Cognitive Linguistics Association, the Society for Neuroscience, and the International Society for Research on Aggression.

Hall's Fall from Glory

By the end of the 19th century, it was obvious that Hall had passed his peak of influence in American psychology. Although his Ph.D. output had been prodigious—by 1898, 30 of the 54 psychology Ph.D.s awarded in America had gone to Hall's students—this would not continue. With Clark impoverished, its psychology department could not compete against the departments at wealthier schools.

In addition, Hall's editorship of *The American Journal of Psychology* damaged his relations with other psychologists. In part, the difficulty lay in his continuing attacks—often through book reviews—of some of his "friends." Hall's insults were frequently personal and often caustic. As an illustration, Hall criticized the haphazard arrangement of material in James's *Principles* by implying "that the book sounded as though it were written with a shotgun or water hose, rather than sharply and cleanly with a rifle. So much did James's personality intrude on his work, that it sometimes reminded one of Rousseau or a cheap popular diarist" (Ross, 1972, p. 233).

The idiosyncrasy of Hall's *Journal* and its exclusiveness led other psychologists to start their own journals. Baldwin and Cattell were the leaders in this effort, founding the *Psychological Review*. When the

Review appeared in 1894, Hall reluctantly took steps to meet the challenge to his *Journal*: He named Sanford and Titchener as co-editors and a cooperative board consisting of his and Titchener's friends and supporters. Unfortunately, Hall's editorial opening the "new" *Journal* hastened his isolation within psychology. In it, he claimed that his influence had been responsible "for the founding of departments of experimental psychology and laboratories at Harvard, Yale, Pennsylvania, Columbia, Toronto, Wisconsin, and many other universities" (Ross, 1972, p. 243). Predictably, this editorial led to letters to *Science* from James, Ladd, Baldwin, and Cattell refuting Hall's claims. Hall's subsequent conciliatory letter to *Science* failed to heal the rift that developed between him and James—and, perhaps, between Hall and the rest of American psychology.

Hall's Research Interests

The research and writing for which Hall is best known combined his interests in psychology, pedagogy, and evolution in the study of child development. Hall's data were collected with questionnaires, which he used so extensively that he is often credited with developing the technique, although the originator was actually Galton (Chapter 9).

Before leaving Boston for Baltimore and Johns Hopkins, Hall gathered questionnaire data on schoolchildren, which was published as "The Contents of Children's Minds" (Hall, 1883). However, the major result of Hall's study of children was his 1904 two-volume *Adolescence: Its Psychology and Its Relations to Physiology, Anthropology, Sociology, Sex, Crime, Religion, and Education. Adolescence* perhaps revealed more about Hall himself than he would have cared to admit. Much of it is filled with comments about sexuality, and Hall frequently coined new terms without adequately defining them. Despite its faults, *Adolescence* is important as perhaps the first systematic recognition in modern times of the period from puberty to young adulthood as a distinct stage in the life cycle.

The book was remarkably successful given its size and topic, selling more than 25,000 copies in America. Although popular reviewers often approved of *Adolescence*, psychologists were less enthusiastic. For example, Thorndike reviewed the book negatively and privately wrote Cattell that Hall's book was "'chock full of errors, masturbation and Jesus. He is a mad man'"(Ross, 1972, p. 385).

In *Adolescence,* Hall described his **recapitulation theory** of child development, which maintains that every human being passes "through all the stages of the race's evolution in his personal development (thus Hall's nickname as the 'Darwin of the mind')" (Schlossman, 1973, p. 143). Accordingly, the child is reliving the period when humans were little more than savages; in this stage, what is needed is drilling in the correct habits—indoctrination, in other words. Adolescence thus becomes "the time for training the will and shaping ideals" (p. 143), and boys' clubs were touted by Hall's supporters as ideal venues for such tuition. For psychology, recapitulation theory died at the hands of Thorndike, who criticized it from a biological standpoint (its parallels are more apparent than real) and concluded that the theory's influence was due more to its rhetorical attractiveness than to its validity.

Although Hall's study of childhood and adolescence amply qualify him as an early child psychologist (Nance, 1970; White, 1990), his interest in development did not end with *Adolescence.* Hall tackled life's last stage in *Senescence: The Last Half of Life,* published in 1922. *Senescence* deals more with old age than with the earlier part of life's last half. In particular, it is a look at the problems of old age and the psychological states they engender. Mirroring earlier works, *Senescence* is a personal record of what it was like for Hall himself to grow old. Currently, gerontology—the study of aging and the aged—is a "hot" topic in psychology, and Hall deserves recognition as an early investigator in the area. Another area in which he deserves more recognition than he has usually gotten is the psychology of religion.

Despite his contributions to religious psychology, Hall's role in its founding is often unrecognized. "In most recent psychology of religion texts, Hall is either conspicuously absent or overwhelmingly dwarfed by James" (Vande Kemp, 1992, p. 296). Although people interested in the psychology of religion usually consider James the field's founder, a case can also be made for Hall, who first offered courses in religious psychology at Hopkins and

taught at least one course on the topic nearly every year after 1900. In 1904, "Hall founded a library department of religious psychology and education to concentrate on acquiring a special book collection and publishing a journal" (Vande Kemp, p. 292). Hall's *The American Journal of Religious Psychology and Education* was published for a decade beginning in 1904, its impetus perhaps partly caused by James's 1902 book, *The Varieties of Religious Experience* (Ross, 1972).

Hall initially edited the journal with two former students—**James H. Leuba** (1868–1946) and **Edwin D. Starbuck** (1866–1947). Leuba was an 1895 Clark graduate who stayed on as a fellow before moving to Bryn Mawr College to head the psychology department. Leuba published the first empirical study of religious conversion and the first book with the title *The Psychology of Religion* (Beit-Hallahmi, 1974). Starbuck was James's student at Harvard before transferring to Clark. Like Leuba, Starbuck stayed at Clark as a fellow after receiving his Ph.D.

In 1917, Hall published *Jesus, the Christ, in the Light of Psychology,* which is primarily "a historical study of Jesus' life and its humane meaning . . ." (Ross, 1972, p. 418). Hall delayed publication because of the possible reaction of fundamentalists and the fear of damaging the rest of his career. "The book was indeed criticized severely in the conservative religious press but taken in stride in other quarters" (p. 418), as "Hall's psychological colleagues were accustomed to his eccentricities" (Vande Kemp, 1992, p. 294).

Hall and Psychoanalysis

Another of Hall's continuing interests was in psychopathology and psychiatry, which led him to invite the Swiss medical researcher and psychiatrist, **Auguste-Henri Forel** (1848–1931), to the 10-year anniversary celebration at Clark. Also known for his studies of ants, Forel spoke in 1899 about hypnotism and cerebral activity and about the work of Breuer and Freud (both Chapter 15). In that same year, Hall's *Journal* favorably reviewed Freud's and Breuer's work on hysteria.

As the 20th anniversary of Clark (1909) approached, Hall decided to invite two "foreign savants" for the psychology conference: Wundt and Freud. Wundt promptly refused Hall's offer of 3,000 marks ($750) and an honorary degree, pleading advanced age as his excuse. More reluctantly, Freud also rejected Hall's initial offer of 1,600 marks ($400), his main objection being when the conference was scheduled (Evans & Koelsch, 1985). Hall's invitation was rejected by Alfred Binet (Chapter 18) as well, but Wundt's slot was filled by Hermann Ebbinghaus (Chapter 8), who, unfortunately, died unexpectedly in 1909.

When Hall changed the conference date, Freud accepted his invitation, which carried with it Wundt's honorarium. The other attending psychoanalysts were Carl Jung, Sandor Ferenczi, Ernest Jones, and A. A. Brill (all Chapter 15). Of the psychoanalysts, only Jung and Freud were scheduled to speak.

Freud's five lectures in German were well received both by the attendees and by the local press,

and a positive article about the meeting subsequently appeared in *The Nation*. Apparently, Hall himself wrote *The Nation* article (Evans & Koelsch, 1985), possibly fearing a repeat of the lack of coverage his 10th anniversary meeting had received. Figure 10–4 is a famous group photograph of most of the attendees at the 1909 Clark Conference.

For Freud, the opportunity to present his work to interested psychologists in the United States was a dream come true. The subsequent publication of his lectures in Hall's *Journal* (Freud, 1910) completed his successful introduction of psychoanalytic ideas to the New World. "The seed of Freudian psychoanalysis, if it had not already been sown in America, was certainly sown now and nurtured through this meeting" (Evans & Koelsch, 1985, p. 947).

Although Hall remained an advocate of psychoanalysis the rest of his life, his public support of Freud ended in 1911. The problem apparently lay in

FIGURE 10–4. Attendees at the Clark Conference.

Beginning with first row, left to right: Franz Boas, E. B. Titchener, William James, William Stern, Leo Burgerstein, G. Stanley Hall, Sigmund Freud, Carl G. Jung, Adolf Meyer, H. S. Jennings. *Second row:* C. E. Seashore, Joseph Jastrow, J. McK. Cattell, E. F. Buchner, E. Katzenellenbogen, Ernest Jones, A. A. Brill, Wm. H. Burnham, A. F. Chamberlain. *Third row:* Albert Schinz, J. A. Magni, B. T. Baldwin, F. Lyman Wells, G. M. Forbes, E. A. Kirkpatrick, Sandor Ferenczi, E. C. Sanford, J. P. Porter, Sakyo Kanda, Kikoso Kakise. *Fourth row:* G. E. Dawson, S. P. Hayes, E. B. Holt, C. S. Berry, G. M. Whipple, Frank Drew, J. W. A. Young, L. N. Wilson, K. J. Karlson, H. H. Goddard, H. I. Klopp, S. C. Fuller.

Source: Archives of the History of American Psychology.

Freud's attribution of sexual symbolism to many different objects and to a highly critical review of Hall's *Educational Problems* in 1911. Upbraided for his apparent preoccupation with sexuality, Hall was probably reluctant to continue to support publicly psychoanalysis's sexual emphasis (Ross, 1972).

As a postscript to Hall's interest in psychoanalysis, he corresponded with Alfred Adler (Chapter 16) beginning in 1914 and at one point considered inviting Adler to the United States (Ansbacher, 1971). Finally, Hall's influence on Carl Jung has been suggested (Hinkelman & Aderman, 1968). When they met at the Clark Conference, Jung was a relatively unknown psychologist and Hall was a well-known university president.

Hall and Subordinates

Hall's interpersonal relationships were often less than satisfactory and were frequently characterized by dissembling when he felt his intellectual superiority threatened. For example, Cattell probably lost his Hopkins' fellowship because he was highly intelligent and brashly confident. Feeling threatened, Hall worked behind the scenes to deny Cattell his fellowship and then repeated his performance with John Dewey, another able graduate student.

Hall did not alienate all of his competent associates, however. Edmund Sanford was both capable and steadfastly loyal to his mentor. In addition, Sanford was always willing to be subordinate to Hall, and this was perhaps the key to their relationship. Hall "recognized ability and nurtured it effectively so long as it remained in a subordinate role" (Sokal, 1990, p. 116). Recognizing the quality of his relationship with Hall, Sanford "wrote late in his life that 'the relation of pupil and teacher was never wholly lost'" (p. 118). Apparently, one reason for Sanford's loyalty was that Hall stood by him during Sanford's frequent illnesses. At a time when a disability such as a loss of hearing could cause dismissal, Sanford's loyalty becomes more understandable. According to at least one source (Goodwin, 1987), Sanford's attachment to Hall cost him recognition he might have had if he had gone his own way.

Another illustration of Hall's support for people in ill health is his hiring of Titchener-trained **John**

Wallace Baird (1873–1919) to head Clark's psychological laboratory. Influenced by the Würzburg school (Chapter 8), Baird shared Sanford's unstable health, as did Lewis Terman (Chapter 18). Terman studied at Clark perhaps because Hall was the only psychologist of note willing to offer a graduate fellowship to "a midwesterner with active tuberculosis" (Sokal, 1990, p. 119).

Hall's need for a dominant/subordinate relationship with students and colleagues may also explain the apparent contradiction between his stated objection to the coeducation of the sexes and the fact that Clark was one of the leading institutions for the graduate education of women in the early 20th century. Hall believed that women needed to be educated apart from men in adolescence to avoid damage to their reproductive organs and to prepare them for their appointed role in life—motherhood. Further, Hall opposed having women teachers in high school, "for it was during adolescence that boys needed the firm hand of a man and a model to emulate" (Diehl, 1986, p. 872).

Although Hall's coeducation position never changed, he was a shrewd administrator of a perennially underfunded institution. In 1909, in response to a request for information about what Clark was doing for the common good that would enable it to keep its tax-exempt status, Hall created an Educational Department that would grant higher degrees to women. Privately, Hall noted the political desirability of continuing to award the occasional Ph.D. to a woman in order to prevent trouble from feminists (Diehl, 1986).

Theodate Louise Smith's (1859–1914) career well illustrates Hall's relationships with women junior colleagues. Born in Hallowell, Maine, Smith earned a Ph.D. from Yale in 1896. After unsuccessfully seeking university employment until 1902, Smith became Hall's research assistant. Apparently, Smith shared Hall's views on the role of women and fulfilled her subordinate role so well that, after her sudden death, "Hall wrote a glowing tribute to her deference to him . . ." (Sokal, 1990, p. 121).

Finally, Hall's last graduate student, **Francis Sumner** (1895–1954), further illustrates Hall's tendency to bring to Clark students and faculty who would have found it either difficult or impos-

FIGURE 10–5. Francis
Sumner.
Source: Howard University.

sible to enter academia elsewhere. Sumner (see
Figure 10–5) was the first black student to earn a
Ph.D. in psychology in the United States. He
developed the undergraduate psychology program
at Howard University, which has graduated more
black psychologists than any other school. Sumner
was also a major producer of entries for *Psychological Abstracts*—a principal library tool for students
of psychology—composing nearly 2,000 for articles written in English, Spanish, French, German,
and Russian.

Hall's Influence

It has been noted frequently that Hall had more
firsts than perhaps any psychologist before or since.
For example, Hall received the first Ph.D. from
Harvard's philosophy department; he was the first
American student at the world's first psychology
laboratory (Wundt's at Leipzig); his *American
Journal of Psychology* was the first exclusively psychological journal in English; his Hopkins' laboratory is considered the first psychological laboratory in
America (James's Harvard laboratory was earlier,
but it began as primarily a teaching laboratory); he
was the first president of Clark University; he was
the main organizer and first president of the
American Psychological Association; he was instrumental in giving American psychology its first look

at Freud and psychoanalysis; he was among the first
to write about both adolescence and senescence; and
he directed the program of Francis Sumner, the first
black to earn a Ph.D. in psychology.

Through his many students, Hall's influence
extended beyond the journals, laboratories, and
institutions he founded. Some of Hall's students
developed unswerving loyalty, and Sanford's comment in his obituary to Hall well illustrates Hall's
effect on this group: "To those who were his pupils,
the inspiration, the illumination, the friendliness are
unforgettable" (Sanford, 1924, pp. 320–321). Others
saw Hall differently and "were baffled by his inconsistent anger or approval, his evidences of harshness,
meanness, and selfishness. His most perceptive student sensed that he was a very accomplished actor"
(Ross, 1972, p. 426).

Hall's influence on his students was perhaps most
effective through his Monday night seminars, which
were held in Hall's home. The seminars' formal structure usually consisted of paper presentations by two
doctoral candidates, with a discussion session following. When questioning slowed, Hall, hitherto silent,
"opened his deceitfully half-closed eyes to express his
interest in the student's research" (Averill, 1982, p.
342). Hall employed Socratic questioning with con-
ceited or ill-prepared students, at first complimenting
the student on the presentation and then asking for
some minor clarification. "Locating the essential
weakness of the paper he blandly followed up his lead
question by question until the man either threw up
his hands or became furiously angry, usually the
former" (Sheldon, 1946, p. 234). According to Averill,
none "of the hundreds of pursuers of the graduate
gleam who ever experienced the intellectual ravish-
ment of these soul-stirring seminars of Stanley Hall
ever forgot them" (p. 342).

Although little recognized, Hall also contributed
importantly to the field of the history of psychology
(Bringmann, Bringmann, & Early, 1992), in the
form of biographies. Hall's historical interests
directly influenced a number of colleagues, including the dean of psychological historians, E. G.
Boring. In fact, Boring's first academic position
was at Clark University under Hall. In addition,
Boring began writing his monumental *A History of
Experimental Psychology* shortly after he left Clark,

and the book contains many stories first mentioned in Hall's writings (Bringmann et al.).

Like the other major figures we have surveyed in this chapter (James and Münsterberg), Hall was a forerunner of functionalism and not a "true" functionalist. Although in part chronological, this distinction is made primarily because each man (and Cattell, as well) was an eclectic thinker. Temperamentally, these pioneers were ill-suited to be constrained by adherence to a formal system—even one as diverse and nondoctrinaire as functionalism.

It is difficult to summarize the accomplishments and character of a person as complex as G. Stanley Hall. As president of Clark University, he created an environment conducive to research, and his broad range of interests gave a wide variety of students an opportunity to express themselves. As a builder, organizer, administrator, and propagandist for the "new" psychology, Hall succeeded.

As a person, he was less successful. A man of immense personal magnetism, Hall's character was all too flawed. "Loyalty to persons is something which Hall probably never had," wrote Lorine Pruette (1926, p. 180), a sympathetic biographer and former student. Noting his lack of consistency with people, Pruette concluded that it "made him appear a greater liar than he really was . . ." (p. 180). Perhaps it is enough to say that despite his flaws, Hall attempted and achieved much.

EARLY STUDIES OF GENDER DIFFERENCES: THE WORK OF LETA STETTER HOLLINGWORTH

Hall's view of women as best suited for subordinate positions was shared by many others of his time. Pioneering American psychologist Leta Hollingworth challenged experimentally one of the tenets upon which the idea of male intellectual superiority rested and found little evidence to support it. Her work provides a brief case study of the contributions made by women to the rise of American psychology.

In the Victorian era, the dominant political and social positions held by men were considered con-firmation that men were more capable intellectually than women. When the first efforts of the mental testing movement failed to find a difference in the average abilities of men and women, believers in the innate inequality of the sexes turned to Darwin. In *Descent of Man,* Darwin had noted that in many species there was more differentiation of secondary sex characteristics in the male, from which he suggested that the male was the more variable sex. "Because variation from the average had already been proposed as a primary evolutionary mechanism, the alleged greater variation among males was seen as a distinct advantage and a sign of the superiority of their sex" (Shields, 1975, p. 853).

Because of the social implications of the variability hypothesis—for example, if women were less likely to possess high abilities, their graduate education was probably a waste of resources—**Leta Stetter Hollingworth** (1886–1939) investigated its validity. Born in a dugout canoe along the White River in northwestern Nebraska (Ware, 1993), Hollingworth received her psychology Ph.D. from Columbia in 1916, with Thorndike as her major professor. Because Thorndike advocated the variability hypothesis, Hollingworth's motive for her studies may have been to prove him wrong. It is a testimony to Thorndike's willingness to face facts, however, that he accepted Hollingworth's experimental results (Shields, 1991). Shortly after earning her Ph.D., Hollingworth joined the faculty of Columbia.

Examining the variability hypothesis, Hollingworth (1913) looked at sex differences in the numbers of mentally retarded women and men, finding that there were more institutionalized men than women, which might be taken as evidence for greater male variability. However, Hollingworth argued that women "belong to a non-competitive and dependent class and are not so readily recognized as defective since they do not have to compete mentally to maintain themselves in the social milieu" (p. 753). From this, she reasoned that women would be more likely to be institutionalized at older ages, when they were too old to be "useful," and she found statistical support for this.

Later, Hollingworth and Helen Montague (Montague & Hollingworth, 1914) examined hospital records of 2,000 neonates (1,000 of each sex), searching for greater physical variability in males. If anything, they found greater variability in the females. For this study and the earlier one, Hollingworth was recognized by feminists as the scientific cornerstone of their cause (Shields, 1975).

Much of Hollingworth's later career was devoted to the study of children at the extremes of ability: for example, two of her books were *The Psychology of Subnormal Children* and *Gifted Children.* Like Hall, she wrote on adolescence, and her textbook, *The Psychology of the Adolescent,* was widely adopted. While at Columbia, Hollingworth influenced several graduate students, including Carl Rogers (Chapter 16). Cattell included her in his 1921 *American Men of Science.*

Hollingworth's husband, **Harry L. Hollingworth** (1880–1956), earned a Ph.D. under Cattell at Columbia and served as head of the psychology department at Barnard College for many years. The author of some 25 books on such diverse psychological topics as abnormal, applied, and educational, Harry Hollingworth was the APA president in 1927. The work of both Hollingworths and their connections to Columbia serve to introduce the next of our major forerunners of functionalism—James McKeen Cattell.

JAMES MCKEEN CATTELL

James McKeen Cattell (1860–1944) was born the year after Darwin's publication of *The Origin of Species,* and the theory of evolution was central to his thinking. As Boring (1950) wrote:

> Evolution had taken hold of American thought, and evolution . . . meant in psychology an emphasis upon individual differences. Cattell was convinced of the importance of the psychology of individual differences even before he went to Wundt. . . . He did not get this idea from Galton, but presumably got it out of the same atmosphere that gave it to Galton. (p. 533)

FIGURE 10–6.   James McKeen Cattell.
Source: Columbia University, courtesy Harvard College Library.

Like Galton, Cattell (Figure 10–6) believed he had inherited ability, but he also realized the importance of his environment. He wrote: "It was my fortune to find a birthplace in the sun. A germ-plasm fairly well compounded [good genes] met circumstances to which it was unusually fit to react" (Sokal, 1971, p. 629).

Cattell was born in Easton, Pennsylvania, into a family that combined ambition, education, wealth, and social connections. His father was a Pres-byterian minister and professor of Latin and Greek at Lafayette College and, from 1863 to 1883, president of the College. Many years later, Cattell noted that, "[i]n my statistical studies I found that one who wanted to become a scientific man had the best chance if he chose a professor or a clergyman for his father. . . . My father was both a professor and a clergyman" (Sokal,

1971, p. 633). An advocate of eugenics, Cattell offered each of *his* children $1,000 if he or she would marry the child of a college professor.

Cattell was admitted to Lafayette College before his 16th birthday, and his genetic and environmental promise was amply fulfilled: "I stood first in my class without much effort" (Sokal, 1971, p. 634). In addition, Cattell maintained a lifelong interest in sports and games, learning to play tennis (at Leipzig with James Mark Baldwin) when there were no courts in America and golf "when there were only three courses in the world" (p. 634).

When Cattell left for Europe in 1880, his knowledge of psychology had come mainly from a moral philosophy book he had used in a course at Lafayette College. His main purpose in the journey was ostensibly to learn to speak French and German, and he went first to Göttingen. Cattell heard Lotze (Chapter 5) lecture at Göttingen and Wundt at Leipzig and was impressed with both men.

In Leipzig, Cattell wrote an essay on the philosophy of Lotze that earned him a fellowship at Johns Hopkins. On his own, Cattell began work measuring simple mental processes, but his fellowship was not renewed; instead it was given to his fellow student and lifelong friend, John Dewey. At the end of Dewey's fellowship year, he too had the fellowship taken away through Hall's machinations. As Cattell subsequently wrote to his parents,

> Dr. Hall has not acted honorably towards me. When I was at [Johns Hopkins] he praised me highly, said there was no one he would so gladly see holding the fellowship, but unfortunately, he had nothing to say in the matter, and Dewey was a great favorite of . . . Pres. Gilman's. He added he hoped the university authorities would grant him an assistant, and if so he knew no one so well fitted for the post as me. Pres. Gilman showed me Dr. Hall's recommendation for the fellowship. Dewey stood first and I fourth. (Cattell to his parents, Oct. 27, 1884, as cited in Ross, 1972, p. 146)

Cattell's year at Hopkins was not wasted, however. In addition to his efforts to measure individual differences, he undertook to "make psychological experiments on stimulant and intoxicating drugs. I have full notes on these, but they have never been published, for on reaching years of somewhat greater discretion I was not altogether proud of my enterprise" (Sokal, 1971, p. 632). Cattell had drunk beer in Germany, but he had never tried other alcoholic beverages, coffee, or tobacco. The intoxication he experienced from hashish was remarkable: "I have a drawing of the brain with all the 'faculties' located as it seemed at the time by actual observation," he wrote, and admitted that the dose he ingested was "perhaps the largest . . . ever taken without suicidal intent" (Sokal, 1971, p. 632).

From Hopkins, Cattell returned to Leipzig in 1883, earning his Ph.D. from Wundt in 1886, having spent part of the time as Wundt's first laboratory assistant. Cattell's Leipzig research was unusual in that he studied problems of his own choice using instruments of his own construction. In addition, he was interested in individual differences, which Wundt pronounced *ganz amerikanisch* (wholly American) but was flexible enough to permit, although not in his laboratory. Cattell received permission to perform his experiments in his room. Perhaps it was just as Cattell wrote to his parents: "Prof. Wundt seems to like me and to appreciate my phenomenal genius" (Letter dated February 13, 1885; Benjamin, 1993, p. 50).

Cattell did not idolize Wundt, despite Wundt's reputation and standing in the scientific community. Disparaging comments were frequent in his letters home:

> Prof. Wundt lectured yesterday and today on my subject—I suppose you won't consider it egotistical when I say that I know a great deal more about it than he does, but you will be surprised when I say that half of the statements he made were wrong. (Letter dated January 16, 1885; Benjamin, 1993, p. 49)

Cattell's research output from 1883 to 1886 matched his egotism. He published nine papers, all on either reaction time or individual differences or some combination of the two topics.

For the next 2 years, Cattell divided his time between Cambridge, England, where he met Galton, and America at Bryn Mawr College and the University of Pennsylvania. Galton confirmed Cattell's long-standing interest in measuring individual differences, and Cattell subsequently called him "the greatest man whom I have known" (Woodworth, 1944, p. 203).

Cattell and Psychology in America

From 1888 to 1891, Cattell was Professor of Psychology at the University of Pennsylvania, a position his father had had created for him (Sokal, 1994). At Pennsylvania, Cattell founded a laboratory and began to administer 10 tests to student volunteers, introducing the term "**mental tests**" to describe the battery (Cattell, 1890). The series included tests of sensation by means of the two-point threshold, just noticeable differences in weight judgments, reaction time for noises, memory span for letters, and rate of movement. Cattell left Lightner Witmer in charge when he departed for Columbia.

For his first decade at Columbia, Cattell continued administering his "mental tests" to entering freshmen. Using Galton's idea of correlation and Pearson's correlation coefficient, in 1901 Cattell's graduate student **Clark Wissler** (1870–1947) tested Cattell's (and Galton's) assumption that measures of physical and sensory ability were assessing intelligence. In fact, the correlations between Cattell's tests and college standing were low, indicating that he had not developed a valid measure of intelligence. Cattell's "mental tests" were soon superseded by Alfred Binet's intelligence tests (Chapter 18), and Cattell abandoned his tests to devote himself to administration, science editing and publishing, and the development of a method for ranking according to merit. Wissler changed to anthropology, where he made a name for himself as an ardent environmentalist.

Cattell first applied his order of merit or ranking method to the psychophysical problem of arranging various shades of gray. Subjects were asked to order by brightness over 200 shades of gray, which differed by almost imperceptible steps from black to white. The method was soon extended to value judgments, and Cattell applied it to the ranking of American men of science. For psychologists, he first made a list of 200 men and women, which he gave to 10 competent psychologists with instructions to rank the names by order of scientific merit.

The 1903 ranking of psychologists did not become public until Cattell's 1929 address as President of the Ninth International Congress of Psychology. In order, the top 10 psychologists in 1903 were James, Cattell, Münsterberg, Hall, Baldwin, Titchener, Royce, Ladd, Dewey, and Jastrow. Mary Calkins ranked 12th, ahead of Thorndike in 16th place, and Christine Ladd-Franklin (Chapter 17) ranked 19th. Cattell used his ranking method to compile the *Biographical Directory of American Men of Science* (plus some women), which he edited through the first six editions. *American Men of Science* continues to be published as a basic reference work, a veritable Who's Who of science.

Cattell's academic career ended with his dismissal from Columbia in 1917. In the midst of American involvement in World War I, Cattell used university stationery to write a letter to Congress protesting the use of conscientious objectors in combat. Cattell had long been an irritant to Columbia President Nicholas Murray Butler, and Butler used the letter as a pretext to rid himself of Cattell. (Ironically, Butler received the Nobel Peace Prize in 1931.) Cattell sued the University for libel and won.

Out of academia, Cattell had many activities to keep him busy. His publishing and editing ventures had begun over 20 years before his dismissal, when, with James Mark Baldwin, he founded *Psychological Review* as an alternative to Hall's *American Journal of Psychology*. *Psychological Review* continues to be one of psychology's premier journals. Baldwin bought Cattell out in 1903.

In 1895, Cattell purchased the floundering journal *Science* from Alexander Graham Bell. Under Cattell, *Science* overcame its financial difficulties and became one of the foremost general scientific publications in the world. In 1900, *Science* became the official publication of the American Association for the Advancement of Science (AAAS).

At one time or another, Cattell edited *Psychological Review, Science, Scientific Monthly* (originally begun as *Popular Science Monthly*), *American Naturalist, School and Society,* and *American Men of Science*. In addition, in 1921 Cattell organized the Psychological Corporation with the mission to promote applied psychology. Over the years, the Corporation has grown, and, in keeping with Cattell's original idea, has returned much of its profits to psychologists for further research. The Psychological Corporation publishes the popular Wechsler intelligence tests (e.g., the Wechsler Adult Intelligence Scale or WAIS, Chapter 18), among many other psychological instruments.

Cattell's Influence

Cattell was one of the APA's founding members and was its fourth president. Shortly after his arrival at Columbia, Cattell joined the New York Academy of Sciences (NYAS), soon persuading the Academy to establish a Section of Anthropology and Psychology. He was elected president of the NYAS in 1902.

In 1924, Cattell was elected president of the AAAS, the first psychologist to achieve this honor. He was also the first psychologist to be admitted to the National Academy of Sciences (1901). But his crowning glory came in 1929 when he was chosen by American psychologists to represent them as President of the Ninth International Congress of Psychology, the first such meeting held in the United States.

Like many great figures in the history of psychology, Cattell is a study in contrasts. As we have seen from his letters from Leipzig, he was supremely confident of his abilities. Less charitable writers might view his self-confidence as arrogance or conceit. Always the diplomat, Woodworth accounted for Cattell's lack of a published autobiography by accepting Cattell's excuse that any

> autobiography such as he would write would land him in the position of defendant in a number of libel suits. He felt sure he could not bring himself to delete all the pungent comments that would occur to him, and he had found by long experience that such comments were not always accepted in the spirit of raillery [good-natured teasing] that motivated them. . . (Woodworth, 1944, pp. 207–208)

By contrast, Sokal (1971) noted that "Cattell's conversation and correspondence were full of sarcasm and 'pungent comments' that were usually taken seriously, for it was never clear whether the 'spirit of raillery' to which Woodworth refers actually existed" (p. 627).

In fact, the "combative and sarcastic" Cattell engendered controversy throughout his career. As we noted, Cattell's dismissal from academia ultimately stemmed from his antagonism of Columbia's president. There was also controversy between Cattell and Baldwin over control of *Psychological Review* and conflict between Cattell and William McDougall (Chapter 12). Of the five-person committee that selected nominees for Carl Murchison's (1930) *A History of Psychology in Autobiography*, three voted for Cattell and two voted against. Cattell's decision not to write an autobiography for Murchison's project was, in large part, the result of controversies he had had with Murchison, who actually voted for Cattell's inclusion.

Cattell's influence on his students was more through his ability to inspire than through his teaching skills. His approach to his graduate students was as nondirective as Wundt's and Titchener's were directive:

> In research it is doubtful if a department has existed in this country where students were thrown more upon their own resources. . . . Cattell pointed clearly the way and said "Go," but the greatest teacher must be able to say "Come." These considerations did not prevent the writer from developing . . . as intense a personal loyalty as he has felt towards any man; and there is reason to suppose him hardly alone in this sentiment. (Wells, 1944, p. 271).

In addition to F. L. Wells, students inspired by Cattell included Thorndike, Woodworth, S. I. Franz (Chapter 17), and E. K. Strong, an industrial and vocational psychologist. Margaret Washburn (Chapter 7), America's first major female experimental psychologist, had studied with Cattell before going to Cornell and earning a Ph.D. with Titchener. She wrote, "I feel an affectionate gratitude to [Cattell], as my first teacher, which in these later years I have courage to express; in earlier times I stood too much in awe of him" (Washburn, 1932, p. 339).

Cattell is important to the stream of ideas in American psychology because he provided a bridge between the British psychology of the individual (idiographic) and the German (including Titchener's) psychology of the generalized mind (nomothetic). Cattell understood and communicated the value of both approaches for a mature psychological system.

With his interest in measuring mental ability, Cattell's psychology was a psychology of human capacity and thus a psychology of function. As we will see, Columbia and Chicago were the centers of functionalism, and during Cattell's tenure, Columbia became the foremost producer of psychology Ph.D.s. At the time of the first international psychology congress held in the United States, there were 704 APA members with doctorates. Of these, 155 had degrees from Columbia, with Chicago a distant second with 91 (Cattell, 1929).

However, Cattell's influence was perhaps greatest through his scientific editing. As the editor of *Science* for half a century, Cattell was able to promote psychology's image as a science. "[T]here is no denying that [Cattell's editorship] significantly enhanced psychology's visibility and status among the older sciences" (Benjamin, 1993, p. 39).

Before we conclude our examination of early American psychology, we will briefly consider the life and career of a man mentioned several times in this chapter and in other places in this text: James Mark Baldwin. APA president in 1897 and fifth on Cattell's list of prominent psychologists in 1903, Baldwin's enthusiasm for evolution and functional view of mind make him well suited for placement as another important forerunner of functionalism.

JAMES MARK BALDWIN

Born in Columbia, South Carolina, **James Mark Baldwin** (1861–1934) spent a year with Wundt in Leipzig and Friedrich Paulsen in Berlin before earning his Ph.D. in philosophy from Princeton in 1889, supervised by the Scottish philosopher James

McCosh. Following an appointment at Lake Forest College in Illinois, Baldwin went to Toronto, where he founded the first laboratory of psychology in Canada. From Toronto, Baldwin returned to Princeton, where he established his second laboratory. A decade later, Baldwin moved to Johns Hopkins, reopening the laboratory Hall had closed when he went to Clark. Baldwin (Figure 10–7) was forced to resign from Hopkins in 1909 in a scandal over his presence in a Boston house of prostitution.

Like many of his contemporaries, Baldwin was an ardent evolutionist. In his autobiographical essay (Baldwin, 1930), one of the contributions he valued most highly was his theory of organic selection, which combined Darwinian and Lamarckian concepts to account for the directedness of evolution, and another was his study of children. Baldwin and Hall are often jointly considered the founders of developmental psychology.

FIGURE 10–7. James Mark Baldwin.
Source: Indiana University, Psychology Department.

Although Baldwin was younger than Hall, his initial book on genetic psychology, *Mental Development in the Child and the Race,* first appeared in 1895. However, despite a variety of publications related to developmental psychology (see Kahlbaugh, 1993), Baldwin's greatest contribution may have been through his influence on Jean Piaget, whose efforts in cognitive development will be examined in Chapter 20.

From Hopkins, Baldwin went to Mexico City, where he helped organize the National University of Mexico and was a consultant on social development to the Mexican president. After 5 years in Mexico, Baldwin went to Paris, where he taught as a professor at *L'Ecole des Hautes Etudes Sociales* until his death in 1934.

CONCLUSIONS

When we think of America's founding, we think of its early leaders, their accomplishments, and of certain themes that capture our country's spirit. The same framework can be used in our consideration of the founding of psychology in America.

Thus, William James, G. Stanley Hall, and James McKeen Cattell were early leaders of psychology in America. James produced a classic text, brought experimental psychology to Harvard, and established an important department of psychology there. Hall's importance lay chiefly in his organizational skills, which are well illustrated by his "foundings": for example, the departments of psychology at Johns Hopkins and at Clark, the first American journal of psychology, and the American Psychological Association. In addition, Hall brought Freud and psychoanalysis to America for the Clark Conference. Like Hall, Cattell was a master publicist of psychology in America. Through his publishing ventures and his association with the American Association for the Advancement of Science, Cattell helped make psychology a respected scientific discipline.

America is often seen thematically as the home of pioneers, who were rugged individualists fighting for the freedom of their beliefs. That same characterization may well apply to James, Hall, and Cattell. Although some limited psychological speculation predated James, he was the first pioneer of American psychology, charting a new intellectual territory. Hall's many "firsts" and "foundings" echo that same pioneer theme, as do the efforts of Mary Calkins and Leta Hollingworth.

Clearly, the people we covered in this chapter were willing to "do their own thing," in today's jargon. This is well illustrated by the brash young Cattell performing his own experiments in his room while studying with the normally autocratic Wundt, by James's sense of fair play in treating both Wundt and his phenomenological contemporaries equally within his *Principles,* and by Hall's eclectic interests from development to psychoanalysis. James, Hall, and Cattell represented no established system, such as structuralism, nor did they found one directly. However, their efforts were all directed toward a psychology of function and laid the foundation for functionalism, America's first native school of psychology.

S U M M A R Y

Evolution was a major theme during the 19th century, and Herbert Spencer's social Darwinism fit American society's mood. Few were more influenced by Darwinism than William James and G. Stanley Hall, who believed that consciousness has a function, although neither man was quite a functionalist. The forerunners of functionalism in America took psychology into study areas avoided by "pure" psychologists such as Titchener.

Early Philosophy and Psychology in America

There was little psychology in America before the publication of William James's *Principles.* Although Jonathan Edwards and Samuel Johnson made contributions in the tradition of Locke and British empiricism, mainly the ideas of the Scottish school and to a lesser degree the German rationalists formed the basis of American psychology before James.

William James

After an unusual childhood and education, James's first academic position was as a Harvard physiology instructor. James soon added a physiological psychology course and contracted to write *The Principles of Psychology,* published in 1890.

In the *Principles,* James argued that psychology should not arise from the study of individual sensations but from the study of complete conscious experiences. James's analysis suggested that consciousness is personal, always changing, continuous, always directed at some object, and selective. Further, James believed that consciousness has evolved because it functions to aid its possessor in adapting to an environment.

For James, habits result from changes in the brain, and he offered practical suggestions for acquiring new habits and for getting rid of old ones. He and Carl Lange independently arrived at what we call the James-Lange theory of emotion, which holds that a stimulus triggers a response and awareness of the response constitutes the emotion. Despite criticisms, the theory's core idea remains a part of the modern psychology of emotion.

After publishing the *Principles,* James wrote on a variety of philosophical topics including pragmatism. Pragmatism replaced the rationalist notion of truth as an objective entity with a functionally defined understanding of truth. According to James, truth is the value of an idea. If an idea works, it is true.

Through his students and his writings, James shaped psychology in America. Both Gestalt psychology and functionalism acknowledged a debt to James, and he was influential in founding the important Harvard psychology department.

Mary Whiton Calkins

One of James's brightest students, Calkins was allowed to take courses at Harvard, but she never received the Harvard Ph.D., despite her superior performance. Calkins spent her career at Wellesley and was the first woman elected president of the APA and of the American Philosophical Association. Her main contributions to psychology include an early psychology laboratory, the paired-associates method for studying memory, and a self-psychology system.

Hugo Münsterberg

Hugo Münsterberg earned his Ph.D. under Wundt, received a Heidelberg M.D., and then founded a laboratory at Freiburg. James secured a position for him in charge of the Harvard psychological laboratory.

Many of Münsterberg's works were major contributions to applied psychology, and he published volumes on forensics, pedagogy, psychotherapy, and industrial psychology. Despite his productivity, Münsterberg is not remembered more favorably because he continued to promote German-American ties when relations between Germany and its neighbors were worsening and World War I was underway.

Granville Stanley Hall

G. Stanley Hall was a man of many firsts, fads, and crazes who helped shape the course of American psychology. Securing a position at Johns Hopkins in 1884, Hall founded an important early psychological laboratory and attracted several noteworthy students. In 1887, Hall founded *The American Journal of Psychology* (the first psychology journal in America).

In 1889, Hall became the first president of Clark University. Most of Hall's outstanding faculty and students left Clark in 1892, the same year that Hall was instrumental in founding the American Psychological Association and was elected its first president.

Hall is perhaps best known for his work in developmental psychology. Using questionnaires, Hall gathered data that led to the writing of *Adolescence,* which included his recapitulation theory of child development. Hall also published *Senescence,* which is about the last part of life.

Like James, Hall was an early contributor to the study of the psychology of religion. He founded a journal in the area, and two of his students were instrumental in developing what some call the Clark School of Religious Psychology.

At Clark's 20th anniversary, Freud's lectures gave America its first look at psychoanalysis. Hall initiated a dialogue with Alfred Adler in 1914, and his influence on Carl Jung has also been suggested.

Hall's relations were perhaps best with subordinates, and this is apparent in his relations with several junior colleagues at Clark. Although Hall and Clark University were responsible for training many female psychologists, this can also be viewed as supporting Hall's need to have relationships in which he was dominant. Hall's last graduate student was Francis Sumner, the first African American to receive a Ph.D. in psychology.

Early Studies of Gender Differences: The Work of Leta Stetter Hollingworth

True to the *Zeitgeist,* Hall viewed women as inferior intellectually to men. Leta Stetter Hollingworth obtained early empirical evidence refuting this view.

James McKeen Cattell

James McKeen Cattell completed his Ph.D. under Wundt in 1886. After meeting Galton in Cambridge, England, Cattell became Professor of Psychology at the University of Pennsylvania. There, Cattell founded a laboratory and developed his battery of mental tests before leaving for Columbia, where he continued his research on "mental" testing. When Cattell-student Clark Wissler found little evidence for a correlation between physiological measures and intelligence, Cattell went into administration and Wissler became an anthropologist.

Cattell developed a ranking method that he initially used in ranking different shades of gray before extending it to the ranking of people in science in terms of scientific merit. In 1903, Cattell assessed the eminence of psychologists, but the results were not released until 1929.

After being fired from Columbia, Cattell continued his publishing and editing ventures. In 1921, Cattell founded the Psychological Corporation, which remains the publisher of several important psychological tests, including the WAIS.

A founding APA member and its fourth president, in 1929 Cattell served as president of the Ninth International Congress of Psychology, which was the first such meeting to be held in America. Cattell's influence was perhaps greatest through his editing of the journal *Science,* in which he was able to promote psychology's image as a science.

James Mark Baldwin

Considered one of the creators of developmental psychology along with Hall, Baldwin founded the first laboratory of psychology in Canada, a second laboratory at Princeton, and reopened the laboratory at Johns Hopkins. An ardent evolutionist, one of the contributions Baldwin valued most highly was his theory of organic selection that combined Darwinian and Lamarckian features to account for evolution's directedness.

CONNECTIONS QUESTIONS

1. Compare and contrast the psychologies and the personalities of Hall and James.
2. How would you connect Cattell's contributions to psychology's present status as an experimental science?
3. Compare and contrast Titchener and Münsterberg. Why is Titchener so celebrated in the history of psychology, whereas Münsterberg is all but forgotten?
4. How did Mary Calkins's and Leta Hollingworth's research contribute to the place of women in American psychology?
5. How does William James connect to the scientific psychology that preceded him in Europe? To the scientific psychology that followed him in America?
6. Hall is remembered for his many firsts. How many connections can you make between Hall and something he initiated for American psychology?
7. Draw a concept map connecting the major psychologists in this chapter with each other, and try showing their connections with evolution, Wundt and the founding of psychology as a science, and phenomenological psychology. Compare your results with one possible solution on p. 565.

SUGGESTED READINGS

Cattell, J. M. (1929). Psychology in America. *Science, 70,* 335–347.
    This is the published version of Cattell's presidential address to the Ninth International Congress of Psychology, and it is an interesting overview of early American psychology from the perspective of one of the pioneers.

Donnelly, M. (Ed.) (1992). *Reinterpreting the legacy of William James.* Washington, DC: American Psychological Association.
    This anthology was born from symposia held at the 1990 meeting of the APA to honor the 100th anniversary of the publication of the *Principles.* In contributions by well-known psychologists, this work makes connections between James and many other persons and topics (e.g., James and Darwin, James and psychic research).

James, W. (1890). *The principles of psychology* (Vols. 1–2). New York: Henry Holt. Any serious consideration of William James's place in the history of American psychology should begin with his magnum opus, the *Principles*. Open the books anywhere and read a paragraph or two, and you may agree with Thorndike who found the work more stimulating than any he had read before or since.

Johnson, M. G., & Henley, T. B. (Eds.) (1990). *Reflections on The Principles of Psychology*. Hillsdale, NJ: Lawrence Erlbaum Associates, Publishers. Johnson and Henley's edited book is a compilation of essays on James's *Principles* written on the 100th anniversary of its publication.

Myers, G. E. (1986). *William James: His life and thought*. New Haven, CT: Yale University Press. Myers's biography is the most current, and perhaps the most exhaustive, available work on William James. Although James has been the subject of many biographical books and articles, the scope and recency of this work make it one we highly recommend.

Ross, D. (1972). *G. Stanley Hall: The psychologist as prophet*. Chicago: The University of Chicago Press. Ross's biography of Hall should be the starting point for anyone who desires a better understanding of a complicated and talented, but ultimately flawed, individual.

Sokal, M. (1971). The unpublished autobiography of James McKeen Cattell. *American Psychologist, 26,* 626–635. Cattell's preliminary draft of an autobiographical essay and Sokal's introduction to it provide a fascinating look at a pioneering American psychologist who "was not a modest man . . ." (p. 629).

Spillmann, J., & Spillmann, L. (1993). The rise and fall of Hugo Münsterberg. *Journal of the History of the Behavioral Sciences, 29,* 322 v –338. The Spillmanns' paper presents an objective but sympathetic look at a man whose contributions to applied psychology are often overlooked in histories of psychology.

Functionalism

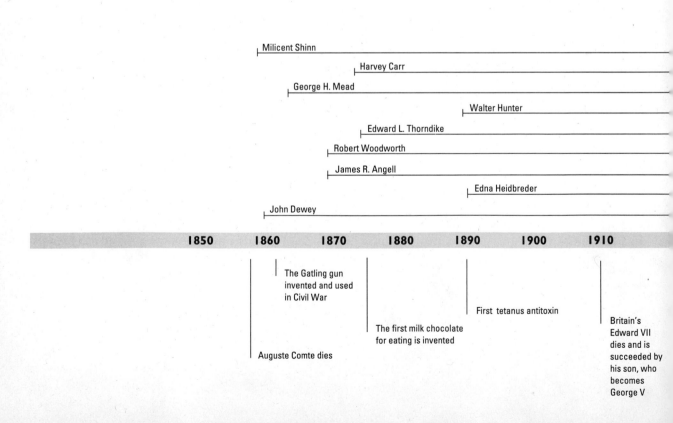

Milicent Shinn

Harvey Carr

George H. Mead

Walter Hunter

Edward L. Thorndike

Robert Woodworth

James R. Angell

Edna Heidbreder

John Dewey

1850	1860	1870	1880	1890	1900	1910

The Gatling gun invented and used in Civil War

First tetanus antitoxin

The first milk chocolate for eating is invented

Britain's Edward VII dies and is succeeded by his son, who becomes George V

Auguste Comte dies

As a formal school of psychology, functionalism was remarkably informal. Unlike structuralism, which was founded and dominated in America by Titchener, functionalism had no central individual. Nevertheless, functionalism represents the first truly American school of psychology and is important in its own right and as a forerunner of behaviorism.

As this chapter will document, functionalism was a diverse school. Drawing on the analogy of America as an ethnic melting pot, American functionalism served likewise as an intellectual smelter. Given functionalism's eclectic nature, historians of psychology typically list several individuals as important influences on functionalism rather than focusing on a founder. As we saw in Chapter 10, James, Hall, and Cattell were all interested in the mind's functions and were psychologists of function without really being functionalists. For example,

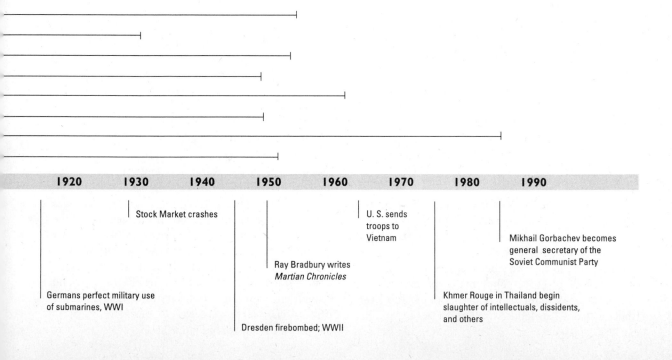

| 1920 | 1930 | 1940 | 1950 | 1960 | 1970 | 1980 | 1990 |

Stock Market crashes

U. S. sends troops to Vietnam

Mikhail Gorbachev becomes general secretary of the Soviet Communist Party

Ray Bradbury writes *Martian Chronicles*

Germans perfect military use of submarines, WWI

Khmer Rouge in Thailand begin slaughter of intellectuals, dissidents, and others

Dresden firebombed; WWII

although James supported the strongly empirical, experimental approach adopted by functionalism, he did not have the temperament to sustain such a research effort. In the end, he imported Wundt-trained Münsterberg to assume command of the laboratory he had established. In turn, Münsterberg's forays into the application of psychology were also compatible with the pragmatic psychology of function. Hall, too, abandoned laboratory science early in his career. Both James and Hall had such diverse interests that they could never become members of a psychological school, even one as loosely knit as functionalism.

Given his single-minded approach to psychology, Titchener (Chapter 7) was better suited to become the founder and leader of a school. Ironically, Titchener is often credited with establishing functionalism as a "formal" school, by objectifying the differences between his approach and the functional approach of others (Titchener, 1898). In differentiating his structural (or experimental) psychology and a functional (or descriptive) psychology, Titchener wrote:

> The primary aim of the experimental psychologist has been to analyze the structure of mind; to ravel out the elemental processes from the tangle of consciousness. . . . His task is a vivisection, but a vivisection which shall yield structural, not functional results. He tries to discover, first of all, what is there and in what quantity, not what it is there for. . . . There is, however, a functional psychology, over and above this psychology of structure. . . . Just as experimental psychology is to a large extent concerned with problems of structure, so is 'descriptive' psychology . . . chiefly occupied with problems of function. (pp. 450–452)

As you can see, Titchener was interested in the "what" of consciousness rather than the "why," or, as it is sometimes expressed, he was interested in the "is" rather than the "is for."

It was clear to Titchener that his structuralism was preferable to the functional approach seen in the work of William James, John Dewey, and later, that of James Rowland Angell and Harvey A. Carr. As he expressed it,

> The burden of the argument has been that there is reasonable agreement, within the experimental camp, as to the postulates of a purely structural psychology, whereas there is pretty radical disagreement among the psychologists of function. . . . I believe . . . that the best hope for psychology lies to day in a continuance of structural analysis, and that the study of function will not yield final fruit until it can be controlled by the genetic, and, still more, by the experimental method. . . (Titchener, 1898, pp. 464–465)

As we revealed in Chapter 10 and as we will show in this chapter, functionalism bore abundant fruit, whereas Titchener's structuralism essentially died with him.

Titchener's 1898 paper was a response to an earlier paper by John Dewey (1896), "The Reflex Arc Concept in Psychology," which is usually honored as functionalism's seminal article. Because the theme of this chapter is functionalism, the first truly American school of psychology, we will begin with John Dewey and his many contributions to the school.

JOHN DEWEY

John Dewey (1859–1952) was born in Burlington, Vermont, the same year that Charles Darwin published *Origin of Species.* A shy youth, Dewey attended the University of Vermont in his hometown, turning to philosophy in his senior year. After graduation in 1879, the year Wundt established his laboratory, Dewey taught all subjects in high school for a few years, where he first developed the interest in the problems and purpose of education that shaped much of his career. Although Dewey is famous for his contributions to the American educational system and to teaching, by most accounts he was himself a poor teacher. "It remains indeed one of the sociological paradoxes of American culture . . . why a man, by the usual outward, visible signs not a good—and indeed by all conventional criteria a poor—teacher, should have so deeply inspired and remade the thinking of crucial individuals in all the professions, teaching above all" (Edman, 1955, p. 24). Dewey is shown in Figure 11–1.

FIGURE 11-1.   John Dewey.
Source: University of Chicago Library, Department of Special Collections.

While teaching high school, Dewey submitted a pair of philosophical papers to the *Journal of Speculative Philosophy.* Both papers were accepted, and the editor suggested to Dewey that he should become a philosopher. With this goal in mind, Dewey enrolled at Johns Hopkins in 1882.

At Hopkins, Dewey took courses from the three men on trial for the position of professor of philosophy: Peirce, Hall, and Morris (as noted in Chapter 10). Of the three, Dewey was most influenced by the Hegelian idealism of Morris. When Morris accepted the chairmanship of the philosophy department at the University of Michigan, one of his first actions was to offer Dewey—who earned his Ph.D. from Hopkins in 1884—an instructorship at Michigan, which Dewey took.

Except for a year at the University of Minnesota, Dewey spent the next 10 years at Michigan, becom-

ing chairman of the philosophy department with Morris's untimely death. In his first term at Michigan, Dewey taught a course in empirical psychology for which he wrote a textbook published in 1886 as *Psychology. Psychology* was a synthesis of the new empirical, experimental psychology with the older, primarily Hegelian, idealistic philosophy. Along with other psychology books of the period immediately preceding James's *Principles of Psychology* (Chapter 10), it was a psychology text written from the viewpoint of a philosopher.

After reading James's *Principles,* Dewey felt encouraged to move toward a more empirical and objective functionalism (Raphelson, 1973), although as Shook (1995) noted, there were other influences, including Wundt. Dewey (1896) expressed his new approach to psychology most clearly in his classic article, "The Reflex Arc Concept in Psychology."

The Reflex Arc Concept

Dewey began by accepting the reflex arc—a stimulus produces a sensation that triggers a response—as a unifying principle in psychology, but he was critical of the conception of the arc as "a patchwork of disjointed parts, a mechanical conjunction of unallied processes" (Dewey, 1896, p. 358). Instead, "what is wanted is that sensory stimulus, central connections and motor responses shall be viewed, not as separate and complete entities in themselves, but as divisions of labor, functioning factors, within the single concrete *whole,* now designated the reflex arc" (p. 358, italics added).

To illustrate what he considered wrong with the division of the reflex arc into three components (sensory stimulus, central activity, and motor discharge), Dewey used the child-candle reflex from James's *Principles.* As usually interpreted, the candle's light is a stimulus leading to the child's grasping response, which produces a burning stimulus that causes hand withdrawal, and so on, the reflex being broken neatly—but perhaps artificially—into its stimulus-response components. According to Dewey, the candle's light is not the beginning of the reflex: "the real beginning is with the act of seeing; it is looking, and not a sensation of light" (pp. 358–359). And the act of seeing is really part of the whole act of seeing and reaching, "because seeing and grasping have been so often bound together to reinforce each other . . . that each may be considered practically a subordinate member of a bigger coördination" (p. 359). When the burning sensation is added, the original seeing and reaching coordination becomes a "seeing-of-a-light-that-means-pain-when-contact-occurs" (p. 360) coordination.

Dewey's point was that the reflex arc, as perceived before his analysis, led to a disjointed psychology because it assumed that sensory stimulus and motor response were separate psychical entities. In reality, the sensory stimulus and motor response "are always inside a coördination and have their significance purely from the part played in maintaining or reconstituting the coördination . . ." (Dewey, 1896, p. 360). In other words, Dewey was arguing against the elementism of Wundt and Titchener (their tendency to divide consciousness into its elements, which they believed to be sensations, images, and feelings). Dewey saw behavior as a total coordination leading to adaptation. The reflex arc should be viewed as a coordinated whole with a purpose or function, not as a series of individual components. In his stress on considering behavior as a total coordination, we will see that Dewey was anticipating one of the central tenets of Gestalt psychology (Chapter 14) and also agreeing with the holistic emphasis of Brentano's act psychology (Chapter 8). Note also the similarity of Dewey's holistic approach to the reflex arc and James's description of consciousness as a stream (Chapter 10). As Boring (1953) noted,

> [Dewey's] 1896 paper on the reflex arc concept is, in a way, a declaration of independence for American functional psychology, but it is also, along with James' *Principles,* one of those wise early American writings which vigorously rejected Wundtian elementism and thus could be exhibited later, when Gestalt psychology crossed the Atlantic to protest about elementism, as American anticipations . . . of Wertheimer's complaints about the Wundtians. (p. 146)

As an index of the importance of Dewey's article for American psychology, the article ranked first in a preferential vote on the first five titles of articles appearing in the initial 50 volumes of *Psychological Review* (Langfeld, 1943).

Although he was no longer interested in teaching psychology courses, as head of the department of philosophy at Michigan, Dewey did not abandon the psychological program he had initiated. Instead, he hired **James H. Tufts** (1862–1942) to teach the psychology courses. Tufts established a laboratory course that enrolled Michigan's president's son, James Rowland Angell (discussed later). When Tufts left Michigan for Chicago in 1891, Dewey was forced by student interest to hire two instructors to replace him, one of which was **George Herbert Mead** (1863–1931). Born in South Hadley, Massachusetts, Mead studied at Oberlin College, Harvard (where he met James), and at the Universities of Leipzig and Berlin. A Hegelian like Dewey, Mead is best known for his concept of the self, and his ideas anticipated movements in both social and clinical psychology, including elements of contemporary humanistic psychology (Chapter 16). One of Mead's most well-known works is *Mind, Self and Society* (Mead, 1934), which purports to be a social psychology from a behaviorist viewpoint. However, as Cook (1977, 1994) emphasized, Mead's social behaviorism was rooted in Dewey's functionalism, not in Watsonian behaviorism (Chapter 12). Mead was also influential in the rise of sociology as a formal academic discipline in America.

At Tufts's urging, University of Chicago President William Harper offered Dewey the position as chairman of the philosophy department, which also included both psychology and pedagogy. Dewey accepted, in part because the position offered possibilities in his three major interests. Mead came with Dewey, and in 1895 Dewey attracted a former Michigan student, James R. Angell, to direct the department's psychological laboratory. With a young and vigorous staff, Chicago's philosophy department flourished.

In 1896, Dewey developed a working laboratory in which he could study the learning processes of children and put his "progressive education" theories into practice. Dewey's approach to education emphasized learning by doing, the importance of a student's interest in a task, and intelligent problem solving rather than rote memorization. The progressive education movement spawned by Dewey's educational approach declined and eventually died in the 1950s (Hilgard, 1987). We will examine a similar approach to education in our discussion of Max Wertheimer's *Productive Thinking* (Chapter 14). It is worth noting that Dewey and Wertheimer had their own radio program in 1935 devoted to such topics as education and anarchy.

Dewey's school was never intended to be a teacher-training school, and this irritated some of the education faculty, who eventually persuaded Chicago's president to merge Dewey's school with the Teacher Training Institute. This action so offended Dewey that, despite being offered the directorship of the School of Education, he resigned in 1904 to take a post at Columbia University secured for him by Hopkins classmate and friend, James McKeen Cattell (Chapter 10). Dewey stayed at Columbia for the rest of his life.

Dewey was one of the charter members of the American Psychological Association and, despite the fact that his career as a psychologist is often said to have ended with his departure from Chicago, he remained an APA member until 1927. Elected APA president in 1899, in 1910 Dewey became the fourth psychologist to be elected to the National Academy of Sciences. "The rôle of philosophers in founding American psychology is shown by the fact that the psychologists who preceded Dewey in election to the National Academy were Cattell (1901), James (1903), and Royce (1906). After Dewey the elections ran: Stanley Hall, Thorndike, James Angell" (Boring, 1953, p. 147). Dewey was also involved in several liberal causes, including the American Civil Liberties Union, the founding of the American Association of University Professors, and in the move in America to give women the vote.

As we have noted, Dewey's formal contact with psychology effectively ended with his departure from Chicago in 1904. His position as nominal leader of functionalism was filled by a former student who became head of the psychology department at Chicago—James Rowland Angell.

JAMES ROWLAND ANGELL

Like Dewey, **James Rowland Angell** (1869–1949) was born in Burlington, Vermont. His father, James

Burrill Angell, was president of the University of Vermont from 1866–1871 and president of the University of Michigan from 1871–1909, and his maternal grandfather had been president of Brown University. As a child in an environment frequented by distinguished political and academic leaders, Angell undoubtedly developed the interpersonal skills that made him well suited for university higher administration, and he eventually became a university president himself.

Angell entered the University of Michigan in 1886, pursuing the classical studies—Latin, Greek, and mathematics—along with history, English, modern languages, and science as fillers. His first psychology course "instantly opened up a new world, which it seemed to me I had been waiting for, and for the first time I felt a deep and pervasive sense of the intellectual importance of the material I was facing" (Angell, 1936, p. 5). This material was the newly published *Psychology* by his teacher, John Dewey.

Angell received his bachelor's degree in 1890 and elected to stay an extra year at Michigan, taking a seminar with Dewey to study James's just published *Principles.* After earning a master's degree in philosophy in 1891, with Dewey's encouragement Angell went to Harvard, where he studied under William James and Josiah Royce (Chapter 10). With James, Angell "enjoyed a peculiarly intimate contact . . ." (Angell, 1936, p. 7), because James turned over to him a mass of material from the American Society for Psychical Research. Although the work did not prove important for psychical research, it put Angell "in direct contact with one of the most inspiring and spiritually beautiful human beings I have ever known" (p. 7).

After earning a second master's degree at Harvard, like so many of his generation, Angell went to Germany. In Leipzig, armed with a letter of introduction from his cousin, **Frank Angell** (1857–1939)—founder of psychological laboratories at Cornell and at Stanford—Angell was disappointed to find Wundt's laboratory full. Moving on to Berlin, Angell heard lectures by Ebbinghaus (Chapter 8) and by Helmholtz (Chapter 6), with whom he was "especially impressed."

After the fall semester, Angell went to Halle, where he wrote a doctoral thesis on Kant (Chapter 5)

while working with philosopher Hans Vaihinger (1852–1933), who exposed Angell to the German idealist tradition. Angell's dissertation was accepted pending its revision into more acceptable German. In a quandary about whether to finish his degree, to take an offer from Minnesota for $1,500 a year, or to accept a Harvard position at significantly less money than Minnesota had promised, Angell chose the Minnesota money and marriage to his fiancée of 4 years. A planned return to finish his degree never materialized, and Angell wrote, "while in after years I was given an honorary degree of Doctor of Philosophy, I never quite completed the formalities for winning it on my own merits. In view of the large number of doctor's degrees I have been instrumental in conferring on others, this circumstance has always elicited sardonic reflections whenever I think of it" (Angell, 1936, p. 10).

A year later, Angell joined Dewey, Tufts, and Mead at the University of Chicago, where his neighbors and friends included the famous physiologist, Jacques Loeb, and the neurologist, Henry Donaldson (both Chapter 12). Angell quickly established a research program at Chicago, and his first paper (Angell & Moore, 1896) clearly showed the importance of research from the functionalist point of view, by successfully addressing the Titchener-Baldwin reaction-time controversy (Chapter 7).

At Leipzig and Cornell, Titchener found that attention to the motor reaction produced reliably shorter reaction times than attention to the sensory stimulus; using naive subjects rather than Titchener's (and Wundt's) highly trained ones, Baldwin (Chapter 10) often obtained the opposite result. Angell and A. W. Moore discovered that without training, subjects produced Baldwin's results—some displayed shorter reaction times when attending to the motor response, whereas others had shorter times when attending to the signalling stimulus. With further experience, subjects produced the kind of reaction times observed by Titchener. The resolution to the Titchener-Baldwin controversy was that both men were right— Baldwin with untrained observers and Titchener with highly trained ones. For the functionalist, however, the study's importance lay in the adaptive change that occurred in subjects during exposure to

the task. Also important was the demonstration of the relevance of individual differences for performance on the task. Structuralists, in their desire to illuminate the generalized mind, considered individual differences a nuisance to be overcome through long training.

Note again that the Titchener-Baldwin controversy and its resolution by Angell shows the importance of the nomothetic (study of the generalized mind)/idiographic (psychology of the individual) distinction we mentioned at the end of the last chapter. Titchener's nomothetic approach led to different results than Baldwin's idiographic work, which Angell and Moore (1896) demonstrated.

Perhaps because of his lack of the Ph.D. degree, during his first 7 years at Chicago, Angell received neither a raise nor a promotion. Beginning to listen seriously to other job offers, Angell was finally promoted to associate professor in 1901. Promotion to professor came in 1904 and with it the promise that he would be made department head when psychology became a department separate from philosophy. The promise was fulfilled the next year.

In 1906, Angell was elected APA president, and at the annual convention, he spoke on "The Province of Functional Psychology." To begin, Angell noted that functional psychology was nothing new. "In certain of its phases it is plainly discernible in the psychology of Aristotle and in its more modern garb it has been increasingly in evidence since Spencer wrote his *Psychology* and Darwin his *Origin of Species.* . . . All that is peculiar to its present circumstances is a higher degree of self-consciousness than it possessed before . . ." (Angell, 1907, p. 62). Angell advanced three main conceptions of functionalism, summarized as follows:

(1) functionalism conceived as the psychology of mental operations in contrast to the psychology of mental elements; or . . . the psychology of the *how* and *why* of consciousness as distinguished from the psychology of the *what* of consciousness.

(2) the functionalism which deals with the problem of mind conceived as primarily engaged in mediating between the environment and the needs of the organism. This is the psy-

chology of the fundamental utilities of consciousness . . .

(3) functionalism described as psychophysical psychology, that is the psychology which constantly recognizes and insists upon the essential significance of the mind-body relationship for any just and comprehensive appreciation of mental life itself. (Angell, 1907, pp. 85–86, italics added)

First, Angell contrasted functionalism's interest in the how and why of consciousness with structuralism's concern over the what—mental activity versus mental content, in other words. Second, Angell saw a functional psychology whose task was to understand the mind's mediation between the environment and the organism's needs. For the functionalist, consciousness is concerned with "accommodation to the novel"; actions frequently repeated become habit, and "the mental direction tends to subside and give way to a condition approximating physiological automatism . . ." (Angell, 1907, p. 72). Finally, Angell conceived of functionalism as "a form of psychophysics," a psychology of the total mind-body organism. Functionalism "finds its major interest in determining the relations to one another of the physical and mental portions of the organism" (p. 80). Functionalism's biological orientation encouraged the further development of animal psychology, which Angell supported at Chicago.

Over the years, administrative duties took more and more time away from Angell's efforts in psychology. From a variety of posts at Chicago, including having been acting president on a number of occasions (Angell could not have become president at the time because of a clause in the University charter requiring the officeholder to be a Baptist), Angell left in 1920 to become the president of the Carnegie Corporation. The Corporation had been created in the United States to promote human welfare, principally along educational lines. After only a year as its head, Angell was offered the position of president of Yale University, at exactly half his Carnegie salary. Angell (Figure 11–2) accepted Yale's offer, serving with distinction from 1921 until his retirement in 1937.

FIGURE 11–2. James Rowland Angell.

Source: University of Chicago Library, Department of Special Collections.

Angell's Influence

With his increasing administrative responsibilities, Angell essentially retired from psychology in 1911. However, his position as president of Yale permitted him to promote psychology and its associated scientific interests. As we have seen, before Angell "retired," he was instrumental in further articulating the functionalist position, most importantly in his 1907 paper. Angell's influence was also felt through his textbook, *Psychology: An Introductory Study of the Structure and Functions of Human Consciousness* (Angell, 1904). Angell's text, which was popular enough to go through four editions by 1908, was initiated in part as a response to the lack of an integrating system in James's *Briefer Course*. Thus, although James had many of the basic ideas and insights of functionalism, it fell to Angell and others to integrate them into a system.

Like James and Hall, Angell attracted loyal followers, and several of the 50 psychology doctorates awarded during his Chicago tenure were received by people who had significant careers in psychology. As we noted in our discussion of Münsterberg in Chapter 10, applied psychology was particularly compatible with functionalism, given the system's focus on pragmatic rather than philosophical solutions. We can see this applied focus in many of Angell's students. For example, **Helen Thompson Woolley** (1874–1947) received a Ph.D. in 1900 and became the director in Cincinnati of the Bureau for the Investigation of Working Children. Her research with children made her an ardent proponent of child welfare reform. In Detroit, she organized one of America's first nursery schools, where she studied child development and the mental abilities of young children and applied what she had learned to the benefit of her charges.

Another of Angell's stars was **June Etta Downey** (1875–1932), who founded the laboratory of psychology at the University of Wyoming. Downey's applied approach resulted in the development of many personality tests, and she became an expert on handwriting analysis (graphology). **Walter S. Hunter** (1889–1953) earned a Chicago Ph.D. in 1912 and then slipped from his functionalist teachings toward the behaviorist movement begun by another of Angell's students, John Watson. Hunter—the 1931 APA president—eventually became the head of the psychology department at Brown University and director of the experimental laboratory, where he developed the **delayed-response problem** to study memory in animals. In the problem, an animal is first shown the problem's solution (e.g., the door behind which a reward is located) and then is restrained for varying time periods before being released. To solve the problem, the animal must "remember" the reward's position during the delay. Hunter was a pioneer in comparative psychology, including the comparison of animals and humans (e.g., Hunter, 1913). Comparative psychology was an area neglected by the structuralists but embraced by American functionalists.

Further important comparative work came from Robert Yerkes (Chapter 12) and his pupil—later his teacher—**Gilbert Van Tassell Hamilton** (1877–1948). Considered a major figure in the history of psychiatry (Sears, 1992), Hamilton was another pioneer in

American comparative psychology (e.g., Hamilton, 1911, 1916), with interests in contrasting animals and humans on the same behavioral phenomena.

Angell himself was also an important figure in the growing interest in "behavior" that came to dominate American psychology (Leahey, 1993). Two years before Watson's "behaviorist manifesto," Angell (1911) wrote the following:

> But there is unquestionably a movement on foot in which interest is centered in the *results* of conscious process, rather than in the *processes* themselves. This is peculiarly true in animal psychology; it is only less true in human psychology. In these cases interest is in what may for lack of a better term be called 'behavior'; and the analysis of consciousness is primarily justified by the light it throws on behavior, rather than *vice-versa.*
>
> If this movement should go forward, we should probably have a general science of behavior . . . (p. 47, italics in the original)

One of Angell's best-known students was Harvey A. Carr, who received his Ph.D. in 1905. Carr eventually succeeded Angell as functionalism's primary spokesperson.

HARVEY A. CARR

Harvey A. Carr (1873–1954) was born on an Indiana farm. After an early education in a county district school, he entered the preparatory school at DePauw University at the age of 18. Two years later, Carr began his university work, majoring in mathematics. As he later reported, he liked physics and was curious about the biological sciences, but there was little taught in the latter at DePauw—rumor had it that school authorities disliked "biology because of its evolutionary implications" (Carr, 1936, p. 69). Illness at the beginning of his third year interrupted Carr's education at DePauw. Carr's recovery was followed by a period of teaching, which Carr (1936) felt was partly responsible for his later specialization in psychology.

Instead of returning to DePauw, Carr entered the University of Colorado, where he intended to resume his studies in mathematics. However, Carr found that he liked the professor of psychology and education and disliked the mathematics instructor, so he opted for psychology.

Carr earned his bachelor's and master's degrees from Colorado, and then went to the University of Chicago to pursue a Ph.D. in experimental psychology. When he arrived at Chicago, Dewey was the department head, and Angell was in charge of the course in experimental psychology. Carr and his fellow students found Angell to be "intensely human, stimulating, encouraging, and genuinely interested in our intellectual and scientific development . . ." (Carr, 1936, p. 75). At the end of Carr's first year, Dewey left Chicago, Angell became head of a separate department of psychology, and John Watson was hired as an instructor.

Carr's first reaction to Watson was "of slight reserve and suspicion," but this soon changed to a spirit of comradeship that lasted many years. After receiving his Ph.D. in 1905, Carr's first university employment was at Chicago in 1908 when he took the opening left by Watson's departure. Carr remained at Chicago, assuming the position as head of the psychology department in 1925. During the period of Carr's association with the department—from 1908 until his 1938 retirement—130 doctorates were conferred. According to Fred McKinney (1978), a student at Chicago from 1929 to 1931, Carr was

> held in special regard by most of the graduate students. . . . To me he was like a favorite uncle: warm, friendly, teasing at times, oblivious to everyone when he was preoccupied. He was a quiet, apparently happy family man who came to the office regularly and did his work unostentatiously. He was no academic prima donna, but was quite comfortable in the background; he seemed emotionally mature and unpretentious. His speech had a nasal twang and he mispronounced some words, but no one doubted the keenness of his intellect or the depth of his concern for students. (pp. 143–144)

Under Carr (Figure 11–3), functionalism at Chicago reached its zenith, and we will consider his approach to psychology in some detail as being representative of functionalism's most mature position.

FIGURE 11–3.   Harvey A. Carr.

Source: University of Chicago Library, Department of Special Collections.

Our discussion will center on the system of functionalism described in Carr's (1925) influential textbook, *Psychology: A Study of Mental Activity.*

Carr's Functionalism

For Carr, psychology was the study of mental activity, whose aim is to manipulate experience in order to achieve a better adjustment between the organism and its environment. Mental activity is a generic term for more specific activities such as perception, memory, feelings, and reasoning. These various mental activities produce adaptive behavior.

For Carr, the **adaptive act** was a key concept consisting of three essential elements: (1) a motivating stimulus, (2) a sensory situation, and (3) a response that changes the situation to satisfy the motivating conditions. Carr saw a motive as a stimulus that dominates and directs behavior until the organism responds in such a way that the motivating stimulus is no longer effective. Resolution of the motive may come in any of three ways: The adaptive act may remove the stimulus, disrupt it by substituting a more powerful stimulus, or the organism may adapt to the motivating stimulus.

As an example of an adaptive act, consider the last time you were hungry. There was a motivating stimulus—for example, hunger pangs, time on the clock; a sensory situation—for example, nothing you wanted to eat in your refrigerator or cupboard; and a response that changed the sensory situation—for example, you got in your car and drove to a fast-food restaurant, where you ordered and then ate something to remove the motivating stimulus. Although our example is oversimplified, each adaptive act consists of a coordinated series of stimuli and responses, with each response altering the stimulus situation. Like Dewey's reflex arc concept, in Carr's adaptive act, behavior is a continuous and integrated process.

Thus, the adaptive act ends when a response removes the motivating stimulus, and this is the basis for learning. "The usual explanation of the adaptive character of our acquired reactions is that of the law of effect, which accounts for the selection and elimination of acts on the basis of their consequents. . . . The law merely accounts for the fixation of the adaptive acts and the elimination of the non-adaptive ones . . ." (Carr; Hilgard, 1991, p. 128). We will see that the law of effect, mentioned first in our discussion of Bain (Chapter 4), was formulated by Thorndike (discussed later), who served as a bridge between the functionalist and behaviorist traditions.

Like most of the psychologists before him—for example, Wundt, Brentano, Titchener, James—Angell saw introspection as a fundamental method of psychology, although their approaches to introspection differed. Carr's mature functionalist position accepted the possibility that mental acts could be either subjectively (through introspective self-report) or objectively observed, without implying that one method was preferable. He considered self-reports necessary to gain knowledge about human mental events, but the subjective method could only be used with "subjects of training and ability." Psychologists must use the objective method (obser-

vation of behavior) in the study of animals, children, primitive peoples, and the insane.

For the Chicago functionalists, experimentation was preferred to naturalistic observation, and learning became a key area for study. A large amount of objective data was obtained through the study of learning in animals by psychologists working in the functionalist tradition. Carr himself had worked with rats early in his career.

Carr's Influence

Carr was eclectic in his view of what mattered in psychology. Thus, Carr's and functionalism's eclecticism permitted the acceptance and development of a variety of disparate areas. Because of their concern for the adaptive nature of mental acts—the uses to which the acts could be put—functionalists were particularly supportive of applied fields such as educational psychology, industrial psychology, abnormal psychology, and mental hygiene, as we have indicated. Put another way, applied psychology, by stressing the application of psychological knowledge for the enhancement of the human condition, is by definition functional (i.e., adaptive).

In addition, because of their nondoctrinaire positions, functionalists tended to be skeptical of the more extreme, although sometimes related, systems such as behaviorism and psychoanalysis. By calling for the study of overt behavior, the behaviorists were merely embracing a position that was included under the functionalist umbrella; the objective, scientific study of animals clearly interested functionalists. When psychoanalysts stressed the importance of motivation for behavior, functionalists could say that motivation had always been important in their conception of adaptive behavior. Because of its inclusiveness, functionalism saw little need for these "new" schools.

Basically, Carr's view was that functional psychology was American psychology, "and he might have included France and Britain too, as well as animal psychology and all applied psychology . . ." (Boring, 1950, p. 559). Unfortunately, by being so catholic in what it accepted, functionalism lost the dynamic that comes in opposing and being opposed.

Still, there were functionalists at places other than Chicago. As we saw in Chapter 10, Cattell, a psychologist of function, if not formally a functionalist, had a career at Columbia spanning over 25 years (1891–1917). In 1904, Cattell brought John Dewey from Chicago, but by this time Dewey was more concerned with philosophy and education than with psychology. Two of Cattell's Ph.D. students were particularly instrumental in imparting a functionalist flavor to psychology at Columbia and for making Columbia—along with Chicago—an important center for American psychology. Both had studied under James at Harvard before taking their Ph.D.s with Cattell. They were Edward Lee Thorndike and Robert Sessions Woodworth.

EDWARD LEE THORNDIKE

Edward Lee Thorndike (1874–1949) was the son of a Methodist minister, who, in the custom of the Methodist church at the time, moved his family every 2 or 3 years to another little New England town. Thorndike's mother was the perfect minister's wife, regarding as wicked such pleasures as dancing and Sunday newspapers. Seriousness and diligence were the order of the day.

Thorndike was a serious and diligent student, and his career at Wesleyan University in Middletown, Connecticut, was a testimony to his brilliance. At Wesleyan, the youthful Thorndike's religious faith yielded to a trust in science. We will see this commitment reflected in Thorndike's scientific productivity, which was prodigious even by the standards of the people we have so far considered.

During his junior year at Wesleyan, Thorndike heard the word "psychology" for the first time, when he took a required course in the subject, for which James Sully's *Outlines of Psychology* was the text. Thorndike considered Sully's book unremarkable, but his reaction was quite different to the chapters of James's *Principles of Psychology* he read for a prize competition, which he won. He found the *Principles* stimulating, "more so than any book that I had read before, and possibly more so than any read since" (Thorndike, 1936, p. 263). As a consequence,

FIGURE 11–4.   Edward Lee Thorndike at Harvard.
Source: From Boakes From Darwin to Behaviourism *(1984) by courtesy of Mary Naylor and Harvard College Library.*

Thorndike (Figure 11–4) bought the two volumes, the only books outside of his English major that he bought voluntarily during his stay at Wesleyan, and chided the psychology professor for not using the *Principles* as a text.

After graduating from Wesleyan, Thorndike enrolled at Harvard, initially planning to major in English and also taking courses in psychology and philosophy. However, work in English was abandoned in favor of psychology in his first graduate year, and Thorndike began to think of himself as a psychology Ph.D. candidate. Thorndike's research training in psychology was primarily directed by **E. B. Delabarre** (1863–1945), who was in charge of the Harvard laboratory in Münsterberg's absence. Delabarre, who had earned an M.A. under James and a Ph.D. from Freiburg, was on leave from Brown University, where he had established a psychology laboratory. Delabarre's main contributions to psychology were in visual perception, particularly the perception of the orientation of lines.

Thorndike's first research was an attempted study of "mind-reading ability" in children. The rationale for the study came from James's belief that "mind reading," if it occurred, resulted from the detection of slight (and unconscious) changes in facial expression or movements. As close observers of their parents and other adults, children might be particularly proficient at detecting these minuscule signals.

In his experiment, Thorndike would think of one of a set of numbers, letters, or objects, and a child, seated across from him, would try to guess the correct item. Thorndike found little evidence for "mind reading," despite rewarding any correct guesses with a piece of candy.

You may recognize similarities between Thorndike's "mind-reading" experiments and Oskar Pfungst's work with Clever Hans, the wonder horse (Chapter 8). Through careful observation, Pfungst found that Hans was using barely discernible changes in the body posture and/or facial expressions of his questioners to answer their questions correctly. When Pfungst used Hans's method in the laboratory with human subjects, many subjects thought he was reading their minds. Specifically, Pfungst asked a subject to think of a number, which Pfungst then tried to guess by tapping it out with his hand. Pfungst would stop tapping when he saw the kind of signal Hans had responded to.

Although the study of Clever Hans occurred nearly a decade after Thorndike's experiment with children, the rationale for the "mind-reading" experiments was the same. Thorndike's lack of results with the children appears to contradict the study by Pfungst, but there is a key methodological difference in the studies. In Pfungst's demonstration, the correct answer invariably occurred in the sequence of his tapping. All Pfungst had to do was stop tapping when he detected the signal that meant he had reached the correct number. By contrast, the children in Thorndike's experiment were only allowed to make one guess of the item Thorndike had selected. If Thorndike had allowed a child to name each of the possible items on each trial, stopping when the correct one was named, then "mind reading" of the Clever Hans variety might have been revealed.

Although the children enjoyed the experiments, the authorities decided they should not be continued, and Thorndike was forced to choose a new thesis topic. "I then suggested experiments with the instinctive and intelligent behavior of chickens as a topic, and this was accepted" (Thorndike, 1936, p. 264). Although never explicitly acknowledged by Thorndike, the reason for his choice seems to be that he was influenced by Lloyd Morgan, as we noted in Chapter 9. Morgan lectured at Harvard in 1896 on his learning studies in chickens, which illustrated the Spencer-Bain principle that behavior is modified by its consequences.

At first, Thorndike kept his subjects in his room, but his landlady's protests forced him to move them to new quarters. When space could not be found at Harvard, James, "with his habitual kindness and devotion to underdogs and eccentric aspects of science, harbored my chickens in the cellar of his own home for the rest of the year. The nuisance to Mrs. James was, I hope, somewhat mitigated by the entertainment to the two youngest children" (Thorndike, 1936, p. 264).

Smarting from a rejected marriage proposal and tired of tutoring a boy to earn money for graduate school, Thorndike accepted a fellowship offer from Cattell at Columbia. In the fall of 1897, he moved to New York, taking with him two educated chickens that he planned to breed for the beginnings of a test of the inheritance of acquired mental traits (Lamarckism; Chapter 9). This project was scrapped when Thorndike realized how long it would take to train and breed several generations of fowls.

At Columbia, Thorndike began the research that established his fame in psychology, training animals, chiefly young cats, to escape from puzzle or problem boxes of his own construction. Because of their importance for behaviorism, we will discuss Thorndike's animal experiments in detail in the next chapter. At this point, we will just note that within 16 months of his arrival at Columbia, Thorndike had written and successfully defended his dissertation, published it as a monograph supplement to *Psychological Review,* and presented his results to both the American Psychological Association and the New York Academy of Sciences.

After a disappointing year at the College for Women at Western Reserve University in Cleveland—where Thorndike had gone partly because a brother expected to go there and partly because of the school's reputation—Thorndike returned to New York to accept a position at Teachers College, Columbia. With the exception of one more brief foray into animal research—he studied monkeys in the period from 1899 to 1901—Thorndike devoted himself to research with humans. The reason for this was his employment at Teachers College—a school with a focus on pedagogy. As he wrote in 1936, "it has been my custom to fulfill my contractual obligations as a professor before doing anything else" (p. 270).

Thorndike's Psychology

For Thorndike, psychology was the study of stimulus-response (S-R) connections, and he assumed that behavior can be analyzed into such associations or connections, as he called them. However, Thorndike's idea of S-R bonds was broader than that often assumed by his critics. Instead of just simple associations between discrete phenomena, Thorndike's conception included the type of associations we saw in Dewey's reflex arc.

> [Connections] often occur in long series wherein the response to one situation becomes the situation producing the next response and so on. They may be from parts or elements or features of a situation as well as from the situation as a whole. . . . The things connected may be subtle relations or elusive attitudes and intentions. (Thorndike, 1949, p. 81)

Of course, quite specific S-R connections were certainly possible in Thorndike's learning theory, and this is what he found in his dissertation research. Highly specific S-R bonds were also found in a famous study in which Thorndike and Woodworth (discussed later) tested the **doctrine of formal discipline**. The doctrine was the then widely held belief that exercising the mind by learning disciplinary subjects such as Latin, Greek, and mathematics

would improve the mind's ability to learn other unrelated subjects. It was the "mind-as-a-muscle" idea: Exercise would strengthen the mind's "fibers" and make them more capable of profiting from future training.

James, Thorndike and Woodworth's Harvard mentor, had informally tested the doctrine by memorizing passages from Victor Hugo and John Milton. Reporting his results in the *Principles,* James (1890) concluded that "*No amount of culture would seem capable of modifying a man's* GENERAL *retentiveness*" (Vol. 1, pp. 663–664, emphasis in the original).

Thorndike and Woodworth (1901) examined the doctrine by training subjects on various tasks such as estimating geometrical areas and then testing the subjects to see whether they had improved in their ability to perform tasks more or less similar to the original. **Transfer of training**—improvement in one task following training on another—proved to be slight. When it did occur, transfer seemed to require "identical elements" between the tasks, not the learning of something unrelated. Thorndike and Woodworth's results helped shift educational practices toward specifically task-oriented teaching and away from nonspecifically disciplinary training—that is, away from the doctrine of formal discipline.

For Thorndike, the S-R connections were formed through what came to be known as trial-and-error learning, although it is more accurate to call it trial-and-success. As we will see in the next chapter, Thorndike's animals demonstrated to him that the strengthening of S-R bonds occurred through the action of the Spencer-Bain principle, which he dubbed the *law of effect*—success strengthens the bond between a stimulus situation and a particular response. Thorndike's learning theory was so influential that even a psychologist who disagreed with it could say: "The psychology of animal learning—not to mention that of child learning—has been and still is primarily a matter of agreeing or disagreeing with Thorndike, or trying in minor ways to improve upon him" (Tolman, 1938, p. 11). B. F. Skinner's learning theory (Chapter 13) is in many ways an extension of Thorndike's, and Skinner acknowledged that his most important contribution to psychology was to take Thorndike's law of effect seriously.

Thorndike's Applied Contributions

Although Thorndike's learning theory was a major contribution to both psychology and education, his influence on pedagogy was also felt in other ways. Thorndike wrote a number of practical educational works that literally changed how children were taught in America. For example, with a concern for how best to teach children to read and spell, Thorndike measured the frequency with which different words occur in print, initially determining the 10,000 most common words. The 10,000 were expanded to 20,000 and finally to 30,000 in *Teacher's Word Book of 30,000 Words*. The point of the word books was that teachers should concentrate on teaching children to read and spell the most common words, not the most obscure.

As an adjunct to his common-word lists, Thorndike revolutionized children's dictionaries. At the time, school dictionaries were made by abbreviating adult dictionaries, omitting words and condensing definitions to a form often incomprehensible to a child. By contrast, Thorndike defined each word with words simpler than itself, and the simplest words were merely used in sentences rather than being defined. Additionally, pictures were widely used to illustrate objects being defined. Thorndike's dictionaries were quite successful, and the principles he used were generally adopted by later producers of dictionaries for children.

After children have been taught to read and to spell, it is desirable to have some measure of their progress, and Thorndike developed scales to measure reading ability, just as he created ability scales for spelling, drawing, handwriting, and arithmetic. Like Galton and Cattell, Thorndike loved to measure things, particularly things that were objectively difficult to measure. According to him, "Whatever exists, exists in some amount. To measure it is simply to know its varying amounts" (Thorndike, 1921, p. 379). Paradoxically for one who so loved to measure, Thorndike recognized the deficiency in his mathematical training, which he "tried to remedy . . . by private study, but something else always seemed more important" (Thorndike, 1936, p. 267). However, he encouraged his children to get a strong mathematical grounding, with the result that

two of his sons earned doctorates in physics, and his daughter received a Ph.D. in mathematics. The "only intellectually disreputable member of the family" (R. L. Thorndike, 1991, p. 141) was the other son—respected psychometric psychologist Robert L. Thorndike.

Consistent with his penchant for measurement, Thorndike developed tests to measure intelligence, culminating in his *Intelligence Scale CAVD*. From his belief that intelligence was not a unitary phenomenon but a combination of many different skills, the *CAVD* measured sentence completion (C), arithmetic ability (A), vocabulary (V), and the ability to follow directions (D). Robert L. Thorndike (1991) used his father as an illustration of the multidimensionality of intelligence: "In abstract intelligence, he was unquestionably in the top fraction of a percent of the population, while in mechanical intelligence he was a slow learner. He never learned to drive a car; I never saw him fix any device" (p. 145). Although this comment about Thorndike may strike you as odd given Thorndike's methodological innovation of the puzzle boxes for studying learning in animals, when you see examples of the actual pieces of apparatus in Chapter 12 (Figure 12–2), the statement will become more meaningful.

As with so many of the early psychologists we have considered, Thorndike was an avowed hereditarian. Like Galton (Chapter 9), Thorndike advocated eugenics. Although a great deal of his research and writing benefited the education of all, Thorndike himself was opposed to universal equal educational opportunities. Different intellectual abilities called for different instruction. As you can see, Thorndike's hereditarian viewpoint was consistent with the intellectual *Zeitgeist*.

Thorndike's Influence

Thorndike was incredibly prolific, averaging one publication per *month* throughout his career, and many of them were textbooks based on his lectures. As he explained, "It has always seemed to me better for an instructor to present his contributions in black and white than to require the labor and risk the errors of note-taking"

(Thorndike, 1936, p. 266). In addition to taking Thorndike swiftly to the top in psychology—a 1921 poll of psychologists for Cattell's *American Men of Science* found Thorndike ranked first—his books earned him a good income. In 1924 alone, his annual income from royalties was five times his salary as a professor.

As a result of his productivity and original contributions, Thorndike received many honors during his lifetime. He was elected APA president in 1912, elected to membership in the National Academy of Sciences in 1917, and received the Butler Medal from Columbia in 1925 in recognition of his contributions to education. Thorndike was the president of the American Association for the Advancement of Science in 1933.

As R. L. Thorndike (1991) put it, his father was "in some ways the original workaholic, reading the *Encyclopaedia Britannica* in bed to locate good passages for reading comprehension tests, not . . . because he was driven to it but because he would rather be getting or analyzing data than most anything else" (p. 151). Although he was not a social person, according to his son, Thorndike could inspire great loyalty. To illustrate, his student Herbert Toops named his first son Edward L. Toops and his second son Thorndike Toops.

Thorndike was particularly influential in educational psychology because of his learning theory, his studies on the learning of specific skills, his many published instructional materials, and his investigations of intelligence and the tools to measure it. Much of his learning theory was derived from the results of his dissertation experiment, a study that began systematic laboratory research in animal learning. His further investigation of human learning resulted in a revision of his learning theory. Thorndike's approach to education became known as the "scientific movement" in contrast to Dewey's "progressive movement."

Thorndike represents a transitional figure between functionalism and behaviorism. His animal research fits well into the behaviorist tradition, as we will see in the next chapter, whereas the bulk of his research had the applied, utilitarian flavor of functionalism. There is little contradiction in our placing Thorndike astraddle the functionalism-behaviorism fence, however, because the behaviorist movement grew out of functionalism.

As we indicated, Cattell's two most important students at Columbia were Thorndike and Woodworth. The two had very different dispositions; where Thorndike was anxious to get on with whatever he was doing—a temperamental necessity if you want to have over 500 publications—Woodworth was more patient and thoughtful. Still, despite their differences, there are similarities in their systematic positions, and the two remained lifelong friends.

ROBERT SESSIONS WOODWORTH

Robert Sessions Woodworth (1869–1962), shown in Figure 11–5, was born in Massachusetts, the oldest son of his father's third wife. His father was a

FIGURE 11–5. Robert Sessions Woodworth.

Source: Archives of the History of American Psychology.

sternly religious Congregational minister, and his mother was an early graduate of Mount Holyoke Seminary (now College). In 1859, she was instrumental in founding a women's seminary in Ohio, Lake Erie College.

For the most part, Woodworth grew up in New England, and he considered his environment the neighborhood more than his immediate family. As he put it, "from the age of six or seven, I had a chum, I had "a girl," I had a group of friends, whose doings loom larger in my memory than what went on within the four walls of home" (Woodworth, 1932, p. 360).

Woodworth earned his bachelor's degree from Amherst College in 1891, with exposure to psychology in his senior philosophy course, taught by Amherst's exceptional instructor, Charles E. Garman (1850–1907). Garman, with a master's degree from Yale, also founded the psychology laboratory at Amherst. James H. Tufts, mentioned earlier in the chapter, was another psychologist with an important early influence from Garman.

For the next 4 years, Woodworth taught mathematics, first at a secondary school, and then at Washburn College. During this period, he recorded two influences that directed him toward a career as an academic psychologist: William James and G. Stanley Hall. Like many of his contemporaries, Woodworth found James's *Principles* stimulating, and a lecture by Hall sent him back to his room, where he inscribed the word "INVESTIGATION" on a card that he hung over his desk. Although his investigations were still mathematical at the time, Hall's influence asserted itself a year later, and Woodworth abandoned mathematics to study psychology and philosophy at Harvard. At Harvard, Woodworth's main teachers were James and Royce. Like his fellow student Thorndike, his experimental training came from E. B. Delabarre.

James set Woodworth to work on the study of dreams, and he thought he saw a pattern of dreaming about matters begun but not completed during the day, which anticipates elements of the Zeigarnik effect (Chapter 14) by more than 2 decades. Motivation was another problem that interested Woodworth during his Harvard days and afterwards, and at one point he said to Thorndike that he was going to try to develop a "motivology," or science of motives.

In 1897, both Woodworth and Thorndike earned master's degrees from Harvard. Woodworth spent a year in physiology at the Harvard Medical School before going to Columbia, and he got his Ph.D. the year after Thorndike (1899).

In the 6 years following his master's degree, Woodworth spent 5 studying or teaching physiology, and as Charles Sherrington's (Chapter 17) assistant at Liverpool in 1903, he was "much minded to make my psychology contribute to a career in brain physiology, rather than vice versa" (Woodworth, 1932, p. 368). Sherrington's physiological work on the reflex and his theorizing about the functional gaps (synapses) between nerve cells were detailed in his 1906 work, *The Integrative Action of the Nervous System.* This monumental publication helped Sherrington win a Nobel Prize and also provided the neurological basis for Dewey's reflex arc concept.

However, at this point, Cattell asked Woodworth to come back to Columbia to "work at experimental and physiological psychology," and after careful consideration, Woodworth decided that this was the work for which he was best prepared. Except for the year of 1912 in Külpe's (Chapter 8) laboratory, Woodworth stayed at Columbia, succeeding Cattell as department head when Cattell was fired in 1917 and retiring in 1942.

Perhaps reflecting his lengthy and varied training before becoming fully committed to psychology— he was 34 when he returned to Columbia to stay— Woodworth was remarkably broad in his concerns. In addition to his interests in experimental and physiological psychology, Woodworth lectured on abnormal psychology, tests and statistics, and social psychology and offered seminars on such diverse topics as movement, vision, thinking, and motivation. He was also interested in the history of psychology as it established itself as a science. His "bogey men"—psychologists who most irritated him—were individuals who tried to dictate method and results, whose aim was to restrict.

Woodworth's Contribution to Functionalism

Woodworth's most systematic contribution to functionalism can be found in his 1918 *Dynamic*

Psychology, revised 40 years later as *Dynamics of Behavior.* In keeping with his eclecticism, Woodworth saw psychology encompassing both the introspectionist tradition and the newer interest in the study of behavior. For him, psychology's subject matter was both consciousness *and* behavior. In other words, he sought a healing of the schism between traditional introspectionism and revolutionary behaviorism, or between the psychologies of his two biggest bogey men—Titchener and Watson.

Woodworth's psychology was not Thorndike's S-R psychology, however. Instead, Woodworth stressed the importance of the state of the organism itself, changing the S-R formula to S-O-R. It is not enough just to describe the stimuli; in order to know what the organism will do, we must know its internal state, its motivation. Here we see Woodworth working to develop his **motivology**, or science of motivation, that he had mentioned to Thorndike 2 decades earlier. To illustrate the importance of the "O" for behavior, a hungry rat will rapidly traverse a maze, whereas a satiated rat, placed into the same maze, may groom itself before falling asleep. The difference is in the O—the organism.

Two of Woodworth's most important concepts were mechanism and drive. **Mechanism** refers to *how* something is accomplished, whereas **drive** indicates *why*. For example, take a hungry rat in a maze. The rat's behavior that leads to the goal box and food—its running and exploring the maze's alleys— is the mechanism that eventually leads to success, whereas its hunger is the drive.

Woodworth also noted that mechanism itself might become a drive. For example, take the case of a woman who works to earn money to satisfy her needs for food, clothing, and shelter. Initially, her work is the mechanism that satisfies her basic drives. At some point, the work may not be necessary to satisfy basic drives; she may have earned enough money to provide for her basic needs with money left over. However, the woman continues to work because the mechanism itself has become a drive.

Woodworth is often credited with coining the term *drive,* but the term actually appeared in print at least several months before *Dynamic Psychology* was published, in an article by Watson and Morgan (1917). Although he did not introduce the word, it is fair to say that Woodworth popularized it.

Woodworth's Other Contributions

In a career that spanned nearly 60 years, Woodworth wrote several major books, almost any one of which would have capped the career of a lesser psychologist. For example, in 1911 he revised G. T. Ladd's (Chapter 10) *Elements of Physiological Psychology,* "which became the standard handbook for this field until 1934" (Boring, 1950, p. 564). We have already mentioned *Dynamic Psychology* in 1918, with its revision 40 years later. In 1921, Woodworth published *Psychology: A Study of Mental Life,* an introductory textbook whose several editions outsold its competition for 25 years.

Woodworth revealed his interest in psychology's history with the publication in 1931 of *Contemporary Schools of Psychology.* His general eclecticism is evident in his even-handed treatment of the various systematic positions; Woodworth denied that any approach to psychology was the *only* approach, even his own. *Contemporary Schools* went through three revisions, the last published with a co-author 2 years after Woodworth's death.

One of Woodworth's students, **Edna Heidbreder** (1890–1985), is best known for her book on the same topic as *Contemporary Schools,* which is entitled *Seven Psychologies.* Heidbreder received her Ph.D. from Columbia in 1924. Following a decade at the University of Minnesota, Heidbreder accepted a position at Wellesley College, where she worked until her retirement. In addition to an interest in systems and theories of psychology, like many other functional psychologists Heidbreder made significant contributions to applied psychology, particularly to the psychological testing movement and personality testing (see Henle, 1991).

Of all his publications, perhaps the one for which Woodworth is best known is *Experimental Psychology,* which first appeared in 1938, although a mimeographed version had been used for nearly 20 years by then. The 1938 version and its revision with Harold Schlosberg in 1954 taught experimental psychology to literally thousands of students, becoming for its generation what Titchener's *Experimental Psychology* had been to an earlier one.

In 1914, Woodworth was elected APA president, and his presidential speech presented his contribution to the imageless-thought controversy that we first mentioned in Chapter 7. Of perhaps greater interest in Woodworth's 1914 presentation was his call for psychology to develop its own technical vocabulary. As Woodworth pointed out, the problem is that many of psychology's technical terms are part of everyday language, with all the imprecision that implies. Terms such as *thoughts, mind, memory, behavior,* and even *psychology* itself have both common and technical definitions, with the former frequently interfering with the latter (for a recent critique of the term *behavior,* see Hibbard & Henley, 1994). Woodworth called for psychology to develop a technical vocabulary, following the lead of physics and chemistry of naming something after its discoverer. For example, you may recall that in Chapter 8 we mentioned Karl Marbe, who, working in the Würzburg school, discovered what he called *Bewusstseinslagen,* or "conscious attitudes."

> [S]ince Bewusstseinslagen were first reported and defined in the work of Marbe and his associates, I would suggest calling them "marbs," the term to be defined for all time by reference to the original description by Marbe. Similarly, since the "thoughts" were gradually brought to light by the school of which Külpe was the guiding spirit, I would suggest calling them "kulps," defining this term similarly by reference to the original works. These terms are certainly beautifully compact and euphonious, and those who can bring themselves to use them will find them very convenient. (Woodworth, 1915/1978, p. 126)

Although the problem Woodworth highlighted is a real one, his technical terms never caught on. That is unfortunate, because drives might have become "woods."

For his many contributions to psychology, Woodworth received a number of honors. In addition to being elected APA president, in 1921 he was elected to the first board of directors of the Psychological Corporation, Cattell's organization to promote applied psychology. In 1956, he received the first American Psychological Foundation Gold Medal Award for his contributions to the growth of psychology.

WOMEN IN AMERICA'S FIRST SCHOOL

Before leaving functionalism, we would like to examine briefly the place of women in America's first school of psychology by highlighting the struggles and accomplishments of one such woman—Milicent Shinn.

Milicent W. Shinn

California native and cousin of Edmund Sanford (Chapter 10), **Milicent Shinn** (1858–1940) entered the University of California in 1874, only a year after it opened its doors to women and just 2 years after it moved to Berkeley. There, she met President Daniel Gilman, the man we mentioned as the president of Johns Hopkins University in the last chapter. Gilman left California for Baltimore in 1875, and in 1879, after a chance meeting with Shinn at a social science convention in the East, began a correspondence with her that lasted for many years. Although Gilman wrote to tell her about opportunities for study at the Harvard Annex, Shinn (Figure 11–6) could not escape the ties of her family. Instead, she assumed the nonpaying editorship of a failing San Francisco literary magazine, *Overland Monthly,* continuing to live on the rural family farm near Niles, California, and commuting to the city.

In 1890, Shinn began a project that eventually led her back to Berkeley as a psychology graduate student. One of her brothers had brought his wife to the family homestead to live, and when their daughter was born, Shinn began keeping a permanent record of the infant's growth and development, which she documented in detail for more than 2 years. This was one of the first systematic descriptions of a child's physical and mental development and established Shinn's place in psychology.

FIGURE 11–6. Milicent W. Shinn.
Source: The Bancroft Library, Berkeley; courtesy Harvard College Library.

In 1893, Shinn was invited to present a paper on her findings at the World's Columbian Exposition in Chicago. Sandwiched among experimental papers in a conference on education, Shinn's "The First Two Years of the Child" was hailed as an outstanding early American contribution to the topic of child development. Convinced by others of the importance of her efforts, Shinn resigned her editorship and entered graduate school at Berkeley in 1894. In 1898, she received the 11th Ph.D. awarded by the University of California and the first given to a woman. Shinn's studies of her niece were published in popular form in 1900 as *The Biography of a Baby*.

However, Shinn's work was not the first systematic description of child development. Darwin (Chapter 9) kept a similar account of the development of his infant son, which he published in 1877 as "Biographical sketch of an infant." After Darwin, but before Shinn, **Wilhelm Preyer** (1842–1897) published *Die Seele des Kindes* in 1882, which was translated and published in 1888–1889 as *The Mind*

of the Child. Preyer's book was based on his observational study of his own son and is sometimes credited with being the first work of modern child psychology (Scarborough & Furumoto, 1987). A physiologist, Preyer was a friend of Fechner (Chapter 6) and one of the original editors of Ebbinghaus and König's *Zeitschrift für Psychologie* (Chapter 8). After 1882, Preyer devoted most of his time to child psychology.

Shinn obtained Preyer's book at the beginning of her observations of her niece, and she later acknowledged being guided and instructed by it. As her observations continued, she diverged more and more from Preyer's method, however. After reading portions of Shinn's dissertation, Preyer acknowledged its value, suggesting in a letter to an American colleague that it should be translated into German so that it could be read by German mothers.

Unfortunately for psychology, after receiving her Ph.D. Shinn abandoned scholarly activity, returning to the family home, where she lived for the rest of her life. As Scarborough and Furumoto (1987) put it, "her sense of responsibility to her family emerges as the overriding factor deterring her from forging a professional identity" (p. 61).

Of course, Shinn was not the only woman of her era to face the dilemma posed by family obligations on the one hand and career on the other. Although Mary Calkins (Chapter 10) enjoyed a successful career in psychology, she did not consider the scholarly life an easy one for a woman. Particularly problematic, in her view, were the conflicting demands of work and social responsibilities.

> In an observation that reflected her own personal experience as well as the existing social norms, [Calkins] remarked [in a 1913 address] that it was an unmarried daughter rather than a son who was likely to become responsible for the care of aging parents. For the woman who chose to marry, the balancing act between career and family demands was even more difficult. (Scarborough & Furumoto, 1987, p. 51)

This was especially true for **Ethel Puffer Howes** (1872–1950), who graduated from Smith College in western Massachusetts in 1891. As you may recall, both Mary Calkins and Theodate Smith (Chapter

10) also earned degrees from Smith. In 1895, Puffer went to Germany to study psychology. Eventually Puffer worked with Münsterberg in Freiberg, where she was essentially adopted by the Münsterberg family. Back in New England on a fellowship she received with Münsterberg's support, Puffer completed the Ph.D. requirements at Radcliffe, which included an examination by a committee that included James, Santayana, and Münsterberg.

For a decade after she received the Radcliffe Ph.D., Puffer held academic positions in the Boston area and served as Münsterberg's laboratory assistant. In 1908, she married Benjamin Howes, a young man she apparently met as one of her students during a year of high school teaching (Scarborough, 1991). For much of the rest of her life, Ethel Puffer Howes fulfilled the role of homemaker.

However, unlike Milicent Shinn, Ethel Howes did not completely relinquish the scholarly life to devote herself to family. At various times, she wrote articles for the popular press, worked for the war effort and for women's suffrage, and had a brief (but exhausting) second career in the 1920s as the director of an institute at Smith College devoted to the study of the status of women.

In her last word on the marriage-versus-career dilemma, it is evident that Howes (1929) no longer believed that it was possible for a woman to have a satisfactory career by making either personal adjustments in her family life or in her attitudes. What was needed instead was a redefinition of the traditional role of the woman, a changing of the inner attitudes of both men and women toward acceptance of the need of educated women for both familial and intellectual satisfaction. Society must change to eliminate "the intolerable choice" of the woman.

CONCLUSIONS

In the last three chapters, we have sketched the antecedents, the rise, and the maturation of that peculiarly American school of psychology, functionalism. Functionalism declined as a recognized school primarily because of the success of its off-spring, behaviorism, which we will examine in the next two chapters. As we have noted on a number of occasions, behaviorism's founder, John Watson, received his training in the functionalist tradition at the University of Chicago.

In a very real sense, Chicago's functionalism, exemplified by the work of James Rowland Angell and Harvey Carr, gave scientific substance to many of William James's pronouncements in the *Principles*. Watson's behaviorism can be seen as a logical outgrowth of the functional psychology to which he had been exposed, stripped of its mentalistic flavor. Although he accepted many of functionalism's loosely held principles—the strongly empirical, scientific approach to psychology, the importance of applied research, the study of animals—Watson rejected functionalism's continued interest in the study of consciousness.

However, despite all the early success of behaviorism, a case can be made for the idea that functionalism was not murdered by its progeny, but lives on in its quiet, informal, nonrestrictive way. For example, in our examination of cognitive psychology (Chapter 20), we will see that studies of human consciousness using both subjective and objective data in a manner perfectly consistent with functionalism are once again popular. As Fred McKinney (1978), one of Harvey Carr's students, expressed it,

> As I look back to the late twenties and then turn to observe psychology today, I conclude that *the functional tradition quietly persists*. Among all the systems of psychology that have emerged, it produced the greatest number of residuals. American psychology (which started with the functionalist William James, was institutionalized by John Dewey and James Angell as functionalism, and was regarded as the mainstream of psychology by Carr) generally continues in that tradition. American psychology serves as the model for psychologists and laboratories arising in the many new departments around the world; as a result, the functional tradition is worldwide. . . . Functionalism, present in the time of Ancient Greece, had its heyday as a school in the twenties and thirties of this century and lives on without the trappings of a school to this very day. (p. 147, italics in the original)

S U M M A R Y

As a school of psychology, functionalism had no dominant individual, and its formal founding is often credited to Titchener's criticism in 1898 of John Dewey's earlier paper. Contrary to Titchener's predictions for it, the study of function proved fruitful.

John Dewey

In 1896, John Dewey wrote the article criticized by Titchener, "The reflex arc concept in psychology." Dewey's analysis of the reflex arc was intended to show that strong distinctions between stimulus and response are artificial and that an event such as seeing a candle, touching the flame, and drawing back in pain are part of one coherent whole. At the University of Chicago, Dewey was able to build a strong functionalist philosophy department, while pursuing his interests in education. Dewey went to Columbia in 1904, where his efforts were directed toward philosophy and education.

James Rowland Angell

Without earning a Ph.D., James Rowland Angell became head of the psychology department at Chicago in 1905. In his presidential address to the APA, Angell characterized functionalism as (1) the study of mental operations in contrast to the study of mental elements, (2) the study of the mind engaged in mediating between the environment and the organism, and (3) the study of the relationship between the mind and the body.

Harvey A. Carr

With a Ph.D. from Chicago, Harvey A. Carr eventually became department head, and under him functionalism at Chicago reached its peak. For Carr, psychology was the study of mental activity, which produces adaptive behavior. A key concept was the adaptive act, which consists of three essential elements: (1) a motivating stimulus, (2) a sensory situation, and (3) a change in the situation that satisfies the motivating conditions. The adaptive act ends when a response removes the motivating stimulus, providing the basis for learning. Under Carr's direction, functionalism supported a variety of methods and applications, although it stood in opposition to the increasingly extreme positions of behaviorism and psychoanalysis.

Edward Lee Thorndike

Probably Edward Lee Thorndike's most important research for psychology was the work he did with animals for his dissertation. Soon after receiving his Ph.D. from Columbia, Thorndike joined the faculty of Teacher's College at Columbia, where he stayed for the rest of his career.

Although Thorndike's psychology can be understood as a psychology of S-R connections, his conception of stimulus and response was influenced by Dewey. Examples of Thorndike's work include his test of the doctrine of formal discipline (with Woodworth). Thorndike and Woodworth found little evidence for the doctrine, and transfer of training seemed to require "identical elements" between the tasks. In his study of animal learning, Thorndike found that success strengthened a bond between a stimulus situation and a particular response, and he dubbed this updating of the Spencer-Bain principle the law of effect.

Much of Thorndike's work dealt with practical matters of education. He made contributions to reading, spelling, children's dictionaries, and the measurement of children's abilities. In addition to Thorndike's important contributions to learning theory, education, and the measurement of intelligence, he represents in many ways the transition in American psychology from functionalism to behaviorism.

Robert Sessions Woodworth

Harvard- and Columbia-trained Robert S. Woodworth's dynamic psychology stressed the state of the organism, changing Thorndike's S-R formulation to S-O-R. To know what an organism will do in a situation, we must know its motivation, and Woodworth is perhaps best known for his motivology, or science of motivation. Motivology concerned the study of the mechanisms (how something is accomplished) and drives (why something is accomplished) that form our motivations.

Woodworth wrote several important textbooks, including *Contemporary Schools of Psychology*, which dealt with psychology's history, but perhaps the textbook for which Woodworth is best known is *Experimental Psychology*. Woodworth also called for psychology to develop a technical vocabulary, but this suggestion has not been heeded.

Women in America's First School

The career of Milicent Shinn illustrates the struggles and accomplishments of women in America's first psychological school. Shinn received the first Ph.D. given to a woman by the University of California at Berkeley. Shinn's primary work concerned her observations of an infant's development across a 2-year span. In Germany, Wilhelm Preyer had done similar work and suggested that Shinn's work should be translated into German. After receiving her Ph.D., Shinn returned to the family home.

Another woman trained in the functional school, Ethel Puffer Howes struggled to combine marriage and a career.

Howes eventually concluded that it was impossible for a woman to have a satisfactory career by making personal adjustments in her family life or in her attitudes. Instead, society needed to redefine the woman's role.

CONNECTIONS QUESTIONS

1. What connections can you make between William James and the major functionalists reviewed in this chapter?
2. What is the connection between Dewey's reflex arc concept and James's stream of consciousness? Between Carr's adaptive act and Dewey's reflex arc concept?
3. What connections can you draw between Thorndike's (and James's) "mind-reading" experiments and Pfungst's work with Clever Hans?
4. What connection can you make between the "founding" of functionalism as a school of psychology and Titchener?

5. What connections can you make between the women pioneers of American psychology? What sorts of common obstacles may they have faced?
6. What connections can you draw between Thorndike and Woodworth?
7. Draw a concept map connecting functionalism and functionalists at Chicago and Columbia with developments in the study of motivation, the study of learning, and applied areas. Compare your results with one possible solution provided on p. 566.

SUGGESTED READINGS

Angell, J. R. (1936). James Rowland Angell. In C. Murchison (Ed.), *A history of psychology in autobiography* (Vol. 3, pp. 1–38). Worcester, MA: Clark University Press.

Carr, H. A. (1936). Harvey A. Carr. In C. Murchison (Ed.), *A history of psychology in autobiography* (Vol. 3, pp. 69–82). Worcester, MA: Clark University Press.

Thorndike, E. L. (1936). Edward Lee Thorndike. In C. Murchison (Ed.), *A history of psychology in autobiography* (Vol. 3, pp. 263–270). Worcester, MA: Clark University Press.

Woodworth, R. S. (1932). Robert S. Woodworth. In C. Murchison (Ed.), *A history of psychology in autobiography* (Vol. 2, pp. 359–380). Worcester, MA: Clark University Press.

These autobiographical essays in Murchison's *History of Psychology in Autobiography* are excellent starting points in the search for information on their authors. In reading Woodworth's autobiographical account, keep in mind that he lived and worked for another 3 decades after writing it.

Angell, J. R. (1907). The province of functional psychology. *Psychological Review, 14,* 61–91. This published version of Angell's

presidential address to the APA in 1906 provides both an excellent overview of a mature conception of functionalism and a glimpse of Angell's tendency toward verbosity.

Dewey, J. (1896). The reflex arc concept in psychology. *Psychological Review, 3,* 357–370. As we noted, this is the paper that is usually credited with initiating functionalism as a separate school of psychology. As a companion piece, it is worthwhile to read Titchener's critique: Titchener, E. B. (1898). The postulates of a structural psychology. *Philosophical Review, 7,* 449–465.

Scarborough, E., & Furumoto, L. (1987). *Untold lives: The first generation of American women psychologists.* New York: Columbia University Press. This is an excellent source for information on early women psychologists. In addition to chapters on Milicent Shinn and Ethel Puffer, Scarborough and Furumoto examine the travails and successes of Mary Calkins, Margaret Washburn, and Christine Ladd-Franklin. Cameo portraits are presented of such early women psychologists as Lillien Martin, Naomi Norsworthy, Theodate Smith, and Helen Woolley.

Animal Psychology and Early Behaviorism

Edward Lee Thorndike

Ivan Pavlov

John Watson

Robert Yerkes

William McDougall

Vladimir Bekhterev

Ivan Sechenov

1820	1830	1840	1850	1860	1870	1880	1890	1900

Darwin publishes
The Descent of Man

Johannes Brahms is born

Wagner flourishes

Cy Young begins his
National League
pitching career

England introduces the first
postage stamp

Robert E. Lee assumes command
of the Army of Northern Virginia

Behaviorism's formal beginning is generally attributed to John Watson's (1913) article, "Psychology as the behaviorist views it." However, as we have seen before, no school of psychology arises in isolation, and behaviorism, like structuralism and functionalism, had many antecedents. One element of behaviorism was the associative psychology advocated by early British and French empiricists (Chapter 4; see also Walsh, 1971). From its beginning, there was a strong French influence upon behaviorism, which we saw first in Descartes's (Chapter 3) and in La Mettrie's (Chapter 4) objective, mechanistic explanations of body and mind. Some authorities (e.g., Fraisse, 1970) have even suggested that a French pioneer such as Henri Piéron (1881–1964) should be credited with behaviorism's founding as a school of psychology.

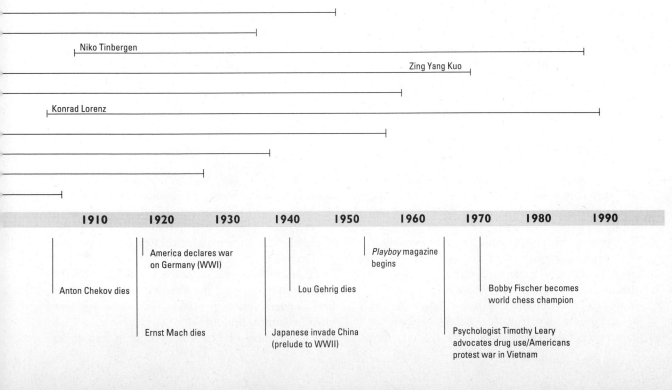

Niko Tinbergen

Zing Yang Kuo

Konrad Lorenz

| 1910 | 1920 | 1930 | 1940 | 1950 | 1960 | 1970 | 1980 | 1990 |

America declares war on Germany (WWI)

Playboy magazine begins

Anton Chekov dies

Lou Gehrig dies

Bobby Fischer becomes world chess champion

Ernst Mach dies

Japanese invade China (prelude to WWII)

Psychologist Timothy Leary advocates drug use/Americans protest war in Vietnam

A few generations after La Mettrie, Comte developed the philosophy of positivism (Chapter 5), which became a major part of the European *Zeitgeist*. Comte's early 19th-century philosophy had at its core his Law of Three Stages, the highest of which was the positivistic or scientific stage. Having advanced to this stage, a field relies on experimentation and observation and tries to explain its phenomena objectively, by the laws of natural cause and effect. Comte did not think a science of the mind that relied chiefly on introspection was possible. Watson also rejected introspection and substituted a science of behavior for a science of the mind. As the wags put it: With Darwin, psychology lost its soul; with Watson, it lost its mind.

In Chapter 5, we saw that the objective approach to science was further developed by the positivists Mach and Avenarius. Subsequently, Carnap and Schlick (both Chapter 5) and other members of the Vienna Circle continued to refine positivism, and positivism's objective approach to science facilitated psychology's takeover by behaviorism—a singularly objective approach.

Evolution was another element of the 19th-century's *Zeitgeist* that was an important antecedent of behaviorism. As we saw in Chapters 9 through 11, evolution was central to the psychology of function, the idea that abilities evolved because they play a part in their possessors' adaptation. Behaviorism was a direct descendant of functionalism, accepting many of its principles—for example, a strongly empirical, scientific approach, the importance of applied research, the study of animals—while rejecting the study of consciousness. As we will see, Watson was trained in the functionalist tradition at the University of Chicago.

Darwinian evolution placed humans squarely in the animal kingdom, and efforts by George Romanes (Chapter 9) to find support for intellectual continuity among animals began comparative psychology, which was further developed by Romanes's protégé—C. Lloyd Morgan (Chapter 9). Although behaviorism was not synonymous with animal psychology, it was critical for behaviorism's development, and Watson's early animal studies contributed significantly to his formulation of behaviorism. After we examine animal psychology's influences on behaviorism, we will describe developments in Russia that importantly anticipated and affected American behaviorism's course.

ANIMAL PSYCHOLOGY

Animal psychology was a relatively small part of the rapid expansion of American psychology at the turn of the century (Boakes, 1984). In fact, some of the most important early contributors to animal psychology were biologists. For example, mentioned in Chapter 11 as Angell's neighbor at the University of Chicago, **Jacques Loeb** (1859–1924) was a major influence on Watson. With an assistantship to study medicine in Berlin, Loeb did his first experimental work on the effects of brain lesions on the behavior of dogs, which he abandoned when inflicting injuries on the animals became too distasteful. With another assistantship in Würzburg, Loeb became interested in the reactions of simple animals to light and also in plant movement, which Würzburg's plant physiologists explained by elementary chemical and physical forces acting on the plant's structure. Loeb extended the idea of tropistic reactions to simple animals such as cockroaches and caterpillars and believed that **tropisms**—directed, mechanical movements—could account for much behavior in higher animals as well (e.g., Pauly, 1981).

With limited employment prospects because of his Jewish background, Loeb emigrated to the United States in 1891. In 1892, he obtained a position at the newly founded University of Chicago, which is where he was when Watson arrived. Loeb eventually became head of the general physiology division at the Rockefeller Institute for Medical Research, a post he held from 1910 until his death in 1924.

Loeb's mechanistic approach to animal behavior was strongly opposed by American biologist **Herbert Spencer Jennings** (1868–1947). Jennings was born in Tonica, Illinois, the son of a physician. The father's reading of Herbert Spencer (Chapter 9) stimulated him to abandon his religious beliefs and so influenced him that he named one son Herbert Spencer and another Darwin.

Entering in 1890, Jennings worked his way through the University of Michigan. From Michigan, Jennings went to Harvard, where he earned his doctorate in just 2 years. A travel fellowship took him to Europe in 1896, where he worked with Max Verworn, a zoologist who had been with Ernst Haeckel (Chapter 9) at Jena. In Verworn's laboratory, Jennings became fascinated with the behavior of the unicellular paramecia. The complexity of this behavior convinced Jennings that Loeb's theory of tropisms was an invalid explanation for the behavior of even simple creatures.

Although Loeb and Jennings disagreed on the fundamental basis for animal behavior, both believed in and popularized the idea that the study of simple creatures would tell much about the behavior of complex organisms. In addition, Loeb and Jennings agreed on the importance of experimental work and on the necessity for the objective description of behavior. Finally, both were important for the training of early behaviorists, Loeb for Watson and Jennings for Karl Lashley (Chapter 17).

Jennings's last behavioral work was performed in 1906, the same year that he published *The Behavior of Lower Organisms,* a review of 20 years of research on protozoa (a group of unicellular, usually microscopic organisms) and other simple multicellular creatures. In his book, Jennings discussed the learning ability of his microscopic animals, although there was little evidence for it. Herrnstein (1969) called Jennings "the most modern of the early behaviorists . . . for his objective use of psychological terms is most like what goes on among today's behaviorists . . ." (p. 60).

Animal research was poorly supported during this period even in biology departments, and Jennings's first permanent post did not come until 1906, when he became a professor of experimental zoology at Johns Hopkins. Jennings switched to work on genetics at Hopkins, following the *Zeitgeist* in biology. Gregor Mendel's (Chapter 9) classic work on inheritance in the pea, the basis for modern genetics, had been rediscovered in 1900.

Thorndike's Animal Research

If animal research was poorly supported in biology departments, it was even less encouraged in philosophy and psychology departments. For example, Edward Lee Thorndike's initial animal study was conducted in William James's (Chapter 10) basement when Thorndike was unable to secure space for it at Harvard. At Columbia, Cattell (Chapter 11) initially supported Thorndike's animal work, but "Cattell's commitment was not long-lasting. After a few short years of animal work, Thorndike followed the professional path of least resistance by turning to educational psychology" (O'Donnell, 1985, p. 192). Thorndike's "few short years of animal work" was the effort for which he is usually remembered outside of education and provided the data that laid the foundation for his learning theory and for the ascendance of behaviorism.

As we noted in Chapter 11, Thorndike is a transitional figure between functionalism and behaviorism. Thorndike's animal research ties in well with behaviorism, and passages from *Animal Intelligence* (1911)—a compilation of his animal research performed around the turn of the century—sound remarkably like what Watson later wrote. For example, on the use of introspection as psychology's primary method, here is what Thorndike had to say:

> So long as introspection was lauded as the chief method of psychology, a psychologist would tend to expect too little from mere studies, from the outside, of creatures who could not report their inner experiences to him in the manner to which he was accustomed. In the literature of the time will be found many comments on the extreme difficulty of studying the psychology of animals and children. But difficulty exists only in the case of their *consciousness.* Their *behavior,* by its simpler nature and causation, is often far easier to study than that of adults. . . . The studies reprinted in this volume produced in their author an increased respect for psychology as the science of behavior. . . (pp. 3–5, italics in the original)

Thorndike's study of animal behavior included the testing of cats in several homemade **puzzle boxes**. The neatly constructed box shown in Thorndike's dissertation is a picture of an idealized

FIGURE 12–1.   Four puzzle boxes actually used by Thorndike.

Source: From the Yerkes Collection, by courtesy Yale University Library.

piece of apparatus. Recall that Thorndike's son, Robert L. Thorndike, wrote that his father had little mechanical aptitude. Evidence for this observation is apparent in Figure 12–1, which shows four boxes actually used in Thorndike's experiments.

Thorndike tested 13 kittens and young cats in 15 puzzle boxes, each box requiring a different response or sequence of responses for its solution. For example, a cat was required to turn a button to open the door in Box C, whereas in Box G, operating a thumb latch freed the cat.

Thorndike's inspiration for the puzzle boxes came from Romanes's claims about the mechanical abilities of cats, which Romanes (1881/1895) published as part of the work for which he is most remembered— *Animal Intelligence.* It is no coincidence that Thorndike titled the version of his dissertation published in *Psychological Review,* "Animal intelligence: An experi-

mental study of the associative processes in animals" and the 1911 book simply *Animal Intelligence.* However, despite the similarity in titles between his work and that of Romanes, Thorndike's approach to the subject was decidedly different from that of his predecessors, as he quickly pointed out:

> Although no work done in this field is enough like the present investigation to require an account of its results, the *method* hitherto in use invites comparison by its contrast, and . . . by its faults. In the first place, most of the books do not give us a psychology, but rather a *eulogy,* of animals. They have all been about animal *intelligence,* never about animal *stupidity.* . . (Thorndike, 1911, p. 22, italics in the original)

Thorndike continued in this vein, charging previous researchers with being biased observers, ruled by "the well-nigh universal tendency in human nature to find the marvelous wherever it can" (p. 23). By contrast, Thorndike aimed for an objective appraisal of animal ability. First, he studied in a systematic, quantitative fashion an animal's ability to escape confinement. Next, he examined animal memory by training animals on the puzzle box task and then testing their retention later. Finally, he examined the possibly beneficial effects of imitation and of passive tuition—guiding a passive animal through the appropriate response.

On each trial, Thorndike placed a hungry cat into a box with food in view outside and then timed the latency of the animal's escape. Thorndike's use of the motive of "practically utter hunger" was widely criticized, with detractors accusing him of starving animals and of experimenting on animals panic-stricken from hunger (e.g., Mills, 1899). Responding to Mills, Thorndike (1899) admitted that many of his animals exhibited "great violence and fury of activity" on early trials, but animals that did not display "mental panic" performed no better than ones that did. Thorndike explained in 1911 that by "utter hunger" he had meant that the animal was hungry enough to eat a hearty meal after the experiments were completed for the day. At that time, "the cats received abundant food to maintain health, growth and spirits . . ." (p. 27).

Thorndike plotted the first animal learning curves, examples of which have been redrawn in Figure 12–2. As you can see, freedom on the early trials in Box A occurred after long latencies, with the cats engaging in many unsuccessful responses before making the correct response by accident. On succeeding trials, the successful movement was performed more and more efficiently until by the end a cat would perform the appropriate response rapidly and smoothly. Cats 3 and 10 both showed excellent memory for the correct response after lengthy intervals without training (38 and 74 days, respectively).

Thorndike concluded that his dissertation research illustrated **stimulus-response (S-R) learning**, the association of "the sense-impression of the interior of the box" with a successful movement. Thorndike stated that the animal did not learn to associate ideas—for example, the idea of confinement with the idea of a movement to produce freedom. Instead, his cats learned "the association of idea or sense impression [S] with *impulse* [R]" (Thorndike, 1911, p. 106). On the issue of animal consciousness, Thorndike was not optimistic:

> The possibility is that animals may have *no images or memories at all, no ideas to associate.* Perhaps the entire fact of association in animals is the presence of sense-impressions with which are associated, by resultant pleasure, certain impulses, and that, therefore, and therefore only, a certain situation brings forth a certain act. (pp. 108–109, italics in the original)

Thorndike's Laws

For Thorndike, association learning in animals was the bonding of sense-impressions (stimuli) with impulses (acts, responses) by the intervention of "resultant pleasure." Correspondingly, Thorndike believed initially that "discomfort" weakened the bond. He called this principle of association the law of effect, which is a restatement of the Spencer-Bain principle (Chapter 9). In 1911, he defined the **law of effect** as follows:

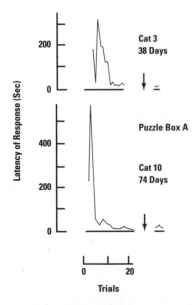

FIGURE 12–2. Examples of the first learning curves; retention is also shown.

Of several responses made to the same situation, those which are accompanied or closely followed by satisfaction to the animal will, other things being equal, be more firmly connected with the situation, so that, when it recurs, they will be more likely to recur; those which are accompanied or closely followed by discomfort to the animal will, other things being equal, have their connections with that situation weakened, so that, when it recurs, they will be less likely to recur. (Thorndike, 1911, p. 244, italics in the original)

In addition, Thorndike stated a second law to account for the learning phenomena he had observed, which he called the **law of exercise**:

Any response to a situation will, other things being equal, be more strongly connected with the situation in proportion to the number of times it has been connected with that situation and to the average vigor and duration of the connections. (Thorndike, 1911, p. 244, italics in the original)

We have encountered the law of exercise in different guises in earlier chapters: for example, in Aristotle's (Chapter 2) statement, "we remember easily what we often ponder," and in much of Ebbinghaus's memory research (Chapter 8). After conducting many human learning studies, Thorndike later modified his laws of effect and exercise (e.g., Thorndike, 1932), concluding that repetition (exercise) without consequences produced little effect and that reinforcement was more important than punishment.

Thorndike realized that his phrases "satisfaction to the animal" and "discomfort to the animal" lacked precision, and he struggled with general definitions for reward and punishment before adopting a behavioral one:

[b]y a satisfying state of affairs is meant one which the animal does nothing to avoid, often doing such things as attain and preserve it. By a discomforting or annoying state of affairs is meant one which the animal commonly avoids and abandons. (Thorndike, 1911, p. 245)

Thorndike's behavioral definition dodges the issue of whether a particular event is inherently satisfying or annoying. If the organism works to obtain the event, then it is reinforcing, no matter how negative the event might be in an absolute sense.

Observations Important for Later Animal Research

In his dissertation, Thorndike cited examples from Romanes's *Animal Intelligence* purporting to show reasoning in cats. From his own research, Thorndike's conclusion was dramatically different. For example, he pointed to the gradual acquisition of associations shown in his learning curves, arguing that reasoning ability should lead to sudden mastery of a complex act, which his animals never exhibited. Instead, everything indicated the gradual strengthening of a bond between an accidental act leading to pleasure and the stimulus situation of confinement in a particular box. "Futile impulses are gradually stamped out. The gradual slope of the time-curve, then, shows the absence of reasoning. They represent the wearing smooth of a path in the brain, not the decisions of a rational consciousness" (Thorndike, 1911, p. 74).

If animals cannot reason, can they learn by imitation or by passive tuition? In experiments with both cats and dogs, Thorndike saw no evidence for imitation, and passive tuition was similarly ineffective, despite widespread belief in its efficacy. When Thorndike (1911) tried passive tuition with his cats, dogs, and a chicken, "[t]he results . . . [demonstrated] that no animal who fails to perform an act in the course of his own impulsive activity will learn it by being put through it" (p. 103).

In his animal research, Thorndike also made a number of observations explored further by later animal researchers. For example, Thorndike's data from cats placed into Box Z raised the question of whether all types of behavior are equally sensitive to reinforcement. All cats had to do to escape from Box Z was to lick or scratch themselves. Because cats ordinarily spend much time in self-grooming, you might expect that the association would be easily formed. However, Thorndike found that the response was learned differently from responses in other boxes.

There is . . . a noticeable tendency . . . to diminish the act until it becomes a mere vestige of a lick or scratch. After the cat gets so that it performs the act soon after being put in, it begins to do it less and less vigorously. The licking degenerates into a mere quick turn of the head with one or two motions up and down with tongue extended. Instead of a hearty scratch, the cat waves its paw up and down rapidly for an instant. Moreover, if sometimes you do not let the cat out after this feeble reaction, it does not at once repeat the movement, as it would do if it depressed a thumb piece, for instance, without success in getting the door open. (Thorndike, 1911, p. 48)

Thorndike's observation and others like it have led to the concept of **learning predispositions**, the idea that evolution has shaped an organism's "associative apparatus" as well as its sensory and motor abilities (e.g., Goodenough, McGuire, & Wallace, 1993; Seligman, 1970). Presumably, hungry cats that groomed themselves instead of seeking food did not survive long enough to pass on this tendency.

Aristotle anticipated Thorndike's observations in *Parva Naturalia,* noting that some experiences are better remembered after only a few repetitions than others often encountered. One example of a biological predisposition in humans is conditioned taste aversion, identified in Chapter 4. Almost all of us have developed an aversion to a particular food, when eating it was followed by illness (e.g., Logue, 1985). This type of conditioning requires only one pairing of the food with stomach upset, and there may be a relatively long interval between the meal and illness (e.g., Klein, 1996). Important research on conditioned taste aversion has been performed by **John Garcia** (1917–), one of the first Hispanic Americans to earn a Ph.D. in psychology. For his contributions, Garcia received APA's Distinguished Scientific Contribution Award in 1979.

Another observation that Thorndike made with his animals that he later explored further with humans was the idea of transfer of training (Chapter 11). Thorndike found that his cats became progressively better at solving new puzzle boxes. The positive transfer that Thorndike's cats exhibited may be seen as an example of **stimulus generalization**, a learning phenomenon extensively investigated by Ivan Pavlov (discussed later). In stimulus generalization, a response associated with a particular stimulus is made to other, similar stimuli. Learning predispositions and transfer of training are only two of

Thorndike's many observations about human and animal learning that remain a part of contemporary learning theory.

Thorndike and Behaviorism

Although we have noted the importance of Thorndike's animal work for behaviorism, the early behaviorists did not consider Thorndike solidly in their camp. Unlike Watson, Thorndike did not reject the study of subjective experience as a part of psychology: He just preferred to study behavior. If support for animal research had been more available when Thorndike completed his classical animal studies, perhaps we would honor him instead of Watson as behaviorism's founder, but Thorndike's employment at Teachers College made him an educational psychologist for most of his career.

Thorndike's dissertation research almost completely overshadowed animal studies performed at about the same time by another psychology graduate student, **Willard Stanton Small** (1870–1943) at Clark University. Small's studies are primarily important for two things they introduced to psychology: the laboratory rat (Small, 1900) and the maze task (Small, 1901).

Unlike Thorndike, Small wanted to study his animals as naturally as possible, and for this reason, he hit upon the idea of the maze as an analog of the burrows of wild rats. For the pattern of his maze, Small constructed a miniature replica of the famous Hampton Court Palace maze. (Near London, Hampton Court Palace was built by Cardinal Thomas Wolsey, who occupied it until 1529. Afterwards, it became a favorite residence of British monarchs, including Henry VIII. Its gardens and its maze are popular tourist attractions. One of your authors well remembers his wife displaying ratlike behavior when frustrated by the Hampton Court maze.) Small's maze and two views of the Hampton Court maze are shown in Figure 12–3.

Small's studies were primarily observational, and his hesitant conclusions were more in Romanes's style than in Thorndike's objective mold. For example, in describing the difference between cats and rats, he wrote:

View from above

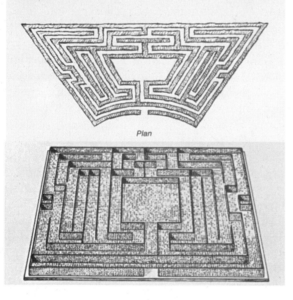

Plan

FIGURE 12–3.   Overhead view and plan of the Hampton Court Palace maze on which Small's rat maze was based.

Source: (top) From Rachlin, Introduction to Modern Behaviorism *(1970) © Her Majesty Queen Elizabeth. (bottom) From Boakes* From Darwin to Behaviourism *(1984).*

The cat, primarily a hunter, is bold, independent, and aggressively open; the rat, . . . primarily the hunted, and only secondarily a hunter, is timid and furtive. His timidity is comparable to

an intellectual obsession. His boldness when displayed is impudent and half apologetic, never self-contained and unconscious like that of the cat. (Small, 1901, p. 208)

In addition to introducing the rat and the maze to psychological experimentation, Small's comments on the rat's olfactory sensitivity and on its ability to traverse a maze without vision led to the question of the sensory mechanisms the rat uses in solving a maze, which Watson investigated extensively.

In his 1898 monograph, Thorndike offered photographs of his apparatus to anyone who requested them, and Harvard graduate student Robert Yerkes sent such a request. Thorndike found Yerkes's interest flattering and eventually sent pictures of several puzzle boxes, which are preserved today in the Robert M. Yerkes Papers at Yale University Medical Library (Burnham, 1972).

Robert Mearns Yerkes

Robert Mearns Yerkes (1876–1956) was the first-born child in a family of farmers who lived near Philadelphia. He described his mother as "a woman of rare sweetness of disposition and unusual ability, beloved of all who knew her . . ." (Yerkes, 1932, p. 382). Yerkes's negative feelings for his father turned him away from the family's agricultural tradition, and the care he received from the family physician, his cousin, during a bout with scarlet fever initially inclined him toward medicine.

In 1892, Yerkes entered Ursinus College in Collegeville, Pennsylvania, and in June 1897, he received his A.B. degree. Offered a $1,000 loan to do graduate work in biology at Harvard, he took it, assuming that he could begin his medical studies in Philadelphia after a year at Harvard. At the end of his first year, Yerkes received another A.B. degree and was given graduate status. With the encouragement of his teachers, he became a candidate for the Ph.D. rather than for the M.D.

Yerkes had another dilemma: He was intensely interested in both zoology and psychology. On the advice of Royce and encouraged by Münsterberg (both Chapter 10), Yerkes decided to combine his interests by devoting himself to comparative psy-

FIGURE 12–4.   Robert Mearns Yerkes in about 1908.

Source: From the Yerkes Collection, by courtesy Yale University Library.

chology. Thus, he transferred from the laboratories of zoology to the laboratory of psychology, and for the next 18 years, Yerkes (Figure 12–4) was associated with Harvard as student, assistant, instructor, and assistant professor. His research was in psychobiology, and he taught courses in comparative and genetic psychology.

Münsterberg's support was crucial, and Yerkes (1932) wrote, "I seriously doubt whether I should have remained in Harvard more than one or two years except for his influence and encouragement" (p. 389). Yerkes received his Ph.D. in 1902 and was offered an instructorship in comparative psychology paying $1,000. When Münsterberg asked him if he could afford to accept the position, Yerkes replied: "No, . . . but I shall, nevertheless" (p. 389).

In fact, remaining at Harvard required true economic sacrifice. As he noted, "To supplement my small and obviously insufficient Harvard salary, . . . I taught in Radcliffe College, Harvard Summer School, and the University Extension Department in Boston" (Yerkes, 1932, p. 392). His low salary and lack of promotion stemmed from Yerkes's continuing interest in comparative psychology. Although this research was supported during President Eliot's tenure, a new administration advised Yerkes that the road to a professorship would be easier if he switched to educational psychology. Thorndike was willing to make the shift, but Yerkes was not, and he was still an assistant professor when he was elected APA president in 1917.

Nevertheless, Yerkes enjoyed his years of animal research at Harvard and especially his associations with his colleagues, which, in addition to Royce and Münsterberg, included William James, George Santayana, Edwin B. Holt, and Ralph Barton Perry. In his research, Yerkes may be said to have worked his way up from primitive creatures to primates, investigating sensory ability, adaptive behavior, and instinct in various invertebrates, amphibians and reptiles, mice, rats, crows and doves, pigs, monkeys and apes, and finally in humans. Yerkes's interests at Harvard later broadened to include human psychopathology and mental testing.

Much of Yerkes's animal research was included in the first animal psychology book written by an American, *The Animal Mind* by Margaret Washburn (Chapter 7). After receiving her Titchener-directed Ph.D. from Cornell in 1894, Washburn taught for several years at Wells College in Aurora, New York, before becoming warden of Sage College, which was the dormitory for women at Cornell. In addition to her administrative duties, Washburn taught a course in animal psychology at Cornell, and she later cited this course as the beginning of her interest in the topic (Washburn, 1932). This interest culminated in *The Animal Mind*, first published in 1908, which was an unbiased, evenhanded, and readable review of experimental studies of animal behavior. Washburn subscribed to Morgan's view that the reason for studying an animal's behavior was to infer its conscious states and the purpose of this was to provide a basis for the analysis of subjective experience in humans.

Many of the studies Washburn reviewed in 1908 reflected the influence of Thorndike's dissertation. In some cases, Thorndike's methods for studying trial-and-error learning were extended to different species, whereas other studies examined his negative conclusions about imitation learning and learning by passive tuition. Nearly all of the experiments Washburn reviewed were conducted at either Clark, Chicago, Johns Hopkins, or Harvard.

Yerkes might have stayed at Harvard, content with his animal research, but in 1917 he received an offer to reorganize psychology and take over the laboratory at the University of Minnesota. He accepted it, and without moving to Minneapolis, he made staffing recommendations, planned the department, and arranged to move the laboratory. At the same time, as APA president, he assumed leadership of psychologists mobilized to support the American war effort in World War I. His group developed the first group intelligence tests, the Army Alpha and Army Beta (Chapter 18).

After the war, Yerkes resigned from the University of Minnesota and stayed in Washington to work in connection with the National Research Council. Yerkes wanted to supervise the completion of the final report on the psychological work during the war, and in addition, he wanted to continue to seek financial support for the use of anthropoid apes in psychobiological research. This lifetime goal came closer to realization when Yerkes accepted a professorship at Yale University.

Supported by Yale President James Rowland Angell (Chapter 11), Yerkes established a laboratory at New Haven to study apes. This was followed by a larger facility at Orange Park, Florida, which Yerkes headed from 1930 until 1942, when the directorship passed to Karl Lashley. From Florida, the primate center moved to Atlanta, Georgia, to become the Yerkes Regional Primate Center of Emory University.

As a result of his primate work, Yerkes and his colleagues and students published many papers and monographs and a few semipopular books (e.g., Yerkes & Learned, 1925). One of his greatest works (Yerkes & Yerkes, 1929) was a compilation of all that was known about apes (in English; German, Russian, and Japanese researchers were also pioneers in primatology) before the opening of the Orange Park facility. *The Great Apes: A Study of Anthropoid Life* was co-authored with his wife, Ada Watterson Yerkes, a Ph.D. biologist.

As a psychologist, or as he preferred, a psychobiologist, of renown in the first half of the 20th century, Yerkes had extensive contact with many people we have considered. For example, a correspondence with

Titchener (Chapter 7) grew out of his teaching of the introductory course in psychology, and Yerkes considered Titchener the most learned psychologist he had ever known. He also corresponded extensively with Watson when the two were working to improve and standardize the methodology for studying vision comparatively in animals.

Although Yerkes and Watson were comfortable collaborators, Yerkes was not a behaviorist. Like Woodworth (Chapter 11), Yerkes objected to people who tried to dictate the "appropriate" method and results. He rejected the extreme objectivism of biologists such as Loeb "because it impressed me as dangerous in its restrictions and negations" (Yerkes, 1932, p. 396), and he rejected Watson's behaviorism on the same grounds. Despite his interest in organic structure and function, Yerkes was not opposed to the study of consciousness and mind, and he credited Titchener with "[w]hatever interest I have in introspection, competence in its use, and appreciation of its results, and whatever I know of the psychology of the self, as contrasted with objective psychology . . ." (p. 392).

Yerkes is also remembered for the **Yerkes-Dodson law**, which holds that the optimal level of arousal depends on task difficulty: For a simple task, high arousal aids performance, whereas for more complex tasks, the optimal level declines. This relation was based on the work of one of the many doctoral students Yerkes supervised at Harvard (Yerkes & Dodson, 1908).

E. G. Boring (Chapter 1) considered Yerkes "the leader in the American movement of comparative psychology, not merely because of his belief in comparative study, but also because of the volume of his work, his persistence, and the way . . . he threw his influence toward the organization of investigation" (Boring, 1950, p. 628). As we have noted, Yerkes contributed significantly to mental testing and to the study of primates, particularly the apes.

In 1909, Yerkes co-authored a paper introducing Pavlov's animal work to an American audience (Yerkes & Morgulis, 1909). The paper carefully discussed Pavlov's method of salivary conditioning in dogs, although the authors failed to see the generality of the Pavlovian method. "It seems, therefore, as if Pawlow's method were especially important in animal psychology as a means to the intensive study of the mental life of a limited number of mammals. The dog evidently is especially well suited to the experiments" (p. 262). (The use of w's rather than v's in the spelling of Pavlov suggests that Yerkes and Morgulis [and American psychologists in general] first discovered Pavlov through German publications [Skinner, 1981].) Pavlov's reflex conditioning became a major part of the psychology of Watson—who recognized its generality—and Russian objective psychology is another important antecedent of modern behaviorism.

OBJECTIVE PSYCHOLOGY IN RUSSIA

Russian objective psychology began not with Pavlov, but with a man born a generation before Pavlov—Ivan Sechenov. Sechenov is also considered the founder of modern Russian physiology.

Ivan Mikhailovich Sechenov

Ivan Mikhailovich Sechenov (1829–1905) was born in a village now called Sechenovo. As a youth, he was fortunate to have a governess who taught him French and German, which he later used on trips to study in Europe. When he was 14, Sechenov entered a St. Petersburg college of military engineering. Because of trouble with the college authorities in his 4th year, Sechenov was forced into an unattractive posting near Kiev. After a disappointing infatuation in Kiev, Sechenov borrowed some money and set out for Moscow to study medicine.

At this point in Russian history, the teaching of medicine was in a sorry state. Lectures on any topic were usually out of date because of efforts to keep out foreign ideas. Sechenov's exposure to stimulating lectures from a professor of physiology convinced him to become a researcher in physiology instead of a physician.

When his mother died during his last year at the university (his father had died earlier), Sechenov sold his claim to the family inheritance and left for Germany to study with Johannes Müller (Chapter 6). Near the end of his life, Müller's lectures on the vertebrate genitals proved disappointing to Sechenov, and

he was more impressed with Émil du Bois-Reymond (Chapter 6), although the latter treated the young Russian with coolness. With little guidance, Sechenov learned all he could about electrophysiological research before departing for Leipzig and Vienna.

From Vienna, Sechenov went to Heidelberg to study chemistry with Bunsen and physiology with Helmholtz (Chapter 6). In 1859, Sechenov returned to St. Petersburg to find that during his time abroad, there had been momentous changes in Russia. Now there was great interest in learning about the new discoveries in physiology. As a result, Sechenov was in demand as the first Russian in years to have returned after extensive training abroad. He became an assistant professor at the Military-Medical Academy, which was part of the University of St. Petersburg. Sechenov is shown in Figure 12–5 in his laboratory at the Military-Medical Academy.

FIGURE 12–5. Ivan Sechenov in his laboratory at the Military-Medical Academy.

Source: From Boakes, From Darwin to Behaviourism *(1984), by courtesy Harvard College Library.*

In 1862, Sechenov left Russia to study in Paris with Claude Bernard (Chapter 6). Sechenov was interested in voluntary control over normally involuntary actions—the ability to avoid scratching an itch, for example—and his Paris research concerned this topic. Earlier, Eduard Weber (1804–1891), Ernst Weber's (Chapter 6) brother, had made an important discovery related to Sechenov's interest: Electrical stimulation of a frog's vagus nerve caused a decrease in the animal's heart rate. Weber had demonstrated that nerve excitation could produce physiological inhibition. Weber also noticed that spinal reflexes were sometimes more reduced in normal animals than in animals without their cerebrums, which led him to theorize that the cerebrum might have inhibitory influences on reflex activity.

Using the reflexive withdrawal of a frog's leg dipped in a mild acid solution, Sechenov extended Weber's finding. He found that stimulation of certain parts of the frog's brain with a salt crystal depressed the withdrawal reflex. This was the first experimental illustration that supported Weber's suggestion that brain stimulation might inhibit reflex activity. Sechenov believed that his demonstration of inhibitory actions in the central nervous system paved the way for a physiological analysis of mental processes.

Returning to St. Petersburg, Sechenov wrote a paper expressing clearly his view that the brain is simply a center for organizing reflexes. Planning initially to call this work *An Attempt to Bring Physiological Bases into Mental Processes,* the St. Petersburg censor required him to change it instead to *Reflexes of the Brain* (1863). The purpose of the change was to make the article seem technical and uninteresting (Boakes, 1984), so that its mechanistic approach to the brain would be little read by people who might have their religious faith undermined.

Actually, *Reflexes of the Brain* was an appropriate title. La Mettrie's materialistic philosophy (Chapter 4) became in Sechenov's hands a physiological theory in which all forms of behavior are reflexes of the brain. Sechenov considered emotional behavior merely reflexes whose intensity is heightened by brain activity. He saw voluntary behavior as reflex chains assembled during development as the result of involuntary learning. We will see Sechenov's view of thought as reflexes with inhibited motor expression (Gray, 1979) echoed in Watson's notion of thought as subvocal activity.

Sechenov learned his psychology from the French philosophers after La Mettrie, and La Mettrie's belief that appropriate tuition would transform an ape into "a little gentleman" is reflected in Sechenov's suggestion that with a European upbringing, various ethnic minorities (e.g., Lapps and Bashkirs) would develop skills and interests little different from that of an educated European. Watson's (1924/1970) pronouncement, "Give me a dozen healthy infants, well-formed, and my own specified world to bring them up in and I'll guarantee to take any one at random and train him to become any type of specialist I might select" (p. 104), makes the same point. Contrast these attitudes with those of Sechenov's British contemporary, Francis Galton (Chapter 9), expressed in *Hereditary Genius.*

Sechenov resigned his St. Petersburg position in 1870 and soon found employment at Odessa. There, he wrote another article on physiology and psychology entitled *Who Must Investigate the Problems of Psychology and How.* In it, Sechenov asked psychologists to abandon the introspective analysis of subjective experience and concentrate on the study of reflexive behavior in animals. He believed that if physiologists turned to the study of psychology, the result might be slow, but real, progress rather than the illusion of rapid progress that he felt characterized psychology. To his question of who must investigate, the answer was the physiologist. To the question of how, the answer was by studying reflexes.

Sechenov's most important contributions for psychology were the idea of inhibitory action in the nervous system, the extension of physiology into the domain of psychology, and his influence on the next generation of Russian neurophysiologists. Although Sechenov's neurophysiological speculations were dazzling, there was little evidence to sustain them. Ivan Pavlov provided the empirical observations needed to flesh out Sechenov's outline.

Ivan Petrovich Pavlov

Ivan Petrovich Pavlov (1849–1936) was born in Ryazan, a small Russian town southeast of Moscow. His father was the town's priest, and his mother was a priest's daughter; from his father, Pavlov developed a love of gardening and of hard physical exercise. Pavlov's position as the oldest of 11 children brought him responsibility and taught him the value of hard work.

A severe fall as a youth delayed his entrance to the local school, and Pavlov spent much of his recuperation with his godfather, the abbot of a nearby monastery. His godfather lived a life devoted to his duties and studies, and as an adult, Pavlov did likewise.

Pavlov began his formal education at the Ryazan Ecclesiastical High School, where he obtained a more progressive education than he would have if he had attended the secular state schools. At this time, a Minister of Education introduced into the state high schools a rigid educational program that excluded the teaching of science. By contrast, in his religious school, Pavlov was exposed to the "literature of the '60s," which included such topics as Darwin's theory of evolution.

In 1870, Pavlov left Ryazan for St. Petersburg University, where he planned to study science. By his third year, he had chosen to be a physiologist. Because Sechenov left St. Petersburg in 1870, Pavlov received his introduction to physiology from Sechenov's successor, Ilya Cyon (Boakes, 1984). Cyon was an excellent researcher and an inspirational lecturer whose unpleasant personality resulted in his eventual expulsion from the university and departure from Russia. Under Cyon's supervision, Pavlov studied the nerves of the pancreas, earning a gold medal and graduating from the university in 1875.

Next, Pavlov studied at the Medico-Surgical Academy in St. Petersburg, where he received his second degree in 1879. Shifting his research interests from the pancreas to the innervation of the heart, Pavlov earned a second gold medal. Because of his exceptional research ability, Pavlov was sought after by doctoral students even before he had earned his own doctorate. Based on his reputation, in 1878 Pavlov was asked to take charge of the small animal laboratory of the director of the academy's medical clinic, Professor Sergei Botkin. Botkin had attended du Bois-Reymond's lectures in Berlin with Sechenov and in the intervening 2 decades had become one of the most influential men in Russian medicine. Botkin's belief in nervism, the pervasive importance of the nervous system to disease, undoubtedly influenced Pavlov's later commitment to the same view.

In 1883, Pavlov received his Doctorate of Medicine, but his financial situation remained precarious. He had gotten married in 1881, and he and his wife Sara (Figure 12–6) suffered extreme poverty for the first several years of their marriage. Their poverty was partly due to the scarcity of decent research jobs and to Pavlov's refusal to allow Sara to work. In addition, their situation was undoubtedly worsened by Pavlov's lack of concern over worldly matters.

In retrospect, some of the stories of Pavlov's impracticality are amusing, but they were undoubt-

FIGURE 12–6.   Ivan and Sara Pavlov at about the time of their marriage.

Source: Babkin Collection; Osler Library, McGill University by courtesy Harvard College Library.

edly not funny to his wife. For example, during their engagement, Sara visited Pavlov in St. Petersburg. Aware of her tendency to spend money too freely, Sara gave all her funds to Pavlov at the beginning of the visit, and he paid for everything during her stay except a pair of shoes that she bought for herself. Unfortunately, Pavlov had spent not only all of Sara's money but all of his own, and Sara returned home in a state of nearly penniless misery. Upon arriving, Sara opened her luggage to find only one shoe inside. Pavlov had kept the other shoe to remember her by (Babkin, 1949).

Pavlov's carelessness with money even extended to a 1923 trip to America.

> Confused by rush and roar he sat for a moment on a seat in Grand Central Station, Manhattan. A small handbag containing much of his money [$2,000] lay on the seat beside him and with characteristic absorption in the seething human laboratory around him, he forgot his worldly goods completely. When he rose to go, the handbag was gone. It had been taken from under his very nose. "Ah, well," sighed Pavlov gently, "one must not put temptation in the way of the needy." (Gerow, 1988, p. 12)

Pavlov's negligence in his personal life was offset by his practicality, ingenuity, and dedication to science. "Pavlov said of himself: 'I am an experimenter from head to foot. My whole life has been given to experiment'" (Babkin, 1949, p. 110). As one illustration of his dedication, on a particular day during the Russian Revolution, Pavlov arrived at his laboratory at 9 A.M., his usual time. An assistant came in 10 minutes late, explaining that he had been delayed by the Revolution and shooting in the streets. Unsympathetically, Pavlov scolded the assistant, admonishing him to get up 10 minutes earlier the next time there was a revolution.

Even Pavlov's final illness illustrates his dedication to his work. After an apparently mild attack of the grippe (influenza), against the arguments of his family, Pavlov went to his laboratory on February 21, 1936, and spent the day there, returning at dinnertime. The next day he awoke with a fever, and his condition worsened rapidly. Pavlov died early in the morning on February 27.

Pavlov's Research on the Digestive System

One of the hallmarks of Pavlov's research was that he almost always avoided *acute* experiments, in which an animal is anesthetized, an organ isolated and studied quickly, and then the animal is sacrificed. Instead, he used *chronic* preparations, in which his animal subjects were conscious, healthy, and capable of being repeatedly observed. Like many animal researchers of the period, Pavlov agonized over experiments employing vivisection. Pavlov felt that his work was justified because the only way humans can learn many of the laws of the organic world is through experimentation and observation of animals. Although he was often criticized by anti-vivisectionists, there is ample evidence of Pavlov's kindness toward and dedication to his experimental animals, and

> On a monument at the Institute of Experimental Medicine to the dogs used in his experiments Pavlov had carved, "The dog, man's helper and friend from pre-historic times, may justly be offered as a sacrifice to science; but let this always be done without unnecessary suffering" . . . (Dewsbury, 1990, pp. 322–323)

Pavlov's research on the mechanisms for the secretion of different digestive juices began in earnest in 1890, when he became a professor of pharmacology at the Military-Medical Academy in St. Petersburg and shortly thereafter was named director of the Physiology Department at the Institute of Experimental Medicine. These appointments gave Pavlov the space and facilities to pursue his interests.

In an early study of the digestive system, Pavlov's chronic preparation involved an operation to create an isolated portion of the stomach, a "gastric pouch," open to the outside of the dog's body so that he could study its contents at will. The German physiologist Heidenhain had nearly accomplished such a preparation, and Pavlov had studied the surgical method in Heidenhain's Breslau laboratory. However, Heidenhain's pouch required cutting nearly all the nerves to the externalized stomach tissue. Because Pavlov believed that most bodily functions were under nervous control (nervism), he sought to preserve the nerves to the isolated stomach tissue. The surgical procedure proved to be difficult, and it was only with iron determination that Pavlov—called by Sechenov the best surgeon in Europe (Gray, 1979)—eventually succeeded.

Pavlov pioneered "sham feeding" experiments, in which a dog was allowed to eat, but the food fell out through an opening cut in the esophagus. Feeding actually occurred through a second opening—or fistula—in the dog's stomach, through which Pavlov could study the animal's gastric secretions.

Pavlov found that the taste of food triggered the release of gastric juices in the stomach even though the food never reached that organ. These "psychical secretions," as Pavlov called them, prepare the stomach to digest the food that normally reaches it. Pavlov demonstrated that psychic secretion release is under nervous system control and in particular, under the control of the vagus nerve. In the days before the ready availability of over-the-counter antacid preparations, Pavlov bottled and sold his dogs' gastric juices as a treatment for human stomach ailments, nearly doubling his laboratory's income (Babkin, 1949).

In 1897, Pavlov published *Work of the Principal Digestive Glands*, which dealt with his research on the digestive system and only incidentally mentioned psychical secretions. From this book, Pavlov gained an international reputation and the Nobel Prize in medicine in 1904. However, by 1904, Pavlov had already begun the research for which he is most famous, and his address at Stockholm was devoted to conditioned reflexes.

The Conditioned Reflex

Pavlov's serious study of psychical secretions or psychic reflexes started in the latter half of the 1890s, at about the same time that Thorndike was engaged in his animal learning experiments. Pavlov later credited Thorndike's research with providing the experimental groundwork for studies of animal conditioning:

> [T]he American School of Psychologists— already interested in the comparative study of psychology—evinced a disposition to subject

the highest nervous activities of animals to experimental analysis under various specially devised conditions. We may fairly regard the treatise by Thorndyke [sic], *The Animal Intelligence* (1898), as the starting point for systematic investigations of this kind. (Pavlov, 1927/1960, pp. 5–6)

Although Pavlov's psychical secretions had been observed in both the gastric glands and the salivary glands, Pavlov concentrated on the latter, using a method one of his colleagues had developed for the long-term study of a dog's salivary glands (Koshtoyants, 1957). The first experiments on psychical secretions were conducted by Stefan Wolfson or Vul'fson (Windholz, 1990), working under Pavlov's direction. (Like many other names in translations of Russian literature [see Bagg, 1972, for a listing of different spellings of Pavlov and others], various spellings of Wolfson can be found. Our spelling is that used in Pavlov [1928].) Wolfson found that the sight of food was enough to elicit salivary secretion. Further, the quantity and quality of the saliva depended on what was actually shown, whether it was edible or inedible, for example.

Similar experiments were conducted by another student, Anton Snarsky. Snarsky interpreted his results introspectively, in terms of the dog's inner world of thoughts, desires, and emotions. In Snarsky's opinion, the dog's salivation was a result of its psychical reaction, and this inner state of the animal was unavailable to physiological investigation.

However, by this time Pavlov had decided to replace the notion of psychical secretion with physiological concepts. As a result, he and Snarsky differed bitterly, and Snarsky was finally forced to leave Pavlov's laboratory. As Pavlov expressed the controversy,

> Snarsky clung to his subjective explanation of the phenomena, but I, putting aside fantasy and seeing the scientific barrenness of such a solution, began to seek for another exit from this difficult position. After persistent deliberation, . . . I decided finally, in regard to the so-called psychical stimulation, to remain in the role of a pure physiologist, i.e., of *an objective external observer and experimenter, having to do exclusively with external phenomena and their relations.* I

attacked this problem with a new co-worker, . . . and from this beginning there followed a series of investigations with my highly esteemed collaborators, which has lasted for more than twenty years. (Pavlov, 1928, Vol. 1, pp. 38–39, italics added)

As an "objective external observer [of] . . . external phenomena and their relations," Pavlov was clearly in the behaviorist mold.

In keeping with his rejection of an explanation of conditioning by appeal to the dog's mental life, Pavlov dropped the term "psychical reflex," using instead the term "conditional reflex." Note that the word is "conditional," not "conditioned." Yerkes and Morgulis (1909) decided to use the "ed" versions because they considered it quite likely that Pavlov himself had sanctioned "conditioned" and "unconditioned" in lectures given in London in 1906. Following Yerkes and Morgulis and many others, we too will use the "ed" forms (e.g., conditioned reflex).

Conditioning was still a side issue for Pavlov until a report was received in 1902 about a momentous finding by two British physiologists, Sir William Maddock Bayliss (1860–1924) and Ernest Henry Starling (1866–1927). Bayliss and Starling found that some information in the digestive system is conveyed by chemical signals, or hormones (a word they coined), and they discovered the first hormone (secretin).

Because of his nervism bias, Pavlov had assumed that signals from one part of the digestive system (e.g., the mouth) to another part (e.g., secretory glands in the stomach) were conveyed by the nervous system. Perhaps some of this information was carried via chemical messages. At first, Pavlov did not accept Bayliss and Starling's work, and when full details of their experiment became available, Pavlov asked one of his assistants to replicate it. It was soon obvious that secretin stimulated secretion from a digestive system organ Pavlov had assumed was completely under nervous control. As a result, Pavlov's study of digestive system physiology decreased and his research on conditioned reflexes increased.

As we indicated, Pavlov's Nobel Prize address was devoted to reflexive conditioning, and the reac-

tion of physiologists to his new work was quite negative. For example, Sir Charles Sherrington (Chapter 17) advised Pavlov to return to "real physiology." However, Pavlov's Nobel Prize insulated him from such criticism, and his work on conditioning continued.

In contrast to Pavlov, University of Pennsylvania doctoral student **Edwin Burket Twitmyer** (1873–1943) had no established position and little economic security when he observed the conditioning of the patellar (knee jerk) reflex to the sound of a bell. Although he reported his observations at the 1904 APA convention, his discovery drew only an uncomfortable silence from the gathered American psychologists. Coon (1982) concluded that Twitmyer's contemporaries, chiefly interested in identifying the contents of consciousness, were poorly prepared to realize the significance of the conditioned reflex. As a physiologist, Pavlov had no qualms about studying a "primitive" reflex as a window on the central nervous system's operations, and Pavlov, not Twitmyer, is recognized as the discoverer of the conditioned reflex.

Research on Conditioning

Pavlov assumed that all behavior consists of reflexes, some depending on inborn anatomical connections between the central nervous system and effectors (muscles and glands), and some that are acquired through experience with the environment. Pavlov systematically studied acquired reflexes for the last 3 decades of his life.

To study reflex conditioning, Pavlov and his colleagues typically used the preparation shown in Figure 12–7, which shows a dog that has had a minor surgical procedure so that its salivation can be precisely recorded. The dog has been trained to stand quietly in the harness.

Note that Pavlov's choice of animal and of the salivary response was essentially arbitrary. He believed that he was studying the general laws of higher nervous activity, which were applicable to any higher animal and to any reflex. Subsequent reflexive conditioning research has tended to sup-

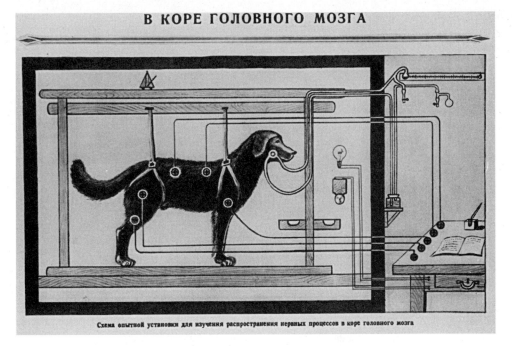

В КОРЕ ГОЛОВНОГО МОЗГА

Схема опытной установки для изучения распространения нервных процессов в коре головного мозга

FIGURE 12–7. Pavlov's dog prepared for conditioning.

Source: Archives of the History of American Psychology.

port this belief, and the principles Pavlov established have been validated over a broad array of different behaviors, in a variety of species.

In a typical Pavlovian study, a conditioned reflex was established by presenting a neutral stimulus (**conditioned stimulus** or **CS**—a stimulus that does not initially trigger salivation) with an **unconditioned stimulus** (**UCS**—a stimulus that innately triggers salivation). Salivation to the UCS is the **unconditioned response** (**UCR**). After several pairings of the CS and the UCS, the CS alone begins to elicit salivation, which is called the **conditioned response** (**CR**).

Pavlov found two conditions necessary for the development of a CR: temporal contiguity and repeatedly pairing the CS and UCS. Contiguity and repetition were first mentioned by Aristotle and developed further by Hume (Chapter 4) and his successors. Further, Pavlov found it important for the CS to precede the UCS; neither strict simultaneity (**simultaneous conditioning**) nor presenting the UCS before the CS (**backward conditioning**) results

in significant conditioning. A slight delay between the CS and UCS (**delayed conditioning**) is often optimal for conditioning, as long as the CS is still present when the UCS begins. If the CS presentation has ended and some time passes before the UCS begins, the conditioning is called **trace conditioning**, which Pavlov found difficult to achieve.

Using the basic procedure, perhaps pairing a tuning fork tone (CS) with meat powder (UCS), Pavlov and his associates elucidated virtually all of the basic conditioning phenomena. For example, Pavlov and a colleague found that once a conditioned reflex has been acquired, repeatedly presenting the CS without the UCS eventually causes the animal to stop salivating to the CS (**extinction**).

In further studies, another colleague, B. P. Babkin, found that the extinguished CR reappears under certain conditions. For example, a dog conditioned to salivate at the sight of a dish of food by being allowed to eat from it had its salivary response extinguished by repeatedly being shown the dish without being allowed to eat from it. Once the CR had disappeared, the animal rested for a few hours, and then the dish was again presented. The CR reappeared at almost full strength, and the phenomenon—reappearance of the CR after a rest interval following extinction—is called **spontaneous recovery**.

Babkin also found that recovery from extinction would occur if he presented another strong, but irrelevant, stimulus. For example, a dog whose salivary response to the sight of a food dish had been extinguished began to salivate again to the dish after Babkin placed a little dilute acid into its mouth. Later study indicated that the irrelevant stimulus did not have to produce the UCR in order for **disinhibition** to occur. A loud sound was sufficient to restore the CR, if it happened during the CS presentation to an animal whose response had been extinguished.

Pavlov and his colleagues also studied the use of a CS as a UCS in further conditioning (**higher-order conditioning**). For example, once a dog has been conditioned to salivate to a tone (CS) by pairing it with meat powder (UCS), another neutral stimulus (e.g., a light) can be paired with the tone to eventually produce the conditioned response. The demonstration of higher-order conditioning was considered essential support for the claim that all behavior represents chains of conditioned reflexes. Although Pavlov did not actually make this claim, others did, including Clark Hull (Chapter 13) and John Watson (Malone, 1991).

Pavlov also called the stimuli that come to signal biologically important events (CSs) the **first-signal system**, that is, the first signals of reality. But humans have a **second-signal system**, language, or symbols of symbols, which are presumably learned by higher-order conditioning. Pavlov used the distinction between a first-signal system and a second-signal system to categorize people into artistic types, dependent on the first-signal system, and intellectual types that depend primarily on the second-signal system.

Other phenomena studied by Pavlov and his co-workers included stimulus generalization—that is, responding to a stimulus similar, but not identical, to the original CS. For example, a dog trained to salivate to one tone also salivates less copiously to a slightly higher or lower tone. If two tones are presented alternately, with one always followed by the UCS and the other never followed by it, eventually the dog learns to discriminate between them (**conditioned discrimination**). That is, the generalized response extinguishes, leaving only the conditioned response.

However, when the discrimination became too difficult for the animal, Pavlov observed a phenomenon important both for his brain function theory and for the generalization of his findings to humans: **experimental neurosis**. Experimental neurosis was first observed in 1921 in visual discrimination experiments performed by one of Pavlov's female students, N. R. Shenger-Krestovnikova. In this study, a dog learned to distinguish a circle from an ellipse, with feeding always occurring after the circle and never occurring after the ellipse. The discrimination was quickly made when there was a large difference between the shapes, but as the ellipse became more circular, discrimination slowed until the animal reached the limit of its discrimination ability. Pavlov (1927/1960) described the animal's subsequent behavior as follows:

> After three weeks of work upon this differentiation not only did the discrimination fail to improve, but it became considerably worse, and finally disappeared altogether. At the same time the whole behaviour of the animal underwent an abrupt change. The hitherto quiet dog began to squeal in its stand, kept wriggling about, tore off . . . the apparatus for mechanical stimulation of the skin, and bit through the tubes connecting the animal's room with the observer. . . . On being taken into the experimental room the dog now barked violently, which was also contrary to its usual custom. . . (p. 291)

Pavlov believed that experimental neurosis developed when his animals experienced a conflict between incompatible conditioned-response tendencies; in this case, between the tendency to salivate at the sight of the nearly circular ellipse or to not salivate to it. As a physiologist, Pavlov incorporated this idea into a theory of brain functioning.

Pavlov's Theory of Brain Function in Conditioning

Pavlov began with the familiar reflex arc, as introduced originally by Descartes. As we noted in

Chapter 11, Dewey's (1896) reinterpretation of the reflex arc concept led to functionalism.

A reflex arc's components consist of (1) a receptor organ (e.g., the rods and cones in the eye's retina) that changes energy from the physical world into messages in the nervous system, (2) conductors or nerve cells that process the information received by the receptor and provide a link to (3) an effector organ (muscles or glands). Following Sechenov, Pavlov held that unconditioned reflexes occur through connections between sensory and motor nerves in the lower parts of the central nervous system—the spinal cord and subcortical brain areas. Pavlov further assumed that conditioned reflexes involve cortical circuitry, because studies of decorticated animals indicated that they were apparently unable to acquire conditioned reflexes involving sophisticated processing of sensory information.

Pavlov combined the reflex arc's first two components into something he called the "analyzer," which includes the receptor organ and the neurons that take information from it to the brain, as well as the brain areas that analyze the information and are responsible for perception. In Pavlov's view, both the CS and the UCS act first on the relevant analyzers, arousing neural activity in their cortical portions. This neural activity is an "excitatory process" that occurs in the different CS and UCS "centers." Further, Pavlov assumed that the excitatory strength of the UCS is stronger than that for the CS and that the most strongly excited center attracts toward itself weaker excitation reaching the system simultaneously. As a consequence, the excitation reaching the CS center will be attracted to the UCS center and a connection between the CS and UCS will be formed, resulting in the CR. Pavlov's notion of the attraction of weaker activity to stronger activity as the basis for the CS-UCS association is similar to James's statement of the basis for his "law of neural habit": "*When two elementary brain-processes have been active together or in immediate succession, one of them, on reoccurring, tends to propagate its excitement into the other*" (James, 1890, Vol. 1, p. 566, italics in the original).

The excitatory processes (or inhibitory processes) spread in a wavelike fashion over surrounding locations, weakening as they get farther from their centers. To explain generalization, Pavlov assumed that stimuli similar to the CS arouse centers that are close to the CS center; increasingly dissimilar stimuli presumably have their centers farther from the CS center, producing correspondingly less CR (i.e., less generalization). On the other hand, discrimination training in which two CSs are presented alternately, with one always followed by the UCS and the other never followed by the UCS, takes effect when the nonreinforced center begins to transmit waves of inhibition instead of excitation. Experimental neurosis occurs when an unavoidable stimulus simultaneously triggers both strong excitation and strong inhibition.

Pavlov's evidence for this theory was completely behavioral. He never actually measured cortical electrical activity to see if it fit his theoretical concepts, and subsequent research into neural functioning has not supported Pavlov's notions. When Pavlov was developing his ideas of brain function in the early 20th century, there were so many unanswered questions that his neurological theorizing was not all that farfetched. For example, a major contemporary theory held that the nerves formed an interconnected network (Chapter 17), in which it was possible to imagine that there could be a spreading of excitation or inhibition as Pavlov hypothesized. It was not until Santiago Ramón y Cajal convincingly described the separateness of neurons that most experts abandoned the idea of the nervous system's unitary nature. Although Pavlov was familiar with Ramón y Cajal's work and with Sherrington's studies showing that spinal reflexes could be analyzed in terms of the actions of specific neurons and their synaptic connections, he failed to modify his explanatory ideas. "[I]t is as though, in 1900 or thereabouts, he stopped listening to what was going on elsewhere" (Gray, 1979, p. 102). Fortunately, Pavlov's importance for psychology does not rest on his theory of brain function.

Personality Types and Psychopathology

In order to appreciate the basis for Pavlov's theory of personality types, you need to recall that he and his colleagues observed the same dogs over long periods, often for years, becoming quite familiar with their dogs' temperaments. Also, each dog's behavior was studied in many different experimental situations, and behavioral consistencies were easy to see.

Pavlov categorized his animals into four temperament types based on three variables: the strengths of their excitatory and inhibitory processes, the balance or equilibrium between the processes, and the mobility or lability of the processes. Pavlov's four temperament types were first proposed by Galen (Chapter 2) and were based on the Hippocratic idea of four humors: sanguine (excessive blood), melancholic (excessive black bile), choleric (too much yellow bile), and phlegmatic (excessive phlegm). Before you conclude that Pavlov was archaic in his categories, note that some modern personality theorists (e.g., Eysenck; Chapter 16) still use these labels and temperaments.

For Pavlov, strong but balanced excitatory and inhibitory processes lead to different types of dogs depending on how easily the processes can be set in motion. Easily triggered processes produce a sanguine dog (lively, readily conditioned); a phlegmatic personality (inert, slow to condition) results from relatively inactive processes. If the excitatory processes are dominant over the inhibitory, the result is a choleric temperament (impetuous, difficulty with discriminations). Finally, weak excitatory and inhibitory processes lead to a melancholic personality (depressed, slow to condition), irrespective of the ease with which the processes can be activated. Note that, for Pavlov, environmental conditioning was mediated by an animal's temperament, which differentiates Pavlov from later behaviorists.

While developing his theory of personality differences, Pavlov was also studying psychopathology. As we indicated, too fine a discrimination caused experimental neurosis in the dogs. The question was, How do stress and personality combine to produce a particular type of mental disorder?

At 80, Pavlov began to visit psychiatric wards, where he observed and discussed the cases with psychiatrists. Soon he began to talk of psychotics and neurotics as though they were dogs whose conditioning had gone awry; his explanations and treatments for the human disorders were based on his theories of brain function. For example, the sedative bromide was assumed to strengthen the inhibitory process, and it became Pavlov's main remedy, along with sleep. Because of Pavlov's recommendation, sleep therapy became popular in the Soviet Union, but it has not caught on in other parts of the world. In general, Pavlov's importance for psychopathology stems more from his method than from his actual findings and theorizing: He was among the first to bring abnormal behavior under experimental investigation (Gray, 1979). Dews (1981) concluded that Pavlov's direct impact on psychiatry was slight and that it was too early to assess his indirect effect.

Pavlov and His Laboratory Coworkers

From 1897 to 1936, Pavlov was assisted by at least 146 different students and colleagues, most of whom were from the Soviet Union (Windholz, 1990). Pavlov excluded women from his laboratory in the early 1900s because of an early conflict with a woman in the laboratory, admitted only 3 women from 1905 until 1910, but after 1910 included them readily among his laboratory personnel. Ultimately, his coworkers in the study of higher nervous activity included at least 20 women, among them his daughter.

New workers in Pavlov's laboratory were required to read previous dissertations, because before the 1920s there was no systematic exposition of the work on conditioned reflexes. They were also assigned to a project and required to attend Pavlov's seminars. Finally, the new worker was given a dog with a fistula in one parotic gland to allow measurement of its salivary response.

According to Jasper Ten-Cate, a Dutch citizen, the atmosphere in Pavlov's laboratories was congenial, and a new worker was quickly made to feel "at home" (Windholz, 1990). Pavlov was not a distant figure to his coworkers, because he spent most of his workday in the laboratory. "Every morning Pavlov would sit in a large room, where any co-worker could approach him. The co-workers would report new experimental findings, listen to his comments and explanations, and occasionally dare to disagree with him" (p. 67).

The reminiscences of former Pavlovians give the impression that having worked with the master was a signal event in their lives. Although Pavlov was often approachable and pleasant, many Pavlovians experienced "Pavlov's loud verbal abuse and threatening gestures" (Windholz, 1990, p. 68). Most of these attacks occurred because of a coworker's failure to follow established procedures precisely. Easily angered, Pavlov was also quick to apologize if he was in the wrong. Boris Babkin (1949), a student and long-time friend, attributed Pavlov's yelling at his associates to the style among Russian officials of the period, who "considered it necessary to instill fear into their subordinates by raising their voices" (p. 120). Despite his fiery temperament, Babkin concluded that Pavlov's closest associates were not afraid of him.

In the 40 years Pavlov devoted to the study of higher nervous activity, he and his coworkers published at least 532 papers (Windholz, 1990). Given the turmoil in Russia during the period of Pavlov's research (e.g., World War I, the Bolshevik Revolution), the output of his laboratories was remarkable and surely a credit to the inspiration of Pavlov himself.

Pavlov's Influence

Pavlov was a great hero to the Soviets, both because of his international scientific reputation and because his materialistic approach to the problems of mind and behavior fit nicely with the Soviet rejection of spiritualism. As evidence of Soviet support, a 1921 decree over Lenin's signature established a committee whose task was to see that the conditions were optimal for the work of Pavlov and his colleagues. By the same decree, Pavlov and his wife received double food rations.

In 1950, Pavlov was in effect canonized by the Soviet Academy of Sciences. As a result, in the ensuing decades there has been a great accumulation of experimental psychological data in Russia but little critical examination of Pavlovian theory.

Outside Russia, Pavlov's influence has gone through several phases. First, behaviorism adopted Pavlov's objective language of conditioned reflexes, without adding his actual methods and theories to its repertoire. In part, this was caused by the early lack of American access to English translations of his major papers. The scarcity of translated material had an even greater effect on the international influence of Pavlov's contemporaries and rivals, such as Vladimir Bekhterev (discussed later) and Lev Vygotsky (Chapter 20).

Behaviorism's interest in Pavlov was reciprocated by Pavlov. He particularly approved of the behaviorist belief that the behavior of people is more important than speculation about their conscious states, and Pavlov almost certainly knew of the similarity between his methods and assumptions and those of behaviorism (Windholz, 1983). Pavlov's approval of Watsonian behaviorism is probably at least partly responsible for Pavlov's extreme reaction to criticisms by Lashley in his 1929 APA presidential address and Edwin Guthrie (Chapter 13) in 1930. Pavlov (1932) responded to both of these critics in a *Psychological Review* article, "The reply of a physiologist to psychologists." Lashley's and Guthrie's criticisms aside, Pavlov fully expected American behaviorism to continue his work on the conditioned reflex.

The second phase of Pavlov's American influence came with Clark Hull's (p. 312) attempt to develop a comprehensive, mathematically formulated learning theory in the 1930s and 1940s. Hull borrowed freely from Pavlov's data and adopted many of his concepts, while discarding any Pavlovian references to brain physiology. As in the earlier influence, Pavlov's methodology was not used to study animal behavior; Thorndike's technique continued to dominate American comparative psychology.

The third phase of Pavlov's influence came in the 1950s and 1960s, when the distinction between Pavlovian (or classical) conditioning and Thorndikian (or instrumental) conditioning had been clearly drawn (Gray, 1979). The distinction led psychologists such as O. H. Mowrer (Chapter 13) to construct "two-factor" theories, which assume that classical conditioning teaches an animal the significance of events in its environment, whereas instrumental conditioning enables the animal to learn to do something about the environmental events. This type of theorizing eventually led to the use of Pavlovian conditioning to explore questions posed by Pavlov over half a century ago, and Gray concluded: "The influence of Pavlov on the study of animal learning is stronger and more direct now than at any time in the past; and it appears still to be growing" (p. 127).

Although we will explore classical conditioning in the context of early American behaviorism in the rest of this chapter and parts of the next, Pavlovian conditioning is by no means extinct. For example, **Robert A. Rescorla** (1940–) won the APA's Distinguished Scientific Contribution Award in 1986 for "[h]is use of Pavlovian conditioning as a representative associative process [that] has enabled him to question and expand the laws of association put forth by Aristotle and the British Associationists" (*American Psychologist,* 1987, p. 285). Rescorla's interest in the Pavlovian paradigm began at the University of Pennsylvania, where he received his Ph.D. in 1966. At Yale, Rescorla's research focused on animal learning, conditioned inhibition, and Pavlovian higher-order conditioning. His more recent efforts have examined the effect of context on learning.

In concluding our look at the life and influence of Ivan Pavlov, we will let Pavlov speak for himself:

> I must say that looking back on my life I would describe it as being happy and successful. I have received all that can be demanded of life: the complete realization of the principles with which I began life. I dreamed of finding happiness in intellectual work, in science—and I found it. I wanted to have a kind person as a companion in life and I found this companion in my wife . . . , who patiently endured all the hardships of our existence before my professorship, always encouraged my scientific aspirations and who devoted herself to our family just as I devoted myself to the laboratory. (Pavlov, 1957, p. 62)

Vladimir Mikhailovich Bekhterev

Although **Vladimir Mikhailovich Bekhterev** (1857–1927) was nearly 8 years younger than Pavlov, he climbed the educational ladder rapidly and received his first degree in medicine in 1878, a year before Pavlov. In 1881, Bekhterev received his M.D. from St. Petersburg and for the next several years, he studied abroad with such notables as du Bois-Reymond, Wundt (Chapter 7), and Charcot (Chapter 15). Bekhterev (Figure 12–8) returned to found the first two experimental psychology laboratories in Russia—in 1886 at Kazan and in 1895 at St. Peters-

FIGURE 12–8.   Vladimir Bekhterev.

Source: From Boakes, From Darwin to Behaviourism *(1984), by courtesy Harvard College Library.*

burg. Most of his career was spent as a colleague of Pavlov's in St. Petersburg.

Throughout his career, Bekhterev was more of a psychiatrist than a physiologist. In Kazan, Bekhterev became convinced that more could be gained from an objective study of a neurotic patient's life than from trying to analyze the neurotic's subjective experience. Bekhterev was also interested in neural localization of conditioning experiences, and his animal research often involved conditioning a dog and then damaging its brain in an effort to see which areas were involved in the conditioning.

Like Pavlov, Bekhterev believed that a study of conditioned reflexes, which he called "associated reflexes," was the key to the scientific study of the mind. Also like Pavlov, Bekhterev was committed to an objective science. The two were completely unlike in virtually every other area, however.

In many respects, Bekhterev's career mirrored that of G. Stanley Hall (Chapter 10). Like Hall, Bekhterev was a great organizer and innovator, with little interest in the repetition and tedium often characterizing laboratory work. Like Hall, Bekhterev was a founder of clinics, laboratories, institutes, and journals. In fact, his *Review of Psychiatry, Neuropathology, and Experimental Psychology,* established in 1896, was the first journal with "experimental psychology" in its title. In addition to editing the journal, Bekhterev was for a time its most prolific author, contributing a third of the first volume's reports.

Bekhterev's dizzying pace had a cost, however. Students and colleagues saw little of him and his family even less. For years he worked 18 hours a day, requiring no more than 5 hours sleep, often writing in bed while his wife slept beside him. The result was that he produced an amazing number of papers and books.

In a 1904 article, Bekhterev argued against introspection in psychology, and like Sechenov, proposed the reflex as a key concept for an objective psychology. Bekhterev expanded the paper into a book that gave a clear presentation of his work on conditioning and animal behavior and should have enhanced his reputation. Its failure to do so can be attributed to controversies between Bekhterev and Pavlov, which Pavlov won.

At issue in the most important controversy was whether destruction of a salivary "center" in the cortex would prevent a dog from re-establishing a conditioned reflex. In Bekhterev's laboratory, this appeared to be the case, whereas Pavlov's results convinced him that dogs with particular cortical ablations could reacquire a conditioned response. The matter came to a head at a meeting at which Bekhterev arranged for a public demonstration to prove he was right. One of Bekhterev's students tested two animals with cortical ablations, and neither showed any signs of salivating to a visual stimulus that had produced a CR before surgery. Testing the dogs himself, Pavlov convincingly demonstrated that with the appropriate technique, conditioned reflexes were easily re-established. After this, Bekhterev's interest in animal research declined dramatically (Boakes, 1984).

In 1917, Bekhterev published a series of lectures in *General Principles of Human Reflexology.* In the lectures, he again argued for an objective approach to psychology's problems and expressed his opposition to mentalistic terms. **Reflexology** was Bekhterev's word for an objective psychology that would study the relationship between behavior and physiological and environmental conditions. However, despite his approximately 600 publications, when Bekhterev died in 1927, his influence rapidly waned.

As you can see, the study of animal behavior and Russian objective psychology were quite compatible with behaviorism. However, as we noted above, American behaviorism's founding is usually marked by Watson's 1913 publication. We will now examine the colorful life and controversial career of behaviorism's founder.

JOHN BROADUS WATSON

By his heredity and his upbringing, **John Broadus Watson** (1878–1958) was different from most of the other American psychologists of his generation. For example, he was from the small Southern village of Travelers Rest, near Greenville, South Carolina. Unlike most of his contemporaries, Watson was not the son of a minister or professional—his father was by most accounts a disreputable character who spent much of his time away from the family.

Watson's mother was the family's strength, moving her six children (Watson was the fourth-born) to Greenville when Watson was 12, because the schools were better in town than in the country. Emma Watson was devoutly religious, and Watson was named for John Broadus, a fire-and-brimstone Greenville Baptist minister. At some point, Emma made Watson promise to become a Baptist minister, probably hoping that he would follow in the footsteps of his namesake (Brewer, 1991). It was a forlorn hope: According to his son, James B. Watson,

Dad was not just without religion; he was an atheist. He had been required to go to church regularly as a child and was steeped in the Baptist religion as he grew up. As he turned to science he rejected religion. . . (Hannush, 1987, p. 148)

Given his circumstances, it is not surprising that Watson was a wild youth. In his autobiographical essay, Watson described himself as "lazy, somewhat insubordinate . . ." (Watson, 1936, p. 271) and a poor student. He was arrested twice, "once for . . . fighting, and the second time for shooting off firearms inside the city limits" (p. 271).

Although we will cite frequently Watson's autobiographical essay, its tone is generally negative, and it is difficult to know how much stock to place in it. Any positive comments are quickly negated. For example, Watson noted that he was the youngest person to receive his Ph.D. from Chicago at the time he finished, and then added, "I got my first deep-seated inferiority at the same time. I received my degree Magna Cum Laude and was told . . . by Dewey and Angell that my exam was much inferior to that of Miss Helen Thompson who had graduated two years before with a Summa Cum Laude" (p. 274).

In 1894, Watson enrolled at Greenville's Furman University as a subfreshman, a status reflecting his lack of preparation for college. Predictably, his performance was undistinguished. His introduction to philosophy and psychology came from Gordon B. Moore, who was up on the latest in psychology after a sabbatical year at the University of Chicago. Although Watson felt that Moore "gave us his best," he still managed to challenge Moore in his senior year. Moore had promised to fail any student who "handed in a paper backwards," and Watson, "by some strange streak of luck . . ." (Watson, 1936, p. 272), committed that very crime. As a result, Watson was forced to stay an extra year, graduating from Furman with an A.M. rather than an A.B. in 1899, with a resolve to become a Ph.D. psychologist so that he could one day get even with Moore. "Imagine my surprise and real sorrow during the second year of my stay at Hopkins, when I received a letter from [Moore] asking to come to me as a research student. Before we could arrange it, his eyesight failed, and he died a few years later" (p. 272).

For a year, Watson taught in a one-room country school, where he impressed the children with his trained rats. In July, 1900, Watson's mother died, and within a month of her death, he applied to the University of Chicago to do graduate work.

Watson in Chicago

In 1900, the distinguished instructors at Chicago included Jacques Loeb, John Dewey, George Herbert Mead, James Rowland Angell (all from Chapter 11), and **Henry H. Donaldson** (1857–1938). Donaldson had been one of Hall's students at Hopkins and was among the first American scientists to work with laboratory rats. As a neurologist, his interest was mainly in their nervous systems, not in their behavior.

Arriving in Chicago with only $50 in his pocket, Watson worked at a variety of jobs to pay his way. One of his jobs was as an assistant janitor, and his duties included taking care of Donaldson's rats. At first, Watson leaned toward Loeb as his dissertation director because he found Loeb's mechanical explanation of behavior through tropisms appealing. However, Angell convinced Watson that Loeb was not a "safe" supervisor, and Angell and Donaldson became his dissertation advisers.

Watson's project combined animal learning and neurology. After establishing a baseline of what infant rats of different ages could learn, Watson then sacrificed different-aged animals and microscopically examined their nervous systems. Watson concluded that increasing behavioral complexity was strongly correlated with increasing maturation of nerve fibers. This was an important finding, and Watson borrowed $350 (which he took nearly 20 years to repay) from Donaldson to have his dissertation published in 1903 as *Animal Education: The Psychical Development of the White Rat*. Watson's work was generally well received (see Dewsbury, 1990).

After earning the Ph.D., Watson stayed at Chicago, first as an assistant to Angell and then as an instructor. In his animal laboratory, Watson investigated the cues that rats use in learning their way through the maze, a problem suggested by Small. Assisted by Carr (Chapter 11), Watson (1907) concluded that vision, audition, olfaction, and sensations from the vibrissae (whiskers) did not play an important role in the rat's mastery of the maze. He suggested that kinesthetic sensations might provide the necessary cues for maze learning; that is, the rats learn a series of muscular movements. To test this idea, he built a maze in which the "straightaways [could] be shortened or lengthened without disturbing any of the *turning* relations" (p. 96). Watson reasoned that if a rat learns to run a particular distance and then turn, the rat should turn into a side wall if the arm has been lengthened or run into the end wall in a shortened pathway. In fact, this is what he and Carr found the next year (Carr & Watson, 1908).

Watson's (1907) paper was viciously attacked by antivivisectionists of the day, many of whom probably had not read the actual report (Dewsbury, 1990). Watson was ably defended by Baldwin (Chapter 10) and by his department head, Angell. Accused of cruelty to his rats, Watson was actually "loving to animals and very sensitive to their needs," according to his son (Hannush, 1987, p. 141). Watson's animal work during his Chicago years also included the study, with Yerkes, of sensory processes in animals and investigations of the behavior of terns (a sea bird). Watson's successful animal work helped establish his name as a rising star in psychology.

In 1904, Watson publicly married Mary Amelia Ickes, a former student of his. He had married her secretly the year before, primarily because of opposition to him by her brother, Harold Ickes, who later became Secretary of the Interior in Franklin D. Roosevelt's cabinet. Watson and Mary had two children, Mary (or Polly) and John. Polly's daughter, John Watson's granddaughter, is the television and stage actress Mariette Hartley.

Although Watson enjoyed his work at Chicago, he was less satisfied with his salary and his academic position—he was still just an instructor in 1908. Thus, when Baldwin offered Watson a position at Johns Hopkins as professor and director of the psychological laboratory at a salary nearly twice what he was making at Chicago, his decision was easy.

Watson at Johns Hopkins

As we noted in Chapter 10, scandal over a visit to a brothel forced Baldwin's resignation from Hopkins in 1909, soon after Watson's arrival. With Baldwin's departure, responsibility for leading the psychology department and for editing *The Psychological Review* fell to Watson, who was only 31 when he moved to

Baltimore. From his new position of power, Watson began to pressure the administration to separate psychology from philosophy and to develop more ties between psychology and biology. In May 1912, Watson was permitted to establish a separate department of psychology with himself as its head (O'Donnell, 1985).

Meanwhile, Watson still taught a Jamesian general psychology course and used Titchener's experimental manuals in his experimental courses, but his animal research was steering him more and more toward behaviorism. In fact, he had broached the idea of the nonintrospective study of behavior to his Chicago colleagues as early as 1904, but their response had not been encouraging.

Watson's dislike of introspection was at least partly caused by his lack of facility at it. In 1936, he admitted,

> I never wanted to use human subjects. I hated to serve as a subject. I didn't like the stuffy, artificial instructions given to subjects. I always was uncomfortable and acted unnaturally. With animals I was at home. . . . More and more the thought presented itself: Can't I find out by watching their behavior everything that the other students are finding out by using [observers]? (p. 276)

Watson now had the freedom and the power base to pursue his ideas aggressively, or, as Angell (1936) wrote, to develop his behaviorism "in such an extravagant manner" (p. 26). In addition, Watson had the influence of **Knight Dunlap** (1875–1949), one of the psychologists Baldwin brought in to bolster the department at Hopkins. Dunlap had earned his Ph.D. from Harvard, working primarily under Münsterberg, and then came to Hopkins in 1906, where he spent the bulk of his professional life. Dunlap's dissatisfaction with psychology's focus on introspection and consciousness encouraged Watson to make the final break with the traditional, introspective approach to psychology. Watson (Figure 12–9) made his break with a vengeance in the famous article, "Psychology as the Behaviorist Views It" (Watson, 1913), which was based on lectures he had given at Columbia in early 1913.

FIGURE 12–9.   John Watson in 1912, voted the most handsome professor by Johns Hopkins students.

Source: The Ferdinand Hamburger, Jr. Archives of the Johns Hopkins University.

Psychology as the Behaviorist Views It

Watson placed his cards squarely on the table in the opening paragraph:

> Psychology as the behaviorist views it is a purely objective experimental branch of natural science. Its theoretical goal is the prediction and control of behavior. Introspection forms no essential part of its methods, nor is the scientific value of its data dependent upon the readiness with which they lend themselves to interpretation in terms of consciousness. (Watson, 1913, p. 158)

Watson described his uncertainty about how to respond when other psychologists asked him about the relevance of his animal work for human psychol-

ogy. The prevailing attitude was that it was essential to fabricate the conscious content of the animal whose behavior had been studied in order to relate the results to human consciousness. Recall that this was what Snarsky had wanted to do in Pavlov's laboratory, and Pavlov had found the approach absurd. For Watson, there were two solutions to the problem of how to handle the gulf that existed between the study of animal behavior and the study of human consciousness: Either animal behavior could be studied independently of psychology or psychology could be changed to the study of behavior. Watson chose to change psychology.

"I do not wish unduly to criticize psychology," Watson (1913) wrote, before noting that "It has failed signally, I believe, during the fifty-odd years of its existence as an experimental discipline to make its place in the world as an undisputed natural science" (p. 163). In Watson's opinion, introspection was the problem, and if psychology continued to use it, future psychologists would still disagree over the conscious mind's basic elements. Thus, psychology should "discard all reference to consciousness . . ." (p. 163).

Watson's criticism was not reserved solely for the structuralists, however. He considered functionalism little different from structural psychology and attacked it on the same grounds, namely for using introspection to study conscious processes. Without consciousness and introspection, psychology would become the objective, positivistic study of behavior.

Although Watson was confident that beneficial changes would come to psychology once consciousness was discarded, he made few specific predictions about what these changes would be. "I am more interested at the present moment in trying to show the necessity for maintaining uniformity in experimental procedure and in the method of stating results in both human and animal work, than in developing any ideas I may have upon the changes which are certain to come in the scope of human psychology," he wrote (Watson, 1936, p. 170).

It would be difficult to overstate the impact of Watson's "manifesto" on psychology. As one illustration of its lasting significance, Skinner (1964) used Watson's article as a point of departure in one of his most famous essays, "Behaviorism at fifty."

More recently, Kimble (1994) began an 80-year report on behaviorism's status using Watson (1913) as his starting point.

Watson worked diligently for the next few years to fill in the gaps in his behaviorist agenda. With Karl Lashley, he spent some time, ultimately unsuccessfully, attempting to study thought as faint contractions in the speech musculature. As Watson envisioned it in 1913, thought was simply subvocal speech.

Watson's next major statement of his behaviorist approach appeared in *Behavior: An Introduction to Comparative Psychology* (1914). After essentially repeating his 1913 manifesto, Watson presented a review of animal behavior work that, except for its theoretical stance, was similar to Washburn's *The Animal Mind*. In addition to claiming that thought was subvocal speech, Watson gave a behavioristic view of feelings, arguing that they were based on sensations arising from the reproductive organs and erogenous zones. To illustrate, Watson gave an example of how the pleasing effect to the male of the sight of a female animal could be explained physiologically. Watson's explicit discussion of sex was ahead of its time.

Behavior was well received as a comprehensive look at contemporary animal behavior and added to Watson's stature at a time when he was campaigning for the APA presidency. In his presidential speech in late 1915, Watson (1916) appealed again for behaviorism. In place of introspection, Watson proposed the use of the conditioned reflex method. After listing difficulties with Pavlov's conditioned salivary reflex, he noted that his work with Lashley had focused on Bekhterev's conditioned motor reflex. The rest of his talk detailed conditioning work that he and Lashley had conducted on human and animal subjects.

Watson at Phipps Psychiatric Clinic

Soon after Watson's APA address, an incident at Hopkins led him to begin research on humans rather than animals. Most of the university moved to a new campus, but the psychology department space was more restricted than before. **Adolf Meyer** (1866–1950), a Swiss psychiatrist and the director of Hopkins' Phipps Psychiatric Clinic, offered and Watson eagerly accepted some space at the Clinic for his animal colony. A leading figure in American psychiatry, Meyer believed in close contact with academic psychology and invented the term "psychobiology" to describe the union of psychological and biological approaches he thought were necessary to solve psychiatric problems.

In a 1916 paper, Watson advocated the application of his ideas on conditioning to clinical problems, and he sent Meyer a prepublication copy. Meyer was enraged at Watson's apparent ridicule of treatment methods other than conditioning, by his ignorance of mental illness, and by his lack of understanding of Meyer's views. When Watson was unable to mollify Meyer, Watson avoided contact with him as much as possible by studying the behavior of newborn infants at a nearby maternity hospital.

Watson had been engaged in this work for about a year when World War I intervened. Watson was called to active duty in September 1917. Because of poor eyesight, he was rejected for service as a line officer and was assigned at first to organize and oversee the aviation examining boards. According to Watson (1936), "This work held my interest until Colonel Bingham . . . was put in charge. His egotism and self-seeking soon made every one in the personnel section of aviation understand why it is that some officers fail to return from expeditions . . ." (p. 277).

Later, while serving with the Aviation Medical Corps, Watson wrote a report critical of a particular testing procedure, and it nearly resulted in his courtmartial. Watson was returned "to Aviation with the notation 'that he be not allowed to serve his country in his scientific capacity, but be sent to the line'; in other words, the wish was implied that I be killed speedily" (Watson, 1936, p. 278). Fortunately, the war ended, and Watson summarized his experiences with the military by writing, "The whole army experience is a nightmare to me. Never have I seen such incompetence, such extravagance, such a group of overbearing, inferior men" (p. 278).

By December 1918, Watson was back at Phipps. Just before his involvement in the war, Watson had published an article in which he talked about three basic emotions in infants from which all others are derived by conditioning (Watson & Morgan, 1917).

Watson's basic emotions were fear, rage, and love. Before training, Watson found that the emotions were triggered by only a limited range of stimuli. For example, fear was elicited reliably only by loud sounds and sudden loss of support (infants were dropped by the experimenter and caught by an assistant). Although many have attributed instinctive fears of darkness and animals to newborns, Watson (like John Locke in Chapter 4) concluded that such fears were conditioned. Afraid of the dark most of his life, Watson revealed what he believed to be his fear's origin by writing: "From time immemorial children have been 'scared' in the dark, either unintentionally or as a means of controlling them (this is especially true of children reared in the South)" (p. 166). Rage was elicited reliably by hampering an infant's movements, and love responses—for example, smiling, gurgling, and cooing—followed "the stroking or manipulation of some erogenous zone, tickling, shaking, gentle rocking, patting, turning upon the stomach across the attendant's knee, etc." (Watson & Morgan, 1917, p. 167).

In 1919, Watson published *Psychology from the Standpoint of a Behaviorist* (Watson, 1919a), in which he presented a clear outline of his behaviorist program. Devoted to solving practical problems, the program would include the study of the development of emotional reactions, the clarification of the basic laws of habit formation, and the effect of such factors as alcohol, climate, sex, and age on human performance. Again, Watson repeated his proposal to study thinking by recording movements of the larynx. Psychopathology, perhaps because Watson was still smarting over Meyer's reaction in 1916, was treated only in the book's final two pages.

Although a central theme of *Psychology* was the development of "conditioned emotional reactions" in the child, Watson had little hard data to present. He soon remedied this deficit with what is surely his most widely quoted (and misquoted) experiment.

Fear Conditioning in Little Albert

In an experiment that would almost certainly not pass institutional review today, Watson and Rosalie Rayner (1920) deliberately attempted to create a conditioned emotional response in an infant. For the study, Watson selected a "stolid and unemotional" son of a wet nurse (a woman paid to nurse another woman's child). Albert B., or **Little Albert**, was afraid only of a suddenly produced loud noise when he was about 9 months old.

Attempts to condition Little Albert began approximately 2 months later. Albert received two training trials on the first day of conditioning. On each trial, a white rat was placed in front of the child, he reached for it, and as soon as he touched the animal, a loud sound was made behind his head by striking a steel bar with a hammer. Albert responded to the second presentation by jumping violently, falling forward, and starting to whimper.

A week later, Albert received five joint presentations of the rat and the loud noise. When the rat was presented alone at the end of the session, Albert began to cry and crawled away so swiftly "that he was caught with difficulty before reaching the edge of the table" (Watson & Rayner, 1920, p. 5).

Five days later, Albert was tested to see if he was still afraid of the rat (he was) and then to see if his fear response would generalize to other similar objects. Albert reacted fearfully to a rabbit, a dog, and a seal fur coat but had little reaction to cotton wool. Albert also reacted negatively to Watson's hair and to a Santa Claus mask. Watson, Rayner, Little Albert, and the white rate are shown in Figure 12–10.

After another 5 days, Albert was again given generalization tests and tests of his reaction to the rat. In addition, Watson decided to strengthen Albert's reaction to various stimuli by making the loud noise in their presence. At the end of the session, the dog was presented to Albert without the loud noise, and the child initially had little reaction. When the animal barked unexpectedly, Albert fell over and began wailing until the dog was removed. Watson and Rayner (1920) wryly reported that the "sudden barking of the hitherto quiet dog produced a marked fear response in the adult observers" (p. 9).

A month later, Albert was given his final test with the stimuli, and the authors concluded that their "experiments would seem to show conclusively that directly conditioned emotional responses as well as those conditioned by transfer persist, although with a certain loss in the intensity of the reaction, for a

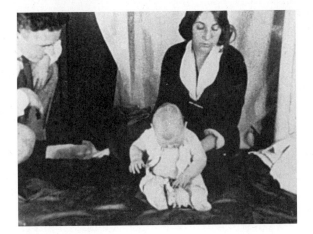

FIGURE 12–10.   Watson, Rayner, Little Albert and a white rat.

Source: Archives of the History of American Psychology.

longer period than one month" (Watson & Rayner, 1920, p. 12). Because Albert left the hospital after these final tests, Watson and Rayner did not try to remove the conditioned emotional response.

In conclusion, Watson and Rayner (1920) suggested that many phobias are either conditioned emotional reactions or their generalizations and ridiculed the possible Freudian (Chapter 15) interpretation of the cause of Albert's fear of seal skin coats:

> The Freudians twenty years from now, . . . when they come to analyze Albert's fear of a seal skin coat . . . analysis at that age—will probably tease from him the recital of a dream which upon their analysis will show that Albert at three years of age attempted to play with the pubic hair of the mother and was scolded violently for it. . . . If the analyst has sufficiently prepared Albert to accept such a dream . . . as an explanation of his avoiding tendencies, and if the analyst has the authority and personality to put it over, Albert may be fully convinced that the dream was a true revealer of the factors which brought about the fear. (Watson & Rayner, 1920, p. 14)

An account of the Little Albert study appears in most introductory psychology textbooks and in most psychology of learning textbooks, although the study's details are not always accurate. Harris (1979) reported that some of the inaccuracies involve minor details such as the child's age and the initial object that Albert was taught to fear (i.e., a rabbit instead of a rat). More significant distortions involve the range of generalized fear items and the story's ending.

Harris (1979) indicated that some of the distortion resulted from Watson's own varied recountings of the study in later publications. In addition, discrepancies about the animal Albert was taught to fear and the study's outcome may have come from a confusion of the Little Albert report with a later project involving Watson, the study of a child named Peter by Mary Cover Jones (Jones, 1924a, 1924b, 1974).

During her last semester as a Vassar undergraduate, **Mary Cover Jones** (1896–1987) attended a lecture by Watson at which he discussed and showed movies of Little Albert's conditioning. By the time Jones became a graduate student at Columbia, where she earned her Ph.D., Watson had left Johns Hopkins and was working in New York City. Because Jones had been a classmate and friend of Rosalie Rayner, by this time Watson's wife, Jones was able to secure Watson's advice on most Saturday afternoons during the project to cure Peter. As Peter was successfully treated by someone associated with Watson, and Peter was initially afraid of rabbits (and rats), you can see how confusion might occur.

Peter was nearly 3 when Jones's testing revealed that he was afraid of a white rabbit, a white rat, and other similar stimuli. Treatment was designed to remove his fear of the rabbit. First, Jones used social imitation (modeling therapy) in which Peter was placed in a room with three other children who played fearlessly with a rabbit. Peter's fear was successfully reduced, but an accidental encounter with a frightening dog brought it back. Jones next adopted a "direct conditioning" procedure in which Peter sat in a highchair eating a preferred food while the rabbit was brought successively closer to him over a several day period. At times, another child joined Peter in these sessions. By the end, Peter showed "a genuine fondness for the rabbit. . . . The fear of the cotton, the fur coat, feathers, was entirely absent at our last interview" (Jones, 1924a, p. 314).

Elsewhere, Jones (1924b) discussed eight different procedures she had tried for removing fear responses, concluding that only direct conditioning and social imitation worked consistently. The methods that were only sometimes successful were verbal appeal (talking about the feared object), elimination through disuse, negative adaptation (stimulation with the feared object until the child grows used to it), repression (punishment by social ridicule), and distraction (using a substitute activity to divert the child's attention from the feared object).

Jones spent most of her career at the Institute of Human Development of the University of California, Berkeley, where she collaborated with her husband, Harold E. Jones, on longitudinal studies of development. However, she is best known for having been the first researcher in modern times—recall Locke's method for removing "vain Terrors"—to use counterconditioning to remove a fear in a child.

From Behaviorism to Advertising

In his autobiographical essay, Watson (1936) treated his divorce and dismissal from Hopkins in three sentences: that is, "I was divorced in 1920 and was married immediately to Rosalie Rayner, of Baltimore" (p. 271) and "All of this work abruptly came to a close with my divorce in 1920. I was asked to resign" (p. 279). Of course, there is much more to the story than that.

By 1920, Watson's career was soaring, but his home life was in shambles. Perhaps describing his own situation, at the end of a 1919 publication, Watson (1919b) wrote about a man with a low level of adjustment who seemed to have a wall around him in terms of his emotional attitudes. Watson suggested that emotionally exciting stimuli might be able to break through the wall. Shortly after writing this, Watson encountered such "emotionally exciting stimuli" in his laboratory assistant, Rosalie Rayner.

Although it is true that Watson and Rayner began a passionate affair before his divorce and their marriage, it is probably not the case that the romance stemmed from a sexual research study in which he and his laboratory assistant were the subjects (e.g., Magoun, 1981; McConnell & Philipchalk, 1992).

After examining a variety of records, including the transcripts of Watson's divorce trial and the private correspondence of university officials and involved faculty, biographer Kerry Buckley (1989) dismissed the sex research allegations as speculation. The truth was that Watson's involvement with a student at Hopkins, particularly one whose prominent family had given significant amounts of money to the university, was offensive to the administration. Combined with his very public divorce, the result was his dismissal from Johns Hopkins. In addition, "after the newspaper publicity, no university could afford to risk the inevitable public outcry by hiring Watson" (p. 129), who became an outcast from academic psychology. Watson and Rayner were married on New Year's Eve in 1920, and he began a new career in advertising.

Out of academia, Watson was confident that he would be able to find employment in the business community. A friend introduced him to Stanley Resor, the head of the J. Walter Thompson advertising agency, which at the time was possibly the largest advertising agency in the world (Kreshel, 1990). Watson, who had said that psychology's "goal is the prediction and control of behavior" (Watson, 1913, p. 158), now had the opportunity to apply that goal.

While Resor checked Watson's references, Watson was given the temporary assignment of "studying the rubber boot market on each side of the Mississippi River from Cairo to New Orleans. I was green and shy, but soon learned to pull doorbells and stop wagons in order to ask what brand of rubber boots was worn by the family" (Watson, 1936, p. 279). Offered a permanent position with the agency, Watson entered J. Walter Thompson's rigorous training program, which was sometimes called a "University of Advertising" (Kreshel, 1990). During his training, Watson spent some time "Yubanning" (selling Yuban coffee to retailers and wholesalers) and clerking at Macy's department store in New York City.

Watson (1936) reported that it took a little over a year for him to find himself in the agency, but after this period, he "began to learn that it can be just as thrilling to watch the growth of a sales curve of a new product as to watch the learning curve of animals or men" (p. 280). He was promoted to a vice presidency in 1924, and he worked at J. Walter Thompson until resigning in 1936 to become a vice president at another advertising agency, William Esty and Company. He retired from Esty in 1947.

At J. Walter Thompson, Watson became a company ambassador, standing in for Resor as a speaker at conventions and conferences (Kreshel, 1990). Watson excelled in this role: He was handsome, articulate, well educated, practiced in public speaking, and he loved the limelight. Furthermore, because he was a former scientist, Watson's hiring showed the business community that the Thompson agency was committed to seeking scientific solutions for marketing problems. Watson's task "was to develop campaigns of mass appeal that would create reliable markets for goods created by mass production" (Buckley, 1982, p. 211).

Watson proved adept at creating markets by applying behaviorist principles. Instead of just giving consumers product information, Watson told the advertising community that the purpose of advertising was to create a society of consumers whose buying activities could be controlled, and this control could be achieved by conditioning emotional responses.

> To insure the appropriate reaction from the consumer, Watson counseled, "tell him something that will tie up with *fear,* something that will stir up a mild *rage,* that will call out an affectionate or *love* response, or strike at a deep psychological or habit need." (Buckley, 1982, p. 212, italics added)

Note that Watson invoked his three basic emotions in this statement, which was taken from an undated typescript in the Watson Papers entitled "Dissecting the Consumer: An Application of Psychology to Advertising."

Using fear, Watson created ads for Johnson and Johnson Baby Powder in which pediatricians stressed the dangers of infection to infants, the "purity" and "cleanliness" of baby powder and its infection-fighting properties, and the need to use the powder frequently to keep the baby well. As an example of Watson's use of love (or sex), an ad for Pebeco toothpaste showed an enticingly dressed young woman smoking a cigarette. The implication

was that smoking enhanced a woman's sex appeal, but at the same time the ad's message was that this appeal would be diminished if the woman did not brush with Pebeco toothpaste to freshen her breath and brighten her smile.

Other techniques that Watson employed effectively included the use of demographic information to target a particular segment of the consumer market and the use of celebrity testimonials. As an example of the former, demographic information was used to target young, upwardly mobile middle-class mothers as consumers of baby powder. As an illustration of the use of testimonials, Watson employed Queen Marie of Romania to endorse Pond's cold cream. Note that celebrity testimonials take advantage of Pavlovian conditioning by pairing a particular product, initially a neutral stimulus, with the image of a famous person, which is like an unconditioned stimulus. Presumably, after several repetitions of the ad, the consumer begins to respond to the advertised product the way he or she responds to the celebrity.

In one of the few experiments he conducted after leaving academia, Watson studied Thompson employees and found that despite specific brand preferences, smokers could not discriminate between cigarette brands. This reinforced Watson's belief that the successful marketing of products depended not on appeals to reason but on the creation of desire. Incidentally, Watson was a smoker who, according to his son, smoked about half a pack a day without ever inhaling. Watson smoked Lucky Strikes until he went to the William Esty Company; because Esty handled the Camel account, he dutifully switched to Camels.

Although Kreshel (1990) cited authors who concluded that Watson's influence on advertising was "nothing short of phenomenal" (p. 54), Kreshel interpreted Watson's advertising career differently. According to her, many of the advertising techniques that Watson supposedly originated had entered the industry long before he was employed by J. Walter Thompson. For example, testimonial advertising was first popular in the late 19th century. Kreshel concluded that "Watson was quite simply an advertising man who became very good at what he did" (p. 54).

As an advertising executive, Watson had the time and the skills needed to present his thoughts on psychology in general and on behaviorism in particular to a new, larger audience. He thereby became one of the first psychologists to package psychology in a digestible form to the general public, that is, to popularize it. From 1922 on, Watson wrote articles for such magazines as *Harper's, McCall's, Collier's,* and *Cosmopolitan.* He was well paid for the articles, which averaged about one per month, and was never rejected until he submitted what he considered a "good" article under the unappealing title, "Why I Don't Commit Suicide" (Brewer, 1991).

Behaviorism and Childrearing

Watson's advertising career provided one opportunity for him to put his behaviorism to the test, and another came with his and Rosalie Rayner's children. The Watsons' behavioristic approach to childrearing was published as *Psychological Care of Infant and Child* in 1928. The book became a controversial bestseller.

Watson's work was controversial not only because of its specific recommendations, which we will explore later, but also because of the changing nature of developmental psychology. As Elkind (1985) noted, the important distinction between children and adults—that is, children are not just little adults—was not fully realized until relatively modern times. One of the first to argue for this distinction was Maria Montessori.

Born into a wealthy home in Rome, **Maria Montessori** (1870–1952) was the first woman in Italy to receive a medical degree (1894). Later study in philosophy and psychology helped her better understand intellectually challenged children, and she helped found a school for retarded children in 1899. Learning from the children and pioneering many educational techniques—often credited to better-known American psychologists—Montessori's legacy remains today in schools employing the Montessori Method.

Two psychologists who focused primarily on the physiological phenomena of maturation—Arnold Gesell and Leonard Carmichael—were closer rivals

to Watson in the area of child development than Montessori, however. Nearly the same age as Watson and with a chronologically overlapping career, Gesell was more interested in children's maturational growth processes than Watson, who, as an extreme environmentalist, was more concerned with changes occurring through learning. **Arnold Gesell** (1880–1961) received his undergraduate degree at the University of Wisconsin, where he was influenced by Joseph Jastrow (Chapter 10) to pursue his Ph.D. under Jastrow's mentor, G. Stanley Hall at Clark. After earning his Ph.D. in 1906, Gesell had brief stints with some of American psychology's best-known researchers—Lewis Terman, Henry Goddard (both Chapter 18), and Lightner Witmer (Chapter 7)—before settling at Yale.

At Yale, Gesell founded a psychology clinic in 1911, completed his M.D. in 1915, and conducted research that established maturational standards for children. Gesell is most remembered for his contributions to the methodology used by developmental psychologists, particularly for the use of photography and observation through a one-way mirror.

Like Gesell and unlike Watson, **Leonard Carmichael** (1898–1973) worked to establish the physiology of maturation. With a Ph.D. from Harvard, Carmichael's disparate accomplishments include the first recording of the electroencephalogram in the United States, being president of Yale, and work at the Smithsonian Institution and the National Geographic Society. He is probably best known in developmental psychology for his editorial work and for his writing in the *Manual of Child Psychology,* subsequently known as *Carmichael's Manual of Child Psychology.*

Watson's approach to childrearing was a harsh regimen that avoided, as much as possible, any expressions of tenderness and affection to the child. As he put it,

> A certain amount of affectionate response is socially necessary but few parents realize how easily they can overtrain the child in this direction. It may tear the heart strings a bit, this thought of stopping the tender outward demonstration of your love for your children or of their love for you. . . . Mothers just don't know,

when they kiss their children and pick them up and rock them, caress them and jiggle them upon their knee, that they are slowly building up a human being totally unable to cope with the world it must later live in. (Watson, 1928/1972, pp. 43–44)

Watson acknowledged how parents would react to his prescription: "Once at the close of a lecture before parents, a dear old lady got up and said, 'Thank God, my children are grown—and that I had a chance to enjoy them before I met you'" (Watson, 1928/1972, p. 69). But, according to Watson, this was the attitude responsible for the unhappiness of children in general—they were too coddled, which made them whiners.

> Treat [children] as though they were young adults. Dress them, bathe them with care and circumspection. Let your behavior always be objective and kindly firm. Never hug and kiss them, never let them sit in your lap. If you must, kiss them once on the forehead when they say good night. Shake hands with them in the morning. Give them a pat on the head if they make an extraordinarily good job of a difficult task. . . . In a week's time you will find how easy it is to be perfectly objective with your child and at the same time kindly. You will be utterly ashamed of the mawkish, sentimental way you have been handling it. (Watson, 1928/1972, pp. 81–82)

Watson and Rayner apparently practiced what they preached on their two sons, Bill and James, although there is evidence that Rayner was not wholeheartedly in favor of strict behaviorist childrearing practices (Duke, Fried, Pliley, & Walker, 1989). However, her untimely death and the effect this had on Watson make it difficult to attribute Bill's and James's subsequent problems solely to their unemotional upbringing. Still, it is interesting to read James Watson's thoughts about the effect of the application of his father's behavioristic principles.

> I have some unhappy thoughts about my upbringing, . . . about the effects of behavioristic principles on my being raised into an adult. It is difficult not to let these thoughts affect my feelings about my father. In many ways I adored him as an individual and as a character. He had

a nice sense of humor. He was bright; he was charming; he was masculine, witty, and reflective. But he was also conversely unresponsive, . . . unable to express and cope with any feelings of emotion of his own, and determined unwittingly to deprive, I think, my brother and me of any kind of emotional foundation. . . . We were never kissed or held as children; we were never shown any kind of emotional closeness. (Hannush, 1987, pp. 137–138)

Bill eventually became a psychiatrist, whereas James finished college in industrial psychology and became a successful executive with Hunt-Wesson Foods. Both brothers experienced bouts of depression; an attempted suicide sent James into psychoanalytic therapy, which he continued for several years after Bill killed himself. According to James,

> I believe [depression] happens to a lot of people who are not raised by behaviorists, but I strongly believe that strict adherence to the principles established in behaviorism, particularly as advocated in some of Dad's earlier books, tends to . . . cause a great deal of difficulty in later life. (Hannush, 1987, p. 139)

Watson's Learning Theory and the Decline of the Instinct Concept in Psychology

As illustrated in *Psychological Care of Infant and Child*, Watson was an extreme environmentalist by 1928. In fact, Watson's ideas about learning and instinct changed over the course of his academic career and beyond. For example, Pavlovian conditioning was not incorporated into his view of learning until 1915, when he endorsed it wholeheartedly. The important aspect of conditioning was that it allowed a stimulus and response to occur together so they could be associated together. Thus, Watson's central learning principle was contiguity. Watson considered Thorndike's law of effect too mentalistic, emphasizing instead repetition and recency. That is, because each trial in a learning situation ends with the animal making the correct response, it is this response that occurs most frequently. In addition, because the trial ends with the successful act, the act's recency results in its being likely to occur the next time the animal encounters the learning situation.

In *Behaviorism* (Watson, 1924/1970)—based on a series of lectures Watson gave at the New School for Social Research—Watson argued for a radical environmentalism in which learning rather than heredity determines behavior. *Behaviorism* contains two chapters entitled, "Are there any human instincts?" Watson's answer was, "There are then for us no instincts—we no longer need the term in psychology" (p. 94).

Of course, Watson's (1924/1970) response to the question of human instincts implies that the term was once needed or used by psychologists. In fact, Darwin's theory of evolution encouraged the search for inherited patterns of behavior (instincts) in animal species including man, and the concept has an even earlier history (Diamond, 1971). William James (1890) defined instinct "*as the faculty of acting in such a way as to produce certain ends, without foresight of the ends, and without previous education in the performance*" (Vol. 2, p. 383, italics in the original). After listing many "special human instincts," including such diverse behavioral tendencies as hunting instinct and acquisitiveness, James concluded that humans have the greatest repertoire of instincts in the animal kingdom.

Another avid proponent of human instincts was a man who considered himself James's successor— **William McDougall** (1871–1938). After becoming a leading figure in British psychology, McDougall came to America in 1920 to fill the Harvard professorship created by Münsterberg's 1916 death. Unfortunately, McDougall left his experimental work behind him and never became fully accepted by American psychologists. McDougall (Figure 12–11) accepted the chairmanship of the psychology department at Duke University in 1927, where his support of **Joseph Banks Rhine**'s (1895–1980) controversial research on extrasensory perception did little to enhance McDougall's image in American psychology.

In *An Introduction to Social Psychology,* McDougall (1908) presented his theory of instincts to explain human behavior. Although his definition of psychology as the science of behavior antedated Watson's manifesto, McDougall was not a behaviorist. Instead, his

FIGURE 12–11.   William McDougall.
Source: Psychology Department, University College, London.

outspoken opposition to mechanistic behaviorism led to a 1924 debate with Watson, which was won by Watson, according to McDougall, because the women in the audience voted overwhelmingly for his handsome opponent (Boakes, 1984).

Debate about the relative contributions to behavior of nature and nurture (e.g., instinct vs. learning, heredity vs. environment) began in earnest around 1920. One of the first papers came from Knight Dunlap, Watson's Hopkins colleague. One problem that Dunlap (1919) identified was that there was a tendency to perceive the instinct labels as something more than they really were. "Having posited a 'pugnacious instinct,' for example, one writer proceeds gravely to infer that war is forever a necessity, as the expression of this 'instinct'" (p. 309). This type of inference would be justified only if the underlying psychological processes were understood. Because they were not understood, Dunlap wrote "that for psychology there are no 'instincts'" (p. 311).

Dunlap was not opposed to the instinct concept in principle, just to the way it was then defined.

FIGURE 12–12.   Zing Yang Kuo.

Source: Archives of the History of American Psychology.

Zing Yang Kuo (1898–1970) opposed the instinct concept in principle. A Chinese psychologist, Kuo (Figure 12–12) studied in the United States. Before receiving his 1923 Ph.D. from the University of California, Kuo (1921) wrote an influential anti-instinct paper in which he stated that the "so-called instincts are in the last analysis acquired trends rather than inherited tendencies" (p. 648).

Kuo's environmentalism was even more extreme than Watson's, based in part on studies in which Kuo demonstrated environmental effects on purportedly inherited behaviors. For example, Kuo (1930) raised kittens under a broad range of conditions to assess environmental effects on rat or mouse killing. In one study, he found that most kittens raised with mothers allowed to kill rats subsequently killed rats before they were 4 months old. By contrast, kittens raised in the same cages with rats never killed their cagemates. Kuo concluded "that kittens can be made to kill a rat, to love it, to hate it, to fear

it or to play with it: it depends on the life history of the kitten" (p. 34).

In the final analysis, three major criticisms were leveled against the instinct concept (Krantz & Allen, 1967). First, there was a tendency for the proliferation of instincts. Whereas McDougall (1908) listed 11 basic human instincts, Angell (1908) listed 17, Warren (1919) listed 26, Woodworth (1921) listed 110, and an early exhaustive literature survey listed 14,000 different instincts that had been identified since 1900 (Bernard, 1924).

A second major criticism was the use of the instinct concept to "explain" behavior, which is the **nominal fallacy**. Instinct proponents tended to attach the label to any poorly understood behavior pattern, which largely accounts for the proliferation of instincts. Often the explanation of a particular instinct became an exercise in tautology or circular definition. An example of a tautology is the following: Why did the woman take poison? Because she had an instinct to commit suicide. How do we know that she had the suicide instinct? Because she took poison.

The third major criticism was that instincts turn out to be merely learned responses when they are properly analyzed. Kuo was initially a proponent of this view, but later his radical environmentalism led him to conclude that both instinct (heredity) *and* habit (learning) should be eliminated from psychology. The research with cats that led to his 1930 paper resulted in his earlier comment that

> A psychology without heredity is a psychology which proposes to do away with not only the concepts of heredity and instinct but also all their related concepts such as habit, trial and error, imitation, insight and purpose. . . . Its view is essentially passivistic in that it considers every action as a 'forced' response to be described solely in terms of the functioning of the environmental stimulation. (Kuo, 1929, p. 199)

Despite the cogency of Kuo's arguments, few were willing to go as far as he did.

By the middle of the 1930s, instinct theory had been driven out of American psychology. As McDougall (1921) realized, the instinct controversy was a disagreement between his purposive view of behavior and Watson's mechanistic paradigm. In this, as in so many areas, behaviorism carried the day but not necessarily the future. The instinct concept was successfully revived by such biologists as the 1973 Nobel Prize winners **Karl von Frisch** (1886–1982), **Niko Tinbergen** (1907–1988), and **Konrad Lorenz** (1903–1989). Von Frisch is best known for his studies of communication by "dances" in honeybees. Considered the founders of the study of animal behavior known as **ethology**, Lorenz and Tinbergen earned the Nobel Prize for their biological explanations of behavior. Tinbergen is perhaps best known for his analysis of the reproductive behavior of the three-spined stickleback fish and other studies of instinct (e.g., Tinbergen, 1951/1969). As many psychology texts note, Lorenz described the form of social attachment (learning) called imprinting, and also studied a variety of phenomena including aggression (e.g., Lorenz, 1963/1966).

Unlike behaviorism, which often used animal models to explore general principles of learning, or comparative psychology, in which different species are contrasted on a particular phenomenon, ethologists study animal behavior for its own sake. Typically, the focus has been instinctive, species-specific action patterns rather than learned behaviors. Also, ethologists favor naturalistic observations over controlled laboratory studies. Although it never achieved the status of behaviorism within American psychology, ethology remains a respected alternative to the study of behavior.

Watson's Influence

Watson's effect on psychology has been immense. As one writer put it, "Second only to Freud, though at a rather great distance, John B. Watson is, in my judgment, the most important figure in the history of psychological thought during the first half of the century" (Bergmann, 1956, p. 265). Bergmann saw Watson as a tarnished idol, however, writing, "His social philosophy is, in my opinion, deplorable. His metaphysics is silly" (p. 266).

According to Bergmann (1956), Watson's greatest contribution was his methodological behaviorism, that is, his advocacy of psychology as an experimental, objective science free from mentalistic concepts and introspection's subjectivity. With Watson, the definition of psychology became "the scientific study of behavior." According to at least one recent textbook of psychology, this "definition lasted until the 1960s, when interest in studying the mind returned and led to the current, broader definition of **psychology** as 'the science of behavior and mental processes'" (Sdorow, 1990, p. 4; see also Henley, Johnson, Herzog, & Jones, 1989).

In 1974, Mary Cover Jones effectively captured the impact Watson had on her generation of psychologists:

> As graduate students at Columbia University, my husband, . . . myself, and other members of our student group were among those to whom Watson "sold" behaviorism. I can still remember the excitement with which we greeted Watson's (1919) *Psychology from the Standpoint of a Behaviorist.* It shook the foundations of traditional European-bred psychology, and we welcomed it. This was in 1919; it pointed the way from armchair psychology to action and reform and was therefore hailed as a panacea. (p. 582)

One benefit of Watson's advertising career was that it provided him a position from which he could advocate his version of psychology without academia's limitations. Watson's popularization of psychology enhanced the public's view of the usefulness of science and particularly of the science of psychology. At the same time, Watson's popularizing of psychology brought him into disrepute within the academic community.

By 1957, the year before he died, a new generation of psychologists had forgotten (or forgiven) Watson's earlier transgressions, and his contributions to psychology were recognized by the APA's Gold Medal Award. In New York to receive the award, at the last minute Watson dispatched his eldest son to the APA convention to accept it. In gratitude for the recognition, Watson dedicated a 1958 reprint of *Behaviorism* to the members of the APA. Bergmann (1956), who saw in Watson both the good and the ill, concluded:

> Yet I have not the slightest doubt that, with all the light and all the shadow, he is a very major figure. Psychology owes him much. His place in

the history of our civilization is not inconsiderable and it is secure. Such men are exceedingly rare. We ought to accept them and appreciate them for what they are. (p. 276)

Although Watson was the founder and driving spirit behind behaviorism, he was by no means the only important behaviorist. In the next chapter, we will review the lives and careers of several psychologists who went well beyond Watson's psychology.

CONCLUSIONS

Without exception, the major anticipators of behaviorism and the first behaviorists began their careers with the study of animals. Obviously, the study of animals is incompatible with introspection. Because animals cannot give subjective, phenomenological reports, studying them requires an objective methodology similar to that used by physicists. Watson recognized that an objective psychology of behavior would make psychology like physics in other ways, as well. Psychology would become a science in the positivistic sense of being grounded in public observations. We will have more to say about the connections between behaviorism and positivism in the next chapter, but note that, armed with the positivist agenda, John Watson vaulted the school of behaviorism to a position of ascendancy in American psychology that it enjoyed for over half a century.

Strongly anticipated by many elements of functionalism—such as Thorndike's animal research—behaviorism began with the work of Pavlov and Watson. It was grounded in a truly scientific methodology (Thorndike's trial-and-error learning, Pavlovian conditioning), and, as Thorndike's work in education and Watson's career in advertising illustrated, behaviorism could be applied outside the laboratory and used to affect people's lives. In the next chapter, we will continue our story of behaviorism with an examination of the important behaviorists after Watson—the neobehaviorists.

S U M M A R Y

Behaviorism's many antecedents include the mechanistic explanations of body and mind of Descartes, La Mettrie, and Cabanis, as well as Comte's philosophy of positivism. Further positivist anticipations of behaviorism came from Mach, Avenarius, and the Vienna Circle, led by Carnap and Schlick. Darwinian evolution set the stage for the animal research of George Romanes and Lloyd Morgan.

Animal Psychology

Although animal psychology was a relatively small part of American psychology at the turn of the century, all of the early behaviorists began as animal researchers. Both Jacques Loeb, with his concept of tropisms, and H. S. Jennings were important influences on the early behaviorists, particularly Watson.

Although Edward Lee Thorndike is usually viewed as a transitional figure between functionalism and behaviorism, his animal research particularly influenced the latter school. In Thorndike's most important animal studies, he tested the ability of cats to escape from puzzle boxes, finding evidence supporting the law of effect—responses followed by satisfaction will be closely associated with the stimulus situation and will be likely to be repeated in that situation—and the law of exercise. Thorndike found no evidence for reasoning in animals or for animal learning by imitation or passive tuition. He did see evidence for stimulus generalization and for learning predispositions in animals, however. Thorndike's animal research overshadowed the contributions of Willard Small, who introduced the maze problem to psychology.

Comparative psychologist Robert Yerkes studied sensory ability, adaptive behavior, and instinct in invertebrates, reptiles, birds, and mammals such as rats, monkeys, and apes. After World War I, Yerkes established a laboratory at Yale to study apes. This was followed by a larger facility in Orange Park, Florida, which was directed by Karl Lashley after Yerkes's retirement. Yerkes is also remembered for the Yerkes-Dodson law, which states that the optimal arousal level for task performance depends on task difficulty.

Objective Psychology in Russia

Ivan Sechenov studied with such outstanding European physiologists as Müller, du Bois-Reymond, Helmholtz, and Bernard. In his research, Sechenov found support for Eduard Weber's suggestion that brain stimulation might inhibit reflex activity, and in *Reflexes of the Brain,* Sechenov expressed the view that the brain is a center for organizing reflexes.

Physiologist Ivan Pavlov won a 1904 Nobel Prize for his research on the digestive processes in the dog. Along the way, he became interested in salivary responses to novel stimuli. The rest of his career was spent studying the conditioned reflex, in which a conditioned stimulus (CS) is paired with an unconditioned stimulus (UCS), which produces an unconditioned response (UCR). After several pairings, the CS by itself elicits the conditioned response (CR). Pavlov found that a slight delay between the CS and UCS was optimal for conditioning.

Pavlov and his coworkers studied such learning phenomena as extinction, higher-order conditioning, stimulus generalization, discrimination, and experimental neurosis. Pavlov believed that his dogs had different personality types—sanguine, phlegmatic, choleric, and melancholic—which were important for ease of conditioning and for mental illness. Pavlov's conditioned reflex became an important part of behaviorism's methodology.

Throughout his career, Vladimir Bekhterev was more of a psychiatrist than a physiologist. Like Pavlov, Bekhterev thought that a study of conditioned reflexes was the key to the scientific study of the mind. The advocate of an objective psychology that he called reflexology, Bekhterev was also a founder of clinics, laboratories, institutes, and journals.

John Watson

Staying at Chicago after he earned his Ph.D., Watson established an animal laboratory, where his studies included the cues rats use in learning their way through a maze. In 1908, he took a position at Johns Hopkins as professor and director of the psychological laboratory.

From his position as leader of the Hopkins psychology department and editor of *Psychological Review,* Watson began behaviorism with the article "Psychology as the Behaviorist Views It." The article called for the abandonment of the introspective method and the study of human consciousness and advocated the objective study of behavior.

After World War I, Watson returned to his observation of human infants at Phipps Psychiatric Clinic. Working with Rosalie Rayner, Watson demonstrated the conditioning of a fear response in Little Albert. Watson found that Albert's fear response to a white rat generalized to similar stimuli. Later, Mary Cover Jones, with Watson's help, developed techniques for removing an abnormal fear response from a child named Peter. Peter was most successfully treated with a counterconditioning method similar to one suggested by John Locke.

In 1920, Watson's affair with his student and assistant, Rosalie Rayner, resulted in his divorce and forced resignation from Johns Hopkins. After marrying Rayner, Watson went to work in advertising, where he successfully demonstrated that behaviorism could be applied to real-world situations. Another application of behaviorism's principles that Watson presented in *Psychological Care of Infant and Child* was less successful.

Watson's central learning principle was contiguity, and in *Behaviorism,* Watson argued for a radical environmentalism, denying that there are any human instincts. Watson's instinct position was consistent with that of most psychologists by the 1930s, due in part to the work of the extreme environmentalist Zing Yang Kuo. Ethologists such as Lorenz, Tinbergen, and von Frisch developed an alternative approach to the study of instincts in animal behavior.

Watson's most important contribution was probably his advocacy of psychology as an experimental, objective science free from mentalism and the introspective method. For the next 40 years after Watson, the definition of psychology became "the study of behavior."

CONNECTIONS QUESTIONS

1. How is behaviorism connected to the *Zeitgeist* of the 19th century? Specifically, what connections can you make between behaviorism and Darwin's theory of evolution? Between behaviorism and logical positivism?

2. How would you connect the following to behaviorism: Aristotle, La Mettrie, Locke, Darwin, Romanes, Morgan, Loeb, and Yerkes?

3. How is the disagreement between Pavlov and Snarsky connected with Pavlov's importance for behaviorism?

4. What are the connections between American function- alism and American behaviorism?

5. Connect Watson's mechanistic behaviorism with the decline of the instinct concept in American psycholo- gy. How is Kuo's research connected to the decline?

6. Sechenov and Watson held extreme environmentalist views. Contrast their views with Galton's ideas on heredity.

7. Draw a concept map connecting positivism, function- alism, animal psychology, and Russian objective psy- chology with American behaviorism, and compare your results with one possible solution provided on p. 566.

SUGGESTED READINGS

Babkin, B. P. (1949). *Pavlov: A biography*. Chicago: The University of Chicago Press. Boris Babkin was a student and long- time friend and associate of Pavlov. Although obviously sympathetic to his subject, Babkin's book provides a balanced consideration of Pavlov's personality, temperament, and work.

Brewer, C. L. (1991). Perspectives on John B. Watson. In G. A. Kimble, M. Wertheimer, & C. White (Eds.), *Portraits of pio- neers in psychology* (pp. 170–186). Hillsdale, NJ: Lawrence Erlbaum Associates, Publishers. Charles Brewer, a professor at Watson's alma mater, Furman University, has become an expert on Watson. His chapter contains background material on Watson not found in other sources.

Buckley, K. W. (1989). *Mechanical man: John Broadus Watson and the beginnings of behaviorism*. New York: The Guilford Press. Buckley's definitive biography is an interesting account of the life, times, and contributions to psychology of a man who was ulti- mately more successful in his careers than in his personal life.

Gray, J. A. (1979). *Ivan Pavlov*. New York: Viking Press. Gray's biography is a brief, highly readable account of the context and contri- butions of one of the world's foremost scientists, Ivan Pavlov.

Pavlov, I. P. (1960). *Conditioned reflexes: An investigation of the physiological activity of the cerebral cortex*. New York: Dover Publications, Inc. (Original work published 1927)

Pavlov, I. P. (1928). *Lectures on conditioned reflexes*. New York: International Publishers. These are the two classical collections of Pavlov's work. The writing (or the translation) is straightforward and easily understandable. The detail and care with which Pavlov and his associates made their observations is evident.

Thorndike, E. L. (1911). *Animal intelligence*. New York: The Macmillan Co. Any career devoted to the study of animal learning should begin with a careful reading of this book. The brashness and self-confidence of the young Thorndike is obvious, and it is also appar- ent why so many animal researchers of the period were offended. Thorndike's dissertation, which is included in this work, can still pro- vide insight into the animal "mind" nearly a century after it was pub- lished.

Watson, J. B. (1913). Psychology as the behaviorist views it. *Psychological Review, 20*, 158–177. Watson's "behaviorist mani- festo" is still must reading for the student of the schools of psychology.

Watson, J. B. (1919). *Psychology from the standpoint of a behavior- ist*. Philadelphia: Lippincott.

Watson, J. B. (1970). *Behaviorism*. New York: Norton. (Original work published 1924) These are two of Watson's best-known books. The first was written while Watson was still in academia, and, as Mary Cover Jones wrote, it "shook the foundations of European-bred psychology." *Behaviorism* was written after Watson had become a suc- cessful advertising executive, and it is pitched at a wider audience than its predecessor. Reprinted editions are readily available.

Watson, J. B. (1936). John Broadus Watson. In C. Murchison (Ed.), *A history of psychology in autobiography* (Vol. 3, pp. 271–281). Worcester, MA: Clark University Press.

Yerkes, R. M. (1932). Robert Mearns Yerkes: Psychobiologist. In C. Murchison (Ed.), *A history of psychology in autobiography* (Vol. 2, pp. 381–407). Worcester, MA: Clark University Press. The autobiographical essays in *A History of Psychology in Autobiography* are often fascinating. Watson's essay is particularly intriguing because of its terseness and its generally negative tone.

Neobehaviorism

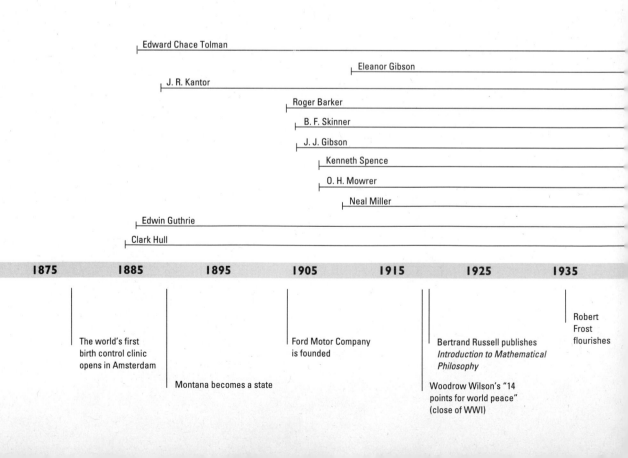

Edward Chace Tolman

Eleanor Gibson

J. R. Kantor

Roger Barker

B. F. Skinner

J. J. Gibson

Kenneth Spence

O. H. Mowrer

Neal Miller

Edwin Guthrie

Clark Hull

1875	1885	1895	1905	1915	1925	1935

The world's first
birth control clinic
opens in Amsterdam

Montana becomes a state

Ford Motor Company
is founded

Bertrand Russell publishes
*Introduction to Mathematical
Philosophy*

Woodrow Wilson's "14
points for world peace"
(close of WWI)

Robert
Frost
flourishes

After Watson, "it seemed as if all America had gone behaviorist. Everyone . . . was a behaviorist and no behaviorist agreed with any other" (Boring, 1950, p. 645). Although behaviorism became American psychology's predominant paradigm, a position it occupied relatively unchallenged for over 50 years, there were many versions of it. Our interest in this introduction will be in what made behaviorism such a dominant school, and in the body of the chapter, we will examine some of its most important versions.

In general, behaviorism can be viewed as the culmination of a line of influences that led to an emphasis on a strongly objective, rigorously experimental psychology. Accordingly, the empirical tradition of Locke and Hume (Chapter 4) represents one early influence, with later influences coming from

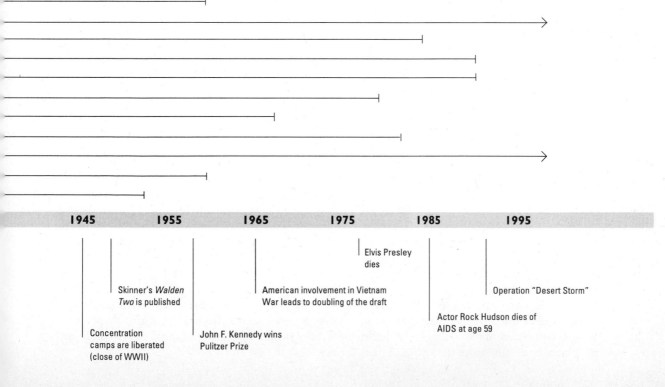

| 1945 | 1955 | 1965 | 1975 | 1985 | 1995 |

Elvis Presley
dies

Skinner's *Walden Two* is published

American involvement in Vietnam
War leads to doubling of the draft

Operation "Desert Storm"

Actor Rock Hudson dies of
AIDS at age 59

Concentration
camps are liberated
(close of WWII)

John F. Kennedy wins
Pulitzer Prize

Darwinian evolutionary theory (Chapter 9) and American functionalism (Chapters 10 and 11).

Additional influences came from the positivism of people like Avenarius and Mach (Chapter 5) and from the later positivism of the Vienna Circle, whose chief members were Carnap, Schlick (both Chapter 5), and Feigl. Herbert Feigl, with a 1927 Ph.D. in philosophy from the University of Vienna, used the term "logical positivism" to describe the Vienna Circle's position and to differentiate it from earlier positivism. Logical positivism considered that all of science's assertions should be analyzed, and only assertions that can be verified empirically, or are connected logically to verifiable assertions, are meaningful.

Mentioned in Chapter 5, **Rudolph Carnap** (1891–1970) was born in Germany and taught in Vienna and Prague before coming to the United States in 1936, where he worked first at the University of Chicago and then at UCLA from 1954 until his death. In describing logical positivism, Carnap proposed that philosophy's proper task is logical analysis, which would be applied to all scientific assertions in order to clarify the sense of each statement and to illuminate how the claims are connected. Of particular importance for psychology, Carnap believed that psychological propositions belong to empirical science just as surely as do the propositions of chemistry and biology. According to him, the language of psychology is reducible to the language of physics; psychology would become an aspect of physics because all science would ultimately reduce to physics.

At the same time that the Vienna Circle was forming, a general approach to science with its roots in positivism was introduced to physics, always psychology's model science, by P. W. Bridgman. **Percy Williams Bridgman** (1882–1961) was born in Cambridge, Massachusetts, and educated at Harvard, where he became professor of mathematics and physics in 1919. Bridgman won the Nobel Prize in physics in 1946. In *The Logic of Modern Physics,* Bridgman (1927) argued for **operationism**, which states that scientific concepts should be defined by the operations used to measure them. An example of an **operational definition** in psychology is to define hunger as the length of time since the last meal or as the number of calories consumed in a meal, that is, by the operations used to measure the concept.

According to operationism, concepts that cannot be tested by observation are pointless, and operational definitions should permit psychology to discard questions that are unanswerable by any available observational tests. Although Bridgman did not say it, the notion of private conscious experience is operationally meaningless. A number of psychologists had taken this view of the study of consciousness by the time that Bridgman's book appeared, which meant that Bridgman's call for operationism in science fell on fertile grounds in psychology.

In 1935, Harvard psychophysicist **Stanley Smith Stevens** (1906–1973) advocated an operational basis for psychology, and by the end of the decade, operationism had swept the field. According to Stevens, "[operationism] insures us against hazy, ambiguous and contradictory notions and provides the rigor of definition which silences useless controversy" (p. 323). He concluded that, "with psychology stabilized on the operational basis, we must expect still to maintain constant vigil against the human tendency to read into a concept more than is contained in the operations by which it is determined. Only then shall we never think of energy or consciousness as a substance; only then are we fortified against meaningless concepts" (p. 330).

Consistent with behaviorism's aims, operationism's acceptance by psychology contributed to behaviorism's domination. As were most psychologists of the period, the major psychologists in this chapter were philosophically attuned to logical positivism and operationism. Because their main contributions came after Watson's, they are, by definition, neobehaviorists. In reviewing the neobehaviorists' psychologies, we will see that neobehaviorism is largely synonymous with learning theory. The reason is that behaviorists studied behavior, which they assumed, following Watson and the abandonment of the instinct concept (Chapter 12), to be learned. If behavior is learned, then a theory of behavior will also be a theory of learning. We will first consider Edwin Guthrie's learning theory, as it is more similar to Watson's (and classical conditioning) than the others.

EDWIN RAY GUTHRIE

Edwin Ray Guthrie (1886–1959) was born in Lincoln, Nebraska, the oldest of five children. Guthrie's father was a minister's son who operated a Lincoln piano store, whereas his mother was the daughter of a newspaperman and had taught school before her marriage.

Guthrie's exceptional scholastic ability was demonstrated early, and he read Darwin's *Origin of Species* and *Expression of the Emotions* while just in the eighth grade. As another illustration of his ability, his high school senior thesis was so insightful that the principal interviewed him to be sure that it was not plagiarized.

Guthrie entered the University of Nebraska in 1903, where he majored in mathematics with an interest in philosophy. In 1907, he received the bachelor's degree in mathematics and philosophy with Phi Beta Kappa honors, having taken only a general course in psychology during his 4-year program.

Guthrie continued as a graduate student at the University of Nebraska, changing his major to philosophy, and he earned his master's degree in 1910. Guthrie's master's program included courses in psychology from Harry Kirke Wolfe (1858–1918), one of Wundt's early Ph.D. students. Wolfe was also the high school principal who interviewed Guthrie about his senior thesis, having served at several high schools during a period when he had been terminated from the University of Nebraska in a "debate over his orthodoxy." Guthrie was the only student in one of his courses with Wolfe, and he later recalled that Wolfe's "views on the philosophy of science were of great interest" (Guthrie, 1959, p. 160).

Guthrie's readings at Nebraska were all philosophical, and he wrote that "Mach and Avenarius were later read with that same conviction that had accompanied reading Darwin's *Origin of Species* and his *Expression of the Emotions . . .*" (Guthrie, 1959, p. 160). Thus, Guthrie, like many others, was strongly influenced by twin aspects of the era's *Zeitgeist*—evolution and positivism.

Guthrie went to the University of Pennsylvania in 1910 to work on his Ph.D. Still a philosopher, his dissertation dealt with symbolic logic and Nobel Prize–winning philosopher **Bertrand Russell**'s

FIGURE 13–1.   Edwin Ray Guthrie.
Source: Archives of the History of American Psychology.

(1872–1970) paradoxes—propositions whose truth implies their falsity, and vice versa. An example is the statement "This proposition is false."

Guthrie received his Ph.D. in 1912, and he taught high school mathematics until he was appointed as an instructor in the department of philosophy at the University of Washington in 1914. In 1919, Guthrie changed to the department of psychology, where he remained until he accepted the position as dean of the graduate school in 1943. After attaining emeritus status in 1951, Guthrie (Figure 13–1) continued to teach and participate in university affairs until his retirement in 1956 (Sheffield, 1959).

At the end of his life, Guthrie wrote that his "chief interest lay in undergraduate teaching, a fact that probably accounts for a strong bent toward simplification which, with some justification, has been described as oversimplification" (Guthrie, 1959, p. 161). In fact, simplicity is the hallmark of Guthrie's learning theory.

One-Trial, Nonreinforcement, Contiguity Learning

Like Watson, Guthrie adopted one main principle for his learning theory—contiguity—which has been embraced by almost every psychologist since Aristotle. As we indicated and Guthrie noted (Guthrie, 1952), the law of association by contiguity has been a key feature of the theories of learning of Berkeley, Hume, James Mill, Hartley, Bain (all Chapter 4), and James (Chapter 10), to list only a few. Guthrie's formal statement of the contiguity principle was: *"A combination of stimuli which has accompanied a movement will on its recurrence tend to be followed by that movement"* (p. 23, italics in the original). Note that there is nothing about the necessity for association of "satisfiers," or reward, or pleasant effects. Guthrie explicitly rejected Thorndike's law of effect as a necessary condition for learning.

Guthrie's point was that an organism will tend to do in a situation whatever it did when it was last in the situation. However, a problem for Guthrie's theory quickly arises: Which of the many things that an organism actually does will it tend to repeat? Guthrie's answer is again simple: The response that will tend to be repeated is the very last one made previously. For example, suppose you are trying to solve a mechanical puzzle. You try many different responses, and you finally hit upon one that works. The next time you pick up the puzzle, Guthrie's theory predicts that you will perform the response that solved it previously—that is, the last thing you did earlier.

Again, this sounds like one of Watson's ideas, the recency principle. Guthrie disagreed with Watson's frequency principle, however. Although Watson thought of learning as the formation of stimulus-response connections that strengthen with practice (frequency), Guthrie saw the bonds as all-or-none. A movement becomes attached to a stimulus situation on the first occasion of its pairing either completely or not at all, and the bond's strength does not change with practice.

But this idea seemingly flies in the face of common sense. If practice does not result in gradual improvement, why else would you spend so much time on the putting green or solving a particular type of math problem? How can all-or-none learning be involved in learning to ride a bicycle or drive a car?

We need to reconsider Guthrie's definition of contiguity: "A combination of stimuli which has accompanied a *movement* will on its recurrence tend to be followed by that *movement*." Guthrie differentiated movements from acts, a movement being a small unit of behavior such as the contraction of particular muscles, whereas an act is a much larger unit consisting of many movements. We tend to think of learning occurring on the level of acts—for example, the act of successfully making a 15-foot putt—when what is learned on each practice putt is to make a specific set of muscle movements in response to the specific set of stimuli in effect on that particular stroke. Guthrie's differentiation between an act and the movements comprising it accounts for how performance improves with practice (repetition, frequency) at the same time that it allows one-trial learning. Learning a particular movement to a specific set of stimuli occurs in one trial, but the act—for example, driving a car, making 15-foot putts—requires many trials for mastery because it consists of many movements.

Like Watson, Guthrie often wrote of human behavior as a mechanical affair. For him, behavior was tightly controlled by stimuli, and the changes in the S-R connections occurred through the action of simple mechanical laws. However, unlike Watson, Guthrie was receptive to concepts like desire and purpose, recognizing that much behavior is goal directed. Guthrie interpreted such concepts in terms of actual movements that may be too minute to be readily detected. He particularly emphasized **movement-produced stimuli**, which are sensations produced by the movements themselves, in maintaining sequential responding. For example, each movement of a rat running a maze produces a stimulus for the animal's next movement, which produces another stimulus, and so on. These movement-produced stimuli are also important in thought (remember Watson's subvocal speech), and in producing trains of responding leading to stimuli that are not present.

As we indicated, Guthrie was a nonreinforcement theorist; he did not consider reinforcement necessary for the S-R bond. For Guthrie, reinforcement is important because it changes the stimulus situation, thereby protecting the S-R bond between a stimulus situation and the last movement before the reinforcement.

Consider a hungry rat in a T-maze. The rat ambles down the long part of the T, comes to the crossing alley, turns right, and discovers food at the end of the alley. The reinforcement stops the rat's movement and changes the situation so that the last behavior before the food was located (turning right on the T) is the last thing done in the stimulus situation and thus is the movement learned. "*What encountering the food does is not to intensify a previous item of behavior but to protect that item from being un-learned*" (Guthrie, 1940, p. 144, italics in the original).

Guthrie's definition of reinforcement as something that changes the stimulus situation so that the last movement is paired with the original stimulus conditions leads to testable predictions. For example, consider a hungry rat that presses a bar to receive tiny food pellets. Guthrie would say that receiving a food pellet changes the situation in the box, and the rat becomes increasingly likely to press the bar because this is the last thing it does before receiving the food. However, simply removing the rat from the box after each bar press changes the stimulus conditions even more dramatically than giving the rat a food pellet. If reinforcement is simply a matter of changing the stimulus conditions, then removing the rat should also increase the probability of the rat's pressing the bar.

Seward (1942) found that rats that received food were much more likely to press the bar than rats taken out of the box. Although this and similar results appear to cast doubt on Guthrie's definition of reinforcement, there are other possible explanations for this study that may save Guthrie. Remember that the animals were hungry. In this case, hunger's effect is to produce and to maintain movement. Thus, removing the rat from the box each time it presses the bar does not change the rat's internal state, because the animal is at least as hungry as it was before being removed. Therefore, pressing the bar is never connected with a change in

the stimulus situation that matters to the animal—its internal state of hunger.

Note that the rat's hunger drive also has not been removed by eating the tiny food pellet. As Guthrie (1939) put it, "The rat at the end of the maze may be given only a small pellet of food, not enough to put an end to the state of hunger which made him restless, but enough to cause the rat to stop and eat" (p. 482).

Another interpretation of Seward's (1942) experiment compatible with Guthrie's theory is that removing the rat from the box was punishment rather than reinforcement. For Guthrie, a punisher was a stimulus that triggers new behaviors incompatible with what was last done in the stimulus situation. "It is what the punishment makes the [animal] *do* that counts or what it makes a man do, not what it makes him feel" (Guthrie, 1934a, p. 458, italics in the original).

Because Guthrie did not believe that reinforcement strengthens S-R bonds, he accounted for the extinction of the conditioned response that occurs with the removal of reinforcement by arguing that the organism has learned to do something else. Similarly, Guthrie's interpretation of forgetting was that habits do not fade away with disuse or lack of practice—they are replaced by other habits. In this interference theory (Chapter 8), forgetting occurs because new learning interferes with previous learning, or vice versa.

Although it is one thing to use reason to confound your critics, it is quite another to provide experimental evidence to support your theory, and this is why the 50-year-old Guthrie embarked on a lengthy study with a colleague, George P. Horton. The result was published in 1946 as *Cats in a Puzzle Box.*

Cats in a Puzzle Box

Like Thorndike, Guthrie and Horton (1946) put cats individually into puzzle boxes and watched them escape. Unlike Thorndike, they were interested in the movements the cats used to escape, not just in whether escape occurred and how long it took. Thorndike believed that his cat experiments revealed a learning curve showing a gradual decline in escape latencies, which is accompanied by a slow increase in the strength of the association between the stimulus situation and the successful response.

By contrast, Guthrie sought evidence for one-trial learning, which he believed would be shown by a stereotyping of behavior. Assuming that the cat learns the last thing it did in the puzzle box, then it should precisely repeat on subsequent trials the movements that freed it. Guthrie and Horton constructed a puzzle box that enabled the experimenters to observe all the animal's movements, as well as allowing them to photograph the successful movement and to record all behavior with a movie camera.

In the puzzle box, there was either a post on the floor or a tube hanging from the ceiling. Contact with this post or tube operated the front door release and simultaneously triggered the shutter of a camera, which photographed the cat's last response before being freed. Guthrie and Horton found striking evidence for stereotyped behavior, and Guthrie (1952) reported that what happens on each trial/escape from the box—one association—differs from what Thorndike thought happened. Instead, in its wanderings in the box on each trial, the animal establishes many associations that are subsequently replaced by others. The "escape routine, the essential movements of escape, are repeated because they remove the cat from the puzzle box and, being removed, *no new associations with the puzzle-box situation are possible*" (p. 270, italics in the original).

However, there is another explanation for Guthrie and Horton's (1946) study. Rather than observing learning in the cat, what Guthrie and Horton may have watched was the cats' species-typical "greeting" reaction of rubbing. Using a similar apparatus and procedure, Moore and Stuttard (1979) reported that "When we watched unobtrusively, the reaction did not occur; but when we were visible [as Guthrie and Horton were], the animals rubbed heads, flanks, or tails against the (convenient) vertical rod" (p. 1032). Further, Moore and Stuttard found that a food reward was irrelevant to the cats' behavior; naive, unrewarded animals performed the same rubbing motions in response to a human observer entering the room.

Guthrie was interested in the demonstration of his theory through real problems of real people, not just in how well the model could predict the behavior of cats in boxes. One illustration of this application can be seen in Guthrie's description of methods for changing habits.

Guthrie's Methods for Breaking Habits

The key to Guthrie's methods for breaking habits is that they are designed to produce a new behavior in the old situation. For example, if the old stimulus situation (e.g., the end of a meal) results in smoking a cigarette, the person trying to "kick the habit" should do something else instead (e.g., eat a piece of fruit). Unfortunately, this does not always work, as illustrated by the following passage:

> I once had a caller to whom I was explaining that the apple I had just finished was a splendid device for avoiding a smoke. The caller pointed out that I was smoking at that moment. The habit of lighting a cigarette was so attached to the finish of eating that smoking had been started automatically. (Guthrie, 1952, p. 116)

Even though Guthrie's methods did not always work as intended for Guthrie himself, their success in breaking habits has resulted in their being adopted by behavior therapists, who usually do not acknowledge their source. One example is the fatigue or exhaustion method.

The **fatigue** or **exhaustion method** is the typical technique used for breaking horses in which an experienced "horsebreaker" saddles, bridles, and mounts the horse, staying aboard while the horse bucks until the horse is too exhausted to struggle any more. At this point, the horse has learned a new habit to replace the old habit of bucking to the weight of a rider on its back.

Using the exhaustion method, a person who wants to quit smoking is placed in a small room and told to chain smoke until he or she exhausts the urge for another cigarette. Of course, nausea may occur, which leads to behavior incompatible with further smoking.

In Chapter 12, we discussed the case of Peter, who had a fear of white rabbits and rats. Mary Cover Jones cured Peter of his fear by exposing the child gradually to the rabbit. The essence of the **toleration** or **threshold method** is the presentation of the cues that trigger the behavior at such a low level that the response does not occur. Then the stimuli are gradually increased, and the threshold for triggering the response is raised.

Another example involves the use of **incompatible stimuli**. In this method, the stimulus for the behavior we want to remove is presented when other aspects of the situation will prevent the response from occurring. Guthrie illustrated the method with a college student who is unable to read in the bustle of the library. If the student starts a study session by reading a book so interesting that it absorbs her full attention, she will quickly become used to the noise around her and later will be able to read study material without being distracted. The situationally maladaptive response of looking up from her reading has been inhibited by the engrossing nature of what she is reading, which results in the cues of the library sounds becoming associated with the response of not looking up.

Guthrie and Pavlov: The Reply of a Psychologist to a Physiologist

Guthrie took a simple idea with a basis in antiquity—that learning occurs through the contiguity of stimulus and response—and from it derived an important theory of learning. Retaining the practical, useful flavor of Thorndike, Guthrie's theory used Pavlov's conditioning terminology but not the conditioned reflex itself. Guthrie (1930) reinterpreted 10 "established facts of learning" in light of his contiguity conditioning theory. In the paper, Guthrie carefully distinguished his conditioning theory of learning and Pavlov's theory of learning in terms of conditioned reflexes. Not surprisingly, Guthrie concluded that all the main characteristics of learning could be understood as examples of conditioning by contiguity.

Pavlov (Chapter 12) was so disturbed at what he perceived as attacks from American behaviorists (Guthrie and Lashley) that he wrote his only article for an American psychological journal (Pavlov, 1932). He began by attacking Guthrie, primarily for not recognizing the need to further analyze condi-

tioning and conditioned reflexes. "Conditioning, association by contiguity in time, conditioned reflexes, even if they serve as the factual point of departure of our investigations, are none the less subject to further analysis" (p. 92). The physiologist and the psychologist differ in their approaches to phenomena, with the psychologist using deduction from logic without verifying by experiment and the physiologist analyzing through investigation every step of the way.

Guthrie (1934b) acknowledged that Pavlov's characterization of the difference between the physiologist and the psychologist was "substantially correct." Guthrie *was* interested in "painting with a broad brush." He discussed each of Pavlov's objections, concluding that

> It is evident that the differences between us do not concern Pavlov's laboratory findings. . . . Our differences concern a strong tendency found throughout Pavlov's reports to interpret the facts in terms of [counterfeit] events and states in the cortex. These events and states are not the characteristics of nerve conduction . . . directly demonstrable in the laboratory. (p. 205)

As we noted, criticism of Pavlov's theory of nervous activity in conditioning was valid; he did have a tendency to propose mechanisms that were problematic in light of then-current knowledge of cortical function. Guthrie's reply to Pavlov ended the exchange.

Guthrie's Influence

The simplicity of Guthrie's learning theory elicited both criticism and praise. The praise has come from psychologists who prefer parsimonious theories; with its one main principle, Guthrie's theory is elegant in its simplicity. Praise has also come from psychologists who dislike jargon. As many have noted (e.g., Bower & Hilgard, 1981; Sheffield, 1959), Guthrie was a master in the use of anecdote and simple terms to illustrate complex theoretical ideas.

But the theory's simplicity has also led to the criticisms of incompleteness and vagueness. There is also the valid criticism that Guthrie often relied on his anecdotes to demonstrate his ideas rather than performing controlled experiments. Recall that

Guthrie's sole research test of his theory came in his study of stereotypy in cats learning to escape a puzzle box (Guthrie & Horton, 1946). It is a testimony to the quality of Guthrie's anecdotes that he was often successful in convincing his readers of the validity of the point he was making. For example, Skinner-trained **William K. Estes** (1919–) found Guthrie's theory so convincing that he developed a statistical theory of learning based on the principle of contiguity (Chapter 18).

Guthrie's influence extended beyond learning theory, with the publication of *The Psychology of Human Conflict* (Guthrie, 1938). Guthrie acknowledged his debt to the writings of Pierre Janet (Chapter 15), and, in fact, he and his wife (Helen Macdonald Guthrie) had earlier translated Janet's *Principles of Psychotherapy. Human Conflict* "was not too well received in some quarters, perhaps because it favored Janet over Freud and took a generally critical attitude toward psychoanalysis" (Sheffield, 1959, p. 646). In addition to *Human Conflict,* Guthrie's influence in abnormal psychology can be seen in the adoption by behavior therapists of many of his suggestions for breaking bad habits.

Guthrie's honors included being elected APA president in 1945 and receiving an honorary doctorate from the University of Nebraska the same year. In 1958, Guthrie was given the American Psychological Foundation's Gold Medal Award for his contributions to the science of learning. The University of Washington honored Guthrie in 1956 by naming a building after him.

EDWARD CHACE TOLMAN

Edward Chace Tolman (1886–1959) was born in Newton, Massachusetts, the son of the president of a manufacturing company and "a warm, loving, but in some areas Puritanical mother . . ." (Tolman, 1952, p. 324). Because of family pressure, Tolman followed his older brother to the Massachusetts Institute of Technology, where he received a B.S. in electrochemistry in 1911. After reading some William James in his senior year, Tolman (Figure 13–2) decided to be a philosopher, and he enrolled in summer school at Harvard planning to become one.

FIGURE 13–2.   Edward Tolman in about 1911, the year he graduated from MIT.

Source: Archives of the History of American Psychology.

Tolman took two courses that summer, one in philosophy taught by **Ralph Barton Perry** (1876–1957) and one in psychology taught by Robert Yerkes (Chapter 12). Perry's course convinced him that he was not bright enough to become a philosopher, and psychology seemed to be a good compromise between philosophy and science. Although it turned him to psychology, Tolman also acknowledged that Perry's course "laid the basis for my later interest in motivation and . . . gave me the main concepts . . . which I have retained ever since . . ." (Tolman, 1952, p. 325). Perry's attitudes toward Watsonian behaviorism were also influential, as he welcomed Watson's methodological objectivity but rejected Watson's reductionism. Anticipating the importance of purpose in Tolman's behaviorism, Perry (1918) suggested a learning process in which purpose was "significantly applicable."

With only the two summer courses as background, Tolman enrolled at Harvard in the fall of 1911 in the joint department of philosophy and psychology. Tolman's graduate research experience presented him with a dilemma: On the one hand, Münsterberg (Chapter 7), who was nominally in charge of the laboratory, often made little opening speeches to the students in which he claimed that introspection was *the* method of psychology. On the other hand, most of the laboratory's research—supervised by Langfeld (Chapter 10)—was quite objective. "If introspection were 'the' method of psychology and we weren't doing it, shouldn't I really go to Cornell where Titchener taught one to do it properly?" (Tolman, 1952, p. 326).

Fortunately, the resolution of Tolman's conflict came in Yerkes's comparative psychology course, which introduced Tolman to Watson's behaviorism. Watson's idea that the true method of psychology was the objective measurement of behavior and not introspection came as a great relief to Tolman.

After his first Harvard year, Tolman went to Germany for the summer to practice the language in preparation for the required Ph.D. examination. Tolman spent part of the summer in Giessen with Kurt Koffka, the Gestalt psychologist (Chapter 14). Tolman's first introduction to Gestalt psychology prepared him to be receptive to Gestalt concepts when they became widely available to American psychology after World War I. In 1923, Tolman returned to Giessen to learn more from Koffka.

Tolman received the Ph.D. from Harvard in 1915 and took an instructorship at Northwestern University in Illinois. Tolman (1952) recalled that he was "self-conscious and inarticulate, and was afraid of my classes" (p. 327), and he was dismissed in 1918 because of "war retrenchment and my not too successful teaching" (p. 327). With Langfeld's aid, Tolman obtained an instructorship at the University of California at Berkeley, where he spent the rest of his career. As he explained it, "Whatever my increasing psychological maturity . . . I like to credit most of it to the social, intellectual, and physical virtues of Berkeley plus an extraordinarily happy marriage" (p. 328).

Arriving at Berkeley in 1918, Tolman learned that it was up to him to suggest a new course. "Remem-

bering Yerkes' course and Watson's textbook I proposed 'comparative psychology.' And it was this that finally launched me down the behavioristic slope" (Tolman, 1952, p. 329).

Purposive Behaviorism

Unlike Guthrie, Tolman relished laboratory research, particularly with rats and mazes. In fact, it can be argued that Tolman thought of the world as a giant maze (Smith, 1990), and he built mazes and used them and his rats to test key elements of the learning theories of Watson and Thorndike and later, Hull.

As a behaviorist, Tolman was concerned with objective behavior—not with conscious experience—and with the effect of external stimuli on behavior. However, unlike Watson and ‹Guthrie, Tolman was little interested in molecular behavior, behavior analyzed in terms of single movements of individual muscles. Instead, he studied molar behavior, which is behavior considered in large units—for example, Guthrie's acts. Examples of Tolman's molar behaviors included

> A rat running a maze; . . . a man driving home to dinner; . . . my friend and I telling one another our thoughts and feelings—*these are behaviors* (qua [as] *molar*). And it must be noted that in mentioning no one of them have we referred to, or . . . even known what were the exact muscles and glands, sensory nerves, and motor nerves involved. (Tolman, 1932/1967, p. 8, italics in the original)

In addition, Tolman stressed the relation of behavior toward goals, recognizing that much behavior is concerned with a search for a goal. In other words, behavior has a purpose, and Tolman's brand of behaviorism has been called "**purposive behaviorism.**" In fact, Tolman (1932/1967) titled his most important statement of his system *Purposive Behavior in Animals and Men* and dedicated it to M.N.A.—*Mus norvegicus albinus* (literally "white Norway mouse," but Tolman meant the white rat). Tolman's self-deprecating sense of humor is immediately apparent: "First, I would ask forgiveness in that, as a presentation of a system, this book is not shorter and more to the point. No mere system is worth so many pages nor deserves so laborious and minute a treatment" (p. xvii). Later, he apologized for all the "neologisms I have introduced" (p. xviii). Many of Tolman's neologisms—newly created words or expressions—have been incorporated into psychology's language. One example is Tolman's "cognitive map."

Purposive Behavior in Animals and Men

Initially, Tolman's attention was attracted to Watson's and Guthrie's denial of the law of effect and to Watson's emphasis on frequency and recency. However, he did not like Watson's atomistic notions of stimulus and response.

> I was already becoming influenced by Gestalt psychology and conceived that a rat in running a maze must be learning a lay-out or pattern and not just having connections between atom-like stimuli and atom-like responses 'stamped in' or 'stamped out,' whether by exercise *or* by effect. (Tolman, 1952, p. 329, italics in original)

Tolman soon saw experimental evidence that argued against the primacy of Watson's ideas of frequency and recency.

With advice from Tolman, Zing Yang Kuo (Chapter 12) gave rats a choice of four different routes leading to food (Kuo, 1922). Kuo's study showed Tolman "that the successive droppings out of the bad routes were in no case due to a preceding greater frequency or recency on the other routes" (Tolman, 1932/1967, p. 349).

Like Watson, Tolman did not believe that the consequence of a response, its reinforcement, is important for learning. However, unlike Watson, Tolman recognized the importance of reinforcement for motivating learning. Thus, he distinguished between learning and **performance**, holding that learning occurs in the absence of reward but that reward is important for an animal's performance—that is, its actual behavior. In other words, learning may have occurred without being evident in the organism's behavior; a reward motivates performance and reveals the learning that has occurred. The key early study that reinforced the learning-

performance distinction was contained in H. C. Blodgett's 1925 dissertation, which provided evidence for **latent learning**.

Blodgett ran three groups of hungry rats in a maze: Group I was fed in the food box at the end of the maze after each day's run; Group II received no reward for the first 6 days and then was rewarded on subsequent days; Group III received no reward for the first 2 days, with reward thereafter. Before receiving reward, rats in Groups II and III showed no evidence for learning. However, errors were halved on the day after the reward was introduced, and by the day after that, animals in Groups II and III were performing as well as the rats rewarded throughout. Tolman concluded that learning had been occurring in the absence of reward—was latent—but an incentive was necessary for the learning to appear in the rats' performance (Tolman, 1932/1967).

Tolman found further evidence to challenge Thorndike's mechanical view of reinforcement's effect on learning. "According to Thorndike, an animal learned . . . merely because a quite irrelevant 'pleasantness' or 'unpleasantness' was . . . shot at it, as from a squirt gun, after it had reached the given goal-box or gone into the given *cul de sac*" (Tolman, 1952, p. 330). According to Tolman, an animal's experience with a particular reward in a particular situation leads to the expectation that in future occurrences of the situation, the particular reward will continue to be encountered.

Perhaps the most dramatic evidence for reward expectancies was observed in monkeys by Otto Tinklepaugh (1928). In a delayed-response task—an animal is shown the reward location but prevented for different lengths of time from obtaining it—Tinklepaugh decided to see exactly what the monkey remembered about the reward by surreptitiously substituting a piece of lettuce for the piece of banana he had shown the animal. Here is Tinklepaugh's description of a typical test:

> After the delay, the monkey is told to 'come get the food.' She . . . rushes to the proper container and picks it up. She extends her hand to seize the food. But her hand drops to the floor without touching it. She looks at the lettuce but (unless very hungry) does not touch it. She looks around the cup and behind the board. She

stands up and looks under and around her. She picks the cup up and examines it thoroughly inside and out. She has on occasion turned toward the observers . . . and shrieked at them in apparent anger. (p. 224)

It is difficult not to conclude, as Tinklepaugh did, that the monkey's memory included a representation of the piece of banana under the container.

Tolman's program also included studies that challenged Carr and Watson's (1908) conclusion that rats learn a sequence of motor responses in a maze. For example, D. A. Macfarlane trained one group of rats to swim through a maze initially, whereas the other group waded through the maze at first. Then, the required responses were reversed, and the "swimming" rats waded, but the "wading" rats were forced to swim. Tolman (1932/1967) noted

> that the results of this experiment were . . . such as to prove surprising to anyone convinced of the old kinesthetic doctrine of maze learning. . . . The kinesthetic impulses received as a result of wading must have been quite different in quality, and very different in quantity, from those received from swimming and *vice versa*, and yet the change from the one condition to the other, although it caused evident disruption, surprise, etc., did not cause any considerable increase in the error scores, per se. The rats still *"knew" where to go*, although at first their behavior was obviously upset . . . at finding free water instead of submerged bottom, or *vice versa*. (pp. 80–81, italics in the original)

That rats typically learn *where* to go in a maze for reward rather than a sequence of specific motor responses was even more dramatically illustrated in a study by Tolman and Honzik. Tolman and Honzik used the maze shown in Figure 13–3, which had three different pathways to the food box: Path 1 was the shortest and most direct; Path 2 was intermediate in length; and Path 3 was the longest.

When Path 1 was blocked at A, the rats backed out of Path 1 and chose Path 2 more than 90% of the time; because Path 2 was second in preference to Path 1, this finding was not surprising. The crucial question was what the rats would do if they found Path 1 blocked at B, which would also prevent them from reaching the goal by Path 2. Would they try

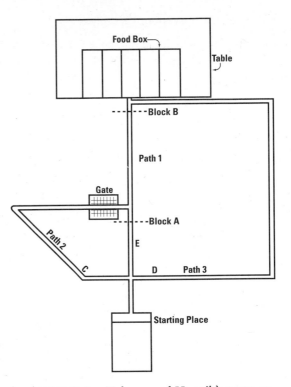

FIGURE 13–3. Tolman and Honzik's maze on which rats demonstrated "insight."

Source: Tolman's (1967) Purposive Behavior in Animals and Men. *New York: Irvington Publishers, Inc. (original work published 1932 by Appleton Century Crofts). Reprinted by permission of Irvington Publishers, Inc.*

Path 2, the simple S-R prediction, or would they be aware of the layout of the maze and select unblocked Path 3? This problem is similar to the *Umweg* or detour problem developed by Wolfgang Köhler (Chapter 14). Köhler visited Tolman's laboratory at Berkeley in the mid-1920s, and the English translation of Köhler's classic work, entitled *The Mentality of Apes,* was published in 1925, well before Tolman and Honzik's experiment.

Tolman and Honzik's results were unequivocal: On the first "test" run, 14 out of 15 rats (93%) selected Path 3. The simple S-R prediction proved incorrect; the rats had gotten the "big picture" of the maze. To use Köhler's term, they had developed "insight." Later studies showed that Tolman and Honzik's results were reproducible but that the "insight" explanation was not as clearcut as it seemed in 1930 (Bower & Hilgard, 1981).

Intervening Variables

As noted, Tolman believed that behavior is goal oriented. A particular goal can be obtained through many different acts, and Tolman's theory was designed to explain the complexity of behavior used to obtain goals. Thus, he considered it essential to take into account the organism's cognitions—its knowledge of the world. This knowledge constitutes behavior space, which is closely related to Kurt Lewin's "life space" (Chapter 14), and Tolman acknowledged his debt to Lewin's ideas in many publications (e.g., Tolman, 1939/1951, 1952).

In accounting for behavioral complexity, Tolman extensively used **intervening variables**, which are constructs that come between the stimulus and the response and are completely defined by the S-R conditions. The intervening variable is a purely abstract behavioral concept, without any presumed physiological mechanism underlying it. Although the exact list of intervening variables changed throughout Tolman's career, we can illustrate the concept with a well-known example: the cognitive map.

In 1959, Tolman wrote that "Learning . . . is conceived by me as the acquisition of . . . connections I have called means-end readinesses or beliefs" (p. 124). The combination of these beliefs becomes the organism's **cognitive map**, which may be defined as an organism's understanding of the layout of its environment. In the case of a rat learning a maze,

> the incoming impulses [sensory stimuli from the maze and its surroundings] are usually worked over and elaborated in the central control room into a tentative, cognitive-like map of the environment. And it is this tentative map, indicating routes and paths and environmental relationships, which finally determines what responses, if any, the animal will finally release. (Tolman, 1948, p. 192)

Note that the cognitive map, which we have called an intervening variable, appears to have a physiological basis. In the quotation, Tolman referred to the "map" as being "elaborated in the central control room," referring to the brain. MacCorquodale and Meehl (1948) differentiated between intervening variables and constructs with more surplus meaning and at least the implication of a physiological basis, which

they called **hypothetical constructs** (Chapter 18). According to MacCorquodale and Meehl's differentiation, Tolman's cognitive map is a hypothetical construct, not an intervening variable. Tolman acknowledged MacCorquodale and Meehl's distinction but disagreed with it.

Tolman's evidence for the rat's development of cognitive maps came from several different types of study. For example, during the period of nonreward in latent learning studies, rats were learning the location of the blind alleys. "They had been building up a 'map,' and could utilize the latter as soon as they were motivated to do so" (Tolman, 1948, p. 195).

Studies of vicarious trial and error (VTE) also support the cognitive map idea. VTE refers to a rat's hesitant, looking-back-and-forth behavior at a maze choice point, or to similar behavior when an animal has to choose between two stimuli in a discrimination test. Tolman (1939/1951) found that the VTEing began to appear at the time the animals started to learn and that VTEing decreased when the learning was established. He concluded that "VTEing . . . is evidence that in the critical stages [of learning] . . . the animal's activity is not just one of responding passively to discrete stimuli, but rather one of the active selecting and comparing of stimuli" (Tolman, 1948, p. 200)—that is, of developing a cognitive map.

Further evidence for cognitive maps came from Ira Krechevsky's so-called **hypothesis experiments** (Tolman, 1948). Krechevsky—later known as David Krech—observed that rats tested on discrimination problems often exhibit systematic responses that appear to an observer to be the result of the rats' testing a particular hypothesis. For example, in a two-choice situation where the stimuli are separated laterally, rats often go to one particular side initially, apparently testing a spatial position hypothesis. If this hypothesis fails to maximize success, rats select another hypothesis, which might be discarded for a third, and so on. Tolman wrote that Krech used the term *hypothesis* to refer to what Tolman had "been calling cognitive maps which, it appears from his experiments, get set up in a tentative fashion to be tried out first one and then another until, if possible, one is found which works" (p. 202).

Finally, the idea that rats develop cognitive maps is supported by **place learning** experiments, in which an animal learns to go to a specific place rather than learning to make a specific sequence of motor responses. Macfarlane's study of swimming and/or wading rats and Tolman and Honzik's blocked-pathway experiment indicated that rats do not learn a specific sequence of motor responses but rather learn about the maze, if they are permitted to do so.

Another type of place-learning experiment directly pitted place learning against response learning to see which was learned more readily by rats. For example, Tolman, Ritchie, and Kalish (1946) used the apparatus shown in Figure 13–4. Half of the animals were reinforced for always going to a particular place on the elevated maze, whereas the other animals were reinforced for always making the same response. That is, if a place-learning rat was being taught to find food at F_1, then it should turn right when started from S_1 but left when started from S_2. A response-learning rat reinforced for always turning right at point C would find food at F_1 when it started from S_1 and at F_2 when it started from S_2. In this experiment, all rats in the place-learning group learned within 8 trials, whereas none of the response learners learned as quickly and several had not attained the criterion of learning after 72 trials.

Subsequent place learning studies gave conflicting results. In resolving the controversy, Restle (1957) noted that there is nothing about the rat that makes it inherently a "place" learner or a "response" learner. Rats use all the cues available to them, and if such cues favor place learning, then the place learners perform better than the response learners. Restle concluded that further "definitive" studies would prove fruitless.

Tolman's Influence

As you can see, Tolman introduced a number of apparently subjective, mentalistic concepts into his accounts of the learned behavior of rats. Although the notion that rats form cognitive maps and that their behavior has purpose seems foreign to Watson's aims for behaviorism, Tolman considered himself a behaviorist. In fact, there is no contradiction. In 1932, Tolman explained how he could employ mentalistic terms such as purpose and cognition while remaining true to behaviorism:

> Finally . . . it must . . . be emphasized that purposes and cognitions which are thus immediately, immanently [directly], in behavior are wholly objective as to definition. They are defined by characters and the relationships which we observe out there in the behavior. We, the observers, watch the behavior of the rat, the cat, or the man, and note its character as a getting to such and such by means of such and such a selected pattern of commerces-with. It is we . . . who note these perfectly objective characters as immanent in the behavior and have happened to choose the terms *purpose* and *cognition* as generic names for such characters. (pp. 12–13)

Thus, Tolman believed it was possible to introduce apparently mentalistic, but common-sense, ideas such as insight, purpose, and expectancy into an objective psychology. In addition, his provocative experimental results challenged contemporary learning theorists—particularly Hull (discussed later)—and forced them to modify their theories in order to deal with his findings.

In Chapter 12, we noted that it was often said that with Watson, psychology lost its mind. Krech (1967) wrote "that it was actually Tolman and his rats who sought to give back to psychology its mind—its insights, its cognitions, its purposes. And this, I believe, played a crucial role in shaping the

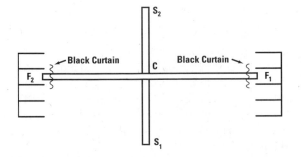

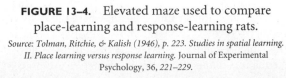

FIGURE 13–4.   Elevated maze used to compare place-learning and response-learning rats.

Source: Tolman, Ritchie, & Kalish (1946), p. 223. Studies in spatial learning. II. Place learning versus response learning. Journal of Experimental Psychology, 36, 221–229.

history of American psychology" (p. xv). By including such apparently relevant concepts as insight, cognition, and purpose, Tolman's behaviorism was less easily dismissed by "people psychologists"—for example, clinical, child, and social psychologists—than Watsonian behaviorism or Pavlovian conditioning. In this sense, Tolman's work "helped to preserve animal experimentation, learning theory, and Behaviorism as viable forces in the development of American psychology" (p. xv). In addition, Tolman's "cognitive behaviorism" was clearly an important influence on modern cognitive psychology (Chapter 20).

Unlike such professional rivals as Hull and Skinner, Tolman did not seek to make converts or disciples of his many students. According to former pupil Henry Gleitman (1991), students "mattered much more to Tolman than his own beliefs, or, rather more than instilling his own beliefs in students" (p. 240). When Tolman learned of Gleitman's brief defection to Hullian theory, his reaction was characteristically straightforward:

> "Gleitman, you son of a bitch, I hear you are becoming a Hullian! So okay. Just be a good Hullian!" (p. 240)

As a result of "the loose, exploratory style of [Tolman's] research and theorizing . . ." (Smith, 1990, p. 248) and Tolman's unwillingness to proselytize, there were no Tolmanians, as there were Hullians and Skinnerians. As Hill (1971) expressed it,

> [Tolman] wanted not so much to build a truly adequate theory as to explore the whole activity of theory building, both playing with it himself and puncturing the excessive claims of others. As a result, he has been widely respected and widely loved, but not widely followed. (p. 129)

Despite his lack of followers, Tolman's professional accomplishments resulted in the APA presidency in 1937, an invitation to membership in the Society of Experimental Psychologists, and an APA Distinguished Scientific Contribution Award in 1957.

Tolman was also widely respected at Berkeley. Toward the end of the McCarthy era, the university attempted to force its faculty to sign loyalty oaths. In 1949–1950, Tolman led the faculty in opposition to

signing. Acknowledging that his refusal to sign would cause him little economic hardship, he advised his younger colleagues to sign the oath and leave the battle to those who could afford to pursue it. For his courageous stand, Tolman received wide acclaim and honorary degrees from several major universities.

Of his career in psychology, Tolman wrote in 1959,

> I have liked to think about psychology in ways that have proved congenial to me. Since all the sciences, and especially psychology, are still immersed in such tremendous realms of the uncertain and the unknown, the best that any individual scientist, especially any psychologist, can do seems to be to follow his own gleam and his own bent, however inadequate they may be. In fact, I suppose that actually this is what we all do. In the end, the only sure criterion is to have fun. And I have had fun. (p. 152)

During the 1940s, Tolman offered a major alternative to Hull's neobehaviorism, which was arguably the dominant view at the time. From Tolman the unsystematic theorist, we turn to Hull, whose "gleam and bent" lay in developing the most systematic learning theory ever attempted.

CLARK LEONARD HULL

Clark Leonard Hull (1884–1952) was born in a log house on a farm near Akron, New York, and grew up on a farm in Michigan, where the family moved when he was very young. Hull attended a one-room rural school until he was 16; he was an able student with a lifelong interest in building machines. At 17, he passed a teachers' examination and taught for a year in the same school, an experience that motivated him to continue his education.

After a year of high school, Hull attended the academy of Alma College in Michigan, where the study of geometry "proved to be the most important event of [his] intellectual life . . ." (Hull, 1952a, p. 144). At the graduation dinner from the academy, he contracted typhoid fever, which nearly killed him and left him with a generalized bad memory for names.

After studying courses at Alma College leading to work as a mining engineer, Hull took a job at the Oliver iron mines in Hibbing, Minnesota. Two months later, Hull contracted polio, which left him with a permanently paralyzed left leg that was supported by a steel brace he designed himself. Hull's disability made a career as a mining engineer impossible, and he briefly considered becoming a minister in the Unitarian Church before turning to psychology. As a preliminary survey of the subject, he read both volumes of James's *Principles of Psychology*. After another brief stint as a teacher, Hull married Bertha Iutzi, and the newlyweds pooled their resources and entered the University of Michigan. At Michigan, Hull's most memorable course was a year in experimental psychology, with W. B. Pillsbury's lectures and J. F. Shepard's laboratory. APA president in 1910, Walter Bowers Pillsbury (1872–1960) was also known as an early historian of psychology.

Hull received his bachelor's degree from Michigan in 1913, at the age of 30. After graduation, he took a teaching position in Richmond, Kentucky. Despite a heavy teaching load, Hull found time to build an exposure apparatus that he later used for his dissertation.

Through Pillsbury's assistance, Hull became a part-time teaching assistant in psychology at the University of Wisconsin, working under Joseph Jastrow (Chapter 10). In his spare time, Hull worked on a series of problems concerning concept formation, using his exposure apparatus. Hull (Figure 13–5) received his Ph.D. in 1918, continuing as a staff member at Wisconsin.

Hull's Three Interests

Although the sequential discussion of Hull's disparate areas of interest—aptitude testing, hypnosis, and learning theory—makes it appear that each interest was developed serendipitously, Triplet (1982) argued that they all fit within a major theme "that ties Hull's life work together as a unified whole" (p. 24). The theme is Hull's ambition to achieve personal recognition for his work. At the time Hull began work on them, aptitude testing,

FIGURE 13–5.   Clark Leonard Hull.

Source: Archives of the History of American Psychology.

hypnosis, and learning theory had not been systematically investigated in a manner that met Hull's stringent criteria. He believed that by employing his talents in these areas, he would attain the recognition he sought.

Aptitude Testing

Hull's interest in aptitude testing began when he was asked to teach a course in psychological tests and measurements. Changing the course name to "Aptitude Testing," Hull found that much of the work in the area was methodologically weak and too little concerned with test validation. "With characteristic energy he set about the task of organizing the field systematically" (Hovland, 1952, pp. 347–348), which he accomplished by publishing *Aptitude Testing* in 1928.

Hull also developed an aptitude test and invented a machine to compute correlation coefficients. As he later explained, "It happens that I am very prone to make small errors in such computations, . . . [and] I conceived the idea of building a machine which would do nearly all of the correlation work automatically" (Hull, 1952a, p. 151). Hull built two machines, one of which is in the Smithsonian Institution in Washington, D.C., but he abandoned aptitude testing when his survey of the field made him pessimistic about the future of such work. However, by this time he had another interest.

Hypnosis

In addition to the aptitude testing course, Hull was asked to teach Jastrow's introductory course in psychology for premedical students. One of Hull's innovations was the topic of suggestion, which he believed was used a great deal in contemporary medicine. Hull began to study hypnotic suggestion, using the quantitative methodology of experimental psychology to make his work more robust than most earlier research (see Chapter 15).

Hull's hypnosis research (performed mostly at Wisconsin) yielded 32 published papers and a major book, *Hypnosis and Suggestibility: An Experimental Approach,* published in 1933. Hull concluded that hypnosis was merely a state of hypersuggestibility differing quantitatively, but not qualitatively, from the normal state. Further, he believed that there were no hypnotic phenomena that could not occur in the normal state, given appropriate suggestion.

Hull's hypnosis research was attacked almost immediately at Yale, where he went in 1929. The opposition came first from medical authorities and then from one of Hull's female subjects, who sued the university. Despite the bizarre nature of the charges, Yale bought the woman's silence, and Hull was forced to pursue a new research interest (Kimble, 1991).

Hypothetico-Deductive Learning Theory

Although Hull was sympathetic with Watson's rejection of introspection and with his desire for objectivity in psychology, he was uncertain about Watson's more dogmatic claims and repelled by the fanaticism on both sides of the debate over behaviorism. Briefly, he was attracted to the Gestalt movement that began at about the same time as behaviorism. In fact, Mills (1988) suggested that the primary motive driving

Hull's development of a learning theory was his need to respond to the Gestaltists' challenge. While listening to Koffka's lectures, Hull agreed with most of Koffka's criticisms of behaviorism. However, exposure to Koffka—Hull had him brought to Wisconsin in 1926–1927—had the opposite effect on Hull that it had on Tolman: "Instead of converting me to *Gestalt-theorie,* the result was a belated conversion to a . . . behaviorism mainly concerned with the determination of the quantitative laws of behavior and their deductive systematization" (Hull, 1952a, p. 154). At the same time, Hull was positively influenced by his study of Pavlov's *Conditioned Reflexes* and by the empiricist approach to animal behavior exemplified by Morgan's and Thorndike's work (Triplet, 1982). Rather than concluding that Gestalt theory was sound, Hull decided "that Watson had not made out as clear a case for behaviorism as the facts warranted" (Hull, 1952a, p. 154). He would remedy Watson's failure with a system of postulates and theorems immune from "the damaging criticisms of Koffka and the other [Gestaltists]" (Mills, p. 397). In other words, he would develop a **hypothetico-deductive learning theory**.

In 1929, Hull was called by President Angell (Chapter 11) to the Institute of Psychology at Yale; the Institute of Psychology soon became part of the Institute of Human Relations. Although he usually conducted a weekly 2-hour seminar, Hull's lack of formal teaching duties gave him freedom to pursue his goal of a systematic learning theory. In addition, his work was aided by the many capable psychologists his seminar attracted, including such subsequent luminaries as Kenneth Spence, Neal Miller, John Dollard, O. H. Mowrer (all discussed later), and Carl I. Hovland (Chapter 19).

In Hull's (1929) first essay into learning theory, he described the conditioned reflex "as an automatic trial-and-error mechanism which mediates, blindly but beautifully, the adjustment of the organism to a complex environment" (p. 498), and the same theme reappears in Hull's later work (e.g., Hull, 1937, 1952b). Around 1930, Hull concluded that psychology is a true natural science and that he could describe its primary laws with equations. As he began to develop his system, Hull realized that it would take at least three books to detail it adequately:

one volume introducing the system and stating its primary principles; a second volume in which he would deduce the more common forms of individual behavior from the primary principles; and a third volume that would provide similar deductions for social or group behavior. Hull's *Principles of Behavior* appeared in 1943, and *A Behavior System* was published shortly after his death. To some degree, the aims of the third volume were accomplished by his students (e.g., Neal Miller).

Fifty years before he died, Hull began a journal of his thoughts on his work, his life's progress, and on things in general. He called these his "idea books," and he had filled 73 of them by the end of his life, with his last entry coming just 18 days before he died (Hays, 1962). In Hull's June 16, 1930, entry, he gave the rationale for and a clear statement of his novel approach to system building:

> Every time I start reading writers of the classic theories of knowledge I am at once struck with the extreme subjectivity of their point of departure. . . . [A]ll have started from introspective experience as the more primary and more basic, and attempted to derive a system with which to explain action and human nature as well. . . . [As a result,] . . . innumerable attempts to derive a satisfactory (i.e., scientific) theory of knowledge and of thought and reason from conscious experience as such have failed. . . . I propose to develop a system which starts from exactly the opposite end. . . . I shall start with action—habit—and proceed to deduce all the rest, including conscious experience, from action, i.e., habit. (Hull, 1962, pp. 836–837)

In his APA presidential address, Hull (1937) listed three requirements for a sound theoretical system: First, there should be a set of postulates with all important terms defined operationally. Next, using logic, a series of interlocking theorems about the field's most important phenomena should be deduced from the postulates. Finally, the theorems should agree with the discipline's known facts. If they agree, the system is probably true; if they do not agree, the system is demonstrably false. If it is impossible to tell whether the theorems agree or disagree, the system is neither true nor false; it is scientifically meaningless. Note the similarity between Hull's conception of a sound theoretical system and the tenets of logical positivism noted early in the chapter.

For Hull, a valid theory was one containing a logical system of postulates from which could be derived theorems. Hull's postulates would not be proven but would be the starting points for subsequent proofs. From them, theorems—as laws of behavior—could be deduced logically. At this point, experiments would be performed to test the theorems; a positive outcome would support the whole theory, whereas a negative outcome would weaken the overall theory, forcing revision.

Hull's (1952b) final learning system contained 17 postulates, several with corollaries, from which he had derived more than 130 theorems, many with multiple parts. Obviously, this was a grand attempt to systematize a particular area of psychology. Because of the complexity of Hull's (still unfinished) system, we will present only a simplified version in order to give you some of the flavor of what he was trying to accomplish.

For Hull, as for others before him, all learned behavior involved stimulus-response connections. Like the functionalist Woodworth (Chapter 11), Hull realized the importance of internal factors that can affect an organism's response to a stimulus, and one of Hull's students wrote: "Hull's S-R diagrams . . . may be thought of as being essentially an elaboration of the S-O-R formula of Woodworth" (Spence, 1952, pp. 645–646). Hull followed Tolman's lead in filling the organism with intervening variables that mediate between stimulus and response.

Thus, Hull's predictive scheme contained four stages: Stages 1 and 4 detailed independent variables and dependent variables, respectively. Stages 2 and 3 consisted of intervening variables assumed to connect the stimuli and responses. A schematic representation of the stages, along with some representative intervening variables, is shown in Figure 13–6.

Note that independent variables—experimenter-manipulated variables—can refer to stimulation the organism is receiving at the moment (e.g., electric shock), stimulation from preceding events (e.g., time since the last meal), or previous experience in the particular learning situation (e.g., number of times the response to be learned has been made).

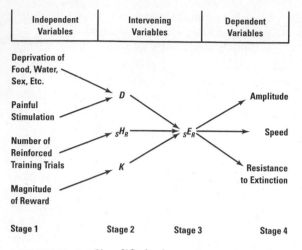

FIGURE 13–6. Simplified schematic representation of the four stages in Hull's system.

Source: Adapted from Figure 5 from Learning: a survey of psychological interpretations, *4th ed. by Winfred Hill. Copyright © 1985 by Harper & Row Publishers, Inc. Reprinted by permission of Addison Wesley Educational Publishers, Inc.*

The different independent variables affect intervening variables in the second stage. For example, food or water deprivation and painful stimulation affect the intervening variable labelled "D" for drive. For Hull, **drive** is an activated state of the organism, and reward is drive reduction.

The number of reinforced training trials affects habit strength ($_sH_R$), one of Hull's most important intervening variables. **Habit strength** is the strength of the S-R connection. "H" stands for habit, which is a permanent connection between the particular stimulus (S) and the response (R). Each time a response occurs in the presence of a stimulus and is quickly followed by reinforcement, the strength of the bond between S and R increases. A simplified version of the equation Hull used to express the relationship between habit strength and the number of reinforced trials is

$$_sH_R = 1 - 10^{-.0305N},$$

where N is the number of reinforced trials. Exact values like the exponent –.0305 generally came from the results of a single experiment. As N grows, the fraction subtracted from 1 becomes smaller so that the limit of habit strength is 1, which is approached

more and more slowly with each additional reinforced trial. Herbart (Chapter 5) thought of psychology as being mathematical, and it has been noted that Herbart's equation to express the rise of a concept in consciousness is similar to Hull's function for the rise of habit strength (Bakan, 1952).

The magnitude of the reward on the previous response affects the intervening variable labelled "K," which was Hull's symbol for **incentive motivation**. K's inclusion as a separate intervening variable was a change in Hull's system from 1943 to 1952. In 1943, Hull treated the quality or quantity of reward as just another aspect of reinforcement—the larger (or more preferred) the reward, the greater the drive reduction and the larger the increase in habit strength. However, experiments showed that increasing the reward resulted in more rapid improvements in performance than would be possible given the slow growth of habit strength. Even more problematic, a decrease in reward actually produced a decrement in performance, suggesting a decrease in habit strength. Such a decrease is impossible assuming a permanent S-R bond whose strength is increased with successive reinforcements, no matter what their size.

Thus, Hull adopted Kenneth Spence's idea of incentive motivation ("K" for Kenneth; Malone, 1991), which is affected independently of habit strength. Finding a large reward on a trial after receiving small rewards previously increases the organism's motivation for the incentive, even though each rewarded trial adds only a small increment to habit strength. Making K separate from $_sH_R$ provided a way to account for dramatic increases or decreases in performance with changes in reward magnitude. Here, note the importance of Tolman's learning-performance distinction; habit strength is a learning variable, whereas incentive motivation is a performance variable. Also, recall Tolman's expectancy effect—animals learn to expect a particular quantity (or quality) of reward, and there are dramatic behavior changes when this expectation is not fulfilled (e.g., Tinklepaugh's monkey discovering lettuce instead of banana).

Now we come to Stage 3 and $_sE_R$, which Hull called **excitatory potential** and **reaction potential** in 1952. Reaction potential is the total tendency to make a particular response to a particular stimulus and is equal to the product of the intervening variables in Stage 2, or

$$_sE_R = {_s}H_R \times D \times K.$$

In other words, the tendency for an organism to make a given response to a given stimulus is the product of habit strength developed through reinforced practice ($_sH_R$), an internal state of the organism (D), and the magnitude of the incentive found on the immediately preceding trial (K).

The fourth stage of Hull's system consists of the dependent variables, which are measurements of behavior. In Figure 13–6, reaction potential ($_sE_R$) determines the amplitude or size of the response, response speed, and resistance to extinction. As reaction potential increases, so does the size of the response, its speed, and how many responses are made before the organism stops responding. A variety of additional variables, such as R_G (goal response) and r_G (anticipatory goal response), were included in Hull's system.

Although you may find it hard to believe, we have barely scratched the surface of Hull's learning theory. In the final analysis, Hull conceded that reaction potential for a given subject on a given learning trial was not a precise value, as it would appear to be from the equation for $_sE_R$. Instead, there is a random variation in reaction potential, which attests to the fact that "[v]ariability, inconsistency, and specific unpredictability of reaction under seemingly constant conditions are universal characteristics of the molar behavior of organisms…" (Hull, 1943, p. 317). Hull's system—for all its complexity and apparent scientific precision—never achieved perfect prediction or control of behavior.

Hull's Influence

Both Hull's mathematical/logical analysis of learning and his propensity to build machines reinforce the idea that for Hull the metaphor of mechanism was central to understanding behavior and advancing psychology (Smith, 1990). Hull was an anticipator of modern cognitive psychology's efforts in artificial intelligence and machine learning (Chapter 20), as you can see from the following comment:

It should be a matter of no great difficulty to construct parallel inanimate mechanisms, even from inorganic materials, which will genuinely manifest the qualities of intelligence, insight, and purpose, and which, in so far, will be truly psychic. (Hull, 1930, p. 256)

Like his contemporary learning theorists, Hull was interested in the general principles of learning, and whether the study object was a rat, a person, or a machine was of secondary importance. In Hull's day, the focus on the general principles of learning per se was used to validate generalizations from animal studies—for example, of rats in mazes—to human behavior. At the present time, the same sort of focus is used to explain how the analysis of computer programs can produce important insights into human learning and cognition.

Hull's dominance during the 1930s and 1940s is shown in Ruja's (1956) examination of reference citations in three major journals during the years from 1949 to 1952. For example, in 183 articles in the *Journal of Experimental Psychology,* Hull received more than twice as many citations as his nearest rival. Perhaps more importantly, the four psychologists below Hull were all Hull's students or associates. Ruja also found that the work most frequently cited was Hull's (1943) *Principles of Behavior.*

Another illustration of Hull's importance can be found in Coan and Zagona's (1962) obtained ratings of psychological theorists. Coan and Zagona received ratings both for the period from 1880 to 1960 and by decades within the period. Overall, Hull was ranked second only to Freud. In the 2 decades from 1930 to 1949, Hull had the highest ranking, with Tolman second. However, Hull's name was not among the top 10 in the decade from 1950 to 1959—Skinner topped the list—and Tolman slipped to ninth. Still, three of Hull's students and associates were included among the top 10 theorists of the decade.

Hull's more tangible honors included election to the APA presidency in 1936, election to the American Academy of Arts and Sciences in 1935, and acceptance into the National Academy of Sciences in 1936. Hull particularly enjoyed attending the meetings of the Society of Experimental Psychologists, and he received the society's coveted Warren Medal in 1945. According to the award citation for the Warren Medal:

> [Hull's] theory has stimulated much research and it has been developed in a precise and quantitative form so as to permit predictions which can be tested empirically. The theory thus contains within itself the seeds of its own ultimate verification and of its possible final disproof. A truly unique achievement in the history of psychology to date. (Hovland, 1952, p. 349)

The line about Hull's theory possibly containing the seeds of its final disproof was prophetic. In an evaluation of Hull's system shortly after his death, Seward (1954) concluded that

> If a building is no more solid than its foundations, neither is a system more stable than its postulates. That Hull's postulates are far from "finished" is obvious from their rate of revision during the past few years. He is said to have remarked, "I reserve the right to change my postulates every morning before breakfast." There is no reason why we should regard them with greater awe. (pp. 155–156)

Although critical of the foundation of Hull's grand system of behavior, Seward acknowledged probably the most important effect of Hull's attempt in his last sentence: "High on any list of his contributions to psychology should go the many challenging targets he gave us to shoot at" (pp. 156–157). By making his theory explicit and testable, Hull stimulated an enormous amount of research in laboratories all over the country.

As we have indicated, Hull's direct influence on psychology did not long survive his death, which came a few weeks before his planned retirement from Yale in 1952. Overly ambitious and mathematically tedious, Hull's learning theory, which truly was a "unique achievement in the history of psychology," has been considered by some to be a failure. "Moreover, his failure has probably discouraged others from attempting such a task. Many observers have noted a trend in learning theory away from . . . all-encompassing theories . . . toward theories of smaller scope designed to explain only certain kinds of learning" (Hill, 1971, p. 157). Although this trend was undoubtedly true for at least a couple of decades

following Hull's death, recent advances in machine learning, of which Hull would have approved, can be seen as a return to a general theory of behavior with several similarities to Hull's system (e.g., Rumelhart, McClelland, & the PDP Research Group, 1986).

Nevertheless, Hull set the stage for the inductive approach to learning adopted by the man who supplanted him in theoretical importance in the decade of the 1950s: B. F. Skinner. Before we examine Skinner's life and accomplishments, we will take a brief look at the careers of a number of Hull's most important students and associates.

Hull was adept at creating disciples who continued to pursue his line of research after they had gone to other universities. In turn, his students motivated their own students to continue similar pursuits, with the result that there were soon "a large number of enthusiastic fourth and fifth generation students [of Hull] throughout the country" (Hovland, 1952, p. 349). The reasons for Hull's ability to inspire unswerving loyalty may be found in the introduction by Ruth Hays (1962), Hull's long-time assistant, to excerpts from Hull's idea books.

> Those who worked with him were deeply conscious of his intellect and ability, his integrity and courage; they respected his sincerity and singleness of purpose; . . . they stood almost in awe of his constant achievements and hard work, often in the face of physical weakness and suffering; and they loved him for his humanness—his forthright likes and dislikes, his keen sense of humor, . . . his quick contempt of sham or affectation or pomposity. Above all they appreciated his unstinting generosity in giving an assistant all or even more than his due or credit in recognition of work done and in the matter of publication. (p. 805)

HULL'S STUDENTS AND ASSOCIATES

Kenneth Spence

Kenneth W. Spence (1907–1967) was raised in Montreal, Canada, where he attended McGill University, earning B.A. and M.A. degrees. Spence went to Yale to work on his Ph.D., which he received in 1933, with a dissertation directed by Robert Yerkes. Although he moved to the University of Texas at Austin in 1964, most of Spence's career was spent at the State University of Iowa. Spence's eminence as a theorist, experimentalist, and methodologist resulted in election to the National Academy of Sciences.

Throughout his career, Spence's name was closely associated with Hull's, and when Hull died, Spence continued his mentor's theoretical efforts. Although their approaches and views differed in significant ways, both Spence and Hull were dedicated to developing an objective theory of behavior based on conditioning. Spence's major contributions were his theory of discrimination learning and his invention and elaboration of incentive motivation.

Discrimination Learning and Relational Responding

Spence's theory of discrimination learning was proposed as an S-R theorist's response to learning experiments by Köhler. In what became known as the transposition problem, which we will discuss in Chapter 14, Köhler (e.g., 1925) trained chickens to peck at a dark gray card and to avoid pecking at a lighter gray card. In order to see what an animal had learned, Köhler tested it with the dark gray card and a still darker card, reasoning that if the animal had learned to make a specific response to a specific stimulus, it would peck at the same card as in original learning. However, if the animal had learned the relationship between the stimuli originally, it would peck at the darker stimulus in the test. Most animals pecked at the darker stimulus.

Spence (1937) developed an explanation for Köhler's results based on the S-R concepts of habit strength, conditioned inhibition, and stimulus generalization that did not require innate tendencies to "get the big picture," as the Gestaltists suggested. Spence's solution to the relational versus absolute responding controversy stimulated much research, and the "decline in [relational responding] with distance [between the stimuli] has indeed been found many times and it provides a difficulty for the relational view" (Bower & Hilgard, 1981, p. 115).

Incentive Motivation

As we noted, Spence suggested to Hull that motivation based on the quantity or quality of a reward should be separated from habit strength, thus giving Hull the idea of incentive motivation (K). When Hull died, K was not completely assimilated into his system, and Spence worked to clarify K's status, eventually making radical changes in Hull's theory that took it closer to the theories of Hull's competitors.

Hull believed that habit strength ($_sH_R$) was a function of the number of reinforced pairings of a stimulus and a response. By about 1950, Spence had decided that the development of habit strength did not depend on reward in the form of drive reduction. That is, he believed that "if the response occurs there will be an increment in [habit strength] regardless of whether a reinforcer does or does not result" (Spence, 1960, p. 96). According to this, the formation of habit became strictly a matter of S-R contiguity, a basic tenet of Guthrie and Watson.

Further, Spence continued to modify his conception of K, eventually suggesting a physiological basis for it consisting of movement-produced stimuli. These movement-produced stimuli help to maintain an animal's movement toward a goal, which is a thoroughly Guthrian concept. But Spence also drifted toward cognitive behaviorism. Incentive motivation can be seen as the anticipation of reward with a physiological basis. The idea of the anticipation of reward is completely Tolmanian.

Neal E. Miller

Neal Elgar Miller (1909–) earned his B.S. from the University of Washington, his M.A. from Stanford, and his Ph.D. from Yale in 1935, with Hull as his adviser. Miller then went to the Vienna Psychoanalytic Institute to learn about Freudian therapy, and his knowledge of psychoanalysis was incorporated into the book, *Personality and Psychotherapy* (Dollard & Miller, 1950), published with his long-time collaborator, the sociologist **John Dollard** (1900–1980).

Returning to Yale after Vienna, Miller was a member of the Institute of Human Relations—as was Dollard—from 1936 to 1950, a professor of psychology from 1950 to 1952, and the James Rowland Angell Professor of Psychology from 1952 to 1966. He then went to New York's Rockefeller University, where he served as a professor and head of a physiological psychology laboratory from 1966 to 1980, acquiring emeritus status in 1980.

Miller's contributions have occurred in several different areas: First, with Dollard, he presented a simplified version of Hullian theory and began social learning theory. Second, starting with Lewin's ideas on conflict (Chapter 14), Miller elaborated and developed a precise account of conflict theory. Third, Miller collaborated with Dollard to apply learning theory to such phenomena as psychopathology and aggression. Fourth, in his physiological research, Miller demonstrated that learning can be motivated by electrical brain stimulation (Miller, 1958) and investigated the conditioning of autonomic responses (Miller, 1969), which was important for the field of biofeedback. Unfortunately, later attempts to replicate some of his earlier work in autonomic conditioning in rats were unsuccessful (e.g., Miller & Dworkin, 1974). We will briefly consider Miller's version of Hull and its application to psychopathology.

Social Learning and Imitation

In 1941, Miller and Dollard published *Social Learning and Imitation,* which contains Miller's adaptation of Hull and provides the impetus for Albert Bandura's social learning theory (Chapter 19). Miller's central concept is drive, which causes an organism to act. Further, a drive always involves a strong stimulus, and any stimulus, if strong enough, can function as a drive. Drive is the basis of motivation.

Drive stimulates activity, and it is possible that one of the organism's responses will reduce the drive's strength. This reduction reinforces whatever response produced it, which means that the response tends to be learned—that is, repeated in a similar stimulus situation. Thus, we have presented the four elements that Miller and Dollard used to anticipate Hull's elaborate postulates and theorems: drive, cue, response, and reward. That is, *drive* causes a *response* in the presence of certain *cues* (the stimulus situa-

tion). If the result reduces the drive, this is *rewarding,* and the response is connected to the cues.

Miller and Dollard used their theory to account for imitation, which they believed is a learned behavior. To illustrate, Miller and Dollard used the behavior of two young boys. On one occasion, the older brother heard his father's footsteps entering the house and ran to greet him. His brother happened to be running in the same direction at the same time. The father gave both boys candy. Thus, this was a learning situation for the younger boy, with his desire for candy the drive, his brother's running the cue, his own running the response, and eating the candy the reward. From this event and other similar ones, the younger boy learned to imitate his brother.

In *Social Learning and Imitation,* Miller and Dollard (1941) presented a wealth of data from animal and human experiments on imitation. From their studies with people, the authors concluded that good human models tend to be similar demographically, older and of higher social status, technically skilled, and more knowledgeable.

Secondary Drives and Neurosis

In addition to primary drives such as hunger, pain, and fatigue, Miller and Dollard were particularly interested in **secondary drives**. A secondary—learned or acquired—drive gains its motivating status from being initially paired with a primary drive and its reduction. For example, money, a secondary reinforcer, and the urge to acquire it, a secondary drive, earn their status from being paired with hunger and its alleviation.

In *Personality and Psychotherapy,* Dollard and Miller (1950) were interested in the learning and unlearning of neuroses. According to them, neurotics have three characteristics: They are unhappy because of their conflicts, at least some of their behavior is irrational because they are acting on unresolved conflicts, and they present a variety of symptoms. At the root of the neurotic's conflicts is the learned drive of fear.

In a classic experiment, Miller (1948) demonstrated that stimuli paired with an aversive reinforcer become capable themselves of motivating and reinforcing behavior—in other words, the stimuli become secondary aversive reinforcers. In the study, rats were placed individually into a box with two compartments, one white with a grid floor and the other black with a wooden floor. Strong shock through the grid floor caused the rats to learn quickly to escape to the black box. After several shock presentations, the rats were placed into the white compartment without shock—all ran to the black chamber. Because pain did not motivate this escape behavior, Miller concluded that the rats had learned a secondary drive of fear, which motivated the escape behavior.

Further, Miller showed that the learned fear could motivate new learning. To do this, he closed the door between the white and the black compartments and made it possible for a rat to open the door by turning a wheel. Over half of the animals learned the response, and the successful learners then acquired a lever-pressing response in order to enter the black compartment. Miller's experiment showed that cues occurring with an aversive stimulus acquire the power to produce fear, and new responses permitting escape from the cues will be reinforced and thus learned.

What does all this animal work have to do with neurotics? According to Dollard and Miller (1950), through maladaptive learning, the neurotic has acquired a fear drive that is triggered by stimuli that are not normally associated with fear. Behavior that reduces the fear is rewarding and is likely to increase. For example, suppose a boy is consistently punished for displays of assertive behavior. The punishment triggers emotional responses, which result in the secondary drive of fear. As a consequence, the child's assertive behavior comes to trigger fear, and submissiveness reduces the fear.

As an adult, the man encounters situations where assertiveness might allow him to receive the goals he wants, but he has learned to fear his assertiveness. This fear produces a conflict between his desire for certain goals and his fear of the assertive behavior that would possibly bring goals. His conflict—with learned fear at its heart—makes him unhappy, causes apparently irrational behavior in some situations, and may produce the symptoms of a disorder.

Because the fear is learned, extinguishing it is the key to curing the man through psychotherapy. If he can be convinced to make assertive responses under nonpunitive conditions, his fear will eventually extinguish. Because the cues for the fear come from his own emotional responses, the responses should be induced weakly at first, gradually building in intensity.

Although we have focused on only a portion of it, Neal Miller has had a long and productive career. His honors include being elected president of the APA (1961) and of the Society for Neuroscience. In addition, he was elected to the National Academy of Sciences and to the American Philosophical Society, and he has received the National Medal of Science, the APA Gold Medal Award, and several honorary degrees.

O. H. Mowrer

The last of Hull's talented students and associates we will consider here is **Orval Hobart Mowrer** (1907–1982), born and raised on a farm near Unionville, Missouri. Mowrer suffered bouts of depression throughout his life, the first coming at 14. This experience motivated his decision to study psychology in college.

As an undergraduate at the University of Missouri, Mowrer studied with Max Frederick Meyer (1873–1967), a staunch behaviorist who had taken his Ph.D. under Carl Stumpf (Chapter 8) at Berlin. For a sociology course, Mowrer constructed a questionnaire that asked, among other things, about attitudes toward premarital sex and divorce. Mowrer was nearly dismissed as a result of the outcry, and Meyer was suspended for a year without pay and fired the next year for giving his interpretation of the incident at a professional meeting. Although the awarding of Mowrer's undergraduate degree was delayed from 1929 until 1932, all was ultimately forgiven, and Missouri honored Mowrer with a Certificate of Merit in 1956 (Hunt, 1984).

Mowrer received his Ph.D. from Johns Hopkins in 1932 and had an appointment from 1934 to 1940 at Yale's Institute of Human Relations. Mowrer's motivation for becoming a psychologist attracted him to the Institute's program geared toward integrating psychoanalysis with learning theory in the hope of achieving a mental health breakthrough. At the Institute, he participated in Hull's psychoanalytic seminar with a number of psychologists that included Dollard and Miller. At Yale, Mowrer made his major contributions to learning theory (discussed later).

From 1940 until 1948, Mowrer was an assistant and then an associate professor in the Harvard Graduate School of Education, with a courtesy appointment in Harvard's Department of Psychology. At Harvard, Mowrer began counseling students on their personal problems, and this eventually led to the development of a type of treatment that he called *integrity therapy*. From Harvard, Mowrer went to the University of Illinois as a research professor of psychology, and he held this position until he retired in 1975. Mowrer was president of the APA in 1954.

At the end of his life, Mowrer concluded that his depression, although frequently distressing, had spurred him to a usefulness that he would not otherwise have had. Three years after his wife died, Mowrer consciously decided to end his own life in order not to deprive his children of whatever financial assistance he might leave them.

Mowrer's Two-Factor Theory

During the era of Watson and Guthrie, little distinction was drawn between Thorndikian and Pavlovian conditioning. Despite obvious procedural differences, it was assumed that the learning was the same in each case. In 1938 (and earlier), Skinner (discussed later) suggested that there was a fundamental difference between Pavlovian conditioning and the type of conditioning he was studying, and Mowrer (1947) further elaborated this distinction.

Mowrer called the two forms of learning sign learning and solution learning. **Sign learning** referred to Pavlovian or classical conditioning of involuntary responses controlled by the autonomic nervous system. Sign learning requires only temporal contiguity of a neutral stimulus (e.g., a white box) and an unconditioned stimulus (e.g., pain from shock). Mowrer called this sign learning because the CS becomes a sign of danger that trig-

gers an emotional response of fear. This was Pavlov's first-signal system (Chapter 12).

Solution learning involved instrumental conditioning of voluntary responses of the striped, skeletal muscles controlled by the central nervous system. Reinforcement for solution learning occurs through drive reduction. Mowrer called it solution learning because the instrumental response solves the problem created by the drive. Incidentally, Hilgard and Marquis (1940) advanced the more familiar terms "classical conditioning" and "instrumental conditioning."

Later, Mowrer's (1960) thinking changed dramatically, and his two-factor theory had only one factor—conditioning or sign learning—with solution learning seen as just a special kind of sign learning. Unlike Mowrer, B. F. Skinner was a two-factor theorist who did not change his thinking.

B. F. SKINNER

Burrhus Frederick Skinner (1904–1990) was born and spent the first 18 years of his life in the small railroad town of Susquehanna, Pennsylvania. Skinner was the first-born son of attorney William A. Skinner and Grace Burrhus Skinner, described by Skinner as "bright and beautiful" (Skinner, 1967, p. 387). She also had rigid standards of right and wrong, and the only physical punishment Skinner received from either of his parents came at her hands: She washed his mouth out with soap and water for using a dirty word.

Skinner described his home environment as "warm and stable," and he and his parents graduated, as salutatorians, from the same high school. Skinner was fond of his younger brother, Edward or Ebbie, who was more athletic and more popular than Skinner. In Skinner's presence, Ebbie died suddenly at the age of 16, probably of a cerebral aneurism (Skinner, 1976).

As a youth, Skinner was a gadgeteer, an amateur inventor who delighted in building things. Skinner also enjoyed school, and he was fortunate to have a teacher named Mary Graves, who taught him art in grammar school and English in high school. She was probably responsible for Skinner's early decision to major in English literature in college and to become a writer.

In high school, Skinner discovered Francis Bacon (Chapter 3) by challenging Shakespeare's authorship of a play his 8th-grade class was reading (some have suggested that Bacon is really the author of the works we attribute to Shakespeare). Miss Graves responded that Skinner did not know what he was talking about, which stimulated him to acquire the knowledge to defend his contention. Many years later Skinner described his attitude toward science as Baconian:

> I reject verbal authority. I have "studied nature not books," asking questions of the organism rather than of those who have studied the organism. I think it can be said, as it was said of Bacon, that I get my books out of life, not out of other books. (Skinner, 1967, p. 409)

Skinner's first year at Hamilton College in New York, which had been recommended by a family friend, was a period of adjustment for him. He pledged the "wrong" fraternity, made few friends, and suffered humiliation over his mispronunciations (e.g., "crick" for "creek"; Bjork, 1993). Then, at Easter break, Ebbie died.

After his freshman year, Skinner became acquainted with the Saunders family through tutoring their youngest son in mathematics. The Saunders were sophisticated and well connected, and the Saunders' large house was "full of books, pictures, sculpture, musical instruments, and huge bouquets of peonies in season" (Skinner, 1967, p. 392). Percy Saunders remained a vital confidant to Skinner long after he graduated from Hamilton.

As a junior, Skinner's anatomy and embryology professor recommended that he read work by Jacques Loeb (Chapter 12), and Skinner was impressed by Loeb's concept of tropism, much as Watson had been earlier. However, his inclination toward a literary career was reinforced by attending the Bread Loaf School of English in Vermont during the summer following his junior year. There he met Robert Frost, who suggested that Skinner send him some of his work. Skinner sent three short stories, and Frost responded positively: "*You are worth twice*

anyone else I have seen in prose this year" (Letter from Frost, 1926; Skinner, 1976, p. 249, italics in the original).

After graduation, Skinner entered his "Dark Year." He built a writer's study at his parent's house and spent his time doing essentially nothing productive—he later decided that he failed as a writer because he had nothing important to say.

Skinner spent the 6 months before he went to graduate school living in New York City's Greenwich Village, where he worked in a bookstore. Much of his reading pointed him toward a career in psychology and particularly toward behaviorism. For example, Bertrand Russell's (1925) *Philosophy* directed him to Watson's *Behaviorism,* which he read. Many years later, Skinner sat across the table from Russell at a luncheon in the philosopher's honor. According to Skinner (1979),

> I told him that his *Philosophy* had converted me to behaviorism. "Good heavens," he said, "I thought it had demolished behaviorism." (p. 224)

After a summer in Europe, Skinner applied to Harvard and was accepted for graduate school in psychology.

Skinner at Harvard

At Harvard, Skinner was apparently less influenced in his interests by the psychology faculty than he was by a fellow graduate student, Fred S. Keller (1899–), with whom he maintained a correspondence throughout his life, and the physiologist William Crozier. A student of Loeb, Crozier studied tropisms in intact lower organisms and also worked with rats. Crozier encouraged Skinner throughout his graduate and postgraduate tenure at Harvard, and Skinner worked independently for several years in a laboratory offered by Crozier in the biology building. However, proximity to biology and physiology did not turn Skinner toward them, and he became more and more convinced that the study of behavior should concentrate on behavior and not on its physiological substrate. Thus, "Skinner would become a 'descriptive' or 'radical' behaviorist precisely because he denied that behavior is determined by processes within the physiology of the organism" (Bjork, 1993, p. 80).

Skinner's Harvard research combined his belief in the orderliness of individual animal behavior with his love of building gadgets. Beginning with a silent-release box designed to prevent a rat introduced into an apparatus from being disturbed, Skinner tinkered until many apparatuses later he had invented what Hull later called the **Skinner box**. In it, a rat could be conditioned to press a lever in order to receive a food pellet, and a cumulative record of the animal's responding could be obtained. In his effort to develop experimental control over an individual animal's behavior, Skinner had constructed an apparatus that recorded behavior with relatively little variability and produced apparently lawful results. Skinner was ecstatic about his accomplishment, writing his parents that it was the best birthday present he had gotten—he was 26.

An accomplished student, at his doctoral oral examination, Skinner suffered only one moment of chagrin: Gordon Allport (Chapter 19) asked him to name some objections to behaviorism, and Skinner could not think of any. After receiving his Ph.D., Skinner stayed at Harvard on a fellowship that lasted for the rest of the academic year. With Crozier's assistance, Skinner spent the next 2 years on a National Research Council Fellowship. On his 29th birthday in 1933, Skinner was interviewed by the Harvard Society of Fellows for the prestigious Junior Fellowship, which he was awarded the following month. This enabled him to stay at Harvard until 1936.

Skinner at Minnesota

Despite Skinner's research accomplishments, finding a university position proved difficult because of the Depression. Finally, with a strong recommendation to a Harvard Ph.D., Richard Elliott, chairman of the psychology department at Minnesota, Skinner found himself in a teaching position for the first time. Staying one step ahead of his students, Skinner began to learn college psychology, and later he wrote that "I have never again been so richly reinforced as a teacher" (Skinner, 1967, p. 400).

Before leaving Harvard, Skinner had met Yvonne Blue, later known as Eve, the daughter of a wealthy ophthalmologist. She had majored in literature at the University of Chicago, had mixed with a bohemian crowd, and had horrified her parents by smoking in public. She and Skinner were married in a civil ceremony in late 1937, and their first child, Julie, was born in 1938.

The Behavior of Organisms

In 1938, Skinner's *The Behavior of Organisms* was published. This work represented the culmination of his research efforts since 1930. Through *The Behavior of Organisms* and earlier papers, Skinner demonstrated that the rat's lever-pressing response was a behavioral unit that could be studied as scientifically as Pavlov's conditioned reflex. In fact, it illustrated a second type of conditioning, which he had identified earlier: "At almost any significant level of analysis a distinction must be made between at least two major types of conditioned reflex" (Skinner, 1935, p. 66). Describing the difference in the two types of conditioning, Skinner noted that Pavlovian conditioning prepared the organism for food, whereas his version—which he dubbed "Type I"—obtained the food for which the organism was prepared.

Polish physiologists Konorski and Miller (1937) criticized Skinner's two conditioning types, renaming them Type I for Pavlovian conditioning and Type II for Skinner's "new type of reflex." Replying to Konorski and Miller, Skinner (1937) introduced another pair of names: Type R for his type of conditioning and Type S for Pavlov's. Further, he wrote that "All conditioned reflexes of Type R are by definition operants and all of Type S, respondents . . ." (p. 274). This was Skinner's first use of the term "**operant**," which he defined as "a kind of response which occurs spontaneously in the absence of any stimulation with which it may be specifically correlated" (p. 274). Operant behaviors operate on the environment to produce consequences, and these consequences determine whether the behavior will be repeated in the given situation. A **respondent** was a reflex in the more traditional sense, involving the correlation between a stimulus and the response to it. Skinner did not claim to have discovered Type R or operant conditioning, noting that "The behavior characteristic of Type *R* was studied as early as 1898 (Thorndike)" (Skinner, 1937, p. 278).

Konorski and Miller (1937) had implied that a conditioning procedure that relied on the spontaneous occurrence of a response could not be universally valid because many responses never occur spontaneously. Skinner (1937) responded by describing **shaping**, in which "elaborate and peculiar forms of response may be generated from undifferentiated operant behavior *through successive approximation to a final form*" (p. 277, italics added).

Most reviewers of *The Behavior of Organisms* thought it contained serious flaws. For example, some reviewers wrote that the title was pretentious, arguing somewhat justifiably that it is an impossible leap from rat conditioning experiments to "the behavior of organisms." Skinner's rebuttal was that in choosing the title he was just following the lead of Pavlov, who had not added "in the dog" to the title *Conditioned Reflexes*. Further, several reviewers criticized Skinner for neglecting previous work on learning and motivation. Skinner's justification was that he had had little success in finding completely relevant material elsewhere because his paradigm was so novel. Other criticisms included the book's lack of coverage of such important psychological fields as perception and thinking, and its lack of statistical fortification.

The Behavior of Organisms was not a profitable publication for either the author or the publisher. As of 1946, there were still 250 copies unsold from the original 800-copy printing. Despite its unprofitability, Keller (1991) considered it Skinner's "most important book, . . . assuring him of an honored place in the history of our science" (p. 4).

Project Pigeon

With World War II underway, Skinner knew about the Nazis' use of the airplane as a potent offensive weapon, and he began to wonder about a missile that would zero in on a bomber. While idly thinking about this problem on a 1939 train ride, Skinner noticed a flock of birds flying alongside the train. "Suddenly I saw them as 'devices' with excellent vision and extraordinary maneuverability. Could they not guide a missile?" (Skinner, 1979, p. 241).

Skinner bought some pigeons and began to train them to guide missiles. Following a successful demonstration, the dean of the Minnesota faculty wrote to Richard Tolman, Edward Tolman's brother, who was affiliated with the National Defense Research Committee (NDRC). Tolman decided not to support the experimentation that would be needed to see if Skinner's pigeons could function under combat conditions.

After the Pearl Harbor attack in December 1941, Skinner resurrected the pigeon project. With graduate students Keller Breland, Breland's wife Marian, Norman Guttman, and later William Estes, Skinner began working on a steerable bomb rather than a surface-to-air missile as before. Again, the dean was supportive, but once more Tolman denied funding. However, Skinner's efforts came to the attention of the chairman of the board of General Mills—two General Mills' engineers believed they could design a missile that could be controlled by a pigeon—and Chairman Bell appropriated $5,000 to fund the project until it could be supported by a governmental agency.

A successful 1943 demonstration led the newly formed Office of Scientific Research and Development (OSRD) to award a contract to General Mills to "develop a homing device" under the name of **Project Pigeon**. Of course, some of the pigeon studies Skinner and his group performed had nothing to do with the project. "The pigeons were there, crude apparatus was available, and we had all the time in the world" (Skinner, 1979, p. 267). In a letter to Fred Keller, Skinner wrote that they had replicated almost all of the work reported "in [*The Behavior of Organisms*] (with a different species) plus oodles of new stuff" (p. 267). Key pecking in pigeons proved to be a more satisfying model than rat lever pressing, and Skinner (Figure 13–7) never returned to rats.

After another successful feasibility demonstration to OSRD officials, Skinner was told that further support of the project would delay other developments that promised more immediate military application. Although the pigeons had performed beautifully, "all our efforts with the scientists came to nothing. My verbal behavior with respect to Washington underwent extinction, and the effect generalized" (Skinner, 1979, p. 274).

FIGURE 13–7.   Skinner demonstrating the operant conditioning of a pigeon.

Source: Reprinted with permission, B.F. Skinner Foundation; from The Shaping of a Behaviorist *(1979).*

In the early 1950s, Skinner acted as consultant on a Navy project on the use of pigeons for missile guidance, which was called Project ORCON (ORganic CONtrol). With the discovery of alternative electronic guidance systems, ORCON was discontinued in 1953.

Skinner at Indiana

In 1940, **Jacob R. Kantor** (1888–1984) asked Skinner if he would be willing to come to Indiana. A Chicago Ph.D., Kantor called his approach **interbehaviorism** and stressed the interactions of an organism with stimulus objects. Both the responding organism and the stimulus objects were considered to be of equal importance.

Skinner rejected the Indiana position in 1940, but he was interested in 1945 when the offer included the chairmanship of the department. Feeling out of the mainstream of psychology in Minneapolis, Skinner accepted Indiana's offer.

The Baby in a Box

Because Yvonne had disliked caring for their first child during the baby's first couple of years, Skinner

suggested that they simplify the care of the new baby that arrived in 1943. He started work on

> a crib-sized living space that we began to call the "baby-tender." It had sound-absorbing walls and a large picture window. Air entered through filters at the bottom and, after being warmed and moistened, moved upward through and around the edges of a tightly stretched canvas, which served as a mattress. A strip of sheeting ten yards long passed over the canvas, a clean section of which could be cranked into place in a few seconds. (Skinner, 1979, p. 275)

When Deborah arrived from the hospital, she was immediately placed into Skinner's **baby-tender** "and began to enjoy its advantages."

Deborah thrived in the box for the first 2 and 1/2 years of her life. Contrary to rumors of insanity and suicide, Deborah was a healthy, happy infant who grew into an accomplished adult. According to her father, "she's actually a happily married woman, living in London at the moment, [and] cooperating in writing a book on the best hotels in England and Scotland" (Trudeau, 1990, p. 10). Although Julie Skinner had not been raised in the baby-tender, she elected to raise her children in one. Debbie is shown playing in the baby-tender in Figure 13–8.

After failing to interest General Mills in developing the baby-tender, Skinner wrote an article describing the device's advantages, which was published in *Ladies' Home Journal* as "Baby in a Box" in the fall of 1945. Although there were some negative letters from people who assumed that Skinner was experimenting on his daughter as he had done on rats and pigeons, there were far more positive letters. "Within a month after the article's appearance, seventy-five to one hundred baby tenders were being built by *Journal* readers" (Bjork, 1993, p. 132).

After further publicity, Skinner was approached by a Cleveland businessman who wanted to build and market "Heir Conditioners." J. J. Weste "came to Bloomington, and I liked him and agreed to put things in his hands" (Skinner, 1979, p. 309). Unfortunately, Skinner soon learned that Weste had disappeared, hounded by lending companies from which he had borrowed money. He had also borrowed money from Skinner and had received advances from a number of potential customers. For

years afterward, Skinner felt the embarrassing effects of Weste's dishonesty.

In the 1950s, Skinner finally became involved in a successful effort to produce baby-tenders (now called aircribs) commercially. In 1957, John Gray's Aircrib Corporation began to manufacture and sell Skinner's invention. Approximately a thousand aircribs were sold by the time Gray died a decade later. Skinner always believed that his first social invention failed to find greater acceptance because of the problem of getting aircribs mass-produced by a large manufacturer. His next venture into social invention came in novel form.

Walden Two

At a party in 1945, Skinner talked to a dinner companion about what young people would do after the war and how it was a shame that they would lose their crusading zeal. Perhaps they should explore new ways of living, as people had done in utopian communities in the 19th century. Skinner's dinner companion asked for details and later suggested that he write it all down.

In June 1945, Skinner began to write what he planned to call *The Sun Is But a Morning Star.* In writing the book, Skinner (1948) adopted a standard utopian strategy by having a group of people visit a community whose concept is described and defended by its founder. The book's narrator is Burris (as in Burrhus), a college professor who has unhappily returned to the classroom after an exciting wartime experience. The community's founder is Frazier, "a self-proclaimed genius who has deserted academic psychology for behavioral engineering, the new discipline upon which the community is based" (Skinner, 1979, p. 296). Skinner speculated that "Frazier" was a combination of "Fred" (either himself or his friend, Fred Keller) and "Crozier," his Harvard mentor.

Skinner's utopian community operates according to the operant conditioning principles its author had discovered. The environment is arranged so that each person can engage in work, hobbies, the arts—all inherently reinforcing activities. Not surprisingly, babies are raised in aircribs. Also not surprisingly, Frazier contends that behavioral science is superior

FIGURE 13–8. A happy Debbie Skinner playing in the baby-tender.

Source: Corbis-Bettmann.

to all other ways of improving the human condition. All that is necessary for the good life is to apply operant techniques to society.

Skinner found that writing the book was cathartic. Frazier was able to "say things that I myself was not yet ready to say to anyone" (Skinner, 1979, p. 298). However, catharsis was one thing—finding a publisher was another. Four large publishing firms rejected it before Macmillan accepted it on the condition that Skinner write an introductory psychology textbook for them. *Walden Two* was published in 1948.

Several early reviews of the novel were quite favorable: for example, "the New Yorker called it 'an extremely interesting discourse on the possibilities of social organization'" (Skinner, 1979, pp. 346–347). Unfortunately, *Life,* a magazine with broad national circulation, published a particularly damning review. Possibly because of such reviews, *Walden Two* sold poorly for many years. However, with a growing interest in alternative lifestyles in the 1960s, sales blossomed, and by Skinner's death in 1990, sales recorded on a cumulative response curve in his study had reached nearly 2,500,000 copies.

Much later in his career, Skinner (1971) made another attempt to advocate social change from the behaviorist perspective in *Beyond Freedom and Dignity.* In it, Skinner argued that only operant science is capable of properly modifying human culture. "A scientific view of man offers exciting possibilities," Skinner concluded. "We have not yet seen what man can make of man" (p. 215).

Negative reactions to *Beyond Freedom and Dignity* were legion, coming from sources ranging from scholarly journals to television and radio talk shows. Most critics objected to Skinner's apparent disparagement of the notions of individual freedom and dignity. More than one suggested that Skinner's approach to individual freedom was compatible with a police state or with Germany and Italy in the late 1930s. Certainly the most colorfully negative critique came from the philosopher/novelist Ayn Rand, whose novels *The Fountainhead* and *Atlas Shrugged* stress the importance for society of the autonomous individual. Rand compared *Beyond Freedom and Dignity* to "'Boris Karloff's embodiment of Frankenstein's monster: a corpse patched with nuts, bolts and

screws from the junkyard of philosophy, Darwinism, Positivism, Linguistic Analysis, with some nails by Hume, threads by Russell and glue by the *New York Post*" (Rand, as cited in Bjork, 1993, p. 205).

Obviously, Skinner struck a sensitive chord with *Beyond Freedom and Dignity.* He was not, as his critics contended, advocating the loss of individual freedom, because he already believed that such freedom was an illusion. As products of our environments, he argued, we should strive to structure our environments to produce behavior that maximizes the benefits to society. Perhaps the novelty of Skinner's argument *shaped* his critics' reactions.

Skinner at Harvard Again

In 1947, Boring (Chapter 1) invited Skinner to give the William James Lectures at Harvard. Skinner agreed, speaking on "Verbal Behavior: A Psychological Analysis." On the strength of the lectures and his many other accomplishments, Skinner was invited to return to Harvard, which he did the following year. He remained there until his retirement in 1974, when, fittingly enough, he was presented a first edition of Thoreau's *Walden.*

Teaching Machines

During a visit to his daughter Debbie's fourth-grade arithmetic class, Skinner observed some students finishing their task early and sitting idly while other students strained with their problems. Afterwards, the teacher collected the papers to grade and return the next day. The situation violated two fundamental learning principles: "[T]he students were not being told at once whether their work was right or wrong (a corrected paper seen twenty-four hours later could not act as a reinforcer), and they were all moving at the same pace regardless of preparation or ability" (Skinner, 1983, p. 64). Skinner responded by building a **teaching machine** that presented arithmetic problems singly, in a fixed order, that the student had to solve before proceeding. A student could work at his or her own pace, and reinforcement—getting the problem right—was immediate.

In fact, Skinner was not the first American psychologist to invent a teaching machine. In 1926, Ohio State University professor Sidney Pressey built a box with a revolving drum. Problems appeared in a slot in the box, and the student responded by pressing one of four buttons. A correct answer caused the drum to revolve and a new problem to appear, whereas an incorrect answer had to be corrected before the drum would rotate. Pressey sent Skinner a bundle of reprints, and the two met at the next APA convention, where, despite his earlier disillusionment, Pressey agreed with Skinner that a brighter future lay ahead.

Skinner's teaching machine was a device to deliver programmed instruction, and this instruction was the key. With several young behaviorists, Skinner began in 1954 to develop instructional programming, and in 1956, the group received a $25,000 grant from the Ford Foundation Fund for the Advancement of Education. By 1957, Skinner's group was allowed to use teaching machines on student subjects at Harvard, and Skinner developed an instructional program for one of his courses. Enrollment in the course increased 70% in a year, and Skinner attributed the increase to the use of teaching machines.

Unfortunately, Skinner's attempts to get his teaching machines mass marketed proved as fruitless as his efforts with the baby-tender. Although Skinner's revolution in American education failed, his ideas have not completely died out. "The seeds he sowed are still alive and, to a limited extent, have been integrated in some computer-learning software" (Bjork, 1993, p. 186). Still, at the end of his life, Skinner was discouraged about the future of American education, calling his efforts to change education his life's greatest disappointment.

Schedules of Reinforcement

Not long after he arrived at Harvard, Skinner established a pigeon laboratory in which he and Charles Ferster worked happily for several years, studying the effects of different schedules of reinforcement on behavior. The result was the publication of *Schedules of Reinforcement* (Ferster & Skinner, 1957).

In *The Behavior of Organisms,* Skinner (1938) had discussed the effect of intermittent or partial reinforcement on behavior and had indicated that intermittent reinforcement could be scheduled in many ways. *Schedules of Reinforcement* was an "exhaustive extension" of that theme. As just one indication of the book's thorough nature, it contains 921 figures, which mostly depict cumulative response curves.

The basic intermittent schedules of reinforcement are either based on time between reinforcements (interval schedules) or the number of responses between reinforcements (ratio schedules). Further, the time between reinforcements can either be fixed or variable, resulting in **fixed-interval** (**FI**) and **variable-interval** (**VI**) schedules. Similarly, the number of responses between reinforcements can be fixed or variable, giving **fixed-ratio** (**FR**) and **variable-ratio** (**VR**) schedules.

Schedules of Reinforcement was an enormous achievement, and a decade later, Skinner (1967) described his collaborative work with Ferster as "the high point in my research history" (p. 405). Cumulative response curves illustrating the basic schedules are shown in Figure 13–9.

Verbal Behavior

In the same year that *Schedules of Reinforcement* appeared, Skinner (1957) finally saw the publication of *Verbal Behavior,* a book that he had begun in 1934 in response to a friendly challenge from Alfred North Whitehead (mentioned in Chapter 2). Whitehead was willing to agree that science might successfully account for all human behavior except for verbal behavior. Naturally, Skinner began work on a behavioristic account of human language.

For the behaviorist, human speech is just another example of behavior, which, like any operant behavior, is controlled by its consequences. We learn to speak by being reinforced for our verbal behavior, and we learn what to say (and what not to say) through reinforcement and punishment. Speech becomes a way to obtain reinforcement from others around us and a way for us to reinforce others. Literature, poetry, and other forms of creative writing are variations of verbal behavior acquired and retained through the principles of operant conditioning.

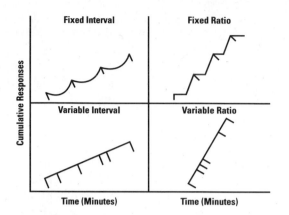

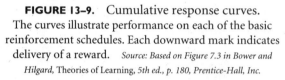

FIGURE 13–9. Cumulative response curves. The curves illustrate performance on each of the basic reinforcement schedules. Each downward mark indicates delivery of a reward.   *Source: Based on Figure 7.3 in Bower and Hilgard,* Theories of Learning, *5th ed., p. 180, Prentice-Hall, Inc.*

Although there were some favorable reviews of *Verbal Behavior*, Skinner received a strongly negative critique from Noam Chomsky. Skinner put the critique aside when the "first pages were not reassuring," but Chomsky's criticisms were published in the journal *Language*, and they soon began to receive more attention than *Verbal Behavior*. According to Skinner (1983), one of his former students was said to have begun a speech with the statement, "'Behaviorism is dead and it was a linguist [Chomsky] who killed it'" (p. 155). We will have more to say about Chomsky's views of language and their impact on the decline of behaviorism in Chapter 20.

Skinner's Influence

In our discussion of Skinner's contributions, we have avoided discussing a theory of learning. This omission is consistent with the conclusion of Skinner's (1950) article, "Are theories of learning necessary?" Skinner noted that although "[t]heories are fun . . . it is possible that the most rapid progress toward an understanding of learning may be made by research that is not designed to test theories" (p. 215). Following Francis Bacon's precept to experiment, Skinner made numerous lasting contributions to many areas of psychology.

In addition to the contributions we have discussed—for example, the identification and study of a second type of conditioning (operant conditioning), the invention of the Skinner box, the elucidation of schedules of reinforcement, the scientific beginnings of programmed instruction, and the illustration of the power of shaping (e.g., in Project Pigeon)—operant conditioning has been used in myriad ways. One example has been its use in testing the psychoactive effects of different drugs and/or the effects on behavior of different types of brain damage (e.g., Aaron & Thorne, 1975; Thorne, Rager, & Topping, 1976). Another example involves the work of students Ogden Lindsley, Nathan Azrin, and others, who have used operant conditioning to treat psychopathology. In one of the best-known studies, Teodoro Ayllon and Azrin (1968) used a **token economy** to treat schizophrenic female patients in a state hospital. The women received small plastic tokens for cooperative behaviors such as making their beds and eating properly. The tokens could be exchanged for privileges (e.g., being allowed to go for a walk on the grounds) or traded for desired items (e.g., candy). Under the token economy, desirable behaviors increased dramatically, and removal of the tokens produced swift extinction of the desirable behaviors.

Skinner's influence can also be seen in the journals and associations his work spawned. The *Journal of the Experimental Analysis of Behavior* came first (1958), followed by the *Journal of Applied Behavior Analysis* (1968). In 1974, the Midwestern Association for Behavior Analysis was organized, and it was followed 4 years later by the Association for Behavior Analysis.

Despite his acclaim, Skinner was never elected APA president, primarily because he did not want the job. The office then and now involves a kind of "political" work for which Skinner considered himself unsuited. Without making him president, the APA did recognize Skinner's research efforts with the Distinguished Scientific Contribution Award in 1958. In addition, shortly before his death, the APA presented Skinner with a Lifetime Contribution to Psychology Award.

Skinner was less successful in changing dramatically certain of society's institutions: for example, education and early childrearing practices. Perhaps Skinner's lack of success came from embracing the Baconian technological ideal, which seeks to control and remake the world (Smith, 1992). In this, Skinner was following Watson's lead in declaring that the aim of behavioral science is the prediction and control of behavior. According to Smith, some historians of science have identified another approach, the Aristotle-originated contemplative ideal, which seeks to understand the natural world and its causes.

Skinner's adoption of the Baconian approach and defense of behavioral technology came at a time in American history when technological advances were being seen as a mixed blessing at best. *Walden Two* was finished shortly before the destruction of two Japanese cities with atomic bombs, an event that raised the specter of humanity's destruction through the unwise application of technology. Rachel Carson's (1962) *Silent Spring* was an early harbinger of the negative environmental effects of modern industrial technology, just as earlier novels such as George Orwell's *1984* and Aldous Huxley's *Brave New World* had cautioned against behaviorism's promise of social engineering.

In a National Public Radio interview shortly before his death, Skinner summarized his successes and failures in this way: "I've had a very good life. It would be very foolish of me to complain in any way about it" (Trudeau, 1990, p. 12). We will let the final comment on this outstanding figure of the 20th century come from a psychologist who probably knew him best, his friend from graduate school—Fred Keller.

> B. F. Skinner, as he signed himself professionally, was a many-sided genius, a product of small-town America, with a liberal education at the hands of a few good teachers, an exposure to some of the finest thinkers of our past, and a natural endowment that permitted him to take advantage of these benefits to the full. He was an independent worker, an expert in self-management, and was undistracted by personal attacks or by high honors (of which there were

very many). He was never an office-seeker or a hail-fellow-well-met, but he played an active part in every group of which he was a member. He was not a do-gooder, but all of his attempts to apply the principles of behavior to practical affairs were aimed at the improvement of the lot of human beings everywhere. (Keller, 1991, p. 5)

It would be impossible to overemphasize behaviorism's importance as a school of psychology, or the importance of Skinner as its leading contributor. Boring's 1950 comment about all America having gone behaviorist was valid, and later it was not just behaviorism, but Skinnerian behaviorism (e.g., Skinner, 1974), that dominated modern scientific psychology.

Behavioral analysis focuses on the environment as the source of stimulus information, and a psychology whose goal is the prediction and control of behavior—the aim of behaviorism—typically involves the study and manipulation of the environment. Instead of unseen mental or biological events, the radical behaviorists provided explanations of psychological phenomena in terms of observable environmental conditions. Not surprisingly, one of the camps of behaviorism focused on analysis of the environment itself, and we will call this camp ecological psychology. Because the ecological behaviorists have been more readily embraced by contemporary cognitive psychology than most other elements of behavioral theory, it seems appropriate to close our consideration of behaviorism with them.

ECOLOGICAL PSYCHOLOGY

We are using "**ecological psychology**" to signify a movement in behaviorism that stressed the importance of examining the environmental conditions and fully understanding the nature of the stimulus in any behavioral event. This attention to the stimulus, and thus to the organism's perception of the information contained in it, paradoxically gives the ideas of the ecological behaviorists a somewhat "cognitive" feel. By expanding the consideration of the stimulus to matters of perception and information, these behaviorists represent a connection to both the underlying physiology of behavior and to phenomena often considered mentalistic (Chapter 20). However, as behaviorists, the ecological psychologists provided alternative explanations for many "cognitive" phenomena.

J. R. Kantor and his interbehaviorism, mentioned earlier, can be viewed as the forerunner to the ecological movement, which we will examine in the work of Roger Barker and James J. Gibson.

Roger Barker

Roger Barker (1903–1990) was born in Iowa and raised in California and Canada. Barker was sickly as a child, an invalid from the ages of 14 to 21, and suffered health problems intermittently throughout his adult life. After starting college at the University of Redlands in California, Barker earned a Ph.D. in psychology from Stanford.

From Stanford, Barker returned to Iowa as a research assistant to the Gestalt psychologists Kurt Lewin and Tamara Dembo (Chapter 14). Barker (1989) specifically acknowledged his debt to Lewin for introducing him to the "stream of behavior" metaphor that Barker made central to his own research (e.g., Barker, 1963). Also, Lewin's concept of the "life space" was adapted by Barker into a more behavioral analysis of the environment and the invitations and constraints it places on our actions.

Leaving Iowa, Barker held positions at Harvard, Illinois, Stanford, and Clark before settling at Kansas. His best-known work, *One Boy's Day* (Barker & Wright, 1951), is a microanalysis of just what the title indicates—one boy's day—and is a methodological masterpiece of environmental analysis. The book also illustrates the main work at the Midwest Psychological Field Station of the University of Kansas, which was established in 1947 by Barker and H. F. Wright in Oskaloosa, Kansas. The Station's aims included the discovery and description of the environments in Oskaloosa for the town's children, the recording of the children's behavior in the environments, and the study of the relations in the town between behavior and environment.

James Jerome Gibson

Like Barker, **James Jerome Gibson**'s (1904–1979) career was shaped by contact with Gestalt psychology. Gibson was a Princeton Ph.D. who studied under Herbert Langfeld. His dissertation on form perception offered a behaviorist alternative to phenomena reported by Gestalt psychologist Kurt Koffka.

Gibson (1966a) credited his interest in behaviorism to H. C. Warren's (Chapter 7) zeal over Watson's ideas and to E. B. Holt's (Chapter 10) motor theory of consciousness, which Gibson thought allowed a place for the study of consciousness within the framework of a behavioral, scientific psychology. Moving to Smith College, Gibson found that one of his new colleagues was Kurt Koffka, a psychologist he came to greatly admire. Professionally, Gibson wrote that "Koffka, along with Holt, was a main influence on my psychological thinking" (p. 131), and the Gestalt tempering of Gibson's behaviorism is clear in his classic works (e.g., Gibson, 1966b, 1979).

J. J. Gibson's primary interests were in the relationship between the perceived properties of a stimulus and behavior. Gibson studied several tasks to demonstrate the importance of the stimulus, of which the best known was his work for the military on the ability to land aircraft successfully (e.g., Gibson, 1947). After the war, which for Gibson was a boon because his research was useful in training pilots, Gibson moved to Cornell, where he concluded his academic career. He was a recipient of the APA's Distinguished Scientific Contribution Award.

Gibson's major work, *The Ecological Approach to Visual Perception,* appeared the year he died. Many believe that Gibson succeeded in presenting a grand, unifying theory of behavior that provides both a behaviorist account of mentalistic concepts and the appropriate conception of the relationship between behavior and physiological processes. In so doing, Gibson may have reduced psychology's three rival modes of explanation—the mentalistic, the physiologically reductive, and the behavioral focus on the environment—into a holistic way of understanding the action of organisms.

Although not everyone is convinced that Gibson succeeded (e.g., Fodor & Pylyshyn, 1981), Gibson's ideas have had an impact both on behaviorism and on cognitive psychology. The core idea of Gibson's final book is **affordance**, which is the information contained in a stimulus that we perceive and respond to directly because of our evolutionary history. From the behaviorist viewpoint, affordance is attractive because of this direct perception; that is, the information is not processed by an unseen mental structure but is interpreted directly by the biological equipment evolved to survive in an ecological niche.

At Smith, Gibson married Eleanor Jack, a former student of his and later one of Hull's Ph.D. students at Yale. A member of the National Academy of Sciences, a fellow of the American Association for the Advancement of Science, and a winner of the APA's Distinguished Scientific Contribution Award, **Eleanor Jack Gibson** (1910–) is best known for her work with the visual cliff.

One illustration of an affordance is infant (human and animal) performance on the **visual cliff**. Studies by Eleanor J. Gibson and others have shown that infant organisms avoid an apparent "cliff" despite a lack of experience with falling, which suggests an evolutionary advantage for an innate association between edges and danger. Humans are tall, and falling is dangerous because it brings the head and the rest of the body to the ground with great force. Thus, we have evolved a visual system vigilant for signals, such as edges, that warn of environmental contexts that can lead to falling. In Gibson's view, the affordance of falling that edges provide is not a consciously mediated event but a direct perception that influences our behavior in a particular situation.

CONCLUSIONS

It would be misleading to suggest that there were no behaviorists of importance after Skinner or Gibson, or that behaviorism's impact faded from psychology with the deaths of the major figures we have examined in the last two chapters. Still, it is undeniably true that although behaviorism was American psychology's pre-eminent school from the 1920s until the 1970s, in the last 2 decades the center of psychology has shifted away from the behaviorist focus on learning theory.

For example, social psychology (Chapter 19) increased dramatically in popularity following World War II, and, as we have suggested in this chapter, the Chomsky-Skinner debate over language was fundamental to the rise of cognitive psychology and perhaps to the fall of behaviorism. Cognitive psychology was not the only critic of behaviorism's hegemony over psychological research, however. The ethologists (Chapter 12) mounted an attack over the proper analysis of animal behavior, and humanistic (often clinical) psychologists (Chapter 16) saw behaviorism as too narrow a perspective to explain adequately the vagaries of human existence.

Broader changes in science and philosophy also contributed to behaviorism's decline. Logical positivism fell from respectability as new problems in physics and further analysis by philosophers of science challenged its core assumptions. In fact, it can be argued that the embrace of positivism by such behaviorists as Watson, Hull, and Skinner was too tight, and behavioral psychologists represent some of the final holdouts to the increasingly discredited positivistic view of science.

It is difficult to know exactly how to conclude our review of behaviorism. Behaviorists have made so many important contributions that seem destined to remain forever in the body of psychological fact that in at least this sense, behaviorism has achieved immortality. Although the ideas of Guthrie and Tolman seem to garner less coverage in each new introductory psychology textbook, we can point to a return of Hullian concepts with modern interest in machine learning. Additionally, principles such as those derived by Skinner from his work on schedules of reinforcement seem to us to be etched in stone. Undoubtedly that perception reflects the timing of our own educations, which have occurred during and immediately following the era of behaviorism.

S U M M A R Y

Behaviorism was the culmination of a line of influences toward a strongly objective, rigorously experimental psychology. These influences included British empiricism, Darwinian evolutionary theory, American functionalism, logical positivism, and operationism. After S. S. Stevens called for operationism in psychology, its principles swept the field, as did behaviorism.

Edwin Ray Guthrie

Guthrie's learning theory can be called one-trial, nonreinforcement, contiguity learning, because he believed that a connection between a stimulus and a response occurs at full strength on each trial, without the necessity of reinforcement, by stimulus-response contiguity. Practice improves performance because the learning of a particular movement occurs in one trial, but an act consists of many movements, each of which must be acquired before the act is performed skillfully.

Based on his theory, Guthrie developed several ways to break bad habits: for example, fatiguing the response. Guthrie recognized that much behavior is goal directed and emphasized the role of movement-produced stimuli in sequential responding. William K. Estes applied a mathematical model to Guthrie's learning theory.

Edward Chace Tolman

Tolman was interested in behavior considered in large units, and he also believed that behavior is goal oriented. In *Purposive Behavior in Animals and Men,* Tolman differentiated learning from performance, holding that learning may occur in the absence of reinforcement, but that reward is necessary for performance. Evidence for the distinction came from studies of latent learning.

From studies of rats in mazes, Tolman believed that animals developed cognitive maps that they could use to achieve alternative solutions when a particular pathway was blocked. Support for the cognitive map idea included studies of vicarious trial and error behavior, hypothesis-testing experiments, and studies comparing place-learning and response-learning rats.

Clark Leonard Hull

Hull's first major interest in psychology was in aptitude testing, and his second major interest was in hypnosis. At Yale, Hull began work on a systematic theory of learning—hypothetico-deductive learning theory. In Hull's final system, there were 17 postulates and over 130 theorems. Like Tolman, Hull used intervening variables in his theorizing, including such variables as drive, habit strength, excitatory potential, and incentive motivation.

Hull's Students and Associates

After Hull's death, Spence continued the experimental efforts of his mentor. One of Spence's main contributions was an S-R explanation for Köhler's demonstration of relational responding in chickens. Over time, Spence's theorizing edged closer to Tolman's and Guthrie's.

With John Dollard, Neal Miller presented a simplified version of Hull's theory in *Social Learning and Imitation.* Dollard and Miller reduced Hull's postulates and theorems to the elements of drive, cue, response, and reward. Miller and Dollard provided a wealth of data for the importance of imitation, and they were also interested in secondary drives—learned drives that gain their motivating status from being paired with primary drives.

O. H. Mowrer proposed a two-factor theory of reinforcement, and, correspondingly, two types of learning. Skinner had earlier distinguished between Pavlovian conditioning and Skinner's type of conditioning, which was based on Thorndike. Mowrer elaborated Skinner's distinction into sign learning (Pavlovian conditioning) and solution learning (instrumental conditioning).

B. F. Skinner

Through a process of development, Skinner invented the Skinner box. In the Skinner box, an organism is conditioned to make a response for reinforcement. Skinner called his version of conditioning operant conditioning because the organism operates on the environment to produce consequences, which determine whether the behavior will be repeated. By reinforcing successive approximations of the desired behavior, an organism's operant behavior can be shaped.

Skinner and his associates demonstrated the power of operant conditioning by training pigeons to be missile guidance systems. A more practical demonstration came in Skinner's development of teaching machines. Skinner's inventiveness also led to the baby-tender, a protected environment for early childrearing. Neither the teaching machine nor the baby-tender achieved commercial success.

At Harvard, Skinner worked with Charles Ferster to study the effects of different reinforcement schedules on behavior. Skinner also developed a behavioristic analysis of language, and its attack by linguist Noam Chomsky may have led to behaviorism's death.

Skinner was often controversial, penning such social commentaries as *Walden Two* and *Beyond Freedom and Dignity.* Skinner's radical behaviorism forms the foundation of modern scientific psychology.

Ecological Psychology

Ecological psychology was a movement in behaviorism stressing the importance of fully understanding the environmental conditions and the nature of the stimulus in any behavioral event. Roger Barker and James J. Gibson were leading ecological psychologists who were influenced by Gestalt psychologists. Gibson was married to Eleanor Jack Gibson, who is perhaps best known for her visual cliff experiments with young animals.

Some psychologists think J. J. Gibson's *The Ecological Approach to Visual Perception* achieved a holistic understanding of the behavior of organisms that combines the mentalistic, the physiologically reductive, and the behavioral focus on the environment. The core idea is the affordance, which is the information contained in a stimulus that we respond to directly because of our evolutionary history.

CONNECTIONS QUESTIONS

1. What were some of the connections Skinner foresaw between behaviorism and how we live in the everyday world?
2. How is Guthrie's brand of behaviorism connected to our everyday lives?
3. What connections can you make between the functionalists and the neobehaviorists?
4. What events in the lives of Hull and Skinner seem to connect with their psychological positions and research interests?
5. What connections can you make to support the claim that Skinner's most important contribution to psychology was to take Thorndike's law of effect seriously?
6. What enduring connections can you make between learning theory (behaviorism) and other areas of psychology such as clinical, social, developmental, and cognitive?
7. Draw a concept map connecting the major neobehaviorists, and compare your results with one possible solution provided on p. 567.

SUGGESTED READINGS

Bjork, D. W. (1993). *B. F. Skinner: A life*. New York: BasicBooks. Bjork was aided in the production of this highly readable biography by interviews with Skinner, his family, and Fred Keller, Skinner's longtime friend. Access to the Harvard Archives and to the "Basement Archives" at Skinner's home were invaluable.

Gibson, J. J. (1979). *The ecological approach to visual perception*. Boston: Houghton Mifflin. This is Gibson's most well-known work. It is foundational reading in ecological psychology.

Guthrie, E. R. (1952). *The psychology of learning* (Rev. ed.). New York: Harper & Brothers, Publishers. Guthrie is considered a peerless user of anecdote and simple terms to illustrate complex theoretical ideas. This book will show you why.

Hull, C. L. (1943). *Principles of behavior: An introduction to behavior theory*. New York: Appleton-Century-Crofts, Inc. If you want to learn more about Hull's learning theory by reading him in the original, this book is less technical and formulaic than his later *Behavior System*.

Hull, C. L. (1952a). Clark L. Hull. In E. G. Boring, H. S. Langfeld, H. Werner, & R. M. Yerkes (Eds.), *A history of psychology in autobiography* (Vol. 4, pp. 143–162). Worcester, MA: Clark University Press. Written shortly before he died, Hull's autobiographical essay is an excellent introduction to the man, providing details about his preprofessional life, his different "careers" in psychology, and his behavior system.

Skinner, B. F. (1967). B. F. Skinner. In E. G. Boring & G. Lindzey, *A history of psychology in autobiography* (Vol. 5, pp. 385–413).

New York: Appleton-Century-Crofts.

Skinner, B. F. (1976). *Particulars of my life*. New York: Alfred A. Knopf.

Skinner, B. F. (1979). *The shaping of a behaviorist*. New York: Alfred A. Knopf.

Skinner, B. F. (1983). *A matter of consequences*. New York: Alfred A. Knopf. Here you have a choice: Skinner's autobiographical essay or his three-volume autobiography. Skinner's autobiographical essay is a remarkably detailed, amusing summary of the contents of his autobiography.

Skinner, B. F. (1974). *About behaviorism*. New York: Vintage Books. *About Behaviorism* is an outstanding collection of Skinner's ideas about most of the topics (e.g., learning, language development, social engineering) we have explored in this chapter.

Tolman, E. C. (1967). *Purposive behavior in animals and men*. New York: Meredith Publishing Co. (Original work published 1932) Despite Tolman's penchant for creating neologisms, this is an entertaining and informative account of much of the early animal research from his laboratory.

Tolman, E. C. (1952). Edward Chace Tolman. In E. G. Boring, H. S. Langfeld, H. Werner & R. M. Yerkes (Eds.), *A history of psychology in autobiography* (Vol. 4, pp. 323–339). Worcester, MA: Clark University Press. Tolman's autobiographical essay gives a summary account of changes in Tolman's thinking 2 decades after *Purposive Behavior*.

Gestalt Psychology

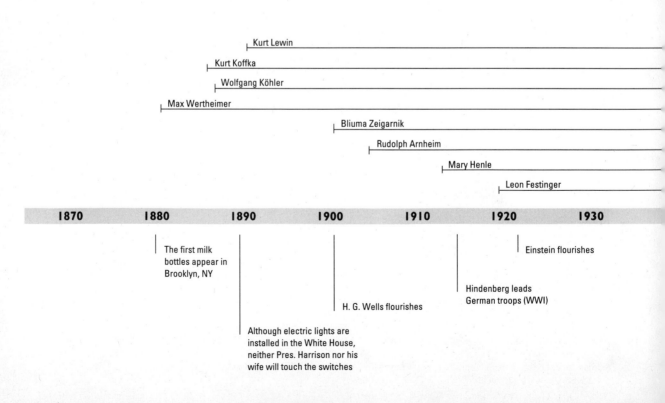

Kurt Lewin

Kurt Koffka

Wolfgang Köhler

Max Wertheimer

Bliuma Zeigarnik

Rudolph Arnheim

Mary Henle

Leon Festinger

1870   1880   1890   1900   1910   1920   1930

The first milk
bottles appear in
Brooklyn, NY

Einstein flourishes

Hindenberg leads
German troops (WWI)

H. G. Wells flourishes

Although electric lights are
installed in the White House,
neither Pres. Harrison nor his
wife will touch the switches

Synonyms for the German word *Gestalt* include shape, form, and configuration, and Titchener (Chapter 7) even suggested configurationism as the name for this German school of psychology. "Total structure" is sometimes included as a dictionary definition, and Boring (1950) indicated that *Strukturpsychologie* (structural psychology) might have been an appropriate name, "since a structure is a whole in which the total organization is altered by the change of any part . . ." (p. 588). Although Boring's suggestion was apt and consistent with a major theme of Gestalt theory, the problem with structural psychology was that the label had already been applied by James (Chapter 10) to contrast Titchener's approach with functionalism. In fact, Titchener's structuralism, with its focus on identifying the elements of consciousness (a molecular

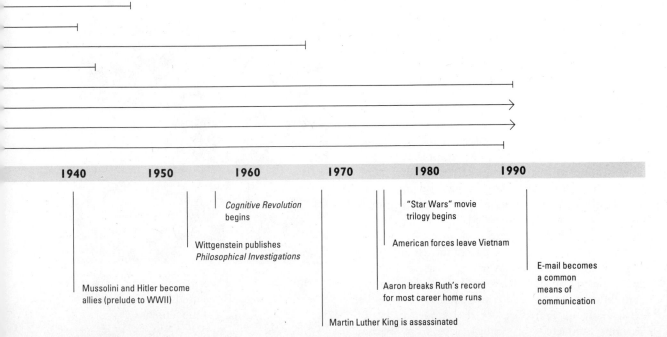

approach), is in a sense the exact opposite of Gestalt psychology's molar approach.

Thus, we are left with the solution taken by most, which is to leave the German word *Gestalt* untranslated. Indeed, the word has become part of our English vocabulary and is usually taken to mean "a structured whole." That is, Gestalt psychology dealt with organized wholes that could not be explained by breaking them into their component parts. Gestalt psychology was particularly opposed to the reductive elementism characteristic of the schools of structuralism and behaviorism. But the school of Gestalt psychology was much more than a group of Germans who opposed structuralism and behaviorism; it was a new way of looking at experimental psychology from the vantage point of rational philosophy, the phenomenology of experience, and early neuroscience.

FOUNDING GESTALT PSYCHOLOGY: THE PHI PHENOMENON

In 1910, Max Wertheimer had an insight that was the beginning of Gestalt psychology. According to the story, Wertheimer was traveling by train from Vienna to vacation in the Rhineland. Along the way, he realized that the phenomenon in which a perception of movement is experienced even though there is no actual movement had great significance for psychology. It must mean that perception does not necessarily correspond on a one-to-one basis with sensory stimulation. Perceptions may have properties that cannot be predicted from the sensations that comprise them. The whole percept is not necessarily equal to just the sum of its sensory parts. Therefore, structuralism was a misguided enterprise.

Wertheimer left the train at Frankfurt and purchased a stroboscope—a popular toy of the period that allowed still images to be projected in a time sequence that resulted in apparent movement of the figures in the images. Wertheimer experimented with the toy in his hotel room before going to the Frankfurt Academy, which was soon to become the University of Frankfurt. At the Academy, Wertheimer contacted an acquaintance from Berlin,

Friedrich Schumann (Chapter 8), who allowed Wertheimer to use his newly constructed **tachistoscope**—a device that flashed lights on and off for very brief intervals. Figure 14–1 shows Max Wertheimer standing by the tachistoscope used in early experiments of apparent motion.

Wertheimer conducted several experiments of apparent motion, which he called the **phi phenomenon**, using as subjects two younger psychologists at Frankfurt, Wolfgang Köhler and Kurt Koffka (both discussed later), as well as Koffka's wife. In a typical experiment, two lights were briefly shone successively, one through a vertical slit and the other through a horizontal slit, in that order. With too-short time intervals between their presentations, both lights appeared to be on simultaneously; with

FIGURE 14–1. Max Wertheimer standing next to a type of tachistoscope he used in the experiments of apparent movement.

Source: Courtesy Dr. Michael Wertheimer.

too-long intervals, the lights appeared stationary, with the vertical light on first, followed by the horizontal light. However, if the time interval was just right, the vertical line appeared to rotate to the horizontal position. Wertheimer's description of his experiments of apparent movement in the 1912 publication, "Experimental Studies on the Seeing of Motion," is often said to mark the formal beginning of Gestalt psychology. The three men, Wertheimer, Köhler, and Koffka, became Gestalt psychology's triumvirate.

What was the significance of Wertheimer's studies of apparent motion? After all, Wertheimer did not discover the phenomenon, and Wundt (Chapter 7) had an explanation for it based on learned eye movements. Wertheimer had nevertheless demonstrated that perceptions were not reducible to sensory stimulation alone and in the process had rendered Wundt's eye-movement explanation untenable with his critical experiment (Figure 14–2). When line "a" was followed by line "b," "the phenomenon of rotation clearly appeared, both to the left and to the right at the same time . . ." (Max Wertheimer, 1912/1968, p. 421). Because the eyes cannot move in two directions simultaneously, it is impossible to explain the apparent movement by sensations from the eye muscles. Thus, the perception of apparent movement where none existed, the phi phenomenon, could not be understood by breaking the phenomenon into its component elements.

Was Wertheimer's initial study of phi a turning point in psychology or merely "a rallying point"? Arguing from the *Zeitgeist* perspective, O'Neil and Landauer (1966) stated that Wertheimer's experiment was no more than a rallying point for like-minded psychologists. In concluding his rebuttal of O'Neil and Landauer, Seaman (1984) observed that all of the major ideas of Gestalt psychology can be found in Wertheimer's 1912 article. Because of this, Seaman saw no reason for not regarding Wertheimer's article as a turning point for Gestalt thinkers rather than simply a rallying point.

GESTALT PSYCHOLOGY'S ANTECEDENTS

Max Wertheimer must have been a "great" person—Abraham Maslow (Chapter 16) believed that he was fully self-actualized—and his 1912 article can be seen as fundamental to modern perceptual theory and to cognitive psychology. Still, what if Wertheimer had gone into another field or had not taken that train ride along the Rhine? Would someone else have had the insight leading to Gestalt psychology? The answer is probably yes. Like the other schools we have considered, Gestalt psychology had many antecedents.

Wertheimer's insight was anticipated in part by both Ernst Mach (Chapter 5) and Christian von Ehrenfels (Chapter 8), the latter a scientist with whom Wertheimer studied. A physicist who developed a version of positivism, Mach studied the nature of sensations and concluded that there were two "new" types—space form and time form—and that these new sensations were independent of their elements. For example, a space form such as a triangle could be large or small, or drawn in red ink or green ink, without losing its triangularity. Similarly, a time form, such as a melody, could be played with different instruments or in another key without losing its essential quality (Mach, 1886/1914).

In 1890, Christian von Ehrenfels published a criticism of Wundt's failure to include another element—***Gestaltqualitäten*** or form qualities—with his triad of sensations, images, and feelings (Heider, 1970). As an example of form qualities, von Ehrenfels, like Mach, pointed to a musical melody. The melody is more than simply a collection of

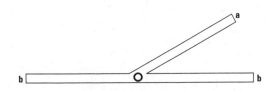

FIGURE 14–2. Experimental figure that resulted in a perception of movement from "a" to "b" in both directions simultaneously.

individual notes, because it can be transposed to different keys or played by different instruments without loss of recognition.

Wertheimer's insight was that the qualities of the whole, the Gestalt or form qualities, determine the characteristics of the parts, rather than the other way around. Form quality was not just another of Wundt's basic elements of consciousness, as von Ehrenfels thought, but a new concept altogether. This was a rationalistic, Kantian (Chapter 5), "top down" analysis rather than the empirical, sensation-based, "bottom up" approach of the structuralists.

Actually, Wundt himself could be considered something of a forerunner to Gestalt psychology. His idea of the creative synthesis of elements—similar to John Stuart Mill's (Chapter 5) mental chemistry—acknowledged the difference between wholes and the sum of their parts. Both Mill and Wundt realized that something new might arise from the combination of elements into a whole, although neither developed the idea as fully as the Gestaltists.

Franz Brentano (Chapter 8) is often listed as one of Gestalt psychology's forerunners. In addition to the profound influence of Brentano on von Ehrenfels, Brentano's use of introspection was quite different from the technique practiced by Wundt and his students. Brentano's introspection tended to be phenomenological, where phenomenology is defined as the study of meaningful, intact experiences without further analysis into smaller, artificial, discrete units. Brentano directly anticipated the kind of analysis of whole and psychologically meaningful experiences practiced by later phenomenologists (Chapter 16), William James, and the Gestaltists.

Oswald Külpe (Chapter 8) also deserves mention. Wertheimer earned his Ph.D. under Külpe's direction, and "Külpe may . . . have had something to do with Wertheimer's progress away from sensationism toward phenomenology" (Boring, 1950, p. 594). All of the major Gestaltists also studied with Carl Stumpf (Chapter 8), with Koffka, Köhler, and Kurt Lewin (below) earning Ph.D.s at the University of Berlin under his supervision. However, despite this obvious connection, the Gestalt psychologists never admitted that Stumpf had directly shaped their thinking, and, conversely, Stumpf denied influencing the Gestalt school.

Edmund Husserl (Chapter 8) has been called the "father" of modern phenomenological psychology. There are many similarities between Gestalt psychology and phenomenological psychology, which suggests that at least the indirect influence of Husserl and Stumpf on Gestalt theory may be more extensive than has been acknowledged. An alternative explanation is that phenomenology borrowed heavily from Gestalt psychology (see Henley, 1988; Schmidt, 1985).

Both William James and John Dewey (Chapter 11), can be considered precursors of Gestalt psychology. In his dislike of elementism and his conception of the stream of consciousness, James was far from structuralism, and the Gestaltists undoubtedly found support in the phenomenological flair of James's (1890) *Principles.* Like James, Dewey argued against the artificial elementism that dominated psychology under the structuralists.

One of James's best-known biographers, Ralph Barton Perry (1935; Chapter 13), developed in detail the thesis that James, even more than Stumpf, was the major influence upon the Gestaltists. However, Mary Henle (1990) suggested that Perry's connection between Gestalt psychology and William James was overblown. Although Henle found many areas of similarity between James and Gestalt theory, she also noted important differences, particularly on such issues as mechanism, atomism, and organization. For example, James's view of the nervous system as a machine (a mechanistic view) prevented him from seeing the more dynamic processes (and organization) the Gestaltists considered necessary to "permit the interactions needed to make understandable many corresponding psychological phenomena" (Henle, p. 79). Although James generally rejected the sort of atomism that the Gestaltists rejected, he often lapsed into it.

Beyond the German phenomenologists and American philosophical psychologists such as James, theorists from Jean Piaget (Chapter 20) and Jean-Paul Sartre (Chapter 16) to J. J. Gibson and Edward Tolman (both in Chapter 13) have been linked to the Gestaltists because of similarities of some of their ideas to Gestalt positions. We can see from this brief survey of antecedents and "relatives" that Wertheimer's insight fell on fertile soil.

These various connections also suggest the thematic elements of Gestalt psychology. First and foremost, it was a rationalistic approach to psychology, consistent with the tradition of Kant, Herbart (Chapter 5), Brentano, Stumpf, and Külpe. Second, Gestalt psychology was concerned with the search for what sort of a priori (innate) structures serve to organize and direct our mental experiences, not just our perceptual experiences, but our learning and thinking, as well. Finally, perhaps more than any other school, Gestalt psychology attempted to provide a synthesis of sophisticated philosophical analysis, physiological data from neuroscience, and our everyday, phenomenological experiences. More than a school about "wholes and parts," Gestalt psychology prospered because of its important advances on long-standing issues such as the mind-body problem and the relationship between perception and consciousness.

Now that we have some overview of Gestalt psychology, we can explore in some detail its major theorists and their contributions. We will begin by returning to the life of Max Wertheimer.

GESTALT PSYCHOLOGY'S TRIUMVIRATE

Max Wertheimer

Max Wertheimer (1880–1943) was born into an intellectual and artistic family in Prague. Wertheimer's father was a financially successful educator, whose success triggered in the son a lifelong interest in the methods of education and gave him the financial independence to pursue his own intellectual interests.

As a child, Wertheimer was gifted in mathematics, philosophy, literature, and especially in music. He played the piano and the violin and composed symphonies and chamber music. As a psychologist, Wertheimer often used musical examples to illustrate his ideas and sometimes even required that a piano be present at his lectures (Michael Wertheimer, 1992).

In adolescence, Wertheimer's interest centered on literature, and he became fascinated with the philosopher Spinoza (Chapter 3). With so many talents and interests, it was difficult for Wertheimer to decide on a career, and he considered law before turning to philosophy and then to psychology.

Wertheimer studied at the University of Berlin from 1901 to 1903, taking classes from Stumpf. He then moved to the University of Würzburg, where he got his Ph.D. summa cum laude in 1904, with Külpe as his adviser. His dissertation was on lie detection, and he developed a word association test that he used to evaluate the truth of legal testimony.

Between 1904 and 1910, Wertheimer was at the Universities of Prague, Vienna, and Berlin. In 1910, his phi phenomenon insight took him to Frankfurt, where he stayed until 1916, with time out for World War I. As a German army captain, he conducted research on sound localization, which ultimately led to the invention of a type of sonar (Michael Wertheimer, 1992). From 1916 to 1929, Wertheimer was a *Privatdozent* at the University of Berlin, where, along with Koffka, Köhler, and neurologist Kurt Goldstein (discussed later), he established the journal *Psychologische Forschung* (*Psychological Research*). He served as editor for the first 20 volumes.

Despite his undisputed contributions to psychology, Wertheimer was not given a professorship until 1929, when he was offered a position at the University of Frankfurt. This delayed promotion was partly caused by his Jewish heritage and partly by his lack of publications. A perfectionist, Wertheimer had great difficulty relinquishing a manuscript. He stayed at Frankfurt from 1929 until September 1933, when he immigrated to the United States to escape the growing Nazi threat that eventually led to World War II and the Jewish Holocaust.

In the United States, Wertheimer took a position in New York City at the New School for Social Research, an institution established to employ refugee scholars from Europe. Along with Köhler, Wertheimer was invited in 1936 to join the prestigious Society of Experimental Psychologists (Chapter 7). Beyond his continued academic affiliations, Wertheimer remained broadly interested in education throughout his life, as indicated by his collaboration on a radio program with John Dewey.

Wertheimer became a U.S. citizen the day before his 59th birthday. He died 4 years later of a coronary embolism at his home in New Rochelle, New York, on October 12, 1943. In 1945, one of his best-known works, *Productive Thinking,* was published. *Productive Thinking* was based in part on interviews with people known for their problem-solving abilities. For example, Wertheimer spent many pleasant and productive hours with one of his friends in America, another Jewish refugee, the Nobel Prize–winning physicist Albert Einstein.

Kurt Koffka

Recalled by his biographers as a charismatic and charming man that women found attractive, Berlin-born **Kurt Koffka** (1886–1941) earned a Ph.D. from the University of Berlin in 1908, under Stumpf's supervision. His Berlin studies were interrupted by a year at the University of Edinburgh, during which he became fluent in English. This language proficiency enabled Koffka to spread the Gestalt message to America, which he did in a 1922 *Psychological Bulletin* article, "Perception: An Introduction to *Gestalt-Theorie.*" Unfortunately, this article led most American psychologists to assume that the Gestalt psychologists were *only* interested in perceptual phenomena, when, in fact, they were interested in philosophical issues, learning, thinking, and many other topics.

It is true that the early publications of the Gestaltists focused on perception. According to Michael Wertheimer (1987), the reason for this is that they were rebelling against Wundt's system, and much of Wundt's work had been in sensation and perception. That is, the Gestaltists studied perceptual phenomena "in order to attack Wundt in his own stronghold . . ." (p. 134).

As we noted, Koffka was at Frankfurt when Wertheimer arrived in 1910. In 1911, Koffka took a position at the University of Giessen, 40 miles from Frankfurt, and stayed there until 1924. He was a visiting professor at Cornell University from 1924 to

1925 and at the University of Wisconsin 2 years later. In 1927, Koffka accepted a position at Smith College, where he remained until his death in 1941.

At Smith College, Koffka befriended J. J. Gibson, who became an important, and increasingly influential, perceptual theorist. Gibson's approach to perception was both strongly nativistic and "behavioristic." However, Gibson's theory can also be seen as an extension and development of Koffka's thoughts on perception, an idea supported by Gibson's (1979) discussions of Koffka in his classic work, *The Ecological Approach to Visual Perception.*

As the most prolific writer of Gestalt psychology's three founders, Koffka was the school's major spokesperson. One of his most important works was a book on child psychology from the Gestalt perspective, which was translated into English as *The Growth of the Mind* (Koffka, 1924). Another major work, *Principles of Gestalt Psychology* (Koffka, 1935), was intended to be a systematic application of Gestalt theory to diverse areas of psychology, such as perception, learning and memory, social psychology, and personality. As originally conceived by Koffka, *Principles* was intended for a lay audience, and it was actually written "for 19 year old girls" (Gibson, 1971, p. 3). This is ironic because, according to Henle (1987), Koffka's *Principles* "was probably read only by professional psychologists . . ." (p. 14) but deserves better. She recommended that "we pay our respects to Koffka's *Principles* . . . not as an illustrious antique, but as a 'fount of questions' and a continuing aid in clarification of contemporary thinking" (p. 20). Koffka (Figure 14–3) dedicated the book to Wertheimer and Köhler.

Wolfgang Köhler

Wolfgang Köhler (1887–1967) was born in Reval, Estonia, but grew up in northern Germany. Like Koffka, he attended the University of Berlin, where he received his Ph.D. in 1909 under Stumpf. At Berlin, Köhler also studied with Max Planck, the famous physicist, and "was always a physicist in his thinking, indebted for stimulus in his student days at Berlin to Max Planck rather than to Stumpf" (Boring, 1950, p. 597). From Berlin, Köhler went to

FIGURE 14–3.   Kurt Koffka.

Source: Archives of the History of American Psychology.

Frankfurt, and a year later he participated in Wertheimer's phi phenomenon experiments.

In 1913, the Prussian Academy of Science sent Köhler to study a colony of apes on the island of Tenerife, one of the Canary Islands in the Atlantic. Although Tenerife is off the west coast of Africa, apes are not endemic to the island; the Anthropoid Research Station Köhler supervised was stocked with animals imported from a German colony in the Cameroons, in west central Africa. Although he expected to stay only a short time, world events intervened, and Köhler was marooned for the duration of World War I.

During the war, Köhler was suspected of being a German spy by British intelligence. In the mid-1970s, Ronald Ley, an American psychology professor, visited Tenerife, and published *A Whisper of Espionage: Wolfgang Köhler and the Apes of Tenerife* (Ley, 1990). Ley concluded that Köhler had "served the cause of the German military through his part in building, maintaining, and operating a concealed radio for the purpose of communicating informa-

tion that would contribute to the German war effort" (p. 253).

Köhler himself summarized his work with the apes and other animals on Tenerife in *Intelligenzprufungen an Menschenaffen* (*Intelligence Tests with Anthropoid Apes*), published in 1917. It was translated into English in 1925 and published as *The Mentality of Apes.* We will discuss Köhler's contributions to learning theory later.

In a brief mention of his time spent on Tenerife, Köhler (in Henle, 1971) acknowledged that during his long stay on the island, he did not always work on animal psychology. Instead, his thoughts turned to the possibility of a connection between what he had learned from the physicist Planck and the Gestalt ideas of Wertheimer. Referring to the antielementism of Gestalt psychology, the desire to study wholes rather than elements, Köhler indicated that he was relieved to find a similar approach in physics. Further, Köhler noted that in studying many specific physical situations, physicists handled the situations as wholes rather than as collections of independent facts.

Köhler returned to Germany in 1920, succeeding first G. E. Müller (Chapter 8) at the University of Göttingen in 1921 and then Stumpf at the University of Berlin in 1922. With his replacement of Stumpf, Köhler attained the academic pinnacle of psychology in that era.

Ley's (1990) investigations included an interview with one of Köhler's students and later his assistant at the University of Berlin—Professor Wolfgang Metzger. Metzger gave Ley "the impression that Köhler did not talk very much about anything, except, perhaps, psychology" (p. 76). In addition, Köhler apparently suffered from stage fright whenever he had to give a lecture, and he later developed a tremor in his hands that his students and assistants used to gauge his mood—the worse the mood, the greater the tremor. Metzger's wife told Ley that Köhler did not like small children, and during the early years of his second marriage, his daughter by his second wife was placed in a foundling home.

According to Metzger, Wertheimer was the exact opposite of Köhler. Whereas Köhler was cold and aloof, Wertheimer was warm and friendly. Metzger also suggested that Wertheimer's slow promotion stemmed from German anti-Semitic attitudes even before the Nazis came to power. Köhler's influence as director of the Psychological Institute at the University of Berlin probably helped Wertheimer achieve his Frankfurt professorship.

During his tenure at the University of Berlin, Köhler made two trips to the United States. In the 1925–1926 academic year, he was a visiting professor at Clark University, and he was the William James lecturer at Harvard from 1934 to 1935. Later in 1935, he was a visiting professor at the University of Chicago.

Unlike some non-Jewish German academics, Köhler staunchly opposed the rise of Nazism and the dismissal of Jews and anti-Nazis from their university positions (e.g., Crannell, 1970). In fact, in 1933, Köhler wrote the last anti-Nazi article published in a German newspaper. In the article, Köhler referred to the great patriotism of the valuable people who had *not* joined the Nazi party and criticized the wholesale dismissal of Jews from universities and other positions by citing examples of outstanding contributions made by such Jews as Spinoza and the experimental physicist James Franck (Henle, 1978a). Such was his renown that he was not arrested, but his position in Germany became increasingly precarious, and he immigrated to the United States in 1935. After the visiting professorships at Harvard and Chicago, Köhler served at Swarthmore College in Pennsylvania until his retirement in 1958. His research and writing continued at Dartmouth College in New Hampshire, where he moved after retirement.

In a revealing footnote, Michael Wertheimer (1987) described Köhler as follows:

> A fastidious, meticulous man with the highest personal standards, Köhler loved to be immaculate in everything he did. The present writer remembers seeing Köhler, bent on recreation, spending a Sunday afternoon during the mid-1940s chopping firewood in his back yard—using a razor-sharp, well-polished axe, and dressed in a spotless white suit, with white shirt and tie. (p. 135)

Soon after coming to America, Köhler became a favorite reader of works in progress by his colleagues because of his superior command of English.

Although we have tried to give you some impressions of Köhler's scientific work and his personality, note that we have merely scratched the surface of this complex man. Köhler's scope was phenomenal, encompassing not only the topics we mention in this chapter but also the mind-body problem (e.g., Köhler, 1966), intelligence, physiology, and philosophy (notably ethics and aesthetics).

Köhler, who survived in the United States much longer than any of the other major Gestalt psychologists, received several awards for his scientific contributions. In 1947, he received the Warren Medal for "his studies on figural after-effects and an approach to a more general theory of perceptual responses" (Wilkening, 1973, p. 94). He received one of the first three Distinguished Scientific Contribution Awards from the APA in 1956 and was elected APA president in 1959. Köhler (Figure 14-4) was selected to

FIGURE 14–4.   Wolfgang Köhler in about 1947.

Source: Friends Historical Library of Swarthmore College.

receive the APA's Gold Medal Award in 1967 but died before he could accept it, and the award is not given posthumously.

PRINCIPLES OF GESTALT PSYCHOLOGY

The Gestalt psychology literature is voluminous, and Harry Helson (1933)—an American supporter of Gestalt psychology and a 1962 recipient of the APA's Distinguished Contribution Award—identified 114 different laws of *Gestalten* assumed to structure perceptions and thinking. Rather than attempting to cover 114 different Gestalt laws of form, we will briefly cover a few of the most important points, beginning with the so-called principles of perceptual grouping.

In 1923, Wertheimer published a paper on visual perceptual grouping in which he tried to show that we perceive objects in a way analogous to the way we see perceived movement in the phi phenomenon. That is, we see objects as unified wholes rather than as elemental sensations. Wertheimer used simple stimuli (e.g., lines, dots, and simple line figures) to avoid the criticism that the meaningfulness of real objects might force their organization in particular ways. That is, meaningless stimuli should not suggest any form of organization. In a sense, this is analogous to the invention of the nonsense syllable by Ebbinghaus (Chapter 8); Ebbinghaus wanted to study verbal learning and memory free from the contamination of the meaning of words. Similarly, Titchener emphasized the use of meaningless stimuli in order to prevent his students from committing the "stimulus error." Following Wertheimer's lead, we will use simple visual stimuli to illustrate the Gestalt perceptual principles of organization.

Gestalt Principles of Perceptual Grouping

Figure-Ground

The **figure-ground relationship** was borrowed from the work of the Danish psychologist Edgar

Rubin (Chapter 8), although it can be traced to a political art form in which faces of the unpopular could be hidden. According to Rubin, the perceptual field is divided into two parts: figure and ground. The figure is the part of the field we are attending to, and the ground is the remainder of the field that we are not attending to. Some factors that distinguish the figure from the ground include the following: The figure's shape is fully defined, whereas the ground appears shapeless; the ground seems to continue behind the figure; and the figure looks both closer and brighter than the ground.

What is figure and what is ground is both dynamic and context dependent. This is clearly illustrated through certain reversible figures, such as the ones shown in Figure 14–5.

Continuity

In **continuity**, there is a perceptual tendency to follow elements that appear to be proceeding in the same direction, to "continue" in the direction they appear to be heading. For example, in Figure 14–6a, we tend to see the figure at the top as a semicircle with a line through it rather than as a combination of the two figures shown at the bottom.

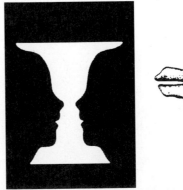

FIGURE 14–5. The figure-ground relationship. Switching of the figure-ground relationship makes each of these figures ambiguous. The figures are called vase/face and duck/rabbit, respectively.

Proximity

According to **proximity**, elements that are close to each other in time or space are seen as belonging together. You see Figure 14–6b as three pairs of lines rather than as six individual lines or a collection of six lines, because of the principle of proximity.

Similarity

The old saying, "birds of a feather flock together," is one way to think of the Gestalt principle of **similarity**. Similar elements are seen as belonging together, and in Figure 14–6c, there is a tendency to see alternating rows of circles and squares rather than columns of mixed circles and squares.

Closure

The principle of **closure** accounts for why we tend to see incomplete figures as complete; we tend to fill in the gaps. You will probably see Figure 14–6d as complete geometric figures (circle, square, and triangle) rather than as collections of unconnected dashes. Closure makes it difficult for many people to to proofread material—they tend to see the material the way it should be rather than the way it really is. Did you catch the error in the previous sentence? If not, closure may have prevented you from seeing it.

Other Gestalt Principles and Phenomena

The Law of Prägnanz

All of the Gestalt principles of perceptual grouping we have considered may be seen as illustrations of a general Gestalt principle, the **law of *Prägnanz***. The law asserts that innate psychological organization tends toward the perception of a "good Gestalt," or that we will perceive a stimulus to be as good and meaningful as prevailing conditions allow. For example, closure works because a completed circle is more meaningful, or a better Gestalt, than a circle with a gap in it. Similarly, we see the semicircle with a line through it in Figure 14–6a because it is more meaningful—a better Gestalt—than the two figures below it.

Note that the law of *Prägnanz* has important implications beyond perceptual organization. Changes in memory over time may also reveal the law's influence, with possible consequences for the validity of eyewitness testimony (Chapter 19). You may recall our discussion in Chapter 1 of a study in which subjects were shown a film of an automobile accident and were later asked questions about the accident. Subjects asked if they saw broken glass in accidents involving cars that "smashed" were more likely to "recall" broken glass than subjects asked the same question about cars that "hit." In reality, there was no broken glass in the film. "Smashed" establishes a context in which broken glass is more likely to be present, and the subjects' responses were consistent with the created context.

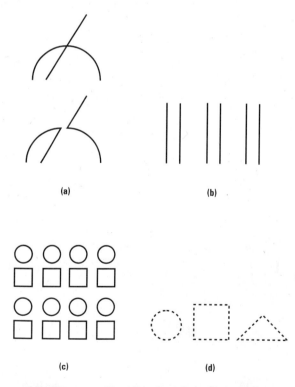

(a)

(b)

(c)

(d)

FIGURE 14–6.   Gestalt principles of perception. Illustration of the Gestalt perceptual principles of (a) continuity, (b) proximity, (c) similarity, and (d) closure.

The Zeigarnik Effect

The **Zeigarnik effect** is another illustration of the law of *Prägnanz* generally and of the principle of closure specifically. The effect is that we tend to remember incomplete tasks longer than finished tasks. The effect was investigated by and named for the Russian-born psychologist **Bliuma Vul'Fovna Zeigarnik** (1890–1990). Zeigarnik did her doctoral work under Kurt Lewin (discussed later). In Russia, where psychotherapy tended to be the province of psychiatrists, Zeigarnik became one of a small number of what we would call clinical psychologists. Her research focused on the psychoses, and she also published papers on the history of abnormal psychology.

Zeigarnik's dissertation research was the first formal test of Lewin's hypothesis that attaining a goal relieves tension, and it was stimulated by an observation Lewin and his students made at a Berlin cafe. During one of their regular meetings at the cafe, someone in Lewin's group called for the bill, and their waiter knew exactly what everyone had ordered even though he had kept no written record. A short time later, Lewin asked the waiter to write the check again. This time, the waiter indignantly explained that he no longer knew what they had ordered because they had already paid the bill. Thus, the unpaid bill (incomplete task) created tension that was relieved with payment (task completion).

To test Lewin's theory, Zeigarnik (1927) gave various tasks to a large number of subjects, allowing the subjects to finish some of the tasks but not others. In a later recall test, many more of the uncompleted tasks were remembered than the completed ones.

Examples of the Zeigarnik effect are easy to find. Assuming you studied and learned the material, you are more likely to remember the test questions you missed—did not complete—than the ones you got right. Have you ever noticed how many TV series end a season with a cliffhanger episode, hoping the lack of completion will force you to tune in next season? Some people have the habit of finishing the sentences of the person speaking to them, which may be another example of the Zeigarnik effect.

Isomorphism

Another important Gestalt principle is called isomorphism, which literally means identical (*iso*) shape or form (*morphism*), and it provides part of the Gestalt answer to the mind-body problem. According to Köhler (1947), "Experienced order in space is always structurally identical with a functional order in the distribution of underlying brain processes" (p. 61). The principle of **isomorphism** assumes there is a direct correspondence between brain processes and mental experiences. The direct correspondence does not mean that brain processes and perception are identical in form, however. For example, it does not mean that when you see a cube, somewhere in the brain there is a neural pattern with the shape of a cube.

One frequently used analogy to illustrate the relationship between neural processes and corresponding perceptions is that of a map and the country it represents. Although the map and the country are obviously not the same, an identity exists in the sense that we can discern much about the country's characteristics from studying the map. The map tells us precisely about the location of cities, about the topography of the country, about the presence of rivers, and so forth, without being in any sense a literal copy of what it depicts.

All three founding Gestaltists accepted the principle of isomorphism, beginning with Wertheimer's 1912 discussion of experiments on the phi phenomenon. Wertheimer noted that the brain processes for apparent motion and for true motion must be essentially the same, because real and apparent motion are experienced as identical. To account for phi, there must be a correspondence between the conscious experience of motion and the underlying neural experience (i.e., there must be a psychophysical isomorphism).

Furthermore, the Gestaltists believed that the fact that we experience our perceptions as coordinated wholes instead of a simple sum of interconnected sensations argues against a telephone switchboard analogy of the brain's structure and function. That is, the phi phenomenon shows that the successive stimulation of neural units that would occur in the perception of the real movement of a line is unnecessary for the perception of apparent movement. Recent advances in machine learning, called neural networks (see Chapter 20), have further strengthened the idea that the nervous system does not have to be organized into interlocking elements. In fact, several authors have discussed the similarity between Gestalt psychology and this new artificial intelligence technology (e.g., van Leeuwen, 1989).

Gestalt Learning Principles

As we noted, Köhler spent several years on Tenerife, at least some of the time studying the behavior of the ape colony established there. In his studies, Köhler developed the problems and learning principles that challenged the prevailing learning theory of the time, Thorndike's (Chapter 12) trial-and-error learning.

Umweg or Detour Problem.   For Thorndike, learning was a process in which an animal made a response and was either rewarded or not rewarded for it. Reward (a satisfier) strengthened the bond between the stimulus and the response, whereas lack of reward (an annoyer) weakened the stimulus-response bond. Learning was a gradual process of trials and errors and trials and successes.

Köhler believed that the nature of Thorndike's task, the problem boxes, made it difficult for Thorndike's animals to see the whole situation. The boxes forced the animals into random activity in order to solve the problem, rather than allowing them to get an overview of it. That is, Thorndike's cats used trial-and-error learning because that was all the task permitted them to use.

Köhler developed tasks for his animals that enabled them to see all the problem elements, although not necessarily in the sequence or format that would permit solution. Solution required a restructuring of the field (i.e., seeing it in a different perspective). Köhler used the term "**insight**" to refer to the sudden behavior change that often occurred when the animal (or human) accomplished the restructuring of the field. Insight occurred when the subject recognized the relationships among the problem's relevant stimuli.

One example of a task used both by Köhler and by later Gestalt psychologists (e.g., Lewin) was the

Umweg or **detour problem**, which allowed an animal to "get the big picture." In the simple version of the *Umweg* task shown in Figure 14–7, the goal is clearly visible to the subject, but the goal cannot be reached directly. The organism must take a detour by initially going away from the goal in order ultimately to obtain it. In one version of the *Umweg* problem, Köhler tested a dog, a child, and a chicken. Although the dog and the child solved the problem readily, the chicken was less successful (Köhler, 1917/1925).

Apes, Boxes, Sticks, and Bananas.   Köhler's ape research provided further evidence for his idea of insight learning. In a typical task, a banana was hung from the ceiling of an ape's enclosure. Boxes and/or sticks were available for the ape to use as tools in obtaining the fruit. The boxes could be stacked by an animal and then ascended like a ladder (see Figure 14–8).

One of the most widely quoted passages from *The Mentality of Apes* involves the insightful behavior of an ape named **Sultan**. Sultan's task required him to rake in a banana placed outside his cage, but neither stick available to the ape was long enough to reach the fruit. The problem's solution required Sultan to join the two sticks together into a longer tool. After Sultan's initial period of failure, Köhler left the ape alone with the keeper. As Köhler (1917/1925) recounted it, animal caretaker Manuel

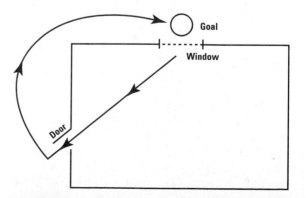

FIGURE 14–7. A typical *Umweg* or detour problem.

González y García described Sultan's development of insight as follows:

> Sultan first of all squats indifferently on the box, which has been left standing a little back from the railings; then he gets up, picks up the two sticks, sits down again on the box and plays carelessly with them. While doing this, it happens that he finds himself holding one rod in either hand in such a way that they lie in a straight line; he pushes the thinner one a little way into the opening of the thicker, jumps up and is already on the run toward the railings, to which he has up to now half turned his back, and begins to draw a banana towards him with the double stick. (p. 127)

Köhler concluded that the insight learning he observed had several important characteristics that differentiated it from Thorndike's trial-and-error learning. Because the solution to a task is based on a perceptual restructuring of the field, it often occurs suddenly and completely, without a gradual accumulation of associations. The learning is all or none, the "aha" phenomenon that in cartoons is drawn as the light coming on over a character's head.

Another characteristic of insight learning is that it does not depend on reinforcement. Sultan had already solved the problem before he raced to the front of the cage to rake in the banana. The banana provided the incentive for his response without being necessary for the learning. Tolman's studies of latent learning and insight learning in rats also showed that learning could occur in the absence of reinforcement, at least reinforcement as traditionally defined. We noted that Tolman always gave credit to the Gestaltists for influencing his thinking.

Problems solved by insight are long remembered, and the solutions are easily generalized to similar problems. Once Köhler's apes had learned to stack boxes to reach a banana or had learned to use a pole to rake in a banana from outside the compound, they were able to apply this knowledge to solve other, similar problems. There was a large amount of positive transfer.

Despite the importance that Köhler and the other Gestaltists attached to the distinction between insight learning and trial-and-error learning, the difference between the two may be less clear-cut than the Gestaltists believed. For example, in one study of "insight" learning, Birch (1945) tested young chimpanzees on a problem like one often used by Köhler: Food was placed outside the animals' cages, and a hoe was available to rake it in. An ape with extensive experience using sticks as tools readily solved the problem. Four animals that could not solve the problem initially were given sticks to play with for 3 days. Although they were never observed using the sticks as rakes, when they were retested with food and a hoe, they soon solved the task. Apparently, in order for insight to occur, the animals must have earlier acquired at least one component skill of the eventual solution (i.e., using sticks as extensions of their arms).

Harry F. Harlow (1905–1981), an experimental psychologist who did extensive research with monkeys at the University of Wisconsin, noted that the

FIGURE 14–8.   Grande stacks boxes to retrieve a banana, while Sultan watches with interest.

Source: American Philosophical Society Library.

typical insight learning problem was one in which the previous experience of the animals with problem components was unknown. Insight sometimes did not occur in animals that did not have some relevant prior experience (Harlow, 1951), just as Birch's (1945) study showed. Harlow's alternative to insight learning was the formation of a **learning set**, or the extraction of one key to the solution of a series of similar problems.

As with so many historical milestones, the idea of insight learning did not originate with the person whose name is so closely associated with it. Instead, the first recorded example may well be the experience of the famous Greek mathematician **Archimedes** (ca. 287–212 B.C.). According to the story, King Hieron gave an artisan some gold to fashion into a crown. The resulting crown weighed as much as the gold the king had supplied, but Hieron suspected that silver had been substituted for some of the gold. The king told Archimedes his suspicions and gave him the crown to test—without damaging it.

Weeks later, Archimedes noticed that as he stepped into the water at the public baths, it overflowed according to how deep he was. This observation led Archimedes to infer that "a floating body loses in weight an amount equal to the weight of the water it displaces. Surmising that a *submerged* body would displace water according to its volume, and perceiving that this principle offered a test for the crown, Archimedes . . . dashed out naked into the street . . . crying out 'Eureka! eureka!'" (Durant, 1939, pp. 630–631), which means "I have found it." Archimedes had exhibited the sudden behavior change that accompanies the insightful restructuring of a field, when he discovered a test for the specific gravity of an object. Because gold and silver have different specific gravities, Archimedes not only showed that the crown's gold had been alloyed with silver, he also told King Hieron exactly how much gold had been stolen.

The Transposition Problem. One of the most interesting tasks that Köhler developed was supposed to contrast directly the Gestalt approach with Thorndike's trial-and-error learning. As noted in Chapter 13, Köhler first trained chickens to peck corn on the darker of two shades of gray paper. If they pecked it on the lighter gray, they were chased away. After hundreds of trials, the chickens were pecking corn only on the darker gray paper. To see what they had learned, Köhler next gave the birds a choice between corn on the dark gray paper from their training trials and corn on a still darker gray paper. S-R theory predicts that the chickens will peck the corn on the reinforced gray paper from the original task, but the Gestalt view is that animals will have learned the pattern or Gestalt. Hence, Köhler predicted that the chickens would choose the new, darker gray paper, demonstrating that they had learned the relations between the stimuli in the original training.

Köhler's chickens generally showed relational responding by choosing the darker of the test stimuli. He called the phenomenon **transposition**, the analogy being that notes from musical melodies do not change their relationship to each other when the melodies are *transposed* to different instruments or to different keys on the musical scale. The darker gray card in the test had the same relation to the dark grey card as the dark grey card had to the light gray card in the training trials.

Dozens of ingenious experiments examined the transposition effect's generality, and the results did not uniformly favor the Gestalt position. However, one effect of the transposition phenomenon was to force the S-R theorists to develop alternative explanations for it. As we noted in Chapter 13, Kenneth Spence developed one elaborate interpretation that enabled him to predict the circumstances under which transposition would and would not occur (Spence, 1937). Further studies sometimes supported the Gestalt relational-responding view and sometimes supported the Hull-Spence absolute stimulus view. Modern learning theorists (e.g., Klein, 1996) conclude that both positions may be valid, with Gestalt relational responding occurring in tasks allowing simultaneous comparison of stimuli and Hull-Spence absolute responding in tasks permitting the subject to see only one stimulus at a time.

Wertheimer and Thinking

Productive Thinking, published 2 years after Wertheimer's death, represents the culmination of his study of thinking. His interest in the topic began much earlier; in fact, Wertheimer published his first article on thinking in the same year (1912) that his famous article on the phi phenomenon appeared.

The case material in *Productive Thinking* ranges from school children solving simple geometric problems to Albert Einstein's thought processes that resulted in his theory of relativity. Applying Gestalt principles, Wertheimer believed that problem solving should proceed from the whole problem down to its parts rather than vice versa. Again, this is a top down or holistic approach in which students should get the "big picture," which, in turn, should help organize the particular details into a "good" or meaningful form. By contrast, the habitual use of repetition and rote memorization as learning techniques leads to a "bottom up," elemental, mechanical performance rather than to creative or productive thinking.

Furthermore, holistic learning should result in comprehension of the principles behind a problem's solution, and these principles can be applied readily to solve future problems. Because Wertheimer emphasized holistic learning, he believed that a teacher should present the whole problem to students from the beginning. This approach contrasted with Thorndike's trial-and-error learning in which the solution to the problem is hidden, and the learner is forced to make errors before "accidentally" selecting the correct solution.

Thus, according to Gestalt principles, learning is based on understanding the nature of the problem. The problem itself creates a cognitive disequilibrium that lasts until it is solved. Recall the observation that led to the Zeigarnik effect—a waiter remembered the details of a bill until it was paid, after which he promptly forgot them. The unpaid bill caused a cognitive disequilibrium that was resolved with payment.

If you have had a social psychology course, you may notice the similarity between cognitive disequilibrium and its resolution and **cognitive dissonance** theory. According to the latter, people cannot tolerate cognitions (beliefs, thoughts, perceptions, etc.) that are in conflict. Something has to give, and the person resolves the inner conflict by revaluing one or more of the conflicting beliefs. Cognitive disso-

nance theory is attributed to **Leon Festinger** (1919–1989), a prominent social psychologist who earned his Ph.D. at the State University of Iowa in 1942—under the direction of the fourth major Gestalt psychologist, Kurt Lewin.

In addition, Gestalt principles suggest that restoring cognitive equilibrium is reinforcing. Earlier, we talked about the reinforcing properties of problem solving in the context of Sultan's insight. The banana Sultan raked in with the joined sticks was not the reinforcement that led the ape to solve the problem; reinforcement came from problem solving itself.

As an example of the benefits of insight learning, Michael Wertheimer (1980) described an experiment in which subjects were permitted to study 15 digits for 15 seconds, the object being to try to remember as many as possible. The digits were 1 4 9 1 6 2 5 3 6 4 9 6 4 8 1. Given only the instruction to try to remember as many as possible, most subjects could remember only a few, and even these were lost after a week.

Instructed to look for a pattern in the numbers, some subjects in another group realized that the 15 numbers are just the squares of the numbers from 1 to 9. With this insight, the subjects then reproduced all the digits correctly both immediately and for weeks afterward. In fact, the insightful subjects probably would *always* be able to recall the 15 numbers, further illustrating the advantage of the insightful approach compared to rote memorization.

In summary, Gestalt psychology contributed significantly to the areas of problem solving and learning. In fact, present-day cognitive psychology (Chapter 20), of which studies of problem solving are a part, can be viewed as a direct descendent of Gestalt psychology (e.g., Gardner, 1985).

KURT LEWIN

Kurt Lewin (1890–1947) was born on September 9, 1890, in the town of Mogilno, Prussia (a former German state). He grew up on a farm, and his family moved to Berlin in 1905. After studies at the Universities of Freiburg and Munich, Lewin began his formal training in psychology at the University of Berlin in 1910. He had completed all the requirements for a Ph.D. under Stumpf by 1914, but because of World War I, he did not receive his degree until 1916. During the war, Lewin rose from private to officer and won the Iron Cross.

After the war, Lewin returned to the Psychological Institute in Berlin. He became a *Privatdozent* at the university in 1921 and an *Ausserordentlicher Professor* in 1927, an advance over his previous rank, but a position without tenure. He was a Visiting Professor of Psychology at Stanford University in 1932, and in the following year he left Germany to escape the growing Nazi threat to Jews.

For the next 2 years, Lewin was an Acting Professor of Psychology at Cornell. This was followed by 10 years as Professor of Child Psychology at the Child Welfare Research Station, University of Iowa. Shortly before his death, he accepted the position of Professor of Psychology and Director of the Research Center for Group Dynamics, Massachusetts Institute of Technology. Lewin died at Newtonville, Massachusetts, of a massive heart attack on February 12, 1947.

Lewin's programs in both Germany and the United States interested women students. Perhaps this was because of his subject matter—the more social elements of cognition and perception, children, applied topics—and the *Zeitgeist* that constrained the place of women and the topics in which they were interested. Four female graduate students began to work with Lewin in 1924: Gita Birenbaum, Tamara Dembo (who came with him to the United States), Maria Ovsiankina, and Bliuma Zeigarnik. Lewin continued to work with women in the United States, but they were not in the majority as they had been in Germany (Ash, 1992).

Almost without exception, people who knew Lewin described him in glowing terms. For example, **Rensis Likert** (1903–1981), a Lewin associate and the developer of the Likert Scale, said that "all who knew him had a singular unanimity of feeling about him. Here was an individual who was a great scientist, a great teacher and a great man" (Likert, 1947, p. 132). According to Lewin-student Jerome Frank (1978), the word best summarizing Lewin's personality is "zest": "He was a little man with an apparently inexhaustible supply of energy. . . .

Although he must often have been seated in my presence, in my memories he is almost always in motion" (p. 223).

Lewin also had a keen intellect and a high degree of mental flexibility; he was always willing to listen receptively to new ideas from any source. Lewin had a talent for attracting capable students, regardless of gender, and his group discussions with them were conducted in an open manner. Lippitt (1947) wrote that "Over and over he made clear that the atmosphere of the discussion must be such that no one had any fears of 'sticking out his neck' in expressing any idea, no matter how unformulated it might seem" (p. 88).

By all accounts, Lewin fit easily into the American way of life. For example, Tolman (1948) referred to an essay Lewin had written about social psychological differences between Americans and Germans. Lewin (Figure 14–9) described Americans as being much more open and communicative than Germans, resulting in

FIGURE 14–9. Kurt Lewin.

Source: Archives of the History of American Psychology.

greater ease and friendliness in ordinary social relations, and greater contact with immediate practical problems in the American, and a more private and idea-centered life in the German. I cite this distinction because Lewin himself was, or became, so very American in the terms of such an analysis. He was so astoundingly open to communication with others, so free from rank or status considerations. (p. 2)

To end his obituary of Lewin, Tolman (1948) predicted:

> In the future history of our psychological era there are two names which, I believe, will stand out above all others: those of Freud and of Lewin. . . . Freud, the clinician, and Lewin, the experimentalist, these are the two men who will always be remembered because of the fact that their contrasting but complementary insights first made of psychology a science which was applicable both to real individuals and to real society. (p. 4)

To the general public, Freud's name is much better known than Lewin's, but to many psychologists, Lewin's contributions are of considerably more than historical interest.

Lewin's Topological Psychology

Lewin is known for applying Gestalt principles to the study of motivation, personality, and social processes. To do this, Lewin developed **field theory**, in which a person is considered to be interacting continually within a field of psychological forces. For Lewin, the behavior (B) of a person (P) is a function of the person's interaction with his or her environment (E); that is, $B = f(PE)$. By environment, Lewin meant the psychological (or psychobiological) environment.

A person's psychological activities occur within a field Lewin called the **life space**, which consists of all the influences on the person at a given time. These influences can include motivational states (e.g., hunger), memories (how good food tastes from a particular restaurant), and sensations (the sights and sounds driving down the road, the smells from restaurants). The only restriction on what is in the person's life space is that it must be something the person is aware of. Lewin called all the influences "psychological facts."

To illustrate the person's life space with its psychological facts, Lewin borrowed symbols from *topology*—a form of mathematics that deals with the unvarying properties of a geometric figure when the figure is changed in certain ways. For example, the relative positions of areas or regions within a bounded form are maintained despite changes in size or distortions of the form. In addition, Lewin invented **hodology**, which he used to show paths of energy within the life space. Lewin used Jordan curves (elliptical shapes) to enclose a person's life space. Psychological facts are contained within the curve; events and objects that are not part of the person's life space lie outside the curve and constitute the foreign hull.

The psychological facts have value (or valence in Lewin's terminology), and this is represented with either a plus (+) or minus (−) sign; a fact with no value to the individual receives no sign. Lewin used vectors to show either impelling or repelling psychological forces acting on a person. To illustrate Lewin's topological psychology in a very simplified way, we will examine some of the concepts Lewin explored in his invited chapter for *A Handbook of Child Psychology* (Lewin, 1931).

One basic concept was that the extent of the life space increases and becomes more differentiated with age. This differentiation occurs temporally as well as physically. That is, the life space of the older child contains not only *present* psychological facts but both past and future psychological facts. The older child begins to plan for the future and also begins to use imagery and fantasy. This means that the child lives to some extent on an irreality level (Lewin, 1936). Lewin used irreality to describe an unrealistic aspect of a person's life space.

In his *Handbook* chapter, Lewin (1931) described three types of conflict experienced by the child (and the adult as well). These are the approach-approach conflict, approach-avoidance conflict, and avoidance-avoidance conflict. Lewin defined conflict "as the opposition of approximately equally strong field forces" (p. 109).

In **approach-approach conflict**, the child must decide between two goals, both with positive valence. In Figure 14–10a, the child (C) must choose between going on a picnic (P) and playing with

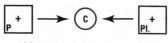

(a) Approach – approach conflict

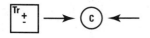

(b) Approach – avoidance conflict

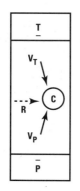

(c) Avoidance – avoidance conflict

FIGURE 14–10.   Lewin's three types of conflict.

Source: from Lewin, K. (1931) "Environmental Forces in Child Behavior and Development." In C. Murchison (Ed.), Handbook of Child Psychology *(pp. 94–127). Worcester, MA: Clark University Press. Reprinted by permission.*

friends (Pl.). The approach-approach conflict is usually easy to resolve because both choices are positively valued, but Lewin noted that once the choice is made, the child often sees the chosen goal as inferior to the rejected goal.

Approach-avoidance conflict occurs when a goal simultaneously has both positive *and* negative valence. Shown in Figure 14–10b, Lewin's example is of a child who wants to climb a tree (Tr) but is fearful of doing so. The length of the vectors can be drawn to indicate which of the impelling and repelling forces is stronger. Thus, if the enjoyment from climbing the tree is likely to be greater than the child's fear of heights, then he or she will climb the tree.

In **avoidance-avoidance conflict**, the child must choose between two goals with negative valence. Shown in Figure 14–10c, in Lewin's example, the child is told to perform an unpleasant task (T) or she will be punished (P). V_T is the vector pushing

the child away from the unpleasant task, and V_P pushes the child away from punishment. The result is often attempted escape from the field, shown in the figure by R, the "sideways resultant." One of the authors well remembers telling his son to do his homework or he would be punished; invariably the son chose the sideways resultant, escaping from the field by falling asleep.

Lewin at the Iowa Child Welfare Research Station (ICWRS)

In Iowa, as in Germany, Lewin was open to the ideas of his group, and daily discussions involved a constantly changing set of participants. In fact, this aspect of Lewin's approach to research was given a special name, *die Quasselstrippe* (the chatter line), and this term appears repeatedly in the reminiscences of Lewin's American students (e.g., Ash, 1992).

From these discussions came the seeds of many important research projects. Two ideas led to especially significant and widely cited studies. According to Dorwin Cartwright, one of Lewin's students, the idea to study the effect of different types of group leadership on the behavior of children probably originated with conversations Lewin had with Ronald Lippitt in 1936 (Ash, 1992). In the most extensive study, Lewin, Lippitt, and White (1939) organized groups of 10-year-old boys. The groups performed various activities under different types of adult leadership: authoritarian, democratic, and *laissez-faire* (not interfering in the boys' pursuits). Authoritarian leadership led to increased aggression within the group and the choosing of a "scapegoat" toward whom much of the aggression was directed. The social atmosphere was friendlier in the democratically led group, and more assigned tasks were accomplished. Little was accomplished in the *laissez-faire* group.

As noted, Lewin believed that the life space of the individual becomes more differentiated with development. Thus, going backward developmentally (regressing) should result in less personality differentiation; in Lewin's terminology, the personality should become dedifferentiated. To study the dedifferentiation hypothesis, Barker, Dembo, and Lewin

(1943) first allowed children to play with ordinary toys including a Teddy bear, a teapot, a cup, a box of crayons, and two pieces of writing paper. During this period, the experimenters rated the constructiveness or destructiveness of the children's play, and each child's play was assigned a developmental age. Next, the children were allowed to play with vastly superior toys on the other side of a screen from their original playthings. The superior toys included a dollhouse large enough to admit a child and "a toy lake . . . filled with real water. It contained an island with a lighthouse, a wharf, a ferryboat, small boats, fishes, ducks, and frogs. The lake had sand beaches" (p. 445). Finally, the children were forced to return to the original toys, but they could see what they were missing through the screen.

The resulting frustration led to regression and dedifferentiation, which was evidenced by a dramatic decline in the children's quality of play. The average rated play age was over 17 months less than originally. Children threw blocks at each other, pounded a toy telephone on the floor, used crayons to scribble on paper rather than to draw or color pictures, had tantrums, and so on. This study provided dramatic evidence for the frustration-aggression hypothesis (Dollard, Miller, Doob, Mowrer, & Sears, 1939).

Lewin after Iowa

After leaving Iowa, Lewin began his "action research" (applied research) that was intended to solve actual problems. Although valuable from the standpoint of positively affecting the human condition, Eng (1978) suggested that Lewin's action research may have been compensation for the "sterility in the long run [of Lewin's field theory] as a paradigm for a new psychology" (p. 232). By contrast, Henle (1978b) did not consider Lewin's field theory approach a failure. She characterized Lewin's work as metatheory rather than theory—Lewin "was writing a *theory of personality theory*" (p. 234, italics in the original)—and concluded that personality theory would be more advanced if its formulators had appreciated Lewin's contribution.

One example of action research dealt with the most effective way to change opinions, particularly

opinions about various food items during World War II. In one study, women either heard a dynamic lecture praising some unpalatable, but abundant, food item or participated in group discussions on the desirability of buying and eating the disliked item. Group discussions and public commitment to changing behavior were clearly more effective than either discussions with individuals or dynamic lectures.

With Lewin's formation of the Research Center for Group Dynamics at MIT, the study of group dynamics became more focused. Some of the concepts that Lewin and his followers studied included group cohesiveness, identification with the group, within-group communication, and group decision processes. After Lewin died, the Research Center for Group Dynamics moved to the University of Michigan. In addition, a National Training Laboratory was begun at Bethel, Maine, to conduct summer workshops to train leaders using the principles of group dynamics. These training groups were called "T groups" and became popular in the 1970s.

We see in Lewin a diverse thinker who made contributions to a variety of areas in psychology. Even today, Lewin's field theory has adherents in both industrial psychology and personality theory.

LESSER-KNOWN GESTALT PSYCHOLOGISTS

In Germany and later America, many other theorists and researchers were associated with Gestalt psychology. For example, David Katz (Chapter 8) was a well-known perceptual theorist in Europe in the 1920s and was always counted as an ally of Gestalt psychology and a contributor to its store of facts. Earlier we mentioned **Kurt Goldstein** (1878–1965) as one of the editors of *Psychologische Forschung*. A pioneer in clinical neuroscience, Goldstein's work with brain-damaged World War I soldiers enabled him to make many substantive contributions to our understanding of the relationship between neurology and behavior within a Gestalt framework.

Karl Bühler (1879–1963) can be associated with several phenomenological movements in Germany,

Gestalt psychology among them. Although little of Bühler's work has been translated into English, what has been translated has been well received by contemporary cognitive psychologists (e.g., Bransford, 1979), as Bühler was a clear forerunner of modern cognitive psychology.

A student of both Wertheimer and Köhler, **Karl Duncker** (1903–1940) was one of the most notable of the Gestalt psychologists with interests in thinking. Duncker's (1945) work on problem solving provides much of the basis for our current understanding of how linguistic relationships constrain human reasoning and for **functional fixedness**. Functional fixedness is defined most simply as whatever is the opposite of creativity, that is, as being unable to use objects to attain a goal in a manner different from their previously established use.

To illustrate how linguistic relationships constrain our thinking, consider the following problem adapted from Duncker (1945): You have a cancer that cannot be operated on or treated with drugs because it is located deep inside the body surrounded by vital tissue. The only option is to destroy it with a laser. However, because the tumor is surrounded by essential organs, a laser beam that would destroy the tumor would also destroy the vital tissue it had to pass through to reach the tumor. A hint from Crovitz (1970) may help you find the solution. Try thinking through the phrase "Take a ray _____ a ray," inserting different prepositions in the blank. Modern work on psycholinguistics has continued to build on Duncker's insights into the importance of relations in human problem solving (e.g., Johnson & Henley, 1992).

Mary Henle (1913–) and **Rudolph Arnheim** (1904–) are two noteworthy modern-day Gestalt psychologists. Although Henle has made a number of research contributions, she is perhaps best known as the "chronicler of Gestalt psychology." Henle has compiled several essay collections (e.g., *Documents of Gestalt Psychology* [Henle, 1961]; *The Selected Papers of Wolfgang Köhler* [Henle, 1971]) and has written articles comparing Gestalt psychology and such things (or people) as phenomenology (Henle, 1979), William James (Henle, 1990), and gestalt therapy. Concerning the relationship between Ge-

stalt psychology and gestalt therapy, Henle (1986) minced few words when she wrote: "The difference is so crucial that I could conclude at this point that there is no substantive relation between Gestalt psychology and gestalt therapy" (p. 26). Henle is currently Professor Emeritus at the New School for Social Research.

Rudolph Arnheim has continued to write articles on classical Gestalt topics (e.g., 1986a), to be a critic of misconceptions of Gestalt psychology (e.g., 1986b), and to take Gestalt psychology in new directions. These new directions have been mostly into art and architecture. *Visual Thinking* (Arnheim, 1969), *Art and Visual Perception* (Arnheim, 1974), and many related articles have pioneered the fields of the psychology of art and of architecture.

GESTALT PSYCHOLOGY'S INFLUENCE

As we indicated, Wertheimer, Köhler, and Lewin all came to America to escape the Nazis. Other, lesser-known Gestaltists left Germany as well, going to Scandinavia, Russia, and to other countries (Henle, 1986). The Gestalt psychologists left behind them in Germany their well-established careers, large laboratories, many students, and a major journal (*Psychologische Forschung*).

The story of how the Gestaltists came to America and found academic positions makes interesting reading. Mary Henle (1984) argued that their immigration and subsequent employment may be attributed primarily to **R. M. Ogden**'s (1877–1959) efforts. Ogden was Titchener's student at Cornell before taking his degree in 1903 with Külpe at Würzburg. While in Germany, Ogden met Koffka, Külpe's assistant at the time (ca. 1909). Returning to America, Ogden taught at Missouri, Tennessee, and Kansas before settling at Cornell. During this time, Ogden kept in contact with Koffka and was instrumental in seeing that Koffka's article introducing Gestalt psychology to America was published in 1922 in the *Psychological Bulletin*.

By the mid-1920s, it was clear that the major Gestaltists were interested in coming to America, and Ogden acted as a facilitator (Freeman, 1977). After considering an offer at Wisconsin, where he had taught in the 1926–1927 academic year (Chapter 13), Koffka settled at Smith College in 1927. In 1929, Ogden arranged for Köhler to give visiting lectures at Cornell after failing to get Wertheimer for them. In 1933, Lewin came to Cornell at Ogden's bidding.

Although all the major Gestaltists except Wertheimer spent brief periods as visiting professors at several major American schools both before and after immigrating to America, the places they eventually chose to stay all had drawbacks. For example, Koffka settled at Smith College. Although his interactions there with J. J. Gibson proved important for perceptual theory, Smith was an undergraduate institution that could not train a new generation of Ph.D.s. (Actually, Koffka did manage to have one Ph.D. student in America: Mary Harrower.) Köhler stayed at Swarthmore, also an undergraduate institution, but he influenced some students (e.g., Mary Henle and Hans Wallach, the latter a 1983 winner of the APA's Distinguished Scientific Contribution Award). Finally, when Wertheimer started at the New School for Social Research, it offered no degrees at all. Wertheimer did not have Ph.D. students in America until very near the end of his life.

Not only did the Gestaltists leave behind their "establishment," their arrival in America coincided with the heyday of American behaviorism. In addition, although seldom stated, the fact that the major Gestaltists were Germans at a time when international tensions with Germany were escalating could not have been beneficial to their careers. Thus, it is easy to see why Gestalt psychology did not prosper in America.

The events around and about World War II played a major role in the fragmentation of Gestalt psychology as a school, leading one social psychologist to comment: "If I were required to name the one person who has had the greatest impact on the field, it would have to be Adolph Hitler" (Cartwright, 1979, p. 84). The major Gestaltists' move to America cost them their place in the sun and relocated them in well-respected, but not powerful, academic settings. Also, because Ameri-

can psychology at the time was deeply rooted in behaviorism, the Gestaltists did not find fertile soil for their ideas.

However, Köhler never gave up the fight for the recognition that Gestalt psychology deserved. He continued to publish and to grow in stature as a psychological theorist and philosopher throughout his long career. Indeed, Gestalt theory as a philosophy of psychology flourished. First exposed to Gestalt psychology by Karl Bühler, Ludwig Wittgenstein (Chapter 20) became the major figure in modern philosophy largely through his later writings in the philosophy of psychology. Wittgenstein frequently used Gestalt principles as his point of departure, and Gestalt figures often appeared in his books, as he grappled with difficult questions about perception, language, and the structure of knowledge.

In Köhler's presidential address to the American Psychological Association (Köhler, 1959), he began by tracing Gestalt psychology from Wertheimer through its then-current works in social psychology by Solomon Asch and Fritz Heider (both Chapter 19). Next, he proposed that the age of the competing schools, such as Gestalt psychology and behaviorism, was waning. Köhler closed by suggesting that the time had come to combine the wisdom of all the schools into one psychology.

In part, what Köhler suggested in 1959 has occurred. Modern cognitive-behavioral therapies and new "cognitive science" advances in learning theory exemplify the combining of disparate areas of psychology. Within 10 years of Köhler's APA address, the last two great schools—behaviorism and Gestalt psychology—were gone. In their place was a loose confederation known as cognitive psychology, which can be viewed as a marriage of both the behaviorist and the Gestalt traditions (e.g., Simon, 1992).

Martin Gardner (1985) traced the origins of the "Cognitive Revolution" in *The Mind's New Science*, in which he referred to Gestalt psychology as "the most direct link" between older works on thinking and modern cognitive psychology. Throughout their careers, many Gestalt psychologists were interested in conception and thinking, in addition to perception.

Obviously, Gestalt psychology has continued to influence modern psychology long after the decline of its status as a formal school. It lives on as a viable perceptual theory and underpins many modern insights in cognitive psychology and social psychology, as we will see in subsequent chapters.

CONCLUSIONS

Gestalt psychology emerged in Germany as the fullest expression of the phenomenological alternative to Wundt's system (see Chapter 8). At its peak just before World War II, Gestalt psychology perhaps represented the most complete and sophisticated system of psychology extant. Unfortunately, the rise of the Nazis resulted in the dismantling of the German academic community, and with it Gestalt psychology. With its principals scattered across Europe and America, Gestalt psychology never regained its former status.

Although introductory textbooks cover the important contributions that Gestalt psychologists made to our understanding of perceptual phenomena, often without giving appropriate credit, equally important contributions to learning, child development, cognition, biological psychology, and social and applied areas are largely ignored. Still, Gestalt psychology did not fade away completely. In America, many of the original Gestalt theorists found a niche, and new students (e.g., Asch, Festinger, Heider), in social cognition. In addition, Gestalt psychology can be seen as an important forerunner of modern cognitive psychology.

Because of the negative effect of world events on Gestalt psychology before it reached maturity, we cannot conclude that Gestalt psychology fully succeeded as a psychological school. However, the impact of Gestalt psychology on the future of psychology should not be underestimated. We are left with the perennial "what if" question: What would the landscape of psychology look like today if the Gestaltists had not been among the casualties of World War II?

S U M M A R Y

The German word *Gestalt* has become part of the English language and is usually taken to mean "whole." Gestalt psychology dealt with wholes unexplained by knowledge of their components.

Max Wertheimer's 1910 insight about apparent movement (the phi phenomenon) was that perceptions may have properties that are different and cannot be predicted from the sensations that comprise them. He studied the phi phenomenon at Frankfurt with Wolfgang Köhler and Kurt Koffka.

The most immediate forerunners of Gestalt psychology were Ernst Mach and Christian von Ehrenfels, who recognized that whole perceptions may have qualities that are independent of the individual sensations comprising them (*Gestaltqualitäten*). Others often mentioned as anticipators include John Stuart Mill, Wundt, Brentano, Külpe, Stumpf, Husserl, James, and Dewey.

Gestalt Psychology's Triumvirate

After studying the phi phenomenon at Frankfort, Max Wertheimer taught at the University of Berlin before

becoming a professor at the University of Frankfort. Coming to the United States in 1933, he was employed by the New School for Social Research in New York City until his death in 1943. His well-known *Productive Thinking* was published in 1945.

Kurt Koffka earned a Ph.D. from the University of Berlin under Stumpf's supervision. Koffka's "Perception: An Introduction to *Gestalt-Theorie*," introduced Gestalt psychology to America.

Wolfgang Köhler earned his Ph.D. from the University of Berlin under Stumpf's supervision. In 1913, Köhler went to Tenerife to study an ape colony, publishing his results in English as *The Mentality of Apes*. Köhler immigrated to the United States in 1935 and held visiting professorships at Harvard and the University of Chicago before settling at Swarthmore College.

Principles of Gestalt Psychology

The Gestalt principles of perceptual grouping include the figure-ground relationship, continuity, proximity, similarity, and closure.

Other Gestalt Principles and Phenomena

The Gestalt perceptual principles may be viewed as special cases of the law of *Prägnanz*. Studied by Bliuma Zeigarnik, the Zeigarnik effect—the tendency to remember incomplete tasks longer than finished tasks—is an illustration of the law of *Prägnanz*. Isomorphism is the Gestalt principle that assumes there is a direct correspondence between brain processes and what is being experienced.

Köhler developed the Gestalt learning principles from his studies of animals solving detour or *umweg* problems, learning to stack boxes or use sticks to get bananas, and being trained and tested on the transposition problem. Animals sometimes showed sudden awareness or "insight" of a problem's solution.

In *Productive Thinking*, Wertheimer applied Gestalt principles to problem solving and learning. Wertheimer favored a holistic approach to problem solving rather than reliance on rote memorization.

Kurt Lewin

Kurt Lewin received his Ph.D. under Stumpf and was at the Berlin Psychological Institute until he immigrated to the United States in the early 1930s. Lewin was at Cornell and in Iowa before becoming the Director of the Research Center for Group Dynamics at MIT.

Lewin applied Gestalt principles to the study of motivation, personality, and social processes, developing field theory in which a person is seen to interact in a field of psychological forces. To illustrate his theory, Lewin borrowed symbols from topology; to show the paths of energy in the life space, Lewin invented hodology.

In an article for *A Handbook of Child Psychology*, Lewin described approach-approach conflict, approach-avoidance conflict, and avoidance-avoidance conflict. In Iowa, Lewin and his colleagues studied groups of boys performing activities under either authoritarian, democratic, or *laissez-faire* adult leadership. Authoritarian leadership led to increased within-group aggression and scapegoating. In another Iowa study, Lewin and his colleagues found that when children were first allowed to play with desirable toys and were then prevented from such play, the resulting frustration caused behavioral regression. In a study during World War II, Lewin found that housewives who participated in group discussions of the benefits of unpopular food items were more likely to use the items than housewives given a dynamic lecture.

Lesser-Known Gestalt Psychologists

Lesser-known contributors to Gestalt psychology include Karl Duncker, David Katz, Kurt Goldstein, Karl Bühler, Mary Henle, and Rudolph Arnheim.

Gestalt Psychology's Influence

All the major German figures in Gestalt psychology immigrated to the United States in the 1920s and 1930s, leaving behind their laboratories, careers, and many students. The institutions where these psychologists eventually settled did not have Ph.D. programs, which, along with behaviorism's popularity, contributed to the failure of Gestalt psychology to prosper in the United States. However, Gestalt psychology lives on in perceptual theory, social psychology, and cognitive psychology.

CONNECTIONS QUESTIONS

1. Name and discuss as many connections as you can between World War II and Gestalt psychology.
2. Who were some of the forerunners of Gestalt psychology and what are some of the connections between them?
3. What connections can you trace between Gestalt psychology and learning theory?
4. Draw as many connections as you can between Gestalt psychology and social psychology.
5. What are some of the connections between Gestalt psychology and cognitive psychology?
6. Defend the thesis that Gestalt psychology is the culmination of a rational approach to psychology.
7. Draw a concept map connecting the main figures and ideas covered in this chapter and compare your results with one possible solution provided on p. 567.

SUGGESTED READINGS

Henle, M. (1961). *Documents of Gestalt psychology.* Berkeley, CA: University of California Press. This volume contains classic papers in Gestalt psychology. Several famous articles are translated and reprinted, and the book includes several essays by the "lesser-known" Gestalt psychologists.

Henle, M. (1986). *1879 and all that: Essays in the theory and history of psychology.* New York: Columbia University Press. Mary Henle has become the chronicler of Gestalt psychology, as well as its leading spokesperson in modern times, and you can also find essays by her on Gestalt psychology in several history anthologies. This volume explores selected elements of the history and theory of Gestalt psychology.

Köhler, W. (1925). *The mentality of apes.* London: Routledge and Kegan Paul. (Original work published 1917) This is the work for which Köhler first became known to American psychologists. In it, he introduced the *Umweg* problem and made other contributions to the study of learning in animals.

Köhler, W. (1947). *Gestalt psychology: An introduction to new concepts in modern psychology.* New York: Liveright. (Original work published 1929) This book provides an excellent overview of Gestalt psychology's key concepts, its stance on several major issues—mind-body, reductionism, molar-molecular analysis—and its relationship to other schools, such as structuralism and behaviorism.

Köhler, W. (1966). *The place of value in a world of fact.* New York: Liveright. (Original work published 1938) This book is included for those of you interested in more philosophical aspects of Gestalt psychology. The essays it includes were first given by Köhler as a series of lectures at Harvard in 1934–1935.

Ley, R. (1990). *A whisper of espionage.* Garden City Park, NY: Avery Publishing Group, Inc. Ley's book is recommended as "fun" reading and as a further introduction to Köhler and some of the other Gestalt psychologists. We will allow you to draw your own conclusions about Köhler's possible role as a German spy in World War I.

Wertheimer, Max (1945). *Productive thinking.* New York: Harper. As we discussed in the chapter, this work explores cognition in a variety of ways, some theoretical and some applied.

Psychoanalysis

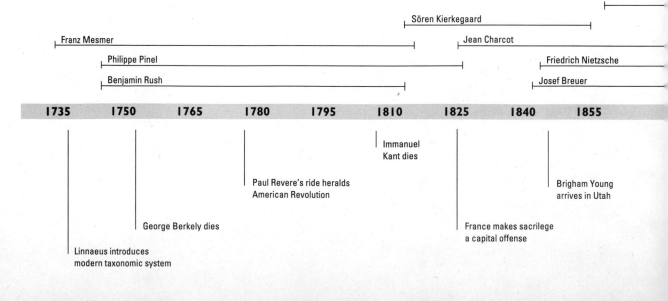

Sören Kierkegaard

Franz Mesmer

Jean Charcot

Philippe Pinel

Friedrich Nietzsche

Benjamin Rush

Josef Breuer

| 1735 | 1750 | 1765 | 1780 | 1795 | 1810 | 1825 | 1840 | 1855 |

Immanuel
Kant dies

Paul Revere's ride heralds
American Revolution

Brigham Young
arrives in Utah

George Berkely dies

France makes sacrilege
a capital offense

Linnaeus introduces
modern taxonomic system

The discussion of the development of psychoanalysis brings us to the last of the schools of psychology. We have saved psychoanalysis for last, not because it is less important than the other schools, but because its origin was quite different from that of structuralism, functionalism, behaviorism, and Gestalt psychology. The other schools were developed within academic settings; with the exception of Watson (Chapter 12), the founders spent much or all of their careers affiliated closely with universities.

By contrast, psychoanalysis focused on human abnormal behavior and how to treat it, obtaining its theoretical concepts primarily from the clinical setting. Quantification of phenomena, experimentation, and the laboratory were key ingredients in the development of the other schools, whereas this was much less important for psychoanalysis.

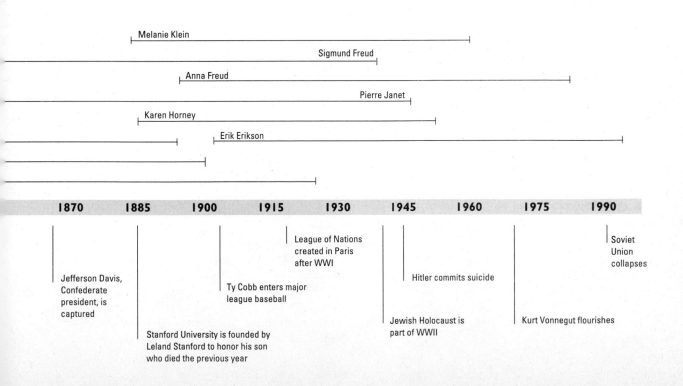

Psychoanalysis grew initially from the clinical experiences of Sigmund Freud. But Freud, like the founders of the other schools, did not develop his ideas in isolation. Five traditions in late 19th-century academia were particularly important influences on Freud's thinking: hypnotism, as practiced and understood by Charcot and Bernheim (discussed later); the Helmholtz School and Brücke's dynamic physiology (discussed later); Darwin's theory of evolution (Chapter 9); German rationalism, especially the works of Hegel and Schopenhauer (both Chapter 5); and contemporary conceptions of the unconscious. Born 3 years before the *Origin of Species* was published, Freud credited Darwinian theory with paving the way for his optimism about the possibility of major advances in understanding the world. More specific connections from Darwin to Freud have also been suggested—for example, from Darwin's *The Expression of Emotions* on Freud's thinking about human emotions (Shakow, 1969).

The idea of unconscious processes was a major part of 19th-century rationalistic, German academia, as we have noted in earlier chapters. In Chapter 5, we discussed Herbart's conception of the apperceptive mass in consciousness, with unconscious ideas incompatible with the mass being prevented from entering it. Similarly, Schopenhauer wrote about the repression of unwanted thoughts into the unconscious, with resistance hindering attempts to retrieve such thoughts. Although Freud credited Schopenhauer with originating this notion, he claimed to have discovered it independently. In Chapter 8, we noted that Ebbinghaus's dissertation was on Eduard von Hartmann's influential *Philosophy of the Unconscious,* with which an educated German-speaking European would almost certainly have been familiar.

Other influences on Freud (Pierre Janet, existential philosophers such as Sören Kierkegaard and Friedrich Nietzsche) will be examined after we have surveyed briefly pre-Freudian concepts of, and treatments for, mental illness. To fully understand the significance of Freud, we must first explore the conceptions of mental illness that were in place before his revolutionary ideas.

EARLY TREATMENT OF THE MENTALLY ILL

Treatment for mental illness is generally consistent with the contemporary concept of the cause of a disorder. Because possession by demons or evil spirits was at times considered the root of abnormal behavior, treatment was aimed at making the demon's habitat as uncomfortable as possible. In prehistoric times, the treatment to exorcise the demon may have involved trephining, or cutting a hole in the skull through which the evil spirit could leave (e.g., Maher & Maher, 1985). At other times, the mentally ill were tortured, subjected to loud noises, forced to drink vile concoctions, flogged, starved, burned, and so on.

In the midst of such barbaric practices, there have been pockets of "enlightened" individuals whose concepts of mental illness suggested more humane treatments. For example, Hippocrates (Chapter 2) attributed illness, including insanity, to natural causes. This led him to prescribe natural remedies such as rest, moderation in food and drink, and sexual abstinence. The Hippocratic approach was generally accepted by the Greeks and Romans, at least through Galen (Chapter 2).

Treatment of the mentally ill during the Middle Ages (from roughly 500 to 1500) was mostly in the hands of the clergy. During the early part of this era, treatment was relatively benign, consisting mainly of prayer, the application of holy water and sanctified relics, and mild forms of exorcism. The more well-developed exorcistic rituals emphasized insulting the devil, and the demons were assailed with every horrible name imaginable in the hope that they would depart from the afflicted.

By the middle of the 13th century, there was the Inquisition, whose goal was to root out heresy, including the practice of witchcraft. For the next several centuries, a populace suffering from famines, plagues, and social unrest became obsessed with the devil as the chief cause of the upheaval. It has been assumed by some historians of psychiatry (e.g., Alexander & Selesnick, 1966) that most of the witches were, in fact, mentally ill, as evidenced by their confessions of having performed impossible acts such as flying. However, although the insane people were often believed to be demonically possessed, the "demoniac was frequently construed as an individual smitten by witchcraft (i.e., bewitched) and was encouraged to accuse the witch who had caused him or her to become possessed . . ." (Spanos, 1978, p. 419). That is, the mentally ill person was often believed to be a witch's victim, rather than a witch. Spanos noted that "there is some evidence that individuals then defined as insane were *less likely* than others to be accused of witchcraft" (p. 425, italics added). Also, the confessions of having performed incredible feats were probably the result of torture, not of mental illness, according to Spanos. Fortunately for people accused of practicing witchcraft, witch hunting began to abate in the early 1600s.

Although histories of psychiatry (e.g., Zilboorg, 1941) have often depicted medieval treatment of the mentally ill as barbaric or worse, the truth may be considerably different (Neugebauer, 1978). Reviewing manuscripts rather than just published documents from medieval and early modern England, Neugebauer found that the mental status of disturbed individuals was measured with common-sense criteria, and in cases of disability, the Crown appointed supervised guardians.

Asylums for the mentally ill were almost unknown before the 15th century, with many of the institutions that would eventually house the insane being used for lepers. As leprosy (Hansen's disease) gradually disappeared from Europe, leprosariums were often converted into insane asylums. Some of the asylums became notorious for their deplorable conditions—for example, filthy surroundings, horrible food, brutality. One of the worst was the priory of St. Mary of Bethlehem in London, which officially became a mental hospital in 1547 when Henry VIII gave it for this purpose to the city of London. Bethlehem, or Bedlam as it became known, "was a favorite Sunday excursion spot for Londoners, who came to stare at the madmen through the iron gates" (Alexander & Selesnick, 1966, p. 154). Tickets of admission into Bedlam to see the violent patients continued to be sold into the 19th century.

Across Europe, the mentally ill began to receive more humane treatment toward the end of the 18th

century. The signal event of this improved care was the action of **Philippe Pinel** (1745–1826). Put in charge at La Bicêtre asylum in Paris, in 1793, Pinel freed the insane men from their shackles and bonds. Pinel improved the lot of the insane women at Salpêtrière the next year.

Pinel's contemporary, **William Tuke** (1732–1822), English Quaker philanthropist, established the York Retreat, which housed the mentally ill in a quiet, religious atmosphere. Samuel Tuke (1784–1857), William Tuke's grandson, was a leading psychiatric reformer, and his son, Daniel Hack Tuke (1827–1895), became an outstanding British psychiatrist. Samuel's published description of the retreat set forth the principles of the "moral therapy" practiced there.

In the United States, **Benjamin Rush** (1745–1813), who had studied in France and Great Britain, encouraged more humane treatment of the mentally ill while he was associated with the Pennsylvania Hospital. In lectures to the medical students at the University of Pennsylvania, Rush expounded a psychology that combined Hartley's associationism and the faculty psychology of the Scottish school (both Chapter 4; Noel & Carlson, 1973). Considered the founder of American psychiatry, Rush was also an "advocate of public schools, free dispensaries for the indigent, higher educational facilities for women, and hospitals for alcoholics" (Alexander & Selesnick, 1966, p. 162). Enlightened in many respects, Rush nevertheless was an ardent proponent of bloodletting, the use of fear to change a mental patient's thinking, and a "tranquilizing chair," on which leather straps around the patient's arms and legs restrained movement. Still, Rush was genuinely concerned with his patients' welfare and represented an important positive force in American psychiatry.

Another American who worked tirelessly for the humane treatment of the insane was **Dorothea Dix** (1802–1887). Forced into early retirement from school teaching by recurring bouts of tuberculosis, Dix began to teach in a women's prison. This exposed her to the shocking conditions in jails and asylums, and for 40 years, Dix was an effective advocate for reform. Through her efforts, hospital conditions were improved in the United States, Canada,

Scotland, and several other countries. Dix was personally responsible for establishing over 30 mental hospitals, and she also served during the Civil War as the superintendent of women nurses in the Union Army.

More humane treatment also followed a change in the suspected basis of mental disorders. Reviving Hippocrates' hypothesis of the bodily origin of illness, in the mid-19th century, German physician Wilhelm Griesinger suggested that the diagnosis of a mental disorder should indicate a physiological cause. One of Griesinger's followers, Emil Kraepelin (Chapter 7), divided mental illness into two major categories—dementia praecox (schizophrenia) and manic-depressive psychosis—attributing the former to a chemical imbalance and the latter to a metabolic defect.

In other parts of western Europe in the 19th century, particularly in France and Austria, mental disorders were thought to be caused by psychic malfunction rather than by physiological disturbance. For reasons that are not entirely clear to us today—although women's constrictive clothing has been blamed—one of the period's most common disorders was hysteria. Major symptoms are sensory or motor problems (e.g., anesthesia of the hand) without a known anatomical basis. Initially attributing hysteria to a physiological cause, the famous Parisian neurologist, **Jean Martin Charcot** (1825–1893), came to view its origin as psychogenic instead. The reason his thinking changed involves the phenomenon of hypnosis.

FIGURE 15–1.   Franz Anton Mesmer.
Source: Corbis-Bettmann.

magnetic fluid that can be used to influence and even cure others. The most important proponent of animal magnetism was a Viennese physician whose name became synonymous with a disreputable methodology.

Mesmerism

Franz Anton Mesmer (1734–1815) graduated in 1766 from the University of Vienna Medical School. His dissertation dealt with the influence of the planets on human physiology. As a Viennese physician, Mesmer (Figure 15–1) developed a method of treating diseases using a magnet. Soon he decided that the magnet was unnecessary and that transmission of a magnetic force from his own body was sufficient to effect cures. When his treatment procedures were not accepted by the medical community, Mesmer was forced to leave in 1778, settling in Paris.

In Paris, Mesmer was spectacularly successful with hysterical patients, whereas the medical

HYPNOSIS

The story of hypnosis begins with another once-mysterious force—magnetism. Swiss alchemist, physician, and mystic **Paracelsus** (1493–1541)—an early opponent of witch hunts and the authority of such ancient physicians as Galen—believed that magnets, like stars, influenced humans by means of a celestial fluid. The Flemish chemist **Jan Baptista van Helmont** (1577–1644) initiated the notion of **animal magnetism**, which was that people emit a community was nearly unanimous in disapproving his activities. Mesmer's treatment was a performance for which he charged the poor nothing and the wealthy exorbitant fees. "Cures" were often obtained.

Patients were generally treated in groups in a dimly lit, carpeted room in which there was soft music and the odor of orange blossoms. The patients joined hands around a covered *baquet* (tub), filled with "magnetized" water. Iron rods protruded from the *baquet*, and Mesmer, clad in a lilac robe, would extract a rod and touch a patient in an afflicted place. Mesmer was trying to induce a "crisis," in which one of the patients would scream and go into convulsions. Generally, other patients followed suit, presumably affected by group suggestion (see Chapter 19).

Although Mesmer tried diligently to convince the medical community of the reality of his animal magnetism, he succeeded with only one doctor, Charles d'Eslon, the physician to Louis XVI's brother. Despite d'Eslon's continuing loyalty, eventually Mesmer came to regard his most influential follower as a rival. Mesmer left Paris in 1781 (Alexander & Selesnick, 1966).

In 1784, he returned to encounter a professional defeat from which he never recovered. Because of pressure from d'Eslon and the Society of Harmony—founded to promote the cause of animal magnetism—Louis XVI appointed a commission to study Mesmer's claims. Headed by Benjamin Franklin, the committee's members included the astronomer Jean Bailly, the famed chemist Antoine Lavoisier, and Joseph Guillotin, after whom the guillotine was named. The Franklin Commission "concluded that Mesmer's animal magnetism was unrelated to physical magnetism and that any beneficial effects were due to pressure of the hands and feet, imagination, or the imitation of other patients" (Hoffeld, 1980, p. 383). After the Franklin Commission's report, Mesmer fled to Switzerland, where he died in obscurity.

Although Mesmer was out of the picture, **mesmerism**—the name given to his treatment method—continued in different parts of the world. One of the practitioners was Mesmer's former student—the **Marquis de Puységur** (1751–1825). In

the same year that Mesmer was investigated by the Franklin Commission, Puységur and his brother began experimenting with animal magnetism on their estate. Puységur found that it was unnecessary to induce a crisis state when one of his servants entered a peaceful trance resembling sleep without having the convulsive fit Mesmer had thought was essential. Puységur called this state "artificial somnambulism" because of its similarity to sleepwalking. Using artificially somnambulistic subjects, Puységur discovered most of the hypnotic phenomena known today, including the subjects' extreme suggestibility, their power to forget what happened during the trance, and their responsiveness to posthypnotic suggestion. Puységur is important for demonstrating that mesmerism occurred and could be studied outside the sensationalistic environment of Mesmer's *baquet*.

Portuguese priest **José Custodio di Faria** (1756–1819) examined a problem with mesmerism that had troubled even Mesmer—why some people are less responsive to "animal magnetism" than others. Faria showed that it was possible to induce deep trance states in some subjects just by commanding them to "sleep." Faria called this trance state lucid sleep, and about 20% of his subjects demonstrated it. He also found that lucid sleep could be induced in appropriate subjects by anyone, even by a child, which suggested that the power to achieve the state lay in the hypnotized person, not in the hypnotizer. Unfortunately, Faria did not successfully promote his ideas, and they faded away after his death (Fancher, 1990).

Mesmerism remained the province of traveling showmen, where it was still connected with magnetism or some occult power. One of the standard demonstrations of such mesmerists was the production of anesthesia in a subject. At a time when chemical anesthetics were unknown, this sort of demonstration piqued the curiosity of a few physicians and surgeons, one of whom was **John Elliotson** (1791–1868), a physician at London's University College Hospital.

No stranger to controversy, Elliotson was among the first to use the newly invented stethoscope to listen to the sounds of the heart. In fact, Elliotson was profoundly distrustful of "old" medicine and always eager to examine the possibilities of the "new." However, when the hospital administrators learned of his plans to study the anesthetic properties of mesmerism, a resolution was passed to prevent mesmerism's use at the institution. Elliotson resigned in protest and never again entered the hospital that he had been instrumental in founding (Boring, 1950).

Elliotson continued to use mesmerism to treat certain conditions, although not for surgical anesthesia, leaving that study to other physicians. For example, a Scottish physician practicing in India, **James Esdaile** (1808–1859), reported a mortality rate of less than 6% in 261 operations on mesmerized patients (Magner, 1992). Unfortunately, back in Scotland Esdaile found that mesmerism was less effective for anesthesia than it had been in India. However, by this time, chemical anesthesia had come to dominate the medical community.

Hypnotism

After losing out to the reliable and universally applicable anesthetic actions of nitrous oxide, ether, and chloroform, mesmerism gained something close to scientific respectability and a new name through the efforts of **James Braid** (1795–1860), a Scottish surgeon. In 1841, Braid attended a series of public demonstrations of mesmerism, becoming convinced at the second demonstration that the mesmerized state was real, and he decided to investigate the phenomenon to bring it into line with scientific physiology.

Braid confirmed the findings of the earlier mesmerists, Puységur and Faria. Like Faria, Braid found that the power to mesmerize lay in the subject, not in the mesmerizer. Also like Faria and Puységur, he thought the trance state resembled sleep, and for this reason, he called it *neurypnology,* which is a contraction of the Greek words *neuro* for "nerve" and *hypnos* for "sleep." Braid later settled on "**hypnotism.**" By presenting his work as an attack on mesmerism, Braid's research was accepted by the scientific community, and hypnotism became a scientific phenomenon that could be studied in the laboratory (Boring, 1950).

Nancy Versus Salpêtrière

Nancy is a town in northeastern France where **Auguste Ambroise Liébeault** (1823–1904) began to practice medicine in 1864. At first, Liébeault charged no fee for hypnotic treatments and a standard fee for orthodox treatment, but he soon found that many of his patients wanted to be hypnotized, and he was forced to "allow" his hypnotic patients to pay whatever they thought was fair. Liébeault's successes attracted the attention of **Hippolyte Bernheim** (1840–1919), a younger physician from Nancy.

Originally an internist, Bernheim decided to visit Liébeault's hypnotic clinic in 1882. Bernheim was so impressed with Liébeault's achievements that he abandoned internal medicine for hypnotherapy. Over the years, his experience with hundreds of hypnotically treated patients led him to conclude that people vary on a general trait of suggestibility and that their hypnotic susceptibility varies accordingly. Bernheim's many books and articles effectively presented the principles of the Nancy school of hypnotism.

Meanwhile, another school of hypnotism was being developed at Paris's Salpêtrière Hospital by Charcot. As we noted, Charcot initially considered hysteria a physiological disorder, but he became convinced of its psychological basis when some of his students hypnotized a normal woman, suggested to her the display of hysterical symptoms, and Charcot believed she was really suffering from hysteria. He then began to concentrate on his hysterical patients, noting their various symptoms, and treating them with hypnosis. He came to regard hypnotizability as a characteristic of hysteria, not part of the normal range of human behavior as Bernheim believed. Charcot was wrong in this, and the "verdict of time has favored the Nancy school . . ." (Boring, 1950, p. 130). However, Charcot's studies of hysteria changed medical thinking about the disorder. In Figure 15–2, Charcot is shown demonstrating hypnotic phenomena.

Medical opinion at the time held that hysterics were probably pretending to be ill, because their symptoms usually did not conform to known neuroanatomy. Physicians who believed in the disorder's reality considered it exclusively a disease of women and attributed it to a defect in their repro-

FIGURE 15–2.   Jean Martin Charcot and hypnotic subject.

Source: National Library of Medicine.

ductive systems. Charcot's observations convinced him that the symptoms were not simulated, and he had examined men outside Salpêtrière with similar conditions, which meant that hysteria could not be caused by a defective female reproductive system. Charcot's opinions greatly influenced two of his pupils: Sigmund Freud and Pierre Janet.

Pierre Janet

Mentioned in Chapter 13, **Pierre Janet** (1859–1947) was born in Paris and was interested in psychology from an early age. At 22, Janet secured a position teaching philosophy at a lycée (a secondary school that prepares students for university study) in Le Havre. Because he wanted to write a thesis on hallucination, Janet asked a well-known physician if he knew of anyone with hallucinations that he might study. In response, the doctor put Janet in contact with a woman named Léonie who had been hypnotized in her youth and "had been observed to perform some curious things with clairvoyance, mental suggestion, and hypnotism from a distance, etc." (Janet, 1930, p. 125).

Janet studied Léonie over a period of years, apparently demonstrating hypnotic somnambulism induced from a distance. For example, on one occasion, Janet found that "16 times out of 20 somnambulism has exactly coincided with a mental suggestion made at a distance of one kilometer" (Janet, 1930, p. 125). In other words, Janet claimed he was able to use thought to cause Léonie to sleepwalk on 80% of his attempts, when the two were over half a mile apart. Repeating Janet's experiments with Léonie, **Charles Richet** (1850–1935) also succeeded in inducing a somnambulistic state from afar. A Nobel Prize–winning physiologist, Richet had concluded that hypnosis was a genuine phenomenon in 1875, and his support helped Charcot decide to investigate hypnosis. Janet's discussion of his work with Léonie, whose interpretation he came to doubt many years later, brought him into contact with Charcot and led to his move back to Paris (Kopell, 1968).

In 1889, Janet was awarded his doctorate at the University of Paris, and, in 1890, he accepted Charcot's offer of the directorship of the psychological laboratory at the Salpêtrière. Janet immediately began to systematize the work on hysteria and to bring it into line with academic psychology, an effort that shows in early form his long-term interest in integrating clinical and academic psychology. The resulting publication earned Janet the M.D. degree, which he received in 1893, the year Charcot died.

Janet went to the Sorbonne in 1895 and then succeeded Ribot (Chapter 4) in 1902 at the Collège de France, where he stayed until his retirement in 1936. As dean of French psychology, Janet was chosen to be the honorary president of the XIth International Congress of Psychology, which met in Paris in 1937.

Janet considered a weakening of psychic energy central to the development of mental disorders. A psychologically healthy person has a stable psychic energy level, whereas fluctuations of psychic energy and lowered mental tension cause an inability to deal with the problems of life, leading to neurosis. The psychic weakness in his hysteric patients resulted in exaggerated suggestibility (increased susceptibility to hypnosis), faulty memory, and fixed ideas. Further, the lack of integration in their personalities meant that there could be a dissociation into conscious and unconscious processes; hence, they could develop multiple personalities. The hysteric's fixed ideas narrowed the focus of consciousness, resulting in the forcing of unacceptable ideas into the unconscious mind, there being nowhere else for them to go. In the unconscious, the unacceptable ideas would be converted into symbolic symptoms.

Janet believed that the psychic weakness of the neurotic might result from negative events in the person's past life.

> These events, which had established a violent emotion and a destruction of the psychological system, had left traces. The remembrance of these events, the mental work involved in their recall and settlement, persisted in the form of lower and more or less conscious psychological processes, absorbed a great deal of strength, and played a part in the persistent weakening. (Janet, 1930, p. 128)

Other potential sources of the psychic weakness included faulty heredity, disease, fatigue, and deficient education.

There is much similarity in Janet's psychopathological system and Freudian psychoanalysis, and Janet believed that the origin of psychoanalysis lay in his and Charcot's work. In addition, controversy arose between Freud and Janet over priority of the concept of the unconscious mind. Janet's 1889 dissertation on "automatic" activities formed the basis for his later claim of priority. Freud argued, apparently with good cause, that Janet's use of the term in 1889 was more or less coincidental and not a serious attempt to establish the concept (Boring, 1950).

Like Freud, Janet thought that the key to treating the hysteric successfully was to make the forgotten, negative experiences conscious, and he used hypnosis to uncover the dissociated memories. Janet found that making the patient consciously aware of the memories often caused the hysterical symptoms to abate.

Whether or not Janet's work significantly influenced Freud's development of psychoanalysis, Freud has received the primary credit for the development of our final psychological school. We will consider Freud's life and work after we examine briefly another source of influence on him: existentialism. Although we will explore the connections between existentialism and psychotherapy in more detail in the next chapter, our discussion of the historical context of the psychoanalytic view of human nature and mental illness would be incomplete without mention of Sören Kierkegaard and Friedrich Nietzsche.

EXISTENTIAL PRECURSORS TO FREUD

Poet, philosopher, theologian, and psychologist, **Sören Aabye Kierkegaard** (1813–1855) was hunchbacked, born into a moderately wealthy Copenhagen family, and educated at the height of Hegel's popularity in Germany and Denmark. Many of Kierkegaard's ideas came from his dissatisfaction with Hegel's system. Kierkegaard (Figure 15–3) came to view Hegel as comic because in trying to capture the structure of reality, Hegel had lost sight of the most important element—personal existence. Kierkegaard is considered the founder of **existentialism**, a philosophy that stresses the isolation of the individual in a hostile universe and emphasizes freedom of choice and responsibility for the consequences of acts.

FIGURE 15–3.   Sören Kierkegaard.

Source: National Historical Museum, Frederiksborg; Philosophical Library, New York.

During his lifetime, Kierkegaard achieved a measure of popularity through his writings. In both philosophy and theology, his stature has continued to grow, but interest in his poetry and psychology has waxed and waned in the time since his death (e.g., Nordentoft, 1972). However, in our search for the origins of modern clinical psychology, Kierkegaard's work on anxiety and despair is important.

Kierkegaard's *The Concept of Anxiety* (alternatively, *The Concept of Dread*) and *The Sickness Unto Death* carefully analyze disorders we might today characterize as an anxiety disorder and as depression, respectively. Kierkegaard was a devout, if iconoclastic, Christian, and his theology permeated his analysis of psychological conditions. Although his association of pathology with sin may seem misplaced, if "sin" is viewed metaphorically as difficulties caused by repressed conflicts or problems of conscience, then Kierkegaard's linkage resembles explanatory mechanisms we will see in Freudian psychoanalytic theory. Given his interest in psychopathology and his position as existentialism's founder, Kierkegaard represents another important element of the European *Zeitgeist* that surrounded Freud.

The connection between Freud and German philosopher **Friedrich Wilhelm Nietzsche** (1844–1900) is even more explicit than that between Freud and Kierkegaard. Although he was considered the next great existential philosopher after Kierkegaard, Nietzsche did not share Kierkegaard's appreciation of theology. Although Kierkegaard was an earnest Christian who feared that organized religion could hamper a personal, meaningful relationship with God, Nietzsche was a self-appointed antichrist who saw religion as central to humankind's problems.

Trained as a philologist, Nietzsche's exceptional scholarship secured for him a chair in philosophy at the University of Basel, Switzerland, at the age of 24, before he had earned his Ph.D. from the University of Leipzig. But a life of scholarship did not satisfy him, and Nietzsche devoted the rest of his productive life—he spent his last 12 years in an asylum—to the development of a philosophy "that would comprise both cool analysis and enthusiastic vision, a synthesis of a new religious creed and merciless criticism. Apollo, the god of lucid wisdom, and Dionysos, the god of orgiastic mysticism, were taken for its symbols" (Runes, 1959, p. 299).

Although "id" and "superego" are Freudian terms, it was Nietzsche who first recognized these opposing psychic forces. The superego (the internalization of external standards of behavior) and the id (our animalistic side) were under scrutiny in Nietzsche's best-known works—for example, *Beyond Good and Evil* (Nietzsche, 1886/1966) and *On the Genealogy of Morals* (Nietzsche, 1887/1967). The superego is the essence of civilization, whereas the id represents baser instincts. Their relationship is that societal rules and religious dictates become our conscience, which keeps us from acting on our immediate impulses. Unlike Freud, Nietzsche viewed this relationship as something humans need to transcend; the superego must be restrained in order for our more fundamental nature to emerge. Nietzsche saw pathology as the submission of our will and nature to the rules of society and religion. Nietzsche's philosophy contains many such provocative ideas, which, if taken literally, seem dangerous or absurd. However, in keeping with the central principle of existentialism, Nietzsche's intent was probably to challenge the reader to place no idea above scrutiny and to think independently.

Nietzsche (Figure 15–4) predated Freud only slightly—his classic works were published mainly in the 1880s—and was well known and controversial enough that Freud undoubtedly was aware of his ideas. As we will show, Freud's views on human nature differed greatly from Nietzsche's, even though the basic psychic elements posited by the two were similar. In fact, Freud admitted that Nietzsche was second only to Schopenhauer as a philosopher who anticipated elements of psychoanalytic theory (Kaufmann, 1974).

Several of the existential and humanistic theorists we will examine in the next chapter acknowledged the influence of Kierkegaard (e.g., Rollo May) or Nietzsche (e.g., Viktor Frankl) on their systems of psychotherapy. In addition, psychologists and philosophers from diverse areas (e.g., social, cognitive) are still exploring the works of these two important and influential pioneers of existentialism. However, Freud felt that neither

FIGURE 15–4.   Friedrich Nietzsche and his mother.

Source: Louis Held, Weimer; Philosophical Library, New York.

Nietzsche nor Schopenhauer were really significant influences on his development of psychoanalysis (Freud, 1925/1963), and we are left with the question: What was the genesis of Freud's system?

SIGMUND FREUD

Sigmund Freud, or Sigismund Schlomo Freud, according to the family Bible, was born on May 6, 1856, in Freiburg, Moravia (which is now part of the Czech Republic). Freud's father was Jakob Freud, a gentle wool-merchant who was loved by all in the family; Freud considered himself a duplicate of his father, both physically and mentally. Freud's mother, Amalia Nathansohn Freud, was Jakob's second wife (or perhaps his third; Gay, 1988), and Freud had two half-brothers from his father's previous marriage. Freud was Amalia's firstborn child (of eight) and her favorite. In fact, Freud was clearly the family favorite—as an illustration, he was the only one to have his own room.

Because of anti-Semitism, a failing business, and limited educational opportunities in a small town, Jakob moved the family to Leipzig in 1859 and then to Vienna the next year. Freud lived in Vienna from 1860 until 1938, when he emigrated to London to escape Nazi persecution. Although Freud was not religious, he identified with Jewish cultural values and ideals throughout his life (e.g., Levin, 1975).

After Freud's early lessons with his mother, Jakob took over his education until Freud qualified by examination for admission to the Sperl Gymnasium. At the Gymnasium, Freud usually ranked first in his class and graduated summa cum laude at 17. For this achievement, his father promised him a trip to England, which he took 2 years later.

Freud was gifted in languages. According to Jones (1953),

> Besides being completely at home in Latin and Greek, he acquired a thorough knowledge of French and English; in addition he taught himself Italian and Spanish. He had of course been taught Hebrew. He was especially fond of English and he told me once that for ten years he read nothing but English books. (p. 21)

Of course, Freud was also a "recognized master of German prose" and was nominated more than once for the Nobel Prize in literature. In 1930, he won the prestigious Goethe Prize.

Entering the University of Vienna at 17, Freud studied medicine. As we noted, Freud took several philosophy courses under Brentano (Chapter 8). In 1876, Freud began the first of several original research efforts with a grant from his zoology professor, the eminent evolutionist, Carl Claus. At Trieste, a northeastern Italian city on the Adriatic Sea, Freud sought the testes of eels. Claus was pleased with Freud's work, but Freud was dissatisfied with his inconclusive findings. As Jones (1953) dryly stated: "One is tempted to . . . remark that the future discoverer of the castration complex was disappointed at not being able to find the testes of the eel" (p. 38).

Despite Claus's excellent reputation, Freud was more impressed by his physiology professor, **Ernst**

Brücke (1819–1892). Brücke's institute at Vienna was part of the movement known as Helmholtz's School of Medicine. The School began with the friendship of Émil du Bois-Reymond and Hermann von Helmholtz (Chapter 6), Karl Ludwig (mentioned in Chapter 10), and Brücke. Its chief purpose was to rid science of Johannes Müller's vitalism—the idea that life involves a vital principle distinct from physical and chemical forces—and, ironically, most of the School's members had studied under Müller. By the time Freud was a student, Helmholtz's School dominated the thinking of German phy-siologists and medical professors and had made impressive discoveries in physiology. Brücke's dynamic physiology, in which organisms were seen as part of a system of forces, became assimilated into Freud's dynamic psychology, and "it can be shown that the principles on which [Freud] constructed his theories were those he had acquired as a medical student under Brücke's influence" (Jones, 1953, p. 45).

In 1876, Freud was accepted into Brücke's institute as a research scholar. Freud's first published work was on the histology of cells in the spinal cord of a primitive fish, which contributed to the work leading to the neuron doctrine (Chapter 17), although Freud is not credited with being part of the discovery.

Freud also developed a new staining technique and, while studying the uses of cocaine, anticipated its use as an anesthetic in eye surgery. Unfortunately, Freud's enthusiasm for cocaine in 1884 proved to be a major embarrassment when its potential for addiction became generally known soon thereafter—for example, by 1891, there were at least 200 reports of cocaine intoxication and 13 reports of death attributable to it (Julien, 1995). Pervasive rumors of Freud's own cocaine addiction seem to be baseless, as Gay (1988) reported that there is no evidence to suggest that Freud ever acquired the habit, although "he continued to use [cocaine] in modest quantities at least until the mid-1890s" (p. 45).

Freud received his M.D. in 1881 and continued to work at the Physiological Institute. In May, he was promoted to Demonstrator, a post with teaching duties. At this point, his long-term plan probably was to work his way through the ranks, eventually becoming Professor of Physiology. However, in June of the next year, Freud decided to become a physician. Brücke's warning that Freud's impoverished financial state could hamper his scientific career (Freud, 1925/1963) and the fact that the normal path of promotion may have contained racial obstacles were undoubtedly factors in his decision.

Accordingly, Freud entered the General Hospital of Vienna to prepare himself for private practice. In 3 years at the Hospital, Freud worked in surgery, dermatology, ophthalmology, and spent 5 months in Meynert's Psychiatric Clinic. A German like Brücke, **Theodor Meynert** (1833–1893) was a pioneer in cytoarchitectonics—the study of cellular architecture—and made the first detailed description of the cerebral cortex. Although Freud agreed with the prevailing opinion that Meynert was an outstanding neuroanatomist (e.g., James, 1890), he was less impressed with Meynert's ability as a psychiatrist. However, in later writings he spoke of following in Meynert's footsteps, and "he always recalled him as the most brilliant genius he had ever encountered" (Jones, 1953, p. 65).

In the spring of 1885, Freud was appointed a *Privatdozent* in neuropathology, a highly prized position affording occasional lectures but no salary. To Freud, the position demonstrated a professional competence that would enable him to secure a medical practice, which would allow him to marry his fiancée, Martha Bernays. He and Martha in 1885 are shown in Figure 15–5.

In late 1885 and early 1886, Freud spent 17 weeks studying under Charcot in Paris, and the experience turned him from neurology to psychopathology. As one among many foreign visitors, Freud probably would have made little impression on Charcot if he had not overheard Charcot complain about a lack of response from the German translator of his lectures (Freud, 1925/1963). Freud wrote Charcot a letter offering to tackle the translation, and his offer was promptly accepted. Freud was so impressed with Charcot that he named his firstborn son Jean Martin after Jean Martin Charcot.

Although he continued to publish and present physiological work for the next several years, Freud returned to Vienna as a clinician. In 1891, Freud published his first book, *Aphasia*, attacking Carl Wernicke's (Chapter 6) model of language deficits

FIGURE 15–5.   Sigmund Freud and his fiancée, Martha Bernays, in 1885.

Source: Corbis-Bettmann.

and challenging Meynert's cortical localization of ideas and memories. Well written and soundly argued, *Aphasia* did not sell and was not cited at the time by others critical of Wernicke's model. A monograph that same year on paralysis in children was more successful and is the work for which Freud is best known in neurology. Freud dedicated *Aphasia* to his friend, Josef Breuer.

Josef Breuer (1842–1925) was a well-respected Viennese physician Freud met in the late 1870s. Breuer's scientific research had earned him an excellent reputation, and like Brücke, Breuer was a follower of the Helmholtz School.

In late 1882, Breuer told Freud of his work with a patient whose story was later published under the name of **Anna O**. Anna O was really **Bertha Pappenheim** (1859–1936), an intelligent, attractive young woman from a distinguished Jewish family. Before seeing Breuer, Anna O had developed several physical symptoms while caring for her gravely ill father. The symptoms included a nervous cough, for which Breuer was consulted. Breuer decided that the nervous character of her cough and the calming effect of his listening to her stories suggested a functional illness, not something organic. Breuer also found that some of Anna's whims disappeared when traced back to their origins.

Because of the cough, Anna was not allowed to tend her father, and some of the additional symptoms she developed included paralyses caused by muscle contractions, tactile anesthesia, vivid hallucinations, and language disturbances. To illustrate the latter, at one point Anna spoke only in English, although she could understand what people told her in German.

The trauma of her father's death triggered a new set of symptoms, and at one point a consulting psychiatrist, **Richard Krafft-Ebing** (1840–1902), was called into the case (Ellenberger, 1972). Although Krafft-Ebing was an expert on forensic psychiatry and sexual pathology, Anna behaved as if he were not there, even when the psychiatrist blew smoke toward her face. Throughout his treatment, Breuer found that getting Anna to talk out her vivid hallucinations under hypnosis brought some relief. Anna called this procedure a "talking cure" or "chimney-sweeping" (Freud & Breuer, 1895/1966).

Finally, Anna developed two personalities, one "normal" and the other "sick," with the "sick" personality existing in time exactly 1 year earlier than the "normal" one. In this condition, Anna told Breuer in reverse order about the appearance of each symptom; when she reached the initial event triggering the symptom, it disappeared.

Although Jones (1953) presented Anna O's story as a classic illustration of hysteria cured by the **cathartic method** or talking cure, in which symptomatic relief is achieved by bringing forgotten memories and feelings to consciousness, the story is more complicated (Ellenberger, 1972). Referring to an unpublished report by Breuer, Ellenberger noted several discrepancies. For example, Anna O was not a hysteric, and "the word catharsis appears nowhere in the 1882 report" (p. 277). Further, Pappenheim

was not cured, and she spent several weeks in the fall of 1882 in a sanitarium in the Swiss town of Kreuzlingen. She eventually recovered and became "the respectable figure of a pioneer of social work, fighter for the rights of women and the welfare of her people . . ." (p. 279).

Freud was fascinated by Anna O's case, and he related it to Charcot at the first opportunity. Charcot, whose mind may have been elsewhere, was not interested. As we noted, Charcot had come to realize that the symptoms of hysteria had a psychogenic origin, and he also recognized that the disorder was not exclusively found in women. Freud was impressed with these new ideas, and on his return to Vienna, he read a paper on male hysteria to the Medical Society. He felt the report was badly received, and his old mentor Meynert challenged Freud to produce a case of male hysteria with the appropriate symptoms. Ironically, on his deathbed, Meynert confessed to Freud that he had been a classical case of male hysteria, a fact that he had always managed to conceal (Jones, 1953). Shortly after his "bad report," Freud found a male hysteric who had developed visual defects after a quarrel with a brother. Along with an ophthalmologist, Freud demonstrated the case to the Medical Society before 1886 ended. For further information on Charcot's influence on Freud's thinking about hysteria, see Libbrecht and Quackelbeen (1995).

At this point, Freud was just beginning to develop a private neurological practice. Unlike the type of patient a neurologist typically encounters today, Freud's patients were primarily neurotics. At first, Freud used electricity to treat them, along with such auxiliary remedies as ice baths and massages. Although he was still using these methods into the 1890s, in late 1887 he began to try hypnotic suggestion.

Freud used hypnotic suggestion with his neurotic patients for 18 months. He soon found that he could not induce a trance in some of his patients and that with others the suggestible state was too shallow for therapeutic purposes. In order to improve his technique, Freud traveled to Nancy in 1889, where he observed the work of Liébeault and Bernheim. While watching Bernheim experimenting with his hospital patients, Freud was struck by the possibility that there might be interesting mental processes unavailable to consciousness. He also learned that Bernheim's success with hypnotic suggestion occurred with his hospital patients, not with private patients. In fact, Bernheim had no more success than Freud with one of Freud's patients who had, at Freud's request, followed him to Nancy. It was obvious to Freud that something more was needed than hypnotic suggestion for the treatment of hysterics.

Initially, Freud used hypnotism to give therapeutic suggestions and to try to uncover the traumatic incident(s) responsible for the illness. In searching for trauma, Freud was still guided by Charcot's teachings. Working with Breuer's—actually Bertha Pappenheim's—cathartic method, Freud would direct the patient's attention to the traumatic scene that had produced the symptom, looking for the psychic conflict that, when brought to conscious awareness, would produce the desired beneficial effect. However, Freud discovered something even more interesting: His efforts to follow his patients' associations to the particular incident led deeper and deeper into the past, continuing back into the earliest childhood memories.

Freud's **free association** method gradually evolved in the period from 1892 through 1895. In a case in 1892, Freud dispensed for the first time with hypnosis. This was also the first case in which he felt satisfied with the "psychical analysis" of the patient, and the case in which Freud began to realize the importance of admonishing the patient to ignore censorship, to say whatever came into her or his mind without trying to make it more socially desirable.

Freud's abandonment of hypnosis has been attributed to a variety of reasons including difficulties in hypnotizing some patients and the fact that hypnotic suggestions were not always effective, particularly with private patients. Schneck (1965) suggested another possibility—Freud's ambition.

> [T]he key to Freud's abandonment of hypnosis may be found in his great ambition and drive for prestige, in his striving for originality and his desire to make a name for himself. It must be remembered that hypnosis had a long tradition behind it and many names were already deeply engraved in its history. (p. 194)

Although he was not using hypnosis, Freud was active in the treatment, questioning, probing, urging the patient to divulge the information needed for a successful outcome. Finally, one of his patients reproved him for interrupting her train of thought, and Freud got the message. Careful listening, without frequent queries, became part of free association.

There is also evidence that Freud's rejection of hypnosis as a method for treating mental illness was not complete. Gravitz and Gerton (1981) cited a little-known autobiography of a Hungarian-born hypnotist, Franz Polgar, as an indication of Freud's continuing interest in the method in the 1920s, long after he had supposedly abandoned it. Polgar reported that in 1924 he watched Freud's method for inducing hypnosis and eventually became the psychoanalyst's medical hypnotist. Freud's negative expressions about hypnosis eventually so undermined Polgar's self-confidence that he returned to Budapest to study psychology.

In 1895, Freud and Breuer jointly published *Studies on Hysteria* (Freud & Breuer, 1895/1966), which contained the case of Anna O, and this is usually considered the seminal event in the beginning of psychoanalysis. Freud's final break with Breuer came within the next 2 years, precipitated by Freud's growing belief in the importance of sex in the origin of neuroses. Freud also decided that the therapeutic relationship between himself and his patients had an erotic basis when a female patient suddenly embraced him. Freud called the phenomenon **transference**, because he thought that the patient had transferred her feelings for a childhood object onto him. Instead of being frightened by transference, as Breuer had been with similar behavior from Anna O, Freud saw it as an important part of the therapeutic relationship and as proof of the neuroses' sexual origin.

Freud's idea of sexual etiology offended more of his friends than just Breuer, and "an empty space soon formed itself about my person . . ." (Freud, 1938a, p. 937). For the next several years, Freud developed his technique and theory of psychoanalysis—a term he first used in a paper published in French in 1896—in relative isolation. Having lost Breuer's advice, encouragement, and financial support, Freud turned to an ear, nose, and throat specialist from Berlin, **Wilhelm Fliess** (1858-1928).

Freud had met Fliess in 1887 through Breuer, and the two men corresponded and met regularly until shortly after the turn of the century. From our perspective, Fliess appears to have been a crackpot. For example, he was a numerologist, believing that it was possible to ground biology in symbolic mathematics. In addition, Fliess considered the nose the body's dominant organ, and "Freud even allowed Fliess to operate on his own nose several times in an attempt to dispel 'neurotic disturbances'" (Grosskurth, 1991, p. 8).

Despite his strange ideas, Fliess was a perceptive and intelligent reader of Freud's manuscripts, supported Freud's ideas of infantile sexuality in publications of his own, and introduced the topic of human bisexuality, which Freud subsequently elaborated. In addition, Fliess served as Freud's informal analyst during the 1890s, along with Freud's sister-in-law, Minna Bernays. Bernays, whose fiancé had died young, eventually came to live in the Freud household. At times, she accompanied Freud—without her sister—on summer vacation trips. Carl Jung's (Chapter 16) rumor that Freud and Minna had an affair lacks persuasive evidence (Gay, 1988).

Freud's isolation was primarily the result of his ideas about the sexual origin of neurosis. Freud later claimed to have gotten such ideas from three people he greatly respected: Breuer, Charcot, and Chrobak, a University of Vienna gynecologist. For example, when Freud was a young hospital doctor, Breuer remarked to him about the neurotic behavior of a female patient, "Those are always secrets of the alcove" (Freud, 1938a, p. 937), meaning that such disorders were always the result of a couple's sexual problems. A few years later, Freud overheard Charcot talking to an assistant about a young married couple in which the husband was impotent and the wife was "a great sufferer." When the assistant appeared astonished, Charcot said emphatically: "*Mais, dans des cas pareils, c'est toujours la chose génital, toujours—toujours—toujours*" (p. 938). (But, in such cases, it is always a genital thing, always—always—always.)

The third incident came when Chrobak asked Freud to take a case for which Chrobak had no time. The patient suffered from debilitating anxiety attacks, and Chrobak "disclosed to [Freud] that the

patient's anxiety was due to the fact that although she had been married eighteen years, she was still a [virgin], that her husband was utterly impotent." Chrobak added, "The only prescription for such troubles is the one well-known to us, but which we cannot prescribe. It is: Penis normalis dosim Repetatur!" (Freud, 1938a, p. 938), which means "repeated doses of a normal penis."

In his work with hysterics, Freud reached the startling conclusion, which he presented in 1896 in an address to the Society of Psychiatry and Neurology entitled "The Etiology of Hysteria," that in every case the disorder was precipitated by a sexual experience occurring before puberty. This is Freud's **seduction theory**, the idea that neuroses are the result of childhood sexual abuse.

Not surprisingly, Freud's 1896 address received an "icy reception." Freud continued to believe in the reality of these childhood memories until the fall of the following year, when he wrote Fliess that he was now convinced the traumatic seductions had never occurred; Freud did not publicly abandon the theory for 9 years, however (Schusdek, 1966). Although much has been written about Freud's abandonment of the seduction theory (e.g., Masson, 1984), his move away from it revealed something new and important about Freud's understanding of the mind: Patients could have fantasized the sexual episodes they thought had really occurred. For Freud, this was further proof of hysteria's sexual origin. Of course, given the current evidence for the widespread nature of childhood sexual abuse, Freud's original version of the seduction theory remains intriguing.

The Interpretation of Dreams

Followers of Freud became psychoanalysts after undergoing an analysis of their personalities conducted with someone else. As the first psychoanalyst, Freud was forced to perform a self-analysis, which he began in 1897, relying primarily on an examination of his dreams. This led to *The Interpretation of Dreams,* which was completed in the summer of 1899 but bears a 1900 publication date. It took 8 years for 600 copies of what many consider Freud's most important book to sell, and Freud received little money for his effort. Although Freud and Ernest Jones—Freud's friend, disciple, and biographer—considered that the book had been overlooked or treated negatively, in fact, the book was extensively and favorably reviewed in Germany when it appeared and was well known to the educated German public (Decker, 1975).

In *The Interpretation of Dreams,* Freud stressed the importance of dream analysis for understanding psychic life: "*[T]he interpretation of dreams is the [royal road] to a knowledge of the unconscious element in our psychic life*" (Freud, 1938b, p. 540, italics in the original). Further, Freud believed that dreams have meaning and that he held the key to understanding them. This key lay in the use of free association to the various dream elements.

Freud believed it was crucial to distinguish the dream's **manifest content**—the details that we remember—from its **latent content**—the dream's true meaning. Dream analysis is aimed at deciphering the latent content from the manifest content.

Freud believed that all dreams represent **wish-fulfillment**, even those in which the manifest content is troubling (Freud, 1938b). The reason that the manifest content may not appear to represent the dreamer's wish is that two psychic forces are the primary cause of a dream's formation: The first system forms the wish expressed, whereas the second system censors the work of the first system, distorting the dream-wish.

This distortion of the dream-wish occurs through "dream work," whose function is to alter troubling impulses and memories to make them relatively innocuous, thereby protecting sleep. A partial list of the principal methods used to disguise the dream-thoughts (latent content) includes condensation, displacement, and symbolization.

Condensation is the tendency for a dream to be abbreviated relative to the ideas expressed in it. As Freud put it, "The dream is meagre, paltry and laconic in comparison with the range and copiousness of the dream-thoughts" (Freud, 1938b, p. 320).

In displacement, "the emotional charge is separated from its real object . . . and attached to an entirely different one" (Stafford-Clark, 1965, p. 77). Displacement means that an innocuous manifest content may conceal great emotion, or vice versa.

Symbolization is the dream work's use of certain universal elements to stand for something else. Although Freud recognized dream symbolism in the beginning of his explorations, he did not consider it important at first. In later editions of *The Interpretation of Dreams,* he added a sizable section on symbols because of the prodding of **Wilhelm Stekel** (1868–1940) and other early followers. Educated at the University of Vienna, Stekel had a brief analysis with Freud in 1902 and became one of the original group of psychoanalysts to gather around him. Stekel's break with Freud around 1912 is undoubtedly responsible for Freud's comment in later editions of *The Interpretation of Dreams* that "[Stekel] . . . has perhaps injured psychoanalysis as much as he has benefited it . . ." (Freud, 1938b, p. 368). Although he added the symbols, Freud warned against overusing them, noting that precedence should be given to the dreamer's associations.

Many of the symbols Freud identified have sexual connotations. For example, weapons, tools, and elongated objects (e.g., cigars and neckties) are phallic symbols, whereas small boxes and vessels represent female genitalia. Castration is represented by baldness, haircutting, and the loss of teeth. The sex act is symbolized by steep inclines, ladders, stairs, and going up or down them. Freud also noted nonsexual symbols, such as "to depart" means death and a traveler's luggage refers to "the burden of sin." In addition, Freud carefully pointed out that the "assertion that *all dreams call for a sexual interpretation . . .* is quite foreign to my *Interpretation of Dreams*" (Freud, 1938b, p. 392, italics in the original).

Freud concluded that,

> The dream is a psychic act full of import; its motive power is invariably a wish craving fulfilment; the fact that it is unrecognizable as a wish, and its many peculiarities and absurdities, are due to the influence of the psychic censorship to which it has been subjected during its formation. (Freud, 1938b, p. 485)

The Interpretation of Dreams was Freud's first comprehensive statement, albeit incomplete, of his psychology. Throughout the book, Freud's belief in psychological determinism is apparent. Therefore, it is fitting that at the same time that he was working on his dream book, Freud was also collecting material for *The Psychopathology of Everyday Life* (1901), another important early volume in which Freud presented many tenets of his psychoanalytic theory.

In *The Psychopathology of Everyday Life*, Freud amassed examples of slips of the tongue or pen, the forgetting of common names, and other examples of behavior previously considered accidental and not worth analyzing. Freud believed that such (Freudian) slips reveal repressed psychic material, and the analysis of "mistakes" became another way, with free association and dream analysis, to understand the patient. As one example of a Freudian slip, Freud wrote,

> Two women stopped in front of a drugstore, and one said to her companion, "If you will wait a few *moments*, I'll soon be back," but she said *movements* instead. She was on her way to buy [a laxative] for her child. (Freud, 1938c, p. 77, italics in the original)

The publication of *The Interpretation of Dreams* and *The Psychopathology of Everyday Life* signaled Freud's emergence from the period of relative isolation that had followed his emphasis on the sexual basis of the neuroses and heralded an important series of new contributions for psychology.

Freud Gains Recognition

Following these publications, Freud's reputation began to grow (e.g., Jones, 1955). In 1902, "a number of young doctors gathered around [him] with the expressed intention of learning, practising, and spreading psychoanalysis. The impetus for this came from a colleague who had himself experienced the beneficial effects of the analytic therapy" (Freud, 1938a, p. 946).

Freud's Inner Circle

Freud's unnamed colleague was Wilhelm Stekel, and the rest of the group consisted of Alfred Adler (Chapter 16), Max Kahane, and Rudolf Reitler. Meeting on Wednesday nights, the group called itself the Wednesday Psychological Society; by 1908, the Society formed the nucleus of the Vienna Psychoanalytic Society.

Freud's circle of disciples continued to grow, incorporating Otto Rank in 1906, Carl Jung, Karl Abraham, Sandor Ferenczi, and Max Eitingon in 1907, and Ernest Jones in 1908. Some of Freud's inner circle eventually broke away from him, usually over matters of theory. For example, Adler resigned from the Vienna Society in 1911, taking 9 of 35 members with him; Stekel followed Adler in 1912. Carl Jung, once Freud's heir apparent, resigned in 1914 from the International Psychoanalytic Association, which had been founded in 1910. **Otto Rank** (1884–1939) was removed from Freud's inner circle after his publication of *The Trauma of Birth* in 1924. Rank's emphasis on anxiety from birth trauma instead of sexual conflict was the theoretical issue on which he and Freud parted company. Rank's place was filled by Anna Freud (discussed later), Freud's daughter.

Karl Abraham (1877–1925) was introduced by Jung to Freud's work. Moving from Zurich to Berlin in 1907, Abraham became the first German psychoanalyst and the founder of the Berlin Psychoanalytic Society. A close collaborator with Freud, Abraham contributed significantly to Freud's theory of the stages of psychosexual development.

Hungarian-born **Sandor Ferenczi** (1873–1933) received his M.D. at the University of Vienna. Ferenczi met and became a follower of Freud in 1908, and he was one of the group accompanying Freud to Clark University in 1909 (Chapter 10), the others being Jung, Jones, and A. A. Brill. Ferenczi founded the Hungarian Psychoanalytic Society in 1913 and collaborated with Rank in writing *The Development of Psychoanalysis* (1924). An Austrian, **A. A. Brill** (1874–1948) was the first practicing psychoanalyst in America and a translator of many of Freud's works into English. He was instrumental in founding the American Psychoanalytic Association.

Ernest Jones (1879–1958) was born in Wales, obtaining his medical degree from University College Hospital in London. Jones came into contact with Freud through neurological research, learned German in order to study Freud's work more closely, and starting in 1908, became a lifelong friend of

Freud. Jones introduced psychoanalysis to Great Britain and founded the British Psycho-Analytical Society in 1913. He was a professor of psychiatry at the University of Toronto from 1909 to 1912, establishing important psychoanalytic connections in North America. Jones's three-volume biography is considered the definitive work on Freud, and Jones arguably became Freud's heir. Carl Jung—Freud's one-time heir apparent—and Alfred Adler will be discussed in Chapter 16.

Freud's Last Years

Despite the growing acceptance of psychoanalysis as an important force in psychology, Freud's last 2 decades of life contained much personal suffering. The years of World War I were particularly stressful because of worry about the safety of his two sons serving in the army, a shortage of food, and a lack of heating during two severe winters. Runaway inflation after the war took Freud's life savings, and it was not until the end of 1920 that he again began to earn a reasonable income.

In 1920, Freud's daughter Sophie died from the influenza pandemic. Freud accepted the news of his daughter's death stoically, writing to his mother,

> She is the first of our children we have to outlive. What [her husband] will do, what will happen to the children, we of course don't know as yet.
>
> I hope you will take it calmly; tragedy after all has to be accepted. But to mourn this splendid, vital girl who was so happy with her husband and children is of course permissible. (Freud, 1920; E. L. Freud, 1992, pp. 326–327)

Unfortunately, Sophie's death was but the first of many that occurred among Freud's family and friends during his lifetime. Perhaps the hardest loss came in 1923, with the death of Sophie's 4-year-old son Heinele from miliary tuberculosis. Freud, who was not one for tears, broke down with the passing of his grandson. "I find this loss very hard to bear," he wrote to friends shortly before the boy died. "I don't think I have ever experienced such grief," he continued, insightfully concluding that "perhaps my own sickness contributes to the shock" (Freud, 1923; E. L. Freud, 1992, p. 344). Diagnosed the same

year Heinele died, Freud's illness was cancer of the mouth and jaw. Freud eventually underwent 33 operations for his malignancy, which was attributed to his cigar smoking. Although he tried several times, Freud was never able to give up his addiction to tobacco.

Lifelong friend and colleague Karl Abraham died at the end of 1925, and Freud's mother died in 1930. In 1933, Freud's books were burned by the Nazis in Berlin, and the German Society for Psychotherapy fell under Nazi control. In March 1938, Austria was invaded by the Nazis, and Freud's apartment was visited first by the SA (*Sturmabteilung*, storm troops) and then a week later by the Gestapo (*Geheime Staatspolizei*, German state police). With the aid of friends and admirers, which included Ernest Jones and President Roosevelt, Freud and his immediate family were allowed to leave, arriving in England in June. Freud's four sisters were detained, and all perished in Nazi gas chambers, a fact that, mercifully, Freud never learned.

Freud received an enthusiastic welcome in England, but his cancer was far advanced. Freud's health grew steadily worse, and further surgery was not an option. He died on September 23, 1939.

Freud's Theory of Personality

As we noted, Freud's conception of human personality was strongly influenced by Brücke's dynamic physiology, which viewed the living organism as a dynamic system. Freud took the same view, considering personality a system in which changes and exchanges of energy are important. From his clinical practice, Freud grew more and more convinced that much of the operation of the dynamic forces within an individual personality occurs unconsciously, and he came to see himself as an explorer of the unconscious. Thus, even in his early work (e.g., *The Interpretation of Dreams*), the unconscious was central to his theory, and Freud conceived of personality in terms of the **unconscious** (the site of relatively irretrievable material, some of which may be repressed), the **preconscious** (antechamber to consciousness, containing relatively accessible material), and the **conscious** (what we are aware of). Later, Freud shifted emphasis from the three levels of consciousness to the three systems of the id, ego, and superego.

In the mentally healthy individual, the three systems work harmoniously, enabling the person to interact in a satisfying way with the environment in the fulfillment of his or her needs and desires. Disharmony among the systems leads to the sort of maladjustment that psychoanalysis was developed to treat.

The Id

The **id** (literally, "it") is the only system present at birth, and it functions to discharge energy released in the organism either by external or internal stimulation. This function satisfies the first principle of life, which Freud called the **pleasure principle**. The pleasure principle strives to eliminate or at least to reduce tension to an acceptably low and stable level. Tension is experienced as discomfort, whereas relief from tension is satisfying, and the aim of the pleasure principle is to seek pleasure while avoiding pain (e.g., Freud, 1920).

The id is a primitive reservoir of energy, which is undifferentiated and derived from the instincts. Freud thought of an instinct as an innate condition imparting direction to psychological processes, and he eventually divided the instincts into two groups: life instincts (*Eros*) and death instincts (*Thanatos*). **Libido** was Freud's term for the form of energy used by the life instincts. Originally, libido was identified with sexual energy, but Freud later broadened the term's definition to include all the life instincts. Perhaps "sensual drive" better expresses Freud's intended meaning.

At first, Freud used the terms "death instinct" and "destructive instinct" interchangeably, "but in his discussion with [Albert] Einstein about war he made the distinction that the former is directed against the self and the latter, derived from it, is directed outward" (Jones, 1957, p. 273). The death instincts strive for the individual's disintegration, whereas the life instincts function to maintain the organism's integration. World War I confirmed Freud's pessimistic view of the ultimate aims of the death instincts.

Of all the components of Freudian personality theory, the notion of death instincts was among the least accepted by other psychoanalysts. Freud himself was not completely committed to it, telling Jones in a 1935 letter, "all this is groping speculation, until one has something better" (as cited in Gay, 1988, p. 402).

The id is initially a reflex apparatus, and if an infant's reflex responses could discharge all the possible tensions aroused by sensory stimulation, no further development would be necessary. However, the organism soon experiences tensions that cannot be reduced by reflexes. For example, at some point, hunger pangs result in tension that produces crying and restlessness in a baby. Because the baby's reflexive responses do not produce food, the pangs increase until either the baby is fed or it becomes exhausted from its unsuccessful efforts.

No matter how diligent the parents, the neonate is bound to experience some frustration in the discharge of tensions. This frustration leads the id to develop the **primary process**, which is the production of a memory image of the object needed to reduce tension. For the hungry baby, the primary process produces the image of food or of the mother's breast. The id does not distinguish between the memory image and the real thing, treating them both as identical. Freud called the formation of an image of a tension-reducing object "wish-fulfillment," suggesting that he considered dreaming an example of the primary process.

Of course, dreaming or imagining something to reduce tension does not work: A hungry infant imagining its mother's breast remains hungry. This failure by the id to satisfy its desires leads to the development of the secondary process, which is an ego function.

The Ego

The id, completely unconscious and functioning either reflexively or by the primary process (imagining, dreaming), often cannot deal effectively with the external environment. As a result, the **ego** (Latin for "I"; the self) develops.

The ego functions according to the **reality principle**, whose aim is to prevent energy discharge until the actual object needed for tension-reduction is produced. The hungry child, as opposed to the hungry infant, has learned to postpone eating until food is located. In order to be able to postpone behavior, the ego must be able to tolerate a certain level of tension. The ultimate aim is still dictated by the id's pleasure principle; in the interest of eventual gratification, the reality principle deals with the environment and tolerates discomfort.

The id's primary process is superseded by the ego's **secondary process**. Instead of fantasizing or dreaming, the ego handles reality by developing an action plan through thought and reason, that is, through cognition. The secondary process corresponds to what we call thinking or problem solving.

In order to deal effectively with the environment, the ego must be able to function on all three levels of consciousness. Like the id, the ego can use the primary process; the difference is that the ego recognizes that its fantasy images are not real. Also like the id, the ego ultimately strives for pleasure. This is not exactly the case for the third system—the superego.

The Superego

The **superego** is the moral component of the personality, striving for perfection rather than for sensual pleasure. It develops from the ego by incorporating the parental and societal standards of appropriate behavior. A child not only learns to obey the reality principle, he or she also learns to obey the moral dictates of parents and society.

The superego has two subsystems: the ego-ideal and the conscience. The **ego-ideal** contains the rules the child perceives that his parents think are right and proper—the "thou shalts," in other words. Helping your neighbor—engaging in altruistic behavior—is an example of a rule that might be in your ego-ideal. If you act according to this rule, you will feel pleasure from a sense of pride.

The **conscience** punishes inappropriate behaviors through a sense of guilt. In it are found the parental (and societal) "thou shalt nots," most of the Ten Commandments, for example. If you cheat on a test, you will feel guilty if your conscience is well developed.

Like the id, the superego's operation is primarily unconscious, and it, too, operates mainly through the primary process. The superego exerts control

over the ego by rewarding or punishing it. In reality, the ego may be punished or rewarded for just thinking of doing something "bad" or "good"; the actual behavior is unnecessary. Like the id, the superego fails to differentiate between subjective and objective reality.

Although we have discussed the three personality systems under separate headings, the boundaries between them are not sharply drawn. The ego develops from the id, and the superego comes from the ego, and the systems continue to be closely associated and interactive throughout life.

Psychosexual Development

As we indicated, Freud believed that the animal instincts provide the energy for the life processes. Although an instinct's aim does not change, its source—bodily excitation—may change during development. This sort of change is evident in the development of the sexual instinct, which Freud considered as a central example for understanding psychic life.

For Freud, the sexual instinct included stimulation of more than just the genitals. In fact, Freud considered any part of the body where sensations become focalized and create tension—which can then be relieved by such actions as stroking and sucking—to be an erogenous zone.

Freud was convinced that childhood sexuality begins long before puberty. The reproductive function awakens at puberty, and people who deny infantile sexuality are "making the mistake of confounding sexuality and reproduction with each other . . ." (Freud, 1920, p. 320). Thus, children have a sexual life divorced from reproduction, which includes the function of receiving enjoyment from the body's erogenous zones. The first of these zones is the mouth.

The Oral Stage.   Initially, all the infant's efforts are centered around obtaining satisfaction through the oral zone, which produces the **oral stage**. Eventually, the mouth develops at least five modes of functioning—taking in, holding on, biting, spitting out, and closing—which are prototypes for different personality traits. Frustration or overindulgence of any of the functions may result in fixation on a prototype, with consequences for adult behavior. For example, anxiety over "taking in" may lead to the adult desire to incorporate such things as love, knowledge, power, money, and material possessions. Biting is the prototype for such adult "biting" as sarcasm and cynicism, and the person may become a movie critic or acerbic essayist (e.g., Hall, 1954).

The adult manifestation may also appear as the opposite of what seems to be dictated by the prototype. Thus, an extremely gullible person ("She'll swallow anything") may have received frustration over either "spitting out" or "taking in." Other typical adult manifestations of oral fixation include excessive eating, smoking, and drinking. The oral stage typically lasts until some time within the infant's second year.

The Anal Stage. Pressure on the anal sphincter and its release with defecation provide for libidinal satisfaction that eventually becomes central for the child at about the age of 2. Toilet training often represents the child's first major experience with external authority. If the parents are too harsh or too lax in their demands, this can result in permanent effects on the child's adult personality in regard to rules and cleanliness.

Excessively punitive toilet training may cause fixation at the **anal stage** leading to adult messiness, irresponsibility, and wastefulness. The opposite is also possible, and the harshly trained child may become a fastidious, compulsive, and overcontrolled adult. By contrast, if the parents extravagantly praise the child's bowel movements, the result may be an adult motivated to create things or to give things away. Alternatively, the lavishly praised child may become a thrifty adult or an adult with an interest in collecting and retaining objects. The anal stage ordinarily lasts until the end of the third or the beginning of the fourth year.

The Phallic Stage. In the third stage, interest centers on the genitals, and the period is called the **phallic stage**, reflecting Freud's emphasis on the male's anatomy and development. Although Freud has in recent times been criticized for focusing on the male, he was merely mirroring the prevailing attitudes of the late Victorian era in which he worked. Nevertheless, to differentiate the events for the sexes, Freud called the two stages "the male phallic stage" and the "female phallic stage."

In the male phallic stage, the boy's love for his mother develops, and he becomes jealous of the control his father has over his mother. Freud called the stage in which the little boy would like to exclusively possess his mother and remove his father as a rival the **Oedipus complex**, after the character in Greek mythology who unwittingly killed his father and married his mother.

The problem is that the father is too powerful to be displaced. Added to the impossibility of defeating the father is the fear that the father will remove the child's genitalia—the little boy may have seen a little girl naked and has discovered that she has no penis. The little boy reaches a horrifying conclusion—the father must have cut off her penis. Called **castration anxiety**, the child's fear motivates the resolution of the Oedipus complex. In the resolution, the little boy represses his desire for the mother and identifies with the father.

At the beginning of the female phallic stage, the little girl, like the little boy, loves her mother, but she does not relate to the father the way a brother might. When she discovers her "missing" penis, the little girl feels cheated by the mother, and her cathexis (attachment) to the mother is weakened. At the same time, the little girl begins to prefer the father, as the possessor of the organ that she lacks. Because her love for her father is mixed with envy—he has what she does not have—the little girl experiences **penis envy**. Where castration anxiety causes the boy to resolve his Oedipus complex, the girl's penis envy introduces her Oedipus complex; now she loves the father and is jealous of the mother. Eventually, **identification** with the mother (unconsciously trying to think, feel, and act like the mother) enables the little girl to experience the father vicariously while partly compensating for her lost love relation with the mother. The complex that we have called the Oedipus complex in both sexes is sometimes called the **Electra complex** in females, after the character in Greek mythology who avenges her father's death by joining forces with her brother to kill their mother and her lover.

The various identifications that end the phallic stage result in the formation of the superego, which is sometimes called the "heir of the Oedipus complex," because it replaces it. At the end of the phallic stage, at about the age of 6, "a standstill or retrogression is observed in the sexual development, which . . . deserves to be called a *latency period*" (Freud, 1920, p. 335, italics in the original). The so-called **latency stage** is followed at puberty by the genital stage.

The Genital Stage.   The first three stages—oral, anal, phallic—are collectively known as the pregenital period. During the pregenital period, sexual gratification is self-directed—autoerotic—because of the child's primary narcissism, or self-love. Secondary narcissism is a feeling of pride when the ego identifies with the superego's ideals. As we noted, the pregenital child's sexual instinct is not directed toward others—reproduction—until puberty.

After the latency period, the adolescent begins to direct the libido outward, toward the opposite sex, and to the ultimate goal of reproduction. The resulting **genital stage** is a period of socialization, marriage, rearing a family, and all such adult activities. Like the earlier stages, the genital stage does not completely replace its predecessors, and activities that satisfy pregenital urges become part of the mating experience. For example, kissing is an activity that clearly involves the erogenous zone that was the focus of the oral stage.

Note that we have spent more time discussing the pregenital stages, which occur in the first 5 or 6 years of life, than we have in discussing the two stages that occupy a much longer period of a person's life. The reason is that the Freudian theory of psychosexual development emphasizes the crucial importance of the first few years of life for later development.

Freud's Influence

With his central interests in sexuality and the darkly aggressive id, Freud was easily and often caricatured. Discussion of sex was a two-edged sword: Although it served to attract attention to his ideas, it also alienated many potential allies. Often Freud used sex as a sensa-

tional metaphor, when he could have couched his ideas in more general and less provocative terms.

Although there was much in the intellectual European *Zeitgeist* with which Freudian thinking is compatible (e.g., evolution, conceptions of the unconscious), Freud made an important break with prevailing opinion in developing a psychological approach to mental illness rather than a physiological one. According to Gay (1988), Freud's "most eminent colleagues in the field of psychiatry were neurologists at heart" (p. 119). For example, Krafft-Ebing published a monograph in 1895 that concluded essentially that psychological suffering was a matter of physiology. Nearly 20 years earlier, American neurologist William Hammond wrote that "The modern science of psychology is neither more nor less than *the science of the mind considered as a physical function*" (as cited in Gay, p. 121, italics in the original). Freud was thoroughly exposed to this physiological point of view through his neurological training, and it is a measure of the independence of his thinking that he was able to break with it.

Although psychoanalysis suffered from Freud's rationalistic, nonexperimental approach, and the system as a whole has experienced devastating critiques in recent years (e.g., Crews, 1996), it is virtually impossible to overestimate the impact of Freud and his ideas on Western civilization. Psychoanalysis has contributed abundantly to our everyday language, where such terms as id, ego, superego, the unconscious, and Freudian slip are immediately recognized. Books on Freud, including major biographies, continue to be published and read. Despite an array of alternatives, psychoanalysis as a method for treating mental illness is still widely used.

In addition to Freud's contributions to personality theory, psychopathology, and the psychoanalytic approach to therapy, he also contributed importantly to such areas as social psychology and cognitive psychology. For example, Freud had a continuing interest in the relationship between an individual's intrapsychic events and a variety of social and cultural concerns. Across a variety of books and essays (e.g., *Character and Culture, Civilization and Its Discontents, Moses to Monotheism,* and *Totem and Taboo*), Freud explored art, humor, political change, religion, and war. Although Freud's writings on pyschoanalysis, personality, and psychopathology remain our first association between Freud and psychology, the scope of Freud's "social psychology" should be underscored. In addition, it is largely through these "nonpsychological" works that Freud's ideas and theories influenced disciplines such as anthropology, literary criticism, and sociology.

Matthew Erdelyi (1985) considered Freud a "grand" theorist, that is, as providing a comprehensive theory of psychology rather than simply making contributions to such selected areas as personality theory and psychopathology. He concluded that Freud was attempting to provide a complete consideration of human existence, and in so doing, Freud anticipated important advances in both social and cognitive psychology.

An ambitious person, Freud was fabulously successful in his quest for personal recognition—as is illustrated by a memorial poem penned by W. H. Auden shortly after Freud's death. Auden mourned Freud's death as he mourned the death of others "who were doing us some good, who knew it was never enough but hoped to improve a little by living" (Auden; Mendelson, 1976, p. 215). As for Freud's method, Auden wrote,

> He wasn't clever at all: he merely told
> The unhappy Present to recite the Past
>   Like a poetry lesson till sooner
>   Or later it faltered at the line where
>
> Long ago the accusations had begun, . . .
> (p. 216)

Auden acknowledged Freud's widespread influence in the passage

> If often he was wrong and at times, absurd,
>   To us he is no more a person
>   Now but a whole climate of opinion
>
> Under whom we conduct our differing lives: . . .
> (p. 217)

NEO-FREUDIANS

Of the many psychoanalysts who came after Freud, some adhered more closely than others to his original teachings. In this section, we will briefly consider the lives and careers of some neo-Freudians who, although they diverged from Freud on certain matters, still remained relatively close to his core theory. Each also shared a special interest in development and sought to embellish Freud's understanding of the developmental process. We will begin with Freud's daughter, Anna Freud, and conclude with an examination of how psychoanalysis is related to such contemporary interests as attachment formation and gerontology.

Anna Freud

The last of Freud's six children, **Anna Freud** (1895–1982) became indispensable to her father and eventually his successor in the continued advancement of psychoanalytic theory. As Freud's illness deprived him of his former speaking abilities, Anna Freud was dispatched to read his papers at international psychoanalytic meetings. This had the dual function of publicizing Freud's ideas and giving her exposure to the psychoanalytic community. Anna Freud also assumed Minna Bernays's role as sympathetic listener and functioned as her father's private nurse toward the end of his life.

Anna Freud was advised by her father at the age of 17 to become more easygoing. Despite this tendency toward seriousness, she did not finish the *Gymnasium* and received no formal scientific training. Initially, she worked as an elementary school teacher, while also attending Freud's lectures at the University of Vienna and meetings of the Vienna Psychoanalytic Society without being a member. Undergoing analysis with her father—a violation of the rules of analytic technique—Anna Freud became a member of the Vienna Society in 1922 and a practicing child analyst the next year. If Anna Freud ever felt deprived of a life outside psychoanalysis, she sublimated it well. Anna Freud in the early 1920s is shown in Figure 15–6.

Anna Freud's Contributions to Psychoanalysis

"During Freud's lifetime Anna Freud was never in her own right a leader in psychoanalysis, but . . . [eventually] she has inherited Freud's throne"

FIGURE 15–6.   Anna Freud in the early 1920s.

Source: Corbis-Bettmann.

(Roazen, 1975, p. 453). After her father's death, Anna Freud became one of the major developers of the psychoanalytic school, making several important contributions, including the popularization of child analysis. For Anna Freud, the main distinction between child analysis and adult analysis was that children are incapable of establishing an adult form of transference. Thus, she did not attempt to treat children in exactly the same way as adults.

Additionally, Anna Freud was one of the earliest of the orthodox psychoanalysts to stress ego psychology and particularly the ego's defensive mechanisms. Freud had introduced the term "defense mechanism" in 1894 but did not use it for the next 30 years (Wolman, 1968). In her best-known work, *The Ego and the Mechanisms of Defence,* Anna Freud (1937) described the mechanisms in detail.

Defense mechanisms are methods the ego uses when it is threatened by conflicting demands of the id and superego. The most basic mechanism is **repression,** defined as an unconscious removal from consciousness of unacceptable ideas, memories, and impulses. The ego forces this unwanted material into the unconscious mind and then expends energy to keep it there. Freud believed that repression accounted for his inability to remember the names of nonpaying patients.

Other defense mechanisms Anna Freud identified include regression, rationalization, projection, reaction formation, displacement, and sublimation. **Regression** is a retreat to an earlier stage of development as a result of traumatic experience. For example, a child may respond to the frustrations of the first day of school by exhibiting such infantile behaviors as crying and thumbsucking. **Rationalization** is the ego's attempt to account for mistakes and failures by providing a reasonable, but untrue, explanation for behavior. For example, a student who does poorly in a course may decide that the professor was biased against her rather than admit that she was not motivated to do well.

Attributing our unpleasant or disturbing desires to others while rejecting them in ourselves is called **projection**. Thus, a woman who no longer loves her husband may accuse her husband of no longer loving her, thereby projecting her own feelings onto him. In **reaction formation**, the person professes the desire for the opposite of what is really wanted. For example, a mother who unconsciously dislikes her child may become overprotective. The excessive display of any attitude (fanaticism) may reveal reaction formation. As Shakespeare expressed it in Act III, Scene II of *Hamlet*: "The lady doth protest too much, methinks."

In **displacement**, emotion is shifted from its real object to a safer object. For instance, a punished child may aggress against a younger sibling or against his or her toys. **Sublimation** is displacement in which the substituted object of the displacement is socially approved. For example, a person with disturbing tendencies may channel the prohibited desires into art, becoming a world-famous painter, such as Van Gogh.

Anna Freud was not the only neo-Freudian with an interest in child analysis. In London, Melanie Klein—an outspoken advocate of analysis for children—became Anna Freud's rival in a conflict lead-

ing to alternative approaches to child analysis that
endure today (Viner, 1996).

Melanie Klein

Initially trained as a nursery school teacher,
Melanie Klein (1882–1960) was first analyzed by
Ferenczi in Budapest and then later by Abraham in
Berlin. Through the intercession of another woman
undergoing analysis with Abraham, Klein's name
became known to Ernest Jones. With an interest in
improving the intellectual quality of the London
psychoanalytic group and in securing the services of
a good child analyst for his children, Jones invited
Klein to come to London, and she settled there in
1926.

Although her personal relationship with Freud
was slight, Klein's ideas were seen by him as a
challenge to those of his daughter, and the arrival
of Freud and his immediate family in England in
1938 caused a rift within the British psychoanalytic
movement. Klein's suffering from the schism was
exacerbated by attacks from her own daughter,
who was also a physician and an analyst. Because
of Klein's outspokenness, "until she died in 1960
the situation in the British Psychoanalytic Society
was tense and difficult. But the fact that psychoanalysis in England is not intellectually complacent
is due in part to her energy and absorption in life"
(Roazen, 1975, p. 488). Klein is shown in Figure
15–7.

Despite the opposition to Klein's views by the
Freud family, her ideas actually conformed rather
closely to an orthodox Freudian framework. One
difference was Klein's emphasis on the pre-oedipal
layers of personality development and her stress on
the importance of the mother's early nurturing of
the child. Although Klein agreed with Freud's concepts of the id, ego, and superego, she thought that
each of them was relatively distinct almost from the
beginning of life.

Because of her emphasis on the importance of the
mother's nurturing function, for Klein the female
breast assumed almost mythic proportions. According to Klein, men experienced not only castration anxiety but also "breast envy." Ironically, Klein

FIGURE 15–7. Melanie Klein.
Source: Melanie Klein Trust, courtesy Harvard College Library.

is reported not to have nursed her own children
(Roazen, 1975).

Unlike Anna Freud, Klein believed that the same
psychoanalytic technique could be applied to both
children and adults. In addition, Klein at one point
advocated universal child psychoanalysis, differing
in this respect from Anna Freud and many others.
Interestingly, many analysts sent their children to
Klein for treatment.

Klein differed from Freud in her approach to
adult psychoanalysis, as well. For example, although
Freud was willing to avoid analyzing certain patient
defenses, Klein believed in leaving nothing uninter-
preted. As a result, her English followers have spoken
of 10-year (or longer) analyses (Roazen, 1975).

Both Anna Freud and Melanie Klein were also
important as pioneering women therapists. As
women became increasingly involved with psychoanalysis, some of the more male chauvinistic elements of Freud's system were challenged. Karen
Horney was an early contributor to the development
of a more "feminine" psychoanalytic theory.

Karen Horney

Karen Horney (1885–1952), née Danielson, was born near Hamburg, Germany, the daughter of a stern, authoritative sea captain. Horney's mother protected her daughter against the father's rigidity and encouraged her to pursue a career, so she entered medical school in 1906. There, she met and married Oskar Horney and subsequently received her M.D. from the University of Berlin in 1915. Horney was psychoanalyzed by Karl Abraham and was associated with the Berlin Psychoanalytic Institute from 1918 until 1932.

In 1932, Franz Alexander (1891–1964)—formerly a student at the Berlin Institute—invited Horney to join him at the Chicago Psychoanalytic Institute, where she became Associate Director. After a couple of years, Alexander's and Horney's incompatibility resulted in Horney's move to New York, where she initially practiced psychoanalysis and taught at the New York Psychoanalytic Institute. Dissatisfaction with a wholly orthodox psychoanalysis led Horney to found, along with others of like mind, the Association for the Advancement of Psychoanalysis and the American Institute of Psychoanalysis. Horney (Figure 15–8) served as dean of the Institute until she died.

FIGURE 15–8.   Karen Horney.
Source: Corbis-Bettmann.

Horney's Version of Psychoanalysis

Although Horney accepted much of Freudian theory, there were some Freudian tenets with which she disagreed. For example, she strongly objected to Freud's notion of penis envy as a determining factor in feminine psychology. As she saw it, the problem was that psychoanalysis was the product of a male genius, and most of its later developers were also men. Hence, it is little wonder that Freudian psychoanalysis was a masculine psychology in which the development of men was more completely portrayed than the development of women. Horney concluded that feminine psychology owed more to a lack of confidence and an overemphasis on the love relationship than it did to a feeling of genital inferiority and jealousy of men.

Like many neo-Freudians, Horney disagreed with Freud's emphasis on the sexual instinct and on the controlling effects of instincts in general, preferring instead to focus on the effects on the individual of cultural and social conditions. Horney considered Freud's basic theoretical contributions to be psychic determinism, unconscious motivation, and the notion of nonrational motives (Horney, 1939).

One of Horney's most fundamental concepts was **basic anxiety**, which is a child's feeling of helplessness and isolation within a potentially hostile world. In general, anything that disturbs the relationship between the child and its parents produces basic anxiety. Unpredictable behavior by the parents, a lack of consistent warmth, and lack of respect for the child's feelings are all potential causes of basic anxiety.

To counteract basic anxiety, the child develops various strategies or defenses, any of which may become permanent personality patterns. Horney identified 10 needs that she considered neurotic in the sense that they represent irrational problem solutions. Of the neurotic needs, Horney found women particularly susceptible to the need for affection and approval, the need for a "partner" to take over one's life, and the need for restriction of one's life within narrow borders. Other neurotic needs include the need for power, the need to exploit others, the need for personal admiration, and the need for perfection and unassailability.

In later work, Horney classified the 10 neurotic needs into three groups: needs that involve moving toward people (e.g., the need for affection and approval); needs that involve moving away from people (e.g., the need for self-sufficiency and independence); and the need for moving against people (e.g., the need for power). Whereas a normal person can effectively integrate the three orientations and reduce his or her conflicts, because of greater basic anxiety the neurotic is unable to achieve a similar integration. Prevention is the best answer to the problem of the conflicts; in a home and society in which there are warmth, security, love, tolerance, and respect, children grow into adults who can either avoid or resolve the conflicts.

As a theorist, Horney did not seek to replace Freudian psychoanalysis. Instead, she aimed to correct the errors in Freud's thinking that she felt were caused by his mechanistic, biological, male-oriented approach. In particular, she sought to replace Freud's portrayal of women dominated by penis envy with concepts that had little to do with a woman's sexual anatomy, that were the result of experience in a male-dominated culture rather than the result of unchangeable biology. Changes to psychoanalysis such as Horney's soon led to new concerns, one of which was the problem of the formation of attachments.

The Formation of Attachments

With the close relation between development and personality assumed by Freud and his followers, the interactions between a child and significant others (e.g., parents, siblings) became a topic of special importance to psychoanalytic theorists, who referred to the general class of relations as **attachments**. For example, **John Bowlby** (1907–1990) and **Mary Salter Ainsworth** (1913–) shared the 1990 APA Award for

Distinguished Scientific Contribution for their work on attachment. Bowlby and Ainsworth's theory of a human attachment behavioral system forms the central thesis of our current view of attachment and the basis for a new connection between child development and personality formation (e.g., Ainsworth & Bowlby, 1991).

Born in Ohio, Mary Salter was raised from the age of 4 in Canada. She received her Ph.D. in 1939 from the University of Toronto, and, following her marriage in 1950, Mary Salter Ainsworth moved to England and secured a position at London's Tavistock Clinic. Under Bowlby's direction at the Clinic, Ainsworth investigated the effects of infant-mother separation on the infant's behavior. In the laboratory, Ainsworth pioneered the "strange situation" methodology for studying mother-infant attachment. By placing a mother/infant pair in a strange room and then having the mother leave the infant and return, Ainsworth was able to examine the type of bond exhibited by a particular pair (i.e., secure attachment, insecure attachment) and the effect of this bond on exploration and learning by the infant.

John Bowlby was born in London, completed his initial studies at Cambridge, and earned his medical degree in 1933, with a specialization in psychiatry and psychoanalysis. After 5 years as an Army psychiatrist, Bowlby resumed his career as a child psychiatrist and accepted a position at the Tavistock Clinic.

Bowlby became an important innovator of modern psychoanalytic theory by turning toward biologically based explanations that better corresponded to the growing data about children and mental health. Bowlby was particularly interested in ethology (Chapter 12), and working with Cambridge ethologist Robert Hinde (1923–), he produced the first outline of his theory of attachment behavior in 1957.

Primate studies of mother-infant attachment, such as those of Harry Harlow (Chapter 14), provided part of the empirical basis for Bowlby's ideas and helped sensitize the psychological community to the importance of proper attachments for developing a healthy personality. Although Bowlby was the central theorist in their collaborations, Ainsworth was primarily responsible for collecting the empirical data to advance the theories. Bowlby and Ainsworth enjoyed 40 years of collaboration that produced a new field of scientific study. In addition to sharing the Distinguished Scientific Contribution Award, Ainsworth received the award for Distinguished Professional Contributions to Knowledge (1987) and was elected a fellow of the American Academy of Arts and Sciences in 1992.

Although interest in developmental issues such as attachment has usually meant work with children, Erik Erikson realized that that did not have to be the case.

Erik Erikson: Life-Span Development

As an artist hitchhiking around Europe in 1927, **Erik Erikson** (1902–1994) got a job painting children who were in analysis with Anna Freud. This work led to Erikson's own analysis with her, and he completed training at the Vienna Psychoanalytic Institute in 1933. Erikson (Figure 15–9) emigrated with

FIGURE 15–9. Erik Erikson.
Source: Archives of the History of American Psychology.

his American wife to the United States, where his rise was meteoric (Roazen, 1975).

Trained as a child psychoanalyst, Erikson is best known for his work in developmental psychology (e.g., Erikson, 1963, 1982). To Freud's psychosexual stages of development, Erikson's additions brought the total to eight: oral-sensory, muscular-anal, loco-motor-genital, latency, puberty or adolescence, young adulthood, adulthood, maturity and old age. Erikson believed that each stage has an accompanying identity crisis, with a desired developmental outcome. For example, the crisis in the oral-sensory stage is one of trust versus mistrust, for which the desired outcome is hope. At the other end of development—maturity and old age—the crisis is over integrity versus despair. If the person considers that his or her life has had meaning, then he or she will gain a sense of integrity. Despair can result if the person feels that his or her life has not been meaningful.

Erikson's additional developmental stages can be linked to a growing modern interest in **gerontology**, the study of aging and the exploration of issues that emerge as we age. Erikson's added stages also anticipate the current interest in a life-span consideration of the development of personality. Life-span approaches to many topics in psychology—for example, creativity, sexuality—are now being studied by psychologists. According to a life-span approach, development is a continuous process that does not stop at puberty or at any other developmental milestone but continues throughout life—that is, across the life span.

In addition to his developmental theorizing, Erikson popularized the "psycho-history," which is a psychoanalytic analysis of a historical figure. His first foray into this arena resulted in *Young Man Luther* (Erikson, 1962), an excellent study of Martin Luther (Chapter 3).

CONCLUSIONS

Compared to the other schools we have considered, which developed out of the academic tradition, psychoanalysis largely developed out of a different culture—clinical medicine. In addition, many of Freud's followers, coming from nonacademic backgrounds, were openly disdainful of "scholarship," with all its apparently stultifying dictates (Shakow, 1969). Thus, the inclusion of psychoanalysis as one of psychology's great schools is problematic.

Nevertheless, the impact of Freud and psychoanalysis has been profound on both psychology and Western society. Academic psychology has added to its repertoire such psychoanalytic conceptions as the goal-directed unconscious, the importance of early experience, and ego psychology, including the defense mechanisms.

Psychoanalysis has clearly made inroads into traditional psychology. Early evidence of this rapprochement can be seen in *Personality and Psychotherapy,* the 1950 book written by Neal Miller, who had studied psychoanalysis at the Vienna Psychoanalytic Institute, and John Dollard (both Chapter 13). More recently, Matthew Erdelyi (1985) has shown that psychoanalysis can be transposed into a cognitive framework, bringing the final integration of psychoanalysis with experimental psychology perhaps a step closer.

Finally, we briefly examined some of the first important women psychoanalysts—Anna Freud, Melanie Klein, and Karen Horney. Following these female pioneers, women have continued to be attracted to clinical psychology and related areas in large numbers. For example, over the decade from 1981 to 1991, "the pool of new entrants into the clinical, counseling, and school psychology workforce was primarily comprised of women (64% of the 1991 new doctorate recipients in these subfields)" (American Psychological Association, 1995, p. 10).

Although Freud was the pioneer of psychoanalysis, as we have seen in this chapter, other people (e.g., A. Freud, Klein, Horney, Erikson) had much to contribute. In the next chapter, we will continue the story of psychoanalysis with a consideration of Adler and Jung, two of Freud's one-time disciples who separated from him to establish successful variations of psychoanalysis. Chapter 16 will also explore existential and humanistic variations to therapy and concludes with a brief summary of other contemporary developments in clinical psychology.

S U M M A R Y

Unlike the other schools of psychology we have considered, psychoanalysis did not develop in an academic setting, arising instead from the clinical experiences of Sigmund Freud.

Early Treatment of the Mentally Ill

The early treatment of the mentally ill was at times barbaric and at other times (and places) relatively enlightened. In the latter part of the Middle Ages, the mentally ill were generally seen as bewitched rather than as witches. By the end of the 18th century, the *Zeitgeist* produced more humane treatment than earlier, with the actions of Philippe Pinel in Paris considered the signal events in this era of improved treatment. In the United States, Benjamin Rush and Dorothea Dix represented important positive forces in American psychiatry.

In the 19th century, Wilhelm Griesinger and his followers, especially Emil Kraepelin, attributed mental illness to organic causes. At the same time, particularly in France and Austria, an approach to etiology grew that considered mental disorders to be caused instead by psychic malfunction.

Hypnosis

Franz Mesmer was an early practitioner of a method of treatment for hysteria variously called animal magnetism, mesmerism, and later, hypnosis. The method was used and studied by such individuals as the Marquis de Puységur, José di Faria, John Elliotson, and James Esdaile, before James Braid gave it a name and scientific respectability.

In the 19th century, competing schools of hypnosis developed in France, with Liébeault and Bernheim at Nancy and Charcot at Salpêtrière Hospital. Pierre Janet used hypnosis to treat hysteric patients and developed a system of psychology with similarities to Freud's psychoanalysis.

Existential Precursors to Freud

Sören Kierkegaard is considered the founder of existentialism, the philosophy stressing the isolation of the individual in a hostile environment while emphasizing freedom of choice and responsibility for actions. Like Freud, Friedrich Nietzsche recognized the opposing psychic forces of the superego and the id; unlike Freud, Nietzsche viewed the relationship between the opposing forces as something that humans need to transcend. Freud considered Nietzsche second only to Schopenhauer as an anticipator of elements of psychoanalysis.

Sigmund Freud

Trained for a neurophysiology career, Freud eventually opened a private practice in psychiatry. Using ideas from a variety of sources, Freud began to develop a method of treatment that became known as psychoanalysis in the latter part of the 19th century. To analyze the unconscious mind of his patients, Freud first used hypnosis, eventually abandoning it for free association and dream interpretation. His analysis of his patients convinced Freud that sex was at the root of most neurotic disorders.

Freud's most important book is often considered to be *The Interpretation of Dreams.* Freud considered dream analysis essential for understanding psychic life, and he further believed that dreams represent wish-fulfillment and that many dream elements are symbolic.

Freud's reputation and circle of devotees began to grow after his turn-of-the-century publications. Early disciples included Alfred Adler, Otto Rank, Carl Jung, Sandor Ferenczi, Karl Abraham, and Ernest Jones. The most conspicuous defectors from Freud's inner circle were Adler, Jung, and Rank.

In Freudian theory, three systems of personality—id, ego, and superego—operate on different levels of consciousness. The storehouse of innate drives, the id seeks pleasure through the primary process, which is fantasizing about the desired object. The ego develops to deal with the environment by means of the reality principle. Striving for perfection, the superego is the personality's moral component.

For Freud, the instincts, and particularly the sexual instinct, provide the energy for life's processes. Development of the personality passes through five stages: oral, anal, phallic, latency, and genital. Fixation at any of the first three stages has consequences for adult behavior. The phallic stage is particularly crucial, because during it the little boy experiences the Oedipus complex and the little girl the Electra complex. Castration anxiety is the impetus for termination of the former, whereas the latter ends because of penis envy.

Freud's influence can be seen in our language (e.g., id, ego, superego), in psychoanalysis as a method of treatment for mental illness, and in the many disciples he created.

Neo-Freudians

Anna Freud, Freud's daughter, became his successor in psychoanalysis. Without academic credentials, she became a child analyst after being analyzed by her father. In her best-known work, Anna Freud described the ego defense mechanisms that her father had earlier identified. Some of the major mechanisms are repression, regression, rationalization, projection, reaction formation, displacement, and sublimation.

Like Anna Freud, Melanie Klein was a child analyst. She became a rival of Anna Freud, and the Freuds' arrival in England produced a rift within the British psychoanalytic movement.

Karen Horney's version of psychoanalysis disagreed with Freud's approach to feminine psychology and with Freud's emphasis on the sexual instinct. Horney identified ten neurotic needs, which included the need for affection and approval, the need for power, the ambition for personal achievement, and the need for perfection.

John Bowlby and Mary Ainsworth studied attachment behavior in children and developed a theory of human attachment. Part of the empirical basis for Bowlby's theory came from primate mother-infant attachment studies, such as those of Harry Harlow.

Analyzed by Anna Freud, Erik Erikson is best known for his work in developmental psychology. To Freud's psychosexual stages of development, Erikson added adolescence, young adulthood, adulthood, maturity, and old age.

CONNECTIONS QUESTIONS

1. Describe as many connections as you can between conceptions of mental illness and treatments for it.

2. How might the social *Zeitgeist* of the late 19th century and the various wars involving Germany be connected to Freud's theory?

3. How are mesmerism and hypnosis connected to psychoanalytic theory and treatment?
4. What effects on Freud's theory might we expect to see from Freud's connection with Brentano? From his association with Meynert? With Brücke and the "Helmholtz School"?
5. What sort of connections can you draw between Freud's work and subfields of psychology such as developmental, Social, and cognitive?

6. What connections can you make between the various neo-Freudians and changes in the psychoanalytic conceptions of development?
7. Draw a concept map connecting the major ideas and people in this chapter, and compare your results with one possible solution provided on p. 568.

SUGGESTED READINGS

Brill, A. A. (Ed. and Trans.) (1938). *The basic writings of Sigmund Freud.* New York: The Modern Library. This collection of Freud's works consists of such classic writings as *Psychopathology of Everyday Life, The Interpretation of Dreams, Totem and Taboo,* and *The History of the Psychoanalytic Movement.* Many similar volumes can be found.

Erdelyi, M. H. (1985). *Psychoanalysis: Freud's cognitive psychology.* New York: W. H. Freeman and Company. This is a scholarly work that advances the thesis that Freud was much more than just a psychotherapist. In addition, it has high intrinsic interest, because many of its examples are drawn from sources such as dreams, religion, and art.

Freud, A. (1937). *The ego and the mechanisms of defence.* London: The Hogarth Press Ltd. This is Anna Freud's most important work, which details the various ways in which the ego seeks to protect itself when threatened by conflicting demands of the id and superego.

Freud, E. L. (Ed.) (1992). *Letters of Sigmund Freud.* New York: Dover Publications. The letters of famous people are good sources of information about them and their times, and this collection of Freud's is no exception.

Gay, P. (1988). *Freud: A life for our time.* New York: W. W. Norton & Company. This is a readable and scholarly biography of Freud. Gay's qualifications for writing the work include the fact that he is a graduate of the Western New England Institute for Psychoanalysis.

Jones, E. (1953–1957). *The life and work of Sigmund Freud* (Vols. 1–3). New York: Basic Books, Inc. One of Freud's most loyal disciples, Jones produced what is considered the definitive biography of his mentor and friend.

Roazen, P. (1975). *Freud and his followers.* New York: Alfred A. Knopf. Roazen's book contains excellent pictures and interesting biographies of all the major, and most of the minor, characters in the history of the psychoanalytic movement.

Shakow, D. (1969). Psychoanalysis. In D. L. Krantz (Ed.), *Schools of psychology: A symposium* (pp. 87–122). New York: Appleton-Century-Crofts. Shakow's essay is an excellent overview of the psychoanalytic movement.

Beyond Psychoanalysis

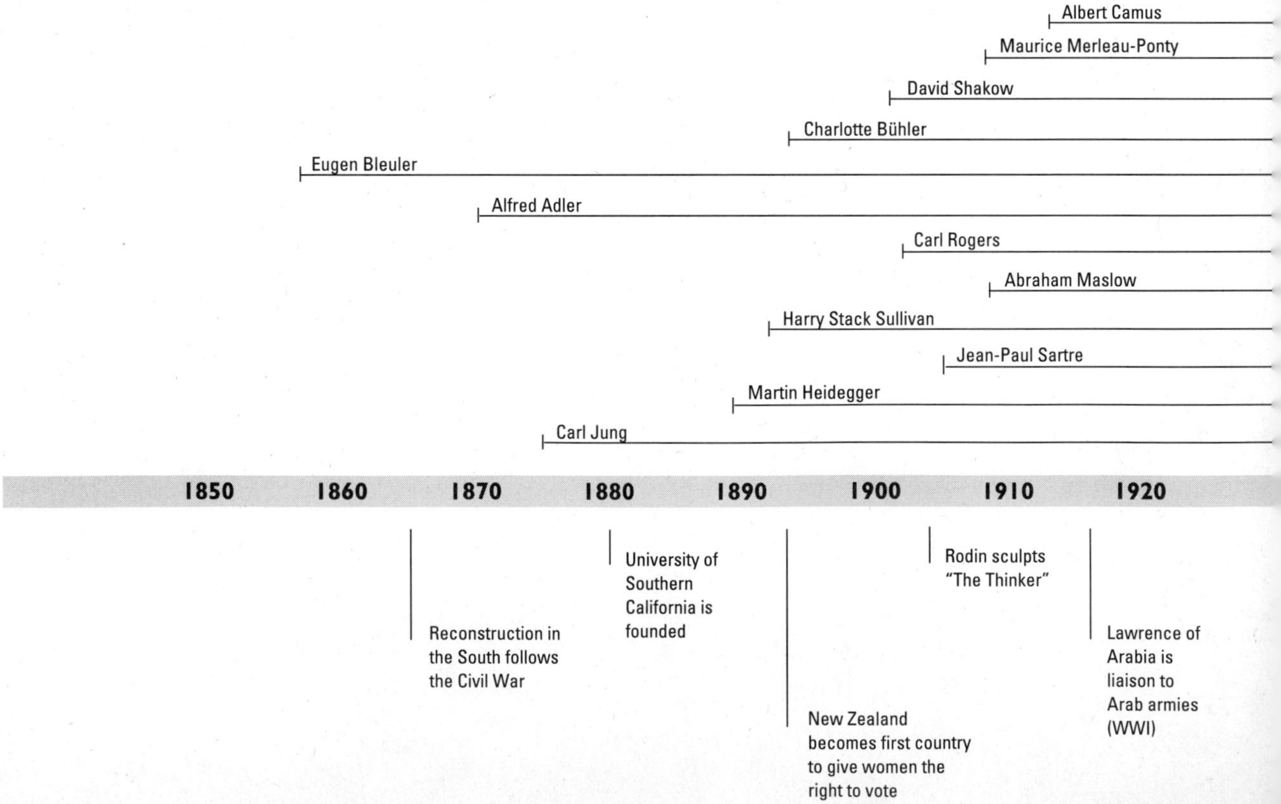

Albert Camus

Maurice Merleau-Ponty

David Shakow

Charlotte Bühler

Eugen Bleuler

Alfred Adler

Carl Rogers

Abraham Maslow

Harry Stack Sullivan

Jean-Paul Sartre

Martin Heidegger

Carl Jung

| 1850 | 1860 | 1870 | 1880 | 1890 | 1900 | 1910 | 1920 |

Reconstruction in
the South follows
the Civil War

University of
Southern
California is
founded

Rodin sculpts
"The Thinker"

Lawrence of
Arabia is
liaison to
Arab armies
(WWI)

New Zealand
becomes first country
to give women the
right to vote

In the last chapter, we examined the work and influence of Sigmund Freud, the patriarch of psychoanalysis. In this chapter, we will consider some of the developments in personality theory and psychotherapy that go beyond Freud's system. Clinical psychology is a broad area, so our coverage will, of necessity, be highly selective. We will explore some of the psychodynamic theories that emerged from the Freudian framework, including various existential and humanistic approaches. In closing, we will review some of the important developments in the practice of clinical psychology, as well as some of the connections between American clinical psychology and the psychiatric community. For example, David Shakow's career (discussed later) began at a time when there essentially were no clinical training programs and ended near the present day—when the number of APA-approved clinical programs exceeds

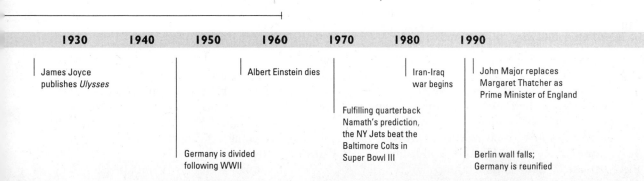

1930   1940   1950   1960   1970   1980   1990

James Joyce publishes *Ulysses*

Albert Einstein dies

Iran-Iraq war begins

John Major replaces Margaret Thatcher as Prime Minister of England

Fulfilling quarterback Namath's prediction, the NY Jets beat the Baltimore Colts in Super Bowl III

Germany is divided following WWII

Berlin wall falls; Germany is reunified

150. Throughout Shakow's lifetime, clinical psychology greatly expanded on its Freudian foundation, with many elements of clinical theory and practice becoming a standard part of academic psychology (e.g., a required course in abnormal psychology).

PSYCHOANALYSIS BEYOND FREUD

At the end of Chapter 15, we discussed one group of neo-Freudians—Anna Freud, Melanie Klein, and Karen Horney—which represents only one set among many. In fact, after Freud, several forms of psychotherapy appeared, and the ones with some connection to Freud's system are now often called either "psychoanalytic" or "psychodynamic." Within the neo-Freudian tradition, further distinctions can be made. For example, where Freud emphasized intrapsychic conflicts pertaining to the satisfaction of basic desires or needs, one of the later approaches emphasizes conflicts based on object relations, which are interpersonal relationships as they are represented in the mind of the individual. This approach is called **object-relations theory** (e.g., Kernberg, 1976). Two other, different variations on the Freudian system were developed by one-time members of Freud's inner circle—Alfred Adler and Carl Jung.

Alfred Adler

Alfred Adler (1870–1937) was born in a suburb of Vienna, the second child in a family of six. His father was a prosperous grain merchant, and Adler was his father's favorite. As a child, Adler suffered from rickets, which prevented him from competing successfully with his older brother and perhaps set the stage for his later conception of organ inferiority and compensation.

At 5, Adler nearly died from pneumonia, and this experience determined his choice of a medical career. With this goal in mind, Adler enrolled at the University of Vienna, receiving his M.D. degree in 1895. Initially, he specialized in ophthalmology, then became a general practitioner, and finally changed to psychiatry, abandoning general practice

because of his distress when young patients died. Two years after he graduated from the University, Adler married Raissa Timofejewna, a Russian, and they had three girls and a boy, two of whom became Adlerian psychiatrists.

According to one biography (Bottome, 1939), Adler gained Freud's attention by defending Freud's book on dream analysis against a highly critical review, although after a "thorough search," Jones (1955) was unable to corroborate this account. At any rate, in the autumn of 1902, Freud sent postcards to the four men—Adler, Kahane, Reitler, and Stekel—who became the nucleus of the Vienna Psychoanalytic Society. Adler quickly became a leader of the group and succeeded Freud as the president of the Society in 1910. At the same time, he and Stekel became co-editors of the newly founded *Zentralblatt für Psychoanalyse*. However, by this time Adler's views on psychoanalysis had evolved, and his separation from Freud was inevitable.

Early in 1911, Adler was asked to present his views to the Society, which he did at meetings in January and February. Two additional evenings were devoted to discussions of Adler's theories, with Freud unstinting in his criticisms. Perhaps trying to smooth over the differences, Stekel voiced the "opinion that there was no contradiction between Freud's theories and Adler's, to which Freud replied that unfortunately for this view both Adler and Freud thought there was" (Jones, 1955, p. 132). Adler immediately resigned his presidency and after a few months resigned from the Society and stepped down as co-editor of the *Zentralblatt*. Although his break with orthodox psychoanalysis was complete, there was some truth to Stekel's observation. We will focus on the differences between Adler and Freud, not on the many similarities.

Adler formed his own group, which soon became known as the Society of Individual Psychology. After World War I, Adler became interested in preventing neurosis by establishing child-guidance centers in Vienna's public schools. Through the 1920s and early 1930s, Individual Psychology attracted many adherents, reaching a peak in Europe just before Hitler came to power.

A prolific author and almost compulsive lecturer, Adler began making regular trips to America in

FIGURE 16–1.   Alfred Adler.
Source: National Library of Medicine.

1925, lecturing to audiences of all types and sizes. In 1932, Adler became Professor of Medical Psychology at the Long Island College of Medicine, and in 1934, he settled permanently in New York City. While on a lecture tour in 1937, Adler (Figure 16–1) died of a heart attack in Aberdeen, Scotland.

Adler's Individual Psychology

Adler's personality theory differs from Freud's in several fundamental ways: First, he de-emphasized sexuality and particularly the idea of infantile sexuality. Second, Adler developed an ego-oriented psychology that made consciousness, not the unconscious, the center of personality. In contrast to Freud's view of behavior ruled by instincts, Adler stressed human social urges, and social interest

molds the Adlerian personality. Although Freud "assumed an innate evil component of human nature . . . which must be suppressed by some power to make life in society possible, Adler in accordance with all democratic and liberalizing tendencies . . . postulated an innate readiness for social living, which through encouragement can be nurtured and developed into a full-fledged social interest" (Ansbacher, 1959, p. 380).

Adler's desire to be in touch with the masses extended to his psychiatric practice: A comparison of the socioeconomic status of Adler's and Freud's patients revealed that Freud tended to treat the upper classes, whereas Adler focused on the middle class and the working poor (Wassermann, 1958). This difference undoubtedly influenced Freud's and Adler's theories, with Freud's upper-class patients exhibiting a "comparatively high degree of sexual misery alongside the freedom from financial cares" (p. 624). By contrast, Adler's working-class patients were more concerned with basic problems of existence. As Wassermann put it, "Where Freud sees nothing but a distressed Eros, Adler finds the drive for success to be the motivating force of the human psyche" (p. 625).

Inferiority and Striving for Superiority.   In 1907, as a physician, Adler addressed the question of why one person develops an illness involving one organ (e.g., the heart), whereas in another person a different organ (e.g., the liver) is at fault. He suggested that organ inferiority is the answer: The heart patient has a basically inferior heart, whereas the liver is inherently defective in the other. Adler also noted that a person with an organ weakness often tries to compensate for this weakness through training. For example, although Demosthenes (384–322 B.C.) stuttered as a child, through practice he became Greece's greatest orator.

Soon, Adler broadened his concept of organ inferiority to include any feelings of inferiority, whether physically based or psychologically based. Initially, Adler equated inferiority with femininity and called the resultant compensation the "masculine protest." This male chauvinistic view was replaced by the idea that inferiority feelings result from incompleteness or imperfection in any realm of life, and the masculine protest became a **striving for superiority**. The feeling of inferiority and the effort to compensate become humanity's great driving forces—people are pushed by the need to overcome inferiority and drawn by the need for superiority.

Adopting a less intense version of Nietzsche's (Chapter 15) "will to power," Adler believed that the striving for superiority is innate, carrying us from one stage of development to the next higher stage throughout life. In addition, what Adler meant by a striving for superiority was that the healthy person strives for a sense of completeness or self-actualization and is not necessarily trying to achieve a position of leadership or eminence. By contrast, the neurotic strives for personal recognition and power, that is, for egotistical or selfish goals.

Soon after his break with psychoanalysis, Adler was greatly influenced by German philosopher Hans Vaihinger's *The Psychology of "As If."* The book suggested that humans live according to many ideas—for example, "the ends justify the means"—that have no counterparts in reality. We treat these fictional goals as if they were real and strive toward them. For Adler, this was the answer to Freud's rigid determinism resulting from constitutional factors and early experiences. Adler believed that we are motivated more by our expectations of the future than by our past experiences.

In striving toward our fictional goals, we develop our own unique style of life. Adler tied his idea of the **style of life** to the concepts we have already discussed in the following way:

> We have seen how human beings with weak organs . . . suffer from a feeling or complex of inferiority. But as human beings cannot endure this for long, the inferiority feeling stimulates them . . . to movement and action. This results in a person having a goal. Individual Psychology has long called the consistent movement toward the goal a plan of life. But because this name has sometimes led to mistakes among students, it is now called a style of life. (Adler, 1929; Ansbacher & Ansbacher, 1956, p. 173)

Each of us has the goal to achieve superiority (completeness), but there are many ways this goal can be attained. The different ways constitute the different possible lifestyles, which are established early in life. Once the individual's lifestyle has been formed, usually by 4 or 5, all subsequent experiences are interpreted and incorporated according to it.

Adler believed in a coherence of the personality and the unity of the individual, concepts with a Gestalt flavor. In fact, he acknowledged that "Gestalt psychology shows a better understanding of this coherence [than psychoanalysis]" (Adler, 1929; Ansbacher & Ansbacher, 1956, p. 175), and Max Wertheimer (Chapter 14) proposed a concept similar to Adler's "style of life."

Adlerian Therapy. According to Adler, psychopathology is the result of a lifestyle that is inadequate for solving problems in the person's current life situation. The task of therapy is to reorganize the patient's style of life. But this involves first giving the patient an understanding of the current lifestyle through the investigation of the person's earliest memories, birth-order position, and dreams.

Adler was interested in a person's earliest memory because it shows "some dominant interest of the individual, since the creative tendency of the imagination always produces fragments of the life ideal . . ." (Adler, 1930, p. 404). Adler found the early-memory method an economical way to assess an individual's personality.

Adler believed that birth order is important for personality, because each child encounters a different environment from its siblings (Orgler, 1963). For example, the first-born child initially receives a lot of attention and spoiling but is dethroned with the next child's birth. Oldest children usually show an interest in the past—when they were the center of attention—and often develop into responsible, protective adults. However, according to Adler, criminals, drunkards, and neurotics are frequently first-born children.

The second-born or middle child may well grow up to be ambitious, because he or she is always trying to compete with the older sibling. In later life, the middle child may become a revolutionary, believing on the basis of his or her earlier striving that there is no power that cannot be overcome.

Spoiled, the youngest child is most likely to have problems in adulthood. One reason for later difficulties is that the youngest child may develop severe inferiority feelings, because the older children are bigger, stronger, and more experienced.

Adler viewed dreams as just another expression of a person's style of life and considered a person's fabricated dream to be as meaningful as a real one, because "the person's imagination cannot create anything but that which his style of life commands" (Adler, 1929; Ansbacher & Ansbacher, 1956, p. 359). Adler considered that dreams have a problem-solving function, connecting the dreamer's problem with its goal of attainment.

For Adler, as for Freud, dreams contain common elements—symbols—that can be interpreted. However, the hallmark of Individual Psychology is that the individual is unique, and we should not look for universal symbols. The same element in two individuals' dreams may have different meanings and must be interpreted in terms of each person's total personality. For example, two people might dream of having an examination. With one, the interpretation might be that the person is not prepared to face some current problem; with the other, the dream may mean that the person enjoys challenges.

Adler's Influence

Adler's contributions to personality theory included an emphasis on social determinants of behavior, an emphasis on the uniqueness of personality (i.e., Individual Psychology), a de-emphasis on the contributions of sexuality to personality, and a focus on consciousness and the ego. Paradoxically, although Adler's concepts have been incorporated into many modern personality theories, including psychoanalytic theories in particular, his contribution has not always been recognized (Ansbacher, 1994).

Adler's approach to theory and therapy is sustained through a number of organizations, including the North American Society of Adlerian Psychology, which publishes a newsletter and the quarterly journal *Individual Psychology.* In Europe, the largest Adlerian society is in Germany, and its

journal is the *Zeitschrift für Individualpsychologie,* published quarterly.

Carl Gustav Jung

Carl Gustav Jung (1875–1961) was born in Kesswil, which is on Lake Constance in Switzerland, the son of a minister in the Swiss Reformed Church. Jung's father was also an Oriental and classical scholar who was described by Jung as kind, tolerant, somewhat conventional, and weak, at least in contrast to Jung's mother. Jung characterized his mother, a minister's daughter, as inconsistent, the possessor of two dispositions: one unstable and mystical and the other more traditional and practical. Jung identified with his mother's mystical side.

For his first 9 years, Jung was an only child in a family plagued by marital discord. Perhaps because of this, Jung "developed a deep distrust of women in general, and an ambivalent attitude toward his mother in particular" (Storr, 1973, p. 2). Another possible residue of his childhood was Jung's ability to leave completely contradictory impressions in the minds of people who knew him. For example, Gay (1988) noted that people found Jung "sociable but difficult, amusing at times and taciturn at others, outwardly self-confident yet vulnerable to criticism" (p. 198). Similarly, Alexander (1991) found Jung (Figure 16–2) described by various people as "arrogant, vain, ambitious, status seeking, competitive, and even untrustworthy . . . ," these negative characteristics occurring alongside such positive designations as "humble, caring, undefensive, even saintly . . ." (p. 157).

Jung's family moved near Basel when he was 4, and Jung went to school there from the age of 11. Entering the University of Basel, Jung intended to become an archeologist. However, there was no one in archeology at the University, and Jung's family was too poor to send him away from home, so he chose a medical career instead.

Jung completed his medical degree in 1900 and had nearly decided to become a surgeon when he encountered a textbook of psychiatry by Krafft-Ebing (Chapter 15). Krafft-Ebing described the field as being in such a primitive state that textbooks

FIGURE 16–2.   Carl Jung.

Source: Archives of the History of American Psychology.

about it were inevitably marked by the authors' subjective assumptions and personality. This description appealed to Jung because of his dual need to be associated with an objective natural science and to have the freedom to pursue his lifelong interests in religious speculation, the search for meaning, and mysticism. Perhaps amorphous psychiatry would afford what he needed (Storr, 1973).

After completing his medical degree, Jung became an assistant to Eugen Bleuler at the Burghölzli Mental Hospital in Zurich. **Eugen Bleuler** (1857–1939) had studied briefly with Charcot (Chapter 15) and is known particularly as an early expert on schizophrenia, a term that he coined. Bleuler had succeeded Auguste-Henri Forel in 1898 as director of the Burghölzli. As you may recall, Forel spoke on hysteria in America at Hall's invitation (Chapter 10).

Bleuler had made the Burghölzli an outstanding center for psychiatric research by the early 1900s, and physicians from other countries often came to

observe the latest in the diagnosis and treatment of mental illness. In addition, Bleuler encouraged the staff physicians to travel, and this gave Jung the opportunity in 1902 to spend a semester at the Salpêtrière psychiatric center that earlier influenced Freud. There, he heard Janet (Chapter 15) lecture on psychopathology.

Shortly after joining Bleuler, Jung was asked to review Freud's *The Interpretation of Dreams* for the staff. From Freud's dream book, Jung became familiar with the concept of repression of material into the unconscious, and this concept dovetailed nicely with work on the study of word associations that he undertook at Bleuler's request. Using Galton's method (Chapter 9), Jung asked individuals to respond to singly presented words with the first word that came to mind, recording both the response and its latency. Jung believed that words a person responded to more slowly than average had special meaning for the person, which could be found in a unified core of ideas in the unconscious accompanied by excessive or inappropriate affect, which Jung called a "complex." These complexes were in the unconscious because of repression.

Jung's discovery of the agreement between his word association studies and Freudian concepts presented him with a dilemma: Should he become a Freudian and risk damaging the academic career he was contemplating—Freud had a negative standing in academic circles at this point—or should he publish his results without mentioning Freud? Jung heeded the inner voice that told him:

> "If you do a thing like that, as if you had no knowledge of Freud, it would be a piece of trickery. You cannot build your life upon a lie." With that, the question was settled. From then on I became an open partisan of Freud's and fought for him. (Jung, 1961, p. 148)

In 1906, Jung sent Freud a copy of the paper on his word association work, and then the following year a copy of his monograph *On the Psychology of Dementia Praecox*, in which he had singled out Freud's "brilliant conceptions." Jung did have one reservation to Freudian ideas, however—he was unwilling to attribute as much significance to youthful sexual trauma as Freud, and this would be the rock on which their relationship eventually foundered. In 1906, Freud and Jung began a correspondence that lasted until 1913 and involved over 300 letters. The following year they had their first meeting, with Jung later reporting that they had "met at one o'clock in the afternoon and talked virtually without a pause for thirteen hours" (Jung, 1961, p. 149).

Although Freud apparently truly liked Jung (Gay, 1988), he was also elated over what Jung brought to the psychoanalytic movement. Jung was young, dynamic, handsome, brilliant, associated with a famous mental hospital, and first and foremost, not Jewish. Heretofore the movement had involved primarily Jewish physicians in Vienna, and Freud saw Jung as a propagandist who would bring significant expansion of psychoanalysis beyond its provincial boundaries. He also saw Jung as his heir to the throne of psychoanalysis, writing him in April 1907: "Your person has filled me with confidence in the future" (as cited in Gay, p. 203).

For his part, Jung saw Freud as a father figure, writing in 1908 to ask Freud "to let me enjoy your friendship not as that of equals but as that of father and son" (as cited in Gay, 1988, p. 202). Despite frequent expressions of affection between the two, throughout their association there were hints of future difficulties. One of the first hints came in 1909, when Freud, Jung, and Ferenczi were waiting to board ship for the voyage to America to attend Hall's Clark Conference (Chapter 10). Jung began talking about prehistoric remains being unearthed in Germany, and Freud, interpreting the topic as a veiled death wish against him, fainted.

In 1909, Jung resigned from the Burghölzli because of a growing private practice, and in 1913 he resigned his University of Zurich instructorship to devote himself to his practice, his writing, his training and research, and his travel. The same year also brought the final separation from Freud and psychoanalysis. Although it is likely that Jung was never able to accept Freud's emphasis on sexuality, other factors ranging from Jung's interest in mystical experiences to jealousy over Freud's writing skills may have contributed to the breakup.

Throughout his relationship with Freud, Jung had sought to expand the meaning of Freudian libido, to make it encompass a general mental energy instead of focusing on the sensual drives. On a 1912 lecture tour in America, Jung divested himself of what he considered psychoanalytic baggage—such concepts as childhood sexuality and the Oedipus complex—and redefined libido. Adding insult to injury, Jung cheerfully told Freud that his revised psychoanalysis had converted many who had been offended by Freud's pansexuality. Although there were brief reconciliations, Freud was exultant when Jung finally resigned as president of the International Psychoanalytic Association.

Freud found the whole affair distressing and considered Jung's departure from psychoanalysis "a great loss," but Jung was even more disturbed. "After the parting of the ways with Freud, a period of inner uncertainty began for me," he wrote in his autobiography. "It would be no exaggeration to call it a state of disorientation" (Jung, 1961, p. 170). Jung's disoriented state included a feeling of inner pressure that seemed to be from "something in the air," which was revealed to him on August 1, 1914, with the outbreak of World War I. In response, Jung began a self-analysis that led to his own personality theory, which became known as **Analytical Psychology**. "The rest of his life was devoted to the elaboration of the insights which he attained during his self-analysis . . ." (Storr, 1973, p. 18). The end of Jung's period of mental turmoil was signalled by the publication of *Psychological Types or the Psychology of Individuation* (Jung, 1921/1923).

Psychological Types

As Jung saw it, the libido is directed either inward by the person or outward. Jung called the inward-directed attitude **introversion** and the outward-directed one **extraversion**. The introvert is oriented toward the inner, subjective world of ideas, whereas the extravert is oriented toward the external, objective world of objects and people. The introvert tends toward self-sufficiency, whereas the extravert needs people around. Both of the attitudes are present in everyone, but usually one is dominant.

In addition to the two attitudes, Jung identified four psychological functions: thinking, feeling, sensation, and intuition. Thinking and feeling are ways of making decisions. The person who predominantly uses thinking decides on the basis of logical and objective considerations, whereas the feeling person decides on the basis of personal, subjective values.

Sensation and intuition are called the perceiving functions because they are two different ways of taking in information. "[S]ensation and intuition . . . are perceptive—they make us aware of what is happening, but do not interpret or evaluate it" (Jung, 1933, pp. 91–92). A person using sensation acquires information through the primary senses, whereas the intuitive individual acquires and processes information unconsciously—through a hunch, for example.

In summarizing the four functions, Jung (1933) wrote that, "[s]ensation establishes what is actually given, thinking enables us to recognize its meaning, feeling tells us its value, and finally intuition points to the possibilities of the whence and whither that lie within the immediate facts" (p. 93). The **Myers-Briggs Type Indicator** or **MBTI** (Myers & McCaulley, 1985) is a personality assessment device developed independently of Jung to implement Jung's type theory. In addition to Jung's attitudes and functions, the MBTI includes the judging-perceiving scale.

Personality Structure

For Jung, the personality, or psyche, consisted of several different, interacting systems. The major systems are the ego, the personal unconscious and its complexes, and the collective unconscious and its archetypes (persona, anima and animus, shadow, and self).

The Ego. The ego is the conscious mind, which is comprised of our perceptions, thoughts, memories, and feelings. It is the mechanism through which we interact with the environment. Before work indicating the importance of the unconscious, the ego was considered to express the psychic totality. Now, the "ego, once the monarch of this totality, is dethroned. It remains merely the centre of consciousness" (Jung, 1939, p. 4).

The Personal Unconscious. The **personal unconscious** is a superficial layer of the unconscious containing experiences that were once conscious but have been repressed, suppressed, or simply forgotten and also experiences that were too weak to affect the ego. Material in the personal unconscious is relatively accessible to consciousness. The personal unconscious contains an unknown number of **complexes**, which are organized groups of memories, thoughts, perceptions, and feelings. "Complexes are autonomous groups of associations that have a tendency to move by themselves, to live their own life apart from our intentions" (Jung, 1968, p. 81).

The Collective Unconscious. Jung believed that there is a deeper layer of the unconscious, which he called the **collective unconscious**. He chose the term "collective" to illustrate that this part of the unconscious is universal, containing "contents and modes of behaviour that are more or less the same everywhere and in all individuals. The collective unconscious, so far as we know, is self-identical in all Western men and thus constitutes a psychic foundation, superpersonal in its nature, that is present in every one of us" (Jung, 1939, pp. 52–53).

The collective unconscious contains the archetypes, a term that Jung noted came from St. Augustine (Chapter 3). An **archetype** is a universal thought-form (idea) that transcends the individual's experience; it is an unconscious, inherited predisposition to perceive or respond in a particular way, the trace of the collective experience of humankind. That is, because throughout time people have encountered the same types of experiences, they have evolved the tendency to respond in a certain way to a particular experience. Myths, fables, dreams, visions, and works of art reveal such archetypes as birth, death, power, magic, God, and the hero.

Although all archetypes can be considered autonomous systems, some are so developed that they may be treated as separate personality systems. These evolved archetypes include the persona, the shadow, and the anima and animus.

The **persona** is the role a person assumes in society, the side of personality for public consumption, which may or may not reveal a person's true nature. If a person becomes too identified with the persona—the judge who can never take off the judicial robes, for example—this is detrimental to the personality because it means that other personality parts are being neglected. An example of such a neglected part is the archetype often paired with the persona—the shadow.

The **shadow** is the residue of the animal nature of the human being, what we have inherited from more "primitive" forms of life. It is the dark side of our nature and is assumed to be responsible for our socially unwanted thoughts, feelings, and actions. The shadow is also a potent source of creative energy.

Jung's recognition of the importance of human sexual duality is evident in the anima and the animus. Simply put, the **anima** is "the woman in a man . . . ," and the **animus** is "the man in a woman" (Jung, 1939, p. 19). By living together through the ages, women have acquired some of the characteristics of men and vice versa. Men and women have the potential to understand each other because of the anima and animus, respectively.

The interactions between the ego and the archetypal realm involve the archetypes we have identified: the persona, the shadow, the anima and the animus. In addition, there is an overall integrating archetype that Jung called the "self."

The self arises through **individuation**, which is the process that makes a person a unique, whole entity. Through individuation, the self becomes the totality of the psyche. "The self is not only the centre, but also the circumference that encloses consciousness and the unconscious; it is the centre of this totality, as the ego is the centre of consciousness" (Jung, 1939, p. 96). The self archetype is revealed in a number of symbols, the primary one being the mandala, or magic circle, which is any of a variety of geometric designs representing the universe.

According to Jung, the ultimate goal of life is the realization of the self, which, often sought, is seldom achieved. Because complete development of the different personality components is needed before the self can emerge, self-realization does not appear, if at all, before middle age. That is, childhood, adolescence, and early adulthood are periods when person-

ality's conflicting components are being reconciled. During middle age, a person seriously begins to strive to reorient the center of the personality from the conscious ego to a region midway between the consciousness and the unconscious, which is the self's domain.

Personality Development

Implicit in much of our discussion has been the importance of opposites for personality development. Jung held that conflict between personality systems creates tension that is the essence of life. Without such tension, personality does not exist. Both Freud and Hegel before him (Chapter 5) were also conflict theorists.

Opposition is seen in Jung's attitudes and functions, between introversion and extraversion, for example. There is further opposition between the ego and the collective unconscious, between the anima and the animus, and so on. Jung saw conflict everywhere in the personality.

Nevertheless, Jung believed that the union of opposites is possible and that the different systems can be integrated into perfect wholeness. This is the ultimate goal of self-realization, revealed to us in symbols found in such venues as dreams, myths, art, and religion.

Unlike Freud, Jung did not detail the stages through which personality develops. Taking an optimistic viewpoint, Jung believed that we are continually striving or trying to progress from a less perfect to a more perfect stage of development. In practice, perfection will not be achieved, but the ultimate goal is the realization of the self, which represents a harmonious blending of the various personality systems.

Jung saw the transition from a youthful, passionate person into a wise, spiritual person as the most important event in life, but one fraught with pitfalls. For example, if the spiritual values of middle age fail to use all the energy the person formerly invested in the aims of early adulthood—for example, acquiring a vocation, marriage, rearing a family—then there will be excess energy that will act against the integration of the psyche. Jung had perhaps his greatest success in treating middle-aged persons whose core problem was a need to find satisfactory outlets for this excessive and undirected energy.

Jung's Influence

Jung's influence on academic psychology has been limited, which is borne out by even a cursory look at histories of psychology. For example, Boring's (1950) *A History of Experimental Psychology* contains six pages devoted to Freud and only six *lines* to Jung. More recently, Fancher's (1990) *Pioneers of Psychology* contains a lengthy chapter on Freud but just two sentences that mention Jung.

There are a number of reasons for traditional psychology's lack of acceptance of Jungian concepts. For one thing, his writing is difficult, at best. Freud wrote gracefully and logically, whereas Jung often wrote feverishly, flinging material together hastily to form a difficult hodgepodge of ideas. In addition, the source of many of Jung's concepts—for example, religion, astrology, alchemy—militates against their receiving an unbiased appraisal from most psychologists. For the same reason, Jung's thinking has had a much greater influence on disciplines outside of psychology, including such diverse areas as literature, film making, and art education (e.g., McWhinnie, 1985). Jung's ideas have also found favor with a nonscientific populace in Western society interested in such phenomena as occultism, mysticism, meditation, and self-fulfillment.

Jung's characterization of personality types is perhaps the work for which he is best known in psychology. Using the statistical technique of factor analysis, Hans Eysenck (Chapter 18), a vocal opponent of psychoanalysis, found evidence supporting Jung's introvert-extravert distinction (Eysenck & Rachman, 1965). Tests to identify personality type based on Jung's work have been developed, and the Myers-Briggs Type Indicator is the focus of a quarterly research journal—the *Journal of Psychological Type*. From his interests in such mysterious phenomena as "synchronicity" to his personality theory, a brief survey of Jung's life and analytical psychology cannot hope to do justice to the breadth of canvas on which he worked.

EXISTENTIAL AND HUMANISTIC APPROACHES

In Chapter 15, we briefly considered Kierkegaard and Nietzsche, two of the better-known existential philosophers of the 19th century. Existentialism in general, and Kierkegaard and Nietzsche in particular, have significantly impacted the evolution of psychology—especially clinical psychology. A humanistic "Third Force" (discussed later) emerged in post–World War II American psychology, which incorporated many ideas from existential philosophy.

The Backdrop of Existential Philosophy

Although Kierkegaard and Nietzsche are remembered as existential philosophy's founders, they also represent the beginnings of something new within psychology. From Kiekegaard's interest in anxiety and depression through Nietzsche's analysis of man relative to society, both philosophers advocated an approach that placed questions about personal freedom and life's meaning at the forefront.

Two themes perhaps best capture existential philosophy's appeal for psychology. The first is that subjective meaning, rather than a third-person account of brain or behavior, should be psychology's central focus. This theme is not peculiar to existentialism, as the same idea can be found clearly in James (Chapter 10), Freud, and other important psychologists.

Existential philosophy's second major theme is that humans have the freedom to make choices and thus must take responsibility for their choices. For Kierkegaard and Nietzsche, this meant resisting the tendency to consider God or society responsible for failures and successes instead of accepting them as the result of freely chosen actions. In the language of contemporary psychology, this theme means resisting reductionistic and deterministic accounts of human behavior that assign the causes of human action either to biology or to the environment. The existentialist is trying to combat the human desire to assign an action's cause to an outside agency (e.g., God, the environment, instincts) rather than assuming personal responsibility for it.

In addition to Kierkegaard and Nietzsche, there are several existential philosophers with important connections to psychology. Two of the best known also won the Nobel Prize in literature: Albert Camus received the award in 1957, and Jean-Paul Sartre declined it in 1964.

Jean-Paul Sartre and Albert Camus

Jean-Paul Sartre (1905–1980) was born in Paris to a military officer father and a mother who was the first cousin of famed theologian/physician Albert Schweitzer. Sartre completed his doctorate in philosophy from the École Normale Supérieure in the late 1920s, with a focus on French philosopher **Henri Bergson** (1859–1941), winner of the 1927 Nobel Prize in literature. Bergson is sometimes called the French William James because his work so closely resembles that of James. Before World War II, Sartre taught philosophy at several prestigious universities in France and studied phenomenology under both Husserl (Chapter 8) and Heidegger (discussed later) in Germany. Captured early in the war, Sartre spent 9 months as a prisoner before being released and joining the French Resistance as an essayist and reporter.

Several of Sartre's major works first appeared during the tumultuous years before and during World War II, including his moving psychological novel, *Nausea* (Sartre, 1938). Sartre's most substantive contribution to theoretical psychology and the philosophy of mind—*Being and Nothingness* (Sartre, 1943)—provides an existential analysis of the structure and function of consciousness. His best-known play, *No Exit* (Sartre, 1947), is a harsh look at the relationship between self and others, which explores how we carefully try to manage the public aspects of our self. After the war, Sartre never returned to a full-time academic position, working instead as a writer in several different forms (e.g., plays, novels) and on an array of topics including philosophy, psychology, and social criticism.

Even without the advantages of a university position, Sartre's influence on French intellectuals and existential philosophy and psychology internationally was enormous. For example, Sartre's long-time associate, **Simone de Beauvoir** (1908–1986), produced pioneering writings in existentialism and feminism. De Beauvoir's *The Second Sex* is a classic work in the psychology of women and illustrates the impact of existential thought on psychology beyond clinical theory. Sartre's own psychological works are perhaps best classified as social psychological—such as his analysis of the dreadful power of the human gaze (How do you feel when someone stares at you?)—or as existential clinical theory.

The son of a farm laborer, **Albert Camus** (1913–1960) was born in Mondovi, Algeria. His father was killed early in World War I, and his mother moved to Belcourt, a suburb of Algiers, to better support the family. An able student and soccer player, Camus nevertheless struggled with tuberculosis.

Before World War II, Camus studied philosophy, completing a thesis on Plotinus (Chapter 3) in 1936. Like Sartre, during the war Camus served as a writer for the French Underground and also produced many of his own classic contributions. These include *The Myth of Sisyphus,* Camus's existential treatise exploring the meaning of life, the nature of absurdity, and the possibility of suicide, and his intensely gripping novel, *The Stranger*. In *The Stranger,* Camus considers in detail a range of psychological phenomena including the causes of aggression, the nature of guilt and grief, and the social aspects of emotional display.

After the war, Camus worked as a writer until his death in an automobile accident. Later works that contributed to Camus's receipt of the Nobel Prize include *The Plague*—which explores the social psychology of quarantine—and *The Fall,* perhaps his most classic statement of such basic existential issues as personal choice and subjective meaning. Although Camus was never closely associated with academia, his short and engaging novels are often required reading for university courses in existential philosophy and existential psychology, with the result that Camus may be the most commonly read of the postwar existentialists.

Sartre and Camus were writers who found Cold War anxieties fertile ground in which to sow the seeds of existentialism for the general public

FIGURE 16–3.   Martin Heidegger.

Source: Philosophical Library, New York.

through works of fiction. At the other extreme, Martin Heidegger was an academician who felt that everyday language inadequately conveyed the ideas of his rich existential, phenomenological, philosophical system.

Martin Heidegger

A student of Edmund Husserl, **Martin Heidegger** (1889–1976) has become an increasingly controversial figure. On the one hand, his contributions to philosophy are considered among the most significant of the 20th century. Unfortunately, questions about his character and about his relations with the Nazis have continued to cast a shadow over his legacy. Heidegger is shown in Figure 16–3.

The son of a Catholic sexton, Heidegger was born in the Black Forest region of Germany. His interest in philosophy and psychology was stimulated by reading Brentano (Chapter 8) when just 17. Struck

by the basic questions of metaphysics, Heidegger began a lifelong quest to understand such fundamental issues as "What is the meaning of being?"

Heidegger began at the University of Freiburg as a theology major, but the influence of Kierkegaard, Nietzsche, and most importantly of Husserl pulled him toward philosophy. After completing a dissertation on Duns Scotus (Chapter 3), Heidegger was Husserl's assistant until he accepted his own position at the University of Marburg in 1922. For the next several years, Heidegger undertook a synthesis of classic existential philosophy and contemporary Husserlian phenomenology, creating his own existential-phenomenology with the publication of *Being and Time* (Heidegger, 1927/1962).

Heidegger succeeded Husserl as professor at Freiburg, thereby becoming the world's leading phenomenologist. He was appointed the Rector of Freiburg in 1933 and declared his support for Hitler in his inaugural address. However, he remained a member of the Nazi party for only a brief period and resigned as Rector in 1934. For the next decade, Heidegger taught courses critical of the Nazi version of philosophy. Officially retired in 1945, Heidegger remained an influential writer and lecturer.

Heidegger's Philosophy. Heidegger's goal was to transform questions about being and existence from abstract concerns into a discussion of the nature and place of humans in the world that would be of interest to almost everyone. Through a deliberate manipulation of ordinary language, Heidegger sought to illustrate that humans alone question "Being" and that only people are aware of their Being.

Heidegger distorted the standard uses of many terms and created new terms in an effort to clarify his ideas. The most important of his new terms was *Dasein*, which in German means "being there," and which Heidegger used to represent humanity. The term *Dasein* was intended to capture the idea that people are always aware, always thinking, and are not like the world's other objects. Humans, *Dasein*, do not exist as things in the world like other things in the world; rather *Dasein* has a **being-in-the-world** (another of Heidegger's linguistic constructions) that differs from all other objects. People exist by being-in-the-world, and conversely, the world as a meaningful reality exists because humans are in it.

Because of their awareness of Being, humans are also aware of the impermanence of their existence. This realization creates the fundamental mood of people, which is anxiety. Humans are "thrown into the world" that is not of their making or choosing and must constantly strive to realize their fullest potentials by making appropriate decisions. In trying to create a worthwhile existence, to live toward death, the person lives an "authentic" life.

Failure to accept death's inevitability leads to an "inauthentic" life, in which the person experiences no sense of urgency to become all that he or she can become. An inauthentic person is always giving away his or her ability to choose. For example, the person may become involved in a social organization in which the rules of behavior are manifestly clear. By doing this, the individual surrenders his or her choices in living life. The person has elected to live an inauthentic life by accepting the decisions of others about how life should be lived.

As you can see from our brief consideration of a small part of Heidegger's thought, his ideas are both intriguing and difficult. Nevertheless, no existential philosopher has had a more direct connection to clinical psychology than Heidegger. The reason for this influence is that a variety of German psychotherapists fashioned approaches to therapy based on Heidegger's *Dasein* concept.

Daseinanalysis. Two of Europe's leading psychiatrists, **Medard Boss** (1903–) and **Ludwig Binswanger** (1881–1966) founded a system of psychotherapy after World War II based partly on Heidegger's existential phenomenology. As is true for Boss and Binswanger, in most cases the humanistic approaches to psychotherapy were developed by people trained in the predominant psychoanalytic (Freudian) school.

Boss was born in St. Gallen, Switzerland, and started his medical studies in Vienna, where he worked briefly with Freud. Returning to Switzerland, Boss completed his training with Bleuler and then studied in London and Berlin with such notables as Karen Horney, Ernest Jones (both Chapter

15), and Kurt Goldstein (Chapter 14). Again returning to Switzerland, Boss became closely associated with Carl Jung and was an "orthodox psychoanalyst" (Craig, 1988).

An encounter with fellow Swiss psychiatrist Ludwig Binswanger led Boss to read Heidegger, whom he met in 1947 at Heidegger's residence in the Black Forest. Binswanger, 22 years older than Boss, had completed his medical degree from the University of Zurich in 1907, before studying with Bleuler and Jung. Although he was considered one of Switzerland's premier Freudian therapists, Binswanger was moving toward a more phenomenological approach based on the ideas of Husserl and Heidegger when he met Boss.

Because of its foundation in existential philosophy, *Daseinanalysis* (existential psychoanalysis) differs from traditional psychoanalysis in placing a greater emphasis on present choices, minimizing the past as a cause of current problems. People are responsible for their lives and are free to make choices about what to do or what not to do. The central fact of existence is being-in-the-world; people cannot live apart from the world or in a world apart from themselves. *Daseinanalysis* aims to help the person experience life itself, to live an authentic life, in other words.

Other Existential Psychotherapies. Existentialism was increasingly a part of the European *Zeitgeist* after World War II, and many psychotherapists began to make connections between existential philosophy and clinical practice. Such a connection is evident in the life work of the German-born Swiss philosopher, psychologist, and psychiatrist **Karl Jaspers** (1883–1969). Jaspers received the M.D. degree from Heidelberg in 1909 and was Professor of Philosophy at the university from 1921 until 1937, when he was dismissed by the Nazis. Undeterred, Jaspers stayed in Germany throughout the war and was awarded the Goethe Prize in 1947 for his uncompromising stand. Somewhat ironically, a year later he became a Swiss citizen.

Although Jaspers indirectly popularized Heidegger by advocating an existential psychology, Kierkegaard was Jaspers's primary point of departure in the development of his approach. In his three-volume *Philosophy,* Jaspers distinguished three modes of being: being-there, being-oneself, and being-in-itself. Being-there refers to the world we know through our observations; being-oneself is the subjective awareness of our own difficulties, wishes, and expectancies; and being-in-itself is the ability to surmount the world and to know other worlds.

Jaspers found such existential, philosophical considerations useful as a framework for structuring psychotherapy and for understanding psychopathology. For Jaspers (e.g., 1932/1969), psychotherapy was a form of *Existenzphilosophie* (analysis of existence), with a focus on understanding a person's existence through an active analysis of the process of consciousness as it relates to the self and to objects in the world. In turn, Jaspers's thought had a strong impact on psychiatry and psychology in the United States, whereas his many comprehensive volumes in the history of philosophy were popular with academicians interested in an existential perspective.

Viktor Frankl (1905–) was another contributor to existential psychotherapy. A Viennese psychiatrist and holocaust survivor, Frankl emerged from his 3 years in Nazi concentration camps—including the notorious Auschwitz—with a renewed appreciation of Nietzsche and other existential philosophers. *Man's Search for Meaning* (Frankl, 1946/1959) chronicles Frankl's experiences during the war and the creation of **logotherapy**, his brand of existential psychotherapy.

Logotherapy involves the search for meaning, focusing on what Frankl calls "the will to meaning" as opposed to Nietzsche's "will to power" or "the will to pleasure" (i.e., hedonism). Frankl believes that many of the ills of our time can be traced to a frustrated search for personal meaning, resulting in the neurotic triad of depression, aggression, and addiction. The logotherapist cannot prescribe meaning for the individual, however. Instead, it "is the objective of logotherapy to *describe* the process of meaning perception by way of a phenomenological analysis, so as to find out how normal people arrive at meaning and consequently at a sense of fulfillment" (Frankl, 1994, p. 350).

Not all of the influential European existentialists were therapists or philosophers, however. In fact,

FIGURE 16–4.   Maurice Merleau-Ponty.

Source: AP/Wide World Photos.

the most influential theorist for an existential-phenomenological psychology, Maurice Merleau-Ponty (Figure 16–4), was primarily a child psychologist, with strong interests in cognition and consciousness.

Maurice Merleau-Ponty

Like Camus, **Maurice Merleau-Ponty** (1908–1961) lost his father in World War I, and like Sartre, he was educated in Paris, graduating from the École Normale Supérieure in 1930. Until he joined the war effort in 1939, Merleau-Ponty was affiliated with various schools and movements, including the structural movement in sociology championed by social anthropologist Claude Levi-Strauss (1908–). Merleau-Ponty's most relevant works for theoretical psychology are *The Structure of Behavior* and *The Phenomenology of Perception,* both first published during the war years.

In *The Structure of Behavior* and *The Phenomenology of Perception,* Merleau-Ponty revealed his interest in understanding the relation between consciousness and human nature. For Merleau-Ponty, the appropriate method for studying consciousness was the phenomenology of perception, and he rejected extreme methodological approaches such as that found in Watson's behaviorism (Chapter 12).

In the late 1940s, Merleau-Ponty taught courses in Gestalt psychology, sociology, psychoanalysis, and the philosophy of language at the University of Lyon and at the École Normale before being named Professor of Child Psychology and Pedagogy at the Sorbonne in 1949. For the next several years, Merleau-Ponty conducted research in cognitive development. In 1952, he accepted what had been Bergson's chair at the Collège de France. From that prestigious position, Merleau-Ponty continued to write about language, consciousness, and existential-phenomenological psychology until his death in 1961.

Although Merleau-Ponty was knowledgeable about both psychoanalysis and philosophy, he left his mark on psychology primarily through his advocacy for an existential-phenomenological approach to experimental psychology. Using less of traditional existential and Husserlian philosophy than most of his contemporaries, Merleau-Ponty built on such starting points as William James and Gestalt theory (Schmidt, 1985). Methodologically, Merleau-Ponty focused on the analysis of perceptual processes and what that revealed about the structure and function of consciousness. His findings suggested that the experience of time, our own bodies, and of other people were primary elements in the organization of our conscious processes.

Merleau-Ponty marks an important transition in phenomenology from its status as a psychologically sophisticated philosophical system (e.g., Brentano and others in Chapter 8) to a school of psychology. Because of his more experimental nature and his connection to established psychological systems, Merleau-Ponty's approach to existential-phenomenology became the most popular among academic psychologists (e.g., Ihde, 1979; Pollio, 1982; Pollio, Henley, & Thompson, in press; Valle & King, 1978).

Other Existential Contributors

Our survey of the philosophical backdrop to a more humanistic psychology has been highly selective. Many people have made important contributions, some of which were far removed from psychology. For example, many historians view Russian novelist Fyodor Dostoevsky (1821–1881) as one of the principal contributors to modern existential philosophy (e.g., Kaufmann, 1956), and college courses on existentialism often list his *Notes from Underground* as required reading. Additionally, the Austrian Jewish theologian and philosopher **Martin Buber** (1878–1965) wrote both clinically relevant articles (e.g., Buber, 1957) and also what has become the classic existential analysis of language use—*I and Thou* (Buber, 1923/1970). Buber's work remains a key volume for clinicians, social psychologists, and cognitive psychologists interested in language.

In America, **Rollo May** (1909–1994) was an early advocate for an existential psychology. Born in Ada, Ohio, May obtained his B.A. from Oberlin College in 1930, a divinity degree from Union Theological Seminary in 1938, and a clinical psychology Ph.D. *summa cum laude* from Columbia in 1949. Battles with tuberculosis partly account for how long May took to earn his Ph.D.

May's dissertation was on the meaning of anxiety, and it drew heavily on Kierkegaard's analysis of dread. May's subsequent publications (e.g., May, 1950) marked the first exposure most American psychologists had to Kierkegaard's ideas. Further books by May included several that focused on Heidegger (e.g., May, 1961), and May became perhaps the most celebrated American existential psychotherapist of his era.

One of May's contemporaries, George Kelly, further illustrates the increasingly humanistic nature of American psychology during and after World War II. Born in Kansas, **George A. Kelly** (1905–1967) completed his Ph.D. in physiological psychology from the University of Iowa in 1931. Following his first appointment at Kansas State College, Kelly spent most of his career at The Ohio State University, where he worked to build the clinical program with the aid of Julian Rotter. **Julian Rotter** (1916–) is known for his construct "locus of control" (Rotter, 1966), which distinguishes individuals who see themselves as the source of what happens to them (internal locus of control) and people who believe that their fate largely rests with forces beyond their control (external locus of control).

Kelly began his academic career during the depths of the Depression. Because he was unable to see how behavioristic S-R psychology or Freudian psychoanalytic theory could help the plight of most Americans during this era, Kelly began searching for a more relevant system, which he detailed in *The Psychology of Personal Constructs* (Kelly, 1955). Where the scientist develops a theory to help predict and control the environment, individuals develop **personal constructs** based on their experience with the world, which they in turn use to organize and make sense of experience. Although originally more "clinical" in nature, Kelly's personal construct theory is similar to contemporary schema theory used by cognitive psychologists (Chapter 20) to explore such things as our perception and understanding of the world.

From a therapeutic perspective, to understand a person's world, it is necessary to understand his or her personal constructs. It is not enough just to examine a person's background (e.g., heredity, environment), because identical backgrounds may produce different personal constructs. According to Kelly, people are free to choose how they interpret the events that affect them and how the events will impact their lives.

In more contemporary American psychology, several well-respected theorists, such as Amedeo Giorgi (e.g., Giorgi, 1970) and Joseph Rychlak (e.g., Rychlak, 1991), have lobbied for a more "humanistic" approach to all psychology, not just to clinical psychology. Articles representing an existential and/or phenomenological orientation can be found in almost every area of psychology, including artificial intelligence, social psychology, and consumer psychology. We will now examine the area of American psychology on which existentialism has had perhaps the greatest impact—humanistic clinical psychology. The result of this impact has been the rise of what some have called the Third Force.

The Third Force

Charlotte B. Bühler (1893–1974)—Karl Bühler's (Chapter 14) wife—made several important contributions before World War II to the area of cognitive development. Bühler, who came to the United States in 1923 on a fellowship to study with Thorndike (Chapters 11 and 12), performed several studies of age-specific cognitive abilities (e.g., Bühler, 1930) that were similar to work often associated with Piaget's stage model (Chapter 20). Bühler's later works anticipated the modern life-span developmental approach of Erik Erikson (Chapter 15). Additionally, her child psychology work is thought to have strongly influenced the American child psychologist Arnold Gesell (Chapter 12).

After 1940, Charlotte Bühler's interests increasingly focused on the new humanistic psychology movement, which Abraham Maslow called the **Third Force** in American psychology, the first force being behaviorism and the second force psychoanalysis. With Maslow, Carl Rogers (both discussed later), and Viktor Frankl, Bühler founded the Association for Humanistic Psychology in 1964, serving as its president in 1965–1966. Bühler is also known for producing one of the first widely read position papers outlining and popularizing this new humanistic approach to psychology (Bühler, 1971).

Humanistic psychology can be defined as a focus on the positive rather than the negative aspects of the self—an orientation that is more concerned with present choices than with past events. Such a definition encompasses people who may or may not have considered themselves humanists. For example, Alfred Adler would be a humanist by this definition and could be considered the founder of modern humanistic psychology. Although some historians and Adlerians would welcome this designation, others would not.

From another perspective, existentialists frequently focused on the self, and existential approaches to clinical psychology are often considered a subset of humanistic orientations. Nevertheless, existentialism—with its roots in European philosophy—is not synonymous with humanism as an approach to clinical psychology in America. To understand what Charlotte Bühler and her colleagues intended, our approach will be to concentrate on some of the individuals involved in a movement that emerged in America in the late 1950s and resulted in the founding of the APA's Division of Humanistic Psychology in the early 1970s.

Several individuals we have recognized in other contexts were part of the humanistic movement in psychology, including the social psychologist Hadley Cantril (mentioned first in Chapter 1), Gestalt neuroscientist Kurt Goldstein, and the novelist Aldous Huxley (mentioned in Chapters 9 and 13). The movement also included the leading existential psychologist in America, Rollo May, and a clinician known for his client-centered therapy, Carl Rogers. We will start by examining the life and contributions of the person most associated with the movement's position as the Third Force in modern psychology—Abraham Maslow (Figure 16–5).

FIGURE 16–5. Abraham Maslow.

Source: Corbis-Bettmann.

Abraham Maslow

Abraham Maslow (1908–1970) was born in Brooklyn, the eldest child in a large immigrant household of Russian Jews. After brief stops at the City College of New York and Cornell, Maslow settled at the University of Wisconsin to earn his B.A. (1930), M.A. (1931), Ph.D. (1934), and first job. At Wisconsin, Maslow worked with Harry Harlow (Chapter 14), and in the early part of his career, Maslow made important contributions to the study of primate social behavior (e.g., Maslow, 1936). From Wisconsin, Maslow returned to New York, first on a fellowship to work with Thorndike at Columbia, and later as part of the faculty at Brooklyn College.

Beginning with his tenure under Thorndike, Maslow's interests shifted to human behavior and eventually into motivation, personality, and clinical psychology. This shift is coincidental with Maslow's association with the refugee psychologists from Germany: for example, Wertheimer and Koffka (Chapter 14) and Horney and Adler. In 1951, Maslow accepted a position at the recently established Brandeis University in Waltham, Massachusetts, where he soon formed a close association with Kurt Goldstein.

Maslow is best remembered for his hierarchy of human needs and his theories of personality and motivation. Maslow's **need hierarchy** is often depicted as a pyramid at whose base are the physiological needs, such as the need for food and water. Next are the needs for safety, which are followed by the needs for belongingness and love. Once the needs to love and be loved are satisfied, the person can begin to satisfy the needs for esteem (e.g., self-esteem, achievement, independence). Finally, after the deficiency needs have been met, the need for self-actualization can be addressed.

Maslow came to believe that subjective experience is central to psychology's subject matter, which implies that animal models are of minimal value for understanding human psychology, as are studies of group tendencies. Maslow felt that psychology should be a future-oriented and applied enterprise and that research efforts should focus on solving real human problems and upon expanding human potential.

As appealing as Maslow's conception of psychology may sound, it was clearly in opposition to many aspects of behavioral and biological psychology seen as fundamental for establishing the discipline as a true science. For example, Maslow and most other humanists would reject reductionistic attempts to study units smaller than a complete human being, or attempts to reduce human existence to elements such as the stimulus and response. Also anathema is the idea that the goal of a psychological science involves prediction and *control* of human nature (e.g., Maslow, 1966).

Maslow's death in 1970 came on the eve of humanism's recognition by the APA, and it is unfortunate that Maslow did not live to see the fruits of his labor. For the humanistic movement, Maslow's demise was a serious blow. The likely candidates to fill his leadership role were Rollo May and Carl Rogers, but neither had Maslow's impressive academic pedigree. Although many in scientific psychology might object to Maslow's specific claims for a humanistic psychology, Maslow's early work in animal behavior and his connections to such scientific stalwarts as Thorndike, Wertheimer, and Harlow ensured that his opponents took him seriously.

Carl Rogers

Born in a Chicago suburb, in his teens **Carl Ransom Rogers** (1902–1987) moved with his family to a more rural farming area. This background led to his first major in "scientific agriculture" (Rogers, 1967) at the University of Wisconsin, but Rogers's interests soon shifted to theology and history.

Rogers was selected for travel to China as part of a student missionary group, and this 6-month trip combined with a 6-month hospitalization for an ulcer delayed his graduation until 1924. From Wisconsin, Rogers transferred to New York's Union Theological Seminary. Leta Hollingworth's (Chapter 10) course in clinical psychology at Columbia was an experience Rogers (1967) later recalled as facilitating his shift from theology to clinical psychology.

In 1926, Rogers started work at the Institute of Child Guidance and began his education in psychology in earnest at the eclectic but psychodynamically oriented program at Columbia. After completing his Ed.D. from Teachers College, Rogers accepted a position at a guidance clinic in Rochester, New York. During the next several years, Rogers developed his approach to psychotherapy, which was based in part on variations of the techniques of Otto Rank (Chapter 15).

In an academic appointment for the first time in 1940, Rogers spent 5 years at The Ohio State University before moving to the University of Chicago. During the 1940s, Rogers's reputation grew quickly, and the psychoanalytic community began to view him as the most serious challenge to their control over American therapeutic practice (Gendlin, 1988). Rogers achieved this notoriety largely through conflicts with the medical community at Chicago, including disputes with the psychology department's head, **James G. Miller** (1916–). Holding both a psychology Ph.D. and an M.D. that he earned simultaneously from Harvard, Miller is noted for his contributions to systems theory—the idea that all things (e.g., cells, people, groups) can be viewed as systems of essential functions.

In 1951, Rogers published *Client-Centered Therapy,* which described his therapeutic approach. By the end of the 1950s, the client-centered (now called person-centered) treatment method was being widely reviewed and discussed by academics and practitioners alike. Rogers assumed that each person has the capacity to become psychologically healthy and self-actualized, and people become maladjusted when they deny important parts of their personalities. The emphasis on trusting the client led to a number of applications at the University of Chicago, which included student-centered educational approaches and providing therapy to children even when their parents did not participate. This latter application was discussed by Virginia Axline (1947) in *Play Therapy: The Inner Dynamics of Childhood.*

Client-centered therapy provides an accepting environment to which the therapist contributes congruence, unconditional positive regard, and empathic understanding. Congruence refers to genuineness on the part of the therapist, who is willing to be transparent in the relationship—to express his or her feelings. Unconditional positive regard means that the therapist respects the client as a unique individual and is willing to accept whatever the client has to say. The therapist displays empathic under-standing by listening to what the client is attempting to communicate, particularly on the feeling level, and then sharing his or her understanding with the client. The therapist's acceptance of the client's feelings as worthwhile helps restore the client's self-confidence and self-image.

Rogers and his associates were instrumental in promoting the attitude that psychotherapy could be studied objectively. By taping therapy sessions and publishing complete transcriptions of the recordings, Rogers opened the previously closed doors of psychotherapeutic interventions and stimulated an enormous amount of research.

In 1956, Rogers was selected along with Wolfgang Köhler (Chapter 14) and Kenneth Spence (Chapter 13) as a recipient of the first APA Distinguished Scientific Contribution Award. Rogers found this award profoundly moving, "to the point of tears," and he "was astonished that psychologists deeply and significantly regarded me as 'one of them'" (Rogers, 1967, p. 375). In 1957, Rogers returned to the Uni-versity of Wisconsin, which proved to be as turbulent an environment as Chicago had been, because the creation of psychology's Third Force was still not universally well received by either of the first two. Rogers soon left academic psychology for California's greater tolerance. From 1964 on, his primary affiliation was with what is now the Center for the Study of the Person at La Jolla.

With his focus on the inner feelings and experiences of people, Rogers's theories were particularly at odds with the emphasis on external behavior and the effects of the environment endorsed by B. F. Skinner (Chapter 13). In fact, the two men held a number of friendly debates at different universities (e.g., Rice University; see Wann, 1964). Audiences at the debates generally received the impression that Rogers and Skinner were not communicating in any productive fashion that could serve to reconcile their positions.

Rogers remained an active contributor to humanistic conceptions of therapy and to the Center until his death in 1987. Because of his lack of interest in renewing his ties with academic psychology, Rogers was a greatly admired but relatively ineffective leader of the humanistic movement following Maslow's death. With the publication in 1961 of *On Becoming*

FIGURE 16–6. Carl Rogers.

Source: ©Charles Schneider in A History of Psychology in Autobiography, Vol. 5.

a Person, Rogers (Figure 16–6) secured his place as a spokesperson for the humanistic movement.

Although the humanistic movement never fully materialized into a Third Force commensurate with behaviorism and psychoanalysis, it did enjoy a decade in the spotlight from the mid-1960s through the mid-1970s and continues to be one important voice among many in modern psychology. In the final section, we will consider some of the elements other than humanism that have helped shape contemporary clinical psychology.

RECENT ADVANCES IN PSYCHOTHERAPY

Because of clinical psychology's connection to both academic psychology and the real-world problem of psychopathology, the influences on it have been diverse. We will conclude our overview by looking at a few connections with psychiatry and by surveying some of the signal events in the field's development. Additionally, we will explore psychometric advances in personality appraisal in Chapter 18.

Psychiatric Influences

Any history of the development of clinical psychology in America should include at least a mention of Lightner Witmer (Chapter 7) and **Morton Prince** (1854–1929). Witmer started the first psychological clinic, named the field (e.g., Witmer, 1907), and began an early journal—*The Psychological Clinic*—in 1907. Prince founded the clinic at Harvard in 1927, is considered the creator of modern psychotherapy in America (Hilgard, 1987), and started the *Journal of Abnormal Psychology* in 1906. With connections to James, Pavlov (Chapter 12), Charcot, and Münsterberg (Chapter 10), Prince was an eclectic theorist with ideas on complexes, conflicts, repression, and symbols that predated Freud (Murray, 1956). Although both Witmer and Prince demonstrate the contributions of American "psychologists," many important developments occurred in psychiatry.

As we have suggested, the psychodynamic approach to clinical psychology was internationally the most influential technique until after World War II. Then as now, a psychodynamic procedure and the ability to prescribe medications and such medical interventions as electroconvulsive shock and psychosurgery have been favored by members of the medical mental health community. As we noted in discussing Carl Rogers, the relationship between psychiatrists and clinical psychologists has not always been harmonious. However, despite the acrimony, psychiatrists and other physicians (e.g., neurosurgeons) have made substantive contributions to psychology. In addition, psychiatry continues to be intimately connected to the practice of clinical psychology through such venues as drug therapy and its guide to diagnosis (discussed later).

In Chapter 15, we noted that Benjamin Rush is considered the father of American psychiatry. Subsequently, **Harry Stack Sullivan** (1892–1949) was one of the important neo-Freudians in the psychiatric community responsible for shaping much of American clinical psychology's theory and practice. Sullivan never earned an undergraduate degree, received his M.D. from a school he later described as a "diploma mill," and except for a few months at Georgetown University Medical School in 1939, did not hold an academic appointment. Unfortunately, Sullivan died from a cerebral hemorrhage before most of his major works were published. Among Sullivan's posthumous publications, his *The Psychiatric Interview* (Sullivan, 1954/1970) remains a primer in client-therapist interaction.

For Sullivan, therapy was an interpersonal process in which the conduct of the clinical interview was crucial. In talking with clients, therapists needed a structured framework for their questions that would ensure that they discovered the clients' patterns, living conditions, and salient experiences. Sullivan's approach established such a framework, which many still consider essential for successful therapy.

Today, the psychiatric community exerts a tremendous influence over all mental health professionals through its publication of the *Diagnostic and Statistical Manual (DSM)*, which is currently in its 4th edition (American Psychiatric Association, 1994). The *DSM* is an important catalog of identifiable mental disorders, and it provides a consistent language mental health professionals can use to communicate with each other and with the public about psychopathology. Additionally, the *DSM* can be used as a guide to the diagnosis of, information about, and possible treatments for each of its recognized conditions.

All editions of the *DSM* have been organized around contemporary conceptions of the cause of mental illness. Early editions assumed more of a psychodynamic basis, whereas the current publication is slanted toward biological explanations for abnormality. This schism over etiology has resulted in continuing tensions between many psychiatrists and psychologists.

A belief in biological explanations has led to a wide panoply of psychiatric medications, which are generally among the most commonly prescribed drugs in the United States. Currently popular are the tranquilizer Xanax and the antidepressant Prozac; just a generation ago, the tranquilizers Valium and Librium topped the list of most frequently prescribed medications. Although we will not trace the history of drug therapy, because of psychiatric influences, new medications will continue to play an important role in the treatment of a wide range of mental disorders.

Some of the most controversial statements about the nature of mental disorders have come from psychiatrists. For example, **Ronald D. Laing** (1927–1989) described psychopathology as something that occurs in a relationship, not in a person. From his study of schizophrenics, Laing (1979) concluded that schizophrenia is not so much a disorder as it is a method invented by the person to deal with an impossible situation. The schizophrenic is no longer able to maintain the false persona society requires, and his or her schizophrenic behavior is viewed as abnormal.

Hungarian-born **Thomas S. Szasz** (1920–) has also been controversial in his discussions of mental illness. Szasz came to America when he was 18 and earned his M.D. from the University of Cincinnati in 1944. He received training in psychiatry at the University of Chicago and in psychoanalysis at the Chicago Institute for Psychoanalysis.

The essence of Szasz's (1961/1974) thesis is contained in the title of his most famous work—*The Myth of Mental Illness.* Seen by many humanists as their most important statement, Szasz asserted that true illness is by definition biological and that the so-called mental illnesses either result from bodily illnesses with mental symptoms (e.g., the organic psychoses) or are not illnesses at all. Most of what psychologists and psychiatrists call mental illness, Szasz would prefer to label "problems in living" with no connections to underlying physiological disturbance. Although most practitioners in both the medical and the psychological communities disagree with his exact thesis, Szasz's work continues to generate discussion and to stimulate research into the nature and practice of psychotherapy.

The Growth of Clinical Psychology

By contrast, the work of clinical psychologist David Shakow was less controversial but perhaps equally

FIGURE 16–7. David Shakow.
Source: Archives of the History of American Psychology.

influential. Shakow (Figure 16–7) is particularly known for his interest in the study of schizophrenia. Our focus on David Shakow as a case study in American clinical psychology will permit us to examine changes that have occurred in the 20th century, as well as recent advances in the field. Shakow was both a clinician and a researcher, and he was active in the American Psychological Association from a time when clinicians were a small subset of psychologists into the period when clinicians came to dominate the APA.

David Shakow (1901–1981) was born on the Lower East Side of New York City. An early fascination with William James led Shakow to Harvard, where he completed undergraduate courses with such figures as Floyd Allport (Chapter 19), Herbert Langfeld (Chapter 10), and William McDougall (Chapter 12). Following his undergraduate degree, lack of funds kept Shakow from immediately pursuing graduate education, so he took a job at the Worcester State Hospital with **Grace Kent** (1875–1973). Kent is best known for her collaborations with psychiatrist Aran Rosanoff in the early development of clinical diagnostic scales (e.g., Kent & Rosanoff, 1910).

In 1925, Shakow returned to Harvard for graduate training, which he took in the standard program in experimental psychology, because the Harvard Psychological Clinic was not yet underway. Shakow's dissertation on subliminal perception under E. G. Boring's (Chapter 1) direction produced such inconclusive results that Shakow was forced to take a job back at Worcester without completing his degree requirements. Fourteen years later, after World War II, Shakow's dissertation on schizophrenia was accepted, and he finally received his Harvard Ph.D.

In 1946, Shakow accepted a faculty position at the University of Illinois Medical School, and in 1948 he added an appointment at the University of Chicago Department of Psychology. In the postwar years, Shakow was involved in a number of clinical education matters, including work for the APA on the nature of clinical training and internship programs. Specific activities included being an original member of APA's Board of Examiners in Professional Psychology, chairman of the APA's Committee on Training in Clinical Psychology, APA's representative to the World Federation of Mental Health, and president of APA's Division of Clinical Psychology.

In 1947, Shakow's Committee on Training in Clinical Psychology report suggested guidelines for training clinical psychologists that included the recommendation that they should be trained first as psychologists—that is, as scientists—and second as practicing clinicians. The Committee's recommendations were formalized in 1949 at a national conference on clinical training held at Boulder, Colorado. Thus, the **Boulder model** of clinical training views the modern clinical psychologist as both scientist and practitioner and serves as a guide in universities where this approach is adopted. Subsequent conferences have been held to explore further the issues of clinical training, including the 1973 meeting in Vail, Colorado. The Vail conference recognized professional clinical training (as distinct

from training as a scientist-clinician) as an acceptable model. In programs devoted to training clinical practitioners, the terminal degree is the Psy.D., whereas the Ph.D. is preferred by programs where the focus is on the development of new knowledge in psychology.

From 1954 until 1966, Shakow served as the director of the National Institute of Mental Health's (NIMH) psychology laboratory. In that capacity, he was able to return to his primary research interest in schizophrenia. In 1966, Shakow retired from his administrative position to become a Senior Research Scientist at NIMH. Among his many honors, Shakow received the APA's 1975 Distinguished Scientific Contribution Award and the Distinguished Professional Contribution Award the next year.

Shakow's professional biography offers a snapshot of the evolution of clinical psychology. His initial Harvard training was ill suited to the practice of clinical psychology, despite his tuition by several major figures in the history of psychology (e.g., William McDougall, Floyd Allport, Morton Prince). When Shakow entered Harvard, an education into the symptoms, causes, and treatment of psychopathology was not available outside of a medical school. In the years after World War II, Shakow played a vital role in the creation of standards for clinical training programs and for clinical research.

At the time of Shakow's entry and before his work within it, the APA was an organization dominated by experimental psychologists (Chapter 10), with little conception of how to oversee clinical practitioners. By the time of his death, the APA situation had changed dramatically, and clinical practitioners had become more numerous than experimental researchers. Shakow himself embodied what many graduate programs today try to encourage—the dual role of scientist and practitioner.

CONCLUSIONS

Modern clinical psychology has often tried to dissociate itself from Freud. For example, one currently popular approach to therapy, the cognitive-behavioral paradigm developed by Albert Ellis and Aaron Beck, has more salient connections to neobehaviorism (Chapter 13) and to cognitive psychology than it does to the fundamentals of Freud's system.

Most historians prefer to attribute the shape of modern psychology to Wundt, James, or perhaps Watson. Nevertheless, the aura and impact of Freud remain with us. Ask any introductory psychology student to name a psychologist, and the response is likely to be "Freud." Perhaps too often these days Freud's seminal role in such areas as development, personality, and abnormal psychology is minimized. Clinical psychology—Freud's legacy—continues to be the most popular and attractive subdiscipline for undergraduate and graduate students alike.

As Freud knew, our world is remarkably dynamic. Because of this, the development of psychoanalysis did not end with Freud, and the work of Adler and Jung demonstrates some of the first substantive changes to Freud's system. Further developments came in World War II, which provided a fertile

ground for existentialism, and subsequently a more humanistic approach to psychotherapy grew in popularity. In America, during the last 75 years or so, clinical psychology has gone from nonexistence to its place of eminence among psychology's subdisciplines.

This chapter also concludes our focus on psychology's great schools: structuralism (and voluntarism), fuctionalism, behaviorism (in its many forms), Gestalt psychology, and psychoanalysis. Arguably, there were also lesser schools, with some such as ethology (Chapter 12) and existential-phenomenology still viable. Nevertheless, as we noted in Chapter 14, the time of the competing schools has passed.

In the next section, we will review some of the more contemporary advances in psychology by topic rather than by school. Specifically, in Chapter 17, we will consider neuroscience, which continues to be a rich source of ideas for the clinical community (particularly its psychiatric elements) as evidenced through current biological explanations of psychopathology.

S U M M A R Y

This chapter surveyed developments in personality theory and psychotherapy that originated in, but went beyond, Freud's system. Important connections between clinical psychology and the psychiatric community were also explored.

Psychoanalysis beyond Freud

After Freud, several forms of psychotherapy appeared. One of the later approaches emphasizes conflicts based on object relations—hence object-relations theory. Two other variations were developed by Alfred Adler and Carl Jung.

Adler's Individual Psychology de-emphasized the sexual instinct and made consciousness the center of personality. For Adler, the great driving forces of humanity were feelings of inferiority and efforts to compensate. Adler also viewed birth order as an important determinant of personality.

Carl Jung's self-analysis led him to develop Analytical Psychology. Jung's conception of psychological types divided people according to the attitudes of introversion and extraversion and the functions of thinking, feeling, sensation, and intuition. For Jung, the personality consisted of several different, interacting systems, the major ones

being the ego, the personal unconscious and its complexes, and the collective unconscious and its archetypes.

Existential and Humanistic Approaches

Two themes from existential philosophy important to psychology are that subjective meaning should be psychology's central focus and that humans have the freedom to make choices for which they should be prepared to take responsibility. The idea of choice represents a resistance to reductionistic and deterministic accounts of human behavior.

Jean-Paul Sartre and Albert Camus were two existentialists whose writings influenced philosophy, psychology, and the general public. Martin Heidegger's philosophy included the idea of humanity as *Dasein*, German for "being there." For Heidegger, the human effort to create a worthwhile existence leads to an authentic life, whereas giving up the ability to make decisions leads to an inauthentic life. Medard Boss and Ludwig Binswanger developed *Daseinanalysis*, a psychotherapy based on Heidegger's philosophy. Karl

Jaspers and Viktor Frankl developed additional existential psychotherapies.

Maurice Merleau-Ponty's primary influence on psychology came through his development of a scientifically respectable approach to a phenomenological experimental psychology. Martin Buber wrote the classic existential analysis of language, and Rollo May provided the first exposure of most American psychologists to the existential ideas of Kierkegaard. May's contemporaries, George Kelly and Julian Rotter, further illustrate the increasingly humanistic nature of American clinical and social psychology during and after World War II. Kelly's most important contribution was his idea of personal constructs.

Charlotte Bühler's work anticipated the life-span developmental approach of Erik Erikson and focused on the humanistic psychology movement that Abraham Maslow called the Third Force. Maslow is perhaps best remembered for his human need hierarchy. At the bottom are the physiological and safety needs, and above these are the needs for belongingness, love, esteem, and finally, for self-actualization.

Carl Rogers developed a client-centered psychotherapy approach in which the therapist provides an accepting environment to which he or she contributes congruence, unconditional positive regard, and empathic understanding.

Recent Advances in Psychotherapy

Psychiatric influences on clinical psychology include the work of Harry Stack Sullivan, the American Psychiatric Association's *Diagnostic and Statistical Manual,* and the controversial statements of Ronald D. Laing and Thomas Szasz.

David Shakow's career traces the evolution of clinical psychology in America, and he was instrumental in the creation of standards for clinical training programs (e.g., the Boulder model) and for clinical research. Shakow exemplified the dual role of scientist and practitioner.

CONNECTIONS QUESTIONS

1. What connections can you make between the rise of existential approaches to philosophy and psychology and World War II?
2. How is Freud connected to the various existential and humanistic approaches to psychology?
3. What is the connection between Heidegger and *Daseinanalysis*?

4. Connect David Shakow's career in psychology with the evolution of clinical psychology in America.
5. In what ways did Adler and Jung "disconnect" themselves from Freud?
6. Draw a concept map connecting the major figures and ideas in this chapter, and compare your results with one possible solution provided on p. 568.

SUGGESTED READINGS

Ansbacher, H. L., & Ansbacher, R. R. (Eds.) (1956). *The Individual Psychology of Alfred Adler: A systematic presentation in selections from his writings.* New York: Basic Books, Inc. This volume includes both interpretation and voluminous citations from primary works and is a good place to begin the study of Adler's psychology.

Frankl, V. E. (1959). *Man's search for meaning.* Boston: Beacon Press. (Original work published in 1946.) The original German edition was published in 1946 as *Ein Psycholog erlebt das Konzentrationslager.* In English translation, *Man's Search for Meaning* is available as a paperback and has been a long-standing international bestseller. Short and readable, this volume is actually two different books. The first is a vivid account of Frankl's personal experiences in the Nazi death camps, and the second is an outline of the existential therapy (logotherapy) Frankl derived from his survival of the Holocaust. This is a book that everyone should read.

Ihde, D. (1979). *Experimental phenomenology.* New York: Paragon Books. This is a delightful little book filled with several simple experiments designed to illustrate basic concepts in phenomenology. These thought-provoking exercises nicely demonstrate some of the methodology used by modern-day phenomenological psychologists.

Rogers, C. R. (1961). *On becoming a person.* Boston: Houghton Mifflin. This book earned Rogers a place as one of the major voices in the humanistic movement. *On Becoming a Person* presented a perspective of psychology's Third Force that proved to be both popular and influential.

Sartre, J.-P. (1947). *Huis Clos [No exit].* Paris: Gallimard. Published in French as *Huis Clos, No Exit* is a short, intensely psychological play that appears in almost any anthology of Sartre's work or any collection of modern drama. Without divulging the plot, we can say that the key line is "Hell is—other people"; in other words, the story is an eye-opener.

Schmidt, J. (1985). *Maurice Merleau-Ponty: Between phenomenology and structuralism.* New York: St. Martin's Press. With only a small amount of biographical information on Merleau-Ponty, this book is rich in its consideration of his thought and work. This is an important work for anyone interested in the origins of existential-phenomenology as a methodology for psychology.

Storr, A. (1973). *C. G. Jung.* New York: The Viking Press. In slightly more than 100 pages, Storr has written a worthwhile overview of the life and theories of one of the psychoanalytic movement's most complex figures.

Szasz, T. (1974). *The myth of mental illness* (Rev. ed.). New York: Harper & Row. (Original work published 1961) Szasz's book challenges many of our basic conceptions about psychopathology and the practice of "mental health" professionals. *The Myth* remains standard reading for first-year graduate students in many clinical psychology programs.

PART III

Beyond the Schools

The examination of psychoanalysis and its relatives brings to a close our survey of psychology's schools. As we noted in Chapter 14, Köhler argued in 1959 that the age of the schools—collections of people subscribing to particular systems of thought—was on the decline. In their place, Köhler suggested that the wisdom of the schools might be combined into one psychology, which appears to be a goal of the "cognitive revolution." We will examine this amalgamation of the last great schools—functionalism, behaviorism, and Gestalt psychology—in Chapter 20.

What role did the schools play in the history of psychology? According to Edna Heidbreder (1933; Chapter 11), the schools had a comforting power, offering their proponents a sense of knowledge in the absence of abundant facts. In addition, the systems on which the schools were based served to organize disparate observations and principles, provided the theoretical basis for stimulating new research, and established boundaries that excluded certain concepts from consideration. As examples of the latter function, behaviorism avoided the study of consciousness, whereas structuralism downplayed the study of animals, children, and abnormal behavior.

With all these benefits, what was wrong with the great schools and the theoretical systems on which they were based? At about the same time that McGeoch (1933) defined a system of psychology as "a coherent and inclusive, yet flexible, organization and interpretation of the facts and special theories of the subject" (p. 2), Heidbreder (1933) observed:

> Psychology, especially in the United States, has risked everything on being science; and science on principle refrains from speculation that is not permeated and stabilized by fact. *Yet there is not enough fact in the whole science of psychology to make a single solid system.* (p. 3, italics added)

In other words, the systems and schools were premature; psychologists did not know enough at the time to establish even one "inclusive and coherent" scheme, much less several.

Today, psychologists are usually identified by their specialized training—for example, as clinical psychologists, cognitive psychologists, industrial psychologists, or physiological psychologists—rather than by adherence to any particular theoretical position. For this reason, we will concentrate on *topics of study* in Part III. First, we will examine the physiological advances in the 20th century in Chapter 17. Intelligence testing, whose antecedents we saw in Ebbinghaus (Chapter 8), Galton (Chapter 9), and Cattell (Chapter 10), will be considered in Chapter 18, along with developments in other areas of psychometrics and applied psychology. Chapter 19 will focus on social psychology, a topic introduced with the Gestaltists and particularly with Kurt Lewin (Chapter 14). Devoted to cognitive psychology, Chapter 20 ends our examination of psychology's history and perhaps anticipates its future.

The Physiology of Behavior in the Twentieth Century

Sir Charles Sherrington

Otto Loewi

Karl Lashley

Georg von Békésy

Shepherd Ivory Franz

Christine Ladd

Donald Hebb

1840	1850	1860	1870	1880	1890	1900	1910

Lincoln's Gettysburg Address follows Confederate loss at that site

President Garfield is assassinated

Tchaikovsky's "Nutcracker" opens

War in Balkans fore-shadows WWI

First Woman's Rights Convention is held

Freud publishes *Psychopathology of Everyday Life*

By the end of the 19th century, physiology had made great strides as an experimental science, and the nervous system was yielding its secrets rapidly. The theme of the 19th-century's investigation of the nervous system—its demystification—had for the most part been accomplished, through increased knowledge of the nervous system's electrical component, measurement of the speed of its information transfer, and discovery of the location of some of its most important functions. Although the nervous system no longer seemed as mysterious at the end of the 19th century as it did just 100 years earlier, much still remained to be discovered about the nerve impulse, the chemistry of the nervous system, and about the localization of functions in the brain. Thus, such issues as the localization or nonlocalization of function remained and were joined by new research focuses, such as the burgeoning interest in

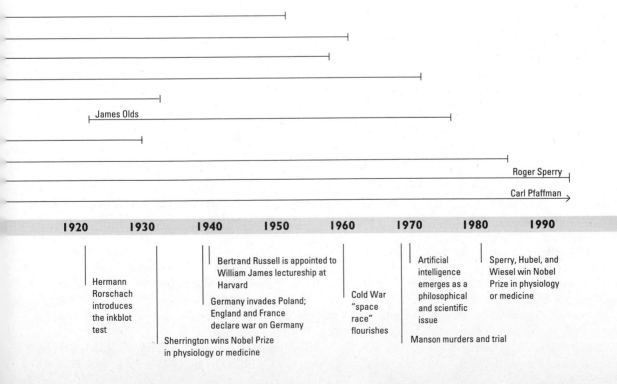

James Olds

Roger Sperry

Carl Pfaffman

| 1920 | 1930 | 1940 | 1950 | 1960 | 1970 | 1980 | 1990 |

Hermann Rorschach introduces the inkblot test

Sherrington wins Nobel Prize in physiology or medicine

Bertrand Russell is appointed to William James lectureship at Harvard

Germany invades Poland; England and France declare war on Germany

Cold War "space race" flourishes

Artificial intelligence emerges as a philosophical and scientific issue

Manson murders and trial

Sperry, Hubel, and Wiesel win Nobel Prize in physiology or medicine the nervous system's chemical mechanisms and the discovery of a central energizing system. Study of the neural bases of the senses continued to be a major research topic because of the importance of sensations as the gateway to the mind.

In the late 20th century, no one questions that the brain is the organ of mind and consciousness. In order to understand fully the nature of mental events, most psychologists deem it essential to understand the biological substrate. The reasons for this desire are both theoretical and practical. Theoretically, knowledge of the operations of the nervous system places limits on explanations. For example, Descartes's (Chapter 6) suggestion that a response occurs when sensory stimulation tightens a thread in a nerve, which opens a pore in the brain allowing animal spirits to flow into a muscle, was shown to be untenable by experiments in which frog muscles continued to contract from nervous stimulation after separation from the body. Similarly, advances in understanding the basic structure of the nervous system did not support the validity of Pavlov's theory of brain function in conditioning (Chapter 12). As a result, we honor Pavlov for his discovery and explication of conditioning, not for his neurological theorizing.

From a practical, applied standpoint, increased understanding of the nervous system and its functions has aided in the treatment of clinical disorders. For example, the finding that people with Parkinson's disease—a major motor disorder characterized by tremors at rest and decreased voluntary movement—display a massive depletion of the brain's neurotransmitter dopamine resulted in at least temporarily successful treatment of many patients with L-dopa, which increases dopamine in the patient's brain. Similarly, increasingly successful pharmacological treatments for such disorders as depression and schizophrenia have stimulated and have been stimulated by enhanced knowledge of the nervous system and its operations.

However, premature application of findings from neuroscience to clinical disorders remains a problem, which is well illustrated by Chapter 1's cautionary tale of Egas Moniz and the prefrontal lobotomy. More recently, interest in grafting tissue into the brain to treat such neurological disorders as Parkinson's disease led to the surgical implantation of a portion of a patient's own adrenal gland (part of the adrenal gland manufactures dopamine). Following preliminary reports of success in treating the disease with such autografts (e.g., Madrazo et al., 1987), physicians at several institutions in the United States and Europe attempted similar procedures, with disappointing results (Lewin, 1988). Unlike the prefrontal lobotomy, autotransplants of adrenal tissue did not become an accepted medical procedure, so in this case at least, history did not repeat itself.

We saw in Chapter 6 that two major methods (i.e., ablation, electrical stimulation) to study the nervous system were developed in the last half of the 19th century. In addition, the brain's anatomy had begun to be studied with chemical stains by the latter part of the 19th century. This technique led to the resolution of a major question about the anatomy of the nervous system: Is the nervous system a nerve net with all nerve cells interconnected, or is it made up of individual nerve cells (neurons)?

NEURON DOCTRINE OR NERVE NETWORK?

In 1891, **Wilhelm von Waldeyer** (1836–1921), German neurologist and anatomist, introduced the term "neuron" to describe the independent nerve unit. This led to the development of the neuron doctrine in opposition to the idea that the nerves form an interconnected network. The network idea was consistent with Flourens's (Chapter 6) nonlocalizationist view of a nervous system in which each major part had a particular function but there was no differentiation of the function within the part. Thus, one of the major effects of the victory of the neuron doctrine over the nerve network idea was to reinforce the concept of functional localization within the brain. In addition, the neuron doctrine appeared to provide an anatomical basis for the multiplicity of ideas formed through associations (e.g., Boring, 1950).

One of the chief proponents of the nerve network theory was **Camillo Golgi** (1843–1926), an Italian histologist and physician whose work ironically led to the downfall of the nerve network notion. Golgi was born in the village of Corteno, in northwest Italy. His father, a country doctor, sent him to study medicine at the University of Pavia, where Golgi received his M.D. degree in 1865. He immediately went to work at a clinic for mental ailments directed by Cesare Lombroso (1836–1909), best known for his theory of a criminal type distinguishable from the normal man.

Golgi experimented with various methods for hardening and staining tissues originally invented by Joseph von Gerlach (1820–1896), Johannes Müller (Chapter 6), and others. He found that osmic acid gave nerve cells and fibers a deep black color, which was well suited for microscopic work. Unfortunately, osmic acid was both scarce and expensive, and Golgi was forced to seek a less costly substitute. In 1873, he announced his invention of a method of staining by immersing hardened brain tissue in a silver nitrate solution.

Golgi's method stains only a few cells at a time in a region, and the stained cells are shown in their entirety. Today, over 100 years later, no one knows exactly how Golgi's stain works to color completely only 1 cell in 100, while leaving the other cells unaffected (Hubel, 1979).

Using Golgi's stain, **Santiago Ramón y Cajal** (1852–1934), Spanish histologist and neurologist, demonstrated that nerve cells are independent cells, contiguous without being continuous. Cajal's work thus supported the neuron theory, undermining Golgi's neural net idea. Golgi and Cajal were joint winners in 1906 of the Nobel Prize in physiology or medicine. Golgi never abandoned his belief in the nervous system's unitary nature, despite Cajal's overwhelming evidence refuting it.

Charles Sherrington and the Synapse

After Cajal's demonstration that neurons are separate units with tiny gaps between them, the key question became: What happens at the gaps? Is the information from one neuron to another carried across the gap the same way it travels the axon (a neuron's relatively long process)? Many properties of transmission across the gap were deduced by

FIGURE 17–1.   Sir Charles Sherrington.
Source: National Library of Medicine.

Charles Sherrington (1906; Figure 17–1) in his book, *The Integrative Action of the Nervous System.*

Born in London, **Sir Charles Scott Sherrington** (1857–1952) was an English physician and physiologist. At Liverpool and then later at Oxford, Sherrington studied the reflex arc, a circuit consisting of at least three neurons: a sensory neuron, a motor neuron, and a neuron connecting the sensory and motor neurons called an "interneuron." Thus, in the basic reflex, a sensory neuron excites an interneuron, the interneuron excites a motor neuron, and the motor neuron stimulates a muscle, which produces the reflex response. As we noted in Chapter 11, Sherrington's study of the reflex arc provided the neurological basis for Dewey's psychological reflex arc, which launched the school of functionalism.

Sherrington called the gap between neurons the **synapse**, which means binding (-apse) together (syn-). Studying the spinal reflex in dogs, Sherrington described several synaptic properties. For example, he found that reflexes were slower than conduction along an axon, suggesting that synaptic transmission introduces a slight delay. In addition, Sherrington found that summation of influences occurs at the synapse; for example, several weak stimuli presented at nearly the same time (temporal summation) or in nearly the same place (spatial summation) produce a greater response than does a single stimulus. For his pioneering work, Sherrington shared the 1932 Nobel Prize in physiology or medicine with another English physiologist, Edgar Douglas Adrian (1889–1977). Lord Adrian was also recognized for his work on the function of neurons.

Otto Loewi and Synaptic Transmission

Although Sherrington correctly deduced many of the properties of the synapse from his experiments, he guessed incorrectly that synaptic transmission is electrical rather than chemical. Although he found that neuronal transmission is slower at the synapse than it is along the axon, Sherrington still believed that synaptic transmission was too rapid to be chemical. Otto Loewi (Figure 17–2) did an experiment in 1920 that showed that Sherrington was wrong.

Born in Frankfurt am Main, **Otto Loewi** (1873–1961) was a German pharmacologist and physician. Until 1921, the prevailing view was that synaptic transmission occurred from the spreading of an electrical wave from the end of the axon (nerve terminal) to an effector organ (e.g., a muscle). Loewi thought this could not be correct because he knew that the stimulation of certain nerves increases the function of one organ while decreasing the function of another, which is inexplicable if synaptic transmission is indeed electrical. As early as 1903, Loewi had the idea that the terminals of some nerves might contain chemicals that are released with stimulation and that these chemicals might carry the nerve impulse across to the effector organs. However, he could not think of a way to test the idea, and it remained dormant for nearly 2 decades.

On the night before Easter Sunday in 1920, Loewi awoke with the plan for an experimental test of the chemical theory of synaptic transmission. He jotted

FIGURE 17–2.   Otto Loewi.

Source: New York University by courtesy of Harvard College Library.

some notes on a slip of paper only to discover the next morning that he could not decipher them. The memory returned at 3 A.M. the following morning, and this time Loewi went to his laboratory and did the experiment. In retrospect, Loewi (1960) wrote, "If carefully considered in the daytime, I would undoubtedly have rejected the kind of experiment I performed. . . . It was good fortune that at the moment of the hunch I did not think but acted immediately" (p. 18).

Loewi first placed two beating frog hearts, one with its vagus nerve attached and the other without its vagus nerve, into a container with a little Ringer solution (Ringer solution is physiological saline with chemicals added that are needed to preserve tissue function). Next, he stimulated the vagus nerve of the first heart, which caused its beating to slow. Loewi then transferred some of the Ringer solution from the first heart to the second heart, and the second heart slowed its beating as though its vagus nerve had been stimulated.

With this simple experiment, Otto Loewi had shown that stimulation of the vagus nerve released a chemical onto the heart muscle that caused its beating to slow. Appropriately enough, he called the mysterious chemical *Vagusstoff*, meaning stuff from the vagus nerve. *Vagusstoff* was soon found to be acetylcholine. For demonstrating that synaptic transmission was chemical and not electrical—that is, for acting on his nighttime hunch—Loewi was a cowinner of the 1936 Nobel Prize in physiology or medicine.

The Discovery of Additional Transmitter Substances

Although Loewi's demonstration that synaptic transmission takes place by chemical means was revolutionary, it did not immediately result in the discovery of a large number of transmitter substances in the central nervous system (brain and spinal cord, abbreviated CNS). In fact, by the mid-1950s, some 35 years after Loewi's demonstration, there was certainty about the neurotransmitter at only one class of CNS synapses: These were cholinergic synapses (synapses where acetylcholine is the neurotransmitter) on a special kind of cell in the spinal cord.

The problem is that the neurons in the CNS are microscopic, and there are literally billions of them. In the peripheral nervous system (PNS, all the nervous structures outside the CNS), organs are usually innervated by large, readily accessible bundles of nerve fibers, all of which use the same neurotransmitter. This neurotransmitter can be collected easily in samples big enough for analysis. In the CNS, the inaccessibility of circuits makes this approach nearly impossible.

In the early 1950s, three developments triggered an explosion of information on neurotransmitters. First, there was the discovery that the brain contains norepinephrine (noradrenalin) and three other chemicals that are similar to norepinephrine in molecular structure: epinephrine (adrenalin), dopamine, and serotonin. Much of the early work on CNS neurotransmission focused on these related chemicals, and they were soon shown to be bona fide transmitters.

The second major development of the 1950s was that methods were developed to detect tiny amounts of suspected neurotransmitters. The third development was increased interest in **psychopharmacology**, the field that uses psychological and pharmacological concepts to investigate the behavioral

effects of drugs. Interest soared in psychopharmacology because of the increased recreational use of drugs (e.g., LSD, marijuana) and because of the discovery of the first major antipsychotic drugs (e.g., reserpine, chlorpromazine). Because of these developments, knowledge in neuroscience has gone in less than 50 years from a few putative neurotransmitters in the CNS to approximately 9 known neurotransmitters and another 40 chemicals that are strongly suspected of being transmitter substances (Pinel, 1990).

Each discovery of another neurotransmitter has resulted in a burst of research activity, but probably no neurotransmitter discovery has stimulated more interest and work than that of the brain's own pain reliever, endorphin. **Endorphin** stands for endogenous (produced within) morphine-like substance.

Beginning in the 1950s, researchers found that many drugs and other natural agents cause their behavioral effects by interacting with receptors for them in the brain. Because the opiates (e.g., morphine, heroin) produce such dramatic effects in humans, it was thought that the brain might contain opiate receptors. Researchers had sought the receptors for years, and they were found in 1973 by scientists working independently in three laboratories: Solomon Snyder and Candace Pert at Johns Hopkins University School of Medicine, Eric Simon of the New York University School of Medicine, and Lars Terenius of Uppsala University in Sweden (Marx, 1975).

Because no one believed that opiate receptors had evolved so that we could be intoxicated by substances taken from the opium poppy, the search was on for naturally occurring opiate-like substances. Within 2 years, John Hughes, working in the laboratory of Hans Kosterlitz at the University of Aberdeen in Scotland, found two endogenous opiates, which he called enkephalins, meaning "in the head." Together, the enkephalins are known as endorphins.

What do the endorphins do? First and foremost, they produce analgesia (pain relief), and their release is suspected in the pain-suppressing effects of both placebos (inactive substances that nevertheless have a physiological effect) and acupuncture (Watkins & Mayer, 1982). In addition, the endorphins, or the receptors for them, are almost certainly involved in the other primary effect of the opiates—euphoria.

The discovery of opiate receptors and the associated endogenous opiates has advanced knowledge of the brain's pain mechanisms and of brain areas concerned with reinforcement. In addition, knowledge of the endorphins has implications for the pharmacological treatment of a variety of conditions. For example, some opiate antagonists prevent all the effects of the opiates, including the drugs' "high." Thus, it might be possible to use an opiate antagonist to treat heroin addiction. Other opiate antagonists prevent most of the opiate effects, but not all of them. Using this knowledge, a drug might be designed with morphine's pain-relieving qualities but without its addictive potential.

Although increased information about neurotransmitter substances and how they are involved in neurological disorders has led to more effective treatments for the diseases (e.g., L-dopa to replace the missing dopamine in victims of Parkinson's disease), often the process has been reversed, with a pharmacologically effective treatment leading to a better understanding of the neurological basis for a disorder (e.g., Kalat, 1995). For example, when it was found that effective antidepressant drugs increased the activity in synapses employing dopamine, norepinephrine, and serotonin as transmitter substances, it was inferred from this that depression might be related to deficiencies at these synapses. Further substances were sought to remedy the suspected deficiencies while limiting the side effects, leading to the development of the tricyclic antidepressants (e.g., imipramine, trade name Tofranil), which target particularly norepinephrine and serotonin.

More recently, antidepressants have been developed that focus on a single neurotransmitter—serotonin—thereby avoiding many of the side effects of the older drugs. Fluoxetine (trade name Prozac) is a currently popular example of this class of drugs, and its effectiveness in treating depression has implications for current thinking on the neurological basis of the disorder. Of course, the fact that Prozac is not universally effective in treating depression and the observation that some people are helped by drugs that target norepinephrine rather than serotonin

suggests that there is not a single neurological basis for the disorder.

The Nerve Impulse

Meanwhile, additional research focused on how nerve cells transmit information axonally. That is, although Otto Loewi demonstrated that synaptic transmission was chemical and many subsequent studies sought to expand the list of transmitter substances, research was also aimed at discovering how the nerve cell delivers the information received by its dendrites and cell body to the synapse.

This research was enormously aided by a discovery in the 1930s by Oxford University scientist John Z. Young: Young found that the squid has neurons large enough to be isolated and studied individually during transmission of the nerve impulse. Much of what we now know about axonal transmission came from experiments on the giant axon of the squid by the British neurophysiologists **Sir Alan Hodgkin** (1914–) and **Sir Andrew Huxley** (1917–), mentioned in Chapter 9. Hodgkin and Huxley, along with **Sir John Eccles** (1903–), received the Nobel Prize in physiology or medicine in 1963. Eccles's research furthered our understanding of synaptic transmission.

LOCALIZATION OF FUNCTION REVISITED

Against the backdrop of research aimed at understanding the nature of the nerve impulse and synaptic transmission, additional studies continued along themes developed in the 19th century. One of these themes involved the question of whether or not functions can be attached to specific brain areas. As we noted in Chapter 6, 19th-century brain investigators successfully localized a number of functions, with only the research of Flourens ostensibly supporting a nonlocalizationist view. In the first half of the 20th century, the work of S. I. Franz and Karl Lashley reawakened interest in the nonlocalizationist position.

Shepherd Ivory Franz

Like many of his era, **Shepherd Ivory Franz**'s (1874–1933) introduction to psychology came through a reading of William James's (Chapter 10) *Briefer Course* (Franz, 1932). This was at Columbia University, where Franz minored in education and anthropology while working on his doctorate with James McKeen Cattell (Chapter 10). Among the students Franz encountered in Cattell's laboratory, the ones who most affected his work included Thorndike (Chapters 11 and 12) and Woodworth (Chapter 11).

After receiving his Ph.D. in 1899, Franz spent an influential 2 years as a physiology assistant at Harvard Medical School. Franz's work at the Medical School necessitated his reading the current and classical literature on brain functions, and this reading directed him toward problems in physiological psychology. In Franz's initial work in the area, he became the first investigator to combine the ablation method of the physiologist with the training methods—based on Thorndike's dissertation work—of the psychologist. Franz used the combination to investigate the functions of the frontal lobes in cats. The resulting publication (Franz, 1902) stimulated a letter of encouragement from Charles Sherrington (Franz, 1932).

From Harvard Medical School, Franz was employed successively at Dartmouth Medical School and McLean Hospital (1901–1906), the Government Hospital for the Insane in Washington, D.C. (1907–1924), and UCLA (1924-1933). Although his interests were remarkably diverse, for many years Franz continued to apply the training/ablation method to the study of brain function. Like Flourens, Franz believed that the recovery of functions initially lost after cerebral destruction argued against a fixed localization of function in the cortex. As he put it, "Everything tended to show that there are not the definite and exact functions for parts of the cerebrum which were posited, but that there is rather a possibility of substitution" (Franz, 1932, p. 103). Ablation work with Karl Lashley in 1916 and Lashley's subsequent brain-ablation research further reinforced Franz's nonlocalizationist position.

Karl Lashley, the "Father of Neuropsychology"

Karl Spencer Lashley (1890–1958) was born in Davis, West Virginia. Lashley went to the University of West Virginia, where he planned to major in either English or Latin. However, an accidental encounter with the neurologist John Black Johnston led Lashley to discover the world of biology. According to Lashley, another accidental encounter, this time with a set of Golgi slides of the frog brain, resulted in his deciding to study behavior. Lashley took the slides to his instructor and naively proposed to work out all the connections, so that "we should know how the frog worked" (Hebb, 1963, p. viii).

Instead of turning immediately to neurology and psychology, Lashley received his M.S. in bacteriology at Pittsburgh and his Ph.D. in genetics with H. S. Jennings (Chapter 12) at Johns Hopkins University in 1914. At Johns Hopkins, Lashley was greatly influenced by John Watson (Chapter 12), with whom he pursued a minor in psychology. Lashley continued to work with Watson after he received his Ph.D., and their 4-year collaboration produced 14 psychology articles (Bruce, 1986). During his work with Watson, Lashley also joined Franz on two studies of cortical ablations and learning in the rat, setting the stage for Lashley's research career.

From 1917 until 1926, Lashley taught and worked at the University of Minnesota. He might have gone from Minnesota to Stanford, except for his appearance. Lewis Terman (Chapter 18) had asked for Lashley to be brought to California, and Stanford's President Wilbur traveled to Minnesota to offer Lashley a position.

> Wilbur did not fulfill his mission because, while walking across the Minnesota campus, a young faculty member riding by on his bicycle was pointed out to him. Lashley's long hair and pince-nez glasses, with a ribbon flowing in the breeze, offended Wilbur who felt that he had to be particularly circumspect in employing psychologists. (Hilgard, 1987, p. 429)

Although Lashley was not approached, Stanford did hire one of his Ph.D.s, **Calvin P. Stone** (1892–1954). APA president in 1942, Stone spent his professional career at Stanford. Perhaps Stone's best-known student was Harry Harlow (Chapter 14).

In 1926, Lashley went to the Institute for Juvenile Research in Chicago, where he began the experiments reported in *Brain Mechanisms and Intelligence* (Lashley, 1929/1963). From 1929 until 1935, Lashley was a professor at the University of Chicago.

In 1935, Lashley moved to a psychology professorship at Harvard. Actually, Harvard had approached Lashley as early as 1927 about a position at the university, and the offer in 1935 was Harvard's third overture (Bruce, 1991). Unfortunately, Lashley quickly became dissatisfied at Harvard. There was more administrative work than he wanted, and promised monetary support was not forthcoming. As a result, Lashley demanded a "roving" professorship, and he was appointed Research Professor of Neuropsychology in 1937.

Still retaining his Harvard affiliation, Lashley (Figure 17–3) became director of the Yerkes

Laboratory of Primate Biology in Orange Park, Florida, in 1942. He retired from this position in 1955 and died unexpectedly in 1958 while vacationing in France.

Lashley's Search for the Engram

Lashley's search for the **engram** (memory trace; the location of specific memories in the brain) began with the "simple aim of demonstrating the soundness of Watson's ideas of . . . the formation of stimulus-response connections through the cortex" (Hebb, 1963, p. viii). In the face of a great deal of conflicting evidence from studies in which he tested brain-damaged rats on a variety of different problems, Lashley abandoned Watson's simplistic idea of transcortical stimulus-response connections (Lashley, 1950). Note that this is another illustration of the importance of neurophysiological research for testing and constraining theoretical notions in psychology. Lashley's search for the engram also led to the development of his best-known concepts: mass action and equipotentiality.

By **mass action**, Lashley meant that the amount of cortical tissue destroyed is more important for complex learning than the location of that tissue. The greater the area of destruction, the greater the negative effect on learning. "Complex learning" is the operative phrase here—mass action is true for learning that involves many different cues and motor responses (e.g., a maze) and correspondingly many different cortical areas.

Equipotentiality was Lashley's term for the idea that any part of a functional area could carry out a particular function. Within a functional area, the parts are equal in their potential to mediate the function. Loss of the particular function requires the ablation of the entire area, and if any part is spared, the function will still be displayed. Lashley (1929/1963) suggested that equipotentiality held only for the so-called cortical association areas (cortical areas that are neither primarily sensory nor primarily motor) and for relatively complex functions (e.g., maze learning).

Note that Lashley did not deny the possibility of cortical localization. For example, when a rat learns a simple brightness discrimination, lesions of the

FIGURE 17–3.   Karl Lashley in the 1930s.

Source: Archives of the History of American Psychology.

posterior cortex disrupt it, whereas anterior cortical lesions have no effect. This is localization of function, but it is localization of a relatively simple function primarily involving one sensory mechanism. Lashley's principles of equipotentiality and mass action held for complex learning involving many sensory cues.

Toward the end of his famous paper, "In Search of the Engram," Lashley (1950) wrote, not totally tongue-in-cheek, "I sometimes feel, in reviewing the evidence on the localization of the memory trace, that the necessary conclusion is that learning is just not possible" (pp. 477–478). However, he reluctantly assigned the memory trace to sensory areas in the cortex, concluding "that the memory trace is located in all parts of the functional area; that various parts are equipotential for its maintenance and activation" (p. 469). As we will see later, one of the many individuals influenced by Lashley came to different conclusions following a similar search for the engram.

FIGURE 17–4.   D. O. Hebb.

Source: Courtesy Mary Ellen Hebb.

Lashley's Students and Colleagues

Throughout his career, Lashley was influential both through his publications and through his many students. We encountered one of his students from the Minnesota days in the first chapter—**Carlyle Jacobsen** (1902–1974). Jacobsen's frontal lobe operations in chimpanzees excited Egas Moniz and resulted in the first prefrontal lobotomies.

Born in Chester, Nova Scotia, **Donald Olding Hebb** (1904–1985) was another of Lashley's students. Hebb (Figure 17–4) received a B.A. degree from Dalhousie University with the lowest grade average possible without failing. After graduation, Hebb first attempted to write novels but, like Skinner (Chapter 13), gave this up and read Freud (Chapter 15) instead. He then went to McGill University as a part-time graduate student in psychology, even though he had no background in the area. At McGill, Hebb read Pavlov and worked with two Pavlov-trained scientists, Boris P. Babkin and Leonid Andreyev. When Hebb became disenchanted with Pavlov, Babkin urged him to study with Lashley. Although Hebb started his graduate work with Lashley in Chicago, he completed his Ph.D. with Lashley at Harvard in 1936. From 1937 to 1939,

he worked with Wilder Penfield (Chapter 6), the neurosurgeon whose cortical stimulation work on human patients was anticipated by Roberts Bartholow (Chapter 6). At Lashley's invitation, Hebb went to the Yerkes laboratories for 5 years (1942–1947).

In 1949, Hebb's *The Organization of Behavior* reawakened interest in psychologists for neurological explanations of behavior. This interest had been dulled by Lashley's work, which seemed to show that the brain was a relatively homogeneous structure in whose parts the principle of equipotentiality reigned. From about 1930 until 1950, theoretical psychology concerned itself with the behavioral aspects of learning, avoiding speculation on learning's neural basis. Hebb's book changed all this.

In *The Organization of Behavior,* Hebb developed hypothetical neural mechanisms (e.g., the *cell assembly,* which is a circuit of neurons firing together in response to a particular stimulus) to account for a wide array of behavior: such perceptual phenomena as reversible images, inverted images, and closure; learning phenomena such as all-or-none learning and insight; motivation; attention; forgetting; sleep;

and emotional disturbance. Because of this inclusiveness, Hebb's book was still being nontrivially cited 30 years later by a variety of authors writing on diverse topics (e.g., sensation and perception, emotion, motivation, cognitive science, physiological psychology) in Hearst's (1979) book, *The First Century of Experimental Psychology*. In fact, present-day theorists interested in machine learning (see Chapter 20) consider Hebb's contributions so important to their work that one element of machine learning is called the "Hebbian rule" (Rumelhart, McClelland, & the PDP Research Group, 1986). The rule is an equation that predicts the learning rate given the number and strength of neural connections.

Hebb returned to McGill in 1947 and assumed the psychology department leadership the following year. He remained at McGill for the rest of his career, serving as the university chancellor from 1970 through 1974. Among his many honors, Hebb was one of the few non-American APA presidents (1960). Hebb also received the gold medal of the American Psychological Foundation for his contributions to psychology.

Frank A. Beach (1911–1988) was another one of Lashley's Chicago Ph.D. students. Beach became well known for his work in human and animal sexual behavior. In a classic paper, Beach (1950) chided comparative psychology for its overemphasis on the behavior of only a few species and particularly the behavior of the white rat. For the most part, his message has been ignored by comparative psychologists.

Lashley also influenced people who did not take degrees with him. For example, Lashley was one of two men to whom Clifford T. Morgan (mentioned in Chapter 10), a Harvard instructor during Lashley's tenure there, dedicated his 1943 book, *Physiological Psychology*. At Orange Park, Florida, Lashley so influenced the practicing neurosurgeon **Karl Pribram** (1919–) that Pribram abandoned his medical practice for an academic career in neuropsychology. While contributing many experimental studies to the literature of physiological psychology, Pribram has also been a theorist of brain function in the Hebbian mold. Pribram's theories have been expounded in major reviews (e.g.,

Pribram, 1960) and books (e.g., Miller, Galanter, & Pribram, 1960; Pribram, 1971), and he remains a leader in the field.

Robert Thompson (1927–1989) was so intrigued with Lashley during a 1-year research assistantship at Yerkes Laboratory in 1951 that he devoted the bulk of a 35-year career in physiological psychology to an attempt to find what Lashley had failed to discover conclusively: the locus of the engram (Thorne, 1995). What spurred Thompson's search was the idea that Lashley may have been looking in the wrong place for the memory trace, by concentrating on the cortex. Perhaps Lashley's (1950) dismissal of subcortical areas had been premature.

Robert Thompson received his Ph.D. from the University of Texas in 1955. At Texas, Thompson and a fellow graduate student, **James V. McConnell** (1925–1990), became the first researchers in modern times to show that it was possible to classically condition the planarian, or flatworm (Thompson & McConnell, 1955). McConnell's career included controversial research on memory transfer in the flatworm, APA's Distinguished Teaching Award, and a light-hearted journal called the *Worm Runner's Digest* (Sommer, 1991). His success in popularizing psychology also led to an attack by the Unabomber (Rilling, 1996). After Texas, Thompson began to study learning and memory in the rat.

In his search for the engram, Thompson adopted Wilder Penfield's idea of a "**centrencephalic system** or **centrencephalon**." Based on clinical evidence, Penfield (e.g., Penfield, 1958) concluded that there is a collection of subcortical structures that coordinates and integrates the activities of the cerebral hemispheres—the centrencephalic system. Penfield attributed to the centrencephalon many of the qualities Descartes claimed for the pineal gland (Chapter 3). For example, if a person wants to perform some particular action, Penfield believed the centrencephalon directs impulses to the cortical area in which the action's instructions are stored (Penfield, 1952).

Using carefully placed cortical or subcortical lesions in rats, Thompson and his students and coworkers amassed a wealth of evidence for a core set of brain structures involved either in the retention of preoperatively acquired tasks or in the post-operative learning of such tasks. Thompson's memory studies culminated in *A Behavioral Atlas of the Rat Brain* (Thompson, 1978), whereas his learning studies produced over 50 articles and the posthumously published book, *Brain Mechanisms in Problem Solving and Intelligence: A Lesion Survey of the Rat Brain* (Thompson, Crinella, & Yu, 1990). A final summary of his centrencephalic system can be found in Thompson (1993).

Thus, Thompson essentially succeeded where Lashley failed, as indicated by Jan Bures of the Czechoslovak Academy of Sciences. In a 1986 letter, Bures wrote that "[Robert Thompson] is a true heir of Karl Lashley" (as cited in Thorne, 1995, p. 129). Unfortunately, Thompson is little known outside a small circle of neuroscientists. One reason for Thompson's lack of name recognition is quite mundane: There is another, better known R. Thompson who also has been engaged in a "search for the engram"—Richard F. Thompson.

In Search of the Engram—Simple Tasks and Simple Animals

Like Robert Thompson, **Richard F. Thompson** (1930–) has had some success in his search for the engram. Thompson received his Ph.D. in physiological psychology in 1956 from the University of Wisconsin, where he also studied with Harry Harlow and did a postdoctoral stint in neurophysiology at the University of Wisconsin School of Medicine. Thompson is currently Keck Professor of Psychology and Biological Sciences at the University of Southern California.

In the 1970s, Thompson began his search for the engram of the classically conditioned eyelid response in the rabbit. Note that where Lashley and Robert Thompson sought the location of the memory trace for relatively complex tasks (e.g., maze running), R. F. Thompson chose a much simpler learning task in the belief that the brain area(s) devoted to it would be more circumscribed. During conditioning of the rabbit's eyeblink to a tone by pairing it with an air puff to the eye, recording the activity of different brain cells indicated that cells in the cerebellum are responsible for the development of the conditioned response. Damage to the particu-

lar cerebellar area abolishes the conditioned response but not the unconditioned response. That is, the animal can still blink in response to the air puff, but the tone no longer elicits the response. Now that the locus of this engram has been well established (e.g., Thompson, 1986), the next step is to work at the cellular level to find the neural mechanisms responsible for coding the memory trace.

Work on the cellular level has been the hallmark of Eric R. Kandel's research on learning in the sea snail, *Aplysia*. Kandel, who graduated from Harvard in 1952 and received his M.D. at the New York University School of Medicine in 1956, began working with *Aplysia* in 1962 while he was a National Institutes of Health special fellow at the Institute Marey in Paris. He was looking for a simple creature in which he could study the mechanisms of learning and memory more directly than is possible in a more complex organism, and the invertebrate *Aplysia* proved to be ideal. Compared to vertebrates, *Aplysia* has fewer neurons, many of the neurons are relatively large, and the nervous systems of different snails are nearly identical. It is possible to identify a particular neuron in a given specimen and then study the same nerve cell in other *Aplysia*, something that so far has proven to be impossible in vertebrates.

Kandel and his associates have studied and successfully identified the cellular changes in habituation (decreased response to repeated exposure to a harmless stimulus), sensitization (an overresponsiveness to any stimulus following exposure to an intense stimulus), and classical conditioning of *Aplysia's* withdrawal response to a touch on different parts of its body (Kandel, 1985). It remains to be seen if the mechanisms for behavioral plasticity Kandel has discovered in *Aplysia* will generalize to vertebrates.

Roger Sperry and the Split-Brain Operation

As we indicated, Lashley's research generally supported nonlocalization of function, particularly of a complex maze-learning task in the rat. However, research by Lashley's students and by people he influenced continued to steer neuroscience toward functional localization. Still, in the middle of the

20th century, no function had been assigned to the most important bundle of fibers connecting the two cerebral hemispheres—the corpus callosum. Lashley himself jokingly speculated that the function of the corpus callosum "'must be mainly mechanical . . . i.e., to keep the hemispheres from sagging'" (Sperry, 1964, p. 42).

Nearly a century before Lashley, Gustav Fechner (Chapter 6) had speculated about the corpus callosum's function. Fechner knew that the brain was essentially symmetrical: Its two hemispheres appear on casual inspection to be mirror images of each other. Because Fechner believed that consciousness is one of the brain's properties, he also thought that splitting the brain in half by cutting the corpus callosum would result in separate streams of consciousness (Blakemore, 1977). Although Fechner was somewhat correct in his speculation, he was wrong in his belief that it would never be tested. The riddle of the corpus callosum, and the question of whether two streams of consciousness result from its transection, began to be answered in the 1950s with Roger Sperry's research program.

Born in Hartford, Connecticut, **Roger Wolcott Sperry** (1913–1994) received his A.B. (1935) and his M.A. (1937) degrees in psychology from Oberlin College. After receiving his Ph.D. in zoology from the University of Chicago in 1941, Sperry was a research fellow at Harvard and at the Yerkes Laboratory of Primate Biology until 1946, where he undoubtedly came under the influence of Lashley and Hebb. Sperry worked at the University of Chicago from 1946 until 1952, was the chief of developmental neurology for the National Institutes of Health from 1952 to 1954, and was Hixon professor of psychobiology at the California Institute of Technology (Cal Tech) from 1954 to 1984. Sperry received a Nobel Prize in physiology or medicine in 1981 (Figure 17–5). Other honors included the Warren Medal of the Society of Experimental Psychologists, the Distinguished Scientific Contribution Award of the APA, the Presidential National Medal of Science in 1989, and the APA's Award for Outstanding Lifetime Contribution to Psychology in 1993.

The first convincing demonstration that the function of the corpus callosum was more than

FIGURE 17–5. Roger Sperry (left) receiving the Nobel Prize from King Gustaf XVI in Stockholm.

Source: AP/Wide World Photos.

mechanical was provided by the doctoral research of Sperry's student, Ronald E. Myers. Working with split-brain cats whose corpus callosum and optic chiasm had been cut, Myers and Sperry (1953) found that learning by one hemisphere of the brain was not transferred to the other hemisphere. In addition, with the corpus callosum split, cats functioned as though they had two independent brains; for example, the left hemisphere could learn a problem whose solution required a response diametrically opposed to the solution of a problem learned by the right hemisphere.

After a series of studies of the **split-brain operation** in animals did not indicate any dramatic impairment of mental abilities, surgeons P. J. Vogel and J. E. Bogen of the California College of Medicine decided to try the operation on humans with uncontrollable epilepsy. The rationale for the operation was that commissurotomy, as it is called, might reduce the intensity of the patients' seizures by limiting them to one hemisphere. Actually, the operation proved quite beneficial, and many commissurotomized patients never had another seizure. Beginning with the first patient in 1961, Sperry and various associates, particularly Michael S. Gazzaniga, studied the patients postoperatively to see if the animal findings generalize to humans.

Amazingly, commissurotomy produces little change in temperament, personality, and general intelligence. In a typical case, Gazzaniga (1967) reported that a patient awakened from the surgery with the comment "that he had a 'splitting headache,' and in his still drowsy state he was able to repeat the tongue twister 'Peter Piper picked a peck of pickled peppers'" (p. 369).

Under ordinary circumstances, the commissurotomized patients appeared normal, but sophisticated testing procedures revealed striking differences in the abilities of the two hemispheres. According to Sperry (1982), the left hemisphere's specialties tend to be verbal, mathematical, and sequential, and because of the language capacity, the left hemisphere is sometimes called the "dominant" hemisphere. The mute right hemisphere typically specializes in spatial and imagistic ability, the kind of ability in which "a picture is worth a thousand words." Block design, discriminating random shapes, and map reading are all tasks at which the right hemisphere excels.

Concerning Fechner's prediction of separate consciousness from splitting the brain, Gazzaniga (1967) wrote: "All the evidence indicates that separation of the hemispheres creates two independent spheres of consciousness within a single cranium . . . .This conclusion is disturbing to some people who view consciousness as an indivisible property of the human brain" (p. 374). But remember that the evidence for separate consciousness in the divided hemispheres comes primarily from the sophisticated testing of researchers like Sperry and Gazzaniga— ordinarily the split-brain patients appear normal.

Sperry went beyond Gazzaniga in discussing the implications of his work for solving the mind-body or mind-brain problem. In his Nobel Prize address, Sperry (1982) said:

> [I]t remains to mention briefly that one of the more important indirect results of the split-brain work is a revised concept of the nature of consciousness and its fundamental relation to brain processing. . . . The key development is a switch from prior noncausal, parallelist views to

a new causal, or "interactionist" interpretation that ascribes to inner experience an integral causal control role in brain function and behavior. In effect, and without resorting to dualism, the mental forces of the conscious mind are restored to the brain of objective science from which they had long been excluded on materialist-behaviorist principles. (p. 1226)

In what is certainly a novel approach for a biopsychologist, Sperry argued for a return to an introspective science of the mind.

> Cognitive introspective psychology and related cognitive science can no longer be ignored experimentally, or written off as "a science of epiphenomena" or as something that must in principle reduce eventually to neurophysiology. The events of inner experience, as emergent properties of brain processes, become themselves explanatory causal constructs in their own right, interacting at their own level with their own laws and dynamics. The whole world of inner experience . . . , long rejected by 20th-century scientific materialism, thus becomes recognized and included with the domain of science. (p. 1226)

Sperry's concern with the mind-body problem was still evident at the end of his life (Sperry, 1994). Sperry's new model of consciousness holds that consciousness has a causal influence. Expanding on the Gestalt maxim "the whole is different from its parts" and the Gestalt understanding of emergent properties, Sperry noted that the "emergent whole . . . constantly exerts downward control over its parts. . . . In the new view . . . things are doubly determined, not only from lower levels upward, but also from above downward" (p. 11). The impetus for this new view of mind has come as a result of the cognitive revolution (Chapter 20). Further important theoretical and philosophical implications drawn from the split-brain research include Jaynes's (1977) consideration of the origin of human consciousness.

A word of caution is in order about the implications of the split-brain research for human abilities, however (e.g., Sperry, 1982). There has been a tendency to apply (and misapply) the research to support popularistic speculations about differential abilities of the two hemispheres, and as Sperry noted, "The left-right dichotomy in cognitive mode is an idea with which it is very easy to run wild" (p. 1225). Further, it should be remembered that, "in the normal state, the two hemispheres appear to work closely together as a unit, rather than one being turned on while the other idles" (p. 1225). Thus, popular works that purportedly teach the reader how to "turn on the right brain's creativity" or how to tap selectively the left hemisphere's analytical prowess are not supported by split-brain research.

From an examination of Sperry's work and its implications for the study of the conscious mind, we turn to an area of study that appeared to identify the physiological basis of consciousness. We begin with a look at sleep research.

SLEEP AND THE BRAIN'S ENERGIZING SYSTEM

One popular theory of sleep was that the nervous system and the body simply became exhausted after a certain amount of activity, and sleep was necessary for recovery. The "passive" theory held that the brain's natural state was sleep and that sensory input was necessary for wakefulness. By contrast, the "active" theory of sleep suggests that the brain is normally active, and there is an inhibitory system that periodically depresses brain areas responsible for consciousness.

The ability to study sleep experimentally took a giant leap forward with **Hans Berger**'s (1873–1941) discovery and recording of the brain's fluctuating electrical potentials—the electroencephalogram or EEG. Berger was a German psychiatrist whose mostly unsuccessful research attempted to establish relationships between physiological measures and psychological states. We have encountered such attempts before in Galton (Chapter 9) and Cattell. While studying such physiological measures as heartbeat, respiration, and the brain's temperature, Berger (1929) placed electrical recording equipment on the scalp and recorded "brain waves." Initial skepticism in the scientific community gave way to widespread use and after

only 15 years, a review chapter listed approximately 450 references (Lindsley, 1944).

Berger's EEG techniques allowed brain researchers to study sleep-wake cycles in laboratory animals subjected to various treatments (e.g., brain damage, drugs). For example, Belgian scientist Frédéric Bremer (1936) studied cats with cuts through different levels of the brainstem. Animals with cuts between the spinal cord and lower brainstem showed EEG signs of waking and sleeping, whereas higher cuts through the midbrain produced animals with persistent EEG sleep patterns. Because the higher cuts permitted less sensory information to reach the cortex, Bremer interpreted them as evidence for the passive theory of sleep. Bremer's conclusion was shown to be wrong by the pivotal experiments of the Italian physiologist Guiseppe Moruzzi and the American anatomist Horace Magoun.

Moruzzi and Magoun (1949) found that stimulation of a brainstem structure called the *reticular formation* because of its netlike appearance (reticular means netlike) produced an alert cortical EEG even in a lightly anesthetized or sleeping cat. In later studies (e.g., Lindsley, Schreiner, Knowles, & Magoun, 1950), destruction of the brainstem reticular formation (BSRF) produced permanently sleeping animals, whereas damage to surrounding areas did not have this effect. This demonstrated that sleep was not simply the elimination of specific sensory information as Bremer had suggested—rather, input to the cortex from the BSRF was critical, and Bremer's higher cuts had blocked this input.

Further study of the BSRF seemed to indicate that all sensory systems sent information to the reticular core and that the core sent fibers to virtually all areas of the forebrain. The BSRF seemed the ideal structure for an energizing system in the brain. Sensory input through the normal channels would also stimulate the BSRF, and the BSRF would arouse the cortex, possibly acting as a filter to stimulate the cortical areas most responsible for dealing with the particular sensory information. Perhaps the BSRF was responsible for consciousness, not just consciousness in the sense of the opposite of unconsciousness, but consciousness in the sense of attending to something. In some speculations, the

BSRF nearly achieved the status of the "little man inside," a director of operations that could recognize immediately every bit of sensory input, decide whether or not to ignore it, and direct it to the appropriate part of the brain if it were allowed to pass through (Milner, 1970). The objection to this kind of function for any brain area is obvious: If the BSRF (or any other area) can make the high-level decisions suggested for it, what is the purpose of the rest of the brain?

Although the BSRF may not have fulfilled all the expectations of early investigators, its discovery stimulated an enormous amount of interest in the search for biological explanations of behavior. Some of the resulting research proved to be at least as important as the eliciting stimulus. This was particularly true for an accidental discovery made by two psychologists at McGill University—James Olds and Peter Milner (Figure 17–6).

James Olds (1922–1976) received his M.A. in 1951 and his Ph.D. in 1952 from Harvard. Olds was trained as a social psychologist and spent the year after he got his Ph.D. lecturing and doing research at Harvard's Laboratory of Social Relations. From 1953 to 1955, Olds was a postdoctoral fellow at McGill University, where he met and collaborated with Peter Milner. Olds and Milner's famous discovery came in an experiment in which the two young men were attempting to investigate the effects of an increased drive state on learning. To increase the drive state, they planned to stimulate the reticular formation in freely moving, unanesthetized rats. A novice brain surgeon, Olds accidentally stuck an electrode in the septal area of a rat rather than in the BSRF (this was a gross error, as the two brain areas are several millimeters apart). The result was a rat that sought out and stayed in parts of the learning apparatus in which it received stimulation. Olds and

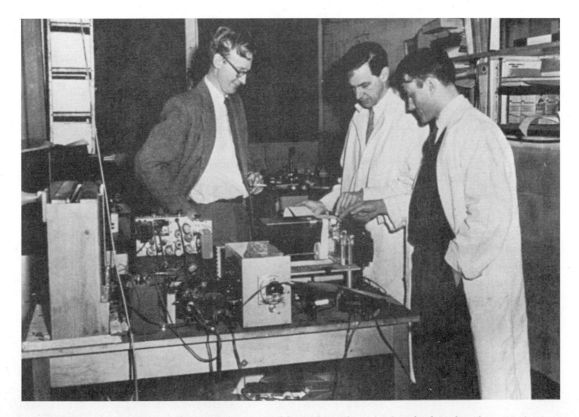

FIGURE 17–6.   (From left to right) James Olds, Peter Milner, and Seth Sharpless (ca. 1955).

Source: M. E. Olds; courtesy Harvard College Library.

Milner (1954) had found brain regions often called **"reward areas"** or **"pleasure centers."**

In the same year, researchers found three areas in the cat brain where stimulation was aversive (Delgado, Roberts, & Miller, 1954). The animals would learn responses in order to turn off stimulation of these negative regions. Since 1954, most of the rat brain has been mapped into positive, negative, and neutral areas. In addition, countless studies have examined the question of whether stimulation of the positive areas mimics natural reward. In some areas, the experimental results point to an answer of yes, and it should come as no surprise that a considerable amount of evidence links the brain's reward areas with the sites of action of such addictive substances as the opiates, cocaine, amphetamine, nicotine, and alcohol (e.g., see Beatty, 1995). Theoretical issues surrounding self-stimulation of the brain have been reviewed by Gallistel, Shizgal, and Yeomans (1981).

James Olds, whose lack of expertise in electrode implantation initiated the study of the brain's reward areas, died in a swimming accident in 1976 (Routtenberg, 1978). One of your authors heard Olds lecture at an APA convention in the early 1970s. He came across as an incredibly exciting person, with boundless enthusiasm for what he was doing. His premature death was a tragic blow to physiological psychology.

On another front, research continued on the sensory mechanisms investigated in the 19th century by Helmholtz, Hering, and others (Chapter 6). With advances in technology, evidence to support or refute 19th-century speculations became available.

SENSORY SYSTEMS

The Visual System

Color Vision

As we noted, Helmholtz revived an earlier color vision theory proposed by Thomas Young in which Young had suggested that perhaps as few as three color receptors are needed to explain our ability to perceive the colors of the visual spectrum. In support, Helmholtz showed that normal observers require only three different primary colors (e.g., red, green, and blue) to match any color stimulus, and the Young-Helmholtz theory became known as trichromatic (three-color) theory.

Physiological evidence for the required three cone pigments did not appear until over 100 years after Helmholtz's revision (Coren, Ward, & Enns, 1994). One technique for studying cone pigments uses an instrument that measures the amount of light absorbed when tiny amounts of light of different wavelengths are passed through a cone. The cone is most sensitive to the maximally absorbed wavelength of light. Using the device, several investigators (e.g., Brown & Wald, 1964) found three different types of cones just as trichromatic theory predicts.

However, a number of color phenomena seem to require opponent processes and a tetrachromatic or four-color theory. Ewald Hering proposed one tetrachromatic theory in 1874 that came to be known as opponent-process theory. After Hering's theory was introduced, several additional color vision theories appeared, of which Christine Ladd-Franklin's became perhaps the best known (Boring, 1950).

Christine Ladd (1847–1930) earned an undergraduate degree from Vassar College in 1869 and was admitted to graduate studies at Johns Hopkins as a "special student." Her "special" status reflected Hopkins's admissions policies that excluded women. Ladd was admitted because a prominent mathematics professor at the university, aware of her already published work, interceded on her behalf. Although she completed the requirements for the Ph.D. degree in 1882, the degree was not actually granted until 1926, when Johns Hopkins celebrated its 50th anniversary. Soon after finishing her work at Hopkins, Ladd married Fabian Franklin, a member of the mathematics department.

A trip to Europe during her husband's sabbatical leave in 1891–1892 brought **Christine Ladd-Franklin** into contact with several outstanding German psychologists and physiologists. With G. E. Müller's (Chapter 8) support, Ladd-Franklin conducted experimental work in vision in his Göttingen laboratory. In addition, she worked in Helmholtz's Berlin laboratory and attended lectures given by

Arthur König (Chapter 8), who supported Helmholtz's trichromatic theory.

Ladd-Franklin's theory was based on the tetrachromatic theory of Franciscus Cornelius Donders, the Dutch ophthalmologist and professor of physiology introduced in Chapter 7 in connection with the study of reaction times. Donders had suggested that color discrimination could be explained by decomposing color molecules stimulating optic nerve fibers. Ladd-Franklin's theory added a developmental focus to Donders's idea. She proposed that white receptors are basic to vision. Some white receptors developmentally split into either blue or yellow receptors, and some of the yellow receptors evolve into either red or green receptors. Ladd-Franklin's attempted reconciliation of the Young-Helmholtz theory with Donders's theory was eventually supplanted by Hering's opponent-process theory.

Hering thought the opponent processes—for example, one process excited by white and inhibited by black, one excited by green and inhibited by red, and one excited by yellow and inhibited by blue, or vice versa—occurred at the level of the receptors. This view was incompatible with trichromatic theory, and Hering's theory did not catch on until L. M. Hurvich and Dorothea Jameson (1957) published an article entitled "An Opponent-Process Theory of Color Vision." Hurvich and Jameson's psychophysical studies were soon supplemented by physiological evidence for an opponent-process theory (e.g., Svaetichin & MacNichol, 1958). In addition, Hurvich and Jameson (1974) constructed a simple diagram (Figure 17–7) to show how three different cones might be "wired" to higher-level visual cells to produce opponent responses.

Most authorities currently accept that both trichromatic and opponent-process theory are correct at different levels of the visual system. Trichromatic theory is valid at the receptor level, and opponent-process theory is correct at higher levels.

Form Vision

Although Descartes (Chapter 3) saw and described the retinal image, the image is not conveyed in any literal sense to the brain's visual areas. Instead, receptor cells are stimulated by the different patterns

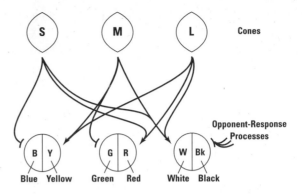
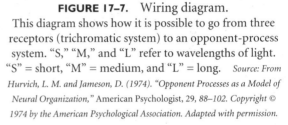

FIGURE 17–7. Wiring diagram.
This diagram shows how it is possible to go from three receptors (trichromatic system) to an opponent-process system. "S," "M," and "L" refer to wavelengths of light. "S" = short, "M" = medium, and "L" = long. *Source: From Hurvich, L. M. and Jameson, D. (1974). "Opponent Processes as a Model of Neural Organization,"* American Psychologist, 29, *88–102. Copyright © 1974 by the American Psychological Association. Adapted with permission.*

and colors of light striking them, some features of the stimulus are encoded, and the coded message is decoded in the cortex. A number of researchers have sought to discover how the different nerve cells in the visual system analyze the visual scene.

The research method used is conceptually simple: While recording from single nerve cells, experimenters have visually stimulated the eyes of their experimental subjects to try to determine the stimulus with the most pronounced effect on the cell from which they are recording. The visual stimuli employed have consisted of light patterns of different sizes, shapes, and colors, moving and stationary patterns, and patterns on different backgrounds. Using this procedure, investigators have mapped the **receptive fields** (patch of receptor cells supplying the nerve cell recorded from) of neurons at all levels of the visual system. This is the neurological equivalent of Titchener's (Chapter 7) search for the elements of visual sensations.

Haldan Keffer Hartline (1903–1983) was the earliest investigator of single optic nerve fibers (e.g., Hartline, 1938). For his pioneering work, Hartline shared the 1967 Nobel Prize in physiology or medicine with Ragnar Granit and George Wald. Like Hartline, **Ragnar Arthur Granit** (1900–) was one of the first to use microelectrodes to study the visual system. A Finnish-born Swedish physiologist, Granit worked at Oxford under Sherrington (1928–1931). In addition to replicating Hartline's work with different animals (e.g., Granit, 1947), Granit was the first investigator to study the response of optic nerve fibers to colored stimuli. **George Wald** (1906–) is an American biochemist who spent most of his career at Harvard. In 1933, he discovered vitamin A in the retina; subsequent work demonstrated that the light-sensitive pigment of the eye is composed of a protein fragment linked to a structure derived from vitamin A.

Improving on Hartline's and Granit's investigation of single optic nerve fibers, Stephen Kuffler (1953) used tiny spots of light to determine more precisely the receptive fields. He found that the fields had a center-surround configuration, with some of the cells having an excitatory center with an inhibitory surround and others having the opposite pattern. This receptive field configuration is also found at the next level of visual processing, so the cells at the first two levels seem to be responding to spots of light in a particular part of the visual field.

At the cortex, most neurons appear to respond best to lines with quite specific orientation. This discovery led to the **feature detector model** of David Hubel and Torsten Wiesel (Figure 17–8), cowinners along with Roger Sperry of the 1981 Nobel Prize in physiology or medicine. **David Hunter Hubel** (1926–) is a Canadian-born American neurophysiologist who studied medicine at McGill University in Montreal, joined Torsten Wiesel in Kuffler's laboratory at Johns Hopkins, and continued his work with Wiesel at Harvard. **Torsten Nils Wiesel** (1924–) is a Swedish neurobiologist who studied medicine at the Karolinska Institute in Stockholm before meeting Hubel at Johns Hopkins.

Working first with cats and then later with monkeys, Hubel and Wiesel found that many neurons in a particular part of visual cortex have receptive fields like their predecessors at earlier levels (e.g., in the optic nerve). But in other layers of the cortex, the cells seem to respond best to lines or slits of light with a particular orientation (horizontal, vertical, or at any angle), in a particular part of the visual field. Hubel and Wiesel called these "line" or "edge" detectors *simple cells* and assumed that the simple

FIGURE 17–8.   David Hubel (eating) and Torsten Wiesel (crouching).

Source: Courtesy of Colin Blakemore, Oxford University.

cells break the visual scene into lines or edges. Again, these cells are presumably the neural equivalent of Titchener's visual sensations.

Next, Hubel and Wiesel found cells with larger receptive fields than seen in the simple cells, which they called *complex cells.* Complex cells seem to respond best to a bar or edge of light with a particular orientation moving across the receptive field. Finally, Hubel and Wiesel described *hypercomplex cells,* which have receptive fields like the complex cells with the addition of a strong inhibitory area at one end of their bar-shaped receptive fields.

Hubel and Wiesel's research suggests that cells in the visual cortex detect increasingly complex features of the visual scene. Carrying the feature-detector model to its extreme, some have argued that there must be cells farther along in the visual system that respond only to images of your grandmother or of your psychology professor. These are sometimes called "grandmother" detectors, and a few studies have reported evidence for them. For example, Gross, Bender, and Rocha-Miranda (1969) discovered cells in the temporal lobes of monkeys that appeared to respond best to the outline of a monkey hand. Unfortunately, few "grandmother" detectors have been found, and some have suggested that a collection of higher-order cells equipped to respond to every complex stimulus that we perceive would require more neural connections than are available in the cerebral cortex (Schneider & Tarshis, 1986).

Without "grandmother" detectors, how is the information from a collection of cells assembled to recognize complex patterns? Again, we come to a restatement of the mind-body problem: What is the relationship between our conscious perceptions and the activity of all the millions of cells in the visual cortex? At present, there is no satisfactory answer to this question. In fact, not all brain investigators are convinced that the feature-detector model satisfactorily describes the way the brain analyzes visual information. Although it is true that cells in the visual cortex respond to lines, edges, moving lines, particular angles, and so on, the cells may actually show a preferential response to some other information supplied by the visual stimulus. For example, a complex visual scene can be described both in terms of lines and angles and in terms of alternating patterns of light and dark. The number of light and dark alternations in a degree of visual angle is called the frequency of the visual stimulus, and Russell DeValois and his colleagues have proposed a **spatial frequency model** (DeValois & DeValois, 1987). Proponents of this model suggest that neurons in the visual cortex perform a spatial frequency analysis rather than breaking the visual scene into component lines and angles. For now, there is no evidence that allows us to decide whether the cells in the visual cortex function primarily as line or edge detectors, as spatial frequency analyzers, or as detectors of some other feature of a visual stimulus.

The Auditory System

As we noted in Chapter 6, Helmholtz's place theory of pitch perception envisioned fibers analogous to piano strings in the inner ear's basilar membrane. When stimulated by a sound, specific fibers tuned to the sound's frequency would vibrate, stimulating the appropriate auditory nerve fiber to produce the appropriate auditory sensation.

Challenging Helmholtz, physicist William Rutherford proposed a frequency theory of pitch in 1886, shortly after the invention of the telephone. Rutherford's theory assumed that the basilar membrane acts like a telephone diaphragm, vibrating in synchrony with the incoming sound wave. The different sound frequencies are encoded by different frequencies of impulses in the auditory nerve. For example, a sound with a frequency of 1,000 cycles per second or Hz would generate auditory nerve impulses at the rate of 1,000 per second. (Hz stands for hertz, the unit of sound measurement named after Heinrich Rudolf Hertz [1857–1894], who studied under Helmholtz.)

American experimental psychologists Ernest Glen Wever and Charles William Bray (1930) discovered apparently definitive support for Rutherford's frequency theory. Recording electrical activity from a cat's cochlea (part of the inner ear), Wever and Bray reported that the activity perfectly matched the stimulating sound. Wever and Bray called this phenomenon the *cochlear microphonic,* because it seemed that the cat's inner ear was acting like a microphone. Unfortunately, it was soon discovered that sounds recorded from the cochlea do not match what is happening in the auditory nerve.

Undeterred from his frequency theory, Wever (1949) recorded from the auditory nerve and found that its frequency of firing matched the sound frequency up to approximately 4,000 impulses per second. However, because 4,000 impulses per second is beyond the maximum rate at which neurons can generate impulses, Wever's explanation for the perception of sound frequencies up to 4 kHz was based on his *volley principle,* which assumes that the auditory nerve contains many sets of neurons that fire out of synchrony with each other. That is, the neuronal sets fire in volleys: While one group is recovering, another group fires. The end result is that the sound frequency is matched by the generation of auditory nerve impulses up to 4,000 cycles per second. However, humans can detect and discriminate sound frequencies up to about 20 kHz or 20,000 cycles per second, well beyond the ability of Wever's volley principle to account for pitch perception.

Above 4 kHz, a version of place theory appears to be the answer. Modern place theory (below) is based on the work of **Georg von Békésy** (1899–1972), who was born in Budapest and received his Ph.D. in physiology in Budapest in 1923. Von Békésy (Figure 17–9) worked as a telephone research engineer in

FIGURE 17–9.   Georg von Békésy.

Source: AP/Wide World Photos.

von Békésy saw that the peak of vibration of the membrane depended on the frequency of the stimulation. High-frequency stimulation caused peaks relatively close to the membrane's base, whereas low-frequency stimulation produced less precise peaks closer to the apex. In other words, the basilar membrane's physical properties produced peaks of vibration that depended directly on the stimulation's frequency. Von Békésy concluded that the place of maximal vibration determines a sound's perceived pitch (Békésy, 1960), and for this, he won the Nobel Prize in physiology or medicine in 1961.

The current theory of pitch perception is a combination theory. For low-pitched sounds, perhaps up to 400 Hz, Rutherford's frequency theory accounts for pitch, with the firing of individual auditory nerve neurons directly matching the sound's frequency. For intermediate pitches, up to 4 kHz, Wever's volley principle is the likely mechanism. Finally, for sounds above 4 kHz, von Békésy's place theory suggests that the place of maximal vibration on the basilar membrane determines the perceived sound. Actually, both the volley principle and place theory are probably engaged for intermediate pitches, which may account for our greater sensitivity to sounds between about 1 kHz and 4 kHz.

Hungary from 1924 to 1946; in 1946, he moved to the Royal Caroline Institute in Stockholm. Von Békésy came to Harvard in 1949 to work as a senior research fellow in psychophysics. Finally, he moved to the University of Hawaii in 1966, where he was a professor of sensory sciences.

Von Békésy's fascination with sound and hearing was triggered by exposure to high-pitched gypsy music when he was a boy. Von Békésy was a genius at devising techniques and instruments to investigate the auditory apparatus. For example, to study the basilar membrane's movement in response to different sound frequencies, von Békésy used the cochleas of recently deceased humans. He would drill a small "observation window" in a cochlea and then sprinkle tiny silver particles on the normally transparent membrane to make it visible through a microscope. Using stroboscopic light flashing synchronously with the frequency of the stimulation,

The Chemical and the Mechanical Senses

Taste

Although the visual and auditory systems have received the bulk of experimental attention, advances also have been made in understanding the chemical (taste and smell) and mechanical (touch and pain) senses. We will begin our survey of 20th-century research on the "minor" senses with a look at the sense of taste.

The contemporary study of taste is nearly synonymous with **Carl Pfaffman** (1913–). Pfaffman studied at Brown University, Oxford, and then at Cambridge as a Rhodes Scholar. Receiving a Ph.D. in 1939, after World War II, Pfaffman returned to Brown University, where he worked closely with Walter Hunter (Chapter 11).

Pfaffman and other taste researchers generally agree on four primary taste qualities—sweet, salty, sour, and bitter—and Titchener also found the same qualities in his research. On the basis of evidence showing that different taste nerve fibers are "tuned" to specific taste stimuli, responding vigorously to a particular taste stimulus but less vigorously to others, Pfaffman proposed a **labeled-line theory** of the encoding of taste qualities. For example, a particular nerve fiber may respond most to a bitter taste, whereas another fiber responds best to a salty taste. If a taste stimulus primarily activates "salty" fibers, then it tastes salty; if it mainly activates "bitter" fibers, then it tastes bitter, and so forth.

Smell

As you may know, much of what we call taste is actually smell. For example, with your eyes closed and holding your nose, you would have difficulty distinguishing a piece of apple, a piece of onion, and a piece of potato.

A Dutch physiologist, **Hendrik Zwaardemaker** (1857–1930) was for many years *the* authority on olfaction. In 1889, Zwaardemaker invented the **olfactometer**—an instrument for the control and measurement of olfactory stimuli—and continued to improve it throughout his research career.

Unlike taste, there is little agreement on the primary olfactory qualities, and several classification schemes have been proposed. For example, Hans Henning suggested a system in 1916 in which smells are defined in terms of six basic odors—fragrant, putrid, ethereal, resinous, burned, and spicy—arranged as points on a prism. Simple odors are placed on the outer surfaces of the prism, with more complex odors on the inside.

More recently, J. E. Amoore (1970) proposed a **stereochemical theory** of smell in which an odorant molecule's shape determines its odor quality. Amoore suggested seven primary odors, with some overlap with Henning's scheme. Amoore's theory has not been established, and other theories include the vibration theory, which is based on the vibration frequency of odor molecules, and the gas chromatographic model, in which rate of movement of an odor molecule across the receptor surface accounts for its smell.

Touch

The physiologist **Max von Frey** (1852–1932) was an early authority on the sense of touch. A contemporary of Stumpf, G. E. Müller, and Ebbinghaus (all Chapter 8), von Frey served successively at Leipzig, Zurich, and Würzburg, confirming and extending the results of earlier workers on the sense. So great was his contribution that "[a]fter von Frey, the writers of psychological textbooks all knew what to say, by section and almost by paragraph, about the skin" (Boring, 1950, p. 425). Von Frey established pain as a separate sense modality in addition to the senses of pressure and temperature.

Pain

Pain is an unusual sensory mechanism for a number of reasons. For one thing, much of the large volume of medically oriented research on pain has focused on how to *eliminate* it. In addition, pain is strongly related to motivational areas of the brain, with the result that much of what we call pain is not so much a sensory experience as it is an emotional response to particular sensations.

One of the most important theories of pain was proposed over 3 decades ago by Ronald Melzack and Patrick Wall. Called the **gate-control theory**, "the theory proposes that a neural mechanism in the . . . spinal cord acts like a gate which can increase or decrease the flow of nerve impulses from peripheral fibres to the central nervous system. . . . When the amount of information that passes through the gate exceeds a critical level, it activates the neural areas responsible for pain experience . . ." (Melzack, 1973, p. 153).

The gate-control mechanism can be influenced by information coming into the pain system from below—from the stimulation of pain receptors in the body—and also from above. The idea that the gate can be opened or closed from above accounts for the influence on pain of such neural activities as those subserving attention, emotion, and memory.

Discovered after Melzack and Wall's theory was introduced, endorphin release provides the chemical basis for downward influence from the brain on the spinal gate.

THE PHYSIOLOGY OF BEHAVIOR IN THE TWENTY-FIRST CENTURY

Although much has been learned about brain-behavior relationships in the 20th century, much remains to be learned. Some of the new technology is already with us that will almost certainly lead to the discoveries that will appear in a future history of physiological psychology. For example, the combination of nuclear physics, computer technology, and medicine has given us incredible new methods for studying the anatomy and function of the living brain. First, there was computerized axial tomography (CT). Now, magnetic resonance imaging (MRI) has almost completely replaced the CT scan (Barnes, 1988). MRI has higher powers of resolution than CT, and psychiatric researchers are using MRI to try to develop an index that will allow them to detect psychiatric patients with brain abnormalities with better than 90% accuracy. If accomplished, this should revolutionize the diagnosis of at least some types of mental illness.

Although CT and MRI are excellent for detecting structural abnormalities in the brain, positron emission tomography (PET) is used to study the metabolic activity of the living brain. For example, with PET, researchers can actually visualize the brain areas most active during panic attacks, when a person is performing mental arithmetic, or when a schizophrenic is hallucinating. Actually, single photon emission computed tomography (SPECT) may be preferable to PET. SPECT is less expensive than PET, and it does not require a cyclotron to create radioactive materials. With it, a researcher can assay metabolic activity or measure neurotransmitter binding in different brain regions. Perhaps the day will come when brain researchers will be able to use techniques like PET and SPECT to solve the problems of functional localization that have intrigued scientists from Gall and Flourens in the

19th century to Lashley and his students and associates in the 20th century.

In addition to the evolution of techniques that permit visualization of the living brain, technology is advancing in other areas. For example, it is now possible to see images of single atoms with the electron microscope. Advances in molecular biology are beginning to reveal the genetic apparatus that controls the development and function of nerve cells. These and other technological achievements will certainly result in greater understanding of the brain and how it works.

CONCLUSIONS

In this chapter, we have explored selected advances in biological psychology and neuroscience in the 20th century. Some of the issues—for example, localization versus nonlocalization of function—we first examined in Chapter 6. Other advances in knowledge, such as the Nobel Prize–winning efforts of pioneers like Sperry, Hubel, and Wiesel, represent exclusively 20th-century work.

Some of the major 20th-century discoveries in neuroscience did not require technology beyond that available in the 19th century. For example, from studies of spinal reflexes in the dog, Sir Charles Sherrington deduced many synaptic properties long before electron microscopy allowed visualization of a synapse. Otto Loewi's proof that synaptic transmission from the vagus nerve to the heart muscle is chemical rather than electrical required no technological advances. Helmholtz could have done the experiment if he had known the right questions to ask.

At the same time, some of the discoveries we have reviewed in this chapter have clearly been technology-bound. For example, the discovery of reward areas by James Olds and Peter Milner required the surgical capacity to implant stimulating electrodes into the brain of a living animal. Similarly, the ability of George Wald and others to prove that the Young-Helmholtz color vision theory was correct on the receptor level required the ability to measure changes in the photochemicals in single cones exposed to light. Without modern technology, Helmholtz had no way to verify the anatomical correctness of trichromatic theory.

As we indicated above, we believe that the technologies are already available that will lead to the signal discoveries of the next century in brain science. The only missing ingredient is a 21st-century Helmholtz, and he or she could be you or one of your classmates.

Of necessity, our coverage of the physiology of behavior in the 20th century has been highly selective and abbreviated. For example, the ethologists mentioned in Chapter 12 (e.g., Lorenz, Tinbergen) also won the Nobel Prize in physiology or medicine for their pioneering work on the relationship between biology and behavior and initiated a field of research that is active today. Similarly, our coverage of issues and discoveries in sensation and perception represents only a small portion of what has been achieved in the last century. From physiological psychology in this chapter, we will move to another active area of psychology in Chapter 18—applied psychology, including psychometrics and intelligence testing.

SUMMARY

Brain research in the 20th century has continued along such 19th-century themes as the localization of function and the study of the senses, and new areas of focus include the nervous system's chemical mechanisms and the brain's energizing system. Reasons to study the biological basis of behavior include the limits that brain function places on psychological theorizing and the practical applications that can be achieved with increased knowledge of neural functioning.

Neuron Doctrine or Nerve Network?

A major debate in the latter part of the 19th century was whether the neurons are separate or whether they form a nerve network. Using a stain developed by Camillo Golgi, Santiago Ramón y Cajal demonstrated that nerve cells are independent cells, thus supporting the neuron doctrine.

From his study of the spinal reflex arc in dogs, Sir Charles Sherrington hypothesized a functional gap or "synapse" between neurons and deduced many of its properties. Pharmacologist Otto Loewi demonstrated in 1920 that synaptic transmission was chemical rather than electrical, but it took several decades before the discovery of large numbers of neurotransmitters in the CNS began to occur. One of the most recent discoveries involves the transmitter substance that binds to the brain's opiate receptors—endorphin. Endorphins produce analgesia and euphoria.

Research on axonal transmission was aided by the discovery of the giant axons of the squid, which were used by British neurophysiologists Hodgkin and Huxley in their Nobel Prize–winning research.

Localization of Function Revisited

The ablation/training research of S. I. Franz and Karl Lashley reawakened interest in Flourens's nonlocalization of function position. Lashley learned his research methodology working with S. I. Franz, who argued against a fixed localization of cortical function. Working with brain-damaged rats in his search for the engram, Lashley derived the concepts of mass action and equipotentiality.

Many of Lashley's students and associates had outstanding careers in psychology. For example, D. O. Hebb published *The Organization of Behavior* in 1949, a book that rekindled interest in neurological explanations of behavior. Another of Lashley's students, Frank Beach became known for his work in human and animal sexual behavior. A Lashley associate, Karl Pribram, abandoned a medical practice for a career in neuropsychology. Another associate, Robert Thompson, devoted the bulk of a 35-year career to a search for the engram in subcortical brain areas.

Using simpler tasks than Lashley or Robert Thompson, Richard F. Thompson has also sought the engram with some success. Eric Kandel's approach has been to seek the locus of learning in a simple animal, the invertebrate *Aplysia.*

Research to answer Fechner's speculation about whether cutting the corpus callosum would produce two minds has been performed by Roger Sperry and his students and colleagues. Sperry's research tended to support Fechner's prediction.

Sleep and the Brain's Energizing System

The experimental study of sleep began with Hans Berger's discovery and recording of the brain's fluctuating electrical activity. Sleep research led to the discovery of alerting functions of the brainstem reticular formation, which in turn led to the serendipitous discovery of the brain's reward areas by James Olds.

Sensory Systems

In the study of sensory systems, the visual system has been the focus for many researchers. Modern research has supported both of the 19th century theories of color vision, the Young-Helmholtz theory at the level of the receptors and Hering's opponent-process theory at higher levels.

Studies of form vision have involved the mapping of the receptive fields of cells in successively higher levels of the CNS. Hartline's study of single optic nerve fibers in the frog led to research by David Hubel and Torsten Wiesel following their association in Stephen Kuffler's laboratory. Hubel and Wiesel found evidence for a feature detector model of visual processing in the cortex, classifying the cells they found there into simple, complex, and hypercomplex categories. Further research has led Russell DeValois to propose a spatial frequency model instead.

In research on the auditory system, pitch perception has been attributed to a frequency or volley coding up to sound frequencies of 4 kHz and a place theory for higher-pitched sounds. Georg von Békésy won a Nobel Prize for his modern version of place theory.

Taste has been studied by Carl Pfaffman, who, like others, has found evidence for four primary taste qualities—salty, sweet, sour, and bitter. In olfaction, there is little agreement on the primary qualities, although various schemes have been proposed, including Amoore's stereochemical theory.

Max von Frey was an early expert on the sense of touch, establishing, among other things, that pain is a separate sense modality. The gate-control theory of pain was proposed by Melzack and Wall over 30 years ago.

The Physiology of Behavior in the Twenty-First Century

Some of the technology that will almost surely lead to important discoveries in the 21st century include magnetic resonance imaging and the study of the brain's metabolic activity with such methods as PET and SPECT. In addition, advances in electron microscopy and molecular biology will undoubtedly result in greater understanding of the brain and its functions.

CONNECTIONS QUESTIONS

1. What connections can you make between advances in technology and advances in our understanding of the biology of behavior?
2. Can you see any themes or connections between the various Nobel Prize winners we have discussed in this chapter?
3. Of the various researchers and techniques covered in this chapter, which seem most connected to the 19th-century fascination with electrical processes?
4. What connections can you draw between advances in neuroscience and advances in perceptual theory?
5. What methodological advances in neuroscience promise to have a dramatic impact on psychopathology, both its conceptualization and its treatment?
6. Draw a concept map incorporating the major figures and discoveries in the chapter, and compare your results with one possible solution provided on p. 569.

SUGGESTED READINGS

Hebb, D. O. (1949). *The organization of behavior.* New York: Wiley. Hebb's book produced a renaissance in the study of the brain and behavior and once was required reading for most graduate students in psychology.

Hubel, D. H. (1979). The brain. In *The brain* (pp. 2–11). San Francisco: W. H. Freeman and Company. Nobel Prize–winner David Hubel edited an issue of *Scientific American* in 1979 devoted to the brain. This is his introduction to that issue, which was published as a book by Freeman and Company. It provides an interesting overview of research on the brain through the late 1970s.

Lashley, K. S. (1963). *Brain mechanisms and intelligence.* New York: Dover Publications, Inc. (Original work published 1929)

Lashley, K. S. (1950). In search of the engram. In Society for Experimental Biology (Great Britain), *Physiological mechanisms in animal behaviour* (pp. 454–482). Cambridge: University Press. *Brain Mechanisms and Intelligence* summarizes a decade of research in which Lashley used the ablation method to study learning and memory in the rat. In Hebb's introduction to the Dover edition, he gave several examples of ideas about brain function seriously considered possible before Lashley's work and concluded that "None of this carefree neurologizing was possible after 1930, at least not for a psychologist" (p. v). "In search of the engram" is Lashley's summary toward the end of his career of much of his lesion work.

Loewi, O. (1960). An autobiographic sketch. *Perspectives in Biology and Medicine, 4,* 3–25. This is a highly readable account of Otto Loewi's discovery that much synaptic transmission occurs chemically.

Olds, J., & Milner, P. (1954). Positive reinforcement produced by electrical stimulation of septal area and other regions of rat brain. *Journal of Comparative and Physiological Psychology, 47,* 419–427. This brief article introduces the discovery of the reward areas in the brain, a discovery that provided some of the anatomical basis for Thorndike's law of effect.

Sperry, R. (1982). Some effects of disconnecting the cerebral hemispheres. *Science, 217,* 1223–1226. This is the published version of the talk Sperry gave in accepting the Nobel Prize in 1981. The article is must reading for anyone who is aware of the left brain–right brain unscientific extrapolations that have been made from Sperry's original work on hemispheric specialization.

Intelligence Testing, Psychometrics, and Applied Psychology

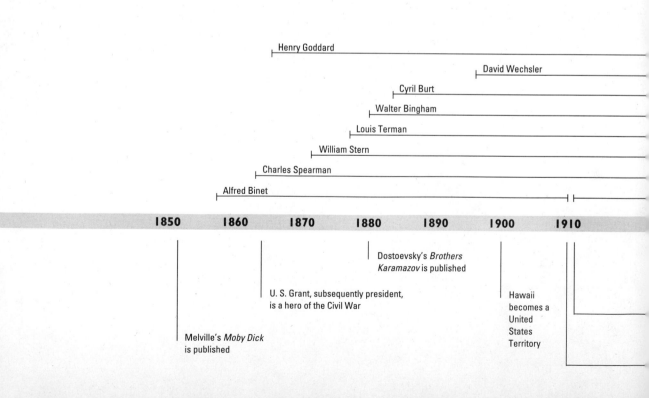

Henry Goddard

David Wechsler

Cyril Burt

Walter Bingham

Louis Terman

William Stern

Charles Spearman

Alfred Binet

1850 1860 1870 1880 1890 1900 1910

Dostoevsky's *Brothers Karamazov* is published

U. S. Grant, subsequently president, is a hero of the Civil War

Hawaii becomes a United States Territory

Melville's *Moby Dick* is published

In this chapter, we continue our topical overview of advances in psychology that are either outside the scope of, or followed the decline of, the great schools. In the last chapter, we examined 20th-century advances in physiology and behavior. This chapter's dominant theme is psychometrics and some of psychology's many applications.

Although contributions to basic research and theory are fundamental for the development of scientific psychology, when psychology was introduced into applied settings such as schools, the military, and later the world of business and industry, the importance of accuracy took on greater weight. For example, misclassification of an individual's mental ability could affect the person's entire life. Thus, applied psychologists often worked to become especially sophisticated in statistics and methodology.

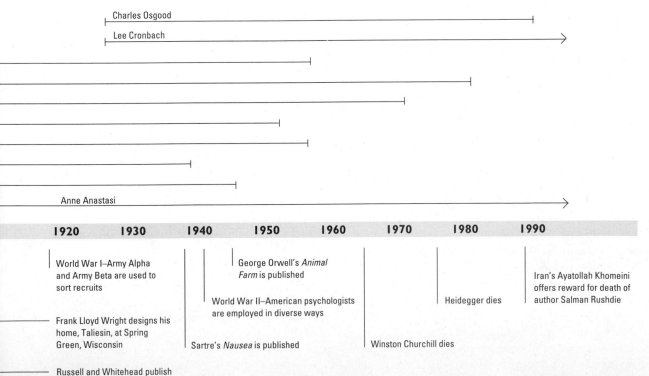

Charles Osgood

Lee Cronbach

Anne Anastasi

1920   1930   1940   1950   1960   1970   1980   1990

World War I–Army Alpha and Army Beta are used to sort recruits

George Orwell's *Animal Farm* is published

Iran's Ayatollah Khomeini offers reward for death of author Salman Rushdie

World War II–American psychologists are employed in diverse ways

Heidegger dies

Frank Lloyd Wright designs his home, Taliesin, at Spring Green, Wisconsin

Sartre's *Nausea* is published

Winston Churchill dies

Russell and Whitehead publish *Principia Mathematica*

In modern psychology, **psychometrics**—literally, measuring the mind—is sometimes used synonymously with statistics and methodology, although it is perhaps better defined as the measurement of mental processes through psychological tests. The most celebrated example of psychometrics and the application of psychological ideas to the "real world" is undoubtedly intelligence testing. Thus, we will begin with a survey of the history of intelligence testing before exploring other developments within psychometrics. The chapter concludes with a consideration of selected elements of nonclinical, applied psychology.

INTELLIGENCE TESTING

A number of historians (e.g., Doyle, 1974) have argued that applied psychological testing began over 4,000 years ago in ancient China, where civil service candidates were given batteries of exams. In the West, reflections on why one person seems more intelligent than another can be traced back at least as far as the Greeks (Chapter 2). For example, Socrates—as reported in several of Plato's dialogues—was concerned with issues we would recognize today as part of the debate about the origins of intelligence (Chapter 9). Plato's *Republic* touches on such practical matters as how a society should handle the variation in the intellectual abilities of its citizens. Subsequently, Aristotle's thoughts about the nature, origin, and organization of intelligence were explored by both Christian and Islamic scholars throughout the Middle Ages (Chapter 3).

As with many other areas in psychology, by the early 19th century the topic of intelligence had mostly ceased being a philosophical discussion and was beginning to be linked with scientific—or in some cases pseudoscientific—advances in measurement. For example, although Gall's phrenological work (Chapter 6) was found to be scientifically bankrupt, it did involve an initial attempt to measure various mental faculties, including intelligence, and from that point onward, such "scientific" measurements were assumed to have the potential for application to business and industry. As we noted,

Orson and Lorenzo Fowler enjoyed successful careers performing phrenological measurements for American businesses. From the very inception of intelligence testing, we see its connection to both psychometrics and applied psychology.

In Chapter 9, we examined in detail Sir Francis Galton's contributions, many of which are important for the history of intelligence testing, psychometrics, and the application of psychology to everyday problems. Galton's interest in measurement and methodology makes him a true pioneer in psychometrics. Additionally, Galton first framed the still ongoing nature-nurture debate over the origins of intellectual ability, favoring the nature explanation.

In American psychology, no one was more influenced by Galton than James McKeen Cattell (Chapter 10), who coined the term *mental tests* to describe the psychometric measurements (including tests of intelligence) that he conducted and popularized in the late 19th century. Additional American pioneers in testing included Joseph Jastrow (Chapter 10), Franz Boas (Chapter 10), and one of Titchener's (Chapter 7) students, Stella Sharp. At Harvard, Hugo Münsterberg (Chapter 10) in some ways represented the continuation of work initiated by German researchers such as Hermann Ebbinghaus and William Stern (both in Chapter 8). As we indicated, Münsterberg was also an important early advocate in America of applied psychology. However, without diminishing the importance of the contributors we have just noted, any serious discussion of intelligence testing best begins with an examination of the work of Alfred Binet (Figure 18–1).

Alfred Binet and the First Intelligence Tests

Alfred Binet (1857–1911) was born in Nice, France, the son of a wealthy physician. Binet was raised by his mother, an amateur artist, after his parents separated. Binet maintained a lifelong fear of his father after an incident in which the man attempted to cure his son's timidity by forcing him to encounter a cadaver (Fancher, 1985).

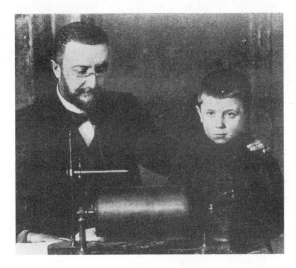

FIGURE 18–1.   Alfred Binet testing an unknown boy.

Source: Archives of the History of American Psychology.

A bright student, Binet was educated at excellent schools in Nice and Paris, where he won awards for his compositions. After completing a degree in law without developing an interest in practicing, Binet turned to medicine. Perhaps predictably, Binet's medical school career was cut short by his psychological conflicts concerning his father and cadavers.

From 1879 through 1883, Binet undertook a course of self-directed study at the prestigious *Bibliothèque Nationale* (National Library) in Paris, focusing on the available works in psychology. Discovering an interest in the work of John Stuart Mill (Chapter 4), Binet sought someone who could further advance his understanding of an empirical, associationistic psychology. The person he found was Charcot (Chapter 15) at the Salpêtrière.

Under Charcot's influence, Binet's interests quickly expanded to include hypnotism and psychopathology. In conjunction with the psychiatrist Charles Féré (1852–1907), these new interests culminated in the book *Animal Magnetism* (1888), which offered some empirical support for Charcot's model of hypnotism.

At the Salpêtrière, Binet continued to broaden his interests, working on such diverse topics as child development, sexual fetishes, and illusions. In addition, he continued to hone his experimental skills

and to publish his findings, producing two additional books and over 20 articles, most of which appeared in Ribot's (Chapter 4) *Revue Philosophique.* During this period, Binet's interest in individual differences and mental tests began as a result of observing and working with his young daughters, Madeleine and Alice.

With a growing personal interest in testing and individual differences, the independently wealthy Binet took a position in 1891 as an unpaid assistant to Henri Beaunis (1830–1921), director of the newly formed Laboratory of Physiological Psychology in the School of Advanced Studies at the Sorbonne. In 1894, Binet replaced the aging Beaunis as laboratory director, establishing himself as one of the foremost experimental psychologists in France.

Binet continued as the unpaid laboratory director for the remainder of his career. Despite completing an advanced degree in natural science in 1894 in order to obtain the standard credentials, Binet was never able to secure a position as a professor. In part, this was caused by the lack of students attracted to a facility that offered no degree. During his Sorbonne tenure, Binet saw the chairs held by Janet (Chapter 15), Ribot, and Bergson (Chapter 16) go to other candidates.

Individual Measurement

In 1895, Binet and his assistant Victor Henri (1872–1940) began a research program they called "Individual Psychology" to identify or create a battery of mental tests that would allow them to examine the individual differences between people in detail. Some tests existed—mostly the work of Galton and Cattell—but whole intellectual faculties remained unexplored. This line of research continued slowly, and for Binet somewhat unsatisfactorily, for nearly a decade.

Beginning in about 1899, Binet's research program gradually evolved into a more specialized consideration of children and intelligence, following a series of applied problems in the French public school system. A new universal education law required that all children be given a certain amount of instruction. Soon, problems emerged with children whose school performance was below average.

In some cases, there was the practical question of what to do with children who could not keep up with their classes, whereas in other cases the problem concerned children who seemed to be of such low intelligence that they could not benefit from a standard education.

In 1899, Binet was fortuitously approached by a young physician—**Théodore Simon** (1873–1961)—who wanted to work with him. Simon had access to retarded subjects, and Binet immediately recognized the value of working with subjects of below-average intelligence.

In 1904, the French government appointed a commission to investigate the problems of educating "weak ones," or students who were retarded, and Binet was named a member. For the government, the problem had become a matter of objectively and impartially identifying children who could not benefit from the standard education the state provided. From the outset, Binet and the government seemed to appreciate the importance of test accuracy, both to be sure that all needy children received special attention and to insure that no normal child was stigmatized as retarded.

The Tests of Binet and Simon

Binet and Simon's first test appeared in 1905 and was based on 30 tasks of varied difficulty. The easiest task required the child to follow a light with his or her eyes, something that very young normal children could do, but that some retarded children could not do. The tasks increased in difficulty through sentence completions that could be solved only by clever 11-year-olds.

Although the test succeeded in identifying retarded children in an objective, empirical manner, Binet saw his first test as merely the starting point of what could be accomplished in the measurement of intelligence in children. Important revisions of the test were made in 1908 and then in 1911, the year of Binet's untimely death. The revisions increased the test's length, reflected research with an ever-increasing subject pool of both normals and subnormals, extended the range of ages of children who could be tested, and most importantly, allowed for more subtle distinctions to be made than simply whether or not the child was retarded. Having developed a test to meet the needs of the government's commission, Binet was moving toward a test that would allow him to state with empirical precision if a particular child was performing at the level of an average child of that age.

For example, suppose that André is 8 years old and performing poorly in school. Binet's test might demonstrate that André's intellectual abilities are only equal to the skills of the average 6-year-old, which would account for his poor performance. Alternatively, imagine Marie, a bright 7-year-old child. Marie's test results might inform her parents and teachers that she is able to score as well as the average 10-year-old on an array of tasks.

Binet was justifiably proud that through the use of experimental research techniques he had demonstrated the utility of psychometrics for solving real problems in the world. Always the empiricist, Binet resisted philosophical speculations about intelligence—such as what the construct actually was or how it should be defined—and even felt that it mattered little what the tests were as long as they were numerous and well designed. In 1911, Binet was 54 and at the height of his public prestige, but his personal life appears to have been in ruin. Fancher (1985) noted that there is evidence that Binet's wife was struggling with mental illness, that Binet himself was growing increasingly more macabre, and that his exact cause of death is not known.

In a discussion of intelligence testing in France after Binet's death, Schneider (1992) contrasted the French understanding of intelligence as multifaceted with the prevailing English notion that intelligence was best understood as a single factor. Charles Spearman was the Englishman most associated with this idea.

Spearman and Factor Analysis

In 1890, **Charles Spearman** (1863–1945) was a decorated British army officer with the curious habit of reading philosophy texts, when, like Binet, his encounter with the works of J. S. Mill put him on the path to a career in psychology. At 34, Spearman started work at Leipzig under Wundt (Chapter 7). Seven years and another stint of active duty later,

Spearman completed his Ph.D. Following a brief tour of the major European psychology laboratories (e.g., Oswald Külpe's, Karl Bühler's, G. E. Müller's [Chapter 8]), Spearman began work in psychometrics at University College in London (Spearman, 1930).

Spearman represents the continuation of the ideas about intelligence and psychometrics conceived by Galton, developed by Pearson (Chapter 9), and systematized by Burt (below). Spearman was an early theorist concerning the nature of intelligence (e.g., Spearman, 1904), and his initially rejected ideas (e.g., Binet, 1905; Thorndike, Lay, & Dean, 1909) were eventually accepted by many of the hereditarians who played an important role in the development of intelligence tests.

Spearman's intelligence tests were unsophisticated, which led to the initial rejection of his work. His method of data analysis is another story, however. Statistically accomplished, Spearman invented a way to analyze and interpret a series of correlations, which was an early form of **factor analysis**, and he applied it to the data obtained from the tasks he assumed were related to intelligence.

What Spearman observed was that people who excel on one measure of intelligence—for example, solving mathematics problems—tend also to do well on other tests such as measures of vocabulary, block assembly, and so forth. This high intercorrelation of scores on the tests indicates the work of an underlying general factor, which he abbreviated "**g**." Spearman also believed that each of the particular tests reflects a specific ability, an "**s**" factor, and his theory can thus be called a *two-factor theory of intelligence,* although this may be somewhat misleading given the importance Spearman and subsequent researchers placed on g.

From Spearman's theory and data analysis came the idea that the most important thing to know about a person's intelligence is the level of g, or general intelligence. As Terman (1932; below) noted, "if Spearman's logic failed to convince me, the originality of his attack commanded my utmost respect" (p. 319). Spearman's notion of "g" continues to anchor one side of the debate over the nature of intelligence (e.g., Jensen, 1985). As Gould (1981) also noted, the widely held belief that the construct of intelligence as measured through intelligence tests actually corresponds to something real—something biological—originated with Spearman. The "Intelligence: One or many debate?" remains active today (and is covered later), and it was also of interest to Ebbinghaus's student, William Stern.

Stern and the Intelligence Quotient

Although the 1908 version of the Binet-Simon test can be seen as the point of departure for all subsequent intelligence tests that we will consider, William Stern introduced both the term "**intelligence quotient**" and the modern concept of an IQ score in *The Psychological Methods of Intelligence Testing* (1912). Note that the abbreviation **IQ** comes from the English words, not from the German equivalent used by Stern, and was introduced by the American Lewis Terman in 1916. Stern undoubtedly will always be remembered for developing the concept of the intelligence quotient, but by the time of his death in 1938, he may well have wished that he had never suggested the use of a single number to represent intelligence (Allport, 1968). As we will see, the IQ idea quickly became controversial.

Stern is one of the individuals who appears in several places in the history of psychology. In addition to his book on intelligence, Stern advanced applied psychology in Germany by founding an early journal in the area. Many of his efforts are perhaps best categorized as either cognitive or developmental psychology (e.g., see also Chapter 20). After establishing himself as one of Germany's leading psychologists, Stern completed his career in the United States at Duke University.

The Psychological Methods of Intelligence Testing provided a detailed and critical review of the early theory and research in intelligence testing—that is, of the work of Binet and Simon, as well as that of Spearman. Stern also presented some of his own ideas, including the concept of an intelligence quotient. The actual formula for the intelligence quotient is simple—mental age divided by chronological age—and follows rather directly from Binet's work. To illustrate, André has a chronological age of 8 (he is 8 years old) and a mental age of only 6 (the age of most children at his skill level); 6/8 = 0.75. By contrast, Marie's chronological age is only 7, but her mental age is 10, which gives her an IQ of 10/7 = 1.43.

As you can see, Stern's approach results in a fractional term that is not quite in the form with which you are probably familiar. Lewis Terman removed the fraction.

Terman and the Stanford-Binet

Born in rural Indiana, **Lewis Madison Terman** (1877–1956) had completed all the formal education that was available to an Indiana farmboy in 1889 by the time he was 12. As the 12th of 14 children, Terman found he had one advantage—older siblings who could tutor him—and the education he received in this way prepared Terman at 15 to start taking classes at the unaccredited Central Normal College in Danville, Indiana. At Central, Terman completed degrees in arts, sciences, and pedagogy while he continued to farm part-time and, starting at age 17, became a full-time schoolteacher.

At 21, Terman was married and principal of a high school, despite having never attended one. For the next 3 years, Terman saved his money to attend the University of Indiana. There, he enrolled in both pedagogy and psychology courses, and in only 3 years completed work at both the bachelor's and the master's levels. Because of his interest in children, education, and intelligence, Terman decided to become a professor of psychology.

In 1903, Terman was made a fellow in psychology and education at Clark University, where he intended to earn a Ph.D. under G. Stanley Hall (Chapter 10). Things seem to have begun well enough, as Hall published Terman's master's thesis and also some early research Terman completed under his direction. However, Terman's desire to work on mental tests began to wear thin with Hall—possibly because of Hall's conflicted relationship with James McKeen Cattell—the person with whom such research was most closely associated in America.

Eventually, Terman broke with Hall and began work with Edmund Clark Sanford (Chapter 10), who was willing to let Terman study intelligence in young boys. Terman completed his doctoral work in

1905 and saw it published in 1906, despite suffering from tuberculosis in the interim. As we noted above, 1905 was the date of the first Binet and Simon test. Although Terman was not seeking to identify the retarded, the conceptual similarity between his initial test and Binet and Simon's first test is striking, providing further evidence for the influence of the *Zeitgeist*.

Terman first realized his ambition to be a professor of psychology at the State Normal School in Los Angeles (now UCLA). In 1910, Terman joined the faculty of Stanford University as a professor of education, becoming over the years head of the psychology department.

At Stanford, Terman modified and consolidated the efforts of Binet and Stern (Terman, 1916). Under Terman's direction, the 1908 Binet and Simon test was translated into English and its content revised to make it better reflect the experiences of American children, creating the **Stanford-Binet**. A score for the Stanford-Binet was obtained by multiplying Stern's intelligence quotient by 100. Applying Terman's slight modification, André has an IQ of 75 (.75 × 100) and Marie an IQ of 143 (1.43 × 100).

In addition to his 1916 publication that created the widely used Stanford-Binet and popularized the use of IQ scores, Terman was involved in two other important research efforts concerning intelligence. First, he was part of the team directed by Robert Yerkes (Chapter 12) that developed the Army Alpha and Beta tests (discussed later) that were used during and after World War I. Terman's other major effort was a longitudinal study of the gifted, with his results released from 1925 through 1959.

Longitudinal studies—research on a group over an extended time period—represent a powerful but difficult methodology. Like Terman, **Nancy Bayley** (1899–) distinguished herself in part through longitudinal studies of intelligence and its stability across a changing environment. Born in The Dalles, Oregon, Bayley completed the B.S. and M.S. at the University of Washington before earning her Ph.D. from the University of Iowa in 1926. In 1966, Bayley became the first woman to win the APA's Distinguished Scientific Contribution Award for her work, which includes the internationally used Bayley Scales of Infant Development.

As for Terman, he initially tested over 250,000 schoolchildren and from this group selected a sample of 1,500 subjects with average IQs of 150. Periodic followups were conducted and have continued through the present time (see Cravens, 1992). In general, the results suggest that the group has been healthier, happier, and more successful than the population from which it came. Terman's study, and other similar research (e.g., Janos & Robinson, 1985), contradict the stereotype of the gifted as weak, sickly, and socially inept "bookworms."

Terman's Stanford-Binet has been through four major revisions and remains one of the most widely used intelligence tests available. Following Binet's original model, the Stanford-Binet has a variety of items—mostly verbal—scaled to various ages. Sample items include questions like: "An inch is short, a mile is _____" (for age 6). The current version is designed for use with both children and adults and includes a wide array of tasks designed to be administered by a psychologist to one individual at a time.

Although we have focused on Terman's work with intelligence, he made substantive contributions to a number of other areas of psychology. For example, his study of marital satisfaction was both epic in scope and groundbreaking in its consideration of women (Terman, 1938). In addition to his research prowess, Terman was an excellent administrator. Hilgard (1987) suggested that Terman's administrative skills as head of Stanford's psychology department were largely responsible for that school's development of one of the foremost psychology programs in America. Terman (shown as part of a group in Figure 18–3) served as APA president in 1923.

The Wechsler Tests

Beginning in 1939, the Stanford-Binet acquired serious competition as the optimal measure of intelligence. That was the year that David Wechsler first released the Wechsler-Bellevue test, which evolved into a series of widely used intelligence tests.

Born in Romania, **David Wechsler** (1896–1981) came to America as a child of 6. He was educated in New York, completing his A.B. at City College and his master's and doctorate at Columbia. At Colum-

bia, Wechsler encountered many psychological luminaries, including some involved in mental testing such as Thorndike (Chapters 11 and 12) and Cattell.

When World War I began, Wechsler was working on a master's degree on the topic of memory loss. He initially served as a volunteer with the psychologists working on IQ testing for the military, and he continued this work after he enlisted. Before completing his tour of duty, Wechsler was sent to England, where he worked with both Pearson and Spearman. After the war, Wechsler spent some time studying psychology in Paris before returning to America in 1922. In 1925, he completed his dissertation at Columbia on the measurement of emotional reactions.

After graduation, Wechsler worked as a psychologist for various organizations, and by 1932, he was the Chief Psychologist at the Bellevue Psychiatric Hospital in New York (a name that may be familiar to you if you watch many New York–based police dramas on TV). Wechsler's first mental test—The Wechsler-Bellevue—had the advantage of being better suited to, and normed for, use with adults than the contemporary version of the Stanford-Binet.

During World War II, Wechsler modified his test to be used with a younger population—military volunteers were often around 16—and after the war further revisions produced first the **Wechsler Intelligence Scale for Children** (**WISC**) and later the **Wechsler Adult Intelligence Scale** (**WAIS**). The WAIS was particularly well received because it was recognized that the Stanford-Binet was better suited for use with children than with adults. The WAIS introduced a more precisely standardized scoring system that established 100 as the mean IQ score and linked other IQ values to percentiles along a normal distribution. This change in calculating the IQ proved to be popular and has been incorporated into the scoring of the Stanford-Binet as well.

The WAIS is composed of 11 subscales divided into two general groups. The verbal group includes measures of general information, vocabulary, and comprehension, whereas the performance subscales include such tasks as picture completion and block and puzzle assembly. Both the WISC and the WAIS

FIGURE 18–2.   David Wechsler.

Source: Archives of the History of American Psychology.

have continued to be revised and today stand alongside the Stanford-Binet as the most widely used intelligence tests (Matarazzo, 1979). Wechsler is shown in Figure 18–2.

The Mismeasure of Mental Ability

For the sake of brevity, our survey of intelligence testing to this point has been quite selective. One way in which it has been selective is that we have focused on contributions that have proved to be advances, omitting several false starts and bad ideas that are part of a complete history of intelligence testing. Nevertheless, some of these false starts and bad ideas deserve mention.

Craniometry

Although modern science has proven otherwise, and modern sensibilities find even the discussion offen-

sive, in the age of Darwin (Chapter 9) it was widely believed that different races represented different levels of evolution between man and ape. Light-skinned northern Europeans were seen as fully evolved humans, whereas darker-skinned groups—particularly the tribal cultures found in Africa and Australia—were sometimes viewed as only a step above the nonspeaking primates (e.g., Gould, 1981).

Evidence for this evolutionary sequence often came from wildly exaggerated caricatures of facial features that illustrated the "obvious" evolution from ape to the Nordic ideal. The efforts in **craniometry**—the measurement of skulls—were ostensibly more scientific, and Gould (1981) surveyed in detail the skull-related evidence that marked the initial attempts at measuring intelligence. Few of the otherwise respectable scientists with an interest in intelligence emerge unblemished. For example, Darwin and Galton, Agassiz (Chapter 10), Broca (Chapter 6), and Binet (among others) all at some point endorsed a racial elitism based in part on craniometric data.

The basic argument was simple: Bigger heads mean bigger brains, and bigger brains mean greater intelligence. In the absence of any real understanding of how brains work, it is possible to sympathize with the assumption that bigger brains equal better brains. Gould's (1981) point was not so much to vilify overzealous craniometrists such as Broca, as it was to show how the initial pseudoscientific mistakes established the groundwork for some of the hereditarian assumptions that followed. Actually, recent work (e.g., Rushton & Ankney, 1996) has called Gould's own efforts into question and has confirmed many of the earlier observations of people such as Broca. Still, one of the most famous (or infamous) examples of "the mismeasure of man" occurred in the study of the Kallikak family by Henry Goddard.

Goddard and the Kallikaks

After completing his undergraduate degree and master's degree at Haverford College in Pennsylvania, **Henry Herbert Goddard** (1866–1957) was employed as a high school teacher and later a principal. At the age of 30, Goddard enrolled under Hall at

Clark University, where he finished his Ph.D. with a dissertation on faith healing. Following a period on the faculty at Pennsylvania's West Chester State Teacher's College, Goddard became the director of the Training School for the Feebleminded at Vineland, New Jersey, in 1906.

With little background in mental retardation, Goddard began to collect information on his charges. His initial efforts brought him into contact with Binet's 1905 test, which he found unimpressive. However, he changed his opinion of Binet after encountering the more sophisticated 1908 test, and Goddard's efforts to translate Binet's testing material anticipated by several years Terman's development of the Stanford-Binet.

Goddard (part of the group in Figure 18–3) was an outspoken supporter of the hereditarian position. Because of his stature in the American intelligence testing community, his closed-mindedness on the inherited basis of intelligence was unfortunate. Goddard's best-known work, *The Kallikak Family: A Study in the Heredity of Feeble-Mindedness,* appeared in 1912. The book's preface noted that for the benefit of educating the public, "we have made rather dogmatic statements and drawn conclusions that do not seem scientifically warranted" (Goddard, 1912, p. x).

The moral of Goddard's (1912) book was simple: If the feebleminded are allowed to interbreed with normal people, their feeblemindedness will spread like a genetic cancer through future generations. Subsequent work by Goddard targeted eastern European immigrants—as Fancher (1985) ironically observed—like David Wechsler. It is noteworthy that terms that today are considered offensive (e.g., feebleminded, moron, imbecile, idiot) once had fairly precise technical meanings for intelligence testers.

Several researchers have raised questions about the accuracy of information presented as fact in Goddard's work (e.g., Gould, 1981). For example, it appears that photos were retouched to make some of the individuals appear sinister and stupid, but it is unclear if anything truly fraudulent was done. Likewise, Goddard's questionable findings about Eastern Europeans have often been linked to the dark eugenic aspects of the U.S. Immigration Act of 1924, although Snyderman and Herrnstein (1983) found little factual basis for the connection.

FIGURE 18–3.   The Committee on the Psychological Examination of Recruits, Vineland Training School, Vineland, New Jersey.

Robert Yerkes, the Chair of the Committee, is in the middle of the back row, with Walter Bingham on Yerkes's immediate right, and Lewis Terman on Bingham's right. Henry Goddard is immediately in front of Yerkes.

Source: Archives of the History of American Psychology.

Army Alpha and Army Beta

The United States entered World War I in 1917, and many psychologists soon became involved in the war effort in a diverse number of ways (for examples, see Mayrhauser, 1989; Popplestone & McPherson, 1994; Samelson, 1977). For example, although Robert Yerkes was primarily an animal psychologist, he did have some experience and interest in intelligence testing. Yerkes was selected to head the committee to create a test for the American military that would serve two functions: (1) to identify mentally deficient individuals who could not be counted on to serve; and (2) to assign individuals to the military service they could be trained to perform given their intellectual potential.

Yerkes recruited five other psychologists to assist in the project, including Terman and Goddard. Although David Wechsler was part of the project, he was not involved in the initial test development. Yerkes's group produced the Army Alpha and Beta tests, and the Committee on the Psychological Examination of Recruits is shown in Figure 18–3.

The **Army Alpha** was similar to Terman's Stanford-Binet test with one important difference: The design was simplified for group administration. Essentially the same test as the Army Alpha, the **Army Beta** was given a pictorial format so that subjects who were unable to read and write English could still be tested. Before the end of 1918, almost 2 million people had been examined, and in some ways the program was a huge success.

First, like Binet's work for the French government, the Army Alpha and Beta demonstrated that psychology could be applied to difficult real-world problems. Second, by using group administered tests, over 200,000 men a month had been tested. The time constraints produced by individual testing had been solved, and the viability of now-familiar pencil-and-paper measures had been established. The idea of intelligence testing and its use in applied settings were here to stay—for good or ill.

In fact, all was not good. With little previous experience, it appears that test administrators may have encountered technical problems that could have adversely affected some scores (e.g., people in the back of the room may have been unable to hear the instructions or see the examiners). Worse, published reports of the results (e.g., Yerkes, 1921) were often misinterpreted by the public as suggesting that many in the military were of below-average intelligence, because the mental age averaged around 14. Actually, mental age stops increasing for most people at 15, so the results were in fact close to what would be expected.

Another problem was more troubling. All of the major American mental testers at the time believed that heredity was the source of intelligence. With this bias, published results were presented as evidence for the intellectual inferiority of some ethnic groups compared to others. Although subsequent research softened the views of some hereditarians such as Terman (Hilgard, 1957), the widely disparate racial results stimulated a great deal of tension. Wild ideas were bandied about by both the media and elitist members of the intelligentsia, and questions such as "Should we really have a democracy where every person has one vote, if some of the races in America are clearly inferior to others?" remained in the public arena for years (e.g., Block & Dworkin, 1976).

Gould (1981) found that some of the claims made by hereditarians based on the Army Alpha and Army Beta data were ludicrous. For example,

> How could Yerkes and company attribute the low scores of recent immigrants to innate stupidity when their multiple-choice test consisted entirely of questions like:
>
> > Crisco is a: patent medicine, disinfectant, toothpaste, food product
> > The number of a Kaffir's legs is: 2, 4, 6, 8
> > Christy Mathewson is famous as a: writer, artist, baseball player, comedian
>
> I got the last one, but my intelligent brother, who, to my distress, grew up in New York utterly oblivious to the heroics of three great baseball teams then resident, did not.
>
> Yerkes might have responded that recent immigrants generally took Beta rather than Alpha, but Beta contains a pictorial version of the same theme. In this complete-a-picture test, early items might be defended as sufficiently universal: adding a mouth to a face or an ear to a rabbit. But later items required a rivet in a pocket knife, a filament in a light bulb, a horn on a phonograph, a net on a tennis court, and a ball in a bowler's hand (marked wrong, Yerkes explained, if an examinee drew the ball in the alley, for you can tell from the bowler's posture that he has not yet released the ball). Franz Boas, an early critic, told the tale of a Sicilian recruit who added a crucifix where it always appeared in his native land to a house without a chimney. He was marked wrong. (pp. 199-200)

Gould's (1981) point was that most of the observed racial differences were artifacts of the tests' cultural biases. Still, in the 1920s, few people recognized such bias in the test items, and the results made sense in light of the hereditarian views of the leading psychologists interested in intelligence at the time. One of the staunchest hereditarians was Sir Cyril Burt.

Sir Cyril Burt

The son of the Galtons' family physician, **Cyril Lodowic Burt** (1883–1971) was born in London. Although he wanted to study science and medicine at Oxford, he arrived there in 1902 on a scholarship in the classics and found that the authorities insisted that he pursue a curriculum appropriate to his award. Fortunately for Burt, Oxford relegated psychology to a subcategory of philosophy—a subject open to him.

In 1904, William McDougall (Chapter 12) arrived to fill the chair in psychology, and Burt found his first mentor. Burt had already come into contact with Galton, Pearson, and Spearman, and his interests in psychometrics were forming at the same time that he continued to study the classics.

Burt's efforts at Oxford led to his receipt of The John Locke Scholarship in Moral Philosophy, which allowed him to continue his studies in psychology more directly. On McDougall's advice, Burt went to Würzburg to work with Külpe. After Germany, Burt returned to England and in 1908 accepted a position teaching psychology to medical students at Liverpool under Sherrington's (Chapter 17) direction.

Subsequent appointments included work for the government and a position at Cambridge. Around 1910, Burt started revising the Binet and Simon test for use in England. His initial efforts included collaborations with Charles Spearman, England's foremost contributor to intelligence testing at that time. The outbreak of World War I—during which Burt worked as a statistician—created in England as in America a greater appreciation for the usefulness of psychometrics and applied psychology. Following the war, Burt resumed his governmental work on intelligence tests for children.

In 1932, Burt accepted the Chair of Psychology at the University College of London, just vacated by Spearman. This prestigious position was created by Galton, first occupied by Karl Pearson, and from it Burt became established as one of the foremost psychological researchers in Britain. His widespread interests included studies of personality, vocational selection, the psychology of aesthetics, and mental telepathy. Outstanding students of Burt included Raymond Cattell and Hans Eysenck, both of whom have made substantive advances in psychological testing and in the study of personality that will be considered later in the chapter.

In 1946, Burt became the first psychologist to receive knighthood (Dorfman, 1978). However, at 63, Burt was suffering from poor health, a failed marriage, and the stresses of war. In addition, his hereditarian views had fallen out of favor with the racial overtones of World War II. Unwilling or perhaps unable (e.g., Kuhn, 1970) to discard his beliefs about the origins of intelligence, Burt found his contemporaries forcing him out of his department and also away from the editorship of his own journal—the *British Journal of Statistical Psychology*. Worse, much of his data had been destroyed during the war. Perhaps some of it was human error, but several sources (e.g., Dorfman, 1978; Gould, 1981; Hearnshaw, 1979) argue that at least part of Burt's postwar research was fabricated, resulting in one of the largest scandals of this century in the scientific community.

As early as the late 1930s, exaggerations, minor inconsistencies, and dubious editorial practices came to be associated with Burt. More serious questions began to arise in the mid-1970s about some of the details in Burt's empirical work (e.g., Jensen, 1974; Kamin, 1974). Of course, Burt was no longer alive to answer the accusations, and Leslie Hearnshaw, a psychologist and Burt supporter, was asked to conduct an investigation. Hearnshaw reluctantly concluded that some of Burt's most famous—and important from the hereditarian standpoint—work on twins appeared to have been fraudulent. Even more disturbing was evidence that Burt possibly published concocted articles supporting his views under false names in his own journal. Finally, there was evidence that as Burt grew older he began to take personal credit for more and more of the early work on factor analysis that was actually pioneered by Spearman (e.g., Lovie & Lovie, 1993).

Although Hearnshaw's (1979) biography of Burt was damning, more recent books (e.g., Fletcher, 1991; Joynson, 1989) make a strong "case that Burt was innocent of outright fraud, and that some of his detractors were guilty of character assassination" (Green, 1992, p. 328). Green concluded that Burt's primary mistake was in not recognizing that the standards for data collection had changed and that the data he had collected were substandard and should not have been published.

With Burt's data suspect and his reputation compromised, you might think that the hereditarian position was weakened. However, the nature-nurture debate remains one of the most heated contemporary issues in intelligence testing.

Contemporary Issues in Intelligence Testing

Intelligence testing remains a vital area of modern psychology and continues to be associated with social and political policy. Recently, some psychologists have damned and some have praised Herrnstein and Murray's (1994) *The Bell Curve,* a book that reconsiders issues we have already discussed, such as the nature-nurture controversy and single-factor versus multiple-factor theories of intelligence. Although Sternberg (1995) scathingly reviewed *The Bell Curve,* our approach will be to look at these major issues as part of the ongoing debate about both intelligence and intelligence testing.

Heredity Revisited

In this chapter, we have noted many people who have taken a hereditarian position on the nature-nurture controversy. On the other side of the issue, we have previously cited the views of environmentalists such as Watson (Chapter 12) and Skinner (Chapter 13). Additional nurturists include George Stoddard (1897–1981) and Beth Wellman (1895–1952)—affiliated with the Iowa Research Station—who in 1940 summarized several research projects and concluded that environmental changes can cause dramatic shifts in an individual's IQ on a standard measure of intelligence.

Florence Goodenough (1886–1959), best known for the Draw-a-Person Test, initiated a lengthy rebuttal to Stoddard and Wellman's work. Through a more sophisticated psychometric analysis, Goodenough challenged Stoddard and Wellman's findings. Not surprisingly, Terman and the Stanford IQ testing community tended to side with Goodenough,

although many developmental psychologists, particularly individuals with ties to Iowa, continued to endorse Stoddard and Wellman. In many respects, the debate degenerated into more of a "turf war" over intellectual development than a meaningful academic exchange. Although a compromise position has emerged as an attractive alternative, and Anne Anastasi (1958; discussed later) offered one in this particular situation, the nature-nurture debate remains a contentious topic.

As we indicated, **Arthur Jensen** (1923–) and **Leon Kamin** (1927–) released the initial reports of errors in Burt's work in 1974 (for an analysis of Kamin's contribution to and credit for the controversy, see Tucker, 1994). Since that time, Jensen and Kamin have come to represent the extreme positions in the continuing debate over the relative roles of heredity and environment in intelligence.

In 1969, Jensen published a highly controversial and critical review of postwar programs such as Head Start, which were designed to improve intelligence and scholastic achievement in America. Jensen suggested that the programs had failed because intelligence was mainly inherited. As evidence, Jensen relied heavily on Burt's research, which had suggested that as much as 80% of the variance in the intelligence of the British public could be linked to heredity. Criticism of Jensen's scholarly work became acrimonious when he raised the topic of race.

Jensen (1969) observed that Blacks have produced distributions with means about 15 points lower than the means of distributions of Whites on almost all measures of intelligence since World War I. Jensen went to some length to explain that these were group means and should not be used to predict individual cases. Additionally, Jensen suggested that environmental factors undoubtedly play a major role in the observed differences. Still, Jensen asked, if the tests are culturally balanced and populations are controlled for economic factors, does not any remaining variance suggest some biological difference? Even some supporters of the hereditarian position feel that Jensen needlessly linked biology and race, observing that any underlying biological determinants for intelligence do not have to be linked to ethnicity (e.g., Jensen, 1980).

In contrast to Jensen, Kamin believed that if Burt's data were fraudulent, the hereditarian position should be virtually destroyed, as Burt was the central figure of that camp. The son of Eastern European immigrants, Leon Kamin was one of the psychologists most directly affected by Senator Joseph McCarthy's hunt for communists in academia during the 1950s. Publicly vilified, Kamin became a persona non grata for American universities, continuing his career in Canada. By 1964, Kamin had become chairman of the psychology department at McMaster University in Ontario. His accomplishments and changes in the political climate allowed Kamin to move to Princeton in 1968.

Perhaps overconfidently, Kamin (1974) advanced several bold claims that often seemed to be based more on conviction and moral principle than on data. His claims typically involved the assertion that the *actual* research with twins suggested little, or perhaps zero, contribution to IQ from heredity.

However, even without Burt's studies, the hereditarians still have abundant data that many find persuasive (e.g., Eysenck & Kamin, 1981; Jensen, 1985). For example, work with twins and nontwins suggests a correlation of about .74 for twins raised apart but only about .16 for unrelated children raised together (Jensen, 1981), strong evidence for a large genetic component in IQ. Increasingly, most psychologists today endorse some sort of intermediate position that includes the effects of both nature and nurture. Although the debate remains a sensitive issue, psychologists like Sandra Scarr (a winner of the American Psychological Society's James McKeen Cattell Award for applied psychology) have advocated a careful balance of evidence from such diverse areas as behavioral genetics and environmental influences on child development (e.g., Scarr & Weinberg, 1978). Scarr has emerged as a respected critic of extremes in psychological theory (e.g., Scarr, 1985), and she contends that nature *or* nurture is a false dichotomy, recognizing that with respect to intelligence and many other phenomena, both nature *and* nurture play a role.

Another factor in the debate concerns the traditional IQ tests themselves, which some see as culturally biased (e.g., Gould, 1981). One way to eliminate this factor might be to develop a biological measure of intelligence. Eysenck (1982) explored different physiological variables and found the most promising to be a measure of brain wave activity called the average evoked potential. An average evoked potential is determined by examining the subject's EEG pattern in response to a brief stimulus such as a sound. Correlations between the average evoked potential and the WAIS have been high, suggesting that average evoked potential may be a useful measure of intelligence. A former APA president and an expert on IQ tests, Joseph Matarazzo (1992) noted that it is possible that future psychological testing may rely increasingly on advanced physiological measures instead of traditional IQ tests.

Intelligence: One or Many?

J. P. Guilford (1897–1987) was perhaps the first to provide a well-articulated, multifactor alternative to Spearman's g. Presumably Spearman's g is summarized by the intelligence quotient, or IQ, the single-number concept first proposed by Stern. Although g is one idea of the nature of intelligence, other psychologists believe that intelligence is composed of many factors. Titchener's student at Cornell, Guilford completed his Ph.D. under Karl Dallenbach (Chapter 7) in 1927 and went on to win the APA's Distinguished Scientific Contribution Award in 1964. Guilford argued that his research suggested more than 100 components of intelligence (e.g., Guilford, 1967, 1985). Guilford's research was indebted to another pioneer in factor analysis, L. L. Thurstone.

Louis L. Thurstone (1887–1955) was born in Chicago, the son of Swedish immigrants who Americanized the spelling of the family name (Thurstone, 1952). Like many others, Thurstone's route to success in psychology was circuitous—before going to college, Thurstone was educated in places as diverse as Stockholm, Sweden, and Centerville, Mississippi. Thurstone's initial college education was in engineering at Cornell, and on the basis of some early work, he was invited to join the laboratory of the famed American inventor Thomas Edison, which he did briefly before starting to teach geometry at the University of Minnesota.

Exposure to some psychology lectures at Minnesota stimulated Thurstone's interest in the subject, and he enrolled for graduate study in psychology with James Rowland Angell (Chapter 11) at the University of Chicago. Thurstone completed his Ph.D. in 1917, having already accepted a position at the Carnegie Institute of Technology, where Walter Bingham (discussed later) was building the first department of applied psychology.

In 1924, Thurstone returned to the University of Chicago to offer courses in statistics and mental tests. At Chicago, his psychometrics laboratory flourished, and eventually Thurstone became the head of the department. In 1952, Thurstone moved to the University of North Carolina, and after his death in 1955, his wife Thelma G. Thurstone (1897–1993) succeeded him there as director of the newly established psychometrics laboratory.

Thurstone's major contributions to psychology came from his advances in factor analysis. As we indicated, Spearman observed that several independent measures of intelligence (e.g., verbal tests, mathematical tests) were highly correlated with each other. This intercorrelation suggested the existence of an underlying factor (g) measured through the various tests. Factor analysis was an attempt to quantify the amount of the effect produced by this underlying factor. A series of variations and inversions of the basic procedure that Spearman and Burt developed led Thurstone to suggest that a group of factors was the basis for the observed correlations.

Thurstone (1938) argued for seven primary mental abilities: verbal comprehension, word fluency, use of numbers, spatial visualization, associative memory, perceptual speed, and reasoning skills. Thurstone's work was fundamental to later advances in scholastic aptitude or achievement testing and to the debate over one or many factors in intelligence. Thurstone is shown in Figure 18–4.

Psychologists such as Robert Sternberg and Howard Gardner are today's leading advocates of what is called the componential view of intelligence, and they have each suggested a more manageable number of components than Guilford. Gardner (1983) identified six components—linguistic, logical-mathematical, spatial, musical, bodily-kinesthetic, and personal—whereas Sternberg (1986)

FIGURE 18–4. Louis L. Thurstone.
Source: Archives of the History of American Psychology.

proposed only three: componential, experiential, and contextual. Sternberg's componential intelligence is our usual conception of intelligence as the ability to think abstractly and to solve word problems and mathematics problems. By experiential intelligence, Sternberg means the ability to formulate new ideas and to find novel relationships by drawing on past experiences. Contextual intelligence—the ability to adapt to changing environmental conditions—has proven to be the most difficult type of intelligence to measure reliably.

Just as with the nature-nurture debate, many psychologists have sought a middle ground on the issue of the number of different types of intelligence. One example of the middle-ground approach came from Burt's student Raymond Cattell (e.g., 1963). Cattell introduced the terms *fluid* and *crystallized,* by which he meant that there is a single, biological factor (called fluid or g) that establishes the broad outlines of our intellectual potential. Within this outline, environmental conditions, life experiences, and other factors determine the specifics (crystallization) of our intellect.

Given the importance of intelligence as a psychological construct, it is easy to understand why its study continues. As we will see in Chapter 20, there is even debate about and interest in computer intelligence. Perhaps at some point in the future you will be involved in trying to create a new version of the Stanford-Binet or the WAIS that can be used to gauge the intelligence of a machine. If so, you will be charting new waters in the field of psychometrics.

PSYCHOMETRICS

If psychometrics is the construction of psychological tests and measures, then all psychologists who ever designed, conducted, or analyzed research were psychometricians in some sense of the word. Although that probably overstates the issue, to the degree that psychology is an empirical, experimental science, a certain level of mathematical and statistical knowledge is essential. Thus, it is not surprising that a number of the individuals we have covered earlier were also pioneers in mathematics and statistics. Descartes (Chapter 3)—the inventor of analytical geometry—is an obvious example, along with Leibniz, an inventor of calculus. Yet another example is Blaise Pascal (mentioned in Chapter 3), who is often considered the "father" of statistics. In psychophysics, we saw important psychometric advances in Fechner's (Chapter 6) measurement of sensory experiences. Similarly, Helmholtz's (Chapter 6) measurement of the speed of the nerve impulse brought psychometrics to physiological psychology. We have also noted Galton's, Pearson's, and Spearman's impact on psychometric methods.

A number of more contemporary psychologists have also made important contributions to data analysis. Some contributors have invented new statistical techniques, whereas others have worked on how to apply existing statistical techniques and standards to psychological phenomena—for example, to intelligence testing. We have already noted one such statistical technique—factor analysis—invented by

Spearman and refined by Burt. Further developments were made by L. L. Thurstone's student, Quinn McNemar.

Advances in Methods of Analysis

Quinn McNemar (1900–1986) was one of the first to ask if a single factor of intellectual ability, or a set of multiple factors (such as Thurstone's primary mental abilities), would do better at predicting some "real world" intellectual event, such as college grades. As it turns out (McNemar, 1964), there is little difference, another reason why the more parsimonious idea of generalized intelligence (g) remains a viable concept.

Born in West Virginia, McNemar completed his Ph.D. under Terman at Stanford and did postdoctoral work with Thurstone at Chicago. Such geographical diversity seems appropriate for a man who hitchhiked from Stanford to Yale in 1929 to attend the International Congress of Psychology. In remembering the Congress, McNemar (1980) reported that he had never heard anyone so "cocksure" as Spearman. Interestingly, Terman (1932) used the same term to describe his initial reaction to Spearman's prose. McNemar's contributions to psychometrics included further refinements of factor analysis, work on the 1937 revision of the Stanford-Binet, and one of the classic texts in psychology, *Psychological Statistics* (1949).

In 1964, McNemar served as president of the American Psychological Association, an honor he received in tribute to his many contributions to psychometrics. McNemar, like Spearman, achieved a certain degree of immortality by having a variation of the chi-square statistical test named after him. Spearman's name is associated with a type of correlation coefficient: the Spearman rank-order correlation coefficient.

Factor analysis is more than just a tool for intelligence testing. Raymond Cattell's 16 PF (discussed later) represents one well-known example of the use of factor analysis in the measurement of personality. A Yale Ph.D., **Charles Osgood** (1916–1991) extended the idea of factor analysis to understanding semantics (word meanings), developing the **semantic differential** (Osgood, Suci, & Tannenbaum,

1957) as a measurement technique to assess word meanings. As a result of his work, Osgood received the 1960 Distinguished Scientific Contribution Award from the APA and was elected APA president in 1963.

In recent years, newer statistical techniques have tended to overshadow traditional factor analysis. In 1988, Frederic Lord (1912–), a researcher at the Educational Testing Service from 1949 to 1985, received the APA's Distinguished Scientific Contribution Award. Lord's major contribution is Item Response Theory, a mathematical advance in test analysis that has been used to determine racially biased items on a psychological test such as an IQ test.

At the present time, some of the most powerful and widely used statistical procedures are path analysis and structural equation modeling, techniques that allow a researcher to make causal inferences from correlational data—and meta-analysis. In meta-analysis, the numerical data from several related studies are combined in order to perform a grand assessment of the phenomenon of interest.

Hilgard (1993) recognized not only the importance of statistical but also of mathematical contributions to the analysis of behavior. For example, as we noted in Chapter 13, William Estes introduced a mathematically formalized version of Guthrie's learning theory. In addition, for recognizing some of the myriad ways in which mathematics can be applied to the analysis of psychological problems, **Wendell Richard "Tex" Garner** (1921–) won the APA's Distinguished Scientific Contribution Award in 1964. Garner's analysis of information and communication (e.g., Garner, 1962) and his applied work in radar jamming illustrate his interests in mathematical psychology.

Introduced in Chapter 13, E. G. Boring's student S. S. Stevens received the APA's Distinguished Scientific Contribution Award in 1960, along with Osgood. Stevens is primarily known for his mathematical refinements of many of Fechner's original psychophysical principles (e.g., Stevens, 1961). More recently, John Swets won the same APA award in 1990 for his extension of **signal detection theory**—a mathematically based theory that assumes the observer in a perceptual experiment is an active decision maker who makes perceptual judgments under conditions of uncertainty—as an alternative to the magnitude estimations of Fechner and Stevens. Swets extended signal detection theory not only to psychophysics (e.g., Swets, 1961), but also to applied areas such as aptitude testing and decision making.

Reliability, Validity, and Generalizability

If you have taken a course in research methodology, you are almost certainly familiar with **reliability** (the consistency of measurement over time), **validity** (the extent to which a test measures what it is supposed to measure), and **generalizability** (the extent to which your sample results apply to different populations). Several psychologists have made important contributions to these and related concepts; we will primarily examine the work of two of the most important contributors: Anne Anastasi and Lee Cronbach.

Anne Anastasi

Anne Anastasi (1908–), shown in Figure 18–5, was born, raised, and educated in New York City. She earned a B.A. degree from Barnard College, the women's college of Columbia, and a Ph.D. from Columbia at the age of 21. Although her initial interests were in mathematics, a course under Harry Hollingworth, Leta Hollingworth's (Chapter 10) husband, and an article by Spearman convinced her that psychology and mathematics could be combined.

Anastasi started at Columbia in the summer of 1928, a time when Columbia was active in psychometrics. Thorndike was there, and some of his students—for example, **E. E. "Ted" Cureton** (1902–1992)—were working on methodological dissertations. Like Anastasi, Cureton made substantial contributions to psychometric issues such as reliability and validity (e.g., Cureton, 1950). Working under Henry Garrett, a psychologist whose interest in methodology resulted in a casebook of classic experiments (Garrett, 1951), Anastasi's doctoral thesis was a factor analytic consideration of memory.

FIGURE 18–5.   Anne Anastasi.

Source: Archives of the History of American Psychology.

After receiving her Ph.D., Anastasi was a faculty member at Barnard until 1939, when she founded the department of psychology at New York's Queens College. In 1933, Anastasi married another Columbia student, John Foley. Anastasi (1980) noted that being married to a psychologist was almost like having a second degree, and through her husband she was exposed to the ideas of Kantor (Chapter 13). In 1947, Anastasi moved to Fordham University, still in New York, where she worked until her 1979 retirement.

Anastasi's contributions include work on test construction and validation (e.g., Anastasi & Foley, 1952), reliability (e.g., Anastasi, 1934), and psychological testing in general (e.g., Anastasi, 1954). In an autobiographical essay, Anastasi (1980) noted that one theme underlying much of her research and publications concerned the effect of environmental and experiential factors on psychological development. As an illustration of this theme, Anastasi and her colleagues carried out a long-term project to examine the role of such factors in the development of creativity in children and adolescents (e.g., Anastasi & Schaefer, 1969; Schaefer & Anastasi, 1968). Anastasi (1964) also wrote a widely used text surveying the various fields of applied psychology. In recognition of her work, Anastasi was elected APA president in 1972.

Lee Cronbach

Lee J. Cronbach (1916–) was born and initially educated in Fresno, California, completing his A.B. at Fresno State College in 1934. This was followed by master's and doctoral degrees in education from Berkeley and Chicago, respectively, and by appointment to the psychology faculty at the State College of Washington.

After World War II, Cronbach was employed first at the University of Chicago and then at the University of Illinois before returning to his native California and a position at Stanford. Like Anastasi, Cronbach has distinguished himself in psychometrics through both classic papers (e.g., Cronbach & Meehl, 1955) and textbooks (e.g., Cronbach, 1949). In addition, the most common statistical measure of the relation between a given scale item and the overall score of a scale bears his name (Cronbach's alpha).

Cronbach's (1957) APA presidential address has also become a classic. In it, he asserted that scientific psychology has produced two very different cultures. One culture consists of researchers from areas well-suited for true experimentation and the discovery of general principles (e.g., psychophysics, physiological psychology). The other includes researchers from areas in which experimental designs are not always practical and individual differences are of interest (e.g., clinical psychology, developmental psychology). Cronbach contrasted and compared the experimental-design approach with the correlational procedure in a variety of ways to illustrate the "two cultures." From his analysis, Cronbach concluded that neither approach in isolation is the path to a complete, and psychometrically sophisticated, psychology. In 1974, Cronbach received the APA's Distinguished Scientific Contribution Award.

In addition to reliability, validity, and generalizability, there are many other philosophical and practical matters relating to psychometrics. Perhaps the most important of these concerns the nature of hypothesis testing and how we apply statistics to psychological data.

Hypothesis Testing and Its Critics

Much of psychology's basic understanding about how to design an experiment and the statistical analyses to perform on the data comes from the work of Cambridge mathematician **Sir Ronald A. Fisher** (1890–1962). Fisher was an innovator in the analysis of variance and a variety of nonparametric statistics, which are techniques that do not require the estimation of parameters (measurable characteristics of populations). The second holder of Galton's chair in eugenics at University College, London (Pearson was the first), Fisher was an outspoken opponent of Pearson's correlational paradigm.

Despite his reliance on agricultural examples, Fisher's 1925 text, *Statistical Methods for Research Workers,* was arguably the first classic book for psychometricians. Fisher's greatest contribution was undoubtedly his conceptualization of testing the null hypothesis. As it is usually explained, the null hypothesis is the opposite of the thesis being tested, so that to reject it is implicitly to support the thesis.

Jacob Cohen has been one of the most relentless watchdogs of the misapplication of statistics in psychology. Cohen's most recent admonition has been against the misuse of Fisherian hypothesis testing. Cohen (1994) noted that, "What we want to know is 'Given these data, what is the probability that [the null hypothesis] is true?' But . . . what [hypothesis testing] tells us is 'Given that [the null hypothesis] is true, what is the probability of these (or more extreme) data?' These are not the same" (p. 997), although psychologists often proceed as if they were.

Cohen (1962) initially achieved notoriety with his critical review of research and data analysis from selected areas of psychology. Cohen reported that as a result of insufficient power, which is a statistical concept involving sample size and effect size, the findings of perhaps half the empirical studies reviewed were dubious. A more recent followup to

Cohen's work reported no improvement (Sedlmeier & Gigerenzer, 1989).

Paul E. Meehl (1920–) is perhaps the foremost critic of psychological methodology (e.g., Meehl, 1967, 1978, 1992). Meehl's concern stems largely from the recognition that psychology's subject matter is often quite different from the subject matter in such natural sciences as chemistry, although psychology's hypothesis-testing procedures are the same. For example, four gold samples are more homogeneous, more readily controlled, and more easily measured than are four samples of most behaviors. However, we frequently analyze the data using the same sorts of statistics and assumptions.

Meehl began his college work at the University of Minnesota in 1938—when Skinner was on the faculty—and entered the graduate program there in 1941 under the direction of Starke Hathaway (Meehl, 1989). Meehl's work following the receipt of his Ph.D. has been both diverse and significant. For example, Meehl's initial publications, often in conjunction with Hathaway, led to the popularity of the MMPI (discussed later). Additionally, his interest in the growing tension between practicing clinicians and academically based experimentalists produced *Clinical Versus Statistical Prediction* (1954), a volume still often selected as required reading. With several other notables, Meehl edited *Modern Learning Theory* (1954), a book that some have said proved the untenability of a grand theory of psychology and is responsible for the absence of any meaningful attempts at a unifying theory of psychology in the last 4 decades.

Perhaps more than any other individual, Meehl has explored the significance of the fact that psychology is dependent upon hypothetical constructs (Chapter 13). With Lee Cronbach, Meehl virtually created the modern understanding of psychological constructs and the concept of validity (Cronbach & Meehl, 1955). In association with the Vienna Circle (Chapter 5) philosopher Herbert Feigl, Meehl was cofounder of the prestigious Minnesota Center for Philosophy in Science in 1953. In addition, Meehl has seen patients as a clinician and developed a theory of schizophrenia, taught courses in law school and published in law reviews, and produced work on the topic of parapsychology. For his efforts, Meehl's honors include the APA presidency in 1962, receipt of the APA's Distinguished Scientific Contribution Award (1958), and being elected a fellow of the American Academy of Arts and Sciences.

Cohen and Meehl represent two contemporary advocates for psychometric sophistication. Perhaps the most important point from their admonitions is that psychologists need to be vigilant in their search for the most appropriate ways to conceptualize their data. Change in psychometric methodology is often resisted: For example, social scientists have only recently begun to implement Bayesian probability, developed by the Reverend Thomas Bayes (1702–1761). A variation of conditional probability theory, Bayes's theorem recognizes that previous empirical findings can be applied to estimations of probability for current events, thus making predictions based on conditional probabilities more accurate. As we noted, nowhere is the need for accuracy in prediction felt more urgently than in applied psychology.

Psychological Testing in Applied Contexts

In modern times, personality theories have been judged primarily by the psychometric sophistication of the instruments they employ to assess personality. The lack of demonstrably reliable and valid personality tests associated with Freudian and neo-Freudian theory (Chapters 15 and 16) has been problematic.

If you can think of a personality characteristic (e.g., Machiavellianism, narcissism, optimism), there is a good chance that one or more tests have been developed to appraise it. Because of the large number of personality tests, we will confine our coverage to some of the more general and widely used ones. To begin our survey, we will examine tests invented by Raymond Cattell and Hans Eysenck.

Raymond B. Cattell (1905–) earned a Ph.D. from Kings College in London, where he was influenced by Spearman and Burt. Cattell created the **16 Personality Factors Test** (**16 PF**) by using Gordon Allport's (Chapter 19) insight that our everyday language about personality traits might be a useful starting point in the study of personality (e.g., All-

port & Odbert, 1936). Cattell and his associates used a number of techniques—including factor analysis and personality questionnaires—to reduce some 4,000 trait descriptions to 16 binary personality factors (e.g., Cattell, 1957, 1973). Although the 16 PF is still used, subsequent personality scales derived from newer factor analytic techniques have suggested that the number of primary traits is less than 16. For example, the **NEO Personality Inventory-Revised** (**NEO PI-R**; e.g., Costa & McCrae, 1992) suggests that only 5 factors are needed to characterize personality: neuroticism, extraversion, openness (to experience), agreeableness/antagonism, and conscientiousness.

Hans J. Eysenck (1916–) left Germany in 1934 in opposition to the Nazis to study in France and England. He earned his Ph.D. in 1940 from the University of London and eventually was charged with starting a profession of clinical psychology in England. His diverse research interests have included personality theory and measurement, intelligence, behavioral genetics, and behavior therapy. Eysenck has suggested that personality can be understood through the use of perhaps as few as two factors (e.g., Eysenck & Rachman, 1965). One component he stresses, sometimes called **neuroticism**, is based on an individual's emotional stability or instability. The other factor is more social and is usually called introversion/extraversion (see Chapter 16). Combining Eysenck's categories of stability/instability with introversion/extraversion produces four personality types that can be mapped readily onto Galen's four temperaments (Chapter 2). Specifically, an unstable, introverted type corresponds to Galen's melancholic; unstable, extraverted to choleric; stable, introverted to phlegmatic; and stable, extraverted to sanguine (Eysenck & Rachman).

Although tests such as the NEO PI-R have many uses, much of the work on personality appraisal has been aimed at developing tests to assist clinical psychologists. The best known and most widely used of these tests is the **Minnesota Multiphasic Personality Inventory** (**MMPI**). Created by **Starke Hathaway** (1903–1984) and J. Charnley McKinley (see Buchanan, 1994), the MMPI has become a vital tool in both the clinical and the research communities. Although the test has been revised recently and a special version for adolescents has been introduced, the inventory's core structure remains intact.

On the MMPI, subjects agree or disagree with 550 simple statements (504 on the original test). The statements range from innocuous items such as "I like to read newspaper editorials" to more obvious clinical probes like "Several people are following me everywhere." Each item is linked to one or more of the test's 10 clinical scales, examples of which are hypochondriasis, depression, psychopathic-deviate, paranoia, schizophrenia, and social introversion. Another feature of the MMPI is the inclusion of three "validity" scales that are designed to detect intentional faking.

A person's profile of scores on the different scales provides a graphic representation of the relations between the various scales, and clinicians are often trained to evaluate the profile according to the two most elevated scales. The MMPI—which is not based on any particular personality theory—has spawned over 500 additional personality scales from its pool of questions (Murphy & Davidshofer, 1988).

Whereas most clinical psychologists greatly respect the "theory-free" MMPI, several well-known measures are more closely linked to a given personality theory and are thus more controversial. Two instruments based on the psychodynamic approach to personality are the **Rorschach Inkblot Test** and the **Thematic Apperception Test** (**TAT**).

Although inkblots had been suggested earlier to assess both personality (e.g., Binet and Henri proposed their use in 1896 for measuring imagination) and medical problems, the use of standardized inkblots as a clinical measure is linked with Swiss psychiatrist **Hermann Rorschach** (1884–1922). Rorschach earned his Ph.D. in Zurich in 1912, with a dissertation supervised by Eugen Bleuler (Chapter 16). Rorschach published the first version of his inkblot test in 1921, and it became immensely popular at a time when the psychoanalytic movement was dominant. As an index of the technique's popularity, during "the Twenties, there appeared 38 titles having to do with the Rorschach Test. This rose to about 230 during the Thirties and after that there were thousands" (Klopfer, 1973, p. 60).

Later, in an era characterized by increasing interest in psychometric precision, the initially attractive free-form nature of the test began to be seen as its biggest problem. Respondents to the test typically describe what they see when they look at the randomly generated, symmetrical images. In scoring the responses, attention is given to how commonplace or unusual they are, to the amount of detail in them, to whether the responses include the whole pattern or just a portion of it, and so forth. Although a reliable and valid approach to Rorschach interpretation appeared to have been developed by Exner (e.g., Exner, 1974, 1993), a recent critical examination has called the Exner scoring system into question (Wood, Nezworski, & Stejskal, 1996). Still, the Rorschach test is widely used by clinicians and particularly by practitioners with a psychodynamic orientation.

The development of the TAT followed a pattern similar to that of the Rorschach, with initial enthusiasm for the test's ambiguity yielding to a desire for psychometric precision in the measure's scoring. The TAT was originally developed in 1935 by Henry Murray and Christiana Morgan. **Henry A. Murray** (1893–1988) began college as a history major at Harvard, earned a B.A., and then transferred to Columbia, where he received his M.D. in 1919. Murray studied embryology at the Rockefeller Institute for 4 years before earning a Ph.D. in chemistry from Cambridge. An interest in Jung sparked Murray's move toward psychology, and he returned to the United States to become Morton Prince's (Chapter 16) assistant at Harvard's newly formed psychological clinic. During World War II, Murray was involved with the government's efforts to develop measures of personality, and he emerged from the war years as the primary American personality theorist.

Even a cursory review of his autobiographical essay (Murray, 1967) leads to the conclusion that Murray was a colorful character; the essay is written as a third-person analysis of "Murr," someone whose passion for the works of the novelist Herman Melville is central to his career as a psychologist. In fact, Murray, a 1961 recipient of the APA's Distinguished Contribution Award and a winner of the 1969 Gold Medal Award of the American Psychological Foundation, planned to analyze Melville's writings, but failing health prevented him from completing the task.

As developed by Murray and Morgan, the TAT consists of 30 pictures depicting ambiguous social situations. In a typical administration, the respondent is shown a subset of cards and is asked to create a story about each picture. The story contents are then examined for common themes. Although various scoring systems exist, problems in developing reliable and valid methods to interpret the TAT's results have contributed to its decline in popularity.

Murray's best-known work, *Explorations in Personality,* first appeared in 1938, just a few years after the TAT, and the book remains a classic analysis of human needs and motives. In it, Murray identified 20 psychological needs, of which the most thoroughly studied has been his "need achievement." This need for achievement represents a desire to excel, "to overcome obstacles, to exercise power, to strive to do something difficult as well and as quickly as possible" (Murray, 1938, pp. 80–81). In many studies of need achievement, it was assessed by analyzing TAT stories (e.g., McClelland, Atkinson, Clark, & Lowell, 1953).

To conclude our survey of personality appraisal, we will briefly examine an approach that once held great interest for the psychological community. However, it is all but forgotten today because of psychometric criticisms leveled against it.

William Herbert Sheldon (1899–1977) was the godson of William James (Chapter 10), and his interest in psychology can be traced to his memory of sitting on James's knee (Hilgard, 1987). Sheldon earned both a Ph.D. and an M.D. from the University of Chicago. Next, Sheldon spent 2 years in Europe, mostly studying with Jung, but Sheldon also visited Freud and German psychiatrist **Ernst Kretschmer** (1888–1964).

Kretschmer divided body type into three categories, and, following Kretschmer's lead, Sheldon's theory of personality was based on three body types: endomorph, mesomorph, and ectomorph. In Sheldon's system, endomorphs have a physique characterized by soft roundness of the body and a large belly compared to other body parts; mesomorphs are hard and rectangular, with a body that is heavier than it looks; ectomorphs are thin and lightly muscled, flat chested, and have a large brain relative to body size.

Sheldon found high correlations between his body types and temperament (i.e., between endomorphy and a love of comfort, social contact, food, people, and affection; between mesomorphy and a love of physical activity, risk-taking, adventure; between ectomorphy and a tendency to be secretive and to love small, enclosed places). In fact, Sheldon's critics found the correlations so high that they assumed his results must have been in error. Additional research in response to the criticisms produced more modest correlations, but Sheldon's results continued to support his general hypothesis of a relationship between body type and temperament. As criticism continued, like Titchener, Sheldon turned to numismatics. His *Early American Cents* (1949), revised as *Penny Whimsy* in 1958, quickly became a classic. With his penchant for measurement, Sheldon developed a scale for grading coins that has been adopted by collectors of U.S. coins. As a result, Sheldon's reputation as a numismatist has waxed as his reputation as a psychologist has waned (e.g., Thorne, 1995).

APPLIED PSYCHOLOGY

In some sense, almost everything that psychologists do can be applied to the "real world." However, endeavors such as personnel selection, treating mental illness, or designing control panels for machines to better fit human perceptual capabilities have a more salient connection to everyday life than analyzing the functions of the olfactory bulbs in rats, for example. One large class of applications of psychology—the one most people think of when they think of psychology—involves the mental health profession. We introduced some of the background to modern clinical psychology in Chapters 15 and 16, and we explored more recent advances in personality appraisal here. Thus, our final focus will be on psychology's nonclinical applications.

The Origins of Applied Psychology in America

Hilgard (1987) suggested 1910 as a convenient starting point for applied psychology in America, noting that Stern founded the first journal of applied psychology in Germany in 1907. Before World War I, interest in phrenological, intelligence, and other kinds of testing was already widespread in America. Some of the first books by psychologists on applied topics had appeared—for example, Münsterberg's *On the Witness Stand* (1909) and Walter Dill Scott's (below) *Human Efficiency in Business* (1910)—and specifically applied programs, such as the one directed by **Walter Van Dyke Bingham** (1880–1952) at the Carnegie Institute of Technology, were being developed. Bingham is shown in Figure 18–3.

Iowa-born Bingham was educated at the University of Chicago in its heyday (1905–1908). James Rowland Angell and George Herbert Mead (Chapter 11) were part of the faculty, and John Watson ran the animal and experimental labs (Bingham, 1952). In 1907, Bingham traveled to Harvard and to Europe to expand his education before completing his dissertation on the nature of melody. In Germany, he visited psychology's leading experts on musicology, Stumpf and von Hornbostel (both Chapter 8); in England, he encountered Spearman and Burt; and at Harvard, his time was spent with Münsterberg and Holt (Chapter 10).

Bingham was an instructor in educational psychology under Thorndike at Columbia, and next at Dartmouth until 1915, when he took the position at Carnegie Tech as head of the Division of Applied Psychology. In conjunction with several businesses, the program at Carnegie soon focused on the psychology of marketing and sales.

During World War I, Bingham was one of the original members of Yerkes's committee that produced the Army Alpha and Beta tests and may have been the person who worked out the details of group intelligence test administration. After the war, Bingham continued at Carnegie Tech until 1924, when the Division of Applied Psychology was suddenly dismantled, in part because a new president was less supportive of the applied program.

From 1924 until 1940, Bingham described his activities as "that of an emissary of psychology to the heathen" (Bingham, 1952, p. 18). In fact, Bingham was promoting the relevance of psychology in fields ranging from economics to engineering.

In 1940, Bingham returned to work for the military on matters of personnel selection. The committee he chaired included Thurstone and Garrett (Anastasi's mentor). Its task was to develop a test to sort recruits into roles for which they were best qualified, and the result was the Army General Classification Test, or AGCT. The AGCT was eventually administered to 10 million men and women recruits.

The duties of the committee were expanded to include consultation on issues in applied psychology (e.g., training and efficiency), and Bingham continued to work with the military until 1947, with the title of Chief Psychologist. Bingham's World War II efforts gave applied psychology an enormous boost.

Walter Dill Scott (1869–1955) was one of Bingham's group at Carnegie before World War I. A Wundt-trained Ph.D. who studied laboratory techniques with Titchener at Cornell, Scott was at Northwestern University when Bingham asked for his assistance. At Carnegie, Scott became one of the first professors of applied psychology. Through a number of books, Scott introduced the use of psychology into the world of work, thereby helping to create the field of industrial psychology.

During World War I, Scott was responsible for the military's initial interest in personnel psychology as distinct from intelligence testing. Although more has been written about Yerkes's committee, it was actually Scott's ideas that endured in the military and shaped the tests given to modern recruits. For his efforts, Scott was awarded the Distinguished Service Medal in 1919.

In 1919, Scott formed his own corporation to do personnel selection and to consult on management issues. Applied psychology was advancing in both academics and the business world—Cattell's Psychological Corporation was founded in 1921, and both Hall and Bingham started journals of applied psychology during the period. Despite Scott's importance to applied psychology, an Eastern European immigrant, Morris Viteles, pioneered the connection between academic psychology and the world of work.

Morris S. Viteles (1898–) was born in Russia just before his family resettled in England (Viteles, 1974). At 5, Viteles came to America and was educated in Philadelphia, eventually attending the University of Pennsylvania. At Pennsylvania, the psychology program was directed by Lightner Witmer (Chapter 7), an applied, clinical psychologist. After completing his Ph.D. under Witmer in 1921, Viteles balanced a successful academic career at Pennsylvania with work for a variety of industries: for example, The Philadelphia Electric Company, The Yellow Cab Company, and The Bell Telephone Company of Pennsylvania. With a foot in both academics and industry, Viteles was well positioned to write some of the early classics in industrial psychology: for example, *Industrial Psychology* (1932) and *Motivation and Morale in Industry* (1953).

The Hawthorne Effect

One of applied psychology's best-known phenomena is called the Hawthorne Effect. The **Hawthorne Effect**—named not for a person but for a place near Chicago—is still used today to suggest that any workplace change that makes people feel important is likely to improve their work performance. Although they are over 50 years old, the studies leading to the Effect stand as perhaps the best examples of the importance of applied psychology. The studies began as a series of experiments conducted between 1924 and 1927 at the Hawthorne Works of the Western Electric Company, a division of American Telephone and Telegraph.

The initial projects consisted of research designed to explore the relationship between workplace lighting and worker productivity and also the effects of changes in rest breaks on productivity. At the completion of the second project, the researchers realized that more was involved in worker productivity than just the physical conditions in the workplace, that is, the research's social impact was far larger than the effect of changes in illumination or breaks.

Actually, the involvement of psychologists in the Hawthorne studies was minimal. Engineers, public health experts, and people from business schools did most of the work. An Australian, Elton Mayo (1880–1949), did have some background in psychology, and it was largely through his participation that the results became popular material (Mayo, 1933). Despite this irony, the Hawthorne Effect remains the standard example of business-related applied psychology.

Advances in Applied Psychology since World War II

Following World War II, several issues within both applied and social psychology (Chapter 19) became topics of public interest, as questions about war and peace, race, and aggression were motivated by the American war experience. Centers for applied psychology began to emerge, and existing institutes hummed with new activity. As one example we noted in Chapter 14, Kurt Lewin founded the Research Center for Group Dynamics at MIT in 1944. Rensis Likert, an associate of Lewin and the developer of the Likert Scale, directed perhaps the most prestigious of the centers for applied psychology, the one at the University of Michigan. In addition to the institutes and centers for applied psychology, many industries have developed a tradition of hiring their own psychologists. Bell Laboratories is perhaps best known for its use of research psychologists, but other firms, such as Honeywell and IBM, have also established themselves as centers of applied psychological research.

Perennial concerns like marketing and advertising (recall our discussion of Watson), as well as personnel selection and worker productivity, have not diminished as part of applied psychology, but applied psychology continues to evolve and expand in new directions. Health psychology—for example, the use of psychological techniques to control chronic pain (among many other things)—is one such area. Social psychologists work on problems like AIDS awareness and drunk driving. Cognitive psychologists now frequently consult on the design of product warning labels, and, as a concluding example, recall the research of Elizabeth Loftus, the cognitive psychologist whose work on memory in applied settings was introduced in Chapter 1.

Psychology and law have enjoyed a long relationship that in recent years has included such new areas as jury selection and the image management of clients. Loftus's own contributions have focused on eyewitness memory (e.g., Loftus, 1979; Wells & Loftus, 1984).

CONCLUSIONS

In this chapter, we have covered a seemingly disparate group of topics—for example, intelligence testing, statistics, applied psychology—that nevertheless are associated closely. Psychometrics understood as mental tests is closely linked with psychometrics understood as advances in statistics and methodology. Mental testing has been just as important for applied psychology as have interests in personnel selection and workplace efficiency. In addition, from its beginnings with Binet and the French government, the effort to measure intelligence has been coupled with the need to do so accurately. As the mental tests have become more complex and our understanding of mental phenomena more complete, advances in how the data are analyzed and reported have also become more sophisticated.

Making recommendations that will influence the lives of people is essential, but tricky, work. Psychologists shaping public policy, consulting in the courtroom, or administering personality and intelligence tests are participating in tasks that our society considers vitally important. The importance to individual lives of many of the tasks in which applied psychologists are involved has undoubtedly fueled debates such as the degree to which nature (heredity) or nurture (environment) affect the development of intelligence.

In the next chapter, we will examine the history of social psychology, which in many ways parallels and at times is intertwined with the material covered in this chapter.

S U M M A R Y

Psychometrics—measuring the mind—is often used synonymously with statistics. Intelligence testing is an example of psychometrics applied to the "real world."

Intelligence Testing

Pioneering efforts in psychometrics were made by Sir Francis Galton and his American disciple, James McKeen Cattell. Ebbinghaus and Stern were also early contributors to intelligence testing.

In 1895, Binet and Victor Henri began research to create a battery of mental tests to identify individual differences between people. After 1900, Binet's work evolved into a consideration of the intelligence of children because of applied problems in the French public school system. Working with Théodore Simon, Binet produced his first test to measure intelligence in children in 1905.

The term intelligence quotient and the modern idea of an IQ score (Lewis Terman invented the abbreviation IQ) were introduced by William Stern. Stern's intelligence quotient was defined as mental age divided by chronological age. Translating the Binet-Simon test into English to produce the Stanford-Binet, Terman eliminated Stern's fractional intelligence quotient by multiplying it by 100.

Terman also was part of the team that developed the Army Alpha and Beta tests during World War I, and he initiated a longitudinal study of gifted individuals in California, which found that the gifted were often superior to the average population.

David Wechsler's initial intelligence test evolved into the Wechsler Adult Intelligence Scale (WAIS) and the Wechsler Intelligence Scale for Children (WISC). The WAIS and the WISC are now among the most widely used IQ tests.

Craniometry—the measurement of skulls—was often used to verify the biases of the measurers. A number of hereditarians misused such measures to show the inferiority of one group relative to another—for example, Goddard and the Kallikaks. Additionally, results from administration of the group intelligence tests, the Army Alpha and Beta, were used to support the inferiority of certain groups. Although Sir Cyril Burt may have falsified data to reinforce his belief in the inheritance of intelligence, it is also possible that he was innocent of actual fraud.

Believing that IQ has a large hereditary component, Arthur Jensen published a controversial review in 1969.

On the other hand, Leon Kamin felt that the removal of Burt's suspect data would destroy the hereditarian position, but this has not happened. Eysenck's successful work on measuring biological intelligence suggests that traditional IQ tests may not be culturally biased.

In the question of one component of intelligence or several, Spearman's work revealed a general factor of intelligence, which he called "g." Other theorists favor a multifactor alternative. For example, J. P. Guilford argued for over 100 different components, whereas Thurstone chose 7, Gardner identified 6, and Sternberg just 3. In a middle-ground approach, Raymond Cattell introduced the terms *fluid* and *crystallized,* with fluid referring to Spearman's g factor and crystallized to specific aspects of intellect.

Psychometrics

In a broad sense, virtually all psychologists can be considered psychometricians. However, this label is more properly applied to people who have attempted to measure mental processes and to people who have made important contributions to data analysis.

Factor analysis was invented by Spearman, refined by Burt, and further developed by L. L. Thurstone and his student, Quinn McNemar. McNemar was one of the first to ask which would do better at predicting a "real world" intellectual event—a single factor of intelligence or multiple factors. The answer—that there is little difference between the positions—supports the idea of a g factor. Factor analysis also has been extended to an understanding of semantics by Charles Osgood, who developed the Semantic Differential.

Anne Anastasi's major contributions have been on test construction and validation. Lee Cronbach is another well-known contributor to psychometrics; the Cronbach-Meehl model of the construct of validity and the validation of psychological constructs is a cornerstone of many psychometrics courses.

Much of psychology's basic knowledge on experimental design and statistical analyses comes from Sir Ronald A. Fisher's work. Fisher's greatest contribution was probably his conceptualization of testing the null hypothesis.

Jacob Cohen and Paul Meehl are critics of the traditional hypothesis testing procedures.

Using factor analysis and other methods, Raymond Cattell reduced a large number of trait descriptions to develop the 16 Personality Factors Test. Further work suggests that even fewer factors are needed to characterize personality, leading to the creation of such personality tests as the NEO Personality Inventory.

The most widely used personality appraisal instrument for assessing clinical populations is the Minnesota Multiphasic Personality Inventory, created by Starke Hathaway and J. C. McKinley. Over 500 personality scales have been developed from the MMPI's question pool.

The most popular tests based on the psychodynamic approach to personality have been Hermann Rorschach's Inkblot Test and the Thematic Apperception Test developed by Henry Murray and Christiana Morgan. Murray is also known for his list of psychological needs, of which the most thoroughly studied is called "need achievement."

William Sheldon created a personality theory based on Ernst Kretschmer's body type theory. Sheldon presented evidence that body type is related to temperament.

Applied Psychology

One of the first applied programs in psychology was developed by Walter Van Dyke Bingham at the Carnegie Institute of Technology. Bingham's work with the military during World War II gave applied psychology an enormous boost. Walter Dill Scott and Morris Viteles were two other early contributors to applied psychology's advancement.

The Hawthorne Effect suggests that any workplace change that makes people feel more important is likely to enhance their work performance. The popularity of the Hawthorne Effect was aided by an Australian, Elton Mayo.

After World War II, centers for applied psychology began to emerge, including the one Kurt Lewin founded at MIT. One of the most prestigious of the centers was directed by Rensis Likert, a Lewin associate. Applied psychology continues to expand in new directions, because the applications of psychology to the real world seem limitless.

CONNECTIONS QUESTIONS

1. How is intelligence testing connected to World War I?
2. What different connections can you make between Francis Galton, James McKeen Cattell, and later intelligence testing?
3. How are Spearman's factor analysis and Stern's concept of IQ related to such ongoing debates as nature versus nurture?

4. How are advances in psychometrics as statistics connected to advances in psychometrics as mental testing?

5. What connections can you make between social and political change and applied psychology?

6. Draw a concept map connecting the major people and ideas covered in this chapter, and compare your results with one possible solution provided on p. 569.

SUGGESTED READINGS

Anastasi, A. (1964). *Fields of applied psychology*. New York: McGraw-Hill.   Although dated, this volume provides a fine overview of the diverse applications of psychology that followed World War II.

Fancher, R. E. (1985). *The intelligence men*. New York: W. W. Norton & Company.   Fancher's work traces the history of intelligence testing from before Binet through the early 1980s. Fancher is a well-known and respected historian, and his book stands out for its objective review of the sensitive topic of intelligence.

Gould, S. J. (1981). *The mismeasure of man*. New York: W. W. Norton & Company.   Gould is one of the premier science writers of our times. Although most of his other works have focused on evolution, this volume is an unbridled attack on the hereditarian position of the origins of intelligence. Even if you disagree with him, Gould remains a delight to read.

Matarazzo, J. D. (1979). *Wechsler's measurement and appraisal of adult intelligence* (5th ed.). New York: Oxford University Press. This book's title implies a narrower scope than is actually addressed. In addition to Wechsler, the book covers all the details of modern IQ testing and has several chapters on the history of both the concept of intelligence and intelligence tests.

Meehl, P. E. (1978). Theoretical risks and tabular asterisks: Sir Karl; Sir Ronald, and the slow progress of soft psychology. *Journal of Consulting and Clinical Psychology, 46,* 806–834. This classic essay has three parts, one of which outlines 20 methodological problems that haunt most research in psychology. It also represents an early attempt by Meehl to provide an alternative to standard hypothesis testing procedures.

Popplestone, J. A., & McPherson, M. W. (1994). *An illustrated history of American psychology*. Madison, WI: Brown & Benchmark. This is a wonderful "picture book" that is great fun to flip through. Several chapters examine the impact of the two world wars on American applied psychology, and the format allows you to actually "see" some of the innovations.

CHAPTER 19

Social Psychology

Albert Bandura

Janet Spence

Stanley Schachter

Eleanor Maccoby

Solomon Asch

Muzafer Sherif

Gordon Allport

Fritz Heider

Gardner Murphy

Floyd Allport

1890	1900	1910	1920	1930

Mark Twain
dies

Atom
is first
split

Basketball is
invented by
James Naismith

Wundt dies

Nobel Prize is first awarded;
President McKinley is
assassinated

United States emerges as
world power following WWI

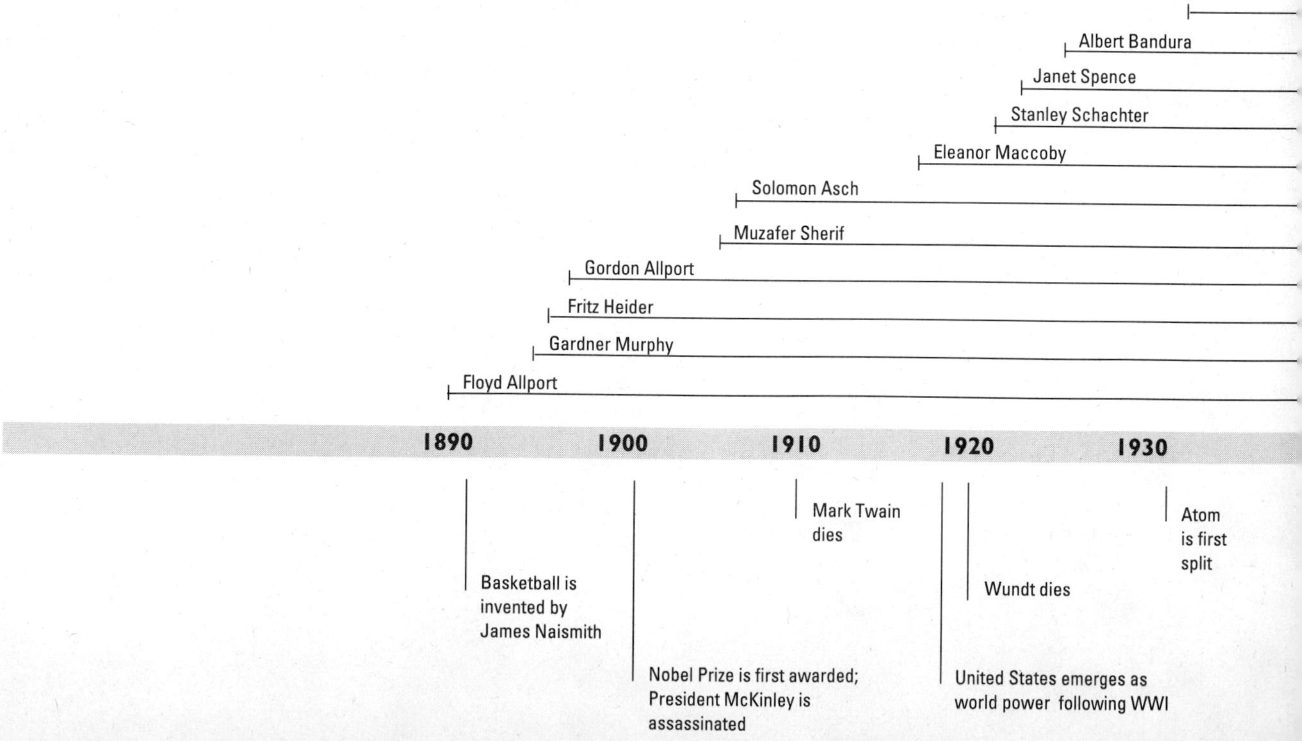

Social psychology is a relatively recent area in psychology, which might lead you to expect that there would be relatively little to survey in this chapter. However, social psychology is broad in scope and includes several topics of interest to both undergraduate and graduate students. In this chapter, we will first examine the origins of the field, concentrating particularly on early American contributors. The remainder of the chapter will focus on some of the classic works that have made social psychology popular and valuable. We will explore a variety of studies to give you a sense of social psychology's diversity and to review some of the area's most important findings.

Modern social science cuts across many academic fields. Political scientists and social philosophers pose theories about society and the individual's rela-

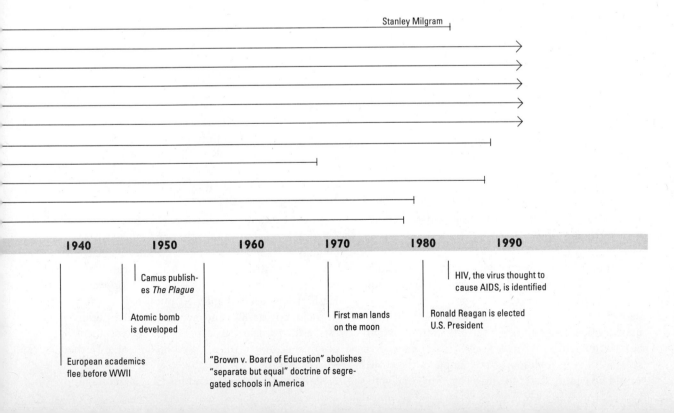

Stanley Milgram

| 1940 | 1950 | 1960 | 1970 | 1980 | 1990 |

Camus publishes *The Plague*

Atomic bomb is developed

European academics flee before WWII

"Brown v. Board of Education" abolishes "separate but equal" doctrine of segregated schools in America

First man lands on the moon

Ronald Reagan is elected U.S. President

HIV, the virus thought to cause AIDS, is identified

tionship to it. Sociologists provide empirical studies of social trends and phenomena within a given society, whereas social psychologists focus on the individuals affected by the social trends and phenomena. At the end of Chapter 18, we noted an overlapping of the histories of applied psychology and social psychology. The period immediately following World War II brought an enormous increase in topics of interest to psychologists, as well as an influx of European psychologists to America.

The idea of using an understanding of human nature to improve the world did not arise de novo after the war, and neither did interest in social behavior. Plato's *Republic* and Marcus Aurelius's *Meditations* (both Chapter 2) contain advice about how the individual should behave with respect to the state and what sort of society would be optimal for humankind. Machiavelli's *The Prince* (Chapter 3), Hobbes's *Leviathan* (Chapter 4), and the political philosophies of Locke and Hume (both Chapter 4) are enduring classics of social psychology, although they anticipate by centuries any formal beginning of the field. Rousseau's (Chapter 5) idea of a social contract, as well as Comte's (Chapter 5) original conception of a science of sociology, are further anticipations of social psychology.

The French jurist **Gabriel Tarde** (1843–1904) was a more recent anticipator of social psychology. Long before Tolman, Miller (both Chapter 13), or Bandura (discussed later), Tarde (1890/1903) was struck by the importance of imitation in human social behavior. In a related development, another Frenchman, **Gustave LeBon** (1841–1931), saw group suggestion as central to social behavior (Faber, 1996).

Although his book *The Crowd* (LeBon, 1895/1960) was possibly the major point of departure for an actual social psychology, LeBon was trained as a physician. Analysis of groups and group behavior led LeBon to assert that people within groups exhibit characteristics different from the individuals comprising the group. Social contagion—the spread of behaviors through a crowd—may occur through unconscious suggestion. A current example might be the movement of the "wave" through sports' spectators. Although few of the people in the crowd would be willing to stand and sway individually, the behavior, and the spreading suggestion to engage in it, often turns the crowd into a single waving entity.

LeBon's views represented a tangible version of ideas about a "group mind," or *Volksgeist* (group mind or spirit), a concept originally popularized by Hegel (Chapter 5). Through his analysis of the crowd, LeBon's impact on later psychologists was substantial. For example, Freud's (Chapter 15) conception of and great interest in social psychology has been linked to LeBon (e.g., Freud, 1921), and the first American to write a textbook concerning social psychology, Edward Ross (1866–1951), was also inspired by LeBon. However, despite LeBon's obvious influence, **Emile Durkheim** (1858–1917), LeBon's contemporary, is credited with founding modern social science as an accepted academic discipline in France.

Durkheim was the pioneer in empirical sociology, although many of his works (e.g., *Rules of Sociological Method* and *Suicide: A Study in Sociology*) are fundamental to social psychology. Durkheim was also one of the many foreign visitors to Wundt's (Chapter 7) laboratory, and later the two corresponded. Perhaps Wundt's career-long interest in the work that led to the *Völkerpsychologie*, a series of volumes devoted to various aspects of social psychology, influenced Durkheim's later interest in social science and sociology.

Although Wundt was important, **Max Weber** (1864–1920) was the leading figure in German social science. Often classified as a sociologist, Weber is best known in psychology for his writings on the protestant work ethic and on charisma (a word Weber coined) in leaders. Both topics illustrate the close association between applied and social psychology.

Thus, we can view the turn of the century (plus or minus a decade) as the time in which social psychology began. In addition to the French and German contributors, the sociological *Zeitgeist* extended to England and America. For example, Herbert Spencer (Chapter 9) published a textbook in sociology in 1876 and popularized the notion of "social Darwinism" to explain the success and failure of social institutions. We noted George Herbert Mead's connection to the rise of sociology in America in Chapter 11, and his Chicago contemporary John Dewey (also Chapter 11) was an outspoken advocate for a recognized subdiscipline of social psychology (Dewey, 1917), as well as an early contributor to the growing literature in the field (e.g., Dewey, 1922).

James Mark Baldwin (Chapter 10) was perhaps the first to use the phrase "social psychology" in an English title (Baldwin, 1897). Like Wundt, Baldwin probably intended the term "social" to indicate an area that he did not think could be studied experimentally. One of Hall's (Chapter 10) Ph.D. students, Norman Triplett is frequently credited with conducting social psychology's first empirical study (Triplett, 1898). Among other things, Triplett investigated the effects of competition on the turning of a fishing reel by children. He found that half of the children (20 out of 40) were positively stimulated by competition and tended to reduce their times on competition trials relative to trials alone. Triplett also found clear evidence for a gender difference in that a higher percentage of girls than boys were stimulated positively by the competition. Triplett's study has been suggested as the first experiment in sports psychology.

As we noted above, Edward Ross was the first American to write a text about social psychology (Ross, 1908). Arguably more of a work in sociology, Ross's text appeared in the same year that William McDougall (Chapter 12) at Oxford produced perhaps the first true textbook of social psychology (McDougall, 1908). Other texts, such as Dewey's 1922 volume and Kantor's (1929; Chapter 13) classic, followed, and social psychology had begun.

AN OVERVIEW OF EARLY ADVANCES IN SOCIAL PSYCHOLOGY

In the introduction, we primarily surveyed some of the connections between early figures in the history of psychology and the rise of social psychology as a recognized subdiscipline. Triplett's 1898 experiment and McDougall's 1908 textbook are commonly cited signals for social psychology's formal beginning. The initial topic of interest remained the group, broadly defined, and there was little agreement in the field

over theory and method. However, following Triplett, other researchers (e.g., Moede, 1920) exper-imentally investigated the effects of the presence of others on an individual's behavior. In general, this research demonstrated that people tend to perform tasks better with other people around. Floyd Allport, one of social psychology's first pioneers, called the effect **social facilitation**.

Floyd and Gordon Allport

Floyd H. Allport (1890–1978) and his younger brother **Gordon W. Allport** (1897–1968) were two of the leading figures in American psychology. Although both Allports had diverse interests and contributed to several areas of psychology, each made a lasting impact on social psychology. Floyd Allport's 1924 textbook, *Social Psychology*, helped solidify the field as an empirical discipline and explicitly associated social psychology with the behaviorist school. The association is not surprising, because, as we noted in Chapter 13, "in the 1920s it seemed as if all America had gone behaviorist" (Boring, 1950, p. 645). Floyd Allport and Gordon Allport are shown in Figures 19–1 and 19–2, respectively.

Floyd Allport was born in Milwaukee, Wisconsin, the son of a businessman who became a country doctor. His father practiced first at Montezuma, Indiana, where Gordon Allport was born, and later near Cleveland, Ohio (G. Allport, 1967). Floyd Allport completed his A.B. at Harvard in 1914 and entered graduate school there with interests in anthropology and psychology. After serving in World War I as a balloon-based observer, he returned to Harvard and completed his Ph.D. in psychology in 1919, the year that Gordon finished his Harvard undergraduate career. Both Floyd (1974) and Gordon Allport (1967) later recalled with fondness several of the Harvard faculty. At that time, the departments of philosophy and psychology were still combined, and luminaries included Langfeld, Holt, Perry, Santayana, Münsterberg (all in Chapter 10), and McDougall.

Münsterberg's applied interests first turned Floyd Allport toward social psychology. After receiving his Ph.D., he stayed at Harvard for a few years before

FIGURE 19–1. Floyd Allport.

Source: *Archives of the History of American Psychology.*

FIGURE 19–2. Gordon Allport.

Source: *Archives of the History of American Psychology.*

moving to the University of North Carolina at Chapel Hill, where his career overlapped with that of John F. Dashiell (1888–1975). APA president in 1938, Dashiell is known for his many methodological contributions to experimental social psychology.

From 1924 until his retirement in 1957, Floyd Allport was at Syracuse University, and it was during these years that his major contributions occurred. In addition to his 1924 textbook anchoring experimental social psychology within the behaviorist framework, his best-known efforts in social psychology include the book *Institutional Behavior* (Allport, 1933) and his work in social facilitation.

In an examination of social facilitation, Floyd Allport (1924) reported that in most cases subjects tested on cognitive tasks (e.g., math problems) and psychomotor problems (e.g., working a fishing reel) perform better when tested with others than when tested alone. Subsequent research has shown that social facilitation is a robust phenomenon across the

spectrum of species from cockroaches (e.g., Allee, 1938) to humans (e.g., Zajonc, 1965).

Floyd Allport (1955) is also remembered for his comprehensive integrative review of theories of perception, *Theories of Perception and the Concept of Structure.* Although *Theories* is usually seen as unconnected with social psychology, it actually was intended as a prolegomenon (introduction) to a complete theory of psychology. Some historians (e.g., Post, 1980) credit Allport with creating modern experimental social psychology by synthesizing and deleting the disparate elements—for example, interest in groups, evolution, sociology—of the *Zeitgeist* that preceded him.

Gordon Allport followed his older brother to Harvard, where he earned his A.B. degree in 1919, having studied psychology and social ethics. Before embarking on graduate studies, Allport spent a year teaching English and sociology in Constantinople, Turkey (now Istanbul). On his return to Cambridge, Allport stopped in Vienna for a visit with Freud. Unprepared for Freud's expectant silence, Allport described an episode that he had witnessed on a tram car on his way to Freud's office, in which a small boy with an obvious dirt phobia kept saying to his mother, "'I don't want to sit there . . . don't let that dirty man sit beside me'" (Allport, 1967, p. 8). When he finished the story, Freud asked, "'And was that little boy you?'" assuming that Allport was revealing something from his own past. Feeling slightly guilty, Allport changed the subject.

Like his brother, Gordon Allport completed his Ph.D. at Harvard (1922). After completing his Ph.D., Allport received a 2-year travel fellowship that enabled him to tour European universities. In Germany, Allport studied with Stumpf (Chapter 8), Wertheimer and Köhler (both Chapter 14), and Stern (Chapters 8 and 18). In England, Allport worked with Frederic Bartlett (Chapter 20) and I. A. Richards. At the end of the European tour, Allport returned to a position at Harvard.

Gordon Allport's primary interest is perhaps best described as a humanistic and social psychological approach to the study of personality. His dissertation was on personality, and his Harvard teaching load usually included courses related to personality and social psychology. After a brief time at Dartmouth, Allport returned to the Harvard faculty in 1928 as the social psychologist, following McDougall's departure to Duke. In 1946, a faction in the psychology department that included Allport broke off and became the cofounders of the Department of Social Relations. The two departments remained almost totally distinct until 1964, the year that he coincidentally retired.

Despite important differences in their theoretical orientations, the two Allports had much in common. For example, each began his career teaching at Harvard, and each for a time edited Morton Prince's (Chapter 16) *Journal of Abnormal and Social Psychology*—an early outlet for social psychology articles. Each Allport also won the APA's Distinguished Scientific Contribution Award, Gordon in 1964 and Floyd in 1965. The two brothers even collaborated on some works, including an early personality scale.

Although he made many contributions to social psychology, Gordon Allport's interests remained varied. His key publications in social psychology include a pioneering chapter on the nature of attitudes (Allport, 1935), possibly the first history of social psychology (Allport, 1954a), and the groundbreaking book *The Nature of Prejudice* (Allport, 1954b). Additional interests resulted in publications on Gestalt psychology, imagery, and issues of war and peace. As is true of many social psychologists, Gordon Allport's work at times drifted into applied topics. The book he cowrote with his student Hadley Cantril (Chapter 1) on *The Psychology of Radio* is just one example.

As Gordon Allport (1967) recalled, many important contributors to psychology passed through the Harvard program. Of those he highlighted, we will consider the contributions to cognitive psychology of Jerome Bruner and Roger Brown in Chapter 20. Later in this chapter, we will cover Stanley Milgram and Kenneth Gergen. Also noted were Gardner Lindzey and Elliot Aronson, who independently have been prolific and respected researchers, and jointly the editors of *The Handbook of Social Psychology* (e.g., Lindzey & Aronson, 1985). The *Handbook* was initially started by **Carl Murchison** (1887–1961), remembered as the editor of several early and long-standing journals friendly to social psychology and the first three volumes of *A History of Psychology in Autobiography*. Finally, Allport gave special recognition to David McClelland, best known for his many studies of achievement and motivation (e.g., McClelland, 1961), which earned him the APA's Distinguished Scientific Contribution Award in 1987.

Gordon Allport's work first introduced the association of a humanistic interest in personality with social behavior. This connection proved fruitful, and one similar line of work was continued by Gardner and Lois Murphy.

Gardner and Lois Murphy

Gardner Murphy (1895–1979) married **Lois Barclay Murphy** (1902–) in 1926. The two are shown in Figure 19–3. At that time, Gardner was on the faculty at Columbia, and Lois was doing postgraduate

FIGURE 19–3.   Gardner and Lois Murphy.
Source: Archives of the History of American Psychology.

work at Union Theological Seminary. Gardner earned his A.B. from Yale in 1916 and entered graduate school at Columbia after World War I. He completed his Ph.D. in 1923 and remained affiliated with Columbia until 1940. Between 1922 and 1925, Gardner also held a fellowship in psychical research at Harvard; you may recall McDougall's interest in this area from Chapter 12.

In 1940, Gardner moved from Columbia to the City College of New York, where he remained through 1950. Gardner was an outstanding teacher, and graduating seniors at CCNY routinely voted him "best-liked teacher." After returning from an extended trip to India, Gardner was named Director of Research at the Menninger Foundation in Topeka, Kansas, a position he held from 1952 until 1972.

Lois Barclay completed her undergraduate work at Vassar in 1923, earned a B.D. at Union in 1928, and completed her Ph.D. in 1937 from Columbia. From 1937 until the move to Kansas in 1952, Lois held a variety of academic positions in the New York area. At the Menninger Foundation, she served as a research psychologist and completed psychoanalytic training (Hilgard, 1987).

At Columbia, Gardner distinguished himself as an emerging leader in social psychology. The social psychology program he created produced such important students as Rensis Likert (Chapter 14), Theodore Newcomb, and Muzafer Sherif (both dis-

cussed later). Gardner's publications at Columbia included a book with Lois on experimental social psychology (Murphy & Murphy, 1931), which became the defining text for the next generation of social psychologists.

Experimental Social Psychology blended biological, social, and personality factors into what the Gardners saw as the proper recipe for social psychology. Like Gordon Allport, the Murphys believed that personality development should be the centerpiece of social psychology. The combining of personality and social psychology was also evident in the works of each of the Murphys individually. For example, Lois Murphy's dissertation was published as *Social Behavior and Child Personality* (Murphy, 1937), and its theme was the interplay between personality and social influences within the developing child.

Gardner Murphy advocated a holistic study of psychological phenomena, seeking to integrate data from such seemingly disparate areas as evolutionary biology and cross-cultural anthropology. His own research was equally aimed at unifying, combining behavioral concepts like needs with Gestalt principles such as fields and more "clinical" elements such as personality. An emphasis on factors such as personality represented just one of the emerging content areas for the new discipline of social psychology. The consideration and analysis of attitudes was another area that quickly rose to prominence in the field.

The Study of Attitudes

To collect data for one of the most widely cited studies of attitudes, Richard LaPiere (1934) traveled across the United States with a young Chinese couple, staying at over 50 hotels and eating at nearly 200 restaurants. After the trip, LaPiere wrote to the hotels and restaurants to ask if Chinese patrons were allowed. Although only one business had refused them service, over 90% of the people who responded to LaPiere's inquiry reported that the Chinese were not welcome in their establishments.

Although LaPiere's work is methodologically flawed (e.g., the people who served them may not have been the people who answered LaPiere's letter), his study illustrates the fascinating early work that was being done with attitudes and the growing interest in the relationship between attitudes and behavior. By the time of Gordon Allport's 1935 chapter on attitudes in the first *Handbook of Social Psychology,* it was clear that research on attitudes had become " . . . the most distinctive and indispensable concept in American social psychology" (p. 798). Early psychometric measures of attitudes were developed by Thurstone (Thurstone, 1928; Thurstone & Chave, 1929) and Likert (1932), both of whom we encountered in Chapter 18.

Understanding and modifying peoples' attitudes clearly has tremendous potential for applied psychology. For example, many of Watson's (Chapter 12) contributions to marketing research can be traced to his recognition that the attitudes people have about a product directly affect their behavior as consumers. As a result of this recognition, much of Watson's applied work involved the development of ways to measure and manipulate consumer attitudes.

Because psychologists were employed in a variety of ways during World War II, it is not surprising that some social psychologists focused on measuring soldiers' attitudes. In much the same way that World War I provided subjects for intelligence testing, World War II allowed psychologists to study attitudes in thousands of young recruits. In fact, just as World War I supplied the boost that made psychometrics respectable, World War II gave social psychology the same sort of lift. Carl Hovland was one of the leading figures in the measurement of soldiers' attitudes during the war (e.g., Hovland, Janis, & Kelley, 1953; Hovland, Lumsdaine, & Sheffield, 1949).

Carl Hovland: The Communication of Attitudes

Carl I. Hovland (1912–1961), a Hull (Chapter 13) Ph.D. from Yale, had been an experimental psychologist with some involvement in industrial research before the war. After the war, Hovland became the leader of Yale's social psychology program. For his many contributions to psychology, he received the APA's Distinguished Scientific Contribution Award

in 1957, just the second year the honor was given. Hovland died from cancer at the age of 49.

Before the war, the Institute of Human Relations at Yale was the site of interaction between Hullian learning theorists and other social scientists. As we indicated in Chapter 13, this interaction produced important collaborations between the sociologist John Dollard and the Neo-Hullian Neal Miller, including their books *Social Learning and Imitation* (Miller & Dollard, 1941) and *Frustration and Aggression* (Dollard, Doob, Miller, Mowrer, & Sears, 1939).

Going beyond many studies conducted during World War II, Hovland revolutionized the study of attitudes by exploring in detail the nature of attitude change. For example, Hovland and Weiss (1951) examined the effects of a communicator's credibility on persuasion. Although being perceived as knowledgeable and trustworthy are beneficial for producing attitude change, there is also the possibility of a **sleeper effect**. With time, the association between the message and its source may fade, with the possible result that the content of the message is remembered after the source has been forgotten. Thus, even if the source is not credible, after a month or so the effects of the message exposure may appear as a change in attitude.

In addition to Hovland, Theodore Newcomb and Muzafer Sherif were winners of the APA's Distinguished Scientific Contribution Award who conducted important early studies on attitudes.

Theodore Newcomb: Change and Stability in Attitudes

Theodore M. Newcomb (1903–1984) began his college career at Ohio's Oberlin College, attended Union Theological Seminary, and then "crossed the street" to complete his Ph.D. at Columbia (Newcomb, 1974). Although Thorndike and Woodworth (both Chapter 11) were also members of the faculty, Gardner Murphy became Newcomb's primary mentor.

After completing his dissertation in 1929, Newcomb was affiliated with a number of schools, most notably Bennington College in Vermont and the University of Michigan. At Bennington, Newcomb performed a longitudinal study on attitude change that remains one of the classics of social psychology. At Michigan, he helped create a prestigious doctoral program that established the school as one of the centers for social psychological research.

Newcomb's Bennington research began in the 1930s and originally involved measuring the attitudes of most of the students at the small women's college. The parents of Bennington students tended to be traditional and conservative, and Newcomb reported the process of attitude change in which the students became more liberal. In his initial study, Newcomb (1943) looked at the variables responsible for attitude change, and he found that attitudes were influenced importantly by an interaction between individual characteristics and group memberships. The results from his 25-year followup study were even more interesting, however.

Newcomb had expected the liberal attitudes to regress as the young women left college and eventually adopted societal roles similar to their parents' roles 25 years earlier. Newcomb's results are important because he found that the liberal attitudes persisted, which he explained by suggesting that the women had selected a lifestyle consistent with their college-developed attitudes. Newcomb's explanation led him to adopt a "balance theory" of attitude formation and change similar to Fritz Heider's theory of cognitive balance (discussed later).

Muzafer Sherif: Social Norms and Group Conflicts

Muzafer Sherif (originally Muzaffer Serif Basoglu; 1906–1988) was born in Odemis, Turkey. Armed with a master's degree, Sherif came to America in 1929. After earning a second master's degree at Harvard in 1932, Sherif traveled to Berlin to study with Köhler. The growing Nazi influence chased him from Germany, and he settled at Columbia to study with Gardner Murphy.

Sherif's 1935 dissertation was published as the *Psychology of Social Norms* (Sherif, 1936), and it soon became one of the key works in social psychology. Returning to Turkey, Sherif was arrested for his outspoken opposition to the Nazis and spent some of 1944 in prison, an experience that may have influenced his later interest in intergroup conflict. Several American social psychologists, including Hadley Cantril and Gardner Murphy, helped facilitate his release and return to the United States.

Sherif was subsequently employed at a number of well-known universities, and by the end of his career, he had written more than 24 books and 60 articles, many with his wife (and fellow social psychologist) Carolyn Wood Sherif (1922–1982). Several of Sherif's works advanced the basic understanding of attitude formation and attitude change (e.g., Sherif & Cantril, 1947; Sherif & Hovland, 1961). However, Sherif is perhaps best known for his research on intergroup conflict (e.g., Sherif, Harvey, White, Hood, & Sherif, 1961), in which he first created, and then alleviated, hostile attitudes between two groups of boys at a summer camp.

Put into direct competition with each other for desirable prizes (medals, pocket knives), relations between the groups quickly deteriorated until the researchers were forced to intervene to prevent serious consequences. The study showed how easily group biases could arise even when group membership was arbitrary and further demonstrated the role of competition in arousing hostility between groups. Sherif et al. also found that intergroup hostility could be removed by introducing situations that forced the groups to cooperate in completing a goal (e.g., restoring a water supply that had been "sabotaged" by the experimenters).

Sherif's return to America is another illustration of the many ways social psychology benefited indirectly from World War II. Further examples include an increased interest in and appreciation of attitude research and innovations in the measurement of attitude change. As we noted in Chapter 14, Hitler's rise forced many of Europe's brightest psychologists to flee (Cartwright, 1979). This led to an outflow of Gestalt psychologists, some of whom came to America and found their niche in the new field of social psychology.

Gestalt Influences and Related Studies

In our discussion of Gestalt psychology, we reviewed Kurt Lewin's work in detail. After Lewin's arrival in America in 1932, his field theory quickly became the most attractive and complete alternative to a strictly behavioral explanation of social phenomena. As we noted, Lewin was also a pioneer in applied social research and in the study of group dynamics, and many of his ideas are still being applied to issues in industrial psychology. In fact, Lewin came to be viewed by other leaders in the social psychological community as "the giant of social psychology" (Hilgard, 1987, p. 604). However, Lewin was by no means the only Gestalt contributor.

In Chapter 14, we also mentioned Solomon Asch, Leon Festinger, and Fritz Heider as three researchers closely affiliated with the Gestalt tradition. Each became a distinguished social psychologist in America; both Asch and Heider were early recipients of the APA's Distinguished Scientific Contribution Award.

Solomon Asch: Social Factors in Perception

Perhaps even more than Kurt Lewin, **Solomon Asch** (1907–), represents the clearest extension of the primary Gestalt ideals into social psychology. A 1932 Columbia Ph.D., Asch first recognized the potential in exploring the social factors related to everyday perception, thus building directly upon one of the major strengths—perceptual theory—of the Gestalt program. Asch also understood that with the behaviorists' control of experimental psychology, the study of attitudes represented a point of attack for Gestalt psychology's more phenomenological and cognitive orientation. In many respects, Asch can be seen as the founder of such contemporary topics as social perception and social cognition, and his work well illustrates why Gestalt theory provided such a fertile breeding ground for the development of social psychology.

Although Asch conducted many studies, the works for which he is best known are probably his demonstration of our willingness to conform our perceptions to match group expectations (e.g., Asch, 1956) and his pioneering studies of impression formation (e.g., Asch, 1946). The latter program represented the first studies in person perception, an increasingly important topic for social psychologists today.

To study conformity, Asch (1956) had a subject come to the laboratory to participate in what appeared to be a study of visual perception, conducted with groups of subjects. Unknown to the real subject, the other 9 or 10 people were actually the researcher's confederates, who had been told how to respond to the stimulus material.

The stimulus material consisted of pairs of large cards. One card in each pair displayed a single black line varying in length from about 6 to 8 inches. The other card had three lines of different lengths, and the task was to say which of the three matched the line on the first card. Although the discrimination was easy, after the first few trials the confederates unanimously began selecting one of the wrong answers. Asch (Figure 19–4) found that fewer than 25% of the subjects resisted conforming their reported perceptions to those of the group on at least some of the trials.

Asch's research on conformity to group pressure is a mild prelude to Stanley Milgram's research on

FIGURE 19–4. Solomon Asch.
Source: Friends Historical Library of Swarthmore College.

obedience. Milgram's work was a conscious continuation of the study of conformity pioneered by Asch (Sabini, 1986).

Stanley Milgram: The Behavioral Study of Obedience

Born in New York City, **Stanley Milgram** (1933–1984) completed his bachelor's degree at Queens College and his Ph.D. at Harvard in 1960, with Gordon Allport in the social relations program as his advisor. Milgram was at Yale from 1960 until 1963, and his famed studies of obedience were conducted during this period. In 1963, Milgram (Figure 19–5) returned to Harvard, moving in 1967 to the Graduate Center of the City University of New York to lead the social psychology program.

At CUNY, Milgram's research focused on urban living, and in addition to the normal academic publications, he wrote and produced an award-winning film—*The City and the Self*—on the topic of life in cities. At the time of his death, Milgram was working with "cyranoids," subjects who speak thoughts that are a confederate's, during a conversation with another person. Typically, the confederate tells the cyranoid what to say via a small radio transmitter. The cyranoid paradigm was developed as an aid to exploring the basic processes of communication and person perception. (The name *cyranoid* comes from a famous play about Cyrano de Bergerac, who put words in the mouth of a suitor to a woman loved by Cyrano himself. The real Cyrano de Bergerac [1619–1655] was a French writer and dramatist who, in his youth, is said to have fought more than a thousand duels because of his enormous nose.)

Although the research on urban living was widely celebrated in social psychology, Milgram's work on obedience brought a greater fame. As a followup to Asch's conformity studies and in response to Nazi war criminals who claimed innocence because "they were just following orders," Milgram decided to explore the boundaries of obedience in normal people. Milgram's initial report on obedience appeared in 1963, and it immediately created a stir. A host of exchanges and subsequent studies followed, resulting finally in Milgram's (1974) book, *Obedience to Authority: An Experimental View,* which provides a complete account of his research and theory on human obedience.

Consider the following thought-experiment, which is similar to one that Milgram presented to many people, including a group of 40 psychiatrists. Your task is to predict the behavior of the person labeled "subject" in the hypothetical situation. Imagine that in the study a subject is seated before a large machine designed to administer a shock to another person as part of an experiment on the effects of punishment on learning. The machine has 30 switches, each delivering a more intense shock. Figure 19–6 will give you a sense of what the subject would see.

An experimenter tells the subject when to flip a new switch to intensify the shock and when the shock is to be administered. Although the subject cannot see the person being shocked, there is auditory feedback. At Switch 6, the shocked person grunts in response, and by Switch 8 the grunts become shouts. After 10 switches are flipped, groans are heard, and the shocked person demands to be freed. At Switch 12, the person cries, "I can't stand the pain!" and with each additional switch the screams become more agonized. After the 20th switch, the person stops responding to the learning task, insisting on being freed at once. The subject is told to treat the lack of response as a wrong answer and to continue to flip the switches, including the last one, which is marked only "XXX" and is beyond the label "Danger Severe Shock."

FIGURE 19–5.   Stanley Milgram.

Source: Courtesy McGraw-Hill, Inc.

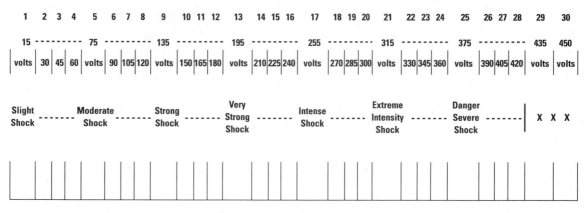

FIGURE 19–6. Adaptation of control panel from Milgram's famous obedience study.

At what point do you think the subject will disobey the researcher and stop shocking the other person? Psychiatrists predicted that most subjects would not go beyond the 10th switch, and that fewer than 4% would reach the 20th switch. The psychiatrists estimated that only 1 person in 1,000 would flip Switch 30 (Milgram, 1992). Actually, in a laboratory test of the hypothetical situation, Milgram found that 62% of the subjects obeyed the experimenter completely, including throwing the final switch.

Although it is often presented as one experiment, Milgram conducted many studies of obedience using the situation we have described. In the studies, subjects were tricked into believing that another person was being shocked as part of a learning experiment. In fact, the only person shocked in Milgram's studies was the subject, who got a mild shock at the beginning to illustrate that the equipment was functional. The "victim" was actually the researcher's confederate, who gave programmed feedback on both the learning task and the "shocks."

Milgram systematically manipulated variables across the studies, and his results changed substantially across the different manipulations. However, even when factors were set to give minimal obedience—for example, having to touch the person being shocked, or the shocked person reporting a history of heart trouble—usually about 25% of the subjects still administered the highest level of shock.

Milgram's purpose in the research was to give people a clear conflict in order to explore the boundaries of obedience. On the one hand, the subjects had been paid a modest fee to participate in a "scientific study" and were being told what to do by a "real scientist" wearing a white lab coat. On the other hand, it was obvious that the other person was in pain and that the subject himself or herself was the source of the pain. Except in situations employing disobedient models, Milgram found that people generally obeyed the authority figure, even when it seemed that the person being shocked was in danger. As the psychiatrists responding to a hypothetical case like Milgram's study demonstrated, the findings were not what most people would predict.

Although many people showed high levels of obedience, you should not assume that they were unaffected by what they had apparently done. Many of the subjects remained upset even after they learned what had really happened. The deception that placed people into this experimental situation quickly became the topic of a heated debate about the ethical guidelines for the use of subjects in psychological experiments (e.g., Baumrind, 1964).

As you have seen, a paper-and-pencil study of obedience—even when trained experts were asked what would happen in a hypothetical study—produced results that were at great odds with what really happened. Thus, a realistic answer to the question of whether people would obey an authority figure required a behavioral measurement of the phenomenon. The key question becomes: Are the results important enough to justify the deception necessary to obtain them?

This is not a simple question, and there are no simple answers. One important result of Milgram's research is that it suggests that under the appropriate conditions, most people will follow orders, no matter how repugnant the results of the orders might be. In addition, Milgram's studies of obedience stimulated discussion and led to the formalization of newer ethical standards dealing with research on human subjects. Although the APA had considered ethical matters before, after Milgram's studies, more precise guidelines for the use of human (and animal) subjects were developed. It is almost certain that a present-day researcher following the APA's ethical guidelines would not be allowed to repeat Milgram's research.

Fritz Heider: Balance and Attribution

In our survey of Gestalt psychology, we briefly summarized Leon Festinger's concept of cognitive dissonance (e.g., Festinger, 1957; Festinger & Carlsmith, 1959). Festinger theorized that people resolve conflicting cognitions by revaluing one or more of them. As evidence, he performed a classic study in which subjects judged a poorly compensated, unpleasant task more favorably than would be expected given the nature of the work. Festinger's conception of cognitive dissonance is closely associated with Fritz Heider's theory of cognitive balance.

Although generally considered an early contributor to social psychology, **Fritz Heider** (1896–1988) spent much of his career as a perceptual researcher in the Gestalt tradition. Heider began his work in psychology with Karl and Charlotte Bühler (Chapters 14 and 16, respectively) in Munich, focusing on methodology and child development. Next, he completed his dissertation in perception under the direction of Alexius Meinong (Chapter 8) at the university in his hometown of Graz, Austria (Heider, 1989). After receiving his degree in 1920, Heider attended the lectures of Köhler, Wertheimer, and Lewin at Berlin, before accepting a position at Hamburg with Stern in 1927.

On Stern's advice, Heider traveled to Smith College, where he worked with Kurt Koffka (Chapter

14) on a series of projects involving deaf children. After World War II, Heider was invited to the University of Kansas by Roger Barker (Chapter 13), who you may recall as an associate of Lewin. At Kansas, Heider met the Murphys (then at Menninger), and about a decade later his classic work in social psychology—*The Psychology of Interpersonal Relations* (Heider, 1958)—appeared.

Despite its title, *The Psychology of Interpersonal Relations* contains a great deal of perceptual theory. Heider offered a phenomenological account of our everyday perceptions of other people based on the Gestalt assumption that some underlying cognitive structure exists to organize the perceptions. The organizing principle is best captured by the concept of **cognitive balance**, which refers to a tendency to perceive information in ways consistent with preexisting beliefs and attitudes.

Heider's balance construct provided a framework within which counterintuitive phenomena from such areas as impression formation (e.g., Asch) and cognitive dissonance (e.g., Festinger) could be explained. Heider's ideas were also fundamental in creating a new research area in social psychology—attribution. **Attribution** refers to how we perceive, interpret, and account for people's actions. Four basic modes of attribution can be illustrated by the common explanations for behavior that we use daily. Specifically, we may attribute "John's" success on a test to *effort* (John did well because he studied), to *ability* (John did well because he was born with an excellent memory), to the *task* (John did well because the test was easy), or to *luck* (John must have gotten lucky for him to have done so well).

Edward Jones (1926–1993) and **Harold Kelley** (1921–) both earned recognition—the APA's Distinguished Scientific Contribution Award—for later work on attribution. Jones (e.g., Jones & Davis, 1965) is perhaps best known for his research on how we modify our attributions as a function of how events directly affect us. This general tendency also predisposes us to evaluate ourselves differently from the way we evaluate other people. In fact, we may tend to blame the situation or bad luck for most of our failures, whereas we may attribute our accomplishments to either our own effort or to natural abilities (e.g., Jones & Nisbett, 1972). Alternatively, for others we may attribute negative situations to the individual, not to the environment or to luck. This inconsistency between how we evaluate ourselves and others is sometimes called the **fundamental attribution error**.

Kelley took a different approach to attribution. He recognized that we frequently incorporate aspects of both the environmental situation and the individual we are evaluating when we make attributions (Kelley, 1972). This insight led him to suggest a system with three key concepts: distinctiveness, consensus, and consistency. For example, if we know that John is doing poorly in other classes, then his excellent performance on a psychology test is *distinctive* and may prevent us from making attributions that would apply to some general or pervasive trait John might have (e.g., high intelligence). *Consensus* refers to our consideration of how other people behaved in the same circumstance—that is, if everybody did well on the test, then it must have been easy. However, if only John did well, then we may appeal to the *consistency* of his past behavior in similar situations. If it turns out that John always does well in psychology courses but poorly in other subjects, we might conclude that John only exerts himself in the classes he enjoys.

We can further illustrate the fertility of attribution theory by briefly considering Stanley Schachter's studies of the attributions of emotions. Incidentally, Schachter, like Milgram, was involved in a controversy over research ethics when he and his colleagues reported data gathered from the infiltration of a doomsday cult (Festinger, Riecken, & Schachter, 1956). The authors and several other observers joined a group that centered around a suburban housewife who believed she was receiving messages from the planet Clarion, which predicted a catastrophic flood. In *When Prophecy Fails,* Festinger et al. reported their observations of the conviction, commitment, and proselyting activity of the people associated with the cult.

Stanley Schachter: Emotions and Social Psychology

The son of eastern European immigrant parents, **Stanley Schachter** (1922–) was born in New York City. He began college at Yale at 17 with some inter-

est in psychology, and a class with Hull sealed the matter. Schachter was drafted about the time he started graduate school and decided not to return to Yale for his Ph.D. after leaving the army. Instead, he went to study with Lewin and Festinger at MIT.

After Lewin's death in 1947, interest in group dynamics faded at MIT, and many of the faculty and students, including Schachter and Festinger, moved to the University of Michigan (Schachter, 1989). The presence of Likert and Newcomb and the infusion from Lewin's MIT group made Michigan the leading center for social psychology in the postwar period. Schachter is shown in Figure 19–7.

Although he has been involved with a wide variety of projects in his long career, Schachter is perhaps best known for his research on the social factors related to the attribution of emotions. Schachter's classic study (Schachter & Singer, 1962) was a response to Walter B. Cannon's (1927) criticism of the James-Lange theory of emotion as discussed in Chapter 10.

FIGURE 19–7. Stanley Schachter.

Source: © William Apple by courtesy Harvard College Library.

In Schachter and Singer's (1962) study, subjects received either a placebo or adrenalin, were either told what to expect physiologically or were misinformed about what to expect, and were exposed either to a euphoric confederate or to an angry confederate while they responded to a questionnaire. The findings supported a two-factor theory of emotion: A stimulus causes arousal, and the emotion experienced depends on how the stimulus is labeled.

Subsequent research on the attribution of emotions (e.g., Zillmann, 1983) has generally supported Schachter's two-factor theory, even demonstrating that it is possible to mislabel emotions. For example, consider a teenaged couple watching the final seconds of an exciting high school football game. After the game, the couple's high state of arousal may persist but now the most salient environmental feature is the presence of the other person, not the football game. In this situation, the teens may experience what Zillmann called "excitation transfer," mislabeling their continued excitement as sexual tension or love.

SELECTED TOPICS IN CONTEMPORARY SOCIAL PSYCHOLOGY

Schachter's and Zillman's research exemplifies the interesting and relevant work that has characterized social psychology in the last few decades. Sex and aggression have emerged as popular research areas, and the study of attitudes, attribution, and groups continues to be central to the field. A number of the APA's awards for distinguished scientific contributions have been made in recent years to psychologists with interests in social phenomena. These awards include the 1978 recognition of the efforts of Robert Zajonc in the area of social cognition, of Paul Eckman in 1991 for work on the communication of emotion, and of Paul Slovic in 1993 for contributions to the study of applied decision making. Although it is impossible to mention even in passing more than a smattering of the work that has shaped the evolution of social psychology, a few classic

studies and contemporary issues should be noted, beginning with social learning theory.

Social Learning Theory

Born in Mundare, Alberta, Canada, **Albert Bandura** (1925–) completed his B.A. from the University of British Columbia in 1949. Because of an interest in Kenneth Spence (Chapter 13), Bandura went to the University of Iowa for his M.A. and Ph.D. degrees, receiving the Ph.D. in 1952. Since 1953, Bandura has been affiliated with Stanford University in various capacities. He was elected president of the APA in 1974 and was honored in 1980 with the APA's Distinguished Scientific Contribution Award.

Bandura's work has often dealt with aggression (e.g., Bandura, 1973), and he has always advocated a social learning theory explanation of phenomena. **Social learning theory** focuses on the role of *modeling* or *imitation* in the acquisition of social behavior. Although much of the empirical basis of social learning theory was developed earlier by behavioral learning theorists such as Edward Tolman and Neal Miller, Bandura's classic research with "BoBo" popularized the ideas behind the theory.

Like Milgram, Bandura actually did a number of studies using basically the same experimental paradigm. The procedural core of Bandura's work was first established in 1961 (Bandura, Ross, & Ross, 1961) and involved the study of children's behavior toward BoBo—a large inflatable toy doll (Figure 19–8)—after the children had observed models aggressing against the doll. As you can see by examining the panels, the children closely modeled some of the aggressive behavior (e.g., Bandura, Ross, & Ross, 1963a).

Bandura and his associates demonstrated that children acted more aggressively toward BoBo after exposure to an aggressive model. Additionally, the model did not have to be present, or even human, as similar results were obtained for films of human aggression and when the aggressive display was a cartoon featuring a cat (Bandura et al., 1963a). Bandura and his colleagues also found that imitative aggression increased when it was rewarded or ignored, but decreased if the model was punished (e.g., Bandura, Ross, & Ross, 1963b).

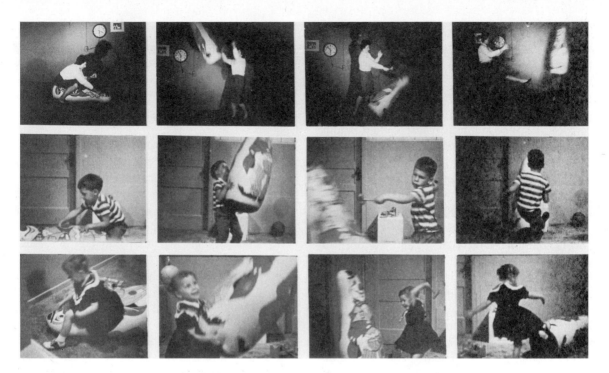

FIGURE 19–8.   The top row of stills show an adult model aggressing against a BoBo doll. The bottom rows show imitative aggressive behavior in two children.

Source: Dr. Albert Bandura.

The implications of Bandura's work were twofold: First, the studies attempted to demonstrate the role of imitative modeling as a source of human learning. Perhaps more importantly, the research addressed the social problem of aggression. Dozens of researchers and hundreds of social activists have used Bandura's work as a point of departure in further considerations of violence.

One of the ongoing debates connected to Bandura's research concerns media violence. Following Bandura's logic, violent films, TV shows, and even cartoons ought to facilitate aggression in children who watch them. In fact, a number of laboratory studies (e.g., Liebert & Baron, 1972) have demonstrated that this facilitation occurs. Popular press coverage of such experimental results has led some to assume that if violence were no longer televised, the problem of aggression would be solved. However, aggression is far older than TV, and across different cultures (e.g., American, Japanese, South African) there seems to be little relationship between levels of media violence and aggressive crimes.

Although it is not the whole story, there is little doubt that children (and adults) learn by imitation and can learn to behave aggressively by observing aggressive models. With the connection of Bandura's work to issues of TV violence, we again see the association between social psychology and applied psychology. Philip Zimbardo's exploration of social roles reveals another element in the learning and aggression story.

Social Roles

Philip Zimbardo (1933–) obtained his B.A. from Brooklyn College of the City University of New York and the M.S. and Ph.D. degrees from Yale, finishing in 1959. From Yale, Zimbardo moved to New York University and then in 1968 to Stanford University, where he is today. Recognized as an outstanding teacher and advocate of psychology,

Zimbardo's research has focused on the nature of social roles.

Zimbardo (1992) provided a vivid narrative of the arrest and processing of nine college students 20 years earlier. Arrested by the police, the students were handcuffed, booked, fingerprinted, strip-searched, sprayed with disinfectant, given degrading uniforms, and locked up in the "Stanford County Prison."

Life in jail was not easy for the students. They were identified only by number and were instructed to address the guards, who wore matching khaki uniforms, reflective glasses, and carried clubs, as "Mr. Correctional Officer, Sir." Failure to obey any rule meant the loss of privileges or worse—as the inmates who were locked in closets or forced to clean toilets with their hands soon learned.

Following an aborted prisoner rebellion, conditions deteriorated. When officials found the prisoners suffering from depression, psychosomatic rashes, and disorganized thinking, they decided that the guards at Stanford County Prison had become too punitive, and the facility was closed only 6 days after it opened.

Although this is a true story, the "rest of the story" is probably not what you think. The Stanford County Prison was a real facility, but it was housed in the basement of the Stanford University Psychology Department. Although the police were real, the guards and the prisoners were drawn from a pool of college student volunteers who had been carefully screened in an effort to prevent the sort of thing that happened. Thus, Zimbardo's account was of events at a simulated prison, not a real correctional institution. The primary official who decided the prison should be closed was its creator, Philip Zimbardo.

Because assignment to the positions of "prisoner" or "guard" was random, Zimbardo and his colleagues concluded that it was the social role and not personal traits that produced the increasingly sadistic guard behavior and the increasingly pathetic prisoner behavior (e.g., Zimbardo, Haney, Banks, & Jaffe, 1973). Zimbardo's demonstration dramatically revealed the power of environmental conditions to shape behavior.

The study of social roles has continued to be central to social psychology from a general, theoretical standpoint and as a vehicle for exploring special situations. One particular situation receiving a great deal of experimental attention in recent years examines the social role of the bystander.

Bystander "Apathy"

At 3:20 A.M. on March 13th, 1964, New York resident Kitty Genovese was returning home from work when she was attacked. She fought off her attacker several times, but in a lengthy struggle, she was finally stabbed to death. At least 38 of Genovese's neighbors later reported hearing her screams, and some even stood at their windows watching her ordeal below them on the street. None came to her aid, and not one neighbor called the police until the attacker was gone for good. The area of research stimulated by this incident became known as the study of **bystander apathy**.

This case and others like it were the center of much attention in the late 1960s. Newspaper and magazine articles, TV specials, Broadway plays, and Hollywood movies attempted to explore how such an event could occur. Although noted writer Harlan Ellison offered a science fictional explanation for the phenomenon (Ellison, 1983), John Darley and Bibb Latané's work led to a better understanding of the unresponsive bystander.

Born in Minneapolis, Minnesota, **John Darley** (1938–) received his B.A. from Swarthmore College, where he worked with Solomon Asch. In 1965, he earned a Ph.D. from Harvard, working with Jerome Bruner. Darley taught at New York University from 1964 to 1972, and he has been at Princeton ever since.

Bibb Latané (1937–) was born in New York but raised in Chapel Hill, North Carolina, where his father was a member of the university faculty. Initially planning to be a lawyer, Latané earned an undergraduate degree from Yale in 1958. Instead of going to law school, Latané began work on a Ph.D. in psychology at the University of Minnesota, where his primary mentor was Stanley Schachter. In an interesting connection, the director of the social psychology program at Minnesota at that time was industrial/vocational psychologist Jack Darley—John Darley's father. In 1961, both Latané and

Schachter accepted positions at Columbia, although Latané did not complete his Minnesota Ph.D. until 1963. Since leaving Columbia in 1968, Latané has held positions at The Ohio State University and the University of North Carolina, and is currently at Florida Atlantic University.

Beginning in the late 1960s, Darley and Latané conducted several studies of bystander apathy (see Latané & Darley, 1970, for an early summary). The researchers theorized that bystander unresponsiveness results from a diffusion of responsibility. **Diffusion of responsibility** refers to a situation in which several individuals have the possibility of acting, but no individual has the clear responsibility to act.

To test their diffusion-of-responsibility hypothesis, Darley and Latané created experiments in which they could stage an apparent emergency, control for the number of bystanders and other variables, and observe the responses of their experimental subjects. For example, in Darley and Latané (1968), the subject was told that he or she was part of a group discussion that was being held via intercom in order to avoid embarrassment. At some point, the primary confederate appeared to be having a seizure. With five other students present, the average delay in seeking aid was 166 seconds, and help was attempted in less than a third of the trials. With two other students, help was sought 62% of the time, with an average latency of 93 seconds. With only 1 bystander—the actual subject—help was obtained in less than 60 seconds on 85% of the trials and eventually in 100%.

Although subsequent studies found that factors such as time pressure inhibited helping (e.g., Darley & Batson, 1973), Latané and Darley's results showed that if an individual recognized a problem and perceived it as his or her responsibility, help would probably be sought. The more people witnessing the emergency event, the less likely that any one person will perceive the incident as his or her responsibility. Hence, diffusion of responsibility delays assistance and accounts for how Genovese could be murdered in full view of many of her neighbors. Because they could see others viewing the incident, each probably assumed that someone else would act or had already acted.

Advances in the Study of Race and Gender

Throughout this book, we have made a conscious effort to highlight the contributions of women and people of color. Unfortunately for our efforts, it is an inescapable fact that the contributions of women and minorities have often been marginalized. With this in mind, we will consider briefly the study of race and gender by social psychologists— areas where contributions by a diverse group of researchers have been recognized.

Race

In Chapter 18, we noted that race and ethnicity emerged as major psychological topics following World War II. Although it is an oversimplification to attribute all of the interest in the study of ethnicity to the war, there is little doubt that the persecution of the Jews in Europe dramatically stimulated the study of racial issues by social psychologists. Gordon Allport's *The Nature of Prejudice* (1954b) is one of the first major works in this area.

Born in Canada, **Otto Klineberg** (1899–1992) received the B.A. from McGill and earned his Ph.D. in psychology from Columbia, where in 1961 he became the first head of the university's social psychology department. In his long tenure at Columbia (1925–1962), Klineberg developed an interest in anthropology, and in *Race Differences,* he described differences between races on a variety of psychological characteristics. Klineberg concluded that the racial differences he observed were primarily culturally determined—for example, the differences in intelligence between Blacks in the northern United States and Blacks in the South were a function of better educational opportunities in the North.

Although the number of minorities in the American academic system historically has been small (Guthrie, 1976), as more people of color have entered psychology in America, they have broadened and stimulated interest in the study of race and cultural differences. From 1920 through 1966, an estimated 8 Blacks received Ph.D.s in psychology out of 3,700 degrees awarded. Of the 8, Francis Sumner (Chapter 10), Hall's student, was the first,

FIGURE 19–9.   Kenneth Clark.
Source: Archives of the History of American Psychology.

receiving his Ph.D. from Clark University in 1920. Earning a Ph.D. from the University of Cincinnati in 1933, Beverly Prossor became the first Black female psychologist. The first Black president of the APA (1971) was **Kenneth B. Clark** (1914–), a social psychologist. Clark received his B.A. and M.S. from Howard University and his Ph.D. from Columbia in 1940. In a famous study of self-concept and racial identification in the late 1930s, Clark and his wife, Mamie Phipps Clark, found that Black preschool children preferred white dolls to black ones. In 1987, Clark (Figure 19–9) received the Gold Medal Award from the APA for his contributions to the public interest.

In recent years, there has been great interest in topics related to race and racial identity (e.g., Parham & Helms, 1985). Additionally, the study of cultural differences has become a popular subdiscipline of social psychology, and journals devoted to special populations (e.g., Asian Americans, Hispanics) encourage research in the area.

Erving Goffman's (1963) *Stigma* is one of the most important works on the general topic of difference and identity. A sociologist, Goffman argued that we all have some sort of stigma that we manage carefully when we present ourselves to others. A stigma can be as obvious as race, gender, or being bound to a wheelchair, or it can be more subtle, such as speaking with an accent, having cancer, or being homosexual.

Although gender can be a stigma, Goffman also considered other issues concerning gender differences and the social presentation of gender. In publications such as *Gender Advertisements*—which explores the portrayal of women in the popular press—Goffman (1976) addressed a variety of gender difference issues. Goffman contended that print and television advertisements reinforce many stereotypes of women (e.g., that they are typically passive, that they function best in the home).

Gender

Any list of the major contributors to modern social psychology's interest in women and gender differences would have to include Janet Spence, elected APA president in 1984. **Janet Taylor Spence** (1923–) received her undergraduate degree from Oberlin College, entered the clinical psychology program at Yale, and completed her doctorate at the University of Iowa in 1949. Among her achievements is the development of the Manifest Anxiety Scale for use in testing a theory she held with her husband, Kenneth Spence, about the interaction of task difficulty with arousal level in determining task performance.

After she moved to the University of Texas at Austin, Spence turned to the examination of differences in men and women, for which she and Robert Helmreich developed the **Personal Attributes Questionnaire** (**PAQ**; Spence, Helmreich, & Stapp, 1974). Reported in *Masculinity & Femininity* (Spence & Helmreich, 1978), their work with the PAQ convinced Spence that the traditional way of looking at the sexes as bipolar opposites (men are men and women are women) is incorrect. Instead, she and Helmreich found that in high school students, college students, and many other groups, masculinity and femininity are essentially independent constructs.

Sandra Bem (1944–) is another pioneer in the exploration of the concepts of masculinity, femininity, and how we acquire our gender-based social roles. A 1968 University of Michigan Ph.D., Bem is perhaps best known for the **Bem Sex Role Inventory** (**BSRI**), a widely used scale that describes the degree to which a person conforms to traditional sex-role stereotypes. The work of Spence and Bem has been at the forefront of the study of sex roles, and their results have challenged many of society's preconceptions about gender by showing that "male" and "female" traits are not always in opposition to each other.

One of the most interesting and controversial issues in the study of gender is over what differences actually exist between the sexes. Beyond the obvious differences in reproductive physiology, do other—more psychological—dissimilarities exist, or are the reputed differences myths that are used as rationalizations for limiting women's roles in such areas as industry and the military? Eleanor Maccoby has been involved in some of the most important attempts to answer this question.

Eleanor Emmons Maccoby (1917–) was born and raised in Tacoma, Washington. Her father was a Purdue-educated engineer, and her mother was a former gospel singer who had toured with William Jennings Bryan. As evidence of her early interest in experimental psychology, Maccoby (1989) recalled that in her youth she wrote to J. B. Rhine (Chapter 12) at Duke, who responded by sending her materials with which to conduct ESP experiments.

Maccoby began her collegiate work at Reed College in Portland, Oregon, in 1934. At Reed, she took her first class in psychology from a former student of Guthrie (Chapter 13). Following a transfer to the University of Washington, Maccoby was able to work directly with Guthrie in her further study of psychology.

At Washington, she married fellow psychology student Nathan Maccoby, and his acceptance of a position at Oregon State College in 1939 complicated her pursuit of the graduate degree. The couple moved to Washington, D.C., during the war, and

Eleanor assisted in some of the survey work psychologists were doing for the government. This experience gave her professional connections that allowed her to complete her graduate work at the University of Michigan in 1950. After Nathan accepted a position at Boston University, Maccoby was associated with Harvard for several years before joining the faculty at Stanford, with her husband, as a professor of psychology.

At Harvard and at Stanford, **Robert "Bob" Sears** (1908–1989) was important for Maccoby's developmental interests. Sears and Maccoby co-authored the classic *Patterns of Child Rearing* (Sears, Maccoby, & Levin, 1957), and Maccoby's subsequent works in sex differences and socialization reflect her continuing interests in developmental psychology. In fact, Maccoby's 1988 APA Distinguished Scientific Contribution Award noted both her efforts in developmental psychology and in social psychology. In 1996, she received the American Psychological Foundation Gold Medal Award for Life Achievement.

Bob Sears and **Pauline "Pat" S. Sears** (1908–1993) met as undergraduates at Stanford and both completed their Ph.D.s from Yale, Bob in 1932 and Pat in 1939. At Yale, Bob Sears was associated with John Dollard and Neal Miller and the growing interest of the Neo-Hullians in connecting learning theory with other areas of psychology (e.g., social, clinical).

From Yale, Bob and Pat Sears moved to Iowa, where Bob Sears directed the Child Welfare Research Station from 1942 until 1949. Pat Sears also became involved with the station's research efforts, collaborating with such notables as Lewin, Dembo, and Festinger (e.g., Lewin, Dembo, Festinger, & Sears, 1944). After a brief period at Harvard, during which Bob Sears served as APA president in 1951, Bob and Pat Sears returned to Stanford in 1953. Following their 1973 retirement, Bob and Pat Sears remained active, continuing Terman's (Chapter 18) longitudinal research on gifted children. In addition, Bob Sears became interested in the psychobiographical analysis of Mark Twain (e.g., Sears, Lapidus, & Cozzens, 1978). For his many contributions to developmental psychology, Bob Sears received the APA's Distinguished Scientific Contribution Award in 1975, and in 1980 Bob and Pat Sears were jointly awarded the American Psychological Foundation's Gold Medal Award.

As for Maccoby, her interest in gender issues grew during the 1960s and early 1970s (Maccoby, 1989), culminating in *The Psychology of Sex Differences,* which she published in 1974 with Carol N. Jacklin (Maccoby & Jacklin, 1974). In *Sex Differences,* Maccoby and Jacklin conducted a comparative review of almost 1,600 studies, using techniques conceptually similar to meta-analysis (Chapter 18). Their review produced evidence for just four unambiguous gender differences: (1) females have better verbal abilities; (2) males have better visual-spatial abilities; (3) males do better on tests of mathematical ability; and (4) females are less aggressive. In addition, Maccoby and Jacklin found tentative evidence for such differences as better tactile sensitivity in females, greater activity levels in males, greater willingness to report anxiety in females, more competitiveness in males, and greater dominance in social situations in males.

Research in gender difference and gender identity continues to be popular in social psychology. Rhoda Unger and Mary Crawford have independently, and jointly (e.g., Unger & Crawford, 1992), emerged as influential authors on these topics in recent years. In addition, they have considered the usefulness of social constructionism as a way to understand better how so many misconceptions about women could have arisen and remained viable for so long (e.g., Unger, 1989).

Postmodernism

Social constructionism is perhaps best understood as one of the psychological manifestations of a theoretical revolution sweeping the humanities and social sciences called postmodernism. To understand postmodernism, we need to identify **modernism**, which refers to a cluster of assumptions that originated with the Renaissance (Chapter 3) and that have structured scientific and philosophical inquiry since. These assumptions include (1) the idea that a self exists, which leads to a distinction between the subject (experiencing self) and object

(external thing experienced), and (2) that truth exists, which fosters the idea that (3) advances in technology are evidence that our theories must be moving closer to this truth.

Postmodernism is a movement that questions modernism's assumptions. In academic disciplines such as literature and philosophy, postmodernism has established a secure foothold and has been effective in challenging the modernist assertions. In social psychology, the impact of postmodernism has been less radical. Social constructionism emerged in the mid-1960s as a theory in sociology (e.g., Berger & Luckmann, 1966), was quickly generalized to all of the social sciences (e.g., Harré & Secord, 1973), and has been popularized most recently in psychology by Sandra Scarr (Chapter 18) and Kenneth Gergen (e.g., Gergen, 1994). Gergen's work has been well received, particularly by psychologists with interests in such topics as race and gender.

Social constructionism in psychology has focused mainly on methodological points. For example, one assertion is that all studies of human behavior are bound by context. That is, rather than assuming that general rules of human behavior exist across space and time, we should acknowledge that the results of every study are relative to the cultural and historical conditions in place when the research was conducted. As Kuhn (1970) noted, the questions asked by a science and what answers qualify as acceptable also appear to be context-specific. Although we will explore Kuhn's ideas about the social construction of science and how it relates to psychology further in Chapter 20, elements of postmodernism have also arisen in contemporary approaches to personality and clinical psychology (Chapter 16).

CONCLUSIONS

Perhaps the most important conclusion that can be drawn from our overview of the field is that the scope and relevance of social psychology are incredibly broad. Humans are social animals, and it is no exaggeration to suggest that a meaningful connection can be found between almost any aspect of human existence and social psychology.

We began this chapter by showing the connections between social psychology and an assortment of other fields and subfields (e.g., sociology, applied psychology). In fact, a number of interesting associations can be made between a variety of sociopolitical philosophies (e.g., Comte, Hegel) through the 19th century and the formal social psychology that emerged in the early 20th century (e.g., Dewey, McDougall). At the same time, it is possible to connect modern social psychology to the real world application of psychology in innumerable ways (e.g., in the study of aggression, consumer behavior, attitudes). Research on race and gender are further examples that have been especially prominent in modern times.

As social psychology has evolved and matured, its original focus on the group has receded as connections have been established with other subfields of psychology. Gordon Allport's and Gardner and Lois Murphy's interest in personality represent one example of this linkage, and the pioneering work of Solomon Asch and Fritz Heider in such areas as social cognition and social perception provide further illustrations.

Amid all the diversity, social psychology has been frequently colorful, often controversial, and almost always socially relevant. Here we would note Darley and Latané's work on bystander apathy, Milgram's obedience studies, and Bandura's research on social learning theory, although many other studies are equally worthy of being highlighted (e.g., Schachter and Singer's study of emotional attributions or Zimbardo's research on a simulated prison experience).

From social psychology, we now turn to our final chapter—cognitive psychology.

S U M M A R Y

Interest in social psychology began long before World War II, although the war and its aftermath produced a dramatic increase in relevant social topics. Some of the early people who demonstrated an interest in social behavior include Plato, Machiavelli, Hobbes, Locke, Hume, and Comte. More recent forerunners include the Europeans Gabriel Tarde, Gustave LeBon, Emile Durkheim, and Max Weber. Americans who contributed to the beginnings of social psychology include George Mead, James Mark Baldwin, and Edward Ross.

An Overview of Early Advances in Social Psychology

Floyd and Gordon Allport were two of social psychology's pioneers. Among other things, Floyd studied social facilitation, in which people perform better when tested with others than when tested alone. Gordon's primary interest can be described as a humanistic and social psychological approach to personality.

Gardner and Lois Murphy continued the association of a humanistic interest in personality with social behavior. Gardner's social psychology program at Columbia produced such important psychologists as Rensis Likert, Theodore Newcomb, and Muzafer Sherif. Much of Lois's work concerned the interaction of personality and social influences on the developing child.

One of the first formal studies on attitudes was performed by Richard LaPiere, who toured the country with a Chinese couple. Although only one business refused them service, over 90% of the people who responded to LaPiere's inquiry said that Chinese were not welcome in their establishments. Continuing the study of attitudes, Carl Hovland explored attitude change, finding evidence for a sleeper effect. Theodore Newcomb examined change and stability in attitudes.

Muzafer Sherif is known for his work on intergroup conflict. Sherif created and then alleviated hostile attitudes between groups of boys at a summer camp.

In addition to Kurt Lewin, Gestalt contributors to social psychology include Solomon Asch, Leon Festinger, and Fritz Heider. Asch became famous for his work in conformity to group pressure, which was continued as the study of obedience by his student, Stanley Milgram. Milgram found that most people would subject other people to apparently harmful electric shock if told to do so by someone in authority.

Fritz Heider's cognitive balance theory is closely related to Festinger's conception of cognitive dissonance. Heider's theory was instrumental in creating the study of attribution—how we perceive, interpret, and account for people's actions—in social psychology. Attribution theory stimulated Stanley Schachter's study in which he found that social factors are linked to the way we attribute our emotions.

Selected Topics in Contemporary Social Psychology

Albert Bandura developed social learning theory, which focuses on the role of modeling or imitation in the acquisition of social behavior. Bandura found that imitative aggression increased when the modeled behavior was reinforced and decreased when the modeled behavior was punished.

Philip Zimbardo simulated a prison environment with normal adults and found that subjects quickly learned social roles appropriate to their status as either guards or prisoners. Zimbardo's work illustrates the power of environmental conditions to shape behavior.

Following Kitty Genovese's murder in 1964, witnessed by many of her neighbors, social psychologists began to study bystander apathy. John Darley and Bibb Latané conducted several experiments that found that bystander unresponsiveness stems from a diffusion of responsibility rather than from a lack of concern for the victim.

The study of race and ethnicity became major psychological topics after World War II. Kenneth Clark is one of a handful of Blacks to earn Ph.D.s in psychology in the period from 1920 through 1966. In 1971, Clark was elected the APA's first Black president.

In *Stigma*, sociologist Erving Goffman considered issues on the general topic of difference and racial identity. One of the issues addressed was that of gender differences. Janet Spence and Sandra Bem are also leaders in the study of gender differences, Spence for her work reported in *Masculinity and Femininity* and Bem for the Bem Sex Role Inventory scale. Eleanor Maccoby concluded from a review of many studies that only four unambiguous gender differences had been demonstrated: less aggression and better verbal abilities in females and better mathematical and visual-spatial abilities in males.

Social constructionism can be viewed as a manifestation of a theoretical revolution in the humanities and social sciences called postmodernism. Postmodernism is a movement confronting the basic assumptions of the modern era, which include the idea of the existence of a self and the idea that truth exists and that our advances in technology are evidence that we are getting closer to it.

CONNECTIONS QUESTIONS

1. How are the social changes in America that began during and following World War II connected to social psychology?
2. What are the connections between the European events leading to World War II, Gestalt psychology, and American social psychology?
3. What is the connection between psychology's founders (e.g., Wundt, James) and social psychology?
4. Describe as many connections as you can between Gestalt psychology and social psychology. For example, what connections can be made between Asch and Milgram in terms of their most well-known research?
5. Support the claim that Thurstone and Likert are among the most important contributors to the rise of social psychology, and tell how Janet Spence Sandra Bem might be connected to their contributions.
6. Draw a concept map connecting the major people and ideas in this chapter, and compare your results with one possible solution on p. 570.

SUGGESTED READINGS

Allport, G. W. (1954). *The nature of prejudice.* Cambridge, MA: Addison-Wesley. This is perhaps the first detailed consideration of racial prejudice by a psychologist. *The Nature of Prejudice* continues to be a relevant source book for researchers interested in race or prejudice.

Berger, P., & Luckmann, T. (1966). *The social construction of reality.* Garden City, NY: Anchor Books. This book was fundamental to the rise of postmodern views in the social sciences, including psychology. The central thesis is that many of our most important social institutions have no reality apart from the people that comprise them.

Goffman, E. (1963). *Stigma.* Englewood Cliffs, NJ: Prentice-Hall. Although Goffman was an academic sociologist, many of his works, including *Stigma,* are required reading in psychology graduate programs. Reading this powerful work may change your outlook on life.

Harré, R., & Secord, P. (1973). *The explanation of social behavior.* Totowa, NJ: Littlefield, Adams & Company. Harré and Secord's book provides a thought-provoking critique of the application of behaviorial theories to social phenomena. It should be read by anyone interested in the nature of theory as it relates to psychology.

Latané, B., & Darley, J. M. (1970). *The unresponsive bystander: Why doesn't he help?* New York: Appleton-Century-Crofts. This book is an early summary of the work done on bystander apathy. Many studies are discussed, in addition to the one on which we focused.

Lindzey, G., & Aronson, E. (Eds.) (1985). *The handbook of social psychology* (3rd. ed., Vols. 1–2). New York: Random House. Considered the definitive source book for social psychologists, *The Handbook* contains a comprehensive review of every major topic within the field. Although it may prove too expensive for your budget, the library's copy should be your first stop when you are exploring any topic in social psychology.

Maccoby, E. E., & Jacklin, C. N. (1974). *The psychology of sex differences.* Stanford, CA: Stanford University Press. This classic work remains basic reading on the topic of gender differences. With its coverage of nearly 1,600 studies, the scope of this work is impressive and probably includes any relevant topic in which you are interested.

Milgram, S. (1992). *The individual in a social world* (2nd ed.). New York: McGraw-Hill. This book surveys the work of Stanley Milgram, with considerable coverage given to his studies of obedience. Other topics include research ethics, urban living, and social cognition.

Spence, J., & Helmreich, R. (1978). *Masculinity & femininity: Their psychological dimensions, correlates, & antecedents.* Austin, TX: University of Texas Press. Spence and Helmreich's book is one of the pioneering works in the social psychology of gender, and it remains an excellent source of information for anyone with interests in the area of gender.

Cognitive Psychology

Herbert Simon

Jerome Bruner

Lev Vygotsky

Jean Piaget

Ludwig Wittgenstein

Frederic Bartlett

	1880	1890	1900	1910	1920	1930

Paul Gauguin paints *Two Tahitian Women*

Adolf Hitler is born

Franz Kafka is born

German torpedoes sink the *Lusitania*, killing 1,198 during WWI

The *Titanic* sinks, over 1,500 drown

The last Allied troops leave the Rhineland

In the first chapter, we briefly mentioned the philosopher of science Thomas Kuhn and his conception of scientific revolutions (Kuhn, 1970). Although Kuhn's thesis was developed to give an account of the evolution of theories and paradigms in the physical sciences (e.g., physics, chemistry, geology), many writers in the history and theory of psychology have attempted to apply Kuhn's work to psychology, especially to the recent waning of behaviorism and the rise of cognitive psychology (Gholson & Barker, 1985; Henley, 1989; Koch, 1975; Palermo, 1971). Kuhn's ideas have even been used to structure history of psychology texts (e.g., Bolles, 1993), although some historians have argued against the use of Kuhn to organize material in the history of psychology (e.g., Leahey, 1992).

Roger Brown

Ulric Neisser

Noam Chomsky

George Miller

1940	1950	1960	1970	1980	1990

The Pentagon is completed during WWII

In the first deployment of U.S. combat troops in Vietnam, U.S. Marines land at Da Nang

AT&T agrees to be broken up

Herbert Simon wins Nobel Prize

Tolkien's *The Hobbit* is published

Hitchcock's "Psycho" opens to bad reviews

For Kuhn (1970), theoretical revolution in science was a matter of evolving paradigms. A science begins with a period of agreement about what a given discipline is, about its subject matter, and about its appropriate methodology. At this point, there is only one paradigm (model or world view). Kuhn called this period of agreement "normal" science, because the period tends to be long, calm, and concerned with working out the details of a grand theory that everyone in the science endorses. During this period, it is clear what needs to be done and how to do it. Staying focused on the task is enforced socially and economically via such rewards as promotion, tenure, publications, and grants.

This period of "normal" science *inevitably* comes to an end when the discipline encounters a phenomenon that is anomalous to the theory. An anomaly is an event that does not fit within the standard pattern, and as Kuhn (1970) observed, an anomaly in a science often requires substantive theoretical change. Discovery of the anomalous phenomenon causes the discipline's veteran researchers to begin patching the holes the phenomenon has created within their theoretical framework. Concurrently, younger researchers are likely to suggest radically different and competing theories to explain the new phenomenon. According to Kuhn, such new theories must be provided by the young, as more seasoned researchers have the old explanatory system at the very core of their understanding of their science.

During the period of instability, competition exists between the old theory and a number of new alternatives. Eventually one of the new competitors will prove to be the most attractive and will emerge "victorious." Once all the old guard have been deposed at granting agencies, editorial boards, and as department heads, a new paradigm and a new era of normal science begins. The new theory in turn will rise, flourish, and prosper, but it too will eventually encounter the anomaly that will be its undoing.

Does Kuhn (1970) help us understand the history of psychology? There are certainly aspects of Kuhn's theory that should seem familiar to you. As they matured, the great schools of psychology acquired some paradigmatic elements: for example, a grand theory, a shared methodology, and a system of rewards. We can view Darwin's theory of evolution, or positivistic conceptions of science, as the anomaly, and the schools can be seen as the young competitors arising to replace long-standing folk theories of human behavior. From the Kuhnian perspective, we might argue that behaviorism emerged as the new paradigm for scientific psychology. Continuing this line of reasoning, language can be viewed as the anomaly that undermined behaviorism, and in turn provided the foundation for a new, cognitive paradigm.

FORERUNNERS TO THE COGNITIVE REVOLUTION

Although the widely used phrase "cognitive revolution" seems to affirm the value of using Kuhn's (1970) theory as a tool for understanding the history of psychology, there are some inconsistencies between Kuhn's model and the historical record. The most important inconsistency may be that the study of cognition did not emerge as a new theory in the latter half of this century, but has a long history of its own. The ideas of Plato (Chapter 2) provide much of the foundation of modern cognitive science, including what could perhaps be seen as its central question—the nature and structure of knowledge.

Descartes, Locke, and certainly Kant (Chapters 3, 4, and 5, respectively) are important—and in Kant's case perhaps essential—stepping stones to modern cognitive science. Descartes's concern with the relationship between mind and body, Locke's analysis of thought and thinking, and Kant's a priori categories each, in turn, advanced our interest and understanding of mental events. Following Kant, German rationalism in all its guises—phenomenology and act psychology (Chapter 8), Gestalt psychology (Chapter 14)—had as its central interest ideas that broadly defined were cognitive. In fact, we suggested several connections between Gestalt psychology and the modern interest in cognition at the conclusion of the Gestalt chapter. Works on thinking by Bühler, Duncker, Wertheimer, and Zeigarnik, as well as several important contributions to social psychology (Chapter 19), which include Asch's work on conformity and Festinger's studies of *cognitive* dissonance, are good examples.

Also in Germany, we must recall the contributions of Ebbinghaus (Chapter 8) for his study of memory, and his student Stern, who helped introduce the term "cognition" into academic psychology. In Chapter 10, we reviewed in detail James's interest in the mind, and both Dewey (Chapter 11) and Münsterberg (Chapter 10) provided works that are arguably cognitive (e.g., Dewey's *How We Think* [1910] and Münsterberg's *On the Witness Stand* [1908]). Tolman's purposive behaviorism (Chapter 13) is the clearest, but by no means the only, example of an interest in cognition on the part of someone we more commonly associate with behaviorism. Clark Hull's (Chapter 13) dissertation was on concept formation, and Jacob Kantor (1936; Chapter 13) produced an early work on psychology and language (*Objective Psychology of Grammar*). In Chapter 15, we noted that even Freud can be viewed as an antecedent to the contemporary study of cognition.

Thus, in earlier chapters we have highlighted many connections to psychology's current interest in cognition. A few additional important antecedents remain to be examined, some from within psychology and some from outside the discipline.

Early Contributors in Psychology

Sir Frederic Bartlett

As can be seen in some of his early works (e.g., Bartlett, 1923), Cambridge psychologist **Sir Frederic Charles Bartlett** (1886–1969) was critical of American behaviorism and its limited focus. Thus, it is not surprising that *Remembering: A Study in Experimental and Social Psychology* (Bartlett, 1932), his magnum opus, was largely ignored in America. Despite its subtitle, *Remembering* represents one of the most important contributions to cognitive psychology ever written. The book marks a departure from thinking about knowledge as occurring in static, atomic bits and focuses instead on larger, meaningful units of information, as well as on the dynamic nature of these knowledge units. The new unit of knowledge is called the **schema**, which can be understood as a mental structure that organizes and summarizes a large number of related experiences. The schemata (schema is singular) allow us to combine many particular experiences—for example, our interactions with dogs—into one composite representation, our dog schema.

Bartlett adapted the term schema from earlier physiological work by Sir Henry Head (1861–1940), a friend and contemporary of Sir Charles Sherrington (Chapter 17). Although Bartlett was not the first to use the term schema, both his work and that of Jean Piaget (discussed later) demonstrated the utility of the concept. Bartlett's methodology included the use of long paragraphs that formed a cohesive, meaningful, whole story. The most famous example is the Kwakiutl Indian tale, the "War of the Ghosts," translated by Franz Boas (Chapter 10).

Bartlett (1932) asked subjects to read the material twice, and then at different time intervals ranging from minutes to weeks, he had subjects attempt to reproduce the story as completely as possible. Bartlett observed that although subjects tended to make omissions of detail, they seemed to recall that the story was a coherent and meaningful narrative and worked to preserve that more "schematic" structure. As they forgot or misremembered actual details of the original story, they reconstructed plausible new elements and connections to maintain a coherent narrative in the story they retold, hence the term "**reconstructive memory**."

For example, an important element near the end of the story read: "When the sun rose he fell down. Something black came out of his mouth. His face became contorted." In one study of serial reproductions, the element became over time:

> When the sun rose he fell down. And he gave a cry, and as he opened his mouth a black thing rushed from it.

> He felt no pain until sunrise the next day, when, on trying to rise, a great black thing flew out of his mouth.

> He lived that night, and the next day, but at sunset his soul fled black from his mouth.

> He lived through the night and the next day, but died at sunset, and his soul passed out from his mouth.

> His spirit left the world. (selections from Bartlett, 1932, p. 127)

The changes suggested to Bartlett (1932) that memory was indeed schematic, with subjects tending to capture the meaningful "big picture" and reconstructing the details based on a combination of what they actually recalled and what, based on other knowledge and similar events, seemed likely to have occurred. Bartlett's research suggests that our reported knowledge of an event can be contaminated by a variety of factors, such as our own interests and prior experiences, an observation similar to that of Francis Bacon (Chapter 3) in his discussion of idols.

In Chapter 1, we mentioned the empirical works of both Ulric Neisser and Elizabeth Loftus (also Chapter 18) and first raised the issue of reconstructive memory in the context of the goodness of source material in writing a history text. In Neisser's and Loftus's work, we see some modern research directly connected to Bartlett's ideas. Bartlett is shown in Figure 20–1.

FIGURE 20–1.   Frederic Charles Bartlett.

Source: Clark University Press by courtesy of Harvard College Library.

Lev Vygotsky

Lev Vygotsky is another forerunner of modern cognitive psychology who deserves mention. Although Vygotsky is not as intimately connected to the modern research agenda as Bartlett, he is a person whose ideas have only recently come of age.

Lev S. Vygotsky (1896–1934) was born into a middle-class Jewish banking family that lived near Minsk in Byelorussia. By age 18, Vygotsky's primary interests were art and Hegel (Chapter 5). Still, his family insisted that he attend the medical school at the Moscow State University. Soon after his arrival in Moscow, Vygotsky transferred from the medical school to the law school and enrolled concurrently at another university to continue his studies in the humanities. Although his goal seems to have been to become a literary critic, it is clear that Vygotsky absorbed a broad and quality education during his university years.

After finishing college in 1917, Vygotsky moved to Gomel, where his parents were then living. The postrevolutionary period was difficult for many, and Vygotsky found humble employment first teaching literature in a high school and then at a teachers' college. This latter position also allowed him to offer lectures in psychology. During this period, Vygotsky educated himself in both psychology and linguistics by reading classic works, including books by James and Freud (Kozulin, 1986). Vygotsky also stayed active in the arts, working in the theater, publishing several articles, and founding the literary journal *Verask.*

In 1924, Vygotsky submitted and delivered his first paper in psychology—a work on the limits of studying the reflex—at the second Psychoneurological Congress in Leningrad. Based on this work, Vygotsky was invited to join the Moscow Institute of Psychology by A. R. Luria. Like Vygotsky, **Alexander Luria** (1902–1977) was an eclectic psychologist. His research on human conflict (Luria, 1932) earned him early acclaim in America. Later studies with a man with a spectacular "photographic memory" (Luria, 1968) and a variety of important works in physiological psychology combined to make Luria arguably the most important Russian psychologist in the post-Pavlov period.

In 1925, Vygotsky submitted what became *The Psychology of Art* as his doctoral thesis to the Institute. Beyond art, Vygotsky worked with children, animals, and investigated such diverse phenomena as intelligence, memory, and cultural influences on cognition. An excellent sample of Vygotsky's writings has been collected and published in English as *Mind and Society* (Vygotsky, 1978). Vygotsky's most famous work, *Thought and Language* (Vygotsky, 1934/1986), was written like most of his publications to contrast and compare divergent opinions from different psychological schools. In the process, Vygotsky attempted to explain the schools' differences and also to offer a new and unifying solution. Thus, William Stern (Chapter 8), Karl Bühler and Wolfgang Köhler (Chapter 14), Jean Piaget (below), and Robert Yerkes and John Watson (both Chapter 12) all played a central role in Vygotsky's attempt to account for the relationship between thought and language.

In many ways, Vygotsky anticipated the "Cognitive Revolution" itself, as his central thesis was that mainstream empirical psychology—the Wundtian program and behaviorism—was not well suited to explain higher cognitive processes. In terms of content, his preference most resembled Gestalt psychology and the works of Stern and the Würzburgers (Chapter 8). Vygotsky's goal was a unified psychology that would provide an account of mind within the context of the other natural sciences and accepted scientific methodology.

Dead of tuberculosis at 38, Vygotsky (Figure 20–2) did not live to see the unified empirical science of the mind he imagined. Much of Vygotsky's work was published posthumously and was not translated from Russian until decades later. *Thought and Language* was banned in the Soviet Union (probably because of anti-Semitism) from 1936 until 1956 and was not translated into English for many years after that.

Until recent times, Bartlett's work on schema theory and Vygotsky's contributions to cognitive development have been overshadowed by another European psychologist's interest in the same topics. That psychologist was Jean Piaget.

FIGURE 20–2.   Lev Vygotsky.

Source: Archives of the History of American Psychology.

Jean Piaget

Jean Piaget (1896–1980) was born in Neuchâtel, Switzerland. In an autobiographical essay, Piaget (1952) recalled that his father was an academic who worked primarily in medieval literature, and he described his mother as having a "rather neurotic temperament," which was an important influence on his development. Perhaps because of his mother's poor mental health, Piaget's first interests in psychology were in psychoanalysis and psychopathology.

Like some others we have encountered—for example, Leibniz (Chapter 5), John Stuart Mill (Chapter 4), and Galton (Chapter 9)—Piaget was incredibly precocious, producing his first scientific paper at the age of 10. Recognizing the boy's abilities and interests, the director of Neuchâtel's natural history museum, an authority on molluscs, took Piaget under his wing. After the director's death, Piaget continued his mentor's research, and he produced over 20 publications on molluscs when he was between the ages of 15 and 19. Piaget's international reputation led one of his readers to offer him a curator's position in Geneva, which Piaget declined because he had not finished high school.

A vacation with his godfather, who aimed to "teach [him] the 'creative evolution' of Bergson" (Piaget, 1952, p. 240), resulted in a profound revelation: "The identification of God with life . . . enabled me to see in biology the explanation of all things and of the mind itself" (p. 240). Piaget dedicated his life to the search for biological explanations of knowledge. Somewhat later, Piaget found that the Nobel Prize winning philosopher Bergson (Chapter 16) had not presented science's last word, as his godfather had led him to believe. "Between biology and the analysis of knowledge I needed something other than a philosophy. I believe it was at that moment that I discovered a need that could be satisfied only by psychology" (p. 240).

After his disappointment with Bergson's philosophy, Piaget began reading everything that came his way, including the work of such philosophers as Kant, Spencer (Chapter 9), Comte (Chapter 5), and Tarde (Chapter 19), and that of such psychologists as James, Ribot (Chapter 4), and Janet (Chapter 15). This reading led to Piaget's "system," which had as its core principle the idea that in all areas of life there are "totalities" different from their parts and that these "wholes" impose organization on the parts. Not surprisingly, Piaget (1952) wrote that, "If I had known at that time (1913–1915) the work of Wertheimer and of Köhler, I would have become a Gestaltist . . ." (p. 242).

Piaget earned his bachelor's degree at 18 and his Ph.D. in biology (with a thesis on molluscs) at 22. In 1918, Piaget spent a year in Zurich, where he worked in Bleuler's (Chapter 16) clinic, studied briefly with Jung (Chapter 16), and continued to study molluscs. In Paris in 1919, Piaget was recommended to Binet's associate, Théodore Simon (Chapter 18), who gave Piaget the task of adapting some of Cyril Burt's (Chapter 18) British work for use with French children. Piaget developed a different approach to children's intelligence than that taken by Binet and Simon, using careful questioning

of the children to tease out their thought processes when they answered test items either correctly or incorrectly. In this way, Piaget discovered that intelligence grows qualitatively with age as well as quantitatively, as Binet had assumed. That is, older children may use cognitive abilities to solve a particular problem that a younger child, without the particular abilities, cannot grasp. In the study of children's cognitive abilities, Piaget had found his niche: He would investigate the biological development of knowledge through the psychogenetic development of the child. Piaget called his program **genetic epistemology**, genetic in the sense of developmental rather than hereditary; epistemology is the branch of philosophy that studies the nature and foundations of knowledge.

On the basis of his initial studies of cognitive development in children, Piaget wrote three articles. Two were published in the *Journal de Psychologie,* whereas the third was accepted by the Swiss psychologist **Edouard Claparède** (1873–1940) for the journal he had founded, *Archives de Psychologie.* Claparède, professor at Geneva and the founder of the Jean Jacques Rousseau Institute for the study of educational science, offered Piaget the position of "director of studies" at the Institute. Piaget took the position, which "changed the course of my life" (Piaget, 1952, p. 245). At the Institute, Piaget had the freedom to perform research in which he was interested and had excellent collaborators, including Valentine Châtenay, whom Piaget subsequently married.

Piaget was professor of psychology at the University of Geneva from 1929 to 1954, and in 1956, he founded the Institute for Genetic Epistemology at the University, where scholars from all over the world can come to discuss issues in cognitive development. The results of their discussions are published annually in the monograph *Studies in Genetic Epistemology.* Always a man of broad interests, Piaget was affiliated with other area universities in contexts ranging from sociology to molluscs.

Although Piaget received some early acclaim in America (e.g., an honorary doctorate from Harvard in 1936), from 1933 until 1950 none of his works was translated into English. After World War II, this neglect was a product primarily of American psychology's behaviorist *Zeitgeist.* With the relative decline of behaviorism and the 1960s growth of interest in cognitive psychology, Piaget was rediscovered. The translation of Piaget's *Psychology of Intelligence* in 1950 was the first of a wave of publications that resulted in his becoming perhaps the world's leading child development theorist. In 1969, Piaget (Figure 20–3) received the APA's Distinguished Scientific Contribution Award.

Piaget's Psychology. Two important components of Piaget's psychology warrant discussion here: his stage model of cognitive development and his contribution to modern schema theory. Piaget's work was not the first of its kind in either case. Several similar stage theories of development predated Piaget's theory, and some alternatives (e.g., Vygotsky's) were perhaps better articulated. Key elements of Piaget's schema theory can be traced not

only to Baldwin (1898; Chapter 10) but also to certain Gestalt psychology principles. Still, Piaget's contributions to both areas were substantial, primarily because it was *his* presentation of cognitive developmental stages and schema theory that eventually was incorporated into mainstream psychology.

On the basis of observations of his own and many other children, Piaget concluded that the child is born with certain simple reflex actions, such as the grasping reflex and the suckling reflex, that it uses to interact with its world. He called these independent reflexes schemata, because they organize the infant's responses to experience. The child also has an inherent predisposition to organize the simple schemata into higher-order ones, such as when the infant combines its grasping schema with its suckling schema and holds the bottle while sucking from it.

Additionally, an infant inherits the processes of **assimilation** and **accommodation**. If an experience fits the individual's schemata, then the experience is taken in or assimilated into the mind. On the other hand, if there is not a match between the experience and existing schemata, then the schemata will be altered to accommodate reality. Piaget called the motive for accommodation **equilibration**. A mismatch between reality and an existing schema produces disequilibrium, which drives the individual to change mental structures to achieve a better match with reality.

To illustrate, a young child initially may have a broad schema for the concept of *dog,* calling all four-legged animals *doggies.* The child soon encounters a quadruped that meows and purrs rather than barks and wags its tail, and this mismatch between the existing schema and reality produces disequilibrium, which is the incentive for the child to refine his or her dog schema (assimilation) and to develop a cat schema (accommodation).

Piaget divided the cognitive development of a child into four stages, which he believed all children go through, although not necessarily at exactly the same ages. Each stage is organized around a dominant theme, and each contains qualitatively different behaviors.

For Piaget, the first stage is the **sensorimotor stage**, which lasts from birth until approximately

FIGURE 20–3.   Piaget and unidentified child.

Source: © Bill Anderson, Monkmeyer Press Photo Service.

age 2. During this stage, the infant is learning the relations between its sensory apparatus and its motor responses. One of the period's defining features is a lack of the concept of **object permanence**. That is, the infant responds as though he or she does not realize that an object continues to exist if it is no longer being sensed. "Out of sight, out of mind" aptly describes the infant's behavior.

From 2 until approximately 7, the child is in Piaget's **preoperational stage**, during which he or she discovers the operations (e.g., plans, strategies, rules) that will be used for solving problems and classifying information. During this stage, the child's thinking is likely to exhibit animism, which is the tendency to attribute life to inanimate objects, and egocentrism, which is the view that the self is the center of everything. The hallmark of the preoperational stage is a lack of the concept of **conservation of quantity**. That is, in preoperational thinking, the child does not realize that the quantity of something remains the same with changes in appearance.

Between the ages of about 7 and 11, the child has developed the concept of conservation when dealing with concrete objects and is in what Piaget called the **concrete operational stage**. That is, as long as a problem concerns tangible things the child can deal with directly, then the child can probably solve it. Problems involving abstract concepts, imagined realities, and symbols require cognitive skills that will not be fully developed until Piaget's final stage.

Piaget's fourth stage is called the **formal operational stage**, and it extends from about 12 or 13 through adulthood. Now the young person can think abstractly and has the cognitive ability to test problem solutions hypothetically and systematically. Consider the following problem to illustrate the difference in cognitive ability of a child in the concrete operational stage and one in the formal operational stage: Lani, Jill, Wanda, and Erin are friends. How many groups of two, three, and four of these friends can be formed, all of which include Erin? In the formal operational stage, the individual has the ability to test the various hypothetical possibilities systematically until he or she discovers that seven groups of two, three, or four friends can be formed, all including Erin.

Piaget's Influence. Piaget's theory of cognitive development of the child has fostered a wealth of research, some of which has disagreed with specific aspects of the theory. For example, it is now considered less certain that the child goes through distinct stages and that children at higher stages have abilities that younger children completely lack. That is, development has been found to be more continuous than Piaget thought. Also, questions have been raised about the degree to which Piaget's hypothesized stages are tied to Western civilization and may not generalize to other cultures.

Although the theory may be wrong in certain details, Piaget's general concepts are still considered valid (e.g., see the July 1996 issue of *Psychological Science* for a recent appraisal of his work). The cognitive abilities of the child are not the same as those of the adult. Through a combination of biological maturation and increasing experience with the world, the child's schemata are altered to better represent reality. In this way, cognitive development occurs.

We will conclude our discussion of Piaget and his contributions with a brief review of the life and work of perhaps his most important student at the University of Geneva and his long-time collaborator, Bärbel Inhelder.

Bärbel Inhelder

Bärbel Inhelder (1913–) was born in St. Gall, Switzerland. From her zoologist father, Inhelder learned pre-Socratic philosophy and Darwin (Chapter 9), whereas her mother, a writer, exposed her to Shakespeare and the German classics (Inhelder, 1989). In 1932, Inhelder began work at the Rousseau Institute in Geneva, where she came into contact with Claparède and Piaget.

Inhelder began a lengthy collaboration with Piaget at the Institute, quickly producing several major publications (e.g., *The Child's Construction of Quantities;* Piaget & Inhelder, 1941) before she found time to complete her doctoral thesis. After completing her degree in 1943, Inhelder continued to work with Piaget, once again producing a number of important efforts (e.g., *The Origin of the Idea of Chance in Children;* Piaget & Inhelder, 1951). In

1948, the Institute's mission was broadened to include the offering of graduate degrees, and Inhelder was named part of the psychology faculty.

The rise of interest in cognitive psychology in America in the late 1960s led to interactions between Inhelder and cognitive pioneers such as Jerome Bruner (discussed later) at Harvard. These interactions facilitated the rediscovery of Piaget's ideas and the discovery of Inhelder's many contributions. Inhelder deserves recognition as one of the first and most important female contributors to cognitive psychology.

Moral Development

When Inhelder first met Piaget in 1932, he had just completed *The Moral Judgment of the Child,* which was his major contribution to the topic of moral development. Although Piaget was an important early contributor to the study of moral reasoning in children, the central figure became Lawrence Kohlberg.

Lawrence Kohlberg (1927–1987) was born in Bronxville, New York. The son of a wealthy businessman and the product of the finest college preparatory schools, Kohlberg joined the Merchant Marines following high school graduation. Perhaps the experience of smuggling Jews from Europe to Palestine was the spark leading to Kohlberg's later interest in differences in moral reasoning.

Returning to America after his Merchant Marine service, Kohlberg completed his B.A. at the University of Chicago in only a year. Based primarily on Piaget's earlier efforts, Kohlberg's 1958 Ph.D. thesis at Chicago signaled the beginning of his lifelong devotion to the study of moral development. Following a brief period at Yale and several interim positions, Kohlberg settled at Harvard in 1967. On a Central American trip in 1973, Kohlberg contracted a disease that ruined his health, produced severe disabilities and depression, and led to his suicide in 1987.

According to Kohlberg's theory of moral development, there are three major stages of moral reasoning, each containing two levels. In the **preconventional stage,** moral behavior is motivated by the avoidance of punishment in the first level and by the desire to be rewarded in the second level.

In the **conventional stage,** moral decisions are motivated by social rules. At the third level, good behavior is behavior that earns the praise of other people, whereas behaving correctly in the fourth level means obeying the laws established by people in power.

In the **postconventional stage,** the individual is guided by internalized moral principles. At the fifth level, these are the principles established by society for the benefit of its members. Finally, at the sixth level, the individual has incorporated and is influenced by universally ethical principles of right and wrong (e.g., by rules such as "Do unto others as you would have them do unto you").

Although Kohlberg's stage theory is still widely taught and respected, it has not escaped criticism. As we noted in our discussion of Piaget, stage theories can always be challenged for de-emphasizing continuous changes in development and for being dependent on the cultural context from which they are derived.

One of Kohlberg's best-known critics, Carol Gilligan, has largely focused on the problem of gender differences in moral development. Gilligan (1982) noted that theorists such as Freud, Piaget, and Kohlberg (with whom Gilligan taught a course on moral development at Harvard-Radcliffe) concluded that women were morally inferior to men because of how they reasoned about hypothetical moral dilemmas. Instead, Gilligan has found that women are more likely to consider the interpersonal context of the problem, probably because they are socialized to be caring rather than judgmental. Gilligan's speculations highlight the importance of experience for moral development and the relevance of gender-based issues outside of personality and social psychology.

Early Contributions Outside of Psychology

Although human development serves as one element of contemporary cognitive psychology, it is not the only one. For example, Claude Shannon (1938) observed that basic logic could be contained in an electronic relay, an insight that gave birth to the modern computer era. From the outset, computing machines and psychology have been related. In 1948, the term **cybernetics** was coined by the applied mathematician Norbert Wiener (1894–1964) to cover the study of the fundamental control processes of behavior in both animals and machines. You may recall that in Chapter 13 we mentioned Hull's thoughts on machines and general principles of learning. By 1950, theorists such as **Alan Turing** (1912–1954), the "father" of artificial intelligence, had already observed both how much of human cognitive activity the computer could be programmed to display and the implications this would have for modeling and studying higher cognitive processes such as language and thought (Turing, 1950).

In an area related to cybernetics, McCulloch and Pitts (1943) showed that the operations of nerve cells could be modeled with symbolic logic. Soon it was understood that this again meant that computers could be used as models of such basic psychological processes as learning and perception.

Thus, several events outside of cognitive psychology, or even psychology per se, also have relevance for the rise of cognitive science. Gardner (1985) stressed the importance of a 1948 meeting at the California Institute of Technology concerning "Cerebral Mechanisms in Behavior." The opening speaker was the eminent quantum theory mathematician John von Neumann, who reviewed the evidence that the brain is analogous to a computer. Gardner credited the third speaker, Karl Lashley (Chapter 17), with outlining a program that became the interdisciplinary new cognitive science.

Although we will revisit the computer later, computer science is not the only area outside psychology that is relevant to the modern interest in cognition. Gardner (1985) listed key changes in linguistics, the philosophy of language (and psychology) as pioneered by Gilbert Ryle (1949) and Ludwig Wittgenstein (1953), the rise of cultural anthropology, and many advances in neurology as being important to the development of cognitive science. Although we cannot explore all of these connections in detail, we will next examine one of the changes in linguistics that was most salient for psychology.

NOAM CHOMSKY

Avram Noam Chomsky (1928–) was born in Philadelphia and completed his undergraduate and graduate work in linguistics at the University of Pennsylvania before joining the faculty at the Massachusetts Institute of Technology (MIT) in 1955. Chomsky is considered the historically most important contributor to linguistics. In addition, his contributions to political theory are held in almost as much esteem.

The interplay between psychology and linguistics before Chomsky was limited. Charles Kay Ogden (1889–1957) represents perhaps the most important and notable bridge (e.g., Ogden & Richards, 1923). An English linguistic reformer, Ogden was an insightful investigator of the relationship between language and thought. However, if there has been a cognitive revolution, no person is more responsible for it than Noam Chomsky (Figure 20–4).

FIGURE 20–4.   Noam Chomsky.
Source: MIT Photo/Donna Coveney.

Although he was not trained as a psychologist, his review of Skinner's *Verbal Behavior* (Chomsky, 1959; Chapter 13) came as a rallying cry to foes of radical behaviorism.

Chomsky (1959) began his response to Skinner's analysis of language by attacking behaviorism's fundamental concepts—reinforcement, stimulus, and so on—as being ineffectual when directed to the topic of human language. Although Lashley had already observed that there seemed to be more to language than the behaviorist analysis revealed, Chomsky popularized a rationalistic, and in his own terms Cartesian (Chomsky, 1966), alternative to the study of language and language acquisition. By Cartesian, Chomsky was referring to Descartes's innate characteristics of the mind, which Chomsky believes include a language acquisition device (**LAD**). For Chomsky, the story of language development has less to do with learning and experience than it does with inherent structures in the mind (or brain) that are preprogrammed for language acquisition.

Chomsky argued that what a child must learn in order to speak correctly and understand a language is too complicated to be acquired through behaviorist learning principles and accounted for through such terms as "stimulus" and "reinforcement." Chomsky insisted that the language spoken to children was too poor a stimulus (his **poverty-of-stimulus argument**) and that reinforcement of correct grammar was too haphazard to provide a satisfactory behavioral account of language acquisition. What psychology needed was a revolutionary way of thinking about language. Chomsky's nativistic alternative was a revitalization of ideas first expressed by Wilhelm von Humboldt (1767–1835). For Chomsky (e.g., Chomsky, 1957), various biological, **syntactic structures** exist that contain the basic grammar rules of human language.

Chomsky's poverty-of-stimulus argument has matured into a widely accepted criticism of Skinner in particular, and behaviorism in general, as a unified theory of all aspects of (human) behavior (e.g., Chomsky, 1980). For many, language proved to be the Kuhnian anomaly that led to behaviorism's downfall. Thus, the task of psycholinguistics was to discover and analyze the inherent mental structures that provide for language, and much of the impor-

tant research has been conducted by psychologists such as George Miller and Roger Brown (both discussed later). Following Chomsky, American psychology's focus has shifted from an almost exclusive analysis of behavior back to the study of mental events. Also, the interaction between psychology and linguistics has remained intact and has strengthened with psychology's new cognitive focus. Currently, the study of figurative language (e.g., metaphor, analogy, irony), as pioneered by George Lakoff (1941–), is an increasingly important area of collaboration between psychology and linguistics; e.g., Lakoff & Johnson, 1980.

JEROME BRUNER AND GEORGE MILLER

Jerome Bruner and George Miller are considered foundational figures in the renewed study of cognition. Bruner and Miller together were founders in 1962 of the Center for Cognitive Studies at Harvard, an event Hilgard (1987) called a "genuine milestone" in the history of cognitive psychology.

Jerome Seymour Bruner

New York–born **Jerome Seymour Bruner** (1915–) was trained initially by William McDougall (Chapter 12) at Duke and by Gordon Allport (Chapter 19) at Harvard, where he completed his Ph.D. in 1941. In a biographical sketch, Anglin (1973) also listed Lashley, Piaget, and Tolman (Chapter 13) as Bruner's intellectual mentors. During World War II, Bruner studied public morale with the Rensis Likert group (Chapter 18) and later surveyed public opinion with Hadley Cantril (first mentioned in Chapter 1) at Princeton's Office of Public Opinion Research.

Bruner returned to Harvard and teaching in 1945 and conducted studies in both social psychology and perception. In the early 1950s, Bruner became interested in thinking and concept formation, and working with host Sir Frederic Bartlett, he assisted in holding one of the first conferences on cognition at Cambridge in 1955 (Bruner, 1980).

Bruner's classic *A Study of Thinking* (Bruner, Goodnow, & Austin, 1956) appeared the next year. The interdisciplinary nature of cognitive science and some of its historical connections are evident from the acknowledgments made in the book's preface. For example, they included the nuclear physicist J. Robert Oppenheimer; the perceptual researcher Egon Brunswick (1903–1955), who worked under Karl Bühler before coming to America at Tolman's invitation; and Herbert Langfeld (Chapter 10).

In another historical connection, Bruner (1986) told about how he first heard of Lev Vygotsky at a 1954 party at Wilder Penfield's home (Chapter 6). Bruner's independently formed ideas about language and memory were similar to Vygotsky's, and Bruner was instrumental in introducing Vygotsky to an increasingly receptive American audience.

Bruner eventually settled at the New School for Social Research in New York, where he was named the George Herbert Mead University Professor. Several recurrent themes in Bruner's writings illustrate both his personal interests and cognitive psychology's broader aims. These themes include (1) the relationship between perception and conception, (2) the developmental aspects of cognition, and (3) applications—such as educational applications—of the study of cognition. As an example, after first calling attention to the more intuitive and creative aspects of knowing decades ago (Bruner, 1962), Bruner's recent works (e.g., Bruner, 1986) have criticized cognitive psychology trends that continue to focus on the logical and systematic aspects of thinking while neglecting other, more flexible and imaginative, aspects of knowing. The recognition of diverse cognitive styles holds promise for how children may be optimally educated. Bruner is shown in Figure 20–5.

George Armitage Miller

George Armitage Miller (1920–) wrote that his first experience with psychology came via a chance conversation with a textbook salesman. About the conversation's subject matter, Miller (1989) recalled

FIGURE 20–5. Jerome Seymour Bruner.
Source: Sue Klemens, Harvard University Press.

that "I could recognize the devil when I saw him" (p. 391).

At the University of Alabama, Miller attended his first psychology seminar, which focused on Kurt Goldstein (Chapter 14). Miller recalled that his focus was more on Katherine James, who soon became his wife (Miller, 1989). After earning a master's degree in speech, Miller stayed at Alabama as a psychology instructor. In 1942, his psychology mentor persuaded him to go to Harvard to work with E. G. Boring (Chapters 1 and 7) and S. S. Stevens (Chapters 13 and 18).

At Harvard, Miller became close friends with Wendell Garner (Chapter 18), and his work conducted for the military on jamming signals was accepted for his dissertation. After graduating, Miller stayed at Harvard until 1951, and his initial contributions were in pioneering "mathematical psychology" in the tradition of Claude Shannon and Norbert Wiener. After 2 years at MIT, where he established a laboratory and a research program in speech perception, Miller returned to Harvard to replace the retiring Boring. Miller's (1951) *Language and Communication* summarized much of his research to that point.

The Magical Number Seven

Miller continued his interest in the intersection of mathematical information theory and human communication. In that context, Miller first presented his famous paper, "The Magical Number Seven, Plus or Minus Two: Some Limits on Our Capacity for Processing Information" (Miller, 1956). The paper's central point was that **short-term memory**—consciousness—has an average capacity of 7 ± 2 **chunks** (items of information) independent of the size of the chunks (recall J. M. Cattell's similar findings from Chapter 7). Although the introduction of the idea of chunking stimulated a variety of related memory studies, another important aspect of the paper was its nativistic implications about the fixed capacity of our ability to process information. In addition, it was a paper about the nature of *consciousness* published during the hegemony of behaviorism.

In 1955, Miller attended the conference that Bruner and Bartlett held at Cambridge, and in 1956 Miller and Chomsky met at a symposium on information theory held at MIT. In 1957, the two began to collaborate on several works (e.g., Chomsky & Miller, 1958). In 1958–1959, Miller was a fellow at the Center for the Advanced Study of the Behavioral Sciences at Stanford. There, he was exposed to the growing interest in and research on language by anthropologists and came into contact with Karl Pribram (Chapter 17) and learned of related advances in neuroscience.

Plans and the Structure of Behavior

In 1958, the Cambridge engineering psychologist **Donald Broadbent** (1926–1993) was one of the first popularizers of the information-processing metaphor with his book *Perception and Communication* (Broadbent, 1958). **Information processing** is the term used to describe the application of cybernetic information and control theories to human behavior and mental events, and the first generation of cognitive psychologists accepted this term as a shorthand for their interests. This work by Broad-bent—who was educated by, worked with, and then replaced the retiring Bartlett at Cambridge—along with Miller's "The Magical Number Seven," are often heralded as the publications by psychologists that marked the beginning of the cognitive revolution.

However, Miller, Galanter, and Pribram's (1960) *Plans and the Structure of Behavior* may be a better candidate for the signal publication. The book introduced the concept of the **TOTE** (acronym for Test-Operate-Test-Exit) unit as the structure of behavior. A TOTE unit is a hypothetical, hierarchical, feedback loop that includes cognitive as well as behavioral components and that is assumed to occupy the same theoretical space as the reflex arc. The TOTE was intended to be a general unit of analysis to explain behavioral processes—*Test* the environment for stimulus information, then *Operate,* or respond, to that information. The TOTE was also designed to include further *Testing* of feedback for the congruence between the organism's planned state and its current state that could continue until the *Exit* conditions were met. If you have ever done any computer programming, you may be struck by how similar the TOTE is to any sort of computational routine that analyzes a variable and then responds differently given the variable's state.

Miller (1989) conceded that the TOTE suffered from the same key problem as the S-R concept: It was too vague. However, it was from this new analysis of human behavior that included a role for the cognitive processing of information that the whole information-processing approach to the study of cognitive phenomena emerged.

Returning to Harvard in 1960, Miller approached Bruner with the idea of establishing a Harvard center to do cognitive work. Bruner was receptive, and in 1962, the Center for Cognitive Studies was formed. Initial work at the Center focused on finding empirical, psychological support for Chomsky's linguistic theories (Chomsky was appointed a fellow of the Center in 1962). Miller (1989) recalled that this was the period in which his presentations began to include an opening 30-minute attack on the narrowness of behaviorism as an approach to understanding the complex phenomena of human cognition. Vygotsky would have been pleased.

By 1965, Chomsky's influence upon Miller was clear, as Miller (e.g., Miller, 1965) blasted behavioral approaches to the study of human communication, including his own 1955 text. Other changes were also in the air. Just a few years after being named head of a department at Harvard that then included B. F. Skinner, Miller left to accept a position at Rockefeller University.

Miller remained at Rockefeller for over a decade, and during his tenure his attention shifted from a Chomskyian interest in syntax to broader issues of language and thought. Miller's *Language and Perception* (Miller & Johnson-Laird, 1976) presented the still-prevailing theory of how information about language is stored in the mind. In 1979, Miller (Figure 20–6) moved to Princeton, where in 1986, he founded the Princeton Cognitive Science Laboratory. Still an active researcher, Miller's current work is a computer-based project known as WORDNET, which represents a continuation of his interest in the structure and representation of language.

CLASSICAL CONTRIBUTIONS

It would be impossible for us to survey all of modern cognitive psychology in the remainder of this chapter. Instead, we will briefly explore some areas and individuals that are representative of modern cognitive research and illustrate some of the changes and trends in the area over the last 3 decades.

Words and Things

We have suggested that the study of language is central to modern cognitive psychology, which is not to say that behaviorists had neglected it. Interest in "verbal behavior" existed before Chomsky and certainly before empirical support for his position. In a Kuhnian fashion, several of the younger researchers during the 1960s made the transition from the study of word associations in the behaviorist paradigm to the new psycholinguistics. For example, James Deese (1965) wrote the swan song on word associations before writing an important early psycholinguistics textbook (Deese, 1970). Irvin Rock (e.g., Rock, 1957) migrated from work on associative learning to other areas, such as perception. William Estes (Chapter 13) is also an important figure in the change from positivism and behaviorism, through statistical learning, into cognitive psychology. Another important language researcher, James Jenkins (1993) has written reflectively about this transition from behaviorism to cognitive psychology.

Many studies in the psychology of language could be highlighted, and although he is not a psychologist per se, we have already noted Noam Chomsky's foundational impact on psycholinguistics, as did the APA when it honored him with the Distinguished Scientific Contribution Award in 1984. Likewise, George Miller is a candidate for the "dean" of psycholinguistics, and so is Roger Brown.

FIGURE 20–6. George Armitage Miller.

Source: John T. Miller, courtesy Princeton University Communications Office.

Born of Canadian émigrés, **Roger Brown** (1925–) was raised and educated in America. He credited his reading of "thousands" of comic books as one positive factor in his early education. As a member of the Navy aboard the USS *Wichita* in the Pacific Theater following the Battle of Okinawa, Brown found time to read John Watson's *Behaviorism,* an event that he feels led him to study psychology after the war (Brown, 1989).

Brown completed his Ph.D. at Michigan and took a position at Harvard in 1952. Although his own teaching and research interests involved social psychology, he was attracted to Bruner's work in cognition, and so Brown, along with Bruner and Miller, attended the conference at Cambridge in 1955. In 1957, he completed *Words and Things* (Brown, 1958), which made his initial mark in the area of psychology and language.

In 1957, Brown moved to MIT, where he came into contact with Noam Chomsky. In 1962, Brown returned to Harvard (where he remains) and began work on two of his best-known publications: *Social Psychology* (Brown, 1965), a classic text in the field that also pioneered social cognition; and *A First Language* (Brown, 1973), which is a careful, empirical analysis of language acquisition in children.

Although Brown has done important work in other areas of cognitive psychology—such as his research on **flashbulb memories** (Brown & Kulik, 1977), which are memories of first learning about a surprising or emotional experience—he has been at the center of the psychological study of language. His work on language acquisition with young children was the first empirical work of its kind and provided much of the research data that fueled the lingering Chomsky-Skinner debate.

Although his own original analysis and stage model of the language development process has been modified over the last 25 years, the changes often have come from his own students' further exploration of phenomena that Brown first recognized (e.g., Maratsos, 1983). Indeed, several of Brown's students have made substantive advances in psycholinguistics. For example, Dan Slobin (1985) performed a cross-cultural study of language acquisition. In addition, Jill de Villiers (de Villiers & de Villiers, 1978) analyzed telegraphic speech (e.g., a

child saying "hungry" to mean "I am hungry"), and Steven Pinker (1984) examined underextensions of words (using a term too narrowly, such as resisting calling a mosquito an animal). Through his continued interest in social psychology, Brown pioneered the expansion of the scope of psycholinguistics from the mere study of words and things into a host of applied settings.

Cognition and Reality

Ulric Neisser (1928–) was born in Germany but educated at Harvard, where he received his undergraduate degree in 1950 and his Ph.D. in 1956. Neisser has taught at several locations, including Cornell, where he was a colleague of James J. Gibson (Chapter 13). Neisser is currently at Atlanta's Emory University, where he remains among the most active and respected of all cognitive scientists.

Although he was already a well-established perceptual researcher (e.g., Selfridge & Neisser, 1960), his *Cognitive Psychology* (Neisser, 1967) was the first widely used textbook devoted to the new study of cognition. The success of the text moved Neisser to center stage, and it was from that position that he published *Cognition and Reality* (Neisser, 1976).

Cognition and Reality advanced the schema concept as the basis of cognitive psychology and used schema theory to provide a general account of human behavior and development through a process Neisser called the **perceptual cycle**. The perceptual cycle suggests that our mental structures (schema) direct our behavior, and our experiences modify our mental representations in an unending cycle.

The book also had three more implicit themes that reflected not only Neisser's interests but also a number of changes that occurred in the field during the late 1960s and early 1970s. The first theme can be characterized as one of critical appraisal. Neisser offered a critical appraisal of many of the ideas he presented in *Cognitive Psychology* and of the initial information-processing approach to the study of cognition that followed Miller's *Plans and the Structure of Behavior.* Neisser advised future cognitive psychologists to be careful that their laboratory experiments have **ecological validity**—that is, that their results will also generalize to the world outside the laboratory. In fact, Neisser advocated studying real-world problems as a necessary element to a mature cognitive psychology (see Neisser, 1991).

The idea of ecological validity dovetails nicely with a second theme of *Cognition and Reality,* which is to focus on applications of cognitive theories. Neisser readily acknowledged the success of behaviorism as a psychological theory that proved itself useful in everyday life and admonished cognitive theorists to follow that lead. For Neisser, the ultimate success of cognitive psychology will rest as much on what it can accomplish outside of academia as with the quality and veracity of its research within academia. Donald Norman's (1988) *The Psychology of Everyday Things* represents perhaps the best example of such a focus on real-world applications. By exploring the cognitive elements in product design, Norman's book has become a widely used volume in both human factors engineering courses and in environmental psychology courses. His examples range from automobiles to kitchen appliances, and throughout the book he shows the relevance of cognitive theory and data (e.g., in areas such as memory, perception, and reasoning) to the design of optimally functional mechanisms.

Like the second theme, *Cognition and Reality*'s third theme has elements of a reconciliation with behaviorism. Neisser advocated a holistic, ecological approach to understanding human nature, and his perceptual cycle includes perception, development, and behavior, as well as cognition. Neisser made extensive use of the work of the self-proclaimed behaviorist James J. Gibson to accomplish the reconciliation. Because Gibson is associated with an ecological approach to perception, Neisser's work is often viewed analogously as an ecological approach to cognition. Neisser is shown in Figure 20–7.

Memory, Categorization, and Reasoning

Since the publication of *Cognition and Reality,* Neisser has also made substantive contributions to two of cognitive psychology's major subfields, memory (e.g., Neisser, 1981; Neisser & Harsch, 1993) and categorization (e.g., Neisser, 1987). We will

FIGURE 20–7.   Ulric Neisser.

Source: © University Photography, Emory University.

briefly examine memory, categorization, and reasoning, noting Neisser's and others' contributions.

Memory

Within the cognitive framework, two important discoveries have been made about memory. First, Bartlett found that memory is often schematic and reconstructive, and memory's reconstructive nature continues to be an active research area. For example, Neisser (1981) explored in detail the memory of Watergate principal John Dean and also the flash-bulb memory college students have of the space shuttle Challenger disaster (Neisser & Harsch, 1993). Both studies provided further support for memory's schematic nature as well as offering new information about the factors and conditions that facilitate misleading reconstructions.

The second vital development in memory research extends from the efforts of Atkinson and

Shiffrin (1968). As we noted earlier, Miller (1956) distinguished short-term memory—information we can keep in mind for a span of about 1 minute or less (e.g., the start of this sentence, so that you know what the whole sentence means when you get to its end)—from long-term memory, events that may have happened to you years ago that you still remember. Nevertheless, it was Atkinson and Shiffrin who provided the first model of memory from the information-processing point of view. Their work attempted to trace a concept from its initial conscious perception, through a short-term memory storage stage, on into long-term memory. The chief importance of this for subsequent memory researchers was not so much the particulars as the recognition that memory was not a unitary phenomenon.

Subsequently, an important, related discovery was the distinction between various memory types, and we associate this finding most clearly with **Endel Tulving** (1927–). Born in Estonia, Tulving listed among his "occupations" (in order) poacher, soldier, prisoner of war, interpreter for the U.S. Army, medical student at Heidelberg, undergraduate psychology major at the University of Toronto, psychology graduate student at Harvard, and, for 35 years, psychology faculty member at the University of Toronto (American Psychologist, 1994). Tulving currently holds the Tanenbaum Chair in Cognitive Neuroscience at Canada's Rotman Research Institute of Baycrest Centre.

Tulving (e.g., 1972) distinguished between two types of long-term memory: **episodic** and **semantic**. Tulving observed that some memories are of isolated, emotionless, atemporal facts; these semantic memories include such things as your student identification number and the capital of Texas. Semantic memories resist forgetting and are probably less subject to reconstruction. In contrast, there are also episodic memories that tend to have lots of associations, often include an emotional sense, and have a temporal, narrative structure. Examples include your memory of your first day of school, your last romantic encounter, or breakfast this morning. These memories seem more likely to be both misremembered and forgotten. Tulving's recent research (e.g., Tulving, 1985) has suggested that the seman-

tic-episodic dichotomy may be too simple and that several further distinctions may be required before we fully understand memory.

Categorization

William James's (1890) *Principles of Psychology* asserted that the fundamental act of cognition is **categorization**. However, Wittgenstein (1953)—like James, a psychological philosopher—introduced the ideas that brought categorization to the forefront of cognitive psychology. **Ludwig Wittgenstein** (1889–1951) was born into a Viennese family of wealth and connection. His brother was the most acclaimed pianist of the era, and his sister facilitated Freud's exodus from Germany.

Wittgenstein was formally educated in mathematics and mechanical engineering, and his initial philosophical work was viewed as an important contribution to both logical positivism and applied mathematics. After his release as a military prisoner following World War I, Wittgenstein returned to Austria, where he became friends with Karl Bühler. During this period, he taught elementary school, worked at a Catholic monastery that he considered joining, and stayed in fairly close contact with the leading European intelligentsia in mathematics and logic (e.g., Bertrand Russell and Rudolph Carnap).

Wittgenstein joined the Cambridge faculty in 1930, and that remained his academic home for the rest of his life. The remainder of Wittgenstein's career was mostly occupied with what we would call the philosophy of language and the philosophy of psychology—two subdisciplines of philosophy that Wittgenstein and Gilbert Ryle (below), his Oxford contemporary, largely founded.

Wittgenstein's magnum opus was *Philosophical Investigations* (Wittgenstein, 1953), whose title is probably a play on the title of Husserl's *Logical Investigations* (Chapter 8). *Philosophical Investigations* is the work that contains Wittgenstein's discussion of **family resemblance**, which is the point of departure for modern cognitive psychology's interest in categorization. Before Wittgenstein's analysis, it was assumed that to be a member of a category required sharing in some defining attribute. Without reflection, we might say that the defining feature of birds is flight. But empirical examination shows us that not all birds fly (e.g., penguins). If we are not attending to defining features, how is it possible for us to recognize the penguin as a bird?

The concept of family resemblance asserts that a category does not have to have a defining feature that all members share. Instead, there can be a set of features that is distributed across the category members, with no one feature essential for inclusion in the category. According to this view, we recognize a member more in terms of its schematic similarity to other members than by perceiving a key trait. The idea of family resemblance helped Wittgenstein solve certain problems he recognized in perception and semantics. Ironically, Wittgenstein died before seeing the impact of his ideas on psychology, which he spent the latter part of his career criticizing.

Over 20 years after the publication of *Philosophical Investigations,* Eleanor Rosch and Carolyn Mervis (Rosch & Mervis, 1975) brought Wittgenstein's family resemblance concept into cognitive psychology. Considering essentially the same problem as Wittgenstein, Rosch found empirical support for Wittgenstein's suggestion that family resemblances, not defining features, are the core of human categorization. Rosch (e.g., Rosch, 1978) continued to explore empirically the structure and function of our categories and made several other significant findings. For example, she discovered that categories exist at three levels: superordinate (such as animal or pet); basic (such as dog or cat), which is the level at which we most often speak and think; and subordinate (such as poodle or pomeranian).

Following Rosch's work, categorization came to be understood (as James had known) as the fundamental act of cognition, the process by which we organize and access all of our perceptions, knowledge, and memory. The structure of the basic level category remains the focus of much research. For example, Neisser (1987) explored how different contexts affect the formation and use of categories, and Lakoff (1987) examined several possible theories for the structure and internal organization of our mental categories, finding support in anthropology and linguistics as well as in cognitive psychology.

Reasoning

Both Wittgenstein and **Gilbert Ryle** (1900–1976) are sometimes called philosophical behaviorists, although that term may be misleading. Neither was a supporter of behaviorism per se, and both felt that the psychology of their day was terribly confused in its conception of mental events. Both Wittgenstein and Ryle advocated a more phenomenological analysis of language—an analysis of what we say and the behavioral and environmental contexts in which we say it—as part of the corrective they offered to psychology.

The editor of Bain's (Chapter 4) journal *Mind* for many years, Ryle (1949) also published *The Concept of Mind,* which was a book about the mind-body problem, which Ryle called "the ghost in the machine." In an attempt to provide a fresh perspective on the nature of mind, Ryle suggested that we reflect on how we talk and think about it—indeed, about how we talk and think in general. In this vein, Ryle's discussion of the **category mistake** became the centerpiece of his book. Ryle related the following story to illustrate a category mistake, and the story by analogy was also intended to illustrate how the mind-body problem had been misconceived.

> A foreigner visiting Oxford or Cambridge for the first time is shown a number of colleges, libraries, playing fields, museums, scientific departments and administrative offices. He then asks "But where is the University? I have seen where the members of the Colleges live, where the Registrar works, where the scientists experiment and the rest. But I have not yet seen the University in which reside and work the members of your University." It has then to be explained to him that the University is not another collateral institution, some ulterior counterpart to the colleges, laboratories and offices which he has seen. The University is just the way in which all that he has already seen is organized. (p. 16)

In other words, Ryle (1949) was suggesting that the mind and body are not at the same "level" of analysis, just as the University and the physical buildings at Oxford are not at the same level, even though philosophers and psychologists have long spoken and theorized about the mind and the body as if they exist on the same plane.

Ryle (1949) made another observation about how we think, and although it is less clever than his discussion of the category mistake, it has had more direct impact on research in cognitive psychology. His observation concerns two types of things we might claim to know: "Knowing that" is an intellectual sort of knowing that includes knowing that a bow is used to play the violin, for example. "Knowing how" refers to procedural knowledge, such as how to use a bow to play the violin. Ryle's point is that much of our knowledge is known only intellectually and not through direct experience. Likewise, there are other things we know—like how to play a tune on the violin—that are difficult to express intellectually with any accuracy; instead, our knowledge is demonstrated through motor skills. With this distinction between "knowing that" and "knowing how," Ryle can be seen as a forerunner to modern cognitive psychology's critical study of human knowledge and reasoning. A more contemporary example of research on reasoning can be found in the work of Daniel Kahneman and Amos Tversky.

Daniel Kahneman (1934–) was born in Tel Aviv and raised in France and Israel. He was educated first at Israel's The Hebrew University and later at the University of California at Berkeley. **Amos Tversky** (1937–) was born in Haifa, Israel, and attended first The Hebrew University and later the University of Michigan. Collaboration between Kahneman and Tversky on research in human reasoning began in 1969.

Kahneman and Tversky's research showed that people do not follow the rules of logic and statistics when they reason about problems in the everyday world. Instead, people use a series of heuristics, or rules of thumb, to process information. This use of heuristics occurs even when subjects actually know the underlying logical and statistical concepts. Unfortunately, the heuristics often produce errors in reasoning and risk assessment.

One example of the sort of heuristic we use is the **representative heuristic**, which concerns the misunderstanding of randomness and such related concepts as base rates and sample sizes (Kahneman &

Tversky, 1972, 1973). For example, research subjects are given information about a character: e.g., that the person is bright and interested in helping others. Then the subjects are asked to select the job that the character might hold. Although subjects usually select options like physician or psychologist, they typically fail to select occupations such as sales, at which many more people are employed. By ignoring the base rates of the various occupations, the subjects may be making a mistake in their choices.

Another case is the **availability heuristic**, which concerns the tendency to base estimates of frequency or probability on information that is easy to remember (because it is familiar, vivid, or recent) instead of on the most relevant information (Tversky & Kahneman, 1973). A little quiz you can give to your friends illustrates this nicely. Prepare a list of 40 names. The list should have 18 or 19 well-known women (e.g., Madonna, Agatha Christie, Hillary Clinton) and 21 or 22 ordinary men's names (e.g., Randy Denton, Sam Burns, Mike Smith). With no special instructions, read the list to your friends and then ask them if there were more women or men. If your results follow Tversky and Kahneman's (1973), about 80% of your friends will say that there were more women. The familiarity of the names presumably makes them more available, and this differential availability misleads us as we reason.

Because of the importance of their work on reasoning, Tversky and Kahneman won the APA's Distinguished Scientific Contribution Award in 1982. We have noted that Chomsky also won this award, and so did Bruner, Miller, Brown, Broadbent, Tulving, and three others among the researchers that we will consider next: Herbert Simon, Alan Newell, and Robert Abelson.

Artificial Intelligence

Herbert Alexander Simon (1916–) was born in Milwaukee, Wisconsin. In 1943, Simon completed his Ph.D. in political science at the University of Chicago. From the beginning, his primary interests were in organizational behavior and decision making, areas that led to his 1978 Nobel Prize in economics.

Postwar advances in cybernetics attracted Simon's interest, and for the remainder of his career he blended psychology and computer models with his original focus areas of economics and management. In 1952, Simon met **Allen Newell** (1927–1992) while both were working at the RAND Corporation. A San Francisco native, Newell completed a degree in physics from Stanford and a Ph.D. in industrial administration at the Carnegie Institute of Technology (now Carnegie-Mellon University). Together, Simon and Newell empirically explored human problem solving, produced computer simulations of their findings, and worked to advance the state of artificial intelligence computing.

Artificial intelligence (**AI**) has two slightly different meanings in the psychological community, and at different times, Simon and Newell's research program was associated with both of them. On the one hand, AI can be understood as the construction of machines that model how humans think, learn, or perceive; on the other hand, AI refers to developing machines that can perform some activity as well as a person, or even as well as an expert at that activity. In the first sense of the term, building and then manipulating such models is viewed as perhaps the most powerful research tool available to cognitive science. In this tradition, Newell and Simon (1972) developed the **General Problem Solver**, a computer program designed to mimic how humans solve a number of diverse problems and logic puzzles. Earlier, in 1955, Simon and Newell collaborated to produce probably the first general problem-solving computer program (Logic Theorist) designed to be in some way analogous to human cognition.

Other programs derived from the General Problem Solver were adapted to specific problems and illustrate the second sense of artificial intelligence, which is perhaps best understood by considering Alan Turing's (1950) original definition of AI. Turing's definition can be seen in the **Turing Test**, a test for "artificial," computer intelligence. In the cited passage, "the problem" is the question of how we would establish the existence of such intelligence in a computer.

The new form of the problem can be described in terms of a game which we will call the "imitation game". It is played with three people, a man (A), a woman (B), and an interrogator (C) who may be of either sex. The interrogator stays in a room apart from the other two. The object of the game for the interrogator is to determine which of the other two is the man and which is the woman. . . . The interrogator is allowed to put questions to A and B thus:

C: Will X please tell me the length of his or her hair?

Now suppose X is actually A, then A must answer. It is A's object in the game to try and cause C to make the wrong identification. His answer might therefore be

"My hair is shingled, and the longest strands are about nine inches long."

In order that tones of voice may not help the interrogator . . . [an] . . . ideal arrangement is to have a teleprinter communicating between the two rooms. . . .

We now ask the question, "What will happen when a machine takes the part of A in this game?" Will the interrogator decide wrongly as often when the game is played like this as he does when the game is played between a man and a woman? These questions replace our original, "Can machines think"? (Turing, 1950, pp. 433–434)

In its general form, the Turing Test can be seen as an empirical, behavioral, pragmatic test. If a computer's performance in a given situation is indistinguishable from human performance in the same condition, then we must conclude that, in the context, the machine is intelligent.

Interest in artificial intelligence was widespread in psychology (and other fields) from the mid-1950s through the early 1970s. Carnegie-Mellon University, Simon and Newell's academic home, was then and remains a center of AI activity. At MIT, Marvin Minsky was a founder of the artificial intelligence laboratory and oversaw a variety of important demonstrational projects. MIT and Minsky continue to be at the forefront of AI research (e.g., Minsky, 1985), as is Roger Schank.

Roger Schank (1946–) arrived at Yale in 1974 and, in collaboration with social psychologist

Robert Abelson (1928–), set about making Yale another center of AI research. Schank and Abelson's (1977) *Scripts, Plans, Goals, and Understanding* demonstrated clearly how the interplay between computer models and cognitive psychology could advance our understanding of human knowledge structures. Abelson (1981) defined a **script** as a special type of schema involving a structured sequence of behavioral events. For example, consider the sequence of events we follow when we dine at a restaurant. We go in, wait to be seated, review the menu, place our order, wait for the food, eat the food, perhaps order dessert, finish our meal, get the check, pay the bill, and exit.

By the way, if we ordered dessert, did we eat it? And if we left a tip, when was that done? These questions do not present problems, because the script has more slots than we illustrated, and as members of this culture, we all know the location of the slots and what their default values are. For example, if someone tells you about eating at a new restaurant and does not comment on the quality of the food or service, you will probably assume that it was acceptable but not outstanding—the default value. Because people share that default assumption, they only need to mention the quality of the food or the service if it was above or below the shared expectation. Moreover, there is a set place in the sequence of telling about the restaurant at which the information is presented.

Schank (1972, 1982) showed that computers can be programmed with scripts, and computers programmed in this way can answer questions and reason through the data available to them in much the same way as people. Schank's research represented a true breakthrough in AI and also in our conception of the structure of human reasoning.

The 1970s saw other advances in AI, especially in the areas of machine understanding and natural language interactions with computers (e.g., Winograd, 1972). There was a widespread sense that truly spectacular computer programs capable of thinking and speaking exactly like people were just around the corner. Alternatively, others saw problems and limits with AI and were not optimistic about its future (e.g., Dreyfus, 1972). Although it is easy to imagine how to program a computer to make a cer-

tain judgment if a particular condition is met (if X, then Y), how can we get a computer to see a family resemblance? As Wittgenstein and Rosch observed, if there are no rules or defining attributes that we use to categorize information, then the computers of the day, rule-based systems, had serious problems.

The truth apparently lies somewhere between the two extremes. Advances in AI programs written as rule-based systems have continued, and probably you have enjoyed the fruits of this labor as you interact with your automated bank teller and play sophisticated computer games. On the other hand, we do not yet communicate with our personal computers in ordinary language, nor do we see computer systems that reason like people outside of the narrow domain in which the computers are programmed to be expert.

Rule-based systems have limits, and one of AI's remaining problems is that humans gain new knowledge by learning, something that most computers do not do, and something that most cognitive psychologists have neglected. Instead, rule-based systems come programmed at the start with all the information that they know and with a program composed of rules governing how to analyze new information. In 1986, **David Rumelhart** (1942–) and his colleagues first published their efforts to resurrect an older computer architecture that had been neglected in recent years (Rumelhart, McClelland, & the PDP Research Group, 1986). This architecture, called variously connectionism, parallel processing, or **neural networks**, represents a non-rule-based alternative to computing.

Parallel processing also represents a return to learning theory and a strengthening of cognitive psychology's ties with neuroscience. Computers are being programmed as models of the underlying neurology, not as models of higher cognitive processes. Indeed, parallel processing brings us back full circle to the initial observations of McCulloch and Pitts (1943) that a computer could be made to simulate neural activity.

Although still in its infancy, connectionism has shown promise in circumventing the limits of rule-based systems, while at the same time allowing us to retain most of the advances discovered under that architecture. For example, machines can learn a family resemblance (Rumelhart et al., 1986). In addition, there are systems that truly (nonmetaphorically) learn on their own by making adjustments to their own neural connections as a function of new experience. Many such systems are already being used in industry and in the military.

CONCLUSIONS

What does the future hold for psychology? Bartlett (1936) concluded his autobiographical essay with these thoughts:

> I will finish with the sort of remark that ought to be perfectly obvious. A psychologist who thinks that his work is done, that all that is now needed is the application of a final scheme to new instances is dead. Psychology will go on and leave him lamenting. Like the reactions it studies, psychology is living and oriented forward: there can be no end to its achievements. (pp. 51–52)

Perhaps some clues can be found by examining the themes that structure our present-day interest in cognition.

At times in this chapter we have talked about cognitive psychology, and at other times about cognitive science. Whether this usage reflects two synonymous terms, or two different fields, is largely a matter of opinion. The term "cognitive science" is often applied to cognitive psychology, although some have defined cognitive science more broadly, viewing cognitive psychology—along with cultural anthropology, computer science, linguistics, neuroscience, and the philosophy of mind—as a component (e.g., Gardner, 1985).

Is this collaboration among disciplines the new trend? Will psychology vanish into fields such as cognitive science and neuroscience, or will the study of behavior always remain? Either way, the modern study of cognition is an interdisciplinary affair, and psychology has come a long way since Wundt (Chapter 7).

As we complete this book, topics such as language, human factors engineering, memory, categorization, reasoning, and artificial intelligence are among the "hottest" in psychology, but how long will it be before another change—a Kuhnian paradigm shift perhaps—sends the focus elsewhere? Does the sort of machine learning being done by the parallel processing advocates and the ecological approach of Neisser represent a reunification in psychology? Will machine learning bring a final synthesis of cognition, physiology, and behavior? Are there trends in areas such as social or clinical psychology that reflect this union?

We began this book with a series of questions, and now we close the same way. The answers to the questions in the first chapter were found in the past. The answers to the questions we have posed in closing lie in the future.

S U M M A R Y

According to Kuhn, theories inevitably encounter an anomaly that the theory cannot explain, and the encounter leads to a theoretical revolution. Language may have been such an anomaly for behaviorism, resulting in the cognitive revolution.

Forerunners to the Cognitive Revolution

Important antecedents of cognitive psychology include Plato, Kant, and Gestalt psychology. Sir Charles Bartlett and Lev Vygotsky were also major early contributors. Bartlett popularized the "schema" as the basic unit of thought and illustrated it through studies of reconstruc-

tive memory. Best known for analyzing the relationship between language and thought, Vygotsky imagined and argued for a scientific study of the mind that resembles modern cognitive science.

Piaget called his program genetic epistemology, because it dealt with knowledge development in children. Based on his research, Piaget believed that children pass through developmental stages that he called the sensorimotor stage, the preoperational stage, the concrete operational stage, and the formal operational stage.

Although Piaget contributed to the topic of moral development, the central figure was Lawrence Kohlberg.

In Kohlberg's theory, the major stages of moral reasoning are the preconventional stage (external rules guide morality), the conventional stage (social rules predominate), and the postconventional stage (moral principles are internalized).

Gardner has noted that important advances outside of psychology have also been important for the cognitive revolution. Specifically, Gardner noted cybernetics—the study of control processes in machines or animals—that became artificial intelligence, the philosophy of mind, and linguistics.

Noam Chomsky

The interplay between psychology and linguistics was limited before Noam Chomsky. Chomsky felt that behavioral explanations for the language acquisition process were inadequate. Chomsky's poverty-of-stimulus argument suggested that behaviorist principles such as "stimulus" and "reinforcement" could not explain language learning. This argument can be expanded to question the completeness of a behavioral explanation of human behavior. As an alternative, Chomsky suggested that we have innate syntactic structures that allow us to acquire language, and the empirical study of language has remained central to cognitive psychology.

Jerome Bruner and George Miller

Jerome Bruner and George Miller's creation of the Center for Cognitive Studies at Harvard in 1962 was a signal event in cognitive psychology. Bruner's early work was in perception and social psychology, but his interests shifted to thinking after a conference on cognition hosted by Sir Charles Bartlett at Cambridge. In his research on thinking, Bruner has stressed the relationship between thinking and perception, the developmental aspects of cognition, applications of cognitive research, and the creative aspects of thought.

George Miller entered psychology via his interest in communication and was interested in cybernetics from the outset. Miller is famous for "The Magical Number Seven," which is an analysis of short-term memory; *Plans and the Structure of Behavior,* which introduced the TOTE concept and popularized, along with Donald Broadbent's work, the information-processing metaphor; and *Language and Perception,* which explores a variety of mental events.

Classical Contributions

Language remains central to cognitive psychology, and Roger Brown is arguably the "dean" of psycholinguistics. Associated with Chomsky, Bruner, and Miller, Brown was the first to provide empirical data for some of Chomsky's claims about language acquisition. Brown is known also for his flashbulb-memory studies and for his contributions to social psychology.

Ulric Neisser's *Cognitive Psychology* was widely used until he published *Cognition and Reality,* which represents a shift away from the information-processing approach toward a more applied, ecological perspective. *Cognition and Reality* further advances the schema as the fundamental unit of thought by making it central to the "perceptual cycle." Also, the book advocates the need for research that generalizes to real-world applications. Neisser has advanced our understanding of the reconstructive nature of memory, which was first noted by Bartlett.

Memory researcher Endel Tulving distinguished between semantic and episodic long-term memory. Episodic memories are eventlike and seem to be the kind of memories on which work on reconstructive memory has focused. By contrast, semantic memories are memories of discrete facts, such as your telephone number.

Modern interest in categorization can be traced to Ludwig Wittgenstein and his analysis of family resemblance. Eleanor Rosch showed that categorizing the information we constantly acquire is the most fundamental act of cognition.

Like categorization, current reasoning research can be viewed as having its roots in philosophy. Like Wittgenstein, Gilbert Ryle was interested in pointing out problems that psychology seemed to have either neglected or misunderstood. Ryle's most famous work concerned the "category mistake," which involves confusing the ontological level of two objects: for example, confusing the buildings that comprise a university with the abstract notion of university. For Ryle, the most important category mistake was the mind-body problem.

In contemporary research in reasoning, Daniel Kahneman and Amos Tversky have focused on our use of heuristics that lead us to make erroneous judgments. One example is the representative heuristic, which often causes us to ignore such important information as base rates.

Artificial intelligence (AI) is a vital component of cognitive science in which Herbert Simon and Allen Newell were pioneers. In psychology, AI may refer to using computers as tools to model cognitive operations, or it can refer to building machines that perform some task as well as a person or expert.

One possible way to determine whether intelligence exists in an entity is to apply the Turing Test. If performance by an entity is indistinguishable from intelligent human behavior in the same situation, then the entity has intelligence. AI pioneers Roger Schank and Robert Abelson programmed machines with scripts—modified versions of schema—and achieved success in both getting machines to perform interesting tasks in ways analogous to people and in using computers to advance our understanding of human cognition.

The most recent innovation in computing technology is often called the neural network because what is being modeled is a basic physiological process rather than a more abstract cognition. Neural networks have overcome some of the limits of the older, rule-based technology.

CONNECTIONS QUESTIONS

1. What connections can you make between advances in other academic disciplines and the rise of cognitive science?
2. What connections can you make between cognitive psychology and technological advances?
3. What are the connections between cognitive psychology and Gestalt psychology? Between behaviorism and the modern study of cognition?
4. What events in this chapter—and the previous ones in this section of the book—do you feel will be most connected to the shape of psychology in the next century?
5. What connections can you trace to support the idea that psychology had a "cognitive revolution" of the Kuhnian variety?
6. Draw a concept map of the central characters and ideas in this chapter, and compare it with one possible solution provided on p. 570.

SUGGESTED READINGS

Gardner, H. (1985). *The mind's new science: A history of the cognitive revolution.* New York: Basic Books. Gardner's book contains a nice sketch of the early events in psychology and other fields (e.g., anthropology, computer science, linguistics, neuroscience, philosophy) related to cognitive science. This work is not highly technical and would be of interest to anyone who enjoys the history of ideas.

Miller, G., Galanter, E., & Pribram, K. (1960). *Plans and the structure of behavior.* New York: Adams-Bannister-Cox. This is perhaps the "signal" work in the cognitive revolution. Although the details are dated, *Plans and the Structure of Behavior* remains a classic look at early cognitive science.

Minsky, M. (1985). *The society of mind.* New York: Simon & Schuster. A cognitive science classic, this book provides a complete theory of human behavior and mental events from the perspective of the cognitive paradigm. Lighthearted, yet informative, the more recent paperback edition should be easy to find.

Neisser, U. (1987). *Concepts and conceptual development.* New York: Cambridge University Press. *Concepts and Conceptual Development* was the first in a series edited by Neisser. This volume focuses on categorization, and the theory and research it contains represents the most current ideas in cognitive psychology about categories and concepts.

Piaget, J. (1952). Jean Piaget. In E. G. Boring, H. S. Langfeld, H. Werner, & R. M. Yerkes (Eds.), *A history of psychology in autobiography* (Vol. 4, pp. 237–256). Worcester, MA: Clark University Press. Like many of the essays in this series, Piaget's makes interesting reading and reveals many of the influences on him that led to his seminal research on child development.

Vygotsky, L. S. (1978). *Mind in society: The development of higher psychological processes.* Cambridge, MA: Harvard University Press. *Mind in Society* is a nice sampler of Vygotsky's work, and it includes a short biographical sketch by Vygotsky's associate, A. R. Luria.

Concept Maps

Precursors to Psychology in Ancient Greece

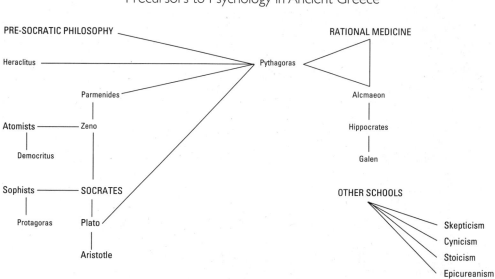

The Roman Period, the Middle Ages, and the Renaissance

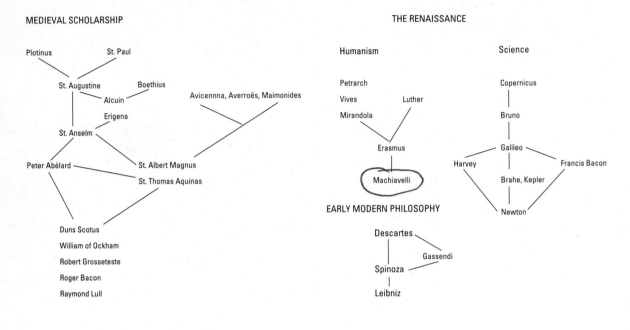

MEDIEVAL SCHOLARSHIP

THE RENAISSANCE

Humanism

Science

EARLY MODERN PHILOSOPHY

Empiricism, Associationism, and Common-Sense Psychology

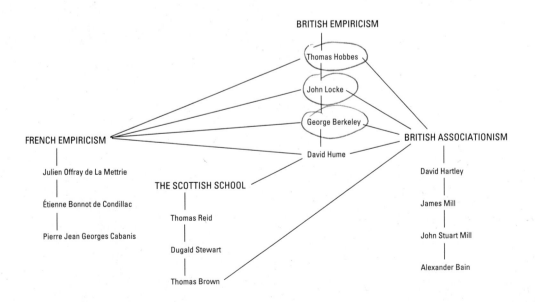

BRITISH EMPIRICISM

FRENCH EMPIRICISM

BRITISH ASSOCIATIONISM

THE SCOTTISH SCHOOL

CHAPTER 5

Continental Philosophies: Rationalism, Positivism, and Romanticism

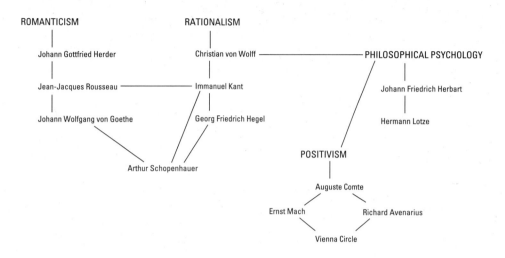

CHAPTER 6

Nineteenth-Century Physiological Influences on the Development of Psychology

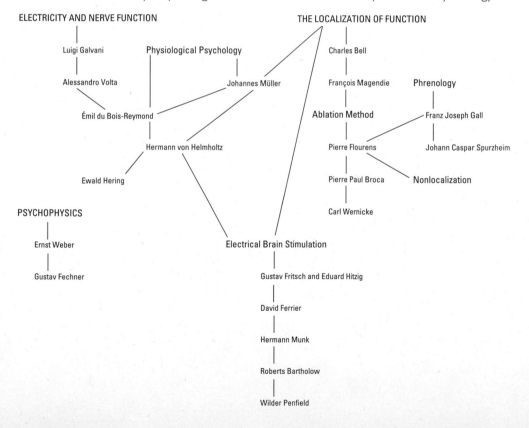

CHAPTER 7

Voluntarism and Structuralism: The First Schools

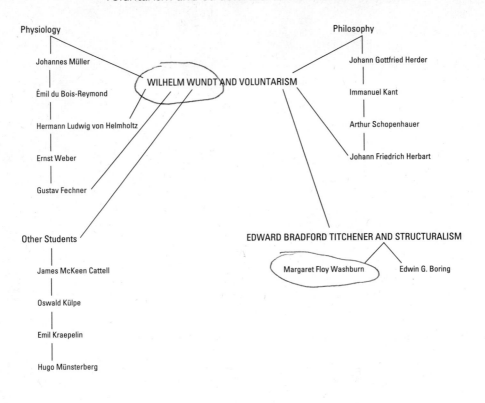

Physiology

Johannes Müller

Émil du Bois-Reymond

Hermann Ludwig von Helmholtz

Ernst Weber

Gustav Fechner

WILHELM WUNDT AND VOLUNTARISM

Philosophy

Johann Gottfried Herder

Immanuel Kant

Arthur Schopenhauer

Johann Friedrich Herbart

Other Students

James McKeen Cattell

Oswald Külpe

Emil Kraepelin

Hugo Münsterberg

EDWARD BRADFORD TITCHENER AND STRUCTURALISM

Margaret Floy Washburn   Edwin G. Boring

CHAPTER 8

Competing Approaches to Psychology's First Schools

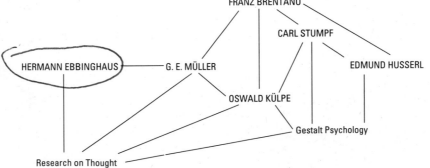

FRANZ BRENTANO

CARL STUMPF

EDMUND HUSSERL

HERMANN EBBINGHAUS   G. E. MÜLLER

OSWALD KÜLPE

Gestalt Psychology

Research on Thought

CHAPTER 9

British Forerunners of Functionalism

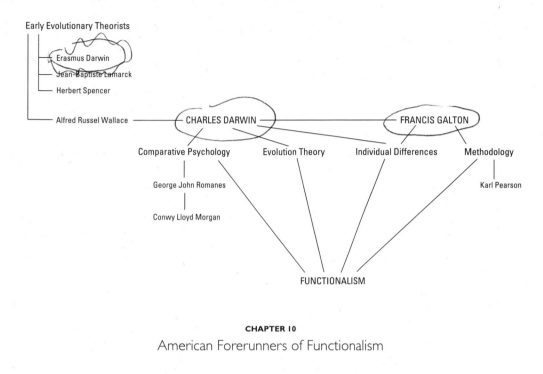

CHAPTER 10

American Forerunners of Functionalism

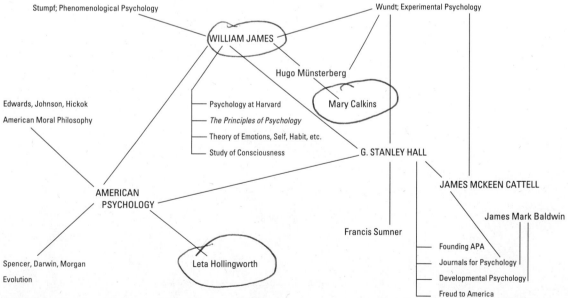

CHAPTER 11

Functionalism

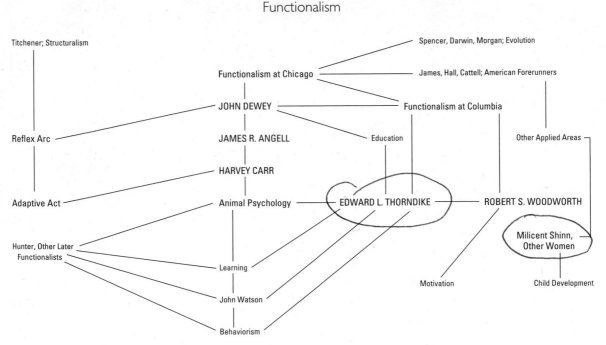

CHAPTER 12

Animal Psychology and Early Behaviorism

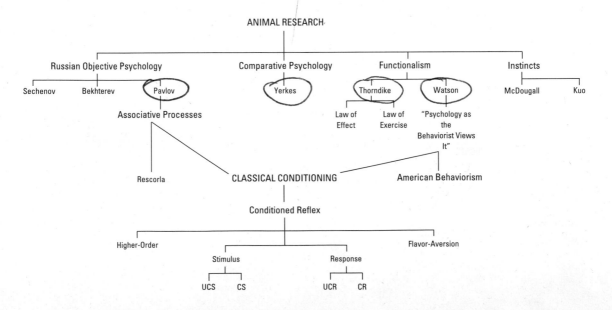

CHAPTER 13

Neobehaviorism

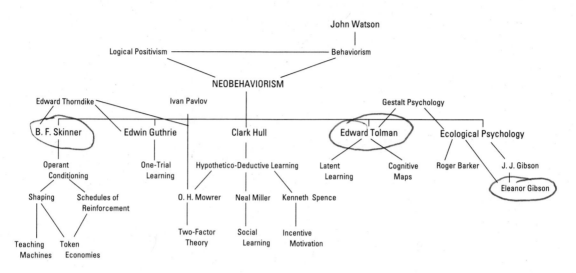

CHAPTER 14

Gestalt Psychology

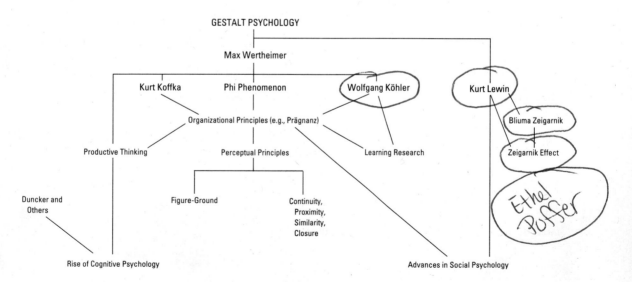

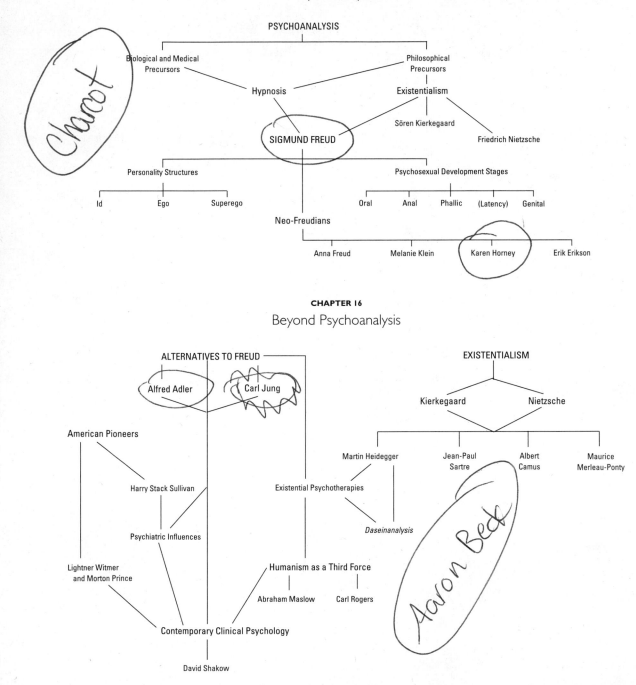

CHAPTER 15
Psychoanalysis

PSYCHOANALYSIS

Biological and Medical Precursors

Hypnosis

Philosophical Precursors

Existentialism

Sören Kierkegaard

Friedrich Nietzsche

Charcot

SIGMUND FREUD

Personality Structures

Id Ego Superego

Psychosexual Development Stages

Oral Anal Phallic (Latency) Genital

Neo-Freudians

Anna Freud Melanie Klein Karen Horney Erik Erikson

CHAPTER 16
Beyond Psychoanalysis

ALTERNATIVES TO FREUD

Alfred Adler Carl Jung

EXISTENTIALISM

Kierkegaard Nietzsche

American Pioneers

Harry Stack Sullivan

Psychiatric Influences

Lightner Witmer and Morton Prince

Existential Psychotherapies

Martin Heidegger

Daseinanalysis

Jean-Paul Sartre Albert Camus Maurice Merleau-Ponty

Aaron Beck

Humanism as a Third Force

Abraham Maslow Carl Rogers

Contemporary Clinical Psychology

David Shakow

CHAPTER 17

The Physiology of Behavior in the Twentieth Century

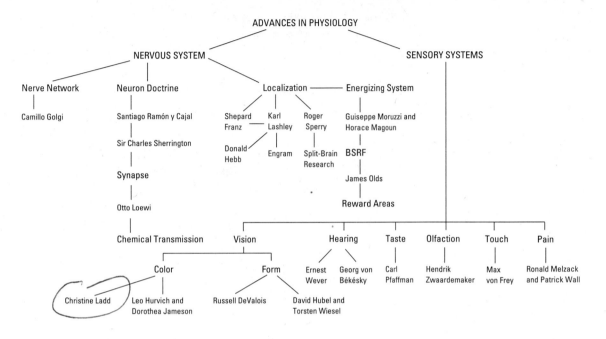

ADVANCES IN PHYSIOLOGY

NERVOUS SYSTEM — SENSORY SYSTEMS

Nerve Network — Neuron Doctrine — Localization — Energizing System

Camillo Golgi

Santiago Ramón y Cajal

Shepard Franz — Karl Lashley — Roger Sperry — Guiseppe Moruzzi and Horace Magoun

Sir Charles Sherrington

Donald Hebb — Engram — Split-Brain Research — BSRF

Synapse

James Olds

Otto Loewi

Reward Areas

Chemical Transmission — Vision — Hearing — Taste — Olfaction — Touch — Pain

Color — Form — Ernest Wever — Georg von Békésky — Carl Pfaffman — Hendrik Zwaardemaker — Max von Frey — Ronald Melzack and Patrick Wall

Christine Ladd — Leo Hurvich and Dorothea Jameson — Russell DeValois — David Hubel and Torsten Wiesel

CHAPTER 18

Intelligence Testing, Psychometrics, and Applied Psychology

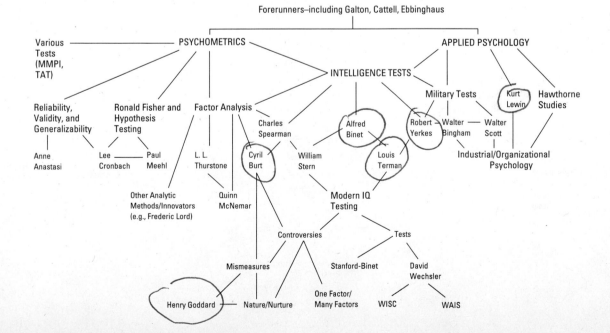

Forerunners–including Galton, Cattell, Ebbinghaus

Various Tests (MMPI, TAT) — PSYCHOMETRICS — APPLIED PSYCHOLOGY

INTELLIGENCE TESTS

Military Tests — Kurt Lewin — Hawthorne Studies

Reliability, Validity, and Generalizability — Ronald Fisher and Hypothesis Testing — Factor Analysis — Charles Spearman — Alfred Binet — Robert Yerkes — Walter Bingham — Walter Scott

Anne Anastasi — Lee Cronbach — Paul Meehl — L. L. Thurstone — Cyril Burt — William Stern — Louis Terman — Industrial/Organizational Psychology

Other Analytic Methods/Innovators (e.g., Frederic Lord) — Quinn McNemar — Modern IQ Testing

Controversies — Tests

Mismeasures — Stanford-Binet — David Wechsler

Henry Goddard — Nature/Nurture — One Factor/Many Factors — WISC — WAIS

CHAPTER 19

Social Psychology

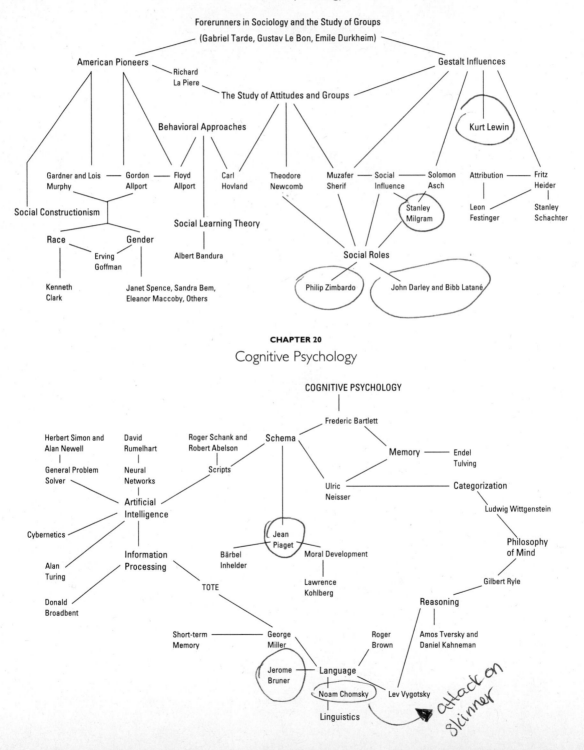

CHAPTER 20

Cognitive Psychology

Glossary of Terms

Ablation The surgical removal of part of the body to study its function.

Academy Plato's school, founded around 387 B.C. and closed in 529 A.D.

Act psychology The name of Franz Brentano's school of psychology that studied psychological acts or functions rather than the contents of consciousness.

Action potential A reversal of polarity across a cell membrane that is the basic means of long-distance communication in the nervous system.

Acts Also known as the functions of consciousness; according to Brentano, mental acts fell into three broad categories: presentation (or ideating), judging, and the acts of desire (or loving and hating).

Adaptive act For Carr, the adaptive act had three elements: (1) a motivating stimulus, (2) a sensory situation, and (3) a response that changes the situation to satisfy the motivating conditions.

Affordance J. J. Gibson's term for a stimulus whose information we perceive and respond to directly because of our evolutionary history.

American Psychological Association Founded in 1892 by G. Stanley Hall and others, one of the primary organizations of psychologists in America.

American Psychological Society Founded in 1988 and organized primarily for experimental and academic psychologists.

Anal stage The second of Freud's psychosexual stages in which pressure on the anal sphincter and its release with defecation provide for libidinal satisfaction that becomes central for the child at about the age of 2.

Analytical Psychology The system of psychology developed by Carl Jung after his break with Freud.

Anamnesis The recollection of knowledge we already possess.

Anima/animus The feminine (anima) and the masculine (animus) aspects of an individual's personality, according to Jung.

Animal magnetism The notion that people emit a magnetic fluid that can influence others.

Animal spirits The substance that many Greeks believed distinguished the living from the dead.

Anthropometric laboratory A laboratory Galton first established for the measurement of man (anthropometric) at the International Health Exhibition in London in 1884.

Apperception Wundt's term for the focus of attention on a particular region of consciousness, resulting in clear perception of that region's contents.

Apperceptive mass For Herbart, a formation of a group of compatible ideas in consciousness.

Apprehension Wundt's term for the first step in the attentional process, the entry of information into consciousness.

Approach-approach conflict Conflict in which the person must decide on one of two goals, both with positive valence.

Approach-avoidance conflict Conflict in which the person is forced to choose whether to pursue a goal with both positive and negative valence.

Archetype For Jung, a universal, unconscious idea transcending individual experience that resides in the collective unconscious.

Army Alpha and **Army Beta** The first IQ tests designed for group administration; the Army Alpha was appropriate for literate takers, whereas the Army Beta was made for illiterate subjects.

Artificial intelligence (AI) The construction of machines that model how humans think, learn, or perceive, and the development of machines that can perform some activities as well as a person.

Assimilation and **accommodation** Two terms in Piaget's psychology: Assimilation refers to the incorporation of experiences that fit the infant's schemata; accommodation refers to the changing of existing schemata to make them conform to reality.

Association of ideas Hume's associative principles were originally resemblance, contiguity, and cause and effect.

Associationism Associationism is derived from empiricism and includes formal rules for the association of ideas in the mind.

Atomism The theory of Leucippus and Democritus that holds that everything is made of tiny, indivisible particles (atoms).

Attachments The general class of interactions between a child and significant others.

Attention For Titchener, an attribute of a sensation, its clearness (vividness, attensity).

Attributes For Titchener, the basic attributes of sensations, images, and feelings were quality, intensity, duration, clearness, and extent.

Attribution Refers to how we perceive, interpret, and account for people's actions.

Availability heuristic The tendency for people to base estimates of frequency or probability on information that is easy to remember instead of on the most relevant information.

Avoidance-avoidance conflict Conflict in which the person must choose between two goals, both with negative valence.

Baby-tender A self-contained box that Skinner built to facilitate the early rearing of children.

Backward conditioning In Pavlovian conditioning, the presentation of the UCS before the CS.

Basic anxiety In Horney's theory, a child's feeling of helplessness and isolation within a potentially hostile world.

Behaviorism A psychological system that stresses the use of objective methods to study the overt behavior of organisms.

Being-in-the-world In Heidegger's existential-phenomenology, being-in-the-world addresses an entity's mode of existence. Heidegger was especially interested in humanity's being-in-the-world.

Bell-Magendie law Independently proposed by Bell and Magendie, the law states that the dorsal root of spinal nerves brings in sensory information, and the ventral root takes out motor impulses.

Bem Sex Role Inventory (BSRI) Developed by Sandra Bem, the widely used scale that describes the degree to which a person conforms to traditional sex-role stereotypes.

Boulder model Named for a 1949 conference at Boulder, Colorado, the model holds that graduate education should train clinical psychologists to be both scientists and practitioners.

Bystander apathy An area of research in which emergency situations are simulated in order to observe their effects on people exposed to them.

Castration anxiety The fear the little boy develops during the Oedipus complex that his father will remove his penis. Castration anxiety is the motive for resolving the Oedipus complex.

Categorical imperative The central a priori principle in Kant's conception of morality. According to it, a person should act in such a way that the rule behind his or her actions could serve as a universal law for all to follow.

Categories of thought According to Kant, the mind's 12 categories of thought that shape but are independent of experience.

Categorization Refers to how we assign objects and concepts to particular groups; William James called categorization the fundamental act of cognition.

Category mistake Introduced by Ryle, this is the idea that errors sometimes occur when concepts are considered together although they actually require different levels of analysis.

Catharsis The purging of negative thoughts or emotions.

Cathartic method A method for treating mental illness in which symptomatic relief is achieved by bringing forgotten memories and feelings to consciousness.

Causality Belief of Hume that causality was a habit of mind in which we infer that one thing causes another when we have seen them constantly together in the past.

Causes Aristotle's belief that to understand anything completely, we must know its four basic causes: material, formal, efficient, and final.

Centrencephalic system or **centrencephalon** Penfield's name for a collection of subcortical structures that coordinates and integrates the activities of the cerebral hemispheres.

Cerebellum The nervous system unit that Flourens thought enabled an animal to coordinate its movements.

Cerebral lobes The nervous system unit Flourens concluded was responsible for voluntary movements and perception.

Chaos theory A modern-day theory that contends that systems may be more complex and variable than we realize. Heraclitus can be seen as a forerunner of this theory.

Chunks A term referring to collected items of information in memory.

Client-centered therapy The name Carl Rogers gave to his humanistic approach to psychotherapy.

Closure The Gestalt perceptual principle that says that people tend to see incomplete figures as complete.

Cognitive balance Refers to a tendency to perceive information in ways consistent with pre-existing beliefs and attitudes.

Cognitive dissonance According to Leon Festinger's theory, people cannot tolerate conflicting cognitions, and one or more of the conflicting beliefs is rejected or revalued.

Cognitive map Tolman's term for an organism's complete understanding of the layout of its environment.

Collective unconscious For Jung, the part of the unconscious reflecting aspects of behavior that are common to all individuals.

Complex ideas Ideas formed by combining simple ideas of both sensation and reflection.

Complexes For Jung, the organized groups of memories, thoughts, perceptions, and feelings contained in the personal unconscious.

Composite portraiture A method developed by Galton for creating a picture of the "average" individual by combining several photographic images onto one picture.

Concrete operational stage The third stage in Piaget's theory of child development, lasting between the ages of about 7 and 11. During this stage, the child displays conservation when dealing with concrete objects but not with abstract concepts.

Conditioned discrimination In Pavlovian conditioning, learning to respond to only one of a pair of similar stimuli.

Conditioned reflex The association of a stimulus that triggers a reflex with a previously neutral stimulus.

Conditioned response (CR) In Pavlovian conditioning, the response made to the conditioned stimulus.

Conditioned stimulus (CS) In Pavlovian conditioning, the initially neutral stimulus that is paired with a stimulus that reliably elicits a reflex.

Conditioned taste aversion A negative reaction to a taste following an illness associated with the taste.

Conscience One of the two subsystems of the superego that contains the parental and societal prohibitions.

Conscious In Freudian theory, the part of the mind that is what we are aware of at any moment in time.

Conservation of quantity In Piaget's developmental theory, the realization that the quantity of something remains the same even with changes in appearance. Conservation of quantity is lacking in children in the preoperational stage.

Continuity The Gestalt perceptual principle that says people tend to follow elements that appear to be heading in the same direction.

Conventional stage The second of Kohlberg's stages of moral reasoning in which moral decisions are motivated by social rules.

Convergence The eyes' inward rotation to keep an object in focus as it nears the observer; as recognized by Berkeley.

Corpora quadrigemina The nervous system unit Flourens thought was necessary for vision.

Corpus callosum The brain's major interconnecting structure.

Craniometry Literally, the measurement of skulls.

Creative synthesis Wundt's term for the possibility that apperceived ideas may be combined in novel ways.

Cybernetics The term coined by Norbert Wiener to refer to the study of the fundamental control processes of behavior in both animals and machines.

Cynicism School of thought advocating a back-to-nature life free from society's conventions.

Dasein Literally "being there"; Heidegger's term representing humanity.

Daseinanalysis A system of psychotherapy based on the existential-phenomenology of Heidegger and popularized by Boss and Binswanger.

Deductive reasoning Reasoning from a known principle to an unknown one; Plato relied on deductive reasoning.

Defense mechanisms Methods the ego uses when it is threatened by conflicting demands of the id and superego.

Delayed conditioning In delayed conditioning, the CS begins before the UCS and continues at least until the UCS begins.

Delayed-response problem Developed by Walter S. Hunter to study memory in animals, an animal is shown the solution to a problem but is prevented from making it immediately.

Derived ideas For Descartes, ideas that come from experience.

Description The most essential step in Husserl's phenomenological method, description involves intense concentration on and analysis and careful depiction of a phenomenon.

Determining tendency For Ach, the tendency that predisposes a subject to have a particular association to stimulus material; also known as *Aufgabe* or *Einstellung*.

Determinist Someone who believes that all events are determined by prior causes.

Dialectic The use of logical argument to arrive at the truth of an issue.

Dialectical movement Hegel's evolutionary concept in which every condition leads to its opposite, and the conflict of opposites produces a new, higher whole.

Diffusion of responsibility Refers to a situation in which several people have the possibility of acting, but no individual has the clear responsibility to act.

Disinhibition In Pavlovian conditioning, the recovery of a previously extinguished CR caused by the presentation of a strong but irrelevant stimulus.

Displacement The ego defense mechanism in which emotion is shifted from its real object to a safer object.

Distributed practice Training with rest periods between repetitions, which Ebbinghaus found to be superior to massed practice.

Doctrine of formal discipline The idea that the study of disciplinary subjects strengthens the mind for future learning.

Doctrine of specific nerve energies Formulated by Johannes Müller, the doctrine's central principle is that the nerves impose their own specific qualities on the sensory information they convey.

Double aspectism The mind-body solution that contends that mind and body are two aspects of the same thing.

Drive As defined by Woodworth, the "why" of motivation as opposed to mechanism, which concerns the "how"; for Hull, an activated state of the organism whose reduction results in reinforcement.

Dualism The mind-body position that says that both mind and body exist.

Duplex idea James Mill's duplex idea results from the uniting of two complex ideas.

Ecological psychology A movement in behaviorism that stressed the importance of examining environmental conditions and fully understanding the nature of the stimuli in any environmental event.

Ecological validity Popularized by Neisser, the idea that laboratory experiments should be generalizable to the world outside the laboratory.

Ego "The self," the personality process introduced to deal more effectively with the environment than the id can.

Ego-ideal One of the subsystems of the superego that contains the rules the child perceives that his parents think are right.

Electra complex The name sometimes given to the Oedipus complex in girls.

Empiricism The search for knowledge through experience rather than through reasoning.

Endorphins The transmitter substances that have the same effect as morphine and its derivatives; endorphin stands for endogenous morphinelike substance.

Engram Another name for the memory trace—the location of specific memories in the brain.

Entelechy The built-in purpose of things, which is complete actuality rather than potentiality.

Epicureanism Founded by Epicurus, a school in which true pleasure was to be found in simplicity and moderation.

Epiphenomenalism The mind-body position that says that the brain's activity produces mind as a by-product.

Episodic memory A type of long-term memory introduced by Tulving that refers to memories for events, such as your first day at school or breakfast this morning.

Equilibration In Piaget's developmental theory, the motive for the process of accommodation.

Equipotentiality Lashley's term for the idea that all parts of a given brain structure are equal in their potential to mediate a particular function.

Ergonomics Also called human factors engineering, the designing of equipment that can be efficiently used by humans; Münsterberg called it psychotechnics.

Ethology The name for the biological approach to the study of animal behavior.

Eugenics The idea that the human race can be improved through selectively breeding people for desirable traits.

Evolutionary associationism Herbert Spencer's idea that frequently made associations can be passed on to future generations.

Excitatory potential (reaction potential) In Hull's system, the total tendency to make a particular response to a particular stimulus; it is the product of habit strength, drive, and incentive motivation.

Existentialism A philosophy that stresses the isolation of the individual in a hostile universe and emphasizes freedom of choice and responsibility for the consequences of actions.

Experimental aesthetics The data-based study of beauty, a field founded by Gustav Fechner.

Experimental neurosis The name for abnormal behavior often observed in Pavlov's dogs when discrimination training became too difficult for them.

Experimentalists, The Titchener's informal club of laboratory directors who met annually to give reports in a "smoke-filled room with no women present"; after Titchener's death was reorganized as The Society of Experimental Psychologists.

Extinction In Pavlovian conditioning, the presentation of the CS without the UCS.

Extraversion An outward-directed attitude that Jung made a central component of his theory of psychological types.

Factor analysis A statistical procedure to analyze and interpret a series of correlations within a data set.

Faculty psychology A position first associated with the Scottish School of common-sense psychology whose adherents believed that the mind can be divided into a number of different powers, or faculties.

Family resemblance A key concept of categorization proposed by Wittgenstein, the idea of family resemblance asserts that a category does not have to have a defining feature shared by all of the category's members. Instead, there can be a set of features distributed across the category members, with no one feature essential for inclusion in the category.

Fatigue or **exhaustion method** One of Guthrie's methods for breaking a habit by forcing its performance until the person could no longer do it.

Feature detector model Hubel and Wiesel's model of what the individual cells in the visual system respond to—that is, to individual features of a visual scene such as edges, angles, and moving lines.

Fechner's law $S = k \log R$, where S is the sensation, which is equal to a constant (k) times the logarithm of stimulus intensity.

Field theory Lewin's social-psychological theory in which a person is assumed to be continually interacting within a field of psychological forces.

Figure-ground relationship Borrowed from the work of Edgar Rubin, the Gestalt perceptual principle in which the perceptual field is divided into two parts: The figure is the part of the field attended to, whereas the ground is the remainder of the field.

First-signal system Another name Pavlov gave to CSs, because he considered them the first signals of reality.

Fixed-interval schedule An operant conditioning schedule in which reinforcements are given after set periods of time.

Fixed-ratio schedule An operant conditioning schedule in which rewards occur after fixed numbers of responses.

Flashbulb memories Memories of first learning about a surprising or emotional experience.

Formal operational stage The fourth stage of Piaget's theory, which extends from about 12 or 13 through adulthood. The person in this stage can think abstractly and has the cognitive ability to test problem solutions hypothetically and systematically.

Forms Plato's universals known fully only through reasoning; also called Ideas.

Fractionating A technique developed by Watt at Würzburg that involved dividing introspections into four distinct periods.

Free association The name given to Freud's "talking cure," in which the patient is told to say anything that comes into the conscious mind, without trying to censor it.

Functional fixedness The inability to see novel uses or possibilities for something.

Functionalism A psychological school that studied the functions of mind and behavior in the context of the organism's adaptation to the environment.

Fundamental attribution error The inconsistency between how we evaluate ourselves and how we evaluate others.

Galvanic skin response (GSR) Named after Galvani; a change in the skin's ability to conduct electricity.

Gate-control theory The theory of pain that proposes that a spinal cord mechanism acts like a gate to increase or decrease the flow of nerve impulses from peripheral fibers into the central nervous system and thereby determines whether or not we experience pain.

General Problem Solver A computer program developed by Newell and Simon and designed to mimic how humans solve a number of diverse problems and logic puzzles.

Generalizability The extent to which sample results apply to different populations.

Genetic epistemology The name Piaget gave to his program of study, which was genetic in the sense of developmental and epistemological because it studied the foundations of human knowledge.

Genital stage The final psychosexual stage in Freudian psychoanalysis during which the person begins to direct the libido outward, toward the opposite sex, and to the goal of reproduction.

Gerontology The study of aging and the exploration of issues that emerge as we age.

Gestalt Synonyms include whole, shape, form, and configuration.

Gestalt psychology A school that held that psychologists should study and discover useful and meaningful laws about the relations between parts and wholes.

Gestaltqualitäten von Ehrenfels's term, which means "a quality of the forms" or "form quality."

Golden Age of Greece The time period between the birth of Pericles (ca. 490 B.C.) and Aristotle's death (322 B.C.).

Habit strength In Hull's system, the strength of the bond between the stimulus and the response.

Hawthorne Effect Derived from a series of studies of workplace conditions and job performance, the Hawthorne Effect suggests that any workplace change that makes people feel important is likely to improve their work performance.

Hedonism The search for pleasure and the avoidance of pain.

Helmholtz-Hering debate A debate over the development of visual space perception, in which Helmholtz took an empiricist approach (it is learned) and Hering argued for the nativist position (it is there from the beginning).

Higher-order conditioning In Pavlovian conditioning, the use of a previous CS as a UCS in further conditioning.

Hodology Term invented by Lewin to show paths of energy within a person's life space.

Humanism The Renaissance focus on the importance of people rather than religion or the natural world.

Humors The bodily fluids Hippocrates thought were distilled from the universe's basic elements. The humors were blood, black bile, yellow bile, and phlegm.

Hypnotism Named by James Braid, a state of heightened suggestibility in humans.

Hypothesis experiments Experiments by David Krech in which rats appeared to test hypotheses about response strategies in order to maximize their success on the task.

Hypothetical constructs Intervening variables with surplus meaning and at least the implication of a physiological basis.

Hypothetico-deductive learning theory The name given to Hull's learning system in which general statements (postulates) gave rise to testable theorems.

Id Literally "it," the totally unconscious, biological storehouse for drives, derived from instincts.

Idealism (immaterialism, mentalism) The point of view stating that the objects of perception are ideas of the perceiving mind and that it is impossible to know whether reality exists apart from the mind.

Ideas The mind's contents, according to Locke, and faint copies of impressions, according to Hume.

Identification Unconsciously trying to think, feel, and act like another, identification ends the Oedipus complex.

Idols The term Francis Bacon used for preconceived notions that contaminate reasoning.

Imageless thought Found by Külpe and others, referred to introspections during problem solving that yielded either no or vague images and feelings. Wundt and Titchener did not believe it was possible, and this led to controversy.

Immediate experience Wundt's term for the direct experience of a stimulus, uninfluenced by any previous knowledge of it. Immediate experience provides the data for experimental psychology.

Impressions The mind's active perceptions, according to Hume.

Incentive motivation Kenneth Spence's idea, adopted by Hull, that the quantity and quality of a reward affects performance.

Incompatible stimuli Guthrie's method for breaking a habit by presenting the stimulus that would normally trigger the undesirable behavior when other aspects of the situation will prevent the behavior's occurrence.

Individuation For Jung, the process through which the self became the whole psyche.

Inductive reasoning Reasoning from the particular to the general; Aristotle used inductive reasoning.

Information processing The term used to describe the application of cybernetic information and control theories to human behavior and mental events.

Innate ideas The ideas that Descartes believed come to mind with certainty and inevitability; they do not come from experience.

Insight A type of learning in which a change in the perception of problem elements results in both the ability to solve the immediate problem and others of a similar nature.

Intelligence Quotient (IQ) Mental age divided by chronological age—a term introduced by William Stern; the abbreviation IQ was coined by Lewis Terman.

Intentionality A concept central to Brentano's act psychology, to be conscious is to be conscious of something (i.e., consciousness always intends something).

Interactionism The mind-body position that says the mind and body are separate but interacting.

Interbehaviorism The name Kantor gave to his psychology stressing the interactions of the organism with stimulus objects.

Interference theory of forgetting The observation by Müller and Pilzecker that new learning can interfere with the memory of previously learned material.

Internal perception (*innere Wahrnehmung*) Used by Wundt rather than introspection, as one method to aid in the study of the lower mental processes.

Interposition One of three depth perception cues in which near objects hide, or partially hide, more distant objects; as recognized by George Berkeley.

Intervening variable A construct coming between the stimulus and the response that is completely defined by the S-R conditions.

Introspection Meaning "to look within"; a method for studying inner experience first suggested by St. Augustine.

Introversion An inward-directed attitude that Jung made a central component of his theory of psychological types.

Isomorphism A Gestalt principle that assumes a direct correspondence between brain processes and what is being experienced.

James-Lange theory of emotion Theory of emotion, which put the physiological expression of emotion before the emotional feeling; proposed independently by William James and Carl Lange.

Just noticeable difference (jnd) The amount that a comparison stimulus must differ from a standard stimulus in order to be reliably detected as different.

Labeled-line theory An idea of how sensory processing works that suggests that each nerve fiber carries a specific piece of sensory information—that is, is labeled.

LAD The acronym for "language acquisition device," Chomsky's term for an innate characteristic of the human mind that enables children to acquire language easily.

Latency stage The relatively uneventful period in psychosexual development that occurs between the phallic stage and the genital stage.

Latent content The dream's true meaning, which may differ from its manifest content.

Latent learning Learning that is assumed to have occurred but is not evident in the organism's performance.

Law of effect Thorndike's statement that responses in a situation followed closely by satisfaction will be more firmly attached to the situation and more likely to recur when the situation is repeated, whereas responses followed by discomfort will have their connections to the situation weakened and be less likely to recur when the situation is repeated.

Law of exercise Thorndike's statement of the long-held belief that repetition of an association strengthens the bond between a situation and the response to it.

Law of *Prägnanz* A general Gestalt principle asserting that any psychological organization will tend toward a "good Gestalt" or good form; the organization will tend to be as good as prevailing conditions allow.

Law of Three Stages According to Comte, the three stages each field of thought passes through: theological, metaphysical, and positivistic, or scientific.

Learning predispositions The idea that evolution has shaped an organism's associative system so that some associations are more easily made than others.

Learning set The extraction of one key to the solution of a series of similar problems.

Libido Freud's term for the form of energy used by the life instincts.

Life space Lewin's term for a field within which a person's psychological activities occur; it consists of all the influences on the person at a given moment in time.

Local sign For Lotze, a particular pattern of stimulation somewhere on the body that carried with it a sense of location.

Localizationists Neuroscientists who hold that specific functions are located in specific brain areas.

Logical positivism A movement started by the members of the Vienna Circle that continued the refinement of positivism through a systematic investigation of the logic of science.

Logotherapy The existential psychotherapy developed by Frankl that involves the search for meaning.

Longitudinal studies Studies performed on a group over an extended time period.

Lyceum The name of Aristotle's school, which came to rival Plato's Academy.

Manifest content The literal details of a dream that a person remembers upon awakening.

Mass action Lashley's term that meant that the amount of loss of function following brain damage was proportional to the amount of damage to the brain, not to its locus.

Massed practice Practice without rest periods that Ebbinghaus found is inferior to distributed practice.

Materialism The mind-body position that says there is only body; the underlying reality is physical; form of monism.

Meaning For Titchener, the context in which something was experienced.

Mechanism As defined by Woodworth, the "how" of motivation, as opposed to drive, which concerns the "why" of motivation.

Mediate experience Wundt's term for the indirect experience that produces the data for physics and the other natural sciences.

Medulla oblongata The first brain structure after the spinal cord; it is essential for life.

Memory drum A mechanical device invented by G. E. Müller and Schumann to systematize presentation of syllables in memory experiments.

Mental chemistry In John Stuart Mill's mental chemistry, an idea is generated by its components rather than consisting of them.

Mental chronometry A method developed by Donders to study the time taken by the mind to perform different mental acts.

Mental tests A term coined by Cattell for his measurements of such things as sensation, reaction time, and memory.

Mentalism (immaterialism, subjective idealism) The mind-body solution that holds that reality ultimately exists in the mind; form of monism.

Mesmerism In psychology, an early name for hypnosis.

Method of expression The recording of physiological changes used by Wundt to study feelings.

Method of limits One of Fechner's psychophysical techniques. In using it to determine the threshold of detection, the subject is presented with an undetectable stimulus that is gradually increased until the person reports it; then, a clearly detectable stimulus is gradually decreased until it is no longer sensed. The average intensity at which judgment changes is called the detection threshold.

Middle Ages The period extending from roughly 500 to 1500—from the fall of the Roman Empire until the beginning of the Renaissance.

Mind A journal of philosophy and psychology founded by Alexander Bain.

Mind-body dualism Descartes's idea that the mind and the body are separate, with the mind unextended and without substance and the body extended and having substance.

Mind-body problem One of the basic issues in the history of psychology that asks whether organisms have both mind and body, and, if so, how the two are related.

Minnesota Multiphasic Personality Inventory (MMPI) Created by Hathaway and McKinley, a personality assessment device consisting of 550 simple statements with which the taker either agrees or disagrees. Each statement is linked to one or more of the test's 10 clinical scales. The MMPI also has three "validity" scales designed to detect faking.

Modernism Refers to a cluster of assumptions—for example, the idea that a self exists and the idea that truth exists—that originated with the Renaissance and have structured scientific and philosophical inquiry ever since.

Monads Leibniz's term for the unextended, uncreatable, indestructible, and immutable particles he thought comprised everything.

Monism The mind-body solution that says there is only one underlying reality, either mind or body.

Morgan's Canon The suggestion that higher mental abilities should not be attributed to the animal mind than are necessary to explain the animal's behavior.

Motivology Woodworth's term for the study of the drives and mechanisms related to motivation.

Movement-produced stimuli Used to explain sequential responding, sensations produced by movements that lead to further movements.

Myers-Briggs Type Indicator (MBTI) A contemporary personality test based on Jung's theory of personality type.

Nativists People adopting a nature position on the nature-nurture controversy.

Nature and nurture A phrase popularized by Galton used to describe the longstanding debate about the relative importance of inherited or environmental influences on human behavior.

Nature-nurture controversy Controversy over how much of behavior is inherited or instinctive (nature) and how much is acquired or learned (nurture).

Need hierarchy The part of Maslow's theory of motivation often shown as a pyramid with basic physiological needs at its base and self-actualization at its apex.

Negative afterimages The perception of the opposite color after prolonged stimulation with a particular color.

NEO Personality Inventory-Revised (NEO PI-R) A personality assessment device suggesting that only five factors are needed to characterize personality—neuroticism, extraversion, openness, agreeableness/antagonism, and conscientiousness.

Neoplatonism A school that tried to combine Plato's views with various theologies.

Neural networks A non-rule-based alternative to AI computing; also called parallel processing and connectionism.

Neural plasticity A phenomenon in which remaining brain areas are believed to assume a lost function when a brain area is ablated.

Neuroticism One of Eysenck's personality components that is a measure of an individual's emotional stability or instability.

Nominal fallacy The mistaken idea that naming something explains it.

Nominalist One who believed that universals, concepts like truth and beauty, existed in name only, not in reality.

Nonlocalizationists Neuroscientists who are impressed with the way the nervous system works as a coordinated unit.

Nonreductionism The position that psychological phenomena can stand on their own, without the need for biological or biochemical explanations.

Nonsense syllable, or **CVC trigram** Consisting of two consonants with a vowel between, the wordlike unit Ebbinghaus created in order to study memory.

Normal curve The bell-shaped curve that is often approximated when the distribution of scores from some physiological or behavioral measurement is plotted.

Noumenal world Kant's term for the world outside our minds, which consists of "things-in-themselves."

Nurturists People adopting a nurture position on the nature-nurture controversy.

Object permanence In Piaget's theory, a child displays object permanence when it responds as though it realizes that an object continues to exist even when it is no longer being sensed.

Object-relations theory A psychoanalytic variation stressing conflicts based on object relations, which are interpersonal relationships as they are represented in an individual's mind.

Occasionalism The mind-body position of Malebranche in which the need to act becomes the "occasion" for God's intervention.

Ockham's razor Belief of William of Ockham that the simplest explanation for a phenomenon is preferred over an explanation with more assumptions; sometimes called the Law of Parsimony.

Oedipus complex Part of the phallic stage during which the little boy would like to possess his mother and remove his father as a rival for her affections.

Olfactometer An instrument invented by Zwaardemaker for the control and measurement of olfactory stimuli.

Ontological argument St. Anselm's argument that says that God is the greatest thing that can be thought, and if God did not exist, then something greater could be thought. Hence, God must exist.

Operant Skinner's term for a spontaneously occurring response.

Operational definition A definition of something in terms of the way it is measured.

Operationism The philosophical approach to science that states that concepts should be defined operationally.

Opponent-process theory Ewald Hering's theory of color vision in which three receptor systems each respond in one of two opposing ways: red-green, blue-yellow, and black-white.

Oral stage The first of Freud's psychosexual stages during which the infant's efforts to achieve satisfaction are centered around the oral zone—the mouth.

Overlearning Continued practice beyond mastery; Ebbinghaus observed that overlearning facilitates retention.

Paired-associates method An experimental technique for studying the nature of association that was introduced by Mary Calkins and further developed by G. E. Müller and others.

Panpsychism The idea that mind or soul pervades the world of nature.

Pantheism The belief that God and the universe are the same.

Parallelism (psychophysical parallelism) The view that mind and body are separate and noninteracting entities.

Pearson product-moment correlation coefficient, or **Pearson r** The standard statistic computed to reveal the degree of relationship (correlation) between two variables.

Penis envy The desire by females to possess the organ that they lack; penis envy introduces the Oedipus complex.

Perceptual cycle Introduced by Neisser, the perceptual cycle suggests that our mental structures direct our behavior, and our experiences modify our mental representations in an unending cycle.

Performance Refers to a distinction first made by Tolman between learning and performance; performance—the organism's actual behavior—may or may not reveal learning that has occurred.

Pericles (ca. 490–429 B.C.) Ruler under whom Athens enjoyed the privileges of democracy and benign dictatorship.

Persona In Jung's system, the part of the self that reflects a person's role in society.

Personal Attributes Questionnaire (PAQ) The questionnaire developed by Janet Spence and Robert Helmreich for use in studying gender differences.

Personal constructs From George Kelly's psychology, a theory an individual develops to help organize and make sense of his or her world.

Personal unconscious In Jungian theory, the layer of the unconscious containing material that was once conscious but has now been repressed, suppressed, or simply forgotten.

Petite perceptions The term Leibniz called perceptions that never reach consciousness.

Phallic stage The third of Freud's psychosexual stages of development during which interest in the child centers on the genitals.

Phenomenal world Kant's term for the inner world created by the intuitions and categories of the mind.

Phenomenology Often defined as the study of intact, meaningful experiences; Husserl defined it as the examination of the data of conscious experience.

Phi phenomenon Wertheimer's name for apparent movement caused by the flashing of lights in the correct temporal sequence.

Phrenology The pseudoscience that held that the mind's "faculties" were related to the bumps on the skull.

Pineal gland The gland in the brain Descartes chose for the point of interaction between the mind and the body.

Place learning Contrasted with response learning, in Tolman's experiments rats were taught either to go to a specific place or to make a particular response; place learning proved to be superior to response learning, at least in Tolman's studies.

Place theory of pitch perception The theory that the place of stimulation on the basilar membrane determines pitch perception.

Pleasure principle The principle by which the id operates to try to eliminate or reduce tension to an acceptably low level.

Positive afterimage A brief image of an object that remains after the object has been withdrawn, which Hartley attributed to continuing vibrations of tiny particles in the brain.

Positivism A philosophical approach in which scientific facts are to be gathered through empirical, objective observations.

Postconventional stage Kohlberg's third stage of moral reasoning in which the individual is guided by internalized moral principles.

Postmodernism A movement that questions modernism's assumptions.

Poverty-of-stimulus argument Chomsky's idea that the language spoken to children is too poor a stimulus and reinforcement of correct grammar is too haphazard to support a satisfactory behavioral account of language acquisition.

Pragmatism A philosophical theory usually associated with William James or with its originator, C. S. Peirce. According to pragmatism, the meaning of an idea or proposition lies in its observable consequences; if an idea works in a context, it is true.

Preconscious In Freudian theory, the part of the mind that is the antechamber to consciousness, containing relatively accessible material.

Preconventional stage The first stage in Kohlberg's theory of moral reasoning in which moral behavior is motivated by the avoidance of punishment and the desire to be rewarded.

Prefrontal lobotomy A brain operation in which the prefrontal lobes were severed from other brain regions.

Preoperational stage The second stage in Piaget's developmental theory, lasting from about age 2 to age 7. During this stage, the child discovers the operations that will be used for solving problems later.

Presentist bias The tendency for historians to discuss and analyze past ideas, people, and events in terms of present issues and contexts.

Primary process The production of a memory image of the object needed to reduce tension.

Primary qualities Qualities inherent in matter (e.g., shape, quantity, and motion).

Principles of association Three principles—similarity, contrast, and contiguity—Aristotle used in describing recall.

Project Pigeon A project devised by Skinner to train pigeons to guide missiles to their targets.

Projection The attribution of our unpleasant or disturbing desires to others while rejecting them in ourselves.

Proximity The Gestalt principle of perceptual grouping stating that elements that are close together are seen as belonging together.

Psyche Term used by Aristotle to refer to a vital principle that differentiated the living from the nonliving. For him, there were three different *psyches*: vegetative, sensitive, and rational.

Psychic determinism The idea that all psychological events are determined.

Psychoanalysis The system developed by Sigmund Freud to study human motivation, personality, and psychopathology, using such techniques as free association and the analysis of dreams and everyday errors.

Psychometrics The measurement of mental processes through psychological tests; the term is sometimes used interchangeably with advances in statistics and data analysis.

Psychonomic Society Founded by Clifford Morgan and others in 1959–1960 in response to a growing perception that the APA was spending an increasing amount of time on concerns affecting primarily clinical psychologists.

Psychopharmacology The field that uses psychological and pharmacological concepts to investigate the behavioral effects of drugs.

Psychophysics Fechner's term for the method he developed to measure the relation between sensation and the stimulus that produces it.

Purposive behaviorism The name given to Tolman's version of behaviorism, which stressed the relation of behavior toward goals.

Puzzle boxes The pieces of apparatus Thorndike built to study learning in animals.

Questionnaire This method to obtain data relevant to psychology was first introduced by Galton and is still popular today.

Rationalism A philosophical approach based on the use of reason to develop knowledge.

Rationalism The use of reason and logic to arrive at knowledge.

Rationalization The ego's attempt to account for mistakes and failures by providing a reasonable, but untrue, explanation for behavior.

Reaction formation The defense mechanism in which the person professes the desire for the opposite of what is really wanted.

Realist In medieval philosophy, one who believed that universals had a "real" existence apart from specific examples.

Reality principle The principle by which the ego operates; its aim is to prevent energy discharge until the actual object needed for tension-reduction is produced.

Recapitulation theory Ernst Haeckel's idea that the development of the individual reprises the development of the species; Hall applied the theory to child development.

Receptive field The receptive field of a cell consists of the group of receptor cells that send information to it.

Reconstructive memory Refers to a tendency to construct plausible, but not necessarily accurate, memory elements when the actual memory details have been lost.

Reductionism In psychology, the search for increasingly elemental explanations of psychological phenomena.

Reflection The perception of the operations of the mind, according to Locke, which included perception, thinking, doubting, and reasoning.

Reflexology The name Bekhterev gave to his objective psychology that would study the relationships between behavior and physiological and environmental conditions.

Regression A retreat to an earlier stage of development as a result of a difficult experience.

Regression toward the mean The tendency over time for the measurements of a variable to come closer to the mean or average for that variable.

Relative size One of three cues to distance perception. When two objects the same size are at different distances from the observer, the near object appears larger than the more distant object; as recognized by Berkeley.

Relativism The theory that truth and moral values are not absolute but relative to the context.

Reliability A test's consistency of measurement over time.

Representative heuristic Refers to a tendency for people to use the wrong sort of heuristic in solving problems because of a misunderstanding of such concepts as randomness, base rates, and sample sizes.

Repression The unconscious removal from consciousness of unacceptable ideas, memories, and impulses.

Respondent Skinner's term for a reflex in the traditional sense; he called Pavlovian conditioning respondent conditioning.

Retroactive inhibition Interference that acts back upon an earlier memory.

Reward areas or **pleasure centers** Regions of the brain where stimulation appears to be pleasurable.

Romanticism A philosophical approach emphasizing the whole person and particularly the person's feelings; romanticism was a reaction against empiricism and rationalism.

Rorschach Inkblot Test Based on the psychodynamic approach to personality, the test assesses a person's responses to a series of inkblots.

Scatter plot A graphic representation of two variables, with one variable plotted on the x axis and the other variable plotted on the y axis.

Schema The schema (plural, schemata) is a mental structure that organizes and summarizes related experiences. Schema theory is central to modern cognitive psychology.

Scholasticism A system of thought based on Aristotelian logic and theology, whose adherents were called schoolmen.

School of psychology A psychological school, consists of all the people who more or less agree with a particular system of psychology.

Scottish School A philosophical school whose members were all Scottish; founded by Thomas Reid in opposition to Hume's skepticism.

Script According to Abelson, a special type of schema involving a structured sequence of behavioral events.

Second-signal system What Pavlov called human language to contrast the system with what he considered the first-signal system, basic conditioned stimuli.

Secondary drive A learned drive that has acquired its motivating status from being paired with a primary drive and its reduction.

Secondary process The process the ego uses to handle reality by developing an action plan through thought and reason; it corresponds to what we call thinking or problem solving.

Secondary qualities Qualities (e.g., color, smell, and taste) that require the presence of a sensing observer.

Seduction theory The idea that neuroses are the result of childhood sexual abuse.

Self-psychology The psychological system developed by Mary Calkins; also known as personalistic psychology.

Semantic differential A measurement technique developed by Charles Osgood used to assess word meanings.

Semantic memory A type of long-term memory introduced by Tulving that are memories of isolated, emotionless, atemporal facts, such as your memory for the name of the capital of Louisiana.

Sensations Locke's term for impressions received by sense organs that are transmitted to our minds.

Sensorimotor stage In Piaget's stage theory of development, the first stage, lasting from birth until about age 2. During the stage, the infant learns the relations between its sensory apparatus and its motor responses.

Shadow For Jung, the residue of the animal nature in humans, which provides a potential source of creative energy.

Shaping An operant conditioning technique in which successive approximations to the desired behavior are rewarded.

Short-term memory Another name for consciousness; refers to a brief memory stage having a capacity of 7 ± 2 chunks.

Sign learning Mowrer's term referring to Pavlovian conditioning in which the conditioned stimulus becomes a signal for an environmentally meaningful event.

Signal detection theory A mathematically based theory that assumes the observer in a perceptual experiment is an active decision maker who makes perceptual judgments under conditions of uncertainty.

Similarity The Gestalt perceptual principle that says that similar elements are seen as belonging together.

Simple ideas Ideas that have their origin in sensations and reflection; they cannot be divided further.

Simultaneous conditioning In Pavlovian conditioning, the presentation of the CS and the UCS at the same time.

16 Personality Factors Test (16 PF) The test created by Raymond B. Cattell, who constructed it by reducing some 4,000 trait descriptions to 16 binary personality factors.

Skepticism The philosophical position holding that we can never know anything with certainty, so the way to avoid believing something false is to not believe in anything.

Skinner box Named by Hull, the apparatus Skinner developed to study operant conditioning in rats and pigeons.

Sleeper effect Refers to attitude changes over time in which the association between the message and its source may fade, with the result that the content of the message is remembered after the source has been forgotten.

Social Darwinism The idea that society and its institutions evolve, facilitating the survival of the fittest.

Social facilitation Floyd Allport's term for the improved performance on tasks when others are present.

Social learning theory The theory developed by Bandura that focuses on the role of modeling or imitation in the acquisition of social behavior.

Solution learning Mowrer's term for instrumental conditioning of voluntary responses.

Sophists Traveling teachers who taught young Greek men logic, science, philosophy, and especially rhetoric.

Spatial frequency model The model proposed by DeValois and his colleagues, which suggests that neurons in the visual cortex perform a spatial frequency analysis rather than breaking the visual scene into component lines and angles.

Spearman's g Spearman's abbreviation for his general factor of intelligence.

Spearman's s Spearman's abbreviation for his specific intellectual abilities factor.

Spencer-Bain principle Spencer's revision of Bain's explanation of voluntary behavior to include evolutionary ideas.

Split-brain operation An operation in which some or all of the major connections between the brain's hemispheres are severed.

Spontaneous recovery In Pavlovian conditioning, the reappearance of a conditioned response following a rest interval after extinction.

Stanford-Binet An intelligence test devised by Terman from the original test introduced by Binet and Simon.

Stereochemical theory The theory of smell in which an odorant molecule's shape determines its olfactory quality.

Stevens's law Law holding that there is a power relation between sensory intensity and stimulus magnitude.

Stimulus error For Titchener, describing the stimulus itself rather than the immediate sensations and feelings produced by the stimulus.

Stimulus generalization A learning phenomenon in which a response made to a particular stimulus is made to other, similar stimuli.

Stimulus-Response learning (S-R) The association of a particular stimulus with a particular response with the result that future encounters of the stimulus will lead to the same response.

Stoicism A school of thought that taught acceptance of whatever comes.

Striving for superiority For Adler, the idea that people are pushed by the need to overcome inferiority and pulled by the need for superiority over their environments.

Structuralism The name often given to Titchener's psychology; the system in which psychologists used introspection to try to find the basic elements of adult, human consciousness.

Study of twins A technique Galton introduced for examining the relative importance of heredity and the environment.

Style of life For Adler, each person's unique response to the goal of achieving superiority.

Sublimation A form of displacement in which the substituted object of the emotional shift is socially approved.

Suggestion Thomas Brown's term for "association." He developed both primary and secondary laws of suggestion.

Superego In psychoanalysis, the moral component of personality, which strives for perfection rather than for sensual pleasure.

Survival of the fittest Spencer's term to indicate that only the best adapted organisms or entities survive.

Syllogism Aristotle's invention of reasoning that begins with a fundamental general statement from which additional statements necessarily follow.

Synapse A gap between neurons, which was hypothesized by Sir Charles Sherrington.

Syntactic structures Chomsky's idea of innate, biological structures that contain the basic grammar rules of human language.

Synthetic philosophy The name Herbert Spencer gave to his comprehensive program for a unified philosophy of science.

System of psychology A collection of ideas defining what is psychological and the methods that will be used to study it.

Systematic desensitization A technique developed by Joseph Wolpe for removing an irrational fear.

Systematic experimental introspection A method used at Würzburg in which subjects performed complex mental tasks and then introspected on their mental experiences during the solution of the task.

Tachistoscope A piece of apparatus used to present visual stimuli for short time periods.

Teaching machine An educational device that Skinner worked on that would present problems to students at their own pace and would provide immediate reinforcement of their responses.

Teleology The idea that everything has a definite end or final purpose.

Thematic Apperception Test (TAT) The test, originally developed by Henry Murray and Christiana Morgan, that consists of 30 pictures depicting ambiguous social situations to which a person responds by creating a story about the situation shown in each scene.

Theory of Forms The belief that there are universal Ideas, or "Forms," that underlie what we know through our senses.

Third Force With behaviorism and psychoanalysis as the first two forces, Maslow argued for a humanistic approach as the Third Force in psychology.

Threshold or **limen of consciousness** Herbart's term for a limit that an idea had to surpass in order to become conscious.

Token economy Derived from operant conditioning, a situation in which patients are given tokens that can be exchanged for privileges, in an effort to shape their behavior.

Toleration or **threshold method** In this method Guthrie introduced for breaking habits, cues that normally trigger the behavior are presented at such a low level that the response does not occur, and then the cues are gradually increased.

TOTE The acronym for Test-Operate-Test-Exit unit, which is a hypothetical, hierarchical, feedback loop that has both cognitive and behavioral components and is assumed to occupy the same theoretical space as the reflex arc.

Trace conditioning In Pavlovian conditioning, the conditioning that occurs when the CS is presented and ends before the UCS occurs.

Transfer of training The improvement in one task following training on another.

Transference An important part of the therapeutic relationship in which the patient unconsciously shifts her or his feelings for something or somebody onto the therapist.

Transposition problem The task Köhler developed to contrast the Gestalt learning approach with Thorndike's trial-and-error learning. Animals often learned to respond to the relationship between the stimuli rather than learning to make a specific response to a specific stimulus.

Tripartite soul Plato's idea that the soul has three parts: reason, spirit, and appetite.

Tropism A directed, mechanical movement of a plant or animal in response to a stimulus.

Turing Test A test for computer intelligence that asks whether or not the computer output is indistinguishable from what would be expected from a human under the same circumstances. If it is indistinguishable, then the conclusion is that the machine is intelligent within that context.

Two-point threshold The minimum distance two simultaneously applied points must be separated before they are experienced as separate touches.

Umweg or **detour problem** The problem in which a goal is clearly visible to the subject, but it can't be reached directly; the subject must make a "detour" in order to get the goal.

Unconditioned response (UCR) In Pavlovian conditioning, the reflex response made to the unconditioned stimulus.

Unconditioned stimulus (UCS) In Pavlovian conditioning, the stimulus that always elicits the reflex response.

Unconscious For Freud, the part of the mind that was the site of relatively irretrievable material.

Utilitarianism A social and ethical philosophy that holds that the goal of all behavior should be to achieve the "greatest good for the greatest number."

Validity The extent to which a test measures what it is supposed to measure.

Variable-interval schedule An operant schedule in which rewards occur after varying periods of time.

Variable-ratio schedule An operant schedule in which reinforcements occur after varying numbers of responses.

Vibratiuncles For Hartley, tiny vibrations in the brain that represented sensory vibrations in the nerves.

Vienna Circle A group of scientists who refined positivism into the movement known as logical positivism.

Visual cliff An apparent "cliff" used by Eleanor Gibson and others to determine if depth perception is innate.

Vitalism The idea that life is caused by a principle different from chemical and physical forces.

Völkerpsychologie A 10-volume work on language, culture, religion, etc., that resulted from Wundt's efforts to study the products of humankind's higher mental processes, as he did not believe that higher mental processes could be investigated experimentally.

Voluntarism Wundt's name for his system of psychology, in which there is a voluntary focusing of attention.

Weber fractions Weber found jnds to be constant ratios of a standard stimulus, and his colleague Fechner called the ratios Weber fractions.

Weber's law Fechner gave the relation Weber found for jnds mathematical form and called it Weber's law, which is

$$\frac{\delta R}{R} = K.$$

Wechsler Adult Intelligence Scale (WAIS) A popular intelligence test invented by David Wechsler for determining adult IQ.

Wechsler Intelligence Scale for Children (WISC) Invented by David Wechsler, an important alternative to the Stanford-Binet test for assessing IQ in children.

Wernicke's model Wernicke's proposal that an area of the temporal lobe converts speech sounds into comprehended language, and this information travels through the arcuate fasciculus to Broca's area for speech production.

Wesensschau The step in Husserl's system that is the cognition of essence: that is, the apprehension of the nature of a thing through a consideration of phenomena. where R (*Reiz*) stands for the magnitude of the stimulus, and δR is the jnd.

Whytt's reflex Named for its discoverer, another name for the pupillary reflex to light.

Will The central theme of Schopenhauer's philosophy, will is in everything and is the driving force of all nature.

Wish-fulfillment Freud's idea that all dreams represent events the dreamer really wants to happen, no matter how troubling the events seem to be.

Word-association experiment An experiment in which Galton looked at each of 75 different words and recorded his associations; the use of word associations was developed further by others, including Wundt and Jung.

Würzburg school A collection of psychologists under Külpe's direction at the University of Würzburg. Much of their research was concerned with thought.

Yerkes-Dodson law The law stating that the optimal level of arousal for performance of a task depends on the difficulty of the task—for example, for easy tasks, a high level of arousal results in superior performance, whereas for difficult tasks, a high level of arousal is detrimental.

Young-Helmholtz (or trichromatic) theory First proposed by Thomas Young and revised by Helmholtz, the theory of color vision proposes that color sensations come from some pattern of stimulation of three different types of receptors in the eye.

Zeitgeist "The spirit of the times"; view of history saying that the historical context plays a major role in determining which ideas are accepted and which are rejected.

References

Aaron, M., & Thorne, B. M. (1975). Omission training and extinction in rats with septal damage. *Physiology and Behavior, 15,* 149–154.

Abelson, R. P. (1981). Psychological status of the script concept. *American Psychologist, 36,* 715–729.

Adler, A. (1930). Individual psychology. In C. Murchison (Ed.), *Psychologies of 1930* (pp. 395–405). Worcester, MA: Clark University Press.

Ainsworth, M. D. S., & Bowlby, J. (1991). An ethological approach to personality development. *American Psychologist, 46,* 333–341.

Albert, R. (1975). Toward a behavioral definition of genius. *American Psychologist, 30,* 140–151.

Alexander, F. G., & Selesnick, S. T. (1966). *The history of psychiatry: An evaluation of psychiatric thought and practice from prehistoric times to the present.* New York: Mentor.

Alexander, I. E. (1991). C. G. Jung: The man and his work, then and now. In G. A. Kimble, M. Wertheimer, & C. L. White (Eds.), *Portraits of pioneers in psychology* (pp. 153–169). Hillsdale, NJ: Lawrence Erlbaum Associates, Inc.

Allee, W. (1938). *The social life of animals.* Boston: Beacon Press.

Allen, R. E. (Ed.) (1966). *Greek philosophy: Thales to Aristotle.* New York: Macmillan.

Allport, F. H. (1924). *Social psychology.* Boston: Houghton Mifflin.

Allport, F. H. (1933). *Institutional behavior.* Chapel Hill, NC: University of North Carolina Press.

Allport, F. H. (1955). *Theories of perception and the concept of structure.* New York: Wiley.

Allport, F. H. (1974). Floyd H. Allport. In G. Lindzey (Ed.), *A history of psychology in autobiography* (Vol. 6, pp. 1–29). Englewood Cliffs, NJ: Prentice-Hall.

Allport, G. W. (1935). Attitudes. In C. Murchison (Ed.), *A handbook of social psychology* (pp. 798–844). Worcester, MA: Clark University Press.

Allport, G. W. (1954a). The historical background of modern social psychology. In G. Lindzey (Ed.), *A handbook of social psychology* (Vol. 1, pp. 3–56). Reading, MA: Addison-Wesley.

Allport, G. W. (1954b). *The nature of prejudice.* Cambridge, MA: Addison-Wesley.

Allport, G. W. (1967). G. W. Allport. In E. G. Boring & G. Lindzey (Eds.), *A history of psychology in autobiography* (Vol. 5, pp. 3–25). New York: Appleton-Century-Crofts.

Allport, G. W. (1968). *The person in psychology: Selected essays.* Boston: Beacon Press.

Allport, G. W., & Odbert, H. S. (1936). Trait names: A psycholexical study. *Psychological Monographs, 47,* (1, Whole No. 211).

American Psychiatric Association (1994). *Diagnostic and statistical manual of mental disorders* (4th ed.). Washington, DC: Author.

American Psychological Association. (1995, October). *Report of the task force on the changing gender composition of psychology.* Washington, DC: Author.

American Psychologist. (1987). Robert A. Rescorla. *American Psychologist, 42,* 285–288.

American Psychologist. (1994). Endel Tulving. *American Psychologist, 49,* 551–553.

Amoore, J. E. (1970). *Molecular basis of odor.* Springfield, IL: Thomas.

Anastasi, A. (1934). The influence of practice upon test reliability. *Journal of Educational Psychology, 25,* 321–335.

Anastasi, A. (1954). *Psychological testing.* New York: Macmillan.

Anastasi, A. (1958). Heredity, environment, and the question "How?" *Psychological Review, 65,* 197–208.

Anastasi, A. (1964). *Fields of applied psychology.* New York: McGraw-Hill.

Anastasi, A. (1980). Anne Anastasi. In G. Lindzey (Ed.), *A history of psychology in autobiography* (Vol. 7, pp. 1–37). San Francisco: W. H. Freeman and Company.

Anastasi, A., & Foley, J. P., Jr. (1952). *The Human-Figure Drawing Test as an objective psychiatric screening aid for student pilots.* USAF School of Aviation Medicine, Project No. 21-37-002, Report No. 5.

Anastasi, A., & Schaefer, C. E. (1969). Biographical correlates of artistic and literary creativity in adolescent girls. *Journal of Applied Psychology, 53,* 267–273.

Angell, J. R. (1904). *Psychology: An introductory study of the structure and functions of human consciousness.* New York: Holt.

Angell, J. R. (1907). The province of functional psychology. *Psychological Review, 14,* 61–91.

Angell, J. R. (1908). *Psychology* (4th ed.). New York: Henry Holt & Co.

Angell, J. R. (1911). Editorial: William James. *Psychological Review, 5,* 78–82.

Angell, J. R. (1911). Topic: Philosophical and psychological usages of the terms mind, consciousness, and soul. *Psychological Bulletin, 8,* 46–47.

Angell, J. R. (1936). James Rowland Angell. In C. Murchison (Ed.), *A history of psychology in autobiography* (Vol. 3, pp. 1–38). Worcester, MA: Clark University Press.

Angell, J. R., & Moore, A. W. (1896). Reaction time: A study in attention and habit. *Psychological Review, 3,* 245–258.

Anglin, J. M. (1973). Introduction. In J. S. Bruner, *Beyond the information given* (pp. xii–xxiv). New York: Norton & Company.

Ansbacher, H. L. (1959). The significance of the socio-economic status of the patients of Freud and of Adler. *American Journal of Psychotherapy, 13,* 376–382.

Ansbacher, H. L. (1971). Alfred Adler and G. Stanley Hall: Correspondence and general relationship. *Journal of the History of the Behavioral Sciences, 7,* 337–352.

Ansbacher, H. L. (1994). Alfred Adler (1870–1937). In R. J. Corsini (Ed.), *Encyclopedia of psychology* (2nd ed.) (Vol. 4, pp. 1–2). New York: John Wiley & Sons.

Ansbacher, H. L., & Ansbacher, R. R. (Eds.) (1956). *The Individual Psychology of Alfred Adler: A systematic presentation in selections from his writings.* New York: Basic Books, Inc.

Appleman, P. (Ed.) (1979). *Darwin: A Norton critical edition* (2nd ed.). New York: W.W. Norton & Company.

Archer, R. L. (Ed.) (1964). *Jean Jacques Rousseau: His educational theories selected from Émile, Julie and other writings.* Woodbury, NY: Barron's Educational Series, Inc.

Arens, K. (1985). Mach's "psychology of investigation." *Journal of the History of the Behavioral Sciences, 21,* 151–168.

Armstrong, P. (1993). An ethologist aboard HMS *Beagle*: The young Darwin's observations on animal behavior. *Journal of the History of the Behavioral Sciences, 29,* 339–344.

Arnheim, R. (1969). *Visual thinking.* Berkeley, CA: University of California Press.

Arnheim, R. (1974). *Art and visual perception.* Berkeley, CA: University of California Press.

Arnheim, R. (1986a). The trouble with wholes and parts. *New Ideas in Psychology, 4,* 281–284.

Arnheim, R. (1986b). The two faces of Gestalt psychology. *American Psychologist, 41,* 820–824.

Asch, S. E. (1946). Forming impressions of personality. *Journal of Abnormal and Social Psychology, 41,* 258–290.

Asch, S. E. (1956). Studies of independence and conformity: A minority of one against a unanimous majority. *Psychological Monographs, 70* (9, Whole No. 416).

Ash, M. G. (1992). Cultural contexts and scientific change in psychology: Kurt

Lewin in Iowa. *American Psychologist, 47,* 198–207.

Atkinson, R. C., & Shiffrin, R. M. (1968). Human memory: A proposed system and its control processes. In K. W. Spence & J. T. Spence (Eds.), *The psychology of learning and motivation: Advances in research and theory* (Vol. 2, pp. 89–195). New York: Academic Press.

Augustine (1963). *Confessions.* New York: New American Library. (Original work published 400)

Augustine (1931). *The city of God* (Book VII). New York: E. P. Dutton & Co., Inc. (Original work published 412–427)

Averill, L. A. (1982). Recollections of Clark's G. Stanley Hall. *Journal of the History of the Behavioral Sciences, 18,* 341–346.

Axline, V. M. (1947). *Play therapy: The inner dynamics of childhood.* Boston: Houghton Mifflin.

Axtell, J. L. (Ed.) (1968). *The educational writings of John Locke.* Cambridge: University Press.

Ayllon, T., & Azrin, N. H. (1968). *The token economy: A motivational system for therapy and rehabilitation.* East Norwalk, CT: Appleton-Century-Crofts.

Babkin, B. P. (1949). *Pavlov: A biography.* Chicago: The University of Chicago Press.

Bagg, R. A. (1972). How do you spell Pawloff?: A note. *Journal of the History of the Behavioral Sciences, 8,* 387–388.

Bain, A. (1859). *The emotions and the will.* London: Parker & Son.

Bakan, D. (1952). The exponential growth function in Herbart and Hull. *American Journal of Psychology, 65,* 307–308.

Bakan, D. (1966). The influence of phrenology on American psychology. *Journal of the History of the Behavioral Sciences, 2,* 200–220.

Baldwin, J. M. (1894). Psychology past and present. *Psychological Review, 1,* 363–391.

Baldwin, J. M. (1897). *Social and ethical interpretations in mental development.* New York: Macmillan.

Baldwin, J. M. (1898). On selective thinking. *Psychological Review, 5,* 1–24.

Baldwin, J. M. (1930). James Mark Baldwin. In C. Murchison (Ed.), *History of psychology in autobiography* (Vol. 1, pp. 1–30). Worcester, MA: Clark University Press.

Bandrés, J., & Llavona, R. (1992). Minds and machines in Renaissance Spain: Gómez Pereira's theory of animal behavior. *Journal of the History of the Behavioral Sciences, 28,* 158–168.

Bandura, A. (1973). *Aggression: A social learning analysis.* Englewood Cliffs, NJ: Prentice-Hall.

Bandura, A., Ross, D., & Ross, S. (1961). Transmission of aggression through imitation of aggressive models. *Journal of Abnormal and Social Psychology, 63,* 575–582.

Bandura, A., Ross, D., & Ross, S. (1963a). Imitation of film-mediated aggressive models. *Journal of Abnormal and Social Psychology, 66,* 3–11.

Bandura, A., Ross, D., & Ross, S. (1963b). A comparative test of the status envy, social power, and secondary reinforcement theories of identificatory learning. *Journal of Abnormal and Social Psychology, 67,* 527–534.

Barker, R. G. (Ed.) (1963). *The stream of behavior.* New York: Appleton-Century-Crofts.

Barker, R. G. (1989). Roger G. Barker. In G. Lindzey (Ed.), *A history of psychology in autobiography* (Vol. 8, pp. 3–35). Stanford, CA: Stanford University Press.

Barker, R. G., Dembo, T., & Lewin, K. (1943). Frustration and regression. In R. G. Barker, J. S. Kounin, & H. F. Wright (Eds.), *Child behavior and development: A course of representative studies* (pp. 441–458). New York: McGraw-Hill.

Barker, R. G., & Wright, H. F. (1951). *One boy's day.* New York: Harper & Row.

Barlow, N. (Ed.) (1958). *The autobiography of Charles Darwin, 1809–1882.* New York: W. W. Norton. (Original work published as part of *Life and letters of Charles Darwin* in 1887)

Barnes, D. B. (1988). Psychiatrists psych out the future. *Science, 242,* 1013–1014.

Bartholow, R. (1874). Experimental investigations into the functions of the human brain. *The American Journal of the Medical Sciences, 67,* 305–313.

Bartlett, F. C. (1923). *Psychology and primitive culture.* Cambridge: Cambridge University Press.

Bartlett, F. C. (1932). *Remembering: A study in experimental and social psychology.* Cambridge: Cambridge University Press.

Bartlett, F. C. (1936). Frederic Charles Bartlett. In C. Murchison (Ed.), *A history of psychology in autobiography* (Vol. 3, pp. 39–52). Worcester, MA: Clark University Press.

Baumrind, D. (1964). Some thoughts on ethics of research: After reading Milgram's "Behavioral study of obedience." *American Psychologist, 19,* 421–423.

Beach, F. A. (1950). The snark was a boojum. *American Psychologist, 5,* 115–124.

Beatty, J. (1995). *Principles of behavioral neuroscience.* Dubuque, IA: Wm. C. Brown Communications, Inc.

Beit-Hallahmi, B. (1974). Psychology of religion 1880–1930: The rise and fall of a psychological movement. *Journal of the History of the Behavioral Sciences, 10,* 84–90.

Békésy, G. von. (1960). *Experiments in hearing.* New York: McGraw-Hill.

Benjamin, L. T., Jr. (1988). *A history of psychology: Original sources and contemporary research.* New York: McGraw-Hill Book Company.

Benjamin, L. T., Jr. (1993). *A history of psychology in letters.* Dubuque, IA: Wm. C. Brown.

Benjamin, L. T., Jr., Durkin, M., Link, M., Vestal, M., & Acord, J. (1992). Wundt's American doctoral students. *American Psychologist, 47,* 123–131.

Berger, H. (1929). Über das Elektrenkephalogramm des Menschen [Concerning the electroencephalogram of humans]. *Archiv für Psychiatrie und Nervenkrankheiten, 87,* 527–543.

Berger, P., & Luckmann, T. (1966). *The social construction of reality.* Garden City, NY: Anchor Books.

Bergmann, G. (1956). The contribution of John B. Watson. *Psychological Review, 63,* 265–276.

Bergström, J. A. (1894). [Review of *Experimentelle Beiträge zur Unter-suchung des Gedächtnisses*]. *American Journal of Psychology, 6,* 299–301.

Berkeley, G. (1837). *The works of George Berkeley.* London: T. Tegg and Son.

Bernard, L. L. (1924). *Instinct: A study in social psychology.* New York: Henry Holt & Co.

Bernard, W. (1972). Spinoza's influence on the rise of scientific psychology: A neglected chapter in the history of psychology. *Journal of the History of the Behavioral Sciences, 8,* 208–215.

Binet, A. (1905). Analyse de C. E. Spearman, "The proof and measurement of association between two things" et "General intelligence objectively determined and measured" [Analysis of C. E. Spearman, "The proof and measurement of association between two things" and "General intelligence objectively determined and measured"]. *L'Année psychologique, 17,* 145–201.

Bingham, W. V. D. (1952). Walter Van Dyke Bingham. In E. G. Boring, H. S. Langfeld, H. Werner, & R. M. Yerkes (Eds.), *A history of psychology in autobiography* (Vol. 4, pp. 1–26). Worcester, MA: Clark University Press.

Birch, H. G. (1945). The relation of previous experience to insightful problem-solving. *Journal of Comparative Psychology, 38,* 367–383.

Bjork, D. W. (1983). *The compromised scientist: William James in the development of American psychology.* New York: Columbia University Press.

Bjork, D. W. (1993). *B. F. Skinner: A life.* New York: Basic Books.

Blakemore, C. (1977). *Mechanics of the mind.* New York: Cambridge University Press.

Blanshard, B., & Schneider, W. (Eds.) (1942). *In commemoration of William James.* New York: Columbia University Press.

Block, N., & Dworkin, G. (1976). *The IQ controversy.* New York: Pantheon.

Blumenthal, A. L. (1970). *Language and psychology: Historical aspects of psycholinguistics*. New York: Wiley.

Blumenthal, A. L. (1975). A reappraisal of Wilhelm Wundt. *American Psychologist, 30,* 1081–1088.

Blumenthal, A. L. (1979). The founding father we never knew. *Contemporary Psychology, 24,* 547–550.

Boakes, R. (1984). *From Darwin to behaviourism: Psychology and the minds of animals*. New York: Cambridge.

Bochenski, I. M. (1961). *A history of formal logic*. New York: Chelsea.

Boethius, A. M. S. (1981). *De consolatione philosophiae* [*The consolation of philosophy*]. Millwood, NY: Kraus Reprint. (Original work published ca. 525)

Bolles, R. C. (1993). *The story of psychology: A thematic history*. Pacific Grove, CA: Brooks/Cole Publishing Company.

Boring, E. G. (1927). Edward Bradford Titchener: 1867-1927. *American Journal of Psychology, 38,* 488–506.

Boring, E. G. (1935). Georg Elias Müller: 1850-1934. *American Journal of Psychology, 47,* 344–348.

Boring, E. G. (1950). *A history of experimental psychology* (2nd Ed.). New York: Appleton-Century-Crofts, Inc.

Boring, E. G. (1953). John Dewey: 1859-1952. *American Journal of Psychology, 67,* 145–147.

Boring, E. G. (1965). On the subjectivity of important historical dates: Leipzig, 1879. *Journal of the History of the Behavioral Sciences, 1,* 5–9.

Boring, E. G. (1966). A note on the origin of the word psychology. *Journal of the History of the Behavioral Sciences, 2,* 167.

Boring, E. G. (1967). Titchener's Experimentalists. *Journal of the History of the Behavioral Sciences, 3,* 315–325.

Boring, E. G. (1969). Titchener, meaning and behaviorism. In D. L. Krantz (Ed.), *Schools of psychology: A symposium* (pp. 21–34). New York: Appleton-Century-Crofts.

Bottome, P. (1939). *Alfred Adler: A biography*. New York: Putnam's Sons.

Bousfield, W. A. (1953). The occurrence of clustering in the recall of randomly arranged associates. *Journal of General Psychology, 49,* 229–240.

Bower, G. H., & Hilgard, E. R. (1981). *Theories of learning* (5th ed.). Englewood Cliffs, NJ: Prentice-Hall, Inc.

Bransford, J. (1979). *Human cognition*. Belmont, CA: Wadsworth.

Bremer, F. (1936). Nouvelles recherches sur le mécanisme du sommeil [New research on the mechanism of sleep]. *Comptes Rendus de la Société de Biologie, 122,* 460–464.

Brewer, C. L. (1991). Perspectives on John B. Watson. In G. A. Kimble, M. Wertheimer, & C. White (Eds.), *Portraits of pioneers in psychology* (pp. 170–186).

Hillsdale, NJ: Lawrence Erlbaum Associates, Publishers.

Bricke, J. (1974). Hume's associationist psychology. *Journal of the History of the Behavioral Sciences, 10,* 397–409.

Bridgman, P. W. (1927). *The logic of modern physics*. New York: Macmillan.

Bringmann, W. G., Balance, W. D. G., & Evans, R. B. (1975). Wilhelm Wundt 1832-1920: A brief biographical sketch. *Journal of the History of the Behavioral Sciences, 11,* 287–297.

Bringmann, W. G., & Balk, M. M. (1992). Another look at Wilhelm Wundt's publication record. *History of Psychology Newsletter, 24,* 50–66.

Bringmann, W. G., Bringmann, M. W., & Early, C. E. (1992). G. Stanley Hall and the history of psychology. *American Psychologist, 47,* 281–289.

Bringmann, W. G., Bringmann, N. J., & Ungerer, G. A. (1980). The establishment of Wundt's laboratory: An archival and documentary study. In W. G. Bringmann & R. D. Tweney (Eds.), *Wundt studies: A centennial collection* (pp. 123–159). Toronto: C. J. Hogrefe.

Bringmann, W. G., Krichev, A., & Balance, W. (1970). Goethe as behavior therapist. *Journal of the History of the Behavioral Sciences, 6,* 151–155.

Broad, W. J. (1981). Sir Isaac Newton: Mad as a hatter. *Science, 213,* 1341–1342, 1344.

Broadbent, D. E. (1958). *Perception and communication*. London: Pergamon Press.

Brock, A. (1993). Something old, something new: The 'reappraisal' of Wilhelm Wundt in textbooks. *Theory & Psychology, 3,* 235–242.

Brooks, G. P. (1976). The faculty psychology of Thomas Reid. *Journal of the History of the Behavioral Sciences, 12,* 65–77.

Brown, P. K., & Wald, G. (1964). Visual pigments in single rods and cones of the human retina. *Science, 144,* 45–52.

Brown, R. (1958). *Words and things*. Glencoe, IL: Free Press.

Brown, R. (1965). *Social psychology*. New York: Free Press.

Brown, R. (1973). *A first language: The early stages*. Cambridge, MA: Harvard University Press.

Brown, R. (1989). Roger Brown. In G. Lindzey (Ed.), *A history of psychology in autobiography* (Vol. 8, pp. 36–60). Stanford, CA: Stanford University Press.

Brown, R., & Kulik, J. (1977). Flashbulb memories. *Cognition, 5,* 73–99.

Bruce, D. (1986). Lashley's shift from bacteriology to neuropsychology, 1910–1917, and the influence of Jennings, Watson, and Franz. *Journal of the History of the Behavioral Sciences, 22,* 27–44.

Bruce, D. (1991). Integrations of Lashley. In G. A. Kimble, M. Wertheimer, & C. L. White (Eds.), *Portraits of pioneers in*

psychology (pp. 307–323). Hillsdale, NJ: Lawrence Erlbaum Associates, Publishers.

Bruner, J. S. (1962). *On knowing: Essays for the left hand*. Cambridge, MA: Belknap Press.

Bruner, J. S. (1980). Jerome S. Bruner. In G. Lindzey (Ed.), *A history of psychology in autobiography* (Vol. 7, pp. 75–151). San Francisco: Freeman.

Bruner, J. S. (1986). *Actual minds, possible worlds*. Cambridge, MA: Harvard University Press.

Bruner, J. S., Goodnow, J. J., & Austin, G. A. (1956). *A study of thinking*. New York: Wiley.

Buber, M. (1970). *I and Thou* (W. Kaufmann, Trans.). New York: Charles Scribner's Sons. (Original work published 1923)

Buber, M. (1957). Guilt and guilt feelings. *Existential Psychiatry, 20,* 114–129.

Buchanan, R. D. (1994). The development of the Minnesota Multiphasic Personality Inventory. *Journal of the History of the Behavioral Sciences, 30,* 148–161.

Buchner, E. F. (1897). A study of Kant's psychology. *Psychological Review, 1* (Monogr. Suppl. 4).

Buckley, K. W. (1982). The selling of a psychologist: John Broadus Watson and the application of behavioral techniques to advertising. *Journal of the History of the Behavioral Sciences, 18,* 207–221.

Buckley, K. W. (1989). *Mechanical man: John Broadus Watson and the beginnings of behaviorism*. New York: The Guilford Press.

Bühler, C. B. (1930). *The first year of life*. New York: Day.

Bühler, C. B. (1971). Basic theoretical concepts of humanistic psychology. *American Psychologist, 26,* 378–386.

Burghardt, G. M. (1985). Animal awareness: Current perceptions and historical perspective. *American Psychologist, 40,* 905–919.

Burnham, J. C. (1972). Thorndike's puzzle boxes. *Journal of the History of the Behavioral Sciences, 8,* 159–167.

Buytendijk, F. J. J. (1959). *Phänomenologica 2: Husserl et la pensée moderne* [*Phenomenologica 2: Husserl and modern thought*]. The Hague: Nijhoff.

Cadwallader, T. C. (1974). Charles S. Peirce (1839–1914): The first American experimental psychologist. *Journal of the History of the Behavioral Sciences, 10,* 291–298.

Calkins, M. W. (1894). Association. *Psychological Review, 1,* 476–483.

Calkins, M. W. (1906). A reconciliation between structural and functional psychology. *Psychological Review, 13,* 61–81.

Calkins, M. W. (1930). Mary Whiton Calkins. In C. Murchison (Ed.), *A history of psychology in autobiography* (Vol. 1, pp. 31–62). Worcester, MA: Clark University Press.

Candland, D. K. (1993). *Feral children and clever animals: Reflections on human nature.* New York: Oxford University Press.

Cannon, W. B. (1927). The James-Lange theory of emotions: A critical examination and an alternative. *American Journal of Psychology, 39,* 106–124.

Carlson, N. R. (1994). *Physiology of behavior* (5th ed.). Boston: Allyn and Bacon.

Carr, H. A. (1925). *Psychology: A study of mental activity.* New York: Longmans, Green.

Carr, H. A. (1936). Harvey A. Carr. In C. Murchison (Ed.), *A history of psychology in autobiography* (Vol. 3, pp. 69–82). Worcester, MA: Clark University Press.

Carr, H. A., & Watson, J. B. (1908). Orientation in the white rat. *The Journal of Comparative Neurology & Psychology, 18,* 27–44.

Carson, R. (1962). *Silent spring.* Boston: Houghton Mifflin.

Cartwright, D. (1979). Contemporary social psychology in historical perspective. *Social Psychology Quarterly, 42,* 82–93.

Cattell, J. M. (1890). Mental tests and measurements. *Mind, 15,* 373–381.

Cattell, J. M. (1928). Early psychological laboratories. *Science, 67,* 543–548.

Cattell, J. M. (1929). Psychology in America. *Science, 70,* 335–347.

Cattell, R. B. (1957). *Personality and motivation: Structure and measurement.* New York: World.

Cattell, R. B. (1963). Theory of crystallized intelligence: A critical experiment. *Journal of Educational Psychology, 54,* 1–22.

Cattell, R. B. (1973). Personality pinned down. *Psychology Today, 7,* 40–46.

Chisholm, R. (1981). Brentano's analysis of the consciousness of time. *Midwest Studies in Philosophy, 6,* 3–18.

Chomsky, N. (1957). *Syntactic structures.* The Hague: Mouton Publishers.

Chomsky, N. (1959). Review of Skinner's *Verbal behavior. Language, 35,* 26–58.

Chomsky, N. (1966). *Cartesian linguistics.* New York: Harper & Row.

Chomsky, N. (1980). *Rules and representations.* New York: Columbia University Press.

Chomsky, N., & Miller, G. (1958). Finite state languages. *Information and Control, 1,* 91–112.

Christie, R., & Geis, F. (1960). *Studies in Machiavellianism.* New York: Academic Press.

Churchland, P. (1988). *Matter and consciousness: A contemporary introduction to the philosophy of mind.* Cambridge, MA: MIT Press.

Clements, R. D. (1967). Physiological–psychological thought in Juan Luis Vives. *Journal of the History of the Behavioral Sciences, 3,* 219–235.

Coan, R. W., & Zagona, S. (1962). Contemporary ratings of psychological theorists. *The Psychological Record, 12,* 315–322.

Cohen, J. (1962). The statistical power of abnormal-social psychological research: A review. *Journal of Abnormal and Social Psychology, 65,* 145–153.

Cohen, J. (1994). The earth is round ($p < .05$). *American Psychologist, 49,* 997–1003.

Commings, S. & Linscott, R. N. (Eds.) (1954). *Man & the Universe: The Philosophers of Science.* New York: Pocket Books, Inc.

Conley, J. J. (1984). Not Galton, but Shakespeare: A note on the origin of the term "nature and nurture." *Journal of the History of the Behavioral Sciences, 20,* 184–185.

Cook, G. A. (1977). G. H. Mead's social behaviorism. *Journal of the History of the Behavioral Sciences, 13,* 307–316.

Cook, G. A. (1994). George Herbert Mead: An unpublished review of John Dewey's *Human nature and conduct. Journal of the History of the Behavioral Sciences, 30,* 374–379.

Coon, D. J. (1982). Eponymy, obscurity, Twitmyer, and Pavlov. *Journal of the History of the Behavioral Sciences, 18,* 255–262.

Copernicus, N. (1965). *De revolutionibus orbium coelestium* [*On the revolutions of the celestial spheres*]. New York: Johnson Reprint Corp. (Original work published 1543)

Copleston, F. (1950). *A history of philosophy* (Vol. 2, Part 1). Westminster, MD: The Newman Press.

Coren, S., Ward, L. M., & Enns, J. T. (1994). *Sensation and perception* (4th ed.). Fort Worth, TX: Harcourt Brace College Publishers.

Costall, A. (1993). How Lloyd Morgan's Canon backfired. *Journal of the History of the Behavioral Sciences, 29,* 113–122.

Cox, C. M. (1926). *Genetic studies of genius: Vol. 2. The early mental traits of three hundred geniuses.* Stanford, CA: Stanford University Press.

Craig, E. (1988). Introduction: *Daseinanalysis:* A quest for essentials. *Humanistic Psychologist, 16,* 1–21.

Crannell, C. W. (1970). Wolfgang Köhler. *Journal of the History of the Behavioral Sciences, 6,* 267–268.

Cravens, H. (1992). A scientific project locked in time: The Terman genetics studies of genius, 1920s–1950s. *American Psychologist, 47,* 183–189.

Crews, F. (1996). The verdict on Freud. *Psychological Science, 7,* 63–68.

Cronbach, L. J. (1949). *Essentials of psychological testing.* New York: Harper & Row.

Cronbach, L. J. (1957). The two disciplines of scientific psychology. *American Psychologist, 12,* 671–684.

Cronbach, L. J., & Meehl, P. E. (1955). Construct validity in psychological tests. *Psychological Bulletin, 52,* 281–302.

Crovitz, H. (1970). *Galton's walk.* New York: Harper & Row.

Cureton, E. T. (1950). Validity, reliability, and baloney. *Educational and Psychological Measurement, 10,* 94–96.

Danziger, K. (1979). The positivist repudiation of Wundt. *Journal of the History of the Behavioral Sciences, 15,* 205–230.

Danziger, K. (1980). The history of introspection reconsidered. *Journal of the History of the Behavioral Sciences, 16,* 241–262.

Darley, J. M., & Batson, C. D. (1973). From Jerusalem to Jericho: A study of situational and dispositional variables in helping behavior. *Journal of Personality and Social Psychology, 27,* 100–108.

Darley, J. M., & Latané, B. (1968). Bystander intervention in emergencies: Diffusion of responsibility. *Journal of Personality and Social Psychology, 8,* 377–383.

Darwin, C. (1958). *The origin of species, by means of natural selection or the preservation of favoured races in the struggle for life.* New York: New American Library. (Original work published 1859)

Darwin, C. (1979). *The expression of emotions in man and animals.* London: Julian Friedmann Publishers. (Original work published 1872)

Darwin, C. (1874). *The descent of man, and selection in relation to sex* (2nd ed.). New York: A. L. Burt, Publisher.

Darwin, F. (Ed.)(1898). *The life and letters of Charles Darwin* (Vol. 1). New York: D. Appleton and Company.

de Villiers, J. G., & de Villiers, P. A. (1978). *Language acquisition.* Cambridge, MA: Harvard University Press.

Decker, H. S. (1975). *The Interpretation of Dreams:* Early reception by the educated German public. *Journal of the History of the Behavioral Sciences, 11,* 129–141.

Deese, J. (1965). *Structure of associations in language and thought.* Baltimore: Johns Hopkins Press.

Deese, J. (1970). *Psycholinguistics.* Boston: Allyn & Bacon.

Delgado, J. M. R., Roberts, W. W., & Miller, N. E. (1954). Learning motivated by electrical stimulation of the brain. *American Journal of Physiology, 179,* 587–593.

Dennett, D. C. (1995). *Darwin's dangerous idea: Evolution and the meanings of life.* New York: Simon & Schuster.

Dennis, W. (1948). *Readings in the history of psychology.* New York: Appleton-Century-Crofts, Inc.

Descartes, R. (1956). *Discourse on method* (L. J. Lafleur, Trans.). Indianapolis: Bobbs-Merrill. (Original work published 1637)

Desmond, A., & Moore, J. (1991). *Darwin.* New York: Warner Books.

DeValois, R. L., & DeValois, K. K. (1987). *Spatial vision.* New York: Oxford University Press.

Dewey, J. (1896). The reflex arc concept in psychology. *Psychological Review, 3,* 357–370.

Dewey, J. (1910). *How we think: A restatement of the relation of reflective thinking to the educative process.* Boston: Heath.

Dewey, J. (1917). The need for social psychology. *Psychological Review, 24,* 266–277.

Dewey, J. (1922). *Human nature and conduct: An introduction to social psychology.* New York: Holt.

Dews, P. B. (1981). Pavlov and psychiatry. *Journal of the History of the Behavioral Sciences, 17,* 246–250.

Dewsbury, D. A. (1990). Early interactions between animal psychologists and animal activists and the founding of the APA Committee on Precautions in Animal Experimentation. *American Psychologist, 45,* 315–327.

Diamond, S. (1971). Gestation of the instinct concept. *Journal of the History of the Behavioral Sciences, 7,* 323–336.

Diehl, L. A. (1986). The paradox of G. Stanley Hall: Foe of coeducation and educator of women. *American Psychologist, 41,* 868–878.

Dobson, V., & Bruce, D. (1972). The German university and the development of experimental psychology. *Journal of the History of the Behavioral Sciences, 8,* 204–207.

Dollard, J. C., Doob, L. W., Miller, N. E., Mowrer, O. H., & Sears, R. R. (1939). *Frustration and aggression.* New Haven, CT: Yale University Press.

Dollard, J. C., & Miller, N. E. (1950). *Personality and psychotherapy.* New York: McGraw-Hill.

Donnelly, M. (Ed.) (1992). *Reinterpreting the legacy of William James.* Washington, DC: American Psychological Association.

Dorfman, D. D. (1978). The Cyril Burt question: New findings. *Science, 201,* 1177–1186.

Doyle, K. O. (1974). Theory and practice of ability testing in Ancient Greece. *Journal of the History of the Behavioral Sciences, 10,* 202–212.

Drayton, H., & McNeill, J. (1879). *Brain and mind* (6th ed.). New York: Fowler & Wells Co., Publishers.

Dreyfus, H. (1982). *Husserl, intentionality, and cognitive science.* Cambridge, MA: MIT Press.

Dreyfus, H. L. (1972). *What computers can't do: The limits of artificial intelligence.* New York: Harper & Row.

Duke, C., Fried, S., Pliley, W., & Walker, D. (1989). Contributions to the history of psychology: Lix. Rosalie Rayner Watson: The mother of a behaviorist's

sons. *Psychological Reports, 65,* 163–169.

Duncker, K. (1945). On problem-solving. *Psychological Monographs, 58*(5, Whole no. 270).

Dunlap, K. (1919). Are there any instincts? *Journal of Abnormal Psychology, 14,* 307–311.

Durant, W. (1939). *The life of Greece.* New York: Simon and Schuster.

Durant, W. (1944). *Caesar and Christ.* New York: Simon and Schuster.

Durant, W. (1950). *The age of faith.* New York: Simon and Schuster.

Durant, W. (1961). *The story of philosophy.* New York: Washington Square Press.

Durant, W., & Durant, A. (1963). *The age of Louis XIV.* New York: Simon and Schuster.

Durant, W., & Durant, A. (1975). *The age of Napoleon.* New York: MJF Books.

Ebbinghaus, H. (1964). *Memory: A contribution to experimental psychology.* (H. A. Ruger & C. A. Bussenius, Trans.) New York: Dover. (Original work published 1885)

Ebbinghaus, H. (1910). *Abriss der Psychologie [A summary of psychology].* Leipzig: Veit.

Eco, U. (1983). *The name of the rose* (W. Weaver, Trans.). San Diego: Harcourt Brace Jovanovich.

Edie, J. (1987). *William James and phenomenology.* Bloomington, IN: University of Indiana Press.

Edman, I. (1955). *John Dewey: His contribution to the American tradition.* New York: Bobbs-Merrill.

Eiseley, L. (1961). *Darwin's century.* Garden City, NY: Anchor.

Elkind, D. (1985). Child development research. In S. Koch & D. E. Leary (Eds.), *A century of psychology as science* (pp. 472–489). New York: McGraw-Hill.

Ellenberger, H. F. (1972). The story of "Anna O": A critical review with new data. *Journal of the History of the Behavioral Sciences, 8,* 267–279.

Ellison, H. (1983). The whimper of whipped dogs. In H. Ellison, *Deathbird stories* (pp. 2–19). New York: Bluejay Books.

Eng, E. (1978). Looking back on Kurt Lewin: From field theory to action research. *Journal of the History of the Behavioral Sciences, 14,* 228–232.

Erdelyi, M. H. (1985). *Psychoanalysis: Freud's cognitive psychology.* New York: W. H. Freeman and Company.

Erikson, E. H. (1963). *Childhood and society* (2nd ed.). New York: Norton. (Original work published 1950)

Erikson, E. H. (1962). *Young man Luther.* New York: W. W. Norton & Company, Inc.

Erikson, E. H. (1982). *The life cycle completed: A review.* New York: Norton.

Evans, R. B. (1972). E. B. Titchener and his lost system. *Journal of the History of the Behavioral Sciences, 8,* 168–180.

Evans, R. B. (1990). William James and his *Principles.* In M. G. Johnson & T. B. Henley (Eds.), *Reflections on* The Principles of Psychology (pp. 11–31). Hillsdale, NJ: Lawrence Erlbaum Associates, Publishers.

Evans, R. B. (1991). E. B. Titchener on scientific psychology and technology. In G. A. Kimble, M. Wertheimer, & C. White, (Eds.) *Portraits of pioneers in psychology* (pp. 89–103). Hillsdale, NJ: Lawrence Erlbaum Associates, Publishers.

Evans, R. B., & Koelsch, W. A. (1985). Psychoanalysis arrives in America: The 1909 Psychology Conference at Clark University. *American Psychologist, 40,* 942–948.

Exner, J. E. (1974). *The Rorschach: A comprehensive system: Vol. 1.* New York: Wiley.

Exner, J. E. (1993). *The Rorschach: A comprehensive system: Vol. 1. Basic foundations* (3rd ed.). New York: Wiley.

Eysenck, H. J. (Ed.) (1982). *A model for intelligence.* New York: Springer-Verlag.

Eysenck, H. J., & Kamin, L. J. (1981). *The intelligence controversy: H. J. Eysenck versus Leon Kamin.* New York: Wiley.

Eysenck, H. J., & Rachman, S. (1965). *The causes and cure of neurosis.* San Diego: Knapp.

Faber, D. P. (1996). Suggestion: Metaphor and meaning. *Journal of the History of the Behavioral Sciences, 32,* 16–29.

Fancher, R. E. (1977). Brentano's *Psychology from an empirical standpoint* and Freud's early metapsychology. *Journal of the History of the Behavioral Sciences, 13,* 207–227.

Fancher, R. E. (1979). A note on the origin of the term "nature and nurture." *Journal of the History of the Behavioral Sciences, 15,* 321–322.

Fancher, R. E. (1985). *The intelligence men.* New York: W. W. Norton & Company.

Fancher, R. E. (1990). *Pioneers of psychology* (2nd ed.). New York: W. W. Norton & Company.

Fechner, G. (1969). *The comparative anatomy of angels: A sketch by Dr. Mises* (H. Corbet & M. E. Marshall, Trans.). *Journal of the History of the Behavioral Sciences, 5,* 135–151. (Original work published 1825)

Fechner, G. (1966). *Elements of psychophysics* (Vol. 1) (H. E. Adler, Trans.). New York: Holt, Rinehart and Winston, Inc. (Original work published 1860)

Ferster, C. B., & Skinner, B. F. (1957). *Schedules of reinforcement.* New York: Appleton-Century-Crofts, Inc.

Festinger, L. (1957). *A theory of cognitive dissonance.* Evanston, IL: Row, Peterson.

Festinger, L., & Carlsmith, J. M. (1959). Cognitive consequences of forced compliance. *Journal of Abnormal and Social Psychology, 68,* 359–366.

Festinger, L., Riecken, H., & Schachter, S. (1956). *When prophesy fails.* Minneapolis: University of Minnesota.

Finger, S. (1988). *Brain injury and recovery: Theoretical and controversial issues.* New York: Plenum.

Fischer, K. (1887). *Descartes and his school.* London: T. Fisher Unwin.

Fletcher, R. (1991). *Science, ideology, and the media: The Cyril Burt scandal.* New Brunswick, NJ: Transaction Publishers.

Fodor, J. A. (1983). *The modularity of mind.* Cambridge, MA: MIT Press/ Bradford Books.

Fodor, J. A., & Pylyshyn, Z. W. (1981). How direct is visual perception? Some reflections of Gibson's "ecological approach." *Cognition, 9,* 139–196.

Føllesdal, D. (1974). Phenomenology. In E. Carterette & M. Friedman (Eds.), *Handbook of perception: Vol. 1* (pp. 377–386). New York: Academic Press.

Fraisse, P. (1970). French origins of the psychology of behavior: The contribution of Henri Pieron. *Journal of the History of the Behavioral Sciences, 6,* 111–119.

Frank, J. D. (1978). Kurt Lewin in retrospect—a psychiatrist's view. *Journal of the History of the Behavioral Sciences, 14,* 223–227.

Frankl, V. E. (1959). *Man's search for meaning.* Boston: Beacon Press. (Original German edition published 1946 as *Ein Psycholog erlebt das Konzentrationslager*)

Frankl, V. E. (1994). Logotherapy. In R. J. Corsini (Ed.), *Encyclopedia of psychology* (2nd ed.) (Vol. 2, p. 350). New York: Wiley.

Franz, S. I. (1902). On the function of the cerebrum: The frontal lobes in relation to the production and retention of simple sensory motor habits. *American Journal of Physiology, 8,* 1–22.

Franz, S. I. (1932). Shepherd Ivory Franz. In C. Murchison (Ed.), *History of psychology in autobiography* (Vol. 2, pp. 89–113). Worcester, MA: Clark University Press.

Freeman, F. S. (1977). The beginnings of Gestalt psychology in the United States. *Journal of the History of the Behavioral Sciences, 13,* 352–353.

Freeman, W. (1949). Transorbital leucotomy: The deep frontal cut. *Proceedings of the Royal Society of Medicine, 42,* Supplement pp. 8–12.

Freud, A. (1937). *The ego and the mechanisms of defence.* London: The Hogarth Press Ltd.

Freud, E. L. (Ed.) (1992). *Letters of Sigmund Freud.* New York: Dover Publications.

Freud, S. (1910). The origin and development of psychoanalysis. *American Journal of Psychology, 21,* 181–218.

Freud, S. (1920). *A general introduction to psychoanalysis* (J. Riviere, Trans.). New York: Washington Square Press.

Freud, S. (1921). *Group psychology and the analysis of the ego.* London: Hogarth.

Freud, S. (1963). *An autobiographical study* (J. Strachey, Trans.). New York: Norton. (Original work published 1925)

Freud, S. (1938a). The history of the psychoanalytic movement. In A. A. Brill (Ed. and Trans.), *The basic writings of Sigmund Freud* (pp. 931–977). New York: The Modern Library.

Freud, S. (1938b). *The interpretation of dreams.* In A. A. Brill (Ed. and Trans.), *The basic writings of Sigmund Freud* (pp. 183–549). New York: The Modern Library.

Freud, S. (1938c). *Psychopathology of everyday life.* In A. A. Brill (Ed. and Trans.), *The basic writings of Sigmund Freud* (pp. 35–178). New York: The Modern Library.

Freud, S., & Breuer, J. (1966). Fräulein Anna O. (Breuer). In J. Strachey (Ed. and Trans.), *Studies on hysteria* (pp. 55–82). New York: Avon Books. (Original work published 1895)

Furumoto, L. (1979). Mary Whiton Calkins (1863-1930) fourteenth president of the American Psychological Association. *Journal of the History of the Behavioral Sciences, 15,* 346–356.

Furumoto, L. (1991). From "paired associates" to a psychology of self: The intellectual odyssey of Mary Whiton Calkins. In G. A. Kimble, M. Wertheimer, & C. L. White (Eds.), *Portraits of pioneers in psychology* (pp. 57–72). Hillsdale, NJ: Lawrence Erlbaum Associates, Publishers.

Gallistel, C. R., Shizgal, P., & Yeomans, J. S. (1981). A portrait of the substrate for self-stimulation. *Psychological Review, 88,* 228–273.

Galton, F. (1971). *The narrative of an explorer in tropical South Africa.* New York: Johnson Reprint Corp. (Original work published 1853)

Galton, F. (1865). Hereditary talent and character. *Macmillan's Magazine, 12,* 157–166, 318–327.

Galton, F. (1874). *English men of science: Their nature and nurture.* London: Macmillan.

Galton, F. (1876). The history of twins, as a criterion of the relative powers of nature and nurture. *Journal of the Royal Anthropological Institute, 5,* 391–406.

Galton, F. (1892). *Hereditary genius: An inquiry into its laws and consequences* (2nd ed.). London: Watts & Co.

Garcia, J., Hankins, W. G., & Rusiniak, K. W. (1974). Behavioral regulation of the milieu internal in man and rat. *Science, 185,* 824–831.

Gardner, H. (1983). *Frames of mind: The theory of multiple intelligences.* New York: Basic Books.

Gardner, H. (1985). *The mind's new science: A history of the cognitive revolution.* New York: Basic Books.

Gardner, R. A., & Gardner, B. T. (1969). Teaching sign language to a chimpanzee. *Science, 165,* 664–672.

Garner, W. R. (1962). *Uncertainty and structure as psychological concepts.* New York: John Wiley & Sons.

Garrett, H. E. (1951). *Great experiments in psychology* (3rd ed.). New York: Appleton-Century-Crofts.

Gay, P. (1988). *Freud: A life for our time.* New York: W. W. Norton & Company.

Gazzaniga, M. S. (1967). The split brain in man. In *Progress in psychobiology: Readings from* Scientific American (pp. 369–374). San Francisco: W. H. Freeman and Company.

Gendlin, E. T. (1988). Carl Rogers (1902-1987). *American Psychologist, 43,* 127–128.

Gergen, K. J. (1994). *Toward transformation in social knowledge* (2nd ed.). New York: Springer-Verlag.

Gerow, J. R. (Ed.) (1988). *Time: Psychology 1923-1988.* Glenview, IL: Scott, Foresman and Company.

Gholson, B., & Barker, P. (1985). Kuhn, Lakatos, and Lauden. *American Psychologist, 40,* 755–769.

Gibbons, A. (1991). Déjà vu all over again: Chimp-language wars. *Science, 251,* 1561–1562.

Gibson, J. J. (Ed.) (1947). Motion picture testing and research. *Aviation Psychology Research Reports,* No. 7 (Washington, DC: U.S. Government Printing Office).

Gibson, J. J. (1966a). James J. Gibson. In E. G. Boring & G. Lindzey (Eds.), *A history of psychology in autobiography* (Vol. 5, pp. 125–143). New York: Appleton-Century-Crofts.

Gibson, J. J. (1966b). *The senses considered as perceptual systems.* Boston: Houghton Mifflin.

Gibson, J. J. (1971). The legacies of Koffka's *Principles. Journal of the History of the Behavioral Sciences, 7,* 3–9.

Gibson, J. J. (1979). *The ecological approach to visual perception.* Boston: Houghton Mifflin.

Gilbert, A. R. (1968). Franz Brentano in the perspective of existential psychology. *Journal of the History of the Behavioral Sciences, 4,* 249–253.

Gilligan, C. F. (1982). *In a different voice.* Cambridge, MA: Harvard University Press.

Gilman, S. L. (1979). Darwin sees the insane. *Journal of the History of the Behavioral Sciences, 15,* 253–262.

Giorgi, A. (1970). *Psychology as a human science.* New York: Harper & Row.

Giorgi, A. (1989). Learning and memory from the perspective of phenomenological psychology. In R. S. Valle & S. Halling (Eds.), *Existential-phenomenological perspectives in psychology* (pp. 99–112). New York: Plenum Press.

Gleitman, H. (1991). Edward Chace Tolman: A life of scientific and social purpose. In G. A. Kimble, M. Wertheimer, & C. L. White (Eds.), *Portraits of pioneers in psychology* (pp. 226–241). Hillsdale, NJ: Lawrence Erlbaum Associates, Publishers.

Goddard, H. H. (1912). *The Kallikak family: A study in the heredity of feeble-mindedness.* New York: Macmillan.

Goethe, J. W. v. (1967) *Faust: A tragedy.* New York: Modern Library. (Original work published 1808, 1832)

Goffman, E. (1963). *Stigma.* Englewood Cliffs, NJ: Prentice-Hall.

Goffman, E. (1976). *Gender advertisements.* New York: Harper & Row.

Goodenough, J., McGuire, B., & Wallace, R. A. (1993). *Perspectives on animal behavior.* New York: John Wiley & Sons, Inc.

Goodwin, C. J. (1987). In Hall's shadow: Edmund Clark Sanford (1859-1924). *Journal of the History of the Behavioral Sciences, 23,* 153–168.

Gouaux, C. (1972). Kant's view on the nature of empirical psychology. *Journal of the History of the Behavioral Sciences, 8,* 237–242.

Gould, S. J. (1981). *The mismeasure of man.* New York: W. W. Norton & Company.

Granit, R. (1947). *Sensory mechanisms of the retina.* London: Oxford University Press.

Gravitz, M. A., & Gerton, M. I. (1981). Freud and hypnosis: Report of post-rejection use. *Journal of the History of the Behavioral Sciences, 17,* 68–74.

Gray, J. A. (1979). *Ivan Pavlov.* New York: Viking Press.

Green, B. F. (1992). Exposé or smear? The Burt affair. *Psychological Science, 3,* 328–331.

Gregory, R. L. (1966). *Eye and brain: The psychology of seeing.* New York: McGraw-Hill.

Gross, C. G., Bender, D., & Rocha-Miranda, C. (1969). Visual receptive fields of neurons in inferotemporal cortex of the monkey. *Science, 166,* 1303–1306.

Grosskurth, P. (1991). *The secret ring.* Reading, MA: Addison-Wesley Publishing Company, Inc.

Guilford, J. P. (1967). *The nature of human intelligence.* New York: McGraw-Hill.

Guilford, J. P. (1985). The structure of intellect model. In B. B. Wolman (Ed.), *Handbook of intelligence* (pp. 225–266). New York: Wiley.

Guthrie, E. R. (1930). Conditioning as a principle of learning. *Psychological Review, 37,* 412–428.

Guthrie, E. R. (1934a). Reward and punishment. *Psychological Review, 41,* 450–460.

Guthrie, E. R. (1934b). Pavlov's theory of conditioning. *Psychological Review, 41,* 199–206.

Guthrie, E. R. (1938). *The psychology of human conflict: The clash of motives within the individual.* New York: Harper & Brothers, Publishers.

Guthrie, E. R. (1939). The effect of outcome on learning. *Psychological Review, 46,* 480–484.

Guthrie, E. R. (1940). Association and the law of effect. *Psychological Review, 47,* 127–148.

Guthrie, E. R. (1952). *The psychology of learning* (Rev. ed.). New York: Harper & Brothers, Publishers.

Guthrie, E. R. (1959). Association by contiguity. In S. Koch, *Psychology: A study of a science* (Vol. 2, pp. 158–195). New York: McGraw-Hill Book Company, Inc.

Guthrie, E. R. (1976). *Even the rat was white: A historical view of psychology.* New York: Harper & Row.

Guthrie, E. R., & Horton, G. P. (1946). *Cats in a puzzle box.* New York: Rinehart.

Hall, C. S. (1954). *A primer of Freudian psychology.* New York: Mentor.

Hall, G. S. (1883). The contents of children's minds. *Princeton Review, 11,* 249–272.

Hall, G. S. (1923). *Life and confessions of a psychologist.* New York: Appleton.

Hamilton, G. V. (1911). A study of trial-and-error reactions in mammals. *Journal of Animal Behavior, 1,* 33–66.

Hamilton, G. V. (1916). A study of perseverance reactions in primates and rodents. *Behavior Monographs, 3* (Serial No. 13).

Handel, S. (1989). *Listening: An introduction to the perception of auditory events.* Cambridge, MA: MIT Press.

Hannush, M. J. (1987). John B. Watson remembered: An interview with James B. Watson. *Journal of the History of the Behavioral Sciences, 23,* 137–152.

Harlow, H. F. (1951). Primate learning. In C. P. Stone (Ed.), *Comparative psychology* (pp. 183–238). Englewood Cliffs, NJ: Prentice-Hall.

Harlow, J. M. (1868). Recovery from the passage of an iron bar through the head. *Massachusetts Medical Society Publication, 2,* 329–347.

Harms, E. (1972). America's first major psychologist: Laurens Perseus Hickok. *Journal of the History of the Behavioral Sciences, 8,* 120–123.

Harré, R., & Secord, P. F. (1973). *The explanation of social behavior.* Totowa, NJ: Littlefield, Adams & Company.

Harris, B. (1979). Whatever happened to Little Albert? *American Psychologist, 34,* 151–160.

Hartley, D. (1966). *Observations on man, his frame, his duty, and his expectations.* Gainesville, FL: Scholars' Facsimiles & Reprints. (Original work published 1749)

Hartline, H. K. (1938). The response of single optic nerve fibers of the vertebrate eye to illumination of the retina. *American Journal of Physiology, 121,* 400–415.

Hastorf, A., & Cantril, H. (1954). They saw a game: A case study. *Journal of Abnormal and Social Psychology, 49,* 129–134.

Hayes, C. (1951). *The ape in our house.* New York: Harper.

Hays, R. (1962). Psychology of the scientist: III. Introduction to "passages from the 'idea books' of Clark L. Hull." *Perceptual and Motor Skills, 15,* 803–806.

Hearnshaw, L. S. (1979). *Cyril Burt, psychologist.* Ithaca, NY: Cornell University Press.

Hearst, E. (Ed.) (1979). *The first century of experimental psychology.* Hillsdale, NJ: Erlbaum.

Hebb, D. O. (1949). *The organization of behavior.* New York: Wiley.

Hebb, D. O. (1963). Introduction to Dover edition. In K. S. Lashley, *Brain mechanisms and intelligence* (pp. v–xiii). New York: Dover Publications, Inc.

Heidbreder, E. (1933). *Seven psychologies.* New York: Appleton-Century-Crofts.

Heidbreder, E. (1972). Mary Whiton Calkins: A discussion. *Journal of the History of the Behavioral Sciences, 8,* 56–68.

Heidegger, M. (1962). *Being and time* (J. Macquarrie & E. Robinson, Trans.). New York: Harper & Row. (Original work published 1927)

Heider, F. (1958). *The psychology of interpersonal relations.* New York: Wiley.

Heider, F. (1970). Gestalt theory: Early history and reminiscences. *Journal of the History of the Behavioral Sciences, 6,* 131–139.

Heider, F. (1989). Fritz Heider. In G. Lindzey (Ed.), *A history of psychology in autobiography* (Vol. 8, pp. 126–155). Stanford, CA: Stanford University Press.

Helson, H. (1933). The fundamental propositions of Gestalt psychology. *Psychological Review, 40,* 13–32.

Henle, M. (1961). *Documents of Gestalt psychology.* Berkeley, CA: University of California Press.

Henle, M. (1971). Did Titchener commit the stimulus error? The problem of meaning in structural psychology. *Journal of the History of the Behavioral Sciences, 7,* 279–282.

Henle, M. (1971). *The selected papers of Wolfgang Köhler.* New York: Liveright.

Henle, M. (1978a). One man against the Nazis: Wolfgang Köhler. *American Psychologist, 33,* 939–944.

Henle, M. (1978b). Kurt Lewin as metatheorist. *Journal of the History of the Behavioral Sciences, 14,* 233–237.

Henle, M. (1979). Phenomenology in Gestalt psychology. *Journal of Phenomenological Psychology, 10,* 1–17.

Henle, M. (1984). Robert M. Ogden and Gestalt psychology in America. *Journal of the History of the Behavioral Sciences, 20,* 9–19.

Henle, M. (1986). *1879 and all that: Essays in the theory and history of psychology.* New York: Columbia University Press.

Henle, M. (1987). Koffka's *Principles* after fifty years. *Journal of the History of the Behavioral Sciences, 23,* 14–21.

Henle, M. (1990). William James and Gestalt psychology. In M. Johnson & T. Henley (Eds.), *Reflections on* The Principles of Psychology*: William James after a century* (pp. 77–99). Hillsdale, NJ: Erlbaum.

Henle, M. (1991). Systems as reconceptualizations: The work of Edna Heidbreder. In G. A. Kimble, M. Wertheimer, & C. L. White (Eds.), *Portraits of pioneers in psychology* (pp. 292–305). Hillsdale, NJ: Lawrence Erlbaum Associates, Publishers.

Henley, T. B. (1988). Beyond Husserl. *American Psychologist, 43,* 402–403.

Henley, T. B. (1989). Meehl revisited: A look at paradigms in psychology. *Theoretical and Philosophical Psychology, 9,* 30–36.

Henley, T. B., & Thorne, B. M. (1992). Eminent psychologists or psychological eminence? *American Psychologist, 47,* 1147–1148.

Henley, T. B., Johnson, M. G., Herzog, H. A., & Herzog, Jones, E. M., (1989). Definitions of psychology. *The Psychological Record, 39,* 143–152.

Henry, L. C. (Ed.)(1955). *Best quotations for all occasions.* New York: Fawcett Premier.

Herrnstein, R. J. (1969). Behaviorism. In D. L. Krantz (Ed.), *Schools of psychology* (pp. 51–68). New York: Meredith Corp.

Herrnstein, R. J., & Murray, C. (1994). *The bell curve.* New York: The Free Press.

Heyd, T. (1989). Mill and Comte on psychology. *Journal of the History of the Behavioral Sciences, 25,* 125–138.

Hibbard, S., & Henley, T. (1994). Is psychology really 'The study of behavior'? A conceptual analysis of 'behavior' and some recommendations on the use of 'behavior' in psychology. *Theory & Psychology, 4,* 549–569.

Hilgard, E. R. (1957). Louis Madison Terman (1877–1956). *American Journal of Psychology, 70,* 472–479.

Hilgard, E. R. (1987). *Psychology in America: A historical survey.* San Diego: Harcourt Brace Jovanovich.

Hilgard, E. R. (1991). Harvey Carr and Chicago functionalism: A simulated interview. In G. A. Kimble, M. Wertheimer, & C. L. White (Eds.), *Portraits of pioneers in psychology* (pp. 120–136). Hillsdale, NJ: Lawrence Erlbaum Associates, Publishers.

Hilgard, E. R. (1993). Which psychologists prominent in the second half of this century made lasting contributions to psychological theory? *Psychological Science, 4,* 70–80.

Hilgard, E. R., Leary, D. E., & McGuire, G. R. (1991). The history of psychology: A survey and critical assessment. *Annual Review of Psychology, 42,* 79–107.

Hilgard, E. R., & Marquis, D. G. (1940). *Conditioning and learning.* New York: Appleton-Century-Crofts.

Hill, W. F. (1971). *Learning: A survey of psychological interpretations* (Rev. ed.). Scranton, PA: Chandler Publishing Co.

Hindeland, M. J. (1971). Edward Bradford Titchener: A pioneer in perception. *Journal of the History of the Behavioral Sciences, 7,* 23–28.

Hinkelman, E. A., & Aderman, M. (1968). Apparent theoretical parallels between G. Stanley Hall and Carl Jung. *Journal of the History of the Behavioral Sciences, 4,* 254–257.

Hobbes, T. (1914). *Leviathan.* London: J. M. Dent & Sons Ltd. (Original work published 1651)

Hodos, W., & Campbell, C. B. G. (1969). *Scala naturae:* Why there is no theory in comparative psychology. *Psychological Review, 76,* 337–350.

Hoffeld, D. R. (1980). Mesmer's failure: Sex, politics, personality, and the zeitgeist. *Journal of the History of the Behavioral Sciences, 16,* 377–386.

Hoffman, R. R., Bringmann, W., Bamberg, M., & Klein, R. (1987). Some historical observations on Ebbinghaus. In D. S. Gorfein & R. R. Hoffman (Eds.), *Memory and learning: The Ebbinghaus Centennial Conference* (pp. 57–75). Hillsdale, NJ: Erlbaum.

Hofstadter, D. R. (1979). *Gödel, Escher, Bach: An eternal golden braid.* New York: Basic Books.

Hohman, G. W. (1966). Some effects of spinal cord lesions on experienced emotional feelings. *Psychophysiology, 3,* 143–156.

Hollingworth, L. S. (1913). The frequency of amentia as related to sex. *Medical Record, 84,* 753–756.

Horney, K. (1939). *New ways in psychoanalysis.* New York: Norton.

Hovland, C. I. (1952). Clark Leonard Hull (1884–1952). *Psychological Review, 59,* 347–350.

Hovland, C. I., Janis, I. L., & Kelley, H. H. (1953). *Communication and persuasion.* New Haven, CT: Yale University Press.

Hovland, C. I., Lumsdaine, A. A., & Sheffield, F. D. (1949). *Experiments on mass communications.* Princeton, NJ: Princeton University Press.

Hovland, C. I., & Weiss, W. (1951). The influence of source credibility on communication effectiveness. *Public Opinion Quarterly, 15,* 635–650.

Howard, G. S. (1992). William James: Closet clinician. In M. Donnelly (Ed.), *Reinterpreting the legacy of William James* (pp. 313–322). Washington, DC: American Psychological Association.

Howes, E. P. (1929). The meaning of progress in the Woman Movement. *Annals of the American Academy of Political and Social Science, 143,* 14–20.

Hubel, D. H. (1979). The brain. In *The brain* (pp. 2–11). San Francisco: W. H. Freeman and Company.

Huguelet, T. L. (1966). Introduction. In D. Hartley, *Observations on man, his frame, his duty, and his expectations* (pp. v-xvi). Gainesville, FL: Scholars' Facsimiles & Reprints.

Hull, C. L. (1929). A functional interpretation of the conditioned reflex. *Psychological Review, 36,* 498–511.

Hull, C. L. (1930). Simple trial and error learning. *Psychological Review, 37,* 241–256.

Hull, C. L. (1937). Mind, mechanism, and adaptive behavior. *Psychological Review, 44,* 1–32.

Hull, C. L. (1943). *Principles of behavior: An introduction to behavior theory.* New York: Appleton-Century-Crofts, Inc.

Hull, C. L. (1952a). Clark L. Hull. In E. G. Boring, H. S. Langfeld, H. Werner, & R. M. Yerkes (Eds.), *A history of psychology in autobiography* (Vol. 4, pp. 143–162). Worcester, MA: Clark University Press.

Hull, C. L. (1952b). *A behavior system.* New Haven, CT: Yale University Press.

Hull, C. L. (1962). Psychology of the scientist: IV. Passages from the 'idea books' of Clark L. Hull. *Perceptual and Motor Skills, 15,* 807–882.

Hume, D. (1955). *An inquiry concerning human understanding.* Indianapolis, IN: Bobbs-Merrill. (Original work published 1748; "My own life," a brief autobiographical sketch, was originally published 1776)

Humphrey, N. (1983). *Consciousness regained.* Oxford, England: Oxford University Press.

Hunt, J. M. (1984). Orval Hobart Mowrer (1907-1982). *American Psychologist, 39,* 912–914.

Hunter, W. S. (1913). The delayed reaction in animals and children. *Behavior Monographs, 2* (No. 6).

Hurvich, L. M., & Jameson, D. (1957). An opponent-process theory of color vision. *Psychological Review, 64,* 384–404.

Hurvich, L. M., & Jameson, D. (1974). Opponent processes as a model of neural organization. *American Psychologist, 29,* 88–102.

Husserl, E. (1931). *Ideas: General introduction to pure phenomenology* (W.R.B. Gibson, Trans.). New York: MacMillan. (Original work published 1913)

Ihde, D. (1979). *Experimental phenomenology.* New York: Paragon Books.

Inhelder, B. (1989). Bärbel Inhelder. In G. Lindzey (Ed.), *A history of psychology in autobiography* (Vol. 8, pp. 209–243). Stanford, CA: Stanford University Press.

Innes, J. M. (1969). A note on the usefulness of biographical material. *Journal of the History of the Behavioral Sciences, 5,* 268.

Irvine, W. (1955). *Apes, angels, and Victorians.* Cleveland, OH: The World Publishing Co.

Jaensch, E. R. (1909). Hermann Ebbinghaus. *Zeitschrift für Psychologie, 51,* i–vii.

James, H., (Ed.) (1920). *The letters of William James.* Boston: The Atlantic Monthly Press.

James, W. (1890). *The principles of psychology* (Vols. 1–2). New York: Henry Holt.

Janet, P. (1930). Pierre Janet. In C. Murchison (Ed.), *History of psychology in autobiography* (Vol. 1, pp. 123–133). Worcester, MA: Clark University Press.

Janos, P. M., & Robinson, N. M. (1985). Psychosocial development in intellectually gifted children. In F. D. Horowitz & M. O'Brien (Eds.), *The gifted and talented: Developmental perspectives.* Washington, DC: American Psychological Association.

Jaspers, K. (1969). *Philosophy* (Vol. 1; E. B. Ashton, Trans.). Chicago: The University of Chicago Press. (Original work published 1932).

Jaynes, J. (1977). *The origins of consciousness in the breakdown of the bicameral mind.* Boston: Houghton Mifflin.

Jenkins, J. J. (1993). What counts as "behavior"? *The Journal of Mind and Behavior, 14,* 355–364.

Jennings, J. (1986). Husserl revisited: The forgotten distinction between psychology and phenomenology. *American Psychologist, 41,* 1231–1240.

Jensen, A. R. (1969). How much can we boost IQ and scholastic achievement? *Harvard Educational Review, 39,* 1–123.

Jensen, A. R. (1974). Kinship correlations reported by Sir Cyril Burt. *Behavior Genetics, 4,* 1–28.

Jensen, A. R. (1980). Précis of *Bias in Mental Testing. Behavioral and Brain Sciences, 3,* 325–372.

Jensen, A. R. (1981). *Straight talk about mental tests.* New York: The Free Press.

Jensen, A. R. (1985). The nature of the black-white difference on various psychometric tests: Spearman's hypothesis. *Behavioral and Brain Sciences, 8,* 193–264.

Johnson, M. G., & Henley, T. B. (Eds.) (1990). *Reflections on The Principles of Psychology.* Hillsdale, NJ: Lawrence Erlbaum Associates, Publishers.

Johnson, M. G., & Henley, T. B. (1992). Finding meaning in random analogies.

Metaphor and Symbolic Activity, 7, 55–75.

Johnson, R. C., McClearn, G. E., Yuen, S., Nagoshi, C. T., Ahern, F. M., & Cole, R. E. (1985). Galton's data a century later. *American Psychologist, 40,* 875–892.

Johnston, T. D. (1995). The influence of Weismann's germ-plasm theory on the distinction between learned and innate behavior. *Journal of the History of the Behavioral Sciences, 31,* 115–128.

Jones, E. (1953). *The life and work of Sigmund Freud* (Vol. 1). New York: Basic Books, Inc.

Jones, E. (1955). *The life and work of Sigmund Freud* (Vol. 2). New York: Basic Books, Inc.

Jones, E. (1957). *The life and work of Sigmund Freud* (Vol. 3). New York: Basic Books, Inc.

Jones, E. E., & Davis, K. (1965). From acts to dispositions: The attribution process in person perception. In L. Berkowitz (Ed.), *Advances in experimental psychology* (Vol. 2, pp. 219–266). New York: Academic Press.

Jones, E. E., & Nisbet, R. E. (1972). The actor and the observer: Divergent perceptions of the causes of behavior. In E. E. Jones, D. E. Kanouse, H. H. Kelley, R. E. Nisbet, S. Valins, & B. Weiner (Eds.), *Attribution: Perceiving the causes of behavior* (pp. 37–52). Morristown, NJ: General Learning Press.

Jones, M. C. (1924a). A laboratory study of fear: The case of Peter. *Pedagogical Seminary, 31,* 308-315.

Jones, M. C. (1924b). The elimination of children's fears. *Journal of Experimental Psychology, 7,* 382–390.

Jones, M. C. (1974). Albert, Peter and John B. Watson. *American Psychologist, 29,* 581–583.

Jones, W. H. S. (1923). *Hippocrates* (Vol. 2). New York: Putnam.

Joynson, R. B. (1989). *The Burt affair.* London: Routledge.

Julien, R. M. (1995). *A primer of drug action* (7th ed.). New York: W. H. Freeman and Company.

Jung, C. G. (1923). *Psychological types or the psychology of individuation* (H. G. Baynes, Trans.). New York: Harcourt, Brace. (Original work published 1921)

Jung, C. G. (1933). *Modern man in search of a soul* (W. S. Dell & C. F. Baynes, Trans.). New York: Harcourt, Brace & World, Inc.

Jung, C. G. (1939). *The integration of the personality* (S. Dell, Trans.). New York: Farrar & Rinehart, Inc.

Jung, C. G. (1961). *Memories, dreams, reflections.* New York: Pantheon Books.

Jung, C. G. (1968). *Analytical psychology: Its theory and practice (The Tavistock Lectures).* New York: Pantheon Books.

Kahlbaugh, P. E. (1993). James Mark Baldwin: A bridge between social and

cognitive theories of development. *The Journal for the Theory of Social Behavior, 23,* 79–103.

Kahneman, D., & Tversky, A. (1972). Subjective probability: A judgment of representativeness. *Cognitive Psychology, 3,* 430–454.

Kahneman, D., & Tversky, A. (1973). On the psychology of prediction. *Psychological Review, 80,* 237–251.

Kalat, J. W. (1995). *Biological psychology* (5th ed.). Pacific Grove, CA: Wadsworth.

Kamin, L. J. (1974). *The science and politics of IQ.* Potomac, MD: Erlbaum Associates.

Kandel, E. R. (1985). Cellular mechanisms of learning and the biological basis of individuality. In E. R. Kandel & J. H. Schwartz (Eds.), *Principles of neural science* (2nd ed.) (pp. 816–833). New York: Elsevier.

Kant, I. (1929). *Critique of pure reason* (N. K. Smith, Trans.). New York: St. Martin's Press. (Original work published 1787)

Kantor, J. R. (1929). *An outline of social psychology.* Chicago: Follett Publishing Company.

Kantor, J. R. (1936). *An objective psychology of grammar.* Bloomington, IN: Indiana University Publications.

Kaufman, W. (1956). *Existentialism from Dostoevsky to Sartre.* New York: World Publishing Company.

Kaufmann, W. (1974). *Nietzsche: Philosopher, psychologist, antichrist* (4th ed.). Princeton, NJ: Princeton University Press.

Keller, F. S. (1991). Burrhus Frederick Skinner (1904-1990). *Journal of the History of the Behavioral Sciences, 27,* 3–6.

Kelley, H. H. (1972). Attribution in social interaction. In E. E. Jones, D. E. Kanouse, H. H. Kelley, R. E. Nisbet, S. Valins, & B. Weiner (Eds.), *Attribution: Perceiving the causes of behavior* (pp. 151–174). Morristown, NJ: General Learning Press.

Kelly, G. A. (1955). *The psychology of personal constructs.* New York: Norton.

Kendler, H. H. (1987). *Historical foundations of modern psychology.* Chicago: The Dorsey Press.

Kent, G. H., & Rosanoff, A. J. (1910). A study of association in insanity. *American Journal of Insanity, 67,* 37–96, 317–390.

Kernberg, O. F. (1976). *Object-relations theory and clinical psychoanalysis.* New York: Aronson.

Kimble, G. A. (1991). Psychology from the standpoint of a mechanist: An appreciation of Clark L. Hull. In G. A. Kimble, M. Wertheimer, & C. L. White (Eds.), *Portraits of pioneers in psychology* (pp. 208–225). Hillsdale, NJ: Lawrence Erlbaum Associates, Publishers.

Kimble, G. A. (1994). A new formula for behaviorism. *Psychological Review, 101,* 254–258.

Kintsch, W. (1985). Reflections on Ebbinghaus. *Journal of Experimental Psychology: Learning, Memory, and Cognition, 11,* 461–463.

Kirk, G. S., Raven, J. E., & Schofield, M. (Eds.) (1983). *The Presocratic philosophers* (2nd ed.). Cambridge: Cambridge University Press.

Klein, S. B. (1996). *Learning: Principles and application* (3rd ed.). New York: McGraw-Hill, Inc.

Klopfer, W. G. (1973). The short history of projective techniques. *Journal of the History of the Behavioral Sciences, 9,* 60–65.

Knight, M. (Ed.) (1950). *William James.* Harmondsworth, England: Penguin Books.

Koch, S. (1975). Language communities, search cells, and the psychological studies. *Nebraska Symposium on Motivation, 23,* 477–560.

Koch, S. (1992). Wundt's creature at age zero—and as centenarian: Some aspects of the institutionalization of the "new psychology." In S. Koch & D. E. Leary (Eds.), *A century of psychology as science* (pp. 7–35). Washington, DC: American Psychological Association.

Koffka, K. (1922). Perception: An introduction to *Gestalttheorie. Psychological Bulletin, 19,* 531–585.

Koffka, K. (1924). *The growth of the mind* R. M. Ogden, Trans.). New York: Harcourt.

Koffka, K. (1935). *Principles of Gestalt psychology.* New York: Harcourt.

Köhler, W. (1925). *The mentality of apes.* London: Routledge and Kegan Paul. (Original work published 1917)

Köhler, W. (1947). *Gestalt psychology: An introduction to new concepts in modern psychology.* New York: Liveright. (Original work published 1929)

Köhler, W. (1966). *The place of value in a world of facts.* New York: Liveright. (Original work published 1938)

Köhler, W. (1959). Gestalt psychology today. *American Psychologist, 14,* 727–734.

Kolata, G. (1984). Puberty mystery solved. *Science, 223,* 272.

Konorski, J., & Miller, S. (1937). On two types of conditioned reflex. *Journal of General Psychology, 16,* 264–272.

Kopell, B. S. (1968). Pierre Janet's description of hypnotic sleep provoked from a distance. *Journal of the History of the Behavioral Sciences, 4,* 119–123.

Koshtoyants, K. S. (1957). Ivan Petrovich Pavlov and the significance of his works. In I. P. Pavlov, *Experimental psychology and other essays* (pp. 23–53). New York: Philosophical Library.

Kozulin, A. (1986). Vygotsky in context. In L. Vygotsky, *Thought and language* (pp. xi–lvi). Cambridge, MA: MIT Press.

Krantz, D. L., & Allen, D. (1967). The rise and fall of McDougall's instinct doctrine. *Journal of the History of the Behavioral Sciences, 3,* 326–338.

Krech, D. (1967). Introduction to the second printing. In E. C. Tolman, *Purposive behavior in animals and men* (pp. xi–xvi). New York: Appleton-Century-Crofts.

Kreshel, P. J. (1990). John B. Watson at J. Walter Thompson: The legitimation of "science" in advertising. *Journal of Advertising, 19,* 49–59.

Kuffler, S. W. (1953). Discharge patterns and functional organization of mammalian retina. *Journal of Neurophysiology, 16,* 37–68.

Kuhn, T. S. (1970). *The structure of scientific revolutions* (Rev. ed.). Chicago: University of Chicago Press.

Külpe, O. (1895). *Outlines of psychology* (E. B. Titchener, Trans.). New York: The Macmillan Co.

Kuo, Z. Y. (1921). Giving up instincts in psychology. *The Journal of Philosophy, 18,* 645–664.

Kuo, Z. Y. (1922). The nature of unsuccessful acts and their order of elimination in animal learning. *Journal of Comparative Psychology, 2,* 1–27.

Kuo, Z. Y. (1929). The net result of the anti-heredity movement in psychology. *Psychological Review, 36,* 181–199.

Kuo, Z. Y. (1930). The genesis of the cat's responses to the rat. *Journal of Comparative Psychology, 11,* 1–35.

Laing, R. D. (1979, July 20). Round the bend. *New Statesman.*

Lakoff, G. (1987). *Women, fire, and dangerous things: What categories reveal about the mind.* Chicago: University of Chicago Press.

Lakoff, G., & Johnson, M. (1980). *Metaphors we live by.* Chicago: University of Chicago Press.

Lamarck, J. B. (1914). *Zoological philosophy* (H. Elliot, Trans.). London: Macmillan. (Original work published 1809)

La Mettrie, J. O. d. (1912). *Man a machine* (M. W. Calkins, Trans.). La Salle, IL: Open Court. (Original work published 1748)

Langfeld, H. S. (1943). Jubilee of the *Psychological Review:* Fifty volumes of the *Psychological Review. Psychological Review, 50,* 143–155.

Langlois, J. H., & Roggman, L. A. (1990). Attractive faces are only average. *Psychological Science, 1,* 115–121.

LaPiere, R. T. (1934). Attitudes versus action. *Social Forces, 13,* 230–237.

Lapointe, F. H. (1970). The origin and evolution of the term "psychology." *American Psychologist, 25,* 640–646.

Lashley, K. S. (1963). *Brain mechanisms and intelligence.* New York: Dover Publications, Inc. (Original work published 1929)

Lashley, K. S. (1950). In search of the engram. In Society for Experimental Biology (Great Britain), *Physiological mechanisms in animal behaviour* (pp. 454–482). Cambridge: University Press.

Latané, B., & Darley, J. M. (1970). *The unresponsive bystander: Why doesn't he help?* New York: Appleton-Century-Crofts.

Laver, A. B. (1972). Precursors of psychology in ancient Egypt. *Journal of the History of the Behavioral Sciences, 8,* 181–195.

Leahey, T. H. (1979). Something old, something new: Attention in Wundt and modern cognitive psychology. *Journal of the History of the Behavioral Sciences, 15,* 242–252.

Leahey, T. H. (1981). The mistaken mirror: On Wundt and Titchener's psychologies. *Journal of the History of the Behavioral Sciences, 17,* 273–282.

Leahey, T. H. (1992). The mythical revolutions of American psychology. *American Psychologist, 47,* 308–318.

Leahey, T. H. (1993). A history of behavior. *Journal of Mind and Behavior, 14,* 345–354.

Leary, D. E. (1978). The philosophical development of the conception of psychology in Germany, 1780–1850. *Journal of the History of the Behavioral Sciences, 14,* 113–121.

Leary, D. E. (1980). The historical foundations of Herbart's mathematization of psychology. *Journal of the History of the Behavioral Sciences, 16,* 150–163.

Leary, D. E. (1982). Kant and modern psychology. In W. Woodward & M. Asch (Eds.), *The problematic science: Psychology in nineteenth-century thought* (pp. 19–21). New York: Praeger.

LeBon, G. (1960). *The crowd.* New York: Viking. (Original work published 1895)

Leibnitz, G. W. (1949). *New essays concerning human understanding* (A. G. Langley, Trans.). La Salle, IL: Open Court. (Original work published 1765)

Levin, G. (1975). *Sigmund Freud.* Boston: Twayne Publishers.

Lewin, K. (1931). Environmental forces in child behavior and development. In C. Murchison (Ed.), *Handbook of child psychology* (pp. 94–127). Worcester, MA: Clark University Press.

Lewin, K. (1936). *Principles of topological psychology.* New York: McGraw-Hill.

Lewin, K. (1937). Carl Stumpf. *Psychological Review, 44,* 188–194.

Lewin, K., Dembo, T., Festinger, L., & Sears, P. S. (1944). Level of aspiration. In J. Hunt (Ed.), *Personality and the behavior disorders* (Vol. 1, pp. 333–378). New York: Ronald Press.

Lewin, K., Lippitt, R., & White, R. K. (1939). Patterns of aggressive behavior in experimentally created "social climates." *Journal of Social Psychology, 10,* 271–299.

Lewin, R. (1988). Cloud over Parkinson's therapy. *Science, 240,* 390–392.

Lewis, R. W. B. (1991). *The Jameses: A family narrative.* New York: Farrar, Straus and Giroux.

Ley, R. (1990). *A whisper of espionage.* Garden City Park, NY: Avery Publishing Group, Inc.

Libbrecht, K., & Quackelbeen, J. (1995). On the early history of male hysteria and psychic trauma: Charcot's influence on Freudian thought. *Journal of the History of the Behavioral Sciences, 31,* 370–384.

Liebert, R. N., & Baron, R. A. (1972). Some immediate effects of televised violence on children's behavior. *Developmental Psychology, 6,* 469–475.

Likert, R. (1932). A technique for the measurement of attitudes. *Archives of Psychology* (No. 140).

Likert, R. (1947). Kurt Lewin: A pioneer in human relations research. *Human Relations, 1,* 131–139.

Lindenfeld, D. (1978). Oswald Külpe and the Würzburg School. *Journal of the History of the Behavioral Sciences, 14,* 132–141.

Lindsley, D. B. (1944). Electroencephalography. In J. M. Hunt (Ed.), *Personality and the behavior disorders* (Vols. 1–2). New York: Ronald Press.

Lindsley, D. B., Schreiner, L. H., Knowles, M. S., & Magoun, H. W. (1950). Behavioral and EEG changes following chronic brainstem lesions in the cat. *Electroencephalography and Clinical Neurophysiology, 2,* 483–498.

Lindzey, G., & Aronson, E. (Eds.) (1985). *The handbook of social psychology* (3rd ed., Vols. 1–2). New York: Random House.

Linschoten, J. (1968). *On the way towards a phenomenological psychology* (A. Giorgi, Trans.). Pittsburgh: Du-quesne University Press.

Lippitt, R. (1947). Kurt Lewin, 1890-1947: Adventures in the exploration of interdependence. *Sociometry, 10,* 87–97.

Locke, J. (1964). *An essay concerning human understanding.* New York: New American Library. (Original work published 1690)

Locke, J. (1964). *Some thoughts concerning education* (F. W. Garforth, Ed.). Woodbury, NY: Barron's Educational Series. (Original work published 1693)

Loewi, O. (1960). An autobiographical sketch. *Perspectives in Biology and Medicine, 4,* 3–25.

Loftus, E. F. (1979). *Eyewitness testimony.* Cambridge, MA: Harvard University Press.

Loftus, E. F., & Palmer, J. C. (1974). Reconstruction of automobile destruction: An example of the interaction between language and memory. *Journal of Verbal Learning and Verbal Behavior, 13,* 585–589.

Logue, A. W. (1985). Conditioned food aversion learning in humans. In N. S. Braveman & P. Bronstein (Eds.), *Experimental assessment and clinical applications of conditioned food aversions* (pp. 316–329). New York: Annals of the New York Academy of Sciences.

Loomis, L. R. (Ed.) (1942). *Plato: Five great dialogues.* Roslyn, NY: Walter J. Black, Inc.

Loomis, L. R. (Ed.) (1943). *Aristotle: On man in the universe.* Roslyn, NY: Walter J. Black, Inc.

Lorenz, K. (1966). *On aggression* (M. K. Wilson, Trans.). New York: Harcourt, Brace & World, Inc. (Original work published 1963)

Lovejoy, A. O. (1936). *The great chain of being.* Cambridge, MA: Harvard University Press.

Lovie, A. D., & Lovie, P. (1993). Charles Spearman, Cyril Burt, and the origins of factor analysis. *Journal of the History of the Behavioral Sciences, 29,* 308–321.

Luria, A. R. (1932). *The nature of human conflict* (W. H. Gantt, Trans.). New York: Liveright.

Luria, A. R. (1968). *The mind of a mnemonist* (L. Solotaroff, Trans.). New York: Basic Books.

Maccoby, E. E. (1989). Eleanor E. Maccoby. In G. Lindzey (Ed.), *A history of psychology in autobiography* (Vol. 8, pp. 290–335). Stanford, CA: Stanford University Press.

Maccoby, E. E., & Jacklin, C. N. (1974). *The psychology of sex differences.* Stanford, CA: Stanford University Press.

MacCorquodale, K., & Meehl, P. E. (1948). On a distinction between hypothetical constructs and intervening variables. *Psychological Review, 55,* 95–107.

Mach, E. (1914). *Analysis of sensations.* La Salle, IL: Open Court. (Original work published 1886)

Machiavelli, N. (1891). *Il principe* [*The prince*]. Oxford: The Clarendon Press. (Original work published 1532)

Mackenzie, B. D. (1972). Behaviourism and positivism. *Journal of the History of the Behavioral Sciences, 8,* 222–231.

MacLennan, B. (1990). *Word and flux.* Unpublished manuscript.

MacNamara, J. (1993). Cognitive psychology and rejection of Brentano. *Journal for the Theory of Social Behaviour, 23,* 117–137.

Madrazo, I., Drucker-Colín, R., Díaz, V., Martínez-Mata, J., Torres, C., & Becerril, J. J. (1987). Open microsurgical autograft of adrenal medulla to the right caudate nucleus in two patients with intractable Parkinson's disease. *The New England Journal of Medicine, 316,* 831–834.

Magner, L. N. (1992). *A history of medicine.* New York: Marcel Dekker, Inc.

Magoun, H. W. (1981). John B. Watson and the study of human sexual behavior. *The Journal of Sex Research, 17,* 368–378.

Maher, W. B., & Maher, B. A. (1985). Psychopathology: I. From ancient times to the eighteenth century. In G. A. Kimble & K. Schlesinger (Eds.), *Topics in the history of psychology* (Vol. 2). Hillsdale, NJ: Erlbaum.

Maimonides, M. (1963). *The guide of the perplexed.* Chicago: University of Chicago Press. (Original work published 1190)

Malone, J. C. (1991). *Theories of learning: A historical approach.* Belmont, CA: Wadsworth Publishing Co.

Maniou-Vakali, M. (1974). Some Aristotelian views on learning and memory. *Journal of the History of the Behavioral Sciences, 10,* 47–55.

Maratsos, M. (1983). Some current issues in the study of the acquisition of grammar. In J. H. Flavell & E. M. Markman (Eds.), *Cognitive development* (pp. 706–788). New York: Wiley.

Marshall, M. E. (1969). Gustav Fechner, Dr. Mises, and The Comparative Anatomy of Angels. *Journal of the History of the Behavioral Sciences, 5,* 39–58.

Marx, J. L. (1975). Opiate receptors: Implications and applications. *Science, 189,* 708–710.

Marx, M. H., & Cronan-Hillix, W. A. (1987). *Systems and theories in psychology* (4th ed.). New York: McGraw-Hill Book Company.

Maslow, A. H. (1936). The role of dominance in the social and sexual behavior of infra-human primates: 1. Observations at Vilas Park Zoo. *Journal of Genetic Psychology, 48,* 261–277.

Maslow, A. H. (1966). *The psychology of science: A reconnaissance.* New York: Harper & Row.

Masson, J. M. (1984). *The assault on truth: Freud's suppression of the seduction theory.* New York: Farrar, Straus, and Giroux.

Matarazzo, J. D. (1979). *Wechsler's measurement and appraisal of adult intelligence* (5th ed.). New York: Oxford University Press.

Matarazzo, J. D. (1992). Psychological testing and assessment in the 21st century. *American Psychologist, 47,* 1007–1018.

Matlin, M. W. (1989). *Cognition* (2nd ed.). Fort Worth, TX: Holt, Rinehart and Winston, Inc.

May, R. (1950). *The meaning of anxiety.* New York: Ronald Press.

May, R. (Ed.) (1961). *Existential psychology.* New York: Random House.

Mayo, E. (1933). *The human problems of an industrial civilization.* New York: Macmillan.

Mayrhauser, R. T. von. (1989). Making intelligence functional: Walter Dill Scott and applied psychological testing in World War I. *Journal of the History of the Behavioral Sciences, 25,* 60–72.

Mazlish, B. (1975). *James and John Stuart Mill*. New York: Basic Books.

McClearn, G. E. (1991). A trans-time visit with Francis Galton. In G. A. Kimble, M. Wertheimer, & C. White (Eds.), *Portraits of pioneers in psychology* (pp. 1–11). Hillsdale, NJ: Lawrence Erlbaum Associates, Publishers.

McClelland, D. C. (1961). *The achieving society*. New York: Van Nostrand Company.

McClelland, D. C., Atkinson, J. W., Clark, R. A., & Lowell, E. L. (1953). *The achievement motive*. New York: Appleton-Century-Crofts.

McConnell, J. V., & Philipchalk, R. P. (1992). *Understanding human behavior* (7th ed.). Fort Worth, TX: Harcourt Brace Jovanovich College Publishers.

McCulloch, W., & Pitts, W. (1943). A logical calculus of the ideas immanent in nervous activity. *Bulletin of Mathematical Biophysics, 5*, 115–133.

McDougall, W. (1908). *An introduction to social psychology*. London: Methuen.

McDougall, W. (1921). The use and abuse of instinct in social psychology. *The Journal of Abnormal and Social Psychology, 16*, 285–333.

McGeoch, J. A. (1933). The formal criteria of a systematic psychology. *Psychological Review, 40*, 1–12.

McKinney, F. (1978). Functionalism at Chicago—Memories of a graduate student: 1929–1931. *Journal of the History of the Behavioral Sciences, 14*, 142–148.

McLeod, R. (1969). *William James: Unfinished business*. Washington, DC: American Psychological Association.

McNemar, Q. (1964). Lost: Our intelligence. Why? *American Psychologist, 19*, 871–882.

McNemar, Q. (1980). Quinn McNemar. In G. Lindzey (Ed.), *A history of psychology in autobiography* (Vol. 7, pp. 304–333). San Francisco: W. H. Freeman and Company.

McWhinnie, H. J. (1985). Carl Jung and Heinz Werner and implications for foundational studies in art education and art therapy. *Arts in Psychotherapy, 12*, 95–99.

Mead, G. H. (1934). *Mind, self and society from the standpoint of a social behaviorist* (C. W. Morris, Ed.). Chicago: University of Chicago Press.

Meehl, P. E. (1967). Theory-testing in psychology and physics: A methodological paradox. *Philosophy of Science, 34*, 103–115.

Meehl, P. E. (1978). Theoretical risks and tabular asterisks: Sir Karl, Sir Ronald, and the slow progress of soft psychology. *Journal of Consulting and Clinical Psychology, 46*, 806–834.

Meehl, P. E. (1989). Paul E. Meehl. In G. Lindzey (Ed.), *A history of psychology in autobiography* (Vol. 8, pp. 336–389). Stanford, CA: Stanford University Press.

Meehl, P. E. (1992). Factors and taxa, traits and types, differences of degree and differences in kind. *Journal of Personality, 60*, 117–174.

Melzack, R. (1973). *The puzzle of pain*. New York: Basic Books, Inc.

Mendelson, E. (Ed.) (1976). *W. H. Auden: Collected poems*. New York: Random House.

Milgram, S. (1974). *Obedience to authority*. New York: Harper.

Milgram, S. (1992). *The individual in a social world* (2nd ed.). New York: McGraw-Hill.

Mill, J. (1967). *Analysis of the phenomena of the human mind* (2nd ed.). New York: Augustus M. Kelley, Publishers. (Original work published 1869)

Mill, J. S. (1973). *A system of logic ratiocinative and inductive, being a connected view of the principles of evidence and the methods of scientific investigation*. London: Routledge & Kegan Paul. (Original work published 1843)

Mill, J. S. (1969). *Autobiography*. Boston: Houghton Mifflin. (Original work published 1873)

Miller, E. F. (1971). Hume's contribution to behavioral science. *Journal of the History of the Behavioral Sciences, 7*, 154–168.

Miller, G. A. (1951). *Language and communication*. New York: McGraw-Hill.

Miller, G. A. (1956). The magical number seven plus or minus two: Some limits on our capacity for processing information. *Psychological Review, 63*, 81–97.

Miller, G. A. (1965). Some preliminaries to psycholinguistics. *American Psychologist, 20*, 15–20.

Miller, G. A. (1989). George Miller. In G. Lindzey (Ed.), *A history of psychology in autobiography* (Vol. 8, pp. 390–418). Stanford, CA: Stanford University Press.

Miller, G. A., & Johnson-Laird, P. N. (1976). *Language and perception*. Cambridge, MA: Harvard University Press.

Miller, G., Galanter, E., & Pribram, K. (1960). *Plans and the structure of behavior*. New York: Adams-Bannister-Cox.

Miller, N. E. (1948). Studies of fear as an acquirable drive: 1. Fear as motivation and fear reduction as reinforcement in the learning of new responses. *Journal of Experimental Psychology, 38*, 89–101.

Miller, N. E. (1958). Central stimulation and other new approaches to motivation and reward. *American Psychologist, 13*, 100–108.

Miller, N. E. (1969). Learning of visceral and glandular responses. *Science, 163*, 434–445.

Miller, N. E., & Dollard, J. (1941). *Social learning and imitation*. New Haven, CT: Yale University Press.

Miller, N. E., & Dworkin, B. R. (1974). Visceral learning: Recent difficulties with curarized rats and significant problems for human research. In P. A. Obrist, A. H. Black, J. Brener, & L. V. Dicara (Eds.), *Cardiovascular physiology: Current issues in response mechanisms, biofeedback, and methodology* (pp. 312–331). Chicago: Aldine.

Mills, E. S. (1974). George Trumbull Ladd: The great textbook writer. *Journal of the History of the Behavioral Sciences, 10*, 299–303.

Mills, J. A. (1987). Thomas Brown on the philosophy and psychology of perception. *Journal of the History of the Behavioral Sciences, 23*, 37–49.

Mills, J. A. (1988). The genesis of Hull's *Principles of behavior*. *Journal of the History of the Behavioral Sciences, 24*, 392–401.

Mills, W. (1899). The nature of animal intelligence and the methods of investigating it. *Psychological Review, 6*, 262–274.

Milner, P. M. (1970). *Physiological psychology*. New York: Holt, Rinehart and Winston, Inc.

Minsky, M. (1985). *The society of mind*. New York: Simon & Schuster.

Mischel, T. (1966). "Emotion" and "Motivation" in the development of English psychology: D. Hartley, James Mill, A. Bain. *Journal of the History of the Behavioral Sciences, 2*, 123–144.

Misiak, H., & Sexton, V. (1966). *History of psychology*. London: Grune & Stratton.

Moede, W. (1920). Einzel und gruppenarbeit [Individual and group work]. *Praktische Psychologie, 2*, 71–78, 108–115.

Moniz, E. (1936). *Tentatives opératories dans le traitement de certaines psychoses* [Tentative surgical methods in the treatment of certain psychoses]. Paris: Masson.

Moniz, E. (1956). How I succeeded in performing the prefrontal leukotomy. In A. Sackler, M. Sackler, R. Sackler, & F. Marti-Ibanez (Eds.), *The great psychodynamic therapies in psychiatry* (pp. 131–137). New York: Paul Hoeber Medical Division, Harper & Row.

Montague, H., & Hollingworth, L. S. (1914). The comparative variability of the sexes at birth. *American Journal of Sociology, 20*, 335–370.

Moody, E. A. (1967). Medieval logic. In P. Edwards (Ed.), *The encyclopedia of philosophy* (Vol. 4, pp. 528-534). New York: The Free Press.

Moore, B. R., & Stuttard, S. (1979). Dr. Guthrie and *Felis domesticus* or: Tripping over the cat. *Science, 205*, 1031–1033.

Moorehead, A. (1969). *Darwin and the Beagle*. New York: Harper & Row.

Morgan, C. L. (1894). *An introduction to comparative psychology*. London: Scott.

Morgan, C. L. (1932). C. Lloyd Morgan. In C. Murchison (Ed.), *A history of psychology in autobiography* (Vol. 2; pp. 237–264). Worcester, MA: Clark University Press.

Morgan, C. T. (1943). *Physiological psychology.* New York: McGraw-Hill.

Moruzzi, G., & Magoun, H. W. (1949). Brain stem reticular formation and activation of the EEG. *Electroencephalography and Clinical Neurophysiology, 1,* 455–473.

Mowrer, O. H. (1947). On the dual nature of learning—a re-interpretation of "conditioning" and "problem-solving." *Harvard Educational Review, 17,* 102–148.

Mowrer, O. H. (1960). *Learning theory and behavior.* New York: Wiley.

Münsterberg, H. (1908). *On the witness stand.* New York: Clark Boardman Co.

Murphy, G., & Murphy, L. B. (1931). *Experimental social psychology.* New York: Harper.

Murphy, K. R., & Davidshofer, C. O. (1988). *Psychological testing: Principles and applications.* Englewood Cliffs, NJ: Prentice Hall.

Murphy, L. B. (1937). *Social behavior of young children: An exploratory study of some roots of sympathy.* New York: Columbia University Press.

Murray, H. A. (1938). *Explorations in personality.* New York: Oxford University Press.

Murray, H. A. (1956). Morton Prince. *Journal of Abnormal Psychology, 52,* 291–295.

Murray, H. A. (1967). Henry A. Murray. In E. G. Boring & G. Lindzey (Eds.), *A history of psychology in autobiography* (Vol. 5, pp. 283–310). New York: Appleton-Century-Crofts.

Myers, G. E. (1986). *William James: His life and thought.* New Haven, CT: Yale University Press.

Myers, I. B., & McCaulley, M. H. (1985). *Manual: A guide to the development and use of the Myers-Briggs Type Indicator.* Palo Alto, CA: Consulting Psychologists Press.

Myers, R. E., & Sperry, R. W. (1953). Interocular transfer of a visual form discrimination habit in cats after section of the optic chiasma and corpus callosum. *American Association of Anatomists: Abstracts of Papers from Platform,* p. 351.

Nance, R. D. (1970). G. Stanley Hall and John B. Watson as child psychologists. *Journal of the History of the Behavioral Sciences, 6,* 303–316.

Neisser, U. (1967). *Cognitive psychology.* New York: Appleton.

Neisser, U. (1976). *Cognition and reality.* San Francisco: Freeman.

Neisser, U. (1981). John Dean's memory: A case study. *Cognition, 9,* 1–22.

Neisser, U. (1982). *Memory observed.* San Francisco: Freeman.

Neisser, U. (1987). *Concepts and conceptual development.* New York: Cambridge University Press.

Neisser, U. (1991). A case of misplaced nostalgia. *American Psychologist, 46,* 34–36.

Neisser, U., & Harsch, N. (1993). Phantom flashbulbs: False recollections of hearing the news about Challenger. In E. Winograd & U. Neisser (Eds.), *Affect and accuracy in recall: Studies of "flashbulb" memories* (pp. 9–31). New York: Cambridge.

Neuburger, M. (1981). *The historical development of experimental brain and spinal cord physiology before Flourens* (E. Clarke, Trans.). Baltimore, MD: The Johns Hopkins University Press. (Original work published 1897)

Neugebauer, R. (1978). Treatment of the mentally ill in medieval and early modern England: A reappraisal. *Journal of the History of the Behavioral Sciences, 14,* 158–169.

Newcomb, T. M. (1943). *Personality and social change.* New York: Dryden.

Newcomb, T. M. (1974). Theodore M. Newcomb. In G. Lindzey (Ed.), *A history of psychology in autobiography* (Vol. 6, pp. 367–391). Englewood Cliffs, NJ: Prentice-Hall.

Newell, A., & Simon, H. A. (1972). *Human problem solving.* Englewood Cliffs, NJ: Prentice-Hall.

Newton, I. (1972). *Philosophiae naturalis principia mathematica* (3rd ed.) [*Mathematical principles of natural philosophy*]. Cambridge, MA: Harvard University Press. (Original work published 1726)

Nietzsche, F. (1966). *Beyond good and evil* (W. Kaufmann, Trans.). New York: Vintage Books. (Original work published 1886)

Nietzsche, F. (1967). *On the genealogy of morals* (W. Kaufmann, Trans.). New York: Vintage Books. (Original work published 1887)

Noel, P. S., & Carlson, E. T. (1973). The faculty psychology of Benjamin Rush. *Journal of the History of the Behavioral Sciences, 9,* 369–377.

Nordentoft, K. (1972). *Kierkegaard's psychology* (B. Kirmmse, Trans.). Pittsburgh: Duquesne University Press.

Norman, D. A. (1988). *The psychology of everyday things.* New York: Basic Books.

O'Donnell, J. M. (1985). *The origins of behaviorism: American psychology, 1870-1920.* New York: New York University Press.

Ogden, C. K., & Richards, I. A. (1923). *The meaning of meaning.* New York: Harcourt Brace Jovanovich.

Ogden, R. M. (1951). Oswald Külpe and the Würzburg school. *American Journal of Psychology, 64,* 4–19.

Olds, J., & Milner, P. (1954). Positive reinforcement produced by electrical stimulation of septal area and other regions of rat brain. *Journal of Comparative and Physiological Psychology, 47,* 419–427.

O'Neil, W. M., & Landauer, A. A. (1966). The phi-phenomenon: Turning point or rallying point. *Journal of the History of the Behavioral Sciences, 2,* 335–340.

Orgler, H. (1963). *Alfred Adler: The man and his work.* New York: Mentor Books.

Osgood, C. E., Suci, G. J., & Tannenbaum, P. H. (1957). *The measurement of meaning.* Urbana, IL: University of Illinois Press.

Palermo, D. (1971). Is a scientific revolution taking place in psychology? *Science Studies, 1,* 135–155.

Parham, T. A., & Helms, J. E. (1985). Attitudes of racial identity and self-esteem of Black students: An exploratory investigation. *Journal of College Student Personnel, 26,* 143–147.

Pauly, P. J. (1981). The Loeb-Jennings debate and the science of animal behavior. *Journal of the History of the Behavioral Sciences, 17,* 504–515.

Pavlov, I. P. (1960). *Conditioned reflexes: An investigation of the physiological activity of the cerebral cortex.* New York: Dover Publications, Inc. (Original work published 1927)

Pavlov, I. P. (1928). *Lectures on conditioned reflexes.* New York: International Publishers.

Pavlov, I. P. (1932). The reply of a physiologist to psychologists. *Psychological Review, 39,* 91–127.

Pavlov, I. P. (1957). Ivan Petrovich Pavlov: Autobiography. In I. P. Pavlov, *Experimental psychology and other essays* (pp. 57–62). New York: Philosophical Library.

Pearson, K. (1914–1930). *The life, letters and labours of Francis Galton* (Vols. 1–3). Cambridge, England: Cambridge University Press.

Peirce, C. S. (1878). How to make ideas clear. *Popular Science Monthly, 12,* 286–302.

Penfield, W. (1952). Memory mechanisms. *Archives of Neurology and Psychiatry, 67,* 178–198.

Penfield, W. (1958). Centrencephalic integrating system. *Brain, 81,* 231–234.

Perry, R. B. (1918). Docility and purposiveness. *Psychological Review, 25,* 1–20.

Perry, R. B. (1935). *The thought and character of William James* (Vols. 1–2). Boston: Little, Brown.

Perry, R. B. (1935). *The thought and character of William James: Briefer version.* New York: George Braziller, Publisher.

Petryszak, N. G. (1981). Tabula rasa—its origins and implications. *Journal of the History of the Behavioral Sciences, 17,* 15–27.

Pettijohn, T. F. (1992). *Psychology: A concise introduction* (3rd ed.). Guilford, CT: Dushkin.

Pfungst, O. (1965). *Clever Hans (The horse of Mr. von Osten)*. New York: Holt, Rinehart and Winston, Inc. (Original work published 1911)

Piaget, J. (1952). Jean Piaget. In E. G. Boring, H. S. Langfeld, H. Werner, & R. M. Yerkes (Eds.), *A history of psychology in autobiography* (Vol. 4, pp. 237–256). Worcester, MA: Clark University Press.

Piaget, J., & Inhelder, B. (1941). *Le développement des quantités chez l'enfant* [*The child's construction of quantities*]. Paris: Delachaux & Niestlé.

Piaget, J., & Inhelder, B. (1951). *La genèse de l'idée de hasard chez l'enfant* [*The origin of the idea of chance in children*]. Paris: Presses Universitaires de France.

Pinel, J. P. J. (1990). *Biopsychology*. Boston: Allyn and Bacon.

Pinker, S. (1984). *Language learnability and language development*. Cambridge, MA: Harvard University Press.

Pollio, H. R. (1982). *Behavior and existence*. Monterey, CA: Brooks/Cole Publishing Company.

Pollio, H. R. (1990). The stream of consciousness since James. In M. G. Johnson & T. B. Henley (Eds.), *Reflections on* The Principles of Psychology (pp. 271–294). Hillsdale, NJ: Lawrence Erlbaum Associates, Publishers.

Pollio, H. R., Henley, T. B., & Thompson, C. (in press). *The phenomenology of everyday life*. New York: Cambridge University Press.

Popplestone, J. A., & McPherson, M. W. (1994). *An illustrated history of American psychology*. Madison, WI: Brown & Benchmark.

Posner, M. I. (1978). *Chronometric explorations of mind*. Hillsdale, NJ: Erlbaum.

Post, D. (1980). Floyd H. Allport and the launching of modern social psychology. *Journal of the History of the Behavioral Sciences, 16,* 369–376.

Pribram, K. H. (1960). Theory in physiological psychology. *Annual Review of Psychology, 11,* 1–40.

Pribram, K. H. (1971). *Languages of the brain: Experimental paradoxes and principles in neuropsychology*. Englewood Cliffs, NJ: Prentice-Hall.

Pruette, L. (1926). *G. Stanley Hall: A biography of a mind*. Freeport, NY: Books for Libraries Press.

Rachels, J. (1986). Darwin's moral lapse. *National Forum, 66,* 22–24.

Rancurello, A. C. (1968). *A study of Franz Brentano: His psychological standpoint and his significance in the history of psychology*. New York: Academic Press.

Raphelson, A. C. (1973). The pre-Chicago association of the early functionalists. *Journal of the History of the Behavioral Sciences, 9,* 115–122.

Restle, F. (1957). Discrimination of cues in mazes: A resolution of the "place-vs.-response" question. *Psychological Review, 64,* 217–228.

Richards, R. J. (1983). Why Darwin delayed, or interesting problems and models in the history of science. *Journal of the History of the Behavioral Sciences, 19,* 45–53.

Rilling, M. (1996). The mystery of the vanished citations: James V. McConnell's forgotten 1960s quest for Planarian learning, a biochemical engram, and celebrity. *American Psychologist, 51,* 589–598.

Risse, G. (1976). Vocational guidance during the Depression: Phrenology versus applied psychology. *Journal of the History of the Behavioral Sciences, 12,* 130–140.

Roazen, P. (1975). *Freud and his followers*. New York: Alfred A. Knopf.

Robinson, D. N. (1989). Thomas Reid and the Aberdeen years: Common sense at the Wise Club. *Journal of the History of the Behavioral Sciences, 25,* 154–162.

Robinson, D. N. (1993). Is there a Jamesian tradition in psychology? *American Psychologist, 48,* 638–643.

Rock, I. (1957). The role of repetition in associative learning. *American Journal of Psychology, 70,* 186–193.

Rogers, C. R. (1951). *Client-centered therapy*. Boston: Houghton Mifflin.

Rogers, C. R. (1961). *On becoming a person*. Boston: Houghton Mifflin.

Rogers, C. R. (1967). Carl R. Rogers. In E. G. Boring & G. Lindzey (Eds.), *A history of psychology in autobiography* (Vol. 5, pp. 341–383). New York: Appleton-Century-Crofts.

Romanes, E. (1896). *The life and letters of George John Romanes*. London: Longmans, Green, and Co.

Romanes, G. J. (1895). *Animal intelligence*. New York: D. Appleton and Company. (Original work published 1881)

Rosch, E. H. (1978). Principles of categorization. In E. H. Rosch & B. Lloyd (Eds.), *Cognition and categorization* (pp. 27–48). Hillsdale, NJ: Erlbaum.

Rosch, E., & Mervis, C. (1975). Family resemblances: Studies in the internal structure of categories. *Cognitive Psychology, 7,* 573–605.

Rosenzweig, S. (1987). The final tribute of E. G. Boring to G. T. Fechner: Concerning the date October 22, 1850. *American Psychologist, 42,* 787–790.

Ross, B. (1981). In memoriam: Robert I. Watson, Sr., 1909–1980. *Journal of the History of the Behavioral Sciences, 17,* 1–2.

Ross, B. (1991). William James: Spoiled child of American psychology. In G. A. Kimble, M. Wertheimer, & C. White (Eds.), *Portraits of pioneers in psychology* (pp. 13–25). Hillsdale, NJ: Lawrence Erlbaum Associates, Publishers.

Ross, D. (1972). *G. Stanley Hall: The psychologist as prophet*. Chicago: The University of Chicago Press.

Ross, E. A. (1908). *Social psychology: An outline and a sourcebook*. New York: Macmillan.

Rotter, J. B. (1966). Generalized expectancies for internal versus external control of reinforcement. *Psychological Monographs, 80* (Whole No. 609).

Routtenberg, A. (1978). The reward system of the brain. *Scientific American, 239,* 154–164.

Rowe, F. B., & Murray, F. S. (1979). A note on the Titchener influence on the first psychology laboratory in the South. *Journal of the History of the Behavioral Sciences, 15,* 282–284.

Ruja, H. (1956). Productive psychologists. *American Psychologist, 11,* 148–149.

Rumelhart, D. E., McClelland, J. L., & the PDP Research Group (1986). *Parallel distributed processing: Explorations in the microstructure of cognition* (Vols. 1–2). Cambridge, MA: Cambridge University Press.

Runes, D. D. (1959). *Pictorial history of philosophy*. New York: Bramhall House.

Rushton, J. P., & Ankney, C. D. (1996). Brain size and cognitive ability: Correlations with age, sex, social class, and race. *Psychonomic Bulletin & Review, 3,* 21–36.

Russell, B. (1925). *Philosophy*. New York: Norton.

Russell, B. (1937). *A critical exposition of the philosophy of Leibniz*. London: George Allen & Unwin Ltd.

Rychlak, J. F. (1991). *Artificial intelligence and human reason: A teleological critique*. New York: Columbia University Press.

Ryle, G. (1949). *The concept of mind*. London: Hutchinson.

Sabini, J. (1986). Stanley Milgram (1933-1984). *American Psychologist, 41,* 1378–1379.

Sahakian, W. S. (Ed.) (1968). *History of psychology: A source book in systematic psychology*. Itasca, IL: F. E. Peacock Publishers, Inc.

Samelson, F. (1977). World War I intelligence testing and the development of psychology. *Journal of the History of the Behavioral Sciences, 13,* 274–282.

Sanford, E. C. (1924). Granville Stanley Hall 1846-1924. *American Journal of Psychology, 35,* 313–321.

Sarton, G. (1954). *Galen of Pergamon*. Lawrence, KS: University of Kansas Press.

Sartre, J.-P. (1938). *La nausée* [*Nausea*]. Paris: Gallimard.

Sartre, J.-P (1943). *L'être et le niant* [*Being and nothingness*]. Paris: Gallimard.

Sartre, J.-P. (1947). *Huis clos* [*No exit*]. Paris: Gallimard.

Savage-Rumbaugh, E. S., Murphy, J., Sevcik, R. A., Brakke, K. E., Williams, S. L., & Rumbaugh, D. M. (1993). Language comprehension in ape and child. *Monographs of the Society for Research in Child Development, 58* (3–4, Serial No. 233).

Scarborough, E. (1991). Continuity for women: Ethel Puffer's struggle. In G. A. Kimble, M. Wertheimer, & C. L. White (Eds.), *Portraits of pioneers in psychology* (pp. 104–119). Hillsdale, NJ: Lawrence Erlbaum Associates, Publishers.

Scarborough, E., & Furumoto, L. (1987). *Untold lives: The first generation of American women psychologists.* New York: Columbia University Press.

Scarr, S. (1985). Constructing psychology: Making facts and fables for our times. *American Psychologist, 40,* 499–512.

Scarr, S., & Weinberg, R. A. (1978). The influence of family background on intellectual attainment. *American Sociological Review, 43,* 674–692.

Schachter, S. (1989). Stanley Schachter. In G. Lindzey (Ed.), *A history of psychology in autobiography* (Vol. 8, pp. 448–470). Stanford, CA: Stanford University Press.

Schachter, S., & Singer, J. E. (1962). Cognitive, social, and physiological determinants of emotional state. *Psychological Review, 69,* 379–399.

Schaefer, C. S., & Anastasi, A. (1968). A biographical inventory for identifying creativity in adolescent boys. *Journal of Applied Psychology, 52,* 42–48.

Schank, R. C. (1972). Conceptual dependency: A theory of natural language understanding. *Cognitive Psychology, 3,* 552–631.

Schank, R. C. (1982). *Dynamic memory: A theory of reminding and learning in computers and people.* Cambridge, MA: Cambridge University Press.

Schank, R., & Abelson, R. (1977). *Scripts, plans, goals, and understanding: An inquiry into human knowledge structures.* Hillsdale, NJ: Lawrence Erlbaum Associates.

Schlosberg, H. (1954). Three dimensions of emotion. *Psychological Review, 61,* 81–88.

Schlossman, S. L. (1973). G. Stanley Hall and the boys' club: Conservative applications of recapitulation theory. *Journal of the History of the Behavioral Sciences, 9,* 140–147.

Schmidt, J. (1985). *Maurice Merleau-Ponty: Between phenomenology and structuralism.* New York: St. Martin's Press.

Schneck, J. M. (1965). A reevaluation of Freud's abandonment of hypnosis. *Journal of the History of the Behavioral Sciences, 1,* 191–195.

Schneider, A. M., & Tarshis, B. (1986). *An introduction to physiological psychology* (3rd ed.). New York: Random House.

Schneider, W. H. (1992). After Binet: French intelligence testing, 1900-1950. *Journal of the History of the Behavioral Sciences, 28,* 111–132.

Schopenhauer, A. (1969). *The world as will and representation* (Vols. 1–2) (E. F. J. Payne, Trans.). New York: Dover Publications, Inc. (Original work published 1844)

Schusdek, A. (1966). Freud's "seduction theory": A reconstruction. *Journal of the History of the Behavioral Sciences, 2,* 159–166.

Schwartz, S. (1986). *Classic studies in psychology.* Palo Alto, CA: Mayfield.

Sdorow, L. (1990). *Psychology.* Dubuque, IA: Wm. C. Brown Publishers.

Seaman, J. D. (1984). On phi-phenomena. *Journal of the History of the Behavioral Sciences, 20,* 3–8.

Searle, J. (1983). *Intentionality.* New York: Cambridge.

Sears, R. R. (1992). Psychoanalysis and behavior theory: 1907–1965. In S. Koch & D. E. Leary (Eds.), *A century of psychology as science* (pp. 208–220). Washington, DC: American Psychological Association.

Sears, R. R., Lapidus, D., & Cozzens, C. (1978). Content analysis of Mark Twain's novels and letters as a biographical method. *Poetics, 7,* 155–175.

Sears, R. R., Maccoby, E. E., & Levin, H. (1957). *Patterns of child rearing.* Stanford, CA: Stanford University Press.

Sedlmeier, P., & Gigerenzer, G. (1989). Do studies of statistical power have an effect on the power of studies? *Psychological Bulletin, 105,* 309–316.

Selfridge, O., & Neisser, U. (1960). Pattern recognition by machine. *Scientific American, 203,* 60–68.

Seligman, M. E. P. (1970). On the generality of the laws of learning. *Psychological Review, 77,* 406–418.

Seward, J. P. (1942). An experimental study of Guthrie's theory of reinforcement. *Journal of Experimental Psychology, 30,* 247–256.

Seward, J. P. (1954). Hull's system of behavior: An evaluation. *Psychological Review, 61,* 145–159.

Shakow, D. (1930). Hermann Ebbinghaus. *American Journal of Psychology, 17,* 504–518.

Shakow, D. (1969). Psychoanalysis. In D. L. Krantz (Ed.), *Schools of psychology: A symposium* (pp. 87–122). New York: Appleton-Century-Crofts.

Shannon, C. E. (1938). A symbolic analysis of relay and switching circuits. *Transactions of the American Institute of Electrical Engineers, 57,* 1–11.

Sheffield, F. D. (1959). Edwin Ray Guthrie: 1886-1959. *American Journal of Psychology, 72,* 642–650.

Sheldon, H. D. (1946). Clark University, 1897-1900. *The Journal of Social Psychology, 24,* 227–247.

Sherif, M. (1936). *The psychology of social norms.* New York: Harper & Row.

Sherif, M., & Cantril, H. (1947). *The psychology of ego involvements: Social attitudes and identifications.* New York: Wiley.

Sherif, M., Harvey, O. I., White, B., Hood, W., & Sherif, C. (1961). *Intergroup cooperation and competition: The Robbers Cave experiment.* Norman, OK: University Book Exchange.

Sherif, M., & Hovland, C. I. (1961). *Social judgement.* New Haven, CT: Yale University Press.

Sherrington, C. S. (1906). *The integrative action of the nervous system.* New Haven, CT: Yale University Press.

Shields, S. A. (1975). Ms. Pilgrim's progress: The contributions of Leta Stetter Hollingworth to the psychology of women. *American Psychologist, 30,* 852–857.

Shields, S. A. (1991). Leta Stetter Hollingworth: "Literature of opinion" and the study of individual differences. In G. A. Kimble, M. Wertheimer, & C. L. White (Eds.), *Portraits of pioneers in psychology* (pp. 243–256). Hillsdale, NJ: Lawrence Erlbaum Associates, Publishers.

Shook, J. R. (1995). Wilhelm Wundt's contribution to John Dewey's functional psychology. *Journal of the History of the Behavioral Sciences, 31,* 347–369.

Silverman, J. (1964). The problem of attention in research and theory in schizophrenia. *Psychological Review, 71,* 352–379.

Simon, H. A. (1992). What is an "explanation" of behavior? *Psychological Science, 3,* 150–161.

Skinner, B. F. (1935). Two types of conditioned reflex and a pseudo type. *Journal of General Psychology, 12,* 66–77.

Skinner, B. F. (1937). Two types of conditioned reflex: A reply to Konorski and Miller. *Journal of General Psychology, 16,* 272–279.

Skinner, B. F. (1938). *The behavior of organisms: An experimental analysis.* Englewood Cliffs, NJ: Prentice-Hall.

Skinner, B. F. (1948). *Walden two.* New York: The Macmillan Co.

Skinner, B. F. (1950). Are theories of learning necessary? *Psychological Review, 57,* 193–216.

Skinner, B. F. (1957). *Verbal behavior.* New York: Appleton-Century-Crofts.

Skinner, B. F. (1964). Behaviorism at fifty. In T. W. Wann (Ed.), *Behaviorism and phenomenology* (pp. 79–97). Chicago: University of Chicago Press.

Skinner, B. F. (1967). B. F. Skinner. In E. G. Boring & G. Lindzey, *A history of psychology in autobiography* (Vol. 5, pp. 385–413). New York: Appleton-Century-Crofts.

Skinner, B. F. (1971). *Beyond freedom and dignity.* New York: Alfred A. Knopf.

Skinner, B. F. (1974). *About behaviorism.* New York: Vintage Books.

Skinner, B. F. (1976). *Particulars of my life.* New York: Alfred A. Knopf.

Skinner, B. F. (1979). *The shaping of a behaviorist.* New York: Alfred A. Knopf.

Skinner, B. F. (1981). Pavlov's influence on psychology in America. *Journal of the History of the Behavioral Sciences, 17,* 242–245.

Skinner, B. F. (1983). *A matter of consequences.* New York: Alfred A. Knopf.

Slamecka, N. J. (1985). Ebbinghaus: Some associations. *Journal of Experimental Psychology: Learning, Memory, and Cognition, 11,* 414–435.

Slobin, D. (Ed.) (1985). *The crosslinguistic study of language acquisition* (Vols. 1–2). Hillsdale, NJ: Erlbaum.

Small, W. S. (1900). An experimental study of the mental processes of the rat. *American Journal of Psychology, 11,* 133–165.

Small, W. S. (1901). Experimental study of the mental processes of the rat. II. *American Journal of Psychology, 12,* 206–239.

Smith, C. U. M. (1987). David Hartley's Newtonian neuropsychology. *Journal of the History of the Behavioral Sciences, 23,* 123–136.

Smith, L. D. (1990). Metaphors of knowledge and behavior in the behaviorist tradition. In D. E. Leary (Ed.), *Metaphors in the history of psychology* (pp. 239–266). Cambridge, England: Cambridge University Press.

Smith, L. D. (1992). On prediction and control: B. F. Skinner and the technological ideal of science. *American Psychologist, 47,* 216–223.

Snyderman, M., & Herrnstein, R. (1983). Intelligence tests and the Immigration Act of 1924. *American Psychologist, 38,* 986–995.

Sokal, M. M. (1971). The unpublished autobiography of James McKeen Cattell. *American Psychologist, 26,* 626–635.

Sokal, M. M. (1990). G. Stanley Hall and the institutional character of psychology at Clark 1889–1920. *Journal of the History of the Behavioral Sciences, 26,* 114–124.

Sokal, M. M. (1994). James McKeen Cattell, the New York Academy of Sciences, and the American Psychological Association, 1891–1902. In H. E. Adler & R. W. Rieber (Eds.), *Aspects of the history of psychology in America: 1892–1992* (pp. 13–35). New York: Annals of the New York Academy of Sciences (Vol. 727).

Sommer, R. (1991). James V. McConnell (1925–1990). *American Psychologist, 46,* 650.

Southern, R. W. (1986). *Robert Grosseteste.* Oxford: Oxford University Press.

Spanos, N. P. (1978). Witchcraft in histories of psychiatry: A critical analysis and an alternative conceptualization. *Psychological Bulletin, 85,* 417–439.

Spearman, C. (1930). C. Spearman. In C. Murchison (Ed.), *A history of psychology in autobiography* (Vol. 1, pp. 299–333). Worcester, MA: Clark University Press.

Spearman, C. E. (1904). General intelligence objectively determined and measured. *American Journal of Psychology, 15,* 201–293.

Spence, J. T., & Helmreich, R. L. (1978). *Masculinity & femininity: Their psychological dimensions, correlates, & antecedents.* Austin, TX: University of Texas Press.

Spence, J. T., Helmreich, R., & Stapp, J. (1974). The Personal Attributes Questionnaire: A measure of sex-role stereotypes and masculinity-femininity. *JSAS Catalog of Selected Documents in Psychology, 4,* 127.

Spence, K. W. (1937). The differential response in animals to stimuli varying within a single dimension. *Psychological Review, 44,* 430–444.

Spence, K. W. (1952). Clark Leonard Hull: 1884-1952. *American Journal of Psychology, 65,* 639–646.

Spence, K. W. (1960). *Behavior theory and learning: Selected papers.* Englewood Cliffs, NJ: Prentice-Hall, Inc.

Sperry, R. (1982). Some effects of disconnecting the cerebral hemispheres. *Science, 217,* 1223–1226.

Sperry, R. (1994). A powerful paradigm made stronger. *Psychological Science Agenda, 7,* 10–13.

Sperry, R. W. (1964). The great cerebral commissure. *Scientific American, 210,* 42–52.

Spiegelberg, H. (1960). *The phenomenological movement: A historical introduction.* The Hague: Nijhoff.

Spillmann, J., & Spillmann, L. (1993). The rise and fall of Hugo Münsterberg. *Journal of the History of the Behavioral Sciences, 29,* 322–338.

Spinoza, B. (1883). *Ethic demonstrated in geometrical order.* London: Trubner. (Original work published 1677)

Stafford-Clark, D. (1965). *What Freud really said.* New York: Schocken Books.

Sternberg, R. J. (1986). *Intelligence applied.* New York: Harcourt Brace Jovanovich.

Sternberg, R. J. (1995). For whom the bell curve tolls: A review of *The Bell Curve. Psychological Science, 6,* 257–261.

Stevens, R. (1974). *James and Husserl: The foundation of meaning.* The Hague: Nijhoff.

Stevens, S. S. (1935). The operational basis of psychology. *American Journal of Psychology, 47,* 323–330.

Stevens, S. S. (1956). The direct estimation of sensory magnitudes—loudness. *American Journal of Psychology, 69,* 1–25.

Stevens, S. S. (1961). To honor Fechner and repeal his law. *Science, 133,* 80–86.

Storr, A. (1973). *C. G. Jung.* New York: The Viking Press.

Stratton, G. M. (1917). *Theophrastus and the Greek physiological psychology before Aristotle.* New York: Macmillan.

Strunk, O., Jr. (1972). The self-psychology of Mary Whiton Calkins. *Journal of the History of the Behavioral Sciences, 8,* 196–203.

Stumpf, C. (1895). Hermann von Helmholtz and the new psychology. *Psychological Review, 2,* 1–12.

Stumpf, C. (1930). Carl Stumpf. In C. Murchison (Ed.), *A history of psychology in autobiography* (Vol. 1, pp. 389–441). Worcester, MA: Clark University Press.

Stumpf, S. E. (1989). *Philosophy: History and problems* (4th ed.). New York: McGraw-Hill.

Sullivan, H. S. (1970). *The psychiatric interview.* New York: W. W. Norton & Company, Inc. (Original work published 1954)

Svaetichin, G., & MacNichol, E. F., Jr. (1958). Retinal mechanisms for achromatic vision. *Annals of the New York Academy of Sciences, 74,* 385–404.

Swets, J. A. (1961). Is there a sensory threshold? *Science, 134,* 168–177.

Szasz, T. (1974). *The myth of mental illness* (Rev. ed.). New York: Harper & Row. (Original work published 1961)

Tamarkin, L., Baird, C. J., Almeida, O. F. X. (1985). Melatonin: A coordinating signal for mammalian reproduction? *Science, 227,* 714–720.

Tarde, G. (1903). *The laws of imitation* (E. C. Parsons, Trans.). New York: Henry Holt, Inc. (Original work published 1890)

Taylor, E. (1990). New light on the origin of William James's experimental psychology. In M. G. Johnson & T. B. Henley (Eds.), *Reflections on* The Principles of Psychology (pp. 33–61). Hillsdale, NJ: Lawrence Erlbaum Associates, Publishers.

Taylor, E. (1992). William James's contributions to experimental psychology. *History of Psychology Newsletter, 24,* 3–6.

Teigen, K. H. (1984). A note on the origin of the term "nature and nurture": Not Shakespeare and Galton, but Mulcaster. *Journal of the History of the Behavioral Sciences, 20,* 363–364.

Terman, L. M. (1916). *The measurement of intelligence.* Boston: Houghton Mifflin.

Terman, L. M. (1932). Lewis M. Terman. In C. Murchison (Ed.), *A history of psychology in autobiography* (Vol. 2, pp. 297–331). Worcester, MA: Clark University Press.

Terman, L. M. (1938). *Psychological factors in marital happiness.* New York: McGraw-Hill.

Terrace, H. S. (1979). *Nim: A chimpanzee who learned sign language.* New York: Knopf.

Thompson, C., Locander, W., & Pollio, H. (1989). Putting the consumer back into consumer research. *Journal of Consumer Research, 16,* 133–146.

Thompson, R. (1978). *A behavioral atlas of the rat brain*. New York: Oxford University Press.

Thompson, R. (1993). Centrencephalic theory, the General Learning System, and subcortical dementia. In F. M. Crinella & J. Yu (Eds.), *Brain mechanisms: Papers in memory of Robert Thompson* (pp. 197–223). New York: The New York Academy of Sciences.

Thompson, R., & McConnell, J. (1955). Classical conditioning in the Planarian, *Dugesia dorotocephala*. *Journal of Comparative and Physiological Psychology, 48*, 54–68.

Thompson, R., Crinella, F. M., & Yu, J. (1990). *Brain mechanisms in problem solving and intelligence: A lesion survey of the rat brain*. New York: Plenum Press.

Thompson, R. F. (1986). The neurobiology of learning and memory. *Science, 233,* 941–947.

Thorndike, E. L. (1899). A reply to "The nature of animal intelligence and the methods of investigating it." *Psychological Review, 6,* 412–420.

Thorndike, E. L. (1911). *Animal intelligence*. New York: The Macmillan Co.

Thorndike, E. L. (1921). Measurement in education. *Teachers College Record, 22,* 371–379.

Thorndike, E. L. (1932). *The fundamentals of learning*. New York: Teachers College.

Thorndike, E. L. (1936). Edward Lee Thorndike. In C. Murchison (Ed.), *A history of psychology in autobiography* (Vol. 3, pp. 263–270). Worcester, MA: Clark University Press.

Thorndike, E. L. (1949). *Selected writings from a connectionist's psychology*. New York: Appleton-Century-Crofts.

Thorndike, E. L., Lay, W., & Dean, P. (1909). The relation of accuracy in sensory discrimination to general intelligence. *American Journal of Psychology, 20,* 364–369.

Thorndike, E. L., & Woodworth, R. S. (1901). The influence of improvement in one mental function upon the efficiency of other functions. *Psychological Review, 8,* 247–261.

Thorndike, R. L. (1991). Edward L. Thorndike: A professional and personal appreciation. In G. A. Kimble, M. Wertheimer, & C. L. White (Eds.), *Portraits of pioneers in psychology* (pp. 138–151). Hillsdale, NJ: Erlbaum.

Thorne, B. M. (1995). Dr. Sheldon's penchant for measurement. *The Numismatist, 108,* 591–594, 619.

Thorne, B. M. (1995). Robert Thompson: Karl Lashley's heir? *Journal of the History of the Behavioral Sciences, 31,* 129–136.

Thorne, B. M. (1996). Edward Bradford Titchener: Numismatist. *The Numismatist, 109,* 833–836, 876–878.

Thorne, B. M. (in press). Can an ape learn a language? In W. G. Bringmann, H. E. Lueck, R. Miller, & C. E. Early (Eds.), *A pictorial history of psychology*. Carol Stream, IL: Quintessence Publishing Co., Inc.

Thorne, B. M., Rager, K., & Topping, J. S. (1976). DRL performance in rats following damage to the septal area, olfactory bulbs, or olfactory tubercle. *Physiological Psychology, 4,* 493–497.

Thurstone, L. L. (1928). Attitudes can be measured. *American Journal of Sociology, 19,* 441–453.

Thurstone, L. L. (1938). *Primary mental abilities*. Chicago: University of Chicago Press.

Thurstone, L. L. (1952). L. L. Thurstone. In E. G. Boring, H. S. Langfeld, H. Werner, & R. M. Yerkes (Eds.), *A history of psychology in autobiography* (Vol. 4, pp. 295–321). Worcester, MA: Clark University Press.

Thurstone, L. L., & Chave, E. J. (1929). *The measurement of attitude*. Chicago: University of Chicago Press.

Tibbetts, P. (1973). Historical note on Descartes' psychophysical dualism. *Journal of the History of the Behavioral Sciences, 9,* 162–165.

Timberlake, W., & Lucas, G. A. (1989). Behavior systems and learning: From misbehavior to general principles. In S. B. Klein & R. R. Mowrer (Eds.), *Contemporary learning theory: Instrumental conditioning theory and the impact of biological constraints on learning* (pp. 237–275). Hillsdale, NJ: Erlbaum.

Tinbergen, N. (1969). *The study of instinct*. Oxford: Oxford University Press. (Original work published 1951)

Tinklepaugh, O. L. (1928). An experimental study of representative factors in monkeys. *Journal of Comparative Psychology, 8,* 197–236.

Titchener, E. B. (1898). The postulates of a structural psychology. *Philosophical Review, 7,* 449–465.

Titchener, E. B. (1901, 1905). *Experimental psychology: A manual of laboratory practice* (4 vols.). New York: Macmillan.

Titchener, E. B. (1910). *A text-book of psychology*. New York: Macmillan.

Titchener, E. B. (1912). The schema of introspection. *American Journal of Psychology, 23,* 485–508.

Titchener, E. B. (1915). *A beginner's psychology*. New York: Macmillan.

Titchener, E. B. (1921). Brentano and Wundt: Empirical and experimental psychology. *American Journal of Psychology, 32,* 108–120.

Titchener, E. B. (1921). Wilhelm Wundt. *American Journal of Psychology, 32,* 161–178.

Tolman, E. C. (1967). *Purposive behavior in animals and men*. New York: Meredith Publishing Co. (Original work published 1932)

Tolman, E. C. (1938). The determiners of behavior at a choice point. *Psychological Review, 45,* 1–41.

Tolman, E. C. (1951). Prediction of vicarious trial and error by means of the schematic sowbug. In E. C. Tolman (Ed.), *Collected papers in psychology* (pp. 190–206). Berkeley, CA: University of California Press. (Original work published 1939)

Tolman, E. C. (1948). Cognitive maps in rats and men. *Psychological Review, 55,* 189–208.

Tolman, E. C. (1948). Kurt Lewin, 1890-1947. *Psychological Review, 55,* 1–4.

Tolman, E. C. (1952). Edward Chace Tolman. In E. G. Boring, H. S. Langfeld, H. Werner, & R. M. Yerkes (Eds.), *A history of psychology in autobiography* (Vol. 4, pp. 323–339). Worcester, MA: Clark University Press.

Tolman, E. C. (1959). Principles of purposive behavior. In S. Koch (Ed.), *Psychology: A study of a science* (Vol. 2, pp. 92–157). New York: McGraw-Hill Book Company, Inc.

Tolman, E. C., Ritchie, B. F., & Kalish, D. (1946). Studies in spatial learning. II. Place learning versus response learning. *Journal of Experimental Psychology, 36,* 221–229.

Traxel, W. (1985). Hermann Ebbinghaus: In memoriam. *History of Psychology Newsletter, 17,* 37–41.

Triplet, R. G. (1982). The relationship of Clark L. Hull's hypnosis research to his later learning theory: The continuity of his life's work. *Journal of the History of the Behavioral Sciences, 18,* 22–31.

Triplett, N. (1898). The dynamogenic factors in pacemaking and competition. *American Journal of Psychology, 9,* 507–533.

Trudeau, M. (1990). An introspective discussion with B. F. Skinner. *Science Agenda, 3,* 10–12.

Tucker, W. H. (1994). Fact and fiction in the discovery of Sir Cyril Burt's flaws. *Journal of the History of the Behavioral Sciences, 30,* 335–347.

Tulving, E. (1972). Episodic and semantic memory. In E. Tulving & W. Donaldson (Eds.), *Organization of memory* (pp. 381–403). New York: Academic Press.

Tulving, E. (1985). How many memory systems are there? *American Psychologist, 40,* 385–398.

Turing, A. M. (1950). Computing machinery and the mind. *Mind, 59,* 433–460.

Tversky, A., & Kahneman, D. (1973). Availability: A heuristic for judging frequency and probability. *Cognitive Psychology, 5,* 207–232.

Unger, R. (1989). *Representations: Social constructions of gender*. Amityville, NY: Baywood.

Unger, R., & Crawford, M. (1992). *Women and gender: A feminist psychology*. Philadelphia: Temple University Press.

Valenstein, E. S. (1973). *Brain control.* New York: Wiley.

Valenstein, E. S. (Ed.) (1980). *The psychosurgery debate.* San Francisco: Freeman.

Valle, R. S., & King, M. (1978). *Existential-phenomenological alternatives for psychology.* New York: Oxford.

van Leeuwen, C. (1989). PDP and Gestalt. An integration? *Psychological Research, 50,* 199–201.

Vande Kemp, H. (1992). G. Stanley Hall and the Clark School of Religious Psychology. *American Psychologist, 47,* 290–298.

Vernon, P. A. (Ed.) (1987). *Speed of information-processing and intelligence.* Norwood, NJ: Ablex.

Viner, R. (1996). Melanie Klein and Anna Freud: The discourse of the early dispute. *Journal of the History of the Behavioral Sciences, 32,* 4–15.

Viteles, M. S. (1974). Industrial psychology: Reminiscences of an academic moonlighter. In T. S. Krawiec (Ed.), *The psychologists* (Vol. 2, pp. 441–500). New York: Oxford University Press.

Vives, J. L. (1963). *De anima et vita* [*Of soul and life*]. Torino, Italy: Bottega d'Erasmo. (Original work published 1538)

Vygotsky, L. S. (1986). *Thought and language* (A. Kozulin, Trans.). Cambridge, MA: MIT Press. (Original work published 1934)

Vygotsky, L. S. (1978). *Mind in society: The development of higher psychological processes.* Cambridge, MA: Harvard University Press.

Walsh, A. A. (1971). George Combe: A portrait of a heretofore generally unknown behaviorist. *Journal of the History of the Behavioral Sciences, 7,* 269–278.

Wann, T. W. (Ed.) (1964). *Behaviorism and phenomenology: Contrasting bases for modern psychology.* Chicago: The University of Chicago Press.

Ware, M. E. (1993, March). *Science and fiction in psychology: Hall and Hollingworth.* Paper presented at the meeting of the Southeastern Psychological Association, Atlanta, GA.

Warren, H. C. (1919). *Human psychology.* Boston: Houghton Mifflin.

Warren, H. C. (1930). Howard C. Warren. In C. Murchison (Ed.), *A history of psychology in autobiography,* (Vol. 1, pp. 443–469).Worcester, MA: Clark University Press.

Washburn, M. F. (1932). Margaret Floy Washburn: Some recollections. In C. Murchison (Ed.), *A history of psychology in autobiography* (Vol. 2, pp. 333–358). Worcester, MA: Clark University Press.

Wassermann, I. (1958). Letter to the editor. *American Journal of Psychotherapy, 12,* 623–627.

Watkins, L. R., & Mayer, D. J. (1982). Organization of endogenous opiate and nonopiate pain control systems. *Science, 216,* 1185–1192.

Watkins, W. H. (1989, March). *Psychological prewarfare: A review of Hugo Münsterberg's dealings in international politics, 1897–1916.* Paper presented at the meeting of the Southeastern Psychological Association, Washington.

Watson, J. B. (1907). Kinaesthetic and organic sensations: Their role in the reactions of the white rat to the maze. *Psychological Monographs, 8*(33).

Watson, J. B. (1913). Psychology as the behaviorist views it. *Psychological Review, 20,* 158–177.

Watson, J. B. (1916). The place of the conditioned-reflex in psychology. *Psychological Review, 23,* 89–116.

Watson, J. B. (1919a). *Psychology from the standpoint of a behaviorist.* Philadelphia: Lippincott.

Watson, J. B. (1919b). A schematic outline of the emotions. *Psychological Review, 26,* 165–196.

Watson, J. B. (1970). *Behaviorism.* New York: Norton. (Original work published 1924)

Watson, J. B. (1972). *Psychological care of infant and child.* New York: Arno Press. (Original work published 1928)

Watson, J. B. (1936). John Broadus Watson. In C. Murchison (Ed.), *A history of psychology in autobiography* (Vol. 3, pp. 271–281). Worcester, MA: Clark University Press.

Watson, J. B., & Morgan, J. J. B. (1917). Emotional reactions and psychological experimentation. *American Journal of Psychology, 28,* 163–174.

Watson, J. B., & Rayner, R. (1920). Conditioned emotional reactions. *Journal of Experimental Psychology, 3,* 1–14.

Watson, R. I. (1971). A prescriptive analysis of Descartes' psychological views. *Journal of the History of the Behavioral Sciences, 7,* 223–247.

Watson, R. I. (1979). *Basic writings in the history of psychology.* New York: Oxford University Press.

Webb, M. E. (1988). A new history of Hartley's *Observations on Man. Journal of the History of the Behavioral Sciences, 24,* 202–211.

Wells, F. L. (1944). James McKeen Cattell: 1860–1944. *American Journal of Psychology, 57,* 270–275.

Wells, G. L., & Loftus, E. F. (Eds.) (1984). *Eyewitness testimony: Psychological perspectives.* Cambridge, MA: Cambridge University Press.

Wertheimer, Max (1968). Experimental studies on the seeing of motion. In W. S. Sahakian (Ed.), *History of psychology: A source book in systematic psychology* (pp. 418–422). Itasca, IL: Peacock. (Original work published 1912)

Wertheimer, Max (1945). *Productive thinking.* New York: Harper.

Wertheimer, Michael (1980). Gestalt theory of learning. In G. M. Gazda & R. J. Corsini (Eds.), *Theories of learning: A comparative approach* (pp. 208–251). Itasca, IL: Peacock.

Wertheimer, Michael (1987). *A brief history of psychology* (3rd ed.). New York: Holt, Rinehart and Winston.

Wertheimer, Michael (1992, March). *Max Wertheimer in America.* Paper presented at the meeting of the Southeastern Psychological Association convention, Knoxville, TN.

Wever, E. G. (1949). *A theory of hearing.* New York: Wiley.

Wever, E. G., & Bray, C. W. (1930). The nature of acoustic responses: The relation between sound frequency and frequency of impulses in the auditory nerve. *Journal of Experimental Psychology, 13,* 373–387.

White, S. H. (1990). Child study at Clark University: 1894-1904. *Journal of the History of the Behavioral Sciences, 26,* 131–150.

Wilkening, H. E. (1973). *The psychology almanac.* Monterey, CA: Brooks/Cole.

Wilshire, B. (1968). *William James and phenomenology.* Bloomington, IN: Indiana University Press.

Wilson, D. S., Near, D., & Miller, R. R. (1996). Machiavellianism: A synthesis of the evolutionary and psychological literatures. *Psychological Bulletin, 119,* 285–299.

Wilson, F. (1991). Mill and Comte on the method of introspection. *Journal of the History of the Behavioral Sciences, 27,* 107–129.

Wilson, M. D. (Ed.) (1969). *The essential Descartes.* New York: Mentor Books.

Windholz, G. (1983). Pavlov's position toward American behaviorism. *Journal of the History of the Behavioral Sciences, 19,* 394–407.

Windholz, G. (1990). Pavlov and Pavlovians in the laboratory. *Journal of the History of the Behavioral Sciences, 26,* 64–74.

Winograd, T. (1972). *Understanding natural language.* New York: Academic Press.

Wippel, J. F., & Wolter, A. B. (1969). *Medieval philosophy.* New York: Free Press.

Witmer, L. (1907). Clinical psychology. *The Psychological Clinic, 1,* 1–9.

Wittgenstein, L. (1953). *Philosophical investigations* (G. E. M. Anscombe, Trans.). New York: Macmillan.

Wolman, B. B. (1968). *The unconscious mind: The meaning of Freudian psychology.* Englewood Cliffs, NJ: Prentice-Hall, Inc.

Wood, J. M., Nezworski, M. T., & Stejskal, W. J. (1996). The comprehensive system for the Rorschach: A critical examination. *Psychological Science, 7,* 3–10.

Woodward, W. R. (1972). Fechner's panpsychism: A scientific solution to the mind-body problem. *Journal of the History of the Behavioral Sciences, 8,* 367–386.

Woodworth, R. S. (1909). Hermann Ebbinghaus. *The Journal of Philosophy, Psychology and Scientific Methods, 6,* 253–256.

Woodworth, R. S. (1978). A revision of imageless thought. In E. R. Hilgard (Ed.), *American psychology in historical perspective* (pp. 119–138). Washington, DC: American Psychological Association. (Original work published 1915)

Woodworth, R. S. (1921). *Psychology: A study of mental life.* New York: Henry Holt & Co.

Woodworth, R. S. (1932). Robert S. Woodworth. In C. Murchison (Ed.), *A history of psychology in autobiography* (Vol. 2, pp. 359–380). Worcester, MA: Clark University Press.

Woodworth, R. S. (1944). James McKeen Cattell (1860-1944). *Psychological Review, 51,* 201–209.

Worcester, E. (1932). *Life's adventure: The story of a varied career.* New York: Scribner.

Wundt, W. (1862). Die Geschwindigkeit des Gedankens [The speed of thought]. *Gartenlaube,* 263–265.

Wundt, W. (1904). *Principles of physiological psychology* (5th ed., Vol. 1, E. B. Titchener, Trans.). New York: Macmillan. (Original work published 1902)

Yerkes, R. M. (Ed.) (1921). *Psychological examining in the U.S. Army.* Memoirs of the National Academy of Sciences (No. 15).

Yerkes, R. M. (1932). Robert Mearns Yerkes: Psychobiologist. In C. Murchison (Ed.), *A history of psychology in autobiography* (Vol. 2, pp. 381-407). Worcester, MA: Clark University Press.

Yerkes, R. M., & Dodson, J. D. (1908). The relation of strength of stimulus to rapidity of habit formation. *Journal of Comparative Neurology and Psychology, 18,* 459–482.

Yerkes, R. M., & Learned, B. W. (1925). *Chimpanzee intelligence and its vocal expressions.* Baltimore: Williams & Wilkins.

Yerkes, R. M., & Morgulis, S. (1909). The method of Pawlow in animal psychology. *Psychological Bulletin, 6,* 257–273.

Yerkes, R. M., & Yerkes, A. W. (1929). *The great apes: A study of anthropoid life.* New Haven, CT: Yale University Press.

Young, R. K. (1985). Ebbinghaus: Some consequences. *Journal of Experimental Psychology: Learning, Memory, and Cognition, 11,* 491–495.

Zajonc, R. B. (1965). Social facilitation. *Science, 149,* 269–274.

Zajonc, R. B., Murphy, S., & Ingelhart, M. (1989). Feeling and facial efference: Implications of the vascular theory of emotion. *Psychological Review, 96,* 395–416.

Zeigarnik, B. (1927). Über Behalten von erledigten und unerledigten Handlungen [On the retention of finished and unfinished acts]. *Psychologische For-schung, 9,* 1–85.

Zilboorg, G. (1941). *A history of medical psychology.* New York: Norton.

Zillmann, D. (1983). Transfer of excitation in emotional behavior. In J. T. Cacioppo & R. E. Petty (Eds.), *Social psychology: A sourcebook* (pp. 215–240). New York: Guilford Press.

Zillmann, D., Katcher, A. H., & Milavsky, B. (1972). Excitation transfer from physical exercise to subsequent aggressive behavior. *Journal of Experimental Social Psychology, 8,* 247–259.

Zimbardo, P. G. (1992). *Psychology and life* (13th ed.). New York: HarperCollins.

Zimbardo, P. G., Haney, C., Banks, W., & Jaffe, D. (1973, April 8). Pirandellian prison: The mind is a formidable jailor. *New York Times Magazine,* pp. 38–60.

Name Index

Subject Index

Brain Mechanisms and Intelligence (Lashley), 466
Brainstem reticular formation (BSRF), 472
Brave New World (Huxley), 367
Breast envy, 423
British associationism, 69–70, 84–92
 Bain and, 91–92
 Hartley and, 84–86
 of James, Mill, 86–88
 of John Stuart Mill, 89–90
 modern psychology and, 98
British empiricism, 70–84
 Berkeley and, 78–81
 Hobbes and, 70–72
 Hume and, 81–84
 of Locke, 72–78
Bromide, Pavlov and, 314
Bystander apathy, 528–529

Calculus
 development of, 5
 Leibniz and, 62
 Newton and, 55
Cambridge University, founding of, 51
Carmichael's Manual of Child Psychology, 326
Carnegie Corporation, Angell and, 177
Carnegie Institute of Technology, 506
Carnegie-Mellon University, AI at, 556
Carolingian Empire, 44
Castration anxiety, 419
Categorical imperative, of Kant, 106
Categories of thought, of Kant, 106
Categorization
 in cognition, 553
 James on, 553
 Wittgenstein on, 553
Category mistake, of Ryle, 554–555
Catharsis
 Anna O and, 411
 Aristotle and, 33
Cats in a Puzzle Box (Guthrie and Horton), 339–340
Causality
 Hume on, 82
 Kant and, 105
 Mill, James, on, 88
Causes, of Aristotle, 30
Celebrity testimonials, Watson and, 325
Center for Cognitive Studies (Harvard), 547
Center for the Advanced Study of the Behavioral Sciences (Stanford University), 549
Center for the Study of the Person (La Jolla), 449
Central energizing system, 460
Central nervous system (CNS), transmitters in, 462–463. *See also* Brain; Nervous system
Centrencephalic system (centrencephalon), 468
Cerebellum, 138
Cerebral cortex, motor areas in, 142
Cerebral lobes, surgical removal of, 138
Change
 Aristotle and, 30–31
 in attitudes, 519–520
 in Heraclitus's philosophy, 20
 Parmenides and, 21

Chaos theory, 20
Character and Culture (Sigmund Freud), 420
Charisma, Max Weber and, 514
Chicago, University of, 253
 J. R. Angell at, 274, 275, 276–277
 Carr at, 279
 Dewey at, 274–275
 functionalism at, 264
 Lashley at, 466
 Loeb at, 296
 James G. Miller at, 448
 Rogers at, 448
 Shakow at, 452
 Thurstone at, 498
 Watson at, 318–319
Chicago Psychoanalytic Institute, Horney at, 424
Child analysis, Anna Freud, and, 422
 Melanie Klein and, 423
Child development. *See also* Child Psychology; Childrearing; Maturation
 Attachments and, 425
 Bruner and, 548
 Darwin and, 289
 Freud and, 418, 418–420
 Inhelder and, 544–545
 language acquisition and, 547
 Murphy, Lois, and, 518
 Piaget and, 542–544
 Preyer and, 289
 Ribot and, 96
 Shinn and, 288–289
 social learning theory and, 526–527
 Thorndike and, 284
 Woolley on, 278
Child psychology
 of Charlotte Bühler, 446
 Darwin and, 217
 group leadership and, 390
 Hall and, 255–256
 Lewin on, 389–391
 of Merleau-Ponty, 444–445
 of Piaget, 543–544
 Stumpf and, 187
Childrearing
 gender and, 531
 Watson and, 326–327
Children. *See also* Child development; Child psychology; Childrearing; Education
 Leta Stetter Hollingworth's studies of, 260–261
 Locke on, 77
 position in family, 434–435
Child's Construction of Quantities, The (Piaget and Inhelder), 544
Child Welfare Research Station (Iowa), Bob and Pat Sears at, 531
Choice
 existentialism and, 440
 Schopenhauer on, 120
Chomsky-Skinner debate, over language, 366, 369
Christian thought
 of Abélard, 47–48
 of Anselm, 47
 Aristotle and, 31, 65
 Augustine and, 43–44
 in later Middle Ages, 47–50

of Thomas Aquinas, 48–49
 Western thought and, 42
Chunks, in short-term memory, 549
City College of New York (CCNY), Gardner Murphy at, 518
Civilization and Its Discontents (Sigmund Freud), 420
Clark Conference, 256–257, 258, 266
Clark University
 Baird at, 258
 Jonas Clark and founding of, 252–253
 Hall and, 252–253
 Small at, 301
 Sumner and, 258
Classification, of animal kingdom, 31
Clever Hans
 Herr von Osten and, 187–189
 Pfungst and, 188
 Stumpf and, 187–189
 Thorndike's "mind-reading" experiments and, 282
Client-centered therapy, of Rogers, 448–449
Client-Centered Therapy (Rogers), 448
Clinical medicine, psychoanalysis and, 426
Clinical psychology
 Boulder model and, 452
 Freud and, 452–453
 growth of, 451–452
 Humanistic approaches to, 446–449
 psychotherapy and, 449–450
 Shakow and, 451–452
Clinical Versus Statistical Prediction (Meehl), 502
Closure, in Gestalt psychology, 382
Clouds, The (Aristophanes), Socrates in, 24–25
Cocaine, Sigmund Freud, and, 409
Cochlear microphonic, Wever, Bray, and, 477
Cogito ergo sum ("I think, therefore I am"), 56
Cognition. *See also* Cognitive psychology; Language
 Brentano and, 185
 categorization and, 554
 Lewin on, 388
 memory and, 552–553
 and reality, 551–552
 reasoning and, 554–555
 Tolman and, 346
Cognition and Reality (Neisser), 551–552
Cognitive balance, 524
Cognitive development, Merleau-Ponty and, 445
 Piaget and, 543–544
Cognitive dissonance theory, 387, 538
Cognitive map, as intervening variable, 346
Cognitive psychology, 537–560. *See also* Language; Psycholinguistics
 as applied psychology, 507
 artificial intelligence and, 546, 555–558
 autobiographical memories and, 6
 Bartlett and, 539–540
 Bruner and, 547–548
 categorization and, 553–554
 Chomsky and, 546–547
 Claperède and, 542
 classical contributions to, 550–558